"Aimed at educated, experienced travellers, the [Berlitz Travellers] Guides capture the flavor of foreign lands."
—*Entrepreneur*

"Filling a needed niche in guidebooks . . . designed to eliminate the cumbersome lists of virtually every hotel and restaurant . . . . Special out-of-the-way places are detailed. . . . The books capture the personality and excitement of each destination."
—*Los Angeles Times*

"There's a different tone to these books, and certainly a different approach . . . information is aimed at independent and clearly sophisticated travellers. . . . Strong opinions give these books a different personality from most guides, and make them fun to read."
—*Travel & Leisure*

"Aimed at experienced, independent travellers who want information beyond the nuts-and-bolts material available in many familiar sources. Although each volume gives necessary basics, the series sends travellers not just to 'sights,' but to places and events that convey the personality of each locale."
—*The Denver Post*

"Just the right amount of information about where to stay and play."
—*Detroit Free Press*

CONTRIBUTORS

MARGARET ADAMS, formerly an editor at the Metropolitan Museum of Art in New York City, now follows the art scene from her home in Paris.

STEPHEN BREWER has edited several guidebooks in this series. He retreats to the South of France regularly, frequently on assignment for magazines and newspapers.

CHARLA CARTER is a freelance fashion editor and journalist in Paris. She has contributed articles on fashion and cultural affairs to American, British, and Australian *Vogue,* to *Elle,* and to *Vanity Fair, European Travel & Life,* and *Paris Passion*.

FRED HALLIDAY divides his time between Paris and Connecticut. He has been a contributor to *The New York Times* and to *Condé Nast Traveler, Travel & Leisure,* and *Food & Wine* magazines.

EDWARD HERNSTADT is a freelance writer who lived in Paris for four years. He has contributed to publications in the United States, France, and Australia.

GEORGIA I. HESSE, for 19 years Travel Editor of *The San Francisco Examiner and Chronicle,* has contributed articles on travel to almost every major North American magazine and newspaper. She was a Fulbright scholar at the University of Strasbourg, and in 1982 she was awarded the *Ordre National du Mérite* by the French government.

AMY HOLLOWELL is an editor at *The International Herald Tribune* in Paris, where she has lived since 1982. She also writes about French cultural and current affairs.

MARION KAPLAN spent 20 years in Africa as a freelance photojournalist working for *Time* and *National Geographic,* among other magazines. She has also lived in Portugal's Algarve province, and is presently based in southwestern France. She is the author of the books *Focus Africa* and *The Portuguese* and contributes to *The Berlitz Travellers Guide to Portugal* and many other publications.

SALLY LEFEVRE, a native New Yorker, has lived in Turkey and England as well as Canada, where she produced a national radio program on tourism. She has now lived in France for more than 15 years and contributes to several U.S. and European publications and guidebooks.

ALEXANDER LOBRANO worked as a writer and editor in New York and London before moving to Paris seven years ago. Formerly an editor in the Paris office of Fairchild Publications, he now freelances for *The International Herald Tribune, The Los Angeles Times,* and *Travel & Leisure,* among other publications.

STEPHEN O'SHEA is a writer and journalist who lived in Paris for many years. He has written for British, American, Canadian, and French magazines and currently lives in New York City.

JENNIFER QUALE, who contributes to many major publications, has written about France for *Food & Wine, The New York Times,* and *European Travel & Life.*

MIMI TOMPKINS is a journalist and broadcaster who has been based in Paris for the last 11 years.

DAVID WICKERS is travel editor of *Marie Claire* magazine and travel correspondent of the London *Sunday Times.* In 1992 he was named U.K. Travel Writer of the Year. He travels to Normandy frequently from his home in London.

THE BERLITZ
TRAVELLERS GUIDES

THE BERLITZ TRAVELLERS GUIDE TO FRANCE

Sixth Edition

ALAN TUCKER

General Editor

BERLITZ PUBLISHING COMPANY, INC.
New York, New York

BERLITZ PUBLISHING COMPANY LTD.
Oxford, England

THE BERLITZ TRAVELLERS GUIDE
TO FRANCE
Sixth Edition

Berlitz Trademark Reg U.S. Patent and Trademark Office
and other countries—Marca Registrada

Published by Berlitz Publishing Company, Inc.
257 Park Avenue South, New York, New York 10010, U.S.A.

Distributed in the United States by
the Macmillan Publishing Group

Distributed elsewhere by Berlitz Publishing Company Ltd.
Berlitz House, Peterley Road, Horspath, Oxford OX4 2TX, England

ISBN 2-8315-1709-5
ISSN 1057-476X

Designed by Beth Tondreau Design
Cover design by Dan Miller Design
Cover photograph by Joachim Messerschmidt/Bruce Coleman, Inc.
Maps by Vantage Art, Inc.
Illustrations by Bill Russell
Copyedited by Kerrin Griffith
Fact-checked in France by Tina Isaac
Edited by Stephen Brewer

THIS GUIDEBOOK

The Berlitz Travellers Guides are designed for experienced travellers in search of exceptional information that will enhance the enjoyment of the trips they take.

Where, for example, are the interesting, out-of-the-way, fun, charming, or romantic places to stay? The hotels described by our expert writers are some of the special places, in all price ranges except for the very lowest—not just the run-of-the-mill, heavily marketed places in advertised airline and travel-wholesaler packages.

We are *highly* selective in our choices of accommodations, concentrating on what our insider contributors think are the most interesting or rewarding places, and why. Readers who want to review exhaustive lists of hotel and resort choices as well, and who feel they need detailed descriptions of each property, can supplement the *Berlitz Travellers Guide* with tourism industry publications or one of the many directory-type guidebooks on the market.

We indicate the approximate price level of each accommodation in our description of it (no indication means it is moderate in local, relative terms), and at the end of every chapter we supply more detailed hotel rates as well as contact information so that you can get precise, up-to-the-minute rates and make reservations.

The Berlitz Travellers Guide to France highlights the more rewarding parts of the country so that you can quickly and efficiently home in on a good itinerary.

Of course, this guidebook does far more than just help you choose a hotel and plan your trip. *The Berlitz Travellers Guide to France* is designed for use *in* France. Our writers, each of whom is an experienced travel journalist who either lives in or regularly tours the city or region of France he or she covers, tell you what you really need to know, what you can't find out so easily on your own. They identify and describe the truly out-of-the-ordinary restaurants, shops, activities, and sights, and tell you the best way to "do" your destination.

Our writers are highly selective. They bring out the significance of the places they *do* cover, capturing the personality and the underlying cultural and historical resonances of a city or region—making clear its special appeal.

The Berlitz Travellers Guide to France is full of reliable information. We would like to know if you think we've left out some very special place. Although we make every effort to provide the most current information available about every destination described in this book, it is possible too that changes have occurred before you arrive. If you do have an experience that is contrary to what you were led to expect by our description, we would like to hear from you about it.

A guidebook is no substitute for common sense when you are travelling. Always pack the clothing, footwear, and other items appropriate for the destination, and make the necessary accommodation for such variables as altitude, weather, and local rules and customs. Of course, once on the scene you should avoid situations that are in your own judgment potentially hazardous, even if they have to do with something mentioned in a guidebook. Half the fun of travelling is exploring, but explore with care.

ALAN TUCKER
General Editor
Berlitz Travellers Guides

Root Publishing Company
330 West Hubbard Street
Suite 440
Chicago, Illinois 60610

CONTENTS

MAPS

THE
BERLITZ
TRAVELLERS
GUIDE
TO
FRANCE

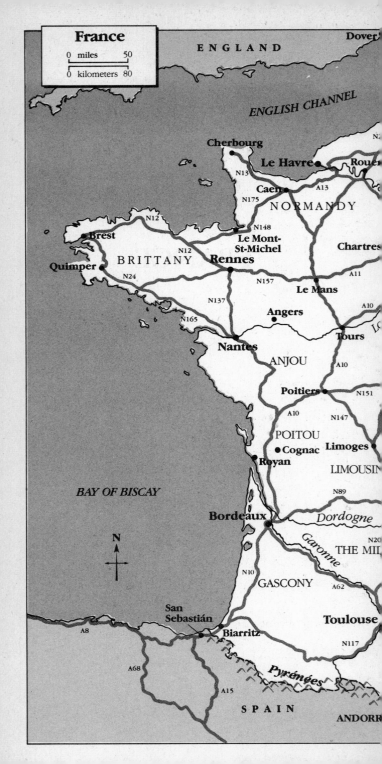

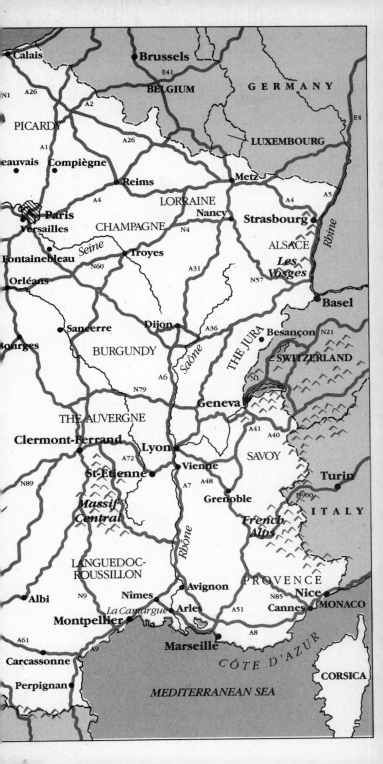

OVERVIEW

By Georgia I. Hesse

Georgia I. Hesse, for 19 years the Travel Editor of The San Francisco Sunday Examiner & Chronicle, *was a Fulbright scholar at the University of Strasbourg. She now contributes articles on travel and related subjects to many magazines and newspapers, including* Diversion, Endless Vacation, Travel & Leisure, The Chicago Tribune, San Diego Tribune, *and* The San Francisco Examiner.

"**A**sk the travelled inhabitant of any nation, In what country on earth would you rather live?— Certainly in my own, where are all my friends, my relations, and the earliest and sweetest affections and recollections of my life. Which would be your second choice? France."
　　　　　　　　—Thomas Jefferson, *Autobiography,* 1821

There are as many reasons to visit France as France has cheeses (265, according to Charles de Gaulle), among them:

- to live *la vie en rose* in Paris, or
- to meander through little villages lost in the snooze of yesteryear, or
- to appreciate art in all its various forms, including the art of living, or
- to transport yourself with haute cuisine (*mousseline de brochet, ragout de homard et morilles à la crème de Sauternes*) or with everyday cooking (*choucroute garnie*), or
- to sit in a shady square in Senlis, north of Paris, and think that "modern" France began there a thousand years ago.

To look at the map of France is to look at the head of a dog, a boxer, perhaps: The scruff of the neck is the Pas-de-Calais on the Belgian border, the head joins the body of

5

Europe along the Alps and the Black Forest. The ears are lower Normandy and Brittany, and the muzzle bites down on Andorra and Spain. It's a very square and handsome head, with Tours as an eyeball.

Ancient as it is in essence, France brought all its parts together only as recently as 1860, when Savoy became the final region to join that whole of which Hugues Capet was crowned king in 987. Of the regions known by their traditional names, such as Alsace or Burgundy, there are today 22, while a Revolutionary "reform" in 1790 established 96 *départements*. (The number of each *département* is used for the last two figures of car registration numbers and the first two of postal codes.)

France for Travellers

Few travellers call upon France without stopping to pay their respects to **Paris**, which, in the last several years, has sprinted forward like a runner from the blocks, leading even Parisians to wonder where all the energy (not to mention the money) is coming from. Jane Kramer (the worthy successor to *The New Yorker*'s Genêt) pinpoints de Gaulle as the last long-distance runner, who, she says, "planned to leave himself to the French, and in a sense he did." Presidents since, however—Georges Pompidou, Valéry Giscard d'Estaing, François Mitterrand—have appeared to share the view, as expressed by Mitterrand, that France cannot have a *grande politique* without a *grande architecture*.

In the race, Parisians, their visitors, and *la culture* are the clear winners. No one knows today's Paris who does not know the Musée National d'Art Moderne (a permanent collection housed in the Centre Georges Pompidou); the Forum des Halles (born in 1979 but still overlooked by many foreigners—not without reason, some might say); the Musée Picasso in the reborn Marais; la Géode (with the world's largest projection screen) at the Cité des Sciences et de l'Industrie (in Parc de la Villette); the controversial and astonishingly successful Musée d'Orsay; the violently debated pyramidal glass entrance to the Louvre by I. M. Pei; the Musée des Arts Décoratifs in the Louvre; the Grande Arche de la Défense, a.k.a. the Tête Défense (also known as Mitterrand's square bagel); or the high-tech tapestry that is the Institut du Monde Arabe (with its fine rooftop restaurant), right on the Seine.

Paris so dominates its immediate region, the **Ile-de-France**, that many of the Ile's riches go unexploited by travellers. After all, the Ile-de-France once *was* France; its lures are as many and as diverse as the autumn leaves in the valley of the Chevreuse: Versailles, Fontainebleau, Chartres, Giverny, et cetera. But France is not just Paris.

France generally is conceived of as a garden carefully tended and trimmed over generations and centuries, a rich, fat land where good things grow, nature made to order. Indeed it is. France is also rugged, untamed, wild, and as mean as a sudden mistral. The hexagonal garden is walled in by hills, massifs, and mountains on several sides: the Vosges and Jura ranges to the northeast; the Alps (at almost 16,000 feet, Mont Blanc is Europe's highest peak) and Alpes-Maritimes to the east; the Pyrénées to the south; and the Massif Armoricain—windblown Brittany—in the northwest. The spine of the Massif Central has helped keep the Auvergne—the high country between Périgord and the Rhône Valley, generally south of the city of Clermont-Ferrand—among the least-trammeled regions of the country.

Following Paris, **Provence** and the Côte d'Azur (the Riviera) lure more non-European visitors than any other part of France, though surely no North American or Australian would go to France for the beaches alone, having more than a sufficiency of better ones at home. No, it's the essence of the region as a whole—the sun falling on old cultures and old stones, the air scented with roses and orange blossoms and basil and thyme and garlic, the welcoming inns with shaded gardens, the hillside picnics of *salade Niçoise* and a chilled rosé (perhaps Tavel) and a regional cheese (Pélardon or Bleu des Causses?), the countrysides that look like Impressionist paintings—and vice versa.

The **Côte d'Azur** is where the fashionable action is and has been since the mid-19th century, when Cannes was discovered and made chic by Baron Henry Peter Brougham and the Brits who followed him there. (Provence proper, on the other hand, is where most of the action isn't, and where almost no one wants it.) Poet-politician Stephen Liégeard called dishes along the Riviera "slices of sun on napkins of sea." Expect the freshest of fruits, vegetables, and seafood, and young, light, fruity wines.

Burgundy and the **Rhône Valley** fit neatly into a Provence–Côte d'Azur itinerary, whether you travel by *autoroute,* by back roads that twist like intestines, or by train. Burgundy is as rich in attractions as the wines that bear its name: a distinctive cuisine for one, more Romanesque churches than you can shake a sculpture at, Gallo-Roman art and archaeology, tiny towns and pine forests, and two major cities, Dijon and Lyon.

Another complete trip could (and should) be confined to the northeast alone, to **Champagne** and **Lorraine and Alsace**, with side trips into Picardie and Franche-Comté. These are the lands of the fatted calf and the stuffed goose, of story-book villages and refreshingly rural pastures and lanes, of a cocktail of cultures ("Let them speak German," Napoléon said of the Alsatians, "as long as they think in French"), the whole seen through a (wine) glass, lightly.

Along the Loire river (". . . mirroring from sea to source a hundred cities and five hundred towers," wrote Oscar Wilde), travellers wander in an oval path from Paris to Brittany, to Normandy, and back again. The **Loire Valley**, with its Renaissance châteaux and its white wines, is serene and civilized, the very essence of the notion of France. This is a land of country wines, little-known outside the region: Gros-plant, Champigny, Coteaux de l'Aubance.

Like Alsace, Celtic **Brittany** is a land of its own, fiercely independent, unbendingly individual, a land of fishermen, saints, standing stones, and a cuisine born of the sea. **Normandy**, on the other hand, is a dream of green, of soft and creamy cheeses (Camembert!), a tapestry of good things growing, torn to the west by the beaches used for the Allied landing in World War II.

South of the Loire and north of Bordeaux-Aquitaine, **Poitou and Les Charentes** stretches inland from the Atlantic beaches, and is renowned for its sunny weather, its brilliant examples of Romanesque art and architecture, and France's most famous spirit, Cognac.

Culinary as well as cultural adventures begin in **Bordeaux** in southwest France, leading devotees into the valleys of the **Dordogne**, the Isère, and the Lot; down into the Guienne and Gascony; to modish resorts and medieval villages; to caves sheltering prehistoric art; and finally to Basque towns climbing the foothills of the **Pyrénées**.

In some respects, southwest France (with names on the map such as Landes, Gers, Tarn, Languedoc-Roussillon) is the largest and most complex of the regions, with an inheritance of linguistic confusions, religious upheavals, and economic and agricultural dislocations. It is also one of the most rewarding. Deeply agricultural, this region feeds much of France, though many of its own dishes are not widely transported: *garbure* (a thick Gascon soup-stew) and various *confits* (meats preserved in their own fat). The hearty, farm-kitchen *cassoulet* is increasingly well appreciated throughout France. And don't forget the great liqueur of the southwest, Armagnac.

The queen city of the central south, **Toulouse** is France's fourth largest and one of the oldest; some scholars say it was founded before Rome. Its climate, its several architecturally remarkable structures, its emphasis on the arts, and its university-inspired liveliness make it a rewarding destination, while it also serves as a convenient jumping-off point for such smart, smaller cities as Auch, to the west in Gascony, Albi to the east, and Castelnaudary and Carcassonne to the southeast, in the direction of Languedoc's Mediterranean coast. South of Toulouse, major routes and little roads as provocative as afterthoughts run through country unfamiliar to most foreigners; here walk the ghosts of prehistoric peoples, of insurgents and heretics, of pilgrims and hermits and troubadours.

Phocaean fleets and Roman galleys called in **Languedoc-Roussillon**, where the landscape rises in theatrical tiers along the Golfe du Lion, from the Spanish border, the Côte Vermeille, and Perpignan in the south, eastward through beaches, marinas, and Montpellier, to Nîmes and its Roman ruins just west of the Rhône. Here, too, are excitements often overlooked: the roads that wiggle inland from Collioure to Céret or through the forests and villages of the Parc National des Cévennes to the natural wonder that is the Gorges du Tarn.

Savoy and **Dauphiné** in winter are empires of ice and snow, of toney resorts such as Chamonix and Megève and Val d'Isère. In summer these places constitute the promised land of mountaineers and lovers of lakes (including Lac du Bourget, France's largest) and Alpine scenery. Pretty spa cities such as Aix-les-Bains and Evian attract those who come "to take the waters"; beautifully sited old Grenoble is an attention-getter in its own right. Cooking in the French Alps tends to be just that—cooking rather than cuisine. The specialties are hearty and filling; *gratin,* for instance, a family of crusty potato-and-cheese dishes. Wines are light, dry, and refreshing as the mountain air.

Franche-Comté fills the space from Alsace-Lorraine to the Rhône-Alpes region with thick woods, quiet lakes, and high pastures that back up against the **Jura** mountains and Switzerland. The "big city" here is Besançon, where Victor Hugo was born and the door opens to the natural beauty of the countryside.

Clearly, France—with 60 million inhabitants occupying a space smaller than Texas—is inexhaustible. So it is that, in one volume, we have not attempted to exhaust, not even to completely cover, France. We are not encyclopedic; we have made choices.

USEFUL FACTS

When to Go

France, like other major European destinations, swarms with
tourists in June, July, and August. The best weather and fewer
crowds make September and October the finest months for
general sightseeing, followed by late April to mid-June (although early spring can be rainy). The Christmas–New
Year's week bring throngs to the ski slopes; plan a ski
vacation for mid-January to early May (depending on resort
altitudes), but *not* during school holidays.

Entry Documents

Holders of valid United States, Canadian, and New Zealand
passports are no longer required to have French visas for
tourism visits of three months or less. Likewise, citizens of
Japan, Switzerland, Sweden, Norway, and other countries, as
well as members of the European Community, are not required to have French visas. Visas *are* required for diplomats, government officials, journalists on specific missions,
and long-term students. In addition, visas are required for
citizens of Australia and many other countries. Anyone with
doubts should check with the nearest French consulate *well
in advance* of a trip.

Arrival at Major Gateways by Air

From North America and elsewhere outside Europe, most
travellers to France arrive at Paris's international airports,
Roissy–Charles-de-Gaulle (25 km/16 miles north of Paris via
A 1 or RN 2) and **Orly** (16 km/10 miles south via A 6 or
RN 7). The third international airport, old Le Bourget, is
served by business aviation.

Note: There are two *aérogares* at de Gaulle, Aérogare 1 and
Aérogare 2. Aérogare 2 has four terminal buildings, A, B, C,
and D. Before arrival and, especially, before departure, it's
wise to check where, precisely, your plane will land or take
off. That's particularly important when you are picking up a
rental car at the airport or when instructing the taxi driver in
Paris where to deliver you.

There are also two terminals at Orly: Orly-Ouest and Orly-
Sud; again, check in advance of arrival and departure. A new
arrival-departure hall at Orly-Ouest has been completed,
and the new electronically automated transport system
(Orlyval) now connects the two Orly terminals with the RER
(Régional Express Métro) to Paris and de Gaulle airport
(more on this below).

Incoming and outgoing passengers at either Charles-de-Gaulle (hereafter CDG) or Orly should know there are restaurants and cafés of all persuasions at the airports: six at CDG 1 (including a branch of Maxim's proper and Grill Maxim's), three at CDG 2A, and three at CDG 2B. Additionally, Aéroport de Paris (ADP) is building a huge business center dubbed "Roissypole," with office towers, exhibitions, and new deluxe hotels at CDG. The duty-free boutiques at CDG's Aérogare 1 offer luxury goods at an average of 31 percent below Paris prices; there's even an antiques shop at Aérogare 1. At Orly-Ouest, the six restaurants include a Maxim's and Jardin d'Orly, while Orly-Sud offers Le Grillardin for upscale meals, as well as a cafeteria.

Free shuttles transfer passengers between airports and on-site hotels such as (at CDG): Sofitel (deluxe), Novotel (first class), and Arcade (standard); and (at Orly): Pullman Paris and Hilton (deluxe), Altéa (first class), and Arcade (standard). The Novotel at Le Bourget has 143 rooms and many amenities, including an outdoor pool.

Currently, almost 100 airlines serve CDG and Orly airports. Be sure to check which Paris airport you're flying into when you purchase your ticket. Air France serves CDG from the U.S. cities of Boston, Chicago, Houston, Los Angeles, Miami, New York, San Francisco, and Washington, D.C.; from the Canadian cities of Montreal and Toronto; from the U.K. cities of Dublin, Edinburgh, and London (Heathrow, Gatwick, London City); and from virtually all other major European cities. Air France serves Orly from Newark. On arrival in Paris, there are convenient connections to major regional cities.

To confirm departing flights you may call the airline directly or the airport: Orly, Tel: 49-75-52-52; CDG, Tel: 48-62-22-80. Many operators speak English.

Among major U.S. air carriers, American flies to Orly from Chicago, Dallas-Fort Worth, Miami, New York, and Raleigh-Durham; Continental has flights to Orly from Newark and Houston; Delta sets down in Orly from Atlanta, Cincinnati, and New York.

Northwest goes to CDG from Boston and Detroit; TWA serves CDG from Boston, Chicago, Los Angeles, New York, San Francisco, St. Louis, and Washington, D.C.; United travels to CDG from Chicago, Los Angeles, San Francisco, and Washington, D.C.

Air Canada flies to CDG from Montreal and Toronto; Canadian International flies to CDG from Toronto; Aer Lingus offers flights to CDG from Dublin, Shannon, and Cork; British Air sets down in CDG from Birmingham, Dublin, Glasgow, London, Manchester, and Newcastle; British Midland serves CDG from Glasgow and London.

Brit Air specializes in flights to airports in Brittany and Normandy out of London-Gatwick, and Regional Airlines (which used to be called Air Vendée), a carrier in western France, has expanded to include London on its flights from Rouen.

Paris has two major in-town airport bus terminals: **Invalides**, at 2, rue Esnault-Pelterie, on the Left Bank near the Pont (Bridge) Alexandre III; and **Porte Maillot/Palais de Congrès**, northwest of the Arc de Triomphe at the end of avenue de la Grande Armée. Invalides occupies a fairly small former railroad station, whereas Maillot sits within a sky-scraping complex that's a veritable town in itself, with shops, a cinema, cafés, a parking lot, a disco, Métro station, etc. In contrast to the other two, the **Etoile** "terminal" is a streetside stop near the Arc de Triomphe on avenue Carnot, not recommended on rainy days or for passengers loaded with luggage. Two giant hotels serve the Porte Maillot/Palais de Congrès complex: the 1,006-room ► **Méridien** (81, boule-vard Gouvion St-Cyr; Tel: 40-68-34-34; Fax: 40-68-31-31; res-taurants include the Clos de Longchamp, which ranks among the best in Paris; the Café l'Arlequin; Le Yamato; and La Maison Beaujolaise) and, just across the street, the 935-room ► **Concorde La Fayette** (3, place Général-Koenig; Tel: 40-68-50-68; Fax: 40-68-50-43; there's a bar on the 34th floor with panoramic views, and restaurants include the highly rated Etoile d'Or, L'Arc-en-Ciel, and, for those who desire a coffee shop, Les Saisons).

Airports are linked to the in-town terminals with frequent departures of Air France buses, or **Le Bus Air France**. These coaches leave from the sidewalks in front of baggage pickup areas at Orly and from, at CDG, Aérogare 1, Porte (Gate) 36; Aérogare 2, Porte 10 at Terminal A, and Porte 6 at Terminal B. Directional signs are well placed, but pick-up points may change without warning. Orly buses arrive at Invalides, CDG buses at Maillot and Etoile.

The trip from CDG to Maillot takes about 30 to 40 min-utes, departs every 15 minutes from 5:45 A.M. to 11:00 P.M., and costs 48 francs. Air France coach service links CDG with the Gare Montparnasse in the 14th *arrondissement* from 6:30 A.M. to 7:30 P.M. Departures are every hour from CDG Aérogare 2 for the 45-minute trip; the fare is 64 francs. Buses between the two airports depart every 20 minutes, take 75 minutes, and cost 64 francs. Such connections are free of charge for connecting flight passengers who pick up vouch-ers at the Connections Desk when deplaning their first flight.

For travellers with considerable luggage, Air France coaches are preferable to the RATP buses discussed below. Both downtown air terminals are more conveniently located for travellers staying around the Champs-Elysées or Place de la Concorde areas than for those going to the heart of the Left Bank or Ile-de-la-Cité.

To make transfers easier, a firm in the United States, **Marketing Challenges International**, sells tickets for the Air France coaches *before* passengers' departure from the U.S. Prices for Le Bus passes are $10 one way, $20 round trip as of this writing. Also available through MCI are the Paris Visite pass for use on the Métro or bus (one day, $9.00; two days, $16; three days, $22; five days, $33); La Carte pass, which covers admission to more than 60 Paris museums and attractions and allows the holder to go to the head of the entry line (one day, $17; three days, $29; five days, $39); and vouchers for sightseeing tours of Paris by day or night through Paris Vision (about $30 per tour).

Marketing Challenges International's address is 10 East 21st Street, New York, NY 10010; Tel: (212) 529-8484; Fax: (212) 460-8287.

RATP (city) buses connect CDG to Paris's Gare de l'Est and Gare du Nord train stations, to Place Nation, and to Place de l'Opéra via the new, very comfortable **Roissybus**; and Orly-Ouest/Orly-Sud—also called **Orlybus**—to Place Denfert-Rochereau (all fares around 35 francs).

Roissy-Rail links CDG by train to the Gare du Nord and such stops as Châtelet, Luxembourg, Port Royal, Denfert-Rochereau, and Cité Universitaire, leaving every 15 minutes from 5:30 A.M. to 11:30 P.M. (30 francs). **Orly-Rail** runs between Orly-Ouest/Orly-Sud and Gare d'Austerlitz with intermediate stops, leaving every 15 minutes from 5:30 A.M. to 8:45 P.M., and after that every 30 minutes until 10:45 P.M. (25 francs). Both rail systems are integrated with city-wide Métro services. (CDG is also linked to the Gare du Nord via **RER**—the suburban commuter train—line B over the French Railways lines.)

In 1991 a new rail line, **Orlyval**, inaugurated service between Orly Airport and CDG via central Paris. From Orly the train runs to the suburban Antony RER station (on the B line). Passengers then board the RER, which serves several in-town stations before continuing on to CDG. The airport-to-airport trip takes 70 minutes; the trip from Orly to the Châtelet-Les-Halles Métro stop takes 30 minutes. Tickets for the entire trip cost about 40 francs. The train operates Monday through Saturday from 6:30 A.M. to 9:15 P.M., and Sundays from 7:00 A.M. to 10:55 P.M., with departures every 4 minutes during the morning and afternoon rush hours and every 7 minutes at other times.

Taxi fares between the airports and central Paris range from between 200 to 300 francs as of this writing, depending upon the airport (CDG is slightly farther out), destination within the city, traffic conditions at the time, luggage surcharges, et cetera. A 10 percent tip is standard. Your hotel concierge will estimate the charge rather accurately.

Arrival by Train

Paris maintains six railroad stations, served by trains from some 6,000 communities in France as well as from all European countries. They are Gare d'Austerlitz (in the southeast of town), Gare de l'Est (east), Gare de Lyon (southeast), Gare Montparnasse (west), Gare du Nord (north), and Gare St-Lazare (northwest). Passengers entering the country may have their passports and visas checked on the train before border crossings.

Major cities and regions served from the stations are as follows: from **Austerlitz**, Tours, Bordeaux, Toulouse, Madrid; from **Est**, Reims, Strasbourg, Frankfurt, Zurich; from **Lyon**, Dijon, Provence, Nice, Barcelona; from **Montparnasse**, Brittany, La Rochelle; from **Nord**, Lille, Brussels, Amsterdam, Hamburg, and also for boat-trains to Boulogne, Calais, Dunkirk; from **St-Lazare**, Normandy, boat-trains to Le Havre, Cherbourg.

Arrival by Sea from Britain

The construction of the railway Eurotunnel under the English Channel has been debated since the turn of the century. The problem-plagued project (the so-called Chunnel) now is well underway and should be completed in May 1994 (though further delays are not unlikely). When finished, as many as 15 million passengers annually will zoom through it at 186 miles per hour.

Several companies maintain ferry, hydrofoil, and Hovercraft services across the English Channel (*La Manche* in French). Crossings may be booked on the spot in Britain, but during the summer season it's wise to reserve well in advance. Travel agents in the U.S. and Canada can do that for you. Not all routes operate year-round.

Operators include **Sealink** (Tel: 0233-64-70-47, Ashford, Kent, and—through BritRail offices—212-575-2667 in New York); **P & O European Ferries** (Tel: 0304-20-33-88, Dover); **Sally Line** (Tel: 0843-59-55-22, Ramsgate, Kent, and 071-409-0536, London); **Hoverspeed British Ferries** (Tel: 0304-24-01-

01, Dover, and 081-554-7061, London, or BritRail offices in
the U.S., see above).

Other major lines are **Brittany Ferries** (Tel: 0705-82-77-01,
Portsmouth); **Truckline Ferries** (Tel: 0705-82-77-01, Poole,
Dorset); and **Sealink-Dieppe Ferries** (Tel: 0273-51-22-66, East
Sussex, or BritRail offices in the U.S., see above). Some of
the companies mentioned above operate services to the
Channel Islands as well.

Roscoff in Brittany is reached from Plymouth by Brittany
Ferries; St-Malo from Portsmouth, Brittany Ferries; Cherbourg from Weymouth and Portsmouth, Sealink, and from
Portsmouth only, P & O Ferries; Caen from Portsmouth,
Brittany Ferries; Le Havre from Portsmouth, P & O Ferries;
Dieppe from Newhaven, Sealink-Dieppe Ferries; Boulogne
from Folkestone, Sealink, and from Dover, P & O Ferries
and Hoverspeed; Calais from Dover, Sealink, P & O Ferries,
and Hoverspeed; Dunkirk from Ramsgate, Sally Line.

Both day and night crossings are offered by the major lines,
particularly P & O and Brittany Ferries. Typically, two- and
four-berth cabins are offered and should be booked well in
advance in high season. (Agents in the U.S. levy a service
charge for reservations, usually about $25.) Hoverspeed Fer-
ries makes the trip in as little as 35 minutes, carrying up to 424
passengers and 55 cars, with 29 round trips daily. For longer
distance crossings, such as Plymouth to Roscoff or Portsmouth to Caen, the trip can take from five to nine hours
(especially overnight).

Around France by Plane

Several airlines operate within the country, including Air
Inter, the domestic carrier within the Air France group. It
serves some 30 major business and resort centers, and
makes an average of 300 trips per day.

In the U.S. Air Inter offers the discount France Pass, while
the Visite France Pass is offered to all visitors from abroad
with purchase of a combined international ticket added to
Air Inter flights. Air Inter's extensive service makes it possible to crisscross France in all directions in an average time
of one hour. Ask for details from a travel agent or an Air
France office.

The largest regional air carrier in France is TAT (British
Airways acts as its sales representative in Great Britain),
which flies between many provincial cities. In 1988 Air
Littoral was formed by the merger of two existing companies, and today operates mainly in the south and southwest.
Regional Airlines (which used to be called Air Vendée) has
served cities in western France for more than ten years and

now joins those routes to a number of foreign cities, including Amsterdam, London, Brussels, and Barcelona.

Around France by Train

French Railways SNCF (*Société Nationale des Chemins de Fer Français*), whose American subsidiary is known as Rail Europe, operates the most advanced rail transportation system in the world with the fastest scheduled service on high-speed **TGVs** (*Trains à Grande Vitesse*). The TGV Atlantique, today the fastest train in the world, can operate up to a speed of 515.3 km (319 miles) per hour, but transports passengers at the commercial speed of 300 km (186 miles) per hour. (All TGV Atlantique services depart from and arrive at the newly reorganized Gare Montparnasse.)

As of this writing the following schedules are maintained on TGVs: Paris–Lyon–St-Etienne (2 hours to Lyon's Part-Dieu station, 10 minutes more to Lyon-Perrache); Paris–Avignon–Marseille–Toulon–Nice (Avignon in 3 hours and 45 minutes, even with multiple stops and trains not yet operating at TGV speeds the entire route; Nice is reached in 6 hours and 58 minutes); Paris–Dijon (1 hour and 36 minutes); Paris–Le Mans (now less than an hour from Paris)–Angers–Nantes–La Baule (about 2 hours to Nantes); Paris–Le Mans–Rennes–Brest (4 hours); Paris–Rennes–Quimper (4 hours and 22 minutes); Paris–Poitiers–La Rochelle (3 hours and 11 minutes); Paris–Nîmes–Montpellier–Béziers (4 hours and 15 minutes to Nîmes); Paris–Aix-les-Bains–either Chambéry or Annecy (3 hours and 30 minutes); Paris–Lyon–Grenoble (3 hours and 16 minutes to Grenoble); Paris–Besançon (2 hours and 30 minutes) or Paris–Beaune–Chalon-sur-Saône (2 hours and 15 minutes); Lille–Douai–Arras–Lyon (4 hours and 30 minutes); Rouen–Lyon (3 hours and 50 minutes); and Lille–Grenoble (5 hours and 50 minutes). To the southwest, TGVs now reach Bordeaux from Paris in 2 hours and 54 minutes, Biarritz in 4 hours and 43 minutes.

TGVs also call in several Swiss cities on runs from Paris to Mâcon and Geneva (between 3½ and 4 hours, depending on intermediate stops) and Paris to either Lausanne or Bern.

It is hoped that by 1997 Paris will be linked to Avignon in 2 hours and 40 minutes, to Nice in 4 hours, and to Barcelona in 4 hours and 30 minutes. Also on line are plans for TGV service to Strasbourg, and beyond Strasbourg the TGV-Est line will connect Paris to Munich in 5 hours. The TGV-Nord system will allow service to Brussels, Belgium, in 1 hour and 20 minutes, and (employing the new Eurotunnel when it's completed) Paris to London in 3 hours.

The new generation of TGVs consists of three first-class

cars per train (meals available at seats), one bar-snack car, and six second-class cars. When run in pairs, as on Paris–Lyon runs, capacity is almost 1,000 passengers. Some first-class cars are arranged for meetings or to accommodate groups; play spaces and nurseries are available in second class; the trains also offer telephone service en route; and access doors between cars have been removed to make moving about easier.

Not all trains, of course, are TGVs: Others include Euro-Cities, Corails, or Turbotrains, all air-conditioned, sound-proofed, and some with complete dining cars. On most night trains (such as the comfortable, traditional Nice–Paris Train Bleu), you may book a private sleeper or a berth in either first or second class. New EuroCity trains are put into service regularly; at the moment, 78 of them serve major cities across the Continent.

Information on all trains and tours as well as discounts described below can be supplied by your travel agent or by the office of **Rail Europe**, 2100 Central Avenue, Suite 200, Boulder, CO 80301; Tel: (800) 438-7245, (800) 848-7245, or (303) 443-5100; Fax: (800) 432-1329. In Canada contact Rail Europe at 2085 Dundas East, Suite 105, Mississauga, Ontario L4X 1M2 (same telephone numbers as above). In the U.K., contact **French Railways, Ltd.**, 179 Piccadilly, London W1 OBA; Tel: (071) 495-4433. In Paris, **SNCF**'s office is located at 10, place de Budapest; Tel: 01-45-82-50-50 (some operators speak English).

Rail Europe is now the general sales agent for railways in the following countries: Belgium, Denmark, Finland, France, Greece, Holland, Hungary, Luxembourg, Norway, Poland, Portugal, Spain, Sweden, and Switzerland. There is not room here to detail all the passes and discount plans available in France, but they are worth inquiry and study: **France Rail-pass, Rail 'N Drive Pass, France Fly Rail 'N Drive Pass**, in addition to the continent-wide **EurailDrive Pass, Eurailpass, Eurail Youthpass, Eurail Saverpass, Eurail Flexipass**. It's im-portant to consider which fits your plans and to purchase your discount pass before leaving home.

Regular discounts on regular runs also are available for those who plan to take just one point-to-point trip and who meet the requirements as members of couples, families, youth groups, et cetera. These are the so-called Bleu-Blanc-Rouge tariffs, which are available on certain days of each month; ask Rail Europe or travel agents for details.

New in North America is a Franco-British railpass known as the **BritFrance Railpass**, which will provide 5 or 10 days of rail travel in both countries, usable over 15 consecutive days for the 5-day pass or one month for the 10-day pass. It includes a round-trip ticket on the Hovercraft for Channel crossings and all supplements for the use of TGVs. All prices are guaranteed in U.S. dollars for the calendar year. For complete information, contact your travel agent or call Rail Europe (see above for contact information) or BritRail in New York at (212) 575-2667.

Rail Europe's brochure *Europe on Track* provides useful information about the various kinds of Eurailpasses. Free copies may be obtained by contacting Rail Europe, P.O. Box 10383, Stamford, CT 06904, Tel: (914) 682-2999, Fax: (914) 682-2821; in Canada, P.O. Box 4000, Station A, Mississauga, Ontario L5A 9Z9, Fax: (416) 602-4198.

Renting a Car and Driving

A valid driver's license from the country of residence is required; minimum age is 23 years, or 21 for credit card holders. All vehicles must be insured; if you are renting a car licensed in France, the rental company will take care of the paperwork. The major rental car companies in France are Avis, Budget-Milleville, Citer, Europcar (affiliated with National Car Rental and InteRent), Eurodollar/Mattei, and Hertz. International car rental credit cards are accepted for payment, with no deposit required. Other cards accepted are American Express, Carte Blanche, Carte Bleue, Visa, Air France, Air Inter, Diner's Club, and Eurocard (MasterCard).

Normally, a good deal of money may be saved by arranging for auto pickups well in advance of the trip when discount plans may be booked. If you are planning to spend a few days in Paris before driving into the country, you may wish to pick up your car when leaving at one of the airports, thus avoiding having to deal with Paris traffic.

The most economical plan for rental periods of one month or more is **Renault's Financed Purchase-Repurchase** lease plan, by which the driver purchases a new Renault, paying basic charges in advance and signing a promissory note for the balance of the cost. The note is discharged upon return of the car in good condition to Renault at an agreed time. The cost includes unlimited mileage, government taxes, factory guarantee, registration, and fire, theft, and nondeductible collision insurance.

For information on Renault Purchase-Repurchase, contact Renault USA, Inc., European Delivery Services, 650 First Avenue, New York, NY 10016-3214; Tel: (212) 532-1221 or (800) 221-1052; Fax: (212) 725-5379.

Unless otherwise signposted, the speed limits under normal conditions (including dry roads) are: 130 km (81 miles) per hour on toll motorways; 110 km (68 miles) per hour on dual carriageways, no-toll motorways; 90 km (56 miles) per hour on other roads (even back roads), and 60 km (37 miles) per hour or less in towns. The limits are considerably lower on wet roads. The sign you frequently see that reads "Rappel" means that the last restriction signposted continues in effect.

River Tourism

France boasts the longest network of rivers and canals in Europe, 5,313 miles of them flowing through all regions of the country. Although barging on canals (especially in Burgundy) has been popular with overseas visitors for years, only recently have larger, more comfortable boats been constructed and put into service.

Vessels come in all shapes and sizes today, from floating homes called house boats (even in French, due to their British origin) that accommodate from 2 to 12 people, to excursion boats carrying up to 500 passengers. House boats offer living room, kitchen, cabin berths, showers, and toilets. On some models roofs can be retracted. Some companies list prices per individual berth; generally, fees include the boat, insurance, bed, and gas. Excursion boats, as their name implies, make trips of one or more hours on lakes and rivers throughout France. Sometimes a meal or entertainment is offered, with fares varying appropriately. Details are available at Offices de Tourisme in areas where such boats operate.

More than 30 hotel barges are now operating; luxurious in accommodation, they provide excellent service and gourmet-quality cuisine and wines. Capacity is usually limited to 12 passengers. Among the most reputable, exciting companies providing barge trips are **Abercrombie & Kent** (on the Seine, the Rhône, barging and biking, etc.), **Charterbarge** (both hotel barge and charter barge trips), **EuropAmerica Cruises** (on the Rhône, other European rivers), **European Waterways** (on the Loire, in Burgundy, Bordeaux, the Midi, Nivernais, Alsace, and Lorraine), **French Country Waterways, Ltd.** (Ile de France, Burgundy), and **French Cruise Lines** (on the Seine from Paris to Honfleur and on the Rhône and Saône rivers from Losne to Avignon). Advance reservations are always necessary. Ask a travel agent's assistance in comparing companies, costs, itineraries, et cetera.

Local Time

Paris is one hour east of Greenwich Mean Time, which means by the clock it's one hour ahead of the U.K., six hours

ahead of New York and the non-Maritime east coast of
Canada, and nine hours ahead of California and western
Canada. Sydney, Australia, is ten hours ahead of Paris. Because different countries go on and off it at different times,
for short periods during daylight savings time there will be
an hour's variance in the differentials mentioned above.

Currency

The basic unit is the *franc,* which is divided into 100
centimes; there are banknotes for 50, 100, and 500 francs and
coins of 5, 10, and 20 centimes and ½, 1, 5, 10, and (new in
1992) 20 francs. When travelling in France, check listings at
major banks or in *The International Herald Tribune* and
other newspapers for current exchange rates.

Telephoning

The telephone area code for Paris is 01; for all other places
in France, the area code is incorporated in the first two
digits of the phone number. When phoning Paris from
outside France, omit the zero from the area code. The
international country code for France is 33. Most telephone
booths in France, both in Paris and in the provinces, operate
on the Télécarte system, which may be new to those who
haven't visited France recently. Instead of coins or those past
jetons, you must use *télécartes;* buy them at post offices and
tobacconists' shops (*tabacs*). The cards are sold for 40F and
96F and have a number of bits (units of calls) that are used
up as you telephone. When you insert your card into the
phone slot, the remaining amount of credit is displayed; it
will decrease as you continue the call. When the card is used
up, you just throw it away and buy another. (Don't forget to
take your card when your call is over.)

In the U.S., *télécartes* are sold (for an additional service
fee) through Marketing Challenges International; Tel: (212)
529-8484.

International calling cards issued by major telephone companies make calling home from France (or elsewhere) easier, more efficient, and less costly than in the recent past.
From anywhere in France, for example, you dial as instructed on the back of the calling card and reach an operator in the United States. The charge is applied directly to
your home or office telephone bill. Although some hotels
will add a surcharge to your bill at checkout time, it will be
the equivalent of U.S.$1 or so and always less than the
horrendous charges often levied by overseas hotels in the

past. The foreign language problem is also eliminated. (International calling cards will be issued by your major telephone company upon request.)

Electric Current

Current in France is 220 V, 50 cycles AC. North American– and British-made appliances require electric current converters and adapter plugs.

Business Hours and Holidays

Most banks in France are open from 9:00 A.M. to 4:30 P.M. every day of the week except Saturdays, Sundays, and holidays. Banks usually close at noon the day before a holiday. Although banks may be closed, currency exchanges are open at Charles-de-Gaulle and Orly airports in Paris (from 6:00 or 6:30 A.M. to 11:30 P.M.) and from early morning until at least 9:00 P.M. at the Austerlitz, Est, Lyon, St-Lazare, and Nord railway stations. Crédit Commercial de France at 103, avenue des Champs-Elysées is open daily except Sundays from 8:30 A.M. to 8:00 P.M. (there is some Sunday service in summer), and Union de Banques à Paris at 154, avenue des Champs-Elysées is open on Sundays and holidays from 10:30 A.M. to 6:00 P.M.

Most department stores are open Mondays through Saturdays from 9:30 A.M. to 6:30 P.M., though some are closed on Monday mornings. They are usually open until 9:00 or 10:00 P.M. one or two evenings a week. Smaller shops close between noon and 2:00 P.M. or later.

Fashion boutiques, perfume stores, and the like are open Tuesdays through Saturdays from 10:00 A.M. to noon and from 2:00 P.M. until 6:30 or 7:00 P.M.

Hairdressers close Mondays and are usually open on Saturdays from 9:00 A.M. to 6:00 or 7:00 P.M. Food shops are open Tuesdays through Sundays from 7:00 A.M. until 1:30 P.M. and from 4:30 to 8:00 P.M. (except bakeries, often open from 2:00 to 8:00 P.M.). Food shops may close at noon on Sunday.

The French in general celebrate 12 national holidays: New Year's Day, Easter, Easter Monday, Labor Day (May 1), Ascension Day, May 8 (end of World War II), Whit Monday, Bastille Day (July 14), Assumption Day (August 15), All Saints Day (November 1), Armistice Day 1918 (November 11), and Christmas Day. Alsace also celebrates Good Friday and December 26.

In addition, some businesses in rural areas may close for some of the hundreds of local celebrations.

Credit Cards

Visa, paired with the French *Carte Bleue,* and MasterCard, affiliated with Eurocard, are the most widely accepted international cards in France in establishments small as well as large, rural as well as urban. American Express and Diner's Club are widely accepted in major shops, restaurants, and hotels. Foreign gasoline credit cards are not accepted.

Room Rates

Hotel room rates listed in the chapters below are for double rooms, double occupancy. Rates are *projections* for 1994 and, unless otherwise indicated, do not include meals. As prices are subject to change, always double-check before booking.

In some seasons, some hotels (usually in resort areas) require guests to stay on a half-pension plan (normally, paying a set price that includes breakfast and dinner as well as the room). If your plans include small seaside inns in mid-summer or ski resorts in winter, be sure you know the hotel's policy well in advance of your stay.

France in Chains

Experienced travellers who don't wish to make all hotel reservations in advance can make the going easier by studying the various groupings of accommodations available and then selecting a "chain" that is suitable in terms of cost, comfort, locations, et cetera. Unlike members of international companies, these "chains" are composed of individually owned and operated properties.

Most luxurious and prestigious are the inns of the **Relais & Châteaux**, many occupying castles and manors (there are 411 members in 40 countries; 153 of them are in France). They are also the most expensive. A catalog is available at some bookstores or by sending $10 to Relais & Châteaux, 11 East 44th Street, Suite 707, New York, NY 10017; Tel: (212) 856-0115; Fax: (212) 856-0193.

On the other hand, the nearly 5,000 small and medium-size family-run inns of the **Logis et Auberges de France** provide warm welcomes, regional character, good comfort, and reasonable prices. Most *logis* are in villages of fewer than 5,000 people. The Logis guide, *Country Hotels & Inns of France,* is sold for about $12 in bookstores, from French Government Tourist offices, or from Logis et Auberges de France, 83, avenue d'Italie, 75013 Paris; Tel: 45-84-83-84; Fax: 44-24-08-74.

Newest of these groups is **La Vie de Château**, which plays host in 134 privately owned châteaux in nine countries, 94 of them in France. The association was created in 1990 by Béraud and Diane de Vogüé; M. de Vogüé's parental home, La Verrerie in the Loire Valley, is one of the châteaux. They offer the opportunity for a hospitable holiday in historic and beautiful homes with the owners as hosts. Rates are remarkably reasonable and are guaranteed in dollars at time of booking. The châteaux can be booked year-round together with car-rental (four-night minimum). Write or telephone **B&V Associates**, 140 East 56th Street, Suite 4C, New York, NY 10022; Tel: (800) 438-4748; Fax: (212) 688-9467. In France, Tel: 05-00-57-47 (toll free) or 48-58-42-73; Fax: 48-58-42-09. In the U.K. contact **Abercrombie & Kent**, Sloane Square House, Holbein Place, London SW1W 8NS; Tel: (071) 730-9600; Fax: (071) 730-9376.

For escapists from noise and wanderers of back roads, the 145 members of **Relais du Silence** provide the kind of calm that may make moving on impossible. Send $5 (which will be credited to your account when a reservation is made) for a guide from: Relais du Silence, 2, passage du Guesclin, 75015 Paris; Tel: 45-66-77-77. In the United States Relais du Silence is represented by H. S. and Associates, 160 East 26th Street, Suite 5H, New York, NY 10010; Tel: (800) 927-4765; Fax: (212) 689-5435. In Canada, the secretariat's address is: Relais du Silence, Auberge des Sablons, St-Irenée, Charlevoix, Quebec F0T 1V0; Tel: (418) 452-8116; Fax: (418) 452-3240.

About 150 hotels in France belong to the **Minotel-France Accueil** group. (*Accueil* means "welcome.") A Euro-Voucher is issued upon request, allowing payment before the trip, making all rooms the same price regardless of the hotel's rank. Some are slick and motel-like, others are cozy country inns. Write Minotel-France Accueil, 163, avenue d'Italie, 75013 Paris. Tel and Fax: 45-84-58-00.

From hotels without restaurants to private castles, the 420 members of **Châteaux-Hôtels Indépendants et Hostelleries d'Atmosphère** exude charm and style. They exist in four classes: hotel-restaurant, hotel *sans* restaurant, restaurant only, and private castle. For information, write Châteaux-Hôtels Indépendants, c/o Adrien Cariou, 15, rue Malebranche, 75005 Paris. Most members are former castles and châteaux, abbeys, or manor houses that have been transformed into comfortable hotels.

Château Accueil includes 70 private châteaux that welcome paying guests. They range from secluded manor homes to bona fide castles; table d'hôte dinners are available by reservation. Château Accueil is now represented by D.M.I.

Tours, 14340 Memorial Drive, Suite 117, Houston, TX 77079; Tel: (713) 558-9933 or (800) 553-5090; Fax: (713) 497-6984.

Another worthwhile group is **ILA Château-Hôtels**, which represents high standards in accommodations, service, cuisine, and surroundings. They are represented in the United States and Canada by Robert F. Warner, Inc.; Tel: (800) 888-1199; Fax: (602) 395-1775 or (212) 725-1762.

An old friend takes on a new name and manner in **Best Western Mapotel**. An advantage of Best Westerns is that you may call a toll-free number in Phoenix, Arizona (Tel: 800-528-1234) to make reservations at any member hotel in France. In France, onward reservations may be made by calling a Paris number; Tel: 01-44-87-40-40.

Some 38,000 holiday homes (part of a house or an entire house), usually on farmland or in small villages, belong to the **Fédération de Gîtes de France** group (called French Country Welcome in English). They can be booked in any season for a weekend, a fortnight, or a month. They are rated by the symbols of one, two, or three ears of corn, and all offer simple, clean, unpretentious accommodations at very reasonable prices. The Fédération publishes two books, available by mail-order, that list thousands of bed-and-breakfast type accommodations in France: *French Country Welcome* ($21.95 in the U.S., $26.95 in Canada, £12.95 in the U.K.; prices do not include shipping charges) and *Prestige Bed & Breakfasts in France* ($18.95 in the U.S., $22.95 in Canada, £11.95 in the U.K.). Distributors in the United States, Canada, and England are: **Ulysses Books & Maps**, 3 Roosevelt Terrace #13, Plattsburg, NY 12901, Fax: (514) 843-9448; **Ulysses Travel Bookshop**, 4176 Saint-Denis Street, Montreal, Quebec H2W 2M5, Canada, Tel: (514) 843-9882, ext. 2232, Fax: (514) 843-9448; **Springfield Books, Ltd.**, Norman Road, Denby Dale, Hudders Field HD8 8TH, England, Tel: (0484) 86-49-55, Fax: (0484) 85-54-43.

An excellent book with photographs and descriptions of some of the most attractive country inns is *Guide des Auberges de Campagne et Hôtels de Charme en France,* listing 466 of them and providing maps for locating them in 18 regions of France. Published by Rivages, 106, boulevard St-Germain, 75006 Paris, the book is available in bookstores in France and may be ordered through travel-oriented bookshops in other countries.

For Further Information

The French Government Tourist Office (FGTO) provides North American travellers with information on travel to continental France and the French West Indies. The France On Call number, 1-900-990-0040, may be called from 9:00 A.M. to 7:00 P.M., Mondays through Fridays, for information on cultural and special events, hotels, transportation, restaurants, tour packages, airlines, car rentals, et cetera. Callers will pay 50 cents per minute and will receive additional information by mail. Within France, a new information number also has been created: Tel: 05-20-12-02; there is no fee for its use. Or you may call the French Government Tourist Office itself at 01-49-52-53-54.

FGTO around the world consolidates its various activities under the umbrella of **Maison de la France**. Offices are located in New York City (628 Fifth Avenue, NY 10020; Tel: 212-757-1125); Chicago (645 N. Michigan Avenue, Suite 630, IL 60611-2836; Tel: 312-337-6301); Dallas (2305 Cedar Springs Boulevard, TX 75201; Tel: 214-720-4010); Los Angeles (9454 Wilshire Boulevard, Suite 303, Beverly Hills, CA 90212-2967; Tel: 310-271-4721); Montreal (1981 Avenue McGill College, Suite 490, Quebec H3A 2W9; Tel: 514-288-4264); Toronto (30 St. Patrick Street, Suite 700, Ontario M5T 3A3; Tel: 416-593-6427); London (178 Piccadilly, WIV 0AL; Tel: 071-491-7622); and Sydney (c/o UTA, BNP Building, 12th floor, 12 Castlereigh Street, N.S.W. 2000; Tel: 02-231-5244).

BIBLIOGRAPHY

HENRY ADAMS, *Mont-St-Michel and Chartres* (1905 and 1913). This classic work goes far beyond its titular subjects into the art, philosophy, and culture of the period.

MICHAEL BAIGENT, RICHARD LEIGH, AND HENRY LINCOLN, *Holy Blood, Holy Grail*. This book has been called revolutionary, astonishing, bizarre, speculative, controversial. Whatever you've thought before about the Cathars, the Knights Templar—or Jesus—this will open your eyes and mind.

DEIRDRE BAIR, *Simone de Beauvoir*. Critics have called this a masterful portrait of one of the most admired and yet most controversial writers of the century; feminists in particular will find much to challenge their preconceptions.

SIMONE DE BEAUVOIR, *Adieux: A Farewell to Sartre*. Frank as always, more fair than seems humanly possible, de Beauvoir details her life spent with an infinitely irritating genius.

JAMES BENTLEY, *Alsace*. Here, town by town, sip by sip, anecdote by recipe, is the Alsace the traveller seeks, presented with restrained passion and unrestrained panache.

FERNAND BRAUDEL, *The Identity of France* (two volumes). No less than the geography, the geology, and the style of history itself are the themes that play through this masterpiece on France's *longue durée*.

SAMUEL CHAMBERLAIN, *Bouquet de France*. Whether he's supping in Strasbourg or climbing about Carcassonne, this epicurean is always entertaining.

RICHARD COBB AND COLIN JONES, *Voices of the French Revolution*. One of history's greatest and most fascinating convulsions is described in the words of its supporters, bystanders, and victims. The American influence upon events is interestingly treated; intriguing illustrations.

ELOISE DANTO, *Undiscovered Museums of Paris*. Small, obscure, and delicious museums—75 of them—including such finds as Edith Piaf's home and a museum of counterfeits.

PIERRE DEUX-LINDA DANNENBERG, *Paris Country*. One of the most provocative, paradoxical, even provincial regions of France is the Ile-de-France, examined here in careful prose and gorgeous photography.

NICHOLAS DELBANCO, *Running in Place*. Provençal culture and history evoked in a personal manner by an English Francophile who returns to Provence with his family.

MARSHALL DILL, JR., *Paris in Time*. From the birth of Paris on the Ile de la Cité to its scrubbing at the hands of André Malraux, here is the great city and how it came to be.

LAWRENCE DURRELL, *Caesar's Vast Ghost*. An adopted son of Provence looks at his quirky homeland with love, admiration, and a saving sense of humor.

MODRIS EKSTEINS, *Rites of Spring*. In a sense, the cataclysm that was the Great War began with the Paris premiere of Stravinsky's ballet, *Le Sacre du Printemps* . . . or so argues the author of this curious, fascinating study of the birth of the modern age.

CAROLLY ERICKSON, *To the Scaffold*. Nobody can read this insightful look at Marie Antoinette without sympathy for her terrible life and her bad press, then and now.

DAVID HUGH FARMER, *The Oxford Dictionary of Saints*. Here are the stories of some of history's most interesting people (many of them French) by an English historian, once a monk.

M. F. K. FISHER, *Two Towns in Provence*. Memoirs of Aix-en-Provence and Marseille by this great food writer are as spicy and delicious as *ratatouille*.

————, *Long Ago in France*. In 1929 M. F. K. Fisher moved to Dijon as a young bride. Intoxicated by the tastes, sounds, sights, and smells, the master of the moment captured holds forth.

NOEL RILEY FITCH, *Sylvia Beach and the Lost Generation*. Literary Paris of the 1920s and 1930s gathered at the book club of Shakespeare and Company. Here's what they did, said, and thought: James Joyce, F. Scott Fitzgerald, et al.

JANET FLANNER (GENÊT), *Paris Journal 1944–1971* (two volumes). No single writer has ever brought Paris's politics, art, and enchantment to life as did Genêt in her columns for *The New Yorker,* excerpted here.

————, *Paris Was Yesterday*. Selected from the journalist's *Letter from Paris* articles in *The New Yorker,* these well-chosen pieces bring to life the people and passions of Paris, from 1925 and the adored Josephine Baker to the *gaieté Parisienne* that preceded World War II.

FORD MADOX FORD, *Provence*. This is less a story of Provence than an evocation of it, a love letter to it; it is a literary *bouillabaisse*.

HUGH FORD, *Published in Paris*. The Lost Generation of American and British writers, printers, and publishers paints the glory years in Paris from 1920 to 1939.

OTTO FRIEDRICH, *Olympia: Paris in the Age of Manet*. This book takes an era—that of the Impressionists, the Third Republic, Baron Haussmann's reconstruction of the city—shakes it, and hands it to the reader entire.

MAVIS GALLANT, *Overhead in a Balloon*. The nuances of life in Paris are revealed in these 12 short stories characterized by finely textured prose.

HELEN GARDNER, *Art Through the Ages*. Published first in 1926, this is the amateur's best introduction to the arts, from cave paintings to Picasso.

FRANCES GIES, *Joan of Arc*. You thought you knew Joan of Arc; have you met Joan of Arc? Here, in a most unusually structured history, Gies makes the real Joan stand up.

————, *The Knight in History*. For six centuries the medieval knight dominated the battlefields and stirred the imagination of the Western world. Here are the Crusaders, the Knights Templar, and individual heroes such as the Breton Bertrand du Guesclin, who changed the world that came after him.

FRANCES AND JOSEPH GIES, *Marriage and the Family in the Middle Ages*. A rewarding turn away from heroes and kings to daily life: What was the family, and how did it bring us to today?

ANTHONY GLYN, *The Seine*. Glyn is the best companion you could want on an amble: easygoing, anecdotal, curious, and thoughtful.

PIERRE GOUBERT, *The Course of French History*. Here's what you've been looking for for decades: the first general, readable, one-volume history of France available in English. It begins with the crowning of Hugues Capet in July 987 and ends with the uneasy *cohabitation* of Jacques Chirac and François Mitterrand in 1986.

MARY ELLEN JORDAN HAIGHT, *Walks in Gertrude Stein's Paris*. The traveller can make five treks, this book in hand, through the years 1900 to 1940 as they were lived on Paris's Left Bank.

————, *Paris Portraits, Renoir to Chanel*. Haight takes strollers on eight walks on the chic side, the fashionable Right Bank of painters, actors, and haute couture.

ERNEST HEMINGWAY, *A Moveable Feast*. Here is the Paris for which the world is nostalgic, the days of wine and cafés.

DENIS HOLLIER (ED.), *A New History of French Literature*. Designed for the general reader, this is an extraordinary collection of essays covering the period A.D. 842 to 1985 by 164 American and European specialists.

JAMES A. HUSTON, *Across the Face of France*. The liberation and recovery of post–World War II France as seen by an American who served there.

PHILIP AND MARY HYMAN AND ROSEMARY GEORGE, *Webster's Wine Tours of France*. Georges Bertrand is one of the talented new winemakers of Corbières, and Aloxe-Corton may be visited daily. This book is as helpful as a *tire-bouchon*.

MICHAEL JACOBS AND PAUL STIRTON, *The Knopf Traveler's Guides to Art*. The volume on France is an essential handbook for the traveller who doesn't want to miss a Gérôme in Vesoul or the tomb of a duke in Dreux.

HENRY JAMES, *A Little Tour in France*. The beautifully reissued "impressions" of the master, written in 1900, will amuse, delight, and sometimes irritate today's Francophile. They don't write books like this any more.

JOHN JAMES, *The Traveler's Key to Medieval France*. This guide and introduction to sacred architecture will be invaluable to anyone who knows that once you've seen one church you haven't seen 'em all.

AMY KELLY, *Eleanor of Aquitaine and the Four Kings*. Beautifully written, endlessly fascinating, this book is more difficult to put down than any murder mystery. The family that created half of 20th-century France still lives.

JEAN LACOUTURE, *De Gaulle, The Rebel 1890–1944, The Ruler, 1945–1970* (two volumes). The difficult genius, the statesman with a poet's love of language, the public hero, and the private visionary are examined in this bold example of contemporary biography.

EMMANUEL LE ROY LADURIE, *Montaillou, the Promised Land of Error*. Peasants who lived more than 600 years ago live once again in the days of the Albigensian heresies; ethnography at its best.

ALEXIS LICHINE, *New Encyclopedia of Wines and Spirits*. This is the classic compendium for the discerning drinker.

A. J. LIEBLING. *Between Meals, An Appetite for Paris*. You may read this humorous tale at one sitting, sometimes laughing aloud; the author does nothing if not whet your appetite for more.

STANLEY LOOMIS, *Paris in the Terror*. A strikingly vivid—read gory—account of Revolutionary zeal gone wild.

H. R. LOYN (ED.), *The Middle Ages*. This is a concise and basic encyclopedia to the people, the institutions, and the pursuits of all medieval Europe, in which France played an enormous part.

PETER MAYLE, *A Year in Provence*. An Englishman's witty memoirs of life on the slopes of the lovely Mount Luberon.

———, *Toujours Provence*. The continuing adventures of the Mayles, their dog Boy, and their neighbors.

W. S. MERWIN, *The Lost Upland*. There's history in every rock in the *causse perdu,* or lost upland of southwestern France, and it is beautifully evoked in these slice-of-life narratives.

TED MORGAN, *An Uncertain Hour*. The disillusion and moral drift of the Vichy government, the Resistance, the persecution and deportation of Jews, and the Klaus Barbie trial will sadden most readers and intrigue them all.

BRIAN N. MORTON, *Americans in Paris*. Where did Henry Adams live and write? Where did Isadora Duncan dance in the gardens? Where did Elsa Maxwell entertain? See Paris in the company of dozens of Americans, from Louis Armstrong to Andrew Carnegie.

FRANCES MOSSIKER, *Madame de Sévigné*. No letter-writer has surpassed Madame de Sévigné's style or substance. Mossiker catches her in full literary flight.

JAMES POPE-HENNESSY, *Aspects of Provence*. A wanderer in the great tradition, educated and urbane, takes us by the hand from Lady Blessington's Nîmes to Merimée's St-Maximin.

DOUGLAS PORCH, *The French Foreign Legion*. All you always wanted to know about the world's most famous and romantic fighting force is here, from its creation by Louis-Philippe in 1831 to its participation in the Gulf War and Bastille Day parades in the 1990s.

JOHN REWALD, *The History of Impressionism*. Specialists will admire and amateurs enjoy this source book on almost everybody's favorite painters. His *History of Post-Impressionism* is of equal interest.

WAVERLEY ROOT, *The Food of France*. The late, great writer-gourmet at his hungry best.

———, *The Paris Edition*. In 1927 the young reporter sailed for Paris and stayed 13 years; this is his memoir of the years 1927 to 1934, filled with good friends, better wines, and all the nasty romance of work on a daily newspaper.

MORT ROSENBLUM, *Mission to Civilize*. The French, they are a funny race; a senior foreign correspondent watches them ticking and tells us how they do it.

JOHN RUSSELL, *Paris*. The erudite art critic for *The New York Times* chooses Dufy, Cartier-Bresson, et al. to help him create the most beautiful and provocative coffee-table book on the world's handsomest city.

GILES ST. AUBYN, *The Year of Three Kings, 1483*. During the dramatic year of 1483, three kings ruled over England—Edward IV, Edward V, and Richard III. Here is the intriguing blood feud of the Wars of the Roses, seen from across the Channel.

SIMON SCHAMA, *Citizens: A Chronicle of the French Revolution*. In a revolutionary look at the French Revolution, the author returns to life the men and women who created the movements that forever altered a continent's—and the world's—history. Studded with humor and anecdotes, this thick volume is almost too fascinating to put down.

KATHERINE SCHERMAN, *The Birth of France*. At once beautifully written, learned, and humorous, this book belongs in the library of everyone who cares about France.

JERROLD SEIGEL, *Bohemian Paris: Culture, Politics, and the Boundaries of Bourgeois Life, 1830–1930*. All the players are here—Verlaine, Baudelaire, Jarry, Satie, Apollinaire, Breton, and others—in this fascinating study of how the famous Bohemia of Paris came to be.

DESMOND SEWARD, *The Hundred Years War*. The endless, spaghettilike tangles and twists of the French-English inheritance struggles from 1337 to 1453 are described in all their fascinating and intricate detail by a precise historian and excellent writer.

———, *Prince of the Renaissance*. No one who meets François I in these pages will ever look at the Loire's great châteaux in the same way again. Here in his finest moments and with flaws revealed lives the man who had more effect on France than any leader since Charlemagne.

———, *Napoléon's Family*. The gossipmongering, backbiting, insatiably amorous Bonaparte clan portrayed in all their ambitious bitterness.

ANDRE L. SIMON (ED.), *Wines of the World*. As readable as it is authoritative, this volume belongs on every imbiber's bookshelf.

OTTO VON SIMSON, *The Gothic Cathedral: Origins of Gothic Architecture and the Medieval Concept of Order* (1956, 1962; many times reprinted). A highly regarded study that is ranked in its evocative power on a par with Henry Adams's *Mont-Saint-Michel and Chartres*. Especially rewarding on the subject of Paris's St-Denis.

FRANCIS STEEGMULLER, *A Woman, a Man, and Two Kingdoms*. The story of a friendship between Madame Louise d'Epinay, a lovely and intelligent Parisienne bluestocking, and Ferdinando Galiani, the priest-diplomat who represented the kingdom of Naples in Paris, opens the window upon the Enlightenment.

BARBARA TUCHMAN, *A Distant Mirror*. Here is the 14th century in all its glittering accomplishments and dreadful agonies; indispensable to an understanding of how modern France came to be.

PATRICIA WELLS, *The Food Lover's Guide to France*. Where to buy olive oil in a working mill, where to bite a *baguette* in Aix: It's all here. There's more of the mouth-watering same in the *Food Lover's Guide to Paris* and *Bistro Cooking,* a collection of recipes.

ANNE WILLAN, *La France Gastronomique*. The founder of La Varenne, the great culinary institute in Paris, takes us by the hand into a rich store of recipes and landscapes.

BRENDA WINEAPPLE, *Genêt*. A wonderful biography of Janet Flanner, who, under her pen name, Genêt, entertained readers of *The New Yorker* for more than half a century describing the culture, the politics, the scandals, and the sensations of life in Paris with incomparable style and perception.

THEODORE ZELDIN, *The French*. A witty writer spies on everyone from the late Yves Montand to François Mitterrand and tells how to deal with them.

PARIS

By Stephen O'Shea

Stephen O'Shea, a writer and journalist who lived in Paris for many years, has written for British, American, Canadian, and French magazines on many aspects of Parisian and French life.

Paris has captivated the Western imagination for so long that even people who have never visited the city sometimes feel nostalgia for it. The mere mention of its river, the Seine, summons up thoughts of beauty, youthful heartbreak, and the creative dissipation that has lured foreigners to the city since medieval times. With its superb restaurants, its districts devoted to high fashion, and its relentlessly romantic vistas, Paris is known throughout the world as Europe's pleasure dome. It is also a city marked by a turbulent past, its rich intellectual, artistic, and religious heritage surviving in museums, galleries, landmarks, churches, and the way Parisians speak and act in everyday life.

The modern metropolis has kept alive one Parisian tradition above all others—the city and its inhabitants remain fascinated by novelty. Anyone travelling to France, whether for the first or the fifteenth time, must have an exceptional excuse not to want to go to its capital.

MAJOR INTEREST

Sights
Notre-Dame, Sainte-Chapelle, Champs-Elysées, Eiffel
    Tower, Hôtel des Invalides

Neighborhoods
Bastille, Latin Quarter/St-Germain, Marais, Opéra–
    Palais Royal

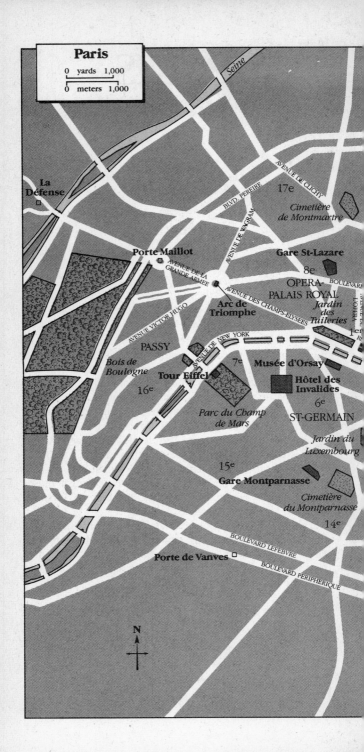

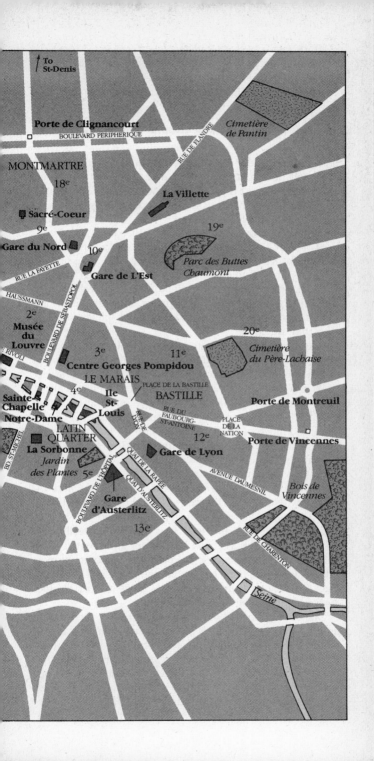

To
St-Denis

Porte de Clignancourt
BOULEVARD PERIPHERIQUE

Cimetière de Pantin

MONTMARTRE

18e

RUE DE FLANDRE

La Villette

📍**Sacré-Coeur**

9e

19e

Gare du Nord

RUE LA FAYETTE

10e

Parc des Buttes Chaumont

Gare de L'Est

HAUSSMANN

BOULEVARD DE SEBASTOPOL

2e

Musée du Louvre

RIVOLI

3e

11e

20e

Cimetière du Père-Lachaise

Centre Georges Pompidou

LE MARAIS

PLACE DE LA BASTILLE

4e

Ile St-Louis

BASTILLE

Porte de Montreuil

Sainte-Chapelle
Notre-Dame

RUE DU FAUBOURG-ST-ANTOINE

RUE DE LYON

PLACE DE LA NATION

Porte de Vincennes

BD. ST-MICHEL

LATIN QUARTER

12e

La Sorbonne

Jardin des Plantes

Gare de Lyon

QUAI DE LA RAPEE

5e

AVENUE DAUMESNIL

Bois de Vincennes

BOULEVARD DE L'HÔPITAL

QUAI D'AUSTERLITZ

Gare d'Austerlitz

RUE DE CHARENTON

13e

Seine

Museums
The Big Three: Louvre, Orsay, Pompidou
Noteworthy: Cluny, Picasso, Rodin, Marmottan

Parks
Bois de Boulogne, Luxembourg, Tuileries

It is best to consider Paris as a performance. Certain districts of the city hold center stage for a time, then step back to let other neighborhoods reappear in the spotlight. The changing nature of this show is a source of both pride and distress to lovers of Paris, fueling countless café-counter arguments and public controversies. A familiar Parisian boast is that one lives or works in a *quartier qui monte,* that is, an area where positive, usually trendy, change is taking place. In present-day Paris, the Bastille district is undergoing such change. Those opposed to the trend point to dubious developments (the underground Les Halles complex, for example) as an indication that their contemporaries have absolutely no idea what they are doing.

Over the centuries a literary cottage industry has sprung up, with distinguished authors bemoaning the imminent destruction of the city's soul. Victor Hugo, in *Les Misérables,* went into loving detail about the warren of medieval alleyways eliminated by the cutting of the boulevards in the middle of the 19th century. However, much of Paris's later fame, and much of its charm, is associated with these broad thoroughfares. In the same way, the Eiffel Tower was almost universally loathed by the literary upon its opening a hundred years ago. Guy de Maupassant said he enjoyed the view from the top of the tower because it was the only place in the city where he wasn't forced to look at the damned thing. Still, successive generations of artists came to use it as a symbol of the city, and it is now almost impossible to imagine Paris without its iron mast. At any given period of its history, Paris has been described as a shadow of its former self or as a disfigured beauty, yet the show still goes on, changing for each generation and, as befits its quarrelsome audience, provoking heated disagreements.

One of the principal reasons Parisians harbor such strong emotions about their city is the accessible, human scale on which it is built. Unlike greater London, which sprawls across miles of the Thames Valley, or even Manhattan, stretching out in a seemingly endless procession of linear neighborhoods, Paris is compact and easy to understand. The Seine, too, is not so much a physical barrier, like the Thames or the East River, as it is a beautiful boulevard for barge traffic. The metropolitan area, with its population of 11 million, may be gigantic, but central Paris, its 20 *arrondissements* (districts) spiraling out from the Louvre district, can easily be crossed on foot in an afternoon.

Even more coherent is the city's growth. From an island settlement of Gauls huddled together in the midst of a watery plain to a 19th-century capital incorporating the hills that hem in the lowlands created by the Seine, Paris has grown outward in ever-widening rings. Roman Lutetia spilled over onto the Left Bank; the 12th-century battlements of Philippe Auguste (King Philip Augustus II) encompassed a bustling town extending from the drained marshes of the Right Bank to the monastery vineyards of the Left; and Louis XVI's Farmers-General Wall, a source of pre-Revolutionary irritation, formed a circuit of customshouses concentric to the present-day perimeter. The city's pie-shape would have a geometric elegance pleasing to all Cartesians, except that the crescent formed by the Seine bisects the circle so unequally that the true focal point of the city lies a little off center, like the human heart. After all, this is Paris.

The Islands

ILE DE LA CITE

The birthplace of the city and the symbolic center of the nation, this small island in the Seine was first settled by the Parisii Gauls in the third century B.C. Long a miniature of French society, with the three Estates of clergy, nobility, and commoners crowded together, the Cité is now inhabited more by presences than by people. It is a place where the legendary and fictional have as great a right to exist—in French, *droit de cité*—as do the historical and factual. In the mind of the modern visitor, Quasimodo and Esmeralda loom larger than Abélard and Héloïse (who lived and loved at 9, quai aux Fleurs) as characters of medieval Paris, and even Inspector Maigret, calmly puffing a pipe in his office at 24, quai des Orfèvres, seems far more believable than the fantastic relics once housed in the Sainte-Chapelle. Romans, Norse, Knights Templar, and Jacobin revolutionaries have all passed this way, remembered not so much in stone as in the imaginative works they have inspired.

There are, however, two other forces that have left a lasting mark on the island. Church and State, wary partners throughout French history, have had dramatic clashes here. On the present-day Cité the standoff between the two is far more benign than it was in the past, but it remains striking

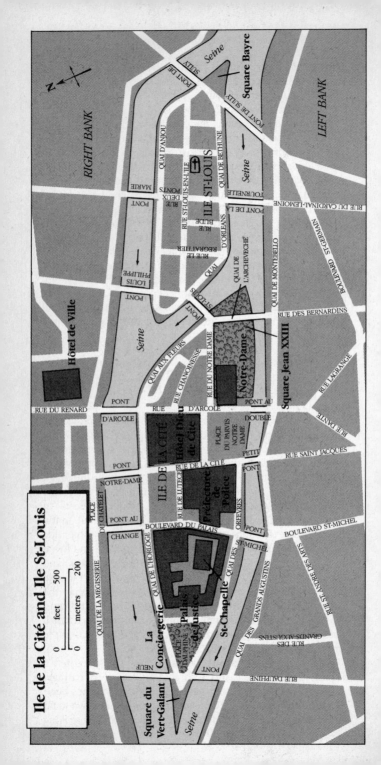

Ile de la Cité and Ile St-Louis

| 0 | feet | 500 |
| 0 | meters | 200 |

RIGHT BANK

LEFT BANK

Seine

Square Bayre

PONT DE SULLY

QUAI D'ANJOU

QUAI DE BETHUNE

PONT DE SULLY

ILE ST-LOUIS

RUE ST-LOUIS-EN-L'ILE

PONTS DEUX

RUE BUDE

RUE LE REGNATIER

RUE ST-LOUIS

QUAI D'ORLEANS

QUAI DE LA TOURNELLE

PONT DE LA TOURNELLE

RUE DU CARDINAL-LEMOINE

PONT MARIE

PONT LOUIS PHILIPPE

QUAI DE BETHUNE

QUAI DE L'ARCHEVECHE

QUAI DE MONTEBELLO

BOULEVARD ST-GERMAIN

Hôtel de Ville

Seine

QUAI AUX FLEURS

RUE CHANOINESSE

RUE DU NOTRE DAME

Notre-Dame

RUE DES BERNARDINS

Square Jean XXIII

RUE DE LA CITÉ

RUE DES

RUE LAGRANGE

RUE DU RENARD

PONT D'ARCOLE

RUE D'ARCOLE

Hôtel Dieu de Cité

ILE DE LA CITÉ

RUE DE LUTECE

PLACE DU PARVIS NOTRE DAME

PONT AU DOUBLE

PETIT PONT

RUE DANTE

PONT D'ARCOLE

PONT NOTRE-DAME

PLACE DU CHÂTELET

QUAI DE LA MÉGISSERIE

PONT AU CHANGE

BOULEVARD DU PALAIS

QUAI DE L'HORLOGE

Prefecture de Police

RUE SAINT JACQUES

ORFEVRES

PONT ST-MICHEL

BOULEVARD ST-MICHEL

Palais de Justice

La Conciergerie

St-Chapelle

QUAI DES GRANDS AUGUSTINS

PLACE DAUPHINE

RUE DES GRANDS-AUGUSTINS

RUE ST ANDRE DES ARTS

PONT NEUF

PONT DAUPHINE

Square du Vert-Galant

RUE DAUPHINE

Seine

nonetheless. Notre-Dame cathedral squares off opposite the sprawling central police station, and the Sainte-Chapelle is dwarfed by a 19th-century courthouse. The Conciergerie, a vestige of the residence of medieval kings, is less a symbol of State power than of its destructiveness: It was used as a prison during the Reign of Terror.

The colorful history of Church–State jostling on the island stretches as far back as Roman times. For more than four centuries the Ile de la Cité was the administrative and spiritual center of the bustling Roman provincial town of Lutetia. Foundations of houses from this period and the street plan of an ancient neighborhood are on view in an artfully designed archaeological crypt beneath the square in front of Notre-Dame. Fittingly, the Roman governor most closely associated with his "dear Lutetia" was Julian the Apostate, a troublemaker in both spiritual and temporal domains. As emperor from 361 to 363, Julian overthrew the Christian orthodoxy imposed on the empire by his uncle, Constantine the Great. When, from his balcony at the Prefect of Gaul's residence on the island, the 29-year-old devotee of the old gods first heard his legions acclaim him sole Augustus of the Roman world, the Cité's long tradition of rivalry between the sacred and the profane was born.

Certain events springing from this rivalry are the stuff of legend. On the western tip of the island, the **Square du Vert-Galant** (now a favorite spot for lovers), Philippe le Bel (King Philip the Fair) brutally put an end to the crusading confraternity of Knights Templar on March 11, 1314, by first torturing its leaders, then burning them at the stake. Legend has it that Grand Master Jacques de Molay, before being consumed by the flames, invoked God to visit a curse on the malevolent king's family. Within a generation the monarch and all his legitimate issue had met violent ends as France and England plunged into the Hundred Years War.

Above this park, on the **Pont Neuf**, stands an equestrian statue of Henri IV, the king whose wedding celebrations were marred by the massacre of his fellow Huguenots and whose reign was marked by an uneasy truce between prelates and certain factions within the nobility. When for dynastic reasons Henri consented to convert to Catholicism (thereby ensuring the continuation of the royal Bourbon line he began), the famous impiety "Paris is worth a Mass" became the catchphrase to describe the depth of his religious conviction. The king was later murdered by François Ravaillac, an ardent Catholic who did not share his cavalier attitude toward the faith. It is fitting that Henri's statue stands on the western, "secular" part of the island.

In 1804 an even more celebrated instance of clerical nose-tweaking occurred on the island, this time at the making of a modern emperor. In the midst of his solemn coronation ceremony at Notre-Dame, Napoléon snatched the crown out of the hands of Pope Pius VII and placed it on his own modest head. So that none of the assembled notables in the devastated church would miss the point about where true legitimacy and power lay, he then crowned Joséphine de Beauharnais his empress. Jacques-Louis David's vivid rendering of the event now hangs in the Louvre.

Sainte-Chapelle

Still, the two great works of religious architecture adorning the Cité attest to periods when Church and State coexisted peacefully. During the long reign of the pious King Louis IX (later canonized as Saint Louis) in the 13th century, a nascent style of architecture, only later stigmatized as "Gothic"—thus, barbarian—by its Renaissance detractors, came to maturity in the Ile-de-France under the supervision of such master builders as Pierre de Montreuil. In 1246 Louis called on Montreuil to build a reliquary worthy of the objects he had obtained from the Holy Lands. A partial inventory: the Crown of Thorns, a piece of the True Cross, a vial of the Virgin's milk, and Jesus Christ's swaddling clothes. Montreuil's construction, the Sainte-Chapelle, erected in 33 months of frantic activity, more than matched the extravagance of the monarch's faith. Even at a remove of seven centuries the chapel inspires awe, with its upper sanctuary seeming to be built entirely of brilliant stained glass. When the sun strikes the building in the late afternoon, especially in the spring and autumn, visitors studying the biblical scenes depicted in the 13th-century windows of this sanctuary will get the distinct impression that they are standing inside a large jewel. The light suffusing the upper chapel at this time of day has not grown any dimmer since the distant age of belief it first illuminated.

Cathédrale Notre-Dame

A more comprehensive example of the spirit of the age is Notre-Dame. Begun in 1163 and not completed until 170 years later, the cathedral is the collective work of generations of architects and craftsmen. At the time of its construction, the symbols of the power and the glory of the Church were being transferred from isolated monasteries in the countryside to the burgeoning cities and towns. Slowly, Romanesque architecture—with its massive pillars, rounded arches, and thick, almost windowless walls that suggested a

fortress Church standing alone against a hostile world—
gave way to the graceful lancets of the Gothic, with innovative flying buttresses strengthening walls that could now be
pierced by huge stained glass tableaux. As naves soared
higher, and such embellishments as statuary and rose windows became ever more accomplished, the great cathedrals
came to serve as spectacular illustrations of the teachings
and ultimate message of the medieval Church. The populace
was both edified and awed by these sanctuaries, learning the
lives of the saints and martyrs from the portals and windows
as their eyes were inexorably drawn heavenward by the
lines of these buildings. The large square cleared in front of
Notre-Dame during the 19th century is an anachronism: The
cathedral's façade was designed to be viewed at close quarters, its balanced composition sweeping the eye up the bell
towers and beyond.

However solemn and instructive its purpose, Notre-Dame
was never a museum. The church served as a refuge from
civil authority in medieval times, sheltering criminals and
vagrants from the law. Markets were set up inside it and
messy everyday life went on beneath the towering vault.
Hence, the Notre-Dame of today, constantly filled with hundreds of people raising dust as they walk and talk their way
around the ambulatory, is not so much a victim of mass
tourism as its beneficiary, marked by the very human informality that reigned within it during the Middle Ages. The
Sunday evening organ recital, jammed with listeners, chatter-
ers, and worshipers, is a particularly good time to visit the
church. So too is the *heure bleue,* when the morning sun
strikes the north rose window and fills the transept with an
otherworldly blue.

A commanding view of Paris is the reward for those hardy
enough to climb the 387 steps of the north tower of Notre-
Dame. The famous gargoyles perched over the void (some of
them 19th-century confections of Eugène Viollet-le-Duc, the
architect who restored the church) look as if they can, indeed,
frighten away demons. Viollet-le-Duc's renovation project
was made possible after Victor Hugo's *Hunchback of Notre-
Dame* had raised public awareness of the cathedral's perilous
state of dilapidation. The Revolution had taken its toll: Most of
the statuary was destroyed, including the façade's 28 kings of
Judah, mistakenly thought to be the kings of France; much of
the glasswork was smashed; the old bells, excluding the 17th-
century Emmanuelle, which still sounds today, were melted
down; and the Goddess of Reason cult, which put a pretty
ballerina atop a pile of dirt in the transept, caused extensive
structural damage. In fact, it was only the cathedral's transfor-

mation into a wine warehouse for military hospitals during
the last phase of the Revolution that prevented it from being
demolished altogether.

The Conciergerie

The spirit of Revolutionary excess is far more palpable at the
Conciergerie. Although the building dates from the 14th
century (as does its remarkable outdoor clock), Parisians
usually associate it with the early 1790s, when it held nobles
and revolutionaries who had fallen from favor. Visitors can
see the cells of Marie Antoinette, Danton, and Robespierre,
as well as the courtyard where women and men prisoners
were momentarily reunited before being led away to their
deaths. A raised corridor at one end of the great Gothic
room is known as the "rue de Paris," a reference to Monsieur de Paris, the name given to the city's executioner. From
this vantage point the beauty of the large hall can be best
appreciated—even if its historical associations are somewhat sinister. The medieval kitchens, with their colossal
hearths for roasting animals on spits, recall the earlier, more
festive days of the Conciergerie.

Place Dauphine

Toward the western end of the Cité lies its most picturesque
residential district, the Place Dauphine. A triangular oasis of
greenery, the spot is known throughout the city for its quiet
charm. The houses lining two of the triangle's sides are a
study in differing styles of architecture. Surrealist André
Breton extravagantly proclaimed the square the "sex of
Paris," which may be why Henri IV, the monarch famous for
his dalliances, seems to be riding expectantly toward Place
Dauphine from his place of glory atop the Pont Neuf.

ILE ST-LOUIS

After the surfeit of history on the neighboring island, it is a
relief to visit Ile St-Louis, a fairly recent creation in a city as
old as Paris. Developed by land speculators and parvenus of
the 17th century, the island is characterized by houses that
have what is called *du ventre,* the bellylike sag of old
constructions. A provincial calm reigns on this small island,
which is best viewed at dawn, when the different shades of
gray (bridges, houses, and river) make it particularly beautiful. A walk around the island on the quais alongside the
Seine is a romantic experience—and useful, if you are
planning to sleep under a bridge. Of the six bridges leading
from the Ile St-Louis, the most remarkable is the **Pont Marie**,
with its elegant stone arches all of a different size.

Now a playground for weekenders in search of mellow but modern restaurants and shops, Ile St-Louis has always been outside the mainstream of Paris life. As its rich occupants left for more spacious accommodations elsewhere in the city, the island became a haven for artists. Its most famous resident was Charles Baudelaire, who used to frequent the Hôtel de Lauzun, where members of the Club des Haschischins ingested hashish in suitably exotic surroundings. Today things are considerably tamer, the consumption of Berthillon ice cream being the islanders' principal sensual indulgence. The resident creative community is consequently less lean than it was during the island's bohemian heyday, with such patrons of the arts as the Rothschilds and the widow of President Georges Pompidou now living in the quaint neighborhood. The best reminder of the island's good old days of poetic self-destructiveness lies across the Pont de Sully on the Right Bank. At the first intersection there is a statue of Arthur Rimbaud in what can only be called a hallucinatory pose. His head and shoulders are dreamily separated from the rest of his body.

The Left Bank

THE LATIN QUARTER

For a long time simply called the Université (the other two districts of Paris were Cité, being the island, and Ville, being the Right Bank), the Latin Quarter embraces the area from Place Maubert in the east to the Odéon in the west, with the Montagne Ste-Geneviève as its southern boundary. Immediately opposite the south flank of Notre-Dame is the **Maubert quarter**, a maze of old streets dotted with restaurants and exotic food shops. Once famed for the rats that infested the tanneries lining the medieval confluence of the Seine and Bièvre (today an underground stream), the area is now the last word in left-wing gentility, housing successful academics, psychoanalysts, and politicians. The uniformed policemen on the narrow rue de Bièvre guard the house of the most successful of them all, François Mitterrand.

Of particular interest to lovers of Gothic architecture is the riverside Square René Viviani. From this tranquil park the south flank of Notre-Dame can be seen in all its gracefully buttressed glory. Directly south of the park stands yet another medieval gem, the tiny church of **St-Julien-le-Pauvre**. One of the first sanctuaries in the Ile-de-France region to have deserted Romanesque for Gothic, it has, since 1889, veered farther to the east in its vocation: St-Julien is the sole church in

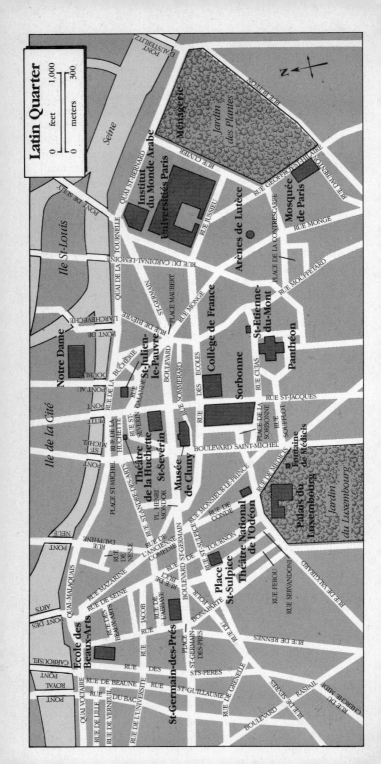

Latin Quarter

feet 1,000
0

meters 300
0

N

Seine

PONT D'AUSTERLITZ

PONT DE SULLY

Ile St-Louis

Ménagerie

Jardin des Plantes

RUE BUFFON

RUE CUVIER

Institut du Monde Arabe

Universités Paris

QUAI ST-BERNARD

RUE GEOFFROY-ST-HILAIRE

Mosquée de Paris

RUE JUSSIEU

RUE MONGE

Arènes de Lutèce

RUE DAUBENTON

QUAI DE LA TOURNELLE

RUE DU CARDINAL-LEMOINE

PLACE DE LA CONTRESCARPE

PONT DE L'ARCHEVÊCHÉ

PLACE MAUBERT

RUE ST-GERMAIN

RUE MONGE

PLACE DE LA CONTRESCARPE

Notre Dame

RUE DE BIÈVRE

RUE MOUFFETARD

PONT DE LA TOURNELLE

St-Julien-le-Pauvre

BOULEVARD

Collège de France

St-Étienne-du-Mont

RUE DE LA BÛCHERIE

RUE GALANDE-DES-ARTS

RUE DE SOMMERARD

RUE DES ÉCOLES

RUE CUJAS

Panthéon

PONT AU DOUBLE

RUE ST-SÉVERIN

Sorbonne

RUE ST-JACQUES

Théâtre de la Huchette

RUE DE LA HUCHETTE

St-Séverin

RUE ST-JACQUES

PONT ST-MICHEL

PLACE ST-MICHEL

Musée de Cluny

BOULEVARD SAINT-MICHEL

PLACE DE LA SORBONNE

RUE SOUFFLOT

Ile de la Cité

PLACE ST-ANDRÉ-DES-ARTS

PL. HENRI MONDOR

RUE DE MÉDICIS

Fontaine de Médicis

PONT NEUF

RUE DAUPHINE

RUE DE NESLE

RUE DE L'ANCIENNE COMÉDIE

RUE DE CONDÉ

RUE MONSIEUR-LE-PRINCE

Théâtre National de l'Odéon

Palais du Luxembourg

Jardin du Luxembourg

PONT DES ARTS

QUAI MALAQUAIS

RUE MAZARINE

RUE DE SEINE

RUE DES BEAUX-ARTS

RUE DE TOURNON

RUE ST-SULPICE

RUE FÉROU

RUE DE VAUGIRARD

Place St-Sulpice

École des Beaux-Arts

PONT DU CARROUSEL

PONT ROYAL

QUAI VOLTAIRE

RUE DE LILLE

RUE DE VERNEUIL

RUE DE L'UNIVERSITÉ

RUE JACOB

RUE DE L'ABBAYE

RUE BONAPARTE

RUE DE BUCI

BOULEVARD ST-GERMAIN

PLACE ST-GERMAIN-DES-PRÉS

St-Germain-des-Prés

RUE DU FOUR

RUE DE SERVANDONI

RUE DE SÈVRES

RASPAIL

PONT

RUE DE BEAUNE

DU BAC

RUE DE BEAUNE

RUE DES STS-PÈRES

ST-GUILLAUME

RUE DE GRENELLE

BOULEVARD

RUE DE RENNES

RUE DU CHERCHE-MIDI

Paris where the mass of Saint John Chrysostom, a Byzantine patriarch, is celebrated for Greek Catholics.

St-Séverin Quarter

Farther downstream, across the old Roman road to Orléans, now called the rue St-Jacques, is another late-medieval quarter that survived the great boulevard-building of the 19th century. Unlike its neighbor, the St-Séverin quarter has nothing genteel about it. It is the area of Paris that counts the most bouzouki players per square foot, and its tiny streets are crammed with Greek restaurants and take-out counters. Before deploring the current commercial state of the neighborhood, detractors should consult historian Robert Darnton's *Great Cat Massacre,* a study of the mock trial and execution of the area's cats that took place on the rue St-Séverin in the 1730s. It gives a fair idea of the grotesque entertainments enjoyed by the scribes, printers, and clerics who used to live and work in these streets. Fittingly, this peculiar neighborhood houses the minuscule theater (**Théâtre de la Huchette**) where nightly performances are given of Paris's longest-running show, two very absurd plays by Eugene Ionesco: *La Cantatrice Chauve* (*The Bald Soprano*) and *La Leçon* (*The Lesson*).

Despite the recent commercialization of the area, the St-Séverin quarter and the slightly more pleasant **St-André district**, on the other side of the busy Place St-Michel, are still associated with eight centuries of student life. Even now, three decades after Paris's universities were dispersed throughout the city, this part of the Latin Quarter remains the symbolic home of student pranks—the hapless stroller or motorist who ventures into the area on Mardi Gras will be pelted with eggs and flour. This offense, however annoying, pales in comparison with the duels, cuckolding, and bawdy singing that once were standard behavior in the district. As early as the 12th century students from the numerous religious colleges on the Cité found respite from their taskmasters in the alehouses of the area. Irreverence was the order of the day, with the inspirational choral singing known as the Ecole Notre-Dame finding its counterpoint in the licentious parodies belted out in Latin Quarter taverns. The best known of these is the collection called *Carmina Burana*. As Latin was the language of instruction and discourse in this quarter (hence its name), students of all nations were in on the earthy pleasantries. A good place to sit down and exchange quodlibets with your travelling companion is the **Café Cluny**, on the busy corner of boulevards St-Michel and St-Germain.

Often tradition was flouted because it impeded knowledge. In Ian Littlewood's anecdotal *Paris: A Literary Companion,* a medieval observer reports stumbling across a group of body snatchers at the St-Séverin cemetery—medical students, one hopes—intent on circumventing the Church's ban on the dissection of cadavers. Such applied skepticism has always been the hallmark of the area, ever since its earliest days when gifted rhetoricians drew crowds with their formal disputations. Pierre Abélard, in particular, was an idol of the neighborhood for his sheer genius in debate, handling contradictions and heckling with elegance and advancing novel ideas on the relation between Reason and Revelation, the central problem of medieval Christian thought. His successors in the 13th and 14th centuries had a far more organized system of colleges at their disposal, and scholasticism found fertile ground for development in the scores of religious institutions then housed in the Latin Quarter. Thomas Aquinas, Albertus Magnus, and many other great thinkers spent stimulating years in the Université, as this collection of schools was called.

The only substantial physical relic of this period is the **Musée National du Moyen-Age/Thermes de Cluny,** a rich repository of art from the Middle Ages housed in a 15th-century mansion on the Place Paul-Painlevé. (The entrance to this museum is on the tiny rue du Sommerard, which leads into the boulevard St-Michel; see also our Museums section, and for historical background, see the Burgundy and the Rhône Valley chapter.) The tapestry series on display in Room XI, *La Dame à la Licorne* (The Lady and the Unicorn), is in itself worth a visit. Illustrated with animals from the allegorical bestiary that inhabited the medieval imagination, the tapestries take as their subject the five senses. The meaning of the sixth and final tapestry in the series remains a beautiful mystery. Within and alongside the museum lie the extensive ruins of the splendid **Roman baths** that in the days of Lutetia occupied this part of the Left Bank. It should be noted that the Cluny, like most state-run museums in the city, is closed on Tuesdays.

The Sorbonne

South of the Cluny are two competing giants of French thought, the Collège de France and the Sorbonne. Now undistinguished in appearance, they have been eminent rivals ever since King François I founded the Collège in 1530 as an intellectual counterweight to the dominant Sorbonne. Even today, the **Collège de France** prides itself on its anti-institutional slant, admitting anyone wishing to attend its public lectures. In recent years, Michel Foucault, Claude Lévi-

Strauss, and Raymond Aron have given lecture series to halls packed with the studious, the curious, and just plain old groupies. All you need to attend is the ability to decipher the arcane timetables posted outside the building.

Although most of its buildings date from the last century, the Sorbonne is one of the oldest universities in the world. Founded in 1253 by Robert de Sorbon, the confessor of Saint Louis, it quickly rose to preeminence among French universities, specializing in the study of theology and the defense of orthodoxy. A latter-day alumnus, Cardinal Riche-lieu, poured funds into restoring its facilities, and it is his impressive mausoleum, a 17th-century chapel, that over-looks the Place de la Sorbonne. Paradoxically, this square, though it bears the name of an academy notorious for its ponderous resistance to change, has come to symbolize youthful revolt in France.

The most spectacular and far-reaching in effect of these outbursts occurred in May 1968, when a carnival spirit reigned in the quarter. The joyful anarchy and explosion of radical political thought almost toppled the central govern-ment. Chafing at the outdated formalism of university life and impatient with an older generation affected by its wartime experience, the *Soixante-huitards* (Sixty-eighters) helped loosen the conservative bonds inhibiting French society. The revolt's climactic moment, both scorned and admired for its utter uselessness, was the occupation of the neighboring Odéon, the theater of an august state company that in the 1960s had been a showcase for contemporary drama under the direction of Jean-Louis Barrault. Although Barrault later lost his job for making clear where his sympa-thies lay, his Odéon will always be remembered for the spread of the movement's most dangerous idea: *L'imagina-tion au pouvoir!* (Power to the imagination!). The legacy of this slogan and the revolt it inspired are still hotly debated in France today. For many Parisians now in early middle age, the acrid smell of tear gas that drifts over the capital from time to time is not so much a nuisance as a fragrant reminder of youth.

THE MONTAGNE STE-GENEVIEVE AND THE CONTRESCARPE

Two peculiar landmarks stand atop the Montagne Ste-Geneviève, a hill named after the fifth-century saint who convinced fleeing Parisians that Attila the Hun would bypass their town (which he did). The **Panthéon**, originally a pious project of Louis XV and Louis XVI, had the singular destiny of reaching completion just as the Revolution broke out. It passed the first century of its existence as an imposing question mark on the landscape, with successive regimes giving it to, then taking it from, the Church. Its definitive role as national mausoleum and temple of the Republic was established with the political stability of the late 19th century, when the body of Victor Hugo was installed with great pomp in its huge crypt. Other illustrious Frenchmen who now lie here are Voltaire and Rousseau (who poetically face each other for eternity), Emile Zola, Jean Jaurès, and Jean Moulin, the Resistance leader murdered by Klaus Barbie's men. The interior of the sanctuary is stridently nationalistic, and the enormous tableaux and other turn-of-the-century celebrations of the spirit of France are unsuited to modern tastes. At the same time that a reactionary Church was elevating its Basilique du Sacré-Coeur (yet another case of dubious aesthetics) on Montmartre, the progressive Third Republic was dressing up the Panthéon in the trappings of secular mysticism. The two domes still compete for attention on the Paris skyline.

The other striking monument on the hill is, indeed, a church, but it suffers from an earlier clash, relating almost entirely to taste. The interior of **St-Etienne-du-Mont** is Gothic—it is the only church in Paris to have kept its rood screen—yet the façade is a mishmash of Renaissance elements. Despite its confusing exterior, the church is of rare beauty and provides a peaceful setting for a regular series of concerts (frequently featuring works by Vivaldi). Blaise Pascal, hedging his bet on salvation, is buried here—not across the way in the Panthéon with the two giants of the Enlightenment.

Mouffetard

Many of the streets winding down from the hilltop have considerable charm, particularly the rue Mouffetard, which follows the old Roman road from Paris to Lyon. Nothing from that distant Roman period exists here today, although *la Mouffe* has kept the 20th century at bay much longer than have most Paris neighborhoods. Its upper stretch near the Place de la Contrescarpe, despite a bewildering number of restaurants and cafés, is prized by sentimental Parisians fond of the local characters who are an enduring part of the human landscape of this quarter. On warm afternoons an elderly bird-lover known in the neighborhood as Madame Pigeon usually can be seen tending her flock, always ready to share her encyclopedic knowledge of *la Mouffe* with passersby. Farther down the street toward its southern end the scene becomes unbearably picturesque, especially when the Mouffetard market opens for daily business. From behind the mounds of fruit and vegetables voluble merchants harangue shoppers in the flat accents of the native Parisian; in the cafés the clocks have stopped at the year 1900. The façade of the building at 134, rue Mouffetard is easily Paris's most elaborately decorated storefront.

The other attractions of this *arrondissement* (the 5th) are notable for their diversity. Near the Seine, the **Jardin des Plantes** is a quiet haven of Enlightenment natural sciences, encompassing a small zoo (where the *sans-culottes* gaped in astonishment at the exotic animals that had been freed from royal menageries), rows of flower beds and herb gardens, mineralogical displays, musty old pavilions, and a cedar of Lebanon that was planted in 1734. In the summer of 1990 several important renovations were made in the Jardin. The Labyrinth regained the aspect originally given it by naturalist Georges Leclerc, the comte de Buffon, in the 18th century. In addition, many tree-lined walks were broadened, and the Alpine Garden, closed for years, reopened. (In June 1994 a gallery of evolution will open in the old zoological gallery.)

Islamic Paris

As is so often the case in this city, history has made strange bedfellows: The immediate neighbor of this Enlightenment garden is an enclave of non-Western values. The spiritual center for the hundreds of thousands of Muslims who have settled in France since the period of decolonization and subsequent North African immigration, the **Mosquée de Paris** is striking not only for its Hispano-Moorish beauty but also for its symbolic importance. As a new multiconfessional, multiracial France takes shape for the future (not without some bitter resistance from antediluvian nationalists), the cultures and customs of North Africa are entering the French mainstream with the maturing of each successive generation. Although admittance to the mosque itself is reserved exclusively for the faithful, the adjoining gardens, tearoom, study center, and *hammam* (bathhouse) have become a meeting place for France and Islam, with Parisians of all backgrounds frequenting the facility. After a sybaritic evening spent in a Paris restaurant, many head to the mosque's soothing hammam for relief. Be sure to pick your night of excess carefully: The bath is open to women on Mondays, Wednesdays, Thursdays, and Saturdays from 11:00 A.M. to 8:00 P.M., and to men on Fridays and Sundays during the same hours; entry costs 65 francs. Movie fans will be interested in knowing that Rita Hayworth married the son of the Aga Khan in this mosque.

The importance of Arab cultures is emphasized further by a new presence along the Seine, a few blocks north of the Jardin des Plantes on the quai St-Bernard: the **Institut du Monde Arabe**. It's open to the public afternoons except Monday and offers fine views and an excellent Middle Eastern restaurant.

Just a javelin's throw from the mosque and the Jardin des Plantes lies the Roman amphitheater of Paris. Much restored, the **Arènes de Lutèce** are an oasis of antiquity in the midst of a busy neighborhood, a perfect place to relax on a warm summer's day and watch men play *boules* or boys torture their younger brothers. For those with a taste for more organized carnage, the last week of June is particularly satisfying, for it is then that a professional stuntmen's association stages mock gladiator battles and other edifying spectacles in the arena.

ST-GERMAIN-DES-PRES AND THE JARDIN DU LUXEMBOURG

The **Pont des Arts**, an aptly named footbridge linking the galleries of the Louvre to the Left Bank, draws visitor and Parisian alike to its unobstructed view of the Ile de la Cité to the east and the often brilliant sunsets over the Seine to the west. The Baroque edifice closing off the perspective to the south—the **Institut de France**—is notable for its dome, which, like Richelieu's chapel of the Sorbonne, serves as a monument to a 17th-century cardinal with a flair for statecraft and intrigue. In this case the ostentatious prelate was Cardinal Mazarin, the gray eminence who ensured the transition from Louis XIII to Louis XIV.

The domed building is also home to the **Académie Française**, which is charged with removing, or at least recording, impurities that have crept into the French language. (In 1992 it was the headquarters of Gallic grumbling when Mickey Mouse occupied the Marne valley.) Admission to the Academy marks the official consecration of a French intellectual during his or her lifetime, although many intellectuals are quick to point out that truly great artists and thinkers have often been passed over in favor of inoffensive mediocrities. This may be a sour-grapes argument or, more probably, the usual Parisian attitude of deference and derision toward the *académiciens*. The Academy's closest neighbors most clearly express these mixed feelings. Opposite the refined reading rooms beneath the dome stand the windswept bookstalls lining the Seine, which carry everything from faded photographs of James Dean to erotic novels and quirky monographs (as in one find, *Women Who Said No to Napoléon*).

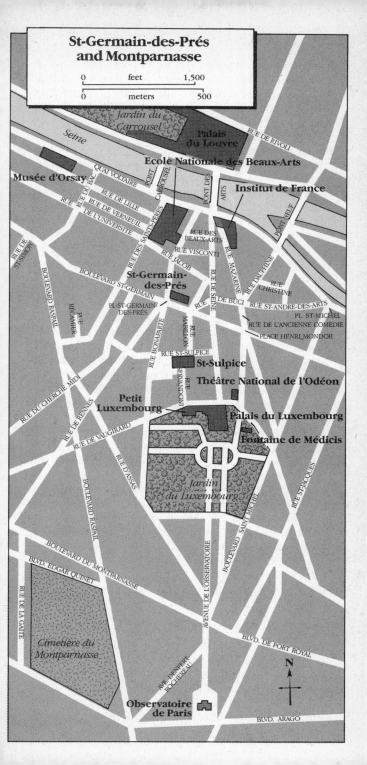

St-Germain-des-Prés
and Montparnasse

0   feet   1,500

0   meters   500

Jardin du Carrousel

Seine

Palais du Louvre

RUE DE RIVOLI

QUAI VOLTAIRE

Ecole Nationale des Beaux-Arts

Musée d'Orsay

RUE DU BAC

RUE DE LILLE

RUE DE VERNEUIL

RUE DE L'UNIVERSITE

PONT DU CARROUSEL

RUE DES SAINTS-PÈRES

PONT DES ARTS

Institut de France

PONT NEUF

RUE DES BEAUX-ARTS

RUE VISCONTI

RUE JACOB

RUE MAZARINE

RUE DAUPHINE

RUE DE SESSIMON

BOULEVARD RASPAIL

BOULEVARD ST-GERMAIN

St-Germain-des-Prés

RUE DE SEINE

RUE DE BUCI

RUE CHRISTINE

RUE RÉCAMIER

PL-ST-GERMAIN-DES-PRÉS

RUE

RUE MABILLON

RUE ST-ANDRE-DES-ARTS

PL. ST-MICHEL

RUE DE L'ANCIENNE COMEDIE

PLACE HENRI MONDOR

RUE BONAPARTE

RUE ST-SULPICE

St-Sulpice

RUE FERRANDON

Théâtre National de l'Odéon

RUE DU CHERCHE MIDI

RUE DE RENNES

Petit Luxembourg

Palais du Luxembourg

Fontaine de Médicis

RUE DE VAUGIRARD

RUE D'ASSAS

Jardin du Luxembourg

RUE ST-JACQUES

BOULEVARD RASPAIL

BOULEVARD SAINT MICHEL

BOULEVARD DU MONTPARNASSE

AVENUE DE L'OBSERVATOIRE

BLVD. EDGAR QUINET

RUE DE LA GAITÉ

Cimetière du Montparnasse

BLVD. DE PORT ROYAL

AVE. DENFERT-ROCHEREAU

N

Observatoire de Paris

BLVD. ARAGO

The *bouquinistes* (booksellers) are Paris's tribute to chaotic erudition, a tradition that is slightly older than the Academy itself: They first set up shop on the nearby Pont Neuf three decades before the founding of the Académie Française in 1635.

Beaux-Arts Quarter

Through a short passageway in the Academy's west wing lies the rue de Seine, the main street of the Beaux-Arts quarter. Two small squares at its lower end contain statues that seem to have been placed here as a parting shot at the Academy: Voltaire, a true immortal, snickers at the *académiciens,* and Carolina, a naked girl, stares defiantly at the temple of official culture. The young nude is doubly appropriate, for she also stands at the entrance to an area given over almost entirely to the study and sale of art. Galleries, art bookstores, and art-supply shops crowd the narrow streets, which are often teeming with students from the nearby **Ecole Nationale des Beaux-Arts**. The cafés here are welcoming and informal, sometimes subjected to impromptu concerts by what may rank as the world's worst brass band, *le fanfare des Beaux-Arts.* The best place to hide from the wayward musicians is at **La Palette**, on the rue de Seine, where you can sample a delicious ham snack jovially named "La Guillotine." This mix of art and frivolity has long made the neighborhood a magnet for aesthetes of all nations. An ailing Oscar Wilde, who said of the rates at his hotel at 13, rue des Beaux-Arts, "I'm dying beyond my means," is also reported to have looked at the wallpaper from his deathbed and sighed, "One of us will have to go."

Parallel to Wilde's street is the tiny rue Visconti, one of the quarter's oldest. Formerly called rue des Marais-St-Germain, it was nicknamed "Little Geneva" for its Huguenot inhabitants in the mid-1500s, and in later periods it housed Racine, Molière, Balzac, Merimée, and Delacroix. Stendhal's masterpiece, *The Red and the Black,* was first printed here. A more recent fictional creation, the loathsome Grenouille of Patrick Süskind's *Perfume,* killed his first red-headed virgin in this street.

St-Germain

The most renowned spot of the Left Bank is the Place St-Germain-des-Prés, from which the visitor can get a good idea of the radical changes Paris has undergone over the centuries. To the north is the Beaux-Arts district with its late-medieval façades; to the west, the 18th-century Faubourg St-Germain and the famous cafés of postwar Paris; to the south, the broad avenues of the 19th century and the tall Tour Montparnasse (a high-rise office tower) of the 20th; and to the east, the **Eglise St-Germain des Prés** itself, a remnant of a time when this area was meadowland (*les prés*) cultivated by Benedictine monks. The Romanesque lines of the distinctive bell tower hint at the sanctuary's considerable age—Pope Alexander III consecrated the enlarged choir of this church only a few days before laying the cornerstone of Notre-Dame. Founded in the times of the Mérovingian kings, the monastery recovered from the ravages of Viking raids in the ninth century and became prosperous around the year 1000, when the Cluniac reform of the Benedictines infused the order with renewed faith and vigor. Since then St-Germain has always figured prominently in the Parisian landscape, for many centuries as a rich country estate just beyond the city walls.

To the modern mind St-Germain-des-Prés is associated with the Paris of the 1940s and 1950s, when prominent artists and intellectuals frequented the **Deux Magots** and **Flore** cafés. Simone Signoret, in her autobiography, *Nostalgia Isn't What It Used to Be,* gives a vivid description of the wartime Flore and its cast of artists, writers, and charlatans living a precarious existence in Nazi-occupied Paris. Just a few blocks away on the boulevard Raspail, the Hôtel Lutetia served as Gestapo headquarters. After the war—perhaps because of it—existentialism and its message of hopelessness as a spur to action became the vogue in these literary cafés and in the nearby **Brasserie Lipp**, the upstairs dining room of which is still a favorite haunt of fast-talking intellectuals and hungry politicians. Thus, in the postwar period Jean-Paul Sartre and Simone de Beauvoir reigned as the undisputed sovereigns of daytime St-Germain. Night was the province of Boris Vian, a gifted writer and trumpeter who celebrated the cult of jazz in the many cellar clubs of the district. As France became embroiled in the Indo-Chinese War and memories of right-wing Vichy collaborators remained fresh, many of the intellectuals of St-Germain turned to Moscow for political inspiration—just as, at the same time, they were turning to New Orleans for enjoyment.

The contradictions are different now, as is the intellectual tenor of café life, but St-Germain has kept faith with some of its traditions. The center of France's publishing industry and, as such, the quarter of Paris with the greatest profusion of bookstores, it is also a popular area for nightlife. The **boulevard St-Germain** is lively well into the small hours of the morning, the crowds growing younger as you head eastward to the Latin Quarter. The two districts converge at the Place

Henri Mondor, a cinema-lined square dominated by a statue of Georges-Jacques Danton, a former resident of the area. Down the rue de l'Ancienne Comédie is the **Procope**, a café (now a restaurant) where revolutions—intellectual and political—have been hatched since the late 17th century. Behind the Procope runs an inconspicuous alleyway called the cour du Commerce-St-André, built alongside the medieval ramparts erected by Philippe Auguste (a vestige of a tower can be seen inside number 4). Nearby, at number 9, a certain Dr. J. I. Guillotin tested a machine that was to inspire terror in royalist and revolutionary alike. Danton, whose statue now stands proudly a few feet away in the square, was one of its many victims.

Slightly off the beaten track and, mercifully, much quieter than the boulevard, is the lovely square and fountain in front of the **Eglise St-Sulpice**. Slightly bombastic in appearance for a simple parish church built for the lay community that had grown up around the St-Germain monastery, St-Sulpice is best viewed at sunset, when the fading light softens the harsh stone and unforgiving classicism of its façade. Among the devotional works inside the church are three striking tableaux by Eugène Delacroix (whose studio on the nearby Place Furstemberg can be visited). The emptiness of the square outside St-Sulpice is relieved only in June at successive antiques and poetry fairs that take place around the central fountain. As befits a literary neighborhood, the given name of this fountain, les Quatre Points Cardinaux (the Four Cardinal Points), is an elaborate pun: Depicting four churchmen facing the four cardinal compass points, the fountain honors prelates whose defense of the Gallican church against Vatican interference guaranteed that they would not rise far in the Roman hierarchy—hence, they were also *point* (which also means "not at all") cardinals. These days such linguistic niceties may be lost, especially at the square's lone watering hole, the **Café de la Mairie**, an ideal spot to pout fetchingly at your fellow customers.

The Jardin du Luxembourg

By far the best way to escape the bustle of both the Latin Quarter and St-Germain-des-Prés is to enter the Jardin du Luxembourg, a large expanse of greenery to the south of these districts that is arguably the city's most entertaining park. In its western reaches, near the Orangerie, old men play interminable games of chess, young couples afflicted with romantic melancholia stroll through the *jardins à l'anglaise,* which are dotted with statues of literary greats (and a miniature Statue of Liberty), and at the Grand Guignol, the French equivalent of Punch and Judy, the real stars of the show are the enthusiastic young spectators. A formal French garden flanked by terraces adorned with statues of great French women of the past makes up the central part of the park. A long prospect to the south opens onto the tree-lined avenue de l'Observatoire, so called for the domed observatory visible in the distance. Yet another institution inspired by the Enlightenment, the observatory fought to make its meridian the division between Eastern and Western hemispheres but lost this honor to Greenwich. As a result, the linear arbor leading from the Luxembourg garden, the Paris meridian, is a rather unremarkable 2° 20′ 14″ E.

The eastern edge of the Luxembourg garden encloses one of the most beautiful spots in the city, a rectangular pond surmounted by a three-tiered fountain on which the lovers Galatea and Acis are watched over by the giant Polyphemus. Overhanging plane trees cover the water with an uneven carpet of leaves, beneath which golden carp swim about languidly. Although the statuary dates from the Second Empire, the Italianate pond, called the **Fontaine de Médicis**, has remained unchanged since the early 17th century, when the widowed queen of Henri IV ordered the construction of the neighboring **Palais du Luxembourg**. Marie de Médicis, who felt no compunction about raiding her late husband's treasury at the Bastille for funds, wanted to reproduce here the Pitti Palace of her beloved Florence. Though thwarted in this grand design, she managed to complete the palace and gardens even while plotting and counterplotting intrigues during the regency of her young son, Louis XIII. Rubens's 21 tableaux depicting her life, now hanging in the Louvre, do not represent Marie's final fate: death in exile, ultimately outfoxed by Richelieu. Her sumptuous palace is now occupied by the French Senate, a powerless but well-remunerated group of legislators. For readers of Dumas *père* uninterested in such contemporary outrages, the place to continue musing about Richelieu's perfidy is in the quiet neighborhood between the Luxembourg garden and St-Sulpice: At 12, rue Servandoni lived the thorn in the cardinal's side, the musketeer D'Artagnan.

Montparnasse

In the 1920s the Jardin du Luxembourg served as the inexpensive alternative to the nearby cafés of Montparnasse. Although still a thriving boulevard dotted with restaurants,

cafés, and movie houses, Montparnasse retains little of the
flavor of its wild days when John Glassco, in his hilarious
Memoirs of Montparnasse, could write about partying with
Kiki (Man Ray's model), cajoling Emma Goldman out of a
post-Bolshevik funk, and drinking heavily with French surrealists and American writers. Café society, especially at the
Coupole and the **Sélect**, can still be slightly subversive, even
if the spread of offices following the erection of the Tour
Montparnasse has made the area more business-minded.
Aside from its Lost Generation lore, which is still powerful
enough to make you self-conscious about writing so much
as a postcard in these cafés, the area has two further attractions: a Breton enclave near the boulevard Edgar Quinet,
with crêperies and cider-fueled merriment, and a small
theater district on the rue de la Gaîté. But Zelda and her
friends have long gone, some of them to the nearby
Cimetière Montparnasse. An avant-garde pantheon from the
19th and 20th centuries, this burial ground shelters the
graves of Baudelaire, Tsara, Zadkine, de Maupassant, and, of
course, Sartre and de Beauvoir.

FROM ORSAY TO THE EIFFEL TOWER

The faubourg St-Germain, the area stretching from the rue
des Saints-Pères to the Hôtel des Invalides, has remained
frustratingly impenetrable to the commoner, its aristocratic
18th-century homes and gardens hidden behind massive
stone gates. Developed when the nobility left the cramped
streets of the old Marais district for the then wide-open
spaces of the Grenelle Plain west of the St-Germain abbey,
the faubourg lost its ancien régime exclusiveness with the
coming of the Revolution and the Bonapartes. The early-
19th-century salons of the lovely Madame Récamier and the
brilliant Madame de Staël restored some of the quarter's lost
cachet, and even today a few fading dynasties match wits and
offspring in the Proustian calm of their faubourg drawing
rooms. Still, most of these fine old homes are now occupied
by government grandees, and the prospect of an elegant
ministry here undoubtedly fuels the ambitions of provincial
politicians. The Hôtel Matignon, its property encompassing
Paris's largest private park, is reserved for the prime minister, the public figure who is expected to thrive best in the
miasma of French party politics. Fittingly, Matignon's fashionable rue de Varenne address was on the calling card of
French history's most formidable political survivor, Charles-
Maurice de Talleyrand.

   If the houses of the faubourg remain closed to the curious, at least some elements of their decor are on view—and

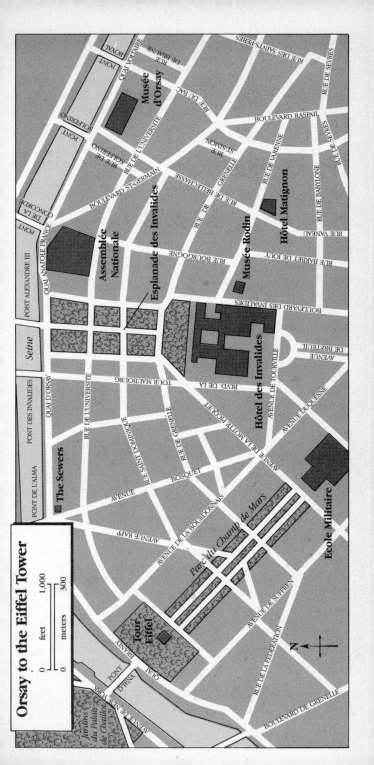

Orsay to the Eiffel Tower

feet	1,000
0	
meters	300
0	

on sale—to the public in the **Carré Rive Gauche**, a grid of streets bordered on the north by the quai Voltaire. Its concentration of antiques and furniture shops makes window shopping here a rewarding pastime, particularly in May, when the *carré*'s Days of the Extraordinary Object give pride of place to some truly weird creations foisted on old and new money alike. An entertaining appraisal of the carré appears in "Old Paris," a sardonic essay by Saul Bellow: "Who would have thought that Europe contained so much old junk? Or that, the servant class having disappeared, hearts nostalgic for the bourgeois epoch would hunt so eagerly for Empire breakfronts, Récamier sofas, and curule chairs?"

Musée d'Orsay

Nostalgia for the 19th century runs even deeper at the nearby Musée d'Orsay, a refurbished Belle Epoque railway terminal that houses the city's rich artistic legacy from the period 1848 to 1914. The creation of this mammoth new way station in the art-lover's tour of Paris brought about the removal here of the collection of French Impressionists from its quaint isolation in the Jeu de Paume pavilion of the Tuileries. In many ways, its transfer to a train station is appropriate, given the Impressionists' conviction that scenes from everyday life, whether in the country or in the city (indeed, the Gare St-Lazare served Claude Monet as inspiration), were worthy subjects for the painter.

Some critics have faulted the Orsay for being indiscriminate in its all-embracing sweep of the 19th century and for giving *pompier* excesses as much exposure as recognized masterpieces. Whatever its contradictions in presentation and contents, Orsay stands as a striking testament to France's continued expertise in converting old buildings to new uses. Whether the result is philistine is a question that visitors must answer for themselves. Those with a taste for coherence can play with the interactive video monitors designed to explain how the social context of France's tempestuous 19th century influenced the bewildering variety of artistic expression housed in the museum. A less intellectual but far headier pleasure is to visit the museum's top-floor coffee shop and walk out onto the balcony—between the train station's mammoth outdoor clocks—for a commanding view of the Right Bank to the north. People visiting Paris with toddlers in tow should know that this museum offers a day-care nursery, where you can make a temporary loan of your offspring to the French State. The service is popular—and not just with kids.

Musée Rodin

The Hôtel Biron, an older example of a successfully converted building and the only 18th-century home in the area that is open to the public, stands at the opposite corner of the faubourg St-Germain. In 1910 the French government reserved this property for the use of artists, among them Isadora Duncan, Henri Matisse, Rainer Maria Rilke, and Auguste Rodin. Rodin later signed an agreement bequeathing his work to the State in exchange for freedom to work and live in the Hôtel Biron at public expense. The result of this ideal arrangement is the Musée Rodin, a quiet, sensual place where such sculptures as *The Kiss, The Thinker,* and *The Burghers of Calais* blend in surprisingly well with their Neoclassical surroundings. Recently, the work of the gifted Camille Claudel, the sculptor's mistress, has belatedly emerged from her lover's shadow and received public recognition in its own right. Claudel's life story—her high-strung genius brought her to a tragic end in an asylum for the insane—is often cited by French feminists as a cautionary tale of great talent frustrated by misogynist times.

Hôtel des Invalides

The Rodin museum's low-key celebration of the arts of love is in contrast to the full-blown cult of martial glory displayed by the neighboring Invalides. An imposing Parisian landmark since its completion in 1706, the Invalides is Louis XIV's legacy to the capital he shunned for Versailles. The king's numerous wars of conquest, although successful in expanding the borders of France and ensuring his reputation as Europe's most powerful monarch, brought about great human misery, some of which this veterans' hospital tried to alleviate. The humanitarian impulse was gradually supplanted by the desire to make the building a showplace for French arms: Indeed, the Revolution, hardly sympathetic to past royal initiatives, made the place a Temple of Mars, and the Invalides became a museum honoring French soldiery. Thus it is appropriate, if anachronistic, that Jules Hardouin-Mansart's superb domed church is principally known as the mausoleum of Napoléon Bonaparte, the greatest soldier France has ever produced. In the eyes of French nationalists, the stature of the two historical figures connected with the Invalides, the Emperor and the Sun King, augments its prestige, making the place a symbol of the grandeur of their country. For those of other political persuasions, the evocation of grandeur is a defense of absolutism and should, like the Invalides itself, be avoided.

These two strong opposing viewpoints, the desire for a

strong central authority and the egalitarian impulse, have been at war in the French mind since 1789, and the struggle is still evident in the contemporary Fifth Republic, in which a multitude of elective offices is dwarfed by the tremendous power of the president. The bridge linking the Esplanade des Invalides to the Right Bank is a more striking illustration of this long-standing ambiguity. Built for the World's Fair of 1900, when many politicians of the Third Republic were fighting the antidemocratic forces of Church and Army (on such issues as public education and the Dreyfus Affair, respectively), the **Pont Alexandre III** honors the most absolutist regime of its time, the Russia of the czars. True, anti-Prussian motives had made France and Czar Nicholas II unlikely allies, yet the mere fact that Paris, the reputedly godless, regicidal capital of a progressive republic, could build such an exuberant monument to an autocrat is still something of a wonder today. It is also our good fortune: The bridge's ornamentation and statuary (the central groups depict the Seine and Neva rivers) make it an overdone Belle Epoque gem and, as such, very photogenic.

Farther downstream the river is spanned by the **Pont de l'Alma**, famous for the Zouave (French-Algerian soldier) standing at its base and acting as the city's unofficial marker of high and low waters. It may come as a relief to know that the bridge's neighboring attractions have nothing to do with art or politics. On the Left Bank is the public entrance to the **sewers of Paris**, a 19th-century engineering achievement that can be visited—whenever the Seine is well below the Zouave's feet—every day except Thursdays and Fridays from 11:00 A.M. to 4:00 P.M. Look for the sign "Musée des Egouts."

Across the river on the Right Bank lies the main embarkation point for the **bateaux-mouches**, the enormous tour boats that ply the Seine year-round. Contrary to the prejudices of seasoned travellers, these boats are not tourist traps. A quick tour of Paris's riverfront is beautiful day or night, provided you can put up with a tiresome recorded spiel in English and every major European language (it's best to sit outside). The dinner boat, however, takes too long to make the circuit but not long enough to allow for a leisurely Parisian feast; far better to take the regular cruise and dine at a good restaurant on shore. For those with a lot of time to kill, there is Batobus (bus-boat), which also plies the Seine. Not quite Italy's vaporetti, the Batobus fleet—old *bateaux-mouches* bought by the city—dallies maddeningly at each stop, making a full circuit of the Seine an afternoon proposition. At 12 francs a stop, it might be better to put up with the multilingual cacophony aboard the commercial *bateaux-mouches*.

In addition to the *bateaux-mouches* and Batobus, various other craft are operated on the Seine and its canals by five other companies. Of particular interest to those who've already "done" the Seine are the three-hour Canal St-Martin cruises of Canauxrama, and the cruises of Paris-Canal boats (also three hours) between the Musée d'Orsay and Parc de la Villette.

The Eiffel Tower

The westernmost part of this large swath of the Left Bank is taken up by the **Champ-de-Mars**, the elegant park that once served as a parade ground for the Ecole Militaire and that has, of late, become an illegal campground for hundreds of impecunious tourists from eastern Europe. When Napoléon was graduated from the Ecole Militaire in 1785, his instructor's prescient evaluation of Bonaparte read, "Will go far, if circumstances permit."

Aside from its military past and its rare status as a Parisian park where you are allowed to sit on the grass (a little beyond the midway point to the river, off the side alleys), the Champ-de-Mars is most famous for its riverside monument, the Eiffel Tower. Built for the World's Fair of 1889, the tower was intended to be the iron icon of France's industrial and engineering might—and to be a temporary structure. Civic pride over having the world's tallest structure at that time forestalled demolition, and the invention of the wireless gave Gustave Eiffel's implausible creation a new lease on life as a radio mast. Its ironwork seems surprisingly light and delicate to 20th-century eyes, particularly when viewed from directly beneath the structure, and recent renovations have been hailed by all Parisians as a success. The nighttime illumination creates the illusion that the tower is covered in cheap gold-colored paint, making it the world's largest souvenir of itself. Long a symbol of the industrial age, the Eiffel Tower is now entering its second century as Paris's most unexpected tribute to Postmodernism.

The Right Bank

THE 16TH ARRONDISSEMENT AND BOIS DE BOULOGNE

There are few places where the performance aspect of Paris is more in evidence than on the Right Bank across the Seine

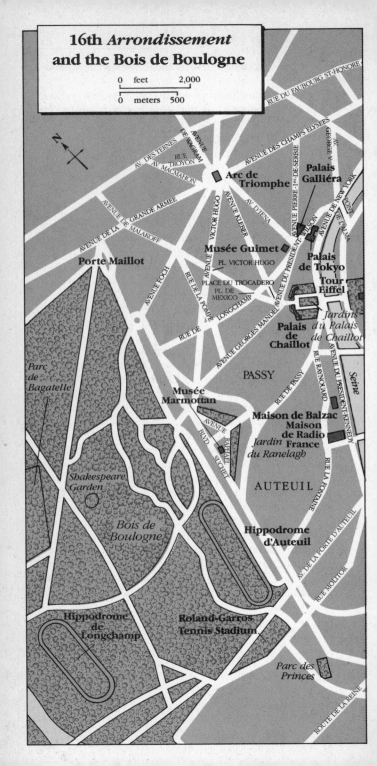

16th *Arrondissement* and the Bois de Boulogne

0 feet 2,000

0 meters 500

N

AVENUE DES TERNES

RUE DU FAUBOURG ST-HONORE

RUE DE WAGRAM

AVENUE DES CHAMPS ELYSEES

AV. GEORGE V

RUE TROYON

AV. MACMAHON

AV. DES TERNES

Arc de Triomphe

Palais Galliéra

AVENUE PIERRE-1er-DE-SERBIE

AVENUE DE GRANDE ARMEE

AVENUE DE LA MALAKOFF

AVENUE D'IENA

AV. D'IENA

AVENUE DE NEW YORK

RUE DE CALM

Porte Maillot

VICTOR HUGO

AVENUE KLEBER

Musée Guimet

PL. VICTOR HUGO

Palais de Tokyo

Tour Eiffel

AVENUE FOCH

PLACE DU TROCADERO

PL. DE MEXICO

AVENUE DU PRESIDENT WILSON

RUE DE LA POMPE

RUE DE LONGCHAMP

Jardins du Palais de Chaillot

Palais de Chaillot

AVENUE GEORGES MANDEL

Parc de Bagatelle

RUE DE

PASSY

RUE RAYNOUARD

RUE DE PASSY

Seine

Musée Marmottan

AVENUE RAPHAEL

Maison de Balzac

Maison de Radio France

AVENUE DU PRESIDENT KENNEDY

BLVD. SUCHET

Jardin du Ranelagh

RUE LA FONTAINE

Shakespeare Garden

AUTEUIL

Bois de Boulogne

Hippodrome d'Auteuil

AV. DE LA PORTE D'AUTEUIL

RUE MOLITOR

Hippodrome de Longchamp

Roland-Garros Tennis Stadium

Parc des Princes

ROUTE DE LA REINE

from the Eiffel Tower. The hilltop **Palais de Chaillot**, built for the 1937 World's Fair at the Place du Trocadéro, forms a large Art Deco backdrop to the play of fountains in the gardens sloping down toward the Seine. Monumental statues adorn these fountains, which send their powerful jets of water spraying out over a long reflecting pool. This area and the terrace above, a striking lookout over the Left Bank, are the playgrounds of roller skaters, skateboarders, and members of other strenuous urban subcultures who suspend their year-round cavorting at Chaillot only for such special occasions as Bastille Day, when the palace is brilliantly illuminated by fireworks.

The Chaillot Museums

The two wings of the palace make up an impressive cultural complex containing a major national theater and three large museums: the **Musée de la Marine** (begun by Louis XIV's minister, Jean-Baptiste Colbert), the **Musée de l'Homme** (the showcase of French anthropology), and the **Musée des Monuments Français** (featuring reproductions of the finest works of art to be found in the French provinces). Down the avenue du Président-Wilson are three other museums of note. The **Musée National des Arts Asiatiques-Guimet** houses a famous collection of art from the Far East, while two neighboring palaces, **Galliera** and **Tokyo**, respectively, exhibit clothing fashions dating from the 18th century and the municipality's modern art holdings. The Palais de Tokyo was built for the 1937 World's Fair and, like its larger contemporary atop the Chaillot hill, serves several purposes. The gallery's photographic exhibits are extremely popular with Parisians, especially during the biennial Mois de la Photo, a citywide celebration of the camera held in November. It also houses France's *cinémathèque,* which contains the celluloid archives of the nation and has several screening rooms open to the public.

Passy

On the southern slope of the Chaillot hill stretches the quiet neighborhood of Passy. Literary pilgrims can visit the house at 47, rue Raynouard where Balzac lived from 1840 to 1847. Constantly beset by creditors, the author of the *Comédie Humaine* became one of its most colorful characters by residing in this suburban hideout expressly to evade bill collectors (an exit at a lower level made it easy for him to disappear at the sound of a door knocker). Balzac's coffeepot, in which he brewed the stuff that kept him awake and writing through the long nights, now sits idly on display.

Passy and its environs have since been swallowed up by the 16th *arrondissement,* the district of Paris known for its splendid isolation. Long a bucolic retreat for aristocrats, artists, and diplomats (Benjamin Franklin spent many years in Passy), the area developed into a fashionable residential quarter at the close of the last century, when most of its stately apartments were built. Today the 16th is home to the Parisians satirically known as the BCBG (*bon chic, bon genre*), the well-scrubbed, well-off, well-dressed conservatives who can be seen, their dogs at their feet, sipping drinks in the fashionable cafés of the Place du Trocadéro and Place Victor Hugo. At night this residential district is dead, especially in the summer months, when its inhabitants answer the call of the civilized and move out to their country homes.

Passy's Jardin du Ranelagh serves as a nursery for the local denizens' impeccably turned-out toddlers and as an elegant antechamber for visiting lovers of Monet—nearby on rue Louis-Boilly is the **Musée Marmottan-Claude Monet**, where many of the painter's greatest works are on exhibit. In fact, the nine canvases lifted one night in 1985 during a stupendous art heist have now been restored to the Marmottan. They include *Impression: Soleil Levant,* the painting that gave the world the label "Impressionism." Found in Corsica, the purloined Monets apparently could not find buyers willing to risk instant recognition and the unseemly reputation that goes along with purchasing hot goods from fences.

The Bois de Boulogne

Although the 16th *arrondissement* is deserted at night, the same cannot be said of the neighboring Bois de Boulogne, which as soon as the sun sets becomes the hunting ground of peculiar human fauna. In the daytime, however, the 2,200-plus-acre park is populated with more innocent pleasure seekers who stroll, jog, cycle (bikes can be rented near the Jardin d'Acclimatation), or ride horses through its maze of forest pathways. On the urging of Napoléon III (in perhaps the only of his many town-planning initiatives to be universally applauded by Parisians), the designers of the Bois set about creating a Hyde Park for Paris, their Anglophilia driving them so far as to plant a Shakespeare Garden at its heart. This enclosure features all of the flora the Bard ever mentioned in his works. Of the park's many attractions (restaurants, artificial lakes, country clubs, children's playgrounds), the oldest is Bagatelle, a country pavilion that the count of Artois constructed in the record time of seven weeks to win a bet with his sister-in-law, Marie Antoinette. However charming this *folie* may be, it is Bagatelle's floral gardens that more truly merit a visit. The azaleas (April) and roses (June and July) draw crowds of admirers whom the resident peacocks assume to be well-wishers. The combination of colorful flower beds and proud peacocks can be quite spectacular.

Peacocks of the human variety are on display at the Bois de Boulogne's most famous attraction, the **Longchamp race-track**. On the first Sunday in October the plumage becomes extravagant at the main event of the season, the Prix de l'Arc de Triomphe, Europe's richest horse race. The Longchamp tradition stretches back to Second Empire days of ostentatious social jockeying and still retains a certain cachet. **Auteuil**, the other track of the Bois, is definitely the poor cousin, although its immediate neighbor, the **Roland-Garros** tennis stadium, has lately risen in social standing, and tickets to the French Open in May are now very difficult to obtain. South of the Bois is another sports venue, the **Parc des Princes**, where French soccer and rugby matches are played.

FROM THE ARC DE TRIOMPHE TO THE TUILERIES

From atop the **Arc de Triomphe**, Napoléon's monument to his military invincibility (completed 21 years after Waterloo), the visitor has a good view of imperial Paris and the 12 avenues radiating from the Etoile (the Star). Far to the west are the towers of La Défense, a suburban business district where striking skyscrapers and wind-tunnel esplanades successfully suggest the might of corporate France. A massive new arch, glorifying communications and media, was splashily opened during France's bicentennial summer at La Défense. It is the final monument in the prospect that runs from the Louvre's Place du Carrousel, up the Champs-Elysées, and out of the city. All told, this triumphal way counts three arches (Napoléon is celebrated by another Arc de Triomphe, smaller and more graceful, at the eastern end of the Tuileries), an Egyptian obelisk (in the Place de la Concorde), and an equestrian statue by Bernini (in the Place du Carrousel). It should hardly come as a surprise that Bernini's horseman is Louis XIV, Napoléon's ancien régime counterpart in the grandeur stakes.

The Champs-Elysées

In fact, the whole failed point of the Champs-Elysées is grandeur. From its beginnings, when Louis XIV's landscaping genius, André Le Nôtre, first laid it out as a tree-lined

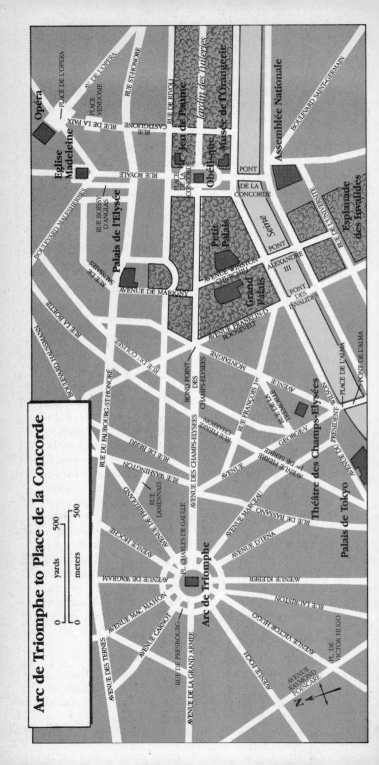

Arc de Triomphe to Place de la Concorde

prospect stretching from the Jardin des Tuileries to a distant, elevated horizon, the avenue was intended to represent the sublime and the permanent. Instead, it has been the theater of the temporary, largely because its development took place during France's stormy 19th century. When the avenue was saddled with a name evocative of the gods walking the Elysian Fields, its fate as colossal irony was sealed. From the Palais de l'Elysée, Louis-Napoléon (the emperor's nephew) engineered the overthrow of the Second Republic in order to set himself up as a mid-century Augustus, leading Karl Marx to remark of this Bonapartist replay on the avenue, "History occurs first as tragedy, then repeats itself as farce." As Emperor Napoléon III, Louis lived in absolutist style in the 16th-century Tuileries palace, only to be run out of the country in 1870 after being utterly humiliated in the war against Bismarck's Prussians. A year later, embittered Parisians put the palace to the torch during the Communard uprising, thereby giving notice that they had had enough of imperial pretensions from their rulers. The avenue's opulent mansions, built by 19th-century capitalists who were as ostentatious as faubourg-St-Germain aristocrats were discreet, gradually fell under the wrecker's ball, to be replaced by office buildings and apartments. (A remarkable survivor stands at number 25.)

Today the Champs-Elysées serves as a stage for Republican spectacles. The French president resides in the **Palais de l'Elysée**, receiving dignitaries in a style that the building's best-known tenant, Madame de Pompadour, would find congenial. On July 14, Bastille Day, the avenue becomes a parade ground for the army, the latest in French weaponry passing in review of the president and thousands of patriotic Parisians. As on other anniversaries of martial significance, a giant *tricolore* hangs from the Arc de Triomphe, giving rise in many hearts to what is sardonically called *"cocorico"* ("cock-a-doodle-do," or chauvinistic nationalism). Whatever misfortunes have befallen the French army in the past century, the grandiose—and to many Frenchmen, moving— sight of the flag billowing above the tomb of the unknown soldier is a reminder of past sacrifices and victories.

Fortunately, the avenue's aspirations to grandeur are overshadowed by its pursuit of the frivolous. Despite its historical significance, the **Etoile** (officially Place Charles-de-Gaulle), for many Parisians, is simply the most exhilarating place in the city to drive, especially at night at a fast clip. (Do not even consider walking across the Etoile to get to the Arc; take the lifesaving underground passageway instead.) The best way to visit the Champs-Elysées is on foot, with occasional stops to watch everybody watching everybody else. Here is where the myth of the extortionate price of coffee in Paris actually has some grounding in fact, so be prepared to nurse a demitasse of espresso for as long as you care to sit and stare. The walker should also cross the street at least once, pausing in the middle of the roadway to get the full effect of the monumental symmetry and the blinking lights of the long lines of traffic. The speed at which this traffic whizzes past accounts for the absence of cyclists: The only time they appear in any number is at the end of July, when the monthlong Tour de France bicycle race concludes here in a blaze of publicity.

For all its bright lights, the modern-day showiness of the Champs-Elysées is fairly empty and need only be taken in once. Cinemas, airline offices, car dealerships, and chain restaurants line the street, with a few shopping arcades scattered about for the benefit of luxury souvenir hounds. Paris City Hall, aware of the avenue's loss of cachet, has recently begun renovation on the Champs-Elysées to try to restore some grandeur to the boulevard. Service lanes are being torn up to allow for underground parking so that pedestrians will have wider, tree-shaded walkways. The eyesores created by the construction trailers and partitions are scheduled to remain through most of 1994.

At number 127, the **Paris Office de Tourisme** provides a mine of information about festivals, concerts, and special events taking place in the city. Near the Franklin Roosevelt Métro stop stands the **Virgin Mégastore**, one of the best cassette and CD emporiums in the world. On the nearby avenue George-V is one of the city's most popular permanent shows, the daring girlie revue of the **Crazy Horse Saloon**, a perennial favorite with visiting potentates from the Middle East.

The area stretching to the east of avenue George-V contains a large number of restaurants and fashionable boutiques, especially in the quarter around the elegant **avenue Montaigne**, which is vying with the rue du Faubourg-St-Honoré (to the north and parallel to the Champs-Elysées) for the title of the city's most exclusive thoroughfare. Faubourg-St-Honoré is longer, older, and more established, but the scents wafting from passersby are just as expensive on Montaigne, and the avenue itself is broad, tree-lined, and uncongested. The street can also lay claim to the fine-art auctioneering facility of Paris, **Drouot-Montaigne**; the theater (**Théâtre des Champs-Elysées**) in which Nijinsky was booed at the premiere of Stravinsky's *Rite of Spring;* and a fashionable mix of diplomats, TV people, and haute couturiers. On the sidewalks of the avenue Montaigne are small plaques commemorating great Parisian designers from the 1920s and 1930s.

Rond-Point des Champs-Elysées

The avenue Montaigne meets the triumphal way at the fountains and flower beds of the Rond-Point des Champs-Elysées. At this midway mark of the Champs, shaded pedestrian alleyways take over from the lively business district. The northern side of the avenue, near the avenue de Marigny, holds a stamp, coin, and antique postcard market on Thursdays, Saturdays, and Sundays, a charming outdoor affair that draws a good number of the city's eccentrics. This green belt, now sedate and often deserted, is forever linked with the most extravagant of Parisian vogues, the *Incroyables* and the *Merveilleux* (the Incredible and the Marvelous) of the post-Revolutionary period. Fashion for strollers through this area at that time dictated outlandish, immodest dress, and a relaxing of morals encouraged the type of libertine behavior that previously had been the preserve of the nobility. Revolutionary fervor even demanded new diction: The rolling French of the aristocracy was so detested and the accent of the Caribbean so admired that the letter "r" was abolished from speech altogether. Couples tempted to be incwedible and mawvelous in the area's secluded shrubbery should remember that times have changed.

The sole intersection breaking up the greenery is impressive for its double vista: the long view up the Champs-Elysées to the west and the broad avenue Winston-Churchill leading south to the distant dome of the Invalides. Flanking this avenue are the **Grand Palais** and **Petit Palais**, pavilions built for the World's Fair of 1900 and now used for the more important temporary art exhibitions and trade shows that come to the city.

A pleasant, inexpensive way to enjoy this imposing urbanism entails catching the **number 83 bus** at the Rond-Point des Champs-Elysées. As this is one of the two routes in the city on which every bus has a rear balcony, the passenger can stand in the open air and watch the show go by. At sunset this ride down the Champs-Elysées, across the Pont Alexandre III, briefly along the quais of the Left Bank, then on to the Jardin du Luxembourg and beyond makes even the most blasé Parisians lift their noses out of their newspapers.

Place de la Concorde

The other major landmark of the Champs-Elysées is the Place de la Concorde, an impressive combination of rushing traffic, beautiful streetlamps, imposing statues of women representing the major cities of France, allegorical fountains, and, of course, the obelisk. The view from the Concorde is special as well. The two buildings on the northern side of the square, occupied by the Hôtel Crillon and the ministry of the Navy, are colonnaded palaces designed by Jacques-Ange Gabriel for Louis XVI. The rue Royale, separating the two buildings, gives onto the Corinthian excess of the 19th-century **Eglise Ste-Marie-Madeleine** (known as La Madeleine). Impossible as it may seem, even more pillars are evident to the south, where the Napoleonic façade of the Assemblée Nationale, France's fractious parliament, stands facing the square from the Left Bank. On the east and west sides equestrian groups by Guillaume Coustou (the *Horses of Marly*) and Antoine Coysevox (the *Winged Horses*) guard the entrances to the Champs-Elysées and Tuileries, respectively.

Like the Champs-Elysées, the Concorde does not live up to its name, for the simple reason that the square has traditionally been associated with discord. During the 1770 wedding celebrations of Louis XVI and Marie Antoinette, 133 people died in a stampede caused by panic over exploding stores of fireworks. In 1793–1794, the square was the Revolution's most prestigious execution site, and 1,119 prisoners rode the tumbrels the length of the rue St-Honoré to their final appointment here. Among those whose heads rolled were Danton, Charlotte Corday (Marat's assassin), Robespierre, Marie Antoinette, and Louis XVI. Two decades later the Bourbons were returned to power and decided to adorn the square with a distinctly apolitical obelisk that Muhammad Ali, Viceroy of Egypt, offered to them. However, by the time the 3,000-year-old gift arrived in Paris, the Bourbons had once again been shown the door and the Orléanist usurper of their throne, King Louis-Philippe, had the pleasure of welcoming the exotic monument to Paris.

In later Republican days the Concorde became the theater of the white-hot *revanchard* sentiment over the loss of Alsace and Lorraine to the Prussians in 1873. The statue of Strasbourg was smothered in flowers for more than 50 years, and the timorous few to oppose the cult of the lost provinces were soon punished. A fashionable ice-cream merchant on the rue Royale had his shop destroyed for daring to put a German flag in his window (his property was quickly snapped up by an enterprising waiter named Maxim Gaillard, and thus Maxim's was born). In 1934 the most violent riot of modern times in France took place at the Concorde, with members of extreme-right groups rushing the Assemblée Nationale to throw parliamentarians into the river. Fifteen died and 300 were wounded, many of them on the **Pont de la Concorde**, the one Paris bridge to have been constructed with building material freed in another memorable riot: Much of its stone comes from the Bastille, demolished in 1789.

The Tuileries

By contrast, the Jardin des Tuileries is almost always associated with the gentler pastime of doing absolutely nothing, although it too was the scene of memorable incidents in the Revolution. A formal French garden designed by Le Nôtre, the Tuileries has been a favorite Parisian promenade since the 17th century, its pools, terraces, and statuary unerringly aligned by landscape geometers. The sole exception is modern: a series of sensual female nudes sculpted by Maillol and scattered about the park's eastern extremity. During the past few years the upkeep of the gardens has been less than careful. Thus, in the fall of 1990, they were made subject (under the auspices of President Mitterrand himself) to an extensive program of restoration and re-creation, which will result in the old Tuileries forming an architectural continuity from the Pyramide du Louvre to the Place de la Concorde. The almost-new park debuted in September 1992.

For those uneasy about idling away too much time on a vacation, however lovely the surroundings, the arcades of the commercial rue de Rivoli that run the length of the Tuileries's northern edge are always ready for shoppers. A more edifying antidote to lazing about the Tuileries can be found at the two galleries near the Place de la Concorde. The **Jeu de Paume**, now bereft of Impressionist glory, holds temporary exhibits, while the **Orangerie**, containing the superb Manet, Cézanne, Renoir, and Douanier Rousseau canvases of the Walter-Guillaume collection, remains one of the city's most surprising—and least visited—small galleries.

THE LOUVRE AND CHATELET

When King Philippe Auguste decided to construct the **Louvre** in order to protect Paris while he was off gallivanting with Richard the Lion-hearted on the Third Crusade, he unwittingly created the architectural hobbyhorse of the French nation. Few buildings in the country have been so assiduously rebuilt, extended, and modified. The result is a glorious monster, glaringly imperfect yet miraculously possessing three fine expressions of the builder's art: the **Cour Carré**, a courtyard built over the course of several reigns that shows the shift from Renaissance to Baroque to Neoclassical styles in French architecture; the **Galerie du Bord de l'Eau**,

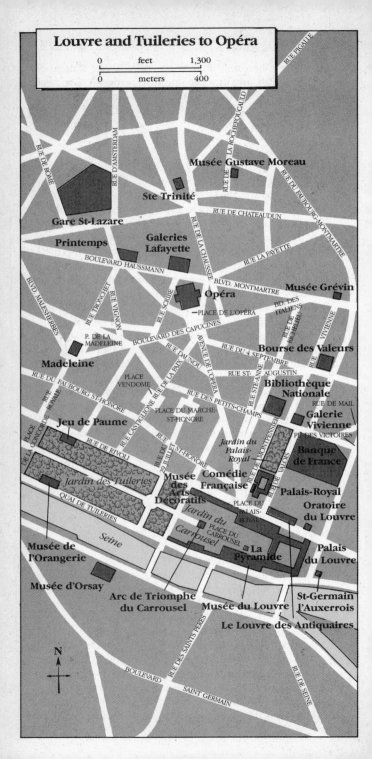

Louvre and Tuileries to Opéra

| 0 | feet | 1,300 |
| 0 | meters | 400 |

RUE PIGALLE

RUE DE LA ROCHEFOUCAULD

RUE DE ROME

RUE D'AMSTERDAM

Musée Gustave Moreau

RUE DU FAUBOURG MONTMARTRE

RUE JEAN

Ste Trinité

RUE DE CHATEAUDUN

Gare St-Lazare

Printemps

Galeries Lafayette

RUE DE LA CHAUSSÉE

BOULEVARD HAUSSMANN

RUE LA FAYETTE

BLVD. MONTMARTRE

Opéra

Musée Grévin

BD. DES ITALIENS

BLVD. MALESHERBES

RUE TRONCHET

RUE VIGNON

RUE SCRIBE

PLACE DE L'OPÉRA

RUE DE RICHELIEU

RUE VIVIENNE

BOULEVARD DES CAPUCINES

RUE DU 4 SEPTEMBRE

Bourse des Valeurs

P. DE LA MADELEINE

RUE DAUNOU

AVENUE DE L'OPÉRA

RUE ST-AUGUSTIN

Madeleine

RUE DU FAUBOURG ST-HONORE

RUE DE LA PAIX

RUE STE-ANNE

Bibliothèque Nationale

PLACE VENDOME

RUE DES PETITS-CHAMPS

RUE DE MAIL

PLACE DE LA CONCORDE

RUE ROYALE

RUE DU FAUBOURG ST-HONORE

RUE CASTIGLIONE

PLACE DU MARCHÉ ST-HONORE

Galerie Vivienne

Jeu de Paume

RUE DE RIVOLI

RUE DU 29 JUILLET ST-HONORE

RUE DE MONTPENSIER

Jardin du Palais-Royal

PL. DES VICTOIRES

Banque de France

Jardin des Tuileries

Musée des Arts Décoratifs

Comédie Française

RUE DE VALOIS

Palais-Royal

QUAI DE TUILERIES

PLACE DU PALAIS-ROYAL

Oratoire du Louvre

Musée de l'Orangerie

Seine

Jardin du Carrousel

PLACE DU CARROUSEL

La Pyramide

Palais du Louvre

Musée d'Orsay

Arc de Triomphe du Carrousel

Musée du Louvre

St-Germain l'Auxerrois

Le Louvre des Antiquaires

N

RUE DES SAINTS PÈRES

BOULEVARD

SAINT GERMAIN

RUE DE SEINE

THE RIGHT BANK 73

the center section of the riverside wing built for Henri IV; and the **Colonnade de Perrault**, the imposing easternmost façade constructed for Louis XIV.

More recent expressions of the 700-year-old tradition of tinkering with the Louvre include an underground concourse of shops, conference rooms, a huge parking garage, and restaurants designed by I. M. Pei, and, as of late 1993, the inauguration of the Richelieu wing on the northern side of the complex, nearly doubling the museum's display space.

Pei's concourse departs from its underground discretion in a tall, pyramid-shaped skylight that rises from the middle of the Cour Napoléon, in an inverted pyramid skylight, and in a commercial mall. However you feel about this daring addition to the Louvre, there can be no doubt that the modern facility meets several needs. It provides a glimpse of the formerly inaccessible medieval palace (visitors can now walk underground through the moats), cleans up the confusion that once reigned in the Cour Napoléon, and, in rationalizing the Louvre's entranceway, gives some order to a museum that has long been notorious among art-lovers for playing hide-and-seek with its cultural treasures. The reorganization of the Louvre's collections, some of which are gathering dust out of view, is expected to continue until the year 2000—that is, if obstacles such as the one encountered in the mid-1980s, when a French finance minister pettishly refused to move his offices from the building's northern wing, can be successfully circumvented. A compromise allowing the minister in question to hang on to his fancy address was eventually struck, but not before Parisians had enjoyed an unseemly fight between private vanity and public interest.

Once inside the Louvre it is easy to forget these recent squabbles and to thank the Revolution for finally opening the building to the public, in 1793. Louis XVI had considered, but never adopted, the idea. The first sight for many visitors, the monumental Daru staircase, crowned by the Victory of Samothrace, is a foretaste of the masterpieces to follow and of the enjoyment to be derived from them, provided, of course, the temptation to sprint through the entire building at one go can be resisted. As many of the paintings come from the private collections of Bourbon and Valois monarchs, it is hardly surprising that the Louvre is particularly rich in art from Italy, the country long synonymous with civilization for France's rulers. As is only natural, French painting is also well represented, particularly in the giant tableaux from the early 19th century. Other famous collections include a priceless selection of Flemish and

Dutch masters and, for classicists, extensive Greek and Roman holdings. France's enduring fascination with the pharaohs, spurred by Napoléon's adventures on the Nile, is evident in the museum's large Egyptology department.

In the northwestern wing of the building, along the rue de Rivoli, is the refurbished **Musée des Arts Décoratifs**. Given over to the traditional arts from medieval times to the present (with an annex devoted to haute couture), this museum forms a practical counterpart to the more famous collection of art for art's sake to be found elsewhere in the palace.

Associated in the modern mind with two women, the Venus de Milo and the Mona Lisa, the Louvre must often have seemed to its royal occupants more aptly represented by another work now in the museum, Hieronymus Bosch's *Ship of Fools*. The history of the Louvre, for seven centuries home to the French court, is rich in incident and intrigue. In the **Petite Galerie** visitors can still see the apartments of the Renaissance Valois monarchs. Their turbulent reign during France's religious wars made the Louvre a nest of plotting noblemen, minions, mistresses, and royal bastards. The 16th-century Louvre was a place of vicious rumor (about sexual and religious practices), suspect foreign connections (the Protestants with England, the Catholics with Spain), and frequent poisonings. Paris, a Catholic fief—it is often forgotten that Saint Ignatius Loyola founded the Society of Jesus on Montmartre—showed little tolerance for the winds of reform reaching France from Geneva, while the Huguenots, disciples of John Calvin, viewed the capital as a sink of corruption under the baleful Italian influence of Catherine de Médicis, the Queen Mother. As the number of Huguenots steadily grew among nobles and commoners alike, many powerful French Catholic clans, led by the Guise family of Lorraine, saw a threat to the secular and ecclesiastical connections that were the sources of their great wealth and power. In 1572, at the wedding of Catherine's daughter, Margaret of Valois, to a Huguenot prince, Henri of Navarre (later Henri IV), the Catholic faction hit upon an expedient solution to the problem posed by French Protestants: Kill them all.

Accordingly, early in the morning of August 23, the eve of the feast of Saint Bartholomew, bells in the rear belfry of **St-Germain l'Auxerrois**, the church opposite the Louvre's eastern façade, chimed the signal for the slaughter to begin. Daggers and swords drawn, the king's men raced through the Louvre killing Huguenot wedding guests in their beds, while armed bands of thugs were dispatched to roam the city and

murder at will. News of this bloodbath sent both Catholic and
Protestant Europe reeling in shock and disgust, no group
more so than the Huguenots themselves, whose aristocratic
spokesmen had suddenly disappeared. Today a statue of the
leader of the movement, Gaspard de Coligny, the admiral of
France murdered by his king on St. Bartholomew's Day, looks
reproachfully at the Louvre's northern façade, his monument
discreetly—perhaps a bit too discreetly—placed behind the
grillwork separating the rue de Rivoli from a Protestant oratory. The Huguenots gained a respite from persecution two
decades later when the bridegroom of that memorable wedding party became King Henri IV, converted to Catholicism,
and promptly decreed religious toleration in the Edict of
Nantes. Unfortunately, his grandson, Louis XIV, set the clock—
and France's development—back by revoking the edict and
driving the Huguenots into exile.

Châtelet
The neighborhood east of the Louvre has lost all trace of its
colorful past, commerce and theater being its principal
modern occupations. The quai de la Mégisserie is the capital's shop for pets and edible animals, with ducks, rabbits,
geese, hamsters, kittens, and white mice competing for attention. The relative scarcity of dogs at this market is puzzling,
for the incautious pedestrian in Paris quickly realizes that
the city's canine population is large and uninhibited. At the
corner of the quai and the Pont Neuf stands the Samaritaine
department store, much like its competitors in all respects
but one: Its circular rooftop observation deck offers, for free,
a superb view of Paris and the Seine.
    The next major intersection to the east is Châtelet, for-
merly the dungeon, torture chamber, and slaughterhouse of
the city. Since the 19th century the square has had a far
gentler vocation: music at the **Théâtre Musical de Paris**,
dance and drama at the **Théâtre de la Ville**. The latter, the
stage on which Sarah Bernhardt reigned as queen of Paris
theater, is the municipality's riposte to the national companies scattered throughout the city: Odéon, Comédie-Française, and Chaillot. Other such state-subsidized theaters as
the Bouffes du Nord (home to Peter Brook productions) and
Ariane Mnouchkine's Cartoucherie, where her imaginative
troupe works out of an old ammunition factory in the
eastern Bois de Vincennes, have received international acclaim for their treatments of exotic epics and Shakespeare
(the Bard is ever popular in France), while the enduring
cocu (cuckold) plot device is alive and well in the farces
staged in the district of the Grands Boulevards. Paris has

scores of theaters, café-theaters (cabarets where Gatling-gun French punning is the rule), and performing-arts venues. To make sense of it all, pick up an inexpensive weekly entertainment guide (*Pariscope* or *Officiel des Spectacles*) at a newsstand.

PALAIS-ROYAL, PLACE VENDOME, AND OPERA

These neighborhoods constitute the Right Bank, an expression synonymous with Parisian elegance, luxury, and liveliness. This is the Paris of fashion magnates and advertisers, of models with slinky legs sliding out of limousines, tripping into stylish shops along the rue du Faubourg-St-Honoré, and strolling down glittering boulevards with a suitably perfect man in tow. Glamour long ago replaced grandeur as Paris's trademark, which is why the triangle formed by the Place Vendôme, Palais-Royal, and Opéra districts is now far more emblematic of the city than the Champs-Elysées. First developed when the Parisian bourgeoisie was shaking free of feudal bonds to king and bishop, this area has significantly few ministries and churches—the presence of two major financial institutions, the Bank of France and the Stock Exchange, indicating its role as the cradle of French capitalism.

North of the Louvre on the rue de Rivoli is the Right Bank's equivalent of the Carré Rive Gauche, the **Louvre des Antiquaires**, today a rich man's flea market, with dozens of shops selling objets d'art and antique curios to collectors. To people of more modest means, the building is perfect for wistful window shopping, especially on those rare muggy days when the facility's most un-Parisian feature, air-conditioning, makes it particularly attractive.

Palais-Royal

There is a far quieter place to loiter across the street at the Palais-Royal, where a garden enclosed on three sides by graceful if neglected apartments has been open to the public since 1784. The present peacefulness of the spot belies its noisy past, for the musty arcades now lined with booksellers and military-memorabilia shops once housed the continent's most raucous cafés. The site served first as Cardinal Richelieu's town house, then as a second home to the monarchs (hence its name), before falling, in 1780, into the hands of Louis-Philippe d'Orléans, a high-living, hard-up nobleman who rebuilt the place and opened it to private businesses. His cousin at Versailles, Louis XVI, is reported to have sniffed, "Now that you're a shopkeeper, we'll no doubt see you only on Sundays."

The Palais-Royal was an overnight success, instantly becoming the city's intellectual center, amusement park, and fleshpot. This last unsavory facet of the place lives on in a skipping rhyme still sung, in all innocence, by French school-girls, *"Le Palais-Royal est un beau quartier/Toutes les jeunes filles sont à marier"* ("The Palais-Royal is a fine neighborhood/All the girls there are ready to wed"). As for the other attractions, the garden's mountebanks, cardsharps, palm readers, and freak shows competed with the strange cafés of the Palais, each of which had its own peculiar novelty. Outside the Café des Mille Colonnes (formerly at 36, galerie de Valois), Madame Rollain, the "most beautiful woman in the world," sat on a raised platform to beguile customers, while at the Café Mécanique (formerly at 121, galerie de Valois) a clever system of dumbwaiters in the center of every table served and cleared drinks without the need for human intervention. The cafés of the Palais-Royal also provided a political forum for encyclopedists, democrats, republicans, and rabble-rousers to discuss the ideas and problems of their day with great freedom.

In the summer of 1789, the air rife with rumors about imminent measures to be taken against the city of Paris and the Estates-General, Camille Desmoulins stood up in the Café de Foy at 46, galerie de Montpensier and incited his listeners to arm themselves against the government. That evening, July 13, they raided the Invalides for guns and later the next day stormed the Bastille, a symbol, if not a true representative (as it then held only seven prisoners), of absolutist repression. Few people thronging the Palais-Royal that evening realized that their revolt would turn into a revolution of unprecedented proportions, bringing down not only a dynasty but also the entire monarchical principle. It is hard to think of the present-day Palais-Royal as a crucible of modern Europe or a place of great social ferment (tellingly, the French Ministry of Culture now snoozes above the galerie de Valois), yet this is where the ancien régime collapsed, the educated yet unenfranchised classes who came here having had enough of the web of privilege woven by aristocracy and clergy. Louis-Philippe d'Orléans, who unwittingly lit the fuse by making his palace a safe house for sedition, was not spared the guillotine, despite the caution he showed by renaming himself Philippe-Egalité.

He might find the spot more to his tastes today, for, curiously enough, France's ultraconservative streak is nowhere more in evidence than it is here. The 300-year-old **Comédie-Française** performs at the Palais-Royal—and is excoriated by its public whenever it experiments. The installation in 1986 of

Les Trois Plateaux, a photogenic artwork consisting of truncated black-and-white columns placed in what had been used as the Palais's parking lot, earned its creator, Daniel Buren, a frightening amount of hate mail. Still, the neighborhood has always been a place of controversy: In the Régence Café that once stood across from the Comédie-Française, Marx and Engels first decided to form a working partnership. It should be noted that both men were initially drawn to the area by the presence of the **Bibliothèque Nationale.** Located just north of the Palais-Royal on the rue de Richelieu, France's national library was first placed here in 1724 by a prescient Louis XV. A complex of 18th-century mansions and Second Empire reading rooms, the "BN," as it is known to its thousands of scholarly regulars, often puts on temporary exhibits of its most precious holdings. (A controversial new national library—dubbed the TGB, or *très grande bibliothèque*—is now being constructed on the Left Bank, behind the Gare d'Austerlitz.)

Place Vendôme

The Place Vendôme has never had the questionable connections of the Palais-Royal; its serenity has been troubled only by the toppling, re-erecting, melting down, and statue-switching effected on the Napoleonic replica of Trajan's column that stands in its center. Playing musical chairs with monuments, however, was something of a national sport in France during the 19th century, so the fate of the Vendôme column was not exceptional. The fame of the square lies more in its ordered Louis XIV elegance (another example is the Place des Victoires, north of the Palais-Royal) and in its prestige. The Ritz, recently refurbished by an Egyptian businessman who also picked up Harrods on a London shopping spree, gives onto the square, as do several of the world's most exclusive jewelers. At sundown, when the streetlamps blink on and the display windows sparkle, Place Vendôme can be captivating, a sensation appropriate to a spot that once housed Dr. Friedrich Anton Mesmer, an 18th-century physician who treated patients simply by staring at them. Many people, however, are spellbound by the square's suggestion of limitless wealth. As every player of the French version of Monopoly knows, the adjoining rue de la Paix is the city's most valuable piece of property.

The Opéra

The rue de la Paix runs north into the Place de l'Opéra, the centerpiece of Napoléon III's scheme to make Paris the "most beautiful capital in the universe." His town planner, Baron Georges Eugène Haussmann, cut swaths through the historic fabric of Paris by driving wide boulevards into the heart of old neighborhoods, much to the dismay of residents. The police were delighted, for the new layout allowed them to isolate disturbances by deploying on the boulevards, putting an end to the age-old insurgent tradition of erecting barricades and scampering to further adventure through the citywide labyrinth of tiny streets and alleyways. The outbreaks of 1830 (portrayed in *Les Misérables*) and 1848 (which ignited the rest of Europe) haunted the emerging ruling classes of capitalist France, who, although at first sympathetic to the risings, did not want to see things get out of hand. The "arsonist-turned-fireman" syndrome, by which each generation of Parisian bourgeois would begin adulthood as constitutional hotheads and finish it as crotchety reactionaries, was commonplace in 19th-century France, as the newly ascendant elites faced a sustained salvo from a wide range of antagonists. Aside from suffering the indignity of Honoré Daumier's withering caricatures (which are beautifully displayed at the Musée d'Orsay), the bourgeoisie of post-Napoleonic times was shaken in its Gallic complacency by the Anglophilia of the French Romantics, and, on another front, attacked in its religious faiths by the writings of such Positivist visionaries as Claude de Saint-Simon and Auguste Comte. The more the business of France became the making of money, the fiercer became the critique of commerce as a sign of moral depravity—a notion that lurks in the back of the French mind even today. Fueling the bourgeois-bashing impulse was class hatred born of economic injustice. The misery of the urban working class, the subject of much of Emile Zola's work, stood in stark contrast to the opulent homes on the Champs-Elysées and to the upper classes' most grandiose riposte to their critics, the Paris Opéra.

Completed in 1875 after 13 years of construction (and five years after its sponsor, Napoléon III, had been deposed), Charles Garnier's Opéra remains Europe's largest theater and still impresses by its sheer excess. Its colorful monumental staircase, tailor-made for gawking at gowns and tiaras, is a riot of marble and statuary. The same holds true for the reception rooms and the great hall itself, dominated by a six-ton chandelier—which has come crashing down on operagoers only once, in 1896—and a ceiling decorated by Marc Chagall in 1964. Tickets to the Opéra are difficult both to obtain and to afford, although guides rattling off impressive figures about kilometers of upholstery and square meters of stage surface conduct tours daily. It is always a challenge to catch a glimpse of the real phantom of this Opéra: good taste. Still, the building has acquired the cachet of underdog since the opening of the very expensive new opera at the Bastille. Garnier's massive stage, once the arbiter of French operatic taste, is now reserved solely for ballet performances.

The Opéra District

The Opéra district was the setting for the 19th-century naughtiness associated with the notion of "gay Paree." To the east stretches the long strip known as the Grands Boulevards (ironically, one of the few broad thoroughfares not created by Baron Haussmann), where the bourgeois, boulevardiers, and soubrettes once came together in a mix worthy of an Offenbach operetta or a Feydeau farce. Today the district is lively but progressively shabbier as you head east, its only real links to the past being its numerous theaters and its **Musée Grévin** (10, boulevard Montmartre), a typical 19th-century entertainment consisting of wax figures, trompe l'oeil devices, and sound-and-light shows. To the west of the Opéra the boulevard des Capucines leads prosperously down to the **Madeleine**, a rectangular church built to look like a Roman temple. Perhaps not surprisingly, French military families have long chosen the Madeleine to mix Mars and Venus at elaborate formal weddings.

To the north of the Opéra the successors to the Second Empire boulevards and the turn-of-the-century Belle Epoque restaurants now pull in the crowds: Such *grands magasins* as Au Printemps and Galeries Lafayette, each a triumph of the 20th-century mass market, line up on the **boulevard Haussmann**. It is difficult to say whether the baron would be flattered or appalled.

Just beyond this bustling commercial neighborhood, hidden in the rue de la Rochefoucauld, one of the oddest expressions of France's 19th-century artistic development can be visited. The three floors of the **Musée Gustave Moreau** house most of the prodigious output of this Symbolist painter, whose work inspired the art-and-artifice worshipers associated with fin-de-siècle decadence. A quiet, peculiar place, where every inch of wall space is covered in darkly sensual paintings, the museum seems out of time, awash in a sensibility that could not have had any bearing on the real-life struggles of Moreau's contemporaries. The warmest praise for the painter's works appeared in J. K. Huysmans's *A Rebours* (*Against the Grain*), a grotesque tale hailed as "the breviary of decadence." It was this book, infused with the esoteric aesthetics of Huysmans and Moreau, that was supposed to have corrupted the youthful Dorian Gray. Thus, the pictures in the museum deserve careful study.

LES HALLES, BEAUBOURG,
AND LE MARAIS

What Zola called the "belly of Paris" is now its hole. The **Halles** district, for eight centuries the central food market of the city, is an undistinguished pedestrian zone with an underground shopping mall, the **Forum des Halles**. It also marks the point where the trendy part of the city begins, the blues and greens of the western Parisian wardrobe giving way to the blacks and grays of the east. In ten years—the time it took the government to decide what to do with the yawning crater left by the demolition of the 19th-century market buildings—the area changed from a charming anachronism in the heart of a traffic nightmare to a shining example of gimcrack urbanism. This is in keeping with a long tradition, for Les Halles has never been a genteel or refined neighborhood.

The peep-show area around the rue St-Denis was once the center of cutthroat Paris, the names of such alleyways as Petite and Grande Truanderie (Little and Big Thuggery) giving a fair idea of the locals' profession. However, the former seaminess of the Grande Truanderie's *Cour des Miracles,* where mutilated beggars by day became whole and hearty by night (simply by taking off their contrived handicaps), pales in comparison to the past squalor of the **Square des Innocents**. Currently known for the never-ending parade of urban fauna filing past its central Renaissance fountain (built by Pierre Lescot, architect for much of the Valois Louvre) and for the designer **Café Costes**, the Square des Innocents long had the dubious honor of being the city's largest cemetery and charnel house and the source of horrific anecdotes. An example: One evening in 1780 the southern retaining wall of the overcrowded Innocents cemetery gave way under the weight of the bodies piled high against it. Tenants sleeping peacefully on the lower floors of the adjacent building (the long, 17th-century construction that still borders the square's south side) were rudely awakened—and almost smothered—by the horde of uninvited and very dead guests crashing into the bedrooms of the living. This disaster spurred efforts to remove the remains from city cemeteries to the catacombs of Denfert-Rochereau—now a ghoulish tourist attraction.

This public health nightmare—an undisciplined graveyard alongside the city's central food market—has now totally vanished, together with almost everything else. The Square des Innocents gives out onto an artlessly landscaped expanse whose saving grace lies in the unobstructed view it provides of the **Eglise St-Eustache**. A 16th-century Gothic behemoth on the outside, St-Eustache impresses even more inside. Its towering nave often resounds with choral singing,

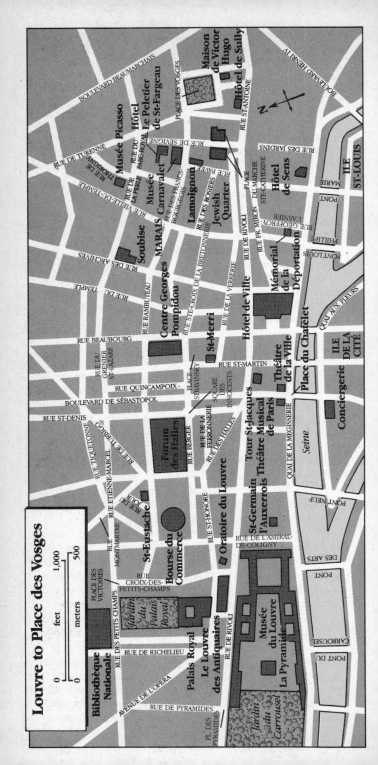

Louvre to Place des Vosges

0   feet   1,000
0   meters   500

Bibliothèque
Nationale

PLACE
DES
VICTOIRES

RUE DE TURENNE

BOULEVARD BEAUMARCHAIS

Musée Picasso

Hôtel
Le Peletier
de St-Fargeau

Maison
de Victor
Hugo

PLACE DES VOSGES

Hôtel de Sully

RUE ST-ANTOINE

BOULEVARD HENRI IV

RUE DE LA PERLE

RUE DE
PARC-ROYAL

RUE DU

RUE DE TURENNE

RUE VIELLE-DU-TEMPLE

Musée
Carnavalet

RUE DE SÉVIGNÉ

RUE DES
FRANCS-
BOURGEOIS

Lamoignon

RUE PAYÉE

PLACE
STE-CATHERINE

DU MARCHÉ

RUE DES JARDINS

ÎLE
ST-LOUIS

RUE DE THORIGNY

Soubise

MARAIS

RUE DES ROSIERS

Jewish
Quarter

Hôtel
de Sens

PONT
MARIE

RUE DES ARCHIVES

RUE STE-CROIX DE LA BRETONNERIE

RUE DE RIVOLI

RUE FR.-MIRON

RUE GEOFFROY-
L'ASNIER

PONT
LOUIS-
PHILIPPE

RUE DU TEMPLE

RUE RAMBUTEAU

Centre Georges
Pompidou

St-Merri

RUE DE LA VERRERIE

Hôtel de Ville

Mémorial
de la
Déportation

QUAI AUX FLEURS

ÎLE
DE LA CITÉ

RUE BEAUBOURG

RUE DU
GRENIER
ST-LAZARE

RUE ST-MARTIN

Théâtre
de la Ville

Place du Châtelet

RUE QUINCAMPOIX

PLACE
STRAVINSKY

SQUARE
DES
INNOCENTS

Conciergerie

BOULEVARD DE SÉBASTOPOL

RUE ST-DENIS

RUE DE LA
FERRONNERIE

QUAI DE LA MÉGISSERIE

Seine

RUE TIQUETONNE

RUE DE TURBIGO

Forum
des Halles

RUE BERGER

RUE DES HALLES

Tour St-Jacques
Théâtre Musical
de Paris

PONT
NEUF

DES ARTS

RUE ÉTIENNE-MARCEL

RUE DU
JOUR

St-Eustache

Bourse
du Commerce

Oratoire du Louvre

RUE ST-HONORÉ

St-Germain
l'Auxerrois

RUE
MONTMARTRE

RUE DE L'AMIRAL-
DE-COLIGNY

PONT

RUE
CROIX-DES-
PETITS-CHAMPS

Jardin
du Palais
Royal

Palais Royal

Le Louvre
des Antiquaires

RUE DE RIVOLI

Musée
du Louvre

La Pyramide

PONT DU
CARROUSEL

RUE DES PETITS CHAMPS

RUE DE RICHELIEU

AVENUE DE L'OPÉRA

PL. DES
PYRAMIDES

RUE DE PYRAMIDES

Jardin
du
Carrousel

and one of its radiating chapels is touchingly dedicated to the butchers, fishwives, and other food merchants who once made up the sanctuary's colorful congregation. Where their stalls once stood, outside the sanctuary's southern flank, is a small hemicycle, dominated by Henri DeMiller's 50-ton sculpture of a head lying on its side, staring off into space. Little imagination is needed to see that the eyes are turned toward the solitary pillar at the western end of Les Halles, an astrological column used by Catherine de Médicis's court seer, Nostradamus.

Beaubourg

Across the boulevard Sebastopol lies the Beaubourg quarter, yet another pedestrian zone. Whereas the neighboring Les Halles is entirely given over to commerce, Beaubourg's vocation is modern art. Galleries line its narrow rue Quincampoix, and its ever-popular **Centre Georges Pompidou** has become Paris's biggest tourist attraction, outdrawing the Eiffel Tower and Louvre combined. Opened in 1977 to groans from Parisians dismayed at seeing a mammoth, multi-colored, glass-and-steel structure erected in a picturesque old quarter, the facility, known locally as "Beaubourg," is now a familiar landmark. Its upper-floor permanent collection, the **Musée National d'Art Moderne**, encompasses an exhaustive range of 20th-century art, although only 1,000 of Beaubourg's 8,000 artworks are on display at any one time, because of space limitations. The museum is unquestionably one of the "musts" of a Paris visit, partly because its outstanding collection—including wonderful works by Picasso, Klee, Modigliani, and such—also has considerable depth in artists not all that well represented outside of France, such as Rouault.

Sharing the center building with permanent collections are a library and *vidéothèque*—chaotically organized victims of their own success—and the occasional mega-show that draws hordes of art-lovers and ensures excruciatingly long lines. The large plaza that has been cleared in front of the museum serves as a stage for street musicians, fire-eaters, contortionists, and crackpots who compete for the attention of the crowds with the neighboring mechanical show, Jacques Monestier's ingenious "Defender of Time" clock (affixed to a wall in the adjacent Quartier de l'Horloge). Overlooking the plaza stands yet another clock, the Nemo design group's Genitron, a digital scoreboard that, since its installation in 1987, has been neurotically counting down the seconds left in our millennium. A good place to watch its melancholy progress is from the terrace of the **Café Beaubourg**, yet another designer bar.

Immediately south of the Pompidou center is the Beaubourg quarter's photogenic showstopper, the **Stravinsky fountain**. The fountain's silly reflecting pool, containing Jean Tinguely's idiosyncratic machines and Niki de St-Phalle's mobile sculptures, forms an irreverent roof to the underground IRCAM complex, noted for its research into experimental music. The unlikely backdrop to the Place Stravinsky is the 16th-century **Eglise St-Merri**. Some critics think its grace is disfigured by the proximity of such an odd neighbor, but the charge betrays ignorance of the history of the church. Its long association with bizarre practices and secretive sects is indicated by the little figure atop the central portal: Baphomet, a grinning hermaphroditic devil.

Nearby, the **Tour St-Jacques**, the lone vestige of a church that was once the starting point of the pilgrimage to Santiago de Compostela in northwest Spain, was a favorite haunt of the mysterious Nicolas Flamel, the alchemist who inspired both fear and respect in 14th-century Parisians. The weird Stravinsky fountain is obviously in good company.

The Marais

From Beaubourg east to the Bastille stretches an area known as Le Marais (The Swamp), a reference to its once-marshy soil. A district totally distinct from the rest of Paris, it has retained a late-medieval flavor, escaping the great changes of the 19th century and narrowly avoiding large-scale demolition in the 20th, thanks to the efforts of culture minister André Malraux in the 1960s. The Marais is studded with magnificent *hôtels particuliers,* aristocratic mansions built when the area was the most elegant urban quarter of France. This was particularly true of the late 17th century, a time of great intellectual ferment in the Marais, the aristocratic *précieuses* holding their salons for the great men of the day: Molière, La Fontaine, Boileau, and La Rochefoucauld. The greatest woman of her time, Madame de Sévigné, lived, wrote, and received in the Hôtel Carnavalet, bequeathing a lively depiction of that glittering milieu in her letters.

The physical evidence of the past is everywhere present in the Marais. Along the rue des Jardins stands a 225-foot-long stretch of the 12th-century city rampart, its original crenellation intact. Bordering a playground, the wall is taken for granted in a neighborhood where stunning courtyards and mansions are commonplace. (If you see an open gate in the

Marais, take advantage of the situation to go in and snoop around.) Four great *hôtels* permanently open for public inspection are grouped around the rue des Francs-Bourgeois and rue des Archives: **Lamoignon**, the historical library of Paris; **Carnavalet**, the very rewarding history museum of Paris, a logical follow-up to a visit to the medieval Cluny museum; **Le Peletier de Saint-Fargeau**, which was renovated in 1989 to absorb some of the Carnavalet's collections, especially the art and artifacts of the Revolution in Paris; and **Soubise**, the national archives, with a permanent exhibition of important French documents from Mérovingian times to the present. On the rue St-Antoine, the **Hôtel de Sully** (named for Henri IV's shrewd finance minister) holds temporary exhibits about other French monuments, although its real interest is intrinsic. Like the interior of the other *hôtels,* the decor of Sully gives the visitor a taste of Baroque splendor. Slightly older than Sully and converted to use as an extraordinary public library is the riverside **Hôtel de Sens**, a half-medieval, half-Renaissance mansion that once served the fanatical Guise family as a Parisian pied-à-terre for hatching their murderous plots. At nightfall especially, this building looks the part.

A popular *hôtel* among modern visitors is Salé, since 1986 home of the magnificent **Musée Picasso**. Created from duties imposed by the French government on the artist's heirs, the collection includes more than 200 paintings and sculptures, handsomely displayed in the 17th-century mansion on rue de Thorigny. The aristocratic neighborhood—the tranquil **Parc Royal** is just around the corner—seems to suit the master.

The only other artist thus honored in the Marais is Victor Hugo, whose former residence at the **Place des Vosges** has been converted into a quirky museum, the **Musée Victor Hugo**, concentrating on the great man's private life. His fame, however, is secondary to that of the square, a graceful 17th-century fund-raising project that Henri IV and Sully dreamed up. In place of the rustic horse-trading market that occupied this spot, a regal square was envisioned, its identical pavilions to be sold off to the highest bidders. The promise of occasional royal occupancy (the queen's apartment in the center of the north side, the king's in the south) was dangled as prestigious bait, which nobles and rich merchants were quick to snap at. The enterprise was a resounding success, proof that business and beauty can coexist.

Aside from its relative antiquity in the Parisian landscape, the contemporary Marais is also known for the variety of its human geography. Affluent professionals clever enough to have picked up apartments when the prices were right (in the 1970s) displaced many of the area's artisans, although quaint businesses still exist alongside dance studios and graphic-arts wonderlands. The rues Ste-Croix de la Bretonnerie and Vieille-du-Temple form the meeting place of the old and new Marais populaces, with gays, trendy designers, and old-time residents strolling past kosher food stores, café-theaters, and antiques shops. Nearby, the Square du Marché Ste-Catherine, a restaurant-dotted expanse in the maze of narrow streets, fills pleasantly on summer evenings, while the Bastille Day Bal des Sapeurs-Pompiers (Fireman's Ball) in the firehall on the rue de Sévigné is by far the most entertaining in the city, with its mix of the comfortably fashion-conscious and the casually fashion-oblivious.

The Jewish Quarter

Completing this mosaic is the age-old Jewish quarter centered on the rue des Rosiers. French Jewry has long maintained a welcoming place for immigrants in the area, once known as the *pletzl* (square) to its Yiddish-speaking newcomers. Today the accents heard here are more likely to be North African, as many Sephardic Jews have moved to France in the wake of decolonization.

The rue des Rosiers, although an anachronistic representative of the French Jewish community, is nonetheless a powerful symbol in a country where a current of anti-Semitism runs deep. Long denied civil rights and subject to sporadic persecutions, the community met its greatest trials in the past hundred years. The turn-of-the-century Dreyfus Affair, which shocked the visiting Viennese journalist Theodor Herzl and strengthened his belief in the need for a Jewish homeland, sullied the French Republic's reputation for tolerance and added further ugliness to the rabid nationalism espoused by such figures as Maurice Barrès. French Jews suffered terribly during World War II, tens of thousands being sent to their deaths by the Nazi occupiers or their French underlings. A monument to the Unknown Jewish Martyr stands on the rue Geoffroy-l'Asnier, and the **Mémorial de la Déportation**, an underground memorial to victims of the Holocaust, can be visited at the easternmost tip of Ile de la Cité. However, the rue des Rosiers, its three blocks teeming with life in an otherwise quiet medieval quarter, remains the most vivid reminder of a hard-won victory over bigotry.

EASTERN PARIS AND MONTMARTRE

The Bastille

The cutting edge of Paris these days is the Bastille district, a neighborhood no longer living paradoxically in the shadow of a demolished building. The Bastille was torn down in the heady days of 1789, and for many years thereafter the area, called the faubourg St-Antoine, was known for furniture manufacture and working-class militancy. Those days are over, too, the old-time *musette* (the Auvergnat accordion music associated with romantic Paris) halls giving way to— or alternating nights with—New Age trendsetters, while the district's warehouses are being converted into lofts, studios, and galleries. Gentrification here, however, is in a far less advanced phase than in the neighboring Marais, and the "hot" street of the Bastille, the rue de Lappe, is still a bit daunting to fainthearted explorers of the night. The Bastille's new **Opéra de la Bastille**— officially inaugurated 200 years less one day after the storming of the Bastille—is a facility that architect Carlos Ott designed to make opera more accessible to a larger public, and points to the future of the area as the cultural laboratory of Paris. Currently the Bastille Opera, a national (i.e., Socialist) company, is being given a run for its money by Châtelet, a municipal (i.e., Gaullist) institution. For the moment, the Bastille is Paris's *quartier qui monte,* possessing a mix of the shabby and the genteel that many young Parisians find compelling.

The improvements in the Bastille area go along with a general redevelopment scheme for the whole of eastern Paris. Long considered the poor cousin of the more historic neighborhoods of central Paris and the wealthy *beaux quartiers* of the west, this large, densely populated section of the city is now experiencing a boom. Slum clearance and renovation here are high on city hall's list of priorities. The canal linking the Bastille to the Seine has been transformed into the Arsenal Marina for pleasure boats, and Bercy, the rough area behind the Gare de Lyon, was chosen as the site for the Palais Omnisports—an all-purpose indoor stadium, a daring new American Center, and a spectacular French Finance Ministry. (The center will open in the spring of 1994 at 51, rue de Bercy to house a library, auditoriums, rehearsal halls, galleries, live and film theaters, a bookstore, travel services, restaurants, and classrooms for an American language program.)

The **Canal St-Martin**, stretching from the Arsenal at the Seine, continues underground for a mile or so north of the Bastille and reemerges as a picturesque waterway threading

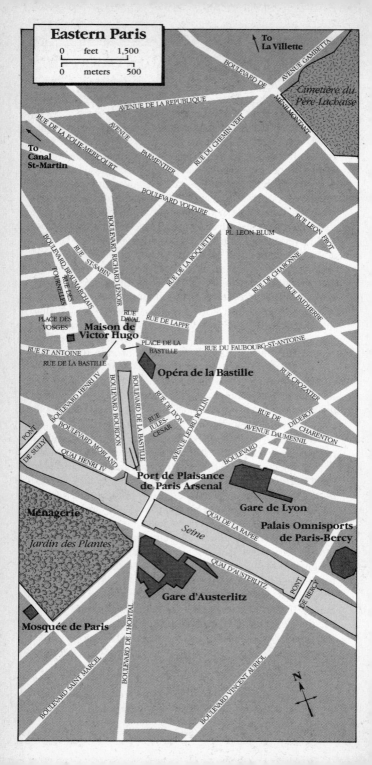

Eastern Paris

0 feet 1,500
0 meters 500

To La Villette

BOULEVARD DE

AVENUE GAMBETTA

Cimetière du Père Lachaise

AVENUE DE LA REPUBLIQUE

RUE DE LA FOLIE-MERICOURT

AVENUE PARMENTIER

RUE DU CHEMIN VERT

BOULEVARD MENILMONTANT

To Canal St-Martin

BOULEVARD VOLTAIRE

PL. LEON BLUM

RUE LEON FROT

BOULEVARD RICHARD LENOIR

RUE ST-SABIN

BOULEVARD BEAUMARCHAIS

RUE DES TOURNELLES

RUE DE LA ROQUETTE

RUE DE CHARONNE

RUE FAIDHERBE

RUE DAVAL

RUE DE LAPPE

PLACE DES VOSGES

Maison de Victor Hugo

PLACE DE LA BASTILLE

RUE ST ANTOINE

RUE DU FAUBOURG-ST-ANTOINE

RUE DE LA BASTILLE

Opéra de la Bastille

RUE CROZATIER

BOULEVARD HENRI IV

BOULEVARD BOURDON

BOULEVARD DE LA BASTILLE

RUE DE LYON

RUE JULES-CESAR

AVENUE LEDRU ROLLIN

RUE DE DIDEROT

CHARENTON

AVENUE DAUMESNIL

BOULEVARD MORLAND

QUAI HENRI IV

PONT DE SULLY

BOULEVARD

Port de Plaisance de Paris Arsenal

Gare de Lyon

Ménagerie

Jardin des Plantes

Seine

QUAI DE LA RAPEE

Palais Omnisports de Paris-Bercy

QUAI D'AUSTERLITZ

PONT DE BERCY

Gare d'Austerlitz

Mosquée de Paris

BOULEVARD SAINT MARCEL

BOULEVARD DE L'HOPITAL

BOULEVARD VINCENT AURIOL

N

through a series of locks and pedestrian bridges; it is now lined with artists' studios and new housing projects.

La Villette

A long, lazy barge tour of the canal leaves daily in the summertime from the Arsenal Marina, allowing visitors to take an unorthodox trip that ends close to the most peculiar of Paris's new attractions, the **Cité des Sciences et de l'Industrie** at La Villette. A textbook example of centralized planning gone awry (the Villette was built as a giant slaughterhouse at about the same time that the central food market was being moved to the southern suburb of Rungis), the complex ended its career as the city's most conspicuous white elephant when billions of francs were poured in during the 1980s to convert it into a showcase for French and European technology. Its most striking feature is the Géode, a spherical cinema that shows stomach-wrenching documentaries. Kids love it, especially because the Villette, Europe's largest technology park, has that most un-Parisian feature: interactive exhibits designed with children in mind. A faster way to reach this far-northeastern corner of Paris is to take the Métro (direction La Courneuve–8 Mai 1945) and get off at the Porte de la Villette station.

Père-Lachaise

The best-known of eastern Paris sights is the Cimetière du Père-Lachaise, a hilltop city of the dead noted for the celebrity of its occupants and the fantasy of its funerary art. A Napoleonic scheme designed to put an end to such horrors as the Innocents cemetery by moving the capital's burial ground outside of the city, the graveyard quickly became the fashionable place for interment—once its caretakers had hit on the publicity stunt of transferring whichever illustrious remains they could get their hands on (e.g., Molière, Abélard and Héloïse) to the then-suburban hillside. Its reputation grew as wealthy Parisian families erected extravagant monuments to their dead and as its roll call of the famous grew longer with the passing of each generation.

It is advisable to tip the gatekeeper in exchange for a map that will help you locate the graves of Marcel Proust, Oscar Wilde, Edith Piaf, Frédéric Chopin, Honoré de Balzac, Sarah Bernhardt, Jim Morrison, Georges Bizet, Gertrude Stein, and scores of others. The strangest tomb of the lot is that of spiritualist Allan Kardec, always covered with flowers and often surrounded by séance holders intent on finding a way to communicate with deceased relatives. In the cemetery's northeastern corner is another pilgrimage site: the wall where, on the night of May 27, 1871, the last of the Communard insurgents were summarily executed after an eerie battle amid the graves. The Paris Commune, a revolutionary city government that lasted three months and ended in savage repression by the army and wholesale arson by the Communards, was the most spectacular uprising of the 19th century, its legacy a continuing bitter division between Right and Left in French society.

Montmartre

The other redoubt of the Communards is associated more with life and art than with death and politics. Montmartre, the northernmost of the city's perimeter hills, was originally a religious refuge, its lovely 12th-century **Eglise St-Pierre** showing its antiquity in a vaulted ceiling that looks ready to topple over at any moment. Monasteries were gradually displaced as the city grew out to meet and engulf this village of wine makers and stonecutters. By the last half of the 19th century its windmills had been converted into dance halls (the 20th would change some of them into condominiums), where absinthe fueled much of the merrymaking and where such painters as Renoir (who frequented and painted the Moulin de la Galette) and Toulouse-Lautrec (the Moulin Rouge) found inspiration. Montmartre became the center of cabarets and bohemia, which, thanks to the new boulevards, more staid Parisians could easily visit for an evening out.

The hill might have stayed a purely local phenomenon had not artists of genius worked a revolution here. At such studios as the Bateau-Lavoir, Picasso, Modigliani, Utrillo, and many others used Montmartre as a subject for experimentation with figurative art, their radical departures defended by the writer Guillaume Apollinaire and often accompanied musically by Erik Satie. The **Lapin Agile**, a cabaret where the avant-garde mixed with the criminal element, still exists, though it is now peopled by the nostalgic rather than the creative. The same might be said of Montmartre itself, a victim of its own fame. The **Place du Tertre** in the warm months is crammed with people looking at the airport art for sale, and the **Basilique du Sacré-Coeur**, a blemish inflicted on the hillside by a vengeful French episcopacy in the wake of the Commune, has become an obligatory stop for every oversize tour bus in Europe. It's best to visit Montmartre in the winter or not at all.

If you do go to Montmartre, by all means visit the narrow strip on the southern slope, between the crush on the summit and the unrelieved sleaze of Pigalle and Clichy at the foot of the hill. The streets leading up from the **Place des**

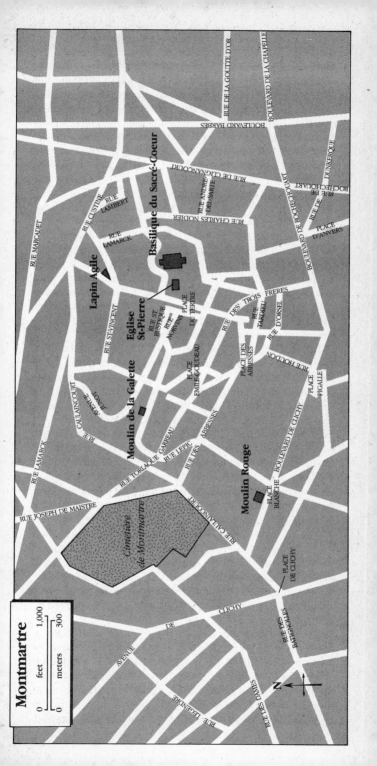

Montmartre

feet 0 — 1,000
meters 0 — 300

N

Basilique du Sacré-Coeur

Lapin Agile

Eglise St-Pierre

Moulin de la Galette

Moulin Rouge

RUE DE LA GOUTTE D'OR
BOULEVARD DE LA CHAPELLE
BOULEVARD BARBÈS
RUE DE CLIGNANCOURT
RUE DE DUNKERQUE
RUE DE ROCHECHOUART
PLACE D'ANVERS
BOULEVARD DE ROCHECHOUART
RUE ANDRÉ DEL SARTE
RUE CHARLES NODIER
RUE CUSTINE
RUE LAMBERT
RUE LAMARCK
RUE MARCADET
RUE DES TROIS FRÈRES
RUE TARDIEU
RUE D'ORSEL
PLACE DES ABBESSES
RUE HOUDON
PLACE DU TERTRE
RUE ST-RUSTIQUE
RUE NORVINS
RUE ST-VINCENT
PLACE ÉMILE GOUDEAU
RUE LEPIC
RUE DES ABBESSES
PIGALLE
AVENUE JUNOT
RUE CAULAINCOURT
RUE GABREAU
RUE TORLAQUE
RUE DES
RUE CAULAINCOURT
RUE LAMARCK
RUE JOSEPH DE MAISTRE
Cimetière de Montmartre
PLACE BLANCHE
BOULEVARD DE CLICHY
PLACE DE CLICHY
RUE DES BATIGNOLLES
RUE DES DAMES
RUE LEGENDRE
AVENUE DE CLICHY

Abbesses are picturesque and quiet, offering lovely, unexpected views over Paris. The rue Lepic, winding up the hill from Place Blanche and the Moulin Rouge, is the site of a charming outdoor market. Here even the most seasoned travellers feel tempted to become maudlin over this extraordinary city, so don't worry if your eyes start misting over. In the springtime bring a handkerchief or, better still, someone you love. This is Paris, after all.

BASILIQUE ST-DENIS

Should you lose your head over Paris while strolling the south slope of Montmartre you'll not be the first person to do so. Denis, a Dark Ages missionary sent to evangelize the Gauls, had his noggin lopped off on Montmartre (hence its name, Mount Martyr)—and then picked it up, tucked it under his arm, and, so the story goes, walked north to what is now the suburb of St-Denis. For the traveller to Paris who has seen and done it all, a visit to St-Denis's historic church and melting-pot neighborhood is perhaps the best way to get a final overview of the turbulent French capital.

To get to St-Denis take line 13 of the Métro (*not* the RER) and be sure the blue terminus sign, St-Denis-Basilique, is lighted on the train. (This Métro line forks and has another terminus, Gabriel Péri Asnières-Gennevilliers, indicated by a yellow light, that is of little interest to the visitor.) Once at your stop—the last stop—it is a short, well-signposted walk to the basilica that, along with those at Chartres and Reims, holds a special place in French history. It was here, just after the turn of the millennium, that Abbott Suger, yet another in the long line of clerics who have held sway in the French court over the centuries, fostered the Gothic revolution in ecclesiastical building and, centuries before Joan of Arc's appearance, gave shape to an inchoate French identity. Suger's massive basilica is thus an artistic, political, and religious milestone. His dominating intellect established that his church should be the mausoleum of French monarchs. As such, the basilica of St-Denis is France's Westminster Abbey—but even more important to the history of architecture. And, France being France, it is also far more scarred by the legacy of revolution.

What the visitor sees today is a magnificent Gothic sanctuary sheltering the carefully restored funerary monuments of the French monarchy. Many are spectacular in their portraiture of the final agonies of death; others, particularly Marie Antoinette's, are robustly voluptuous. The actual bones of these worthies were, *noblesse désoblige,* disinterred by the revolutionaries, just as much of the statuary was smashed.

The Bourbon Restoration that followed on the heels of Napoléon undertook to find and gather the shattered royal remains into a suitably dignified setting. It is in the crypt of St-Denis that the irony becomes inescapable: The bones of dozens of divine-right monarchs—including those of the Sun King himself—are now jumbled together in a common grave.

As if to reinforce the contradictions inherent in the story of France, the basilica's immediate neighbors are refreshingly inappropriate. On one side of the timeless church the municipality of St-Denis has erected an ugly town hall, designed according to the tenets of fall-apart flashiness that has marred such old cities as Montpellier. On the other side of the church the Baroque edifice that once housed the monks who grew wealthy from royal patronage is now an enclave of Republican privilege—it is a private lycée for daughters of members of that most Napoleonic order, the Legion of Honor.

Yet St-Denis does not stop there. Walk across the square in front of the town hall/basilica/lycée and you enter the rue de la République, a lively business district frequented by a crowd so polyglot as to make Ellis Island seem like a country club. Algerians, Malians, Vietnamese, Poles, Moroccans, Senegalese, Iranians—most of them French—jostle past the shops and cafés to the subway and their jobs in the city. The well-informed visitor, now far away from the tranquil waters plied by the *bateaux-mouches,* may realize that this, after and above all else, is the Paris of today.

GETTING AROUND

By Air

As Paris is a major world capital, there is no mystery to getting there. Charles-de-Gaulle airport in Roissy to the north handles regular international flights, while Orly to the south takes charters, domestic flights, and a number of overseas carriers (American Airlines, Continental, and a few others). Both facilities are served by **Air France buses** that go to the central city terminals at Invalides and Porte Maillot (the latter being a modern hotel and convention center complex to the east of the city). In addition, **Orlybus,** a regular city transit line, provides an efficient service to Denfert-Rochereau, and a new train link, called **Orlyval,** will whisk you to Antony, a suburban stop on the RER commuter railway line. (From Antony take the RER B route north to central Paris.) From Roissy take the RER (look for the sign *Paris par le train*) that follows the B route directly and quickly to the Gare du Nord, Châtelet–Les Halles, St-Michel–Notre-Dame, Luxembourg, and Denfert-Rochereau. The cost for all the above is in the 30 to 40 francs range, whereas taxi fare from either airport to the center of Paris runs from 200 to 300 francs, with generous tip included. (See Useful Facts, above, for more details.)

By Train
Paris is well serviced by France's efficient SNCF railway system. The city's six major train stations (St-Lazare, Nord, Est, Lyon, Austerlitz, and Montparnasse) are all served by the Métro, city buses, and taxis.

On Foot
When in Paris, walk; it is the best way to see and enjoy the city. Pedestrians usually ignore traffic signals. Avoid the busier streets between 5:00 and 7:00 in the evening—the pollution can be overwhelming. If you like cycling, this is not the city for you.

The Métro
The public transit system is excellent. The Métro (subway) is open from 5:30 A.M. to 1:00 A.M. every day. The different lines are indicated by their termini; thus, you should know the direction in which you are going—*the name of the terminus*—rather than the number or color of the line. A Métro station is usually exited by way of glass doors (a natural mistake is to push the metal frame of these doors—which will not open them—instead of the green glass marked *Poussez*). A book of ten Métro tickets (a *carnet*) costs about 40 francs. Each ticket is good for one ride regardless of the number of transfers made. If confronted by a ticket inspector—a rare occurrence, except at the Louvre stop in the summer—you must have a valid ticket or a 100-franc banknote to pay the fine. For those staying in Paris for an extended period, weekly and monthly passes are available.

The RER
The RER system provides even faster transit within the city, the four lines (A, B, C, D) having far fewer stops in Paris than the Métro. Thus, to go from the easternmost Bois de Vincennes to the central Châtelet–Les Halles transfer station on the RER entails only two stops. If you stay within Paris on the RER system, regular Métro tickets can be used, the only novelty being the need to insert them in turnstiles on leaving RER

stations. (Never throw away your ticket in the Paris underground.) Leaving Paris on the system (on a day trip to Versailles, Malmaison, or St-Germain-en-Laye, for example) requires purchasing a ticket, the price of which varies according to the length of your journey. As with the Métro, you must know the terminus of the line you wish to take in order to find the correct platform. Once there, make sure to check the electric signboard: Although RER trains do not skip stops within Paris, once in the suburbs they may become superexpresses.

You should closely examine the easy-to-read Métro maps posted at each station to determine which Métro lines connect with the RER (which are marked on the map with wider lines and bolder colors). Also, to save time when taking the RER out of town, it's fairly easy to use an automatic ticket dispenser. Look for one that has an illuminated green *Je rends la monnaie* ("I make change") sign. Then press a destination button (all stops outside Paris are listed alphabetically), followed by the button for first or second class (*2e classe place entière* is the normal adult fare), and finally the button for a one-way (*aller simple*) or return (*aller retour*) ticket. The machine displays the sum required. Deposit your money, and a ticket, as well as change, will be issued. Despite the length of this explanation, it is an effortless, fast way to avoid RER ticket agents, who are known, even among irascible Parisians, for their less than rosy view of the world.

RER trains are identified both by destination and by a letter. To add to the confusion, trains on line C—which serves Versailles—also have *names* (CORA, for example). Ignore the names; it is enough to follow the destination and letter, making sure, of course, that your desired station is on the platform sign that lists the stops for the incoming train.

By Bus

The buses use the same green tickets as the Métro, although there are no transfers between the two systems or even between different bus routes. According to the length of your bus trip, you have to punch one, two, or three tickets in the little box located directly behind the driver. This number is determined by the number of zones you will pass through, as shown on the route map affixed to your bus stop. Information about times, frequency, and last bus runs should also be there. You can always ask fellow bus passengers: They tend to be more civil than the Métro riders (although Britons should not expect to see an orderly queue at a bus stop).

By Taxi

Contrary to Francophobe legend, Paris taxi drivers are not swindlers. It is true, however, that they drive like maniacs and that they sometimes have to be persuaded to take a customer who is not going their way. At cab stands the driver cannot refuse you—even if you're just going around the corner. You should know that hailing a cab in the central business districts between 6:00 P.M. and 7:00 P.M. is an enterprise only for the extremely patient or the irresistibly beautiful. Parisian cabbies are few in number—complaints from tourists and locals alike flow into City Hall every year—and when the demand for cabs is high (at rush hour and at 1:00 A.M., just after the Métro closes), the customer is most definitely not the king.

By Car

Driving into Paris on the major expressways should present no problem except on Sunday nights or the last evening of holiday weekends, when long traffic jams are a certainty. The ring road (called the boulevard Périphérique) can sometimes involve drivers in a challenging game of chicken, especially when merging cars exercise their right of way, unique to this expressway, and zip into traffic without a moment's hesitation or notice.

If you insist on driving in Paris, forget your manners and behave like a spoiled child. For all their admirable qualities, Parisians tend to become arrogant and impatient behind a steering wheel. Avoid driving on weekend evenings, and in central Paris be prepared to spend a good deal of time looking for a parking space. Cars are parked illegally everywhere, but at the high risk of being towed away. A very pleasant experience is to drive around Paris after eleven or so on a weeknight, past all the floodlit monuments. Cruising down the boulevards and around the Concorde and Etoile is pure, unadulterated fun.

—*Stephen O'Shea*

MUSEUMS

Paris is a city with a past—and it has a hundred-some museums in which to showcase its long-gone glories as well as the highest-tech, most avant-garde manifestations of the present. The nearest Métro stop follows each address in parentheses. Regular closing days, if any, follow each entry; unless otherwise noted, museums are open from 10:30 A.M. to 6:00 P.M. For special exhibitions consult listings in current periodicals. Ticket prices are often reduced on Sundays; lines are correspondingly long.

Centre Georges Pompidou, 19, rue Beaubourg, 75004 (Rambuteau). A maze of brightly colored steel pipes surrounds the glass walls of this futuristic building, where paintings, drawings, and sculptures from 1905 to the present fill the **Musée National d'Art Moderne.** The Center also houses a library, cinema, industrial design center, children's workshop, and other public facilities. Closed weekday mornings and Tuesdays; open evenings until 10:00 P.M.; free admission Sundays 10:00 A.M. to 2:00 P.M.

    Cité des Sciences et de l'Industrie, Parc de la Villette, 30, avenue Corentin Cariou, 75019 (Porte de la Villette). This state-of-the-art science and technology museum—set in a 124-acre park bordered by canals—is part of an ambitious government building program. The imaginative and educational exhibits let you take a trip through the human body, "fly" an airplane, and stargaze in the planetarium; in the Cité des Enfants (basically "Kiddie City") your child can even produce a television show. Closed Mondays.

    Grand Palais, 3, avenue du Général-Eisenhower, 75008 (Champs Elysées–Clemenceau). Constructed with its neighbor, the Petit Palais, for the 1900 World Exposition, the building is used exclusively for temporary exhibitions. Closed Tuesdays; open evenings until 8:00 P.M., Wednesday evenings until 10:00 P.M. Opens at 10:00 A.M. Reduced ticket prices Mondays.

    Institut du Monde Arabe, 1, rue des Fossés St-Bernard, 75005 (Jussieu or Cardinal Lemoine). Permanent and temporary exhibits and a multimedia center present art and ethnology of the Arab world in a building noted for its architectural innovations. Closed Mondays; open 10:00 A.M. to 6:00 P.M.

    Maison de Balzac, 47, rue Raynouard, 75016 (Passy or La Muette). Engravings, manuscripts, and other mementos pay tribute to the author of *La Comédie Humaine* in the charming house that he occupied from 1840 to 1847. Closed Mondays. Open 10:00 A.M. to 5:40 P.M.

    Maison de Victor Hugo, 6, place des Vosges, 75004 (Chemin Vert or St-Paul). The rooms of the 17th-century *hôtel particulier* where Victor Hugo lived from 1832 to 1848 overlook the exquisite Place des Vosges, the city's oldest square. The writer's passion for interior decoration comes through in the memento-filled interiors re-created from his various homes. Closed Mondays. Open 10:00 A.M. to 5:45 P.M.

Maison Renan-Scheffer: Musée de la Vie Romantique, 16, rue Chaptal, 75009 (St-Georges). In 1830 the Dutch painter Ary Scheffer took possession of this enchanting house, where for almost 30 years he entertained artistic and literary luminaries of the day; Chopin, Ingres, Liszt, Delacroix, Lamartine, and others met at his popular salons. The residence is now a museum devoted to the romantic period, with a delightful collection of George Sand memorabilia, and temporary exhibitions. Closed Mondays. Open 10:00 A.M. to 5:45 P.M.

Musée de l'Armée, Hôtel des Invalides, 75007 (Varenne or Latour-Maubourg). Extensive displays of arms, armor, and military artifacts occupy the vast galleries of the stately Hôtel des Invalides, built to house wounded soldiers during the reign of the Sun King, Louis XIV. Napoléon's tomb lies in the magnificent Eglise du Dôme. Open 10:00 A.M. to 6:00 P.M.

Musée d'Art Juif, 42, rue des Saules, 75018 (Lamarck-Caulaincourt). Devotional objects, paintings, models of synagogues, and other items related to the cultural and religious heritage of the Jewish people are on view. Closed Fridays and Saturdays; open Sundays through Thursdays 3:00 P.M. to 6:00 P.M. Closed August.

Musée d'Art Moderne de la Ville de Paris, 11, avenue du Président-Wilson, 75016 (Alma-Marceau or Iéna). Dufy's *La Fée Electricité* (The Electricity Fairy), which spans an entire room, is among the Cubist, Fauvist, School of Paris, and other 20th-century masterworks installed here. Closed Mondays; open Tuesday through Friday noon to 7:00 P.M. and weekends 10:00 A.M. to 7:00 P.M.

Musée des Arts d'Afrique et d'Océanie, 293, avenue Daumesnil, 75012 (Porte Dorée). African and Oceanic arts and crafts are not all this museum has to offer; underwater life thrives in a tropical aquarium located in the basement. Closed Tuesdays; open 10:00 A.M. to 5:30 P.M. weekdays, 12:30 to 6:00 P.M. weekends.

Musée National des Arts Asiatiques-Guimet, 6, place d'Iéna, and 19, avenue d'Iéna, 75016 (Iéna). Chinese porcelains, Khmer carvings, Japanese prints, and Indian miniature paintings are but a few of the fine objects in the National Museum of Asian Art. Open 9:45 A.M. to 5:15 P.M. Closed Tuesdays.

Musée des Arts Décoratifs, 107, rue de Rivoli, 75001 (Palais-Royal–Musée du Louvre). Hand-painted antique plates, opulent Louis XIV furniture, and a chic suite of rooms designed for couturière Jeanne Lanvin—all this and much, much more traces the varied history of French decorative arts from the Middle Ages to the present. This outstanding collection occupies galleries in the Pavillon de Marsan, part of the Palais du Louvre. Closed mornings and Mondays and Tuesdays.

Musée des Arts de la Mode, 107, rue de Rivoli, 75001 (Palais-Royal–Musée du Louvre). Houses only temporary exhibits.

Musée des Arts et Traditions Populaires, Bois de Boulogne, 6, avenue du Mahatma-Gandhi, 75016 (Sablons). Folk art, regional costumes, and scenes re-creating everyday activities depict life in pre-industrial France. Closed Tuesdays. Open 9:45 A.M. to 5:15 P.M.

Musée Bourdelle, 16, rue Antoine-Bourdelle, 75015 (Falguière or Montparnasse-Bienvenüe). The rambling house and gardens of Rodin's student Antoine Bourdelle provide the setting for hundreds of his sculptures, including a series of Beethoven portrait busts. Closed Mondays. Open 10:00 A.M. to 5:40 P.M.

Musée du Cabinet des Médailles et Antiques, Bibliothèque Nationale, 58, rue de Richelieu, 75002 (Bourse). The kings of France began the superb collection of 400,000 coins, medals, cameos, antiquities, objets d'art, precious stones, and other treasures here. Open 1:00 P.M. to 5:00 P.M. The Bibliothèque Nationale (known to Parisians simply as the BN) frequently mounts temporary exhibits of its own vast holdings.

Musée Nissim de Camondo, 63, rue de Monceau, 75008 (Villiers). Fine 18th-century furniture by the era's most distinguished cabinetmakers graces the beautifully appointed rooms of this elegant town house adjacent to the lovely Parc de Monceau. Tapestries, porcelain, carpets, objets d'art, and original *boiserie* complete authentic period interiors. Closed noon to 2:00 P.M. and Mondays and Tuesdays.

Musée Carnavalet, 23, rue de Sévigné, 75003 (St-Paul or Chemin Vert). Madame de Sévigné, known for her lively accounts of 17th-century aristocratic life, lived in this beautiful *hôtel particulier,* now a museum of the history of Paris. A fascinating array of objects traces the city from prehistory to the present day; Marcel Proust's bedroom and a jewelry shop designed by Art Nouveau master Alphonse Mucha are among the delights found in the recently annexed galleries of the Hôtel Le-Peletier-de-St-Fargeau. Closed Mondays. Open 10:00 A.M. to 5:40 P.M.

Musée Cernuschi, 7, avenue Velasquez, 75008 (Villiers or Monceau). Chinese art—archaic bronzes, Neolithic pottery, funerary statues, and contemporary paintings—is on display in this attractive 19th-century house near the Parc de Monceau. Closed Mondays. Open 10:00 A.M. to 5:40 P.M.

Musée de la Chasse et de la Nature, 60, rue des Archives, 75003 (Hôtel de Ville). The great 17th-century architect François Mansart built the handsome *hôtel particulier* that now contains antique firearms and hunting trophies as well as paintings, tapestries, and other works of art depicting the hunt and outdoor scenes. Closed 12:30 to 1:30 P.M. and Tuesdays.

Musée du Cinéma Henri-Langlois, Palais de Chaillot, Place du Trocadéro, 75016 (Trocadéro). Movie posters, costumes, film clips, set designs, and photographic equipment unreel the history of the silver screen from its 1880s origins to the present. Guided tours only. Closed 1:00 to 2:00 P.M. and Tuesdays. Last tour begins at 4:00 P.M.

Musée Cognacq-Jay, 8, rue Elzévir, 75003 (St-Paul or Chemin Vert). A specially renovated *hôtel particulier* in the Marais is the new home of the collection of 18th-century art bequeathed to the city by the founder of the Samaritaine department stores. Paintings, furniture, porcelain, and objets d'art portray the sumptuous lifestyle of the upper classes during the age of kings and revolution. Open 10:00 A.M. to 5:45 P.M.; closed Mondays.

Musée Dapper, 50, avenue Victor Hugo, 75016 (Victor Hugo). African art fills these galleries a few blocks away from the Arc de Triomphe. Open every day 11:00 A.M. to 7:00 P.M. Admission free on Wednesdays.

Musée National Eugène-Delacroix, 6, rue de Furstemberg, 75006 (St-Germain-des-Prés). The painter lived and worked on the small, tree-shaded Place de Furstemberg in this quiet house, where he died in 1863. On view is a selection of his minor works and memorabilia. Open 9:45 A.M. to 5:15 P.M.; closed Tuesdays.

Musée d'Ennery, 59, avenue Foch, 75016 (Porte Dauphine). Far Eastern art collected by the 19th-century playwright Adolphe d'Ennery and shown in its original Second Empire setting features hundreds of netsukes—small carved figures in wood or ivory used as toggles on pouches and belts. The same building houses a museum of Armenian art. Open Thursdays and Sundays, 2:00 to 5:00 P.M. Closed August.

Musée Grévin, 10, boulevard Montmartre, 75009 (rue Montmartre). Arresting scenes depict 500 historical and contemporary personalities in this century-old wax museum. A branch devoted to the Belle Epoque is located in the Forum des Halles, 75001 (Châtelet–Les-Halles). The main museum is closed mornings during the school year; the Forum branch, on Sunday mornings.

Musée de l'Homme, Palais de Chaillot, Place du Trocadéro, 75016 (Trocadéro). The exotic trappings of distant cultures, the fossilized remains of early man, and other intriguing artifacts from the fields of anthropology, ethnology, and prehistory are exhibited for young and old alike. Open 9:45 A.M. to 5:15 P.M. Closed Tuesdays.

Musée Jacquemart-André, 158, boulevard Haussmann, 75008 (St-Philippe du Roule or Miromesnil). This former private collection features Renaissance and Baroque paintings and European decorative arts. Closed for remodeling; Tel: 45-62-39-94.

Musée du Jeu de Paume, Place de la Concorde at the rue de Rivoli, 75001 (Concorde). The Jeu de Paume's entire collection of Impressionist and Postimpressionist paintings was transferred to the Musée d'Orsay in 1986; the museum now hosts temporary exhibitions of contemporary art. Closed weekday mornings and Mondays; open Tuesdays until 9:30 P.M.

Musée Kwok On, 41, rue des Francs-Bourgeois, 75004 (St-Paul or Chemin Vert). Costumes, masks, puppets, and other items evoke the fascinating world of Oriental theater. Open 10:00 A.M. to 5:30 P.M. Closed Saturdays and Sundays.

Musée du Louvre, Palais du Louvre, 75001 (Palais-Royal–Musée du Louvre). This former royal palace—one of the world's largest—houses a vast collection of paintings, drawings, sculpture, and decorative arts from antiquity through the first half of the 19th century. Hordes of people jockey for position in front of the Mona Lisa, but don't miss the additional rare Leonardos often overlooked by the eager crowds. In November 1993 the northern wing—formerly government offices—of the immense Louvre structure opened as the Richelieu wing of the museum. The new wing, which is as big as the entire Musée d'Orsay, houses Near Eastern and Islamic antiquities, French sculpture, French paintings through the 17th century, and other collections. Extensive reorganization is scheduled to continue until 2000. The main entrance is now through I. M. Pei's controversial glass pyramid in the Cour Napoléon. Closed Tuesdays; open 9:00 A.M. to 6:00 P.M. and Mondays and Wednesdays until 9:45 P.M. Salle Napoléon and temporary exhibitions open evenings except Tuesdays until 10:00 P.M.

Musée de la Marine, Palais de Chaillot, Place du Trocadéro, 75016 (Trocadéro). Naval memorabilia and artifacts, model ships, and marine paintings are among the many attractions that captivate children and adults. Closed Tuesdays.

Musée Marmottan-Claude Monet, 2, rue Louis-Boilly, 75016 (La Muette). Lovers of Monet should not miss this museum, where a large bequest by the artist's son enriched an already impressive collection that included *Impression:*

Soleil Levant. This work, which inspired the term Impressionism, is back on view along with eight other paintings stolen in 1985. Here also are French furniture, European paintings, and illuminated manuscripts. Closed Mondays.

Musée de la Mode et du Costume, Palais Galliera, 10, avenue Pierre-I-de-Serbie, 75016 (Iéna or Alma-Marceau). Temporary exhibitions drawn from a broad range of carefully preserved antique and modern dress and accessories depict fashion history from 1735 to the present. Closed Mondays and between exhibits.

Musée de la Monnaie, 11, quai de Conti, 75006 (Odéon). The mint museum, housed in the splendid 18th-century Hôtel des Monnaies, displays coins, medals, and related material dating from antiquity through modern times. Closed mornings and Mondays; open Wednesdays until 9:00 P.M.

Musée du Vieux Montmartre, 12, rue Cortot, 75018 (Lamarck-Caulaincourt). Art works and memorabilia, charmingly arranged in an old house overlooking the city's only working vineyard, evoke the colorful history of this former village and its many famous residents. Closed Mondays.

Musée National des Monuments Français, Palais de Chaillot, Place du Trocadéro, 75016 (Trocadéro). The 19th-century architect and medievalist Viollet-le-Duc conceived this museum, where reproductions of monumental sculpture and wall paintings trace the evolution of these art forms in France. Closed Tuesdays.

Musée Gustave Moreau, 14, rue de La Rochefoucauld, 75009 (St-Georges or Trinité). The home of this Symbolist artist teems with hundreds of his paintings, drawings, and watercolors. Old-fashioned displays, narrow staircases, and a late-19th-century ambience exude an eccentric charm in keeping with the works of art. Closed 12:45 to 2:00 P.M. and Tuesdays; open Mondays and Wednesdays from 11:00 A.M. to 5:15 P.M.

Musée National du Moyen-Age/Thermes de Cluny, 6, place Paul-Painlevé, 75005 (Cluny–La Sorbonne). One of the few Gothic houses remaining in Paris now serves as a museum of medieval art; its collection includes the magnificent tapestry series *La Dame à la Licorne* (The Lady and the Unicorn). Ruined Roman baths adjoin the 15th-century house and are a rare example of the city's Gallo-Roman architecture. Closed 12:30 P.M. to 2:00 P.M. and Tuesdays.

Musée de l'Orangerie, Place de la Concorde at the quai des Tuileries, 75001 (Concorde). Monet himself designed the oval configuration for his masterful *Nymphéas,* part of the Water Lilies series he executed at Giverny. These treasures have been moved across the river to the Musée d'Orsay, but many beautiful canvases by Cézanne, Renoir, and other French artists of the 19th and 20th centuries remain. Closed Tuesdays. Open 9:45 A.M. to 5:15 P.M.

Musée d'Orsay, 1, rue de Bellechasse, 75007 (Solférino). A converted railroad station facing the Seine is a spacious setting for art from the mid-19th through the early 20th century. One of the city's most popular visits, the museum's comprehensive collection encompasses painting, sculpture, decorative arts, architecture, photography, and graphic arts, and contains the Impressionist and Postimpressionist paintings formerly in the Jeu de Paume. Closed Mondays; open Thursdays until 9:45 P.M.

Musée du Petit Palais, avenue Winston-Churchill, 75008 (Champs Elysées–Clemenceau). On view in this ornate fin-de-siècle building is a fine array of 19th-century French paintings as well as a varied selection of art through the ages. Closed Mondays.

Musée Picasso, 5, rue de Thorigny, 75003 (Chemin Vert). Paintings, sculpture, drawings, ceramics, and other works, handsomely installed in the recently restored Hôtel Salé, give an overview of Picasso's prodigious career. His personal collection—including canvases by Braque and Cézanne—is also on display. Closed Tuesdays.

Musée de la Poste, 34, boulevard de Vaugirard, 75015 (Montparnasse-Bienvenüe). Issues of all French stamps since 1849 and a variety of other objects dating back to the Middle Ages recount the sometimes surprising history of postal services in France. Closed Sundays.

Musée de la Publicité, 107, rue de Rivoli, 75001 (Palais-Royal–Musée du Louvre). An ever-changing exhibition schedule highlights selections from the thousands of posters and other items preserved in this lively museum of advertising, where TV and movie-theater commercials are also part of the program. Opens at noon; closed Mondays and Tuesdays.

Musée Rodin, 77, rue de Varenne, 75007 (Varenne). The 18th-century *hôtel particulier* called Hôtel Biron where the sculptor lived and worked is the setting for some of his best-known pieces. Large bronzes—among them *The Thinker, The Burghers of Calais,* and the monumental *Gates of Hell*—stand in the lovely garden. Closed Mondays.

Musée Zadkine, 100 bis, rue d'Assas, 75006 (Vavin). The Russian-born sculptor known for his Cubist works occupied this Montparnasse house and studio, a tranquil haven from the bustling streets outside and filled with a number of his sculptures. Closed Mondays. Open 10:00 A.M. to 5:30 P.M.

Muséum National d'Histoire Naturelle, Jardin des Plantes, 18, rue Buffon, 75005 (Monge or Gare d'Austerlitz). Dinosaurs, fossils, minerals, precious stones, exotic insects, and other scientific specimens are on exhibit in several buildings bordering the Jardin des Plantes, a botanical garden that flourished in the 18th century under Buffon, author of the multivolume *Histoire Naturelle.* The enormous 19th-century Galerie de Zoologie, closed to the public since 1965, is scheduled to open in June 1994 as a museum of evolution, the first of its kind in the world. Closed Tuesdays.

Palais de la Découverte, 4, avenue Franklin D. Roosevelt, 75008 (Franklin Roosevelt). Demonstrations and exhibits explain the wonder of scientific discoveries, and a planetarium gives a glimpse of the stars. Closed Mondays.

Palais de Tokyo: Centre de la Photographie et du Patrimoine Photographique, 13, avenue du Président-Wilson, 75016 (Iéna or Alma-Marceau). An exciting range of photographs—from the embryonic work of Nièpce to the stylishly provocative images of Annie Leibovitz—is shown in temporary exhibitions. Closed Tuesdays.

—*Margaret Adams*

ACCOMMODATIONS

Like any world capital, Paris brims with hotels that range from the exquisite to the execrable. The top end offers incomparable luxury and impeccable service; the bottom end is not worth talking about. Unfortunately, prices fit the same pattern. The hotels listed below are divided into two groups: the palace hotels, as they are called, where willing patrons pay at least 2,000 francs per night for a double room and far more for a suite or apartment (the most deluxe of which can reach 50,000 francs); and the rest, which generally cost between 400 and 1,500 francs per night. The rates given below are *projections* for 1994. Rates are for a double room, double occupancy, and do not include meals. As prices are always subject to change, double-check before booking.

The hotels also fall into three geographic regions: the area around the Arc de Triomphe; the center, stretching from the Opéra to the Marais; and the Left Bank from the Place Maubert to the Invalides.

The telephone country code for France is 33; the city code for Paris is 1.

THE PALACES

▶ **The Ritz** is so classy that its name has become synonymous with sophistication. Owned now by an Egyptian businessman, the hotel has lost none of the charm, elegance, and snob appeal that made it famous—its neighbors on the exclusive Place Vendôme include several of the world's most exclusive jewelers. In fact, the new owner created the Ritz-Hemingway literary award (winners so far include Marguerite Duras and Peter Taylor), a real-life paean to the man who claimed to have "liberated" the Ritz bar in 1944 and then decimated its cellars. The first hotel with bathrooms in the rooms, the Ritz now offers such comforts as window awnings that can be worked while you are still in bed, Jacuzzi bathtubs, an exclusive nightclub downstairs—and an excellent restaurant, too.

15, place Vendôme, 75001. Tel: 42-60-38-30; Fax: 42-60-23-71; in U.S., (212) 838-3110 or (800) 223-6800. 3,350F–4,150F.

Designed by Garnier of Paris Opéra fame, the ▶ **Inter-Continental** is the largest of the palace hotels, though its size takes away nothing from its level of comfort. Seven courtyards break up the massive building (one of them is a delightful garden café), and the industrious staff negotiates miles of corridors to ensure that everything is just so. The very advanced business center—with fax, computer, and secretarial facilities—and a central location bordering the Tuileries gardens make it popular with the international business set, and VCRs are available for those unwilling to leave the luxury of their rooms.

3, rue Castiglione, 75001. Tel: 44-77-11-11; Fax: 44-77-14-60; in U.S., (800) 327-0200. 2,500F.

Whenever he came to Paris, Salvador Dalí would swagger through the ▶ **Meurice** lobby sporting a cape swirling from his shoulders and brandishing a silver-headed cane, which says a lot about both the hotel's service—to keep such a demanding patron—and its personality—to attract such a commanding one. A block from the Ritz, the Meurice has a long and distinguished tradition; in the 19th century Edmund Rostand and Talleyrand favored it, and today Liza Minnelli and Shirley Temple Black like to visit. Recent renovations include air-conditioning and remarkably elegant and modern bathrooms. The personal service inspires great loyalty in the customers.

228, rue de Rivoli, 75001. Tel: 44-58-10-10; Fax: 44-58-10-15; in U.S., (212) 935-9540 or (800) 221-2340. 2,500F–2,900F.

The Taittinger Champagne family owns the ▶ **Crillon**, and the hotel is suffused with a vivaciousness that recalls the days when men refused to step out-of-doors without a top hat and women felt naked without a triple strand of pearls. The stunning setting—bounded on one side by the Place de la Concorde, with views of the Assemblée Nationale and the Eiffel Tower across the river—is matched by a sumptuous decor: Glowing 18th-century wood paneling and marble bathrooms are standard. The personalized service draws such patrons from the diplomatic and political ranks as Edward Kennedy and Richard Nixon. Try to get a room with a balcony overlooking the Place de la Concorde.

10, place de la Concorde, 75008. Tel: 44-71-15-00; Fax: 44-71-15-02; in U.S., (212) 752-3900, (800) 223-6800, or (800) 888-4747; in U.K., (0800) 181-591. 3,000F–4,000F.

The softly lit white façade a block from the Champs-Elysées seems to promise exactly the sort of transcendent service the ► **Bristol** in fact supplies. From the sixth-floor swimming pool to bathrooms brightened by Lalique windows and shower doors to the vivid bouquets of flowers everywhere, this hotel is particularly strong at what the Bristol management considers the basics—for almost anyone else the height of comfort. There are several fine dining rooms and a very pretty garden behind, which contribute to the calm, assured atmosphere. The Bristol is popular with the idle rich and well-heeled business people, as well as Bruce Springsteen. Lovely Art Deco decor.

112, rue du Faubourg-St-Honoré, 75008. Tel: 42-66-91-45; Telex: 280961; Fax: 42-66-68-68; in U.S., (201) 265-5151 or (800) 628-8929. 3,600F–4,300F; suites 6,500F–9,300F.

The discreet entrance of the ► **Plaza-Athénée** a few doors from the Place d'Alma modestly guards what is probably the most beautiful of the palace hotels. In the spring, red geraniums blanket the building's façade, and the public rooms on the inside are alive with extravagant floral arrangements. The rooms are large and perfectly appointed, and not a whisper of traffic from the street below is allowed to reach them. During the fall and spring Paris fashion shows, the Plaza-Athénée is packed with the most haute of the haute couture crowd (the hotel is reserved for two years in advance), and the Art Deco grillroom supplies top designers from the *quartier* with their daily nourishment. Sour notes and missed cues are illegal at the Plaza-Athénée, which has satisfied such guests as Mata Hari and Katharine Hepburn as well as just about everyone else who ever stayed there.

25, avenue Montaigne, 75008. Tel: 47-23-78-33; Telex: 650092; Fax: 47-20-20-70; in U.S., (800) 225-5843 or (800) 223-6800. 2,700F–4,100F.

Like the Ritz, the ► **George V** has become synonymous with luxury. The building, situated between the Champs-Elysées and the Seine, was constructed when Art Deco was at its most popular; its architecture is majestic yet completely un–Art Deco. Antiques fill the rooms, and an art gallery is necessary to supply paintings grand enough for the dining room. Recent management changes have restored the hotel to the top rank; today the front entrance is always lined with expensive foreign cars, and a virtual mink farm of coats swings through the main revolving door every night. Large extended suites can be created on certain floors, so this hotel is a favorite for big parties or for people with retinues, and the basement conference rooms draw major meetings and fancy balls.

31, avenue George-V, 75008. Tel: 47-23-54-00; Fax: 47-20-06-49; in U.S., (800) 225-5843 or (800) 223-6800. 2,000F–3,800F.

THE RIGHT BANK

Champs Elysées and Trocadéro

Named after a great 15th-century general, Louis II de la Trémoille, ▶ La Trémoille is anything but warlike. Situated in a lovely, late-19th-century building, this lavishly and tastefully decorated hotel provides clients with a private, elegant retreat from the city (Orson Welles once stayed several months and almost never left his room), complete with balconies alive with flower boxes. An intimate, wood-paneled bar leads to an even more intimate dining room with a crackling fire.

14, rue de La Trémoille, 75008. Tel: 47-23-34-20; Telex: 640344; Fax: 40-70-01-08; in U.S., (800) 225-5843 or (800) 223-6800. 1,900F–2,870F.

The ▶ Raphaël is like a slightly smaller, slightly clubbier version of the Trémoille. The wood paneling is dark rather than light, the plaster moldings are a bit more elaborate, and thick Oriental rugs cover the marble floors. The very large rooms are favored by high-flying business people and those needing personalized service. A very pretty, very distinguished hotel.

17, avenue Kléber, 75116. Tel: 44-28-00-28; Telex: 645356; Fax: 45-01-21-50. 1,900F–2,400F; with salon 2,900F–3,400F; suites 3,900F–6,800F.

Nearby is the ▶ Hôtel Vernet, which, after a total overhaul in 1990, is one of the best-value "baby grand" hotels in Paris. The renovators succeeded in renewing the plumbing—almost every room here is equipped with a whirlpool bath—and the ventilation systems but knew to leave the charming cage elevator alone. The public areas, with lots of marble, Oriental carpets, crystal chandeliers, and good Louis-something furniture, communicate a pleasantly unthreatening but thorough idea of traditional French good taste and luxury. Pleasant staff, and an excellent restaurant (see Dining: Expensive and Moderate).

25, rue Vernet, 75008. Tel: 47-23-43-10; Fax: 40-70-10-14. 1,450F–2,200F.

The ▶ **Lancaster** is another smaller but no less luxurious option to the palace hotels. Just off the Champs-Elysées, in a gracefully designed building with a stained glass ceiling in the entry and a tranquil garden courtyard complete with fountains and statues, the Lancaster offers affluent travellers a graceful home away from home—if you happen to live as Santiago Drake del Castillo did when he built the house in 1899. Run by England's Savoy group.

7, rue de Berri, 75008. Tel: 43-59-90-43; Fax: 42-89-22-71. 1,950F–2,550F.

Up the block from the Elysée palace, home to the French president, the ▶ **Hôtel de l'Elysée** is a very reasonably priced possibility in an expensive neighborhood. The rooms are lovely; some have terrific balcony views, and the ones on the top floor have cozy dormer windows and wood beams. Restoration decor with lots of trompe l'oeil murals.

12, rue des Saussaies, 75008. Tel: 42-65-29-25; Fax: 42-65-64-28. 660F–1,270F.

The Louvre and Opéra

With its marble floors, gilded chandeliers, and extraordinarily well preserved Belle Epoque woodwork framing graceful beveled glass windows, the elegant entrance of the ▶ **Hôtel Regina** belies the slightly faded splendor of its very spacious rooms. Built in the waning days of the Second Empire, the Regina's convenient location just opposite the Tuileries (a two-minute walk from the Louvre's glass pyramid) and airy rooms are its best features. Every room is well equipped with modern comforts, including double-paned windows to muffle the traffic sounds below, and a cozy bar and pretty little courtyard garden round out the charming amenities.

2, place des Pyramides, 75001. Tel: 42-60-31-10; Fax: 40-15-95-16. 1,400F–1,800F.

The ▶ **Normandy**, a few steps from the Louvre and the Palais-Royal, is a gracious, well staffed hotel that has lost little of its Belle Epoque charm since it opened as the height of fashion in 1877. Fortunately, a recent renovation carefully preserved everything that makes this intimate 140-room hotel so special. The old sleigh beds and commodious armoires have been spruced up, roomy old armchairs have been reupholstered, attractive new fabrics in subdued tones of rose, gray, and gold grace the walls and windows, and huge double sinks and deep bathtubs remain in the replumbed bathrooms. Corner rooms, with French windows opening on three sides, are especially roomy and bright. The clubby, paneled bar off the lobby is a fine spot for refreshments at the end of the day.

7, rue de l'Echelle 75001. Tel: 42-60-30-21; Fax 42-60-45-81; in U.S., (800) 223-9832. 1,375F–1,580F.

Wedged between the Louvre and the Comédie-Française, facing the famed shopping street rue du Faubourg-St-Honoré and peering up the avenue de l'Opéra, the ▶ **Louvre-Concorde** could hardly be more central. Its severely formal two-story lobby shimmers under a huge crystal chandelier; a formal staircase leads to the high-ceilinged, comfortable, and fairly expensive rooms. The mirrored dining room can be confusing, but a good outdoor café looks out onto the busy square and Palais-Royal.

Place André-Malraux, 75001. Tel: 42-61-56-01; Telex: 220412; Fax: 44-58-38-01; in U.S., (800) 888-4747 or (212) 752-3900; in U.K., (0800) 181-591. 1,300F–2,000F.

A former 18th-century convent named after its most famous resident, the ▶ **Baudelaire Opéra** is a much more reasonably priced option in the Opéra area than the Grand. The rooms are plain, with an occasional touch of splendor. The sparkling lobby is dominated by a somewhat Roman fresco, a theme that is halfheartedly repeated throughout the hotel. Conveniently located between the Opéra and the Palais-Royal.

61, rue Ste-Anne, 75002. Tel: 42-97-50-62; Telex: 216116; Fax: 42-86-85-85. 450F–600F.

Maybe it isn't as opulent as its MGM namesake, but ▶ **Le Grand Hôtel** on the Place de l'Opéra is pretty grand indeed, especially its white-marble and mahogany lobby. The recently renovated rooms are nicely done up and on the whole tasteful (especially the suites), and the columned and gilded l'Opéra dining room and La Verrèrie garden restaurant are spectacular examples of Second Empire excess. The Grand is very large, on the expensive side, and at times a little impersonal, but the service is generally quite good. A duplex health spa has recently been installed.

2, rue Scribe, 75009. Tel: 40-07-32-32; Telex: 220875; Fax: 42-66-12-51; in U.S., (800) 327-0200. 2,500F.

Les Halles, Marais, Bastille

Smack in the heart of Les Halles, the ▶ **Prince Hôtel Forum** provides character and service at moderate cost in a lively neighborhood. Rooms are soundproof, so proximity to the action won't interfere with your sleep at night. With pleasant, recently remodeled rooms in a very old building, the hotel has a full range of services.

83, rue Rambuteau, 75001. Tel: 42-36-15-90; Fax: 40-13-03-41. 570F–650F.

Just behind the St-Merri church, which bounds the Stravinsky fountain next to the Centre Georges Pompidou (yes, it is central), the small, cozy ▶ **Saint Merry** hotel offers an eccentric decor that seems to draw a very attractive clientele. Everything—bedspreads, wallpaper, curtains, even the wastebaskets—bears the same pattern. Several of the church's flying buttresses launch themselves through rooms, which can pose a danger for sleepwalkers or sudden wakers. Fun and very reasonably priced.

78, rue de la Verrerie, 75004. Tel: 42-78-14-15; Fax: 40-29-06-82. No credit cards. 400F–950F.

The ▶ **Hôtel de la Bretonnerie**, in the heart of the Marais, is the perfect headquarters for people who love wandering the *quartier*'s ancient, charming streets. The moderately priced rooms are neat and pleasant, though decorated with less than complete attention to matching colors and patterns, and each has a comfortable bathroom. The rooms on the airshaft are a bit dim, so it's best to avoid them. Redolent of a somewhat dated Paris bourgeois life. The management is quite cheerful.

22, rue Ste-Croix-de-la-Bretonnerie, 75004. Tel: 48-87-77-63; Fax: 42-77-26-78. 620F–730F.

Mere minutes from the Place des Vosges, a 1682 structure has been transformed into the ▶ **Hôtel Saint-Paul le Marais**. Two partners diligently oversee this small (there are only 27 equally small rooms) but spotless and comfortable family hotel. The bathrooms are modern, if cramped, and the breakfast room in the restored *cave* is contained within comfortable stone arches.

8, rue de Sévigné, 75004. Tel: 48-04-97-27; Fax: 48-87-37-04. 620F.

The historic Place des Vosges houses only one hotel, an honor reserved for the ▶ **Pavillon de la Reine**. This quiet, attractive, and luxurious hotel with a garden courtyard and interestingly decorated rooms and suites (a mix of modern and antique that can be fairly oppressive) is a favorite of those looking for high style and privacy. There is a nice fireplace in the wood-paneled lounge, but no restaurant.

28, place des Vosges, 75003. Tel: 42-77-96-40; Fax: 42-77-63-06; in U.S., (212) 477-1600 or (800) 366-1510. 1,650F–1,950F; suites 1,300F–1,950F.

Within sight of the Place de la Bastille and surrounded by worthwhile restaurants, the ▶ **Hôtel Bastille Spéria** is an inexpensive option in a very hip part of town. There's no old-world charm, as it's quite new, nor any real views, but the small rooms are spotless and crammed with features such as minibars and televisions that come as a surprise considering its low rates. The location cannot be beat and the mattresses are firm.

1, rue de la Bastille, 75004. Tel: 42-72-04-01; Fax: 42-72-56-38. 500F–600F.

Montmartre

Montmartre offers the modern ▶ **Timhôtel**, a very conveniently located member of a medium-priced chain. Bordering the picturesque and quiet Place Emile-Goudeau, the hotel has tasteful rooms, with those on the fourth and fifth floors offering extraordinary views of Paris. Picasso's and Braque's one-time studio, the Bateau-Lavoir, is next door (not open).

11, rue Ravignan, 75018. Tel: 42-55-74-79; Fax: 42-55-71-01. 410F.

The 18th-*arrondissement* charm almost entirely absent from Sacré-Coeur and the Place de Tertres blossoms in full on the pretty Place des Abbesses and the little market streets bordering it. ▶ **Regyn's Montmartre**, overlooking the *place,* benefits from both its location and the lovely garden courtyard within the hotel (request rooms on the courtyard away from the incessantly ringing church bells). The rooms are pleasantly priced and renovated, and the breakfast room is as bright and cheerful as the friendly and helpful staff, who are more than willing to assist visitors with getting to know the *quartier.*

18, place des Abbesses, 75018. Tel: 42-54-45-21; Fax: 42-23-76-79. 415F–500F.

The Islands

The ▶ **Hôtel du Jeu de Paume** is a welcome and comfortable addition to the charming Ile St-Louis. The dramatic cathedral-like lobby, framed by the same 17th-century wood beams that once housed a royal *jeu de paume* (an indoor court for an old game similar to tennis), gives patrons a delightful sense of old Paris. The rooms, while on the small side, are graciously decorated and packed with all the modern comforts. The marble-filled bathrooms are especially luxurious. Room 109 has a nice view of the pretty little Italian garden, but wherever you stay, take the glass elevator to the top floor for a panorama of the ancient game hall, or go down to the basement and enjoy the newly installed sauna.

54, rue St-Louis-en-l'Ile, 75004. Tel: 43-26-14-18; Fax: 40-46-02-76. 870F–1,130F.

The 17th-century hotel ▶ **Deux-Iles**, old-fashioned and

quaint, features a very welcoming lobby with flowered couches and white-painted beams. Ask for the biggest room in the house, because they are all very small. The ▶ **Saint Louis**, another charming hotel in the same vein just down the street, specializes in long stays and is charmingly and tastefully decorated.

Deux-Iles: 59, rue St-Louis-en-l'Ile, 75004. Tel: 43-26-13-35; Fax: 43-29-60-25. 750F–850F. Saint Louis: 75, rue St-Louis-en-l'Ile, 75004. Tel: 46-34-04-80; Fax: 46-34-02-13. 750F–850F. No credit cards at either hotel.

The ▶ **Henri IV** is a tiny, ancient hotel on a tiny, ancient square, the Place Dauphine on the Ile de la Cité. The management is very nice and the rooms are clean, if not particularly tasteful. Be sure to ask for one on the *place,* as the airshaft rooms are rather bleak. It's cheap, central, fun, and always packed with younger travellers. Write for a reservation.

25, place Dauphine, 75001. Tel: 43-54-44-53. No credit cards. 165F–195F.

THE LEFT BANK
Left Bank hotels tend to be smaller and more intimate than those across the Seine, and are usually less expensive.

St-Michel and the Latin Quarter
▶ **Esmeralda**, named after Quasimodo's bohemian flame, has the slightly eccentric, slightly funky character you might expect from such an inspiration. A block from both the Shakespeare & Co. bookshop and the Seine, the structure was built in 1640. The tiny lobby, with its stone walls and huge wood beams, leads to a handful of uniquely decorated rooms—and a sauna. Such actors as Julie Christie and Jane Birkin, who obviously appreciate a good bargain, have come here for the pleasantly odd atmosphere.

4, rue St-Julien-le-Pauvre, 75005. Tel: 43-54-19-20; Fax: 40-51-00-68; in U.S., (212) 254-2217 or (800) 755-9313. No credit cards. 340F–470F.

The ▶ **Hôtel de Nesle** is one of the most colorful places to stay in Paris. The expansive, friendly proprietress takes a personal interest in the young, decidedly Anglophone crowd that populates this small hotel on a short side street near the Seine. The office is more like a lounge or library, with a very Oriental feel. The rooms are adequate and quite cheap, and any shortcomings are overcome by the Nesle's vivacious personality.

7, rue de Nesle, 75006. Tel: 43-54-62-41. No credit cards. 260F (breakfast included).

In the heart of the Latin Quarter, the hotel ▶ **St-André-des-Arts** offers rooms ranging from tiny and cheap on the top floor to spacious and inexpensive on the lower floors. The inner rooms are somewhat shielded from the rollicking street outside, and the clientele runs to artists, dancers, and models.

66, rue St-André-des-Arts, 75006. Tel: 43-26-96-16; Fax: 43-29-73-34. No credit cards. 410F (breakfast included).

If you don't mind breakfasting at a Formica table and sharing a bath down the hall, you will be able to enjoy the ▶ **Hôtel Marignan** for its good qualities: dead-central location near the Latin Quarter, low prices, friendly, English-speaking staff (the owner is married to an American), and cheerful atmosphere. Come early in the day or call ahead—this hotel is often *complet*.

13, rue du Sommerard, 75005. Tel: 43-25-31-03. 260F (breakfast included).

Located just around the corner from the Jardin des Plantes (Paris's botanical gardens) and Les Arènes de Lutèce (the Roman arena), the ▶ **Hôtel des Grandes Ecoles** is a well-kept secret tucked away in an inexpensive corner of the Left Bank. The amenities here are rudimentary—rooms are equipped with not much more than quaint furnishings and functional baths—but you are paid back in charm: The hotel's three buildings surround a tree-filled garden and a terrace where you can have breakfast or tea, and the slightly worn air of the place suggests its many years of housing a devoted clientele, including visiting professors and intellectuals who come to Paris to speak at the nearby Sorbonne.

75, rue du Cardinal-Lemoine, 75005. Tel: 43-26-79-23; Fax: 43-25-28-15. 450F–600F.

Place de l'Odéon

The ▶ **Relais Christine**, opposite a repertory movie house a block from the Seine, is only a half-step behind L'Hôtel (see St-Germain-des-Prés, below) in terms of luxury. An abbey in the 16th century, the building features a handsome courtyard and a lovely garden. Breakfast is served in an ancient vaulted cave, and cocktail hour takes place in a clubby, wood-paneled lounge. Medieval artifacts—including beams that still bear traces of their original paint job, tapestries, and suits of armor—set the tone. Most of the bathrooms have been redone in marble, but ask especially for a finished one if only stone will do.

3, rue Christine, 75006. Tel: 43-26-71-80; Fax: 43-26-89-38; in U.S., (212) 254-2217 or (800) 755-9313. 1,350F–2,500F.

The ▶ **Grand Hôtel des Balcons** is named for its distinctive ironwork balconies, but what really sets this hotel apart is its good-natured and slightly eccentric staff. They, combined with the early-1900s decor in the lobby and stairwells (rooms are less dramatic but comfortable), make this an out-of-the-ordinary and very pleasant option in the heart of the bustling Latin Quarter, just seconds away from the Place de l'Odéon and the Luxembourg Garden.

3, rue Casimir-Delavigne, 75006. Tel: 46-34-78-50; Fax: 46-34-06-27. 395F–450F.

Between the graceful church of St-Germain-des-Prés and the massive St-Sulpice church, the medium-priced ▶ **Hôtel de l'Odéon** features a wood-beamed lobby, a warm reception, and some outstanding four-poster beds. Even the smaller rooms have an old-fashioned charm. The location is excellent. Half the rooms overlook the street, which is generally quiet at night, and half overlook the courtyard.

13, rue St-Sulpice, 75006. Tel: 43-25-70-11; Telex: 206731; Fax: 43-29-97-34. 580F–830F.

The ▶ **Récamier** is a simple hotel with a dated French decor (flowered wallpaper, pseudo-antique furniture) right on the Place St-Sulpice and a three-minute walk from the Luxembourg Garden. Nothing special, except that it is solid, dependable, moderately priced, and superbly located. Ask for one of the five rooms with windows on both the square and the courtyard—the light is great.

3 bis, place St-Sulpice, 75006. Tel: 43-26-04-89. No credit cards. 530F–600F (breakfast included).

Also near the Luxembourg Garden, the ▶ **Bonaparte**, like Napoléon's parceling out of Europe, is a family affair (the same family has kept patrons happy for several generations). Pleasant rooms and a homey salon have exposed beams and a dash of oddness to give them character. The Bonaparte is a good, less expensive option, although prices have risen somewhat after recent renovations.

61, rue Bonaparte, 75006. Tel: 43-26-97-37; Fax: 46-33-57-67. 520F–630F (breakfast included).

St-Germain-des-Prés

▶ **L'Hôtel** is the grandest accommodation on the Left Bank, a sliver of a building on a street crammed with art galleries and character, near the Place de l'Odéon. Each of the 27 luxuriously appointed rooms has a different decor, and the superb service is as straightforward as the name. There is an excellent piano bar in the hotel. It was here that Oscar Wilde spent his last days dying beyond his means.

13, rue des Beaux-Arts, 75006. Tel: 43-25-27-22; Fax: 43-25-64-81; in U.S., (212) 254-2217 or (800) 755-9313. 950F–2,100F; suite 3,600F.

One of Louis XIV's architects designed the ▶ **Hôtel des Saints-Pères** in 1658, and the structure reflects the period's fondness for rich decor—including some terrific frescoes and painted panels and a very pretty little garden courtyard. In warm months, breakfast and tea are served outside; there is a small, comfortable bar off the foyer. Friendly in a faintly formal way and relatively inexpensive.

65, rue des Saints-Pères, 75006. Tel: 45-44-50-00; Telex: 205424; Fax: 45-44-90-83. No American Express. 700F–1,000F.

Nestled between the Ecole des Beaux-Arts and the Faculté de Médecine, the rue Jacob boasts the ▶ **Marronniers** (Chestnut Trees), a lovely little hotel complete with a garden patio for breakfast. Ask for a room on the top floor, amid the mansards and cornices, for a view of the bell tower of the church of St-Germain-des-Prés, or for a room just above the garden. Quiet, reasonably priced, personable, and charming, the Marronniers is just right for a few romantic days in the Latin Quarter.

21, rue Jacob, 75006. Tel: 43-25-30-60; Fax: 40-46-83-56. No credit cards. 620F–680F.

An ancient façade cloaks Paris's most modern hotel interior at ▶ **La Villa**. The relentlessly designed rooms, with their quirky stools, built-in beds, and glamorous chrome-and-glass bathrooms, clash with the spirit of the *quartier,* but not with anyone interested in contemporary French design. Though not overly spacious, the rooms are well equipped, and no one can fail to appreciate the numbers beamed onto the carpet in front of each door. The ground-floor bar is a good place to meet for a drink.

29, rue Jacob, 75006. Tel: 43-26-60-00; Fax: 46-34-63-63. 800F–1,200F.

Called the ▶ **Angleterre** because it once housed the English embassy—Benjamin Franklin refused to enter its doors to sign a treaty because it was British territory—this affordable hotel retains many touches of its former splendor. Canopy beds adorn the deluxe suites, and ancient wood beams stretch across their ceilings. Rooms 40, 42, 47, and 49 are huge and worth the slight surcharge, so reserve well ahead. The lobby sports a bar and piano lounge, and there is a lovely flower-filled patio. Hemingway once lived here.

44, rue Jacob, 75006. Tel: 42-60-34-72; Fax: 42-60-16-93. 750F–1,000F.

The ▶ **Quai Voltaire** hotel is nestled on the quai from which it takes its name, the square between the Biblio-thèque Mazarin and the Musée d'Orsay. Most rooms have superb views of the Seine and unfortunately good acoustics:

The traffic from the street below can get loud. The building is old and not all the rooms are in tiptop shape, but it still has the charm—and the rates—that drew the composers Wagner and Sibelius.

19, quai Voltaire, 75007. Tel: 42-61-50-91; Fax: 42-61-62-26. 650F–700F.

The ► **Ferrandi** offers 19th-century charm in a period house, which means that some of the rooms tread a delicate balance between pretty and kitschy. Others, though, are truly beautiful, such as rooms 33 and 43, which are large and sport canopy beds, and rooms 40 and 49, done in a neat Baroque style. Well kept and well run in a quiet neighborhood in the southwest corner of the 6th *arrondissement*.

92, rue du Cherche-Midi, 75006. Tel: 42-22-97-40; Fax: 45-44-89-97. 540F–920F.

The ► **Lutétia** was refurbished and rejuvenated a few years ago to recapture much of the Art Deco glory that made it famous (especially the stunning paneling in the excellent **Le Paris** restaurant). Some of the rooms are very large (a luxury for which you will pay) and have pretty views of the tree-filled Place Boulicaut at Sèvres-Babylone across the street. There are imposing yet comfortable sitting rooms off the lobby, and its **Brasserie Lutétia** is a pretty, if predictable, restaurant.

45, boulevard Raspail, 75006. Tel: 49-54-46-46; Telex: 270424; Fax: 49-54-46-00; in U.S., (212) 752-3900 or (800) 888-4747; in U.K., (0800) 181-591. 1,500F–2,050F.

A true writer's hotel should be slightly seedy and on a bustling egalitarian street, and it should charge egalitarian prices. ► **Louisiane** qualifies. It housed Sartre and Jacques Prévert in the old days, and it is home to a few real-life writers today. Overlooking the rue de Buci market, Louisiane is perhaps not the quietest of hotels, but the lively rows of fruit stands, greengrocers, butchers, and more are worth the bustle. Ask for the round rooms; they embody the absence of sharp edges one finds here.

60, rue de Seine, 75006. Tel: 43-29-59-30; Fax: 46-34-23-87. 600F (breakfast included).

Faux marbre walls in the corridors and trompe l'oeil murals in the breakfast room may give you the impression that the ► **Duc de St-Simon** is not for real. It is, being a very tasteful hotel in a late-17th-century *maison particulier*. The rooms, some with small terraces, are quite pretty, and the suites are very comfortable. There is a garden on the first floor, and the street is particularly picturesque.

14, rue St-Simon, 75007. Tel: 45-48-35-66; Telex: 203277;

Fax: 45-48-68-25. No credit cards. 1,000F–1,400F; suites 1,450F–1,800F.

Sixty years ago the ▶ **Lenox-St-Germain** was a *pension* favored by such folks as James Joyce and Ezra Pound. Later the Lost Generation prowled its halls. Today the small lobby is still welcoming, and the rooms are very nice (especially 22, 32, and 42) and nicely priced. For a splurge ask for the duplex suite. The cozy Art Deco bar is a quiet place for a late drink.

9, rue de l'Université, 75007. Tel: 42-96-10-95; Fax: 42-61-52-83. 530F–870F.

Old France retains some vigor in the pretty little ▶ **Hôtel de l'Université**, a 17th-century *hôtel particulier* with exposed wood beams and a general air of charm and discretion. The rooms are small but well appointed, and the comfortable bathrooms have marble tubs. Try for the room with the fireplace that overlooks the pretty courtyard or one of the two top-floor rooms with a terrace. Breakfast at the long table off the lobby is communal.

22, rue de l'Université, 75007. Tel: 42-61-09-39; Fax: 42-60-40-84. 850F–1,300F.

Invalides

A stone's throw from the Eiffel Tower, ▶ **La Bourdonnais** is a good option for those who prefer calm but still want to be near the main sights. Housed in a former private apartment building, the Bourdonnais is in the heart of the residential area of the elegant 7th *arrondissement*. The decor is somewhat heavy-handed with antiques and thick carpets, but the overall effect is cozy and comfortable, and the staff is quite friendly.

111, avenue de La Bourdonnais. No American Express. Tel: 47-05-45-42; Fax: 45-55-75-54. 650F.

The ▶ **Hôtel Saint Dominique** is nestled in the middle of one of the more picturesque market streets in Paris. The rue St-Dominique runs from the Champ-de-Mars to the Invalides through the 7th *arrondissement,* and is lined with gourmet food shops, clothing boutiques, and good restaurants. The hotel is slightly cramped in size, but its rustic charms make up for the lack of square footage. Ask for the room on the fourth floor with the view of the Eiffel Tower.

62, rue St-Dominique. Tel: 47-05-51-44; Fax: 47-05-81-28. 460F–500F.

Those tired of the unrelenting old-world feel of the city should take a room in the ▶ **Montalembert**, a model of the best in modern French design. This newly refurbished hotel in the heart of the city's literary quarter is quickly attracting a hip crowd from city capitals around the world. Star French designer Christian Liaigre redid the entire hotel, right down to the new curlicue door handles, but some rooms have maintained the occasional antique French touch so you don't forget where you are. It's worth dropping by for a coffee in the downstairs lounge, especially on a rainy day— the piles of magazines and the crackling fire make it one of the more inviting spots in town.

3, rue Montalembert, 75007. Tel: 45-48-68-11; Fax: 42-22-58-19. 1,525F–2,000F.

—*Edward Hernstadt and Mimi Tompkins*

DINING

Paris has long had a justly earned reputation for its superb cuisine. But in a city of some 20,000 restaurants and cafés, eating well is a surprisingly difficult challenge. Guidebooks are a must: The seemingly similar cafés and small brasseries that line almost every street are too often similar in their mediocrity as well, and many visitors leave Paris sadly dissatisfied. With a little care, though, you can dine as beautifully as the city's fame promises.

Paris haute cuisine, though more expensive than ever, still sets the world standard for sublime and inventive meals served with an emphasis on extreme comfort. The resulting pool of talented chefs means that there is also a reasonably broad range of restaurants that are distinctly less costly (250 to 500 francs per person, rather than 550 francs and up), yet offer innovative and tasty dishes.

Bistros and brasseries still form the solid middle level of Paris restaurants in terms of price (100 to 300 francs), originality, and tastiness of the food. If you want to eat after the witching hour (for most restaurants and cafés, 10:30 P.M.), these old-time eateries are the best and often only bet.

Wine bars take two forms: the modern, which offer *nouvelle* dishes along with a selection of wines, and the traditional, where it is customary to munch on cheese or sausages and Poilane bread. In both, a satisfying repast for less than 130 francs is standard.

Cafés and tearooms fall more or less into the same price range as wine bars: The former feature such traditional snacks as *croques monsieur* and baguette sandwiches, while the latter emphasize tarts (both sweet and with vegetables) and quiches.

HAUTE CUISINE

Gloriously refined meals in sumptuously appointed rooms; attentive waiters hovering discreetly just out of sight; magnificent wines glowing in balloon glasses as one astoundingly subtle and elegant dish succeeds another: the stuff of dreams, perhaps, but not in Paris. In fact, the *haute gamme* food business is raging on vigorously, ignoring the death of *nouvelle cuisine* and such subspecies as *cuisine de terroir* (almost unrecognizably refined "country" food) and "light" dishes for dieters.

Today the world of fine dining is ruled by chefs rather than by restaurant owners or the great "names," the Maxims, of yore. Some chefs, like Joël Robuchon at Jamin, are very low-key, content to remain sequestered in the kitchen, rarely even showing themselves at the end of a service. Others, like Alain Senderens, have cultivated a reputation away from the cutting board (Senderens enjoys his role of "philosopher/chef," making weighty declarations on the state of cooking and frequently sporting ties and eyeglasses of a matching color). But the best chefs, in any guise, are worth the 550- to 1,000-franc bill that is standard at their restaurants, as well as the straining waistline and general aura of peace on earth and good will toward men that suffuses your amble home. For all of these, reserve at least five days in advance, if not far earlier.

Haute Cuisine: 16th and 17th Arrondissements

Jamin (Joël Robuchon), at 59, avenue Raymond-Poincaré in the 16th *arrondissement* (Jamin moved from rue de Longchamp in late 1993), is unquestionably the best mix of the mysterious ingredients that signal greatness in a restaurant. The small main room is intimate and elegant. Huge bouquets of flowers and folding screens of vaguely ancient origin isolate the tables; Roman busts, dated engravings, and tasteful red velvet banquettes contribute to the refined and harmonious ambience. The food is truly sublime: roast duck with spices for two, cooked in an enormous copper casserole with a ring of pastry baked around the rim to seal in every molecule of flavor; *purée de pommes de terre* (the world's best mashed potatoes, with a hint of garlic); boned leg of lamb baked in a salt and thyme crust; langoustines, either in ravioli or with cabbage. The wine list is extensive and excellent, and everyone, from the wine steward to the maître d'hôtel, is remarkably courteous and down-to-earth. The bad news? Reserve at least two months in advance. Tel: 47-27-12-27. (Closed weekends and July.)

Henri Faugeron has redone the strange, dark decor of his restaurant with a restrained and harmonious feel—soft blues and yellows and gilded Deco touches—without changing in the least the consistently notable caliber of his cooking. His creations are less gaudy and thus perhaps less outstanding than those of some of his compatriots, but dishes like the house-smoked salmon, shrimp and cabbage salad, the several versions of roast duck, and *ris de veau* with lentil-stuffed ravioli are delectable. The solid cooking (though in these circles, that means eye-opening) and relaxed atmosphere make Faugeron a popular spot. The service, as is usual for any of these restaurants, is dedicated. Faugeron and three other chefs, Les Toques Gourmands, banded together to buy wine in bulk and rented a huge underground warehouse to store their now vast communal cellar, which means that the wine list is quite good, though best on the more recent vintages. 52, rue de Longchamp, 75016. Tel: 47-04-24-53; Fax: 47-55-62-90. (Closed weekends, August, and Christmas through New Year's.)

On the other side of the Arc de Triomphe, at 18, rue Troyon in the 17th *arrondissement,* **Guy Savoy** continues to minister to the hungry in what was once Le Bernardin (now in New York). This is wonderful, because his former headquarters in the rue Duret was just too cramped to contain the faithful who flocked to experience the monklike Savoy's marvelous mixture of country, traditional, and completely inventive cooking. This young chef is constantly experimenting and growing in the kitchen. Your best and most adventurous move here: Order *le menu dégustation* and try Savoy's latest original and beautifully presented dishes. He has a sure touch with langoustines and lobster, and his variations on duck are all winners. The cheeses are particularly good, and for dessert have the *mille-feuilles* (what in the United States and often in the United Kingdom is served in a heavy-handed and limited version as "napoleon")—they are always works of art. Avoid lunch, which is made almost drab by the multitudes of somber-suited business people. His three bistros are also top-notch (see Bistro de l'Etoile, below). Tel: 43-80-40-61; Fax: 46-22-43-09. (Closed Saturdays for lunch, Sundays, and weekends from Easter through September.)

Michel Rostang has side-by-side restaurants in the 17th *arrondissement* (see Bistrot d'à Côté Flaubert, below) and comes to the trade by blood: His father and younger brother run the wonderful La Bonne Auberge in Antibes. Rostang's first-string restaurant, with its formal, fancy, and, to the delicate, perhaps oppressive decor, is a mighty work indeed.

The cuisine is varied and moves from the classic bour-geois—ambrosial ravioli stuffed with goat cheese in a chicken broth—to the otherworldly—quails' eggs poached inside sea urchins. The delicate, rosy lamb, redolent with herbs, is exactly what you dream lamb should be. One possible drawback to a quiet, intimate, oh-so-French dinner is the number of Anglophones, though the dollar's relative weakness has alleviated this problem in all of Paris's great restaurants. Order the Pantagruelian menu if only a seven-course feast will suffice. The cheeses and desserts are deli-cious, the wine list ample, and the refined atmosphere conducive to those who take their pleasure at the table. 20, rue Rennequin. Tel: 47-63-40-77; Fax: 47-63-82-75. (Closed Saturdays for lunch, Sundays, and first two weeks of August.)

When Philippe Groult left the large, stone-walled Manoir de Paris to open his own restaurant, he changed everything but the excellence of his cooking, which has only improved with his move to independence. **Amphyclès** is a tiny, very pretty room overflowing with flowers and friendly, spirited service at 78, avenue des Ternes in the 17th *arrondisse-ment*. Groult sticks to the basics in his cuisine, with the superb *raviolis de pigeon* a good example of his craft: chunks of pungent, earthy pigeon folded into a giant, melt-ing ravioli with creamy morsels of foie gras and hints of truffles. Each ingredient enhances the particular delicacy and character of the other, the whole exceeding its parts. Order the most interesting and exotic dishes on the menu, as the more standard items tend to be just that: extremely well executed standards. The cheese tray is fabulous and desserts are worth saving room for, especially the *pot de crème*. The wine list is both a bit pricey and a bit limited, though there are some good bargains, and the sommelier is a real pro. Very good value for the money. Reserve; Tel: 40-68-01-01; Fax: 40-68-91-88. (Closed Saturdays for lunch, Sundays, and three weeks in July.)

Rounding out the sedate 17th *arrondissement* is **Apicius**, at 122, avenue de Villiers. The cool, rather small room, the young and attractive Madame Vigato, and the lively atmo-sphere make Apicius a place for you and friends to eat extremely well and make some noise doing it. Jean-Pierre Vigato is another one of those young and creative chefs who has moved well past the strictures of *nouvelle cuisine* and simply cooks what he thinks is tasty. Not everyone agrees with his very personal approach—grilled pig's trotters and exquisite sautéed foie gras sit side by side on the menu. Such juxtapositions are heaven for some, hell for others. Other usual winners include the frog's legs, succulent *coquilles St-Jacques* reminiscent of those at the old Ambroisie, and a lovely, meaty rabbit that is so good you will forever after think of "bunny" as a consumable dish. The varied wine list includes some fairly reasonably priced bottles, but the service, mood, and desserts here could stand some sprucing up. Though still quite good, Apicius has slipped a notch or two within the past few years. Note, though, that Vigato has also opened a second, less expensive restaurant just outside the city gates (see La Manufacture, below). Tel: 43-80-19-66; Fax: 44-40-09-57. (Closed weekends, August, and Christmas.)

Haute Cuisine: Champs-Elysées

There is probably a greater concentration of immodestly expensive restaurants in the 8th *arrondissement* than anywhere else in Paris, though unfortunately that does not mean an equal concentration of culinary wonders. Still, three stops in particular are worth the weighty checks: Taillevent, Les Ambassadeurs, and Lucas-Carton.

If style, class, and a dignified atmosphere are as important as cooking, **Taillevent** is the best restaurant in Paris. Set in a well-preserved Second Empire *hôtel particulier* at 15, rue Lamennais, Taillevent better defines the art of dining out than that of eating well. The tasteful wood-paneled walls and crystal chandeliers in the main room, or the ornate yet unimposing grandeur of the smaller room; the perfect, understated service (you rarely see a waiter until, alerted by some imperceptible gesture or stray thought, one sweeps up to the table an instant before being signaled); the gracious welcome of Jean-Claude Vrinat, the restaurateur who should be a template for all restaurant owners (Vrinat is so gracious, and confident, that he insists the food at Robuchon is the best in Paris); the vast, varied, and surprisingly affordable wine list—these embody the Taillevent dining experience.

Unfortunately, magical, inventive cuisine was left off the list. The food, by Claude Deligne, is awfully good but cannot live up to the experience of eating it. The ingredients are always fresh, the dishes of a modified classicism, and the menu changes frequently (upon request, the house will give diners an outdated one). Order according to what rings true or ask Monsieur Vrinat for his recommendations—everything is tasty, especially the desserts. The bill will be appropriately serious, but you need no longer fear for your safety carrying an immense sheaf of 500-franc bills: Taillevent finally accepts Visa. Reserve at least two months in advance for dinner, less for lunch. Tel: 45-61-12-90; Fax: 42-25-95-18.

(Closed weekends, the last week of July, and the first three weeks of August.)

A different kind of style typifies **Les Ambassadeurs**, the majestic dining room of the Hôtel Crillon at 10, place de la Concorde, a stone's throw from both the U.S. and British embassies. The hotel itself was built in 1758 by the architect Jacques-Ange Gabriel and was used as a residence until 1920. Entrance to the restaurant is through the hotel's opulent front hall, past the piano bar and courtyard—which in the summer is itself a delightful spot to lunch—and into a room that looks exactly like what it once was: the imposing grand salon of a fabulous *hôtel particulier*. Red, beige, and white Sienese marble walls and floors greet the eye, and the vast 30-foot windows look out onto the Place de la Concorde and the illuminated Egyptian obelisk that sits placidly on the same spot where thousands died during the revolution of 1793–1794, their heads sliced from their bodies as neatly as Les Ambassadeurs's chef now dices zucchini.

The atmosphere is formal (famed food critic Henri Gault advises that "if you don't wear a tie you will be shot, with a look, anyway, and someone will bring you one") but not at all oppressive. It's as if the staff assumes that if one dines at Les Ambassadeurs, one is a member of an elite club and due all privileges granted thereby, which is a far cry from the haughtiness of the staffs of some top Paris restaurants. The food by chef Christian Constant completes this sense of privilege. Constant is particularly gifted with fish: Try his delicious tiny *rouget* filets roasted in fennel oil and served with a small tart of tomatoes and mozzarella or the John Dory in a sauce of parsley and aromatic spices. Go to the Crillon for a romantic and anachronistic meal; the surroundings give you a sense of the extreme luxury that defined the ancien régime. Tel: 44-71-16-16; Fax: 44-71-15-02. (Open every day of the year.)

Lucas-Carton is perhaps the most controversial great restaurant in Paris; master chef Alain Senderens does his best to ensure that. The reservation list is long (at least a month for dinner), the portions can be minute, the dishes can miss the mark, and the prices are monumental (a group of eight Americans is alleged to have spent 55,000 francs on a meal—most of it on rare wines). Nonetheless, Senderens prepares some of the best food in the world; order well and a successful meal at Lucas-Carton is as memorable as a feast hosted by Tolstoy's Count Ilya Rostov.

The magnificent Belle Epoque decor announces that something special is at hand: rich, burnished, wood-paneled walls by Louis Majorelle; comfortable, dark brown banquettes separated into individual dining spaces by carved wood and glass dividers; tall, beveled mirrors; and huge floral arrangements. Senderens, who perhaps considers himself the best-dressed chef in Paris, has outfitted his many waiters, stewards, and captains in sober tuxedos, the different pastel shades of the requisite bow tie alone distinguishing each staff member's station.

Senderens is no stranger to the long-renowned restaurant at 9, place de la Madeleine: He worked in the kitchen there more than 30 years ago. In a sense, his return to his beginnings in the mid-1980s mirrors his philosophy at the stove, where he constantly revives and updates ancient recipes (like the famous honey-and-spice-covered *canard Apicius*, which dates back at least 2,000 years). Today Senderens continues to innovate—he was perhaps the first to impose Oriental combinations and ideas on French cuisine—and his masterpieces are extraordinary indeed. Anything with langoustine, foie gras (such as the warm foie gras salad latticed with sheafs of truffles), lobster (such as the miraculous lobster in vanilla sauce), or game is bound to be impeccable and original. The service has gotten better (that is, less pretentious and pressured), and the wine list is extensive. Senderens's latest obsession is the "marriage of food and wine," so it behooves you to try a *menu dégustation* with selected wines included, or the cheese dish consisting of five cheeses and five (usually unexpected) wines. Be prepared to cash in your Christmas Club fund before you go. Tel: 42-65-22-90; Fax: 42-65-06-23. (Closed Saturdays for lunch, Sundays, and three weeks in August.)

Haute Cuisine: Center

Alain Dutournier has settled in beautifully in his polished, eccentric Place Vendôme restaurant, the **Carré des Feuillants** at 14, rue de Castiglione in the 1st *arrondissement*. Moreover, Dutournier has continued to grow in the kitchen, daily showing himself to be one of the most consistently brilliant and imaginative chefs in Paris. The new restaurant cost a fortune to build, with its odd, half-majestic, half-absurd stone entrance hall—featuring an ice-filled sarcophagus that is used to cool Champagne and bunches of plastic grapes housing light fixtures—striking blond wood walls, and sober, surreal paintings of monstrous fruits and vegetables being carried to market. At first this lavish expense—a far cry from his more modest 12th *arrondissement* gem Au Trou Gascon (see below)—put a heavy financial burden on Dutournier, which may explain the occasionally hurried service or dishes that didn't live up to the very high expectations his cooking had raised.

Today *chez* Dutournier is a marvel, and it is perhaps the only great restaurant in Paris that exhibits its owner's sense of humor in addition to his commitment to the highest cooking standards. The cuisine is a fascinating mix of south-western traditional and innovation. All the duck dishes are wonderful, as are the foie gras creations (especially the sublime *risotto au foie gras*). Dutournier is especially good at using rustic foods in a sophisticated way, perhaps evidenced most remarkably by his appetizer of cold lentils mixed with fresh raw oysters under a layer of wafer-thin slices of raw sea scallop. The extremely pleasant sommelier, Jean-Guy Loustau, sports one of the most distinguished mustaches in Paris and makes a point of recommending lesser known (and less expensive) wines. Despite its growing pains, the Carré des Feuillants is an extremely enjoyable place to dine. Tel: 42-86-82-82; Fax: 42-86-07-71. (Closed Saturdays for lunch and Sundays; closed Saturdays in July, and all of August.)

Since Bernard Pacaud moved his restaurant **L'Ambroisie** from its cramped home down the block from the Tour d'Argent to refined and sumptuous quarters at number 9 on the venerable Place des Vosges, the resoundingly imaginative chef has reaped the recognition his wonderful and quintessentially tasteful (you can detect the full flavor of any ingredient Pacaud chooses to use) cooking deserves.

This restaurant is particularly inviting: The high ceilings, massive chandelier, stone walls, and floral displays transform its two rooms into a sanctuary of fine dining. But the fare is the feature here. Pacaud, like Dutournier, revels in renovating and adapting traditional recipes and ingredients in dynamic ways. For years his red pepper mousse dominated discussion of his cooking. Pacaud uses the now-trademark dish as an *amuse-bouche* (literally "amuse your mouth"—an appetizer before the appetizer to get the salivary glands flowing), but try the huge, succulent sea scallops or the meaty, complex wild duck and foie gras "cake." The wine list is pricey but good. Tel: 42-78-51-45. (Closed Sundays and Mondays; also three weeks in August, two weeks in February.)

Haute Cuisine: Left Bank
Partly because of its former working-class and bohemian character, and also because it's so solidly residential, the Left Bank boasts very few truly great restaurants. Within recent years, however, the quai in front of Notre-Dame has become

something of a nursery for rising culinary stars. Bernard Pacaud's L'Ambroisie was born on the quai de la Tournelle, as was Gilles Epié's restaurant, Miravile, which later moved across the river to the quai de l'Hôtel-de-Ville; and Philippe de Givenchy, whose La Timonerie remains on the waterfront, is very much a young talent to watch. Gilles Epié obviously remains convinced by this location, as his very popular and very good new restaurant, Campagne et Provence, occupies the same quai-side quarters that formerly housed Miravile. (Miravile, La Timonerie, and Campagne et Provence are discussed below.)

Characteristic of a certain rather sad breed of Paris restaurant—those whose international renown has brought in a drove of clients with newly fattened wallets and the indifferent palates that are the bane of any really great chef—is the **Tour d'Argent**, which, like Maxim's and L'Orangerie, is now an experience that has more to do with money than food. Michelin still gives the Tour d'Argent its mythic three-star rating, but that must be on the basis of price rather than quality. Certainly the view—of Notre-Dame's spotlit flying buttresses—is unparalleled. And the history is undeniable: Relics include the table where three emperors—Alexander II, the Czar of Russia; his son, Alexander III; and Wilhelm I of Prussia—and Chancellor Bismarck of Prussia once dined; and the signatures of famous customers, including Richard Nixon, that paper the foyer and elevator. But even a postcard recording forever the serial number of the particular duck—rather boringly prepared—that you consumed, or a phone booth that was once a palanquin can't make up for the uninspired food and unbelievable prices (such as a truffle salad for $140, a lobster appetizer—last seen being fed to one diner's hound—for $110, or a dish of clear soup for $45). Perhaps after an enormously costly meal the unwary diner won't, as did Jean-Baptiste Grenouille's first master in *Perfume,* fall into the Seine and drown, but he will feel as if his bank account had. (If you don't know this excellent novel by Patrick Süskind, pick up a copy; the plot, which turns on the malodorousness of medieval Paris, will really nourish your imagination *sur place.*)

Alain Passard, once a student of Alain Senderens, becomes more the equal of his former master every year. With the recent and successful redecoration of **L'Arpège**, in quarters that once housed Senderens's Archestrate, Passard seems to have really come into his own. Is there perhaps even a little symbolism in the fact that Senderens's dark, mirrored surfaces have been replaced by Passard's relaxed and airy blond-wood wall screens and chairs and rosy walls? Who's to say, but it's becoming increasingly less necessary to qualify the restaurant at 84, rue de Varenne in the 7th *arrondissement* by mentioning that it once housed L'Archestrate. While it is true that L'Arpège is one of the best restaurants for the price in Paris, especially the bargain lunch menu, it would be worth visiting at twice the price. The menu is full of wonderful-sounding and delicious-tasting dishes, including a remarkable rosemary lobster in leek leaves, cabbage stuffed with crab meat, and a duck cooked "according to my mother's recipe." Also delectable are the hare and the pigeon. The wine list is somewhat limited, but who cares? Tel: 45-51-47-33; Fax: 44-18-98-39. (Closed Saturdays and for lunch on Sundays.)

Some people find the excellent cooking at **Jacques Cagna** a little unimaginative, while others think the decor borders on the too self-consciously refined, but no one can deny that this 17th-century town house is one of the most charming restaurants in Paris. Admitted through the dark red door, you climb a narrow staircase to the main dining room, an intimate, comfortable space under huge old beams that's done up in blond oak, salmon-colored fabric, and Flemish school still lifes; the overall effect is welcoming yet elegant—people dress up for dinner here as they do for a meal at Lucas-Carton. It's true that Cagna has a horror of the kind of *creative* cuisine that's currently popular, so you won't find lobster in vanilla sauce on his menu. Rather, Cagna provokes with his subtlety, evidenced in a dish like Mediterranean brill stuffed with oysters and served with a watercress sauce, or in the quality of his simpler dishes. His *côte de boeuf*, for example, is aged Angus beef from Aberdeen and is served with a superb potato purée that's doused with a sauce of marrow and shallots. The desserts, such as the luscious chocolate cake with walnuts, are excellent. The enormous wine list is top-heavy with pricey bottles, but there are still a few good choices to be made for 150 francs or less. 14, rue des Grands-Augustins, 75006. Tel: 43-26-49-39; Fax: 43-54-54-48. (Closed Saturdays for lunch, Sundays, and August; open two Saturday evenings per month.)

EXPENSIVE AND MODERATE

Unfortunately, *les crèmes de la crème* are often completely booked up or just too expensive. But there is a second tier of restaurants in Paris that are almost as good as the finest, definitely more accessible, and often far less costly (200 to

500 francs). Some, like the Jules Verne in the Eiffel Tower, are exceptional for their location or view, while others, like Le Divellec, feature cuisine of a very high standard.

Expensive and Moderate: Right Bank

Pile ou Face takes its name—"heads or tails"—from its proximity to the Paris stock exchange, the Bourse. But a meal here is no gamble: The fresh ingredients (many of which come from the owner's Norman farm) and careful, frequently original preparation guarantee a toothsome repast. It is also one of the pleasantest restaurants in Paris, situated at 52 bis, rue Notre-Dame des Victoires, in the 2nd *arrondissement,* on two tiny floors in three tinier rooms—none of which has more than five tables. Lunchtime crowds are dominated by huddled stockbrokers plotting their afternoon trades, but at dinner Pile ou Face's true charm comes into play. The lighting is muted, and soft classical music wafts gently through the charming rooms. The comfortable 1930s decor adds to the romantic atmosphere. The service is attentive enough, and the rabbit with rosemary is especially tasty. Tel: 42-33-64-33; Fax: 42-36-61-09. (Closed weekends, August, and Christmas week.)

The sign outside **Pharamond** promises a "true" tripe from Normandy, and a genuine *tripe à la mode de Caen* is exactly what you get—one of the best in Paris. But even if you don't favor that particular specialty, this little restaurant in the heart of the changing Les Halles neighborhood in the 1st *arrondissement* is still worth a visit. The turn-of-the-century decor (mirrored windows, bright ceramic tiles portraying fruits and flowers, a delicate restored steel staircase leading up to the second floor) and the immaculate table settings and formal service are a joy. So too is the food, with delicious duck and many typical Normandy dishes. The apple cider, also from Normandy, is outstanding. 24, rue de la Grande-Truanderie. Tel: 42-33-06-72; Fax: 40-28-01-81. (Closed Sundays, for lunch Mondays, and three weeks in August.)

Though the food at **Le Domarais** is very good, its remarkable decor, unique in Paris, is also a compelling reason to try this small restaurant near the National Archives in the Marais district. Passing through a rather nondescript courtyard, you enter what was once the first auction hall in Paris, built during the reign of Louis XVI. The small room is dominated from above by a magnificent glass dome, and intimacy results more from the vertical spaciousness than from the distance between tables. A circular staircase on one side leads up to a catwalk overlooking the opulent salon where auctioneers' jewels and precious objets d'art were once displayed. The cuisine is a fine, slightly *nouvelle* rendering of such standard dishes as veal with foie gras, roast duck with fruit or *au poivre,* and an excellent puff pastry with wild mushrooms. The classical music completes the sensation of dining in long-gone splendor. 53 bis, rue des Francs-Bourgeois, 75004. Tel: 42-74-54-17. (Closed for lunch Saturdays, Sundays, and Mondays.)

The delicate fin-de-siècle glass conservatory dome over the intimate dining room of **Les Elysées du Vernet**, a palm-trees-in-planters kind of place in the Hôtel Vernet, is very handsome but offers no clue as to the cuisine. Chef Bruno Cirino does a brilliant job putting a spin on traditional plates from his native Nice and elsewhere on the Riviera and in Provence. An example: sautéed rouget filets served in anis-scented coconut milk and garnished with parmesan shavings. Not *nouvelle* but inventive, the food here is superb. Other gastronomic beauties include the crab meat with pumpkin gnocchi, roasted sea bass with saffron potatoes, and, as a finale, the preserved yellow plums with cinnamon ice cream. In what is currently a rather quiet corner of Paris—so good for a serious or secret meal—this restaurant is one of the city's best buys. 25, rue Vernet. 75008. Tel: 47-23-43-10. Closed weekends and July 23 to August 24.

A very successful restaurant in a colorful part of town (at 2, place d'Anvers in the 9th *arrondissement,* a block from Pigalle, one of Paris's more notorious red-light districts), **La Table d'Anvers** features inventive cooking in a funky, slightly tacky room dominated by lacquered oranges and grays and leafy plants. The cook and staff are young and tend to be slow, but they are full of charm and have a will to please. The food is very pleasing indeed, with a delectable oyster salad, plump roast fish, and a very tasty roast shoulder of lamb. Tel: 48-78-35-21; Fax: 45-26-66-67. (Closed Saturdays for lunch, Sundays, and three weeks in August.)

It's not easy to get a reservation at the **Port Alma** restaurant, and it's easy to see why. This beautifully decorated, traditional-style seafood restaurant on the river at 10, avenue de New-York in the 16th *arrondissement* not only has a splendid view of the Eiffel Tower from its main dining room, but also serves some of the best seafood in Paris. Start with baby clams in thyme-flavored cream or the excellent salad of scallops and mixed greens and then maybe split the luscious *bar* (sea bass) baked in a crust of salt. Desserts such as figs stuffed with whipped cream and raspberries are very good, too, as is the service; the hostess speaks English, which is a help for those who aren't familiar with the different array of fish that come from European waters. Tel: 47-23-75-11. (Closed Sundays and August.)

In terms of relatively new restaurants with talented young chefs, Marcel and Marie-Noëlle Baudis of **L'Oulette** have recently done the nearly impossible: They've received an enormous amount of laudatory publicity without allowing it to upset the kitchen. A pretty, spacious room at 15, place Lachambeaudie in the 12th *arrondissement,* L'Oulette is one of the better things to happen to Paris dining in years. Young master Baudis and his wife have created a restaurant that is intimate, homey, fun, reasonably priced, and blessed with food that is extraordinarily good and screaming with character. To start, the *escabèche,* carpaccio, or escargots are exquisite yet soulful, and the *pintade* and roast duckling make your palate ache with pleasure. The service, proffered in large part by Madame Baudis (who recommends the restaurant's small, very reasonable, southwest-dominated wines), is perfect. Call a week in advance for a reservation or write ahead. L'Oulette is a must. Tel: 40-02-02-12. (Closed Saturdays for lunch, Sundays, and August.)

To catch another rising star, come to Muriel and Gilles Epié's **Miravile**, which recently moved from the Left Bank to handsome new quarters on the quai de l'Hôtel-de-Ville. The new restaurant is stylish and cozy, with pretty trompe l'oeil walls that are a perfect foil to the much-acclaimed cuisine here. What has drawn the raves is a lively and imaginative twist on many Paris restaurant standards. Rather than serving smoked salmon, for example, Miravile offers a *jambon de canard,* thin slices of smoked duck breast served with fresh mango, and similarly reinvents *hachis Parmentier,* the homely but delicious dish of ground meat with a potato crust, by using cod instead of beef. Desserts, such as a coffee-whiskey tart, are superb, too. Miravile recently introduced a 220-franc lunch menu, and new specialties include a *beignet de fois gras caramelisé au porto* (fois gras caramelized in port wine) and *aiguillettes de canard au sang pâtes fraîches* (strips of wild duck with fresh pasta). 72, quai de l'Hôtel-de-Ville, 75004; Tel: 42-74-72-22; Fax: 42-74-67-55. (Closed Saturdays for lunch and Sundays.)

Deep in the heart of the 11th *arrondissement,* a vast and, for most tourists, untravelled region, lies **A Sousceyrac**, a restaurant redolent of an old-time dedication to solid, grand bourgeois cooking and a neighborly atmosphere. The bright interior, divided neatly into smaller areas by the ancient oak wainscoting, is as welcoming as the chef, Gabriel Asfaux, who routinely wanders out from the kitchen to gossip with the regulars and make sure newcomers are happy. The food is traditional and leans heavily to game—especially the restaurant's renowned, and today hard-to-find, *lièvre à la royale,* a heady mix of hare, shallots, onion, and cinnamon wrapped around foie gras and truffles. The menu also features such dishes as a particularly rich cassoulet, sausage, foie gras, and a handful of newer creations. To dine in this honest and pleasant restaurant at 35, rue Faidherbe is to enjoy the special character of an idyllic French eating experience. Tel: 43-71-65-30; Fax: 40-09-79-75. (Closed Saturdays for lunch, Sundays, and August.)

Despite Alain Dutournier's defection to posher quarters near the Place Vendôme (see Carré des Feuillants in the Haute Cuisine section, above), **Au Trou Gascon**, with chef Jacques Faussat at the helm, is still a wonderful place to eat. The bustling bistro, with now-decorative brass coatracks behind the banquettes and lovely plaster half-columns, is as lively as ever, and the food is almost as good as when the Gascon master himself patrolled the kitchen. It is difficult to imagine a more exquisite duck breast: rich, succulent, graced with a fatal half-inch of crackling skin and fat so precisely cooked that it's like a single heavy wafer of manna. The same care and quality mark all the other dishes, from the delectable salmon to the exquisite foie gras and truffle ravioli in consommé to the escargot and cèpe pancake. The cheeses, both of them, are perfectly ripe, and the wine list is excellent. The collection of Armagnacs is one of the best in Paris. 40, rue Taine, 75012. Tel: 43-44-34-26; Fax: 43-07-80-55. (Closed weekends, August, and Christmas week.)

As is well known, Paris has a way of inducing even the most stolid of characters into a romantic swoon. If this is your objective, and you also want to have a superb meal, plan a repast on the shady, flowered terrace at **Le Pré Catelan**, which may be the most seductive restaurant in the city. Located in the heart of the Bois de Boulogne, a good 20-minute cab ride from central Paris, it's also the perfect answer to a *déjeuner sur l'herbe* mood without leaving town. Even in winter, and especially at Christmas, chef Gaston Lenôtre's flagship restaurant (he's almost equally famous for his chic catering service and his chocolate shop) is lavishly furnished with plants and flowers. The cooking on the seasonally varying menu is usually sublime, too. Start with the herb-roasted langoustines dressed in lemon-seed oil, and then maybe move on to veal sweetbreads served with foie gras and asparagus, but be certain to pace yourself with a dessert in mind. Pick one of the two stars: a *millefeuille* of strawberries and raspberries, with the fruit and whipped cream interleaved into the fragile layers of pastry, or the warm chocolate soufflé. This is an expensive meal—and the wine list is a bit overpriced—but a long lunch or a late dinner here is one of the most ecstatic ways imaginable of celebrating the good weather in Paris. Bois de Boulogne, Route de Suresnes, Tel: 45-24-55-58; Fax: 45-24-43-25. (Closed Mondays and for dinner Sundays.)

Expensive and Moderate: Left Bank

Dominique Nahmias is one of the stars of the limited roster of first-rate female chefs in Paris; it was her talent that animated both the kitchen and dining room at Olympe. She's since moved on, however, and is now running the kitchen of the restaurant at the Virgin Mégastore (tapes and records) on the Champs-Elysées, with mixed results. Despite the loss of Nahmias, **Olympe** is still an excellent restaurant, and the dishes that made Nahmias's reputation, especially the lobster ravioli, remain outstanding since the kitchen and dining room came under the control of Albert Nahmias, her ex-husband. Once formidably expensive, the menu has become more reasonable lately. There's an excellent 200-franc prix-fixe menu that includes such treats as *raviolis de canard,* chicken with a white Bordeaux wine sauce, and even a carafe of very good Bordeaux or Chardonnay. The great glamour of this place has subsided, though; once the haunt of the likes of Mick Jagger and Paloma Picasso, it's now become a more local restaurant, drawing an older and very bourgeois crowd, and somehow the plush decor seems a little silly since the starlight has dimmed. 8, rue Nicolas-Charlet, 75015. Tel: 47-34-86-08; Fax: 44-49-05-04. (Closed Mondays and for lunch on weekends.)

The rough, wood-paneled walls and bright quai-side location opposite Notre-Dame make the tiny **La Timonerie** seem more like a welcoming country kitchen in chef Philippe de Givenchy's (yes, that fashion family) native Brittany than a very fine little restaurant. But the precisely cooked fresh pastas and fish creations soon clear up any misapprehensions. Excellent desserts, a very satisfactory wine list, and friendly waiters sensitive to those on diets and tight budgets alike (they will split dishes without a murmur) round out a pleasant and reasonably priced dining experience. 35, quai de la Tournelle, 75005. Tel: 43-25-44-42. (Closed Sundays, Mondays, and for three weeks in August and February.)

Le Divellec is far more expensive than most of the places mentioned here—but rightfully so, since it almost matches the ethereal standards of the "greats." The bright blue-and-white decor promises the sea, which chef Jacques Le Divellec delivers as he knows best: in the form of interesting and stunningly fresh fish dishes—sautéed, poached, steamed, or raw. The oysters with seaweed are particularly good, and Le Divellec never destroys the flavor of a fish with too heavy a sauce. Rather frosty service and a lengthy wine list complete the experience. 107, rue de l'Université, 75007. Tel: 45-51-91-96; Fax: 45-51-31-75. (Closed Sundays, Mondays, and August.)

La Cagouille, at 10, place Constantin Brancusi in the 14th *arrondissement,* is another haven for fish-lovers, though far less formal than Le Divellec. Chef Gérard Allemandou does the shopping himself at the fish markets near Orly airport, and this care shows in the impeccable freshness of his creations. Allemandou cooks like a man whose heart is pure: Simple, straightforward dishes—like his two-inch tuna steaks seared on the outside and sushi-raw at the center—are prepared with grace and devotion, untainted by any sauce that might diminish the natural glory of the fish. The somewhat iconoclastic restaurant has a good, if limited, selection of wines and old-fashioned desserts. Tel: 43-22-09-01; Fax: 45-38-57-29. (Closed Sundays, Mondays, one week in May, and two weeks in August.)

Jules Verne is for the romantic who doesn't let the possibility of doing something "touristy" get in the way of having a good time (the kind of soul who can appreciate kitschy but great *bateaux-mouches* rides on the Seine). On the second "floor" of the Eiffel Tower, this darkly elegant restaurant features all the touches such a hybrid—half monument, half deluxe eatery—ought to. What's missing is outstanding cuisine. The food is actually better than might be expected, but it doesn't live up to the impossible standards set by the truly remarkable views (especially at night, when the shimmering plain of Paris is broken only by spotlit church towers). How could it? But the comfortable black leather chairs and banquettes, somehow more appropriate to the first-class section of an airplane than to a restaurant; the odd paper orchids and designer lamps that grace each table; and the pianist in the bar all add up to a seductive atmosphere. Jules Verne is first and foremost a spot from which to drink in the heady wine of Paris from a truly romantic perspective. Tel: 45-55-61-44; Fax: 47-05-94-40.

Martin Cantegrit's Le Récamier is truly a restaurant for all seasons. The small, attractive Napoléon III–style dining room, a snug place on a winter's night, overlooks a spacious terrace in a tiny cul-de-sac. And on a warm spring night banks of flowers set off some of the most sought-after outdoor tables in Paris. Featuring the specialties of Cante-grit's native Burgundy (dishes like *mousse de brochet sauce Nantua*—fish dumplings in a crayfish truffle sauce—and fricassee of snails and wild mushrooms), the menu changes frequently to offer the perfect meal year-round. Dining by candlelight on a soft July night, you might start with the excellent lobster salad, big chunks of lobster served on an interesting sherry-vinegar-and-walnut-oil-dressed *mesclun* (a mixture of at least seven different multishaded salad greens) and vegetables, and then share a perfectly pan-roasted chateaubriand, the large portion of the best French beef flattered by a light but earthy sauce of red wine, shallots, butter, green peppers, and mushrooms. On a chilly autumn night nothing could possibly be more satisfying than the *boeuf bourguignon,* lean chunks of beef and mush-rooms in a deep, luscious wine gravy, served with *tagliatelle.* Le Récamier also has one of the best wine cellars in Paris; the starred selections on the wine list indicate bottles that should be opened at least an hour before serving. Many of the regulars here, who run to government officials and ambassadors, book publishers, writers, and artists, order their wine when they make their reservation. 4, rue Récamier, 75007. Tel: 45-48-86-58; Fax: 42-22-84-76. (Closed Sundays.)

Unlike their fellow 17th *arrondissement* master chefs Guy Savoy and Michel Rostang, Jean-Pierre and Madeleine Vigato followed up the success of their *haute gamme* flagship restaurant (Apicius, see above) not with a bistro, but with the very chic and young **La Manufacture**, just south of the city gates. The high-ceilinged, whitewashed room once housed a to-bacco plant and is now home to giant, colorful paintings, sharp Art Deco chairs and plates, and a collection of odd paintings crowned by the enormous Egyptian palm that centers the room. The menu is plain but interesting, with an emphasis on imaginative dishes at moderate prices. The very fine yet simple renditions of market-fresh fish and dangerous mashed potatoes are convincing. The wine list is small but carefully selected and excellently priced. Skip the boring cheeses. Well worth the trip one mile past the Porte de Versailles south of the 15th *arrondissement.* 20, esplanade La Manufacture (across from 30, rue Ernest Renan), 92130 Issy-les-Moulineaux. Tel: 40-93-08-98; Fax: 40-93-57-22. (Closed two weeks in early August, Sundays, and for lunch Saturdays.)

FASHIONABLE RESTAURANTS
In a city as committed to eating and as populated with restaurants as Paris, it is inevitable that every year a genera-

tion of slick new restaurants springs up in the dining-out marketplace. But it is important to note that in Paris, high-tech, chic restaurants make up only a fraction of the new additions. As opposed to New York, say, where the city's frenetic, revolving-door culture compels new ventures to be as up-to-date and as instantly popular as possible, new Paris restaurateurs have long gastronomic traditions to guide them. Thus hundreds of restaurants imitating existing genres open their doors yearly, leaving the culinary avant-garde open to a brave few.

It should come as no surprise, then, that having no working model of their own, fast-track entrepreneurs have co-opted ideas found in New York or elsewhere, transplanting them more or less Frenchified, more or less successfully, to Paris. Providing more inspiration for would-be local restaurateurs is the proliferation of international chain restaurants. Paris now has a Hard Rock Café and, more ambitiously, a Bice, which has come to mean something very different from the Milan original; the Paris version is expensive, slick, and not much fun. Bear in mind, too, that fashionable restaurants here are often just what the name implies—places where the fashion crowd hangs out—and that many Parisians reject the whole see-and-be-seen concept that underlies them in favor of something more subtly fashionable, like Sunday night supper at the Brasserie Balzar, for example. Still, some of the fashionables are better than others; here is our selection.

Fashionable Restaurants: Right Bank

Fashionable Parisians suddenly love getting grilled; a new wave of rotisserie-grill restaurants has opened to almost instant popularity. Most of them offer a simple and reasonably priced prix fixe menu that includes an appetizer, a grilled or roasted main course, with lamb, chicken, veal, and salmon as the usual starring attractions, and a dessert, for about $30. It's not difficult to deconcoct the success of this formula, as it requires very little real cooking (meaning few expensive employees), it's "light" (the French are succumbing to lite-mania, too), and, finally and vitally, in the economically earthbound nineties, it's good value for the money. La Rotisserie d'en Face, Jacques Cagna's new annex, defines the genre (see Fashionable Restaurants: Left Bank), but the appeal of this cooking is also influencing other trendy new spots, like Guy Savoy's fourth and latest restaurant, **La Butte Chaillot**. A pleasant, spacious place with a vaguely high-tech decor, the restaurant offers a menu that features a daily rotisserie special, along with other superb dishes such as a salad of baby snails to start and then maybe a rosemary-stuffed breast of veal. Very popular at lunch, this place is agreeably calmer in the evening. 112, avenue Kléber, 75016. Tel: 47-27-88-88; Fax: 47-04-85-70. Open every day.

If you're curious to catch a glimpse of the very heart of the fashion world in Paris, and also want some very good if rather expensive Italian food, reserve for lunch at **Stresa**. This clubby but friendly little restaurant on a back street just off the avenue Montaigne, the Wall Street of French fashion, draws all the major players from Christian Dior, Pierre Balmain, Louis Vuitton, and the other luxury brand-name houses in the area, along with a good sprinkling of movie stars, models, and socialites. Though this gilded crowd generally feigns indifference to food in favor of their waistlines, here they let go for the spinach-stuffed ravioli, the excellent scampi, and the fillet of sole sautéed in olive oil. 7, rue Chambiges, 75009. Tel: 47-23-51-62.

Fashionable restaurants can be a lot of fun, and one of the best venues at the moment is **404**, a lively and good Moroccan place just north of Les Halles. Handsomely decorated in a style that might be called Postmodern Orientalism (the owners brought back a lot of antiques from Morocco and illuminate them skillfully, and pierced alabaster screens set off the old stone walls), 404 is frequented by young designers, models, and photographers who come here for the excellent couscous and *tagine,* a dish of lamb or chicken garnished variously with preserved lemons, raisins, or olives, among other choices, that's then braised in a domed crock. There's a nice selection of North African wines, too. 69, rue des Gravilliers, 75003. Tel: 42-74-57-81. (Closed Sundays and for lunch on Saturdays.)

The creator of **The Studio** is very French, but his perfect southern accent (he lived in Dixie for several years) carries over to the impeccable Tex-Mex decor and country & western music. The Studio exemplifies the restaurant *à l'Américain* in Paris, and is a place to go for good times more than gastronomy. Tucked away in an ancient courtyard at 41, rue du Temple in the 4th *arrondissement,* one of Paris's oldest neighborhoods, The Studio is packed nightly and also has one of the city's great summer courtyards; a fun place to watch people or, when feeling nostalgic, to sup on tacos and nachos while listening to the Flying Burrito Brothers. Reserve; Tel: 42-74-10-38; or wait in the courtyard with a margarita.

Go to **La Perla** to drink as much as to eat; the atmosphere is equally conducive to both. The menu is straightforward Mexican, but the owners are civilized enough to place a shaker of cayenne pepper on every table; the drinks menu is extensive and meant to be taken seriously. There is a rack of tequilas on the wall and frozen margaritas for the homesick. The best thing about the place is its atmosphere: La Perla manages to retain its neighborhoody ambience and be sort of chic at the same time. 26, rue François Miron, 75004. Tel: 42-77-59-40.

The Bastille area is the center of gentrification in Paris. No street shows this more than the 11th *arrondissement*'s rue de Lappe, and no dining spot exemplifies it better than **Tapas Nocturne** at number 17. A sliver of a restaurant just down the block from the very stylish dance spot Balajo (discussed below), it specializes in the dainty and tasty appetizers called *tapas*. It can be quite entertaining, but go early, because after 9:00 P.M. even the chic wait in line. No credit cards. Tel: 43-57-91-12. (Closed Sundays.)

Another sign that this neighborhood is coming of age is the opening of the **Blue Elephant** at 43–45, rue de la Roquette, a luxurious Thai restaurant that debuted in Brussels and that now has branches in London and Copenhagen. Small portions and relatively stiff prices notwithstanding, this lavishly decorated restaurant—under an intricate teak ceiling—quickly became packed with fashionable Parisians of all stripes. An "elephant" system—three elephants means that a dish is very hot, two, rather hot, and one, spicy— protects those with a timid palate, although the food is really rather tame. The best choices here are the seafood appetizers and any of the shrimp dishes. Tel: 47-00-42-00. (Closed for lunch Saturdays.)

Fashionable Restaurants: Left Bank

Aside from an excellent location, very good food for a fair price, and an attractive decor, another reason that **La Rôtisserie d'en Face**, Jacques Cagna's bistro annex (his *grand restaurant* is just across the street) is such a huge hit with chic Parisians is that the chef/owner is on hand every night and is obviously having a fine time with this latest venture. "I wanted to create a place where my friends would come," the genial chef explains. What his friends and everyone else like to eat here are the excellent artichoke-and-leek salad dressed with walnut oil, salmon roasted with rock salt and served with sautéed spinach, or spit-roasted lamb with *dauphinois* potatoes, among other good choices, and the pistachio ice cream–stuffed profiteroles in hot chocolate sauce. 2, rue Christine, 75006. Tel: 43-26-40-98. (Closed Saturdays for lunch and Sundays.)

Gilles Epié is one of the most innovative chefs in Paris. Not only is the menu at his Miravile (See Expensive and Moderate Dining: Right Bank) one of the most innovative in town, but he has just offered the capital an excitingly fresh and original take on Provençal cooking at his new restaurant **Campagne et Provence**, 25, quai de la Tournelle, in the 5th *arrondissement*. This is, in fact, the same space that formerly housed Miravile, and the simple decor has been retained. The menu is small, simple, and reasonably priced, and features such superb updates on southern classics as assorted vegetables (zucchini, tomatoes, etc.) stuffed with *brandade,* the garlicky creamed salt cod so beloved from the Midi to the Mediterranean, and a luscious tuna steak served on a bed of olive-studded semolina. Good desserts, too, including a rare and excellent blueberry ice cream, as well as an interesting wine list. Tel: 43-54-05-17. (Closed Saturdays for lunch and Sundays.)

The fashion crowd has a new canteen: **Marie et Fils.** Marie Steinberg, the ex-wife of British playboy Eddie Barclay, and her son Guillaume run an extremely popular new bistro in the heart of St-Germain, and, rather unusual for a chic restaurant, the food is delicious: rabbit terrine, a steamed vegetable salad, tuna steak with provençal sauce, red mullet with black olives, excellent desserts, and a good wine list. Marie knows her way around Paris, which means that friends like the wordly press attaché from Yves Saint Laurent and Catherine Deneuve are likely to brighten the antiques-accented dining room—otherwise filled with high-powered arts and media types and the BCBG (Bon chic, Bon genre, or the right people with the right stuff)—of a given evening. 34, rue Mazarine, 75006. Tel: 43-26-69-49.

In many ways **La Maison** defines the whole category of fashionable restaurants in Paris. The latest venture of night-club impresario Claude Aurensan, who used to run Le Palace, this place is more about famous faces and frivolity than food. The food's okay, though, and during the summer, when you sit outside on a quiet terrace—a rarity in traffic-choked Paris—under the catalpa trees at candlelit tables, it tastes even better. Come here some night if you want to catch a glimpse of Paloma Picasso or Catherine Deneuve while you're eating your lamb chops. Reservations are essential, and because the place functions as sort of a public private club, service can be distracted and/or a little frosty. 1, rue de la Bûcherie, 75005. Tel: 43-29-73-57. (Closed Mondays and for lunch Tuesdays.)

FOREIGN DINING

Like any city with a large population of immigrants and refugees, Paris enjoys an abundance of foreign restaurants. Some are the fruit of France's traditional ties, either colonial—Vietnamese, North African, and West African—or cultural. Others are the inevitable beachheads established by immigrant communities digging in far from home. A good rule of thumb when considering a foreign restaurant: The more exotic, or chic, the better (outstanding Italian food, for example, just doesn't exist in Paris). The better ventures, though, can be both cultural and culinary adventures.

North African and Middle Eastern

In the aftermath of Algeria's 1954 war for independence, a wave of pro-French Algerians emigrated to France, many of them settling in Paris. Moroccans, too, have moved in by the thousands (Morocco was a French protectorate from 1912 to 1956), as have Lebanese, leaving a troubled land for the city many already considered their spiritual home. Paris's profusion of North African and Middle Eastern restaurants reflects these demographics, and there are now some particularly worthwhile dining spots among them.

The **Timgad**, in the 17th *arrondissement,* is Paris Central for authentic North African dishes in a classy and romantic North African setting. Rough stones, a fountain, and carefully dimmed lighting provide the background for excellent couscous, *tagine,* and *pastilla.* 21, rue Brunel; Tel: 45-74-23-70; Fax: 40-68-76-46. **Le Baalbek**, an authentic Lebanese restaurant at 16, rue Mazagran, tucked away in the heart of Paris's small Turkish quarter in the 10th *arrondissement,* is a must for fans of true exotica. Such standard Middle Eastern fare as shish kebabs and *houmous* is accompanied by a spectacular show: Belly dancers writhe around the room, vendors come to the tables with jasmine, and everyone laughs loudly and cavorts to his heart's content. Reserve; Tel: 47-70-70-02. (Closed Sundays.)

For a more decorous Levantine feast, many people consider **Al-Dar** to be the best Middle Eastern restaurant in Paris. Come to this large, well-lit place with at least two other people, because the fun begins by covering the table with an assortment of some of the more than 40 *mezzes* (starters), including *kébé boulettes,* savory balls of ground lamb and pine nuts enrobed in a deep-fried whole-wheat crust, and the many varieties of Lebanese sausage. Right away you'll be served hot pita bread, a tray of fresh cucumbers, tomatoes, peppers, and lettuce and another of pickled vegetables, along with a pitcher of ice water garnished with a sprig of fresh mint. Order a bottle of rosé de Provence—skip the expensive and unremarkable Lebanese wines. The mixed grill—including lamb and chicken en brochette, lamb chops, sausage, and long strips of grilled ground lamb—is a feast that's served to a minimum of three and eaten with quarters of pita bread filled with tomatoes, onions, and parsley. For dessert order an assortment of the excellent Lebanese pastries that are baked on the premises. 8–10, rue Frédéric-Sauton, 75005. Tel: 46-34-64-46 or 43-25-17-15.

Vietnamese and Thai

Vietnamese settlers came to Paris in two waves: after France's humiliation at Dien Bien Phu and subsequent withdrawal from Indochina in 1954; and then in the 1970s after the American withdrawal from the country. As a result, there are many Vietnamese restaurants in Paris, including some with Cambodian or Thai accents.

Le Palanquin is all Vietnamese. Delicate Oriental screens and a gracious welcome set the atmosphere, and the food is well presented and delicious. The Tran sisters run the comfortable wood-beamed room, at 12, rue Princesse in the 6th *arrondissement,* with quiet charm and complete efficiency. Pleasure awaits in the form of crab claws in lemon sauce or the other specialties of the house. Tel: 43-29-77-66. (Closed Sundays and two weeks in August.)

Tan Dinh, at 60, rue de Verneuil in the neighboring 7th *arrondissement,* features high-quality products imported directly from Vietnam. The dishes that result from these links to the homeland are among the most honest and successful in Paris. The soothing red-and-black lacquered decor is both traditional Eastern and obliquely French. Reserve; Tel: 45-44-04-84. (Closed Sundays and August.)

Chieng-Mai, at 12, rue Frédéric-Sauton in the 5th *arrondissement,* is popular with the city's fashion and media crowds; it also happens to serve some of the best and most authentic Thai food in Paris. Among the regulars' favorites are the chicken and coconut milk soup and spicy beef salad as starters, and the grilled giant prawns and barbecued beef as main courses, all washed down with excellent Thai beer. Tel: 43-25-45-45. (Closed Sundays, first two weeks of August, and last two weeks of December.)

Chez Rosine/Les Folies is a bit off the beaten track, but it's worth the effort for the delicious Cambodian cooking of the jovial, witty Rosine Elk. She custom cooks every dish herself, and the whole effect is like being fed by the Cambodian grandmother you never knew you had. Her salads and grilled catfish are especially delicious. This comfortable, quiet place has a following of neighborhood regulars but also draws creative types from all over the city. 101, rue Saint Maur, 75011. Tel: 43-38-13-61.

Afriques-Antilles

France's former colonial ties with West Africa (Côte d'Ivoire, Benin, Senegal) and the Antilles (Martinique and Guadeloupe) account for most of Paris's black population. And though the cultures and histories of these two areas are completely different in restaurants and nightclubs they are often hyphenated: Afriques-Antilles.

Unquestionably, the *boîtes de nuit* (nightclubs) are the most exciting representatives of African culture in Paris. The restaurant **Babylone**, however, is an exception to the rule. The walls and ceiling are covered with leopard and other animal skins, and an enormous wood carving completely fills one wall. Plants add to the veld atmosphere, as does the hot young crowd, a mixture of Africans resident in Paris and photographers, models, and wannabes. Babylone is open until 8:00 A.M. for those who prefer to dine late. 34, rue Tiquetonne, 75002. Reserve; Tel: 42-33-48-35.

A meal at **La Villa Créole**, at 19, rue d'Antin in the 2nd *arrondissement,* is like an instant visit to the islands. This pretty, festive place, frequented by the most prosperous members of the city's Antillais community, is decorated plantation style with lots of lacy white wood; the airy mood is enhanced by a pianist who plays the sunny music of the Caribbean. Start with one of the imaginative rum-based cocktails, and then try the deep-fried fish balls, barbecued baby pork, stuffed crab, or one of the many good fish dishes. Tel: 47-42-64-92. (Closed Saturdays for lunch and Sundays.)

The modern façade of **La Plantation Paris** fronts an equally modern interior made tropical by the glorious island-blue that dominates the room. The menu is as exotic as the Antilles themselves, featuring a cuisine that mixes Caribbean accents and ingredients with French style at the stove. A well-heeled crowd is drawn by the restaurant's combination of colorful food and dignified atmosphere. The desserts are great. 5, rue Jules-César, 75012. Tel: 43-07-64-15. (Closed Sundays.)

American

For some completely unknown reason, "American" food, especially the Tex-Mex part of the spectrum, continues to become more and more fashionable in Paris. Even as Parisians love to mock American cooking and eating habits (sometimes understandably, since the idea of drinking a Coke, for example, with a rich, deeply simmered plate of *boeuf bourguignon* is pretty revolting), they are increasingly to be found meeting friends for a (mediocre) cheeseburger at Joe Allen's in Les Halles or tucking into some refried beans at **Le Texan**, the best of the burgeoning number of Tex-Mex places. With branches in Avignon and Monte Carlo—Princess Stephanie (or "Steph," as the French wryly call her) and Prince Albert pop in from time to time—this place is the rare Tex-Mex where the crowd's more French than foreign. And the food— nachos, burritos, and the like—is also vastly better here than it is in other such spots in Paris, as elsewhere it too often just sits on the table as sort of a scary prop or an ugly excuse to have another margarita. 3, rue St-Philippe-du-Roule, 75008. Tel: 42-25-09-88. (*Même genre,* see The Studio and La Perla in Fashionable Restaurants.)

Beyond Tex-Mex, the only American restaurants worth bothering with here are the two local branches of the **Chicago Pizza Pie Factory,** one of the many star-spangled theme restaurants on both sides of the Channel that have been opened by Bob Payton, a U.K.-based Yank. They do a decent Chicago-style pie, but the real reason to come here is that you might meet some locally based Anglophones who'll turn you on to the latest cheap bistro, which should remain, a vicious attack of homesickness notwithstanding, the gastro goal of any Paris visit. 5, rue de Berri, 75008, Tel: 45-62-50-23; 9, boulevard Edgar-Quinet, 75014. Tel: 43-21-73-06.

Chinese

Though the Chinese community in the 13th *arrondissement* includes several fine restaurants and is quite fascinating to explore, and the Bellevue *quartier* in the 18th is home to many ethnically fascinating spots, no one restaurant stands out in either neighborhood. For highbrow Chinese cuisine, though, **Chez Vong** in Les Halles—one of an international chain—takes the prize. The deluxe comfort of the small private rooms, Oriental pottery, lacquer finishes, and subtle lighting is matched by sophisticated, carefully prepared Chinese cuisine. The *dim sum* is especially good. 10, rue de la Grande-Truanderie, 75001. Reserve; Tel: 40-39-99-89. (Closed Sundays.)

Conveniently located right in the heart of St-Germain, and therefore good to know about if you've lingered late in one of the local cafés or been to a movie in the neighborhood, is **Le Canton,** which serves simple but tasty food to a hip, young, French crowd. The somewhat austere decor evokes Chinese restaurants of the 1950s, but the service is prompt and friendly and the prices low by local standards. Try the steamed ravioli or *nems* (deep-fried miniature Vietnamese egg rolls) to start and then the chicken with lemongrass or shrimp in spicy sauce. 5, rue Gozlin, 75006. Tel: 43-26-51-86. (Closed Sundays and August.)

Jewish and Middle Eastern

For centuries before World War II, the Marais area was home to most Parisian Jews. Nazi raids (aided by the collaborationist government and French police) nearly decimated the community, which has slowly regained some of its former vigor through the influx of Sephardic Jews from North Africa and the Middle East. The rue des Rosiers in the 4th *arrondissement* is the gastronomic center of this community, featuring a row of kosher restaurants, butchers, fish-sellers, and a pizzeria.

Jo Goldenberg at 7, rue des Rosiers is probably the best-known restaurateur in the Marais. The food—pastrami and smoked fish, of course—is tasty and honest (though not really of New York caliber), the matzoh ball soup is nurturing, and Goldenberg's has the best deli department in the neighborhood. **Chez Marianne**, also in the 4th, at 2, rue des Hospitalières-St-Gervais, has more of a Middle Eastern menu: *tarama, falafel,* stuffed grape leaves, et cetera. There's also a barrel of pungent, homemade pickles from which the sensitive of nose should keep their distance. Service is very warm; for takeout as well. (Closed Fridays and Jewish holidays.)

Tucked onto a narrow street in the Marais, **Esther Street** is a comfortable, well-lit place that serves up motherly portions of lovingly prepared Eastern European and Sephardic food. From the rich stuffed cabbage to the marvelous meat-filled kreplach to the tangy garlic pickles, every dish is tasty, satisfying, and heartwarming. A great spot for a zesty, well-cooked meal. 6, rue de Jarente, 75004. Tel: 40-29-03-03. (Closed Fridays and Saturdays for lunch.)

Japanese

As perhaps a further sign of their low-key but enormous wealth and power in Europe, the Japanese have effectively colonized the environs of the avenue de l'Opéra, especially the rue Ste-Anne. This influx has nothing in common with the bawdy pre–World War II Anglo-Saxon invasion, either. The Japanese aren't here to escape prying great aunts or write "smutty" novels; they've come to make money, and not seeming to relish their expatriation much, they assiduously and gratefully frequent the city's mostly rather unremarkable sushi counters and noodle shops.

For some years **Isse**, at 56, rue Ste-Anne in the 2nd *arrondissement,* has been the Japanese address of preference here—it regularly appears in French magazines with a postage-stamp-size picture of its most famous patron, the invariably grinning Paris-based Japanese fashion designer Kenzo—but spoiled by all of this attention, the restaurant has become indifferent. All of which means that Paris is not a great place to eat Japanese food. Compounding the problem is that Japanese is billed as an upmarket, expensive cuisine in Paris, and the quality is much better in New York, L.A., London, or Toronto. One address for desperate sushi fiends is **Kinugawa**, a fiercely expensive place at 9, rue du Mont-Thabor in the 1st *arrondissement* favored by the big-name Euro-Japanese designers—Yohji Yamamoto and Rei Kawakubo (Comme des Garçons) dine here when they're in town. Tel: 42-60-65-07. (Closed Sundays, and December 23–January 7.)

The cult film *Tampopo* introduced Western audiences to a different breed of Japanese restaurant: the noodle shop frequented by working- and commuting-class diners in Japan. **Higuma**, at 32 bis, rue Ste-Anne, also in the 1st *arrondissement,* is a bustling example of this eating experience. Free of cute Oriental ornaments, save the racks of Japanese comic-book literature in the middle of the three rooms, Higuma is devoted to the art of the noodle. The noodles are freshly made each day in the huge steaming caldrons that dominate the front room and are served in a soup or stir-fried, with pork, vegetables, or calamari. Dumpling fans won't be disappointed, and the toothpicks are . . . special. No need to reserve; just come and wait. Tel: 47-03-38-59.

Eastern European

Eastern Europe has probably the most romantic history of involvement with Paris. Artists such as Frédéric Chopin and Franz Liszt left Warsaw and Budapest for the French capital; Czarist Russia (Napoléon's invasion notwithstanding) had strong ties with France; and such writers as Ivan Turgenev, Eugène Ionesco, and Milan Kundera have made their homes here. Little wonder, then, that a host of restaurants representing the region's several cuisines sprinkles the streets of Paris.

Of the many Russian choices, which range from inexpensive restaurants serving blinis, *tarama,* and brochettes to very elegant caviar emporiums, one of the nicest is **Le Coin du Caviar**. Just off the Place de la Bastille at 2, rue de la Bastille in the 4th *arrondissement,* this refined and tastefully decorated restaurant features hot and cold Russian specialties, including delicious blinis, smoked fish plates, and caviar worth the not insignificant price tag. The atmosphere is quiet and pre-Revolutionary, and vodka is served in carafes frozen in a block of ice. Reservations may be necessary; Tel: 48-04-82-93. (Closed Sundays and for lunch on Saturdays.)

The **Mazurka** is quite a different enterprise. With two charming little rooms in a slightly seedy part of town in the 18th *arrondissement,* this Polish restaurant serves healthy portions of hearty country dishes, including great stews and stuffed cabbage. Everyone, from the waiters to the cooks (who look like stereotypes of Polish housewives waiting in line outside a shoe store) to the musicians who sing at the tables, is either a Pole or a near neighbor, so there's an unrestrained Eastern European air to the place. No credit cards. 3, rue André-del-Sarte. Tel: 42-23-36-45. (Closed Wednesdays.)

BISTROS AND BRASSERIES

Bistros and brasseries are perhaps the most typical French restaurants, offering the most traditional dishes and liveliest atmosphere. With some few exceptions (Hemingway eating potato salad and drinking beer at the Brasserie Lipp, or Jean-Paul Sartre dining at his customary table at La Coupole), there is no great literary tradition associated with these kinds of restaurants—for centuries they have been too crowded with the well-fed bourgeoisie and more expensive than the lower-rent cafés favored by the ink-stained. Today meals will cost between 100 and 350 francs, depending on the quality of the food or grandeur of the decor.

Contemporary bistro and brasserie menus share many of the same dishes. Generally, bistros serve the rustic dishes Mom and Dad used to cook up, with a devoted emphasis on stews (*pot-au-feu,* cassoulet, *daube*), duck (*confit de canard, magret de canard,* foie gras), internal organs, all the varied and wondrous parts of pigs (including knuckles, feet, ears, sausages, hams—cooked, smoked, or aged—and kidneys), lamb (including the rack, shoulder, saddle, feet, and head), and veal (the standard cuts, liver, kidney, pancreas, feet, and head; one critic, in fact, warns readers away from a restaurant because the owner "insists on buying the head ready-rolled, so you miss out on the brains and tongue"). This hearty and sometimes heavy fare goes down best in fall and winter months, though of course poultry, rabbit, fish, and many of the lighter meats are delicious year-round, especially when washed down with plenty of good wine.

Brasseries take their name from the word for "brewery" and are predominantly Alsatian, or advertise themselves as such, so beer and Riesling wine are plentiful. They tend to stay open later than bistros and often feature fresh seafood and shellfish, *choucroute* (assorted sausages and cuts of pork served on a bed of sauerkraut), chicory salad with bacon and a poached egg, and the like.

Understandably, the area surrounding the old Les Halles food market, until 1968 Zola's "belly of Paris," features a number of excellent bistros and brasseries. Some are still open all night, as they were when hungry farmers and butchers refreshed their weary bodies with liters of beer and wine and huge plates of rich country cooking at 5:00 A.M. Unfortunate victims of the market's move to Rungis, near Orly airport, include the row of colorful brasseries on the rue Coquillière, such as the Pied de Cochon, once a magnet for top-hatted society seeking a plebeian meal after a night's revels, all now renovated, refurbished, and reduced beyond all recognition (though the Pied de Cochon *is* still quite fun in the wee hours, glitter and all). Most of the other good spots are spread around the Right Bank, from the Porte Maillot to Nation, with only a cluster of restaurants representing the Left Bank.

Bistros and Brasseries: Les Halles

Chez Denise (or A la Tour de Montléry, to the uninitiated) is a good example of a bistro. The woman behind the cash register is as formidable as her longtime partner's luxuriant mustache, but the food is great and the portions enormous. The salt pork with lentils could feed a nuclear family or a starving merrymaker wandering in for a dawn feast. The (three) wines offered are fine, and the decor—hams swinging from the rafters, signed posters, and sketches of the mustachioed man out front—is eclectic and warm. 5, rue des Prouvaires, 75001. Reservations are a must, and even a basic knowledge of French is a big help here; Tel: 42-36-21-82. (Closed weekends first three weeks of August.)

On the other side of the rue du Louvre, at 25, rue Jean-Jacques Rousseau, is the **Epi d'Or**, one of the most typical bistros in Paris. From the mimeographed menu to the check-ered tablecloth to the knickknacks placed around the room to the gracious hosts, everything bespeaks the warmth and care that is at the heart of bistros. Portions are particularly healthy, and everything is hot and hearty. Desserts are worth-while, and little touches like the peach wine evidence the restaurant's conscious effort to keep up with new develop-ments while maintaining its traditional form. Tel: 42-36-38-12. (Closed for lunch on weekends and in August.)

Five minutes away, still in the 1st *arrondissement,* the **Fermette du Sud-Ouest** would be cloyingly rustic if the dishes turned out here weren't so authentic and soul-warming. The very high quality of this bistro makes it with-out question one of the finest in town. Set on two floors at 31, rue Coquillière, with enough wooden beams and rough stone to build a real farm, the Fermette has exceptionally good sausages of all types, including *boudin* and *andouillette* (a rough tripe sausage that is exquisite when made well and inedible when not). It's best to reserve; Tel: 42-36-73-55. (Closed Sundays.)

At 1, rue de Mail, near the fashionable Place des Victoires (home to several high-toned clothing shops) in the 2nd *arrondissement,* **Chez Georges** continues a tradition as well: that of the utterly dependable neighborhood bistro. The long, somewhat stark, mirrored room with its white tile floor and bright lights is made welcoming by the sweet, motherly waitresses in black dresses and white aprons. The menu is standard and the food quite tasty—in season, the garlicky sautéed cèpes are delicious. During the day patrons are a mixed crowd of stockbrokers, bankers from the nearby Banque de France, and fashion people. The homier evening crowd is made up mostly of locals. Chez Georges serves an impressive collection of Bordeaux wines. The checks have grown somewhat out of proportion, and no credit cards are accepted. Tel: 42-60-07-11. (Closed Sundays.)

Chez Pauline, a block from the Palais-Royal, onetime home to Cardinal Richelieu, D'Artagnan's bane, is understandably pretty swank. The charm of the classic decor, complete with stern, avuncular waiters and plenty of flowers, compensates somewhat for the fact that it's a bit overpriced, as do the excellent *boeuf bourguignon* and rice pudding. More modern dishes, anathema to many bistro chefs, are also available. Chez Pauline is popular with just about everyone. 5, rue Villédo, 75001. It's best to reserve; Tel: 42-96-20-70. (Closed Saturday nights and Sundays, and one week in August.)

Bordering Les Halles to the north, **Aux Crus de Bourgogne** is one bistro that has never seen the need to inflate its prices; what the French lovingly call the *rapport qualité-prix* (quality–cost ratio) is very high here. Just off the rue Montorgueil, one of Paris's finest market streets, at 3, rue Bachaumont in the 2nd *arrondissement,* this lovely old room with long communal tables and private booths brightened by red-checked tablecloths and boisterous waiters would cheer even the most morose boulevardier, with good stews, dishes with luscious wild mushrooms (cèpes and morels), and, in season, wild game (from duck to boar). The langoustines are great, and are easily the most affordable in town. Very reasonable wines are served. No credit cards. Tel: 42-33-48-24. (Closed weekends.)

A short stroll down the block at 50, rue Montorgueil, those wacky Bretons who oversee the rambunctious beverage consumption at Le Baragouin (see Bars) have opened a diminutive and marvelously spirited restaurant. **Le Brin de Zinc**, which refers to the beautiful old zinc bar, is populated by waiters whose exuberant personalities are rivaled by the hearty, artery-clogging bistro fare. And while the waiters make you feel like an old friend, the beautifully restored decor makes you wish they were. Nothing spectacular, just rich, tasty dishes prepared with love and served with heartfelt care. Very good little wine list. Tel: 42-21-10-80. (Closed Sundays.)

If restaurateurs prone to flirtation amuse you, **Chez Pierrot**, 18, rue Etienne-Marcel, in the 2nd *arrondissement,* is the place. Monsieur Losson's ministerings are meant to add to the lighthearted atmosphere of this bright, bustling bistro, not to offend. And he ministers to the stomach as well, with vast portions of everything: an entire plate of sausages to cut from at will; a vat of chocolate mousse from which to scoop spoonfuls to your heart's content. The crowd is unified only in its good humor, with business people and fashion mavens such as Jean Paul Gaultier rubbing elbows over their leeks in vinaigrette sauce, *daubes,* and chicken fricassees. No credit cards. Tel: 45-08-05-48. (Closed weekends.)

Benoît is an extremely elegant version of the bistro, and prices are constructed accordingly. From the shrubs outside that protect diners from inquiring eyes, to the fresh, white foyer and gracious welcome, to the impeccable decor (unchanged since the restaurant opened in 1912), to the heaping portions of perfectly prepared dishes such as the *salade de boeuf,* braised-beef stew, and roast red mullet, everything is of the highest quality. Benoît is so pretty and the food so good that it's quite popular despite the astronomical prices. No credit cards. 20, rue St-Martin, 75004. Reservations are a necessity; Tel: 42-72-25-76. (Closed weekends and August.)

Bistros and Brasseries: Right Bank

Like the remnant of a richer past, **Chez Georges**—this one at 273, boulevard Péreire in the 17th *arrondissement*—maintains its 60-year-old bistro traditions in the face of the poured-concrete modernity of the Palais de Congrès hotel/shopping mall/theater center that has transfigured the Porte Maillot across the street. The dining room, created and redone by Art Deco design king Slavik, is run with care by Roger Mazarguil, who has carried on the appetite-enhancing policy of carving succulent slabs of roast beef and leg of lamb right at the table. It's easy to enjoy the high quality, careful preparation, and atmosphere suggestive of successful people congregating, though the prices are a little steep. Tel: 45-74-31-00. (Closed August.)

Michel Rostang has taken a gorgeous old *épicerie fine* (gourmet grocery store for Proust's crowd) and transformed it into one of the best bistros in town (his talent wouldn't let him do otherwise). At 10, rue Gustave-Flaubert in the 17th *arrondissement,* a few doors down from his eponymous temple of haute cuisine (see Haute Cuisine: Right Bank, above), **Le Bistrot d'à Côté Flaubert** is a small tile-and-wood room filled with old-fashioned candy jars, ceramic plates, mismatched tables and chairs, and a variety of other antiques (most are for sale). This attention to detail is mirrored in the service and the food, which is rigorously of the bistro genre—in itself an act of imagination for such an inventive chef. There's a pleasant terrace, and an excellent repast is guaranteed. Best to reserve; Tel: 42-67-05-81.

Guy Savoy, like Michel Rostang, reached out from his marvelous, likewise eponymous restaurant to create a bistro (and then another) that specializes in perfecting the art of this unpretentious cuisine. The **Bistro de l'Etoile**, a cramped, lively room, serves up fairly modest portions of superbly prepared traditional bistro dishes with occasional modern touches. Everything comes hot from the oven, and the ingredients are particularly fresh. The newer branch, on avenue Niel, is larger and features a terrace. 13, rue Troyon, 75017, Tel: 42-67-25-95 (closed weekends); and 75, avenue Niel, 75017, Tel: 42-27-88-44 (closed Sundays).

The **Cochon d'Or** is a small, gorgeous hideaway in the bowels of the 19th *arrondissement* at 192, avenue Jean-Jaurès. The deep red banquettes, richly paneled walls, stained glass lamp shades, long mirrored wall opposite a perfect zinc bar, and starched white linens all fill you with a confidence easily confirmed by the meal to come. The restaurant is a near neighbor of La Villette, the slaughter-yards-turned-science-center, and meat has been the name of the game since the Ayral family opened the Cochon's doors in 1924. The gorgeous slabs of beef, heady kidneys that are flavorful without being astringent, and the rich sauces are enough to make anyone feel that the trip to the hinterlands was worthwhile. Reserve; Tel: 42-45-46-46.

Across the street from the Gare du Nord, the penultimate stop for battalions of young men on their way to the trenches of the Somme, the **Terminus Nord**'s lovely design suggests not the slaughter of World War I but Art Deco's calm postwar precision. Large, airy, sprawling rooms with numerous bouquets of flowers and a huge bar in the center play host to the featured seafood platters, light fish dishes in butter sauces, and other standards. 23, rue de Dunkerque, 75010. Tel: 42-85-05-15.

Though the mythic Antoine Magnin no longer tends the stove in the cramped kitchen at **L'Ami Louis**, little has changed. The splendidly decrepit decor (which looks as if paintbrushes were banned from the premises before the war) is as shabby as ever, and the slabs of foie gras remain as monstrous. The service is haphazard and the renowned game dishes (pheasant, wild duck) are sometimes disappointing. But the new management has maintained the cuisine at about the same level, and the snails, foie gras, and sometimes surreal atmosphere are still addicting. The only real change, in fact, is that the insanely high prices have risen to an even more mind-numbing level. L'Ami Louis today is a place where you can pay more than you ever thought possible for a fun meal. 32, rue du Vertbois, 75003. Reserve; Tel: 48-87-77-48. (Closed Mondays and Tuesdays.)

Better just to call it **Chez Philippe**, like everyone else: Auberge Pyrénées-Cévennes might be too difficult to remember, and this very fine bistro is not one to forget. Stone walls the color of spicy mustard and red-tiled floors make a comfortable setting for the locals and well-to-do business people who depend on Philippe Serbource to provide them with regular doses of his excellent foie gras and cassoulet. It is easy to make a pig of yourself over the delicious *cochonnailles* (sausages)—customers are free to serve themselves—but it's best to save room for the tasty stews and southwestern specialties. Count on spending about 300 to 350 francs per person. No credit cards. 106, rue de la Folie-Méricourt, 75011. Tel: 43-57-33-78. (Closed weekends and August.)

In the 3rd *arrondissement,* five minutes from Chez Philippe and bordering the Place de la République at 39, boulevard du Temple, **Chez Jenny** offers a different kind of fare but with a similar honesty and enthusiasm. A monument to traditional Alsatian garb and cuisine, Jenny features one of Paris's most authentic *choucroutes*—succulent sausage and sharp sauerkraut—rather than the tasteless, stringy affair many brasseries pawn off on unwary diners. The huge, wood-paneled dining area is well staffed with buxom, costumed waitresses eager to plunk a liter of Alsatian beer on the table. There's also fresh shellfish, a little out of place amid the cabbage, and a fine roast lamb. While the atmosphere may be a little too fairy tale, the very reasonable prices are not. Tel: 42-74-75-75.

Most demonstrations in Paris gather at the Place de la

République and march to the Place de la Bastille, the St. Peter's Square of French revolutionary spirit since 1789, when enraged *sans-culottes* destroyed the ominous Bastille prison, a symbol of monarchal arbitrariness, and joyously marched the handful of mostly insane prisoners through the streets of Paris. Today an occasional tourist still asks directions to the long-gone prison; he or she would do better to ask the way to **Bofinger**, a block from the *place,* at 5, rue de la Bastille in the 4th *arrondissement.* Most of Paris regularly visits the restaurant's two delightfully restored rooms (the larger graced by a stunning glass dome put up in 1919), paying homage to the long zinc bar where in 1864 Paris's first draft beer was served. Tel: 42-72-87-82.

The recently refurbished decor of the **Train Bleu** at the Gare de Lyon epitomizes the grandeur of the high Belle Epoque: comfortable banquettes with plenty of space between them for luggage; seriously romantic blue-dominated murals on all the walls; molded plaster on the ceiling that encloses even more intricate murals; and sometimes infrequent, kindly waiters (a special 45-minute menu is available if you have a train to catch). The food and wine list are pretty good as well, but it is really the eye-boggling decor that makes this grand restaurant worth visiting. Gare de Lyon, 20, boulevard Diderot, 75012. Tel: 43-43-09-06.

Bistros and Brasseries: Left Bank

Twenty years ago Allard reigned as one of the great bistros in Paris. Since then Monsieur Allard has died and Fernande, his wife and longtime chef, has retired. But the spirit and high-quality food that had made this deluxe bistro a watchword among gastronomes since 1903 remain; **Allard** is still a culinary force to be reckoned with. The two dining rooms, separated by the kitchen and shimmering zinc bar, are much brighter when you are within, looking past a floral arrangement out the lovely etched windows, rather than gazing in through the dreary cast-iron bars that protect the windows from high-spirited passersby. People come here to feast on the generous portions of the very well prepared stews (such as the delicious *navarin d'agneau* or *coq au vin*), escargots, or specials (such as the dozen grilled pig kidneys a table of serious diners has been known to consume). It's on the expensive side, but it's a pretty place with high standards. 41, rue St-André-des-Arts, 75006. Tel: 43-26-48-23. (Closed weekends and August.)

It's best not to waste a meal on the Brasserie Lipp, where the reservation system remains as snooty as ever and the food too often teeters on the edge of barely acceptable. Go

instead to the **Brasserie Balzar**, just across the street from the
Sorbonne at 49, rue des Ecoles, in the 5th *arrondissement*.
One of the liveliest and most popular restaurants on the Left
Bank, the Balzar serves what many consider to be one of the
better *choucroute garnie* in Paris. The bacon and pork are
grilled and the sausages, too often bloated and waterlogged
elsewhere, are simmered to perfection. Such attention to
detail continues with a juniper berry or two to be found in
the sauerkraut and a generous serving of firm, freshly boiled
potatoes. Many of the pretty young things dining here with
professorial types look for something lighter, though, and
choose the expertly roasted chicken—you get a choice of an
aile (breast) or a *cuisse* (leg and thigh)—that's served with a
generous portion of crispy *pommes frites;* order the fresh
spinach or *haricots verts* (string beans) as a side dish. With
genial waiters in long white aprons, lace curtains, globe
lights, huge Victorian urns filled with flowers, and strategically placed mirrors, the Balzar is the kind of place you'll
wish were found on every other block. The only real problem here is that the Balzar's popularity often overwhelms a
poorly organized reservations system, so you may find yourself cooling your heels in the narrow sidewalk café longer
than you'd like, but be patient—it's worth the wait. Tel: 43-
54-13-67. (Closed August.)

La Cafetière, a cozy little spot tucked away in the middle
of one of the oldest Left Bank neighborhoods, attracts a
diverse and spirited crowd of book editors, bons vivants,
writers, and longtime expatriates. A collection of antique
metal coffeepots, which gives the restaurant its name, lines
one wall, and the low lighting creates an intimate atmosphere. The food is simple and good, with the *sole greno-
bloise* (capers and lemon), deviled chicken, and steak with
shallots among the better dishes. Start with a salad, either
raw mushrooms or watercress with bacon, croutons, and a
poached egg, and drink one of the good Bourgueils or
Brouillys. 21, rue Mazarine, 75006. Tel: 46-33-76-90.

Because good fish has become so expensive in Paris, the
moderately priced **Bistrot du Dôme** has been a big hit ever
since it opened a few years ago. The scaled-down version of
the Café du Dôme, the grand and expensive seafood restaurant just across the street, the *bistrot* orders its superb fish
from the same supplier. The menu in the sunny, yellow-
painted dining room changes every day, but the succulent
sautéed baby clams with thyme and the delicious fried
galette of grated potatoes and cod are usually available.
1, rue Delambre, 75014. Tel: 43-35-32-00.

Perhaps it's not as cheap as it used to be, but the **Restaurant des Beaux-Arts** is still one of the best deals in town: respectable, sometimes excellent cuisine at bargain prices and an atmosphere that immediately recalls the days at the nearby Ecole des Beaux-Arts (or so you might imagine after reading too much Baudelaire) when hungry artists would throw down the brushes and quit the turpentined haven of the studio for a big *boeuf bourguignon* and many bottles of rough red wine, arguing endlessly whether that Delacroix fellow was a genius or a charlatan. The good old days are gone, but the mood still remains, fueled by an energetic young crowd and a warm decor (enormous canvases cover the walls). At 11, rue Bonaparte, in the 6th *arrondissement,* this bistro is a good time. No credit cards. Tel: 43-26-92-64.

Le Petit Plat is a simple Left Bank bistro with superb food—terrine of rabbit in tarragon aspic, sausage with potato salad in shallot vinaigrette, excellent roast chicken, a good steak with delicious sautéed potatoes—that has become very popular among fashionable Parisians looking for a good feed in a low-key setting. It's a tiny place with wooden chairs and tables and apricot-painted walls accented by old stone, and it's packed every night. Excellent wine list—including a very good and unusual country red from the Ardèche region—selected by Henri Gault of Gault-Millau (his daughter is one of the three owners). 3, rue des Grands-Degrés, 75005. Tel: 40-46-85-34.

The prix fixe menu has made a big comeback in Paris recently, and the best one in the city is the 160-franc offering of young chef Yves Camdeborde at his outstanding restaurant, **La Regalade.** Camdeborde was formerly second chef in the excellent kitchen of the Hôtel Crillon, and when he opened his own place a year ago it quickly became a new reference for the capital's gourmets. He's a gifted, classically trained chef who embellishes traditional bistro dishes with a stylish flourish of contemporary haute cuisine. The menu changes regularly depending on what strikes Camdeborde's fancy, but his *pissaladière de thon micuit* (a flaky square of pastry topped with thin slices of barely cooked tuna and sautéed onions, served with a fine sauce of black olives) is usually available, and is a good expression of Camdeborde's talents. The dining room itself is small, simple, and a bit drab, but the crowd here is too happy with their food and the excellent wine list to really need more props for their festivity. 49, avenue Jean-Moulin, 75014. Tel: 45-45-68-58.

Jean-Paul Bucher Bistros

Jean-Paul Bucher has succeeded in creating a chain of restaurants that share almost identical menus, wine lists, and style of service without making them dreary and repetitious. How? By taking old brasseries, each with its own unique history and decor, carefully renovating them, and limiting the cuisine to the foie gras, Riesling, fresh shellfish, and good grilled meats God intended brasseries to serve. His abysmal and horrifying "renovation" of La Coupole is the sole exception.

One warning: Make reservations, and better early or late (all the chain's restaurants are open until 2:00 A.M.), since even patrons with reservations are irritatingly obliged to join the hordes waiting for tables at the bars of each of these restaurants.

The **Flo**, two long, low rooms with dark, polished wood walls, stained glass beer-hall windows, and a pretty zinc bar, was the first to open. Overtly Alsatian, it's the most traditionally brasserie-esque of the five and emphasizes its sometimes mediocre *choucroute*. There is often a Rolls-Royce parked out front, watched over by the trays of fresh oysters, clams, crabs, and other shellfish. 7, cours des Petites-Ecuries, 75010. Tel: 47-70-13-59. (Flo has also opened a brasserie in Printemps, the *grand magasin* on boulevard Haussmann, providing shoppers with sustenance that is certainly a cut above most department-store fare.)

Julien, whose fabulous 1889 Belle Epoque decor was created only three years after the more somber rooms of the Flo, is a loud, bright restaurant that looks out of place amid the surrounding markets and exotic fast-food shops. Its two rooms are separated by a marble bar; the smaller front space is all crisp white linens and crushed velvet banquettes, whereas the main dining area is capped by a magnificent stained glass dome and made larger by the vast mirrors bracketed by ornate period hats. 16, rue du Faubourg-St-Denis, 75010. Tel: 47-70-12-06.

Probably the most civilized of Bucher's eateries, the **Vaudeville** does not suffer from its nearness (20 yards) to the business of the Bourse. The very pretty 1925 marble-and-mirror walls reflect the chatter of a rather chic crowd, all digging into trays of fresh oysters (and their shellfish brethren) and thick steaks. In the summer the terrace, which looks out onto the stock exchange's imposing columned façade, is especially fun. 29, rue Vivienne, 75002. Tel: 40-20-04-62.

The **Boeuf sur le Toit**, an Art Deco masterpiece, is the most historic of the bunch. In its heyday, creative types from all fields (e.g., Jean Cocteau and Pablo Picasso) were drawn to this gorgeous restaurant, with its innumerable mirrors, symmetrical staircases, and little hidden nooks. Because of its beauty and location (not far from the Champs-Elysées), it is probably the most popular as well. 34, rue du Colisée, 75008. Tel: 43-59-83-80.

La Coupole once defined Montparnasse dining, but we include it here to emphasize the sacrilege and destruction Jean-Paul Bucher has wreaked in its once-hallowed confines. After buying La Coupole—the monument that was once home to the most special ambience in Paris—in 1988, Bucher and his butchers proceeded to "improve" the restaurant. Modifications include: destroying the perfect bar by ripping away the partitions that hid it from the restaurant proper and allowed you to eat with your mate and have cocktails with your lover in the same evening; "upgrading" the familiar, worn, maroon banquettes by covering them with material of an unfortunate shade of brown; and entirely replacing, it seems, the professional troupe of colorful, avuncular waiters and captains with inferior, witless "Flo" clones (that is, the "Flo" design that was successful in reviving dead restaurants, imposed on the still vibrant Coupole). Other "improvements" are just as grating: the tedious "Flo" menu, smaller and far less personable than the old Coupole one; the same "Flo" glasses and tableware; the patented "Flo" crush of patrons; and worst, a bustle that vaguely recalls the Coupole, but without that establishment's humor and grace. To be fair: The food is just as good if not better than before, and the restaurant is still packed. And even the harshest critic must admit that Bucher did a good job cleaning the splendid Deco pillars that punctuate the restaurant—though they are invisible through the tears that cloud the eyes of anyone yearning for what was once the essence of Parisian dining. Try it out if you are strong of spirit. 102, boulevard du Montparnasse, 75014. Tel: 43-20-14-20.

WINE BARS AND WINE BISTROS

For all the hoopla in France about wine, wine *bars* are a fairly recent innovation. Wine *bistros*—and there is a difference—have been a Paris institution since a Russian soldier allegedly shouted *"Bistro!"* ("Hurry!") in an attempt to speed up a laggard barman (circa the Napoleonic wars). The latter, honest *bistrots à vin,* are usually grimier and more personable than what the high-tech 1980s termed a wine bar. Modern, cloned mini-chains can be worth visiting—like the six named L'Ecluse, which serve only Bordeaux; the three named Le Pain et le Vin, created by four chefs who joined together to buy wine (including Henri Faugeron and Alain Dutournier, both mentioned above), which feature some interesting wines and understandably excellent snacks; and Les Domaines, where the Philippe Starck design is so modern it hurts. But these new drinking spots simply lack the character and comfort of Paris's original wine bars and some other newcomers.

The **Taverne Henri IV** is a good place to sample an old-style *bistrot à vin*. On the western end of the Ile de la Cité facing the large equestrian statue of Henri IV, the well-liked king whose assassination in 1610 probably caused many mourners to visit wine bars, the Taverne specializes in crisp whites from the Loire Valley, a selection of fine Beaujolais, and the rare Jura region wines. Add to this farm-fresh cheeses, hams, and sausages, mix in a boisterous owner and a clientele devoted to all of the above, and the result is a terrific place to lunch or taste wines of an afternoon. 13, place du Pont-Neuf, 75001. (Closed Sundays and August.)

People flock to **Jacques Mélac** for four reasons: the moderately priced wines, the lively crowds, Mélac's luxuriant mustache, and the annual harvest of the house grapevine, for many locals a festive occasion inspiring the consumption of vast quantities of wine. The bar is tucked away in the 11th *arrondissement* at 42, rue Léon-Frot, but it is worth the trip: There are fine Côtes-du-Rhône and tempting platters of charcuterie and cheese. Many of the wines can be bought to take out. Tel: 40-96-55-31. (Closed Monday nights, weekends, and August.)

On a small side street in the gritty 11th *arrondissement,* **L'Ange Vin** embodies all that is wonderful about neighborhood wine bars. Host Jean-Pierre Robinot's jovial exuberance is matched only by the care with which he selects the delicate, sweet white wines from lesser-known regions and vineyards that are the bar's specialty. A former wine critic, he employs the same attention when choosing red wines, but *vins mousseux* (sparkling wines), he claims, leave him helpless, and are the glasses he presses on his willing patrons. Lunch is either a plate of vibrant mountain ham and some of the great cheeses or a toothsome daily special. The bread is great and the atmosphere designed for those who love wine. Open for lunch and dinner on Tuesdays and Thursdays (and until 2:00 A.M. for an after-dinner tasting). 24, rue Richard-Lenoir, 75011. Tel: 43-48-20-20. (Closed Monday, Wednesday, and Friday evenings, weekends, and July.)

La Tartine would be hard-pressed to have a more interesting history: It kept the leaders of the Russian Revolution fed and oiled. Trotsky lived right around the corner, and Lenin and Tito were also frequent hangers-out. But La

Tartine today is the same modest café/*bar à vin* it was then, and its past speaks for itself. Such contemporary luminaries as Gérard Depardieu and Nathalie Baye frequent the bar these days, as do a wonderfully mixed crowd of locals, workers, business people, and foreign students—all of them fans of the large wine list (drawn from the nearly 30,000 bottles in the cellar below) and the peasant-bread sandwiches. The atmosphere is warm yet anonymous. 24, rue de Rivoli, 75004. Tel: 42-72-76-85. (Closed August and for lunch on Tuesdays and Wednesdays.)

Two upstart establishments have earned the label "true wine bar" by dint of hard work, a deep knowledge of the Côtes-du-Rhône, and sharp, dry English wit. **Willi's Wine Bar**, named not after acerbic English owner Mark Williamson but after one of Colette's husbands, broke new ground in the Paris wine world. Williamson has created a bar/restaurant with great charm, excellent food, and a weekly choice of often little-known wines by the glass. The rough stone walls and wood beams play host to an international crowd, fans of both the very large selection of fine wines and the atmosphere. Willi's has been renovated recently, with new bathrooms and a sleek, chic decor. 13, rue des Petits-Champs, 75001. Tel: 42-61-05-09. (Closed Sundays.)

Williamson, with partner Tim Johnston, went on and opened **Juvenile's** (named, oddly enough, after another of Colette's husbands) just around the corner from Willi's, at 47, rue de Richelieu. The wines are less rarefied here, though no less carefully selected, with an eclectic mix of French, Spanish, Italian, Californian, and even Australian—the best collection of Australian wines in the country, in fact. The bar's faintly Spanish (though quite Anglicized) air is evident in the *tapas* and the selection of sherries, which is one of the best in town. Juvenile's is basically a lower-key, lower-priced alternative to Willi's. (Despite having English owners, neither bar is an expatriate haven.) Tel: 42-97-46-49. (Closed Sundays.)

Despite its neighborhood—the chic Marché-St-Honoré—**Le Rubis** is as honest and old-fashioned as wine bars get. From the emptied half-barrels that serve as tables outside the always crowded bar to the broad choice of affordable Côtes-du-Rhône to the very high quality cheeses and charcuterie to the wise and wisecracking waitresses, Le Rubis is like the movie set of some imagined 1950s *bistrot à vin*. As you might expect, it is easy to have a good time here. 10, rue du Marché-St-Honoré, 75001. Tel: 42-61-03-34. (Closed Saturday evenings and all day Sunday.)

Tucked away in the far reaches of the 20th *arrondissement,* the **Bistrot-Cave des Envièrges** exemplifies what a radical with a passion for wine can do when the Socialists have been elected and prove no better than the Gaullists. A former *Soixante-huitard* (member of the revolutionary 1968 movement) has translated his commitment to political struggle to more genteel turf—the grape—in this exceptionally friendly and personable *bistrot*. The large selection of wines leans to the Loire Valley and includes many rare and fascinating bottles, all at very good prices. Lunchtime platters are invariably of the freshest ingredients and built to satisfy the deepest hunger. The atmosphere is as special as the wines; political discussion leaning to the left is standard, and social awareness extends even to deliveries of wine, when the bar empties out on the street and everyone pitches in to help unload the truck. Don't miss the spectacular view of Paris at the end of the street. 11, rue des Envièrges; Tel: 46-36-47-84. (Closed Sunday nights and Mondays and Tuesdays.)

La Micro Brasserie is no wine bar. It is, however, the only beer bar in Paris with a brewery on the premises. The extremely tasty house brew—Morgane by name—ages in the huge steel vats visible behind the bar, mellowing even as you sip. Special seasonal varieties are offered at Christmas (Noël beer) and on the bar's birthday. The menu contains only dishes cooked with beer, such as *coq à la Kriek* or *tarte chaude Morgane*. Fascinating. 106, rue de Richelieu, 75002. Tel: 40-20-98-20. (Closed Sundays.)

SALONS DE THÉ

Tearooms are the romantic, warm, and welcoming hideaways for those looking for a light lunch or a cozy spot to dawdle. Calmer than restaurants, quieter than cafés, usually graced with classical music and a relaxing atmosphere, tearooms are for foul weather—or for any day when only a spot of comfort will cure what ails.

Salons de Thé: Right Bank

There are tearooms and there are tearooms. The **Plaza-Athénée** falls in the latter category. Which is to say that tea is taken quite seriously at the Plaza, thank you, either in the Relais, a quiet room washed with gentle harp music, or in the hall, where the famous and the wealthy come to refresh themselves after a long day of being famous and wealthy. 25, avenue Montaigne, 75008. Tel: 47-23-46-36.

A morning *café crème* and a fresh croissant at **La Durée** is one of the most delightfully Parisian experiences anyone can have, and one that no one should miss. Everything here pleases and reassures, from the sturdy marble tables and ancient velvet drapes to the graceful antique brass racks at the pastry counter to the starched uniforms of the wait-resses; the superb macaroons and other pastries complete the experience. La Durée is busy all day, especially in the afternoon when Parisian ladies stop in to recover from the rigors of shopping with a pot of tea and tiny sandwiches. It opens at 8:30 A.M. every day (except Sundays), and that early morning hour is when you should stop by. If you're staying in the neighborhood, skip the expensive lukewarm coffee and rubbery baguette too typical of hotel breakfasts and make this part of your daily routine. 16, rue Royale, 75008. Tel: 42-60-21-79. (Closed Sundays and August.)

A. J. Liebling remembers growing up at **Angelina** when it was called Rumplemeyer's (until 1948). Thousands of French haute-preppies spend their lives here at number 226, down the street from the W. H. Smith bookshop on the rue de Rivoli in the 1st *arrondissement,* as does a broad segment of "beautiful" Paris. History and habitués apart, the famous old room with its green marble tables and mirrored walls is quite pretty, and the hot chocolate should be picketed by the staff of the heart disease center. Tel: 42-60-82-00.

The Ritz offers the most classic tea in town; it is served in a lovely, high-ceilinged room just off the main lobby, com-plete with formal waiters and table settings, soft music waft-ing from a grand piano, and a fireplace. The scones and cakes are just fine, but don't expect anything uniquely Ritz-y here—you'll be disappointed. Dress for the part, both for the hotel, which takes ties as seriously as teas, and for yourself. 15, place Vendôme, 75001.

Another swanky spot to have a cuppa is the stunning interior courtyard of the recently renovated lobby of the **Grand Hôtel**, which once again warrants its name after a multimillion-dollar renewal of its Napoléon III charm. This sunlit space manages to be elegant (white marble) and cozy (lots of mahogany) at the same time; the service is good and the pastry cart alluring. The best measure of this locale is that it is increasingly frequented by Parisians again after having been abandoned to tourists for years. 2, rue Scribe, 75009. Tel: 40-07-32-32.

On a lighter note, **Tea Follies**, on a tree-filled square in the suddenly gentrifying 9th *arrondissement,* typifies the kind of tearoom that is visited for many reasons. Go for lunch and the tasty quiches or chicken pie, for Sunday brunch and the raisin and bran scones and spinach quiche, or on any afternoon to read the stack of papers that builds up over the course of the day and to look over the month's art show, with works accepted only from customers. A wel-coming place, at 6, place Gustave-Toudouze.

A Priori Thé is the best place in town to sit outside on a rainy summer day. It's in Paris's most beautifully restored covered passageway, the Galerie Vivienne, off the rue des Petits-Champs in the 2nd *arrondissement* (sharing space with the likes of fashion designer Jean-Paul Gaultier), so all you suffer is the relaxing sound of rain pattering on the gallery's glass roof. There are comfortable white wicker chairs and rough wood tables, daily lunch specials, and an inviting, equally comfortable atmosphere.

At the unfashionable end of the rue St-Honoré in the 1st *arrondissement* (number 91), **Rose-Thé** is hidden in a court-yard complex of antiques shops. The one small room looks like an antiques shop itself: None of the tables or chairs, which range from deep, overstuffed armchairs to spindly Louis XVI imitations, matches. Because tables are given out on a first-come-first-served basis, some amusing seating ar-rangements have ensued, with overstuffed patrons perched precariously on thin-legged chairs. Rose-Thé has terrific tarts (especially the meat), salads, and desserts. Very pleasant. (Closed Sundays and August.)

Down the block from the Centre Pompidou, but on a street so tiny and aged it appears a world away, **Quincam-bosse** features some of the best and most intricate salads and tarts in town. The raw stone walls have character, though occasional art exhibits take away from their natural beauty. Great for lunch, less great for sitting around. 13, rue Quincampoix, 75004.

The **Loir dans la Théière** (Lewis Carroll's dormouse in a teapot), on the other hand, is a great place for hanging around. At one end of the rue des Rosiers—number 3—in the Marais, this rumpled, comfortable tearoom looks like the common room of some ideal social club. Mismatched tables and chairs, including huge, gratifyingly form-fitting ones near the door, set the tone, and a fairly young crowd that seems to have time on its hands makes for a pleasantly lackadaisical air. Good lunches and cakes.

A pair of tearooms in the Marais reaffirms that neighbor-hood as one of the best in which to wander in all of Paris. The truly serious tea connoisseur should absolutely not miss a stop in **Mariage Frères**, perhaps the most serious *salon de thé* in town. Its sober wood-paneled exterior and handsome front room—bulging with hundreds of jars of tea, a vast array of tea services, and every other tea-related machine known to civilization—promise exactly the sort of comfortable, skylit room you find in the back. The only disappointment here is that the cakes and sandwiches are so mediocre, and the service could use a bit of discipline, too. The 1930s delivery van you occasionally spy rumbling about Paris is, however, a joy. Open every day but Mondays until 7:30 P.M., at 30–32, rue du Bourg-Tibourg, 75004. Also on the Left Bank at 13, rue des Grands-Augustins, 75006.

The **British Colonies** recalls a different era, with its Raj decor of tall, leafy plants, dark wood walls, and general air of gentility. They do a high tea of sorts, and serve tasty sandwiches, tarts, soups, and salads all afternoon. The room is for nonsmokers only, and features a Sunday brunch. 40, rue Vieille-du-Temple, 75004.

The plate glass windows at the **Flore-en-l'Ile** afford a magnificent view of Notre-Dame's flying buttresses, summertime sunbathers, and the organ grinders, storytellers, and mimes who inhabit the pedestrian bridge leading from the Ile St-Louis to the Ile de la Cité. The food is pretty good, and the Flore stocks the famed Berthillon ice cream, which is handy, as lines at the store stretch for blocks during the summer. 42, quai d'Orléans, 75004.

Salons de Thé: Left Bank

Hidden away at 59–61, rue St-André-des-Arts in the 6th *arrondissement,* not far from the Place de l'Odéon, **La Cour de Rohan** is a pretty little tearoom in greens and whites with good furniture. Soothing classical music and fine tarts and pastries make it a nice spot for those rendezvous you hope will linger on. Quite English and yet romantic. Often crowded. (Closed Mondays.)

The **Mosquée de Paris**, the first mosque built in Paris, contains a restaurant, a steam bath, and, of course, a tearoom. And what a tearoom! If it weren't so crowded with students from the nearby university, it would be easy to dally all day, sipping small glasses of sweet, fresh mint tea, staring at tiled floors and exotic Eastern architecture. 1, rue Daubenton, and 39, rue Geoffroy-St-Hilaire, 75005. (Closed August.)

CAFÉS

Cafés are the traditional Paris spots for a quick lunch, a rendezvous, or just to while away a few hours with a book or a diary. And rightly so. The city is rich with these half-bar/half-restaurants: They come in a variety of guises, offering a wide range of settings, atmospheres, and pleasures. The best are graced with a fascinating history and aspects of the character that originally made them historical.

Cafés: Right Bank

Fouquet's (pronounced, in the English fashion so popular during the Belle Epoque, foo-KETS) is technically a café, though of the rarefied sort. Snacks do not come cheap here, but Fouquet's is one of the last remnants, and certainly the classiest one, of the glory that was once the Champs-Elysées before fast-food emporiums, automobile showrooms, and movie theaters overran the avenue. James Joyce was a regular back when dinner was affordable, and today artists of a different sort (journalists and actors) still pack the lively terrace and dining room. The coffee is pretty good, and Fouquet's is an excellent vantage point for people-watching, as well as a fun place. 99, avenue des Champs-Elysées, 75008. Tel: 47-23-70-60.

Another relic, though with less of its former grandeur, the **Café de la Paix**—the sidewalk presence of the Grand Hôtel—still dominates the large square in front of the Opéra. Like Fouquet's, it is now a national monument, so it is likely neither to disappear nor to improve. But most of the civilized world passes by at one point or another, so a good afternoon's examination of what Parisians look like this year can be made.

The **Bon Pêcheur**, at 12, rue Pierre-Lescot in the 1st *arrondissement,* was the first café brave enough to open after the unfortunately ugly Les Halles shopping mall debuted in the late 1970s. Today it is one of the pleasantest in the *quartier:* small, cool (the waiters sport Hawaiian shirts and sunglasses that are at least as chic as the customers'), and personable. The *bouffe* ("chow") is good as far as café fare goes, and the location is ideal for a sunny afternoon's reading of the paper. A mime who is somewhat less annoying than the norm often provides entertainment, following and imitating innocent passersby.

When the **Café Costes** opened its doors at 4, rue Berger, on the Square des Innocents in the 1st *arrondissement* in early 1985, it set off a citywide design revolution. Philippe Starck's hard-edged neo–Art Deco interior was an instant success, and suddenly everyone opening a bar or restaurant either wanted Starck to design it or mimicked his approach (Costes's tables and chairs, logo, coffee cups, and more were created by Starck). Today the design still stands up—a little cold, perhaps, but coherent and attractive. As you might expect, Costes is one of the most chic cafés in Paris (and charges accordingly). In warmer months a well-dressed crowd—a veritable sea of designer sunglasses and men with ponytails—pack the terrace tables facing Square des Innocents (once an overcrowded cemetery). All the same, Costes can be a fun place to hang out.

A few hundred yards away, at 100, rue St-Martin, on the Place Beaubourg, another Costes has set up shop in another very trendy café. The **Café Beaubourg**, opened by Gilbert Costes and his brother Jean-Louis, takes up where the Café Costes leaves off. Total design is, again, the emphasis, but here comfort seems to have been taken into account. There are different areas with different chair designs to suit the needs of a range of customers. Upstairs, private nooks shield the romantic from inquiring eyes; opposite the bar downstairs, a pile of the week's papers in several languages (French, German, Italian, and English) awaits those settling into the most comfortable chairs for a long stay. The food is particularly good here, especially the breakfast egg dishes and the *café crème*. In sort of an echo of the seesaw rivalry for popularity that has long existed between the Café de Flore and Aux Deux Magots in St-Germain, the Café Beaubourg is currently the chicer of this pair; many trendy types now consider the Café Costes to be too *looke,* or obviously, egregiously fashionable.

Of the many cafés in the Marais, two stand out: **Ma Bourgogne** and the Fer à Cheval. The former is nestled under the red brick arches that make up the arcade of the perimeter of the Place des Vosges, once the home of Henri IV. The old-time rattan chairs afford a view of a beautiful little park, where the very fashionable neighborhood's young mothers bring their children to play and where other locals, young and old, come to sunbathe and read in the summer. Inspector Maigret would wander over here from his Ile de la Cité office to drink coffee and ponder his surprisingly light caseload. The **Fer à Cheval**, which was a wine shop in the 1800s and for nearly a century one of the most popular cafés in the *quartier,* takes its name from the lovely horseshoe-shaped marble bar that dominates the small room. A center for troublemakers during the May 1968 student uprising, it's still an excellent hangout. 30, rue Vieille-du-Temple, 75004.

One of Paris's odder cafés, the **Clown Bar** is a fairly seedy spot next to the Cirque d'Hiver (Winter Circus), and the bar's name, decor, and patrons take their cue from this location. Photos of circus stars share wall space with decrepit murals of clowns and bareback riders. Although the food and coffee aren't great, the Clown Bar is worth visiting for its warm, run-down atmosphere. 114, rue Amelot, 75011. (Closed Sundays.)

One of the more pleasantly livable hipster joints in and around the Bastille is the **Café de l'Industrie**. It occupies a big, sprawling space with a funky, haphazard, vaguely thirties decor and attracts some of the rarest, maddest, and most beautiful fauna to its watering hole. Actually, there's a good mixture of Parisian tribes here, along with a good selection of beers and wines by the glass. You can also get a light meal, such as a plate of charcuterie. 16, rue St-Sabin, 75001. Tel: 47-00-13-53. (Open daily.)

Cafés: Left Bank

A grand old café with dark wood walls and a long, classic zinc bar, **La Palette** is still a favorite with art and other students. And well it should be. Good, cheap sandwiches; an open, bustling atmosphere; and plenty of history to inspire fantasy ("What famous painter, then as unknown as myself, could have sat right here?")—all make for a café that seems to define the genre. 43, rue de Seine, 75006. (Closed Sundays and August.)

The Deux Magots and Flore are the kings of St-Germain-des-Prés café life. They've been homes away from home to more artists, writers, and thinkers than the Académie Française, and today they remain beacons for the intellectually prominent.

Aux Deux Magots, opposite the church of St-Germain-des-Prés, is the more boisterous, and touristy, of the two. (It was behind the church monastery that D'Artagnan, about to duel Athos, Porthos, and Artemis, joined the Musketeers against the cardinal's men who suddenly appeared.) A favorite hangout of Cubists and other arty types, Deux Magots became after World War II the second office of Jean-Paul Sartre. Today the prices keep starving artists away, but many glitterati still frequent its hallowed red banquettes. Street musicians serenade the café during summer months.

The nearby **Café de Flore** (the two cafés are always thought of together) has a more literary tradition, though Picasso did move here after the war. Sartre, Camus, and de Beauvoir made the café the headquarters of existentialism, though today few of the literary set go there to ponder questions of being and nothingness, unless it's to ponder their status as cultural icons. A fine place for a coffee or beer, a breakfast of soft-boiled eggs, or the best Welsh rarebit in town.

Because the grand St-Germain cafés have become so expensive—these are where you'll find the six-dollar cup of coffee everyone always complains about—their clientele has grown steadily older and less Parisian. So unless you want the once-in-a-lifetime experience or are indifferent to big markups that come from global notoriety, do what the locals do and seek out a café off the boulevard. One of the best in this neighborhood, the **Café de la Mairie**, at the corner of the rue des Canettes and the Place St-Sulpice, attracts an interesting mixture of young artists and preppies. It's delightful to dawdle over a *kir* here during the summer, especially at night when the fountain in the middle of the square is lit up; and come winter, the second floor, which was just featured in Christian Vincent's hit comedy film *La Discrète,* is electric with eye contact. (Closed Sundays.)

The **Sélect** is the only member of the Montparnasse pantheon of cheap cafés still living and breathing as it once did. The Dôme has been over-renovated and is now more of a restaurant than a café, and the Coupole has been thoroughly disfigured. But the Sélect (with the Deux Magots and the Flore, the 6th-*arrondissement* epicenter of all that life had to offer for the Lost Generation) has retained some of its former glory. The grand terrace, at number 99, lets onto the ravaged boulevard du Montparnasse, now housing a procession of movie theaters and overshadowed by the drab Montparnasse tower, and is filled with a young crowd reading books and soaking up the sun.

—*Alexander Lobrano and Edward Hernstadt*

Paris Restaurants by Arrondissement

For descriptions of each of the following restaurants, turn to the sections indicated in parentheses.

1st Arrondissement
Angelina (Salons de Thé: Right Bank)
Bon Pêcheur (Cafés: Right Bank)
Café Beaubourg (Cafés: Right Bank)
Café Costes (Cafés: Right Bank)
Café de l'Industrie (Cafés: Right Bank)
Carré des Feuillants (Haute Cuisine: Center)
Chez Denise (Bistros and Brasseries: Les Halles)
Chez Pauline (Bistros and Brasseries: Les Halles)
Chez Vong (Chinese)
Epi d'Or (Bistros and Brasseries: Les Halles)
Fermette du Sud-Ouest (Bistros and Brasseries: Les Halles)
Higuma (Japanese)
Juvenile's (Wine Bars and Wine Bistros)
Kinugawa (Japanese)
Pharamond (Expensive and Moderate: Right Bank)
The Ritz (Salons de Thé: Right Bank)
Rose-Thé (Salons de Thé: Right Bank)
Le Rubis (Wine Bars and Wine Bistros)
Taverne Henri IV (Wine Bars and Wine Bistros)
Willi's Wine Bar (Wine Bars and Wine Bistros)

2nd Arrondissement
A Priori Thé (Salons de Thé: Right Bank)
Aux Crus de Bourgogne (Bistros and Brasseries: Les Halles)
Babylone (Afriques-Antilles)
Le Brin de Zinc (Bistros and Brasseries: Les Halles)
Chez Georges (Bistros and Brasseries: Les Halles)
Chez Pierrot (Bistros and Brasseries: Les Halles)
Isse (Japanese)
La Micro Brasserie (Wine Bars and Wine Bistros)
Pile ou Face (Expensive and Moderate: Right Bank)
Vaudeville (Jean-Paul Bucher Bistros)
La Villa Créole (Afriques-Antilles)

3rd Arrondissement
L'Ami Louis (Bistros and Brasseries: Right Bank)
Chez Jenny (Bistros and Brasseries: Right Bank)
404 (Fashionable Restaurants: Right Bank)

4th Arrondissement
L'Ambroisie (Haute Cuisine: Center)
Benoît (Bistros and Brasseries: Les Halles)
Bofinger (Bistros and Brasseries: Right Bank)
British Colonies (Salons de Thé: Right Bank)
Chez Marianne (Jewish and Middle Eastern)
Le Coin du Caviar (Eastern European)
Le Domarais (Expensive and Moderate: Right Bank)
Esther Street (Jewish and Middle Eastern)
Fer à Cheval (Cafés: Right Bank)
Flore-en-l'Ile (Salons de Thé: Right Bank)
Jo Goldenberg (Jewish and Middle Eastern)
Loir dans la Théière (Salons de Thé: Right Bank)
Ma Bourgogne (Cafés: Right Bank)
Mariage Frères (Salons de Thé: Right Bank)
Miravile (Expensive and Moderate: Right Bank)
La Perla (Fashionable Restaurants: Right Bank)
Quincambosse (Salons de Thé: Right Bank)
The Studio (Fashionable Restaurants: Right Bank)
La Tartine (Wine Bars and Wine Bistros)

5th Arrondissement
Al-Dar (North African and Middle Eastern)
Brasserie Balzar (Bistros and Brasseries: Left Bank)
Campagne et Provence (Fashionable Restaurants: Left Bank)
Chieng-Mai (Vietnamese and Thai)
La Maison (Fashionable Restaurants: Left Bank)
Mosquée de Paris (Salons de Thé: Left Bank)

Le Petit Plat (Bistros and Brasseries: Left Bank)
La Timonerie (Expensive and Moderate: Left Bank)

6th Arrondissement
Allard (Bistros and Brasseries: Left Bank)
Aux Deux Magots (Cafés: Left Bank)
Café de Flore (Cafés: Left Bank)
Café de la Mairie (Cafés: Left Bank)
La Cafetière (Bistros and Brasseries: Left Bank)
Le Canton (Chinese)
La Cour de Rohan (Salons de Thé: Left Bank)
Jacques Cagna (Haute Cuisine: Left Bank)
Mariage Frères (Salons de Thé)
Marie et Fils (Fashionable Restaurants: Left Bank)
Le Palanquin (Vietnamese and Thai)
La Palette (Cafés: Left Bank)
Restaurant des Beaux-Arts (Bistros and Brasseries: Left
    Bank)
La Rotisserie d'en Face (Fashionable Restaurants: Left
    Bank)

7th Arrondissement
L'Arpège (Haute Cuisine: Left Bank)
Le Divellec (Expensive and Moderate: Left Bank)
Jules Verne (Expensive and Moderate: Left Bank)
Le Récamier (Expensive and Moderate: Left Bank)
Tan Dinh (Vietnamese and Thai)

8th Arrondissement
Les Ambassadeurs (Haute Cuisine: Champs-Elysées)
Boeuf sur la Toit (Jean-Paul Bucher Bistros)
Chicago Pizza Pie Factory (American)
La Durée (Salons de Thé: Right Bank)
Les Elysées du Vernet (Expensive and Moderate: Right
    Bank)
Fouquet's (Cafés: Right Bank)
Lucas-Carton (Haute Cuisine: Champs-Elysées)
Plaza-Athénée (Salons de Thé: Right Bank)
Taillevent (Haute Cuisine: Champs-Elysées)
Le Texan (American)

9th Arrondissement
Café de la Paix (Cafés: Right Bank)
Grand Hôtel (Salons de Thé: Right Bank)
Stresa (Fashionable Restaurants: Right Bank)
La Table d'Anvers (Expensive and Moderate: Right
    Bank)
Tea Follies (Salons de Thé: Right Bank)

10th Arrondissement
Le Baalbek (North African and Middle Eastern)
Flo (Jean-Paul Bucher Bistros)
Julien (Jean-Paul Bucher Bistros)
Terminus Nord (Bistros and Brasseries: Right Bank)

11th Arrondissement
A Sousceyrac (Expensive and Moderate: Right Bank)
L'Ange Vin (Wine Bars and Wine Bistros)
Blue Elephant (Fashionable Restaurants: Right Bank)
Chez Philippe (Bistros and Brasseries: Right Bank)
Chez Rosine/Les Folies (Vietnamese and Thai)
Clown Bar (Cafés: Right Bank)
Jacques Mélac (Wine Bars and Wine Bistros)
Tapas Nocturne (Fashionable Restaurants: Right Bank)

12th Arrondissement
Au Trou Gascon (Expensive and Moderate: Right
   Bank)
L'Oulette (Expensive and Moderate: Right Bank)
La Plantation Paris (Afriques-Antilles)
Train Bleu (Bistros and Brasseries: Right Bank)

14th Arrondissement
Bistrot du Dôme (Bistros and Brasseries: Left Bank)
La Cagouille (Expensive and Moderate: Left Bank)
Chicago Pizza Pie Factory (American)
La Coupole (Jean-Paul Bucher Bistros)
La Regalade (Bistros and Brasseries: Left Bank)
Sélect (Cafés: Left Bank)

15th Arrondissement
Olympe (Expensive and Moderate: Left Bank)

16th Arrondissement
La Butte Chaillot (Fashionable Restaurants: Right
   Bank)
Henri Faugeron (Haute Cuisine: 16th and 17th
   Arrondissements)
Jamin (Haute Cuisine: 16th and 17th
   Arrondissements)
Port Alma (Expensive and Moderate: Right Bank)
Le Pré Catelan (Expensive and Moderate: Right Bank)

17th Arrondissement
Amphyclès (Haute Cuisine: 16th and 17th
   Arrondissements)
Apicius (Haute Cuisine: 16th and 17th
   Arrondisements)

homage, and many of these legendary institutions are found
on or around the streets radiating from here: **Lalique** crystal,
a few doors down from Maxim's restaurant at 11, rue Royale;
Christofle silver, which supplies much of the world's remaining royalty with its flatware, at number 9; and the city's most
glorious—and costly—florist, **Lachaume**, across the street at
number 10. Farther up the rue Royale are a number of chic
fashion boutiques: **Façonnable** and **Cerruti 1881** for classically inclined men (with a small Cerruti women's boutique
in between), **Gucci** and **Mario Valentino** for flashy Italian
shoes and leather goods, and the American new kid on the
block, **Ralph Lauren**, at 2, place de la Madeleine. On the
other side of the *place* at number 11 is a recently installed
Baccarat crystal showroom. Tucked off the rue Royale in the
Cité Berryer (a passageway lifted straight from the pages of
Zola) is **The Blue Fox** bar, which offers quiche, salad, and a
glass of Bordeaux to an attractive lunchtime crowd of well-
dressed shoppers, fashion-press attachés, and stockbrokers
from the nearby Place Vendôme.

The prestigious saddlery-turned-leather-goods house of
Hermès is a two-minute walk away, at 24, rue du Faubourg-
St-Honoré. Hardened indeed is the heart that doesn't leap at
the sight of a brown-ribboned orange box from Hermès
containing one of the house staples: a silk scarf, a "Kelly"
handbag (made famous by its most celebrated advocate,
Princess Grace), or the ultimate status accessory, Hermès's
pigskin Métro ticket holder. If your notion of high fashion
translates as high profile, you'll want to check out **Gianni
Versace**'s glitzy Neoclassical-style emporium down the street
from Hermès at 62, rue du Faubourg-St-Honoré.

Sitting smugly in the midst of all this luxe is the magnificent Hôtel de Crillon, at 10, place de la Concorde. Its
Obélisque Bar, reached by the hotel's rue Boissy-d'Anglas
side entrance, used to be a watering hole for journalists in
the prewar Paris of Janet Flanner and is still an irresistibly
romantic rendezvous spot.

Just beside it is the kind of shop that collectors of the rare,
the wonderful, and even the slightly kitschy come to Paris
for: **Au Bain Marie**, at 12, rue Boissy-d'Anglas. Specializing in
l'art de la table, Au Bain Marie's huge interior is chocka-
block with antique and reedited items for the kitchen and
dining room: turn-of-the-century silverware purchased from
defunct hotels, antique Daum and St. Louis crystal glasses,
Memphis dishes and 1930s Bakelite tableware, and exquisite
vintage and modern table and bed linens. For those caught
up in the mystique of the Orient Express there's its shop,
Orient Express Collection, at 15, rue Boissy-d'Anglas, which

sells replicas of the logo-stamped tea service and dinner plates, linen towels, and even the terry cloth bathrobes passengers find on that luxury train.

Place de la Madeleine: Food
In a country where food has been elevated to the status of religion, it seems only fitting that Paris's highest concentration of luxury food shops be found in the shadow of one of its most illustrious temples, La Madeleine. Here, clustered around the Place de la Madeleine, are some of the world's most dazzling names in gastronomy. The windows alone of **Fauchon**, at 26, place de la Madeleine, are an ode to gluttony. Inside, myriad culinary delights await: fresh foie gras and Beluga caviar, flavored oils and out-of-season tropical fruits, as well as a stock of more pedestrian imported goods catering to homesick Americans. Across the street at Fauchon's stand-up lunchroom you can wash down a frothy *pâtisserie* with a cup of some of the best coffee in Paris.

On the other side of the *place,* at number 21, is **Hédiard**, *épicier par excellence,* specializing in exotic fruits and vegetables, its own selection of teas, honeys, spice blends, and fresh fruit jellied candies known to every Parisian hostess as *les pâtes de fruits de chez Hédiard.* **Caviar Kaspia**, at 17, place de la Madeleine, offers caviar, smoked salmon, and blinis to go (an upstairs restaurant serves the same thing), and next door **La Maison de la Truffe** supplies fresh truffles from November to March (out of season they are available dried or preserved for less rarefied palates).

The adjacent rue Vignon boasts the quintessential *fromagerie,* **La Ferme St-Hubert**, at number 21, which in addition to its vast selection of cheeses also serves cheese dishes at its tiny adjoining restaurant. While on the rue Vignon don't miss **Pulcinella**, a small shop with a persimmon awning at number 10 that sells wonderful antique jewelry and other collectibles, or number 11, **Jean Lafont**, one of Paris's oldest and most renowned optometrists, specializing in Clark Kent–style, mock-tortoiseshell spectacles. On the corner of rue Vignon and rue de Sèze is the French equivalent of the old corner drugstore, **Pharmacie Leclerc**, whose fine face powders, alcohol-free tonics, and grandmother's-recipe face creams are favorites with Paris-based models and other fashion fauna.

Rue Tronchet and the Grands Magasins
The rue Tronchet is a bustling commercial artery leading north from the Place de la Madeleine to the Parisian *grands magasins,* Au Printemps and Galeries Lafayette. On the

second floor of number 13 (the third floor, to Americans), celebrated hatmaker **Jean Barthet** concocts fanciful headgear for Paris couturiers as well as provincial mothers-of-the-bride. At the intersection of rue Tronchet and boulevard Haussmann is another throwback to a more genteel era, **Aux Tortues** (at 55, boulevard Haussmann), whose caramel-colored marble façade decorated with bronze elephants has stood since 1864. Although its once-standard stock of tortoiseshell-backed boar-bristle brushes, ivory pocket combs, and eyelash brushes is dwindling (there is, apparently, no longer a clientele for tortoiseshell hand mirrors at 8,500 francs), Aux Tortues still has the best selection of polished Baltic amber necklaces and ivory and coral chokers in town.

Paris's two major department stores, **Au Printemps** and **Galeries Lafayette**, at numbers 64 and 40, boulevard Haussmann, are wonders of Belle Epoque architecture: Galeries Lafayette's stained glass dome bathes the entire store in pastel light, and Printemps's top-floor terrace restaurant is known for its elaborate 19th-century decor. They are Paris's answer to New York's Bloomingdale's (at least the Bloomingdale's of ten years ago) and London's Harrod's. Both *magasins* have been recently renovated, and a shopper short on time can find at them Paris's best names in beauty, fashion, and interior design. Both stores accept most major credit cards and are open Mondays through Saturdays, Au Printemps from 9:30 A.M. to 7:00 P.M. and Galeries Lafayette from 9:30 A.M. to 6:45 P.M.

Note: Possibly the world's most exhaustive selection of hardware and household bits and pieces—from hinges, locks, and doorknobs to wooden shoe trees and typically Parisian mailboxes—can be found at Paris's **BHV** (Bazar de l'Hôtel de Ville) department store, at 52–64, rue de Rivoli. Open Mondays through Saturdays from 9:00 A.M. to 7:00 P.M.; open Wednesdays until 10:00 P.M.

A distinct advantage for foreigners shopping at one of Paris's department stores is the ease in garnering the *détaxe*—the refund of the French excise tax to which visitors from abroad are entitled on a single purchase of minimum 4,200 francs if they live within the European Community, or on purchases from 2,000 francs if they live outside the EC. Shoppers from outside the EC must fill out a special *détaxe* form—with receipts of purchases made within a period of six months—which they surrender to customs for stamped approval when they leave France. Paris's *grands magasins* all have special *détaxe* departments that help demystify this all too often bewildering process.

Place Vendôme

Check out the labels on a Parisian dandy and chances are that at least one thing he's wearing comes from **Charvet,** *the* Paris men's haberdashery, located a few minutes' walk from *les grands magasins,* down the rue de la Paix at 28, place Vendôme. A seven-floor sanctuary on the majestic, 17th-century Place Vendôme, Charvet has offered everything for the impeccable man—and for such women enamored of masculine classics as the novelist George Sand, who used to have her shirts made here—since 1838.

Clustered around the Place Vendôme are France's most prestigious names in *haute joaillerie,* the centuries-old family jewelers **Chaumet, Boucheron, Mauboussin, Van Cleef et Arpels**—and **Cartier,** just up the street on the rue de la Paix. With the graceful, curved awnings of the Hôtel Ritz rimming one side, the glittering storefronts of these distinguished jewelers the other, the Place Vendôme on a spring afternoon is the closest approximation of Proust's Paris that the city can offer today.

A visitor can prolong the remembrance of Paris past at two neighboring boutiques: **Annick Goutal**'s glorious, gilded scent shop at 14, rue de Castiglione, and **Cassegrain,** 422, rue St-Honoré, stationers and engravers to Paris since Proust's times. Those nostalgic for the more genteel days of steamship and rail travel should stop by **Morabito,** at 1, place Vendôme, whose windows are perennially, defiantly piled high with gleaming black crocodile luggage (which some countries prohibit under customs laws).

Place du Marché St-Honoré

A *place* no less charming, but of an entirely different nature, is the Place du Marché St-Honoré, which you can reach by making a left onto the rue St-Honoré from the Place Vendôme's southern end and turning left again on the narrow rue du Marché St-Honoré. A fire station occupies the place of honor here, and around it is a jumble of colorful restaurants and boutiques. **Jean-Charles Castelbajac,** at 31, place du Marché St-Honoré, is a designer-clothing store where fashion often blends couture and cartoon; and wacky accessory designer **Philippe Model,** with side-by-side shops at number 33, supplies rose-trimmed toques, tasseled suede gloves, and fuchsia silk pumps to Parisiennes with the wit—and the self-assurance—to wear them. A note of austerity recently added to the *place* is the **Comme des Garçons** furniture boutique at 23, place du Marché St-Honoré, whose minimalist steel creations are the interior design equivalent of Japanese fashion label Comme des Garçons' purist fashions. **Corinne Cobson** sells sleek, sexy, and affordable fashion separates at number 28.

Rue de Rivoli

Do an about-face on the rue du Marché St-Honoré and it becomes—in yet another one of Paris's inexplicable street name changes—the rue du 29-Juillet, which leads onto the colonnaded rue de Rivoli. If you're looking for gilt Eiffel Towers, Mona Lisa sweatshirts, and Paris-monument-printed acetate scarves to take home, any one of the closet-size souvenir shops on the rue de Rivoli will be able to provide them.

Exceptions to the general tourist-trap ambience of the rue de Rivoli are the English bookshops **W. H. Smith** at number 248 and **Galignani**, said to be the oldest English-language bookshop in Paris, at number 224. Visitors hoping to take home with them more than just a memory of Paris streets should check out **Galerie d'Architecture Miniature**'s tiny, handmade faïence reproductions of Paris buildings (206, rue de Rivoli). And **Angelina**, at number 226, Paris's tearoom *par excellence,* is the gilt-and-mirrored meeting place for chic Parisians, a must for anyone seeking to understand French *belles manières.* Sipping a cup of Angelina's sinfully rich *chocolat l'africain*—poured in dollops from tiny porcelain pitchers—over an equally rich chestnut-and-cream Mont Blanc *pâtisserie* is many a Parisian's way of whiling away a long winter afternoon. For wonderful, offbeat mementos, **Destination Paris**, at 9, rue du 29-Juillet, offers artisan-made and generally wacky souvenirs of the City of Light.

If big-game antiques are your bag, **Le Louvre des Antiquaires**, left off the rue de Rivoli, at 2, place du Palais-Royal, is a well-stocked hunting ground. In this highly civilized three-story gallery are 250 shops devoted to fine French furniture, rich leather-bound books, and heavy bronzes. Unlike the tiny *brocanteurs* you find along the Left Bank's rue du Bac or rue Jacob, whose wares are reminiscent of *grandmère's* attic treasures, Le Louvre des Antiquaires's offerings are of a decidedly grander sort—and carry price tags to match. Most of Le Louvre des Antiquaires's shops accept major credit cards, but note that although they are open on Sundays, stores here traditionally close Mondays.

Men for whom the traditional pleasures of smoking and hunting remain as compelling as they were in earlier centuries will find two boutiques here to their liking: **A La Civette**,

157, rue St-Honoré, a *tabac* that has been providing smokers with the tools of their vice—fine Havana cigars, aromatic tobaccos, handmade pipes—since the 17th century, and **Faure le Page**, 8, rue de Richelieu, which sells arms and munitions and other hunting and shooting accessories. This shop, located on the same corner as the Comédie-Française since 1716, holds no charm for those who don't share its passion, but it carries a noteworthy distinction: It was here, in 1789, that the Paris mob stole the gunpowder with which they blew up the Bastille.

Palais-Royal
Off the Place du Palais-Royal are the tree-lined gardens of the Palais-Royal, whose graceful stone arcades have stood since 1780, when Louis-Philippe of Orléans built this ground-level shopping mall in Paris's first recorded get-rich-quick building scheme. Colette lived and died in one of the sumptuous apartments overlooking the gardens; the **Grand Véfour** restaurant, which began life here as a café in 1760, boasts a menu with a Jean Cocteau sketch on the cover and has a small brass plaque indicating Victor Hugo's habitual dining place. Old mosaic floor tiles outside still proclaim long-gone shop-owners' names, their places now occupied by a mixed bag of unusual boutiques.

Here are cloistered shops selling old stamps, antique jewels, beribboned medals and orders. **Didier Ludot**, 22–24, rue de Montpensier, sells one-of-a-kind antique leather accessories: Hermès bags and belts, crocodile wallets, and shoes. Next door at number 19–20 is Ludot's vintage couture clothing annex. **Costea**, 63–64, galerie Montpensier, offers geometrically shaped *objets d'art* for home and office in stark ebony wood and ivory, tortoiseshell, and shiny nickeled bronze.

On the northern end of the gardens at 9, rue de Beaujolais is **Anna Joliet**, a delightful boutique that sells music boxes both old and new. Just behind it are the turn-of-the-century glass-roofed shopping "malls," galeries **Colbert** and **Vivienne**. The galerie Vivienne, in addition to an assortment of tearooms, clothing boutiques, and interior design shops and the oldest bookstore in Paris—the **Librairie D. F. Jousseaume**—counts **Jean-Paul Gaultier**'s post-high-tech baroque boutique among its tenants. Childhood nostalgics shouldn't miss **Si Tu Veux**, at 62, galerie Vivienne, which sells charming traditional toys and games—wooden alphabet blocks, farm animal cardboard cutouts, and "real" teddy bears for parents and children weary of computerized fun. And for those who think (mistakenly) a shirt is a shirt is a shirt there's **Moholy-Nagy**, a minuscule shop at 2, galerie Vi-

vienne selling imaginative variations on the shirt theme—
in cotton, wool, or linen—for both men and women. The
newly renovated galerie Colbert's **Bibliothèque Nationale
Gift Shop**—France's national library is right next door—
offers distinctive souvenirs, all adapted from the library's
archives.

Within walking distance of the Palais-Royal gardens, off
the rue Croix-des-Petits-Champs, is another glass-covered
19th-century shopping arcade worth checking out: the
Galerie Véro-Dodat. It boasts exquisite tiled floors, beautiful
carved-wood shop façades, and some amusing shops: **Robert Capia**'s antique doll boutique; 1930s and '40s decorative
arts galleries **Pierre Passebon** and **Eric Philippe**; and, at the
other end of the *passage,* young shoe designer **Christian
Louboutin**'s wacky wares.

Place des Victoires

Where the rue des Petits-Champs meets the rue Etienne-
Marcel sits the Place des Victoires, an elegant 17th-century
place with an equestrian statue of Louis XIV in its center.
Circling it are some of Paris's best fashion storefronts:
Kenzo, Thierry Mugler, Stéphane Kélian, Enrico Coveri,
Charles Chevignon, Victoire, and American import Esprit. Its
overflow has spilled onto the high-tech rue Etienne-Marcel,
which has become the Paris address for the Japanese designers **Comme des Garçons** and **Yohji Yamamoto**, active-wear
designers **Marithé and François Girbaud**, the British knit-
wear house **Joseph Tricot**, and the French ready-to-wear
house **Cacharel**. At number 50, rue Etienne-Marcel is **La
Galerie en Attendant les Barbares**, a showcase for naturalis-
tic furnishings from the "New Barbarians," the group of
young designers who are currently redefining avant-garde
Paris interiors. And at 49, rue Etienne-Marcel is **Chevignon**'s
megastore, France's ultra-successful purveyor of American
1950s nostalgia—leather aviator jackets, chinos, moccasins,
and plaid flannel shirts—displayed with an unmistakable
French twist. The small streets radiating from the Place des
Victoires—the rue Croix-des-Petits-Champs, the rue du Mail,
the rue Hérold, and the nearby rue Coquillière—are full of
interesting, affordable fashion boutiques for both men and
women.

Les Halles

Next stop on the Right Bank shopping tour is the neighborhood known as Les Halles, which has been the subject of
much controversy in the past decade. Out of the rubble of
what Zola once called the "belly of Paris" and in the place of

the sprawling market that for more than 800 years supplied the housewives, restaurateurs, and market stalls of Paris with fresh produce has risen an ultra-modern shopping complex, Le Forum des Halles. Though totally lacking in charm, this chrome-and-glass monument to modern consumerism does have something for everybody: bookshops, sporting-goods stores, fashionable clothing boutiques, cinemas—if you can find your way around the elaborate labyrinth of escalators. One shop that stands out is the **Boutique Paris-Musées**, a showcase for innovative French design wares (some unusual ideas for presents to take home) at the entrance to the underground Forum at 1, rue Pierre-Lescot.

The surrounding *quartier* is an eclectic mix of chic boutiques and sex shops, trendy bars, and fast-food establishments that draws a particular species of Parisian whose characteristic dress often includes black leather, combat boots, and tin can lid–size hoop earrings. Les Halles's other shopping options are a stone's throw from the Centre Pompidou, whose entrance, with its motley congregation of fire-swallowers, African drum bands, and mimes, resembles a medieval fairground. The Place Ste-Opportune and the rue de la Ferronnerie are pedestrian areas bustling with enterprising boutiques; the rue du Cygne and the rue Pierre-Lescot are the streets to comb for 1950s and 1960s *fripes,* or secondhand clothes. The **Papeterie Moderne**, at 12, rue de la Ferronnerie, is the place to find life-size copies of Paris's green-trimmed, blue-metal street signs as well as the bona fide plastic *pâté de campagne* and *terrine de lièvre* signs of French charcuteries. Next door, **Opox Rapax**, also at 12, rue de la Ferronnerie, is *the* Paris address for big, bulky, hand-knit sweaters.

The rue du Jour, in the shadow of the imposing St-Eustache church, where Louis XIV celebrated his first communion and Molière was baptized, is the bastion of Paris's wildly successful ready-to-wear designer **Agnès B**. The designer makes simple, relatively inexpensive clothes for men, women, and children, and each category has its own boutique here. Also worth checking out on the rue du Jour: **La Droguerie**, at number 9, a treasure trove of yarns, ribbons, buttons, and beads where teenage Parisians come to find parts for their funky earrings; **Pom d'Api**, at number 13, for amusing sneakers and other original shoe styles for tots (the "grown-up" store, **Free Lance**, is nearby, at 22, rue Mondétour); at number 7, Jean-Paul Gaultier's **Junior Gaultier** boutique; **Claudie Pierlot** and **Oblique**, at numbers 4 and 19, for reasonably priced fashion separates. For those tin can lid–hoop earrings, check out **Scooter**, at 10, rue de Turbigo, which also sells ethnically inspired, funky sportswear for men and women.

Gourmet Equipment

A five-minute walk away are two establishments for aspiring Cordon Bleu chefs: **A. Simon**, 36, rue Etienne-Marcel, and **E. Dehillerin**, 18–20, rue Coquillière (off rue du Louvre), both vestiges of the days when Les Halles was the city's wholesale market. A. Simon is a family-run business that has been providing restaurateurs and hoteliers with kitchen and dining equipment since 1884. A vast selection of traditional French table items can be purchased here at almost wholesale prices, from the utilitarian stainless-steel-and-glass salt, pepper, and mustard-pot sets found on any Paris bistro table to a select choice of Baccarat crystal at a 10 percent saving; also available are Villeroy and Boch porcelain dinner services at 25 to 30 percent less than in Paris department stores. Across the street, at 48, rue Montmartre, is A. Simon's kitchenware annex, where a stock of Sabatier and Tour Eiffel knives and Cousances and Le Creuset enameled cast-iron cookware await the would-be kitchen wizard. Pots and pans are E. Dehillerin's specialty: shallow cast-iron crêpe pans, weighty steel frying pans, and the shiny copper pots of French country kitchens.

Le Marais

East of Les Halles, tucked in among the jumble of crooked streets, kosher delicatessens, and splendid, half-hidden 17th-century town houses that make up Paris's historic Marais quarter, are several unusual boutiques that reflect the *quartier*'s unique character. Stroll along the rue Vieille-du-Temple, a street that has retained much of its old flavor. At number 26 is a delightful shop, **A La Bonne Renommée**, which sells spools of embroidered ribbons, reams of calico, and everything that could be concocted from a combination of the two. At number 47 the smell of fresh-ground coffee wafts from **La Maison des Colonies**, a gleaming emporium of imported coffees and exotic teas. At number 58, **Jean Lapierre** offers 18th-century carved-stone mantelpieces and blackened 17th-century iron coats of arms ferreted out from demolished buildings. **Casta Diva**, next door, is an opera- and ballet-lover's nirvana: a red-carpeted, red-walled boutique specializing in records, books, magazines, and photographs on opera and dance.

On the adjoining rue des Francs-Bourgeois (which got its name, "the men who pay no tax," in 1332 from the almshouses built there for the poor) is **Janine Kaganski**, at number 41, a mother-and-daughter shop selling 18th- and 19th-century wood furniture from Bavaria and Alsace painted in polychrome patterns of flowers and fruit. At number 45, **A l'Image du Grenier sur l'Eau** has more than a million vintage postcards for sale—from kitsch to classic 1950s film stills—lovingly amassed by the shop's owner over ten years. Artga's charming orange paper–wrapped map of the Marais can be purchased at **Marais Plus**, a bookstore-cum-tearoom at 20, rue des Francs-Bourgeois. **S.M.A.R.T.**, at 22, rue des Francs-Bourgeois, offers artisan-made, hand-painted ceramic tiles for bathrooms, kitchens, or floors—including *tommettes,* the clay-colored floor tiles so popular in Provençal homes. S.M.A.R.T. will also produce tiles of your own design and ship them. At number 17, the idiosyncratic **Jean-Pierre de Castro** sells silver-plated cutlery by the kilo, as well as unusual jewelry fashioned from old knives, forks, and spoons. You'll find a dazzling display of beautiful antique glassware on **L'Harlequin**'s dusty, floor-to-ceiling shelves at number 13. **Carnavalette**, at number 2, is the place to find the ideal Marais souvenir: an old bound copy of Madame de Sévigné's *Lettres,* which chronicles the day-to-day events of aristocratic 17th-century Paris, or an 18th-century *gravure* of the nearby Place des Vosges. And catering to idle Sunday shoppers (the Marais is one of the rare shopping areas in Paris open on Sundays) is France's version of Banana Republic, **Autour du Monde**, at number 12.

Place des Vosges, the oldest square in Paris, awaits you at the end of the rue des Francs-Bourgeois. Once the scene of elegant courtly parades, raucous festivities, and duels at dawn, the Place des Vosges—known in the days of Henri IV as the Place Royale—is today a quiet park where children play and old men reminisce on sun-warmed benches. Rows of antiques shops, restaurants, and boutiques have sprung up under its stone arcades; don't miss Franco-Italian fashion designer **Popy Moreni**'s clean, geometric, three-floor shopping space at number 13; **Les Deux Orphelins**, a *brocanteur* filled with amusing bric-a-brac at number 21; Japanese designer boutiques **Issey Miyake** and **Paco Funada** at numbers 5 and 17; and **Jardin de Flore**'s limited re-editions of antique illuminated manuscripts and exquisite copies of 17th-century Venetian globes at number 24. Music-lovers and those who admire fine workmanship no matter what the craft should stop by **André Bissonnet**, just off the north end of the Place des Vosges, at 6, rue du Pas-de-la-Mule. Here, in an erstwhile butcher's shop (decor intact), the erstwhile butcher himself, André Bissonnet, restores and sells an intriguing array of antique musical instruments: an 18th-century viola, a 17th-century harp, even carnival hurdy-gurdies that have seen better days. For players of string instruments, **François Perrin's Lutherie**, at 4, rue Elzévir, also in the Marais near the Picasso Museum, buys, restores, and sells violins, violas, harps, and other old string instruments.

Just off the serene garden of the Hôtel Le Peletier de Saint-Fargeau at 4, rue du Parc-Royal is **Delisle**, a centuries-old lighting manufacturer whose lamps adorn Versailles and that today sells convincing reproductions of a variety of period lighting fixtures. **Christian Gibeaux**, at number 6, is a master at making *faux* marble lamps, tables, and other objects from wood and resin.

In the past few years the Marais area has become the domain of many of Paris's young, trendy designers. **Lolita Lempicka**, who dresses many fashionable Parisians in witty, feminine dresses and suits, is at 13 bis, rue Pavée (her "younger," better-priced line, **Lolita Bis**, is sold at a shop of that name just across the street), and **Alain Mikli**'s avant-garde eyewear is sold at 1, rue des Rosiers. **Azzedine Alaïa**, one of the Marais's very first "fashionable" tenants, has moved recently to new—and giant—premises a few streets westward, behind the BHV department store at 7, rue de Moussy.

The rue des Rosiers, once the heart of Paris's traditional Jewish quarter, has become a shopper's mecca. **Jo Goldenberg**, the capital's best Jewish deli, still stands at number 7, and **Sacha Finkelsztain** has been supplying bona fide bagels, piroshki, and cheesecake "*de père en fils, depuis 1946,*" but both are now flanked by trendy fashion boutiques. There's **Autre Chose**, at number 2, and **Tehen** at number 5 bis, with **Charles Kammer** shoes and **Olivier Chanas** hats just across the street. At number 4, in the massive building that once housed the neighborhood *hammam* (bathhouse), **Chevignon** has installed an emporium offering U.S. Southwest–style Navajo rugs, hand-hewn "Taos" furniture, and other Santa Fe– and American country–style pieces for the home. On the nearby rue Malher are more amusing hats at **Anna Kaszer**, number 7, and **Paule Ka**'s Audrey Hepburn–style black cocktail dresses at number 20. One street over, at 46, rue de Sévigné, is Italian designer **Romeo Gigli**'s Paris boutique, across the street from Paris's most enchanting history museum, the Musée Carnavalet.

La Bastille

The Bastille area, a ten-minute walk eastward from the Marais, has emerged in recent years as the latest candidate for the title of "the insider's Paris." The controversial Bastille Opera House was inaugurated in July 1989 for the bicentennial of the French Revolution, and the *quartier*—once a humble working-class neighborhood—really spruced itself up for the occasion. La Bastille now offers a lively selection of offbeat restaurants and gutsy P.M. fare for those in search of alternative forms of entertainment. It's no wonder, then, that **Pom Pin Disques**, a record shop specializing in hard-to-find collector's records from reggae to funk, New Wave to Edith Piaf, at 17, rue de Lappe, sometimes stays open until 2:00 A.M. By day this area rife with artists' ateliers and galleries welcomes art amateurs and collectors in search of contemporary alternatives to Picasso and Gauguin. **Galerie Bastille**, at 28, rue de Lappe, which opened in 1979 when La Bastille was still primarily a furniture wholesalers' district, now includes John Cage, Ruffin Cooper, and Michel Faublée among its stable of artists. **Franka Berndt Bastille** devotes its high-ceilinged, cool white-and-gray gallery at 11, rue St-Sabin to constructivist works; and **Lavigne Bastille**, 27, rue de Charonne, to new painters and sculptors.

In a space the size of a walk-in closet, **Duelle** (21, rue Daval) displays another kind of art, avant-garde jewelry: papier-mâché bangles in paint-box colors and resin earrings translucent as uncut stones. "I'm on the lookout for pieces with humor," says the lavender-locked owner, Claude Deilhes. Farther down at number 26, where the rue Daval becomes the rue de Lappe, is a shop devoted to the gentleman's game of billiards. **Le Maître Billiardier** can supply the well-equipped game room with everything from cushioned bistro stools and antique mechanical pianos to the ubiquitous billiard table—from a run-of-the-mill 45,000-franc model to a claw-footed 450,000-franc Charles X antique.

Rue du Pont Louis-Philippe

Double back from the Place des Vosges (south on rue de Birague off the *place,* then a right turn) on the rue St-Antoine and trace the rue François-Miron to where the rue du Pont Louis-Philippe leads to the Seine. Number 68, rue François-Miron is the 17th-century mansion built for Anne of Austria's first woman of the bedchamber in return for her having initiated the 16-year-old Louis XIV in the delights of love. Although fallen into disrepair, the Hôtel de Beauvais is still majestic; its curving, carved-stone staircase is magnificent.

Facing each other on the rue du Pont Louis-Philippe are two boutiques for lovers of beautiful stationery: **Papier +**, at number 9, which sells heavy handmade papers, fabric-covered notebooks, and photo albums; and **Mélodies Gra-**

phiques, at number 10, which carries Florence's famous "Il Papiro" stationery items made from marbleized endpapers.

The Left Bank

Just across the bridge lies the Latin Quarter. Although this medieval *quartier* retains its status as the intellectual heart of Paris—the Sorbonne, the Beaux-Arts, and the *grandes écoles* are all located here—Sartre's table at Aux Deux Magots is likely to have been usurped by a weary shopper, so dense is the concentration of boutiques in the area. The maze of streets nearest the river—the rues des Sts-Pères, de Lille, du Bac, de Verneuil, Bonaparte, and Jacob—are a paradise for the antiques and art-gallery aficionado.

On the river itself, not far from the Ecole des Beaux-Arts, at 3, quai Voltaire, is **Sennelier,** an art-supply shop smelling of chalk and linseed oil that Paris painters have known and loved since 1887. Just behind it, **Robert Montagut** (15, rue de Lille) is a perfectly reconstructed antique Provençal *pharmacie,* whose gleaming niches hold antique apothecary jars of all shapes and sizes on sale for 1,500 to 150,000 francs! Balletomanes will find a spiritual home at 14, rue de Beaune, where **La Danse** offers books, magazines, prints, and watercolors on dance, even Degas-esque bronze statuettes of graceful ballerinas. **La Rose des Vents,** at 25, rue de Beaune, sells old ships' wheels, antique brass compasses, and other ancient nautical treasures. **Le Temps Libre,** down the adjacent rue de Verneuil at number 9, offers children's playthings rescued from attic trunks: odd bits and pieces of porcelain dolls and their houses, long-forgotten board games, and other juvenile oddities. Next door at number 7 is **Parsua,** where Parisian housewives bring their heirloom carpets to be restored and where you can pick up a length of 18th-century Lyonnaise silk for an appropriately princely sum.

On the other side of the rue du Bac, at 47, rue de Verneuil, is the quirky **Galerie Jacques Fischer-Chantal Kiener,** an almost-secret source for affordable 19th-century drawings, paintings, and sculpture. And down the street, at 60, rue de Verneuil, is **Epoca,** an intriguing treasure trove of arcane objects for the home, many of them of Far Eastern origin. Aficionados of contemporary interior design should stop by the **Galerie Mougin,** at 30, rue de Lille, which displays one-of-a-kind furniture and objects by *créateurs* André Dubreuil, Tom Dixon, Christian Astuguevieille, and others.

The rue Bonaparte leads to the Place St-Germain-des-Prés and its surrounding cluster of bookshops. At 31, rue Bonaparte, the **Librairie Bonaparte**'s window is lined with books in many languages on *le spectacle*—ballet, theater, modern dance. The imposing **Librairie F. De Nobele**, next door at number 35, specializes in old tomes and literature related to *les beaux-arts:* fashion, art, design. On the corner of the rue de l'Abbaye and the rue Bonaparte is **Le Divan**, whose name (the kind of tongue-in-cheek reference French wags delight in) means "the couch," indicating this bookseller's bent for psychology and philosophy titles. And sandwiched between the celebrated Parisian cafés Aux Deux Magots and Café de Flore is the no less celebrated **La Hune** bookstore, at 170, boulevard St-Germain, with its wealth of "humanist" books—on poetry, photography, architecture, literature, music, theater, cinema, and fashion. **Elbé**, the best place in Paris for old prints, is up the boulevard at 213 bis. And those on the trail of Hemingway's Paris shouldn't miss **Shakespeare & Company**, near St-Germain's Place Maubert at 37, rue de la Bûcherie. Although today's bookshop is not the Sylvia Beach original, American expatriate owner George Whitman has faithfully reproduced its namesake's bohemian literary atmosphere, offering poetry readings, upstairs beds for itinerant writers, and a mixed bag of English, American, German, and other European-language books.

On the other side of the boulevard St-Germain are hundreds of boutiques. The rues Bonaparte, du Four, St-Sulpice, de Rennes, du Cherche-Midi, des Sts-Pères, and de Sèvres are all showcases for the latest Paris fashions and accessories. A determined shopper short on time can start at the rue du Four and, following the rue de Grenelle westward, encounter an inexhaustible lineup of clothing and shoe shops: Sonia Rykiel, Prada, Boutique d'Emilia, Charles Kammer, Chacok, Christian Aujard, Stéphane Kélian, Miss Maud, Odile Lancon, Claude Montana, Tokio Kumagai, Cerruti 1881, Kenzo, and more. **Cassegrain**, suppliers and engravers of fine writing paper since 1919, has its Left Bank branch at number 81, rue des Sts-Pères, the place to order those oh-so-French outsize *cartes de visite*. Next door, but sharing the same address at number 81, is whimsical hat- and shoemaker **Philippe Model**'s new Left Bank outpost.

Another St-Germain street attracting a concentration of interesting, affordable fashions is the tiny rue du Pré-aux-Clercs, which begins life just off the boulevard St-Germain as the rue St-Guillaume. Boutiques that sell inexpensive ready-to-wear clothes are **Irié**, **Michel Klein**, **Corinne Sarrut** (an ex-Cacharel designer), and **Anvers**, a shop highlighting the fashions of young Belgian designers.

Art and antiques buffs should not miss the quaint rue de Seine and the parallel rue Mazarine. Both are lined with galleries selling some of Paris's finest 1920s and 1930s antiques, old prints, and contemporary art. The side-by-side **Vallois** galleries specializing in Art Deco at number 41, rue de Seine, are a must. (And when you've tired of tramping the cobblestones, stop for a glass of Beaujolais at **La Palette**, one of Paris's oldest and most picturesque cafés, at the corner of rue Jacques-Callot.)

Other unique boutiques in the area are **Soleiado**, at 78, rue de Seine, which carries reams of colorful Provençal-print cotton fabrics and a selection of household and fashion accessories made from them; **Piccolo Teatro**, a whimsical little antiques shop selling 18th-century bits and pieces at 7, rue de Condé; and **Beauté Divine**, 40, rue St-Sulpice, a reconstructed 19th-century store specializing in beauty and bathroom items from bygone eras: Baccarat crystal perfume flacons, ivory nail buffers, antique porcelain pitchers. Another plush turn-of-the-century replica, **Diners en Ville**, at 89, rue du Bac, focuses once again on that popular French preoccupation—dining—but with an emphasis on originality and color. Here are the amusing trompe l'oeil plates the French call *barbotines,* vintage glass and crystal carafes, and refurbished antique paisley tablecloths.

For the kind of lingerie trousseaux are made of, visit **Sabbia Rosa**, 71–73, rue des Sts-Pères, where sumptuous, lace-trimmed satin nightgowns, camisoles, and sexy tap pants hang in languid pastel rows against lacquered gray walls. For sheer delight, visit **Madeleine Gély**, 218, boulevard St-Germain, a doll-size boutique—crammed full of umbrellas, parasols, and canes both old and new—that has been in existence since 1834. Gély will still custom-make umbrellas for too-short or too-tall clients in their choice of fabric, and with wood, ivory, or horn handles. For a crash course in traditional Parisian pint-size elegance, there's **Bon Point** (67, rue de l'Université; furniture at 7, rue de Solférino), which sells the same navy blue coats, gray flannel shorts, and smocked dresses French children have been wearing for decades. For sleek suede and kid gloves and, especially, unique scents sold in a gilded 18th-century-style setting, don't miss **Maître Parfumeur et Gantier** at 84 bis, rue de Grenelle.

Avenue Montaigne

Coming full circle, you will return to the Right Bank by the Pont de l'Alma near the Eiffel Tower and, via the avenue Montaigne, enter a world of unbridled luxury. If your stay in Paris has still not converted you to the gilded life, a stroll down the tree-lined avenue Montaigne will. This is home to much of the haute couture—Dior, Emanuel Ungaro, Guy Laroche, Hanae Mori, with Yves Saint Laurent and Givenchy nearby.

The crimson-awninged, geranium-banked Hôtel Plaza-Athénée presides over the avenue like a serene princess. Its Relais Plaza grill room, with a 1930s ocean liner decor, is the lunchtime spot for Paris's *beau monde,* and postprandial shoppers need only turn left outside the door to check out Italian jeweler **Bulgari**'s latest creations (27, avenue Montaigne). **Valentino** is just next door, at 17–19, avenue Montaigne; **Chanel** is at 42, avenue Montaigne, with its watch and shoe shops just down the street. **Louis Vuitton**'s newest boutique is at number 54. At number 16 is an extraordinary accessory shop, **Isabel Canovas**, a cobalt-blue, mirrored Ali Baba's cave filled with artisan-made jewel-studded cuff links and earrings, brilliant silk-velour shawls, and embroidered bags. At number 14 model-turned-entrepreneur **Inès de la Fressange** has opened up an eponymously named place that sells chic, classic women's and men's fashions and select, hard-to-find items (like double-bed-size, antique-style linen sheets) for the home. **D. Porthault**, at 18, avenue Montaigne, is where house-proud Parisians buy their bed, bath, and table linens; the store's fresh, floral-print cotton percale bedsheets are world famous. **Parfums Caron**, at 34, avenue Montaigne, dispenses Caron perfume classics from gold-etched Baccarat crystal urns. **Puiforcat**, at 22, rue François-Ier, next door to **Fouquet**'s 65-year-old sweet shop, sells re-edited versions of the streamlined sterling silver table settings and tea and coffee services that made them so popular in Paris in the 1930s.

A few streets up from the Plaza-Athénée at 45, rue Pierre-Charron is **Hobbs,** a shop specializing in quality Scottish cashmere sweaters in a rainbow of 50 colors and a variety of amusing patterns. Just around the corner at number 33, rue François-Ier, is the perfume and fashion house of **Rochas**, with its Riccardo Bofill–designed Neoclassical façade, offering a wealth of 18th-century-style fashion accessories, *objets* for the home, and a complete women's ready-to-wear clothing line. (A Rochas boutique for men is located at 29, avenue George-V.) And for the best classic men's fedora, there is the 1887-vintage **Motsch et Fils**, a five-minute walk away at 42, avenue George-V, a hat shop that also sells panamas, homburgs, and hunting caps, in addition to sporting one of the most beautiful wood-paneled storefronts in town.

Although the nearby avenue des Champs-Elysées still inspires awe, the profusion of pinball halls, flashy cinemas, and fast-food establishments has robbed it of its past standing as Paris's ultimate chic shopping avenue. The fragrance house **Guerlain**, at 68, avenue des Champs-Elysées, is a staunch exception: Its marble walls and atmosphere of hallowed luxe make it an obligatory stop for those on the trail of typically Parisian old-world luxury. An addition to "the Champs" is the monumental **Virgin Records**, a bank-turned-music-emporium at 52, avenue des Champs-Elysées.

Flea Markets

No shopping devotee could leave Paris without a pilgrimage to one of Paris's *marchés aux puces,* or flea markets: the **Porte de Montreuil** for antique clothing and odd bits of furniture; the **Porte de Vanves** for bric-a-brac; and especially the **Porte de Clignancourt**, with more than 3,000 stands selling everything from used clothing to gilded Regency furniture. All the flea markets are located in the northern, southern, or eastern outskirts of Paris, "Porte" referring to one of the gateways to the Périphérique (the highway circling the city). For serious antiques hunters, the Porte de Clignancourt's 200-stand Marché Biron sells what is generally considered to be the *crème de la crème* of the *puces:* old silver- and bronze-framed mirrors, Limoges porcelain, and other treasures. Don't miss Stand 232, Allée 6, of the Porte de Clignancourt's Marché Paul-Bert. The Marché St-Paul is a scavenger's dream, offering a mixed bag of chipped crockery, old dentists' mirrors, brass candlesticks; and for fabulous vintage Louis Vuitton steamer trunks (complete with old hotel stickers).

Be warned: Although most flea-market shopkeepers will arrange shipping of these sometimes unwieldy souvenirs back home, depending on weight and choice of air mail or slow boat, transport could almost double the price of your Paris "bargain."

—Charla Carter

ILE-DE-FRANCE
DAY TRIPS FROM PARIS

By Edward Hernstadt and Amy Hollowell

Edward Hernstadt is a freelance writer who lived in Paris for four years. He has contributed to publications in the United States, France, and Australia. Amy Hollowell is an editor at The International Herald Tribune *in Paris, where she has lived since 1982. She also writes about various aspects of life in France.*

Paris is a city of marvels: old and new, secular and religious, vulgar and exquisite. Its 23 centuries of continuous occupation have left a mark on the surrounding countryside as well. Today the Ile-de-France, as the region is called, encompasses Paris as well as the towns and castles around it: the medieval villages that traded with or provided a refuge from the city; the religious centers that spread the word of God; the hunting lodges and country houses of France's kings; and the grand châteaux of the French nobility.

A day in the country can provide both an enriching perspective on the history of Paris as well as the opportunity to spend some time in beautiful valleys and forests, away from the congestion of the city. Many destinations are accessible by train; others are best reached by car. Most are on the tourist-bus circuit, but this option could prove constricting, as organized tours are often crowded and don't allow time for dawdling. Finally, all these destinations are within 90 minutes of the capital, and any one will provide a pleasant day's outing.

MAJOR INTEREST

West of Paris
Versailles
Rueil-Malmaison
Château St-Germain-en-Laye, gardens, and forest
Monet's home and gardens at Giverny
Château Thoiry and game park
Cathédrale de Chartres

South of Paris
Fondation Cartier in Jouy-en-Josas
Vallée de Chevreuse
Château Vaux-le-Vicomte
Barbizon
Fontainebleau

East of Paris
Medieval town of Provins
EuroDisney
Château-Thierry and Bois Belleau battle sites

North of Paris
Compiègne and Pierrefonds châteaux
Forêt de Compiègne armistice site
Roman and medieval town of Senlis
Chantilly
Cathédrale Beauvais
Auvers-sur-Oise, Van Gogh's final home

A brief note on the chief players in the Ile-de-France: François I, the Ramses II of France, built or added to many of the châteaux mentioned, as did Louis XIV. Louis Le Vau and Jules Hardouin-Mansart were the predominant architects of the 17th century, Charles Le Brun, the preeminent decorator; and André Le Nôtre is arguably the most important landscape artist in the history of France.

West

VERSAILLES
Versailles, 20 km (12 miles) from Paris, is as much a conviction as a château—the conviction that bigger *is* better and that moral ostentatiousness *is* more tasteful. The château is enormous, imposing, imperial, and rock solid, and still conveys Louis XIV's message of French omnipotence and his own glory. This is not an unpopular message with the French, who have long struggled to reconcile their longings

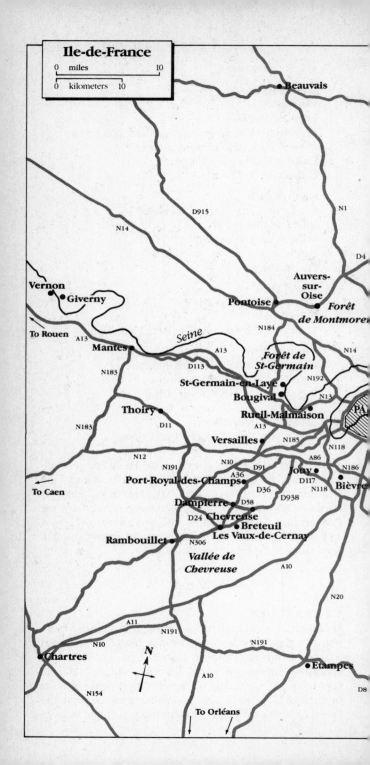

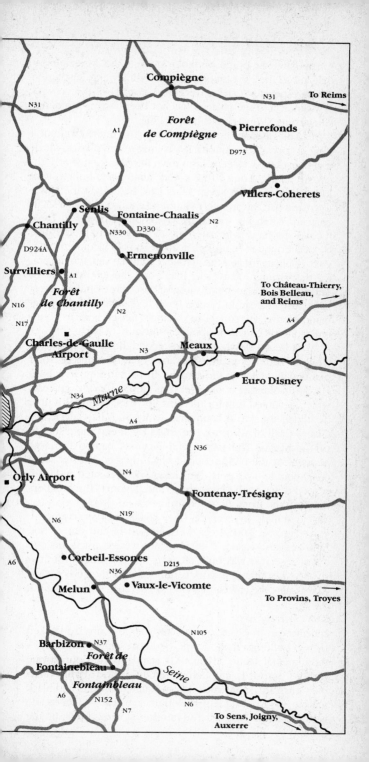

for monarchical pomp with their pride in the egalitarianism that led to the Revolution. Not surprisingly, the Revolution struck especially hard at Versailles, symbol of the crown's arrogance, and the château has not been a royal residence since Louis XVI was beheaded in 1793.

Versailles is one of the few châteaux in France without a long history of renovations; it was built in two phases, which together turned a sleepy farm town into the apogee of 17th-century luxury. Louis XIII enjoyed hunting and built a small lodge here in 1624. Seven years later he bought the entire town and had the architect Philibert Le Roy construct a small château. When his son Louis XIV assumed power in 1661, the new monarch's first step was to outdo mere mortals like Nicolas Fouquet, whose château at Vaux-le-Vicomte he envied. Louis instructed the architect Louis Le Vau, the decorator and painter Charles Le Brun, and the landscape artist André Le Nôtre to build the grandest, most opulent, most expensive château in France. Louis had another, more pragmatic motive: He sought to distance himself and his courtiers from the dangerous political intrigues of Paris.

Work began slowly. Le Vau extended the existing château while Le Brun commanded an army of artisans and Le Nôtre planned and laid out the gardens. In 1678 the architect Jules Hardouin-Mansart took over the design of the château, which occupied him for the next 30 years; during this time he added the two monumental wings and the Galerie des Glaces (Hall of Mirrors). The artists faced enormous logistical problems: The palace and grounds had to be large enough for the entire court—which then comprised some 6,000 people—yet everything had to be decorated and landscaped down to the last cornice and begonia. The numbers that resulted from these requirements are almost too vast to have parallels in everyday life: 36,000 workers were involved; some 3,000 trees were moved in and out of hothouses every season; 1,400 fountains were constructed; and a vast reservoir was built to store water diverted from the river Seine. Although work continued until the end of Louis XIV's reign, the château was in use by 1663.

The Courtyards

A heavy cast-iron gate opens onto a large courtyard flanked by two buildings that once housed government ministers. A monumental statue of Louis XIV stands in the **Cour Royale** (Royal Courtyard), and behind it the **Cour de Marbre** (Marble Courtyard), constructed from squares of white and black marble, is surrounded by the original château, whose façade is by Hardouin-Mansart. The ministerial wings break up the building's nearly half-mile-long façade. From behind, however, the perspective is striking, with the center of the château set forward to add relief. Statues and vases break the line of the balustrade, and statues of Apollo and Diana cap the central, royal, section.

The Apartments

The apartments are relentlessly luxurious. Marble, gilt, moldings, and frescoes are everywhere. It is difficult to understand how any business requiring concentration could have been accomplished in the palace—the sheer mass and ostentation of the decor is distracting. It is also superbly crafted: Le Brun's team of talented artisans executed his designs with precision and grace. The château may be pretentious, but its decor is the most completely realized of the period.

The **chapel**, a sumptuous study in white and gold with intricately carved pillars, is one of Hardouin-Mansart's masterpieces. On the second floor, the **Grands Appartements**, where Louis XIV and his court ate, played pool, and listened to concerts, consist of a series of rooms dedicated to Mars, Venus, Mercury, and Diana; the throne room belongs to Apollo. The staggering **Galerie des Glaces** was in its heyday a ballroom. The mirrored walls reflect Le Brun's ceiling frescoes, which describe Louis XIV's early years, and were designed to show off the wildly expensive costumes of the ladies and courtiers.

Two events that determined the contours of Europe took place in the Galerie des Glaces. In 1871, after soundly defeating France in a war engineered by Otto von Bismarck to unify the various states of Germany under the leadership of Prussia, Germany announced the German Empire to the world from Versailles. This new Germany also seized the disputed territories of Alsace-Lorraine at the war's end, thus augmenting the tensions that resulted in World War I. And it was here in 1919 that the defeated Germany signed the Treaty of Versailles, the unbalanced document that led indirectly to World War II.

The Gardens

After the showy luxury of the apartments, which were designed primarily to celebrate the importance and majesty of Louis XIV, the planned beauty of the gardens is a delight. Directly behind the château, steps lead down to two large basins. To the right the Parterre du Nord stretches through flower beds to the **Neptune fountain**, the largest at Versailles. To the left the Parterre du Midi leads to the **Orangerie**, where hundreds of orange and palm trees bloom every summer. Paths lined with statues thread through the garden, which is divided into areas dominated by different geometric patterns. A long central path, the Tapis Vert (Green Carpet), runs from the center of the château to the Grand Canal. It, too, is bounded with statues, and the view of the château façade over gardens and fountains is stunning. The Grand Canal extends to the horizon from the perspective of the château, and, as it is laid out on an east–west axis, the setting sun is reflected in it. The gardens behind the Trianons (see below) are more rustic; designed in the country style favored in the 18th century, the winding paths are almost emblematically pastoral and lovely to walk along.

The Trianons
Other buildings occupy the grounds, notably the Grand Trianon, the Petit Trianon, and the Hameau. Louis XIV first constructed the Trianon de Porcelain, where he escaped the court with his first mistress, Madame de Montespan. By the time he replaced her with Madame de Maintenon (whom he secretly married after the death of his wife), the porcelain had decayed. So, in 1687 Louis built the pink-marble **Grand Trianon**. It was used principally for receptions by succeeding kings, and in 1962 Charles de Gaulle restored it as a residence for visiting dignitaries. Among those who have enjoyed the royal lodgings are Queen Elizabeth II of England and Leonid Brezhnev. Today it is furnished in the 19th-century style of the Restoration kings. Highlights include the malachite room, which takes its name from the malachite vases and candelabra Czar Alexander gave Napoléon at Tilsit, and the *galerie,* filled with crystal and paintings of the gardens as they looked in the 17th century.

Louis XV commissioned the **Petit Trianon**, and it became a favorite retreat of Louis XVI and Marie-Antoinette. This frivolous queen also built the **Hameau** (Hamlet), a charming, idealized reproduction of what the wealthy imagined farms to be, and she loved to pretend to herd sheep there. Ironically, she was near the Hameau when a messenger brought word that rebellious Parisians were marching on Versailles. Marie-Antoinette fled and never saw the Hameau again. Napoléon III's empress, Eugénie, who sympathized with her, collected many of the late queen's possessions in a little museum there.

Elsewhere in Versailles
Other important sites are spread throughout Versailles, including the **Menus-Plaisirs**, at 22, avenue de Paris (not open to the public), and the **Salle du Jeu de Paume**, just off the rue Satory (restored and open to the public on Saturdays from

June 1 through September 30; hours may vary; Tel: 30-84-76-18 or the local tourist office, Tel: 39-50-36-22). When the Estates-General (the three estates of the clergy, the nobility, and the bourgeoisie) convened in 1789, they met in a makeshift structure erected in the courtyard of the building housing the King's entertainers, the *menus-plaisirs*. Many of the dramatic events that led to the first stage of the French Revolution took place here, including the drafting of the constitution and the Declaration of the Rights of Man. And the Estates-General took the famous "Tennis Court Oath," vowing not to disband until a constitution was accepted by the crown, during the three days they met at the Salle du Jeu de Paume.

Staying and Dining in Versailles

Travellers who would like to make themselves at home almost within the royal purlieu should consider the stately ▶ **Trianon-Palace** on the edge of the gardens. The hotel's 119 rooms have been renovated and a swimming pool and fitness club added to the premises. A luxurious meal in the very refined mansion that houses **Les Trois Marches**, one of the Ile-de-France's most respected restaurants, at 1, boulevard de la Reine, may be a perfect conclusion to a day spent in the opulence of the château (Tel: 39-50-13-21; closed Sundays and Mondays). Specialties include a wondrous foie gras, filet of beef with truffle sauce, and marinated filet of sole. Many other cafés and small restaurants in Versailles offer fine meals. Or you might bring a picnic; it would be hard to find a more inviting picnic spot than the gardens at Versailles.

Versailles is open every day but Mondays, from 9:00 A.M. to 6:00 P.M. April 1 to September 30 and from 9:00 A.M. to 5:30 P.M. October 1 to March 31. You can reach Versailles, about half an hour from Paris, by car via A 13, N 185, or N 10, or in about 20 minutes by RER, line C, direction Versailles-RG (the château is visible from the station).

RUEIL-MALMAISON

For Napoléon and Joséphine, Malmaison was first a house and then a place of refuge. Joséphine bought the pretty brownstone château, in the town of Rueil-Malmaison, 14 km (8½ miles) from Paris, in 1799, when Napoléon was still first consul, and in it he escaped the pressures of the capital in the frivolous, completely unpolitical atmosphere Joséphine created. The house and extensive, beautiful grounds, which are threaded with peaceful paths and rose gardens, remained Joséphine's favorite retreat after Napoléon proclaimed himself emperor in 1804. After their divorce in 1809 she retired to a life of relative calm at Malmaison, living out her days where she had been most content.

Napoléon, too, returned to Malmaison, first in triumph after his escape from Elba in 1814, and then during the darkness that followed his defeat at Waterloo and final exile on the island of Saint Helena. Napoléon III also owned the château, and it was his wife, the Empress Eugénie, who conceived the idea of the museum devoted to Napoléon and Joséphine that eventually opened here in 1906.

The château itself, built in a lovely, symmetrical style, is fairly modest as châteaux go. Because it is small, a satisfying tour can be completed in 45 minutes, allowing ample time to wander through the now reduced, but still appealing, park and gardens. The most interesting rooms are the council chamber, which is dressed up to look like a campaign tent and is where Napoléon plotted some of his early victories; the library, a heavy, serious room packed with tomes on the art of war; and Joséphine's bedroom, an overdecorated boudoir that reveals both her vanity—it's full of mirrors, toiletries, and jewels—and her extravagance—receipts for some of her luxurious gowns are on display. Occasionally, international horse shows are held on the château's grounds.

Cafés are well hidden in the town of Rueil-Malmaison, but a fine lunch can be had on the lovely terrace at **El Chiquito** (126, avenue Paul-Doumer), a rather expensive restaurant specializing in seafood. Reservations are recommended; Tel: 47-51-00-53. (Closed Saturdays and Sundays.)

The château is open every day except Tuesdays from 10:00 A.M. to noon and from 1:30 to 5:30 P.M. You can reach Malmaison in about 20 minutes on the RER, line A; go in the direction of St-Germain-en-Laye and get off at Rueil-Malmaison. Take bus 144A, 144B, or 431 from the station; it's then a short walk to the château. By car leave Paris on the N 13; the drive takes about 20 minutes.

ST-GERMAIN-EN-LAYE

The long and involved history of the town of St-Germain-en-Laye, 23 km (14 miles) from Paris, is reflected in its château. Originally constructed in the 12th century by Louis VI, who thought the commanding hillside site would be ideal for repelling unwelcome guests, the castle was destroyed, rebuilt, and added to for the next five centuries. England's Black Prince, Edward, eradicated the original structure (except for the chapel erected by pious Saint Louis in 1230) during the Hundred Years War, and Charles V rebuilt it in 1368. François I redesigned the castle in 1539, retaining only

Charles's dungeon and the chapel. In addition to the kings of France, inhabitants have included Mary Queen of Scots, before her brief marriage to François II, and James II, after England's 1688 Glorious Revolution. Louis XIII died here, and Henri II, Charles IX, and Louis XIV were born here.

In its current (and probably final) form, the castle is shaped like an unbalanced pentagon. None of the rooms is open to the public; most are storerooms and offices for the château's **Musée des Antiquités Nationales**, which is open to the public every day except Tuesdays. The museum was created by Napoléon III to house prehistoric, Celtic, and Gallo-Roman artifacts. This magnificent collection traces French history from the Paleolithic era to the Middle Ages and is arranged on two levels: the mezzanine, which is devoted to the prehistoric and protohistoric periods, and the first floor, which houses the Gallo-Roman and Merovingian artifacts. There are marvelous objects—weapons, tools, jewels, vases—from the various periods, as well as works of art. The Salle de Mars, formerly the château's ballroom, is devoted to comparative archaeology, and has a remarkable collection of artifacts from throughout the world. Saint Louis's chapel, almost certainly built for him by Pierre of Montreuil, who later constructed the Sainte-Chapelle in Paris, is also open to the public; the bare stone church offers only the beauty of its solemn architecture. The castle's plain stone façade is enlivened by red brick windows and chimneys, and massive stone urns punctuate the balustrade that runs along the roof.

The Gardens and Forest

The gardens are the main reason to visit St-Germain. Enter through the gate to the left of the château's main door. A large graveled space opens to lawns, flower beds, and what was once a fountain. To the right, carefully laid out paths wind through chestnut trees to the more dramatic English garden, where curving paths swing through well-tended lawns (lawns that you actually can sit on, something of a rarity in France) and more flowers. Le Nôtre's masterful **Grande Terrasse** (about a mile and a half long) borders the ridge. It is one of the most famous promenades in the Paris area and overlooks a steep hill and the Seine. In 1547 a duel was fought on the parterre that splits the two gardens and leads to the terrace, one of the last of those contests appealing to God's judgment. The formidable La Chataigneraie, one of Europe's great swordsmen, fell to a certain Monsieur Jarnac, who employed a devious Italian ruse and switched his sword to his left hand to administer the killing blow. La Chataigneraie might have survived, but he was so infuriated by defeat that he refused all help and perished on the spot.

To the north, virtually bordering on the château grounds, lies the vast and beautiful **Forêt de St-Germain**, a superb place for hikes and picnics. Several interesting buildings are in the forest, including a former hunting lodge rebuilt by Jules Hardouin-Mansart that now serves as a retreat for members of the Legion of Honor. The Forêt de St-Germain was originally part of an immense forest that covered much of the Ile-de-France. In the 16th century François I had paths carved through the woods to facilitate his hunting. A century later Louis XIV left his mark on the forest, having Le Nôtre plant five and a half-million trees in the southern part.

Staying and Dining in St-Germain-en-Laye

St-Germain-en-Laye is quite pretty and merits at least a stroll; it has attracted the Parisian aristocracy since the 12th and 13th centuries. A refuge from the capital and a base for hunting in the vast forest, St-Germain-en-Laye became a *ville royale* (royal town), and evidence of this aristocratic status can be found throughout the town today: Superb *hôtels particuliers* line the narrow pedestrian streets, many now housing fine boutiques and charming antiques shops. The square facing the château (where the RER exits, and built over a convenient underground parking lot) shows signs of the 1990s with its videocassette outlet, a "western" shop, and an American restaurant. A couple of the town's other restaurants, however, offer more sophisticated cuisine. The ▶ **Pavillon Henri IV**, at 21, rue Thiers (Tel: 39-10-15-15), set within the smart confines of the 45-room hotel of the same name, is the most historic of these: Louis XIV was anointed here, and Alexandre Dumas wrote both *The Three Musketeers* and *The Count of Monte Cristo* while he was a guest. The classic **Cazaudehore** has a pretty garden (1, avenue du Président-Kennedy; Tel: 34-51-93-80; closed Mondays). At **La Feuillantine**, on a pedestrian street near the château (10, rue des Louviers; Tel: 34-51-04-24), the menu changes regularly, depending on what the chef finds at the market. Reservations are recommended at all three restaurants.

You can reach St-Germain-en-Laye in half an hour via the RER, line A; by car take N 13 from Paris.

GIVERNY

It seems that every visitor to Paris makes a pilgrimage here, to the home of the artist Claude Monet on the banks of the Seine, 76 km (47 miles) from the capital near the town of

Vernon. In the last weeks of autumn, just before the house
and gardens close for the winter and after most of the
flowers have died, the parking lot at Giverny is still full of
tour buses. Even if you shy away from tourists and prefer to
discover sites in relative solitude, Giverny is worth visiting.

Monet made Giverny his home from 1883 until his death
in 1926. Monet's son left the house to the Académie des
Beaux-Arts, which opened the restored property in 1980 as a
museum. An enormous amount of work went into replant-
ing the gardens to re-create the palette of colors Monet
himself created and then depicted in hundreds of paintings.

His studio—called the Nymphéas (Water Lilies)—and
house have also been renovated; the former is filled with
reproductions of his most famous works as well as period
photographs that show him in the studio during the 1910s,
when the originals of those same works hung on the walls.
The house is a more typical museum. The artist's collection of
Japanese prints as well as additional reproductions of his
works are hung as the originals were when he lived here, and
the rooms look as if Monet had just stepped out to go to the
bakery. This exactitude is almost spooky, but the house is
actually quite lovely and the kitchen looks, today, like something out of a "do your own rustic look" catalogue.

The raison d'être of the place, though, is the garden: a
glorious, floral candy shop in shades of blue, pink, yellow,
red, white, and purple. Monet moved through it like a
bearded Druid, addressing the flowers by name and coaxing
ever more brilliant colors from them. Across the road is the
water garden, complete with the Japanese footbridge, weeping willows, and water lilies that inspired so many canvases.

Because of the number of tourists, picnics are not allowed, although plenty of suitable spots can be found in the
woods behind Giverny. A tearoom and flower shop share the
museum's parking lot, and there are several cafés in Vernon.
For a traditional regional lunch try **Les Fleurs**, an old-style
bistro in Vernon between the train station and Giverny that
features good fish and a wonderful apple tart (71, rue
Carnot; closed Sunday nights and Mondays; Tel: 32-51-16-
80).

*The museum and gardens are open from 10:00 A.M. to
6:00 P.M. Tuesday through Sunday from April 1 through
October 31. You can reach Giverny in about an hour via
SNCF from Paris's Gare St-Lazare to Vernon; from the station
it's a brisk walk of about 4 km (2½ miles) along the Seine to
the house. Taxis or buses are available, and bicycles can be
rented at the station. By car take A 13 from Paris; the 77-km
(48-mile) drive takes about an hour.*

THOIRY

The vicomtesse de la Panouse (information director for the Château Thoiry and wife of the comte de la Panouse, whose family has owned and lived in the house since 1564) is quick to call Thoiry a marvel, and she is right. The Château Thoiry, 40 km (25 miles) from Paris, is an astounding mixture of history, kitsch, aggressive marketing, physical beauty, and unrestrained imagination.

Where to start? In the African game park, where camels, zebras, bears, lions, and other creatures cavort on the château's ancestral grounds? Or perhaps in the museum of gastronomy, where those whose eyes are bigger than their stomachs can view replicas of extraordinary desserts? Or maybe in the reptile house, where snakes and alligators slither in the dark cellars beneath the parterre designed by Le Nôtre? The park also has a pond filled with swans and flamingos, a "city of apes," a children's zoo, and assorted tigers, wolves, and hyenas.

Tours are conducted of the house and its treasures, which include a Sèvres pitcher and basin once used by Marie Antoinette, and a small, fascinating archives museum, filled with four centuries of correspondence between the comtes de la Panouse and various prominent international figures. The whole place is actually quite amazing, and the spectacle of the visitors, many of whom are children, is as enjoyable as the château. The stables have been converted into a restaurant, tearoom, and conference facility. Classical concerts (with dinner) are offered year-round, most frequently during the summer.

The game park and museums are open every day from 10:00 A.M. to 6:30 P.M. year-round. You can reach Château Thoiry from Paris in an hour by car via A 13, N 183, then D 11. By train, leave from Gare Montparnasse and get off at the Villiers Neauphle Le Château stop; the château is 4 km (2½ miles) away.

CHARTRES

Today's visitors to Chartres, 88 km (55 miles) from Paris, see the same awesome vista that has greeted pilgrims for centuries: a towering cathedral rising from rough fields, emerging slowly as you near the town and gradually dominating the horizon and countryside. The area has remained as proportionally rural as it was when Edward III laid siege to the town during the Hundred Years War, or when the prince of Condé attacked it as a center of Catholicism. It is something of a mystery why so magnificent a cathedral, one that set the standard for Gothic cathedrals all over Europe, sprang up so far from any major commercial center.

Chartres has always been a place of worship and a place of pilgrimage. Churches have stood on the same spot as the cathedral for more than two millennia. Before the birth of Christ, Chartres was a center of Druidic rites. When the Romans conquered the Gauls, they built a temple to the Earth Mother here. With the rise of Christianity, the icon of this goddess was interpreted as a prefigure of the Virgin Mary, renamed Notre-Dame-sous-Terre, and consigned to a special chapel. Today the ninth-century **Chapelle Notre-Dame de Sous-Terre**, in the crypt below the cathedral, is still devoted to this pagan idol. Worship of her successor, the Virgin, has long been strong at Chartres: Charles the Bald saw fit to give the church the sacred Tunic of the Virgin in 876.

The first Christian church on the site dates from the fourth century, and successive buildings have been erected and subsequently destroyed by raiders. The present **Cathédrale de Chartres** was initiated by the bishop of Chartres, Saint Fulbert, after a fire destroyed an earlier structure in 1020. The upper church, crypt, and ambulatory were completed by 1134, when another fire damaged the façade and bell tower. Work then began on the north tower, the impressively Gothic one on the left. It is known as the "new bell tower" (although it is actually older than the Romanesque south tower) because its spire wasn't erected until 1506. In 1194 yet another fire destroyed the entire church except for the façade, towers, and crypt. This tragedy rocked the international Christian community, because by then the pilgrimage to the Virgin of Chartres was one of Europe's most popular pastimes.

An appeal was made, and local church authorities pledged their tithes for three years, while the area's burghers responded in kind. A spirit approaching frenzy fueled the reconstruction of the cathedral, and most of the work was finished by 1220 in a record 26 years; the outside towers were completed 40 years after that. The relative speed with which it was built gives the church a rare coherence of style: It was rebuilt from a single set of plans, and construction was directed by a single, unknown master-builder.

The Towers and Interior
If you regard the cathedral from the Place Jean Moulin (named after the World War II French Resistance leader who was murdered by Klaus Barbie), the striking main towers will draw your eye first. The towers were begun and completed within ten years of each other (north: 1134–1150;

south: 1144–1160), yet the architectural styles are startlingly dissimilar. The north tower is a superb example of early Gothic techniques; the pious severity and balanced proportions of the south tower, one of the world's great examples of the Romanesque style, contrast dramatically with the sweeping lines of its mate.

The cathedral is famous for its sensitively carved figures. The main, or "royal," portal dates from the mid-12th century, and it is another masterpiece of Romanesque art. Originally designed as the narthex of an 11th-century structure, it later became the main entrance to the cathedral. In hundreds of naïve sculpted figures, the three doors depict Christ's birth, ascension, and second coming. To the right is the story of Mary, culminating in the birth of Jesus; to the left is the story of his betrayal and ascension; the central door is devoted to the Day of Judgment. The figures are carved with an unusual intensity of expression and a wealth of charm.

The south portal, on the right side of the cathedral, is a fascinating mix of sobriety and gore. At the center of the central bay, a peaceful Christ (the "Beau Dieu") oversees acts of charity, with the Twelve Apostles ranged behind him, each bearing the instrument of his martyrdom (or, in the case of Saint Peter, his symbol). The left bay depicts a host of martyrs in the act of being slaughtered; note particularly John the Baptist being beheaded and Saint Blaise being flayed alive. In the right bay saints performing acts of charity and miracles are depicted.

Inside the cathedral two features are particularly outstanding: the beautiful choir screen, consisting of sculptures depicting the lives of Mary and Christ; and the sublime stained glass windows. These windows, built in the 12th and 13th centuries (with some later additions), are among the finest in France. Their astounding "Chartres blue" is an intense, luminous shade that has never been reproduced.

The Medieval Town

While the town surrounding the cathedral has grown greatly over the centuries, it is still quite charming. The stained glass museum (just behind the cathedral), the **Centre International du Vitrail**, is worth visiting. The narrow, picturesque streets are lined with well-preserved 16th- and 17th-century buildings. The medieval splendor of Chartres is particularly evident in the 12th-century **Eglise St-André** and the 12th- and 13th-century **Eglise St-Pierre**. You can pick up a map of old Chartres at the Office de Tourisme, across from the cathedral. A number of cafés and tearooms surround the cathedral. A nearby restaurant of note is **La Vieille Maison**, at 5, rue au Lait. The menu of simple local fare changes regularly according to what the chef finds at the market. Tel: 37-34-10-67.

You can reach Chartres by car via A 10, A 11, and then N 10, or by train from the Gare Montparnasse, in a little more than an hour. You'll be able to see the cathedral from the train station; the cathedral is open every day from 7:00 A.M. to 7:30 P.M.

South

FONDATION CARTIER

In the mid–18th century Baron C. P. Oberkampf opened a cloth factory that eventually employed 1,200 Indian workers and manufactured an instantly popular fabric that put both the baron and the town of **Jouy-en-Josas**, 22 km (14 miles) from Paris, on the map. Louis XVI gave him a title; Napoléon approved of his methods; and all of France clamored for his *toile de Jouy,* a cretonne print. Today the Fondation Cartier, opened in 1984, has taken over Oberkampf's estate and shows works of very contemporary art in an imaginative way on grounds that the baron's wife landscaped in the English fashion.

You can make your way around the park in less than an hour, which gives you time to gawk at such permanent works as the monumental *Long Term Parking,* a gigantic upright rectangle of wrecked cars and poured concrete at least 200 feet tall, by Arman, one of the cofounders of New Realism. On summer days the wide lawns are perfect for lolling and tanning or reading a book. There's a bookstore, a library, and a very high-tech café, furnished by Pascal Mourgue, that's open on weekends for lunch.

The Fondation, which is open every day from June 19 to October 4, noon to 7:00 P.M., is 6 km (4 miles) from Versailles. You can reach Jouy-en-Josas via train from Paris's Gare d'Austerlitz; on the RER, take direction Sceaux to Massy-Palaiseau; change there for direction Versailles-Chantiers and get off at Jouy, where signs point toward the park. By car follow N 118 to Bièvres, then drive west to Jouy via D 117; the trip takes less than half an hour.

VALLEE DE CHEVREUSE

The Vallée de Chevreuse is actually a series of valleys in 25,000 hectares (61,000 acres) of forest, with the quaint town of Chevreuse, 45 km (28 miles) from Paris, as its center. The only way to see the valley properly is by car or bicycle (and those who favor the latter should be warned that the terrain is extremely hilly). The region is justly famous for its great beauty: narrow roads lined with cypress trees winding through lush forests, streams, and small farms; solemn ruins of medieval castles and abbeys; and several very lovely châteaux. To bike, from Paris take line B of the RER to St-Rémy-les-Chevreuse; get off one stop before, at Courcelle-sur-Yvette, where bikes can be rented on weekends and holidays by the hour or the day.

Touring the Valley by Car

To reach the valley by car follow N 306, direction Rambouillet, to A 36. Then head west for 5 km (3 miles) to D 91, then south 3 km (2 miles) to Port-Royal-des-Champs, where you can wander through the ruins of the once-famous abbey. Port-Royal reached its peak under the leadership of Mother Angelica, an austere nun who became mother superior in 1602 at the age of 11 and subsequently reformed the practices of the abbey. Later in that century the abbey became the center of Jansenism in France and as such was notorious in Catholic circles. A doctrinal system that denied free will, Jansenism maintained that human nature is corrupt and that Christ died for the elect and not for all people. Blaise Pascal's sister Jacqueline entered the convent here in 1651; Pascal himself was a defender of Jansenism (especially in his masterful *Lettres Provinciales*). Louis XIV decided to close the troublesome abbey in the late 17th century, and a crew of king's musketeers evicted the remaining nuns (who were denounced by the sisters at the Paris Port-Royal Abbey) in a final expulsion some 30 years later.

From Port-Royal follow D 195 southeast about 6 km (3½ miles) to D 938 and turn west onto N 306 for 2 km (1¼ miles) to Chevreuse. After a walk around Chevreuse and a visit to the beautiful little **Hôtel de Ville**, continue west for 6½ km (4 miles) on D 58 to Dampierre.

Dampierre

The Château de Dampierre is one of the most charming in the region. Designed by Hardouin-Mansart in 1683 for the duc de Luynes, it is smaller than most châteaux and set at the lowest point of a gentle valley so that the wooded hills behind dominate and frame the house. The Luynes family still lives here and has opened one of the two wings to tourists. The 45-minute tour (with no chance of escape) provides some insight into how the nobility actually lived. The rooms still exhibit the exquisite workmanship (especially of the wood panels and parquet floors) and classic design of the era. Part

of the house was redecorated in the desperately overdone
Third Empire style—all trompe l'oeil murals and gilt.

Le Nôtre designed the gardens and park, which are lovely
to walk in; stroll along the formal parterre, feed the ducks
and swans in the pond or the carp in the moat, and then hike
in the woods behind the opulent château, so comfortably
placed in this tranquil setting. The stables have been transformed into a fine **restaurant** (oddly decorated with hundreds of mounted animal trophies, many from Africa). The
tiny village offers a few unexceptional restaurants, all within
a five-minute walk. The house is open from 2:00 to 6:00 P.M.
every day from April to mid-October.

One kilometer (about half a mile) to the south is the **Parc
Floral**. Its extensive gardens were created to feature the
seasonal brilliance of hundreds of flowers, especially summer roses—there are 150 varieties, including some very old
strains.

Les Vaux Valley

From Dampierre continue south for 5 km (3 miles) on D 91
to **Les Vaux de Cernay**, a beautiful valley in which you can
walk beneath ancient oaks along the Vau stream, past a small
waterfall, and perhaps have a picnic beside the Cernay pond.
Along D 91, a nice place to leave the car and head off on foot
is just after Garnes, at a spot called the **Moulin des Rochers**.
A footpath here leads to the pond and the ruins of the **Abbé
Vaux-de-Cernay**, about a two-hour walk through lovely forest. From Les Vaux de Cernay, N 306 north leads to **Breteuil**,
another very pretty château, about 4 km (2½ miles) away.

The Breteuil family is one of the oldest in France and
has occupied the château since its construction in 1550. An
early Norman ancestor, Raoul, possessed a voice so powerful that he once set the entire French army to flight with it.
His son William was a compatriot of William the Conqueror, who gave the family its title after the Battle of
Hastings. The château was constructed in the simple but
imposing architectural style favored by Henri IV. Set on a
small promontory in the middle of a park, it presents a
formal grandeur to motorists driving up the tree-lined
avenue. The building, of tan stone and red brick, houses an
excellent collection of period furniture and china, as well
as the family's own wax museum, which depicts famous
visitors and momentous events in the life of the Breteuils.

VAUX-LE-VICOMTE

Vaux-le-Vicomte, 40 km (25 miles) from Paris, is arguably the
most perfectly realized château in France. Nicolas Fouquet,

minister of finance under Louis XIV, built the first completely planned château and gardens in the country as a monument to his exalted position in France. When Cardinal Jules Mazarin, then first minister, appointed Fouquet finance minister in 1653, the royal treasury had just declared bankruptcy and defaulted on its enormous debts. Fouquet was given the daunting task of reestablishing the crown as a viable credit risk. He proved himself to be one of the most brilliant, able, and loyal ministers ever to work for the crown, yet ambition (his own and that of others), naïveté, and carelessness led him to disaster.

Fouquet's fall came in 1661 after years of conspicuous spending and a period of courting a woman Louis XIV wanted for himself. He held a ball for the king that gave the word ostentation new meaning: His guests ate off 6,000 silver plates, served themselves from 432 large silver platters, and wiped their mouths with 1,440 linen napkins. Louis was so enraged and envious—he'd just been forced to sell his own silver to pay for one of his many wars—that he wanted to arrest Fouquet on the spot. Remembering his obligations as a guest, though, he graciously refrained and 19 days later sent a musketeer to haul the unfortunate minister off to jail.

The Château and Gardens

Five years earlier, Fouquet had given Le Vau, Le Brun, and Le Nôtre—the architect, decorator, and landscaper whom Louis XIV, intending to surpass Vaux-le-Vicomte's splendor, later enlisted to create Versailles—the rare opportunity to design a landscape from scratch. He bought a 1,500-acre expanse on which he changed the course of one river and razed three small towns to make the land "virgin" again. The three artists, the greatest of the era, responded by fashioning a house of matchless grace, with an interior that was exquisitely Baroque yet not disturbingly flamboyant, and a park that was the first and is still the finest example of the "French" garden.

Le Vau's design is ornate yet harmonious. The Grand Salon, which was unfinished at the time of Fouquet's arrest and remains so today, gives the clearest evidence of his plan's clarity and coherence. Le Brun's paintings, frescoes, trompe l'oeil murals, and cameos are better than anything he did at Versailles. They fill the house's magnificent rooms, as do period furnishings, tapestries, and rush mats (which were widely used in the 17th century, when carpets were still rare). The château is so impeccably preserved that it warrants the one- to two-hour tour, and you can easily spend an entire day in the incomparable gardens. That the estate still exists is due to some quick thinking by the comtesse during the Revolution—she convinced the arts commission to declare it a national monument. In 1875 Alfred Sommier, a sugar magnate and patron of the arts, purchased and restored Vaux after it had been abandoned.

The château is open every day of the year from 10:00 A.M. to 6:00 P.M. Candlelight tours are given Saturday evenings at 8:30, May through October, and elaborate fountain shows are held at 3:00 P.M. on the second and last Saturdays of each month, June through September. You can reach the château, an hour (50 km/31 miles) southeast of Paris, via N 6 to Melun, following N 105 to N 36, and then D 215 east. At the sign, turn down a long, elegant, tree-lined avenue and prepare yourself for the sight of this stunning château on the right. There is a café in the refurbished stables.

BARBIZON

Barbizon, 57 km (35 miles) from Paris, is a small, quaint town between Vaux-le-Vicomte and Fontainebleau that is best known as the home of most of France's great mid-18th-century artists. Théodore Rousseau, Jean-François Millet, and Jean-Baptiste-Camille Corot would pack palettes and canvases and head into the idyllic countryside around the town to paint. Charles Baudelaire attacked the Barbizon School, as this group of painters was called, for merely reproducing landscapes; he wrote, "In this silly cult of nature unpurified, unexplained by imagination, I see the evident signs of a general decline."

The surrounding country is still quiet and very lovely, as is the Fontainebleau forest, which bounds one side of the town and offers marvelous walks. On Barbizon's single main street, the rue Grande, are the former studios, now **museums**, of Millet and Rousseau; both artists are buried in the local cemetery. The **Auberge de Ganne**, where the artists used to congregate to eat, drink coffee, and chat with neighbors George Sand and the Goncourt brothers, is also a museum. (The museums are open every day except Tuesdays from 10:00 A.M. to noon and 2:00 to 5:30 P.M.)

If you want to stay the night, the ▶ **Bas-Bréau**, right in town, is a beautifully restored farmhouse with rustic, comfortable, well-appointed, and expensive rooms and an excellent restaurant. Leaders of the Seven Nations Economic Group stayed at the inn during their 1984 summit. Just down the street, at 26, rue Grande, is **La Flambée**, a country auberge featuring simple, hearty fare such as grilled meat and baked potatoes (Tel: 60-66-40-78). For a fine meal overlooking the Fontainebleau forest, try **Au Grand Veneur**, a rustic hunting lodge–like restaurant about a mile outside of

Barbizon via N 7 at 63, rue Gabriel-Séailles. Reservations are recommended; Tel: 60-66-40-44.

You can reach Barbizon via A 6, or by train from the Gare de Lyon to Melun and then by taxi.

FONTAINEBLEAU

Fontainebleau, 65 km (40 miles) from Paris, has been a royal residence since the 12th century and was originally a hunting lodge. Louis VI and Saint Louis came here to hunt stag and boar in the magnificent forests, and Philippe le Bel (Philip the Fair) died here after a fall from his horse. While the town center is a bit rundown in places, there are many beautiful houses, and France's most prestigious business school, INSEAD, is located here as well. The main post office and town hall are quite pretty, and there are some noteworthy buildings along the rue Grande as well as a variety of bakers and *traiteurs* (gussied-up delis, basically).

The Palais

The main entrance is from the Place du Général de Gaulle, where a gilded cast-iron gate leads to the Cour de Cheval Blanc, or the Cour des Adieux (Court of Farewells), so named because it was from this courtyard that Napoléon left for exile on Elba. The courtyard is divided into four squares of perfectly manicured lawn bounded by sculpted pine trees. The minister's wing on the left is one of a pair constructed by Gilles Le Breton, whom François I commissioned to rebuild the palace after he pulled down most of an earlier medieval castle. Its mate was destroyed by Louis XV, who had Jacques-Ange Gabriel build the existing wing. The opposing styles make for a good comparison of 16th- and 18th-century architecture.

The central building, which was expanded by every king from François I to Louis XV, is dominated by the handsome Fer-à-Cheval (Horseshoe) staircase (a Louis XIII production); it was from this majestic podium that Napoléon, the general who decimated two generations of French youth, bade farewell to his beloved guards, asking them always to look after France: "Her happiness," he said, "is my only thought." While emperor, Napoléon lived at Fontainebleau and not Versailles, where the ghost of the Sun King challenged his position in the pantheon of great Frenchmen. The Louis XV wing now houses the **Musée Napoléon**, which displays uniforms and mementos from the reigns of both Napoléons.

The palace itself is a remarkable monument to the incredible luxury with which the kings of France surrounded themselves. The sheer richness of the decor, which covers every imaginable surface in three centuries' worth of decorative styles, stirs even the most jaded. It is less coherent than Versailles because it is the work of master artists from several centuries, but its variety gives a sense of the wastefulness of French rulers who destroyed superbly crafted rooms and buildings not because they were in need of repair (though this was sometimes the case) but merely because they were unfashionable.

Highlights of the *grands appartements*, which you can visit without a guide, include the fantastically decorated **Chapelle de la Ste-Trinité**, every surface of which is covered with gilt, paint, or carved wood, and the gorgeous **Galerie de François I**. This long hall is made entirely of carved wood, stucco, and painted panels—a style that was created by the Italian decorator Francesco Primaticcio (known in France as Le Primatice), who belonged to the Fontainebleau School. The enormous **Salle de Bal** (Ballroom), with its 40-foot ceiling and wood panels and its exquisite view of the Cour de la Fontaine (Fountain Court) and pond and park behind, is undoubtedly the most spectacular room in the palace. Built by François I and completed by Henri II, the room is bathed in light and inspires visions of gowned women swinging on the arms of bewigged men in a space awash with music, splendor, and an indomitable belief in the future. The less fascinating *petits appartements* and those of Pope Pius VII are open only to guided tours.

The Park and Forest
The large, pretty park and English garden are well tended and perfect for an afternoon stroll. Together, they offer a choice of atmospheres: wild (the garden, with its sweeping paths and inviting lawns) or ordered (the carefully geometric park). The Etang des Carpes is filled with large carp; feeding them and watching them splash for the food is a favorite Fontainebleau sport. Pony rides around the parterre are popular among younger visitors to the palace.

The vast wooded expanse of the **Forêt de Fontainebleau** is 25,000 hectares (61,000 acres) of natural splendor. Once a royal hunting ground, the forest is now a favorite of hikers and rock-climbers. Among the predominant oak, beech, and pine trees are scattered 5,000 different species of plant life. Wildlife is also diverse and abundant, ranging from deer and wild boar to wild cats and falcons. There is horseback riding along paths once reserved for kings, as well as mushroom picking (in season) and beautiful walks. Picnic spots abound. The forest is also home to the world's premier "boulder garden"—groups of rocks that climbers use to train or improve their technique.

Fontainebleau palais and the Musée Napoléon are open every day except Tuesdays from 9:30 A.M. to 5:00 P.M. Tickets must be purchased at least 45 minutes before closing. You can reach Fontainebleau in about 35 minutes by train from the Gare de Lyon; get off at Fontainebleau-Avon and take a bus to the château (they run regularly). By car go via A 6; the 65-km (40-mile) drive takes about 45 minutes.

East

PROVINS

The medieval city of Provins, 86 km (53 miles) southeast of Paris, rises from the surrounding fields like a quiet acknowledgment of the earth's long memory. The first records of the village date from the ninth century. In 1120 it provided refuge for Pierre Abélard, one of history's best-known and most unfortunate lovers. His audacious philosophical positions were unpopular with the authorities and he was forced to flee Paris, leaving the heartbroken Héloïse behind. By the end of the 12th century Henri le Libéral had solidified the commercial importance of the town, and for 200 years the annual fair of Provins was a major marketplace for merchants from Italy, Germany, Holland, Marseille, and Spain. In the mid–13th century Edmund of Lancaster, whose coat of arms included the then-rare red rose, was sovereign of Provins, and today the town is famous for the radiant rose gardens below the old ramparts. (It was the red rose of Lancaster that battled the white rose of York in the Wars of the Roses, 1455–1485.)

Enter the **Ville Haute**, the medieval town, through the **Porte St-Jean**, a 12th-century gate in the 30-foot-thick ramparts. The reinforcements, archers' slits, and walkways along the top of the wall are visible from the gate. Follow the road to the central square, the Place du Châtel, where an ancient well is covered by an iron gate. The **Tour de César**, a 12th-century dungeon, still dominates Provins; climb the stairs for a terrific view of the entire region. The **Eglise St-Quiriace**, behind the tower, dates from 1140 but wasn't completed until the 17th century. It is in use today, and the sound of hymns on a Sunday does much to emphasize the tangible medieval quality of this town (ask for the key to the church at the tourist bureau; Tel: 64-00-05-31). Beautiful restored houses, barely visible over their protective walls, share the rest of the hill. French filmmaker Louis Malle thought the town so unspoiled he used it for the setting of his award-winning 1987 film, *Au Revoir les Enfants*. Several cafés bound the Place du Châtel.

You can reach Provins by train from the Gare de l'Est (there are not many trains that go directly to Provins; if necessary, switch at Longueville and take an additional five-minute train ride to Provins) or in about an hour and a half by car on N 19 from Paris; exit at the Porte de Bercy.

EURODISNEY

Amid much fanfare and even greater polemics, EuroDisney, the ultimate American cultural extravaganza, set up shop in 1992 on what was for centuries rich farmland 32 km (20 miles) east of Paris. Many French and Francophiles are skeptical of the incursion, hoping some of these visitors will wander off from Disney's ersatz château, mountains, waterfalls, and other imitation sights and sounds, in which life is but another theme, to take in some of Europe's real treasures.

EuroDisney can be reached from Paris by the RER A4 line, to Chessy/EuroDisney, in about 40 minutes. By car, take A 4 east, direction Metz–Nancy, and then follow the EuroDisney signs.

CHATEAU-THIERRY
AND BOIS BELLEAU

The château that gave the small town of Château-Thierry, 96 km (60 miles) east of Paris, its name once commanded the plain of the river Marne from the hill that rises steeply behind the town. The original castle was built in the early eighth century and gradually fell into ruin. Château-Thierry is most interesting for its involvement in the Napoleonic Wars and both world wars. One major battle was fought below its walls, and the town was invaded and liberated three times.

The English came first, conquering the city during the Hundred Years War. Joan of Arc then liberated it in 1429. In 1814 Napoléon fought off the Russo-Prussian army commanded by Marshal Gebhard von Blücher. Then in 1914 the German army held Château-Thierry for a week before they were forced to retreat. During the last great offensive of the war, the Germans took it once again and this time held it for almost two months. American troops helped push back the "pocket" of German forces that had penetrated deep into the Marne valley. Both times the attacking army sacked the town.

Château-Thierry has another, more pacific, claim to fame: Jean de la Fontaine, the poet and writer of fairy tales and fables, was born here in 1621. His house is open to the public, and some mementos are on display.

The town features the usual assortment of local cafés and restaurants. Of note, however, is the **Auberge Jean de la Fontaine**, across the river from the château at 10, rue du Filoirs, which serves fine cuisine and wines from the nearby Champagne region. Reservations are recommended; Tel: 23-83-63-89.

Bois Belleau

A few kilometers to the north, three monuments commemorate the battles that raged during World War I in the expanse of the Bois Belleau. The **Aisne-Marne memorial** rests on a knoll overlooking the river Marne. A small road winds through placid fields to the massive structure, a symbol of "friendship and cooperation between French and American armies." Families now picnic on the lawns that sweep down from the memorial to the hill's edge, and men play *boules* on the gravel paths. French youths play Frisbee or, more appropriately, baseball instead of their fathers' traditional game. The only impediments to the view of the valley are the chemical plants along the river.

The **American cemetery** is about a thousand feet away at the end of a tree-lined avenue. Impeccably tended lawns and rosebushes guard the footpath to the memorial chapel, on whose walls are inscribed the names of every American who fell in the vicious battle for the wooded hill behind the cemetery. The neat rows of crosses and stars extend far into the distance, marking the graves of the 2,288 men who died here. The graveyard's beautiful location, flush against a hill and under towering trees, is a tranquil and powerful reminder of the war that was supposed to end all wars, the war that so many Americans have forgotten.

Within eyesight a second, almost unmarked cemetery honors the dead of the army that lost. The 8,625 Germans who fell in the battle are buried here. Only a small plaque on one of the two stone buildings that front it marks their presence. The ironies of World War I, which abounded during the conflict, are clearly still with us.

Château-Thierry is open every day; guided tours are given weekdays at 11:00 A.M. and 4:00 P.M. You can reach Château-Thierry, a little more than an hour from Paris, by train from the Gare de l'Est, or by car via A 4 and then D 1 south. For a more leisurely drive you might follow N 3 from Paris. Many of the roads throughout the Marne valley area are very pretty.

North

COMPIEGNE

The town of Compiègne, 80 km (50 miles) from Paris, has been a favorite residence of French kings since Charles the Bald established a palace here in 873. By the 13th century a bustling town had grown around the castle, and in 1374 Charles V built a château on the site of the current palace. It was at Compiègne, in 1430, that Joan of Arc's inspired military career came to an end when a risky sortie across the river to scout English positions resulted in her capture. Louis XIV, dissatisfied with the accommodations at Compiègne, made additions to the château, claiming that "At Versailles I live like a king, at Fontainebleau like a prince, and at Compiègne like a peasant." His great-grandson, Louis XV (Louis XIV reigned for 72 years, outliving both his son and his grandson), completely rebuilt and enlarged the palace so that his entire court could live here in comfort. Jacques-Ange Gabriel, who built the *hôtels particuliers* facing the Place de la Concorde in Paris, oversaw the work and is responsible for the château's classical lines. Wars and revolutions repeatedly interrupted construction—Louis XVI made only one visit to the partially renovated château before the exigencies of the incipient revolution called him back to Paris—and it wasn't until Napoléon chose it as his imperial residence that the building was finally finished.

Today Gabriel's imposing façade, which resembles, not coincidentally, many government offices in Paris, faces the pretty Place du Palais. The north wing has been given over to an automobile museum, and the rooms at the end of the courtyard, including the Salle des Gardes (Guardroom) and the striking Escalier d'Honneur (Grand Staircase), now house changing art exhibits. Entrance to the château's most beautiful apartments, those of Napoléon and Marie-Antoinette, is just to the right. As you might expect, the rooms are luxuriously decorated in a grand mix of royal styles. The Salon des Cartes (Map Room) contains a fascinating collection of maps of the forest, which Louis XV used to consult for his hunts. The apartments have a stellar view of the well-tended, flower-filled gardens and the park, which extends to the forest.

The **Eglise St-Jacques**, where Joan of Arc took communion on the day of her capture, dates from the 13th century and has a very pretty bell tower. The **Hôtel de Ville**, a good example of Gothic architecture, boasts one of the country's oldest clocks. The town itself is lovely, and a brief stroll through its older sections, with their Tudor buildings and ancient walls, is in order. Many small restaurants and cafés, as well as expensive shops, dot the streets; a good omelette *paysan* is available at the charming **Café des Lombards**, on the street of the same name.

The Forêt de Compiègne

The vast and beautiful Forêt de Compiègne is another example of the wild beauty of the terrain around Paris. Napoléon treated the forest as the château's garden. At his request, the wall separating the château's Petit Parc from the forest was removed and replaced with a smaller fence, creating the pleasant impression that the forest runs right up to the château. Nobles once hunted game in the forest, and today it's a beautiful area through which to drive or bicycle (bicycles can be rented weekdays at Place du Château and on weekends at the Carrefour Royale): Ruins of abbeys, stands of ancient oak trees, and hills offering spectacular views of the forest abound. One particularly fascinating stop is the **Clairière de l'Armistice**, a clearing where on November 10, 1918, Marshal Ferdinand Foch and representatives of the Allied armies and Germany met in the marshal's train car to sign the armistice ending World War I. The site of the rolling battle headquarters has been preserved as a monument to the French military, and a giant statue of Foch, the savior of France, stands here. The display makes no mention of a second armistice signed on this spot: In 1940 Adolf Hitler ordered that occupied France capitulate here in the original train car in which Germany surrendered at the end of World War I. The train car was destroyed in 1945 near Berlin, perhaps to prevent yet another surrender in the Compiègne forest; the car on display now is a reproduction.

A nice spot for lunch in Compiègne is **Le Chat qui Tourne**, in the ▶ **Hôtel de France**, which serves classic cuisine at reasonable prices (17, rue Eugène Floquet; Tel: 44-40-02-74). The hotel, founded in 1665, has pleasant rooms with Louis XVI furnishings. In St-Jean-aux-Bois, 11 km (7 miles) southeast of Compiègne via D 332, is one of the region's finest restaurants, the ▶ **Auberge à la Bonne Idée** (Tel: 44-42-84-09). The auberge, which is also a lovely hotel, features local specialties, such as escargot stew, and classic dishes, including a fresh foie gras in honey.

Château de Compiègne is open every day except Tuesdays from 9:30 A.M. to 5:00 P.M. You can reach Compiègne by car in about an hour via A 1 from the Porte de la Villette in Paris, or by SNCF from the Gare du Nord. From the station, cross the bridge into town, turn left at the church of St-

*Jacques, and continue to the château. A tourist office is
located in the Hôtel de Ville.*

PIERREFONDS

Set on a commanding hilltop on the southeastern edge of the
Forêt de Compiègne, Pierrefonds is one of the most striking
châteaux in France. If you drive here from the north or west
you'll wind through small valleys until, quite suddenly, you'll
see the majestic towers and battlements of this restored
medieval fortress rising before you. The château was first
erected in the 12th century, then was rebuilt by Louis d'Orléans, brother of King Charles VI and regent of France during
the Hundred Years War until his assassination by Jean the
Fearless in 1407. Eventually the château became the property
of François d'Estrées. When he imprudently and unsuccess-
fully rebelled against the crown, Pierrefonds was partially
pulled down and fell into a state of such disrepair that Napoléon was able to buy it in 1813 for only 3,000 francs.

In 1857 Napoléon III, taken with the feudal magnificence
of the setting, decided to rebuild the house at great expense,
a move that was criticized by those who felt the fortress's
ancien régime roots should remain buried. Eugène-Emmanuel Viollet-le-Duc, who directed the restoration, based his
design on the walls that remained, and re-created the massive medieval structure.

And an overwhelming edifice it is. Huge, compelling,
secure, and self-contained, the castle commands the entire
valley by virtue of its strategic location and its imposing
appearance. In design, it is true to 14th-century principles:
Only a handful of windows open to the outside, and the
eight towers and many archers' slits determine the fortress's
interaction with the world. The towers are crowned by (and
named after) massive sculptures of King Arthur, Charlemagne, Alexander the Great, and Caesar, among others. The
castle entrance crosses a drawbridge and passes through 15-
foot-thick walls into a central courtyard. The chapel and the
Escalier d'Honneur in the courtyard are both Second Empire; the rest of the buildings and interior, however, are
reasonably accurate reproductions of the original castle.

The town of Pierrefonds is rather small; a pretty lake with
rowboats for rent is at its center. A pleasant café/restaurant,
Le Chalet du Lac, offers lakeside lunches.

*The château is open every day except Tuesdays from 10:00
A.M. to noon and 2:00 to 6:00 P.M.; open Sundays until 7:00
P.M. You can reach Pierrefonds by car from Compiègne in a
quarter of an hour via D 973, or from Paris by SNCF from
the Gare du Nord to Compiègne and then by taxi or bus.*

SENLIS

Senlis, 50 km (31 miles) from Paris, was a major town in
Gallo-Roman times—a first-century amphitheater and the
old walls still mark the Roman presence—and, for centuries,
was the religious center of France, a bishop's seat until 1901.
Today it is a well-preserved little hilltop village with cobblestone streets that echo with history. It was at a gathering of
feudal lords in Senlis castle in 987 that the archbishop of
Reims proposed Hugues Capet as the first king of France.

What makes Senlis special and worth visiting is the palpable sense of antiquity and continuity the town exudes. It's
very small, and often crowded, so a few hours are enough to
explore the entire village. Wandering through the ancient
streets, under Roman gates and past Renaissance houses,
you might share the sharp and certain feeling that centuries
ago people traversed the same stone paths past the same
buildings.

The **Cathédrale de Notre-Dame** here was begun ten years
before Paris's Notre-Dame and is an excellent example of
both early Gothic architecture and the evolution of the style
through succeeding centuries. The cathedral is built on a
smaller scale than its more famous Parisian namesake. Another church in Senlis, **St-Pierre**, exhibits both Romanesque
and Gothic design. The town's **château** is rather modest
(perhaps that explains why kings preferred the comforts of
Compiègne; Henri IV was the last to stay here), as is the
park behind it. The grounds also include a hunting museum.

Ermenonville

Jean-Jacques Rousseau lived in Ermenonville, 13 km (8 miles)
southeast of Senlis via N 330. A pilgrimage to his memorial on
the Ile-des-Peuples remains de rigueur, although his body
now rests in Paris's Panthéon. You can follow beautiful paths
through the woods the philosopher loved (once the grounds
of the château in which he died) and across the odd **Mer de
Sable**—a vast expanse of sand. In a geologic fluke, the climatic warming that ended the glacial era also opened holes in
the vegetation here, baring the underlying layer of sand,
which dates from the Tertiary period—approximately 70
million years ago.

A nice lunch can be had on the edge of the woods
between Senlis and Ermenonville at the **Auberge de Fontaine** in Fontaine-Chaalis (22, Grand'Rue; Tel: 44-54-20-22;
Fax: 44-60-25-38). From Ermenonville take N 330 northwest
4½ km (about 3 miles) to D 126 and follow that road for just
a few more kilometers north.

You can reach Senlis by car in half an hour from Paris via A 1 (the N 17 is a slower, more scenic option), or by SNCF from the Gare du Nord; get off at Chantilly and take a bus to Senlis. From the station, walk up the hill to the old town.

CHANTILLY

Chantilly, 41 km (25 miles) from Paris, has one of the prettiest settings of any château in France: It rises almost ethereally from the tranquil lagoon that encircles it. Built and rebuilt in fits and starts over seven centuries, the château has seen more than its share of sieges and sacks, and the history of its occupying families is particularly interesting. In the 14th century Pierre d'Orgemont, then chancellor of France, purchased the property and erected a fortified castle on the ruins of a tenth-century château that had been destroyed in the Jacquerie (the peasant uprising of 1358).

The Montmorency family bought the estate in 1450, and Anne (a man) demolished the fortress and built what is now called the Petit Château—then separated from the main structure by a moat. As high constable of France, Anne was a man of tremendous wealth, energy, and influence—he was a friend and adviser to every king from Louis XII to Charles IX. At home he was responsible for enlarging the grounds of the estate, as well as building the elegant square that fronts the château. He died at age 70 in a battle with Protestants at St-Denis, and it took five stab wounds, two slashes to the head, and a bullet to the spine to kill him.

Henri II was the last Montmorency to rule at Chantilly; he was beheaded at Toulouse for leading a revolt against Cardinal Richelieu. In the tradition of his ancestor, it took 18 wounds, including five bullets, to convince Henri to surrender. In his will, Henri left the cardinal the two Michelangelo *Slaves* that now stand in the Louvre. Henri II de Bourbon-Condé, who married Montmorency's daughter, inherited the estate, thus initiating the era of the Condés, the longest-lasting and best-known residents of Chantilly. The Grand Condé, Louis II, hired André Le Nôtre to design the renowned gardens and began yet another renovation of the château according to plans by Jules Hardouin-Mansart. The vain Sun King, Louis XIV, was said to be envious of Henri's fountains, which were deemed the most beautiful in France. Henri made Chantilly a center of the arts in France by attracting such writers as Jean-Baptiste Molière, Jean de la Fontaine, and Jean Racine. Henri's chef, Vatel, also elevated cooking to the highest levels, at least in terms of artistic temperament: Distraught that a batch of fish hadn't arrived in time to feed Louis XIV and the 5,000 courtiers who accompanied him everywhere, Vatel fell on his sword. Later it was discovered that the fish had, in fact, come. The Château d'Enghien, the last main addition to the house, was built in 1767 for the presumptive heir, the duc d'Enghien.

The estate was pillaged during the Revolution; the family fled and later died off. Today the castle owes its excellent condition to the duc d'Aumale, fourth son of King Louis-Philippe. A Bourbon like the Condé family, he devoted himself to completing the restoration begun by his predecessor and repairing the ravages of both time and revolution. Aumale died without an heir and left both the castle and his collections to the Institut de France.

The Interior and Grounds

The château, now the **Musée Condé**, houses little of the art that belonged to the family; the bulk of the collection was scattered during the Revolution. The interior is extraordinarily rich, with marble staircases, glowing parquet floors, and ornate tapestries. The museum's collections include a gorgeous 15th-century illuminated manuscript (the Limbourg brothers' famous *Très Riches Heures du Duc de Berry*) and works by Botticelli and Raphael. In the Petit Château a long gallery is lined with canvases depicting the military victories of the Grand Condé. The museum is open every day except Tuesdays from 10:00 A.M. to 6:00 P.M.

The château's grounds are also outstanding; their manicured lawns and immaculate paths invite leisurely strolls through the relaxed English garden, the wooded park, or along the great canal.

The monumental **Grandes Ecuries** (stables) across the road from the château constitute one of the best examples of 18th-century architecture in the country and are also open to visitors. The stables are still in use and house a horse museum (closed Tuesdays), complete with dressage demonstrations and Shetland ponies. Racehorses that train on the track are also stabled here. The stables and tracks have made Chantilly one of France's equestrian centers, and on the second Sunday of June the **Prix de Diane**, the most important race in the world for three-year-old fillies, attracts the most beautiful of the beautiful people to the track, their antique Rolls-Royces, colorful summer suits, and formal top hats filling the infield.

The attractive old château village, which is entered through a large gate connected to the stables, has many restaurants and cafés; one of the best is the **Relais Condé** opposite the racetrack at 42, avenue du Maréchal-Joffre. The

Captainerie du Château in the castle's courtyard is a pleasant tearoom; Tel: 44-57-15-89.

You can reach Chantilly by car in less than an hour from Paris via A 1 to Survilliers, and then D 924A, or via N 16 for a more pleasant drive, or by SNCF from the Gare du Nord. From the station you can take a bus or walk up the avenue du Maréchal-Joffre, turn right on the rue du Connétable, and continue on to the château. The walk takes about 30 minutes.

BEAUVAIS

Much of Beauvais, 75 km (46 miles) from Paris, was destroyed by savage bombing during World War II, but the mammoth cathedral—the world's tallest—survived. Actually, the town has an appealingly stormy history. The Romans dismantled it first after defeating the army of Gaul. In 1429 the bishop of Beauvais was run out of town by honest burghers for supporting England in the Hundred Years War; one year later he condemned Joan of Arc to the stake. In 1472 Beauvais got its own heroine, when Joan of the Hatchet rallied the town to repulse an invasion by the duke of Burgundy. While her townspeople ran along the city walls, panicked by the huge army facing them, Joan took a hatchet to an enemy soldier carrying a banner and hacked him off the wall. The townspeople, inspired by her courage, regrouped and resisted the attack.

The **Cathédrale St-Pierre**, which dominates the town (and is in fact the only real reason to visit Beauvais, now a modern provincial outpost laden with neon and roadwork), is a marvel. Some call it a miracle that defies the law of gravity; others call it an act of extreme hubris. The plans were so grandiose and costly that when construction was abandoned four centuries after work began in 1225, the building still had no towers. As it turned out, the structure could not support the weight of the stonework, and by 1284 the cathedral had begun to collapse. Only constant patchwork and jerry-rigging kept it—and keep it—standing.

Inside, however, the audaciousness of the design seems justified. Majestic, sweeping columns support a ceiling that seems to be miles away, reaching perhaps to heaven. The stained glass windows are sublime, especially the southern rose window, depicting the creation, and the windows along the north transept, showing ten sibyls, who face ten prophets on the south wall.

From Paris you can reach Beauvais in about 90 minutes by car via N 1 from the Porte de la Villette, or by SNCF from the Gare du Nord. From the station take a bus or taxi, or

*make the half-mile walk up the avenue de la République,
then turn right onto the rue Malherbe; the cathedral will be
visible on your left.*

AUVERS-SUR-OISE

If the record-breaking prices of Vincent van Gogh's paintings
are any indication, it will not be long before the somewhat
sleepy little town of Auvers-sur-Oise, 36 km (22 miles) from
Paris, where the artist spent his last days, is awakened. A
century after Van Gogh committed suicide in Auvers, the
artist and his work have taken on mythic proportions. Yet
Auvers, where Van Gogh produced 70 paintings in the final
70 days of his life, remains off the beaten tourist track.

Van Gogh arrived in Auvers in May 1890 to be treated by
Dr. Paul Gachet, a physician, painter, and art patron. Before
Van Gogh, Gachet had welcomed other Impressionist paint-
ers, including Cézanne, Pissarro, Sisley, Guillaumin, and
Renoir; and before them, and before Gachet, Daubigny and
Corot worked here as well.

Scenery in and around Auvers has been the subject of
many famous works, and the sites of various paintings are
signposted throughout the town. And so a visit to Auvers is
best accomplished as a walking tour, with a map that you can
pick up at the Syndicat d'Initiative on rue de Sansonne (Tel:
30-36-10-06). Recommended stops include the Romanesque
church, the cemetery where Vincent and his brother, Théo,
are buried, Gachet's house, and the **Auberge Ravoux**, where
Van Gogh lived and died. (On July 27, 1890, Van Gogh shot
himself in a nearby field; wounded, he was brought to his
room at the auberge, where he died two days later.) The
auberge, also known as La Maison de Van Gogh, reopened
on September 20, 1993, as a restaurant and small museum
and library after being restored by the Institut Van Gogh, a
private, nonprofit group.

There are a few cafés and restaurants in Auvers, but none
is extraordinary. Picnic sites abound, however, in the surrounding countryside or on the banks of the river Oise,
along which the town is built.

*Auvers can be reached in about an hour by SNCF from the
Gare St-Lazare or Gare du Nord, with a change at Pontoise;
from Pontoise you take the train headed to Creil and get off
in Auvers. By car take N 328 for 22 km (13½ miles) northwest from Paris.*

GETTING AROUND

Although it intersects with the Métro at some stations, the
RER is an entirely separate network and has its own plat-

forms. RER trains are identified both by destination and by a letter. To add to the confusion, trains on line C—which serves Versailles—also have *names* (CORA, for example). Ignore the names; it is enough to follow the destination and letter, making sure, of course, that your desired station is on the platform sign that lists the stops for the incoming train.

Maps can be acquired at any Métro or RER station; tickets can be purchased at the ticket window in RER stations or from a machine at the stations. To use the machines, which give change, punch the button corresponding to your destination (Versailles RG, for example) and the type of ticket that you want (first or second class). After the price appears on the screen, insert your money. The ticket and your change will then follow.

On August 1, 1991, the Métro went egalitarian: First-class cars were eliminated. On RER and SNCF trains, however, the class system remains in effect.

ACCOMMODATIONS REFERENCE

The rates given below are projections for 1994. Unless otherwise indicated, rates are for a double room, double occupancy, and do not include meals. As rates are always subject to change, double-check before booking.

▶ **Auberge à la Bonne Idée.** 60350 **St-Jean-Aux-Bois.** Tel: 44-42-84-09; Fax: 44-42-80-45. 440F–560F.

▶ **Bas-Bréau.** 22, rue Grande, 77630 **Barbizon.** Tel: 60-66-40-05; Telex: 690953; Fax: 60-69-22-89; in U.S., (212) 856-0115; Fax: (212) 856-0193. Member, Relais & Châteaux. 950F–1,500F.

▶ **Hôtel de France.** 17, rue Eugène Floquet, 60200 **Compiègne.** Tel: 44-40-02-74; Fax: 44-40-48-37. 290F–325F.

▶ **Pavillon Henri IV.** 21, rue Thiers, 78100 **St-Germain-en-Laye.** Tel: 39-10-15-15; Fax: 39-73-93-73. 400F–1,900F.

▶ **Trianon-Palace.** 1, boulevard de la Reine, 78000 **Versailles.** Tel: 30-84-38-00; Fax: 39-49-00-77. 1,500F–3,500F.

CHAMPAGNE

By Mimi Tompkins with Fred Halliday

Mimi Tompkins is a freelance print and broadcast journalist who has lived in Paris for the past ten years. Fred Halliday, who writes about food, wine, and travel for many magazines and newspapers, divides his time between Connecticut and Paris.

Champagne is arguably the most famous and prestigious drink in the world. The greatest charm of the vast stretch of land that produces it—running all the way from Burgundy in the south to Belgium in the north, bordered by the outskirts of the Ile-de-France to the west and Lorraine to the east—lies without a doubt in the thousands of rolling, vineyard-clad acres that surround the valley of the Marne river.

Hundreds of prosperous villages carefully cultivate, blend, and bottle the precious grapes to make Champagne. You can test small vintages on site, or tour the miles of underground cellars in the prestigious Champagne houses in the cities of Reims and Epernay. Aside from this bounty of the vine, Champagne is also a land full of physical contrasts, where dense forests and flat open plains and fields meet leafy vineyards and meandering rivers. The best time to visit is in high season, from May to September, when the leaves on the vines are full and the temperatures reasonably warm. During other months in the year, while the grapes lie dormant, the atmosphere can be rather sad and dreary.

The region's chalky soils have been host to more than just the ancient vine over the centuries. They've also served as an arena for decisive European battles, and for turning points in French history—from the passage of the Barbarians and Attila the Hun in the fifth century, to the bloody massacres on the front lines of World War I and the bombings of World

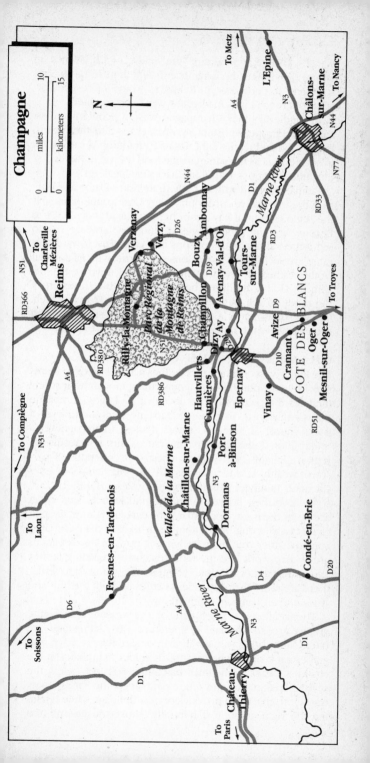

Champagne

0 miles 10

0 kilometers 15

N

To Metz

L'Epine

Châlons-sur-Marne

To Nancy

N3

N44

N77

RD33

RD3

Marne River

D1

N44

Verzenay

Verzy

D26

Bouzy

Ambonnay

D19

Avenay-Val-d'Or

Tours-sur-Marne

Reims

N51

RD366

Parc Régional de la Montagne de Reims

Rilly-la-Montagne

Champillon

Dizy Ay

COTE DES BLANCS

D9

Avize

D10

Cramant

Oger

Mesnil-sur-Oger

To Troyes

Epernay

Vinay

RD51

RD380

To Charleville Mézières

N51

A4

Hautvillers

Cumières

RD386

To Compiègne

N31

Vallée de la Marne

Châtillon-sur-Marne

Port-à-Binson

Dormans

N3

To Laon

A4

Fresnes-en-Tardenois

D6

To Soissons

Marne River

D4

Condé-en-Brie

D20

D1

A4

Château-Thierry

N3

To Paris

War II. The region became the cradle of Christianity in France, leaving us the magnificent cathedrals in Laon, Soissons, and the grandest, in Reims, to which successive corteges of French kings made their way to be crowned.

In medieval times Champagne was an economic crossroads of Europe, enormously prosperous and the host to major food and textile fairs. This rich tradition is carried on in such events as the summertime food festival in Reims and the famous puppet festival in Charleville-Mézières.

Reims, crowned with its Cathédrale Notre-Dame and built atop the impressive *caves* of its many Champagne houses, is the region's central city. From here we head down N 51 to Epernay and the wine villages around the Marne or west to the cathedral towns of Soissons and Laon. East toward Lorraine are such places as Châlons-sur-Marne, with its unusual Gothic cathedral, and the small medieval town of l'Epine, with its Gothic basilica. Then we turn in the direction of Burgundy to the medieval market town of Troyes, which, though somewhat of a trip south of Châlons-sur-Marne and even farther south of Reims, has many delights to offer.

CHAMPAGNE, THE GRAPE

The kings who once led processions across France to Reims may be gone, but if there's a new ruling monarchy, it surely includes the owners of the dozen or so large Champagne houses that lord over the Champagne region and over a good chunk of France's export market. Champagne is a multibillion-dollar industry in France, and as a result the region contains one of the highest concentrations of personal wealth in the country. All the big names—Veuve Clicquot, Taittinger, Mumm, Pommery, Piper-Heidsieck, Lanson—have their houses in and around Reims. Their *caves* are by far the most spectacular wine *caves* in France, deep in chalk quarries dug by the Romans, who used the material to construct their buildings at what is now Reims. As Reims grew, *cave* work became more extensive, reaching farther and farther under Reims and out into the countryside. Today there are more than 120 miles of *caves* beneath the hills and dales of the Champagne region.

The chalk is a large part of the reason Champagne grapes are so special. Temperatures in Champagne are often chilly—the average annual temperature is 51° F, and grapes can't ripen when it's much colder than that. But the chalky subsoils, sometimes extending 800 feet below the surface, retain the sun's heat and keep the vines' roots warm; the chalk also provides perfect drainage while retaining the right amount of humidity. Above the ground, the

Champagne slopes vary in altitude and exposure to the sun, creating many different microclimates. The grapes love all these stressful conditions, and high-quality product is the result. Every autumn, nearly 100,000 workers descend on the region to handpick the grapes, which are carted off to the press houses to be squeezed, then to the cellars to be fermented, blended, and fermented again. They are then mollycoddled for years by highly trained professionals, until the contents of the bottles transform themselves from wine into the delectably unique bubbly.

The big houses, and some smaller ones too, are more than happy to explain the whole process in detail. They'll give you a tour of their miles of *caves,* and in many cases a glass of some of their best at the end. It's advisable to phone ahead for tour times, and to wear nonslip shoes and perhaps a sweater or jacket—it can be humid and chilly down there.

MAJOR INTEREST

Reims
Cathédrale Notre-Dame
Palais du Tau
Musée St-Denis
Musée-Hôtel Le Vergeur
Basilique St-Remi
The Champagne *caves*

Cathédrale St-Etienne in Châlons-sur-Marne
Basilique Notre-Dame de L'Epine
Cathedral towns of Soissons and Laon

Epernay and the "country" villages of Champagne,
    especially Hautvillers

Troyes
Cathédrale St-Pierre-et-St-Paul
Musée d'Art Moderne
The ancient St-Jean quarter

Reims

Reims was the capital of Gallic Belgium when Paris was a mere village, and its wines were so renowned, it is boasted, that in A.D. 92 the Roman emperor Domitian ordered the vines destroyed because they were unfair competition to those of Italy. Throughout the course of its 2,000-year history, Reims has never lost hold of its title as the greatest city in the Champagne region—despite the successive pound-ings of wars and invasions that have swept through this exposed city on the plains.

Reims owes its name to a Gallic tribe, the Rèmes, but its Roman conquerors dubbed it Durocortorum and made it the capital of Lower Belgium. From the third to the eighth century Reims served as a veritable cradle of saints, producing at least 13, including Remi (properly, Remigius; A.D. 440–533). On Christmas Day 496, Remi baptized Clovis, the Mérovingian king of the Franks, on the site where the Cathédrale Notre-Dame stands today. Later kings wished to be consecrated in the same place and with the same oil as was Clovis, and according to history 37 of them were, down to Charles X in 1825.

Julius Caesar admired the hardworking nature and political independence of the people of the colony, whose descendants to this day maintain their reputation for being industrious and refined, with a strong sense for business. "A fine and measured spirit par excellence," wrote the 19th-century French philosopher Hippolyte Taine. Reims's respected university has helped perpetuate an intellectual tradition, and the region has produced some of France's finest poets and writers, from Arthur Rimbaud to Jean de La Fontaine, Jean Racine, and Denis Diderot.

It was in Reims that Napoléon saw his last victory, when he regained the city from the Russians in March 1814. But the city was nearly leveled during the two world wars of the next century. During World War I the trench lines formed a buckle around Reims on three sides. General Dwight D. Eisenhower put an end to World War II on the European front when he signed the German surrender on May 8, 1945, in a school in Reims.

Quite apart from the vines, saints, and kings, Reims has another life. It is also a university city, full of busy sidewalk cafés, pedestrian zones, and interesting shops. As a sign of its sophistication, it has a great metropolitan newspaper, *L'Union,* which grew out of the Resistance and which serves the north of France.

Geographically, the cathedral of Notre-Dame is the heart of the city; from it, most notable attractions are within walking distance, with the exception of the basilica of St-Remi to the south and the Champagne *caves* to the north and the southeast.

CATHEDRALE NOTRE-DAME AND THE MUSEUMS

Dominating the heart of the city, Notre-Dame bore the brunt of the world-war battles that raged on the plains around

Reims, but this massive and graceful structure is still one of the most beautiful cathedrals in the world. Construction began in 1211 and wasn't completed until a century later; the two towers weren't put up until the 15th century. The bombings of World War I dealt a severe blow to a large part of the structure and its riches: Much of the stained glass was blown to bits in 1914, and subsequent bombings caused large parts of the roof to collapse and destroyed many of the statues both inside and out.

Painstaking repairs over the past several decades have restored the cathedral to its near-original state. The 13th-century stained glass—one of the glories of the cathedral—has been reset and new glass added, including three modern windows by Marc Chagall. The masterpiece, though, is still the great rose window on the front façade, especially beautiful in late afternoon when the brilliant colors of the glass come to life in the rich gleam of the slanting sun. Near the window, above the north portal, you can also bask in the happy grin of the cathedral's best-known statue, the "Smiling Angel." All the detail work on the cathedral is impressive—walk around the outside for a close look, especially at the statues in the portals dating from several schools of French sculpture.

Unfortunately, Notre-Dame is suffering today from the aggressive attacks of car exhaust and other pollution. But with funds from France's ministry of culture and the long-established Champagne houses in the city, the cathedral is now undergoing yet more renovation.

Many of Notre-Dame's original sculptures and tapestries, as well as several coronation robes, are housed in the **Palais du Tau**, built in 1690 as the archbishop's residence. The collections include many admirable statues from the Champagne school, among them a fine Coronation of the Virgin and a Goliath. Of the many worthwhile tapestries, one honoring the life and times of King Clovis stands out. The two rooms that constitute the treasury of the Palais du Tau are rich in religious artifacts, talismans, chalices, reliquaries, and objects used in the ceremony of Holy Communion. The **Musée des Beaux-Arts** (known as the Musée St-Denis until a few years ago), next to the cathedral at 8, rue Chanzy, houses a small but excellent collection of paintings, drawings, and ceramics from the Renaissance to the 20th century; David's famous painting of the Revolutionary leader Jean-Paul Marat dying in his bath from a stab wound is here, along with a small number of Impressionist works.

PLACE ROYALE TO
PLACE DE LA REPUBLIQUE

The 18th-century **Place Royale**, just behind Notre-Dame, was built in a fit of urban renewal under Louis XV, but never completed, because of a lack of public funds. The city's English-language bookstore is around the corner at 53, rue Cérès, with a limited but excellent selection of fiction and nonfiction. The staff will be happy to fill you in on what constitutes an Anglophone life in Reims.

A block north of Place Royale, the remains of the city's third-century **Roman forum** still stand in the Place du Forum. The handsome **Musée-Hôtel le Vergeur**, across the street, is a historic monument dating from the 13th through 17th centuries that houses artwork and furnishings from the days of old Reims.

Several blocks northwest of the Place du Forum along rue Colbert and rue de Mars you'll come to the **Porte Mars** (Mars Gate), the largest monumental arch in the Roman Empire, and the only one remaining of four erected in Reims around A.D. 200.

The **Salle de Guerre**, just on the other side of the busy Place de la République (really just a vicious traffic circle) at 12, rue Franklin-Roosevelt, is the preserved map room of General Eisenhower's World War II headquarters, where the German forces signed their surrender on May 7, 1945.

PLACE DROUET-D'ERLON

Most of the city's street life swirls northwest of the cathedral along the rue de Vesles and the elongated Place Drouet-d'Erlon; this is not really a square but rather a small series of interconnected streets signposted with tubs of flowers and trees and lined with restaurants and cheap cafés. The *place* gives you the best chance to catch some of the spirit of the town. Try the **Gluepot**, a café practically under the windows of the offices of *L'Union*. The students you will meet here are superior; Reims has a reputation as one of the finest academic facilities in Europe. Ironically, it is less well known in North America than are many other French universities with less stringent academic standards.

BASILIQUE ST-REMI

It's a temptation to stay put in the Reims city center, where everything is within walking distance, but it's worth a trip to the southern edge of town to the Quartier Fléchambault and the beautiful basilica of St-Remi, the saint who converted Clovis and crowned him as king (from the cathedral, follow the rue du Barbatre south about ten blocks). Built in the 11th and 12th centuries atop the saint's tomb, it has endured several reconstructions necessitated by war and is the repository of the remains of many early archbishops and kings of France; the tomb of Remi is behind the altar, which was reworked in 1847.

THE CHAMPAGNE HOUSES

Most of the houses are to the north and southeast of the old city. **Pommery**, at 5, place du Général-Gouraud, offers daily visits to its 11 miles of more than 120 connecting *crayères* (chalk caves). Down a flight of 116 steps, more than 20 million bottles of Champagne lie in various stages of maturation. The *caves* are "decorated" with a series of 19th-century bas-relief sculptures carved out of the chalk walls. Call in advance for tour times; Tel: 26-61-62-55.

Ruinart, at 4, rue des Crayères, was founded in 1729, and is the oldest house in Champagne. Its *caves* have the sole distinction of being classified by the French government as a historic monument. Tours are given here on weekdays and by appointment only, with preference given to wine professionals. Tel: 26-85-40-29.

For a more high-tech trip through the *crayères*, try **Piper-Heidsieck**, at 51, boulevard Henry-Vasnier: They've rigged up a visit in which you ride an electric car through a set (designed by the people who brought us the decor in *Raiders of the Lost Ark*) that dramatically shows the stages of Champagne making, from field to bottle. Tel: 26-84-43-00.

STAYING AND DINING IN REIMS

In keeping with the character, the style, and the crowd of d'Erlon is **Le Continental**, 95, place Drouet-d'Erlon. This is everyone's favorite old restaurant: The Rémois (those from Reims), tourists, Champagne-industry insiders, and wine lovers keep coming back for the simple but high-quality classic dishes, the attentive waiters, the bustling atmosphere, and the dining room's worn-at-the-heels but comfortable elegance. Try the *sole meunière* (it will be a true sole, not a flounder), the *chateaubriand béarnaise* (again, the real thing, a cut from the center of the filet), or the *coq au vin rouge de Bouzy*. The service is swift and friendly and the prices are easy. For quality-to-cost ratio it is the best bet in the region; the set menus are 91, 156, and 169 francs, the à la carte prices about 260F. Tel: 26-47-01-47.

Le Forum, 34, place du Forum, is a favorite with local

businesspeople and government employees from the nearby Hôtel de Ville, who fill the tables quickly at lunchtime. Try the hearty *pavé au poivre flambé au Cognac,* or if it's winter, their Raclette or fondue *savoyarde.*

Another busy spot is the spacious and recently renovated 1920s **Brasserie du Boulingrin**, located behind the Hôtel de Ville at 48, rue de Mars, in the former market district. The bustle inside this restaurant, which has been a favorite in the city for years, seems out of place in the quiet of the deserted warehouse area outside. But this neighborhood won't be silent for long. The area is slated to become an avant-garde art district: The national ministry of culture has plans to build a huge media and modern-art center here in the next few years. In the meantime, the Boulingrin is one of the few restaurants in Reims that serves after 11:00 P.M. Tel: 26-40-96-22.

For a more subdued and refined meal, try **Le Florence**, along the elegant boulevard Foch around the corner, facing the city's shady public garden. If the weather is nice, sit out on the restaurant terrace and enjoy a wonderful fish specialty, such as the lobster and sole duo in a Champagne sauce. Tel: 26-47-12-70.

Hotels on the Place Drouet-d'Erlon seem to have had their heyday immediately following World War II and are rather dreary today. But the ▶ **Hôtel Continental**, recently renovated, is elegantly decorated and its staff is pleasant and efficient. Some of the bathrooms in the more expensive rooms are enormous even by North American standards.

Surrounded by cafés and stores ranging from chic to utilitarian, the ▶ **Hôtel de la Paix** is perhaps the best headquarters for in-town meandering. It offers pleasant and comfortable rooms, a pool, sauna, and health club, a locally respected restaurant, and a bar that is a meeting place for local businesspeople as well as visitors.

One of Champagne's most elegant hotels and one of the country's best restaurants is ▶ **Boyer "Les Crayères."** This perfectly restored and tastefully decorated 18th-century mansion built by the Pommery family, at 64, boulevard Henry-Vasnier, is surrounded by a well-manicured 19-acre park (complete with helicopter pad for visiting V.I.P.s). Gérard Boyer is considered one of the country's best chefs; the menu changes every few months, but house specialties like *noisettes d'agneau aux herbes et jus au coulis de champignons* (morsels of lamb cooked with herbs, served in its natural sauce with purée of mushrooms) are always very good—and, like the rooms upstairs, very expensive.

Near Reims

While most visitors sooner or later make their way south from Reims into the Champagne vineyards along the Marne river (see below), many of the region's other enormously interesting attractions are within an easy drive from the city.

CHALONS-SUR-MARNE AND L'EPINE

Châlons, 45 km (28 miles) southeast of Reims just off A 4 or N 44, is a proper town with memories of Attila the Hun, Napoléon, and Nazi bombings. This eclectic past is apparent in the odd mix of architectural styles that greets the visitor when strolling about this busy little town. Ugly modern government buildings pop up everywhere—Châlons today is the administrative center of the region—nudging for room next to picturesque medieval half-timbered houses, Roman bridges and arches, and 19th-century churches.

The pride of Châlons is the **Cathédrale St-Etienne**, towering above the banks of the Marne with a beautiful Romanesque tower and superb stained glass windows from the 13th through 17th centuries. The small but remarkable 12th-century **Eglise Notre-Dame-en-Vaux**, several blocks northeast on the rue de la Marne, houses an important collection from the church's original, sadly demolished cloister.

L'Epine, 7 km (4 miles) east of Châlons on N 3, is a tiny medieval outpost on today's highway, with its Flamboyant Basilique Notre-Dame soaring dramatically on the flat horizon. In the Middle Ages hundreds of thousands of pilgrims made their way to the basilica, which is constructed on the site where shepherds stumbled on a statue of the Virgin in a burning thorn bush. Charles VII, Louis XI, and René of Anjou all made pilgrimages to the cathedral, and Nicolas Froment was moved enough to create the famous *Buisson Ardent* (Burning Bush) triptych now in the cathedral of Aix-en-Provence.

Constructed in Flamboyant Gothic style in the 15th century, the basilica is the size of a major cathedral. Its façade presents a fantasy, almost a riot, of architectural details, in particular gargoyles, which in wonderfully varied shapes symbolize the faces of evil and of wicked spirits. The liveliness of the basilica's exterior is belied by its somber interior, the choir enclosed by a beautiful 16th-century rood screen. If you arrive during services you will be struck by the spine-tingling sounds from the Renaissance organ bank.

Staying and Dining in and Around Châlons

The 18-room ▶ Hôtel d'Angleterre in Châlons not only is a comfortable and elegant place to spend the night but also houses one of the best restaurants in the area. Its chef, Jacky Michel, has concocted five different menus to show off his specialties: veal kidneys in red Bouzy wine with garlic, sole filets in cream sauce with sea urchins, and a *matelot* of frog legs and freshwater fish with green sauce. Be sure to book well in advance, especially in high season—the hotel and the restaurant are often full weeks ahead.

Somewhat surprisingly, tiny L'Epine is home to a pleasantly decorated 37-room hotel, reasonable in price, that prizes quiet and prides itself on its kitchen: ▶ Aux Armes de Champagne. The food here tends to the elegant, though it isn't what the French call *fad* (meaning "without character"). Choose the fish, and especially the turbot, when it is offered. The dining room is formal but cozy, overlooking the recently sandblasted basilica. Dining here, watching the cathedral façade change color as the sun sets, is an experience that warrants a memorable Champagne; try a 1985 Pol Roger. Tel: 26-69-30-30.

Gourmets who aren't put off by driving the 43 km (27 miles) farther northeast of Châlons on N 3 to **Ste-Menehould** are well rewarded: This is the pigs'-feet capital of the world. There are signs along the road into town pointing to where you may bite into the juicy, fatty nuggets. **Le Pied d'Or**, across the street from the 17th-century Hôtel de Ville and the post office where Louis XVI and Marie Antoinette were thwarted in their attempt to flee the country during the Revolution, serves up some of the best. The enormous trotters here are stewed for more than 72 hours to bring out their flavor.

From Ste-Menehould it's 78 km (48 miles) back to Reims on N 3 and RD 31.

SOISSONS AND LAON

As a town, Soissons (56 km/35 miles west of Reims on N 31) doesn't warrant much attention, but it's worth a stop here to visit the magnificent Gothic **Cathédrale St-Gervais-et-St-Protais**. Most of Soissons was leveled by shelling during World War I, but somehow the cathedral escaped substantial damage. Such good fortune didn't befall the nearby **Abbaye St-Jean-des-Vignes**. All that remains now is a large chunk of the elegant 13th- and 14th-century façade.

If you head northeast for 30 km (19 miles) on N 2, it's hard to miss **Laon**. The town sits atop a plateau, a bizarre mound on the flat plains, dominated by the five towers of the 13th-century Gothic **Cathédrale Notre-Dame**—which explains the town's nickname, "The Crowned Mountain." If you don't like driving up steep, circuitous streets, leave your car at the bottom of the hill and take the cable car up to the old medieval city. You can stroll lovely streets and visit some of the 80 buildings that the French government has designated as historic monuments. Of special note is the **Chapelle des Templiers**, a 12th-century chapel on the grounds of the town museum (which has a beautiful collection of Greek vases, Gallo-Roman antiques, and 17th- and 18th-century paintings).

Into Champagne Country

On the sloping hills and sweeping plains south of Reims are the great jewels of the Champagne region: the hundreds of small and prosperous wine villages nestled in a picturesque landscape. A vast patchwork of well-tended vineyards rolls out into the distance, a carpet of green leaves and knotty vines is broken by strips of white, chalky soil, and clumps of dark green forest line the hills in the distance.

The stretch makes up three distant areas fanning out from the Marne river: the Montagne de Reims, north of the river and south of Reims; the Vallée de la Marne; and the Côte des Blancs, to the south of the river. But for the locals, the area has one name: the Sacred Triangle of Champagne. These are the vineyards that produce the Pinot noir, Pinot Meunier, and Chardonnay blanc grapes that when blended and distilled create the only drink in the world that may legally carry the name Champagne.

The Champagne fields have been producing their treasure since at least A.D. 280, when the emperor Probus ordered the vineyards planted. François I and Henry VIII of England had personal vineyards here, near Ay. Today the vineyards are divided into parcels that are owned by a select group of prestigious big names, such as Moët & Chandon, Taittinger, and Krug, or by smaller growers who sell to the larger firms, bottle their own, or band together to form the growing numbers of successful cooperatives.

Our routes into the heart of Champagne country take you through the most scenic countryside and villages, which for the most part fall in the Montagne de Reims and Vallée de la Marne areas. The Côte des Blancs, south of Epernay on D 10, is a less interesting region to explore. The landscape here is flatter, the villages more modern. If it's Champagne rather than scenery you're in search of, the villages to head for are Cramant, Avize, Oger, and Le Mesnil-sur-Oger, all of which produce top-of-the-line Grand Cru Champagne.

EPERNAY

The place to begin an expedition into the Champagne vine-yards is Epernay, 26 km (16 miles) south of Reims on N 51 (it's only 20 minutes between the two cities by train). Why is it that even though Reims is the official capital of the prov-ince of Champagne, most people consider this much smaller city on the Marne to be the capital? The answer: Epernay's **avenue de Champagne**.

On this single street, which leads from the Place de la République up to the fertile plain of Seran about five miles away, is assembled the greatest concentration of Champagne wealth in the world: the houses of Moët & Chandon, Pol Roger, Perrier-Jouët, Charbaut, and Mercier. (So often was Winston Churchill received at Pol Roger that the British prime minister dubbed the avenue de Champagne "the best drinking address in the world." For an appointment, call ahead; Tel: 26-59-58-00.) The municipal museum on the north side of the avenue opposite Caves Mercier is really three **museums**: one of wine (with a great collection of labels), another of regional archaeology (glassware, arms, and the finds from tombs), and a third of pottery.

The story of Champagne and how it is made (with a free tasting at the end) is told at many of the great houses in the course of a visit to their *caves*. Moët has a squadron of permanent guides conducting free tours of miles of under-ground galleries all day long, seven days a week from April to October (Mondays to Fridays the rest of the year), and in all major languages.

THE MONTAGNE DE REIMS

This high plateau, covered with vineyards and dense forests, covers much of the territory between Reims and Epernay. We approach the ring of pleasant villages surrounding the plateau from Epernay, though many of them are also quite close to Reims.

Ay and Avenay

Just north of Epernay, across the Marne on D 201 and D 9, respectively, are Ay and Avenay-Val-d'Or. Ay, just 3 km (2 miles) south of Reims on D 201, is the home of Bollinger, James Bond's Champagne, and of Deutz. Avenay, 4 km (2½ miles) farther down the road, is a luscious wine town sur-rounded by vineyards. An American GI who arrived here with General George Patton's forces stayed to marry a local girl and now bottles Ricciuti-Revolte, which you can buy at his *chais* (winery). Avenay is a good destination for the first taste of morning, when the mist is on the Marne but the sun is already on the vineyards stepping up the hill.

Verzy and Verzenay

Continuing north through the vineyards up D 26 from Ambonnay for 11 km (7 miles), you'll come to Verzy and, just outside the village, the lookout atop **Mont Sinai**. This marks the highest point of the Montagne de Reims, and the views over the Champagne plains are terrific. The road up to the lookout skirts the Faux de Verzy, a forest with bizarrely twisted and knotted beech trees, some a century old, that only a gnome could truly appreciate.

If you want to soak up the atmosphere of life in a small, traditional wine-making community, you have only to poke your nose 2 km east of Verzy along D 26 as it leads into **Verzenay**. This village of 1,200 inhabitants has made a comfortable living for itself with more than 500 hectares of *grands premiers cru Pinots noir* grapes. Lanson and Veuve Clicquot are both major owners here. The road into Verzenay is dominated by the village's famous windmill, built in 1820 and a historic monument since World War II, when it was used as a lookout.

Bouzy

Bouzy, 11 km (7 miles) east of Avenay on D 9 and D 19, gives its name to the most famous still wine to come from Champagne. Elsewhere the wine is overpriced, so the town is undersold. But Bouzy offers Bouzy at prices that are guaranteed to put cases in your car. Three wineries to try here: **Champagne Paul Bara** (Tel: 26-57-00-50), **George Vesselle** (Tel: 26-57-00-15), and **Champagne Barancourt** (Tel: 26-57-00-67). In France it's always best to phone ahead, even if it's from a booth on the corner; most wineries offer free visits from April to October.

Hautvillers

Here's one vineyard town nearby that no lover of Champagne and its history should miss. In Hautvillers, 6 km (3½ miles) north of Epernay on N 51 and RD 386, the intimate relationship between the vine and the people can be explored close up. From its steep side streets Hautvillers affords stunning views of the plantings, with the looping course of the Marne far below. The river seems sleepy and tranquil now, a far cry from 1914 when a French army was sent up from Paris in taxicabs to stop the Germans along its banks. They fought for four years. Reims was hit by the

German long guns and the cathedral was damaged, but the Germans never got across the river. In 1940 the Germans came again, this time with tanks. They crossed at Port-à-Binson, 15 miles west of Epernay (see below), and were soon in Paris. Four years elapsed before a major crossing over the Marne was made again—this time by General Patton. (A small escutcheon marks the square in Epernay, a town that his Eighth Army liberated.)

Like the Marne, the streets of Hautvillers are quiet now, but still precipitous and narrow—no place for a car—so it's a good idea to park, stroll around, and get in touch with what constitutes a successful wine village. The streets are impeccably clean, the houses well kept, the gardens full of carefully tended flowers. It's obvious an effort—right down to the antique, wrought-iron signs above the shops—has been made here to show off the village to the constant flow of tourists.

It was in Hautvillers during the 17th century that the sightless Dom Pérignon worked as a cellarmaster, and the Benedictine abbey where he labored still stands, transformed by Moët & Chandon into a museum. Here the traditional story of the step-by-step development of Champagne is told on the very spot where much of it first happened. Like many happy accidents, the discovery of Champagne resulted partly from effort and partly from blind luck. Pérignon had long been immersed in the dark arts of vinification and double fermentation, and it was here that the old monk first announced his immortal words, which rank with those of Marconi and Alexander Graham Bell: "Come quickly—I'm drinking stars!"

THE VALLEE DE LA MARNE
To the west of Epernay a lovely drive unfolds along the Marne whether you take D 1 on the north bank or N 3 on the south bank. Both routes will take you through tiny, well-kept villages, with hilly vineyards on one side of the road and the pretty Marne river running along the other. If you take N 3 west from Epernay, then D 222 south, in about 7 km (4 miles) you'll come to **Boursault**, where the majestic family château makes an appearance from the depths of the forest on the hill.

Châtillon-sur-Marne to Château-Thierry
Continue another 13 km (8 miles) west on N 3 to Port-à-Binson, which boasts the last bridge over the Marne to fall in 1940, and cross the river to Châtillon-sur-Marne, whose abbot Michot, an important Resistance fighter during World

War II, saved the lives of many an Allied bombing crew. An enormous, 100-foot-tall statue of Urban II, the 11th-century pope from Champagne—considered to be an instigator of the First Crusade—overlooks the valley from a belvedere that affords a great view of 22 villages nestled along the river. Back on the other side of the river, N 3 continues another 7½ km (4½ miles) to **Dormans**, where another wonderful vista may be had from the very pretty **Chapelle de la Reconnaissance** in the park of the town's 17th-century château. The Chapelle was built to commemorate the deadly battles along the Marne during the two world wars. In the town of **Château-Thierry**, 25 km (16 miles) down the river, a monument marks the participation of the American forces in the two world wars. More than 2,200 American soldiers lost their lives in the trenches here during World War I. Their bodies now rest in the cemetery just west of town in the **Bois Belleau**, where a memorial commemorates General Patton.

STAYING AND DINING IN CHAMPAGNE COUNTRY

Many hotels in Champagne accommodate guests in manor houses and serve superb renditions of the local cuisine. What's local in Champagne? There are those who will argue there is no such thing as a "gastronomic" regional specialty, and that what constitutes a Champagne *plat* is in fact a French classic with a shot of bubbly thrown in. But the region does have its special dishes, including the *potée champenoise,* a stew slowly simmered with pork and vegetables; *pieds de porc,* breaded pig's feet served with mustard; and *andouillette,* the famous tripe sausage from Troyes. However, try all manner of *crudités,* as well as ham, turkey, smoked wild boar, and thrush pâté. There are haunch of venison, quail in embers, filet of sole in Champagne, chicken in Champagne, *petits-gris* (very small snails) in herb butter, and, of course, icy flutes of Champagne. Two cheeses to try, here and in the north, are Boulette d'Avesnes and Maroilles.

In and Around Epernay

The **Restaurant Chapon Fin** on Place Mendès-France is a reasonable and lusty place to sample local wines, while for accommodations a good choice is the 42-room ▶ **La Briqueterie** in Vinay, just south of Epernay on D 11. Its food sometimes approaches the memorable, and the *carte des vins* is excellent. In Epernay proper there are a nice hotel and restaurant, the kind that the French take their dogs to, and it's on a nice street as well. All three have the same name: ▶ **Les Berceaux**, at 13, rue des Berceaux. On a little gem of a side street, the hotel/restaurant is almost a secret place. You can pass its understated brick façade as quick as a wink, but step inside and you are entering a 19th-century *maison particulier*. The stairs and balustrade are of polished wood, and there are thick Persian rugs everywhere. Upstairs, the rooms are comfortable without being posh or modern; downstairs, the restaurant and bar will make you feel as if you had come to visit a rich French relative. The kitchen turns out daily specials, such as *turbotin* (turbot) *au Champagne*. The bar is in effect a wine bar where you can taste your way around the world as well as around Champagne itself. Best of all, the prices are quite reasonable.

The ▶ **Royal Champagne**, 6 km (3½ miles) north of Epernay on N 51 in **Champillon**, is, if not the best restaurant in the region, certainly the most admirably situated. Here, in a restored 18th-century post house, you can drink a red Cumières while gazing at the vineyards. The surrounding picture windows bring the countryside into the restaurant with CinemaScope-like reality, and what is brought to your table seems alive with the fields of Champagne.

The Royal was started by David Desvignes, one of the grand old men of Champagne, who truly appreciated the region and its fruits. Though he is gone now, his firm hand seems to hover in the restaurant still. The menu is traditional *champenois: truite bleue,* Chaource cheese, and glorious Philipponat Clos des Goisses Champagne. It would be a grave mistake, in responding to the pressure of more modish urges, for the visitor to Champagne to miss the Royal. The rooms, although expensive, provide breathtaking views over the Montagne de Reims countryside. Tel: 26-52-87-11.

In the Montagne de Reims Region
Some 15 km (9 miles) north of Epernay on N 51 in the town of **Montchenot** is the newly renovated restaurant **Auberge du Grand Cerf** (Tel: 26-97-60-07). Here you are practically on top of the mountain of Reims. The cuisine is imaginative and the *menu dégustation,* with its tempting tiny tidbits, is completely satisfying. Ask to be seated at one of the tables at the back of the restaurant, which offer a view of the vineyards.

It's worth the trip to tiny Sillery, 27 km (17 miles) northwest of Epernay on N 51, D 26, and D 33, and the **Relais de Sillery**, a restaurant in a converted turn-of-the-century post office sitting on the edge of a lake. Run by one of France's few woman chefs, the restaurant specializes in fresh fish (sometimes five different fish are used in one *plat*), mixed salads with the freshest local produce, and filets of beef and liver. (You could also easily make the trip out here for a meal from Reims, only 10 km/6 miles northwest on N 44.) Tel: 26-49-10-11.

For a stay in the lap of Saint Vincent (the patron saint of wine growers), try the ▶ **Auberge Saint Vincent**. Try it as a hotel, a restaurant, or a bar, for it's all three. It's only 11 km (7 miles) south of Verzy on the bountiful D 26 in the village of **Ambonnay**, a town that flaunts its charm. The ten-room Auberge Saint Vincent, newly renovated in 19th-century style, tries hard to be authentic but falls shy of the mark. In the restaurant, though, the auberge earns its spurs. The menu revolves around a cuisine neither modish nor classical, but regionally Champagne. And that means fresh, for the produce is local.

In the Vallée de la Marne

For a memorable meal or overnight stay follow the Marne west on N 3 for 27 km (17 miles) to Dormans, then follow D 6 for 25 km (16 miles) northwest to **Fère-en-Tardenois**— where, because of the microclimate, springlike days can be enjoyed even in February. Here at the site of the ruins of a medieval château is a park of considerable beauty and the spacious ▶ **L'Hostellerie du Château Fère-en-Tardenois**, an impeccable 19-room hotel with a charming restaurant whose cuisine is not too *nouvelle*.

Troyes

Nicknamed "The Champagne Cork" because of the shape of its *centre ville,* Troyes is a market town, its streets aswarm with shoppers, sightseers, and diners. Its antique riches are evident in museums, churches, and handsome old houses. Yet many visitors to the region overlook this town, perhaps because it sits beside the Seine at the southern fringes of the Champagne region just off the direct Sens-to-Burgundy route. (Troyes is 111 km/69 miles south of Reims on A 4 and N 77.)

In the 12th and 13th centuries things were different. Along with Lagny-sur-Marne, Provins (both now considered within the greater environs of Paris), and Bar-sur-Aube, about 30 miles to the east, Troyes staged an annual Champagne fair that attracted merchants from all over civilized Europe and established standards for continent-wide commerce. (Troyes gave its name to our system of troy-weight measurements.) Old Troyes—the part of the city that has the distinction of being shaped like a Champagne cork—is divided into three medieval quarters: the Quartier de la

Cité, the northeastern section (the top of the cork) that is embraced in a broad curve of the Seine; the Quartier St-Jean, where most of the medieval fairs were held; and the Quartier Vauluisant. The city is best seen on foot, and many streets are closed to motor traffic.

QUARTIER DE LA CITE

The most logical place to begin a tour of Troyes is the **Cathédrale St-Pierre-et-St-Paul** (off the Place St-Pierre). The façade was ornately sculpted by Martin Chambiges, who also worked on the cathedrals of Beauvais and Sens. A beautiful Flamboyant rose window remains, but the statues in the portals were destroyed during the Revolution (Flamboyant style features window tracery with a flamelike rhythm). Joan of Arc visited the cathedral in 1429 on her way to the crowning of Charles VII.

Among the fine stained glass from the 13th to 16th centuries here is a curious window that portrays Christ stretched out across the planks of a wine press as the blood pours out of the wound in his side into a handy chalice. Meanwhile, a vine stalk grows out of his chest, and the Twelve Apostles sit on its branches. In fact, Troyes is famous for its beautiful stained glass, and is known as "The Sacred City of Windows." The city is also a leading force in the art of restoring and protecting the precious material; many windows in the cathedral are equipped with electronic surveillance equipment that analyzes and protects the glass around the clock.

The impressive **Musée d'Art Moderne** (a.k.a. Musée Levy) is housed in the renovated bishop's palace next to the cathedral. In 1976 Pierre and Denise Levy presented a part of their enormous art collection to Troyes, their home town. Of most significance are the 1,500 paintings of the late 19th and 20th centuries, representing almost every major French artist of the period, including works by Bonnard, Cézanne, Gauguin, Matisse, and Picasso. Also on display are prints, drawings, bronze and African sculptures, ceramics, and glassware.

Directly on the other side of the cathedral, the 17th-century **Abbaye St-Loup** (named for the fifth-century bishop whose virtues persuaded Attila the Hun not to sack the town) now houses two museums, one devoted to natural history and the other, **Musée des Beaux-Arts et d'Archéologie**, mainly to regional archaeology.

QUARTIER ST-JEAN

Recently revitalized with remarkable preservation work, the Quartier St-Jean is just southeast of the cathedral; follow the rue de la Cité a few blocks and cross the canal. The 16th century is revisited here, from the smartly turned turrets atop the Maison de l'Orfèvre to the recobbled, archaic-looking ruelle des Chats. The great church of the quarter is the **Basilique St-Urbain**, off the Place de la Libération, with a superb Gothic choir.

QUARTIER VAULUISANT

The **Musée Historique de Troyes et de Champagne**, in the superb Renaissance Hôtel de Vauluisant, illustrates the city's history and possesses the only hosiery museum in France. (The museum and many of the quarter's other sights are on the rue Emile-Zola, which cuts a swath through the center of old Troyes.) Stockings, gloves, and hats were even more important to medieval Troyes than was *andouillette* (tripe sausage), which was extremely popular in the 16th century—so much so, in fact, that Royalist troops who were supposed to be attacking the city sat down to gorge in the *andouillette* quarter (St-Denis) and were set upon and massacred by Troyes's defenders. Today only the reputation for sausage survives.

Of the quarter's churches, the most remarkable are **St-Pantaléon** (next to the Hôtel de Vauluisant), with its Renaissance altar screens and statues, and the oldest church in Troyes, **Ste-Madeleine** (on rue du Général-de-Gaulle not far from the railway station). The church's treasures include a 16th-century rood screen in Flamboyant style and a statue of Sainte Marthe dressed as a common woman, the best example of the Champagne school of that century.

STAYING AND DINING IN TROYES

Troyes's best restaurant is generally considered to be **Le Bourgogne**, at 40, rue du Général-de-Gaulle near the church of St-Remy. Le Bourgogne's pike mousseline and duck slivers in Bouzy are featured, as is game in season (Tel: 25-73-02-67). A pleasant choice, and more modest, is **Le Valentino** on cour de la Rencontre near the Hôtel de Ville (Tel: 25-73-14-14), with a 55-franc menu.

As is often the case in provincial French towns, a good hotel is right near the railway station—the ▶ **Grand Hôtel** on avenue Maréchal-Joffre. It is quite reasonably priced and boasts three restaurants, each good in its category: **Le Champagne**, a formal dining room; a grill called **Jardin de la Louisiane**; and the **Pizzéria Grill Aquarius**. You can taste-test the local *andouillettes* for yourself at ▶ **Le Royal**, at 22, boulevard Carnot, near the train station. They offer a choice of menus and pride themselves on their preparation of the sausage. Le Royal is also a hotel in a recently renovated building, with plain but comfortable rooms.

COLOMBEY-LES-DEUX-EGLISES

There's one last piece of Champagne to visit, 67 km (42 miles) east of Troyes via N 19: Colombey-les-Deux-Eglises, the resting place of France's greatest 20th-century soldier-statesman. Here, in his country house, La Boisserie, Charles de Gaulle died on November 9, 1970. From his study you can gaze across a rolling green landscape and read the words of the general and president: "This part of Champagne is impregnated with calm, vast, worn, and sad horizons; melancholy woods, pastures, crops, and lands lying fallow; tranquil and rather poor villages of which nothing, for a millennium, has changed the soul. . . . "

Outside town, on a rise simply called "The Mountain," a Cross of Lorraine (the general's symbol) dominates—as did the general himself—the landscape. A celebration of his memory should properly be made here.

GETTING AROUND

The fastest way from Paris to Champagne is by train from the Gare de l'Est to Reims or Epernay; there are several a day. Those who prefer to drive a more scenic route can begin by leaving A 4 near La Ferté-sous-Jouarre, then taking D 969 along the Marne via Château-Thierry.

The **Route de Champagne** (brochures are available in English at tourist offices) is divided into three routes designated by colors: blue (the Montagne de Reims), red (the Marne Valley), and green (the Côte des Blancs). The blue route, about 50 miles long, departs Reims on N 51 in the direction of Epernay and passes through such villages as Rilly, Verzy, and Bouzy. The route ends in Ay (visits to Bollinger by appointment only).

The red route, 41 miles along the Marne Valley, starts in Tours-sur-Marne on D 1 and winds through Hautvillers (via RD 386), then past Châtillon-sur-Marne to Dormans and back to Epernay.

The green route winds for 31 miles along the Côte des Blancs from Epernay on RD 51 in the direction of Troyes, then to Monthelon and Bergères-les-Vertus (via D 240 and D 9) and back to Epernay. Most of the small producers are open only by appointment, which may be arranged through tourist offices in Reims or Epernay.

The **Champagne Air Show** offers ballooning trips of one, two, or three days, with accommodations in a château hotel (office at 15 bis, place St-Nicaise, 51100 Reims; Tel: 26-82-59-

60). At the same address, you can make arrangements for custom-tailored canal cruising. Champagne bus tours are available from travel agents in Paris.

ACCOMMODATIONS REFERENCE

The rates given below are projections *for 1994. Unless otherwise indicated, rates are for a double room, double occupancy, and do not include meals. As rates are always subject to change, double-check before booking.*

▶ **Aux Armes de Champagne.** 51460 **L'Epine.** Tel: 26-69-30-30; Fax: 26-66-92-31. 490F–800F.

▶ **Auberge Saint Vincent.** 51150 **Ambonnay.** Tel: 26-57-01-98; Fax: 26-57-81-48. 290F–360F.

▶ **Les Berceaux.** 13, rue des Berceaux, 51200 **Epernay.** Tel: 26-55-28-84; Fax: 26-55-10-36. 330F–440F.

▶ **Boyer "Les Crayères."** 64, boulevard Henry-Vasnier, 51100 **Reims.** Tel: 26-82-80-80; Telex: 830959; Fax: 26-82-65-52; in U.S., (212) 856-0115; Fax: (212) 856-0193. Member, Relais & Châteaux. 1,040F–1,880F.

▶ **La Briqueterie.** Route de Sézanne, 51200 **Vinay.** Tel: 26-59-99-99; Fax: 26-59-92-10. 900F.

▶ **Grand Hôtel.** 4, avenue Maréchal-Joffre, 10000 **Troyes.** Tel: 25-79-90-90; Fax: 25-78-48-93. 365F.

▶ **L'Hostellerie du Château Fère-en-Tardenois.** 02130 **Fère-en-Tardenois.** Tel: 23-82-21-13; Telex: 145526; Fax: 23-82-37-81. 970F–1,130F.

▶ **Hôtel Continental.** 93, place Drouet-d'Erlon, 51100 **Reims.** Tel: 26-40-39-35; Fax: 26-47-51-12. 280F–450F.

▶ **Hôtel d'Angleterre.** 19, place Monseigneur Tissier, 51000 **Châlons-sur-Marne.** Tel: 26-68-21-51; Fax: 26-70-51-67. 450F–600F.

▶ **Hôtel de la Paix.** 9, rue Buirette, 51100 **Reims.** Tel: 26-40-04-08; Telex: 830974; Fax: 26-47-75-04. 400F–500F.

▶ **Le Royal.** 22, boulevard Carnot, 10000 **Troyes.** Tel: 25-73-19-99; Telex: 842964; Fax: 25-73-47-85. 365F–395F.

▶ **Royal Champagne.** 51160 **Champillon-Bellevue.** Tel: 26-52-87-11; Telex: 830111; Fax: 26-52-89-69; in U.S., (212) 856-0115; Fax: (212) 856-0193. Member, Relais & Châteaux. 830F–1,350F.

ALSACE-LORRAINE

By Georgia I. Hesse

The hyphen that forever binds these two distinct provinces is also what divides them: the Vosges range, a granite-and-sandstone spine that slices the land north to south from Wissembourg and the German border to Belfort. The Vosges are old, comfortable mountains suited more to rambling than rappeling, to *piques-niques* than pitons. In their thick, dark forests you would not be surprised to stumble upon Hansel and Gretel. The highest point, the Grand Ballon, rises less than 5,000 feet. More French than foreigners take time to divert themselves in this pleasant land of lakes (the largest is Gérardmer; the deepest, Blanc) by fishing, camping, swimming, boating, and, in season, casual, unchallenging skiing.

West of these mountains lies the plateau of Lorraine, an expanse rich in forests, lakes, and croplands that reaches toward Champagne and the Paris basin. To the east of the Vosges is the narrow plain of Alsace, a region thick with grapevines and half-timbered villages bordered by the Rhine river and facing the homeland of those ancient antagonists the Alemanni, a tribe whose name became synonymous with *Allemagne,* the French name for Germany.

The late food writer Waverley Root lumped the two lands together in his so-called Domain of Fat, a happy description for today's traveller, who will find here a wealth not only of hearty cooking but also of history, natural beauty, art and architecture, local traditions and cultures, and important industries (glassmaking in the village of Baccarat in particular).

Both Celtic countries, Lorraine and Alsace have shared a lineage of conquest and liberation almost two thousand years long, from their occupation by Roman legions in 58 and 52 B.C. to the devastating battles of 1914–1918 and 1939–1945. These frequent struggles have resulted in today's resolute pride in being French, although in both cases that nationality is a surprisingly recent phenomenon. France acquired Alsace in 1648 by the Treaty of Münster (except for Strasbourg, which remained independent until 1681) and annexed Lorraine in 1766 upon the death of Stanislas Leszczyński, the former king of Poland, duke of Lorraine, and, not incidentally, father-in-law of Louis XV. Acquired by Germany in 1871 as spoils of the Franco-Prussian War, Alsace and Lorraine were restored to France in 1919 under the Treaty of Versailles following World War I.

This intertwining of Germanic and Frankish inheritances gives Lorraine and, especially, Alsace much of their contemporary fascination: the village architecture, imported from beyond the Rhine, of half-timbered houses and wood-sculpted oriels (encorbelled windows) projecting over the street; the substantial Germanic peasant fare of wine-cured sausages and sauerkraut (*choucroute garni*); the Rhenish art created by German masters; the folkloric costumes, songs, and pilgrimages unlike any others in France; even the traditional arts and crafts that are more closely related to those of Germany's Black Forest than to those of the Ile-de-France.

MAJOR INTEREST IN LORRAINE

Nancy
Place Stanislas
Musée des Beaux-Arts
Palais Ducal (Musée Historique Lorrain)

Near Nancy
Cathédrale St-Etienne in Toul
Eglise St-Etienne (with macabre tomb sculpture) in Bar-le-Duc; Sacred Way
Domrémy-la-Pucelle (birthplace of Joan of Arc)
Vittel-area spas

Elsewhere in Lorraine
Cathédrale St-Etienne (notable for its stained glass windows) and Musée d'Art et d'Histoire in Metz
Battlefields and monuments of Verdun
Village of Avioth and its 13th-century basilica
Lunéville (Petit Versailles)
Baccarat (crystal museum, workshops, and sales)
Lac de Gérardmer

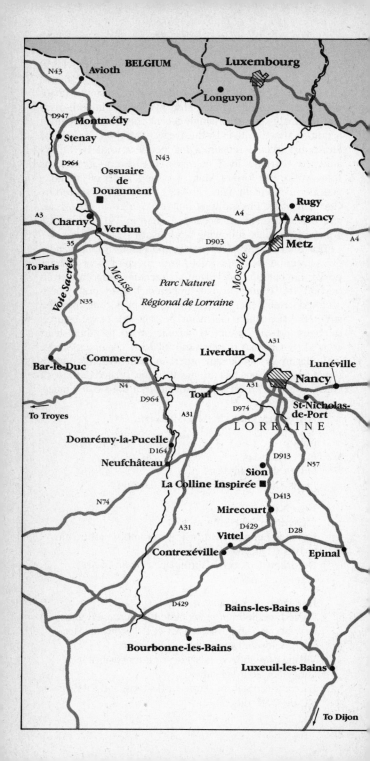

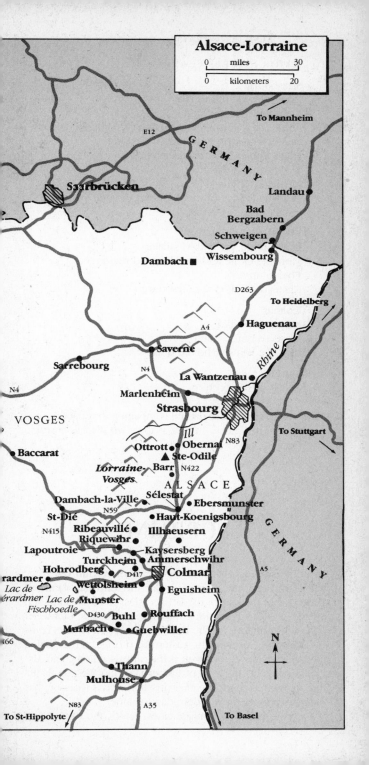

MAJOR INTEREST IN ALSACE

Strasbourg
Boat rides on the Ill river
Cathédrale Notre-Dame
Musée de l'Oeuvre Notre-Dame (pre-Roman, Roman,
    medieval, and Renaissance artworks)
Palais Rohan and its museums
Winstubs and *bierstubs*
Musée Alsacien
La Petite France (ancient quarter of town, featuring
    half-timbered houses)

Elsewhere in Alsace
La Route du Vin and its villages
Mont-Ste-Odile and the Hohwald region
Ebersmunster
Château du Haut-Koenigsbourg

Colmar
Musée Bartholdi·
Musée d'Unterlinden
La Petite Venise (the old quarter)

Munster Valley
Eglise de Murbach

Alsace and Lorraine are natural companion destinations on a
trip to eastern France. In this chapter we discuss Lorraine
first, because it is closer to Paris.

LORRAINE

Lorraine owes its name to the Treaty of Verdun (843), by
which Charlemagne's empire—all the Christian lands of
Western Europe except the British Isles, southern Italy, and
Sicily—was divided among his three grandsons. Charles II
(Charles le Chauve, or the Bald) took western France, Louis
II (Louis the German) the eastern territories, and Lothair I
the lands in between, as well as the capitals at Rome and Aix-
la-Chapelle and the title of Emperor of the West. Lothair's
turf, named Lotharingia after his son and successor, has
metamorphosed into modern-day Lorraine.
    Lorraine boasts two major cities, Nancy, the capital, and

Metz, both of which offer historical, artistic, and culinary attractions in plenty. In addition, the region is rich in the delights and benefits of *thermalisme,* or, as it used to be called, "taking the waters." Happily, Americans and other Anglophone visitors are now beginning to savor these spa vacations, long the province of Europeans. Another major interest centers upon the sad and powerful reminders of World Wars I and II: the battlefields, cemeteries, memorials, and monuments.

We begin in Nancy and proceed south to the ancient Celtic site known as La Colline Inspirée and to the spa towns; then to such towns and sites west of Nancy as Toul, Domrémy-la-Pucelle, and the Parc Naturel Régional de Lorraine. Finally, we travel north to Metz, Verdun, and the Basilique d'Avioth on the Belgian border.

FOOD AND DRINK OF LORRAINE

Excellent restaurants abound in the area. Here you may sample such delicacies as quiche Lorraine; a hearty pork stew named *potée lorraine* that immortalizes the great, floppy-eared Celtic breed of hog; *tourte à la lorraine,* a fine marinated meat dish cooked in a crusty cloak; and *boudin,* or blood pudding, which the food writer Waverley Root said may be the oldest dish on the French menu, since it seems to have been invented in Tyre by the Assyrians. Other regional specialties include *géromé,* Lorraine's most famous cheese, and Marcel Proust's muse, the *madeleine,* born in Commercy (buy some there at **Maison Grojean** on Place Général-de-Gaulle). Bar-le-Duc is renowned for its jams and jellies, particularly those made of currants.

The *vins gris* native to Lorraine are rosés; the best come from Toul, due west of Nancy. They don't compare with the wines of Alsace but get along well with regional fare, as do the beers. Lorraine also produces several fruity *eaux-de-vie,* the finest of which is probably Mirabelle de Lorraine, distilled from plums.

Nancy

Nancy is a pretty, informal town, its people much given to ambling and café-sitting; in conversation they appear to accept—but with some resentment—the greater fame of Strasbourg. In style, in appearance, and in essence, Nancy, the seat of the dukes of Lorraine, lives in the 18th century, the era of its master-builder, Stanislas Leszczyński. This former king of Poland was the father of Marie Leszczyńska, who wed Louis XV and became queen of France. Upon this marriage Louis installed his father-in-law as the duke of Lorraine and Bar, with the understanding that upon Stanislas's death, those lands were to pass to Marie and thus to France. And so it was.

Nancy is 307 km (190 miles) east of Paris via A 4 and A 31, or for those who like to avoid autoroutes, N 4 and A 31.

By rail, it's a three-hour run between Paris and Nancy via Bar-le-Duc, and there are several trains per day. (No TGVs operate on this route yet.)

18TH-CENTURY NANCY

Most of the elegant provincial city Leszczyński created remains. Forming the heart of the town is the harmonious, majestic, and aptly named Place Stanislas, lying between the old town to the north and new, commercial Nancy to the south, and this is where you should begin a tour of the city.

Place Stanislas

Originally called Place Royale out of loyalty to the crown, this large square was once the site of a statue of Louis XV that was pulled down during the Revolution. Of the superb palaces around Place Stanislas, the largest is the **Hôtel de Ville**, with its grand architectural details and its wide-angle views over the square.

On the west rim of the *place,* the **Musée des Beaux-Arts** is devoted to European paintings from the 14th century to the present; particularly interesting in this setting is Delacroix's *Death of Charles the Bold at the Battle of Nancy.* Ironically, neither Claude Lorrain (born Claude-Gellée) nor Georges de La Tour—both were native Lorraine artists—is well represented in town.

Some of the gilded wrought-iron grills that so distinguish this *place* from any other in France enclose extravagant fountains at the north end of the *place;* the Office de Tourisme is nearby at 14, place Stanislas (Tel: 83-35-22-41).

A few steps north off the *place* will bring you before the **Arc de Triomphe**, a copy of that of Septimius Severus in Rome, built to honor Louis XV. Passing through the central arch, you enter the Place de la Carrière.

Place de la Carrière and Palais Ducal

This elongated *place,* once an exercise course for horsemen, is today linked by handsome 18th-century houses flanked by rows of shade trees; it's a natural spot for a slow promenade. At its north end, across the small Place Général-de-Gaulle, stands the Palais du Gouvernement, former residence of the governors of Lorraine, which now houses various city offices. To the east of this formal urban composition is **La Pépinière**, a 57-acre garden in the style the French call English, offering a zoological park, pretty terraces, and a statue by Rodin of artist Lorrain.

The 13th-century **Palais Ducal** (Ducal Palace), directly west of the Palais du Gouvernement, has endured neglect, sacks, and several reconstructions during its long history; fortunately its remarkable *porterie* (gatehouse), in mixed Flamboyant and Renaissance styles, bearing an equestrian statue of Duc Antoine de Lorraine, remains beautifully intact.

The palace houses the **Musée Historique Lorrain** (the entrance is at 64, Grande-Rue), where the collections illustrate with style and depth the history of Lorraine and its individual folklore. Of particular interest are the archaeological gallery, the medieval sculptures on the ground floor, and the tapestries and possessions of the dukes on the first floor.

Eglise et Couvent des Cordeliers

The Eglise et Couvent des Cordeliers (Church and Convent of the Cordeliers) is just a few steps north of the museum along the Grande-Rue. Paris has its St-Denis; Nancy has the Cordeliers. In its crypt lie the remains of all the dukes of Lorraine, most of their tombs carved by the finest artists of the Renaissance in this region. Two superb works are the tomb effigy of Philippa de Gueldre, second wife of René II, in the nave, and the tomb of René II against the southern wall.

The adjoining convent and its cloister have been restored and now house the worthwhile **Musée d'Arts et Traditions Populaires**, one of those fascinating reconstructions of regional interiors, complete with country kitchens, bedrooms, tools, and furnishings.

A little farther north up the Grande-Rue, you will come to the **Porte de la Craffe**, a large gateway that survives from the 14th-century fortifications. Until just after the Revolution, the interior held prison cells. Today, they show off an informal collection of medieval sculptures and instruments of torture.

OUTSIDE THE CENTER

Between 1871 and 1918 the city welcomed so many refugees as a result of various regional upheavals that a new Nancy grew up to the west; here you'll find (with some difficulty) the **Musée de l'Ecole de Nancy**, with collections that embody the indigenous style that became a precursor of the so-called modern French style. The museum houses an exciting collection of late-19th- and early-20th-century furniture, glassware, and faïence and other ceramics by refreshingly unfamiliar artists. To reach this worthwhile museum, drive west of Place Stanislas on rue Stanislas until it meets rue Victor-Hugo. Turn south and continue to rue de Mon Désert, on which you turn west to rue Sergent-Blandan, then south; the museum is at number 38-46, only about a 20-minute drive from Place Stanislas—if you don't get lost. On the same street as the museum, farther along at number 107, the city auction house occasionally offers interesting buys in antique furniture.

South of town proper in the small, resolutely industrial suburb of **St-Nicolas-de-Port** is—unexpectedly—the superb **Basilique St-Nicolas** in Flamboyant Gothic style, built on the site of an earlier sanctuary that once possessed a most precious ancient relic, a finger bone of Saint Nicolas. Joan of Arc knelt here to ask help on her expedition, as have faithful travellers ever since.

STAYING AND DINING IN NANCY

The best and most atmospheric accommodations in town are found in an 18th-century palace at 2, place Stanislas, the ► **Grand Hôtel de la Reine**, with its **Restaurant Stanislas** (Tel: 83-35-03-01). There's great charm to the Louis XV decor and rich wood paneling in the public rooms and the period furnishings in the 45 guest rooms. This palatial hotel is the work of 18th-century architect Emmanuel Héré; ask for a room overlooking his other masterpiece—the *place* itself. There is a garage. The 185-room ► **Mercure Altéa Thiers**, close to the railway station on rue Poincaré, is a pleasant alternative to the Grand Hôtel de la Reine. It has a good restaurant, **La Toison d'Or** (Tel: 83-39-75-75), as well as a garage and facilities for meetings.

Just west of the Hôtel de Ville at 31, rue Gambetta, the quite modern restaurant **Capucin Gourmand** is as popular today for its Lorraine specialties as it was back in the 1950s with the wandering gourmet-writer Samuel Chamberlain. Reserve; Tel: 83-35-26-98. Tops in town today, **Le Goéland**, 27, rue des Ponts, near the Eglise St-Sebastian (stop to admire its Baroque façade), specializes in seafood. Reserve; Tel: 83-35-17-25. Another good dining spot is **La Gentil-hommière**, a short distance west of the Arc de Triomphe at 29, rue des Maréchaux. Tradition says Victor Hugo's ancestors dwelt upon the spot where today *filet de sole* is a specialty (Tel: 83-32-26-44). At Flavigny-sur-Moselle, 16 km (10 miles) southeast via N 57, the highly rated ► **Le Prieuré** serves notable salmon and langoustine; four rooms are available for those who can't bear to leave. Reserve; Tel: 83-26-70-45.

Near Nancy

Rewarding excursions can easily be made from Nancy as day trips; the only practical way to do these, and the most pleasant, is by car.

SOUTH

La Colline Inspirée

A drive of 34 km (21 miles) south from Nancy on D 913 and a jog of 4½ km (3 miles) west on D 58 bring you to the hamlet of **Sion** and La Colline Inspirée (Hill of Inspiration). This lonely place was long said to be sacred to the gods of war and peace, and prayers have been offered up here for more than two thousand years.

Celts worshiped here first in what must have been all but total seclusion. Since then the hill has been a pilgrimage site for followers of the Crusades, those liberated from German domination, the faithful freed of the Prussian yoke, the French writer Maurice Barrès (who gave the spot its name), enthusiasts of French unity, and, in 1973's Peace Festival, thousands of former prisoners of Nazi concentration camps.

Atop the hill (actually a crescent-shaped limestone mesa), three sites are worth a short visit: the **archaeological museum** in Sion, where the history of the spot is outlined; the **Signal de Vaudémont**, an overlook above the Lorraine plateau with an orientation chart; and the ruins of the 11th-century **Château de Vaudémont**, cradle of the family of the dukes of Lorraine. There is even an unpretentious hotel, the 15-room ▶ **Notre Dame** in Sion, where you can have a modest meal.

Vittel and Other Spas

The current health fad favoring fancy bottled waters has made the name Vittel popular with outsiders who know their waters if not their spas. Wanderers have come here to cure various ills since the days of the Romans; when those bath-happy occupiers departed, the springs were forgotten, to be rediscovered only as recently as 1845. The plains and uplands of the Vosges some 45 miles south of Nancy are rich in healing springs both cold and hot, and the waters emerge both with and without natural carbonation. There is something quaint, turn-of-the-century, self-consciously healthful, and studiously manicured about spa villages. They offer a slightly skewed version of French life that is overlooked by many foreigners.

To reach spa country, you could speed 70 km (43 miles) west and then south from Nancy via autoroute A 31 and take the marked turnoff at Bulgnéville. Better, follow the somewhat shorter and slower but prettier D 913 directly south from Nancy; it merges with D 413 north of Mirecourt and from there to Vittel becomes D 429. (Vittel is only 5 km/3 miles east of Contrexéville.)

Of the spa towns—Vittel, nearby Contrexéville, Bains-les-Bains, Bourbonne-les-Bains, and Luxeuil-les-Bains—Vittel is the largest (with 6,500 or so permanent residents) and best known, and offers the possibility of tours and tastings at the bottling factory.

Staying and Dining at the Spas

The best hotels are in **Contrexéville**, once a favorite retreat of Stanislas Leszczyński and a good headquarters for relaxing excursions in the wooded countryside, whether or not you are interested in taking the waters. The two smartest hotels, and those with the most facilities, are the ► **Grand Hôtel Etablissement** and ► **Cosmos**. The former, in the town park just off the rue de la Grande Duchesse and next door to the baths, has 39 rooms and the posh **Restaurant du Casino**, while the Cosmos, on the rue de Metz, has 75 rooms, six apartments, and an outdoor swimming pool. (It should be noted that *thermalisme* is a seasonal pursuit, and spa towns virtually close down in the off-season. Contrexéville's hotels, for example, open in early April and close the last day of September.)

Epinal

Epinal, 41 km (25 miles) east of Vittel en route to Alsace via D 429, then D 28 and D 166, is home to the **Musée des Vosges et de l'Imagerie**. The museum houses local Roman and Gallo-Roman works, including a very fine mosaic, medieval sculptures, and exhibitions of daily private life in the Vosges region. There are also a few outstanding paintings, many drawings, and a display of the history of printmaking from the Middle Ages to the present.

On the Wednesday before Easter the children of Epinal draw lighted boats along a large pond near the Hôtel de Ville for the Fête des Champs-Golots; in June there is an international printmaking festival during which prints and printmaking techniques are displayed.

WEST

Toul

Toul, a little city of almost 18,000 Toulois, is 22 km (14 miles) west of Nancy on A 31. Three centuries were devoted to the construction of its former **Cathédrale St-Etienne**, which has not been returned to its former status since being severely damaged during the battles of 1940. Its façade—on the Place du Parvis—and its Gothic nave are still admirable, however. It's a little east of the center of town, just inside the old ramparts.

A pleasant walk west of St-Etienne, the **Eglise St-Gengoult** near the Place du Marché is a proud example of the Gothic school of Champagne, raised from the 13th to the 15th century. Most appealing is the 16th-century Flamboyant-style cloister. A lovely Renaissance house replete with gargoyles, just to the east of the church on rue Michâtel, was the home of the 17th-century prelate Jacques Bossuet. Several other treasured Renaissance houses stand on rue de Général-Gengoult, a couple of streets west of the church.

Bar-le-Duc

Bar-le-Duc, 59 km (37 miles) west of Toul on N 4 and N 135, is only slightly larger than Toul but plays a much greater commercial role, as befits its status as a county capital more than a thousand years ago. The town boasts a fairly interesting art-and-archaeological museum, **Musée Barrois**, on the west side of town, but almost everybody stops only to visit the **Eglise St-Etienne**. For some reason Anne de Lorraine, widow of René de Châlon, prince of Orange, commissioned one Ligier Richier to depict her husband's body in stone as the decomposed corpse would look three years after his death (he was killed in 1544 during the siege of St-Dizier). The macabre, not to say repellent, *Le Squelette* is the treasure of St-Etienne.

Regional specialties recognized nationwide are the seedless red-currant preserves produced in Bar-le-Duc, which are good to pack along for picnics and are available almost everywhere.

Staying and Dining in Toul and Bar-le-Duc

If the luncheon hour should toll during your sojourn in Toul, consider the small but comfortable **La Belle Epoque**, on the western edge of town at 31, avenue Victor-Hugo, near the Marne canal (reserve; Tel: 83-43-23-71). Try the Côtes de Toul wines, among the best in Lorraine; they are rosés, locally called *gris*, or gray. For finer fare seek out **Le Dauphin**, to the north of town in the direction of Verdun. A specialty here is a *mille-feuille* of potatoes and foie gras. Reserve; Tel: 83-43-13-46.

Across the street from the clock tower is a small, pleasant

café in a former monastery at 1, rue François-de-Guise, **La Meuse Gourmande** (reserve; Tel: 29-79-28-40). There are two small hotels in town for those who wish to make a stopover, but a better choice is the ► **Auberge de la Source**, about 10 km (6 miles) southwest via D 3 in Trémont-sur-Saulx. It offers 25 rooms and a pretty garden.

Domrémy-la-Pucelle

The pilgrimage to Domrémy, 58 km (36 miles) southwest from Nancy, is made easily via D 974 to N 74 to Neufchâteau, then north on D 164. (The Colombey just down the road is not de Gaulle's town; Colombey-les-Deux-Eglises is quite a bit farther on.)

With fewer than 300 inhabitants, this village is as sleepy today as it was in 1412 when Isabelle Romée and her husband, Jacques d'Arc, gave birth to Joan (Jeanne in French), the humble peasant girl who was to lead an army, give France a king, and burn at the stake in one of history's most famous martyrdoms. Joan's story has inspired the French for half a millennium; Charles de Gaulle adopted the Cross of Lorraine as the emblem of a Free France besieged.

According to the historian Frances Gies, Joan was called Jeanette in the village, and was sometimes given her mother's surname of Romée, as was the country custom. During her military career and for a century afterward, however, she was known as Jeanne *la Pucelle* (the Maid). Although a peasant, Jacques d'Arc was prosperous: His thick-walled house was built of stone in a time when most were of timber. Restored in the 19th century to eliminate side structures that had been added throughout the years, it is simple, solid, unpretentious, and firm—very much like Joan herself.

The village church has been much reworked since Joan's day, but several vestiges the Maid would recognize remain, the basin for holy water and the baptismal font among them. About a mile away the **Basilique du Bois-Chenu**, consecrated in 1926, rises rather pretentiously above the spot where Joan heard the voices that inspired her mission, those of Saints Catherine, Marguerite, and Michael.

Travellers interested in Roman antiquities should inquire at the local Syndicat d'Initiative near the post office in Neufchâteau for directions to **Grand**, despite its name a minute village not located on many maps, about 23 km (14 miles) west of Neufchâteau. Among the many ruins and excavations here is the largest Roman mosaic in France, in the town's basilica.

NORTH

Parc Naturel Régional de Lorraine

Established in 1976 to, among other purposes, introduce the urban populace of the province to the joys of the outdoors, the Parc Naturel Régional de Lorraine spreads across 1,147 square miles. Its headquarters are in Pont-à-Mousson, 27 km (17 miles) north of Nancy via N 57.

The park caters to health-and-fitness-conscious visitors with hiking trails, horseback riding, bicycling, picnicking, and bird-watching. It is rich in lakes, ponds, and their resultant bird life. Maisons du Parc (Visitors' Centers) provide information on the park and on such important characteristics of life in Lorraine as artisan and craft activities, community arts and rural traditions, and even the production of salt, a valuable regional product.

METZ

Metz, a city of about 118,000 citizens (known as Messins), has been important almost forever—or at least since the sixth-century days of the Merovingian ruler Theodoric I, the son of Clovis I and king of Metz. Under Sigibert I and his famous wife, Brunhild, Metz became the capital of Austrasia, one of the two major Merovingian kingdoms, the other being Neustria (with Soissons as its capital). Set as it is at the confluence of the Moselle and Seille rivers, Metz was strategically of great importance to the Romans. Here their great highways from the coast of the English Channel (La Manche) to the Rhine and from Trier (in today's Germany) to Italy met, their course marked by today's major shopping street, rue Serpenoise.

Today this port on the Moselle river 53 km (33 miles) north of Nancy via A 31 is an industrial town, but a less grim one than most of its northern neighbors. Metz's major attractions are churches, of which it boasts an inordinate number for its size, and museums.

Between 1871, when the Prussian armies invaded Lorraine, and the ejection of German troops in 1944, the townscape of Metz became increasingly defensive, monumental, and austere. Today, however, it is rich in promenades and renowned for the number and quality of its parks and gardens. Most of old Metz lies east of a spur of the Moselle river, arranging itself around the Cathédrale St-Etienne, one of the finest Gothic edifices in France, where you would do well to begin a tour of the city. (The classical 18th-century Hôtel de Ville is just opposite, across the Place d'Armes.)

THE CATHEDRALE ST-ETIENNE

The nave of St-Etienne soars highest in France after those of St-Pierre in Beauvais and Notre-Dame in Amiens. While the exterior is very richly detailed, it is the interior, with its stunning ensemble of **stained glass** ranging from the 13th and 14th centuries up to the 20th, including the Earthly Paradise series by Marc Chagall, that makes the church remarkable. Because of the glass, the cathedral has been nicknamed the Lantern of God. The building's curious design results from the 12th-century linking-together of two churches, Notre-Dame-la-Ronde and St-Etienne, across a tiny road. Most of old Metz lies east of a spur of the Moselle river, arranging itself (as is so often the case) around the cathedral. The regional tourism office is in front of the cathedral on the Place d'Armes.

THE MUSEUM COMPLEX

From the Place d'Armes on the east side of the cathedral, it's a short walk up rue Chanoine-Collin to an extraordinary grouping of historical buildings: a 17th-century Carmelite convent, a robust 15th-century cereal granary, and, in the basements, vestiges of the Roman thermal baths. The entirety comprises four worthwhile museums. Premier among them is the **Musée d'Art et d'Histoire**, a treasure trove of relics from archaeological digs in the region that have revealed the importance of this Gallo-Roman crossroads town, which became a center of culture under the Carolingians. Exhibits include evidence of the Romans' skill in engineering baths and sewers. The three other museums are **Beaux-Arts** (paintings, engravings, polychrome wood statues), a **military collection**, and a **natural-history-and-zoological collection**.

PORTE DES ALLEMANDS

The Porte des Allemands (Gate of the Germans) and a vestige of the ancient city wall are a pleasant stroll east of the Place d'Armes. Leave the southeast corner of the *place* and follow rue des Allemands to the great gate.

Actually, these are two gates: the 13th-century, double-towered *porte* with pepper-pot roofs on the city side, and the 15th-century crenellated towers facing into the countryside. They are joined by an arcaded gallery that spans the waters of the Seille. On the same street, the **Eglise St-Eucaire** is worth a short look for the enormous pillars in the nave.

THE ESPLANADE

Most of the green "heart" of Metz lies in the western half of town in the park-promenade known as the Esplanade, a rather long but pleasant stroll from the Place d'Armes. Depart the *place* to the south on rue Ambroise-Thomas and turn east into rue du Palais. In a short distance, turn south into the pedestrian area along rue des Clercs, which leads directly to the Esplanade.

In good weather stroll around the Esplanade (a park-promenade area), the adjoining Place de la République, and the banks of an offshoot of the Moselle river called **Lac des Cygnes** (Swan Lake), where, on Friday, Saturday, and Sunday evenings in summer a *son-et-lumière* performance is staged. The **Eglise St-Pierre-aux-Nonnains**, within the Esplanade off the boulevard Poincaré, is thought to be the oldest church in France. It was founded by Benedictines in the seventh century on the site of a fourth-century Roman edifice. Visiting the church usually requires the permission of the regional tourism office. Toward the end of August and beginning of September, singers and dancers in folk costumes and decorated carts march in the Fête de Mirabelle to celebrate the little plum from which the fiery liqueur is made.

STAYING AND DINING IN METZ

The treasures of Metz can be appreciated in a day trip from Nancy. If you decide to spend the night in town, however, there is no shortage of hotels. Perhaps the most atmospheric is the ▶ **Hôtel du Théâtre**, just back from the waters of the Moselle in Port St-Marcel. Within walking distance west of the cathedral, it has 31 rooms and four suites; there's parking right at hand. The restaurant, **Pont St-Michel**, has served traditional Lorraine dishes since 1649; Tel: 87-30-12-29. Other possibilities are the 112-room ▶ **Mercure Altéa St-Thiébault**, with its restaurant, **Les Quatre Saisons**; and the 75-room ▶ **Royal-Concorde**, with its restaurant, **Le Caveau**. At Rugy, 12 km (7½ miles) northeast of Metz via D 1, a 16th-century estate has been transformed into ▶ **La Bergerie**, a 42-room hotel and grill set on rolling lawns.

As for dining in Metz, **Des Roches**, at 29, rue des Roches (Tel: 87-74-06-51), is a pleasant restaurant near the cathedral; there's outdoor service in season. Also near the cathedral is the very traditional **La Ville de Lyon** nearby at 7, rue des Piques (Tel: 87-36-07-01). Try the crêpes suzette. **Maire**, on the very tip of the large Ile Chambière at 1, rue Pont des Morts (Tel: 87-32-43-12), also offers outdoor dining. It can be reached by walking about 15 minutes across the Moyen Pont (Middle Bridge), from which there is a good view of the

arms of the Moselle and its various islands. Farther out, on
the next island to the west, sits the restaurant **La Dinanderie**,
at 2, rue de Paris. Because of its distance from downtown, be
sure to make a reservation; Tel: 87-30-14-40.

Neither of the area's two most highly praised restaurants
is in the city proper, however. **Crinouc**, at 79, rue du
Général-Metman, 3 km (2 miles) east of Metz near the
suburb of Bellecroix, is renowned for its veal sweetbreads,
among other traditional dishes. Reserve; Tel: 87-74-12-46. **Le
Jardin de Bellevue**, also 3 km east of Metz but in the suburb
of Borny at 58, rue du Pange, serves smoked Scottish salmon
and lobster with oyster gratin (in season, November to
April). Reserve; Tel: 87-37-10-27.

Verdun

In 1916 Verdun, about 65 km (40 miles) due west of Metz on
D 903 (and 93 km/58 miles northwest of Nancy), was, along
with Toul, the most stubborn French stronghold. Its strategic
position had commanded battle lines since the days of the
Gauls and then the Romans, under whom it was called
Virodunum Castrum. To visit the sites where hundreds of
thousands of soldiers from both sides died in the epic struggle of World War I is to look back in sadness. That may be why,
as years pass and fewer of the dead remain living in memory,
fewer foreign visitors make this particular pilgrimage.

THE TOWN

The **Citadelle**, in the heart of town near the cathedral, was
the work of perhaps the most renowned military architect in
Europe since the days of the Romans, Sébastien le Prestre de
Vauban (1633–1707). In his characteristic star-within-a-star
design (the best example of which is in Lille), the Citadelle
sits atop the remains of a tenth-century abbey, houses a **war
museum**, and gives access to the famous tunnels that once
sheltered the defensive army. (For anyone who wishes to
survey the theater of combat from the air, Verdun's Aero-
Club de Rozelier organizes flights over the battlefields; inquire at the Office de Tourisme on Place Nation.)

The **Cathédrale Notre-Dame**, east of the Citadelle on the
town's highest point, was begun after a fire in 1048 wiped
out the existing church. Its most interesting aspects include
some Romanesque survivors of the World War I bombard-
ments, the cloister, and the Palais Episcopal, the 18th-century
bishop's residence.

The **Musée Municipal** occupies a part of the Hôtel de la
Princerie and devotes several rooms to collections from

prehistory; Greek, Roman, and Etruscan antiquities; evidences of the Gallo-Roman and Merovingian epochs; and
objects from medieval and Renaissance times.

THE COMBAT THEATER
AND MONUMENTS

Although decades have passed since the Great War and
memories of even greater struggles are fresher in American
and European minds, the scars of war remain on the land
outside Verdun.

The fierce Battle of Verdun (1916–1917) took place in
some parts of the city itself, but mostly along the right and
left banks of the Meuse along a front of more than 124
square miles. To inspect the sites in the most logical and
efficient fashion, pick up a map from the Office de Tourisme
in Place Nation on the right bank (east across town from the
cathedral) and leave town on N 3 to the east, following
avenue de la 42e-Division, then avenue du Maréchal-Joffre.
Drive from one site to another in a counterclockwise direction; the circuit is 21 km (13 miles).

The Right Bank

The right bank was known as the Red Zone of the long
battle, where its decisive decisions were made and actions
taken by both sides. Just beyond town is the **cemetery of
Faubourg-Pavé**; the body of an unknown soldier was taken
from one of the 5,000 tombs here to repose beneath the Arc
de Triomphe in Paris. From here, follow D 112 for 6 km (3½
miles) to the Maginot Monument, then D 913 and D 913ᴬ in
the direction of the **Fort de Vaux**. (A little bit off the road but
accessible by car, the **Monument des Fusillés de Tavannes**
honors soldiers killed by a firing squad on this spot in 1944.)

The fort at Vaux held out for almost three months against
the German onslaughts of 1916; more interesting than Vaux
is the nearby **Mémorial-Musée de la Bataille de Verdun**,
which illustrates the various phases of the battle.

Nearby are the ruins of the village of Fleury, which was
captured and recaptured 16 times during World War I. A
museum opening this year will present shows and exhibits
on the life (and death) of the region.

From Fleury, D 913ᴮ takes you to the **Fort de Douaumont**.
Return to D 913 toward the **Ossuaire de Douaumont**, the
most important World War I memorial in France, housing
the bones of some 130,000 French and German soldiers in a
vast necropolis. From here, take D 913 west across the river
in the direction of Charny.

The Left Bank

From Charny, continue in the direction of Chattancourt and the battlegrounds of the left bank of the Meuse. A short road leads north from D 38 at Chattancourt to the wooded summit known as **Le Mort-Homme**, where in March 1916 every one of the German assaults was beaten back. Next to a monument to the French 40th division, a sign on the pedestal of another monument reads, *"Ils n'ont pas passé"* ("They did not pass").

Returning to Chattancourt, turn west on D 38 and just beyond Esnes-en-Argonne take D 18 toward Montfaucon. In 2 km (1¼ miles), take the short marked cutoff to **La Cote 304**, where for more than 14 months the Germans hurled ferocious attacks, all of which were turned back at enormous cost.

Turning back to D 18, turn north and continue in the direction of **Montfaucon**, where, atop a butte, the First American Army under General Pershing beat back an offensive that lasted from September 26 to November 11, 1918. In the memorial commemorating the victory, a great staircase leads to a column 187 feet tall, topped by a statue of Liberty. Climb the 235 feet to the top for a spectacular look over the battlefields north of Verdun, the rolling hills along the Meuse, and the Ardennes Forest to the north in Luxembourg.

Back on D 18, drive north to **Romagne-sous-Montfaucon** and the American cemetery, about 37 km (23 miles) northwest of Verdun. Some visitors are deeply moved, others visibly shaken by the spot: 128 acres of shady lawns, a mirrorlike pool, and flowery terraces where lie, under 14,000 marble crosses, the remains of the American fallen.

Rather than retracing their route to Metz or Nancy, students of World War I may wish to drive along the Voie Sacrée, now the 43-km (27-mile) stretch of N 35 south from Verdun to Bar-le-Duc. This was the dangerous stretch of road along which supply convoys rolled night and day during the Battle of Verdun in 1916, supplying French defenders in spite of the constant threat—and reality—of death and destruction.

AVIOTH

About 40 km (25 miles) north of Verdun via country roads, near the Belgian border, you come upon the hamlet (100-odd inhabitants) of Avioth. More truthfully, you don't come upon it without some effort, since its name rarely appears except on large-scale regional maps. From Verdun, follow D 964 north to Stenay, angle east on D 947 to Montmédy, and pick up directional signs to Avioth, 8 km (5 miles) to the north of Montmédy on N 43 and D 110.

Those who persist in search of hidden treasures will be rewarded by a magnificent **basilica** founded in the 13th century, some 200 years after the discovery of a miraculous statue of the Virgin Mary at the site. Construction continued for another 200 years or so. Were the stones then as warm and golden in hue as they appear today? Who knows? Gilded in soft late-afternoon light, the 70 figures of the Passion seem harmonious and real, as if they had been frozen alive and preserved throughout time, the little angels sounding their trumpets down through the centuries.

STAYING AND DINING IN VERDUN AND AVIOTH

Verdun may well be explored in one long day out of Metz; otherwise, a good hotel choice is the ► **Hostellerie Coq Hardi**, well regarded for decades, with its excellent restaurant featuring regional specialties. Even if you don't spend the night, try the Coq for luncheon. Always reserve; Tel: 29-86-36-36.

A very pleasant place to stay in the country is ► **Hostellerie du Château des Monthairons**, in its own park 13 km (8 miles) south of Verdun on D 34. It offers nine reasonably priced rooms, three apartments, and a good kitchen with seasonal outdoor dining.

Visitors to the American monument and cemetery near Romagne-sous-Montfaucon can lunch nearby at the informal, pleasantly rustic **Auberge du Coq Gaulois** in the little town. Reserve in high season; Tel: 29-85-14-24.

An outstanding restaurant with 12 cozy rooms, ► **Lorraine et Restaurant Le Mas** is located in the small town of Longuyon, 30 km (19 miles) east of Avioth via N 43, and is a handy stop for visitors to the basilica. (It's 48 km/30 miles north of Verdun via N 18.) It's right across from the local railroad station. A hearty dish for chilly weather is pot-au-feu of foie gras with garlic purée; Tel: 82-26-50-07.

En Route to Alsace

Of the many roads that cross the Vosges from Lorraine to Alsace, the most rewarding for the first-time traveller who wants to sightsee along the way would be a combination of N 4 (Nancy to Lunéville), N 59 (Lunéville to Baccarat and St-Dié), and N 415 (St-Dié to Colmar over the Col du Bonhomme—at which crest you have entered Alsace—and through the villages of Lapoutroie and Kaysersberg).

LUNEVILLE

From Nancy to Lunéville (population: 23,231), a distance of about 30 km (19 miles), N 4 runs through the Lorraine plateau, nearly flat, fairly uninspiring country, skirting the Forêt de Vitrimont for the last few miles. Lunéville owes its 18th-century appearance—wide streets, the spacious Parc des Bosquets, many monuments—in large part to Léopold, duke of Lorraine, who liked to vacation here and, from 1702 to 1714, took it upon himself to mold the town into a minicapital. A great admirer of Louis XIV and of Versailles, he hired as architect one Germain Boffrand, a pupil of Mansart, to construct a modest (though hardly humble) replica of that imposing royal abode at the north edge of town.

The Lunéville Château

In the château and on its grounds Léopold staged dances, games, and theatrical extravaganzas that soon made Lunéville the social center for the nobility and its hangers-on.

Léopold was followed in his enthusiasm for Lunéville by Stanislas Leszczyński, who brought to his favorite residence artists and writers of distinction: Voltaire, Montesquieu, and the like. He also embellished the park and redecorated the château so that Lunéville gained the nickname Petit Versailles; he died there in 1766. Upon Stanislas's death the château became the property of the military; it was taken over by the city in 1936 after almost two centuries of inattention. Restoration began after World War II, and what we see today closely resembles what courtiers admired in the 18th century.

Of greatest interest within the château is the **Musée de Faïences**, of which there is an important collection, as well as calligraphy, Flemish painted leather hangings, and 19th-century paintings. In addition, an audiovisual display describes the works of Georges de La Tour, who painted in Lunéville in the 17th century; there's a cavalry exhibition here as well.

Some visitors may enjoy the **Musée de la Moto et du Vélo** (Motorbike and Bicycle Museum), which displays more than 200 models of two- and three-wheelers with and without motor dating from 1865—some of which are very rare and very curious. The museum is just west of the château on rue de la République. The **Eglise St-Jacques** on Place St-Rémy, a short walk south of the museum, is worth visiting for its fine Regency woodwork.

BACCARAT

The crystal factory in this small town, 25 km (16 miles) southeast of Lunéville on N 59, was established in 1764 and has been making news and quality glassware ever since. A visit to the **Musée du Cristal** makes the most nonacquisitive traveller acquisitive. Old and new pieces are on display, their production is extremely well documented, and a sales shop lies conveniently at hand, with prices somewhat lower than in shops elsewhere in France.

ST-DIE

St-Dié, 25 km (16 miles) southeast of Baccarat on N 59, in a little valley at the foot of pine-studded hills, grew up around a seventh-century Benedictine monastery and today calls itself, with some pride, the "birthplace of America." U.S. citizens aware of the association usually make their way to the **Bibliothèque Municipale**, near the cathedral, and its Gothic cloister and ask to be directed to the rare 16th-century book, *Cosmographiae Introductio,* a kind of early atlas. In the *Cosmographiae,* a work of Vosgian academics, credit is given to Amerigo Vespucci for the discovery of a new continent, and the word "America" is inscribed upon a map of it for the first time.

From St-Dié, you can choose to cross the Vosges via Ste-Marie-aux-Mines (a fine stepping-off place for hikers) to Sélestat or, on a more southerly course, via the Col du Bonhomme, Lapoutroie, and Kaysersberg to Colmar. In the first case, it's a 43-km (27-mile) drive on N 59. In the second, it's a 57-km (35-mile) wind along N 415 through forests of beech and conifers and past small, steely-gray lakes. The second route offers more dramatic sights.

STAYING AND DINING
IN EASTERN LORRAINE

The eight-room ▶ **Château d'Adomenil** is a gourmet retreat just 5 km (3 miles) southwest of **Lunéville** on D 914. Set in a pretty park with century-old trees, it's known for seafood and regional wines. Reserve; Tel: 83-74-04-81.

To get away from it all at a modest price, drive 19 km (12 miles) east of **St-Dié** to the ▶ **Auberge du Spitzemberg**, a hillside retreat of 11 rooms in the Vosges forest near Provenchères-sur-Fave. From St-Dié, it's a short, easterly swing on N 59, then north on N 159. The cooking is traditional, simple, and good.

Gérardmer

An alternate route to Colmar via the summer resort of
Gérardmer and its clear, mountain-edged lake is quite
scenic, winding over the Col de la Schlucht through some of
the prettiest Vosges countryside. If coming from St-Dié, take
N 415 and then D 8 for 27 km (17 miles) directly south.
Gérardmer (pronounced jay-rard-MAY) may be a good place
to stop for a few days: It is both a summer resort for water
sports, climbing, and hiking, and a ski center employing the
slopes of the Vosges. A tour of the lakeside can be made on
foot (6 km/3½ miles) or by car; motorboats, sailboats, and
pédalos (small crafts equipped with seats and pedals) are
available for rental.

Visitors in search of an idle idyll might settle down in ▶ **La
Réserve**, just off the gardened lakeside esplanade. The 24-
room inn boasts a one-star kitchen, and meals are served on
an outdoor terrace in season; a regional specialty is mountain ham in a cream–Alsatian wine sauce. Within walking
distance from the village center on the Place du Tilleul is the
61-room ▶ **Grand Hôtel Bragard**, with its own swimming
pool set in a private park.

Four kilometers (2½ miles) south of Gérardmer via D 486
in tiny Bas-Rupts, the chef-owned ▶ **Hostellerie Bas-Rupts**
attracts guests who enjoy walks in pine forests and fields
gilded with wildflowers. Try the duck *confit* in the Michelin-
starred restaurant. The chef is Sylvie Philippe, one of the few
woman members of the Jeunes Restaurateurs d'Europe.
There are 30 rooms in the inn and its Annexe Chalet Fleuri.

On the Sunday nearest April 20, Gérardmer stages its
Jonquil Festival, with various musical groups parading
through the beflowered town. A giant fireworks display
lights up the night and the lake in mid-August.

ALSACE

France's most distinctive and, to some eyes, most picturesque province is a green corridor 120 miles long and 32
miles wide wedged between Lorraine to the west, Germany
to the north and east, and Switzerland to the southeast.

A long history of independent kingdoms, duchies, and
other regional entities constitutes one of France's greatest
attractions: her deep and lasting variety. Within that diversity

Alsace seems still foreign, a land unto itself, with its own culture, cooking, architecture, tradition, even language.

Even more than Lorraine's, Alsace's history is one of turmoil and tempest between Germanic and Frankish peoples. Though Alsatians today are proudly French, their inheritance is strongly Germanic; witness the Alsatian dialect, which sounds something like Swiss-German and offends or amuses the ears of almost everyone who doesn't speak it. The name Alsace itself derives from *Illsass,* the dialect word meaning "country of the Ill river."

We begin our coverage of Alsace in Strasbourg, a fascinating, historic city and the principal gateway for trips in the region. One of the most scenic trips follows the Route du Vin, the 210-km (130-mile)-long road through wine-making villages that runs south from near Strasbourg to Thann, near Mulhouse and the Swiss border. We follow the wine route and the many side trips that can be taken off it, and end our coverage in the city of Colmar and the nearby Munster Valley.

ALSATIAN FOOD AND DRINK

There is an earthiness, a naturalness, a refreshing absence of vanity to eating and drinking in Alsace. That is not to say there is no haute cuisine to be found, however. In fact, **L'Auberge de l'Ill**, in Illhaeusern (reserve well in advance; Tel: 89-71-83-23), is considered by many epicures to be the finest restaurant in the country.

The province's specialties are soul- as well as stomach-satisfying: the irresistible *choucroute,* wine-cured sauerkraut buried under ham hocks, sausages, smoked bacon, pork slabs, and potatoes; the fatted goose that yields up its liver as foie gras, giving gastronomy *pâté de foie gras en croute;* roasted suckling pig; fried carp and game; *tarte à l'oignon; kugelhopf,* a large, breadlike cake resembling a Teuton prince's crown; *tuiles,* thin, delicate pastry sheets shaped like roof tiles; *tartes mirabelles,* employing a small, rosy plum; fir-tree honey; and creamy Munster cheese.

Vines have been cultivated in Alsace since A.D. 222. Unlike the standard procedure in Bordeaux, Burgundy, and elsewhere, wines here are labeled after the grape: Sylvaner, Pinot (*blanc* and *noir* and even *gris*), Riesling, Muscat, Traminer, Chasselas. Gewürztraminer means simply a spicy (*gewürz*) Traminer; Tokay d'Alsace is a Pinot Gris; a table wine of blended grapes is called Zwicker, and a Zwicker of blended fine grapes is Edelzwicker. The sparkling Crémant d'Alsace is made by the *méthode champenoise* from the Pinot Blanc or

Riesling grape. Rosé d'Alsace is rather well known, but Alsatian reds from Ottrott and Marlenheim are rare.

In 1975 legislation created the Grand Cru appellation in Alsace, and it has been awarded to 25 vineyards. In 1984 late-harvest wines—Vendanges Tardives—were recognized. Deep and rich in flavor, they are reminiscent of heavy Sauternes. Even rarer is the sweet Sélection des Grains Nobles, produced only in great years from individually selected grapes affected by "noble rot," the fungus mold *Botrytis cinerea,* which enhances their flavor. The *eaux-de-vie* (brandylike liqueurs) are forceful but refined. Best known are framboise (raspberry), mirabelle (plum), kirsch (cherry), and myrtille (blueberry). The Gilbert Miclo Distillery in Lapoutroie, on the route from St-Dié to Colmar, is one of the best. Kronenbourg, an Alsatian beer, is widely known and one of the best commercial brands.

Markets and Festivals in Alsace

Every day of the week except Sunday it's market day somewhere in Alsace: Wednesdays in Gérardmer; Fridays in Haguenau and Strasbourg; and Saturdays in Colmar, Mulhouse, Munster, Strasbourg, and Wissembourg.

Orbey's Fête de la Tarte au Fromage (Cheese Tart) takes place from late June to early July. Hoff's Fête du Fromage Blanc et des Traditions Rurales (White Cheese and Folklore) is held in August; Ribeauvillé's Foire aux Vins et Fête Folklorique in July; Thann's Fête de la Poitrine Farcie (Stuffed Veal Breast) in July; Haguenau's Fête du Houblon et Semaine Gastronomique (Hops Festival and Food Week) in August; Colmar's Foire aux Vins et Représentations Folkloriques in August; and Obernai's Fête des Vendanges (Grape Harvest) in October.

STRASBOURG

The capital of Alsace, seat of the Council of Europe since its foundation in 1949, and one of the three capitals of the European Parliament (the other two are Luxembourg and Brussels), Strasbourg is resolutely international and business-minded in outlook and focus. Strasbourg is the sixth-largest city in the country and the second-largest port on the Rhine (Rotterdam is the largest). Yet Strasbourgeois are also attached to their glorious past, evidence of which is what draws most visitors here. Strasbourg is 490 km (304 miles) east of Paris on A 4 (Autoroute de l'Est), 4½ hours from the capital by train.

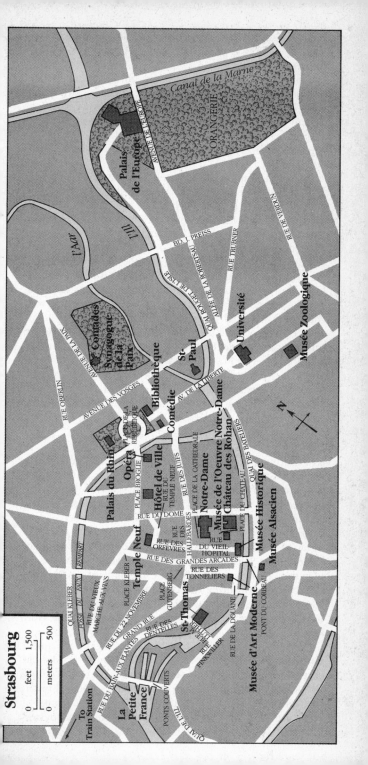

Strasbourg

0	feet	1,500
0	meters	500

To Train Station

La Petite France

RUE DU BAIN-AUX-PLANTES

PONTS COUVERTS

QUAI TURCKHEIM

RUE DES DENTELLES

GRAND RUE

RUE DU 22 NOVEMBRE

PLACE KLEBER

MARCHE AUX VINS

RUE DU VIEUX

FOSSE DU FAUX

QUAI KLEBER

REMPART

RUE OBERLIN

AVENUE DE LA PAIX

Comades

Synagogue de la Paix

AVENUE DES VOSGES

PLACE DE LA REPUBLIQUE

Palais du Rhin

Opéra

Bibliothèque

Comédie

St-Paul

Université

Musée Zoologique

RUE TRUBNER

RUE DE VERDUN

BD. J. PREISS

QUAI FOCH

ALLEE DE LA ROBERTSAU

AVENUE DE L'EUROPE

Palais de l'Europe

ORANGERIE

Canal de la Marne

l'Aar

l'Ill

AV. DE LA LIBERTE

QUAI DE L'ISLE

PLACE BROGLIE

Hôtel de Ville

RUE DU TEMPLE NEUF

RUE DES TUIFS

RUE DU DOME

PLACE DE LA CATHEDRALE

Notre-Dame

Musée de l'Oeuvre Notre-Dame

Château des Rohan

PLACE DU CHATEAU

QUAI DES BATELIERS

Musée Historique

Musée Alsacien

RUE DES HALLEBARDES

RUE DES ORFEVRES

Temple Neuf

RUE DES GRANDES ARCADES

RUE DU VIEIL-HOPITAL

RUE DES TONNELIERS

PLACE GUTENBERG

St-Thomas

RUE MARTIN LUTHER

RUE FINKWILLER

Musée d'Art Moderne

RUE DE LA DOUANE

PONT DU CORBEAU

QUAI DU

N

Visiting Strasbourg

The enormous public garage underneath Place Kléber is the best place to park while exploring the city, though the *place* itself is not particularly interesting. Walk from the *place* directly up rue des Grandes Arcades to Place de la Cathédrale, where you should begin a tour of the city. To return to your car from La Petite France, walk north on rue du Fossé des Tanneurs.

Offices de Tourisme are located near the train station and at 10, place Gutenberg, near the cathedral. (For the latter, Tel: 88-52-28-22.) Regularly scheduled boat sailings on the Ill depart the Palais Rohan, across the Place du Château from the cathedral, every half hour in summer, both day and night, and last 75 minutes or two hours (with meal service). Less frequent but longer sailings on the Rhine depart from the Promenade Dauphine on the Bassin Dusuzeau near the Place de l'Etoile. Except in midwinter, minitrains take visitors on a 45-minute tour that begins near the cathedral, with commentary in English, French, or German.

Strasbourg accords great importance to music, staging the **International Music Festival**, Europe's oldest, in June. In addition to enjoying concerts by the Strasbourg Philharmonic and the Percussions of Strasbourg, travellers may be seduced by performances by the Opera of the Rhine, Strasbourg National Theater, Rhine Ballet, Alsatian Theater, and the satirical cabaret Barabli.

History

Strataburgum, as its Roman name suggests, has been a European crossroads since its founding. Born in 10 B.C. as Argentoratum, the Roman stronghold that is now Strasbourg was renamed Strataburgum under Clovis, king of the Franks, and developed into a major crossroads of commerce, warfare, and Christianity. In the sixth century Scottish monks began to worship on the site of today's church of St-Thomas, where Albert Schweitzer once served as an organist.

In the 11th century Strasbourg came under the rule of the Hapsburgs, and during the Crusades Frederick Barbarossa had many fortresses and convents built in the region; in 1201 Strasbourg was sanctioned as a free city of the Holy Roman Empire.

From 1336 onward the privilege of staging an annual European fair was granted to Strasbourg, and it is still held here, during the first half of September. The 14th century also saw the city's emergence as a center of Rhenish mysticism and then, in the 15th and 16th centuries, as a capital of humanism and Protestantism. Johann Gutenberg perfected the printing press in Strasbourg between 1434 and 1444. A statue of him commands today's Place Gutenberg; the American Declaration of Independence is for some reason engraved on its pedestal.

In 1681 Louis XIV brought Strasbourg under French rule; in 1871 it was ceded to Germany, but in 1919 it again became French; in 1940 the Germans claimed it, and they held it until 1944, when it was once again declared part of France.

Old Strasbourg

The heart of old Strasbourg is an egg-shaped parcel of land cradled within the arms of the Ill river and its canals. At its western end, the quais, canals, and half-timbered houses of the old quarter of La Petite France doze in a picturesque haze of nostalgia, while in the east, beyond the Place Broglie, the Théâtre Municipal (seat of the Opéra du Rhin), and the Hôtel de Ville, bridges link the old city to the Germanic 19th century across the river.

Inside the oval, most major attractions are within ambling distance of one another: Place Kléber, somewhat off-center to the west; the Cathédrale Notre-Dame and a cluster of museums to the southeast, right off the river; and several worthwhile churches in the western half of the city.

THE CATHEDRAL QUARTER

The **Cathédrale Notre-Dame** will stop zealous cathedral visitors in their tracks. Begun in the Romanesque style in 1015 on the site of a temple to Hercules, it was not declared finished until 1439, by which time it had become mostly— and superbly—Gothic.

The Cathédrale Notre-Dame faces the Place de la Cathédrale, with the Place du Château on its south flank, in the southeastern quarter of the ancient heart of the city. It is the natural place to begin a tour of the town, most of which may be seen on foot.

Strasbourg's life has been intimately entwined with that of its cathedral. Martin Luther's 95 theses were posted here as well as on the church door in Wittenberg, Germany, and during the ensuing Reformation (1520–1689), Strasbourg became a center of the Protestant movement; Protestants and Catholics battled beneath the 14th-century Wise and Foolish Virgins sculpted on the church's right-hand portal. Only in 1681, when the city was seized by Louis XIV, was its cathedral returned to Catholicism.

It was here, in 1725, that Louis XV married Marie Leszczyńska, and here, too, in 1770, that Marie Antoinette arrived from Vienna en route to her marriage to the future Louis XVI. At the same time a university student named Johann Wolfgang von Goethe was climbing to the top of the tower and looking woozily into space in an attempt to cure his dizzy spells.

In addition to its famous spire and façade, Notre-Dame's treasures include 12th- to 14th-century stained glass windows (the finest were removed, piece by piece, during World War II, and found afterward buried in salt mines in Wurtemberg), the pulpit in Flamboyant Gothic style, the 17th-century tapestries, and the **astronomical clock**. The clock runs slow by half an hour and now goes through its daily noon celebrations at 12:30 P.M. Crowds assemble to watch at least half an hour in advance.

A *son-et-lumière* production in the cathedral illustrates Strasbourg's two thousand years of history every night except certain annual holidays; the program is given in German at 8:15 P.M. and in French at 9:15 P.M.

Museums Near the Cathedral

The **Musée de l'Oeuvre Notre-Dame**, across the leafy Place du Château from the cathedral, is devoted to Alsatian arts from the Middle Ages and Renaissance, original sculptures from the cathedral (because of weather damage, many of the pink sandstone figures have had to be replaced), Roman and pre-Roman sculptures, and paintings of the Alsatian school. The most celebrated item is a head of Christ, the oldest figure known in stained glass (1070).

The **Palais Rohan**, constructed in 1704 for Cardinal Armand de Rohan-Soubise, bishop of Strasbourg, is also on the Place du Château, just south of the cathedral. It now houses the Musée des Beaux-Arts, the Musée Archéologique, and the Musée des Arts Décoratifs. Renaissance painters and primitives of the Italian school are particularly well represented in the **Musée des Beaux-Arts**, with less emphasis on the Spanish (aside from a wonderful El Greco Virgin) and the Dutch-Flemish (but one superb Pieter de Hooch). The collection of still lifes is highly touted. The **Musée Archéologique** devotes itself largely to prehistoric discoveries made in Alsace but also has fine displays of Roman and Merovingian relics. The finest grouping of ceramics in France is on show at the **Musée des Arts Décoratifs**, including fine faïence from 18th-century Strasbourg, the best of which comes from the famous "blue" period. In addition to the museums, the château houses a stamp-and-art library.

South of Notre-Dame, on the north bank of the Ill, the **Musée Historique** (in the 16th-century slaughterhouse) and the **Musée d'Art Moderne** (in the reconstructed custom-house) face each other across the bustling rue des Grandes Arcades. The former is fascinating to visitors interested in arms, armory, uniforms, and other trappings of war; the latter to enthusiasts of modern French painting, including works by Jean Arp, a Strasbourgeois, and stained glass by such craftsmen as Jean Lurçat.

Across the Ill via the Pont du Corbeau, a pleasant bridge from which, in the Middle Ages, child murderers and parricides were suspended in iron cages until they drowned, is the **Musée Alsacien**, at 23, quai St-Nicolas. Occupying three adjoining 16th- and 17th-century houses, it displays to perfection the Alsatian past in costumes, bedchambers, and kitchens—all the essentials of everyday life.

LA PETITE FRANCE

Once upon a time tanners, fishermen, and millers made this quarter in the western part of the old town their own. Now, with its narrow streets that wind along the Ill and its canals lined by beautiful 16th- and 17th-century half-timbered houses, La Petite France is the most picturesque part of Strasbourg. The excellent restaurants and small art and gift shops of the district attract a sizable permanent population as well as a touristic one.

The "main" street of this quarter is the rue du Bain-aux-Plantes, but all are worth strolling. Arguably, the most picturesque walk in the quarter takes you across the Ill and what remains of the ancient ramparts on the **Ponts Couverts**, three bridges, each topped with a 14th-century tower. There are two long, absorbing routes from the Cathédrale Notre-Dame into La Petite France. The first follows rue de la Mercière west from Place de la Cathédrale (the 13th-century **Pharmacie du Cerf**, at the beginning of the street, is thought to be the oldest pharmacy in France) to Place Gutenberg. (Stop to inspect the statue of Johannes Gutenberg, who refined his world-altering invention, the movable-type press, in Strasbourg.)

From Place Gutenberg, continue west along rue Gutenberg and then Grand'Rue, lined with pastry and clothing shops. Turn south at rue du Fossé des Tanneurs into La Petite France.

You can also walk west along the quais on the south banks of the Ill to the Pont St-Martin, where you turn north to rue des Dentelles and follow it into La Petite France. (At rue Martin-Luther, detour north a block to the Protestant **Eglise St-Thomas**, which houses the marvelously sculpted tomb of the Maréchal de Saxe; Albert Schweitzer is said to have played the organ here.)

New Strasbourg

Begin a walk through this handsome, sprawling part of town in Place Broglie, north from the cathedral via rue du Dôme and east of Place Kléber along the bustling rue de la Mésange.

Place Broglie, a long rectangle lined by trees in stiff, paradelike rows, was laid out in 1742 by the Maréchal de Broglie, governor of Alsace. The handsome 18th-century **Hôtel de Ville**, former mansion of the counts of Hanau-Lichtenberg and then of the landgraves of Hesse-Darmstadt, graces the south side of the square. The **Opéra du Rhin** is at the east end of the square; next to it is the **Hôtel de Klinglin**, with its magnificent 18th-century façade.

The bridge behind the Klinglin crosses the canal (Fossé du Faux Rempart) to the Place de la République and the 19th-century world of "new" Strasbourg.

Beginning in about 1870, the Germans erected grand public buildings in an attempt to create a modern city center: bold, audacious, and—inevitably—Prussian. **Place de la République** is a vast square with a beautiful central circular garden. To the north of the *place* stands the Palais du Rhin; to the south, the Théâtre National de Strasbourg (home of the Comédie de l'Est) and the Bibliothèque Nationale. To the north, avenue de la Paix leads to the Synagogue de la Paix and to a park known as Les Contades, where free concerts by the Strasbourg music society are held weekly from May to September.

THE UNIVERSITY

From Place de la République, avenue de la Liberté leads a few blocks east to the Pont de l'Université over the confluence of the rivers Aar and Ill to **Place de l'Université**, with its terraces, gardens, fountains, and a statue of Goethe; the Protestant **Eglise St-Paul** casts its Neo-Gothic silhouette upon the waters. Strasbourg's vitality stems in great part from its university, since its founding in the 17th century one of the foremost in France. Perhaps among its 35,000 students today there is another Goethe, a Napoléon, or a Metternich. The imposing building dominating the Place de l'Université is the Palais Universitaire, another bow to 19th-century strictness, somewhat softened by a dash of Italian Renaissance. Most of the university buildings stretch to the southeast.

From the *place,* you may follow allée de la Robertsau, lined by aristocratic houses, or quai Rouget de l'Isle several blocks to the **Orangerie**. Laid out by the architect André Le Nôtre in 1692, these formal gardens were reworked in 1804 for a visit by Empress Joséphine. The **Palais de l'Europe**, home to both the Council of Europe (21 member states) and the European Parliament (434 members representing more than 270 million people), is at the eastern edge of the Orangerie. Guided tours are available.

SHOPPING IN STRASBOURG

The winding streets to the northwest of Notre-Dame are chic shopping country; Strasbourg is one of the smartest of French cities as far as style is concerned. Particularly attractive are the rue des Hallebardes, rue du Dôme, and rue des Orfèvres, this last gaily decorated with banners representing the cities and regions of Alsace. Specially packaged gastronomic souvenirs—foie gras, sausages, *choucroute,* cheeses, mustards, honey, chocolates, wines, and liqueurs—are found in rich plenty at places on the rue des Orfèvres.

On rue de la Mercière near the cathedral, **Villeroy & Boch** sells smart tableware, including services featuring the Alsatian figures of the famous caricaturist, Hansi. A flea market is held Wednesdays and Saturdays just off rue de la Mercière on rue du Vieil-Hôpital. Shops, touristic and otherwise, line the arcades around the Place Kléber, including a branch of the popular London department store **Marks and Spencer**.

DINING IN STRASBOURG

Just a few steps east of the Place Kléber at 10, rue de l'Outre is **Le Crocodile**, considered by gourmets to be the best restaurant in Strasbourg and, indeed, one of the best in France. Chef-owner Emile Jung presents seasonal cuisine in a most refined setting. Try the saddle of venison St-Hubert (June to January). Reservations are always necessary; Tel: 88-32-13-02.

Also a short walk away, to the north, is **Valentin Sorg**, on the 14th floor of a rather off-putting skyscraper at 6, place de l'Homme-de-Fer. Valentin Sorg has been well regarded locally for decades for its classic dishes and panoramic views. Tel: 88-32-12-16.

One of the city's best classic restaurants, **Julien**, is at number 22, quai des Bateliers. Reserve; Tel: 88-36-01-54.

Around the Cathedral

Good restaurants in varying degrees of informality cluster near the cathedral, of which **Maison Kammerzell–Hôtel Baumann** (built between 1467 and 1589) is the best known, largely because of its stunning woodwork. It is a fine place in which to sample regional specialties (reserve; Tel: 88-32-42-

14). Old Alsatian decor and quiet characterize **Zimmer**, a perennial favorite with the Strasbourgeois that is located at 8, rue du Temple Neuf (Tel: 88-32-35-01).

Winstubs, historic, informal places suited to settling the world's problems over long lunches of traditional fare, also abound in the cathedral quarter. The best are **Zum Strissel**, 5, place de la Grande-Boucherie; **Tire-Bouchon**, 5, rue des Tailleurs-de-Pierres; and **Au Pigeon**, 23, rue des Tonneliers, an amiably rustic spot that has been in business since the Middle Ages.

Three top *winstubs* that cater more to tourists are the brasserie-like **Le Dauphin**, right across from Notre-Dame; **Aux Armes de Strasbourg**, 9, Place Gutenberg, with the best French fries in town; and **L'Ancienne Douane**, 12, rue de la Douane, which has a terrace overlooking the Ill. (*Winstubs* and *bierstubs* are alike in their informality, simplicity of traditional fare served, and coziness in cold weather. Originally, as their names imply, *winstubs* were directly in or connected to individual wineries, while *bierstubs* bore the same relationship to breweries. Today they usually have no physical relationship to a production site but may serve chiefly one brand of drink.)

Of the many *bierstubs,* among the best is **Les Douze Apôtres** on rue de la Mercière (the short street that leads directly to the cathedral from Place Gutenberg), where special brews from around the world are served. The same street also boasts the city's most elegant *salon de thé,* **Christian**.

La Petite France

Some of the most atmospheric dining in Strasbourg is to be enjoyed in this old quarter on the river Ill.

La Maison des Tanneurs, in perhaps the prettiest old house in La Petite France at 42, rue du Bain-aux-Plantes, offers a warm welcome and excellent regional cooking, including *choucroute au Champagne* (reserve; Tel: 88-32-79-70).

L'Ami Schutz, at 1, rue des Ponts Couverts (Tel: 88-32-76-98), is a good, informal *bierstub-winstub.* Of the several other welcoming retreats in the neighborhood, the most attractive, because of its curious *orgue de Barbarie* (an antique player piano), is **Lohkäs**, at 25, rue du Bain-aux-Plantes (Tel: 88-32-05-26). Students in winter and tourists in summer pack the four-story restaurant **Au Pont St-Martin** (13, rue des Moulins; Tel: 88-32-45-13) to enjoy the large terrace and panoramic view.

Behind the Ponts Couverts a *péniche* (moored barge) serves as a floating disco known as **La Péniche–Le Fantasc** (Tel: 88-36-22-90), which draws an older crowd than **Rocks**, a bar-club-disco a ten-minute walk north at 56, rue du Jeu-des-Enfants; Tel: 88-32-31-22.

A walk through the Orangerie is preparation for a meal at **Buerehiesel** (reserve; Tel: 88-61-62-24), where chef Antoine Westermann serves highly rated cuisine in a rustic, tradi-tional Alsatian house beautifully sited right in the park. Westermann ranks among the Maîtres Cuisiniers (Master Chefs) de France, as does his colleague Jung at the aforemen-tioned Le Crocodile.

STAYING IN AND AROUND STRASBOURG

Just off Place Kléber on rue des Francs-Bourgeois, the ▶ Hô-tel Maison Rouge bears the mantle of one of France's classic turn-of-the-century grand hotels that was torn down in pre–World War II days and rebuilt on a smaller scale in a location near the original. It also inherited many of the Belle Epoque furnishings and artworks. To that collection modern facilities and a sense of color and light have been added. There are 140 guest rooms and the informal café **Le Caveau**; meals also may be taken at the aforementioned L'Ancienne Douane, the town's oldest brasserie, a short walk away.

West of Place Kléber on rue du Vieux-Marché-aux-Vins near an arm of the canal, the ▶ **Relais de Strasbourg** has 72 rooms but no restaurant.

Just off the Place de la Cathédrale, the ▶ **Hôtel des Rohan** offers 36 stylish rooms furnished in Louis XV fashion or regional rustic decor, but with up-to-date conveniences. If you're bothered by street noise, ask for a room at the back. Right on the *place,* at number 12, the ▶ **Cathédrale** occu-pies a recently restored Alsatian mansion. The 28 guest rooms are tastefully appointed in contemporary fashion. Recently, owner Guy-Pierre Baumann installed nine guest rooms to the noted restaurant Maison Kammerzell near the cathedral, changing the name of the establishment to ▶ **Mai-son Kammerzell–Hôtel Baumann**. In striking modern con-trast to the antique restaurant, the rooms overlook the cathedral square and old city streets.

▶ **Europe** is a 60-room charmer in the heart of La Petite France on rue du Fossés-des-Tanneurs. The ancient half-timbered house has been completely renovated; no restau-rant.

The ▶ **Hôtel Terminus-Plaza**, right across from the rail-way station at 10, place de la Gare, is the choice of travellers who like their inns elegantly turned out in the Old World manner yet unpretentious and welcoming. It has 68 rooms and the popular Brasserie for meals. ▶ **Monopole-Métro-**

pole, also convenient to the railway station, on rue Kuhn, is a traditional family inn decorated in typical Alsatian decor. The 94 rooms are furnished with antiques; there is no restaurant.

The 36-room ▶ **Régent-Contades** enjoys an unusual location near the Place de la République on the bank of the Ill at 8, avenue de la Liberté. Housed in a distinctive old mansion, it offers a sauna, solarium, Jacuzzi-type baths, and 24-hour room service; there are a breakfast room and bar, but no restaurant. In a quiet neighborhood south of the Ill, the 32-room ▶ **Hôtel du Dragon** occupies a 17th-century house, now determinedly contemporary in decor. There is no restaurant, but breakfast is served in the pretty Café Coste.

The pleasant suburb of **La Wantzenau,** 12 km (7½ miles) north of Strasbourg via Route de la Bischwiller (D 468), has long been popular with travellers seeking a quiet retreat near, but not in, the city proper. ▶ **Le Moulin de La Wantzenau,** in an old mill on the banks of the river Ill, offers its guests serenity and a pretty garden. There are 20 rooms and a salon with a fireplace and easy chairs that invite settling down with a book from the inn's library. Golf can be arranged on La Wantzenau's 18-hole course. The restaurant, **Au Moulin,** is across the street and independently run by chef Philippe Clauss, a member of the Jeunes Restaurateurs de l'Europe; Tel: 88-96-20-01. Not far away is the ▶ **Relais de la Poste,** a handsome half-timbered house with 19 rooms. Its restaurant lures many Strasbourgeois on pleasant afternoons.

Visitors to Strasbourg often choose to stay in the bucolic village of Obernai or other villages on the Route du Vin (see below). Obernai is just 31 km (19 miles) to the southwest via D 392, N 422, and D 426.

La Route du Vin

A drive down the 130-mile so-called Wine Road from **Marlenheim** in the north (due west of Strasbourg) to **Thann** in the south ranks among the most intriguing excursions in Europe. People have been known to do it in one day, but they can't have been satisfied with that. Three days should be the minimum. Altogether, the Route du Vin covers eight different roads, but because of very clear signposting it is not difficult to follow. You begin at Marlenheim on D 422 and for the longest portion of the route, from Rosheim to Kaysersberg, you follow D 35. Leaving Strasbourg on N 4 to the west, in 20 km (12 miles) you will reach Marlenheim and the beginning of the route.

Every twist and turn of the road seems to demand a stop to

photograph hill-climbing vineyards, Renaissance town halls and oriels, busy markets, medieval walls, châteaux in ruins and various states of disrepair, Romanesque clock towers, Gothic churches, streets dressed in brilliant flowers, folk festivals, and shop windows full of good things to eat and drink.

There are 46 villages and one city, Colmar, along the Route du Vin; all are glorious to drive through. In addition, six inviting side trips lead off the route; we cover the route itself first, north to south, then describe the side trips and Colmar at the end of our Route du Vin coverage. (We strongly recommend you pick up a map of the Route du Vin at one of the Offices de Tourisme in Strasbourg.)

Marlenheim to Obernai

From the beginning of the route in Marlenheim, it's a skip of 1½ km (1 mile) to pretty **Wangen**, where on the Sunday after July 3 the city fountain runs with wine. In **Molsheim**, 14 km (8½ miles) south of Marlenheim, photographers and enthusiasts of architecture will want to follow the *Centre Ville* signs to the Place de l'Hôtel de Ville to admire La Metzig, a graceful, highly ornamented Renaissance edifice that personifies Alsatian style.

Ottrott, 18 km (11 miles) south of Molsheim on D 422, then D 35, a wide spot in the route, boasts a surprising collection of gracious inns (see "Staying and Dining" at the end of the Route du Vin coverage). (From Ottrott, you can also make a circular, 8-km/5-mile excursion to Mont-Ste-Odile on D 109; see below.) The route leads east from Ottrott 4 km (2½ miles) to **Obernai**, a delicious old town whose sinuous streets curl around the Place du Marché.

Obernai boasts as many handsome half-timbered houses as do the smaller villages, and, in the seventh century, was the birthplace of Saint Odile, patron saint of Alsace. Look for the traditional pottery, glassware, and wooden handicrafts of Alsace at **Dietrich's**, on the attractive Place du Marché.

Barr to St-Hippolyte

Wine enthusiasts will want to stop 8 km (5 miles) south of Obernai (on D 35) in **Barr** to taste and buy at prestigious Maison Willm (Klevner de Heiligenstein from the rare Sauvignon Rosé grape is a tasty novelty). The 18th-century town house known as the **Folie Marco** today houses a museum of 17th- to 19th-century furniture, faïence, porcelain, and pewter. (Barr is a good place from which to make a round-trip side trip into the beautiful forest country of the Hohwald; see below.)

Only 2 km (1¼ miles) farther along the route is little

Mittelbergheim, with its pretty Renaissance houses and vineyards coming almost into town. Vines have been cultivated here, it is said, since Roman days.

Dambach-la-Ville, about 11 km (7 miles) south of Mittelbergheim, retains its old ramparts and handsome half-timbered houses in the city center. (Dambach is the easiest village from which to make an excursion to the remarkable abbey of Ebersmunster; see below.)

The next natural stopping place is **St-Hippolyte**, 14 km (8½ miles) south of Dambach. (From St-Hippolyte, it's easy to make side trips to both the castle of Haut Koenigsbourg and the classic town of Sélestat; see below.)

Ribeauvillé

Ribeauvillé, 7 km (4 miles) south of St-Hippolyte, is generally considered to be among the most picturesque of the villages along the Route du Vin. It is also the home of the prestigious 150-year-old **Manufacture d'Impression sur Etoffes**, a textile firm that has printed fabrics for the Galeries Lafayette department-store chain and specialized boutiques in France, as well as for Neiman-Marcus, Bergdorf Goodman, and Bullocks Wilshire. Their tablecloths and napkins are extremely well priced at the factory outlet store; walk down Grand'Rue past the 13th-century Tour des Bouchers and go a few hundred feet toward Ste-Marie-aux-Mines. Don't leave Ribeauvillé without stopping at the tasting rooms of **F. E. Trimbach**, one of the best producers of Rieslings.

From Riquewihr to Kaysersberg

Riquewihr, just 4½ km (3 miles) south of Ribeauvillé, would be the most provocative village along the route were it not for the horrendous crowds that throng through the tiny, irresistibly picturesque streets. **Dopff "Au Moulin,"** one of the finest houses in Alsace, is here; ask to try (and buy) the late-harvest wines.

In the short 14½-km (9-mile) distance between Riquewihr and Kaysersberg, the next important stop, the flowery villages follow one another like blossoms on a lei: Beblenheim (one home of the rare Tokay d'Alsace), Mittelwihr (especially known for Gewürztraminers), Bennwihr, Sigolsheim, and Kientzheim.

Kaysersberg is the perfect medieval vineyard town, just as attractive and photogenic as the tinier villages but big enough to allow the crowds to disperse. This was the birthplace in 1875 of Albert Schweitzer, theologian, philosopher, musician, physician, missionary in Africa. His birthplace, at

124, rue du Général-de-Gaulle, at the western end of the town's main street, is now an interesting cultural center.

A clear stream called the Weiss curves through the town, crossed near the Schweitzer house by a fortified, crenellated bridge between old houses—a site that stops photographers in their tracks. A fine place to try wines is *chez* **Madame Théo Faller et Ses Filles** (consider the Tokay–Pinot Gris). The route continues from Kaysersberg through **Niedermorschwihr**, where many beautiful houses line the main street, and in just 3 km (2 miles) comes to Turckheim.

Turckheim to Thann
Tradition lives in **Turckheim**, just west of Colmar, where at 10:00 on summer evenings the last night watchman extant in Alsace passes through quiet streets in his greatcoat, carrying halberd, lamp, and trumpet and calling out the hour and "All's well." The city of Colmar (see below) is just 5½ km (3½ miles) east on D 417, but the Route du Vin continues southeast to **Eguisheim**, about 3 km (2 miles). This is one of the underrated, still-medieval towns along the route, complete with cobbled streets, squares, wooden oriels, half-timbered houses, Renaissance fountains, outside staircases, and tiny wall niches. For a taste of the local wine you should stop at **Léon Beyer**, family-owned vineyards since 1880; standouts are the Cuvée des Comtes Gewürztraminer and Cuvée des Ecaillers Riesling.

From Eguisheim the road leads through several more villages before arriving, after about 30 km (19 miles), in **Thann**, the final stop on the Route du Vin. Thann is a place of ancient legends that boasts the second-largest church in Alsace after Strasbourg (and the most beautiful, say the locals): **Collégiale St-Thiébaut**, with a remarkable portal on its west façade, superbly carved choir stalls, and stained glass windows from the 15th century.

Side Trips off the Route du Vin

MONT STE-ODILE
Something about the deep green, worn old Vosges inspires brooding, and a good place to indulge in that lonesome mood is this 2,500-foot mount dedicated to the patron saint of Alsace. When you leave Ottrott to the west on D 426, the round trip up the mountain and back is about 15 km (9 miles). Ste-Odile and its convent, restored many times over the centuries, are well worth the journey.

The setting is a fine one for the telling of the tale of Odile, a blind and weak child born in the seventh century in the village of Obernai just down the hill. She was the daughter of the sullen and loathsome Duke Adalric, a.k.a. Etichon, who, because of Odile's miserable condition and because she was, in any case, a girl, ordered her put to death.

The story twists and turns like today's road up the mountain. Suffice it to say the wicked Etichon lost in the war of life; Odile won and founded a convent in her father's château, Hohenbourg. She also established the nearby abbey of Niedermunster, which served after her death and throughout the Middle Ages as a great pilgrimage site. In the 16th century a fire destroyed most of the ancient structures in the area; these were replaced in the 17th century, but an 11th-century chapel survived, and there the ashes of Etichon remain; those of Odile repose in an eighth-century stone sarcophagus next door.

The Convent

The convent complex atop the mount is built around a quiet court dominated by linden trees. It consists of the convent building; the convent church, reconstructed after a fire in the 18th century; and the Chapelle de la Croix (Chapel of the Cross), the oldest part of the complex, dating from the 11th century and housing a sarcophagus with the ashes of Etichon. Through a low door covered with Carolingian sculptures, you enter the little Chapelle de Ste-Odile, raised in the 12th century over the site where the saint is thought to have died, to shelter her eighth-century stone sarcophagus.

Off the terrace, with its wide views over the plain of Alsace and the Black Forest in Germany, are two more chapels, the Chapelle des Larmes (Chapel of Tears), with a paving stone where Odile is believed to have knelt for daily prayers, and the Chapelle des Anges (Chapel of Angels), with a beautiful modern mosaic (1947). It is said a young woman who walks around its nave nine times will find a husband within a year.

The Pagan Wall

About half an hour's walk to the south of the convent of Ste-Odile (a marked path leads the way), the so-called Pagan Wall (Mur Païen) curves through the forests. This wall of immense stone blocks once must have belted a camp, a fortification of some sort, in the days before French memory. Was it Gallic? Was it Celtic? Nobody knows, but it makes the Roman road nearby look positively new. You can

also drive to the wall on D 33, past the Fountain of Saint
Odile (Fontaine de Ste-Odile), where pilgrims to the Mont
once washed their sore eyes.

INTO THE HOHWALD

From Barr, you may want to leave the Route du Vin for a trip
into this intensely rural region of shadowy forests, vineyards,
and charming villages. Depart south on GR 5 and D 62 toward
Andlau, then follow D 425. The circuit of the area is about 102
km (63 miles) and should take most of a lovely day. The
Hohwald offers small inns and restaurants, hiking trails,
creeks, streams, and hidden corners in which to picnic.

ABBAYE D'EBERSMUNSTER

Dambach is the best place from which to approach Ebersmunster; follow D 210 east toward Ebersheim on N 83, drive
north 1 km (½ mile) on N 83, and follow the marked turnoff
east on D 210 again to the abbey. It's a total drive of only 9
km (5½ miles).

Only in the Swiss Vorarlberg will you find Baroque abbeys comparable to Ebersmunster's. This burst of Baroque
exuberance was associated with the Counter-Reformation
and the desire of Catholic crusaders to move the Church
away from the Gothic style, which had begun to seem
barbaric. Here is richness that stops short of excess, embod-
ied in a magnificence of gold leaf, stucco ornamentation, a
sumptuous high altar, frescoes and paintings in glowing
pastels, floral abstractions, garlands and sculptures, and angels as plump as Italian *putti*. The woodwork is remarkable
as well, particularly in the choir stalls and in a pulpit supported by Samson, his brow wrinkled with effort. The superb organ is the 18th-century creation of André Silbermann; concerts in May show it off.

The history of Ebersmunster, which today has fewer than
500 inhabitants, is as old as that of Christianity in Alsace and
edges back into legend. Etichon, the father of Saint Odile, is
said to have constructed an abbey here, perhaps to atone for
his meanness.

HAUT-KOENIGSBOURG

The restored feudal castle in Haut-Koenigsbourg, considered to be the most important in the Vosges, was raised in
the first part of the 12th century by the German princely
family of Hohenstaufen and after a hectic history was burned

down by Swedish invaders in 1633 during the Thirty Years'
War. Today it provides some observers with grounds for the
argument that ruins can be more satisfying than restorations.

From St-Hippolyte, take D 1[B1] west and wind upward to
the château; it's only 6½ km (4 miles). (There is an uphill
walk of several minutes from the parking lot.)

Haut-Koenigsbourg is the very model of a *château-fort,*
that stronghold intended for defense rather than for gracious living. After its immolation in 1635, the decaying pile
of stones became the property of the nearby town of Sélestat
in 1865, still a decaying pile of stones. In a curious political
twist, it was restored by German emperor Wilhelm II and a
self-taught architect named Bodo Ebhardt, who turned it
into an idealized example of Romantic German glory. The
inscription on the mantelpiece in the Great Hall reads, "I did
not want this." Supposedly, it was written by a regretful
Wilhelm II.

Sélestat

From Haut-Koenigsbourg you may choose to continue on to
this town 10½ km (6½ miles) east on D 159. In the late
Middle Ages, Sélestat was a spiritual center, a capital of
Humanism in Alsace, for since the 15th century it had
boasted a Latin school famous throughout Europe. Even
Erasmus of Rotterdam, the greatest philosopher of his time,
came here to teach. Today a thriving industrial city, Sélestat
retains in its heart a prosperous, peaceful, medieval appearance.

Bibliophiles are drawn to Sélestat because of its **Bibliothèque Humaniste** (Humanist Library), one of the great
cultural treasures of Alsace. At its core is the private collection of local Humanist scholar Beatus Rhenanus, who bequeathed it to the town upon his death in 1547. It is installed
in the former Halle aux Blés (Corn Hall) in the north-central
part of town on rue de la Bibliothèque, a few steps west of
the Gothic Eglise St-Georges. Mérovingian and Carolingian
manuscripts, a Book of Miracles of Ste-Foy (12th century),
some charters of Charlemagne: These are among its written
masterpieces whose value is beyond calculation. There are
other wonders, too: medieval woodcarvings, altarpieces, jewels, vases, and faïence.

Some of Alsace's treasures may be tasted in town, too, at
Restaurant Jean-Frédéric Edel, 7, rue des Serruriers. From
the "back" of the Bibliothèque on Place Gambetta, turn left
and you'll be on Serruriers. Seafoods are a specialty, enjoyed
by a blazing fire in winter, on a terrace in summer; Tel: 88-
92-86-55.

MURBACH

"Proud as the dog of Murbach" was a saying understood for the thousand years that the **Eglise Murbach**, bearing upon its coat of arms a silver greyhound, reigned over the region of Guebwiller and enjoyed the protection of Charlemagne and the Holy Roman Empire. The church is 5½ km (3½ miles) west of Guebwiller. Take D 430 to Buhl, then tiny D 40[11] to Murbach.

Proud indeed. Founded, according to legend, by Saint Pirmin in 727, it was the repository of the riches of one of the great lords of the day, Count Eberhard of Eguisheim. Murbach's monks were knights; its armies looted and raided and exacted tribute in good feudal tradition, and only ranking nobility could enter its doors. The abbey even minted its own money.

Great imagination is required today to summon up the lost might of Murbach, and imagination is aided only by the serenity of the site, a remote and wooded valley in the foothills of the Vosges. What remains of the abbey are the choir and the transept, with its twin 12th-century towers; the nave has vanished.

STAYING AND DINING
ON THE ROUTE DU VIN

A gourmet stop in **Ammerschwihr**, 4½ km (3 miles) southeast of Kaysersberg on N 415, is ▶ **Aux Armes de France** at 1, Grand'Rue. It's a prestigious Alsatian house presided over by chefs Philippe and Simone Gaertner. The menu is a subtle mix of classic and contemporary cooking styles. The house also offers ten cozy rooms.

Outside of **Guebwiller** along the short Buhl-Murbach road, you may screech to a stop and grab your camera when you spot the flowery garden of 17-room ▶ **Hostellerie St-Barnabé**. The rooms are cozy, there's tennis nearby, and the warm welcome of Clémence and Eric Orban may encourage you to stay on, and on, and on.

At 9, rue Général-de-Gaulle in **Kaysersberg**, the 20-room ▶ **Résidence Chambard** is a sparkling, quiet inn with a distinguished restaurant. Try the warm *langoustines* in parsley and garlic cream. It has been said that the *mousse au chocolat Chambard* is the best in the world; Tel: 89-47-10-17. Among hotels in **Obernai**, the best are the tranquil, 43-room, moderately expensive ▶ **A la Cour d'Alsace**, or ▶ **Le Parc**, with 50 rooms, a garden, exercise rooms, and indoor and outdoor pools.

There are several pleasant inns in **Ottrott**: ▶ **Clos des Délices**, with 25 rooms, a pretty park, an exercise room, and an indoor pool; ▶ **Hostellerie des Châteaux**, 60 rooms at the edge of a forest, with sauna, indoor pool, and exercise room, as well as highly reputed regional cuisine; and ▶ **Beau Site**, with 15 rooms and a good dining room.

The 12-room, three-apartment ▶ **Hôtel Le Clos St-Vincent**, 1½ km (1 mile) north of **Ribeauvillé** via D 1^B in the direction of Bergheim, is set in the calm and beauty of Riesling vines. It boasts a fine dining room (meals served outdoors in good weather) and indoor swimming pool. Almost all rooms overlook the rich plain of Alsace. For more formal dining, ▶ **Les Vosges**, at 2, Grand'Rue, serves excellent cuisine accompanied by a selective wine list; Tel: 89-73-61-39. There are also 18 rooms. Among the most attractive restaurants in town is **Zům Pfifferhüs**, at 14, Grand'Rue, serving regional dishes and wines. Reserve, especially in high season; Tel: 89-73-62-28.

One way to enjoy **Riquewihr** in relative peace is to arrive in late afternoon when the tour buses have begun to snort away and take a room at ▶ **Hôtel la Couronne** in the heart of the village. This 15th- to 16th-century patrician residence has 36 rooms and four suites, a bar, and a billiards room; breakfast is served, but there is no restaurant. In the morning, you will feel you have stepped into a fairy tale—until around 10:30, when the tours arrive again.

One of the most attractive inns in Alsace is the 37-room, three-apartment ▶ **Château d'Isenbourg** in **Rouffach**, with wide views over the countryside, an exercise room, indoor and outdoor pools, tennis, and an outstanding kitchen; Tel: 89-49-63-53. Rouffach also is home to the acclaimed **Philippe Bohrer** restaurant on rue Poincaré; Tel: 89-49-62-49. Near Rouffach you can also stay in a 10-room *winstub,* the ▶ **Hôtel Gilg**, with quiet, warmly decorated rooms (request the *chambre rose,* with a truly unusual bathroom). The traditional kitchen serves such dishes as curried lamb.

In **Wettolsheim** you'll find another of those restaurant-inns that make travel in Alsace so delightful (and so slow): the 32-room ▶ **Auberge du Père Floranc**. The two couples of the Floranc family charge themselves with providing celebrated cuisine in an authentically Alsatian setting. There are 13 rooms in the main auberge and 18 rooms in an annex, Le Pavillon. Reserve for meals; Tel: 89-80-79-14.

In **Zellenberg**, just down the Route du Vin from Kaysersberg, the 36-room ▶ **Hôtel au Riesling** is on the top of a hill and completely bordered by vines. The rustic dining room serves traditional Alsatian cooking. Ask for a room in the modern part of the hotel (some have balconies) and avoid room number 8.

OTHER SCENIC ROUTES IN ALSACE

In addition to the Route du Vin at least nine routes throughout Alsace have been designed for travellers with special interests: **Route des Crêtes** (mountaintop road); Route Fleurie (for those interested in gardens, parks, decorated homes); **Route de la Plaine et des Forêts** (North Vosges regional park, local color and folklore); **L'Assaut des Vieux Châteaux** (Assault on Old Castles—for enthusiasts of medieval ruins); and others devoted to open spaces, tobacco, cheese, liqueurs, and even fried carp. Maps of these itineraries are available from the Offices de Tourisme in Strasbourg and in Colmar.

Colmar

In the days when Charlemagne kept a regal residence on the banks of the Lauch river, a hamlet of workers and farmers grew up around the villa's tower and its dovecote. The Villa Columbaria, or House of Doves (*colombes*), was to give its name to the growing town. Today Colmar's popularity with some travellers surpasses even that of Strasbourg's, in part because it is comfortably smaller (population: about 63,500) and less an industrial and business center than a vital repository of art and Alsatian architecture.

In Colmar there is a strong sense of connection with the United States: In 1986 many Americans celebrating the centennial of the Statue of Liberty made pilgrimages here to visit the home of the statue's sculptor, Frédéric Auguste Bartholdi. During the dreadful winter of 1944–1945, the Third and Seventh American Armies, joined by the First French Army, fought in the famous Pocket of Colmar, driving the Germans back across the Rhine in February 1945.

You can include Colmar on a trip down the Route du Vin or as a separate trip from Strasbourg or even from Paris. From Strasbourg, it's a 70-km (43-mile) drive south on A 35 and N 83. There are frequent trains between Strasbourg and Colmar and between Paris (Gare de l'Est) and Colmar. You can also fly to Colmar-Houssen Airport from Paris (Orly-Ouest).

Colmar demands to be seen on foot, and, indeed, much of its old center is today zoned for pedestrians. The two handiest parking lots for visitors are at Place Rapp (north of the railway station and along the west side of avenue de la République) and next to the Collégiale (collegiate church) St-Martin.

It's possible to see all the major sites of Colmar in one long day's stroll, but this is not recommended. The best plan is to divide the town into two tours to be taken on successive days, thus allowing time to appreciate the city's art and architecture and to enjoy the leisurely luncheons for which Colmar is well known. Visitors to Colmar who find walking difficult may see much of the old town by taking a tourist minitrain for a 50-minute trip that departs from the Hôtel de Ville on rue des Clefs six times daily; ask your hotel concierge for precise times. Unfortunately, the tours are guided in French or German only.

OLD COLMAR

Musée d'Unterlinden

By far the most important site in Colmar is the Musée d'Unterlinden in the Place d'Unterlinden. Installed in the former convent of the Unterlinden Dominicans, and comprising its chapel and 13th-century cloisters, Musée d'Unterlinden alone is worth the trip to northeastern France. Its greatest treasure is the 16th-century Issenheim Altarpiece of Matthias Grünewald. Grünewald is not well known outside expert artistic circles, perhaps because only 20 of his paintings are in existence, including the nine on the panels of this altarpiece. Suffice it to say, however, that no one who visits the Unterlinden museum could forget him. Grünewald's supreme achievement, so dramatic that some art historians have ranked it "the most moving of all western religious paintings," stuns with its mixture of mysticism and brutally realistic execution of the agony of Christ on the cross. Its impact is immediate, whatever one's beliefs.

The museum also houses paintings by local artists, items of historical and folkloric interest, winepresses, stone engravings and sculptures, and some superb stained glass. Because the Unterlinden is one of the most visited museums in all of France, it can be uncomfortably crowded on summer weekends; try to go on a weekday, whatever time of year, and don't be in a hurry.

Across from the museum at 4, rue d'Unterlinden is the Office de Tourisme.

Maison des Têtes to Collégiale St-Martin

As you leave the museum and walk west on rue des Têtes, you'll come, at number 19, to a beautiful Renaissance house (1608) called **Maison des Têtes**, so named for the many sculpted heads (*têtes*) featured in the gables of its façade. Also notable are the oriels, sculpted loggias that admit light and air to an interior while affording privacy to residents watching the goings-on in the street below. Today the Maison des Têtes houses a restaurant specializing in traditional Alsatian dishes; the atmosphere is lively and informal. Tel: 89-24-43-43.

Turning east into rue des Boulangers, you'll soon come to the **Eglise des Dominicains**, the first stone of which was laid in 1283 by Emperor Rudolph of Hapsburg. Its treasures include superb 14th-century stained glass windows and, at the entry to the choir, a Schongauer masterpiece, the Virgin of the Rose Bush.

The rue des Serruriers brings you south to the Place de la Cathédrale and the noble **Collégiale St-Martin**. Constructed in the Gothic style during the 13th and 14th centuries, the church is particularly admired for the sculptures on the St-Nicolas portal, through which you enter, and a 14th-century sculpture of the Crucifixion in a chapel in the apse. Concerts are played on the famous 18th-century Silbermann organ (restored in 1980) on Tuesdays at 8:30 P.M. in summer.

Musée Bartholdi

The Musée Bartholdi, just south of the Collégiale St-Martin, is installed in the family home where the sculptor was born. Examples of his sculpture abound in the museum, but even more interesting are his paintings and the porcelain, furniture, family portraits, project models, and other personal effects. All over town the walker will encounter the works of Bartholdi: the statue of Général Rapp in the *place* of the same name; the Roesselmann fountain, dedicated to local heroes; the winegrowers' fountain; and other monuments. A statue of Bartholdi himself—chisel in hand, his elbow resting on his workstool near a tiny Statue of Liberty—sculpted in 1907 by the Parisian Louis Noël, stands in a pretty garden near the court of appeals. (There's an extraordinary **Bartholdi grave monument** in the city's cemetery that shows a brave soldier trying, in death, to struggle out from under the cracked lid of his tomb. It is unsettling, and worth a detour. The cemetery is on the northeastern edge of town; follow rue Ladhof.)

Leaving the Musée Bartholdi, admire the **Ancien Corps de Garde** (Guard House) across the street. Built in 1575, it presents a lovely Renaissance loggia from which, in those days, sermons were preached and degrading punishments were pronounced upon civic offenders.

Some of Colmar's oldest houses are clustered near the Musée Bartholdi on rue des Marchands. The ornamentation of frescoes and medallions makes the 16th-century **Maison Pfister** the most photogenic house in old Colmar; today it is occupied by a pharmacy. Just behind it is the **Maison Adolphe**, the city's oldest house (1350).

LA PETITE VENISE

Frequently the term "La Petite Venise" is misused to define much of the southeastern quadrant of Colmar—east and south, that is, of the Grand'Rue. La Petite Venise actually comprises three distinct areas: the Quartier des Tanneurs (Leather Tanners), the Quartier de la Krutenau, and La Petite Venise (so called because of its many canals) proper. Although Colmar was little damaged by the assaults upon the region in World War II, a spirit of modernization that swept France in the 1950s almost succeeded in the demolition of this part of the city. Under laws promulgated by novelist André Malraux (minister of culture during Charles de Gaulle's Fifth Republic), however, money provided for the preservation of old city centers saved Colmar.

Petite Venise and nearby areas were restored and refurbished; where that was impossible, new buildings were constructed in the old style. As a result of all the work in the late 1960s and early 1970s, Colmar was awarded the gold medal of the European Foundation for Historical Preservation and Quality of Life.

Today, the preserved antique atmosphere has made this an area for strolling, shopping, dining, and what the French call *petit commerce* (i.e., no shopping centers, no supermarkets).

Begin your walk at the **Eglise St-Matthieu**, on Grand'Rue just south of the Place Jeanne d'Arc (a few blocks east of the Place d'Unterlinden). Originally of Franciscan denomination, it is today a Protestant church; it's worth a short stop to see the 14th- and 15th-century stained glass. Continue south on the Grand'Rue to **Place de l'Ancienne-Douane** (Customshouse). Here, the **Koïfhus** is the city's most important civic building remaining from the Middle Ages (1480). The square is a gathering of half-timbered houses at the feet of Bartholdi's figure of Lazare de Schwendi, who fought in Hungary, captured the town of Tokay, and introduced the grape of that name to Alsace.

The Old Quarters

From here take the petite rue des Tanneurs or its neighbor, the rue des Tanneurs, into the **Quartier des Tanneurs**, a true village within a city. Wander here and there and then cross the picturesque Lauch river on rue des Tanneurs.

At this point you enter the **Quartier de la Krutenau**, in early days a fortified suburb, today populated by truck gardeners. Turn right and follow the quai and the rue de la Poissonnerie. At the next corner turn right and detour across the Lauch again to have a look at the **Fontaine du Vigneron** (designed by Bartholdi), which speaks of the joys of the wines of Alsace with a grinning, pixilated bacchanal figure. At the corner of the rue de la Poissonnerie and the rue de Turenne, turn left for the **Muséum d'Histoire Naturelle**. Housed in a 17th-century mansion, the collections offer a summary of the region's fauna, geology, and ecology.

Retrace your steps up the rue de Turenne and take the rue de la Herse to the left, then follow the pretty little promenade along the riverbank to the Pont St-Pierre. From here there's a lovely view over the heart of Petite Venise, where the Lauch enters the old town, backed by the rue de Manège, with the tower of St-Martin as a backdrop.

Across the bridge turn north again on the rue du Manège to the Place des Six Montagnes-Noires and its Fontaine Roesselmann. (The view from the bridge to the right offers another photogenic perspective.) The rue du Manège becomes the rue St-Jean, which meanders between beautiful houses back to the Place de l'Ancienne-Douane.

MARKETS AND FAIRS

On Saturdays the Colmar market is particularly interesting because it attracts producers from a wide area and offers a flea market in addition to food stalls. In early August the Foire aux Vins et Représentations Folkloriques lures people from all over eastern France, while the first three Saturdays in September, an ideal season for visiting, bring Les Journées de la Choucroute (Sauerkraut Days). During June the Colmar festival features concerts of classical music.

THE ECOMUSEE D'ALSACE

To step into the past, visit the Ecomusée d'Alsace, about 21½ km (13 miles) south of Colmar via A 35 to Eguisheim, then 4 km (2½ miles) west via D 4 *bis*. More than 50 traditional houses and workshops have been built or brought to the site to replicate the styles and interior designs of the past. Old crafts have been reborn: blacksmithing, clog-making, baking, weaving, and the like. In addition, regional dishes and wines are served, and picnic areas are accessible. Ecomusée is open year-round, from 10:00 A.M. to 6:00 P.M. in spring and summer and from 11:00 A.M. to 5:00 P.M. in fall and winter; Tel: 89-74-44-74.

DINING IN AND AROUND COLMAR

For its size, Colmar boasts a remarkable number of truly outstanding restaurants. Best in town usually is agreed to be the elegant **Schillinger**, at 16, rue Stanislas. Located off the Place de Lattre-de-Tassigny, west of the old town, the two-star restaurant ranks among its special dishes the freshwater *sandre*. Reserve; Tel: 89-41-43-17. (See also **Rendez-vous de Chasse**, below.)

Da Alberto is a green oasis in the heart of town at 24, rue des Marchands, serving outstanding Italian cuisine in a garden (in season). Specialties include crayfish salad (May to July) and tripe Parmigiana style (October to March). Reserve; Tel: 89-23-37-89. In the same category of excellence, the **Fer Rouge**, at 52, Grand'Rue, a couple of corners south of the Musée d'Unterlinden and set in a handsome, typically Alsatian house of the 17th century, combines the freshest of products in both traditional and contemporary dishes; Tel: 89-41-37-24. Informal and welcoming, the small **Caveau St-Pierre**, at 24, rue de la Herse, is a pleasant hideaway for a typical Alsatian menu in La Petite Venise; Tel: 89-41-99-33. For less formal dining, the **Maison des Têtes**, in a historic house in the old city, is a delight, offering traditional dishes in a lively, regional atmosphere; Tel: 89-24-43-43.

Across the square from the Ancienne-Douane at 2, place de l'Ancienne Douane, **Au Koïfhus** takes pride in its preparation of traditional Alsatian specialties, and in pleasant weather serves in an attractive summer garden. Reserve; Tel: 89-23-04-90.

Two rustic *winstubs* (for some reason called *wistubs* in Colmar) that are good for snacks and friendly atmosphere are the **Fontaine Schwendi**, at 23, Grand'Rue (try the *tarte à l'oignon*), and **Flory**, at 1, rue Mangold, off Grand'Rue across from the Eglise St-Matthieu (try the salmon in Riesling sauce).

The finest cuisine in Alsace, and perhaps the most meticulous in France, is prepared at the **Auberge de l'Ill** in Illhaeusern, 17 km (11 miles) north of Colmar; take N 83 to Guémar and then just a few kilometers east on D 106 to Illhaeusern. There's no need to be intimidated by anticipating a grand setting, however; the Auberge de l'Ill is understated and restrained. In good weather you may dine in the garden by the little river Ill, shaded by weeping willows. Any dish you select will surely be delightful; consistently triumphant is the salmon soufflé (salmon filet filled with a soufflé of pike). Reservations always should be made weeks in advance; faxing before leaving on your trip is recommended. Tel: 89-71-83-23; Fax: 89-71-82-83.

STAYING IN AND AROUND COLMAR

The best hotel in Colmar is the handsome, cozy ▶ **Terminus-Bristol**, near the railway station, with its popular restaurant, **L'Auberge**, and the formal, award-winning **Rendezvous de Chasse**, where you should reserve well in advance (Tel: 89-41-10-10) and, from July to December, order the saddle of venison with *airelles* (European blueberries). The Bristol has 70 rooms, some with balconies, and is within walking distance (for the energetic) of the city center.

On the banks of a canal in the historic quarter of Petite Venise, the 31-room ▶ **Hostellerie le Maréchal** occupies four lovely old half-timbered houses, now joined to create a stylish, comfortable ambience of yesteryear with the conveniences of today; ask for rooms above the canal. The dining room, just above the calm waters, serves such specialties as *choucroute* with fresh duck livers; Tel: 89-41-60-32.

The ▶ **Grand Hôtel**, on a mountain slope west of Colmar in the excursion center of Les Trois-Epis, offers splendid views over the Vosges forests and the plain of Alsace. It has 45 beautifully decorated rooms, an indoor swimming pool, an exercise room, an excellent kitchen, and an efficient staff. Leave Colmar on the Route d'Ingersheim toward the northwest and continue through Ingersheim on D 11 to Les Trois-Epis. It's a distance of only 12 km (7½ miles), but you'll be far away from city lights.

The ▶ **Auberge Les Alisiers** in Lapoutroie, 21 km (13 miles) from Colmar, is an old, 13-room farmhouse above the Rhine with splendid views over the Vosges massif and the river valley. The handsome, woody dining room serves regional specialties, leaning heavily (and happily) on Munster cheese.

The Munster Valley

In the seventh century Irish monks retreated into the rich and quiet valleys west of Colmar, establishing there a monastery, or *munster*, that has been famous since the 15th century for its production of the cheese that bears its name. The village of **Munster**, 19 km (12 miles) southwest of Colmar along D 417, is a modest holiday spot with a handful of small, unpretentious inns, as is **Hohrodberg**, just north of Munster on D 5 *bis*, which is substantially higher in altitude. The best time to visit Munster is in June during the **Albert Schweitzer Music Festival**, when concerts are held in the Romanesque church in Munster. The gem of the whole region is the small circular lake called **Fischboedle**.

Out of Munster you can follow the official **Route du**

Fromage (Cheese Road) if you are truly dedicated to the Munster variety. Ask for a map in town at the Office de Tourisme on the central Place du Marché. The route passes the two dozen or more farms that make the cheese, famous since the Middle Ages; at some you can stop to watch the work. If you're really dedicated, you can walk a network of cheese footpaths covering about 400 km (248 miles). Munster cheese is at hand in all the villages of the area.

GETTING AROUND

Lorraine

The major autoroute from Paris to Nancy passes through Reims and cuts south through Metz; take A 4 to Metz, then A 31 to Nancy. A more direct route, though probably no faster, follows E 17 through Vitry-le-François. French National Railways maintains several daily services from Paris's Gare de l'Est via Bar-le-Duc and/or Metz. A new international airport, about equidistant between Nancy and Metz, opened in 1991.

Lorraine's canal network is extensive, encompassing 438 miles of waterways including the Marne-Rhine Canal and the Moselle river. Self-drive boats can be rented through Lorraine Fluvial in Pagny-sur-Moselle. For barge cruises, see below. For horseback riding and other outdoor touring, see A.R.T.E. Lorraine, Dombrot-le-Sec, 88140 Contrexéville.

Alsace

The fastest route from Paris to Strasbourg is A 4 via Metz. Drivers coming from Nancy and other points in Lorraine may choose from among several routes of varying persuasions; the two major ones are via Sarrebourg to the north and via St-Dié to the south.

Air Inter maintains several daily flights to Strasbourg from both Orly-Ouest and Charles-de-Gaulle in Paris as well as from other cities in France and Europe (including London); there are daily flights between Orly-Ouest and Colmar. TAT, a regional airline, serves Colmar, Nancy, and Metz from Paris Orly. The Euro-airport serving Mulhouse–Basel (Switzerland)–Freiburg (Germany) receives daily flights from Paris (both Orly-Ouest and Charles-de-Gaulle). Several trains leave Paris's Gare de l'Est daily for Strasbourg and for Colmar.

A car is essential for exploring Alsace. Five rental companies maintain offices in Strasbourg; Avis is on the railroad square, and Hertz, Budget, Europcar, and Citer are available as well. Autos may also be rented in Colmar and Mulhouse. Maps of the **Route du Vin** and other itineraries are available from the tourism offices in Strasbourg and Colmar (see text, above, for details).

Alsace-Lorraine is one of the most popular areas of France for luxury **barge cruising. European Waterways** cruises the eight-passenger hotel-barge *Stella* from Strasbourg to Mittersheim via Waltenheim, Saverne, Lutzelbourg, and Xouaxange in Alsace; and the six-passenger *La Vancelle* from Nancy to Mittersheim via Liverdun, Maixe, Lagarde, and Gondrexange in Lorraine. For information contact B&V Associates, 140 East 56th Street, Suite 4C, New York, NY 10022; Tel: (800) 438-4748 or (212) 688-9538; Fax: (212) 688-9467.

Rhine cruises of from three to seven days may be booked through **Alsace Croisières**, 12, rue de la Division Leclerc, 67000 Strasbourg; Tel: 88-32-44-55; Fax: 88-32-49-96. For sailings of from one to four hours or a daylong cruise on the Rhine, the Marne-Rhine Canal, or the Ill river, inquire at **La Péniche Pourquoi Pas**, Poste Restante (Tel: 88-36-71-31); or **Port Autonome de Strasbourg**, 15 rue de Nantes (Tel: 88-84-13-13), all in Strasbourg.

Self-drive boats on the Marne-Rhine Canal can be rented through **Blue Line Alsace/Lorraine**, Port du Canal, Hesse, 57400 Sarrebourg (Tel: 87-03-61-74); or **Locaboat Plaisance**, Quai du Port au Bois, 89300 Joigny (Tel: 86-91-72-72).

ACCOMMODATIONS REFERENCE

The rates given below are projections *for 1994. Unless otherwise indicated, rates are for a double room, double occupancy, and do not include meals. As rates are always subject to change, double-check before booking.*

▶ **Aux Armes de France.** 1, Grand'Rue, 68770 **Ammerschwihr.** Tel: 89-47-10-12; Fax 89-47-38-12. 310F–460F.

▶ **Auberge Les Alisiers.** 5 Faudé, 68650 **Lapoutroie.** Tel: 89-47-52-82; Fax: 89-47-22-38. 260F–350F.

▶ **Auberge du Père Floranc.** 9, rue Herzog, Wettolsheim 68000 **Colmar.** Tel: 89-80-79-14; Fax: 89-79-77-00. 330F–520F.

▶ **Auberge de la Source.** Trémont-sur-Saulx, 55000 **Bar-le-Duc.** Tel: 29-75-45-22; Fax: 29-75-48-55. 250F–430F.

▶ **Auberge du Spitzemberg.** La Petite-Fosse, 88490 **Provenchères-sur-Fave.** Tel: 29-51-20-46; Fax: 29-51-10-12. 240F–320F.

▶ **Beau Site.** 67530 **Ottrott-le-Haut.** Tel: 88-95-80-61; Fax: 88-95-86-41. 260F–620F.

▶ **La Bergerie.** Rugy, 57640 **Argancy.** Tel: 87-77-82-27; Fax: 87-77-87-07. 280F–350F.

▶ **Cathédrale.** 12, place de la Cathédrale, 67000 **Strasbourg.** Tel: 88-22-12-12; Fax: 88-23-28-00. 420F–750F.

► **Château d'Adomenil**. 54300 **Lunéville**. Tel: 83-74-04-81; Fax: 83-74-21-78. 550F–850F.

► **Château d'Isenbourg**. 68250 **Rouffach**. Tel: 89-49-63-53; Fax: 89-78-53-70; in U.S., Tel: (800) 927-4765; Fax: (212) 689-5435. 900F–1,300F.

► **Clos des Délices**. Route Klingenthal, 67530 **Ottrott**. Tel: 88-95-81-00; Fax: 88-95-97-71. 480F–680F.

► **Cosmos**. Rue de Metz, 88140 **Contrexéville**. Tel: 29-08-15-90; Fax: 29-08-68-67. 350F–400F.

► **A la Cour d'Alsace**. 3, rue Gail, 67210 **Obernai**. Tel: 88-95-07-00; Fax: 88-95-19-21. 670F–780F.

► **Europe**. 38, rue du Fossés-des-Tanneurs, 67000 **Strasbourg**. Tel: 88-32-17-88; Fax: 88-75-65-45. 340F–480F.

► **Grand Hôtel**. 68410 **Les Trois-Epis**. Tel: 89-49-80-65; Fax: 89-49-89-00. 680F–990F.

► **Grand Hôtel Bragard**. Place du Tilleul, 88400 **Gérardmer**. Tel: 29-63-06-31; Fax: 29-63-46-81. 400F–580F.

► **Grand Hôtel Etablissement**. 88140 **Contrexéville**. Tel: 29-08-17-30; Fax: 29-08-68-67. 395F.

► **Grand Hôtel de la Reine**. 2, place Stanislas, 54000 **Nancy**. Tel: 83-35-03-01; Fax: 83-32-86-04; in U.S., (800) 888-4747; in New York, (212) 752-3900; in London, (0800) 181-591. 600F–840F.

► **Hostellerie Bas-Rupts**. 88400 **Gérardmer**. Tel: 29-63-09-25; Fax: 29-63-00-40. 340F–700F.

► **Hostellerie du Château des Monthairons**. 55320 **Dieue-sur-Meuze**. Tel: 29-87-78-55; Fax: 29-87-73-49. 450F–900F.

► **Hostellerie des Châteaux**. 11, rue des Châteaux, 67530 **Ottrott**. Tel: 88-95-81-54; Fax: 88-95-95-20. 450F–650F.

► **Hostellerie Coq Hardi**. 8, avenue Victoire, 55100 **Verdun**. Tel: 29-86-36-36; Fax: 29-86-09-21. 450F–620F.

► **Hostellerie le Maréchal**. 4-6, place des Six Montagnes Noire, 68000 **Colmar**. Tel: 89-41-60-32; Fax: 89-24-59-40. 550F–800F.

► **Hostellerie St-Barnabé**. 68530 **Murbach**. Tel: 89-76-92-15; Fax: 89-76-67-80. 365F–685F.

► **Hôtel Le Clos St-Vincent**. Route de Bergheim, 68150 **Ribeauvillé**. Tel: 89-73-67-65; Fax: 89-73-32-20. 680F–925F.

► **Hôtel la Couronne**. 5, rue de la Couronne, 68340 **Riquewihr**. Tel: 89-49-03-03; Fax: 89-49-01-01. 280F–355F.

► **Hôtel du Dragon**. 2, rue de l'Ecarlate/12, rue du Dragon, 67000 **Strasbourg**. Tel: 88-35-79-80; Fax: 88-25-78-95. 500F–590F.

► **Hôtel Gilg**. 1, route du Vin, 67140 **Mittelbergheim**. Tel: 88-08-91-37; Fax: 88-08-45-17. 270F–380F.

► **Hôtel Maison Rouge**. 4, rue des Francs-Bourgeois,

67000 **Strasbourg**. Tel: 88-32-08-60; Fax: 88-22-43-73. 540F–580F.

▶ **Hôtel au Riesling**. 3, route du Vin, 68340 **Zellenberg**. Tel: 89-47-85-85; Fax: 89-47-92-08. 230F–310F.

▶ **Hôtel des Rohan**. 17, rue du Maroquin, 67000 **Strasbourg**. Tel: 88-32-85-11; Fax: 88-75-65-37; in U.S., (212) 254-2217 or (800) 755-9313. 400F–595F.

▶ **Hôtel Terminus-Plaza**. 10, place de la Gare, 67000 **Strasbourg**. Tel: 88-32-87-00; Fax: 88-32-16-46; in U.S. and Canada, Tel: (800) 528-1234; in U.K., (081) 541-0033. Member, Best Western International. 530F.

▶ **Hôtel du Théâtre**. Port St-Marcel, 57000 **Metz**. Tel: 87-31-10-10; Fax: 87-30-04-66. 450F–700F.

▶ **Lorraine et Restaurant Le Mas**. Place de la Gare, 54260 **Longuyon**. Tel: 82-26-50-07; Fax: 82-39-26-09. 290F.

▶ **Maison Kammerzell–Hôtel Baumann**. 16, place de la Cathédrale, 67000 **Strasbourg**. Tel: 88-32-42-14; Fax: 88-23-03-92. 580F–630F.

▶ **Mercure Altéa St-Thiébault**. 29, place St-Thiébault, 57000 **Metz**. Tel: 87-38-50-50; Fax: 87-75-48-18; in U.S. and Canada, (800) 221-4542. 450F–630F.

▶ **Mercure Altéa Thiers**. 11, rue Poincaré, 54000 **Nancy**. Tel: 83-39-75-75; Fax: 83-32-78-17; in U.S. and Canada, (800) 221-4542. 475F–600F.

▶ **Monopole-Métropole**. 16, rue Kuhn, 67000 **Strasbourg**. Tel: 88-32-11-94; Fax: 88-32-82-55. 360F–580F.

▶ **Le Moulin de La Wantzenau**. 27, route de Strasbourg, 67610 **La Wantzenau**. Tel: 88-96-27-83; Fax: 88-96-68-32. 295F–395F.

▶ **Notre Dame**. Sion, 54330 **Vézelise**. Tel: 83-25-13-31; Fax: 83-25-16-12. 150F–220F.

▶ **Le Parc**. 169, rue Général-Gouraud, 67210 **Obernai**. Tel: 88-95-50-08; Fax: 88-95-37-29; in U.S., (800) 927-4765; Fax: (212) 689-5435. 400F–700F.

▶ **Le Prieuré**. Flavigny-sur-Moselle, 54630 **Nancy**. Tel: 83-26-70-45; Fax: 83-26-75-51. 600F.

▶ **Régent-Contades**. 8, avenue de la Liberté, 67000 **Strasbourg**. Tel: 88-36-26-26; Fax: 88-37-13-70. 800F–1,200F.

▶ **Relais de la Poste**. 21, rue du Général-de-Gaulle, 67610 **La Wantzenau**. Tel: 88-96-20-64; Fax: 88-96-36-84. 300F–500F.

▶ **Relais de Strasbourg**. 4, rue du Vieux-Marché-aux-Vins, 67000 **Strasbourg**. Tel: 88-32-80-00; Fax: 88-23-08-85. 330F–370F.

▶ **La Réserve**. Esplanade du Lac, 88400 **Gérardmer**. Tel: 29-63-21-60; Fax: 29-60-81-60. 400F–500F.

► **Résidence Chambard**. 9, rue Général-de-Gaulle, 68240 **Kaysersberg**. Tel: 89-47-10-17; Fax: 89-47-35-03. 650F–850F.

► **Royal-Concorde**. 23, avenue Foch, 57011 **Metz**. Tel: 87-66-81-11; Fax: 87-56-13-16; in U.S. and Canada, (800) 888-4747 or (212) 752-3900; in U.K., (0800) 181-591. 520F–600F.

► **Terminus-Bristol**. 7, place de la Gare, 68000 **Colmar**. Tel: 89-23-59-59; Fax: 89-23-92-26; in U.S. and Canada, Tel: (800) 528-1234; in U.K., (081) 541-0033. Member, Best Western International. 400F–850F.

► **Les Vosges**. 2, Grand'Rue, 68150 **Ribeauvillé**. Tel: 89-73-61-39; Fax: 89-73-34-21. 295F–390F.

NORMANDY

By David Wickers with Fred Halliday

David Wickers is travel editor of Marie Claire *magazine and travels to Normandy frequently from his home in London.*

There is, of course, a single Normandy, one defined by its administrative boundaries, which stretch from Le Mont-Saint-Michel in the west to beyond the forest of Lyons in the east and from the Channel coast—known to the French as La Manche, the Sleeve—in the north to just above Le Mans. But such a definition misses the point: Normandy is the sum total of amazingly diverse parts. The enormous pleasure of travelling around Normandy is to dip into its rich countryside, from the flat-as-a-breadboard floodplain of the river Seine, to the hummocky highlands of the verdant terrain known as the Suisse Normande, from meadows where cattle sink up to their knees in grass, to the open heathland of the Cotentin peninsula.

You'll soon see why the Impressionists preferred Normandy, for its countryside, for its coast (especially the chalk cliffs that sweep along the Channel between the busy ports of Dieppe and Le Havre, as well as the almost stage-set harbor at Honfleur), and for the fine light that suffuses all this glorious landscape. Deauville, a resort since the turn of the century, promises worldly pleasures. Move on toward the Cotentin peninsula and the coast echoes with weighty memories, its string of museums recalling the Allied landings.

The word "invasion" has played a key role in Normandy's history: From about the ninth century A.D., the Norsemen sailed from their Scandinavian fjords to what is now Normandy, along with much of the rest of the Western world, pillaging, despoiling, and claiming territory. (The word "Norsemen" came into French as *Normands,* hence the English-language rendering "Normans.") In 911, with Paris

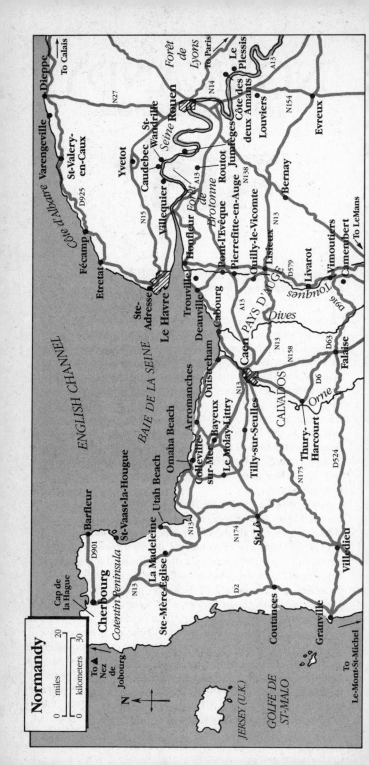

and even Chartres threatened, a peace agreement was finally reached: The king of France ceded all the territory then occupied by the Normans to the Viking Rollo, and the duchy of Normandy was born.

MAJOR INTEREST

Dieppe and the Côte d'Albatre

Le Havre
City planning
Musée des Beaux-Arts André Malraux
The Valley of the Seine

Rouen
Medieval quarter around rue du Gros-Horloge
Cathédrale de Notre-Dame
Museums
Deauville
The Pays d'Auge
Suisse Normande

Caen
Abbaye aux Hommes and Abbaye aux Dames
The château

Bayeux
Tapestry

The D-day landing beaches

Cherbourg and the Cotentin peninsula

Le Mont-Saint-Michel

EATING AND DRINKING IN NORMANDY

Normandy's countryside yields some wonderful products. It all comes down to grass, the great growth industry of Normandy. Deep green and thick as a lion's mane, it would send most of the world's cattle into a fit of envy. Humans, as a result, graze on some of France's finest cheeses—Livarot, Camembert, and Pont l'Evêque. Long may these cheeses reign; their future is jeopardized by European Community pasteurization regulations, but these smelly delicacies could not ask for a better champion: Prince Charles has lobbied for their survival.

Indeed, a great part of the joy of touring Normandy lies in eating, and not only its famous cheeses: sole from Dieppe, duck from the marshes of the Seine Valley, oysters from St-Vaast-la-Hougue, and other shellfish best enjoyed in a teetering display of *assiette des fruits de mer*. If anywhere truly merits the title of "The Big Apple," it is Normandy. The fruit is grown not in regimented orchard rows but on a pretty scattering of trees all over the landscape. Early May, when the trees blossom, is one of the prettiest times to be in Normandy, but any season is a feast of apple tarts, cider, and the apple in its most powerful format, Calvados.

Calva, as its lovers call it, is to the apple what Cognac is to the grape. This distillate of cider is aged in wood and bottled in grades. The least expensive is plain Calvados; next is Calvados Pays d'Auge Reglémentée. Aging is a factor in grading, and within each grade there are the usual variations of quality according to the bottler. One of the finest is Vieux Calvados from the house of Jean-Louis Favennec.

You may see people around you quaffing Calvados during the meal; in fact, it is quite correct to do so. This is the *trou normand* (Norman hole) of which you may have heard, the idea behind the vivid phrase being that because a Norman meal is very heavy, you have to punch a hole in it—with some Calvados—and then proceed to fill it.

There is likewise a reason to drink Calva at the end of the meal, and a phrase to go along with it. The coffee is *coiffé*, the Normans say, and *recoiffé*, or spiked, with the brandy. One final word on behalf of Calvados: Many people who say they cannot drink brandy because it keeps them awake at night report that drinking Calva induces sound sleep—with wild dreams.

Our route follows the Normandy coast, from Dieppe in the north to Le Mont-Saint-Michel on the Brittany border, with forays through lush countryside to the great Norman towns and cities of the interior.

DIEPPE AND THE COTE D'ALBATRE

The port of Dieppe, well connected to Paris by road and rail, and to the United Kingdom by ferries, is a convenient and scenic place to begin a tour of Normandy. This picturesque town lies at the eastern end of a magnificent 75-mile-long coastline called the Côte d'Albatre (Alabaster Coast) for the chalk cliffs that rise from the sea along its length—in fact, for many observers, and not all of them French, the cliffs along the Côte d'Albatre put the White Cliffs of Dover across the Channel to shame.

Dieppe

Parisians have long called the route to Dieppe, 169 km (105 miles) from the capital, the "Road to the Sea," because it is their favorite seaside retreat. In turn, Dieppe puts out the welcome mat by calling itself the "Plage (Beach) de Paris." Not only is Dieppe convenient to Paris, but it also happens to be one of the prettiest coastal towns in France, with old stone houses on narrow streets that cluster around the harbor and behind a long pebble beach. Allied bombers let the town off lightly, unlike so many of Dieppe's neighbors, during World War II, with the result that Dieppe, particularly where it claws around the fishing boats in its natural harbor at the mouth of the river Béthune, retains a charm that is unblemished by modern intrusions.

Ever since the Vikings came and exclaimed "Dyepp!" (Norse for "deep water"), the town has had a high maritime profile. Between the 15th and 17th centuries, Dieppe was the most important port in France. It still has a major fishing fleet, which provides a clue to what awaits you at the table here. Half the scallops eaten in France, in fact, come from Dieppe.

Port it may be, but Dieppe is also France's oldest resort, popularized by the duchesse de Barry when she made sea bathing a socially acceptable pastime for ladies two centuries ago. The town rapidly became a fashionable haunt for both the British and French aristocracy, who came in droves—often to conduct clandestine affairs, the most famous being that between British king Edward VII and his mistress. This royal visitor also left his mark on the town in the shape of a pink-granite, two-tiered drinking fountain in the central Place Camille Saint-Saëns; the upper trough was designed for horses, the lower trough for dogs. Dieppe's turn-of-the-century casino, facing a seafront from the boulevard de Verdun, is still one of the largest in France, open year-round for roulette, baccarat, chemin de fer, and other entertaining ways to squander your hard-earned francs.

THE OLD QUARTER
Dieppe is a town to wander through randomly, ducking in and out of narrow streets and alleyways. The place to begin is the oldest part of town, the **Quartier Ste-Catherine**. The quarter clusters around the 13th-century **Eglise St-Jacques**, hiding behind its well-weathered façade with decorative pinnacles and turrets. A number of fine wooden statues pepper the square in front of the church; Canadian wood-

carvers donated them to the Dieppois in 1982 to commemorate the 40th anniversary of the Allied troop landings.

Every Saturday, at the church's heels and spilling along
the Grand-Rue just to the north, Dieppe stages one of the
best markets in Normandy. Fishermen and farmers from the
environs bring wonderful produce to sell, everything from
moules (mussels) to pâtés, fat rabbits to local cheeses. The
nearby shops are also worthy of a browse, especially the
Epicerie Olivier, famous for its vast selection of Normandy
cheeses, just around the corner from the church on the rue
St-Jacques.

When you've stocked up on food you should fuel up at
the **Café des Tribuneaux** at the top of the Grande-Rue, a
Dieppe institution whose dark, 18th-century interior has
seen the likes of Monet, Renoir, Whistler, Beardsley, and
other artists who have come to Dieppe to relish its light.
This popular watering hole also bore witness to the sad sight
of Oscar Wilde in exile.

THE SEAFRONT AND THE CHATEAU
The old quarter huddles just south of the sea and a deeply
shelving beach backed by a gusty promenade and a broad
swath of grass known as **La Pelouse**. Dieppe's 15th-century
château lies high above the shore on the western edge of La
Pelouse. The scale and elaborate design of the château say a
lot about the wealth and power the sea once bestowed on
Dieppe. Now considerably restored, the château houses a
gallery with paintings by Pissarro, Dufy, Monet and other
Impressionists, as well as prints by Georges Braque, who
spent his last years nearby, and a museum containing a
unique collection of locally made ivory carvings. In the 17th
century there were more than 300 ivory carvers in Dieppe.
Now there is just one.

STAYING AND DINING IN DIEPPE
The best hotels in Dieppe face either the seafront or the
harbor. Many of the rooms at the old ▶ **Windsor**, across
from La Pelouse on boulevard de Verdun, are massive and
face the sea; its staircase is hung with evocative paintings of
the grand transatlantic liners. The rather eccentric, old-
fashioned rooms at ▶ **Hôtel des Arcades**, on the arcade de
la Bourse, have harbor views. If you're in the mood for
modern luxury, the place to stay is ▶ **La Présidence**, above
the sea near the château end of La Pelouse.

La Présidence has an excellent restaurant, a good place to
sample sole à la dieppoise, fish filets poached in white wine

with mussels and shrimp and garnished with truffles, and
scallops caught the same day; sea gulls with avaricious stares
will perch on the windowsills as you eat. Several other
seafood restaurants face the harbor from the arcaded buildings along the quais. The **Marmite Dieppoise**, at 8, rue St-
Jean, is small and popular with the locals, a good indication
of the quality of the seafood that's served here. This is the
place to experience the restaurant's namesake, *marmite
Dieppoise,* a type of bouillabaisse.

Along the Côte d'Albatre

The Côte d'Albatre begins at Dieppe and, broken by some 40
beaches, culminates at the magnificently eroded arches and
the famous hollow needle at Etretat at its westernmost end.
With many *pointes de vue,* official and otherwise, and a
string of villages hidden away in deep cleavage between
folds of land along the way, the coast invites a leisurely drive
down its length.

VARENGEVILLE

Varengeville, whose charm has been recognized by many a
great artist, is the first place west of Dieppe worth pausing
for—just 5 km (3 miles) away on the narrow coast road,
D 63. Georges Braque had his studio here, and you can still
see the "Tree of Jesse" window he executed for the church.
You can also visit the artist's grave, in a lonely cemetery on
the cliff edge; half of the cemetery has already been lost,
eroded by the action of the waves on the cliff face below.

Joan Miró also spent a good deal of time in Varengeville,
and Michel Ciry composed a great work dedicated to solitude and the quest of God here. But you don't have to suffer
such creative pressures to enjoy this relaxing little village.
One of the most pleasant corners is the **Parc des Moustiers**,
an estate that is now a public garden in a valley next to the
sea. The English architect Sir Edwin Luytens designed the
tall, creeper-covered house in the 19th century for an American woman, Guillaume Mallet. The house is surrounded by a
sea of sweeping lawns, flowers, cedars, and rhododendrons,
landscaped by the famous British gardener Gertrude Jekyll.

One of the nicest ways to see this stretch of coast is to
climb to the first-floor platform of the **Ailly lighthouse**,
about 1 km (½ mile) west of Varengeville on D 75A. In clear
weather, you'll have a magnificent view almost 40 miles up
and down the coast. The lighthouse is open from 8:00 A.M. to
approximately one hour before the light is lit.

ST-VALERY-EN-CAUX

Officially classified as a *village fleurie* on account of its
superb gardens of lovingly cultivated flowers, St-Val, as it is
colloquially known, straddles a river, and the two sides of
the town, 20 km (12 miles) farther along the coast from
Varengeville, are connected by a drawbridge. Though not as
attractive as the *fleurie* label might imply, the town has safe,
sandy beaches and a yacht harbor, and out of the sea rise
spectacular rock formations, actually boulders that have
fallen from the cliffs above. For a nice meal on a hot day,
head for the garden tables of the **Pigeon Blanc**, next to the
church. Tel: 35-97-90-22.

FECAMP

Fécamp, a large, busy cod-fishing port 38 km (24 miles)
southwest of St-Valery, leaves the passing motorist with the
impression of ships, sawmills, lumberyards, and little else by
way of instant eye appeal. However, the famous Benedictine
liqueur distillery, founded by Benedictine monks in the 15th
century, is one of the most popular stops along the coast.
The mock Gothic palace that houses the distillery, in the
hands of the Le Grand family since 1863, dominates the town
center. The eclectic collections of the **Musée de la Bénédic-
tine**, entered through massive wrought-iron gates and Gothic arcades, include row upon row of bottles of imitations.
(The original recipe, a well-guarded secret, is based on 27
plants and spices.) The spacious Salle des Abbés is presided
over by stone statues of 16 former abbots, and the monk
who rediscovered the formula for Benedictine (it was once
lost) is depicted, with a trumpeting angel and a bottle of the
elixir, in a stained glass window. Guided tours, in English,
are arranged on the spot, and there's a free sample and a
chance to buy "at the source" at the end.

Fécamp was also the home of Guy de Maupassant, and
many of his short stories are imbued with the atmosphere of
its streets. Cod fishing is no longer a local industry, but the
marina is still interesting, and the quai de la Marine receives
massive quantities of other fish, as well as cargoes of raw
chemicals and timber bound for French sawmills. Along the
wharves are canneries, fish-dressing plants, and drydocks for
boat repairs.

In its length the 12th- to 13th-century **Eglise de la Trinité**
on the Place du Général-Leclerc rivals the longest churches
in France, being less than ten feet short of Notre-Dame de
Paris, and its spire is the quintessence of Norman towers.
Any of the cafés on the *place* is suitable for lunch or a snack.

For something more comfortable there is ► **L'Auberge de la Rouge**; Tel: 35-28-07-59. Menus start at 190 and 260 francs, the rooms at 280F.

ETRETAT

Etretat, 20 km (12 miles) southwest of Fécamp along the coast road, D 211 and D 11, is a quiet family resort wedged between two white cliffs, the **Falaise d'Amont** to the east and the **Falaise d'Aval** to the west. This is a picturesque place where Eugène-Louis Boudin, Claude Monet, Henri Matisse, Raoul Dufy, and Georges Braque painted, inspired by the spectrum of light falling differently on the chalk cliffs at various times òf day and seasons. Jacques Offenbach came to compose, Guy de Maupassant to write; today Parisian holidaymakers come to bask on the pebble beach.

Well-known golfers also come, to test the town's famous cliff-top golf course. The 12th-century **Chapelle Notre-Dame-de-la-Garde** is high atop the Falaise d'Amont near a monument to two doomed French aviators, Nungesser and Coli, who tried to cross the Atlantic and were last seen from the cliff top. Nature has also provided the town with a famous chalk arch, the **Porte d'Aval**, carved by the sea, and a needle-shaped rock, **L'Aiguille**, which rises menacingly 200 feet out of the water.

The ► **Hôtel des Falaises** provides simple but comfortable accommodations near the sea on boulevard René-Coty.

Le Havre

Le Havre, the second-most-important port in France (first for containers) and third-largest in Europe, lies at the western end of the Côte d'Albatre, 28 km (17 miles) south of Etretat on D 940. There is frequent ferry service from Le Havre to the U.K. (Portsmouth) as well as train service to Paris.

If you like your France to reflect the heritage of some ancien régime you might not, it has to be said, like what you see. By the end of World War II, Le Havre had won the title of Europe's most war-damaged port; 146 bombing raids resulted in the death of 4,000 people and the destruction of nearly 10,000 homes.

After the war, architect Auguste Perret transformed Le Havre into a sleekly modern city, succeeding in raising his checkerboard grid of reinforced concrete buildings well above the drab and dreary through the liberal use of grand boulevards, tree-lined avenues, manicured lawns, parks, and flower beds.

But back to beginnings. After the silting up of the older

harbors of Honfleur and Harfleur, in 1517 the authorities under King François I decided to build a new port, *Le Havre-de-Grâce* (the Haven of Grace). It was not until the American Revolution, when cotton, sugar, tobacco, and other commodities from the rebellious colonies were distributed from Le Havre to all parts of Europe, that the port rapidly grew in importance. By the beginning of the 20th century, when the population had grown to 100,000, Le Havre had become the leading port for American trade and a center for the cotton and coffee markets. Just before World War II its fame was glorified as the home port to the world's largest ocean liner, the *Normandie*.

THE MODERN CITY

The main arteries of Le Havre are the arcaded **rue de Paris**, which cuts south through the city toward the ferry terminal and, lined with elegant shops, is known to Parisian aspirants as the city's rue de Rivoli, and **avenue Foch**, a Champs-Elysées–like boulevard that runs east and west (the city's major beach is at the western end) and is divided by a central lawn. They meet in the center of the city at the huge **Place de l'Hôtel-de-Ville**, one of the largest squares in Europe, with proportions that would by no means look lost even in a major capital. Six 10-story tower blocks are dominated by the 17-story Hôtel de Ville, which, wearing the regulation *tricolore,* forms the hub of Perret's new town.

The **Musée des Beaux-Arts André Malraux**, facing the sea south of the *place* near the foot of the rue de Paris, is built entirely of glass and steel, and its different levels are linked by gangways rather like those on board a ship, a concept in keeping with the maritime essence of Le Havre. (If it's pouring with rain, this glass box is a good, dry place from which to view the town.) The permanent collection includes work by Eugène Boudin and Raoul Dufy, both favorite sons, and an important collection of Impressionists. Many of the paintings are of Norman scenes.

In its concrete maze, Le Havre is vast and confining, with arms of the sea blocking this street and that. The best way to see it is by boat. Tours are detailed and fascinating and leave frequently but irregularly (depending on how many people show up) all day long from the quai de la Marine, near the western end of avenue Foch at Porte Océane.

STE-ADRESSE

The writer Casimir Delavigne, when looking at the view over the Seine estuary from the Le Havre suburb of Ste-Adresse, saw "Paris and Naples in one picture" and declared that "after

Constantinople, there is nothing more beautiful." Ste-Adresse is primarily a residential area, a ten-minute walk from the center of Le Havre atop seaside cliffs that offer grand views across the estuary. Colloquially known as "Le Nice Havrais" because of its villas climbing the hillside of Cap de la Hève, sandy beach, and general holiday mood, Ste-Adresse was originally built to rival Deauville; the oddest fact of its life is that it was the capital of Belgium during World War I. Although it has been slowly engulfed by the expansion of Le Havre over the years, Ste-Adresse has still managed to retain a delightful, separate atmosphere. Don't miss it.

STAYING AND DINING IN LE HAVRE
For those overnighting for the ferry, the hotel ► **France et Bourgogne**, 19–21, cours République, also has a reasonable restaurant; the ► **Astoria** hotel, on the same street at number 13, is even more reasonable. For a seafood lunch or dinner try **Cambridge**, 90, rue Voltaire. You'll find more stylish cooking at **Le Montagne**, on the Isle St-François near the Bassin du Commerce.

In **Ste-Adresse**, the small and reasonably priced ► **Hôtel des Phares** accommodates guests in a pretty white villa with some rooms in a chalet-style annex. The best place for a meal in Ste-Adresse is the **Beau Séjour**, with excellent fish and enormous views of the bay, at 3, place Clemenceau.

ALONG THE SEINE TO ROUEN

Napoléon once declared that Le Havre, Rouen, and Paris were "but a single town of which the Seine is the main street." The 87-km (54-mile) route from Le Havre to Rouen is a joy, hugging the grand meanders of the Seine, but you must be patient. It takes a while before you finally shake off the grim and smelly landscape of oil refineries and the general industriousness of outlying Le Havre. These final miles of the Seine's journey across 465 miles of French soil are perhaps the most interesting part of the trip. The river curves and carves several lazy loops of wide, white banks in the limestone soil, making a trail that Lindbergh picked up from the air and followed to Paris. Because of its broad strokes of geography, history, and topography as well as the contents of its abbeys and towns, the valley of the Seine is perhaps the most compelling of sights in the interior of Normandy.

The word *seine* comes from the Celtic word "squan," meaning "to curve," and curve it does, gently falling at the rate of just one foot for every mile of meander. By the time you reach the curious white cliffs at **Tancarville** (28 km/16 miles west of Le Havre along the north shore of the river on the parallel A 15 or D 982), with its massive suspension bridge, the scenery is exclusively rural. (Note that as of late 1994 or early 1995, the first bridge across the Seine out of Le Havre will be the new one to Honfleur, a massive engineering project.)

VILLEQUIER TO THE FORET DE BROTONNE

Villequier, 27 km (17 miles) upriver from Tancarville on D 982 and D 81, spreads pleasantly along the river beneath a forested hill. The novelist Victor Hugo's daughter, Léopoldine, and son-in-law drowned nearby in 1843, in a boating accident six months after their marriage, and the **Musée Victor-Hugo** is filled with mementos of the family. At **Caudebec-en-Caux**, situated on a broad elbow of the Seine 7½ km (4½ miles) farther along the river, you'll come to the flamboyantly Gothic **Eglise Notre-Dame**, built between 1425 and 1539 and described by Henry IV as "the most beautiful chapel in my kingdom." The ferocious reverse tide of the river is clocked at Caudebec as it backs up from the sea, a full 18 miles away. Just upstream you cannot fail to spot the enormous suspension bridge of Brotonne, a 4,000-foot, highly futuristic span, the highest humpback bridge in the world, linking the north bank of the Seine with the **Forêt de Brotonne** (Brotonne Forest), a landscape of oaks, beeches, and pines crooked in a long bend of the Seine.

THE ABBEYS AT ST-WANDRILLE AND JUMIEGES

At St-Wandrille-Rançon, just beyond the Brotonne bridge and barely 2 km (1 mile) east of Caudebec-en-Caux on D 982, are the remains of the Benedictine **Abbaye du Bec-Hellouin**, founded in 649. Directed by a succession of renowned abbots, including Einhard, the contemporary and historian of Charlemagne, for centuries the community here supported brilliant scholarship. The carved cloisters remain, but the incumbent monks, famous for their Gregorian chant and homemade honey and beeswax candles, now worship in a 15th-century wooden tithe barn that they brought, bit by bit, from its original location some 50 miles away.

The **Abbaye de Jumièges**, one of the most magnificent ruins in France, its bones as delicate as lace, its silences broken by the haunting cries of crows, sits on a promontory above a graceful meander of the Seine about 15 km (9 miles) beyond St-Wandrille on D 982 and D 143. Its imposing, 170-foot-tall, 11th-century towers and roofless nave and cloisters, with a lopsided yew tree growing in the middle, are wonderful sights. The heart of Agnès Sorel, mistress of Charles VII, is supposedly buried in the north transept.

From Jumièges, a final riverside amble up D 65 to D 982 brings you to Rouen in 27 km (17 miles).

Rouen

Rouen, the tenth-century capital of the duchy of Normandy, is a crown studded with the gems of France's history and character. Here is the passion of Joan of Arc, the very square where she was burned at the stake; here is the cathedral Monet found so irresistible that he painted it many times in many different shades of light. Here is a maze of medieval streets and buildings to explore on foot—car traffic is banned in much of the city. (The railroad station, to the north of the old city at the end of the rue Jeanne-d'Arc, is a good place to leave your car.) The Norman loves to dine, and so there are excellent cafés and restaurants, with the best Bordeaux lists outside the Médoc.

ALONG THE RUE DU GROS-HORLOGE

A good place to begin your tour of Rouen is the rue du Gros-Horloge, a quarter-mile amble of old cobblestones that runs through the heart of the old city, which partly escaped the war and was partly reconstructed in its aftermath. Except for a few modern refurbishments, mostly of glass and Lucite, appearances would make the average person think that nothing had changed here for 500 years. The rue du Gros-Horloge is overhung with stucco-and-beam houses, work called *colombage*. Because buildings were originally taxed according to the street space they took up, they were generally constructed with a small ground floor, and upper floors—which were not taxed at all—were built to jut out over the street.

Originally a commercial thoroughfare, the rue du Gros-Horloge has retained its hustle-and-bustle character with cafés, sweetshops, and little boutiques that make it worth a trip just for window shopping. When strolling here remember that Rouen has wonderful chocolates and caramels, and many of the sweetshops you find along the street will be happy to send packages home. (There are no emulsifiers, so be sure to specify air mail lest your chocolate arrive white.)

Halfway down the street is its namesake, the **Gros Horloge** itself, a big clock (with only one hand) spanning the street like a bridge. Catercorner to the clock is a **bell tower**.

If it's open, according to a complex schedule, you can visit a collection of clocks and clockworks inside. From the top of the tower a sparkling view gives out over the whole museumlike city. Just to the north, on rue aux Juifs, is the late-Gothic **Palais de Justice**. Blown apart in World War II, it was restored most successfully. To the east there's the quiet medieval neighborhood of the **rue Martainville**, lined with half-timbered houses and cloisters. An amble down this narrow street leads past 15th-century wooden houses, notably the **Aître St-Maclou** at number 184–186, one of the last charnel houses from the host of plagues in the Middle Ages. Its courtyard posts are covered with a frieze of figures, skulls, and skeletal parts in a *danse macabre*.

At the western end of rue du Gros-Horloge is the wide, bustling **Place du Vieux-Marché**, where Joan of Arc was burned at the stake in 1431. A cross in front of the Eglise de Ste-Jeanne-d'Arc marks the spot. Unfortunately, in the 1950s the site was completely remodeled in concrete, and is now a wasteland so far as a visitor's experience of history is concerned.

CATHEDRALE NOTRE-DAME-DE-ROUEN

This massive cathedral, dating almost entirely from 1201, looms at the eastern end of the rue du Gros-Horloge. Monet never tired of painting its splendid Gothic logic in all its sunlit variations. The cathedral presented to the painter, as it does to visitors today, one of the most immense façades in all of Gothicdom, bristling with design detail and flanked by two towers of dissimilar style and appeal—the tower of St-Romain on the left and the Tour de Beurre (Butter Tower) on the right. The St-Romain tower, at nearly 900 years of age, is older and represents a more primitive Gothic style. The Butter Tower, so called because those who contributed to its construction were permitted to eat dairy products otherwise taboo during a certain religious observance, was finished 400 years later. Instead of a cross, a crown of 56 bells lies on top.

Inside the cathedral is a 13th-century choir of great beauty and simplicity, and just to its left is the 15th-century **Escalier de la Librairie**, a wood-carved staircase resembling booksellers' stalls.

EGLISES ST-MACLOU AND ST-OUEN

Eglise St-Maclou, a block west of the cathedral on rue St-Romain, was begun in the 15th century and completed in the mid-16th century. It is an example of Gothic Renaissance architecture, but its soaring Gothic elements are simplified, allowing for a building that was doubtless easier to construct, though still with a "flying," if less massive, aspect. The center and left panels of the three-door portal are celebrated for the excellence of their scenes depicting the life of Christ.

The first-time visitor to Rouen might mistake the imposing 14th-century **Eglise de St-Ouen** for the city's cathedral. Several blocks north up the rue de la République from St-Maclou and in its own pedestrian zone, St-Ouen has perhaps more eminence than the cathedral. Its northern façade presents what might be the longest unadorned surface in Christendom, parading a power of unbroken line. Along this side is the cloister, which opens onto a surprise of gardens bordering on city hall, affording a view of St-Ouen's *chevet* (the rotunda of windowed chapels at the rear of the church). Work on St-Ouen was begun a century later than on Notre-Dame, and so the church reflects a later style of Gothic that can be seen in its flying buttresses, its arch supports, and the radiating chapels of its *chevet*.

ROUEN MUSEUMS

Just a few blocks west of St-Ouen along rue Thiers is the **Musée des Beaux-Arts**, which houses works by several name-brand Impressionists as well as pictures by David, Velázquez, and Rubens, and Norman painters such as Poussin. The interesting collections of the adjacent **Musée le Secq des Tournelles** are housed in the deconsecrated Eglise St-Laurent. Just across Square Verdrel from the fine-arts museum is the **Musée de la Céramique**. Rouen was long an important originator of painted stoneware, and the museum's collection of ceramics, which dates from the 16th to early 19th century, is particularly fine, rivaling any ceramic collection in Europe. The porcelain and stoneware (faïence) of Rouen have a fine reputation in France and are among the bargains for shoppers. Particularly attractive are the large serving pieces.

The **Musée Corneille**, on rue de la Pie, just off the Place du Vieux-Marché, and the **Musée Flaubert** at 51, rue de Lecat (follow the avenue Gustave Flaubert west of the *place*), are also worth visiting (both writers were natives of Rouen). Pierre Corneille is considered to be the master of French Classical tragedy. The museum honoring him occupies the house where he was born in 1806. Flaubert's father was a surgeon, so the family mansion is a surgical-history museum as well as one of writing. But the *grand musée* in Rouen is really its streets. Indoors await the pleasures of the Norman table.

STAYING AND DINING IN ROUEN

The place to order pressed duck, known in France as *canard à la rouennaise*, is **Le Quatre Saisons** (Tel: 35-71-96-00), in the ▶ **Hôtel Dieppe**, just across from the railroad station on Place Bernard-Tissot. As the menu will explain, the duck is a special variety, taken from a nearby backwater of the Seine where the local wild breed, the *col vert*—a type that resembles the mallard—crosses quite naturally with the domestic duck and then remains sedentary. The results are happy, as in delicious. The Quatre Saisons is one of those places that awaken us to the truth: how good the top *centre ville* restaurant can be anywhere in the provinces. The guest rooms upstairs are unusual, shaped by the outline of their particular cranny or hall.

There is also a good restaurant at 31, place du Vieux-Marché: **La Couronne**, housed in a 14th-century building and the oldest inn in France, a big place with several rooms that can hold 200 diners. The food is hearty, with the "local" menus the best choices, at 150 and 270 francs. (Tel: 35-71-40-90.)

THE COTE FLEURIE:
HONFLEUR TO DEAUVILLE

From Rouen, you can make your way back to the coast—to an especially appealing, well-kept stretch just south of the mouth of the Seine known as the Côte Fleurie (the Flowery Coast)—on autoroute A 13. Leave it for D 180 at the well-marked exit for Honfleur; the trip from Rouen to Honfleur is 80 km (50 miles).

Honfleur

This historic port, lined with sleeping yachts, halyards chattering against their masts, is like an Amsterdam in cameo. At first sight it doesn't look genuine, more like a fantasy set for a boat show, but it is, right down to the ancient pharmacist's sign painted on a slated wall recommending "cures for seasickness."

Honfleur has a rich maritime history. In the 16th and 17th centuries the town was a busy fishing and commercial port and the birthplace of numerous navigators, including Samuel Champlain, who on one of many Canadian voyages from here established Quebec in 1608. With the gradual silting up of the Seine, the town's importance dwindled while neighboring Le Havre grew in stature. Honfleur is still a thriving fishing port, threaded with nets to trip the unwary and echoing to the screams of scavenging sea gulls. But the historic port, the **Vieux Bassin**, is now the home of pleasure yachts, and the language of the yellow-booted mariners on the quai is (usually) more refined than that of the peg-leg-and-parrot salts of bygone times.

Narrow, tile-faced, historic houses, some seven stories tall, many with cafés, restaurants, antiques stores, and galleries on their ground floors, sit tightly packed around the three sides of the Vieux Bassin. They are the subject of many an artist's canvas, as well as tourist's camera, especially the one at the northern end of the basin, the **Lieutenance**, the twin-turreted remains of Honfleur's 16th-century governor's house.

Just behind the Lieutenance and Vieux Bassin lie the steeply sloping cobbled streets and alleyways around the **Eglise Ste-Catherine**. Apart from its foundations, the 15th-century church was built entirely of wood by the port's shipwrights, the nave actually constructed with ships' hulls in the shape of a keel. As a summer treat it, along with the weatherboarded belfry, is floodlit.

THE IMPRESSIONISTS IN HONFLEUR

There are those who say that Impressionism began in Honfleur. Certainly this claim is supported by the fact that its leading practitioner, Claude Monet, began to paint here, and that his mentor, the outstanding pre-Impressionist painter Eugène Boudin, was a native son. Honfleur has all the basic ingredients for Impressionistic painting: water, sky, flowers, a port that is as pretty as any ever pictured on a postcard, and something the artists called white light, a quality in the sunlight that seems to let the colors of things stand out in their purest form. Honfleur was also close to Paris, the major art market, and the Norman character afforded neighbors who minded their own business.

Honfleur didn't appeal only to Impressionists. Seurat and Signac broke down the white Norman light into seven colors, painting only with these and giving birth to Pointillism. The bold colors of Fauvism followed these Impressionist and Postimpressionist palettes. Twentieth-century painters continued to live and work in Normandy: Félix Vallotton, Albert Marquet, and Raoul Dufy.

The **Musée Eugène-Boudin**, several blocks behind Ste-Catherine on Place Erik Satie, is filled with works by Boudin, his friends, and his artistic offspring. The Musée des Beaux-Arts André Malraux in Le Havre contains a more comprehensive collection (see above).

STAYING AND DINING IN HONFLEUR

There are more than sufficient working boats in the outer harbor to guarantee an excellent seafood meal, the catch on the menu being landed, in some cases, no more than 20 yards from the sidewalk tables. Apart from the restaurants surrounding the Vieux Bassin there is a row of others along quai de la Quarantaine with acres of outdoor spring-to-autumn seating. But the highest accolades are reserved for ▶ **La Ferme St-Siméon**, a Relais & Châteaux restaurant (with rooms) where the Impressionists dined (contrary to their impoverished reputation?). It stand on the cliffs above town, with sea-gull views of the harbor. Unfortunately, the farmhouse where they discussed the superb colors and quality of light outside has been redecorated and much of its original character has been lost, and prices are much steeper than they were when Old Mother Toutain set a table for the starving types Boudin always seemed to be attracting.

The ▶ **Hôtellerie le Belvédère**, at 36, rue Renouf, is really a restaurant with rooms; eat here and you'll long remember the experience. Rooms are simple and quiet. ▶ **Le Castel Albertine** is a 19th-century manor-house hotel that offers its guests the pleasures of a lovely garden.

Deauville

Deauville, just 15 km (9 miles) southwest along the coast from Honfleur on D 513, is Paris on the sea, its 21st *arrondissement,* an honorary suburb for its wealthier citizens, a fresh-air zone for their dusty lungs. One wall in the Office de Tourisme carries a huge sepia photograph showing the sweep of Deauville's sandy beach with the Eiffel Tower rising from the middle distance. It's a trompe l'oeil, of course, but there's nothing unrealistic about it in spirit.

Deauville is elegant, exclusive, and expensive, a seaside unlike anywhere else. Its main square, Place de Morny, is amed for the illegitimate half brother of Louis-Napoléon who started it all in 1860. The duc de Morny's plan for a seaside resort was an instant success. The rich brought their checkbooks and mistresses, and saucy "Tangoville," as Deauville came to be known, flourished.

Start your Deauville visit on the terrace of the **Bar du**

Soleil, sheltered from the stiff sea breeze by glass screens. *Très sportifs* leisure suits are de rigueur, a poodle on the lap an optional extra. The café is on **Les Planches**, Deauville's wooden promenade. Beyond Les Planches, the wide, sandy beach, lapped by a calm but frigid sea, is all but covered by red, blue, and yellow canvas windbreaks and rows of lounges whose occupants seem far more interested in one another than in the sea. To the east, Les Planches ends at the town's marina, Port-Deauville, filled with sleek yachts.

After you've done Les Planches—many Deauville regulars walk its length several times a day trying to spot a famous face and checking out who's sailed into town—turn inland to take in the chic shops of the Hermès-Gucci ilk. Most are in the environs of the ▶ **Hôtel Normandy**, the smartest address in town, a couple of blocks inland from Les Planches on the rue des Villas. The casino next door is a splendid, Belle Epoque wedding cake of a building, entered at substantial risk to your bank account; don't worry, though: Only serious players are allowed into the high-rolling baccarat rooms.

Deauville is a thousand-horse town. There are fewer hotel bedrooms than horse stalls and, during August, more horses check in at the tiny local airport than people. Horses are bred, sold, and trained here, cantered through the surf at low tide, and raced at the two racecourses—**La Touques**, which takes up a third of the town center and has a mile-long straight, the longest in Europe, and the smaller **Clairefontaine**, just south.

In your wanderings about town you'll soon notice that Deauville's architecture is not particularly distinguished; all in all, it's a fairly ordinary-looking place. Cachet is what sets Deauville apart from other seaside resorts. Keep in mind, though, that Deauville really glitters only in the summer. Come winter, even the casino leaves its opulent palace for smaller *hiver* quarters across the street, and all of Deauville has the air of a ghost town; Les Planches is patrolled only by an occasional mink-enrobed stroller.

TROUVILLE

Flaubert, the French novelist, complained that "the beach where I once ran around naked is now adorned with policemen and there are demarcation lines for the two sexes." He was writing during the early 19th century, when Trouville, Deauville's neighbor across the river Touques, became a fashionable retreat with its own salon and bathing cabins for ladies to take to the waters in privacy. How things have changed. Today Trouville is predominantly a family holiday resort, a poor person's Deauville: It has a wide, sandy beach, the north end of which harbors reasonably priced family hotels, the type the French call "correct," and a casino and swimming pool—which may tell you something about the temperature of the sea. There is also a commercial fishing fleet docked along the Touques, giving the spa a nice water-front animation off-season. The shopping streets are clean and well ordered, the buildings still low enough to allow sunlight to reach the pedestrians. The stroller gets the feeling that Trouville is a town that has kept up-to-date but has not let progress run rampant.

STAYING AND DINING IN DEAUVILLE

Despite its glitz, there's not much in Deauville to detain you for longer than an afternoon. If you decide to spend a night or two here in style, the top choices are the Normandy (discussed above) and the equally luxurious ▶ Hôtel Royal, on the other side of the casino. The ▶ Hôtel Hélios and ▶ Hôtel Continental are both comfortable compromises near the center of town, but Deauville really isn't a place to accept less than the very best—you may be better off moving to less glamorous parts.

The choice for dinner is Ciro's, a restaurant on the promenade that looks like a humble beach café from the outside but can claim that its tables have been occupied by Lord Mountbatten, the duke of Windsor, the shah of Iran, King Farouk, the Aga Khan, Liz Taylor, and their rich and famous likes. Tel: 31-88-18-10. Le Kraal, a few blocks east of the Normandy on Place du Marché, is a pleasant, less expensive alternative. The wide range of crustaceans on the menu comes fresh daily from the fish stalls of the market outside the front door. Tel: 31-88-30-58.

PAYS D'AUGE: FROM DEAUVILLE TO THE LANDING BEACHES

Drive south from Deauville and you'll enter cheese country, Normandy's Pays d'Auge, whose farm and factory *fromageries* produce the four regional cheeses—Livarot, Pont-l'Evêque, pavé d'Auge, and Camembert. This sun-dappled *bocage,* with cows grazing on slopes that are as green as parsley, is what most people imagine when they think of Normandy. You can enter the Pays d'Auge, a 30-mile-long and 15-mile-wide valley of brooks, hills, and farms, from Deauville on N 117. Sections of the way are posted with *La*

Route du Fromage signs, and several *fromageries* offer the option of buying fresh, newly ripened cheese.

PONT L'EVEQUE

Pont-l'Evêque is just 12 km (7½ miles) south of Deauville. Bombed during World War II, the Pont-l'Evêque of today is far from a medieval experience. Yet there are a few buildings left that give an authentic taste of what was old Norman town style, with a courtyard for animals and food stocks attached. On the rue St-Michel a nest of old buildings huddles around such a court bordering a stream, which made for easy provisioning. And who can know France without knowing her classic cheeses? Pont-l'Evêque's special variety was being eaten well before Columbus reached America. Modern marketing techniques, however, have made overseas connoisseurship difficult if not altogether impossible. Nowadays many cheeses are produced at factories, and those earmarked for overseas sale are made to pass various regulations, including (horrors!) taste tests to ensure that they will satisfy differing foreign markets. Particularly hard hit by all this are the fermenting cheeses such as Camembert, Livarot, and Pont-l'Evêque, which are tamed for the trip to faraway markets and for "international" tastes. Even the milk for this kind of production is standardized, coming in the main from high-yield, low-butterfat producers—Holstein cows that feed on grain. But in the Pays d'Auge the visitor can taste the genuine item made from the milk of the original *race normande* breed, which grazes purely on grass, not in feedlots. These cheeses will surprise you with their renowned richness, only the barest hint of which exists in the mass-produced products that bear their names.

LISIEUX

Your next call should be Lisieux, the hub of the region, 17 km (11 miles) south of Pont-l'Evêque on D 579. A turn west onto D 47B just north of the town will take you to the incomparable manor of **Coupesarte**, with its moat and fortified wall. Just a bit farther on is the **Château Grandchamp**, a 16th-century example of Norman privacy ringed by earthen levees meant to protect livestock and granaries against invaders and wind. From a distance the manors look like verdant oases, hedged with oaks or elms and floating on a sea of grass. However, you can enter neither place. At Coupesarte they'll give you a tour around the outside—a satisfactory visit, really—for a donation. At Grandchamp you are expected to keep your distance.

The town is rather dreary, but worth a visit for the giant **Basilique Ste-Thérèse**, dedicated to the number-two patron saint of France—it contains bones from her right arm—and modeled on the Sacré Coeur in Paris. The long-suffering Carmelite sister is commemorated by mosaics, photographs—even a laser show—as well as tasteless souvenirs in town.

INTO CAMEMBERT COUNTRY

From Lisieux it's 27 km (17 miles) south on D 579 to Vimoutiers, the capital of the Camembert-producing region. You may want to stop en route at the cheese-making school in **Livarot**, 18 km (11 miles) south of Lisieux, for a taste of the area's different cheeses; the town is a picturesque little place on the banks of the river Vie.

The road between Pont-l'Evêque and Lisieux is particularly picturesque following the river Touques. In Pierrefitte-en-Auge, about 5 km (3 miles) south of Pont-l'Evêque, the **Auberge des Deux Tonneaux** (Tel: 31-64-09-31) is a good place to stop for refreshments, and the innkeeper can provide you with the key that unlocks the local church. **Ouilly-le-Vicomte**, where one of the oldest churches in Normandy—parts from the tenth century still survive—can be seen on its lovely islet in the river Touques, about 9 km (5½ miles) downstream. In the center of Vimoutiers stands a statue of Marie Harel, the farmer's wife to whom, in the late 18th century, a priest presented the secret recipe for this now-famous cheese. The excellent **Musée du Camembert** houses one of the biggest collections of cheese labels in the world. The village of Camembert, where Madame Harel lived, is about 5 km (3 miles) south on D 246.

Camembert tastes best, of course, in the place of its birth. In a local bistro or café, the Camembert to ask for is Camembert *fermier,* which is made on the farm and has little to do with the perfumed and pasteurized dandies the big cheese factories concoct. The one consumed in this area is rich, with a creamy kick, and is well worth the trip.

THE SUISSE NORMANDE

From Vimoutiers head for **Falaise** (37 km/23 miles west on D 916 and D 83), birthplace of William the Conqueror. The town lies at the edge of some of the most spectacular scenery in northern France, the Suisse Normande.

The Suisse Normande is a landscape of rolling forests and

meadows that dip and rise around the valley of the river
Orne. A good way to enter this pleasant corner of Normandy
is to follow D 6 northwest 27 km (17 miles) from Falaise to
Thury-Harcourt. You can leave your car at a marked area just
outside of town for a pleasant three-mile walk high above
the so-called **Boucle du Hom**, a deep loop in the river Orne.
The spectacular views are a good introduction to the region.

From Thury you can follow the Orne valley south for
about 30 km (19 miles) on the well-marked **Route des
Crêtes** to the most mountainous terrain in the Suisse Normande, the **Roche d'Oëtre**, rising high above the gorges of
the Orne. To continue on to Caen from the Suisse Normande, simply retrace your steps to Falaise, and from there
follow N 158 for 34 km (21 miles) north.

Caen

In the heart of Calvados countryside, Caen, the capital of
lower Normandy, spreads out from the confluence of the
rivers Odon and Orne. What was once a tiny settlement grew
to prominence in the 11th century, when it was nurtured,
protected, and fortified by William the Bastard, later known
as the Conqueror.

British and Canadian bombers, attempting to reclaim the
nearby seaport of Ouistreham in 1944, laid waste to nearly
three quarters of the town, and the retreating Germans
finished the job. But although much of the town's historic
beauty was lost, a lot of time, money, and energy was spent
on Caen's renaissance. Today, remains of historic buildings
stand at ease alongside high-tech edifices, mostly built of the
same soft, mellow, honey-colored local limestone that centuries ago William the Conqueror shipped to England to build
Canterbury Cathedral and the Tower of London.

The town has also been designed with a sense of spatial
generosity, landscaped with parks, attractive streets that are
closed to most vehicles, and broad avenues shaded by trees.
An arm of surrounding countryside penetrates deep into the
heart of Caen as a huge park, **La Prairie**. When you look at a
map of Caen, spread across the page in gulping proportions,
the city poses an alarming prospect for the visitor. But
despair not. The suburbs sprawl for miles and everything
worth seeing is contained within a square mile immediately
south of the château built high above the town by William in
the 11th century. The train and bus stations are south of this
section of the city, just across the river Orne.

ABBAYE AUX HOMMES
AND ABBAYE AUX DAMES

The pope strongly disapproved of William the Conqueror's marriage to Matilda of Flanders (William and Matilda were cousins) and excommunicated the couple. William won back papal approval by promising to found an abbey exclusively for men, while Matilda would do the same for women. The Abbaye aux Hommes (with its Eglise de St-Etienne) and Abbaye aux Dames (with its Eglise de la Trinité) are the magnificent results of their promises. Both were built in Normandy's predominating 11th-century Romanesque style and finished off in Gothic a century later.

Throughout the Battle of Caen the Allies deliberately avoided bombing the two abbeys, knowing from the Resistance that hundreds of civilians were using them for refuge: At least 1,500 were living in the Abbaye aux Hommes, and the Abbaye aux Dames housed a hospital and hospice. Today, the enormous gray profiles of the abbeys dominate the city, Aux Hommes to the west of the château, Aux Dames to the east.

The **Abbaye aux Hommes** is a good place to begin your exploration of Caen. It lies at the western edge of the old city, at the end of the busy rue St-Pierre. Although William died in Rouen, he was buried within the abbey's sanctuary 900 years ago, beneath an imposing tomb on which he is described as duke of Normandy and king of England, in that order. Huguenots stole his remains from the tomb in the 16th century; all that's left is a thighbone. You can still visit the abbey's **Eglise St-Etienne**, a superb example of High Romanesque, a style that William's prior-cum-secretary Lanfranc, the builder of Aux Hommes, modified when he carried it over the Channel and built Canterbury Cathedral. But part of the original abbey, the adjacent conventual building housing the parlor, cloister, refectory, chapter house, main staircase, and guardroom, now serves as the Hôtel de Ville and is open only for guided tours. Set back from the square, its flag-lined driveway and huge, manicured gardens and picturesque flower beds give it the air of a palace rather than the HQ of local government.

Queen Matilda's **Abbaye aux Dames**, with its crypt borne up by 16 massive pillars, is a more compact building, rebuilt in the Classical style in the 17th century. Aux Dames is about a kilometer (half a mile) across town from Aux Hommes via rue St-Pierre to rue des Chanoines. You can visit Matilda's tomb in the choir of the church. After years of faithful service as an old-people's home, the abbey is now also a local government building, newly restored since January 1986, when it opened to visitors for the first time. Matilda's tomb lies in the choir of the **Eglise de la Trinité**, whose elegant spires were sadly destroyed in the war.

THE PLACE ST-PIERRE
AND THE CHATEAU

William's 11th-century château is high above the town, half-way between the two abbeys and reached by a ramp off the lively Place St-Pierre. The highly ornamented **Eglise St-Pierre** here is the parish church of the city merchants; its original 80-meter belfry caught a direct hit from a shell fired by H.M.S. *Rodney* but was later reconstructed. The Office de Tourisme is also on the *place,* in the beautiful mansion of a 16th-century merchant, the **Hôtel d'Escoville**. This and a few other *hôtels particuliers* are among the many Renaissance mansions the nobility built in Caen; the survivors are a striking reminder of how beautiful Caen must have been before World War II.

Another piece of Caen's architectural heritage lies a few blocks south along avenue du 6 Juin: The **Eglise St-Jean**, just off the Place de la Résistance, is Caen's Tower of Pisa look-alike—it was never completed because of the unstable, marshy ground beneath it, and today the whole church leans rather unnervingly, as do the pillars inside. Its bold appear-ance, like some craggy gray mountain rising from a sea of neatly trimmed grass and flower beds, still proudly flying the Norman flag—two leopards against a red background—was paradoxically enhanced by the wartime disappearance of the buildings that once surrounded it. Cross the drawbridge, pass under the mile-long ramparts (the longest in France), and inside you'll find a surprise of trees, gardens, a chil-dren's play area, and two museums.

The **Musée des Beaux-Arts** has impressive galleries of Italian, Flemish, and French painters, including Veronese, Tintoretto, Rubens, Poussin, Monet, and Bonnard. There are enamels from Limoges, 18th-century miniatures and tapes-tries, and an exceptional collection of 50,000 engravings, including works by Dürer and Rembrandt. The **Musée de Normandie**, in a 14th-century house that was once home to governors of Caen, evokes Normandy through the ages with scale models of farms, field layouts, machinery, costumes, crafts, and a detailed study of how the rural folk worked, from the making of buttons to boxes for Camembert. Also within the château walls are the **Salle de l'Echiquier** (Hall of the Exchequer), the Chapelle St-Georges, and a *jardin des* *simples* filled with examples of medical and aromatic plants cultivated in the Middle Ages.

STAYING AND DINING IN CAEN

Caen competes with Rouen as the gastronomic capital of Normandy, producing one of France's most famous dishes, *tripes à la mode de Caen*. Made from beef guts and calves' feet—to which vegetables, garlic, herbs, and cider are added—it was perfected in the 14th century by a chef called Benoît; and even though Caen has changed a lot since then, the recipe has changed little.

The people of Caen have a genuine affinity for their Anglo-Saxon brothers-in-arms. Their welcome is as warm as their Calva, and the *trou normand* is a common practice here. Without doubt the most atmospheric place in town for food and drink is **La Bourride**, housed in a beautiful mansion near the castle at 15, rue Vaugueux. The two menus are priced at 290 francs and 420 francs, not including wine (Tel: 31-93-50-76). Specializing in fish, **Le Dauphin** is an amiable restaurant near the château, at 29, rue Gemare. Tel: 31-86-22-26.

The ▶ **Hôtel Moderne**, in the heart of town, is the place to stay in Caen. Its rooms are comfortable, spacious, and individualized. There is also a wonderful panorama from the fifth-floor dining room, where you can take your breakfast.

At Audrieu, a few kilometers south of N 13 on D 158 between Caen and Bayeux, and within easy distance of both, is the ▶ **Relais Château d'Audrieu**. The hotel is an 18th-century building within its own park and provides deluxe accommodations, a swimming pool, and a restaurant with an intriguing menu. Try the snail-and-lobster soup.

Bayeux

After the modernity of Caen, Bayeux (23 km/14 miles north-west on N 13) looks like it's trapped in a time warp. Just inland from the landing beaches, Bayeux was the first major town to be liberated by the Allies and escaped serious war damage, leaving its limestone houses (many dating from the 14th century) beautifully intact along cobbled streets. This small, ancient, and extremely pretty town is the capital of the Bessin, a meadowy, pastoral subsection of Calvados. Bayeux is famous for its pottery, its lacemaking, and its graceful, medieval **Cathédrale Notre-Dame**—more decorative than Caen's austere abbeys and the best example of the region's exuberant, ornate Gothic-Normand architecture—and oh yes, for its tapestry.

THE BAYEUX TAPESTRY

In 1066 William the Bastard, as he was affectionately known (being the illegitimate son of Robert the Devil), with his fleet of some 800 vessels, the greatest invasion force ever to have crossed the Channel, mounted his successful conquest of Britain. The invasion, and the events leading up to it, is chronicled in what the French call *La Tapisserie de la Reine Matilde,* though it is neither, technically quibbling, a tapestry nor the product of either Queen Matilda's hand or design. It is nevertheless impressive.

This "cartoon," 231 feet long and little more than a foot and a half wide, is a band of linen, embroidered in a trillion stitches of colored wool, and made in England by William's half brother, Bishop Odo. It was brought to Bayeux to decorate the nave of the cathedral on feast days. Half a million people come to the **Centre Guillaume-le-Conquérant** (William the Conqueror Center)—housed in one of Bayeux's fine old mansions, just west of the cathedral on rue de Nesmond—each year to pay their respects, following a tedious, tantalizing, circuitous route through a theater, background displays, and slide presentations before coming face to face with the real thing. Which goes on, and on, and on. If you are confused about who's who, the English are the lads with the mustaches.

STAYING AND DINING IN BAYEUX

The best hotel in town is the ▶ **Lion d'Or,** a 17th-century coaching inn near the center of town on rue St-Jean built around a courtyard, with a Michelin-starred restaurant specializing in roast lamb that draws diners from miles around (Tel: 31-86-22-26). In the center of the town, the ▶ **Luxembourg,** 25, rue des Bouchers, also a former post-road relay station, is another place to stop. Its rooms have charm, its restaurant—**Le Quatre Saisons**—has clout, and its prices are not at all steep (except for a suite).

The Landing Beaches

The Allied action that took place on D day, June 6, 1944, is well documented and needs no repetition here. The beaches—and the war museums—form a line west from Ouistreham, just 14 km (8½ miles) north of Caen on D 515. To visit them, but more specifically to stand at the headlands above the beaches and just look out, will give an idea of the difficulties encountered that day that no amount of reading or film viewing can offer.

The roll call of coast towns rings out with names of beaches that were assaulted: Ste-Mère-Eglise; Omaha Beach (at Colleville); Utah Beach (at La Madeleine); Sword, Juno, and Gold beaches (from Arromanches to Ouistreham). There are markers where the actions took place; here and there broken blockhouses loom. There's a film show at Arromanches and white crosses dotting the green carpets that roll down toward the sea at Omaha Beach.

After the landings the fighting continued. The Battle of Normandy, as it was called, quickly became a desperate struggle. The British, Americans, and Canadians fought so as not to stall and then be thrown back into the sea; the Germans, of course, fought to keep the Allies from advancing. More than 200,000 homes were destroyed in the onslaught; ports and crossroads like Le Havre, Rouen, Caen, and Lisieux were virtually flattened. After ten weeks of attack and counterattack, the Battle of Normandy ended on August 19. The Germans had lost about half a million men against relatively light Allied losses, the route to Paris was open, and the world was about to be reordered into the one we know today.

You could spend a large part of a Normandy trip visiting all the landing beaches, their museums, and cemeteries; indeed, many war veterans make this the focus of their visits.

ARROMANCHES

Otherwise, you may prefer to just get a sense of the campaign; this is arguably best experienced at Arromanches, 10 km (6 miles) north of Bayeux on D 516.

The high point in the hitherto uneventful history of this quiet fishing village–cum–resort at the mouth of the tiny Arro river was its choice in 1944 as the site for the artificial harbor the Allies built to facilitate the landing. Today many tourists swell the number of its 400 or so inhabitants, especially on the anniversary of D day, when they climb to Asnelles to get the best view of the vast remnants of harbor, such as breakwaters and floating metal piers, that still lie in the bay and to visit the **Musée du Débarquement** (Disembarkment Museum) at the eastern end of the town. The excellent displays of Royal Navy and American film, artillery remains, and other memorabilia will tap either sentiment or imagination, depending on the generation.

Tours of the disembarkment beaches, resorts, Bayeux, and more are offered by several outfits from June 15 to September 15. Reserve with Fournier, Calvados Voyages, SNCF, or Verney at the Office de Tourisme on Place St-Pierre.

THE COTENTIN PENINSULA AND LE MONT-SAINT-MICHEL

The Cotentin peninsula, the stubby thumb of Normandy that jauntily protrudes into the Channel, is bordered on three sides by sea. There are no big cities, no polluting industries, no heavy traffic; there are, however, superb scenery, good walks, long, sandy beaches, comfortable hotels, and fishy restaurants. Still off the tourist track, the Cotentin is often referred to as the Cherbourg peninsula, since all roads lead south from its biggest town, at the tip of the peninsula 120 km (74 miles) west and north of Caen on N 13.

Cherbourg

Although the harbor at Cherbourg was heavily blitzed by the retreating Germans, much of the town survived the ravages of World War II. Many of the buildings date to the 16th and 17th centuries, and several of the narrow, cobbled streets are closed to traffic for the benefit of shoppers. Pretty well everything of interest to the visitor is contained within the compact heart the old town, an island of interest hugging the waterfront and surrounded by the tall structures of postwar Cherbourg.

On the wall of Cherbourg's Office de Tourisme, on the busy waterfront at 2, quai Alexandre III, hangs a massive old relief map showing two ocean liners leaving town, one heading across the Channel for Southampton, the other *vers les Amériques*. The *Queen Elizabeth II,* among other liners, still visits half a dozen times a year, but the town's role as a port of call for the great transatlantic giants came to an end with the advent of jet airplanes. The liners have been replaced by cargo ships and less stately ferries bringing passengers from Britain and Ireland.

THE OLD TOWN

The **Musée Thomas-Henry**, a few steps off the quai, houses an important collection of the paintings of Jean-François Millet, who was born in nearby La Hague. Cherbourg's theater, which occupies one side of the Place du Général-de-Gaulle just north of the museum, is a richly sculpted building, a fin-de-siècle *gâteau* that would perhaps be more comfortably accommodated in the Place de l'Opéra in Paris. An open-air market monopolizes the whole of the square, known locally as Place Château, on Thursdays, and is a brilliant exhibition of flowers, fruit, vegetables, chickens, rabbits, cane furniture, cheeses, and *charcuteries*. The tall and narrow **Eglise Notre-Dame-du-Voeu**, with its pair of distinctive towers divided by a statue, stands at the southern edge of the old town in the charming, peaceful Place Notre-Dame-du-Voeu, surrounded by white-shuttered houses.

STAYING AND DINING
IN CHERBOURG

The best hotel in Cherbourg is the ▶ **Mercure**, brash, modern, and low on character, but affording terrific views of the sea and harbor from its waterfront location at the Gare Maritime. For a memorable fish meal, head for the **Café de Paris**, overlooking the port from the quai de Caligny; it's the place with the huge fishing net and live crabs in the window. Tel: 33-43-12-36.

AROUND CHERBOURG

The Eastern Peninsula

Just 6 km (3½ miles) east of Cherbourg, the Renaissance **Château de Tourlaville** is set in several acres of formal gardens with subtropical plants, lakes, and waterfalls. This turreted, fairy-tale castle is well known in these parts as the scene of a tragic love affair between a brother and a sister, Marguerite and Julien de Ravalet, whose incest eventually led to their execution on the Parisian gallows.

The coast at the eastern edges of the peninsula is peppered with hamlets and small fishing ports. One of the most pleasant is **Barfleur**, 27 km (17 miles) east of Cherbourg on D 901, the departure point for William the Conqueror's invasion of England. A bronze plaque duplicating the seal of the *Mora*, William's hardy vessel, is stuck like a limpet to the side of a large rock near the jetty. **St-Vaast-la-Hougue** is well worth the trip of 12 km (7½ miles) south and east of Barfleur on D 902 and D 1: The town's oyster beds are said to yield the tastiest oysters in France.

Cap de la Hague

The moody Cap de la Hague (this northwestern tip of the Cotenin peninsula is 28 km/17 miles west of Cherbourg on D 901) is a heather-covered moorland carved by twisting valleys and stark, bluestone cottages. This wild, granite coastline, with rocky cliffs and sandy beaches, is one of the most dramatic parcels of France.

You will probably want to give the nuclear-processing plant at Jobourg a wide berth, but don't skip the wuthering heights of the **Nez de Jobourg**, where the highest cliffs in France (457 feet) tower above churning, treacherous waters, affording views all the way to the island of Guernsey.

Le Mont-Saint-Michel

According to how the sands at the mouth of the estuary have shifted, this wonder of the medieval world, built over a span of three centuries, is either in Normandy or in Brittany. Right now it's in Normandy, although, lying a mere 50 km (31 miles) east of St-Malo, it would fit well in a tour of Brittany's northern coast. Le Mont-Saint-Michel is 119 km (74 miles) southwest of Caen on N 175; if you wind your way down the Cotentin peninsula, the Mont is 96 km (60 miles) southwest of Cherbourg; it's 24 km (19 miles) across the salty flats of the coast on N 175, D 43, and D 275 from Avranches, at the southwestern base of the peninsula, to the Mont.

Plan your itinerary to arrive during daylight. The outline of the island and its spindle-shaped spire visible from afar form one of the most memorable sights in all of France and must not be missed. To enjoy your visit you must come at a time when the Mont isn't awash in crowds. Arrive in the early morning or late afternoon, to avoid the day trippers. And by all means, never venture anywhere near the Mont on a French holiday.

THE ABBEY

Both fortress and religious shrine, during the Middle Ages the Mont was especially rich in pilgrims' gifts. It was protected against sack and invasion by the ferocious tide, which comes roaring in with the speed of a racehorse and with enough power to splatter besieging armies against the seawall. This fact of nature, along with a hearty band of monks, was the only defense the pyramiding spires of Mont-Saint-Michel—collectively called, as they are, "the miracle"—ever needed. "Miraculous" is the word that best describes the superb Gothic ensemble of the uppermost north façade of the islet.

The structures are built in a heavenly ascent from earth to sky. They begin, above the rampart wall, with the Aumonerie, the great residence of chaplains and monks, on one side. On the other is the great hall of knights. The next tier is the cloister, with arcades and galleries that seem to hover in the sky. There are wonderfully worked sculptures to see in these walks—busts and whole human shapes, and animals, too, amid the decor of surrounding leaves. The arcades overhead are suspended by the lightest and airiest of spindle columns.

This large, luminous refectory has long, narrow windows, and everything that enters is bathed in a sanctifying light. Here the whole host of knights (on pilgrimage) and monks assembled. Eating here must have seemed celestial.

And above all this was the final step on the way to the final reward, as it is the final statement in Mont-Saint-Michel's architecture. There, atop an esplanade of terraces and buttresses, soars the church, its spire thrusting 500 feet into the sky, the final achivement in the architectural ensemble and in the ascent of Western medieval man.

STAYING AND DINING
AT MONT-SAINT-MICHEL

The hotel of note on the Mont is ▶ **La Mère Poulard**; it's comfortable and atmospheric, but there's not a French voice to be heard among the guests. Lamb—the area's sheep feed well in the coastal salt marshes—omelettes, and dessert soufflés are specialties in the wood-beamed dining room. A quieter choice would be the ▶ **Relais du Roy**, 2 km (1 mile) off the Mont on D 976.

GETTING AROUND

By car, Normandy is easily reached from Paris on A 13 (Autoroute de Normandie) to Rouen, and from there on to Le Havre and Dieppe on N 27.

Trains run regularly from the Gare St-Lazare in Paris to Rouen, Caen, Le Havre, and all other major cities in Normandy. Air Atlantique flies from Paris to Cherbourg and Le Havre. By boat from the U.K., the major points of entry in Normandy are Caen, from Portsmouth; Cherbourg, from Portsmouth and Weymouth; and Dieppe, from Newhaven. There is limited air service from London to Normandy cities on Brit Air, which flies from Gatwick Airport to Caen, and Regional Airlines, which flies from Gatwick to Rouen.

ACCOMMODATIONS REFERENCE

The rates given below are projections *for 1994. Unless otherwise indicated, rates are for a double room, double occupancy, and do not include meals. As rates are always subject to change, double-check before booking.*

▶ **Astoria**. 13, cours République, 76600 **Le Havre**. Tel: 35-25-00-03; Telex: 190075F; Fax: 35-26-48-34. 180F–280F.

▶ **L'Auberge de la Rouge**. 76400 **Fécamp**. Tel: 35-28-07-59; Fax: 35-28-70-55. 300F.

▶ **Le Castel Albertine**. 19, cours Albert-Manuel, 14600 **Honfleur**. Tel: 31-98-85-56; Fax: 31-98-83-18. 340F–560F.

▶ **La Ferme St-Siméon.** Route Adolphe-Marais, 14600 **Honfleur.** Tel: 31-89-23-61; Telex: 171031; Fax: 31-89-48-48; in the U.S., Tel: (212) 856-0115; Fax: (212) 856-0193. Member, Relais & Châteaux. 1,350F–2,120F.

▶ **France et Bourgogne.** 19–21, cours République, 76600 **Le Havre.** Tel: 35-25-40-34; Fax: 35-24-35-93. 330F.

▶ **Hôtel des Arcades.** 1–3, arcade de la Bourse, 76200 **Dieppe.** Tel: 35-84-14-12. Fax: 35-40-22-29. 235F.

▶ **Hôtel Continental.** 1, rue Désiré-le-Hoc, 14800 **Deauville.** Tel: 31-88-21-06; Fax: 31-98-93-67. 360F–430F.

▶ **Hôtel Dieppe.** Place Bernard-Tissot, 76000 **Rouen.** Tel: 35-71-96-00; Telex: 180413; Fax: 35-89-65-21. 495F–610F.

▶ **Hôtel des Falaises.** 1, boulevard René-Coty, 76790 **Etretat.** Tel: 35-27-02-77. 270F–380F.

▶ **Hôtel Hélios.** 10, rue Fossorier, 14800 **Deauville.** Tel: 31-88-28-26; Fax: 31-88-53-87. 460F.

▶ **Hôtellerie le Belvédère.** 36, rue Renouf, 14600 **Honfleur.** Tel: 31-89-08-13; Fax: 31-89-51-40. 250F–350F.

▶ **Hôtel Moderne.** 116, boulevard Maréchal-Leclerc, 14000 **Caen.** Tel: 31-86-04-23; Fax: 31-85-37-93. 320F–630F.

▶ **Hôtel Normandy.** 38, rue Jean-Mermoz, 14800 **Deauville.** Tel: 31-98-66-22; Telex: 170617; Fax: 31-98-66-23; in U.S., (212) 254-2217 or (800) 755-9313. 1,700F–2,000F.

▶ **Hôtel des Phares.** 29, rue Géneral de Gaulle, 76310 **Ste-Adresse.** Tel: 35-46-31-86; Fax: 35-54-36-08. 140F–260F.

▶ **Hôtel Royal.** Boulevard E. Cornuché, 14800 **Deauville.** Tel: 31-98-66-33; Fax: 31-98-66-34. 1,500F–2,000F.

▶ **Lion d'Or.** 71, rue St-Jean, 14400 **Bayeux.** Tel: 31-92-06-90; Fax: 31-22-15-64. 270F–900F.

▶ **Luxembourg.** 25, rue des Bouchers, 14400 **Bayeux.** Tel: 31-92-00-04; Fax: 31-92-54-26. 420F–470F; suites 1,200F.

▶ **Mercure.** Gare Maritime, 50100 **Cherbourg.** Tel: 33-44-01-11; Fax: 33-44-51-00. 360F–610F.

▶ **La Mère Poulard.** 50116 **Le Mont-Saint-Michel.** Tel: 33-60-14-01; Fax: 33-48-52-31. 400F–950F.

▶ **La Présidence.** 1, boulevard de Verdun, 76200 **Dieppe.** Tel: 35-84-31-31; Fax: 35-84-86-70. 455F.

▶ **Relais Château d'Audrieu.** Tilly-sur-Seulles, 14250 **Audrieu** (13 km/8 miles south of Bayeux on Route D 158). Tel: 31-80-21-52; Fax: 31-80-24-73; in U.S., Tel: (212) 856-0115; Fax: (212) 856-0193. Member, Relais & Châteaux. 785F–1,200F.

▶ **Relais du Roy.** La Digue, 50116 **Le Mont-Saint-Michel.** Tel: 33-60-14-25; Fax: 33-60-37-69. 385F.

▶ **Windsor.** 18, boulevard de Verdun, 76200 **Dieppe.** Tel: 35-84-15-23; Fax: 35-84-74-52. 290F–345F.

BRITTANY

By Alexander Lobrano with Fred Halliday

Alexander Lobrano worked as a writer and editor in New York and London before moving to Paris seven years ago. Formerly an editor in the Paris office of Fairchild Publications, he now freelances for The International Herald Tribune, The Los Angeles Times, *and* Travel & Leisure, *among other publications.*

While many parts of France gently win you over with their subtle charms, Brittany greets you with a clap on the back. This large and westernmost province of France is a hale and hearty place, shaggy and green, with fresh, bracing air that reminds you constantly of what lies at the core of its identity—the Atlantic Ocean. For centuries the Bretons have earned their living from these rough, cold, green waters, which have also served to isolate or, depending on your point of view, protect it from the rest of the country: Two of Brittany's three borders are with the sea—the English Channel and the Atlantic Ocean—and the third, as the Bretons would have it, is with France.

Since the arrival of the TGV Atlantique, the Breton branch of France's admirable high-speed train service, which now whisks you in two hours from Paris to Rennes, Brittany's capital, or Nantes, its largest city, this isolation is no longer absolute—a fact that many Bretons regret. This new proximity has not yet done anything to blunt the province's indelible culture; the Bretons still cling to the Celtic heritage they share with the Irish and the Welsh, their own cuisine and their own fast food (crepes and *galettes*), as well as their own language—Brezhoneg, which shares the same roots as Cornish and Welsh. (Only about 800,000 people still speak Brezhoneg, but it's currently enjoying something of a revival.) The TGV Atlantique pushes ever onward, and thus promises that the province will become more popular with the French themselves—it's already a favored destination for the Germans, Belgians, Dutch, and British. Additionally, many Bretons fear that the Channel Tunnel, which when completed will link England with Normandy, will disgorge hordes of Brits in search of second homes, as has happened in "Normandyshire" already, even through existing cross-Channel links. Should this come to pass, however, Brittany will more fully warrant its name—"Little Britain," as it was grabbily dubbed by the British Celts who drifted into the region in successive waves around A.D. 460—than it has for the past 15 centuries.

So, the province—one of the most distinctive and beautiful in France—is poised for change, and many of its unself-conscious fishing villages may eventually become well-known resorts. But the metamorphosis won't happen overnight, and it's unlikely that anything will ever change the implacable Breton character, which is as solid, craggy, and picturesque as Brittany's wave-battered coasts.

The interior of the region is a pleasing mélange of forests and farms—most of France's green beans, cauliflower, and artichokes are grown here—and is dotted with small villages and some remarkable medieval art, especially the *calvaires,* granite monuments in parish closes illustrating Christ's Passion. But it is the coastline, with its bays and boulders, cliffs and many islands, that most exhilarates the visitor. Seeing the best of it requires careful planning, as Brittany is large and you'll invariably be tempted to linger in one favorite spot before going on to discover another.

MAJOR INTEREST

SOUTHERN COAST

Nantes
Musée des Beaux-Arts
Cathédrale de St-Pierre et St-Paul
Château des Ducs de Bretagne
Old town pedestrian zone

La Baule, fashionable beach resort

Vannes
Cathédrale de St-Pierre and surrounding medieval
  streets
Golfe du Morbihan and its islands

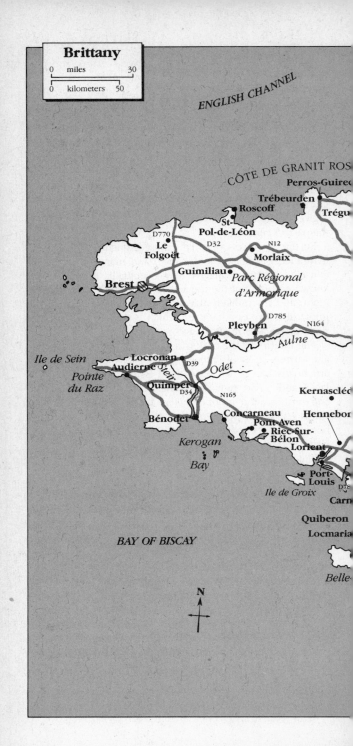

Brittany

| 0 | miles | 30 |
| 0 | kilometers | 50 |

ENGLISH CHANNEL

CÔTE DE GRANIT ROS

Perros-Guirec

Trébeurden

Roscoff

Trégu

St-
Pol-de-Léon

D770

D32

N12

Le
Folgoët

Morlaix

Guimiliau

*Parc Régional
d'Armorique*

Brest

D785

N164

Pleyben

Aulne

Ile de Sein

Locronan

D39

Odet

Audierne

Steir

*Pointe
du Raz*

Quimper

D34

N165

Kernascléd

Bénodet

Concarneau

Hennebor

Pont-Aven

Riec-Sur-
Bélon

Kerogan

Lorient

Bay

Port-
Louis

D78

Ile de Groix

Carn

Quiberon

Locmaria

BAY OF BISCAY

Belle-

N

Locmariaquer and Carnac, prehistoric megaliths
Quiberon, lively resort town with seawater spas and
    good beaches; ferry to Belle-Ile
Concarneau, medieval citadel

Quimper
Cathédrale de St-Corentin
Old city
Musée des Beaux-Arts
Musée Breton

Pointe du Raz, the westernmost point in Brittany
Locronan, picturesque medieval village

Parc Régional d'Armorique
Pleyben and Guimiliau, spectacular *calvaires*

NORTHERN COAST

Roscoff, busy fishing port
St-Pol-de-Leon, cathedral and Kreisker chapel
Morlaix, circuit of local *calvaires*
Le Folgoët, 15th-century Cathédrale de Notre-Dame
    de Folgoët, and Guimiliau
Trébeurden and the Côte de Granit Rose
Tréguier, Cathédrale de St-Tugdual
Paimpol and the Ile de Bréhat
Cap Fréhel, Dinard, and the Côte d'Emeraude
Ramparts of St-Malo and oysters of Cancale

RENNES

Parlement de Bretagne
Musée de Bretagne
Musée des Beaux-Arts
Old houses in the pedestrian zone

A thumbnail history of Brittany explains why the Bretons to
this day consider themselves to be a different people from
the French. This peninsula has been inhabited since 4500
B.C., and has some of the most spectacular prehistoric sites
in Europe. But it was the arrival of the first Celtic tribes
around 300 B.C. that laid the foundations of a Celtic "nation."
These Celts were eventually overwhelmed by five tribes of
Gauls, who called the region Armorica (L'Armorique, in
French; *Armor* is Celtic for "Country of the sea") and left
their names behind; the Veneti were from what is now
Vannes, the Namnetes from Nantes, and the Redones from
Rennes. The Romans conquered these Gallic tribes in 56 B.C.
and ruled the area for 400 years, until their empire came

under attack in Britain by invading Angles and Saxons. This led to the key event in Breton history: the migration in A.D. 460 of the British Celts from England to Brittany.

As the Gallo-Romans withdrew, the Celts organized the land into kingdoms, and wove it into their legends. Much of the Breton interior was once covered by the forest of Broceliande, known today in its much diminished form as the Forêt de Paimpont, and it was in these misty acres where big thickets of ferns grow in the shade of ivy-entwined oaks that Merlin, the sorceror of King Arthur's court, is said to have disappeared. Beloved of the fairy Viviane, the "Lady of the Lake," he is said, according to some versions of the Arthurian tale, to have vanished because Viviane cast a spell on him, appeasing her doubts about his reliability by imprisoning him inside an oak or a stone. The knights of King Arthur's Round Table also wandered these woods in their quest for the Holy Grail.

After subsequent incursions by the Frankish kings were repulsed, Brittany remained essentially independent until 1488, when Charles VII of France defeated François II, the last duke of Brittany, at the Battle of St-Aubin du Cormier. To further ally the province with France, Anne de Bretagne, François's heiress, was forced to marry Charles VIII and, after his death, his successor, Louis XII. Anne attempted to secure the province's independence within the kingdom of France, but these efforts came to an end with the marriage of her daughter, Claude, to François I, the future king of France. During the 16th century the province clung to its few remaining autonomous privileges and the region thrived as its trade with the New World expanded and the ship-building industry flourished.

Almost a millennium of independence is not forgotten in a century or two, however; when the new French Republic started passing unpopular legislation after the Revolution, the Bretons revolted, a failed uprising known as the Chouannerie. Afterward, the French worked assiduously to dissolve Breton culture, and students were forbidden to speak Brezhoneg in school, where all instruction took place in French. This fostered a resentment that simmered for several generations and that was ultimately exploited by the Germans during World War II, with sad results. Under German occupation Breton culture was revived and encouraged as a way of permanently weakening France; the Germans recruited Breton nationalists to serve in the region's puppet government. After the war many of these recruits fled to neutral Ireland to escape retaliation, and remained there until an official pardon was issued by Charles de Gaulle.

A major road-building program began in 1968, and this, along with other substantial government investments in the region, roused the province from its postwar slumber. Today the province continues to produce a major part of the French oyster harvest, and fishing trawlers operating from Breton ports land one of the largest and most valuable catches in the country every year; indeed, many chefs in top Paris restaurants personally visit their suppliers in Roscoff and other ports on a regular basis to ensure their supply of the top-quality Breton catch. Agriculture, especially in the form of truck gardens, employs many Bretons, too, but the region is slowly becoming more and more industrial. Brest—a fine natural port that has been the home of the French Atlantic fleet for centuries—is the headquarters of the French nuclear-submarine fleet and a major naval base. (It was completely leveled after being occupied by the Germans during World War II and so for today's traveller is nearly devoid of interest.) Rennes, Brittany's capital, is a garment-producing center and Nantes, near the mouth of the Loire, a wine town; the vineyards surrounding Nantes produce Muscadet and Gros Plant, the flinty white wines that marry so well with Breton shellfish.

TOURING BRITTANY

Where you begin your Breton tour depends on how much time you have and what parts of Brittany most appeal to you. Unless you are arriving by ferry from Great Britain or Ireland at Roscoff or St-Malo, you should take the TGV from Paris. Since expansion of TGV service to the area has put Nantes within two hours and Lorient within three and a half hours of Paris, you will spare yourself a long, tedious drive by taking the train. Both of these cities are also perfect jumping-off points for tours of the southern coast and Le Finistère, the westernmost tip of Brittany. If you are eager to begin on the northern coast (St-Malo, etc.), travel by TGV to Rennes and transfer to regular train service.

How you choose to tour Brittany will vary according to where you set your holiday dial—on total culture (churches, museums, monuments, etc.) or total leisure (beachcombing, sunbathing, swimming, windsurfing, sailing, etc.), with just plain sightseeing falling near the middle of the band.

Nantes, almost at the mouth of the Loire at the very southernmost corner of the province, is a pretty and historic city that well merits a visit, but the great attraction of the Nantes area is the celebrated beach resort of La Baule.

From Nantes it's an easy drive north to some of Brittany's

most celebrated attractions, including the menhirs of Carnac and the Golfe du Morbihan, and the towns of Pont-Aven and Concarneau.

In designing your itinerary, remember that Brittany offers a delightful variety of different holidays. Ready for an idle and restorative week by the sea, you may wish to nibble on Brittany by heading directly for the most accessible part of the northern coast and dumping yourself on the beach in Dinard, just 72 km (45 miles) north of Rennes, perhaps making excursions to nearby Dinan and St-Malo. Likewise, a week on Belle-Ile, 18 miles off the southern coast from Quiberon, is about as *tonique* (a word the French love, meaning "toning" and "fortifying") a week as you'll find anywhere in France. If, however, you're more interested in touring than in relaxing, you can omit a few resorts— perhaps La Baule and Quiberon—and so gain time to visit other towns and regions. Just remember, Brittany is big and you can't "do" scenery the same way you can museums.

For a good sampling of the area, plan to cover it as we do, beginning at the south coast from Nantes west to the Pointe du Raz, then cutting north to St-Roscoff on the northern coast and making your way east toward St-Malo. (Note that Le Mont-Saint-Michel, though technically in Normandy, is just about 50 km/30 miles east of St-Malo.) Rennes, the region's main railhead, is almost equidistant from the southern and northern coasts; we dip down to it from the north as a last stop in Brittany.

Deciphering Breton Road Signs

With the advent of a more integrated Common Market making Breton nationalism less threatening to France itself, and because the embryonic European government in Brussels is sympathetic to such distinctive regions, the French government (perhaps realizing the tourist potential) has become friendlier to the public usage of Brezhoneg, the local tongue. Consequently you'll see more and more road signs in this language. This poses a special problem to travellers, however—most standard-issue road maps of France are, of course, in French. Here are some of the terms you'll come across most often: *bihan:* small; *braz:* big or large; *coat, goat, haot,* or *hoet:* woods; *coz, goz, koz:* old; *dol:* table or plateau; *his:* long; *illis:* church; *kempter:* river junction; *ker:* village; *kroaz:* crossroads, cross; *lann:* consecrated ground, hermitage; *loc, log:* holy ground or site; *men:* stone; *meur:* big, huge; *minihy:* monastery; *mor:* sea; *penity:* place of penance, hermit's retreat; *pl, pleu, plou, plu, ploe, ple, poul:* former parish territory under the protection of a

Breton saint; *relec:* relics; *roc'h:* rock; *toul:* hole; *ty:* house (as in Ty Coz, or old house, a sign you'll see all over Brittany).

THE BRETON TABLE

A few words of advice before you sit down for your first Breton meal: The real glory of the food in Brittany lies in its freshness, and generally you'll eat better in simple places with straightforward menus than you will in the grander Parisian-style spots. You should almost invariably skip the "à la"–type dishes and concentrate instead on the superb oysters from Bélon near Pont-Aven; sweet, firm langoustines; big, meaty crabs; all kinds of fish (but especially sole, skate, sardines, and tuna); and, maybe most of all, the succulent lobster. The only sure exception you should make to the keep-it-simple rule is lobster *à l'américaine,* or variously, *à l'armoricaine,* a regional specialty of boiled, split lobster served in a sauce of butter, Cognac, white wine, and tomatoes—delicious. Neither carnivores nor vegetarians will go hungry in Brittany; look for the *pré-salé* lamb, whose luscious flavor comes from the salt-grass meadows where the sheep graze, and for cauliflower, tomatoes, potatoes, string beans, and artichokes harvested the morning of the day you taste them.

Bear in mind, too, that one of this land's most venerable and ubiquitous institutions, the *crêperie,* will unfailingly offer you a cheap, fast, and delicious meal. Such a meal usually involves two courses: first a savory crêpe made from *sarrasin* (buckwheat flour) that may come with such fillings as cheese, ham, mushrooms, or shellfish, among many other combinations, and then a *froment* (white-flour) crepe, plain, or perhaps smeared with jam or chocolate or stuffed with fresh or preserved fruit. The beverage of choice is cider made from apples or pears, which is lightly alcoholic, vaguely sweet, and very refreshing; look for the Kerne brand in particular.

Finally, a short course on ordering oysters, as a real Breton oyster tasting is one of the musts when you are in Brittany; it is part of the culture, and in no other place in the world can you do it as well. Oysters in France are sized and priced according to a ubiquitous grading system. The largest size is described on a menu as "000." These are seldom seen. The next are "00"; most menus begin with this size, and these are the costliest. Six will usually do. The next size, the "0," is smaller by about a third. Note that the price of the oyster will decline with size, but only within its type; oyster variety is the other price consideration. *Cancales* and *bélons*—the *plat* (flat) oysters—are usually the most expensive types, followed by *fines de claire* and *papillons*. (An oyster expert, of which there are of course many in France, can taste the difference between a *cancale* and a *bélon* as surely as a wine expert discerns the difference between a Bordeaux and a Burgundy.) All are ordered by the dozen in "0" size.

THE SOUTHERN COAST
Nantes

If you have any prior associations with Nantes, you're either a big fan of Muscadet, which is produced in its environs, or you know something about the Edict of Nantes. The decree, sponsored by Henri IV and signed here in 1598, guaranteed freedom of religion to France's beleaguered Protestants. It was later revoked, forcing many French Protestants (the Huguenots) abroad, but became a point of legal reference for burgeoning democratic movements in both Europe and the United States.

This attractive, leafy old city straddles the Loire river, and though officially it has been detached from Brittany and made part of a new region called Pays de la Loire, it remains a vital center of Breton history. Most of its important sites are an easy walk from the train station, which is on the eastern edge of town, right across the street from the Jardin des Plantes. Follow the cours John Kennedy and cours Franklin Roosevelt into or out of town. The main Office de Tourisme is downtown in the Place du Commerce (Tel: 40-47-04-51), but from June 15 to September 15 a satellite office is open just behind the cathedral, only about a ten-minute walk from the station; Tel: 40-48-56-19.

IN AND AROUND OLD NANTES

From the station walk north up rue Baudry past the **Jardin des Plantes** to the **Musée des Beaux-Arts** on rue Georges Clemenceau. One of the best provincial art museums in France, it has in its collection works by Ingres, De La Tour, Rubens, and Monet. (The museum is closed Tuesdays and national holidays.) Just ten paces from the museum is the **Cathédrale de St-Pierre et St-Paul**. This Gothic charmer, which dates from 1434, contains the tomb of Duke François II as well as other sculptures by Michel Colombe, who is considered Brittany's greatest sculptor.

Right next to the cathedral is the **Château Ducal**, a wonderful, formerly moated 15th-century pile that was the seat of the dukes of Brittany for several centuries; today it contains three museums of middling interest: **Musée d'Art Décoratif**, **Musée des Salorges** (colonial and commercial history), and **Musée d'Art Populaire Régional**. After all this culture it might be pleasant to wander in the pedestrian district of old streets around the 17th-century **Eglise de Ste-Croix**, where there are numerous half-timbered houses. The church is a few blocks west of the château on rue de la Barillerie.

Nantes was an important colonial port and a center of "triangular trade," a commercial sailing geometry in which manufactured goods were exchanged for slaves in Africa, who were then sold in Louisiana and the West ·Indies to purchase sugar that was brought back to France. The splendid 18th-century mansions built by the merchants of this lugubrious commerce are on what was formerly **Ile Feydeau** (the river has since been filled in) just a few blocks south of Ste-Croix.

The **Musée Thomas Dobrée**, on Place Jean V in the western part of the city, houses the eclectic collection of prehistoric artifacts, medieval objects, and Flemish paintings assembled by Thomas Dobrée, a private collector during the 19th century. The building itself is a creation of Viollet-le-Duc. Closed Tuesdays.

STAYING AND DINING IN NANTES

If you decide to spend the night in Nantes, do so at the ▶ **Hôtel Graslin**, a pleasant hotel run by Monsieur and Madame Roche on rue Piron, not far from the Musée Dobrée. This is the type of place that makes travel in France such a pleasure; it's homey yet efficient, and quite reasonably priced. For dinner try **Les Maraîchers**, at 21, rue Fouré, an appealing modern restaurant specializing in seafood. Or, if you're feeling gastronomically ambitious, head for the elegant **La Châtaigneraie**, at 156, route de Carquefou, in suburban Sucé-sur-Erdre, a few miles away. The successful contemporary cuisine—the turbot in a sauce of Muscadet is notably delicious—is served in a handsome 19th-century manor house on the banks of the Erdre river, an especially nice spot in fine weather (Tel: 40-77-90-95).

North Along the Coast
to Quimper

LA BAULE

How much time you spend in La Baule, on the coast 74 km (46 miles) northwest of Nantes, depends on the season and

on where you are in your travels by the time you get here
(of the many routes between Nantes and La Baule, the
quickest takes you on N 165 to N 171). If, say, you've just
spent a week in Paris, you might need a beach day or two; if
this is the case, you'll love La Baule. With three miles of
white-sand beach, a pleasant flower-lined promenade, and
an array of sophisticated, high-quality hotels and restaurants,
La Baule is the most popular resort in Brittany, and a particular favorite of Parisians. There are no real sights to see either,
which may come as a relief. But even if you're keen to get on
with seeing the rest of Brittany, at least pass through here
and stop for lunch.

Staying and Dining in La Baule

Because La Baule is an upscale destination the hotels tend to
be expensive, but most of them are worth the price. Overlooking the beach, the ▶ **Hermitage** is an imposing seven-
story structure that combines eclectic Breton architecture
and classic French luxury; with its comfortable traditional
decor and good service, this is the place to stay if you decide
to stop over. Guests have use of an 18-hole golf course, 28
tennis courts, and a heated seawater pool. But the best
amenity of all is that white-sand beach. If you're just passing
through, treat yourself to lunch at the terrace restaurant
overlooking the red-canvas beach cabanas.

Parc Régional de Brière

En route from La Baule heading northwest to Vannes you
might want to pause in **Guérande**, just 6 km (4 miles) north
of La Baule. Guérande is the main town of the **Grand Brière**,
a vast and misty bogland that was declared a national park in
1970. Though the marshes are steadily depopulating, the
inhabitants, an aloof people who made their living for centuries by fishing, cutting peat, and herding sheep, intrigued
the writer Chateaubriand, himself a Breton from St-Malo.
You can look out on this strange country from the Porte St-
Michel, one of the gates in Guérande's old (15th-century)
walls.

The Brière also produces one of the French chefs' most
prized basic ingredients: Sel Gris du Paludier, natural sea
salt that is still harvested by hand from salt pans, shallow
tidal reservoirs where salt crystallizes as the water evapo-
rates. If you're curious about this process, visit the **Maison
des Paludiers** on rue du Ber in the town of Saillé, just
outside La Baule on D 774, a tiny museum that explains the
life of the salt-marsh workers through exhibits of tools,
costumes, and other furnishings. (This salt, which is sold all

over Brittany, makes a nice gift for a serious—or not so serious—cook back home, too.)

If you wish to explore the park further—there are a 70-acre bird sanctuary and boat trips through the marsh that leave from Les Fossés Blancs on the northern edge of the park—head for the visitors' information center in Ile de Fédrun, a town just off D 50 about 10 km (6 miles) north of St-Nazaire.

VANNES

Vannes, 70 km (43 miles) north and west of La Baule via D 774 and N 165, is a very pleasant little city (population: 45,000) with such a quaint medieval appearance that it has an almost fairy-tale feeling. Much of this atmosphere is created by its 14th- to 17th-century walls and by the lopsided half-timbered houses along the **rue de la Monnaie** in the old quarter, near the **Cathédrale de St-Pierre** (the cathedral dates from the 13th century, but it was greatly altered in the 18th). Don't miss the tomb of Saint Vincent Ferrer in the cathedral's chapel, which is hung with 17th-century tapestries depicting the miracles he performed; in the adjoining chapter house there's an exquisite 12th-century marriage chest painted with scenes from the daily life of medieval nobles. The capital of Brittany from 826 to 1532, Vannes still comports itself with a sense of importance, though it has since become simply a prosperous, modern market town.

A few steps south of the cathedral, along rue des Halles, you'll find the **Musée Archéologique** in the 15th-century Château Gaillard. Its rich collections of jewelry, weapons, and objets d'art from megalithic excavations in the region make it indispensable to enthusiasts of prehistory.

Vannes is an easy place to visit. Start down at the harbor and from there head for the Porte St-Vincent and turn right inside the walls for a wonderful view of the old ramparts before continuing on to the 17th-century Porte-Poterne.

Golfe du Morbihan

The city's charms notwithstanding, Vannes is also the best place from which to make a brief foray into the Golfe du Morbihan, a 1,000-square-mile inland sea (Morbihan means "the little sea" in Brezhoneg) that is one of the great attractions of Brittany. Liberally dashed with islands, 40 of which are inhabited, and subject to powerful tidal flows and currents, the spectacularly beautiful gulf is almost a miniature version of Brittany. You could easily spend several days exploring the islands here, but just to get an idea of the area, pack a picnic and take the ferry from Conleau to the **Ile**

d'Arz, where you can rent bicycles and pedal around to
enjoy the fine views of the mainland from all sides of the
island. The ferries run every 45 minutes and take about 15
minutes. For precise information, call the Office de Tourisme; Tel: 97-47-24-34.

Staying and Dining in Vannes

You can do no better than to settle in at the ▶ **Hôtel Le
Roof**, a homey place with just 11 rooms, on the little island
of Conleau, just south of town. Plan on **Regis Mahe** (Place de
la Gare; Tel: 97-42-61-41) for dinner. It's located in the
workaday neighborhood surrounding the train station, but
this is forgotten once you start eating—the food is extremely
good. Try the sea bass in black pepper and wine sauce.

LOCMARIAQUER AND CARNAC

From Vannes take D 101 15 km (9 miles) west toward Auray,
skirting the Golfe du Morbihan, and then head south on D
28 to D 781 for about 13 km (8 miles) toward Locmariaquer,
the site of several of Brittany's most important prehistoric
monuments.

These monuments—a massive 60-foot-long menhir
("menhir" is a Breton word meaning "standing stone")
weighing 350 tons, now broken and lying on the ground in
four pieces, and a dolmen (a tablelike structure in which a
large flat rock is supported by several smaller ones) known
as the **Table des Marchands**—are appropriate hors
d'oeuvres to the spectacle of Carnac just down the road.
Archaeologists remain generally puzzled as to the age and
exact purpose of these monuments, but have been able to
date them roughly from 2000 B.C. and have ascribed to them
some unknown religious significance, although it has been
noted that the monuments at Carnac also served certain
primitive astronomical functions. Getting out of the car and
staring at these rough old stones is baffling at first; they
mean next to nothing unless you let your imagination off the
leash. (Finding the monuments will present no problem, as
they are well signposted. The town of Locmariaquer itself is
an unremarkable resort with mediocre beaches.)

Remember to use your imagination as well when you get
to Carnac, which is 8 km (5 miles) west of D 28 along D 781.
The monuments in the area around Carnac are much more
impressive than those at Locmariaquer. A sense of mystery
pervades, stretching your ability to measure time or even to
conceive of the civilization that erected the 1,099 menhirs in
11 half-mile-long lines that begin at **Ménec** (just north of
Carnac) or the other two similar groupings in the immediate

vicinity (the **Kerlescan Lines**—579 menhirs—and the **Kermario Lines**—982 menhirs—which stretch along D 196 northeast of Carnac and Ménec). Lacking the humanity of Greek or Roman ruins, the menhirs, standing rough and blunt in heather-covered fields, possess an exhilarating power.

You might also visit the nearby **Tumulus de St-Michel** (just northeast of Carnac off D 781), two burial chambers dating from 3000 B.C. on top of which a chapel has been built. The **Musée Miln-Le-Rouzic**, a museum of prehistory in the center of Carnac, helps put everything into some perspective.

If musing about menhirs makes you hungry, consider lunching at the pretty garden restaurant of the beachfront **Diana** hotel at 21, boulevard de la Plage. Tel: 97-52-05-38.

QUIBERON
From Carnac it's a pretty and brief (15-km/9-mile) drive down to Quiberon on D 768. The town, a lively and popular resort with many thalassotherapy (seawater) spas, lies at the end of a long, narrow peninsula known as Presqu'île de Quiberon, the ocean-facing flank of which is known as the **Côte Sauvage** (Wild Coast)—something to bear in mind if you stop for a swim. From the road leading into town you can see at once both the Baie de Quiberon (to the east) and the ocean (to the west); depending on the wind, the waves, usually edged with fleeting white foam, are likely to be dotted with the bright spinnakers of Windsurfers, as these are some of the most popular beaches for this sport in France.

Quiberon is younger, trendier, and potentially less expensive than La Baule or the resorts on the north coast; the cafés are busy until late at night and every season brings a new crop of discos and clubs. It's a mixed-age resort, though, because there are a fair number of retirees here, and people of all ages come for the thalassotherapy spa treatments. (The logic behind these treatments is to use seawater first to cleanse the body of its impurities and then to restore it through the absorption of all sorts of marine minerals. For some reason it all seems to work; even the skeptical find the whole process wonderfully relaxing.) The most elaborate treatments are offered by the spa in the rather unappealingly modern **Sofitel** hotel on boulevard R. Cassin (Tel: 97-50-20-00).

Belle-Ile
During the high season ferries make the 45-minute trip from Quiberon to Belle-Ile, the largest island in Brittany, several

times a day; car passage is possible but should be booked in advance (Tel: 97-31-80-01 for fares, reservations, and sailing times). A popular turn-of-the-century resort that was made fashionable by Sarah Bernhardt, Belle-Ile is an idyllic place with fields running down to cliffs that drop to the sea below. Best toured on bicycle, the interior of the island is dotted with potato farms and little stone-house villages where you can stop for a lunch of crepes and cider.

Staying and Dining in Quiberon and Belle-Ile

The ► Hôtel Bellevue, a short walk from the beach in Quiberon, is a pleasant, quiet, traditional place with a pool. The hotel ► Castel Clara, part of the Relais & Châteaux chain, is the best place to stay if you decide to spend the night on Belle-Ile. A relaxed, modern sort of chalet, it's perched over a stunning heather-upholstered cove where only gulls break the view to the horizon as it fades into the sea. The food is outstanding, too; try the grilled lobster or the *pré-salé* lamb. The lamb, which is raised on the island, gets its special taste from grazing in the island's salt meadows.

AROUND HENNEBONT

On your way north from Carnac to Pont-Aven, which is 70 km (43 miles) up the coast, stop about halfway at this rather nondescript town 37 km (23 miles) northwest of Carnac on D 781 and D 9. There's not too much of interest in Hennebont itself, except for Notre-Dame de Paradis, a 16th-century cathedral, but there are several interesting things to see nearby. The Musée de la Compagnie des Indes in Port-Louis, 14 km (8½ miles) south of Hennebont on D 781, is housed in an impressive 17th-century fortress that once guarded the harbor; the collections here tell the story of the French West India Company and other colonial trading concerns engaged in commerce between France and North America, the West Indies, Africa, India, and China during the 17th and 18th centuries.

From Hennebont you can also make a detour inland to Kernascléden, a rather difficult-to-get-to village that claims one of the great treasures of 15th-century French painting. The most direct route is to take D 769 north for 30 km (19 miles) to D 782, which you then take east for another 10 km (6 miles); but if you have time, a more scenic option would be to leave D 769 at Plouay and take the rustic D 178 for about 11 km (7 miles) north instead. Here at Kernascléden, in an exquisite Gothic chapel built between 1420 and 1464, are arresting frescoes that depict the life of the Virgin and of

Christ, the Dance of Death, and Hell itself. What lends this art
its power is the sensation that the artistic talent was fueled by
a devout passion.

Staying and Dining Near Hennebont

The ▶ **Château de Locguénolé**, a handsome 18th-century
manor house and now one of Brittany's most charming
hotels, overlooks the Blavet river 4 km (2½ miles) south of
Hennebont on D 781. Rooms (which come at a high price)
are furnished with antiques, and the atmosphere is very
much like that of a private home; the attractively landscaped
swimming pool will come as a relief if you've been in the car
all day. The château's restaurant is excellent as well—the
clam minestrone is a good example of how innovative the
kitchen is with top-quality Breton seafood.

PONT-AVEN

Pont-Aven is a pretty, somewhat coquettish village that was
the home of Paul Gauguin before he shipped out to the
South Seas. Gauguin attracted a number of other artists to
Pont-Aven and founded what has come to be known as the
School of Pont-Aven. To learn more about the town's glory
days as an artists' colony, visit the **Musée de la Ville de Pont-
Aven**, which houses a permanent exhibition of old photographs that document the arrival and lives of the artists,
several canvases by lesser-known artists from the same period as Gauguin, and changing shows of regional painters.
The only other apparent "attraction" of Pont-Aven is a boat
trip down the estuary to the sea, which is relaxing and
pleasant, if you have the time.

   Don't leave Pont-Aven without picking up a tin or two of
the meltingly good Breton *galettes,* or butter cookies, that
are made by the **Traou Mad** bakery. You can find them in
card and curio shops along the main streets in town; packed
in tins decorated with paintings by Gauguin and other artists, they make good gifts. If you're pulling together a picnic,
stop by the **Patisserie Kersale** (Place de la Hôtel-de-Ville; Tel:
98-06-00-61) and pick up a *kouign-amann,* the province's
best-known pastry. When well made, as it is here, it's a
luscious, buttery, flaky, sugared yeast cake; when commercially produced, however, it's often fearsomely leaden.

Staying and Dining In and Around Pont-Aven

Don't dismiss the quiet pleasure of having the place to
yourself after the tour buses have roared off into the sunset.
If you can, book one of the five simple but comfortable
rooms at the ▶ **Moulin de Rosmadec**, a tastefully restored

old mill in the middle of the boulder-strewn Aven river and today one of the best restaurants in Brittany. The special delight of staying here is listening to the water sluice through the rocks all night long. If you can't get a room at the Moulin, try the ▶ **Auberge Les Grandes Roches**, a pretty, old farm that's been converted into a hotel in nearby (8 km/5 miles west) Trégunc, and head back to the Moulin de Rosmadec for lunch or dinner. The grilled lobster at the Moulin is succulent and perfectly prepared, and in season you can get a lobster with delicious, firm red roe; the langoustine-stuffed ravioli and the artichoke hearts with morels are two memorable starters, and the desserts are quite good as well.

If you're lucky enough to be in the area for several meals, another good restaurant to try in Pont-Aven is **La Taupinière** (Tel: 98-06-03-12), a stylish, modern, California-style brasserie that does a delicious tuna carpaccio, among other good seafood dishes. Once you've eaten your fill, go for an after-dinner ramble on the path that winds back and forth across the rushing Aven river.

In **Riec-sur-Bélon** (about 5 km/3 miles southeast of Pont-Aven on D 783), you'll find **Chez Jacky** (Tel: 98-06-90-32), one of the best-known and, indeed, best seafood places in Brittany (follow Rive Droit signs when you get into town). This is a wonderfully but politely rough-and-tumble place in the American tradition of Cape Cod clam shacks, New Orleans oyster bars, and the waterfront restaurants in San Francisco or Seattle. The point of being here is to eat as much shellfish, especially oysters, as you possibly can—you'll rarely find them as fresh as they are here, when they have just come from the Bélon river. You may already recognize the name Bélon, as it's one of the great varieties of French oyster; this is its native habitat.

CONCARNEAU

Concarneau's fame derives from its 13th- to 14th-century walls surrounded by the sea, but today the same august citadel contains a profusion of what must be some of the world's best-protected souvenir shops. If you're in the mood for something sort of kitschy, Concarneau, 15 km (9 miles) west of Pont-Aven on D 70, will fill the bill: Shop here for oyster-shell-shaped candles, Breton *coiffes* (the tall, tubular, lace bonnets that were once a handmade feature of every Breton lady's holiday dress but are now machine-made in Korea), and plastic crabs, among other curiosities. Apart from all this tourism run amok, the walk around the ramparts is still very agreeable, and if you find yourself here at mealtime you can let up on the credit cards by going to one of the very simple fishermen's and dockworkers' cafés on the commercial waterfront outside the walled city. Try **Le Chalut** (20, quai Carnot; Tel: 98-97-02-12) for a delicious *salade de chalut,* a generous helping of very fresh langoustines garnished with rice salad, tomatoes, and hard-boiled eggs. You'll notice, though, that the rather ruddy clientele seems to prefer *grillades* (grilled meat)—maybe you would, too, if you'd been hauling around big crates of raw fish since before sunrise.

Quimper

Though it's never been a capital of Brittany, Quimper (population: 61,000) is the most essentially Breton of all the province's cities—an appealing, slightly aloof place where your curiosity will be rewarded with insights into the Breton character. This is not to say that the Quimperois are brusque, only that as the chief town of the **Finistère** (which means "Land's end"), perhaps the least modernized and hence most Breton region in the province, this small city has a vital life of its own, its well-groomed tourist attractions notwithstanding. Quimper, 24 km (15 miles) northwest of Pont-Aven on D 24 and N 165, follows and straddles the banks of the river Odet; it's a tidy, attractive place with many flower beds that attest to the pride and affection that the residents have for their city. The solid, ornate, turn-of-the-century theater in a park on the river also says much about the mentality of this city, declaring as it does with some architectural seriousness the cultural aspirations of the population.

AROUND THE CATHEDRALE DE ST-CORENTIN

Much of what will interest you is within easy walking distance of the **Cathédrale de St-Corentin**, which was built in stages between the 13th and 16th centuries. Quimper boasts two very good museums, both of which flank the cathedral. Paintings by the Pont-Aven school of artists in addition to works by Rubens, Fragonard, Boucher, and Corot are the highlights of the collection of the **Musée des Beaux-Arts**, in the Hôtel de Ville at 40, place St-Corentin (closed Tuesdays). The **Musée Breton**, in the former bishop's palace next to the cathedral, features Breton art as well as the art of such other Celtic regions as Cornwall (closed Mondays).

Just in front of the cathedral, along rue Kéréon, is the **old town**, more interesting than the old quarters in some other

Breton cities because the medieval buildings here are not only well preserved, but their street-level floors are occupied with modern commerce—which means, not surprisingly, that Quimper is a good place to shop.

Shopping for Quimper-ware

The most sought-after buy here is Quimper-ware, properly called simply Quimper, the daintily hand-painted stoneware that is known the world over. Emblematic of the traditional designs of this pottery are Le Petit Breton, a man in a wide-brimmed hat, and La Petite Bretonne, a woman in an apron and lace cap. The best places to go for Quimper are **L'Art du Cornouaille**, right across the street from the cathedral, and **Faïencerie Keraluc**, at 71, rue du Président Sadet. L'Art du Cornouaille carries not only Henriot (the best-known Quimper producer) but the products of many other Breton manufacturers, as well as grandfather clocks, lace, and other antiques, and they'll pack and ship anything you buy. You might also think of visiting the **H. B. Henriot** factory, just outside the old town, to have a look at their seconds; some days they have wonderful things for sale and others the selection's a bit thin. Be sure to take time out from the ardors of shopping at **Rolland Padou**, at 13, rue Kéréon, a good place to try the pastry *kouign-amann*.

STAYING AND DINING IN AND AROUND QUIMPER

▶ **Le Griffon**, at 131, route de Bénodet, is an attractive, modern hotel with a heated swimming pool just 2 km (1 mile) south of Quimper. In town at 29, rue des Réguaires, **Le Capucin Gourmand** is a good and reasonably priced restaurant that does a luscious seafood pot-au-feu—shrimp, scallops, and various other fish cooked with vegetables in a ginger sauce (Tel: 98-95-43-12). You may also choose to stay in Audierne or Locronan, both scenic towns near Quimper (see below).

Side Trips from Quimper

When you're finished touring the city, the two-and-a-half-hour cruise from quai de l'Odet to **Bénodet**, a well-known yachting and sailing port, and back is a very agreeable way to spend the afternoon; the boat follows the river Odet past numerous châteaux, and the riverbanks are planted with camellias, rhododendrons, and tulip trees.

AUDIERNE

Audierne, on the coast 35 km (22 miles) west of Quimper via D 784, is a small, ungentrified working fishing port that specializes in langoustines, the eating of which is, along with the eating of lobster and oysters, one of the greatest pleasures of a trip to Brittany. How different they are here—big, firm, and sweet—from the sorry specimens you too often get in Paris at twice the price. The place to eat them, and to stay overnight as well, is ▶ **Le Goyen**, a hotel and restaurant right on the waterfront. Book one of the pretty, recently renovated floral-chintz doubles that faces the port and watch the fleet going out to sea, or, early in the morning, landing its catch on the quai. Specialties of the restaurant are excellent roast sea bass and lobster served in a mushroom cream sauce in a pastry case.

After dinner go for a stroll and have a coffee or Calvados in one of the two cafés that look out on the port. They're charmless places in and of themselves, with pinball machines and video monitors, but the crowd is friendly. Furthermore, these are good places for amateur anthropology: The Bretons actually look very different from the French. You'll see a lot of red hair, blue eyes, and freckles, and the manner of these people is open and spontaneous, even though they're often initially shy with foreigners.

POINTE DU RAZ

Stuck out like a finger and carved by the furious wind and sea, with a 300-foot drop at the end, this westernmost point in France, about 60 km (37 miles) west of Quimper on D 784 (it's just 15 km/9 miles beyond Audierne), is one of the world's most dramatic seascapes. Climbing the cliffs here can be dangerous, so tours are organized. The *tour de la pointe* (July and August only) leaves from the parking lot where you must leave your car when you arrive, and starts whenever the guide has five people willing to go. The tour, strenuous but exciting, takes an hour; wear non-skid shoes. Among the highlights of this hardy little hike is the **Baie des Trépasses** (Bay of the Dead), so named, according to legend, because the Druids who once inhabited the point and its environs were taken from here to the Ile de Sein, seven miles offshore, for burial; also because onshore currents used to bring the bodies of drowned sailors to the bay and its beach from wrecks off the point. Adding further mystery to the sinister reputation of these waters is the fact that many believe that the legendary Celtic city of Ys lies offshore. Ys was ruled by King Gradlon (or Grallon) during the fourth or fifth century when the spicy high jinks of his daughter Dahut (or Ahes) brought down the wrath of heaven in the form of an engulfing flood. Some speculate that the roots of this legend may lie in the destruction of an actual city in the region by a tidal wave of some sort. Looking carefully at the sea here, you may notice the roiled waters caused by the *raz,* a perilous riptide that races between the Ile de Sein and the point.

Even if the cliffside expedition is too much for you, the spectacular panorama of the Atlantic and the Ile de Sein from the bluffs above merits the visit. There is, unfortunately, a little tourist village here—shops, cafés, and restaurants—but somehow the salt air and the majesty of the setting render this honky-tonk inoffensive.

Wherever you're headed from here, take the little secondary road (D 7) from the point, maybe stopping at the Réserve du Cap Sizun, a bird sanctuary on the north coast of the peninsula about 15 km (9 miles) east. The road winds through lush green countryside, tiny villages, and neatly tended farms, with the sea always on the horizon and in the nostrils.

LOCRONAN

In the 16th and 17th centuries Locronan, which is just 17 km (11 miles) northwest of Quimper on D 39/63, thrived from the manufacture of canvas for ships' sails; the mills here supplied the Spanish navy, the port of nearby Brest, and the French West India Company. This industry has long since disappeared, but the splendid, mossy, granite Renaissance houses around the tiny main square remain as testament to the wealth it generated. The main revenues today come from tourism, which is easy to understand: Locronan is one of the most attractive and architecturally harmonious villages in Brittany. Set up on a low ridge just a few miles inland, it's a tiny place surrounded by forests and tidy, bright-green pastures. The main sight here is the 15th-century **Eglise de St-Ronan** and the adjoining **Chapelle de Le Pénity**, which contains the 16th-century tomb of Saint Ronan, who came to Locronan from Ireland in the fifth century. But the pleasure of any visit comes from rambling around the place, taking your time and turning left, or right, with no predetermined itinerary. If Locronan looks familiar to you, by the way, it might be because Roman Polanski's *Tess* was filmed here.

Right on the church square, the **Maison des Artisans** displays linen-weaving looms and sells various handwoven items and wooden sculptures, including some good copies of antiques. The **Atelier St-Ronan,** a similar workshop, is located at the intersection of the Douarnenez and Quimper roads.

The Pardon of Locronan

Should you happen to be in the area on the second Sunday in July, you'll also have the opportunity to witness the Pardon of Locronan. Almost every Breton town has a *pardon,* a religious procession that usually goes from or to the tomb of the local saint along a route encompassing various other chapels and crucifixes; a *pardon* is an occasion for a local holiday. The pardon at Locronan covers two or three miles and includes almost everyone in the village, dressed in traditional Breton clothing, making their way through the thick bracken that covers much of the surrounding countryside to the Kador St-Ronan, a block of granite that many locals believe was once the boat in which Saint Ronan travelled from Ireland to Brittany. (Other Breton pardons to note in this area are: Le Folgoët, the first Sunday in September; Rumengol, the first Sunday after Pentecost; Tréguier, the third Sunday in May; Ste-Anne-d'Auray, July 26; Josselin, September 8; and Ste-Anne-la-Palud, the last Sunday in August.)

Staying and Dining Near Locronan

Locronan has a good pastry shop, **Le Guillou-Nicholas Jean,** right in the main square, which sells *kouign-amann, galettes,* and crepes *dentelles* (fluted fruit-filled wafers), but the best places to stay and eat are both a few minutes outside town. Your choice here depends upon your preference—the beach or the countryside. If you want the sea, the ► **Hôtel de la Plage** just to the northwest at Ste-Anne-la-Palud is delightful; it's a small, comfortable old place with a vaguely nautical theme in the public areas, and a bar and very good restaurant that look out on a vast, flat sand beach. Not surprisingly, the specialty here is seafood, which is prepared in perfect simplicity. Should you yearn for the woods instead, the ► **Manoir de Moëllien,** just 4 km (2½ miles) north of Locronan in the hamlet of Plonévez-Porzay, is a comfortably restored and furnished stone château that was built in 1642. It's set in a spacious and tranquil park that looks out on surrounding farmland. The restaurant here is best with such simple dishes as grilled lamb chops, so if you want seafood you might be better off booking for dinner at the Hôtel de la Plage.

PARC REGIONAL D'ARMORIQUE

After visiting Locronan, if you have a quiet day to spare, you might pack a picnic and drive around the craggy and lushly green **Parc Régional d'Armorique (Partie Est)**, the very essence of Brittany. The park is about 40 km (25 miles) north of Locronan on D 63. The most attractive area in this park is around **Huelgoat**, where there is a beautiful forest and a large—for Brittany—lake. You should also visit the **Chaos du Moulin**, a rockfall, and the **Chapelle de St-Herbot**, the patron saint of cattle, dating from the 15th to 16th centuries and distinguished by an intricate figured cross. Otherwise, just pull off the road somewhere and hike and/or loll around all afternoon.

PLEYBEN

Pleyben, 25 km (16 miles) northeast of Locronan on D 7, then N 164, or 30 km due north of Quimper on D 785, has one of the most impressive *calvaires* (calvaries) in Brittany, an amazing sculptural depiction of the Crucifixion dating from 1555 on a raised stone platform in front of an equally handsome stone church (1564). What's most striking about the church is the contrast between its original style and its soaring Renaissance bell tower.

Touring this part of the Finistère, you'll find that many of the churches and churchyards are the repositories of an astonishingly powerful and affecting religious art. Most churches include a parish close, an area adjacent to the church, often walled, that includes a cemetery, a charnel house (where bones were once gathered), a grouping of stone crosses, and, most magnificently, an elaborate calvary. These calvaries are often surrounded by dozens, sometimes even hundreds, of figures grouped in scenes from the Old and New Testaments, the lives of saints and martyrs, and, occasionally, a moral tale, as they often served to illustrate the substance of the sermons offered by the parish priest.

THE NORTHERN COAST

The Channel coast of Brittany is generally rougher and wilder than the flank that faces the Atlantic, and centuries of wind and waves have gnawed away at the cliffs here to create some spectacularly vivid seascapes. This coast is also dotted with fishing ports, such as Roscoff, Trébeurden, and Tréguier; stylish resorts, such as Dinard and St-Malo; and well-preserved medieval villages and towns, the most impressive of which is probably Dinan. Aside from geography, if anything differentiates this area from the rest of Brittany it's the subtle sensation that England is nearby; facing Cornwall, its Celtic sister just across the sea, this part of Brittany historically has had the most intense interaction with Great Britain.

If you're coming by car from the south you'll begin your northern tour at Roscoff (about 100 km/62 miles north of Quimper on D 785 to D 58), which might also be your terminus if you've come by ferry from Britain or Ireland. Should you have decided to visit this coast exclusively, take the train from Paris to Rennes (see below) and transfer at Rennes for the trip to Morlaix, where you should pick up your rental car. We explore the coast from west (the fishing town of Roscoff) to east (St-Malo, the best Breton port of all). Don't bother to visit Brest, the largest town on the northern coast of Brittany (64 km/40 miles west of Roscoff) unless you're an amateur urbanologist; after the Germans made it their main Atlantic U-boat base during World War II it was almost completely leveled by the Allies, and, aside from a major concentration of rather worn-out and unsuccessful postwar architecture, there's very little left to warrant your time navigating the city's heavy traffic.

Roscoff to Paimpol

ROSCOFF
Roscoff, a snug little port, is one of the most important specialty fish markets in France; many well-known chefs, such as Alain Passard of Arpège in Paris, are supplied exclusively by the Roscoff fleet. You'll have no particular obligations here—there are no "sights" per se—so just wander around and drink in the atmosphere of a working port. In late morning you'll find the waterfront busy as the day's catch is weighed and shipped everywhere from Paris to Copenhagen and Chicago, and the cafés filled with weary sailors tossing back a Calvados with a coffee before heading home for lunch and a nap.

INLAND NEAR ROSCOFF
Several interesting, nearby places may lure you inland again before you continue east along the coast.

Le Folgoët
Le Folgoët is a bit out of the way (it's 36 km/22 miles southeast of Roscoff on D 788), but that didn't deter the thousands of pilgrims who made their way here during the 15th century, nor does it deter those who continue to come today. The object of the pilgrims' journey was and is the

Basilique de Notre-Dame de Folgoët, which was erected from 1422 to 1460 after the miracle of the crazy one: Folgoët is a Breton name that translates as *le fou de bois* in French, and in English, roughly, as "the crazy one of the woods." The epithet refers to a simple soul named Solomon, who lived in the woods and passed his days in constant repentance. After his death a lily grew on his grave; stunned to see that the lily bore the message "Ave Maria," the locals investigated and found that the flower sprang from the mouth of Solomon. A miracle thus proved, the basilica was built in honor of the Virgin, and it became the object of an important local pilgrimage. Inside and out the basilica is quite beautiful, but the rose window in the choir is perhaps most impressive.

Guimiliau

From Le Folgoët take D 32 southeast for 25 km (16 miles) to Guimiliau. This small village possesses one of the most impressive churches and churchyards to have been produced in this area during the Counter-Reformation period in the late 16th century, which was the high point of the local artistic movement that produced all the *calvaires*. There are more than 200 figures in the calvary here, which recounts the life of Christ. Note also the triumphal gate, a fine work of Renaissance art that was created by local stoneworkers who took their inspiration from books detailing works of the architect Philibert Delorme, who designed the palace of the Tuileries in Paris. Nearby **St-Thégonnec** claims a calvary that rivals that of Guimiliau—the two villages competed for two centuries to produce ever more splendid ecclesiastical monuments. From Guimiliau it's only about 30 km (19 miles) north back to Roscoff on D 11, D 69, and D 788.

ST-POL-DE-LEON AND MORLAIX

St-Pol-de-Léon lies just 5 km (3 miles) down the road (D 769 and D 58) from Roscoff through the artichoke fields that are its main business; the plants are especially beautiful when they flower in late July. Named after the Welsh monk who came here as an evangelist in the sixth century, St-Pol-de-Léon is a lovely little city that's best seen on foot. Start in the Place du Petit-Cloître, where you'll see a striking prebendary house dating from 1530 in which the canons of the cathedral once lived; there's another such house at 2, rue de la Rosière. Follow rue Général-Leclerc, the town's main street, which is filled with handsome old houses, to the **Chapelle Kreisker** (14th to 15th centuries). You'll probably have already noticed this church, since its 15th-century bell tower is an impressive 246 feet high, with an open-worked spire that set the style for this area. The town's magnificent **cathedral** (13th to 16th centuries), built of pale Norman limestone, is a few blocks north of the chapel on Place Budès de Guébriant and houses a rare Renaissance organ and carved choir stalls that date from 1512. In the cathedral, note the wooden statue of Sainte Apolline; the patron saint of dentists, she had all of her teeth pulled out by torturers.

The main reason to visit Morlaix, 20 km (12 miles) southeast of St-Pol-de-Léon via D 58, is to stop in at the Office de Tourisme (Place Otages; Tel: 98-62-14-94) for a guide map to the best calvaries in the area; this is a very pleasant and slow circuit, for which you should allow an afternoon. Otherwise, the town is known for its enormous viaduct and good antiques dealers along the rue de Paris.

TREBEURDEN AND TREGUIER

From Morlaix head for the little seaside town of Trébeurden, the first (or last) town along **La Côte de Granit Rose**. Trébeurden, 44 km (27 miles) northeast of Morlaix on D 786 and D 63, is known for the huge pink granite stones that line its coast, a sight that is common enough along the 30-mile littoral from Trébeurden northeast to the resort of Perros-Guirec to warrant the romantic sobriquet. Many of these massive stones resemble odd, abstract sculptures, especially at the village of Ploumanach, about 15 km (9 miles) from Trébeurden.

Tréguier, 27 km (17 miles) east of Trébeurden, is complemented by a host of attractive beaches, most notably the one at **Perros-Guirec**, about 20 minutes away. But it is Tréguier itself that holds the ultimate interest. If you've come this far you will have begun to know Brittany, and so you must see Tréguier; here you'll find the major elements of the region's mystique: a saint, the sea, and the products of the sea, all of which are centered around the cathedral.

A good time to catch all French markets at their liveliest is an hour before mealtime—just the time it takes the locals to go to the market, see what's fresh, and take it home and cook it. Because this is Brittany, the market on Tréguier's Place du Martray offers primarily fish. To visitors the produce and its plenty is astonishing. Everything is raw, cold, and fresh, and heaped in baskets and barrels: sole, mullet, turbot, rays, sea bass, and mackerel; oysters, mussels, clams, lobsters, *langoustes,* and more sea creatures. If you have a camper or a boat with a freezer, Tréguier is a good place to fill more than your eyes.

Cathédrale de St-Tugdual

One of the most beautiful churches in Brittany, in both its scale and its rapport with the town, the Cathédrale de St-Tugdual and its attached cloister rise from the center of the great **Place du Martray** in the middle of town, where none of the surrounding buildings is close enough to hem them in. The visitor thus gets a vertical view of the cathedral and its spire, which soars like a ship's mast above the marketplace. All towns in Brittany have their churches, but this cathedral is one you should definitely explore—not only for the windows, sculpture, and architecture, or out of devotion, but for the story it tells of the region.

Erected from the 13th to the 15th centuries, the cathedral has three towers that mark three points of the cross, one with a spire and one containing a magnificent rose window. Everywhere the granite is worked with a lightness and finesse that is now a lost art. The two Christ figures, carved in wood, are particularly fine, but it is the statue of Saint Yves that is especially noteworthy here.

This may be Saint Tugdual's cathedral, but it is Saint Yves who is the more popular. Indeed, he is the most popular saint in Brittany, where he is known as "Monsieur Saint-Yves." Yves was born in nearby Minihy-Tréguier in the middle of the 13th century. After becoming a priest and finishing his studies in Paris, he returned to Tréguier as the bishop's assistant and did legal work for the poor. Yves argued their cases so well and so purely that he was canonized a hundred years later as the patron saint of lawyers. Along with a page from his prayer book, the cathedral possesses Saint Yves's skull, a relic whose closely spaced eye sockets still convey the bony stare of a lawyer. A *pardon* from Tréguier to Minihy-Tréguier (about half a mile) is held every May 19.

PAIMPOL

Paimpol, 15 km (9 miles) east of Tréguier, was celebrated in song and in literature as the most typically Breton town of all. The hero of Pierre Loti's novel *Pêcheur d'Islande* (*An Iceland Fisherman*) comes from here (Breton fishermen make the storm-tossed voyage to Iceland routinely, even in winter); Loti did for Paimpol what Marcel Pagnol did for Marseille. Yet Paimpol is pleasingly sleepy and isolated among its rocks. The wild pinks and *bleuets* that bloom here are not trampled under tourists' soles; the stone pier that juts into the sea to welcome the fishing fleet—and a well-sheltered cove it creates, too—does not groan under the crush of humanity. You can find your place in the sun here, and under the pretty parasols that line the beach you can sip a cider, watch the boats, or read a book in peace.

The town, like the rocks, is in eternal sunset, or sunrise, being built entirely of pink granite—right down to the quaint church.

Ile de Bréhat

As the song goes, when in Paimpol follow *la Paimpolaise*. And where does she go? Why, to the Ile de Bréhat. This magical floating garden of an island, less than two miles long, is very near—ten minutes from the Pointe de l'Arcouest, which is just 6 km (3½ miles) north of Paimpol on the sea—and automobiles are forbidden there. You can spend several hours climbing the slopes and drinking in a surprising variety of wild Breton flora: cedars, fig trees, and even palm trees. There are great rock crevices down by the sea that in low tide can be used for swimming holes—an ideal way to recharge the spirit after the wear and tear of the road. A little town, **Port Clos**, and citadel are huddled around a lovely enclosed harbor, where cafés offer light refreshment to those visitors without picnics.

ROSCOFF TO PAIMPOL: STAYING AND DINING

To sample the catch of the day in **Roscoff** within a few hours of its having been drawn in—an experience that will completely redefine your idea of many fishes—try the restaurant **Le Temps de Vivre** in the hotel Le Corsaire on Place Eglise (Tel: 98-61-24-44). If you're planning to stay the night here, the hotel ▶ **Le Brittany** on boulevard Ste-Barbe offers comfortable, traditional rooms in a seafront location in an old and quiet part of town.

A very pleasant hotel at **Trébeurden** is the ▶ **Manoir de Lan-Kerellec**, an 18th-century granite manor house perched above the sea. The hotel's restaurant, with its peaked wooden ceiling shaped like the hull of a ship, is quite good, too; try the St-Pierre (known in English as John Dory) in cider or tournedos of salmon in red wine.

Another good hotel in this neck of the woods is the ▶ **Hôtel des Rochers** in **Ploumanach**, 13 km (8 miles) north of Trébeurden on D 788. The hotel has only 15 simple but comfortable rooms, but many have sea views and, weird plastic chairs notwithstanding, its dining room is superb; try the medallions of monkfish in a sauce of squid and wild mushrooms (much better than it may sound); Tel: 96-91-44-49.

Try the ▶ **Kastell Dinec'h** for an overnight stay in **Tré-**

guier. A small, comfortable, and reasonably priced traditional hotel with a pool set in well-tended gardens, it's just 2 km (1¼ miles) from town on the route to Lannion.

The ► **Hôtel Le Barbu** at the Pointe de l'Arcouest near **Paimpol** is a pleasant place to spend a night in the area. It has a small, attractive garden and beautiful views of Ile de Bréhat and the sea. Grander, and more expensive, is the luxurious ► **Hôtel des Pins-Relais Brenner** near the Pont de Lézardrieux, just outside of Paimpol as you head west. Set in a quiet, pretty, well-landscaped park on the Trieux river, it has a pool and a good restaurant.

Côte d'Emeraude

East of Paimpol stretch the beaches of the Côte d'Emeraude, a progression of dramatic seascapes, cathedrals, colorful fishing fleets, and quaint villages. There's a family beach at **St-Brieuc**, 45 km (28 miles) southeast of Paimpol on D 786, as well as a fortified church, and another charming beach at **Le Val-André**, 26 km (16 miles) farther up the coast. Then in another 25 km (16 miles) comes what is arguably the most splendid lookout on a whole coast of splendid lookouts: **Cap Fréhel**, a panorama of sky and sea with plumes of spray shooting off the end of the point. The red and gray stone cliffs are dense with ferns and wildflowers, and on a clear day you can see the Channel Islands off in the distance. From here you can also look north toward England, whence the Bretons came, or westward to America, where many went. It is one of the great natural wonders of Brittany, and one that gives some understanding of this region's hazards.

Beyond Cap Fréhel the Côte d'Emeraude begins in earnest. Just a few kilometers to the east is the **Fort la Latte**, a beautifully situated and romantic fortified castle that was built by a pirate family during the Middle Ages and restored in the 17th century by Vauban, Louis XIV's great military architect. With its double drawbridges and sheer stone walls, the fort is a fearsome place, especially impressive at sunset.

After several twists in the road you come to **St-Cast-le-Guildo**. With seven beaches and two superb lookout points, this is a popular place with the locals. After more twists comes **Lancieux**, cheek by jowl with **St-Briac-sur-Mer**, both quiet family places. Just around the bend is **St-Lunaire**, with two elegant beaches, tennis courts, a long promenade out to the sea, and the **Grotte de la Goule-aux-Fées** (Grotto of the Sirens), a hole in a rock through which the wind howls mournfully.

DINARD

Dinard, the gem of the Côte d'Emeraude, is 4½ km (3 miles) east of St-Lunaire. This is a small, chic resort with a delightfully old-fashioned atmosphere that dates back to its original development by English entrepreneurs around 1870. It reached a crest of popularity among British aristocrats at the end of the Victorian era, but it retains a decidedly Edwardian architecture and tone and has been consistently fashionable ever since.

Beyond this aura of refinement, Dinard also has one of the best beaches in Brittany, the **Grande Plage**, an astonishing sweep of sand that is filled with a comely assortment of bathers. The bikini may be a French invention, but there are plenty of American and English accents here. On the other side of the little peninsula is a beach with a serpentine walk called the **Promenade du Clair de Lune** (Moonlight Promenade).

Spend some time exploring Dinard. There are villas niched into its coves, and green hills enveloped by the balmy breezes of a mild microclimate. The Gulf Stream ends around here and, having ended, flirts.

Down the Rance by Boat

An excursion not to be missed is a trip down the Rance. Boats leave from Dinard at the river's mouth and follow the estuary, gulf-size at first, until it narrows to barge-canal width. This hour-and-a-half journey will show you what the North Breton coast is all about: the river and the sea and, in between, the steep forested folds that rise to mountainous heights. Back near Dinard at the mouth of the Rance is a technological wonder: French engineers have harnessed the dramatic tides that run upriver and converted their power to electricity at the **Marémotrice de la Rance**, the world's first tidal-energy station. (If you haven't time for the boat trip, you can drive from Dinard to the power station on D 168, which runs along the high dam and connects Dinard to St-Malo. The station is open to visitors; its entrance is near the lock on the downstream side and there is parking available nearby.)

DINAN

Dinan, not to be confused with Dinard and inland 21 km (13 miles) due south on D 766, is a village filled with so much medieval charm that, were it indoors, it could pass for a museum. In fact, it *is* almost small enough to qualify, which makes it all the easier to see. The town's crooked old streets (see especially the rue du Jerzual) and antique houses, timbered and overhanging the street, are interspersed with gardens and trees. There are ramparts, a massive château, and a great clock tower; Dinan is an excellent place to rest and watch the hands of its 15th-century clock turn.

STAYING AND DINING ON THE COTE D'EMERAUDE

Dinard's ► **Hôtel Reine Hortense**, a splendid place that was originally commissioned by a Russian prince and named in honor of Queen Hortense de Beauharnais, Napoléon III's mother, is convenient to both beaches. This is a special, genteel, fly-in-amber sort of place, where the rooms are mostly decorated in Napoléon III (Empire) style; one of the rooms still contains the big silver-plated bathtub installed for Queen Hortense herself.

The best place to stay in Dinan is the ► **Hôtel d'Avaugour**, a charming old house, perfectly located in the middle of town, that's been done over into a small, very comfortable and stylish hotel. You have a choice of views: In front you can look out on the pretty but sometimes noisy square, and in back, on a little garden with a large fountain. The restaurant here is good as well.

Another fine restaurant-hotel in Dinan, if a bit pricey and touristy, is ► **La Caravelle**, at number 14, place Duclos. The attractive dining room has wainscoting and wooden chairs that create a fin de siècle ambience, a version of which also characterizes the 11 simple rooms in a nearby annex. Try the perch stuffed with crayfish and, in season (fall), any of the superb game dishes such as jugged hare; Tel: 96-39-00-11. For a simpler meal, there's the excellent **Crêperie des Artisans** at 6, rue du Petit Fort (Tel: 96-39-44-10).

St-Malo

St-Malo, a Renaissance city surrounded by a wall and the sea—a virtual fort—is the Breton port to see. The Breton corsairs, the men of St-Malo, declared themselves "neither French nor Breton, but Malouïn." If there was ever a Venice of the north of France, a place where seafaring commerce was king, this is it. The wall was the Malouïns' attempt to protect themselves against their competition and against raids by the English.

The best way to experience this old port, which is directly across the Rance estuary from Dinard, is to enter through the ramparts, find a bakery, buy a bag of glazed chestnuts (those of St-Malo are easily the best in France) or some *craquelins de St-Malo,* an oversize, sugared local version of puffed wheat, climb atop the ramparts, and, munching and marching, walk the entire circumference of the wall. Here is an opportunity to take a tour of some of the loveliest Renaissance architecture in France at its second-story level. The height advantage exposes rooflines and other details—extravagant chimney pots, for example—seldom seen in homes of the upper bourgeoisie, as well as a view of the maritime life below. All the while you will be refreshed by the sea, which almost completely rings the city. The spectacle is best when the tide reaches its 30-foot height, for then the sea is at its wildest, but at any time you will get a close-up view of the many old buildings, now successfully rebuilt after their almost total destruction during World War II. A sort of second resurrection of St-Malo is currently visible in the many mansions marked by recent gentrification; wealthy landowners from the surrounding countryside are now flocking to buy vacation homes here, precipitating a flight *to* the city instead of the usual other way around.

THE CATHEDRAL AND MUSEUMS

Wandering the pedestrian streets inside St-Malo's old city you'll see more crêperies than you ever believed could exist, all manner of nautical and pirate-theme souvenirs, and also the **Cathédrale de St-Vincent**, a hodgepodge of architecture from the 12th through the 18th centuries, with its vivid modern stained glass windows. This church is also the center of the pardon of the Newfoundland Fishing Fleet, should you find yourself here in February. You might also visit the city's very good **aquarium**, built into the walls at Place Vauban, near the Porte St-Thomas.

The **Musée St-Malo** in the great keep of St-Malo **castle**, between Porte St-Thomas and Porte St-Vincent, sheds some light on the city's rowdier past. Exhibits in this pentagonal stone fortress, which was constructed from the 14th to the 17th centuries and was once called the Bastille of the West, focus on the Malouïn pirates, especially Duguay-Trouin (1673–1736), who captured more than 300 British ships between 1689 and 1709, and Surcouf (1773–1827). These men were once the bane of shipmasters in the English Channel; exhibits here display souvenirs of their "trade." The more productive and somewhat more law-abiding lives of other mariners, particularly those who sailed three-masted ships around Cape Horn, are the theme of the **Musée International des Long Cours Cap Hornier**, housed in the 14th-century Tour Solidor, which dominates the Rance estuary in the adjacent resort of **St-Servan-sur-Mer**. The exhibits here display maps, ship models, and navigating tools from the great age of the clipper ship. (St-Servan has a good, sandy bathing beach, a lovely spit of forest, and elegant buildings.)

Any great city, especially a port, has its own special mystique. Along the wall thrust out into the harbor is St-Malo's statue to Jacques Cartier, the first native son to cross the Atlantic, braving the wild seas that begin at the foot of the wall. On his second such voyage Cartier was amazed to find a Breton fishing fleet already in Canadian waters; news of a good fishing spot travelled far even then. The Breton fleet still puts in appearances on the Grand Banks in quest of the singular salmon and cod.

The small **Ile du Grand-Bé**, with its fortified tower and the tomb of native son François Chateaubriand, is accessible at low tide across the sand flats to the northwest. Note, too, by the way, that St-Malo is a good base from which to visit the Channel Islands of Jersey, Guernsey, and Sark (Tel: 99-56-42-29 for information on hydrofoil service).

STAYING AND DINING IN ST-MALO AND CANCALE

St. Malo

Those visitors who want to stay *intra muros* (within the walls) of this fascinating town could do no better than the ▶ **Hotel Central**, a fine downtown hotel, with its restaurant **La Frégate**, which serves Breton seafood. The Central, part of the Mapotel chain, has been completely renovated recently; rooms are comfortably furnished with modern, color-coordinated furniture. The restaurant **La Duchesse Anne** (5, place Guy La Chambre; Tel: 99-40-85-33) offers Breton grilled lobster, *fruits de mer,* and fresh foie gras, which has nothing to do with Brittany but everything to do with gastronomy. At any hotel in town, pick a room on an upper floor; building elevations are regulated and your room will be filled with sunshine.

Cancale

Along this bay- and inlet-riddled coast the tides are so monstrous that it is often possible to wade a quarter of a mile out to sea with the water remaining at your ankles. Here in its most productive beds is that most celebrated of Breton shellfish, the oyster. It couldn't be better met than in one of the region's famous oyster towns, Cancale, 14 km (8½ miles) east of St-Malo.

There's really only one place to feast on them while you're here, the elegant **Maison de Bricourt** at 1, rue Duguesclin (Tel: 99-89-64-76; closed Tuesdays and December 15 to March 15). It's expensive but well worth it as one of the very best restaurants in the whole province; reserve well in advance, too, as it's quite popular. Chef Olivier Roellinger has installed his restaurant in the old stone house where he grew up, and with its pink decor, wall murals, and old tile fireplaces it's both cozy and chic at once. Gently warmed fresh oysters are an obvious first course, but there are many other temptations as well: a succulent salad of smoked salmon and scallops, and tantalizing mussels in Muscat wine with fenugreek. Roellinger may have created the most unusual roast lobster in Brittany; his version is delicately seasoned with an intriguing mélange of spices from the Spice Islands, as Indonesia was once known, a delicious display of his enthusiasm for exotic flavors. Desserts are superb here, too; try the *gratin d'abricots,* apricots and green and yellow plums baked in an almond-infused cream.

If you choose to dine at the Maison de Bricourt you should also book a room in the ► **Hôtel de Bricourt-Richeux**, an intimate six-room granite villa on a bluff overlooking the sea, just half a kilometer from the restaurant. Depending on the weather, you can take some air in the garden here after your meal and enjoy sweeping views of the Baie du Mont-Saint-Michel. (Le Mont-Saint-Michel itself is discussed in the Normandy chapter, above.) But whether you stay the night at the Bricourt or not, you should complement this final glorious Breton feast with a stroll by the sea. Well-fed and with the province's briny air still in your nostrils, you'll be in fine form if it's time for you to cross the border, now a real boundary, back into France.

RENNES

At the end of a tour of Brittany, Rennes (population: 200,000) surprises: It doesn't look at all like other Breton towns and cities. (Rennes is 69 km/43 miles due south of St-Malo on N 137.) Blame this on a tipsy carpenter who upset an oil lamp, à la Mrs. O'Leary's Chicago cow, causing a blaze that devoured the place in 1720. Since then the concentration of power and money in the capital of Brittany has produced an atmosphere of administrative "blandeur" rather than grandeur, and the city doesn't match the liveliness of Nantes, its ancient rival. Even so, Rennes's homeliness is part of its unpretentious appeal, and it's actually a very interesting city—further, Rennes has some very good restaurants and can comfortably be visited during the course of an easygoing

day. The train station here is on the south side of town; by
car or on foot, take the avenue Jean Janvier to or from the
heart of town; this avenue leads from the station to the most
important museums. The main Office de Tourisme is downtown at Pont de Nemours, very near the main post office; Tel:
99-79-01-98.

THE MUSEUMS AND OLD RENNES

Head for the heart of the city, the Place du Palais de Justice,
where you'll find the **Parlement de Bretagne**, a handsome
17th-century building in gray granite that was designed to
reannounce loudly but tastefully the importance of the Breton parliament to the French crown. A visit to the **Musée de
Bretagne** (closed Tuesdays) on the adjoining quai Emile
Zola, with its exhibits of history, art, and folklore, provides a
good introduction to the province; right next door is the
Musée de Beaux-Arts, one of the finest provincial museums
in France. It was founded in 1801, along with 14 other
provincial museums, as part of a postrevolutionary desire to
decentralize the country's cultural treasures. Among the
highlights of its collection are a celebrated painting by
Georges de La Tour called *The Newborn Child,* and a good
sampling of canvases by artists of the Pont-Aven school.

After the museums, wander over to the **Halle de la
Poissonnerie** on the rue de Nemours; one of the most
important fish markets in France, it's a lively, bustling place,
and it has some spectacular Art Nouveau tiles by the artist
Emmanuel Le Ray. You might also have a look at the typically
Breton half-timbered houses (17th- and 18th-century) along
the rue St-Georges, a couple of blocks north.

STAYING AND DINING IN RENNES

For lunch, try **Le Palais** (7, place Parlement de Bretagne; Tel:
99-79-45-01) near the Parlement for a grand, vaguely nouvelle feed, or **L'Ouvrée**, in an old Breton house at 18, place
Haut des Lices, for something more traditional (Tel: 99-30-
16-38). **Le Piré**, which occupies a beautiful Napoléon III–
vintage house in a wooded park downtown at 23, rue
Maréchal-Jaffre, is another excellent restaurant that's popular
with local *fonctionnaires* and *hommes d'affaires* who come
here to eat roast turbot and baby pigeon in cabbage. Tel: 99-
79-31-41. Closed Saturday lunch and Sundays.

Should you decide to spend a night in Rennes, there are
ho-hum branches of the big, modern French hotel chains—
Altea, Novotel, and Mercure. The ▶ **Anne de Bretagne**, at
12, rue Tronjolly, has a little more personality; it's a pleasant,
sort of old-fashioned hotel with a good downtown location

that makes it favored by prosperous commercial travellers and a perfectly comfortable spot for an overnight stay.

GETTING AROUND

The gateway to Brittany is Rennes, 350 km (217 miles) from Paris via A 11 (Autoroute de l'Océanne) and A 81; and now only two hours from Paris by the TGV, which goes on to Brest on one trunk, and to Nantes and Le Croisic on the other. There are frequent flights on Air Inter from Paris to Nantes, Rennes, Lorient, Quimper, and Brest. (Seats are hard to come by, so reserve far in advance.) Brit Air flies from London's Gatwick Airport to Quimper and Rennes, but most travellers coming from England cross the Channel to St-Malo on the ferries from Plymouth and Portsmouth.

Buses of the French National Railroad network connect Rennes with the major seaside resorts. The best way to see the countryside, though, is by car. Hertz, Avis, Europcar, and other major car-rental firms have offices in Rennes, Nantes, and Vannes.

Nantes, in Brittany's southwest corner, is served by the new TGV Atlantique (two hours) from Paris. The TGV whisks you from Paris to Quimper in four hours and 21 minutes.

Brittany Ferries runs daily service from Plymouth, England, to Roscoff (6 hours), and from Portsmouth to St-Malo (8 hours). Tel: 98-29-28-28 for more information in Roscoff; Tel: 99-40-64-41 in St-Malo. It's wise to make reservations for car crossings (through Roscoff office only) well in advance during peak season, from June to September.

ACCOMMODATIONS REFERENCE

The rates given below are projections *for 1994. Unless otherwise indicated, rates are for a double room, double occupancy, and do not include meals. As rates are always subject to change, double-check before booking.*

▶ **Anne de Bretagne**. 12, rue Tronjolly, 35000 **Rennes**. Tel: 99-31-49-49; Fax: 99-30-53-48. 360F–440F.

▶ **Auberge Les Grandes Roches**. 29910 **Trégunc**. Tel: 98-97-62-97; Fax: 98-50-29-19. 250F–520F.

▶ **Le Brittany**. Boulevard Ste-Barbe, 29680 **Roscoff**. Tel: 98-69-70-78; Fax: 98-61-13-29. 390F–840F.

▶ **La Caravelle**. 14, place Duclos, 22100 **Dinan**. Tel: 96-39-00-11. 200F–230F.

▶ **Castel Clara**. Port-Goulphar, 56360 **Belle-Ile-en-Mer**. Tel: 97-31-84-21; Fax: 97-31-51-69; in U.S., (212) 856-0115; Fax: (212) 856-0193. Member, Relais & Châteaux. 860F–1,045F.

▶ **Château de Locguénolé.** Route de Port-Louis, 56700 **Hennebont.** Tel: 97-76-29-04; Fax: 97-76-39-47. 790F. Closed January.

▶ **Le Goyen.** The Port, 29770 **Audierne.** Tel: 98-70-08-88; Fax: 98-70-18-67. 420F–850F.

▶ **Le Griffon.** 131, route de Bénodet, 29000 **Quimper.** Tel: 98-90-33-33; Fax: 98-53-06-67. 400F.

▶ **Hermitage.** Esplanade François André, 44500 **La Baule.** Tel: 40-60-37-00; Fax: 40-24-33-65. 1,250F–2,500F. Closed November to April.

▶ **Hôtel d'Avaugour.** 1, place du Champ-Clos, 22100 **Dinan.** Tel: 96-39-07-49; Fax: 96-85-43-04. 420F (low season)–480F (high season).

▶ **Hôtel Le Barbu.** Pointe de l'Arcouest, 22500 **Paimpol.** Tel: 96-55-86-98; Fax: 96-55-73-87. 500F–700F.

▶ **Hôtel Bellevue.** Rue Tiviec, 56170 **Quiberon.** Tel: 97-50-16-28; Fax: 97-30-44-34. 410F–670F. Closed November to April.

▶ **Hôtel de Bricourt-Richeux.** 1, rue Duguesclin, 35260 **Cancale.** Tel: 99-89-64-76; Fax: 99-89-88-47. 750F–1,250F.

▶ **Hôtel Central et Restaurant La Frégate.** 6, Grande Rue, 35400 **St-Malo.** Tel: 99-40-87-70; Fax: 99-40-47-57; in U.S. and Canada, (800) 528-1234; in U.K., (081) 541-0033. 425F–630F.

▶ **Hôtel Graslin.** 1, rue Piron, 44000 **Nantes.** Tel: 40-69-72-91; Fax: 40-69-04-44. 280F–350F.

▶ **Hôtel des Pins-Relais Brenner.** Pont de Lézardrieux, 22500 **Paimpol.** Tel: 96-20-11-05; Fax: 96-22-16-27. 600F–1,800F.

▶ **Hôtel de la Plage.** Ste-Anne-la-Palud, Plonévez-Porzay, 29136 **Locronan.** Tel: 98-92-50-12; Fax: 98-92-56-54. 650F–950F. Open April 1 to October 12.

▶ **Hôtel Reine Hortense.** 19, rue Malouine, 35800 **Dinard.** Tel: 99-46-54-31; Fax: 99-88-15-88. 750F–1,300F. Closed mid-November to mid-March.

▶ **Hôtel des Rochers.** Port de Ploumanach, 22700 **Ploumanach.** Tel: 96-91-44-49; Fax: 96-91-43-64. 400F–500F.

▶ **Hôtel Le Roof.** Ile Conleau, 56000 **Vannes.** Tel: 97-63-47-47; Fax: 97-63-48-10. 320F–620F.

▶ **Kastell Dinec'h.** Route de Lannion, 22220 **Tréguier.** Tel: 96-92-49-39; Fax: 96-92-34-03. 350F–470F.

▶ **Manoir de Lan-Kerellec.** 22560 **Trébeurden.** Tel: 96-23-50-09; Fax: 96-23-66-88. 410F–950F.

▶ **Manoir de Moëllien.** Plonévez-Porzay, 29136 **Locronan.** Tel: 98-92-50-40; Fax: 98-92-55-21. 320F. Closed January to April.

▶ **Moulin de Rosmadec.** 29930 **Pont-Aven.** Tel: 98-06-00-22; Fax: 98-06-18-00. 470F.

THE LOIRE VALLEY

*By Georgia I. Hesse, Jennifer Quale,
and Sally Lefèvre*

*Georgia I. Hesse also contributes to several other sections of
this guidebook. Jennifer Quale has written about France for*
Food & Wine, The New York Times, *and* European Travel &
Life. *Sally Lefèvre has lived in Turkey and England as well as
Canada, where she produced a national radio program on
tourism. She now resides in France, where she has lived for
more than 15 years, and contributes to several U.S. and
European publications and guidebooks.*

The Loire river, which seems to have few raisons d'être
other than enchantment, flows through land that by any
name—the garden of France, château country, the playground of kings—is infused with spring and summer richness. The Loire Valley suggests idling, an afternoon picnic
under leafy trees, back roads scented by lilacs and *glycines*
(wisteria), light wines, and perhaps a nap. This is not country
to be hurried through, though one-day tours out of Paris
exist for that very purpose.

The traveller's Loire includes 15 *départements,* but historical regional names more truly reflect the cultures, habits,
and allegiances of the people: Orléanais, Touraine, Anjou
(the old capital of which was Angers), Maine, and maybe, by
pushing things slightly, Berry.

THE LOIRE CHATEAUX
Despite the beauty of its landscape, the Loire Valley may be
even more famous for the châteaux the aristocracy built on
and near the river's banks over the centuries. In the 15th and

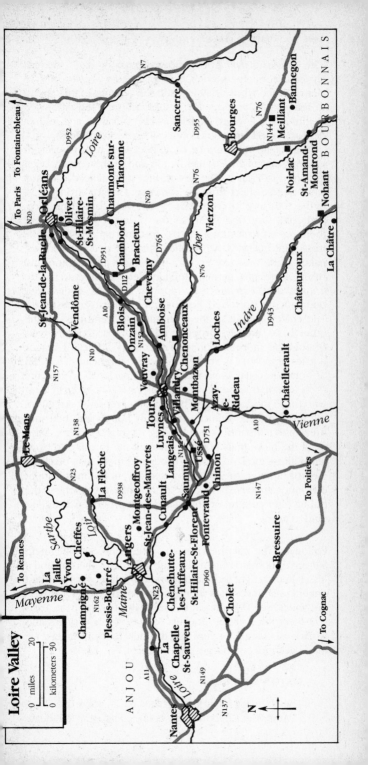

16th centuries everybody who was anybody had to have a
château, from Hurault de Cheverny (who was *chancelier* to
Henri III and whose classic castle still belongs to the family)
to François I (who needed at least a dozen and employed
Cellini as his jeweler, Raphael as his portraitist, and Andrea
del Sarto and Leonardo da Vinci as his court painters).

The Italian Renaissance in architecture, which began in
Florence around 1420, had by the end of the century been
exported to France. The newer, Italian-influenced châteaux
were quite distinct from the *châteaux forts,* or strongholds,
of the 10th and 11th centuries, which were dark, dank, dirty,
and cold. Over the centuries the *châteaux forts,* some of
them veritable fortified towns, metamorphosed from fortresses into palaces. Arrow slits grew into proper windows,
naked stone was covered with panels in a fan of colors and
complex designs, genuine military defense structures were
translated into architectural caprices, and new castles were
built not on protected heights but on great greenswards.
The châteaux built in the 17th and 18th centuries, on the
other hand, are less properly châteaux than country seats
(though far more elaborate than country homes or manor
houses of today). Like their Renaissance forebears, a handful
of hoteliers today collect châteaux to parlay them into the
most sumptuous hotels outside of Paris. Other châtelains,
with more modest budgets but equal entrepreneurial gusto,
are turning their centuries-old family homes into bed-and-
breakfasts nonpareil—thus beating the high property taxes.

Of the more than 1,000 châteaux in the forests and park-
lands along the Loire and its tributaries there may be about
300 major ones; the following text covers the most significant and attractive. Typically, many châteaux open to the
public offer cultural or sound-and-light programs as well as
guided tours.

Following the curving river's course, you could begin in
Sancerre (home of the brisk white wine, a lovely rosé, and a
lesser-known light red) in the east and wander via Tours and
Angers to about Nantes (home of the seafood-lover's Muscadet wines; see Brittany) in the west. But driving from Paris
you meet the Loire at Orléans. So, we start at Orléans and
work west along the river Loire through Tours to Angers. We
then backtrack to Bourges and Sancerre.

MAJOR INTEREST

The six most remarkable châteaux: Chambord, Blois,
Amboise, Chenonceaux, Loches, and Azay-le-Rideau

Other important châteaux: Villandry, Langeais,
   Chinon, Chaumont, Cheverny, Ussé
Fontevraud-l'Abbaye (Plantagenêt tombs)
Eglise Cunault
Châteaux to stay in
Regional wines (Vouvray, Chinon, Sancerre,
   Bourgueil, Montlouis, etc.)
River fish (notably, perchlike *sandre*) with *beurre
   blanc,* local *chèvres* (including Crottins de
   Chavignol), and produce

Orléans
Musée des Beaux-Arts (fine 18th- and 19th-century
   portraits)

Tours
Cathédrale de St-Gatien
Musée des Beaux-Arts

Angers
The château (Apocalypse tapestries)
Cathédrale St-Maurice
Musée Turpin de Crissé

Bourges
Cathédrale St-Etienne
Palais Jacques-Coeur

Noirlac
Cistercian abbey

Sancerre

Orléans

A trade and business center since its very beginnings, Orléans (130 km/81 miles from Paris via the A 10 autoroute) is
today of little interest to the tourist, possibly because its
center was severely damaged by fire during World War II.
Luckily, several medieval and Renaissance façades remain,
lending a certain charm to an otherwise austere city. Orléans
is built in the form of a semicircle on the right bank of the
Loire, centered around the Cathédrale Ste-Croix and the
statue of Joan of Arc on the Place du Martroi. Trains from the
Gare d'Austerlitz in Paris (24 a day) arrive in old Orléans at
the Place Albert I, where the Office de Tourisme is also
located.
   Were it not for Joan of Arc, the "Maid of Orléans," who
came to town to relieve it from the English siege in May
1429, probably even fewer Loire-bound travellers would

now stop here. Orléans's one star shines everywhere: on the rue Jeanne d'Arc, in the Maison de Jeanne d'Arc, the Joan of Arc school, the statue of Joan of Arc in the Place du Martroi, the chapel and stained glass windows of Joan of Arc in the cathedral. Then, of course, there are the stores that do a brisk business in Joan of Arc memorabilia (including Joan of Arc key chains) and the inevitable Café Jeanne d'Arc. The festival of Joan of Arc, which dates from 1435, is held each year on May 7 and May 8.

There is an Orléans beyond the Maid, however. The **Musée des Beaux-Arts**, in the same square as the cathedral (Place Ste-Croix), makes up in modern functionalism for what it lacks in style. Among the early paintings those of Velázquez, Louis Le Nain, and Georges de La Tour are standouts, but there are also fine 18th- and 19th-century French canvases, particularly portraits. The **Cathédrale Ste-Croix**, almost the size of Paris's Notre-Dame, is notable chiefly for the magnificent 18th-century woodwork in its chancel. In 1568 Protestants partially destroyed the 13th-century cathedral. Henri IV rebuilt it in the Gothic style, and work continued until the 19th century under Charles X. Late-19th-century stained glass windows in the side aisles of the central nave depict the life of Joan of Arc.

STAYING AND DINING IN ORLEANS

About 7 km (4½ miles) to the southwest in St-Hilaire–St-Mesmin, the peaceful, 20-room ▶ **Escale du Port Arthur** offers a pretty location and franc-wise rates. Another reasonable find is the small ▶ **Le Rivage** in Olivet, about 5 km (3 miles) south of Orléans. Here, at this grand old house on the banks of the Loiret, you can expect good meals as well as attractive accommodations.

The restaurant scene in Orléans is smarter than the hotel scene. Vying for the top spot are **La Crémaillère** (34, rue Notre-Dame-de-Recouvrance; Tel: 38-53-49-17) and **La Poutrière** (8, rue de la Brèche; Tel: 38-66-02-30), both somewhat expensive (and both closed Sunday nights and Mondays). What the setting at La Crémaillère lacks in pizzazz, the respected Breton chef more than compensates for with such seafood specialties as his *gigot de mer* with garlic. The cozier La Poutrière (*poutre* means "beam") offers classic cuisine, such as peppered salmon in watercress sauce, with original touches in its mirrored dining room or outside on a lovely garden terrace. **Les Antiquaires**, at 2, rue au Lin (Tel: 38-53-52-35), draws a loyal clientele with its caring service, comfortable surroundings, and affordable prices—as well as fish fresh from the Loire.

From Orléans to Blois

As you set out from Orléans in search of châteaux, the route will first take you southwest to Chambord and Cheverny, then north across the river to the town of Blois and its château.

CHATEAU DE CHAMBORD

Chambord, 45 km (28 miles) southwest of Orléans via D 951 and D 112, is the valley's biggest and perhaps most incredible château, built for King François I with 440 rooms, 365 chimneys, and a fantasy of turrets, dormers, and gables. Chambord has a renowned octagonal staircase, a double helix in stone that allows people (or, in its time, horses) ascending to see but never meet those descending. Some say Leonardo may have been the architect of Chambord, but because he died before serious construction began and because his sketchbooks give no details, the odds are on Domenico da Cortona, who may well have shown his model to Leonardo.

The king was passionate about Chambord, which he began just four years after being crowned in 1515, continuing to build through good times and bad (at one point he ordered work to continue even though he lacked the cash to ransom his son from Spain). Once he even considered diverting the Loire to have it run by the château.

If it is true that Chambord was intended mainly as a hunting lodge, it continues to function as planned, for it commands a giant 13,000-acre reserve, **le Parc de Chambord**, which has been set aside for hunting but also has platforms for viewing deer and wild boar at feeding times.

In 1670 Molière's *Le Bourgeois Gentilhomme* premiered at Chambord. These days a sound-and-light performance on the life of François I is held at the château in summer, although it's recommended that you call first for information; Tel: 54-50-40-00. The château is open to visitors daily year-round; guided tours are available upon request from October 1 to March 31.

Staying at the Château de Colliers

On the grounds adjoining Chambord's northeastern edge is the Château de Colliers, the private home of Marie-France and Christian de Gelis, who accommodate guests in six pleasant rooms; each has a superb view of the Loire, including a new one added this year with a private *terrasse*. The château has been in the de Gelis family for more than 200 years; before that it was owned by the marquis de Vaudreuil, the governor of Louisiana and French Canada until 1779. The dinner menu at the château is punctuated by such memorable dishes as *canard aux pêches*. Sports-minded visitors will enjoy the public jogging path that runs in front of the property and continues for four miles along the Loire, as well as the swimming pool and tennis courts.

CHATEAU DE CHEVERNY
This classic château about 17 km (10½ miles) southwest of Chambord via D 112 and D 102, constructed in a single, continuous stroke, is more elegant, better dressed, and altogether more warming and welcoming as a residence than any of its castle colleagues. For one thing, it retains almost entirely the 17th-century furnishings and decorations from the days of its builder, Hurault de Cheverny. For another, it is still kept within the family, the possession of a descendant of the builder, the marquis de Vibraye.

The home, which is open daily year-round, boasts five Gobelins tapestries and several valuable paintings; the kennels for hunting dogs and a hunting museum are also open to the public. More than 2,500 sets of deer antlers testify to the good aim of several generations of Chevernois. A sound-and-light show entitled "The Dreams of Sologne" is performed here in July and August.

Blois

Blois is built along the northern banks of the Loire, 13 km (8 miles) northwest of Cheverny on D 765. Its steep medieval streets twist around the château on the west and the cathedral on the east of old Blois. In its blue slate roofs, white façades, and red brick chimneys, you can almost see the tricolored French flag. (Blois's train station, near the château, is well served by frequent trains from Paris; parking is available near the château on Place Victor Hugo.)

Serene and hospitable, Blois makes for easy strolling. Take a café au lait or pink beer (flavored with grenadine syrup) at the outdoor **Bar Louis XII** across from the château and watch the youngsters surf the ramparts' edge on roller skates and boards.

The old quarter around the Cathédrale de St-Louis is worth exploring for its picturesque Renaissance houses, the beautiful gardens of the **Bishops' Palace**, and the statue of the Huguenot Denis Papin, the inventor of the pressure cooker. The 12th- to 13th-century **Eglise St-Nicolas**, one block south of the château on rue St-Laumer, is the most interesting in Blois; the intricate Benedictine design of the capitals in the chancel are especially worthy. The church adjoins the former Benedictine abbey of St-Laumer, which extends to the Loire. Stop by the open-air market held Tuesdays, Thursdays, and Saturdays on the Place Louis XII, especially when strawberries and asparagus are in season.

CHATEAU DE BLOIS

Originally, a fort designed to thwart the attacks of the Vikings stood upon this defensive site. Of that, only the 13th-century **Tour du Foix** and **Salle des Etats** remain. To circle the courtyard with your eyes is to see the history of French architecture through the Gothic and early Renaissance periods of Louis XII, past the pure Renaissance style of François I, to the severely classical **Gaston d'Orléans wing**, the work of François Mansart for Louis XIII.

Blois Château's fairly dull interior, the result of a 19th-century restoration by a pupil of Viollet-le-Duc, pales by comparison with the exciting exterior, save for the fact that so much drama was played out within the walls.

This was the home, after all, of Charles d'Orléans (1391–1465), son of Louis d'Orléans, who was taken prisoner by the English at Agincourt and held for 25 years. On his return to France in 1440 Charles married Marie de Clèves; he was 50 years old, she 14. Charles had a part of the old fortress torn down and more livable quarters raised, in which he created a kind of *beaux-arts* court. He was 71 when his son—the future Louis XII—was born.

Louis XII took over from Charles VIII in 1498 when Charles, on his way to a tennis match at his castle at Amboise, struck his head upon a door lintel (he measured all of five feet, two inches) and died a few hours later. Louis married Charles's widow, Anne de Bretagne, moved the court to Blois, and began building. His contributions are the brick and stone **Galerie Charles-d'Orléans**, the **Chapelle-St-Calais** (of which only the chancel remains), and the **Louis XII wing**. Each has a delightful, airy, informal quality, even though they were too heavily restored—to some tastes—in the 19th century.

Soon after Louis XII's death in 1515, his daughter, Claude de France, married François I, who ascended to the throne. Claude died at Blois in 1524, having borne François' seven children in eight years. She was 25. The best parts of Blois date from this period, especially the carved, white stone spiral **Grand Escalier** (Grand Staircase) in an octagonal well.

In 1588 the sniveling Henri III (son of Henri II, who lived at Blois during the Wars of Religion) saw to the murder of his rival the duc de Guise here, and the following year his

remarkable mother, Catherine de Médicis (Catherine of the
Bad Press, it could be said now), died here. In the wood-
paneled study visitors are dutifully shown the cabinets,
opened by levers ingeniously hidden in the baseboards, in
which Catherine is supposed to have secreted her poisons.

The château is open daily year-round and includes a
beaux-arts museum and the Robert Houdin gallery; the
magician Henry Houdini named himself after this master
illusionist, who was a native of Blois. Between mid-May and
September the *son-et-lumière* program "Spirits Prefer the
Night" is shown (in English and French) twice each evening,
retracing the history of the château.

STAYING AND DINING
IN AND NEAR BLOIS

Although the local restaurant scene has been bleak, now **La
Bocca d'Or**, in a delightful 14th-century vaulted cellar at 15,
rue Haute, gives reason to look forward to dining in Blois;
Tel: 54-78-04-74. **L'Orangerie du Château**, at 1, avenue Jean-
Laigret, a few steps from the Office de Tourisme and one
block north of the château in a 15th-century *monument
historique,* specializes in game; Tel: 54-78-05-36.

You may also want to drive 18 km (11 miles) southeast on
D 765 and D 923 to Bracieux, where Bernard and Christine
Robin prepare regional specialties in an old coaching inn at
1, avenue Chambord. Indeed, the **Bernard Robin–Relais de
Bracieux** ranks among the best (and most expensive) restau-
rants in the Loire Valley. Hats off to its fish and game dishes.
Reserve; Tel: 54-46-41-22.

The 18th-century ▶ **Château de Breuil** is set in 60 acres of
gardens and forests, 9 km (5½ miles) southeast of Blois on
D 765 in the village of Cour-Cheverny. There are 15 elegant
rooms and two suites, and a restaurant specializing in game.
Another top hostelry in the vicinity (Blois proper, of almost
50,000 people, offers little) is the ▶ **Domaine des Hauts de
Loire**, reflected in the swan pond of its own park just 17 km
(10½ miles) southwest of Blois via N 152 and D 58 along the
river and 15 km (9 miles) inland in **Onzain**. A genteel air
pervades the ivy-covered manor, known for understated
elegance in both its decor and its cuisine. There are tennis
courts on the property, and the Bonnigal family, who own
the hotel, will gladly make arrangements for fishing, golf,
and horseback riding. Nearby, the small ▶ **Château des
Tertres**, a bed-and-breakfast on a leafy knoll about a kilometer and a half east of Onzain proper on D 58, is a pleasant,
less expensive alternative, though it is modest by château
standards.

From Blois to Amboise

You may well want to break up the trip between these two riverside towns with stops at three of the Loire Valley's most evocative châteaux.

CHATEAU DE CHAUMONT

Just 17 km (10½ miles) downriver from Blois on D 751, Chaumont is the fortresslike château, complete with drawbridge and cylindrical dungeon, that Catherine de Médicis gave to her rival Diane de Poitiers when Catherine took Chenonceaux (see below). Chaumont isn't undesirable, but Diane was spoiled, and she sulked and betook herself to more gracious Anet, closer to Paris.

Students of symbols and inscriptions will immediately take note on the façade and throughout the château of the intertwined Cs of Charles d'Amboise (one of the 16th-century owners) and of his wife, Catherine; the emblem of *chaud mont* (a volcano or, literally, "hot mountain"); and the intertwined Ds of Diane de Poitiers that, with the hunting horn here and there, suggest Diane as the classical Diana the Huntress. Then there are the coat of arms of France, the initials of Louis XII and Anne de Bretagne, the hat of Cardinal d'Amboise, and the coat of arms of Charles d'Amboise.

Chaumont also has an American connection: In the 18th century it was owned by a financier named Le Ray, who supported American independence. Benjamin Franklin, when he was minister to the French court, was frequently entertained at the château. Franklin was able to persuade Le Ray to support freebooter John Paul Jones and thus to become instrumental in the creation of the American navy.

The château, park, and the famous *écuries* (stables) are open to visitors daily throughout the year except on major holidays. A one-and-a-half-hour cruise along the Loire on the *Leonardo da Vinci* departs Chaumont at 3:00 and 5:00 P.M. daily in July and August, and on Sundays and holidays until October 31.

CHATEAU DE CHENONCEAUX

At one time Chenonceaux, 26 km (16 miles) southwest of Chaumont on D 114 and D 176, like most other great châteaux along the Loire, came under the sign of the salamander (the symbol of François I). François was not its builder, though; the structure that is admired today is the 16th-century creation of his tax collector, Thomas Bohier. If you were to explore but a single castle in the Loire, a good choice would be Chenonceaux.

The story of Bohier reads somewhat like a Balzac novel, but six women star in the story of the château: Catherine Briçonnet, Bohier's wife; Diane de Poitiers, Henri II's famously beautiful mistress; Catherine de Médicis; Louise de Lorraine, wife and widow of Henri III, who after the king's murder lived out her life dressed only in black and white; Madame Dupin, who employed Rousseau as tutor to her son—Rousseau's *Emile* was written at Chenonceaux—and whose kindness to the local peasantry saved Chenonceaux from destruction during the Revolution; and Madame Pelouze, who restored the whole to its original state.

No castle is more stunning on first glimpse (if you can overlook the rows of parked tour buses; get here as close to 9:00 A.M. as possible to avoid the crowds) and few of the Loire châteaux are as sumptuously furnished. Up a superb avenue flanked by plane trees, you approach the great keep, the 15th-century donjon of the original structure. To the left blooms the **formal garden of Diane**. Diane was the rival of Henri II's wife, Catherine, whose garden to the right is somewhat smaller. Behind the keep Diane's marvelous **Grande Galerie** (topped off by the image of Catherine, as it happens) spans the river Cher in five bounds. After Henri's death in a jousting tournament, Catherine took spiteful pleasure in tossing Diane out of plush Chenonceaux into medieval Chaumont.

Chenonceaux's *son-et-lumière* program, "In the Times of the Women of Chenonceaux," is presented daily from mid-June to mid-September. The château is open daily year-round.

Staying at Château de Chissay

About 5 km (3 miles) east of Chenonceaux in the Cher valley, the ▶ **Château de Chissay** offers perhaps the most tastefully (and often whimsically) furnished accommodations in the Loire Valley. This is one château with a soul. In addition to the trendy staff and clientele and large pool (only Eskimos would agree it's heated), the guest quarters bedazzle even the most jaded of travellers, who have included Charles VII, Louis XI, the duc de Choiseul, and, more recently, Charles de Gaulle. Stop by the 13th-century chapel on your way up to the dungeon suite—if you can stand the stone-wedge staircase to the topmost tower—the most unusual digs around, with its transparent bathroom floor looming over the luxurious bedroom. Only the French could pull this off with good taste. If you're in the area for just the day, make a point of having a meal (albeit a pricey one) at the château's outstanding restaurant, whose chef offers Loire *sandre* in a *beurre blanc* sauce.

LOCHES

If Chenonceaux seduces with grace, Loches, 25 km (16 miles) south of Chenonceaux on D 80 and D 31, strikes right between the eyes with its dungeons, turrets, keep, torture chambers, round towers, and ramparts: all the discomforts of home in the Middle Ages.

The town of Loches (about 7,000 people), at the foot of what was once a medieval entrenched camp on the banks of the river Indre, played a prominent role in the history of the great feudal families of Anjou and Plantagenêt. Henri (England's Henry II) created fortifications here; his son John Lackland had it wrested away from him by Philippe Auguste; John's brother Richard the Lion-hearted, returning from prison in Austria, was so angry he took it back in a three-hour battle; and when Richard died, Philippe Auguste took it back again.

Joan of Arc was here in 1429 when she came to persuade Charles VII to be crowned in Reims, but the real *dame du château* is Agnès Sorel, mistress of Charles VII and benefactor of a very good pun: She was known as *la dame de Beauté,* not entirely because of her good looks but more because Charles gave her an estate known as Beauté-sur-Marne. Respects may be paid at Agnès's tomb in the château, where angels support the recumbent figure's head and lambs her feet.

Everything in the medieval enclosure of Loches is open to visitors daily from February through November (except Wednesdays off-season), including its dungeons and cells. Louis XI liked to put his prisoners into wooden and iron cages here and then suspend them from the ceiling of the **Tour Ronde**. One prisoner is said to have dangled there for 11 years. Ludovico Sforza, the duke of Milan, spent eight years in the dungeons of **Martelet** (the most oppressive in the complex); Sforza wrote and painted on its walls and fell dead the moment he observed the sunlight of freedom. On a lighter note, Loches was also the birthplace of the writer Alfred de Vigny.

A sound-and-light show, *La Peau d'Ane,* a story by Charles Perrault, is presented at the château on Fridays and Saturdays in July and August.

Staying and Dining in Loches

A good choice for accommodation in Loches is the modestly priced 15th-century ▶ **Hôtel George Sand**, with its own lovely garden restaurant. Sand frequently stopped here en route from Paris to her country home. A slightly more expensive possibility is the ▶ **Hôtel de France** on rue

Picois, a tastefully transformed postal inn. The two-story suites that overlook the attractive courtyard are especially nice.

For a special meal in the area, **La Belle Epoque** offers inviting local fare in a lovely setting overlooking a small castle and church in the town of Chanceaux-Prés-Loches, 5 km (3 miles) northwest of Loches on D 21 (Tel: 47-59-38-16).

Amboise

Amboise, 37 km (23 miles) due north of Loches on D 31, lies on the south bank of the Loire, with its château, perched on a rocky plateau, dominating the picturesque village below. Photographers will get their best shots from the bridge on the north bank of the river. In town, stop at **Le Clos-Lucé**, the Renaissance manor on rue du Clos-Lucé where Leonardo da Vinci spent the last years of his life. (It's a five-minute walk east of the château's entrance along rue Victor-Hugo—best to go in the morning; afternoons really bring in the crowds.) The Mona Lisa sojourned here with her master during that time, keeping her smile despite the long journey from Rome over the Alps by mule. Le Clos-Lucé is now a museum furnished with 15th- and 16th-century antiques. No originals are displayed, but models from Leonardo's drawings show the extraordinary talents he had as an engineer. There are also small-scale displays, an armored tank, a helicopter, and a drawbridge among them. Le Clos-Lucé is open every day except the month of January.

Stop by to see Armand and Janine Langlois at **Galerie Atelier Langlois**, just across the street at 5, rue du Clos-Lucé. Experts in refined French folk arts, they combine their talents to produce wooden creatures of the forest masquerading in Renaissance finery—at prices far less than boutiques abroad command.

CHATEAU D'AMBOISE

There is something irresistible about this castle, 2 km (1 mile) north of Amboise on D 31, although what remains is only a part of the dominant fortress that stood here in the 16th century. Perhaps it's the handsome setting above the town, or the glittering artistic history, or the fact that Leonardo worked and died here.

Charles VIII was born to Louis XI and Charlotte of Savoy at Amboise. Only 13 years old when he assumed the throne, Charles began rebuilding and new construction of the château in 1492, eventually creating one of the finest royal residences on the Loire. The masterpiece from this period is the Gothic **Chapelle St-Hubert**, dedicated to the patron saint of the hunt. The chapel, at one time a portion of the apartments of Queen Anne de Bretagne, is rich in decoration; the stained glass windows that were destroyed in 1940 have been suitably replaced by Max Ingrand. From an expedition to Italy (which was undertaken to conquer Naples for the House of Valois), Charles returned with an abundance of artworks, furniture, fabrics, and people: decorators, gardeners, artists, even a chicken breeder.

When Charles died in 1498 (see Bourges), the boy who would become François I moved to Amboise with his mother, Louise of Savoy. François later enlarged Amboise and made it more magnificent, but his greatest accomplishment was the importation of Leonardo da Vinci, who brought with him his *Mona Lisa* and *Virgin of the Rocks,* both now in the Louvre. This one-man Renaissance spent the last three years of his life in a manor house a cobble's toss from the château and died there on May 2, 1519 (see above).

War, however, has always been insensitive to artistic greatness: That August, Leonardo's bones were buried in the cloister of the church of St-Florentin in Burgundy, as he had asked, but during the Wars of Religion his remains and those of hundreds of others were dug up and tossed away. A plaque in the north transept of the Chapelle St-Hubert claims Leonardo's bones are there with others, but nobody knows for sure.

The château is open daily to guided tours only; Tel: 47-57-00-98 for times. A dazzling 100-minute *son-et-lumière* show, "At the Court of King Francis," featuring 420 citizens in period dress, plays from the end of June until the beginning of September on Wednesdays and Saturdays.

STAYING AND DINING IN AMBOISE

Walk three minutes south from Clos-Lucé (everything is easily accessible in Amboise) and you'll find **Le Manoir St-Thomas** at Place Richelieu (Tel: 47-57-22-52), which serves memorable meals in a pretty garden. If you want to stay in Amboise overnight, a good (but pricey) choice is ► **Le Choiseul**, whose entrance is on the quai Charles-Guinot on the riverbank. Its 25 rooms, pool, and two lovely dining rooms, one overlooking the Loire (and, unfortunately, a campground across the river), draw a slightly older crowd. Chef Pascal Bouvier's specialties are *persillé de saumon* in local Montlouis wine, and a fruit soup for dessert.

► **Château de Pray**, just northeast of the village via D 751, is a charming place to stay. Each of its 16 medium-priced rooms, many of which overlook the expansive park, is named after one of the many dignitaries who have graced the château since 1244. A particularly nice room is the duc de Choiseul's, with its large canopy bed. The château also boasts a commendable, reasonably priced restaurant.

TOURS

From Amboise it is a drive of only 25 km (16 miles) along the Loire to the region's largest city. In the days of the Pax Romana, under the name of Caesarodunum (Caesar's Hill), Tours became a prosperous free city with an administrative center, baths, arenas, and other Roman necessities near the site of the cathedral of St-Gatien. By the fourth century, Tours (named for a Celtic tribe, the Turones) was the bustling center of Roman Gaul in the west. Five roads, reaching from Spain to Roman settlements in the far north, met in Tours, which allowed for important land commerce in addition to that provided by the river. By the late eighth century, Tours—more specifically, the monastery that Saint Martin founded in the fourth century just outside Tours in Marmoutiers on the northern banks of the Loire—had become one of the greatest centers of culture and learning in all Europe.

There are more than 138,000 (253,000 including suburban areas) Tourangeaux today, working mostly in various medium and heavy industries. An industrial zone between the north bank of the river and the airport has permitted important construction for electronic and metallurgic industries. So far, however, the vital industrial element of the city has been prevented from impinging on the traditional cultural attractions that lure travellers.

Tours is also a college town. As throughout its long history, the university of Tours remains a significant institution, and Tourangeaux continue to boast and believe that the French spoken here is the purest in France. Tours is just 50 minutes from the Gare Montparnasse in Paris on the TGV Atlantique. The station and Office de Tourisme are near the Cathedral.

The Old City

Vieux Tours centers on **Place Plumereau**, originally a marketplace for hatters. Most of the area is off-limits to vehicles, resulting in pleasurably winding streets lined with a variety of chic boutiques that offer everything from traditional arts and crafts to *au courant* toys and fashions.

The 15th-century half-timbered houses and gabled fa-

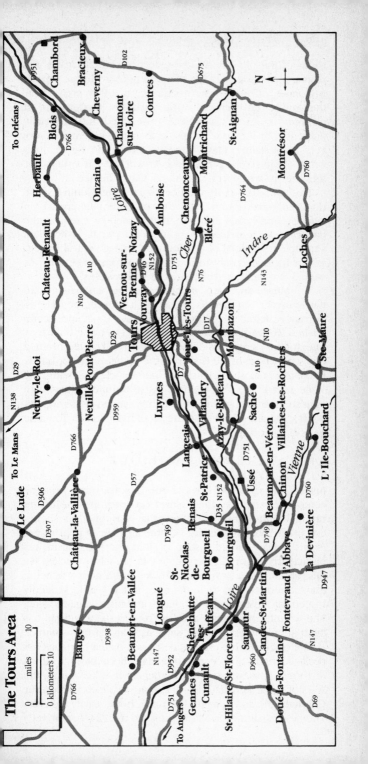

The Tours Area

0 miles 10

0 kilometers 10

N

To Orléans

To Le Mans

To Angers

Chambord
Bracieux
Cheverny
Contres
D102
D951
Blois
D675
Herbault
D766
St-Aignan
D760
Chaumont-sur-Loire
Onzain
Loire
Montrichard
Montrésor
Château-Renault
Amboise
Chenonceaux
A10
N10
D764
Bléré
Vernou-sur-Brenne
Noizay
D952
Vouvray
N152
D751
Cher
Indre
Tours
Neuillé-Pont-Pierre
Joué-Lès-Tours
Loches
D29
N138
D29
D7
D17
N143
Nazelles-le-Roi
Neuvy-le-Roi
D959
D57
Luynes
Villandry
Montbazon
N10
Le Lude
D306
D766
Château-la-Vallière
Langeais
Saché
A10
D307
St-Patrice
Azay-le-Rideau
Villaines-les-Rochers
Ste-Maure
D749
Benais
D35 N152
Ussé
Beaumont-en-Véron
Chinon
Vienne
D760
L'Ile-Bouchard
Beaufort-en-Vallée
D938
St-Nicolas-de-Bourgueil
Bourgueil
D749
La Devinière
Baugé
Longué
Chênehutte-les-Tuffeaux
Fontevraud-l'Abbaye
D947
N147
Gennes
Cunault
Saumur
Candes-St-Martin
D960
Doué-la-Fontaine
D69
St-Hilaire-St-Florent
D751
D952
N147

çades of the old city shelter seductive sidewalk cafés and restaurants. Various styles of town houses cluster on rue Briçonnet, off the northern side of Place Plumereau, near the **Musée du Gemmail**. The relatively modern art of *gemmail,* colored glass pieces assembled and artificially lighted from the back or inside to create a contemporary version of stained glass, was invented by the painter John Crotti (1878–1958). Works of *gemmail* may be original or they may re-create frescoes, mosaics, and the like.

This tangle of streets also houses the **Hôtel Gouin** (on rue du Commerce, four blocks east of Place Plumereau), an ornate Renaissance mansion that somehow survived the battering the area underwent in World War II. Visitors can view the collections of the Touraine archaeological society, which includes prehistoric and Gallo-Roman treasures as well as late-medieval sculptures and other items.

The **Musée du Compagnonnage**, on rue Nationale next to the Eglise de St-Julien, is housed in a 16th-century monks' dormitory. It traces the history, techniques, tools, and accomplished works of artisans in the region. (Its name is a happy one: It joins derivatives of the Latin *com* and *panis,* meaning one with whom bread is shared; the French slang for buddy is *copain,* and the English *companion* clearly shares the same root.) The 13th-century **Eglise St-Julien** glows with light shining through the 20th-century stained glass windows of Max Ingrand; there's a museum of the wines of Touraine in its cloister cellar.

THE ANCIENNE BASILIQUE ST-MARTIN

Just off the rue des Halles at rue Descartes and near the central marketplace, the basilica occupies the site of the original fifth-century sanctuary that was built to shelter the saint's remains and that became a center of pilgrimages in his honor. Named bishop of Tours in 372, Martin was particularly beloved because of his homely miracles. He died at Candes in November 397, and as his body was being transported by boat to Tours, trees in the region suddenly leaped into leaf, flowers bloomed, and birds began to sing. The warmth that comes after the first frosts of autumn has been known in France ever since as Saint Martin's summer.

The original structure was destroyed by the Normans but replaced in the 13th century by a magnificent basilica, which in turn was sacked by the Huguenots in 1562 during the Wars of Religion. What's left of *that* are two towers, the **Tour Charlemagne** and **Tour de l'Horloge**, both heavily restored. The new basilica of St-Martin, finished in 1924, comprises a corner of the former structure and claims to preserve the tomb of the saint in its crypt, the exact spot where it lay in antiquity.

As the cult of Saint Martin grew its constituency prospered, and the influence of the monastery he had founded at Marmoutiers began to spread. The first French historian, Gregory of Tours, became bishop of the see in 573. In the late eighth century Charlemagne brought the Anglo-Saxon monk Alcuin out of England to be the leading spirit in the soon-to-be emperor's drive to spread learning and bring some unity to the teaching of Christianity. In this Alcuin was vastly successful—in what we know as the Carolingian Renaissance—and was named abbot of Saint Martin's monastery in 796. It was under Alcuin and his successors at Tours that the abbey produced such notable illuminated manuscripts as the *Bible of Charles the Bald*. Tours remained an extremely important religious and cultural center until the Normans invaded. Modern visitors can see the scanty remains of the original monastery, which was ravaged by the Normans in the middle of the ninth century, just across the river north of the center of Tours in what is still known as Marmoutiers (today a suburb); a convent occupies the site.

The **Musée St-Martin** at 3, rue Rapin (one block south of the Basilique de St-Martin) depicts the main events of the saint's life, giving visitors a deeper understanding of the churches dedicated to Martin and insight into the devotions made to him by the faithful. Fragments from Martin's tomb, constructed by Perpetus around 470, are among the treasures of this little museum, which is open every day except Mondays and Tuesdays from mid-March to mid-November.

Quartier St-Gatien

From Old Tours it's a pleasant walk east on rue Colbert toward the cathedral and the less touristic quarter of St-Gatien. Enthusiasts and collectors of antiquities will not be able to pass by the cluster of antiques shops on rue Colbert and parallel rue de la Scellerie, particularly **Bruneau**, for its paintings.

THE CATHEDRALE DE ST-GATIEN AND MUSEE DES BEAUX-ARTS

Begun in the 13th century and not completed until the 16th, the cathedral of St-Gatien, on the Place de la Cathédrale at the corner of rues Colbert and Lavoisier, shows off the entire extensive genius of the Gothic style, most of the evolution being visible on the recently restored façade. Romanesque

sits in the form of towers upon a Gallo-Roman wall; Flamboyant dances on the façade; Renaissance triumphs in the turret
towers. Inside, the premier attractions are the 13th- to 15th-
century stained glass windows. The top of the south tower is
a good spot for taking photographs. On the grounds adjoining the cathedral, the **Cloître La Psalette** (where one sings
psalms) boasts fine 15th- and 16th-century frescoes. The
Musée des Beaux-Arts, located in a 17th- to 18th-century
palace of the archbishops on the other side of the cathedral,
has attempted to bring alive, in several completely outfitted
rooms, the styles of the 18th century: Regency, Louis XV,
Louis XVI. This is one of the most comprehensive art museums in the Loire Valley, with French paintings from the 15th
to 19th century displayed chronologically; the early Italian
works are particularly interesting.

The 12th-century **Tour de Guise**, one block north on rue
Lavoisier, off quai d'Orléans, is all that remains of the Château de Tours, in which the young duc de Guise was imprisoned after the murder of his father by Henri III; Joan of Arc
was received here by Charles VII. The **Historial de Touraine**,
a wax museum within the château, is worth a short stop, as is
the small **aquarium** also on the premises.

MARKETS AND FESTIVALS IN TOURS
Markets are held daily in Tours, either at the Marché des
Halles or Place Velpeau, and are said to be best on weekends. Porcelain, pottery, and wickerwork may be among the
finds at the flea market on Place des Victoires on Wednesdays and Sundays. A garlic and basil fair puts Tours in good
odor near the end of July.

Music is important to the life of Tours: A summer's schedule will include jazz, rock, and classical concerts. The Grand
Théâtre, located on rue de la Scellerie three blocks west of
the Musée des Beaux-Arts, devotes itself, in the main, to
symphonic and choral productions; recitals are held in several churches and in the Salle des Tanneurs; chamber orches-
tras frequently perform in the Salle des Fêtes of the Hôtel de
Ville.

For ticket and other information, inquire at the Comité
Départemental de Tourisme, 9, rue Buffon, near the railroad
station; Tel: 47-31-47-31. The famous choral festival Florilège
Vocal, celebrating its 21st year, is held in May. The classical
music festival, *Fêtes Musicales en Touraine,* is staged in late
June and early July at the **Grange de Meslay**, a 13th-century
ensemble of farm buildings, 10 km (6 miles) north via A 10
(Tel: 47-21-65-08). Another event not to miss is the *Académie*

Internationale d'Art Musicale festival, which is held for three weeks in July (Tel: 47-22-97-08).

STAYING AND DINING IN TOURS

Dining is most expensively done in Tours at ▶ **Jean Bardet**, on rue Groison just across the Pont Wilson on the north bank of the Loire (Tel: 47-41-41-11), a bright and airy restaurant that consistently wins rave reviews for exemplary up-to-the-minute cuisine. Bardet also offers 15 luxurious rooms and suites in its early-19th-century villa—as well as a heated pool. Cooking courses in English are offered here off-season. In this same neighborhood of gastronomical delights is the **Jardin du Castel** (part of the Hôtel de Groison), at 16, rue Groison, just down the street from Bardet. Try the "menu surprise" created by master chef Guy Tricon in his most attractive dining room (Tel: 47-41-94-40). Within walking distance, at 101, avenue de la Tranchée, the venerable **Charles Barrier** (Tel: 47-54-20-39) continues to serve impeccable classical dishes in its hush-hush formal dining room.

Near the Tour de Guise at 19, rue Lavoisier, on the southern bank just across the Pont Suspender, less extravagant local fare is offered at the rustic **Les Tuffeaux**, including *blanc de turbot au vin de Layon et melon* (turbot with sweet white wine and melon). Master chef Gildas Marsollier turns out irresistible pastries (Tel: 47-47-19-89). The sumptuously decorated **Le Palmier** at 22, rue Bretonneau, one block west of Place Plumereau, serves delicious Moroccan food; there's a floor show on Thursdays. Tel: 47-64-60-49.

Centrally located on the wide boulevard Heurteloup, the old-fashioned ▶ **Univers** is perhaps Tours's best choice of accommodations in a city with many good hotels. If you're looking for a bargain, stay at the modest but spotless ▶ **Hôtel Italia** at 19, rue Devilde, two streets east of the Barrier restaurant on the northern bank. What the Italia lacks in aesthetics, it makes up for with the friendliness of its kind hosts and rock-bottom prices.

Tours is about the only place in the Loire with any degree of nightlifer; a good spot to get a drink at midnight is the **Relais de Cicognes**, on a corner of the Place Plumereau.

COUNTRY HOTELS AND CHATEAUX NEAR TOURS

Travellers in search of serenity (and who don't mind then having to drive into town to sightsee) would prefer the ▶ **Domaine de Beauvois**, a lovely 15th-century manor house, and its fine restaurant, 13 km (8 miles) west of Tours on

N 152 in Luynes. Beauvois, with its knowledgeable staff (particularly the good-natured British concierge, Brian Byron), draws lots of American and English guests. Done up in comparatively bright colors, this is one manor house where you can wear jeans and not worry about offending history. Tennis, fishing, swimming, and ballooning are offered on the immense wooded estate, along with a library and TV (in the rooms) for rainy days. Especially appetizing on the restaurant's menu are the *paupiette de sandre* in bacon and leeks and the Touraine chicken with light cream sauce and herbs by chef Daniel Dauvel. The wine list is as impressive as the dinner menu. After dinner, classical music quartets lull satisfied guests before they retire to their tastefully appointed rooms.

Another good summer choice because of its access to public tennis courts and swimming pool next door is the ▶ **Château de Beaulieu**, 5 km (3 miles) southwest of Tours via D 86 in Joué-lès-Tours. The rooms are small and simple, but manager and master chef Jean-Pierre Lozay and his lovely Scottish wife couldn't make you feel more at home. Their noted restaurant specializes in such culinary treats as hot oysters in white leek sauce and wild duck in truffle butter.

Vouvray

Oenophiles and would-be cave dwellers can head to Vouvray, just east of Tours on the north bank of the Loire. Renowned for its *pétillant* (bubbly) and *tranquille* (still) wines, the village itself lacks character, but its landscapes, gentle rolling hills and soft hues of cherry blossoms and lilacs in spring, still possess the charm often described by Balzac, a native of Tours, in *La Comédie Humaine*. ▶ **Les Hautes Roches**, 2 km (1 mile) east of Tours on N 152 in Rochecorbon, has turned old troglodyte quarters into luxurious—though not for the claustrophobic—guest rooms and a commendable restaurant specializing in seafood to draw more than curiosity seekers.

A good quick-stop lunch in Vouvray can be had at the little roadside café **B. Loré** on route N 152 (look for the ten-foot-high green wine bottle stuck in the driveway). The proprietors sell their own wine, but the place to sample and buy Vouvray is at **Daniel Jarry**, off route N 152 at 99, rue La Vallée Coquette, or **Daniel Allias**, just up the road at Le Petit Mont.

Just a few minutes east of Vouvray via D 46 and D 1 in Vernou-sur-Brenne is the modest, ivy-covered ▶ **Hostellerie les Perce-Neige** (meaning "snowdrops"). Although the rooms and bathrooms have been renovated with rather bizarre taste, the lovely setting amid a wisteria and lilac garden and the low prices more than compensate. The restaurant is cozy and offers excellent local fare, also at a good price. In summer the outdoor *terrasse* is a treat, as is the pool.

If you feel more in the mood for castle dwelling, by all means stay at the ▶ **Château de Noizay**, just five minutes farther east via D 1. Like many châtelains wishing to maintain their homes, Monsieur Hubert André has transformed his family château of generations into a full-fledged luxury hotel, and a superb one it is. The reception rooms are gracious and personalized with many family heirlooms, and each of the 14 bedrooms is graced with period furniture. At the château's fine restaurant chef Didier Frebout offers creations such as *langoustine aux choux croquants* in a curry and saffron sauce. The château offers a pool, a tennis court, bicycles, and a putting green. Balloon flights can also be arranged.

Montbazon

Among the most regal hostelries in France is the ▶ **Château d'Artigny**, just a couple of kilometers southwest of the village of Montbazon, which is 10 km (6 miles) south of Tours on N 10. It's smart, stylish, and feels like a big-city hotel, if not a stage set for a period costume drama (*musicales* are in order on weekends). D'Artigny reeks of opulence and draws an appropriately international clientele that revels in the château's meticulously landscaped park along with the heated pool, putting green, and tennis courts. The cuisine of master chef Francis Maignaut is excellent (try the curried *mignon* of veal), the dining room festooned with gilt, and the regional wine list among the area's most comprehensive (and pricey).

About 2 km (1½ miles) north of Montbazon via N 10 and D 287, the family-run ▶ **Domaine de la Tortinière** presents a less formidable, more soothing château in a private park overlooking the river Indre and a ruined tenth-century tower on the opposite bank; there are 21 quiet rooms (including seven suites) and an outstanding kitchen, where cooking courses are offered off-season. Just to the west of town, nestled on the banks of the Indre, is the ▶ **Moulin Fleuri**, small (12 rooms) and intimate. Travellers who don't mind the flimsy mattresses love this spot for its winsome setting and no-frills cooking at extremely reasonable prices.

If you're in the mood to drop a bundle (even the artistic furniture is for sale), head to the elegant 16th-century ivy-covered **La Chancelière** (Tel: 47-26-00-67) on Place des Marronniers in Montbazon. No other restaurant in the Loire

Valley has risen so high or fast in the estimate of French
"foodies," who carry indelible memories of its oyster-stuffed
ravioli and warm foie gras.

From Tours to Chinon

A meandering drive west and south of Tours brings you to a
string of châteaux. They are close enough to Tours to be
visited on separate excursions or on one scenery-filled
drive.

VILLANDRY

The original Château de Villandry, some 20 km (12½ miles)
west of Tours via D 7, was built in the 16th century by Jean le
Breton, secretary of state under François I. Today only the
dungeon remains from the original fortress. In 1906 Dr.
Joachim Carvallo, a Spaniard, bought the château, bringing
with him a 13th-century Moorish ceiling from Toledo and a
collection of 16th- to 18th-century paintings—rather startling in the heart of French château country!

The remarkable element of Villandry is not the interior,
however, but the gardens. Nothing like them exists elsewhere. Perfectly manicured and maintained by six full-time
gardeners who are supervised by descendants of Dr. Carvallo, and set on three rising terraces, these are ornamental
gardens you would consider eating. Flowers are plentiful,
but there are also geometrical, color-coordinated growths of
chard, cabbage, fruit trees, aromatic herbs—all the good-
looking vegetables except the potato, which had yet to arrive
in France in the 16th century.

The château is open to visitors from mid-March to mid-
November; the gardens are open daily year-round.

There's a decent restaurant in this village of about 780
inhabitants: **Cheval Rouge**, in an old house with an odd
modern façade and a pretty garden terrace in the rear.
Although the cuisine is classic Loire fare, the chef has a flair
for creating attractive dishes from fresh seasonal vegetables
and fruits (Tel: 47-50-02-07).

AZAY-LE-RIDEAU

On an autumn afternoon when the air is as golden as the
leaves, the pretty promenade to the **Château d'Azay-le-
Rideau**, in its island setting of woods and water 28 km (17
miles) southwest of Tours (take D 751) and 10 km (6 miles)
south of Villandry on D 7 and D 39, seems an invitation to a
dream—an elegant escape that was translated from Gothic

to Renaissance perfection. You might feel as if you lived here in another, more serene life.

Constructed by financier Gilles Berthelot between 1518 and 1529, Azay is a superb example of medieval defenses that have become less useful than graceful, not deadly but decorative. The château today is a fine Renaissance museum with beautiful furnishings and tapestries. From late May to late September, a nightly *son-et-lumière* program, "Since We Have No Other Image of You," features a walk around the château with the disembodied voices of five actors. The château itself is open to visitors daily year-round, except on major religious holidays.

The lazy river Indre winding through Azay renders the village one of the loveliest in the Loire Valley. A morning market is held on Wednesdays, and there's an apple fair in late October. If it's lunchtime head for a table on the terrace at ▶ **Le Grand Monarque**, an unpretentious vine-covered hotel with a kitchen specializing in fine local fare, such as green salad in walnut oil vinaigrette, grilled *sandre,* goat cheese (from nearby Ste-Maure), and crunchy *baguettes.* The owners of the 18th-century hotel make the most of its rustic charms and have christened each of the 30 rooms after a different château.

Only 5 km (3 miles) south of Azay via D 57 at Villaines-les-Rochers, the basket weavers of **La Vannerie** have been turning out beautiful wicker goods for generations (even Balzac fancied them) and are happy to ship them overseas.

Saché

At the château in Saché, 7 km (4½ miles) east of Azay-le-Rideau by a back road (off D 17), you may pay respects to Honoré de Balzac, who wrote all or part of *Le Père Goriot, La Recherche de l'Absolu,* and other works there. Balzac's bedroom/workroom remains as it was in the mid-19th century; the whole is a small museum. Each weekend in July 120 actors perform a sound-and-light show called "Balzac and the Lily." The château is closed in December and January and on Wednesdays off-season. Alexander Calder (1898–1976) lived and worked on his mobiles and stabiles near Saché from 1953 until his death. Keep an eye out for homegrown kiwis and *noix* (walnuts) sold on the side of the smaller roads.

LANGEAIS

The harmony of this medieval residence (its appearance from the outside bespeaks more a feudal fortress) results from its having been built in the relatively short time of five years or so. Fortunately, also, it has never undergone substantial restoration. The ruins of a tenth-century keep stand in the gardens. Within, the *appartements* are unusually well furnished and precisely descriptive of life in the 15th century; Gothic furniture and Flemish tapestries abound. Charles VIII married Anne de Bretagne in the Grand Salon. Intricate wax figures depict the wedding scene in perfect detail. The costumes are works of art. Note the wide shoes of Charles VII: He was blessed with six toes on each foot. Langeais castle is open to visitors daily year-round, except for Mondays in the off-season.

Langeais, on the north bank of the Loire 25 km (15½ miles) west of Tours via N 152 and 10 km (6 miles) north of Azay-le-Rideau on D 57, is the idyllic town you've been looking for, with narrow streets that wind around the château, fetching shops, and flower boxes bedecking every window and balcony. If your visit here coincides with lunchtime, try **Le Langeais** on rue Gambetta. It's known for chef Jacques Hosten's grilled Loire baby eels and the *blanquette de sole et turbot* (Tel: 47-96-70-63). Stop by the small pottery shop on the Place de l'Eglise and admire the fine workmanship of Patrice Collat, whose studio is on the premises. The **Musée Robert-Keyearts**, located at the lovely Château de Planchoury in St-Michel-sur-Loire, just 4 km (2½ miles) west of Langeais on N 152, has the largest collection of Cadillacs outside the United States. (Closed January and Tuesdays off-season; Tel: 47-96-81-52.)

Drive 2 km (1¼) west along the Loire on N 152 and D 35 to the ▶ **Hostellerie du Château de Rochecotte** in the village of St-Patrice, once Talleyrand's country estate and now a family-run hotel with what are surely the valley's only 18th-century interiors ablaze with uplights. Further, Rochecotte's cuisine comes off with unexpected dash and finesse. Even dogs are welcome in the palmy dining salon, as long as they don't attempt to sing along with the tapes of Pavarotti and other operatic greats.

One of the region's best wineries, producing the currant-scented, tannic Bourgueil wine, is located about 10 km (6 miles) west of St-Patrice, just north of D 35 in the wee village of **Benais**. Look for **La Croix Rouge**, the house and bottling plant of the amiable vintner Pierre-Jacques Druet.

CHATEAU D'USSE

For some reason this massive, fortified, rather grim château, 30 km (19 miles) southwest of Tours on D 7 and 16 km (10 miles) across the Loire and downstream from Langeais on D 57 and D 7, does not play the feature role it should within its company. It often catches photographers with their lenses down (the best shots are from the small bridge on D 113), yet it is the very model of fairy-tale writer Perrault's *Sleeping Beauty* keep (waxwork tableaux in the attic illustrate the story). The château bristles like a brush with turrets, clock towers, chimneys, dormers, roof trapdoors (the better for pouring boiling oil), and so forth. In comparison with the fairly fierce exterior, the interior rooms are comfortable, even gracious. The château was built in the 16th and 17th centuries on the foundations of a medieval fortress. It is open daily, but closed November 15 to March 15; a small tearoom opposite the château serves light lunches and snacks.

Chinon

The town of Chinon, about 40 km (25 miles) southwest of Tours on D 751 and 14 km (9 miles) south of Ussé on D 7 and D 16, is surrounded by the fertile river Vienne and is dominated by its partially destroyed, three-sectioned castle. The château (open to visitors daily, but closed December and January) is a fortress that played major roles in the nearly endless Anglo-French fights. Here Charles VII retreated when the power of Paris really belonged to England's Henry IV, and here Joan of Arc came to announce the mission her "voices" had commanded. The "château" you see today is really three adjoining ruins above the river Vienne: **Fort St-Georges**, of which little remains but memories of the death of Henri II; **Château du Milieu**, entered through the still impressive Tour de l'Horloge and housing the Musée Jeanne d'Arc; and the **Fort du Coudray**, where the Maid resided. Opposite the château a walled vineyard of Chinon grapes flourishes on a sloping plateau, producing one of the finest wines in the Loire Valley—Clos de l'Echo—which can be tasted and purchased at the **Maison Couly-Dutheil**, 12, rue Diderot in the old town.

The Middle Ages still can be sensed in the town, particularly along rue Voltaire (where the Office de Tourisme is located) and at the crossroads known as **Grand Carroi**, heart of the medieval action and today the center of ambience. (The old days are restaged on the first weekend in August at the annual medieval market festival.)

It is believed that *Gargantua and Pantagruel* is actually the autobiography of François Rabelais; it was written in his birthplace, a modest manor home, **La Devinière**, about 5 km (3 miles) southwest of Chinon just off route D 117. La Devinière is now a museum devoted to Rabelais's life and work; open daily except Wednesdays off season.

STAYING AND DINING
IN AND AROUND CHINON

An excellent restaurant choice in Chinon is the ► Hostellerie Gargantua, named after Rabelais's famous character.
This 500-year-old stone mansion is said to be where the
writer's father practiced law. Be sure to order the famous
house omelette whipped up by chef Girault; the recipe has
remained a secret for more than 200 years. If your French is
good enough, spend a few minutes with the gregarious
owners, Monsieur and Madame Fossé, who have many tales
to tell. If you can, book a table on Friday or Saturday evening
when the staff is decked out in medieval costumes. Eight
pleasant guest rooms are also available at reasonable rates.

Another good choice in Chinon is **Au Plaisir Gourmand**,
at the foot of the château. Master chef Jean-Claude Rigollet
and his wife Danielle are well known in the region for the
superb cuisine and warm welcome found in their 16th-
century dining room. Tel: 47-93-20-48.

Just 7 km (4½ miles) south of Chinon via D 116 is the
► **Château de Marçay**, surrounded by its own vineyards on a
wide, open plain. Everything about the handsome 15th-
century fortress bespeaks good taste. Marçay, with 38 guest
rooms, abounds with terraces for dining, sunning, and reading, and the swimming pool, bicycling, hot-air ballooning,
and tennis courts attract a young, zippy clientele. Its restaurant, actually a pair of dining salons, is decorated with
exquisite taste and serves commendable fare such as *feuil-
leté* of farm pigeon from Druye. Perhaps most impressive at
Marçay is its wine cellar, with 35,000 vintage wines under the
close supervision of sommelier Corinne Gaudian, named
1992's Woman in Wine of the year.

A hotel worth considering in Beaumont-en-Véron, 5 km
(3 miles) northwest of Chinon on D 749, is ► **La Giraudière**,
nestled happily in the beautiful Chinon region countryside.
Rooms and suites with kitchenettes are very simple, and so
the prices are extremely low; a modest restaurant offers
typical French cooking at low prices. This is a popular
choice for the young and hearty (bicycle groups often stay
overnight).

Fontevraud-l'Abbaye

Richard the Lion-hearted seems almost fanciful, the overstated hero, the Superman of antiquity. His tomb (and that of
his parents, Henry II Plantagenêt, king of England, and
Queen Eleanor of Aquitaine) is in the town of Fontevraud,
12 km (7½ miles) northwest of Chinon on D 117 and D 147.

The tiny town (Fontevrault, in the old spelling) grew up to support the royal abbey, one of the finest examples of monastic architecture.

In 1099 (when Jerusalem was captured during the First Crusade), a hermit named Robert d'Arbrissel settled in the forested valley of Fontevraud near a formidable spring. Eventually convents were built at the site: St-Lazarus for lepers and Ste-Magdalene's for women. An abbess was put in charge and given absolute power. From the 12th century into the 18th century, 36 abbesses, all of royal descent, ruled over Fontevraud.

Today the traveller marches single-mindedly through the Romanesque church, past the high altar—which survived the Revolution and is now enduring extensive archaeological digs at its base (they're searching for old tombs and will continue to do so well into the next century)—and into the transept room, where, recumbent upon their tombs, lie effigies of Richard, Eleanor, Henry, and their daughter-in-law, Isabelle d'Angoulême, third wife of King John Lackland. Behind a protective glass wall they are splendid in peeling polychrome limestone (Isabelle is in wood); Eleanor in death, as in life, reposes with a book.

Other elements of the abbey—the chapter house, the cloisters, the refectory—are excellent, but the most curious is the old **kitchen**, the only one extant from the Romanesque period in France. It is octagonal, with semicircular attached towers topped by upside-down witches' hats in tiles. Inside, a staff of cooks worked over six hellishly hot wood-fire hearths; smoke soared 90 feet and exited through 20 flues.

Highly recommended for lunch or dinner is **La Licorne**, a restaurant in the center of Fontevraud-l'Abbaye. Summer travellers can enjoy a meal in the attractive garden; Tel: 41-51-72-49.

STAYING IN AND AROUND FONTEVRAUD

Leaving in the evening you may hear church bells in the distance and look back 700 years. It's the headquarters of the Cultural Center for Western France and subsidizes on the premises a hotel, the ► **Hostellerie du Prieuré St-Lazare**, with 52 simple but comfortable rooms in former nuns' cells. The restaurant is part of the 12th-century chapel and is surprisingly elegant, as is the summer *terrasse* where meals are also served.

More luxurious lodgings can be found across the river at the privately owned ► **Château des Réaux**, 15 km (9 miles) northeast of Fontevraud on D 947 and N 152. The dynamic

Florence Goupil de Bouillé has decorated the eight guest rooms in her 15th-century château with warmth and style. A copious breakfast is served in the cheerful blue-and-yellow dining room. Lovely accommodations can also be found in nearby St-Nicolas de Bourgueil, 5 km (3 miles) northwest of Les Réaux on D 759 and D 35, at the ▶ Manoir du Port Guyet, the former hunting lodge (1420) of the French poet Pierre de Ronsard. Here, Ronsard composed his best poems to the great love of his life, Marie. Owner Geneviève Valluet Deholin has restored this lovely manor to perfection, furnishing it with fine antiques, including bathroom fixtures from the royal suites of the former Claridges Hotel in Paris. The house, which has only three guest rooms, is classified as a *monument historique*.

Saumur

Saumur, 11 km (7 miles) west of Chinon on D 751, is a stately town of 18th-century houses with wrought-iron balconies overlooking the river that has always been renowned for its wines (especially the *mousseux*—sparkling—ones, such as Crémant de Loire), its mushrooms, and its cavalry school. It is also Europe's foremost maker of masks for Carnival.

The 14th-century Château de Saumur sits high above the Loire in grace and majesty, its towers and turrets conjuring up the classic fairy-tale French castle.

SAUMUR MUSEUMS AND OTHER SIGHTS

Two fine and distinct museums are housed in the château: the **Musée du Cheval** (Museum of the Horse) and the **Musée des Arts Décoratifs**. In the first, the horse rides through all ages and countries, bareback, saddled, bridled, spurred, and stirruped. The Musée des Arts Décoratifs is notable for its collection of fine ceramics. (The château and museums are closed on Tuesdays and from November 1 to March 31.) Sherman and Patton tanks, the British Conqueror, German Panzers, and landing craft from D-Day are among the items in the **Musée des Blindés** (armored vehicles), near the river and the northern corner of the large Place du Chardonnet. The **Musée de la Cavalerie** shows off historic swords, sabers, uniforms, and other military memorabilia. Guided tours are available in the afternoons; ask for written authority to enter at the office of the cavalry school in the same building (entrance off avenue Foch).

The unusual **Musée du Champignon** (Museum of the Mushroom) is in neighboring St-Hilaire–St-Florent, 1 km (½ mile) west of Saumur on D 751, where Louis Bouchard grows the fragrant fungus in the darkness of underground caves. Local mushrooms account for 70 percent of the national production.

The **Eglise de Cunault**, about 12 km (7½ miles) northwest of Saumur via D 751, is thought to embody the finest elements of Romanesque architecture in the Loire Valley. Sculpted figures on the 200 column capitals demand a close look with a long camera lens or binoculars. Some traces of the medieval painted decoration remain.

STAYING AND DINING
IN AND AROUND SAUMUR

The best place to stay and dine in Saumur is the ► Hôtel **Anne d'Anjou**, on the quai Mayaud overlooking the château. The 18th-century building houses 50 elegant guest rooms and a widely acclaimed restaurant, **Le Menestrels**, overlooking the gardens of the hotel and château. A suit of armor in the tiny lobby reached by a narrow, spiral stone staircase greets guests at ► **Le Prieuré**, a restored Renaissance manor (with a disappointing motel-style wing) in nearby Chêne-hutte-les-Tuffeaux, 8 km (5 miles) west on D 751. Set on a wooded hillside high above the river, the 37-room hotel offers staggering views of the terrain (especially from the rooms with private terraces). The rather large dining room provides, along with exquisite cuisine, an additional panorama. Try chef Lumineau's *pigeon d'Anjou* with smoked mushrooms, served with a glass of sweetish wine from nearby Layon.

One of the finest bed-and-breakfasts in the region is about 13 km (8 miles) northwest of Saumur on D 751 (watch for the *chambre d'hôte* sign in the drive). ► **Beauregard** is the lovely home of Monsieur and Madame Tonnelier, both musicians. Two beautifully decorated guest rooms are filled with antiques (one has a splendid view of the Loire) and are so reasonably priced it's best to book at least a month in advance.

Sharp-eyed drivers who travel around the riverside cliffs near Saumur—and in other areas on the north bank of the Loire—will spot dozens of centuries-old dwellings of present-day troglodytes; some of the caves are carpeted and outfitted with electricity, heating, and running water.

ANGERS

The old capital of the counts and dukes of Anjou is at the western end of the traditional Loire Valley sightseeing region, 45 km (28 miles) northwest of Saumur on D 952. The city occupies a splendid (and easily defensible) site above the banks of the river Maine, about five miles from its confluence with the Loire. During Roman times Angers was called Juliomagus, and Tacitus mentioned the existence of an ancient people on a local site called Andes or Andecavi, but very little is otherwise known of this prehistoric culture. By Roman times the town served as a crossroads for routes from Rennes, Nantes, and Tours. Some second-century baths remain from Gallo-Roman days, as do some portions of the third-century ramparts.

The first House of Anjou (10th to 12th century) and the second (13th to 15th century) were separated by the dynasties of the Plantagenêts and Capets. Anjou became part of the French domain in 1204, though England and France battled over it until the Hundred Years War (1337 to 1453) had come to an end.

The small city (about 142,000 Angevins) and its surroundings deserve an exploration of at least three days; Angers is less known but more inviting than either Tours or Orléans.

Angers is a pleasant place to idle away a day by café sitting, ambling along the river, or even indulging in nine holes of golf at nearby **St-Jean-des-Mauvrets**, 7 km (4½ miles) southeast of town on D 751. Markets are held in Angers daily except Mondays. An *entrepôt* for wines, liqueurs (Cointreau), flowers, and agricultural products, Angers hosts an annual wine fair in late September. Known as an arts center since the Renaissance, Angers also stages the cultural festival of Anjou in July. Angers is 95 minutes from Paris on the TGV Atlantique; the station and Office de Tourisme are just south of the château.

The Old Town

The **Château d'Angers**, on the eponymously named Place du Château, looms high above the Maine just to the west of the city's center—a formidable feudal retreat that looks as if it might even today defeat any conventional-weapons attack. Still standing are the 17 mighty towers, between 130 and 195 feet high, that were once capped by what were called pepper-pot roofs (*poivrières*). Formal medieval gardens bloom in the impressive moat. Inside, magnificent tapestries from the 14th to the 17th century are displayed, including the remarkable **Tenture de l'Apocalypse**, the oldest and largest tapestry known, a 14th-century marvel 551 feet long and more than 16 feet high, woven in seven sections.

From the château, follow rue Toussaint east for four blocks to the center of the city, Place Freppel, where the **Cathédrale St-Maurice**, dating from the 12th and 13th centuries, epitomizes Plantagenêt-Angevin style; the 12th-century tympanum above the porch is particularly fine. Close observers will note that the Gothic vaulting of the nave—the earliest in Anjou—is rather unusual because of its exceptional width, about twice the usual size. The stained glass windows provide a review of the history of this art in France from the 12th to the 18th century. (No stained glass from before the 12th century is known.)

Collections of Greek and Etruscan vases, amphorae, Renaissance art and furnishings, engravings, Chinese and Japanese objets d'art, and enamels are displayed in the **Musée Turpin de Crissé** in the Renaissance mansion known as L'Hôtel Pincé, just a few blocks northwest from the cathedral up rue Chaperonnière on rue Lenepveu.

In the former 13th-century abbey **Toussaint** (All Saints), a block from the cathedral down rue Toussaint, the David d'Angers gallery displays the works of this native son and sculptor (1788–1856), including statuary and some 500 medallions (round bronze wall plaques) d'Angers crafted of his contemporaries from the Romantic period (Hugo, Goethe, Chateaubriand, Balzac, and others).

OTHER ANGERS SIGHTS

Just on the other side of the Maine from the city center, one block west of the Pont de la Haute Chaîne on boulevard Arago, is the 12th-century **Ancien Hôpital St-Jean**, the oldest hospital in France. It houses the **Musée Lurçat**, with ten tapestries, known collectively as *Song of the World,* by the artist Jean Lurçat (1892–1966).

Château de Montgeoffroy, about 24 km (15 miles) east of Angers via D 147, has remained in the family since it was built in the 18th century. Its signed pieces of furniture by Gourdin, Garnier, and Durand, and paintings by Van Loo, Rigaud, and others, haven't budged a centimeter since their arrival two centuries ago. The kitchen is also beautifully preserved. The château is open to the public daily year-round.

The Mayenne River cuts a winding course from northern France south to join the Loire near Angers. The river is navigable and in summer is full of pleasure boats. One of the most pleasant spots along the river is the seignorial **Château**

de Plessis-Bourré (20 km/12 miles north of Angers on D
107), with its exquisite 18th-century furniture and fascinating ceiling in the guard room, which is painted with outra-
geous depictions of fables and proverbs. (Do not confuse
this château, which is not a hotel, with the Château du
Plessis, discussed below, which is.)

STAYING AND DINING
IN AND AROUND ANGERS

Fish from the Loire is particularly well cooked and served at
Le Toussaint, 7, place Kennedy (Tel: 41-87-46-20). Of local
hotels, the best is the ▶ Anjou, with its restaurant La
Salamandre, on the boulevard du Maréchal-Foch. This comfortable 53-room hotel is centrally located, near the attractive Jardin du Mal. But it might be nicer to try a country
retreat.

Châteaux Hotels and Restaurants

The ▶ Château de Noirieux overlooks the Loir (no "e," an
affluent of the larger river) 14 km (9 miles) north of Angers
on D 52. Guest rooms are divided between the château and
an adjacent 15th-century manor house. This is a pleasant
place to relax by the pool or to ride bikes or horses across
the lovely countryside. Excellent local cuisine is served in
the elegant dining room. The lushly set ▶ Château de
Teildras is about 23 km (14 miles) north of Angers on D 107
and D 74 in the village of Cheffes-sur-Sarthe, just east of the
town of Plessis-Bourré. Overlooking its own pond, the château boasts 11 rooms in a 16th-century country house that's
intimate and more livable than many châteaux hotels. Some
complain about the curt service while others revel in the
company of the young, spirited châtelaine and her American
writer husband. Regardless, the tiny dining room serves
tantalizing cuisine.

The ▶ Château des Briottières is in the small village of
Champigné, 26 km (16 miles) north of Angers via D 107 to
the town of Plessis-Bourré and from there 6 km (4 miles) on
D 74 and D 768. François and Edwige de Valbray offer eight
splendid rooms in their magnificent 18th-century château, in
the de Valbray family for more than 200 years, to paying
guests. (*Impromptu,* the film about the passionate love affair
between George Sand and Frédéric Chopin, was shot here.)
The young owners—who have five small children—manage
to receive guests for dinner, organize seminars and receptions, and sell local wines (at reasonable prices), all with
great ease and warmth. Guests are encouraged to help

themselves to the open bar after a swim at the château's pool, a game of tennis, a round of golf at a nearby course— or perhaps even hot-air ballooning. Children are welcome here.

Simone and Paul Benoist own the ► **Château du Plessis** in La Jaille-Yvon, 4½ km (3 miles) north of Chambellay on D 187. (From Angers, you can make the trip of about 30 km/19 miles in no time on N 162, turning off for the village onto D 189.) This 16th-century home boasts eight superb guest rooms, all tastefully decorated with period furniture. Especially recom-mended is the room called Arc-en-Ciel (meaning "rainbow"), which overlooks the well-landscaped 28-acre park on three sides. Monsieur Benoist is actively involved with the Château Accueil group of private château owners (see Useful Facts, above), whose philosophy is based on exceptional hospitality. Madame Benoist is an expert chef, serving salmon with *beurre blanc* and *canard à l'orange*. The Benoists are shining exam-ples; they go out of their way to help visitors organize their stay in the Loire Valley. They've even managed to get the best deal in the area on hot-air ballooning, a delightful way to discover château country. You're in for a real treat if you decide to stay here.

At the ► **Château de la Mazure**, 42 km (25 miles) north of La Jaille-Yvon in the heart of the Mayenne valley, you can stay at a 19th-century castle while learning French with the outgoing owner, André Le Marié. You can also stay at this estate, set in a lush forest, and enjoy the impressive collec-tion of tapestries without taking the French course.

The ► **Château de la Jaillière** is just outside the village of La Chapelle St-Sauveur, 35 km (22 miles) west of Angers via N 23 and D 30. The comtesse d'Anthenaise, who was mayor of St-Sauveur for more than 25 years, owns the château. She will personally greet you in her 50-room home (four bedrooms and a suite are available for guests), which was built during the 19th century on the site of the original castle that's been in the same family since the 15th century. The countess raised her ten children at the châ-teau, and now has numerous grandchildren who enjoy, as do her guests, the swimming pool, tennis court, lovely gardens, and fine cuisine of their dynamic *grandmère*. Parts of this vast estate are in need of a face-lift, but the overall feeling here is grand. Breakfast is served in the wood-paneled dining room overlooking the château's grounds, with a mountain of raspberries fresh from the gardens. Well-behaved children are welcome here; families should request the Marie Antoinette suite, which has two bed-rooms adjoined by a bathroom.

BOURGES

Bourges, 110 km (65 miles) south of Orléans on the A 71 autoroute and 153 km (95 miles) east of Tours on N 76, and its nearby attractions make a rewarding side trip out of the Loire Valley. If you want to backtrack to Bourges from Angers or other places in the western Loire Valley, follow the river back to Tours on D 952 and N 152. Even today, Bourges, capital of the old region of Grand Berry–Limousin, is a stranger to most foreigners and to many French. The little city of about 80,000 Berruyers sits somewhat off the tourist trails of Burgundy to the east, the Loire to the north, and Brittany–Normandy to the west.

In truth, Bourges is the heart of the matter, only 22 miles north of the hamlet of Bruère, the measured center of this measured land. That fact did not interest Stendhal at all; he saw Bourges as "surrounded by plains of a bitter ugliness." Only someone born near the up-thrust magnificence of the Alps around Grenoble could feel that way. George Sand had a more traditional opinion about the region: "Happiness exists here as an idea, if not as a reality. As for me? I admit my native horizon can lull to sleep all bitterness." It's been said that life here is so harmonious that the rate of divorce is a thousandth of that of Paris.

In 52 B.C. Roman armies massacred some 40,000 Celtic citizens of what Caesar had called one of the "most beautiful cities in Gaul." Bourges prospered under the Romans (though the slaughter remains unforgotten), becoming a major city of Aquitaine, a vital marketplace, and the site of a great amphitheater (at today's Place de la Nation). By the third century the city was hemmed in by a wall crowned with almost 50 towers; remnants of the wall may be seen along rue Bourbonnoux.

After Pépin the Short (Charlemagne's father) conquered the territory in 762, Bourges became the southern base of the Capetian kingdom.

Jean, duc de Berry, third son of Jean II, returned from captivity in England in 1356 and was awarded, among other territories, the region of Berry. A man of great taste and even greater extravagance, Jean decorated his "empire" with palaces, princely residences, collections of manuscripts, tapestries, rare animals and birds, and jewels. It was he who hired the Flemish artist Pol de Limbourg and his brothers to create *Les Très Riches Heures du Duc de Berry,* perhaps the most exquisite illuminated manuscript known, now in the Condé museum in Chantilly.

When Jean died at age 76, Charles VII took over. Disinherited from the throne, with half the lands of France in English and Burgundian hands, he endured with fairly good grace the nickname king of Bourges. Luckily, he had as minister of finances the nimble-minded Jacques Coeur, a canny merchant whose fleet of trading ships made him the most illustrious financier of his age. His brilliance resulted in France's increasing supremacy among trading nations in the East.

Many travellers pay their respects at a handsome half-timbered *pâtisserie* at the corner of rue d'Auron and rue des Armuriers that some guidebooks—and an inscription on the place—cite as his natal home. However, it's more likely that the present building dates from only the early 16th century, and the house it replaced came to Coeur only after his marriage.

Today's town will come as a happy surprise to anyone who has planned to see only "the reds of Bourges" in the stained glass windows of the cathedral and the rich decorations of the Palais Jacques-Coeur and then skip away. It is a town not to visit quickly but to meander through and then use as a base for exploration of a countryside as yet unplundered by mass tourism.

The Old City

The heart of the well-preserved old city is contained within the old city walls and is centered around the cathedral. Many half-timbered houses still stand to the north of the cathedral in the vicinity of the **Gallo-Roman wall**. Rue Bourbonnoux debouches into Place Gordaine with its bustling little park, sidewalk cafés, and the magnificent Renaissance **Hôtel Lallemant,** now a museum of decorative arts (open year-round; closed Sunday mornings and all day Mondays). The house itself is a major attraction, heightened by collections of 16th- and 17th-century furnishings, tapestries, paintings, and marquetry, in addition to ivories, enamels, and the like. Smart and trendy shops line the **rue Mirabeau,** veering off Place Gordaine, interspersed with fast-food places such as Lucky Burger Luke.

CATHEDRALE ST-ETIENNE

"One must see the reds of Bourges and the blues of Chartres," a student of stained glass once said. Well, the blues of Bourges aren't so shabby either. In fact, the 13th- to 16th-century windows of the cathedral of St-Etienne will cause the stiffest of necks to swivel: This is one of the most astonishing collections in France. Here the impious of the Middle Ages could see moral misbehavior writ large, as in the window depicting the bad rich man, who turns aside from a beggar named Lazarus dying with ulcers and then dies himself. In agony, he begs Father Abraham for pity, only to be told, "Look, you got yours in life and so did Lazarus. Now your roles are reversed." Or words to that effect.

If the windows are the initial lure of St-Etienne, the Gothic interior—with four side aisles in the place of transepts—is of almost equal interest. Jean, duc de Berry lies entombed in the 12th-century **crypt**. Circling up the steps of the **north tower** is recommended to enthusiasts of city overviews, photographers who enjoy taking shots of double-winged buttresses through pseudo arrow slits, and others stout of heart. (This is also called the Butter Tower, because it was built with funds donated by citizens in return for dispensations allowing them to consume butter and milk during Lent.)

PALAIS JACQUES-COEUR

Also within the old city, three blocks west of the cathedral on rue Jacques-Coeur, is one of the handsomest, richest, and most elegant and precisely turned private structures of the Gothic period in France: the Palais Jacques-Coeur, begun in 1443 and completed in fewer than ten years. Seen from its entrance on the Place Jacques-Coeur, it seems a fortress that's taken a fanciful turn, with two sculpted false windows on either side of the entrance from which stony heads spy out—servants, or perhaps Jacques and his wife, Macé.

Whatever was beautiful, practical, or inventive was what Coeur wanted and what he got. The Palais Jacques-Coeur contains 43 rooms, of which visitors are permitted to visit 15 or 16 daily year-round. The most impressive elements are the monumental ornamental fireplace in the banquet room; the storage-loft ceiling shaped like an upside-down ship's keel; the several painted ceilings and secret chapels; and— far from least—an engineering system that provided water for hot baths.

One of the mottoes of the man of the house is inscribed on the central tower: "*Dire, Faire, Taire*" (loosely translated "Say it, do it, shut up"). Having inherited no great coat of arms, the master merchant invented one and had it placed on the palatial façade: a cockleshell for Jacques (reminiscent of the pilgrimages to Santiago de Compostela in Spain; Santiago is Spanish for St. James, or Jacques in French), a heart (*coeur*), and the words (in translation) "To a valiant heart nothing is impossible."

FESTIVALS IN BOURGES

In 1963 the first of several Maisons de la Culture was inaugurated in Bourges by André Malraux and Charles de Gaulle, charged with devotion to and promotion of theater, cinema, music, dance, arts and crafts, expositions, and scientific and cultural conferences. Today the maison, located on Place André Malraux, *naturellement,* is a home for such happenings as *Le Printemps de Bourges,* which in late April brings French and foreign singers and songs to the public, putting special emphasis on the discovery of new talent. It houses as well the festival of electro-acoustical music near the end of May and beginning of June.

Other annual goings-on include the *Fête de la Vieille Ville* (Old Town Festival) near the end of May, featuring concerts, plays, and folkloric events; a national fair and exposition during the last half of June; and the Foires Jacques Coeur, with travelling shows and entertainment, held in Place Séraucourt, near the Maison de la Culture, from mid-June to mid-July.

STAYING AND DINING IN BOURGES

Just a few steps from the Palais Jacques-Coeur at tiny Place Quatre Piliers, the old ► **Hôtel Angleterre** is a good place to stay. Accommodations here are reasonable and have been renovated, and the Angleterre's central location makes it a convenient base for exploring the town. The Angleterre also boasts a pleasant, small dining room. Another good choice is the newish ► **Hôtel de Bourbon**, centrally located and built within the grounds of the Abbaye St-Ambroix. Its restaurant, **Le Saint-Ambroix**, is already widely acclaimed by locals; both hotel and restaurant are in the medium-range price category. Or you might prefer staying at the attractive 15th-century hotel ► **Le Grand Argentier**, on rue Parerie; Jacques Coeur was allegedly born here, though the hotel is not the only place in town that makes this claim. Dinner is served to hotel guests only.

You can have a pleasant luncheon at the **Bar Remparts**, between the old walls and the Hôtel Lallemant on the rue Moyenne. The **Jacques Coeur**, on the *place* of the same name, is a pleasant small restaurant; Tel: 48-70-12-72.

Around Bourges

Out of Bourges, the enthusiast of castles and history may wish to drive the Jacques-Coeur tourist route, which shows off more than a dozen châteaux, manors, Noirlac abbey, and so on. A booklet in the *Routes de Beauté* series is available at the Palais Jacques-Coeur in Bourges, where the tourist office will also be happy to supply a map.

THE CISTERCIAN ABBEY OF NOIRLAC

About 40 km (25 miles) south of Bourges via N 144, Noirlac is the embodiment in pure white regional stone of the simple and austere regimens of the Cistercian movement. The stone can also be seen as a reflection of the soul of Saint Bernard, who wished to return his church—which he considered fat and fraught with excesses—to the leanness of earlier Christianity.

The founding Cistercian monks, under their leader, Robert de Clairvaux (a cousin of Saint Bernard), suffered many privations during their first years (the order was founded in 1130). The 13th century brought success, but this would be supplanted by the Hundred Years War, the Wars of Religion, and the Revolution. The abbey was eventually sold to a manufacturer of porcelain.

Restoration began in the 1950s and proved enormously expensive. Today, however, the abbey stands again as one of the best built and most complete of its kind in the country. (Sénanque, near Gordes in Provence, is another top competitor in the rigorous Cistercian race.)

Noirlac is as perfect in its manner as a Gregorian chant.

CHATEAU DE MEILLANT

About 10 km (6 miles) northeast of Noirlac on N 144 and D 92, on the other side of a dense forest, Meillant is an important stop along the route Jacques-Coeur because of its Renaissance western façade, its face of a feudal fortress on the south, and its touches of Gothic and Flamboyant. About a dozen of the 75 rooms in the château, richly decorated and furnished with Cordovan leather hangings, Louis XIV chairs, Bruges tapestries, and Turkish carpets, are open to the public daily (closed mid-December to the end of January).

NOHANT

Upon the death of her father, young Aurore Dupin went to live with her grandmother in the château of Nohant, some 70 km (43 miles) southwest of Bourges via N 144 and D 940, near the small town of La Châtre. The author of *Indiana* became George Sand with the publication of that first novel in 1832, and though she lived in Paris, having left her husband and two children for several famous liaisons, she returned often to the calm and serenity of Nohant, where she died in 1876.

Despite her stormy romances and her many novels featuring the villages and folk of the Berry region, Sand was known in La Châtre as the Good Lady of Nohant, even serving the villagers from time to time as a local doctor.

The château has become a museum (open daily, but closed in January) memorializing Sand and her famous guests, which included, at one time or another, Chopin, Liszt, Balzac, Delacroix, and Flaubert. The Good Lady (and better novelist) is buried in the family cemetery on the château grounds.

SANCERRE

Outsiders have no image of the town of Sancerre, which lies near the Loire about 46 km (29 miles) northeast of Bourges, other than that of a dry derivative of the Sauvignon Blanc grape. Sancerre is an informal, everyday wine, to be drunk young and inexpensively; while it is predominantly thought of as being white, some reds and rosés also exist, from Pinot grapes.

Sancerre, a tiny, ancient village atop a beehive-shaped hill, is as sweet as the wine grown from the vineyard-covered hills that run down to the Loire and Niverois rivers. Visit the 14th-century dungeon and 15th-century tower of the fiefs here. Sancerre is a natural stopping place for eastward-bound drivers heading from Bourges into Burgundy. They usually park near the Esplanade de la Porte César to inspect the view over the vineyards, and perhaps they have lunch at the modest **Auberge Alphonse Mellot** (Tel: 48-54-15-01) to try Sancerre on its home ground. The local goat cheeses (try Crottins de Chavignol) and herb cheeses made from cow's milk are delicious.

Annual fairs are held at Sancerre in honor of cheese (the first week in May), wine (around Pentecost and the last Sunday in August), and oysters (the end of October).

GETTING AROUND

The main road from Paris that proceeds through the Loire Valley is Autoroute 10, which cuts around Orléans (127 km/ 79 miles from Paris) and edges near Blois, heading for Tours. If you drive like the French you can reach Blois, the heart of the Loire, in two hours. Major route N 20 sweeps south from Paris via Etampes to Orléans, then runs south of Vierzon for Bourges. From Orléans, regional route N 152 leads to Blois and Tours. As is almost always the case, however, the best choices if you have time are the local routes.

The Loire Valley is reached by train from Paris's Gare

d'Austerlitz, with about 24 daily trains to Tours, and ten to twelve to Bourges. The TGV Atlantique, with ten daily trains, whisks travellers from the Gare Montparnasse in Paris to Tours in about 50 minutes at 320 km per hour (185 mph). Rental cars are available at train stations (and can be booked through Avis and Hertz in the United States).

If you don't have a car, be forewarned that public transportation can be difficult. If you take the train, start at Tours and then connect with local trains to the various châteaux towns. Bicycles can be rented at most train stations and are a great way to see château country. Minivans with English-speaking chauffeurs can be hired through Touraine Evasion (Tel: 47-60-30-00), or why not hire a bilingual chauffeur to drive you in a Rolls-Royce (Tel: 47-28-30-81)? Guided bus tours can be arranged through the Office de Tourisme in Tours (Tel: 47-05-58-08; Fax: 47-61-14-22).

The following may be of special interest to travellers to the Loire Valley:

The **Château Accueil** group has 12 private châteaux in the Loire Valley area. These can be booked directly through the château owners as listed below, or in the United States; Tel: (713) 558-9933 or (800) 553-5090; Fax: (713) 497-6984. **Castle and Cottage Vacations/Chez Vous** in the suburbs of Paris (Tel: 53-40-85-54; Fax: 53-40-86-30), under the expert guidance of Mike Farraday, can also book Paris apartments, villas, and bed-and-breakfasts.

Five- to ten-day **ballooning adventures** are offered in the château country–Loire Valley region by **Bombard Balloon Adventures**. Contact them at 6727 Curran Street, McLean, VA 22101 (Tel: 703/448-9407 or 800/862-8537) or in France under the name of **Société Bombard Air Adventure** at Château de Laborde, 21200 Meursanges (Tel: 80-26-63-30; Fax: 80-26-69-20). One- to three-day **helicopter tours** with accommodations in châteaux are arranged by **Abercrombie & Kent**, 1520 Kensington Road, Suite 212, Oak Brook, IL 60521 (Tel: 708/954-2944 or 800/323-7308), or Sloane Square House, Holbein Place, London SW1 W8NS; or **Map Travel** in Paris (Tel: 46-34-16-18).

In Tours, A.R.T.E. Val-de-Loire-Centre supplies itineraries and makes arrangements for **horseback tours**, while **hiking trips** can be arranged along some 750 miles of the Loire by Fédération Française de la Randonnée Pédestre (National Committee for Long-Distance Footpaths) in Paris. Bicyclists flock to the Loire for its generally flat terrain and endless back roads; tours are planned by **La Fédération Française de Cyclotourisme** in Paris and by such high-ticket operators as **Butterfield & Robinson**, 70 Bond Street, Toronto, Ontario

M5B 1X3; Tel: (800) 387-1147 (in U.S.), (800) 268-8415 (in Canada), or (416) 864-1354.

Language courses are widely available, especially out of Tours, where it is said the best French is spoken. The **Institut d'Etudes Françaises** organizes intensive courses for foreigners (Tel: 47-05-76-83; Fax: 47-20-48-98).

A list of **captain-it-yourself boats** is supplied by Syndicat National des Loueurs de Bateaux de Plaisance, Port de la Bourdonnais, 75007 Paris. The best organization for canal cruising on luxurious barges along the Lateral Canal of the Loire is the **Crown Blue Line**, 18320 Marseilles-les-Aubigny; Tel: 48-76-48-01. More luxurious cruising, on the *Fleur de Lys* barge, can be arranged in the United States through Abercrombie & Kent; see "helicopter tours," above, for their contact information.

Another fun way to discover the region on summer weekends is by **steam-driven trains** (Tel: 47-58-12-97).

The Loire Valley is rapidly becoming a center for **golf**, with 30 courses, five of which opened in 1990. Several offer accommodation on the premises. Inquire at the Comité Régional du Tourisme, 9, rue St-Pierre-Lentin, 45041 Orléans; Tel: 38-54-95-42; Fax: 38-54-95-46.

ACCOMMODATIONS REFERENCE

The rates given below are projections *for 1994. Unless otherwise indicated, rates are for a double room, double occupancy, and do not include meals. As rates are always subject to change, double-check before booking, especially during the winter months, as closing dates change.*

► **Anjou**. 1, boulevard du Maréchal-Foch, 49100 **Angers**. Tel: 41-88-24-82; Telex: 720521; Fax: 41-87-22-21; in U.S., (212) 254-2217 or (800) 755-9313. 375F–575F.

► **Beauregard**. 49350 **Cunault**. Tel: 41-67-92-93. 300F, including breakfast.

► **Château d'Artigny**. Route de Monts, 37250 **Montbazon**. Tel: 47-26-24-24; Fax: 47-65-92-79; in U.S., (212) 856-0115; Fax: (212) 856-0193. Member, Relais & Châteaux. 760F–1,260F (low season); 945F–1,575F (high season). Closed December to mid-January.

► **Château de Beaulieu**. 1, route de l'Epend, 37300 **Joué-lès-Tours**. Tel: 47-53-20-26; in Paris, 40-68-77-37; Fax: 47-53-84-20. 380F–750F.

► **Château de Breuil**. 41700 **Cheverny**. Tel: 54-44-20-20; Fax: 54-44-30-40; in U.S., (212) 254-2217 or (800) 755-9313. 705F–830F.

► **Château des Briottières**. 49330 **Champigné**. Tel: 41-42-

00-02; Fax: 41-42-01-55. 550F–7,500F. Closed late February to mid-March.

▶ **Château de Chissay.** Chissay-en-Touraine, 41400 **Montrichard.** Tel: 54-32-32-01; Telex: 750393; Fax: 54-32-43-80; in U.S., (212) 254-2217 or (800) 755-9313. 690F–920F.

▶ **Château de la Jaillière.** La Chapelle St-Sauveur, 44370 **Varades.** Tel: 40-98-62-54; Fax: 40-98-61-97. 550F–700F. Closed mid-October to mid-May.

▶ **Château de Marçay.** 37500 **Marçay.** Tel: 47-93-03-47; Fax: 47-93-45-33; in U.S., (212) 254-2217 or (800) 755-9313. 495F–1,295F. Closed mid-January to mid-March.

▶ **Château de la Mazure.** 53260 **Force.** Tel: 43-53-55-63; in Paris, 40-68-77-37; Fax: 43-67-03-49. 620F–730F, breakfast included. Closed November through March.

▶ **Château de Noirieux. Noirieux.** Tel: 41-42-50-05; in U.S., (212) 254-2217 or (800) 755-9313. 750F–1,100F.

▶ **Château de Noizay.** 37210 **Noizay.** Tel: 47-52-11-01; Telex: 752715; Fax: 47-52-04-64; in U.S., (212) 254-2217 or (800) 755-9313. 660F–1,100F. Closed mid-November to mid-March.

▶ **Château du Plessis.** 49220 **La Jaille-Yvon.** Tel: 41-95-12-75; Fax: 41-95-14-41. 600F–750F, including breakfast. Closed November through February.

▶ **Château de Pray.** 37400 **Amboise.** Tel: 47-57-23-67; Fax: 47-57-32-50; in U.S., (212) 254-2217 or (800) 755-9313. 550F–750F. Closed January to mid-February.

▶ **Château des Réaux.** 37140 **Chouzé-sur-Loire.** Tel: 47-95-14-40; in Paris, 40-68-77-37. 450F–950F.

▶ **Château de Teildras.** Tiercé, 49125 **Cheffes-sur-Sarthe.** Tel: 41-42-61-08; Fax: 41-42-17-01; in U.S., (212) 856-0115; Fax: (212) 856-0193. Member, Relais & Châteaux. 620F–995F. Closed January 1 to March 1.

▶ **Château des Tertres.** 41150 **Onzain.** Tel: 54-20-83-88; Fax: 54-20-89-21. 350F–460F. Closed November 1 to Easter.

▶ **Le Choiseul.** 36, quai Charles-Guinot, 37400 **Amboise.** Tel: 47-30-45-45; Fax: 47-30-46-10; in U.S., (212) 856-0115; Fax: (212) 856-0193. Member, Relais & Châteaux. 415F–960F (low season); 520F–1,200F (high season). Closed end of November to mid-January.

▶ **Domaine de Beauvois.** Route de Cléré-les-Pins, 37230 **Luynes.** Tel: 47-55-50-11; Telex: 750204; Fax: 47-55-59-62; in U.S., (212) 856-0115; Fax: (212) 856-0193. Member, Relais & Châteaux. 850F–1,130F (low season); 870F–1,360F (high season). Closed early January to end of March.

▶ **Domaine des Hauts de Loire.** 41150 **Onzain.** Tel: 54-20-72-57; Telex: 751547; Fax: 54-20-77-32. 900F–1,300F. Closed December 1 to March 1.

▶ **Domaine de la Tortinière.** 37250 **Montbazon.** Tel: 47-26-00-19; Fax: 47-65-95-70. 575F–825F; suites 900F–1,250F. Closed mid-December through February.

▶ **Escale du Port Arthur.** 205, rue de l'Eglise, 45160 **St-Hilaire–St-Mesmin.** Tel: 38-76-30-36; Fax: 38-76-37-67. 270F–350F. Closed first two weeks of January.

▶ **La Giraudière.** 37420 **Beaumont-en-Véron.** Tel: 47-58-40-36; Fax: 47-58-46-06. 270F–350F.

▶ **Le Grand Argentier.** 9, rue Parerie, 18000 **Bourges.** Tel: 48-70-84-31; Fax: 47-58-46-06. 370F.

▶ **Le Grand Monarque.** Place de la République, 37190 **Azay-le-Rideau.** Tel: 47-45-40-08; Fax: 47-45-46-25. 310F–500F. Closed mid-December to mid-January.

▶ **Les Hautes Roches.** 86, quai de la Loire, Rochecorbon, 37210 **Vouvray.** Tel: 47-52-88-88; Fax: 47-52-81-30; in U.S., (212) 254-2217 or (800) 755-9313. 600F–1,025F. Closed mid-January to mid-March.

▶ **Hostellerie du Château de Rochecotte.** St-Patrice, 37130 **Langeais.** Tel: 47-96-90-62; Fax: 47-96-90-59; in U.S., (212) 254-2217 or (800) 755-9313. 500F–830F. Closed February.

▶ **Hostellerie Gargantua.** 73, rue Haute-St-Maurice, 37500 **Chinon.** Tel: 47-93-04-71. 480F–600F. Closed November 1 to March 15.

▶ **Hostellerie les Perce-Neige.** 37210 **Vernou-sur-Brenne.** Tel: 47-52-10-04; Fax: 47-52-05-96. 250F–320F.

▶ **Hostellerie du Prieuré St-Lazare.** Abbaye Royale de Fontevraud, B.P. 14, 49590 **Fontevraud-l'Abbaye.** Tel: 41-51-73-16; Fax: 41-51-75-50. 430F.

▶ **Hôtel Angleterre.** 1, place Quatre Piliers, 18000 **Bourges.** Tel: 48-24-68-51; Fax: 48-65-21-41; in U.S., (212) 254-2217 or (800) 755-9313. 375F.

▶ **Hôtel Anne d'Anjou.** 32–33 quai Mayaud, 49400 **Saumur.** Tel: 41-67-30-30; Fax: 41-67-51-00. 260F–640F.

▶ **Hôtel de Bourbon.** Boulevard de la République, 18000 **Bourges.** Tel: 48-70-70-00; Fax: 48-70-21-22. 480F–610F.

▶ **Hôtel de France.** 6, rue Picois, 37600 **Loches.** Tel: 47-59-00-32. 250F–350F. Closed January to mid-February.

▶ **Hôtel George Sand.** 39, rue Quintefol, 37600 **Loches.** Tel: 47-59-39-74; Fax: 47-91-55-75. 260F–450F. Closed late November to mid-December.

▶ **Hôtel Italia.** 19, rue Devilde, 37100 **Tours.** Tel: 47-54-43-01; Fax: 47-97-98-98. 196F.

▶ **Jean Bardet.** 57, rue Groison, 37000 **Tours.** Tel: 47-41-41-11; Fax: 47-51-68-72; in U.S., (212) 254-2217 or (800) 755-9313. 700F–1,300F (double); 1,500F–1,850F (suites). Closed late February to mid-March.

► **Manoir du Port Guyet**. 37140 **St-Nicolas de Bourgueil**. Tel: 47-97-82-20; Fax: 47-97-98-98. 450F–650F.

► **Moulin Fleuri**. Veigne, 37250 **Montbazon**. Tel: 47-26-01-12. 270F.

► **Le Prieuré**. Chênehutte-les-Tuffeaux, 49350 **Gennes**. Tel: 41-67-90-14; Fax: 41-67-92-24; in U.S., (212) 856-0115; Fax: (212) 856-0193. Member, Relais & Châteaux. 900F–1,000F (low season); 1,000F–1,300F (high season). Closed January to mid-March.

► **Le Rivage**. 635, rue de la Reine Blanche, 45160 **Olivet**. Tel: 38-66-02-93; Fax: 38-56-31-11. 350F–430F.

► **Univers**. 5, boulevard Heurteloup, 37000 **Tours**. Tel: 47-05-37-12; Fax: 47-61-51-80; in U.S., (212) 254-2217 or (800) 755-9313. 750F.

BURGUNDY AND THE RHONE VALLEY

By Georgia I. Hesse

The traveller (as distinct from the geographer) can scarcely tell where Burgundy begins: with a first sight of Vézelay and its hilltop basilica of Ste-Madeleine, where Saint Bernard preached the Second Crusade, perhaps; or with the first sips of Montrachet slipping seductively down the throat (Alexandre Dumas said this princely elixir should be drunk on your knees with hat off); or even when you first stand before the enormous vessel known as the Treasure of Vix, in Châtillon-sur-Seine, and mentally stumble backward into dim memories of Vercingétorix and first-year Latin.

Burgundy is a bouquet of good things to eat, to drink, to touch and see and feel. It is very sensual country with nothing abstemious about it (except for the considerable world of the Cistercians).

When Charles le Téméraire (the Rash, or, as usually rendered, the Bold), last of the Grand Dukes of Burgundy, died in battle in 1477 before the walls of Nancy, his dukedom held sway over Holland, Luxembourg, Flanders, much of today's Belgium, Artois on the English Channel, Picardie, Lorraine, and Franche-Comté. In fact, his dukedom was larger than the kingdom of France, which it separated from the Germanic Roman Empire.

Burgundy has, of course, shrunk to a more comprehensible size: physically speaking, from about Sens in the north to

Charlieu and Mâcon in the south, from the Loire in the west to the Saône river in the east, with Dijon as its principal city. After covering Dijon this section will concentrate on the quadrant north and west of Dijon, then will move south to the Autun-Beaune area.

From Dijon, we first cover the area roughly to the *north:* the source of the Seine, Alise-Ste-Reine, Semur, Fontenay, Tonnerre, and Châtillon-sur-Seine. Then we go *west* from Dijon to Saulieu, Vézelay, Auxerre, Chablis, and Sens. Finally, we cover the heart of the Burgundy wine region *south* of Dijon, from Beaune—between Dijon and Beaune you'll be encountering names such as Gevrey-Chambertin, Clos de Vougeot, Nuits-St-Georges, and Vosne-Romanée—down to Tournus (with a detour west to Autun), Cluny, Mâcon, and down the Saône (through Beaujolais country) to Lyon and the Rhône Valley.

The Rhône Valley, for its part tied to Burgundy by gastronomy and travellers' traditions, reaches south from Mâcon and the Beaujolais country to Orange (which is covered in the chapter on Provence), and from the Auvergne region in the west to the Jura mountain country east of Lyon; its center, for the visitor, is the city of Lyon.

MAJOR INTEREST IN BURGUNDY

Food and wine
Romanesque architecture

Dijon
Palais des Ducs and the Musée des Beaux-Arts
Eglise Notre-Dame
Cathédrale St-Bénigne and crypt
Musée Archéologique

NORTH FROM DIJON

Semur-en-Auxois
Abbaye de Fontenay
Château Bussy-Rabutin
Châtillon-sur-Seine and Treasure of Vix
The châteaux of Tanlay and Ancy-le-Franc

WEST FROM DIJON

Saulieu
Basilique St-Andoche

Vézelay
Basilique Ste-Madeleine

Auxerre
Cathédrale St-Etienne
Excursion to village of Chablis

Sens
Treasury at Cathédrale St-Etienne

SOUTH FROM DIJON

Beaune
Center of wine trade
Hôtel-Dieu

Autun
Tympanum sculptures at Cathédrale St-Lazare
Musée Rolin

Tournus
Eglise St-Philibert

Remains of the abbey at Cluny

MAJOR INTEREST IN THE RHÔNE VALLEY

Roman remains
Food

Lyon
Basilique Notre-Dame-de-Fourvière
Roman theater and Musée de la Civilisation Gallo-
    Romaine
Walking tour of Old Lyon (especially *les traboules*
    passageways)
Museums: Beaux-Arts, Textiles, Decorative Arts

The walled village of Pérouges

Vienne
Temple d'Auguste et de Livie
Roman theater
St-Romain-en-Gal, Gallo-Roman city
Excursion to Mont Pilat and to Gouffre d'Enfer for
    scenic views

BURGUNDY

The ample evidence of the long, diverse history of Burgundy
will repay your wanderings both in the beautiful countryside

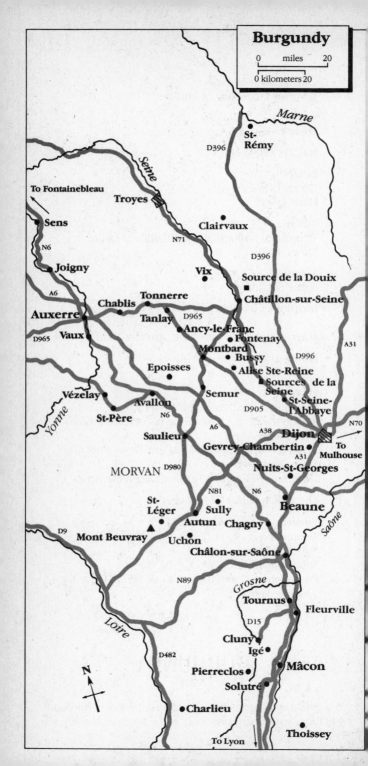

and in the streets and museums of the major towns. Before the Gallo-Romans, before Saint Bernard and the Romanesque period, before the House of Burgundy, and even before the Celts, prehistoric peoples lived, worked, and worshiped in this antique land.

The Celts

Before the Roman Empire, the Celts—barbarians, war-mad, but highly accomplished artisans—inhabited vast reaches of Europe stretching from Romania to Ireland, from the Rhine to the Pyrénées.

Gaius Julius Caesar finally conquered the Celts of Gaul in the seven years from 58 to 51 B.C. He found a valiant opponent in Vercingétorix, leader of the Arverni tribe. "A man of boundless energy," Caesar wrote of his enemy, "he terrorized waverers with the rigors of an iron discipline."

Vercingétorix and an independent Celtic Gaul found their particular Waterloo on the battlefields of Burgundy at Alésia, today's Alise-Ste-Reine, in 52 B.C.

The House of Burgundy

Burgundy, the name on the land, is derived from the Burgundi, or Burgondiones, a people of Germanic origin who, as a result of wars against the Alemanni tribes, were forced in 411 to take refuge in Gaul under the leadership of their chieftan, Gundicar. The major towns of this first kingdom were Vienne, Lyon, Autun, Mâcon, Besançon, and Geneva. Except for the last two, these towns still come within the territories of Burgundy and the Rhône Valley.

The House of Burgundy as one thinks of it today, however, began in 1031 when Robert, son of the king of France, by heredity became the Capétian duke of Burgundy. For the next three centuries Burgundy stood as a bastion of Christianity under the rules of the abbey of Cluny, followed by the monasteries of Cîteaux, Clairvaux, and some 350 others. The shining light of the whole movement was Saint Bernard (1091–1153), whose eloquence and genius dominated the 12th century. He alone established 160 Cistercian abbeys.

The Romanesque Period

During the period known as Romanesque (roughly from the 11th to the 12th century), dramatic changes led to an increase in the mobility of the typical European. Feudal wars slackened, new lands were exploited, new villages built. With the advent of two major influences—the cult of relics and the Crusades—great numbers of people began to travel over roads and under conditions that today would be considered impassable and impossible. All this energy led to a flood of construction of churches and abbeys. Architecture became to the Romanesque period what painting was to the Italian Renaissance.

Nowhere can a traveller interested in Romanesque art and architecture enjoy a bigger banquet than in Burgundy, with no fewer than 100 *major* Romanesque churches. (Offices de Tourisme in Dijon and other major towns can supply descriptive brochures in English.) The ornamental, often fantastic, sculptural detailing of these churches, especially in column capitals—which enraged the ascetically minded Saint Bernard—delights visitors today.

The historical Burgundy that is best known, however, is that of the proud and powerful Grand Dukes of the West, who ruled from 1364 to 1477: Philippe le Hardi (Philip the Bold), Jean sans Peur (John the Fearless), Philippe le Bon (Philip the Good), and Charles le Téméraire. Carl Rudolf Friml's musical *The Vagabond King* thus enshrined this worthy dynasty: "And bow down to Burgundy."

BURGUNDIAN FOOD AND WINE

The cooking and wines of Burgundy are synonymous, in many minds, with French cuisine itself. The fare is lusty, sturdy, basically simple, a triumph of *cuisine bourgeois* (peasant fare): *boeuf bourguignon* (beef Burgundian-style; France's best beef comes from the Charolais steer, raised in that little village near Mâcon); *escargots* (snails; the best feed on grape leaves); *pommes lyonnaises* (potatoes Lyon-style, i.e., cooked with onion); *saucissons de Lyon* (small sausages eaten *very* hot).

Other specialties are *jambon persillé* (cold poached ham layered with parsleyed gelatin); *volaille au foie gras* (chicken with foie gras); *quenelles* (fish dumplings); *foie de veau à la lyonnaise* (veal liver with onions), and on and on. The cheeses are famous, too: Epoisses, Montrachet, Charolais, Soumaintrain, Saint-Marcellin, and the like.

And the wines! Their names ring on the imagination as their tastes stir the palate: Vosne-Romanée, Nuits-St-Georges, Meursault, Puligny-Montrachet, Pommard, Volnay, and more, more.

The jewels in the crown of Burgundian gastronomy are the chefs renowned in France as *Les Six:* Michel Lorain of A la Côte St-Jacques, in Joigny; Marc Meneau of L'Esperance, in St-Père-sous-Vézelay; Bernard Loiseau of Côte d'Or, in Saulieu; Jacques Lameloise of Lameloise, in Chagny; Jean-Pierre Billoux of Jean-Pierre Billoux, in Dijon; and Georges Blanc of Georges Blanc, in Vonnas. Even if you aren't able to dine at their tables, you will also dine very well elsewhere in Burgundy.

DIJON

The good Dijonnais—merchants, local leaders, university professors and students, wine growers and mustard makers—think of their city as a French, even a European, *plaque tournante,* or turntable, at the center of great commercial routes leading from Paris, the Mediterranean, across the Rhine from Germany, and over the Alps from Switzerland and Italy.

It is true that motorways from all directions appear to lead to Dijon, that you can whisk here from Paris in an hour and 40 minutes aboard a TGV, that five international airports make for easy access to the region (though Dijon proper has only a small civil airport, with daily flights from both Paris-Orly and Paris–Charles-de-Gaulle).

It is also true that the Dijon Agglomération boasts properly bustling and traffic-tied industrial and commercial zones to the northeast and to the south of town, where emphasis falls less on Flemish sculpture and half-timbered houses than upon food-processing plants, automobile parts (Peugeot), and pharmaceutical research.

Yet here in the heart of things, at the site of the Roman camp called Divio, a visitor can still summon up the days of the dukes, a period of economic and artistic dominance that for more than a hundred years inspired the envy of states across Europe, especially the kingdom of France.

Dijon is handsome, for one thing, which most metropolises are not. It centers on the hemispheric **Place de la Libération** (the former Place Royale), a pretty, 17th-century layout by Jules Hardouin-Mansart, the architect of Versailles.

It is difficult to imagine that after the death of Charles le Téméraire in 1477 the ducal palace was neglected, ignored, and all but abandoned for 200 years. Then, in the 17th century, Louis XIV reinstituted the ducal title for a short time, and Burgundy controlled a government within a government, a *pays d'états* (a kind of parliament of estates, consisting of clergy, nobility, and other citizens). Dijon's grand days came in the 18th century, when it became a center of commerce and culture.

Old Dijon

Dijon shows the world two distinct faces. One is the classic, Renaissance, monumental look of proud public buildings and grand mansions, set off broad streets and squares or noble gardens and courtyards. The second is the more secretive, intimate face of narrow lanes bordered by medieval-looking corbeled and half-timbered housefronts. It is interesting to note that these dissimilar faces present themselves cheek by jowl, as it were, rather than existing separately in different reaches of the city, as is the case in Paris and in Lyon.

THE PALAIS DES DUCS AND ENVIRONS

A good place to begin your tour of Dijon is at the former Palais des Ducs et des Etats de Bourgogne, a part of which today houses the Hôtel de Ville, just north of the central Place de la Libération. Only a portion of the palaces—the two towers (Tour de Bar and Tour Philippe-le-Bon), the guardroom (Salle des Gardes), and the kitchens—represents the original complex. These remnants are almost entirely enclosed within the current structures, built in the 17th and 18th centuries.

Musée des Beaux-Arts

The east wing of the complex, near the Tour de Bar (named for its most illustrious prisoner, Good King René, duc de Bar and Lorraine and comte de Provence), houses the Musée des Beaux-Arts, among the richest and most unusual in France. The entrance is on the Place de la Ste-Chapelle at the eastern end of the palace. Taking precedence over the painting and sculpture galleries are the magnificent **tombs** of Philippe III, le Hardi (the Bold), and Jean sans Peur (buried along with his wife, Marguerite of Bavaria) in the Salle des Gardes, obsequies in stone, witnesses in great part to the genius of the Flemish sculptor Claus Sluter. There is nothing elsewhere like the alabaster "cloister" of Le Hardi's catafalque, around which parade 41 *pleurants* (mourners)—relatives, friends, soldiers, clergymen—carved from life, heads covered in stony sorrow. Juan de la Huerta reproduced that inspiration for the tomb of Jean and Marguerite.

The tombs so dominate the room that other masterworks might be missed: a scale model of Sluter's *Puits de Moïse* (Well of Moses) from Dijon's Chartreuse (Charterhouse) de Champmol (see below) and the painted Nativity by Melchior Broederlam, also from Champmol. The emphasis on sculpture in the museum is due to both Claus Sluter and to Dijon native François Rude (responsible for Paris's Arc de Triomphe sculptures). Paintings are displayed according to schools: Italian, German-Swiss, Flemish, 19th-century French.

Banquets famous throughout the dukedom were prepared in the kitchens, which date from 1435. Six enormous chimneys surround a central, even larger one from which smoky air soared several stories. The well-stocked bookshop, near the information desk, has a good selection of books on history and art in English.

Musée Magnin and Palais de Justice

Leaving the museum, turn south for a few steps and cross the Place de la Libération to rue des Bons Enfants and, in a handsome 17th-century town house at number 4, the Musée Magnin. Decorated in elegant mid-19th-century fashion, the museum displays the extraordinary grouping of Northern European, Italian, and French paintings from the 16th to the 19th centuries, as well as some extremely rare furniture, that two Dijonnais, Jeanne and Maurice Magnin, gave to the nation in 1937.

A few steps to the south, rue Philippe Pot leads past the Hôtel de Vesvrotte (with extraordinary sculptures on its façade) to the Palais de Justice, formerly the Burgundian parliament. A superbly worked door beneath a loggia in the gabled Renaissance façade is a copy of the one by a pupil of Leonardo da Vinci that you may have admired in the Musée des Beaux-Arts. There's a remarkable paneled ceiling inside the vast lobby and another from the 17th century in the Assize courtroom.

Musée Rude and Eglise St-Michel

From the Palais de Justice, follow the rue du Palais a block to the **Bibliothèque Municipale** (City Library), which houses more than 210,000 volumes, some luxurious 18th-century furnishings, and illuminated manuscripts, including some from the 12th-century Cîteaux monastery.

What remains of the former St-Etienne abbey buildings, including the 15th- to 17th-century church (today the chamber of commerce) is directly east of the Palais des Ducs on rue Vaillant. Its northern transept now houses the Musée Rude, which honors the sculptor François Rude, a local son.

Eglise St-Michel, across from the museum in the Place St-Michel, was begun in the 15th century in Flamboyant Gothic style and completed in full-flowing Renaissance, with a wonderful Last Judgment on the tympanum.

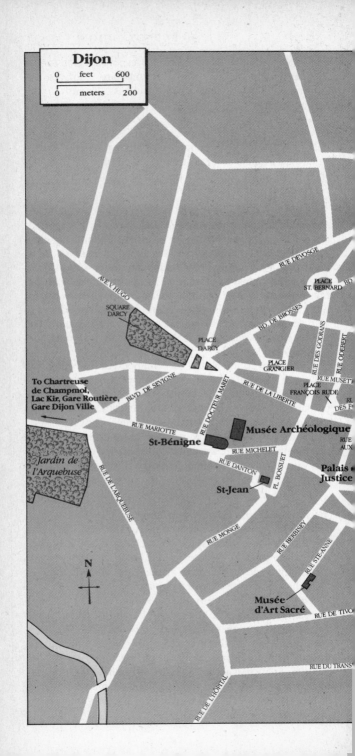

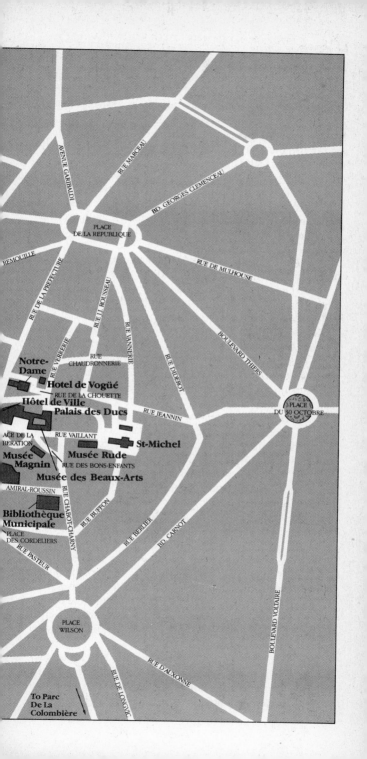

Place St-Michel to Notre-Dame

From the Place St-Michel, rue Vannerie leads north past two 18th-century mansions at numbers 39 and 41, with Rococo-Baroque decoration that seems almost excessive (although delightful) in a town so classical in spirit.

Turning west into rue Chaudronnerie, stop at number 28 to admire the 1603 **Maison des Cariatides**, where caryatids and telamons (Atlas figures) keep watch between every pair of windows, and continue west a block to rue Verrerie, where you'll suddenly step into a medieval world of half-timbered and corbeled houses. The street is lined with seductive little shops (this is the quarter for antiques dealers); the houses at numbers 8, 10, and 12 are particularly attractive.

Rue Verrerie leads to rue de la Chouette and the **Hôtel de Vogüé**, a 17th-century mansion and the finest private home to have been built in Dijon. It is solemn, aristocratic, and grand, from its pink stone Italianate portico to the green, gold, and black mosaic-tiled roof.

Just beyond you'll come to the north wall of the 13th-century Gothic **Eglise Notre-Dame**. Search the wall until you spot, on a pillar, the tiny carved owl (*chouette*) that is the mascot of the town. It becomes more difficult to notice as the years go by; the Dijonnais believe they will gain wisdom and happiness by rubbing it.

The west façade bears two arcaded galleries and three tiers of astonishing fake gargoyles ("fake" because they're not working rainspouts) that form a motley crew of earthly and heavenly figures: virtues and vices; gluttony and a condemned soul; scandalmongers and the avaricious; goodness and charity; an eagle and a monkey.

The **Jacquemart clock** atop Notre-Dame is the oldest clock in France to include automatons. When Philippe le Hardi brought the clock to Dijon in 1382 from a church in Courtrai (in today's Belgium) after his suppression of a Flemish rebellion, the clock bore only the Jacquemart figure, a man with a pipe who struck a bell to mark the hours. In the 17th century the Dijonnais decided to give their Jacquemart a wife, Jacqueline. In the next century the couple was given a son, Jacquelinet, whose hammer strikes a small bell on the half hour, and a daughter, Jacquelinette, who sounds the quarter hours.

The chief treasure within Notre-Dame is an 11th-century **Black Virgin**, one of the oldest wood sculptures in the country. Two tapestries honor deliverances from war: one from Tournai, Belgium, dedicated after the lifting of a

16th-century siege of Dijon by the Swiss; the other a
Gobelins dedicated to the liberation from German occupation on September 11, 1944.

Around Place François Rude

From the south side of Notre-Dame, rue des Forges leads
west toward the Place François-Rude. Until the 18th century,
the rue des Forges was Dijon's main street and is lined by a
parade of medieval and Renaissance houses. The most outstanding is the **Hôtel Chambellan** at number 34, a gem of
Flamboyant Gothic built in the 15th century by a rich family
of drapers. The courtyard, with its spiral staircase in lace-
work stone, is the home of the Office de Tourisme. In the
same street, also take note of number 38, the Renaissance
Maison Milsand; number 40, the Hôtel Aubriot, built in the
13th century by the first banking family; and numbers 52, 54,
and 56.

The Place François-Rude, which is surrounded by sidewalk cafés, opens to the south into rue de la Liberté, the
fashionable shopping street where the Dijonnais go to keep
themselves *en chic*. No gallivanting gastronome can keep
from popping in at number 32, where the smart **Grey-
Poupon** shop sells and celebrates mustard, a regional re-
source since the days of the great Gallo-Roman spice route.
Considering the hand-painted, museum-quality porcelain
containers on display, it's difficult to exit with just a mere jar
of familiar *moutarde de Dijon*. On the same street, at number 16, the **Mulot et Petitjean** store offers another traditional
Dijonnais specialty, *pain d'épice* (spice bread), in several
varieties.

WEST OF THE PALAIS DES DUCS

From rue de la Liberté follow rue Bossuet south past the
Coin du Miroir (Mirror Corner), where the Maison des Trois
Faces (House of Three Faces) has stood for 500 years, to the
Place Bossuet, with several splendid mansions.

Walk west from Place Bossuet on rue Danton and within a
few steps you'll come to **Eglise St-Jean**, where the great
prelate and orator Jacques-Bénigne Bossuet was christened
in 1627. This mid-17th-century church has lived many lives,
the current one as a theater called Le Parvis St-Jean.

Shortly beyond, at the corner where rue Danton becomes
rue de la Prévote, the mid-12th-century **Eglise St-Philibert**
has long been deconsecrated and closed, but rich carvings
still adorn the right-hand doorway.

Cathédrale St-Bénigne

The Gothic Cathédrale St-Bénigne, topped by an elegant
19th-century spire and a roof of colorful tiles, stands in the
Place St-Bénigne, just west of St-Philibert off rue de la
Prévote. The superb treasures of St-Bénigne (Benignus was a
local, second-century martyr) are the crypt (what remains of
a tenth-century basilica) and its rotunda with massive, squat
pillars, some still retaining their capitals carved with palm
leaves, personages, and monsters.

Almost elbowing St-Bénigne at 5, rue Dr-Maret, the **Musée
Archéologique** is a treasure trove for enthusiasts of Burgundian history. Displays cover the Neolithic period (there are
thongs used for catching horses) through Gallo-Roman
times. The most interesting objects here are a head of Christ
from the Well of Moses (see below) and, in the 11th-century
cellars, limestone and wooden effigies of pilgrims and other
votive offerings found in the sanctuary at the source of the
Seine (see below).

Square Darcy

From St-Bénigne, continue north up rue Dr-Maret to Place
Darcy and the 18th-century Porte Guillaume, which marks
the entry into rue de la Liberté. Place Darcy takes its name
from the engineer who brought drinking water to Dijon in
1839 and is laid out atop a great underground reservoir. Just
west of the traffic-ridden *place,* the Square Darcy is a public
garden with terraces, balustrades, waterfalls, ponds, and
little lakes; all the Italianate elements so popular in the days
of Napoléon III.

Jardin de l'Arquebuse

A fairly long stroll along the boulevard de Sévigné southwest
of Place Darcy or a slightly shorter one west of St-Bénigne
on rue Mariotte will bring you to the lovely Jardin de
l'Arquebuse (Dijon's botanical garden), which owes its
name to the former 16th-century barracks of the Company of
Harquebusiers. The *arquebuse* was a gun of matchlock or
wheel-lock mechanism much used by the Spanish, Italians,
and French in the 15th and 16th centuries. Arquebuse is also
the name of a fiery liqueur, which its adherents prefer to call
a vulnerary, since, they modestly claim, it can cure anything.
It is very difficult to find; inquire at the wine shop called **La
Cave du Clos** on rue Jeannin, which is south of rue Verrérie.

The **Muséum d'Histoire Naturelle** is at the north corner of
the garden, where boulevard Sévigné meets avenue Albert I
and rue de l'Arquebuse.

Chartreuse de Champmol

West along avenue Albert I you'll come to the grounds of a psychiatric hospital where, in 1383, Philippe le Hardi founded the charter-house now known as the Chartreuse de Champmol as a quasi-royal necropolis and filled it with works of the best artists from around his vast lands. The entrance is at 1, boulevard Chanoine-Kir. Visitors are admitted to the grounds to see the doorway to the chapel and the **Puits de Moïse** (Well of Moses) in the courtyard. Both are works of Claus Sluter. On the door Sluter represented in statue form Philippe le Hardi, his wife Marguerite of Flanders, their patron saints (John the Baptist and Catherine), and the Virgin and Child. The "well" is really the multicolored base of a *calvaire* made between 1395 and 1405 to decorate the font of the charter-house cloisters. Six strikingly realistic statues face outward: Moses (seemingly staring the observer in the eye) and the prophets David, Jeremiah, Zachariah, Daniel, and Isaiah.

OTHER MUSEUMS

Three other Dijon museums cater to visitors with special interests and may be reached by taxi or public bus (ask at your hotel or the Office de Tourisme for proper routings).

The **Musée de l'Hôpital** occupies the former 15th-century chapel of the town's general hospital in the southwest corner of town off rue de l'Hôpital. It contains a collection of *objets d'art* and illuminated manuscripts tracing the hospital's history.

The **Perrin de Puycousin Musée de la Vie Bourguignonne**, slightly southwest of the center of town at 17, rue Ste-Anne, houses a gallery with some 2,000 ethnographical items, including the reconstruction of a domestic kitchen from nearby Bresse. The urban section attempts to depict everyday life in Dijon in the 19th century through the re-creation of shops.

Next door, at 15, rue Ste-Anne, the late-17th-century Eglise Ste-Anne houses the **Musée d'Art Sacré**, with a collection of vestments and other liturgical items from the 12th to 19th centuries.

STAYING IN DIJON

Two of Dijon's best inns are the ▶ **Pullman La Cloche** (76 rooms), at 14, place Darcy, with beautiful views of the Darcy gardens (ask for a large room on the second floor), and ▶ **Chapeau Rouge** (30 rooms), at 5, rue Michelet, near the Cathédrale St-Bénigne.

There has been an inn on the site of La Cloche since the

15th century. Chef Jean-Pierre Billoux practices his culinary artistry at the one-star restaurant that bears his name, located on the premises of La Cloche; here's a good place to enjoy the famous Burgundian *escargots* at their best. Reservations are always necessary; Tel: 80-30-11-00. The highly ranked restaurant at Chapeau Rouge specializes from July to September in a warm soufflé of red fruits for dessert; Tel: 80-30-28-10.

The 27 rooms of the ▶ **Hôtel Wilson** (a restored 17th-century post house) open off a courtyard near the traffic circle in south-central Dijon named Place Wilson. A superb restaurant adjoining the hotel, **Thibert**, wins praise for its rabbit and pork dishes. Tel: 80-67-74-64. The ▶ **Hôtel du Nord** (29 rooms) enjoys a good location on the Place Darcy; its **Restaurant de la Porte Guillaume** has a good local reputation for regional dishes.

The walled Parc de la Colombière, a short drive southeast of Place Wilson on rue de Longvic, was laid out in the 17th century by Louis II de Bourbon, prince de Condé, then governor of Burgundy. Within the park, where green lawns are intersected by flower-bordered paths and a small portion of the Roman Via Agrippa that led from Lyon to Trèves remains. The small hotel-restaurant ▶ **Du Parc de la Colombière**, at 49, cours du Parc, has 39 comfortable, simple rooms and a pleasant outdoor dining terrace; Tel: 80-65-18-41.

Staying Near Dijon

Châteaux hotels outside of Dijon are pleasant retreats from the city but within easy driving distance. The ▶ **Château de Saulon la Rue** is a tranquil hideaway just outside of Dijon, near the village of the same name 10 km (6 miles) south via D 996. Contemporary decor has been added to a 17th-century château in the heart of its own 67-acre park.

Another country choice is the ▶ **Château de Longecourt** near Longecourt-en-Plaine, where Comtesse Bertrand de Saint-Seine welcomes visitors to her four guest rooms; dinners available. It's about 16 km (10 miles) southeast of Dijon via D 996 and D 968. The ▶ **Hostellerie du Château** in Châteauneuf, about 35 km (21 miles) west on A 38 and D 977 (follow narrow D 18 from the village to the château), occupies a 15th-century presbytery. The ▶ **Château de Ste-Sabine** in the village of the same name, about 50 km (31 miles) west via A 38 and A 6 or by any number of country roads, occupies a former monastery overlooking the Ouche river. The ▶ **Château de Chailly**, about 40 km (25 miles) west on A 38 and D 77, has been relentlessly restored, with 45 rooms, two restaurants, swimming, tennis, and golf. Though the château dates from the 16th century, the modern decor will not delight traditionalists. One of the smartest retreats in the region, the ▶ **Château de Gilly**, is at Gilly-lès-Cîteaux near the hamlet of Vougeot. It's a 38-room, eight-apartment marvel set in an ancient Cistercian abbey. The kitchen matches the stunning setting. Take the Vougeot turn-off about 18 km (11 miles) from Dijon as you drive south on N 74. Gilly is 2 km (1¼ miles) east via D 251.

DINING IN DIJON

One of the most unusual places to dine in Dijon is **La Toison d'Or**, at 18, rue Ste-Anne, across the street from the Musée d'Art Sacré. (If you take a taxi, be sure you specify the restaurant La Toison d'Or. In the northern outskirts of the city, there's a leisure park of the same name; for the park, take RN 74 in the direction of Langes.) It joins gastronomy to culture in a 15th- to 16th-century town house with a private museum containing medieval figures and vineyard tools (reserve; Tel: 80-30-73-52). The museum-cum-restaurant also houses an inn called ▶ **Hôtel Philippe le Bon**, with 27 rooms attractively decorated in rural fashion.

In the heart of town, near the Palais de Justice at 39, rue Chabot-Charny, **Le Rallye** serves especially good meals at moderate prices (Tel: 80-67-11-55).

For a meal near the Palais des Ducs, the **Pré aux Clercs et Trois Faisans** serves coq-au-vin and other down-to-earth regional specialties. It's at 11–13, place de la Libération; Tel: 80-67-11-33. **Au Peche Mignon** is a pleasant tearoom near Notre-Dame at 4, rue de la Chouette. Across the street at number 1, **Restaurant La Chouette** serves fine food in a pleasant, provincial atmosphere; Tel: 80-30-18-10.

Dining Near Dijon

For a brief surcease from the city, drive or take the *autobus* (ask directions at the Office de Tourisme) about 4 km (2½ miles) west of town on D 10 to the hamlet of Plombières-lès-Dijon on the north bank of the river Ouche, which was dammed in the 1960s to create Lac Kir. The lake is the center for delightful walks, and you may lunch outdoors in clement weather at pretty **Le Cygne**; Tel: 80-41-02-40. The lake was named for the late Canon Félix Kir, a local priest who doubled for many years as the Communist mayor of Dijon and, during World War II, languished for two months in a Gestapo cell as punishment for aiding in the escape of French prisoners. While you watch canoes, kayaks, and small boats at play, salute the mayor with his favorite drink, a *kir,* classically one-third Dijonnais *crème de cassis* (a black-currant liqueur) and two-thirds white Burgundian Aligoté.

(The *kir* is popular throughout France today; a *kir royale* uses Champagne, while the *kir communiste* is made with red wine—what else?—preferably a Gamay or Beaujolais.)

As this is Burgundy, you can count on finding fine places to dine in the countryside all around Dijon. One of the most careful, refined cuisines is produced by Joël Perreaut at his **Restaurant des Gourmets**, at 8, rue du Puits-de-Têt, in the village of Marsannay-la-Côte, 8 km (5 miles) south of the city on D 122. The restaurant is next to the church; an unusual specialty is foie gras with pears (Tel: 80-52-16-32).

NORTH FROM DIJON

Many of the man-made and natural wonders of the Burgundian plain lie just north of Dijon. We explore them from south (those closest to the city) to north. We also give directions from Dijon for each, so you can explore any of them as separate day trips from the city.

THE SOURCE OF THE SEINE

On N 71 about 27 km (17 miles) northwest of Dijon is **St-Seine-l'Abbaye**. Turn north from there in search of *les sources de la Seine,* not the easiest spot to find. (Inveterate church inspectors will stop at St-Seine itself, which marks the transition from Romanesque style to Gothic, and is named not for the river but for a sixth-century Benedictine monk, Saint Seigne, who appears in one of the church frescoes in his black monk's robe.) Continue north on N 71 for about 8½ km (5 miles), then turn west on D 26 (the turnoff is marked) for about 2 km (1 mile) to the source. (In French, *source* means not only "source," but also "spring," "fountain," or "fountainhead.")

The name Seine derives from that of Sequana, a Roman goddess who was worshiped in the remote and wooded valley where the river rises. For 300 years, until the third century A.D., the goddess worked her miracles. On the site, two temples succeeded the first clay-and-wattle hut, and in the center a spring gushed forth. Slightly downstream, a bathing pool almost 200 feet long lured the faithful from all over Gaul to wash in the holy waters. The disabled and the merely curious came to cure themselves or to sell nostrums, votive offerings, and knickknacks, as do pilgrims to Lourdes today. Archaeological digs here have unearthed thousands of items of tribute, today on show in Dijon's Musée Archéologique as well as several other museums in Burgundy. The temple was smashed and the site desecrated, possibly by invading Burgundians (the Burgondiones), and what had been a hive of worshipers reverted to an empty, rather mournful valley.

Surrounded by signs announcing that the source is the property of the City of Paris, the Seine emerges from a small bubbling pool surrounded by an ugly, artificial grotto with a a fat water nymph reclining on a rock. From the pool a trickle of water runs away through the cow pasture, on its way to Paris and the sea at Le Havre.

ALISE-STE-REINE

The heart of the Gallic empire beat its last in 52 B.C. near today's little town (fewer than 800 inhabitants) of Alise-Ste-Reine. The town is 26 km (16 miles) west of the source of the Seine, reached by following N 71 about 5 km (3 miles) north to D 6 and turning west on D 10. It's about 60 km (37 miles) northwest of Dijon on D 905.

Next to Alise was **Alésia**, a hilltop fortress chosen by Vercingétorix for what he planned to make the final rout of the Romans. Tactician though he was, he was no match for Caesar. As Katherine Scherman writes, "Caesar built siege works all around the base of the hill, and in a short time Vercingétorix's big army had exhausted the garrison supplies. In the fierce battle that finally ensued—in which Caesar himself took part, conspicuous to his own men and the enemy alike in the scarlet cloak he always wore in action—the Celtic troops were thoroughly routed and many of them simply ran away and went home." The great Gaul surrendered himself and his horse to Caesar, who, though admitting his enemy's prowess, humiliated him by imprisoning him in Rome and then parading him through the streets. Vercingétorix was finally executed at the foot of the Roman capitol.

Caesar was a creative conqueror; after all, he wanted a trouble-free Gaul. Celts of rank were awarded Roman citizenship, the Roman monetary system was established, and the Latin language was introduced. "He laid the groundwork for a Roman Europe," says Scherman, "that would fuse the continuing classical Greco-Roman tradition with the fresh Celtic-Teutonic ethos." In a deep sense, classical France was born in these Burgundian fields.

Excavations (*fouilles*) of the Gallo-Roman camp and town are still in progress. What you will see is exciting: a Mérovingian basilica dedicated to Sainte Reine, the early-second-century tiered theater, the law courts, a house with underground heating and the base of a portico, and a series of shops. Objects found during the digs are exhibited in the

Musée Alésia. (A ticket to the museum, open from the end of March to mid-November, also allows entrance to the digs.) Dijon's late mayor, the aforementioned Canon Kir, was born in Alise and is buried in the town cemetery.

On the Saturday and Sunday nearest to September 7, Alise celebrates Sainte Reine with a morning parade in Gallic or Gallo-Roman costumes and an afternoon production of the *Mystère de Sainte-Reine*. Local residents march with torches on the eve of the festival, one of the most attractive of the rural representations in Burgundy. It has been staged by the villagers since A.D. 866.

CHATEAU BUSSY-RABUTIN

Marie de Rabutin-Chantal, Marquise de Sévigné, was not the only pithy writer in the family. Her cousin Roger de Rabutin, comte de Bussy, had as pointed a pen and as developed a nose for naughty news. Unfortunately, Rabutin could not keep his wit to himself and was exiled by Louis XIV to his château in far-off Burgundy (far from Paris, that is, and therefore from civilization; Bussy-Rabutin is about 5 km/3 miles northeast of Alise-Ste-Reine via D 954; like Alise, the château is a drive of about 60 km/37 miles up D 905 from Dijon, with a turn east onto D 954). His crime: having ridiculed, in a series of irresistibly amusing couplets, the king's affair with Marie Mancini.

In exile Rabutin kept up a lively correspondence with his beautiful and talented cousin (whom he alternately adored and maligned) and wrote a chronicle titled "The Amorous History of the Gauls," satirizing the scandalous goings-on at court. As a result, he was imprisoned in the Bastille for more than a year and then exiled to the country again. Once challenged on his own purity of motives and behavior, Rabutin wrote, "Let me remind you, sir, that I condone only such scandals as I have myself occasioned."

The first castle at Bussy, constructed in the 13th century, had become a powerful fortress under the Rochefort family and passed into the hands of François de Rabutin in 1602. Roger, his grandson, devoted his years of country confinement to enlarging and beautifying his golden cage.

Of all the public and private rooms, several decorated by Rabutin himself in flights of original fancy, the most interesting may be the master bedroom, with furniture and woodworks of the day, highlighted by 26 portraits of women, among them Madame de Sévigné. Bussy-Rabutin's masterpiece, however, is the **Tour Dorée** (literally "gilded tower," though it makes up only one floor of the structure), which is entirely overwhelmed by paintings that feature mythological subjects as well as contemporary gallants accompanied by cutting, cynical couplets.

SEMUR-EN-AUXOIS

Just when you think Burgundy can come up with no more tempting little towns, you round a hill and there stands Semur-en-Auxois, an outsize storybook city of about 5,500 Sémurois situated on a pink granite outcrop above the valley of the river Armançon, 11½ km (7 miles) west of Alise-Ste-Reine on D 9.

Semur demands to be painted or at least photographed at once: a bridge that leaps the river toward a parade of picturesque old houses; round towers and ramparts (now a promenade); medieval gates and the soaring spire of Notre-Dame; and gardens blooming around ancient stones.

In the 14th century Semur's ramparts supported 18 towers, and as each third of the town was encircled by its own wall, the whole was believed to be impregnable. The treasure was, and is, the **Eglise Notre-Dame**, founded in the 11th century, restored in the 13th and 14th; eventually it, too, was restored by Viollet-le-Duc. An Entombment in the second chapel on the left ranks among the most beautiful created during the late Middle Ages; its monumentality is reminiscent of the work of Dijonnais sculptor Claus Sluter.

The **Musée Municipal et Bibliothèque**, in the former convent of the Jacobins (17th century), exhibits geological and paleontological finds as well as paintings and sculptures from the 13th to the 18th centuries. The library owns manuscripts and incunabula of great value, including a tenth-century illuminated manuscript, the Missal of Anne de Bretagne, and a work from the Gutenberg press.

Semur is a lively little place and stages several happenings during spring and summer: the Course des Chausses et des Desmoiselles (since 1369) in late May; the Fête de la Bague (since 1639, the oldest horse race in France) on May 31; and the Course à la Timbale d'Argent, around May 31. (A *course* is a race, of people or animals.)

Lovers of cheese will detour from the route to **Epoisses**, only 12 km (7½ miles) northwest of Semur via D 954, perhaps not so much because of its château as for a taste of its renowned, buttery Epoisses cheese, produced originally by Cistercian monks. For tasting and buying for picnics, stop in at **Fromagerie Berthaut** on the central Place Champs-de-Foire; try Epoisses with the fiery liqueur marc de Bourgogne.

FONTENAY

When Saint Bernard, then abbot of Clairvaux, came to the countryside near Montbard to seek a site for the foundation of a hermitage, he must have felt Nature had designed with him in mind. Set in a deep valley of intense green 20 km (12½ miles) north of Alise-Ste-Reine via D 905 and east on D 32, broken in autumn by outbursts of red and golden leaves, the **Ancienne Abbaye de Fontenay** and its grounds are eminently suited to meditation, contemplation, and quiet pursuits. (From Dijon, follow D 905 about 80 km/50 miles northwest to the D 32 turnoff; the abbey is just 3 km/2 miles east.)

Originally Fontenay was home to only 12 monks, but that number increased quickly, and the present abbey was constructed and waxed exceedingly prosperous from the 12th through the 15th century. Its buildings consisted of chapel, bakery, dovecote and kennel, church (with dormitories), cloister, infirmary, forge, and hostel.

Decline began in the 16th century, largely due to the devastating effects of the Wars of Religion, and further aggravated by a system of appointing, by royal favor, abbots who were uninterested in the traditional roles of abbeys. With the Revolution, Fontenay became a paper mill. It was resold in 1820 to Elie de Montgolfier (of the pioneering family of balloonists). In 1906 a Montgolfier son-in-law, Edouard Aynard, acquired the abbey, dismantled the factory, and began restoring it to its original appearance. The Aynard family currently lives at the abbey and maintains it as a historical monument. In 1981 UNESCO declared Fontenay a Universal Heritage site.

In the history of Cistercian architecture, Fontenay ranks as one of the most successful examples of form joined to monastic ideal (along with Noirlac, in Berry, and Sénanque, in Provence). What was desired, and here achieved, is a reduction of the unnecessary in a creation of admirable proportions—a severe but harmonious simplicity.

Even on a summer's day the visitor shivers slightly in the communal dormitory and tries to imagine monks sleeping on straw mattresses in midwinter; heat was allowed only in the copying room, where, near a great fireplace, manuscripts were transcribed. The abbey is open year-round, with guided tours given on the hour from 9:00 A.M. to noon and 2:30 to 6:30 P.M., and more frequently on afternoons in July and August.

Montbard

Georges Louis Leclerc, comte de Buffon and author of the classic 44-volume *Natural History,* was born in nearby, pretty

Montbard in 1707 (Montbard is just 6 km/4 miles west of Fontenay via D 32 and D 905). His gardens and study, in what had been a stronghold of the dukes of Burgundy, are open to the public. An association was founded in 1978 to restore Buffon's 18th-century ironworks, and so far it has completed the employees' lodgings, the stable, the blast-furnace hall, the refinery, and the foundry. It's all quite fitting, since Montbard today is a metallurgical center specializing in steel tubing. One of the most pleasant diversions here is an amble in Parc Buffon, smack in the center of town.

The Montbard Regional Fair is held during the first half of September.

Staying and Dining Around Fontenay

A lunchtime excursion 4 km (2½ miles) north of Montbard along D 905 (watch for the turnoff to the west) will bring you to the village of St-Rémy on the banks of the Burgundy-Brenne canal, where the woody **Le St-Rémy** restaurant is a happy oasis; Tel: 80-92-13-44.

If an excuse were needed to spend a night or so in the heart of the lovely Fontenay valley, it might be the presence of the quiet, 22-room ▶ **Château de Malaisy**, a 17th-century retreat in Fain-lès-Montbard, 5½ km (3½ miles) southeast of Montbard on D 905, with a 37-acre park, an outdoor pool, and an exercise room; from the kitchen come such delights as *escargots au Chablis* and *tournedos Malaisy*. If you haven't the time to stay the night, consider dining here anyway; Tel: 80-89-46-54.

TANLAY AND ANCY-LE-FRANC

In the 16th century Burgundian architecture began to change, having come under the influence of Renaissance arts imported from Italy. Unlike the Loire Valley, Burgundy had not seen a burgeoning of châteaulike country mansions until this period, to which Tanlay, 27 km (17 miles) north of Fontenay on D 905, and nearby Ancy-le-Franc, belong. (These châteaux are about 100 km/62 miles northwest of Dijon on D 905.)

Tanlay is in essence a comfortable palace, elegant yet unimposing, the kind of noble dwelling most commoners would be happy to call home. It was erected sometime around 1550 on the remains of a feudal fortress.

Several of the handsomely furnished rooms are open to visitors, and the most interesting of them is in the tower where Huguenot conspiracies were hatched during the Wars of Religion. The vault is covered with a most curious fresco from the Fontainebleau school, featuring—together—notable Catholics and Protestants. (Guided tours 45 minutes long are offered from late March to early November, mornings and afternoons; closed Tuesdays. Some tours are given in English during high season, and an English-language brochure makes it easy to follow a tour in French. Ask a hotel concierge or inquire at an Office de Tourisme for precise hours.)

Sébastien Serlio, an Italian architect brought to the region (as were so many other artists) by François I, designed ▶ **Château d'Ancy-le-Franc** (south of Tanlay via D 118 and D 905) for Antoine III de Clermont-Tonnerre in the mid-16th century. It is a harmonious composition of four major structures linked by corner pavilions, the original model of pure Renaissance style in France. Among the 25 beautifully decorated rooms open to the public, the chapel, with its carved woodwork, is most notable. (Ancy is open every morning and afternoon from early April to early November. Guided tours are available but are not mandatory. There are carriage rides through the park in fine weather.) An exceptional opportunity is available here: Four bedrooms, two suites, and two apartments (but no meals) may be booked for receptions, seminars, or weekly rentals between April 1 and October 30. Address Monsieur Jean de Menton (see Accommodations Reference).

TONNERRE

Tonnerre, 10 km (6 miles) west of Tanlay via D 965, is little known to foreigners except to passengers aboard the luxury hotel-barges that cruise the canals of Burgundy. It is worth a stop, however, en route from the châteaux of Tanlay and Ancy-le-Franc to Auxerre, largely because of the beautiful 13th-century **Ancien Hôpital** that somehow survived ruinous fires in the 16th century.

Built at the order of Marguerite de Bourgogne, widow of Charles d'Anjou, the hospital is similar in style and purpose to the Hôtel-Dieu in Beaune. The chapel near the high altar contains a very moving *mise au tombeau*, a 15th-century form of Burgundian sculpture that is also called a *saint sépulcre* and, in English, an entombment. This one in Tonnerre, the one at Notre-Dame in Semur-en-Auxois, and another in the hospital in Dijon are the three most arresting examples of the form; the one in Tonnerre features a semi-recumbent Christ being laid upon his tomb by seven mourning figures.

(A *hôtel-Dieu*, or God's mansion, was, and is, a hospital maintained by the Church to care for the sick, poor, homeless, etc.—rather like a hospice. Virtually every town of every size has one. Because they were maintained by the Church they were used to spread the Good Word and to care for souls as well as bodies. Generally, the *hôtel-Dieu* was located near the cathedral or main church.)

Another reason to linger in Tonnerre is the outstanding restaurant and 15-room inn (including five suites) of the ▶ **Abbaye Saint-Michel**, which occupies a Benedictine abbey of the tenth century set in its own manicured park. The cooking is under the control of Christophe Cussac, one of the heralded Jeune Restaurateurs d'Europe. His cuisine is thoroughly original within the classic tradition: foie gras with rhubarb in a pastry shell; brill with chives and onions. For wines, try the regional Epineuil or Irancy, and always reserve; Tel: 86-55-05-99. This is a good base from which to explore the region.

(Note that Auxerre and Chablis are a short distance west of Tonnerre via D 965; they are covered below as part of the route west and northwest from Dijon.)

CHATILLON-SUR-SEINE

Châtillon-sur-Seine, 49 km (30 miles) east of Tonnerre on D 965 and 85 km (53 miles) north of Dijon on D 71, and 58 km (36 miles) north of the Seine, straddles the lazily flowing river, its flowered bridges, pretty houses, winding streets, and coquettish air suggesting that nothing much ever has happened here.

Sadly, that's not true. During World War II the town center was badly mauled; in September 1914 Général Joseph Joffre set up headquarters here so that his retreating French troops could counterattack the charging German army; and, just a hundred years before that, Napoléon chose the spot for a congress with the enemies allied against him during the famous Hundred Days.

Today this town of fewer than 8,000 inhabitants is home to one of the most interesting small museums in the country, the **Musée Municipal**. The handsome 16th-century Renaissance Maison Philandrier houses collections from protohistoric sites in the region: fifth-century ceramics from Mont-Lassois, a bronze alms basin from the chariot tomb at Ste-Colombe, votive sculptures from the sanctuary of Essarois, and Gallo-Roman everyday tools and utensils from Vertillum (Vertault).

Most sensational are the finds from the tomb of Vix, discovered in 1953 at the foot of nearby Mont-Lassois. These consist of the remains of a woman (most likely a Celtic princess) who died in the sixth century B.C. and was buried with goods probably intended to accompany her into the next world (a golden diadem, earrings, bejeweled bracelets); a huge ceremonial chariot, and—one of the most majestic finds of contemporary archaeology—the **Treasure of Vix**. This last is a giant vase five and a half feet high, weighing 460 pounds, and capable of holding 1,162 quarts of liquid (wine, perhaps). A masterpiece of Archaic Greek bronze style, it is thought to have been created in about 500 B.C. It is richly decorated with a frieze featuring helmeted warriors and horse-drawn chariots, with Gorgon heads on the handles.

The calm, gentle nature of the countryside between the waters of the young Seine and those of the rivers Ource and Aube off to the east lends itself to pleasant, easygoing activities much enjoyed by families. Should you want information about outdoor activities or "rambling" on a portion of the long-distance footpaths in the region, inquire at the Office de Tourisme on Place Marmont in the center of town; Tel: 80-43-42-12.

Before departing Châtillon, stop near the **Source de la Douix** at the foot of a rocky hill where waters bubble up from the limestone earth at a rate of up to 800 gallons a second to mingle, slightly farther along, with those of the Seine. The site is reminiscent of the Fontaine de Vaucluse in Provence but is much less tourist-ridden.

The ▶ **Côte d'Or** in Châtillon offers 11 recently redecorated rooms in an old post house on rue Charles-Ronot. Since the rooms vary widely in size and style, ask to see what's available before you book (six have toilet only; no bath or shower). The garden is quiet, fragrant, and shaded by century-old trees, breakfasts are taken in the small corner bar, and the surprisingly good kitchen serves trout with *escargots, jambon persillé châtillonnais,* and chicken with *morilles.*

WEST FROM DIJON

A drive west from Dijon takes you first through an intensely agricultural region called the Morvan, where fields and pastures are divided by hedgerows, then on to a string of such wonderful places as the hilltop town of Vézelay and, at the western boundary of Burgundy, Sens.

COMMARIN

One of the most elegant of the stately residences in Burgundy is the 18th-century château in the tiny hamlet of Commarin, 35 km (22 miles) west of Dijon on A 38 and D 977. In the part of the home open to the public—the family still lives here—the chapel and the spacious Grande Salle show off Burgundian art, woodwork, decor, and furniture. Guided tours (45 minutes) are given mornings and afternoons except Tuesdays from early April to late October; for current hours, inquire at the Office de Tourisme in Dijon.

SAULIEU

In 177 Saint Andoche and two companions, Thyrse and Félix, were martyred at Saulieu, a small, pleasant town 72 km (45 miles) west of Dijon via A 38, D 977 *bis,* and N 6. A church was erected on the spot in 306, only to be destroyed before long by the Saracens. The present **Basilique St-Andoche**, in the center of town, was begun in the 12th century and has endured several indignities during its long life, including fires that destroyed the choir and transept during the Hundred Years War and the mutilations of the Revolution. The glory of St-Andoche is the remarkable set of powerfully carved column capitals somewhat reminiscent of those in Autun (see below), featuring grinning monsters, incredible foliage from an imaginary jungle, and biblical scenes.

Next to St-Andoche, the **Musée Régional** (sometimes called the Musée François-Pompon) exhibits a fine collection of Gallo-Roman stelae and medieval, Renaissance, and classical sculptures. Today Saulieu supplies much of France and the rest of Europe with Christmas trees from the forests of the Morvan. The woods near the town also serve for picnics, provisioned in part by **Laiterie Overney** in town for some of the things good picnics are made of, such as a five-week cheese washed with local Chablis. Shops in nearby **Nontron-le-Beau** sell the pleasing handicrafts—pottery and ceramic figures—created by Jean-Louis Pasquet, a well-known regional artist.

Staying and Dining in and Around Saulieu

Saulieu's gastronomic reputation was well established as early as the 17th century, when it became an important post stop on the route between Paris and Lyon. Rabelais wrote of the good living here (on which, of course, he was an authority), and Madame de Sévigné was made absolutely tipsy by the quality and quantity of food and drink. Today the major attraction here is still a restaurant, ▶ **Bernard Loiseau-La Côte-d'Or**—for gastronomes, a place of pilgrimage. Michelin awarded its coveted three stars to chef-owner Bernard Loiseau and his wife, Chantal, whose kitchen is devoted to purity, lightness, and creativity. Specialties include *sandre* (a pike-perch) with a shallot and red-wine sauce, and chicken breasts with warm foie gras and truffles. Dinner now averages more than $100 a person, without wine, which may well be some of the finer Chablis that belie the very ordinary quality of bottlings under that name in the United States. Reservations are required several weeks in advance. Tel: 80-64-07-66; Fax: 80-64-08-92.

Côte d'Or is also a popular overnight stop, with 16 tastefully decorated rooms, four apartments, and three rather new duplexes.

The welcoming, 25-room ▶ **Auberge des Brizards**, on a forest-ringed lake near Saulieu, is a more modest retreat. Take D 977 *bis* west of Saulieu a very short distance, then jog on D 6 a bit to D 10 and follow it north to Quarré-les-Tombes, about 15 km (9 miles).

VEZELAY

The abbey at tiny (fewer than 600 inhabitants) hilltop Vézelay, about 90 km (56 miles) west of Dijon (fastest route: A 38 to E 15-A 6 to Avallon, then west on D 957 for 16 km/10 miles), was consecrated by Pope Jean VIII in 878 and remained significant throughout the glory years of the 12th and 13th centuries.

Mostly pilgrims in search of art and history arrive now, climbing uphill in cars from the Place Champs-de-Foire along a skinny one-way street, but their destination is the same: the Basilique Ste-Madeleine, dominating a village of brown-roofed houses and among the most impressive of all the Romanesque churches in Burgundy.

In the ninth century Girart de Roussillon, a Burgundian count, founded a settlement of nuns in the valley below, where St-Père-sous-Vézelay sits today. When that location was repeatedly attacked by Norman invaders, it was decided to reestablish the monastery atop a nearby, more defensible hill. The relics of Sainte Madeleine (Mary Magdalen) and the miracles accredited to them lured so many pilgrims in the 11th century that the town's population swelled to 10,000 and the church was expanded. Then in 1120 a terrible fire broke out on the eve of July 22, the date of a traditional pilgrimage and the feast day of the saint, destroying the nave and more than a thousand of the faithful with it.

On March 31, 1146, Saint Bernard, the man of most consequence in Christendom, came to stand on Vézelay's "inspired hill" to preach the Second Crusade to a worshiping crowd that included France's Louis VII. Vézelay was by then an origination point for the most important pilgrimage route, that to Santiago de Compostela, in Spain.

It was from Vézelay that France's Philippe Auguste and England's Richard the Lion-hearted departed for the Third Crusade in 1190. In the next century Saint Francis of Assisi founded the first brotherhood of Franciscans in France, the

Frères Mineurs, here. In 1248, when the Seventh Crusade began, Louis IX (Saint Louis) made pilgrimages to Vézelay on several occasions. In the late 13th century, however, with the discovery of more relics of Sainte Madeleine in Provence, proud Vézelay began to decline; then came the Wars of Religion, the ravages attributed to the Huguenots, and the destruction wrought by the Revolution.

The Basilique Ste-Madeleine

Had Eugène-Emmanuel Viollet-le-Duc not been employed in 1840 to restore the whole to its ancient excellence, Vézelay now would attract no more curiosity than a pile of rocks. The basilica's façade, which was almost entirely reconstituted in the 19th century, is not universally applauded, but the interior contains artworks acknowledged to be among the finest in the Western world. The central **tympanum of the Pentecost** depicts a gigantic Christ in Glory from whose hands the rays of the Holy Ghost reach out to the Apostles. To the right and left, the people of the world await the Word. These are wonderful, fantastical figures, since the artists of the day knew little of the world and thus imagined most of it: Some characters appear with the heads of dogs, some with pendantlike ears, others more monster than man. The column capitals are even more entertaining and as beautifully and imaginatively carved. David defeats a lion; Jacob wrestles with an angel. On the right, the bad rich man dies in agony; on the left, Absalom is decapitated. (You can buy copies of these capitals around town.)

The crypt, which sheltered the tomb of Mary Magdalene during the pilgrimages of the Middle Ages, was reworked in the 12th century and today holds only a few of the saintly relics. A climb of 200 steps to the tower offers a grand view over the valley.

Staying and Dining in and Around Vézelay

Follow the narrow, crabbed streets of Vézelay to lunch or spend the night at ▶ **Hôtel Poste-Lion d'Or**, a fairly modest but most comfortable hideaway of 48 rooms set in a garden. Another inn in town, ▶ **Le Pontot**, offers ten rooms and a garden with delicious views over the countryside. Both are closed from early November until the end of March.

Today food aficionados make their pilgrimage to the hamlet of **St-Père** (some 350 inhabitants) at the foot of Vézelay's hill to dine at the celebrated ▶ **L'Espérance** (chef Marc Meneau has earned three Michelin stars for his work; reserve well in advance; Tel: 86-33-20-45). L'Espérance prides itself on a sophisticated bar-lounge with leather armchairs and couches where you may relax to study the menu; if oysters *en gelée,* salmon in lobster sauce, grilled lamb, or wild duck are listed, consider yourself most fortunate. The 18-room hotel and restaurant are housed in a large, unpretentious, white stone manor of the 19th century, its severity softened by window boxes overflowing with color. Many experienced travellers rank L'Espérance among the two or three top country retreats in France and don't mind paying top dollar for the quality.

While in St-Père, take a look at **Eglise Notre-Dame**, begun in the 13th century and restored in the 19th century by Viollet-le-Duc; the **Musée Archéologique Régional** houses the finds from digs at nearby Fontaines-Salées, where Gallo-Roman baths have been unearthed. ▶ **Le Moulin des Templiers** in **Pontaubert**, 5 km (3 miles) east of Vézelay on D 957, has 15 comfortable though modest rooms, and the ▶ **Château de Vault de Lugny** in Lugny, 2 km (1¼ miles) farther east, accommodates guests in 11 luxuriously appointed rooms and arranges ballooning, fishing, and tennis.

In Avallon, 13 km (8 miles) east of Vézelay on D 957 and worth a call in its own right for its ramparts and Eglise St-Lazare, the ▶ **Hostellerie du Moulin des Ruats** occupies a renovated mill. It has 27 rooms and a highly praised restaurant with a great view over the river.

Auxerre

Auxerre (locally pronounced O-sair) is one of the oldest towns in France, known at its beginning as Autricum to the Gauls, Autessiodurum to the Romans. It lies along the great trade route from Lyon to Boulogne, about halfway between Paris and Dijon, the latter being some 150 km (93 miles) to the south and east via the speedy autoroutes A 6 and A 38. (Dijon and Auxerre are also well connected by train service.) By the end of the fourth century Auxerre was an important center, and even today retains a wealth of art and business activity worthy of a much larger city. Unlike some provincial cities, Auxerre is growing younger: 60 to 65 percent of the population is less than 40 years of age.

Auxerre is known throughout France as the birthplace of the great Saint Germain, who was born in 378 to noble parents. He studied and practiced law in Rome and then returned to Gaul, married, and won a high official post. Germain paid little heed in early life to religion. In 418 he was elected bishop of Auxerre by the clergy and the people, much against his will. He changed his life immediately, however, devoting himself to prayer and action in defense of the Church. When Saint Germain died in Ravenna, his body was returned to Auxerre and buried with pomp and circumstance under the abbey church that bears his name.

Saint Germain knew and supported Sainte Geneviève, now the patron saint of Paris. He is memorialized in Paris in the church of St-Germain-l'Auxerrois, behind the Louvre, and he is not to be confused with another Saint Germain, a sixth-century bishop of Paris named Germanus, who lies in St-Germain-des-Prés.

THE MEDIEVAL TOWN

There is a pleasant capriciousness to the daily life of Auxerre, a sturdy and bourgeois business approach joined to a hat-in-the-air, youthful exuberance. Today the entire city is classified as a national protected site, with the result that it's a joy to stroll about its ancient monuments and numerous houses and mansions from the 15th, 17th, and 18th centuries. The easiest way into the city is via avenue Jean-Jaurès across the Yonne river by Pont Paul-Bert (from which there's an excellent view of the city). From the bridge turn north along the quai de la République; there are parking lots in the center of town atop the river bluffs. (The Office de Tourisme is on the quai at number 1-2.)

The Cathedral and Abbey

The place to begin a tour is at the **Cathédrale St-Etienne**, the fifth structure built on the site of the original sanctuary founded in 400 by Bishop Saint Amâtre, the result of some 500 years of architectural forays. The south tower never has been completed.

Among the remarkable achievements here are the 13th-century stained glass windows and the 11th-century Romanesque crypt with its superb frescoes, including the unique portrayal of Christ Triumphant astride a white horse surrounded by angels, also on horseback. The treasury holds valuable manuscripts, books of hours, ivories, miniatures, and enamels.

From the cathedral walk north up rue Cochois to Auxerre's other medieval treasure, the **Abbaye St-Germain**. What you see first is the Gothic 13th- to 15th-century church; what you will remember is the **crypt**, which essentially constitutes the sixth-century church erected in Saint Germain's honor by Clothilde, Christian wife of the Frankish king Clovis of the Mérovingian dynasty. The oldest frescoes yet discovered in France are here, dating from 858 and depicting the martyrdom of Saint Etienne (Saint Stephen). Still in place, and still bearing weight, are beams of oak that are more than 1,100 years old. A museum and cultural center in this building make up one of the most valuable historical resources in the country.

Around the Place de l'Hôtel de Ville

From here retrace your steps to the bustling center of town, the Place de l'Hôtel de Ville. This *place* and streets leading off it (rue Fécauderie, rue de l'Horloge) show off fine half-timbered houses, most of them occupied by smart shops and banks. Just west of the *place* is the 15th-century **Tour de l'Horloge** (Clock Tower), a graceful structure in Flamboyant style built atop the Gallo-Roman wall and now the heart of the shopping area. One face of the clock features the movements of the sun and moon, while the other counts the hours. Step into Place Charles-Lepère just west of the clock tower and then amble north on rue de la Draperie and rue de Paris. Shoppers will find many temptations in this area, which is studded with 16th-century half-timbered houses and some fine Renaissance mansions.

A revival of the arts of pottery, ceramics, and faïence so celebrated here in the Yonne region during the 18th and 19th centuries is under way today, and shops selling such crafts have sprung up everywhere. In Auxerre, you can find these works for sale near the Tour de l'Horloge; the creations of Pierre Merlier are especially attractive.

The Vineyards at Clos de la Chaînette

What remains of the region's famous vineyards grows on the grounds of Clos de la Chaînette, a psychiatric hospital just outside town to the northwest. Take rue des Migraines, named for a once-famous vineyard (we can only wonder what it produced!). These few rows of grapes (producing whites and rosés) are the only survivors of Auxerre's great seventh-century vineyards. At the beginning of the 19th century Alexandre Dumas regarded the local production as among the greatest of French red wines, mentioning it in the same breath as Château Margaux and Romanée Conti. The phylloxera crisis of the 19th century and increasing urban pressures caused virtually all the other prestigious local vineyards to disappear, but some are being reborn several kilometers away in the environs of **Vaux**.

STAYING AND DINING IN AUXERRE

The best restaurant in town today is **Barnabet**, in a garden setting near the riverfront at 14, quai de la République. It's a good place to try *sandre,* the pike-perch. Reserve; Tel: 86-51-68-88. Another outstanding restaurant in the area is **La**

Chamaille, located in an old farmhouse on the banks of the Yonne river in the village of Chevannes, 8 km (5 miles) southwest of Auxerre (reserve; Tel: 86-41-24-80). Also good are the **Jardin Gourmand**, at 56, boulevard Vauban in Auxerre (reserve; Tel: 86-51-53-52), and **La Petite Auberge**, in nearby Vaux (reserve; Tel: 86-53-80-08). The **Restaurant Le Maxime** in Auxerre, next to (but not part of) the Hôtel Le Maxime, is quite good and informal, and puts an emphasis on regional dishes and fresh fish from nearby rivers (reserve; Tel: 86-52-04-41). The ▶ **Hôtel Le Maxime**, a 25-room inn right on the river, is the finest hotel in town and the best located for walking.

Chablis

"I would give a fortune and all my titles to intoxicate myself on a mixture of Chablis and oysters," Eugène Deschamps once wrote. Or, he might have said, Chablis and turbot . . . or *sole meunière* . . . or *escargots* . . . or St-Marcellin cheese.

Chablis, 19 km (12 miles) east of Auxerre via D 965, is one of the most famous wine names in the world—and one of the most misused. Outside France it is often employed as a generic name for any white, frequently those of little distinction.

However, as wine expert Alexis Lichine pointed out, "Used correctly, it refers to one of the world's rarest great wines—to the steadily decreasing quantity of magnificent flinty, dry white wines which are made from grapes grown on hilly acres in and around the Burgundian town of Chablis."

At one time Chablis boasted some charming old houses and was most picturesque during harvest. Unfortunately, on a clear June night in 1940 some far-afield Italian flyers unloaded their bombs on the heart of the unsuspecting and unstrategic town. Fortunately, Chablis's real treasure grows in the rolling hills beyond, where pockets of bituminous clay lend the wines of the region their distinctive taste.

Chablis today is a natural stop on a day's excursion out of Auxerre, and it is refreshing, since there's little to do here but sip Chablis (for maximum appreciation, you should request a grand cru—Les Bouguerots, Les Blanchots, Les Clos) and lunch or dine at Michel Vignaud's ▶ **Hostellerie des Clos** (reserve; Tel: 86-42-10-63). A conversion of an ancient *clos des hospices,* the *hostellerie* offers 26 quiet, comfortable bedrooms overlooking gardens to those in search of a real hideaway. (If you require a historical stop in town, you can admire the 12th-century Eglise St-Martin and its Romanesque doorway.)

A festival of regional wines is held in Chablis the fourth
Sunday in November.

(The town of Tonnerre and the châteaux of Tanlay and
Ancy-le-Franc lie not far to the east of Chablis. They are
discussed as part of the route north from Dijon, above.)

Sens

Travellers stop in Sens to visit the Cathédrale St-Etienne and
its treasury. Sens is 58 km (36 miles) north of Auxerre on N 6
and about 206 km (128 miles) north of Dijon via A 6 and N 6.
The town, counting some 27,000 Sénonais, takes its name
from one of the strongest Gallic tribes, the Senones. Its
history is proud: The Romans made Sens the capital of one of
the provinces of Lyonnaise. It was later the seat of an archbish-
opric when Paris had only a bishop, and when Pope Alexander III was in residence from 1163 to 1164 Sens effectively
became the capital of Christianity. It was at Sens that Abélard
was condemned, and Saint Louis married Marguerite de
Provence in the cathedral here. It was also in Sens (as well as
in the abbey of Pontigny, nearer Auxerre) that Thomas à
Becket lived six years in exile from England and Henry II.

CATHEDRALE ST-ETIENNE

The Sénonais are likely to tell visitors that their cathedral
represents the birth of Gothic architecture in France—an
opinion that is more enthusiastic than accurate. The choir of
the Cathédrale St-Denis in the Paris suburb of that name is
universally acclaimed as the birthplace of Gothic; what *is*
certain is that St-Etienne ranks among the first great Gothic
edifices in France. Interestingly, the choir of St-Etienne became a model for the rebuilding of the eastern end of
England's Canterbury Cathedral following the disastrous fire
there in 1174. Note the early-Gothic Saint Etienne on the
central portal (wearing deacon's garb and carrying the Gos-
pel) before entering the nave, where light streams through
superb 12th- to 17th-century stained glass windows.

The cathedral has always been renowned for the value of
its **treasury**, one of the most highly regarded in Europe (along
with those of Ste-Foy, in Conques, and St-Maurice, in Switzerland). Other great collections are housed nearby in the **Palais
Synodal** in the Dépôt Lapidaire.

Since 1985 many works formerly dispersed throughout
the city have been joined together in the **Musées de Sens**, a
restoration of part of the cathedral complex. The collection
includes relics, antique textiles, liturgical ornaments, tapestries, mosaics, and silver, ivory, and enamel works; particular

attention should, however, be paid to the **vestments of Thomas à Becket**. They appear to have been fitted to a man extremely large and powerful for his time. Among other treasures are a 15th-century Flemish tapestry showing the Adoration of the Magi; a gold and bejeweled fibula (brooch) from Mérovingian times; a remarkable carved ivory reliquary, the *Sainte Chasse;* and an eighth-century shroud depicting a gigantic Gilgamesh, the hero of the ancient Babylonian epic.

Joigny

A fine headquarters for exploring all of northwest Burgundy is ▶ **Résidence de la Côte Saint-Jacques** in the town of Joigny, about halfway between Auxerre and Sens on the river Yonne (30 km/19 miles southeast of Sens on N 6). On a grassy terrace above the river, equipped with some private balconies and an indoor pool with doors opening to the terrace, this cultivated oasis has 25 rooms and four suites that bespeak country elegance, and the kitchen, under chef Michel Lorain, is one of the very best in France. The fish called *bar,* lightly smoked and served with cream of caviar, is not to be passed over. Reservations are essential; Tel: 86-62-09-70.

Anne Willan, who runs the highly reputed La Varenne cooking school in Paris, now accepts guests for one-week classes at her renovated 17th-century ▶ **Château du Fey**, in a 100-acre setting above the valley of the Yonne; a resident chef provides the best of the land's culinary riches at dinner.

The Château du Fey is just outside the village of Villecien, 8 km (5 miles) north of Joigny via N 6.

SOUTH FROM DIJON

The principal routes we follow south from Dijon are N 74 to Beaune, with a detour to Autun to the west via D 973, and N 6 south to Tournus, Cluny, Mâcon, and, finally, Lyon and the Rhône Valley.

Beaune

The oenophile approaches Beaune, 45 km (28 miles) south of Dijon on N 74, reverentially, admiring the rich slopes of hills and the names on the land: from Dijon, Gevrey-Chambertin, Vougeot, Vosne-Romanée, Aloxe-Corton; from Mâcon in the south, Chassagne-Montrachet, Puligny-Montrachet, Meursault, Volnay, Pommard, and more, all along N 74.

Beaune lives up to the nobility of the neighboring vineyards. "This is one of the most soul-satisfying of towns," wrote Samuel Chamberlain, "the pure essence of rural France—civilized, bourgeois, unruffled. Its fat chimneys bespeak a well-fed race." To the traveller Beaune comes as a respite: It doesn't bustle, it strolls; it doesn't shout, it chants; it is less chic than comfortable. Beaune, after all, is scarcely an upstart; this town of fewer than 22,000 Beaunois is enjoying a respected old age. Beaune was a sanctuary for the Gauls, then the Romans, and, finally, the Grand Dukes of Burgundy, before they seized upon Dijon as their capital. Its 14th-century walls and some towers remain, rich with artworks and other evidences of the good life. Central Beaune is small enough to be seen comfortably on foot.

THE HOTEL-DIEU

The Hôtel-Dieu, also known as the Hospices de Beaune, was founded in 1443 by Nicolas Rolin, the chancellor of Burgundy under Philippe le Bel (the Fair), as a charity hospital. Rolin's intentions may not have been quite so splendid as the architecture: Louis XI of France is said to have sniffed, "It is indeed just that having made so many people poor, Rolin should now construct a hospital to shelter them."

Whatever. The hospice catered to the souls as well as the sores of the poor—and in style—for more than 500 years, and the last patients didn't move out until 1971; part of the building still houses the aged. The look of the place has scarcely changed since architect Jehan Wiscrère created its Flamboyant design, the most striking elements of which are visible only after you step past the sober, somewhat formidable façade into the courtyard. The multicolored tile roofs, the small towers from which Rapunzel might let down her hair, the ranks of inviting dormer windows, the eccentric weather vanes—all conspire to put you in the mood of a storybook rather than sickness.

The **Grand'Salle** served as a ward as well as a church, designed so that patients could share the Mass without leaving their beds. (Beds were scarcely king size, as the visitor will notice, and several people were squeezed into each one, probably with infectious results.) Among the other installations that can be seen, the most interesting are the kitchen and the pharmacy.

The *chef d'oeuvre* here is the immense **Last Judgment** by Flemish painter Roger van der Weyden, which occupies a room especially built for it in the late 1980s in the Hôtel-

Dieu's central hall. On the covers of the panels, Rolin and
his wife, Guigone, appear as they did in life, no warts or
wrinkles overlooked. (At the push of a button a giant
magnifying glass moves back and forth in front of van der
Weyden's work, allowing visitors to inspect details.)

Chancellor Rolin willed his vineyards to the hospital, and
today, the holdings slightly increased, income from the annual wine auction goes to preserve and implement its good
works. The mid-November auction is the central event of Les
Trois Glorieuses, a three-day festival of feasting watched
over by the merry group known as the Confrérie des Chevaliers du Tastevin.

In season, the only way to see the Hôtel-Dieu and its
museum is on guided tours (45 minutes long) conducted
mornings and afternoons year-round. Out of season, visitors
are sometimes allowed to enter on their own.

THE PLACE DE LA HALLE
AND HOTEL DE VILLE

Leaving the Hôtel-Dieu, walk a few steps north up rue de
l'Hôtel-Dieu into the Place de la Halle. The local Office de
Tourisme is here, and on Saturday mornings you can enjoy
an explosion of color, action, scents, and colors when the
outdoor market fills the square. Walking north into the Place
Fleury you'll spot the Hôtel de Saulx, with a pretty tower.
The avenue de la République begins here. At the first corner
on your right, follow the sign toward the **Musée du Vin de
Bourgogne**, a former mansion of the dukes, a handsome
wood-and-stone structure from the 15th and 16th centuries.
The history of winemaking is outlined by artworks, tools,
costumes, and photographs. From the wine museum, the
short rue d'Enfer leads a few steps northeast to the **Collégiale Notre-Dame**, begun about 1120, and worth visiting
particularly for its collection of tapestries in the choir behind the high altar. Titled *The Life of the Virgin,* the collection appears to have one artistic foot in the Middle Ages and
one in the Renaissance.

From the back of the church, rue Marey leads east a short
distance to the Place Monge, dominated by a statue of the
geometrician Gaspard Monge by François Rude, and just
beyond, a lovely collection of 16th-century homes along rue
de Lorraine. Veer east into rue du Collége and you'll come to
the Hôtel de Ville, installed in a former convent of the
Ursuline nuns and housing two museums, the **Musée des
Beaux-Arts**, with a good collection of Dutch and Flemish
paintings, and the **Musée Etienne-Jules Marey**, devoted to
early photography.

One of the nicest strolls in Beaune is atop the ramparts on the walls encircling the town. Beginning at the Bastion St-Jean, on rue du Château at the east side of the old town, you can follow the wall for about a mile, with the rooftops on one side and the moat, planted with orchards and gardens, on the other.

SHOPPING IN BEAUNE

Shopping in Beaune runs less to fashion than to food, kitchenware, and table accessories. Mustard is the king of French condiments, and some of the best (and hottest) is made not in Dijon but in Beaune. (The dukes of Burgundy never set forth to battle without a mighty supply; perhaps that's why they were so successful.)

In Beaune, the place to shop for mustard is **Fallot et Compagnie** at 31, rue du faubourg Brétonnière, a short drive southwest of the ramparts; the shop will ship internationally.

Buy your picnic supplies, especially a few slices of delicious *jambon persillé,* the cold, poached ham that's cubed and layered with parsleyed gelatin, and other products—mustards, sherry-wine vinegars, capers, etc.—at **Roger Batteault**, 4, rue Monge, a few steps northeast from the Place de la Halle.

STAYING AND DINING
IN AND AROUND BEAUNE

▶ **Belena**, on boulevard Foch just around a corner from the Place de la Halle, offers 34 rooms and six duplexes. Its distinguished restaurant **Jacques Lainé** turns regional ingredients into haute cuisine: Try pigeon from Bresse in a red wine sauce or *escargots* sauteed in a garlic mousse. Reserve; Tel: 80-24-76-10.

The stylishly comfortable and old-fashioned ▶ **Le Cep**, within easy ambling distance of the town center on rue Maufoux, is an old favorite with visitors to Burgundy, with 49 rooms and three apartments. Next door is the fine **Bernard Morillon** restaurant, at 31, rue Maufoux; try fine regional wines from the large cellar. Reserve; Tel: 80-24-12-06. Right near the northern ramparts of Beaune, next to the old church of St-Nicolas at 138, route de Dijon, the ▶ **Hôtel Le Home** is a more modest hideaway with 22 pretty, comfortable rooms set in a green and flowery garden.

▶ **Hôtel de la Poste**, just west of the ramparts on boulevard Clemenceau, is a grand old place with 21 rooms, nine apartments, and a pleasant garden.

Just beyond the outer boulevards, ▶ **Henry II** is a well-managed, modern, 50-room place on rue du faubourg St-

Nicolas, which leads north to N 74, the road to Dijon. ► **Hôtel de la Paix**, east of the moat and ramparts on rue du faubourg Madeleine, has only ten rooms but two popular restaurants, **Le Bouchon** and **La Rôtisserie**. Reserve for La Rôtisserie; Tel: 80-22-33-33. **L'Ecusson**, just across the Place Malmédy, specializes in seafood; if it's offered, order the roast turbot in a smoked onion cream sauce. Tel: 80-24-03-82.

Right in the center of things, on the north side of the Place de la Halle, the reasonably priced **Auberge de St-Vincent** is an excellent spot for lunch on a day of sightseeing; it serves traditional dishes in a venerable setting (Tel: 80-22-42-34). **Le Jardin des Remparts** is another handy luncheon stop, in a very pretty site at the foot of the ramparts at 10, rue de l'Hôtel-Dieu.

The ► **Hostellerie de Levernois**, 5 km (3 miles) southeast of Beaune near the village of Levernois via D 111, is a 25-room inn in its own ten-acre park; chef Christophe Crotet presents his refined two-star cuisine and wines. Among other triumphs, try the pigeon *poêlé* with foie gras. Reservations always are required; Tel: 80-24-73-58.

At the ► **Ermitage de Corton**, 4 km (2½ miles) north of Beaune in the village of Chorey (follow N 74 to D 20), André Parra prepares light, delicate dishes suited to contemporary tastes. Order the crayfishlike langoustines with curry butter when they're on the menu, and try the local Chorey-les-Beaune or the more expensive Aloxe-Corton wines. Tel: 80-22-05-28. There are also two rooms and eight apartments in a calm, green setting.

Autun

Autun and Rome—today little of one would suggest the slightest inkling of the other. Pleasant, calm (indeed, half-asleep might be a better description) little Autun, with about 16,000 citizens, snoozes on its slope below the wooded hills of the Morvan, 48 km (30 miles) west of Beaune on D 973.

Autun owes its existence to the demise of Bibracte, a Gallic *oppidum* (fortified camp) at the summit of Mont Beuvray (an easy excursion about 17 km/11 miles west from Autun on N 81 and north on D 61 to St-Léger; follow the signs from there) and capital of the Eduen tribe, where Vercingétorix held a council of war in 52 B.C. It was at Bibracte that he took command of the Gallic armies and organized his troops against Julius Caesar.

In the days of Emperor Augustus (27 B.C. to A.D. 14), Bibracte was abandoned. Autun was established as Augustodunum and matured into a flourishing city, an impor-

tant stop on the trade and defensive routes from Lyon to
Boulogne. Indeed, road maps from the period show Autun
as the hub of a six-spoked wheel.

During the late Roman Empire (180 to 395) the fame of
Autun's schools was widespread, its diocese was one of the
oldest in Gaul, and it was the premier suffragan of the
mother church in Lyon. Over the centuries an impressive
number of abbeys flowered in Autun, including that of St-
Martin, founded in the sixth century by the Mérovingian
Queen Brunhild. It defended its independence even in the
face of Cluny.

Brunhild, hardened by her harsh life (her husband was
murdered as a result of the wicked machinations of her
sister-in-law, Frédégund), used to retreat from the troubles
of her regency to the relative serenity of Autun. (The quarrels of the two queens and the downfall of Brunhild's husband, King Sigibert I, are said to be the stuff of the medieval
German epic *Niebelungenlied;* Autun is thought to have
been the home of the Niebelungs, and Sigibert metamorphosed into Siegfried.)

After the decline of the Gallo-Roman world Autun slept for
a while, only to awake to new prosperity in the Middle Ages.
The town is liberally endowed with vestiges of its long past.
You might begin a tour by exploring Autun's medieval sights,
in the southern end of the city.

MEDIEVAL AUTUN

Leave your car in the **Champ de Mars**, in the center of town.
Take a look at the *grilles* (wrought-iron grill works) on the
façade of the Lycée Bonaparte on the north side of the
square; they are splendidly adorned with gilded medallions,
globes, and lyres. The library of the **Hôtel de Ville**, on the
north side of the square near the Office de Tourisme, has a
fine collection of manuscripts and incunabula.

From the Champ de Mars, follow rue des Cordeliers south
to the Palais de Justice on the Place d'Hallencourt and turn
west into the Place St-Louis, dominated by the cathedral.

Cathédrale St-Lazare and Environs

The tall stone spire that marks this cathedral, in its entirety
one of the most important examples of the Romanesque in
Burgundy, dates from the 15th century, but the church itself
is one of the major works of Cluniac art, constructed between 1120 and 1146 and consecrated by Pope Innocent II
in 1130. Its artistic marvels are the sculptures (in local gray
stone) on the **tympanum** of the central portal, the Last

Judgment, and its column capitals in a stippled stone containing mica.

Probably it was for the best that Autun again declined during the Renaissance; otherwise "renovations" of these triumphs might have been made, as happened elsewhere. The tympanum is a true sermon in stone, designed by the artist to be "read"—and paid heed to—by illiterates. (Following medieval habit, public works of art were usually anonymous, but the tympanum is signed: "Gislebertus hoc fecit.") An inscription carved in Latin advises, "Let this horror appall those bound by earthly sin." In the center, Christ sits in Byzantine majesty, a figure not yet capable of seeming human. All around him there is wicked and wonderful action: three children bound for Paradise hold on to an angel; a woman headed for Hell is being eaten by serpents; Saint Peter holds the hand of a nude soul; Saint Michael tries to weigh the good and bad honestly, even as Satan pulls the scale down in his direction.

A *son-et-lumière* performance is held at the cathedral on Fridays and Saturdays from mid-May through June, daily except Sundays and Mondays from July to late September.

The **Musée Rolin** occupies the 15th-century town house built for Nicolas Rolin, the founder of the Hôtel-Dieu in Beaune, just across the square from St-Lazare. The collections include some superb Gallo-Roman artifacts, French and Flemish primitive paintings, and a 15th-century Nativity by the so-called Master of Moulins. The **Muséum d'Histoire Naturelle**, about three blocks northeast along rue St-Antoine, is a nice collection of fossils and other evidence of the region's rich geology.

ROMAN AUTUN

Autun's Roman remains are spread throughout the northern part of the town; you may want to drive. Whether on foot or in a car, from the Champs de Mars follow rue Guérin north for about a fifth of a mile to rue de Paris and the **Musée Archéologique**, housed in a 12th-century Romanesque chapel, with many Roman remains in the cloisters and gardens. There are also some medieval objects.

Back on rue Guérin, continue northeast (the street becomes boulevard Mazagran) to a traffic circle and rue Théâtre Romain. A jog to the east brings you to the **Théâtre Romain** (Roman Theater), once the largest theater in all Gaul, with seating for 15,000 spectators. The ruins, impressive in scope, are pleasantly melancholy in these landscaped surroundings. From the theater you can walk atop the ramparts all the way to the Tour des Ursulines, a 12th-century keep, back in the southern part of town; you could also use the ramparts as a scenic route from the Cathédrale St-Lazare to Roman Autun.

If you retrace your steps up rue Théâtre Romain you will come, just past the traffic circle, to the **Porte St-André**, one of four gateways and 62 semicircular towers in the Gallo-Roman fortifications. Tradition says it was near this gate that Saint Symphorien, one of the most revered martyrs of Roman Gaul, was beheaded as his mother shouted condolences to him from the wall.

From here, follow rue de Gaillan northwest to the avenue de la République. Then turn north on rue de Paris to the **Porte d'Arroux**. Beautifully proportioned and well preserved, it was built in the time of Constantine. It gave access to Agrippa's Way, which once linked Lyon with Boulogne. Just beyond, in the middle of a plain beyond the Arroux gate, only a square tower remains of what was once the **Temple de Janus** (actually, the temple was dedicated to an unknown god).

STAYING AND DINING
IN AND AROUND AUTUN

Just beyond the Porte d'Arroux, Dominique Tarel's **Hostellerie du Vieux Moulin** serves outstanding meals (outdoors in summer) in a restored mill. This is the best place to dine in the immediate neighborhood; Tel: 85-52-10-90. For another superb dining experience, drive 43 km (27 miles) east on D 973 and D 6 to **Chagny** and the three-star restaurant ► **Lameloise**, which occupies an elegantly reworked Burgundian home with 20 rooms for overnight guests (dining reservations are important; Tel: 85-87-08-85). An unusual dish to try is *ravioli d'escargots de bourgogne*.

The best hotels are also outside the town. The ► **Hostellerie Château de Bellecroix**, a delightful 21-room inn near Chagny, has its own park and outdoor swimming pool. (Drive 3 km/2 miles south of Chagny on N 6, then take the Bellecroix turnoff.) The 14-room ► **Chez Camille** in the old town of Arnay-le-Duc, 28 km (17 miles) north of Autun on N 81, occupies a 16th-century mansion, with 11 rooms in a new annex. Reserve well in advance and request room number 17.

The mansion's central court has been converted into a dining room that resembles a winter garden; the cuisine of Armand Poinsot is as admirable as the setting. The capon (a Burgundian specialty) cooked in his house manner is delectable. Accompany it with one of the regional wines, Hautes Côtes de Beaune.

A 17th-century almshouse in the town's center is now a gallery for the exhibition and sale of regional crafts and specialties. Arnay is surrounded by deeply rural countryside.

UCHON AND SULLY

The **Signal d'Uchon** is a circular drive of about 70 km (43 miles) that affords views of the exterior of the lavish Château de Sully, northeast of Autun, and also takes in the hamlet of Uchon, 24 km (15 miles) south of Autun. To make the drive to Uchon and its panoramic overlook, leave Autun by the little road to the south marked D 120, veer west on D 256, and follow clearly marked D 46 and D 228 to the village of Uchon. Wiggle south and uphill on D 275 for about a mile. There's a little hotel and a parking lot near the top; leave the car and follow the path for a few yards to the marker at 2,133 feet. The village of **Uchon** is most photogenic; note the oratory with a figure of the Virgin Mary atop its column, where pilgrims came in the 16th century to pray for the end of the Black Death.

The **Château de Sully** is on the northeastern perimeter of the circuit. Should you wish to go there directly from Autun, take D 973 east of Autun to a point just west of the hamlet of la Drée, where D 26 turns north for the 5-km (3-mile) run into Sully. The château, often called the Fontainebleau of Burgundy, may remind you in its Renaissance beauty of Ancy-le-Franc. For complete details about the château, ask at the Office de Tourisme in Autun, at 3, avenue Charles-de-Gaulle near the Hôtel de Ville; Tel: 85-52-20-34.

Tournus

The traffic thundering along N 6 tends to bypass Tournus. Perhaps that is why the little city (about 7,000 Tournusiens) 57 km (35 miles) south of Beaune seems antique and slumbering. It deserves to slumber; it was a settlement of the Eduen tribe long before the Romans built a camp in the area. Around A.D. 180, Saint Valerien came to Tournus as an evangelist and was martyred on a hill overlooking the river Saône. History ignored the settlement, it seems, until the ninth century, when monks from Ile de Noirmoutier, off the coast of Brittany, fled Norman invaders and arrived in this quiet spot to shelter the relics of their founder, Saint Philibert.

Your first stop in town should be the **Eglise St-Philibert**; take rue Albert-Thibaudet east off N 6 and pass between two round towers into the Place de l'Abbaye. Begun in the late tenth or early 11th century and completed by the end of the

12th, this grand example of early Romanesque style is older than the better-known abbey at Cluny. The thick-walled crypt and the narthex, with its short, powerful pillars—solid, strong, and impressive—are the two oldest elements of the abbey. The nave, with its alternating pink and white stones and unusual arrangement of transverse bays and very tall masonry pillars, soars with a lightness unusual in the Romanesque.

The **Musée Greuze**, a short walk south of St-Philibert on rue A. Bessard, houses archaeological collections and canvases by local painter Jean-Baptiste Greuze, whose works may seem overly sentimental to today's eyes. There are reconstructions of old Burgundian home interiors, in the **Musée Perrin-de-Puycousin**, directly across the narrow street north of the church in the 17th-century treasury building.

STAYING AND DINING IN TOURNUS

A couple of good hotels, ▶ **Hôtel de Greuze** and ▶ **Le Rempart**, make Tournus a pleasant stop for excursions into the countryside, particularly to Cluny. De Greuze offers 19 rooms and four suites just across the street from the remarkable abbey, and is not related to the well-known **Restaurant Greuze** a couple of doors away, where chef Jean Ducloux commands as much respect as the better-known, aforementioned, "Les Six." Restaurant Greuze is renowned for its pike *quenelles* and pâté *en croûte;* it's fairly expensive (reserve; Tel: 85-51-13-52). Le Rempart, right at the old wall across a little park south of De Greuze, has 31 rooms, six suites, and its own fine kitchen, starring a salad of roasted spiny lobster (reserve; Tel: 85-51-10-56).

Cluny

Cluny nestles among woods and fields in the green valley of the meandering Grosne southwest of Tournus. (The best way to reach Cluny from Tournus is to follow N 6 south for about 14 km/8½ miles to Fleurville, then take the turnoff via D 15 west for another 24 km/15 miles.) Today, its battles over and out of the spotlight, Cluny is a peaceful and small country town of Romanesque and Gothic houses and fewer than 5,000 Clusinois.

In the Middle Ages, though, Cluny, "as dark as the hood of a monk's cloak," as poet Alphonse de Lamartine had it, dominated the religious, artistic, intellectual, and political life of Western Europe. Its struggle with the Cistercians and Saint Bernard from the early 12th century split Christianity in ways still in evidence today. Saint Benedict created the order that bears his name at Montecassino, in Italy, about 529, but its greatest monastery did not appear in the wilds of Burgundy for another 400 years. The Benedictine abbey at Cluny was founded on September 11, 910, by Guillaume le Pieux (the Pious), duc d'Aquitaine. Less than a hundred years later it had achieved immense power and prestige: Some 1,500 brotherhoods across France and in England, Germany, Spain, Switzerland, and even Poland depended on Cluny. "Wherever the wind blows," went a saying of the time, "the abbot of Cluny owns."

THE BENEDICTINE ABBEY

The immense abbey was conceived by one of Cluny's abbots, Saint Hugues de Semur, who laid the first stone in 1088. Major construction was completed in only 20 years, but building went on until 1130. Cluny was the physical as well as spiritual pride of Christendom, remaining the largest church in the world for 500 years until it was exceeded (and then by only ten yards in length) by St. Peter's in Rome.

The Benedictine rule made liturgical prayer the primary occupation of monks, to be complemented by sacred reading, manual labor, practice of the arts, and *opus divinum* (praising God) through the splendor of churches and the beauty of liturgy and hymns. The rule came to be recognized as the fundamental monastic code of Western Europe. Cluniac houses—the first at Barnstaple, the second at Lewes—were introduced to England by William the Conqueror; by the 13th century there were 40 dependencies in England.

"You are the light of the world," Pope Urban II said to Cluny abbot Saint Hugues in 1098. The greatness of Cluny sprang from the genius of its seven great abbots (Pontius is usually excepted) over 250 years. When Peter the Venerable died in about 1157, slow decline set in, perhaps the inevitable result of riches and international power.

Serious decline set in for Cluny in the 14th century; the Wars of Religion in the 16th century almost struck a death blow, and the Revolution completed the job. The abbey was closed in 1790, and in 1798 the whole was sold to a merchant from Mâcon, who demolished the nave. By 1823 only the near ruins visible today were left of Cluny's medieval magnificence. (In 1330 the abbey of Cluny bought land in Paris to build a residence for abbots attending a college near the Sorbonne; what remains of the luxurious residence constitutes today's **Musée National du Moyen-Age/Thermes de Cluny**; see the Paris section.)

THE ABBEY REMAINS
What remains of Cluny today are the two Baraban towers at the entrance to the narthex, part of the porch, bits of the south side aisle, a chapel on the south side of the lesser transept, an octagonal belfry known as Clocher de l'Eau Bénite (Holy Water), and the south end of the larger transept. These remains manage to transmit a sense of the strength, daring, and splendor of the immense abbey. (Hour-long guided tours from July to late September, in French only, are an invaluable aid to understanding what Cluny really was; an English-language self-guiding brochure is available.)

In the **Farinier**, once the flour or meal barn, remnants of the abbey are displayed, including some capitals from the choir, masterpieces of Romanesque sculpture.

CLUNY TODAY
Cluny affords not much more than a pleasant ramble down its old streets. The **Musée Ochier** houses paintings, architectural remnants, and other *objets* from the collections of the 19th-century Ochier family. Climb the 120 steps of the Tour des Fromages for a view over the countryside. A music festival, Les Grandes Heures, is held in Cluny in August.

Staying and Dining in Cluny
The town's serenity makes it a nice place to stay for a night or two. Across from the abbey's ruins the ▶ **Hôtel de Bourgogne** has an eminently satisfactory restaurant and 15 guest rooms furnished in cozy country fashion. It sits at the edge of pretty gardens in which stands an ancient lime tree called "the lime of Abélard." The philosopher-monk took refuge here near the end of his life. Only 11 km (7 miles) east via D 134 is the ▶ **Château d'Igé**, a handsome retreat in the tiny village of Igé that offers seven rooms and six suites in a fortified château built by the dukes of Mâcon in the 13th century.

Discriminating travellers have for years sought out the hotel ▶ **Chapon Fin et Restaurant Paul Blanc**, about 35 km (22 miles) southeast of Cluny in the village of Thoissey. (Take D 980 5 km/3 miles south from Cluny to Berzé-le-Châtel, then head southeast on N 79 to its juncture with A 6, then south to the Thoissey turnoff.) Perhaps it's the warm welcome of the Blanc-Maringue family that does the trick, or the elegance of its 20 rooms, the relaxed setting, or the excellence of the kitchen. Try the crayfish ravioli in herb butter, from June to December, or chicken fricassee with creamed *morilles*. This is also a good place in which to introduce yourself to the Mâconnais wine named St-Véran. Tel: 74-04-04-74.

Mâcon

From Cluny it's a 26-km (16-mile) run south and east on D
22 and N 79 to Mâcon, not far from Solutré, one of the most
intriguing archaeological sites of all prehistory.

Mâcon is worth a stop during a day's drive (perhaps to
Bourg-en-Bresse, below), even if you don't wish to spend
the night. The reason to visit is the **Musée des Ursulines**,
installed in the 17th-century convent of the Ursuline order.

Entering town from the north (probably on N 6, if coming
from Cluny), you'll be on the avenue de Lattre de Tassigny.
Watch on the right for rue du 28-Juin 1944, take it west to the
Place Gardon, and turn south on the cours Moreau. When
you arrive at the green Square de la Paix near the Hôtel-
Dieu, look for a place to park. The museum is a couple of
winding streets east on rue des Ursulines.

All the collections here are worthwhile, but what you have
come to see is the prehistory room with its stunning presentation on the excavations at Solutré, where the finds were
great enough to give their name to a period of the Stone
Age, the Solutrian Era. Three rooms describe the Celtic and
Gallo-Roman eras with ceramics, stelae, and the like. There
are also Gallo-Roman and Mérovingian arms. At least see the
ground floor, even if you haven't time for more contemporary works also housed here.

Walk from the museum to have lunch at **Rocher de
Cancale**, about four blocks east along the Saône at 393, quai
Jean-Jaurès; Tel: 85-38-07-50.

Bourg-en-Bresse and Brou

In a land so rich in artistic, culinary, and architectural triumphs as Burgundy, perhaps it is inevitable that some wonders are overlooked. So it is in the case of Bourg-en-Bresse
and Brou, slightly off the tourism lanes on the way to the
Jura and Switzerland.

Whether you are driving south from Tournus or east from
Cluny, take N 79 east from a turnoff just north of Mâcon; N 79
merges into D 975 just outside the Bourg city limits.

Something about Bourg (pronounced "Bourk") makes
you wonder why you haven't heard much about it before.
It's a busy, bustling place, but one with a decent respect for
the undisturbed luncheon and the glass or so consumed at
the sidewalk café. It's particularly exciting on market days,
Wednesdays and Saturdays, from 8:00 A.M. to noon on the
large Champ de Foire, on the northeast edge of downtown

along avenue Maginot (Wednesday's market is the bigger of the two).

As you amble about the heart of town (the streets just west of Notre-Dame), window shop for the Bresse country furniture in traditional styles, made of walnut, wild cherry, cherry, and pear trees. Bresse enamels and Meillonnas pottery are good regional buys.

Dining in Bourg

Bourg derives its fame from its chickens, widely admitted to being the finest in France. (They consume a diet rich in corn, and before being eaten are bathed in milk and then powdered, so that they go to market glistening white.) In Bresse itself the chicken usually is simply roasted in order to best preserve its delicate flavor; so done, it appears on menus as *poularde* rather than *poulet de Bresse.*

A major excuse for visiting Bresse is thus to dine upon chicken, which can best be done at **Jacques Guy**, 19, place Bernard, a few steps east of Notre-Dame and near a parking lot. It is always thronged, so reserve; Tel: 74-45-29-11. If you'd like simpler surroundings, try the modest **Le Français** at 7, avenue Alsace-Lorraine (the main street; the Office de Tourisme is at number 6). It's a popular local brasserie, friendly and unfussy, where you can accompany your *poularde* with a potato *gratin,* good local cheeses, and a bottle of simple Burgundy. Tel: 74-22-55-14.

THE CHURCH AT BROU

What makes Bourg a real destination, however, is not chicken but a masterwork of Flamboyant Gothic, the church at Brou. Once a small village that grew up around a Benedictine monastery, Brou is now part of the southeastern suburbs of Bourg, reached by driving out of town on the boulevard de Brou.

Everything about this church (now secularized) is remarkable (including its romantic history, which should be read on the spot; brochures and booklets are available in English at the tourism office and at the church). The church and monastery were built in the 16th century in one sustained creative burst. Its exterior is richly sculpted, and the light from the clerestory bathes the white limestone of the nave. But neither matches in evocative power the rood screen and the choir, with its richly detailed stalls, stained glass windows, and three monumental tombs in Carrara marble of Margaret of Bourbon, Margaret of Austria, and Philibert the Handsome. Almost as wonderful are the chapels and oratories. A fine **museum** is installed in the greater cloisters.

Staying and Dining in Brou

If on leaving the church you feel faint from hunger and the exhausting effects of fine art, you have only to step across the street to the **Auberge Bressane** to restore yourself with local dishes, perhaps in the café's pleasant garden. Reservations are necessary only in the height of the tourist season; Tel: 74-22-22-68. The immaculate and handsomely furnished 14-room ▶ **Le Prieuré** is the best inn in the immediate region; it's just north of the church at 49, boulevard de Brou.

Leaving Bourg-en-Bresse, you can retrace your steps to Mâcon or drive 62 km (38 miles) southwest to Lyon via N 83.

THE RHONE VALLEY

Since the beginning of recorded history in Europe, the Rhône, its tributaries, and its valley have constituted a major highway system for invaders, traders, civilizers, and conquerors. As long ago as 20,000 B.C. Paleolithic man left engravings on the rock walls of caves. Many sites bear witness to the occupations of Neolithic times (around 8000 B.C.), and by the time of the Bronze Age (2000 B.C.) the Rhône had become a watery thoroughfare for the transportation of amber and tin.

In 121 B.C. Roman legions established camps on the east bank of the river at the site of today's Vienne. Lyon was established (as Lugdunum) in 43 B.C. and soon became the capital of the Gauls.

The Burgundian tribes likewise selected Vienne as their capital, in the fifth century, while in the Middle Ages various French kings attempted to seize control of the valley. In 1419 the future Charles VII established the first fairs in Lyon, making the town one of the world's great commercial centers. The fairs lost much of their importance after Medieval times, but the one at Lyon was revived in 1916.

During World War II Lyon was a headquarters of the Resistance; retreating German armies destroyed many of the river's bridges in 1944.

For the traveller's purposes, the valley of the Rhône stretches from Mâcon in the north to Orange in the south (for Orange, see the Provence chapter), from the regions of Auvergne and Causses in the west to the Alps in the east. Most visitors to the Rhône Valley confine themselves to the

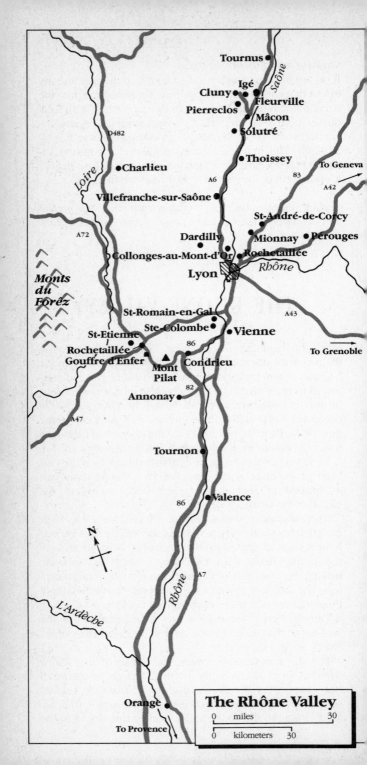

Tournus

Saône

Igé
Cluny
Fleurville
Pierreclos
Mâcon
Solutré

Thoissey

To Geneva

Charlieu

83

A42

Loire

D482

A6

Villefranche-sur-Saône

St-André-de-Corcy

A72

Dardilly
Mionnay
Pérouges
Collonges-au-Mont-d'Or
Rochetaillée

Lyon
Rhône

Monts
du
Forêz

St-Romain-en-Gal
A43

Ste-Colombe
Vienne

St-Etienne
86
Rochetaillée
Gouffre d'Enfer
Mont
Pilat
Condrieu

To Grenoble

82

Annonay

A47

Tournon

86

Valence

N

A7

L'Ardèche

Rhône

Orange

To Provence

The Rhône Valley

| 0 | miles | 30 |

| 0 | kilometers | 30 |

cities along the river corridor—Lyon, Vienne, Valence—at
the same time complaining about over-industrialization. Yet
to the east and particularly to the west of A 7, the rough
plateaus, the woods, and the glacier-sliced valleys are almost empty of inhabitants, certainly of travellers.

Just to the north of Lyon and east of the river, in the
region called La Dombes, the landscape remains serene,
punctuated with little glacier-carved lakes that reflect the
blue sky and dotted with forests. South of Lyon the Rhône
runs between the Monts du Lyonnais in the west, a region
of high, grassy hills, piney woods, and fertile lands well
suited to vegetable-growing. In the east stretches the Bas-
Dauphiné, a high plateau stretching off to the foot of the
Alps. Continuing southward the river cuts between the
volcanic crests of the Vivarais in the west and the plains of
Valence in the east, where the winds seem to blow north
from Provence and the Mediterranean. Some fascinating
drives may be made through this region, especially in the
valley of the Ardèche, north of Orange.

LYON

It is not easy to evade Lyon. Autoroutes from the north (A 6),
from the south (A 7), from the east (A 42) and southeast (A
43), from the west (A 47), and through-routes from all
directions are sucked into the maw of the city like so many
strands of spaghetti. The third-largest city in France, with a
population of about half a million and a metropolitan area
comprising almost 1.25 million, Lyon is today less and less a
city that people need to make excuses for as they would for
some well-intentioned but dull old relative. The visual bourgeois stolidity of the city, once perceived by many as a curse,
suddenly seems, in the midst of our own fin de siècle, to be
of great value for the aura of authenticity it generates. This
city's architectural harmony is much appreciated by travellers as a fine example of a rare, major French urban center
that hasn't been ham-handedly and hysterically modernized.

Yet in some ways Lyon is just an overgrown village. Away
from the high-rises and commercial centers that have sprung
up during the last two decades or so, the narrow lanes of Old
Lyon give you the sense of Paris in the 1930s, the one familiar
from the works of Gertrude Stein, Hemingway, Joyce, and
Ford Madox Ford.

To orient yourself to Lyon, imagine it as if you were
looking down from a helicopter, with its peninsula cradled
in the arms of the Saône river to the west and the Rhône to

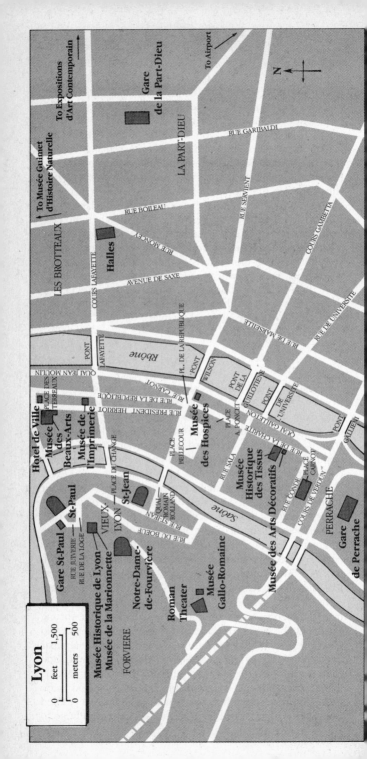

the east. Centered over the old railway station near the tip of the peninsula, you would look directly down at Perrache, in the 2nd *arrondissement;* ahead is the smartest district, Bellecour, also in the 2nd; just north of that is Cordeliers/ République and Place de la République, where the 1st and 2nd *arrondissements* meet; then there's Terreaux, a division of the 1st *arrondissement,* with Place des Terreaux and the Hôtel de Ville. Far beyond is a meeting of the 4th and 1st *arrondissements* in Croix-Rousse, where the silk industry first flourished.

Off to the left, you would spot Vieux-Lyon/Fourvière (5th *arrondissement*), while to the right is Guillotière (7th–3rd *arrondissements*), Part-Dieu (3rd *arrondissement,* the new railway station, shopping centers, etc.), and—on the eastern horizon—Gerland (7th *arrondissement*) and the international airport at Satolas.

THE HERITAGE OF LYON

As the story goes, two Celtic princes stopped one day at the dramatic meeting place of the Saône and Rhône rivers and deemed it a propitious spot for a city, so they began to dig. A cloud of ravens swept up and over them. Taking that as a sign from Providence, they dubbed their new town Lugdunum, hill of the ravens.

In 43 B.C. the Romans made Lugdunum their base for the conquest of Gaul. Agrippa built five great roads extending out from it, and Augustus later built aqueducts, temples, and a theater. Tiberius Claudius Drusus was born in Lugdunum on August 1, 10 B.C., during Augustus's reign. Considered a booby as a child, he nonetheless became Claudius, emperor of Rome, in A.D. 41, as which he conquered most of Britain and accomplished much else besides. After a fire in 59, Nero reworked and beautified the city, and succeeding emperors continued the job.

In 177 Marcus Aurelius ordered the slaughter of local Christian leaders in the amphitheater, an act followed 20 years later by Septimius Severus's massacre of some 18,000 Christians, including Irenaeus, bishop of Lyon. His shrine remained in the church of St-Irénée until it was destroyed by Calvinists in 1562.

The 15th century saw the installation of the great fairs that made Lyon a commercial hub, so that when silk manufacturing spread (it was until the 16th century a purely Italian craft), Lyon jumped into the industrial world. New fabrics were invented: silks woofed with wool, watered silks, poplins, moirés, and so forth.

The tradition of the literary salon may seem to have been

confined to Paris, but it flourished in Lyon from time to time as well, most spectacularly at the end of the 15th century in the days and nights of Louise Labé, la Belle Cordière. (She married Ennemond Perrin, a rope maker, or *cordier*.) Accomplished in several languages, beautiful, a musician and poet, la Belle Cordière, a precursor of Madame de Sévigné, held open house for the intelligentsia of her day.

By 1548 there were more than 400 printing studios in town, as well as a host of painters, sculptors, and ceramicists. Rabelais published his *Gargantua and Pantagruel* in Lyon, to be sold during the annual fairs.

Lyon always has been in the forefront of France's political life. In 1793 widespread resistance against the Convention resulted in a terrible reaction by Robespierre and, subsequently, the Terror. Hundreds of Lyonnais were murdered, beautiful old houses around Place Bellecour were put to the torch, and the very name of the town was changed, to Commune Affranchie (Free Community).

The creator of the wooden puppet named Guignol and thus of all the Grand Guignol shows in France was Laurent Mourguet, a Lyonnais weaver born in 1769. The wide-eyed handpuppet Guignol always dresses in a black silkworker's cap and tunic. His sidekick, the red-nosed, Beaujolais-drinking Gnafron, and Guignol's wife, Madelon, are the principals in a slapstick comedy of errors that is played out regularly in both indoor and outdoor puppet theaters around France.

Guignol came to life when a post-Revolution decline in the demand for silk put many Lyonnais *canuts* (piece workers, including Mourguet) out of work. Mourguet set up shop as a street dentist, manipulating his marionette to distract patients from their pains. Successful as an entertainer, he gave up dentistry and replaced his marionette with a soft, hollow-bodied doll—the world's first handpuppet. Guignol performances are given most days of the week at the Nouveau Guignol de Lyon at the Palais du Conservatoire, rue Louis-Carrand. Inquire about precise times at your hotel.

André-Marie Ampère (1775–1836), a locally famous physicist and absent-minded professor, gave his name to the basic unit of electrical current. The Musée Claude Bernard in nearby St-Julien-en-Beaujolais honors the creator of experimental medicine. In 1896 Louis and Auguste Lumière debuted their first films here, and the world witnessed the birth of cinematography.

In the early 19th century J. M. Jacquard introduced a loom here by which a single worker could do the work of six in creating elaborate fabrics. Homes became factories for *canuts* to whom silk makers supplied fabrics. The center of this activity was today's Croix-Rousse district.

Lyon never has ceased to build upon its industrial inheritance; today's enterprises are grouped in contiguous suburbs. Lyon is also a center for scientific research, engineering, and communications, and it has an international airport at Satolas, a fairly new Métro system, and TGV traffic to and from Paris and the south.

Touring Lyon

If you arrive in Lyon from Paris by train, your first sight of the city will be the Part-Dieu railroad station and shopping complex, east of the shopping-dining heart of the city. (The TGV whizzes from Paris to Lyon in two hours.) The first site you explore, however, will be that of Roman Lyon.

FOURVIERE, THE ROMAN HILL

The view from the terrace of the 19th-century **Basilique Notre-Dame-de-Fourvière** is what the Romans saw in the second century—the joining arms of the Saône and the Rhône rivers and, off in the distance, the mountainous horizon that rises to become the Alps. In the foreground, however, those builders saw no metropolis, no industrial suburbs, no towers or hotels or railroad stations testifying to the importance of COURLY (Communauté Urbaine Lyon). To reach Fourvière, on the west side of the Saône, take a funicular to either Notre-Dame-de-Fourvière or the Roman theaters. The large **theater**, the oldest in France and about the size of those in Orange and Arles, still serves as a venue for performances of music and dramatic arts from about mid-June to mid-July.

If you see nothing more in Lyon than Fourvière's **Musée de la Civilisation Gallo-Romaine**, adjoining the Roman theater, the trip will have been worthwhile. Opened in 1975, it is an unsurpassed repository of prehistoric, Gallic, and Roman art in France: Paleolithic and Neolithic tools, a chariot from the early Iron Age, a Gallic calendar engraved in bronze, magnificent mosaics, antique glass, pottery, and kitchen utensils.

Perhaps the most valuable find from modern digs in the city was that of the **Claudian Tables**, an inscription on bronze of a speech by Claudius delivered in A.D. 48 before the Roman Senate, in which the Lyon-born emperor urged that the chiefs of Gallic nations might succeed in their attempts to be elected as Roman magistrates.

VIEUX LYON

It is in the narrow streets and charming courtyards of Vieux Lyon, below and north of the Fourvière hill on the banks of the Saône river, shadowed by tall houses, that you feel, finally, comfortable in a city that without this heart would seem disjointed and difficult to comprehend. There is a sense, in Old Lyon, of neighborhood, of a villagelike intimacy where you greet the corner grocer by name, meet friends for lunch at a family restaurant, and buy fresh flowers to spruce up the apartment.

The principal artery of the quarter is rue St-Jean, which slices it neatly in two from about the Gare St-Jean in the south (near the terminus of the funiculars up the Fourvière hill) to the Place du Change in the north, from which rue de la Lainerie continues to the *place* and the Gare St-Paul. It's a walk of about a kilometer (half a mile), not counting detours to the left and right through *traboules*—the narrow passageways left over from the Middle Ages—that debouch into minuscule market squares, beautifully decorated courtyards, or even, surprisingly, upon the openness of a river quai. In Vieux Lyon, and in the smart peninsular region between the Saône and Rhône rivers, the *traboules* form a network of passages tunneling under, through, and around the ancient houses. *Traboule* derives from the Latin *trans ambulare,* "to walk through." The Lyonnais even employ a verb otherwise unknown in French, *trabouler.*

Cathédrale St-Jean

Begun in the 11th century, the Cathédrale St-Jean, near the southern end of rue St-Jean, is a Gothic mass rising upon a Romanesque base; it was the seat of the primate, or first bishop, of Gaul. The façade owes its fine decorations to the 14th century. Inside, the greatest treasure is the 12th-century choir, and some beautiful 13th-century stained glass has survived. On the north side of St-Jean, excavations of a much earlier church are under way.

Along Rue St-Jean

Walking up this beautiful street, you will spot marvelous architectural details: sculpted gables, corridors with pointed arches (ogives), outcrops of little towers, Italianate galleries, statues of the Virgin high up in niches, wrought-iron signs. Among the most famous and amusing of the last is that of a bull at the corner of, appropriately, the rue du Boeuf and the Place Neuve-St-Jean; it is the work of sculptor Giovanni Bologna (1529–1608, known in France as Jean de Bologne). A delightful little Adoration of the Magi on the façade of the nearby 17th-century Maison du Crible is also accredited to Bologna.

The old town preserves a wealth of at least 300 houses dating from the Renaissance. Along rue Juiverie, rue de la Loge, rue de Gadagne, and around the Place du Change these proud houses stand shoulder to shoulder, representing the end of the Gothic period, the Italian-inspired Renaissance, the French Renaissance, and pre-Neoclassic days.

A Walk Through the Traboules

To experience the *traboules* in this quarter, enter the narrow passageway at number 19, rue St-Jean, and emerge in moments on the rue des Trois-Marie. Walk north, hesitating to admire the houses at numbers 5 and 7, where small statues in niches represent the Virgin and a Christ between two female saints, into the charming Place de la Baleine and rejoin rue St-Jean on the west. Continue up the street (north) a few steps to the Place du Gouvernement with, in its northeast corner, the **Hôtel du Gouvernement**. Follow the traboule right through it and you will come out on the quai Romain Rolland, where there's a handsome view across the Saône. Walk again to your left and enter the traboule at number 8. You will find yourself in a beautiful Renaissance courtyard and exit at number 9, back on rue St-Jean.

At this point, turn left into the courtyard of the building at number 11, one of the most striking in Vieux Lyon, notable for its Flamboyant decoration and a stairway twisting up for eight floors.

PLACES BELLECOUR AND DES TERREAUX

Place Bellecour and its peninsula, between the Saône to the west and the Rhône to the east, is the heart of contemporary Lyon and one of the largest such squares in France, bordered on east and west by handsome, symmetrical Louis XVI houses. It sits atop a large parking garage, a handy place to leave your car. Place Bellecour is within walking distance of several hotels (in various price ranges), museums, and shopping streets.

Smaller than Bellecour but also more animated, Place des Terreaux was near the confluence of the rivers in Roman times. Today it's the confluence of sidewalk cafés; its fountain is the work of Bartholdi. Walks in the area of Terreaux reveal several curious *traboules,* the Musée des Beaux-Arts (discussed below), pretty squares, and a collection of renowned restaurants.

A Walk Near Place des Terreaux

An intriguing walk through one of the least "spoiled" neighborhoods of Lyon begins and ends just north and east of the Place des Terreaux, in the Place Tolozan on the banks of the Rhône. It takes about an hour and a half to amble along these narrow, old ways where you can easily imagine the incessant click-clacks of hand-operated machines used by some 30,000 *canuts* (silk weavers) in the 19th century.

Begin on the northwest edge of the Place Tolozan at number 19, where a short traboule leads to petite-rue des Feuillants. Crossing that street, enter number 5, and after a longer passage you will exit at number 5 on the parklike Place Croix-Paquet. Veer to your left around the point of the *place* and enter number 11, quickly exiting at number 32, rue Leynaud.

From there, stroll to west on Leynaud to the **Eglise St-Polycarpe**. Facing the church, an entry at number 25 leads into the passage Mermet, inside which a stairway leads to rue Burdeau. Cross the street and veer right and up the montée du Perron along the delightful Place Chardonnet. You'll find at the northeast corner of this *place* a stairway on the rue des Tables-Claudiennes. Walk up and enter the traboule at number 55. You will come out at 20, rue Imbert-Colomès.

Crossing Imbert-Colomès, enter again at number 29. You will then traverse a series of four courtyards at different levels (take the stairs in the first one and enter number 14 *bis*). Exiting at 9, place Colbert, follow the montée St-Sebastien north to boulevard de la Croix-Rousse and, on your right (east), you'll see the so-called Gros Caillou (Big Boulder). The stone was deposited here during glacial times, when the site of Lyon was being shaped, and is very popular with the Lyonnais as a symbol of sturdiness.

The return is much less complicated—and downhill. Walk around the "back" (east) of the Gros Caillou into the Place Bellevue and take the stairway on the left down to rue Philibert-Delorme and slightly east to rue des Fantasques, at which point there's a lovely view over the Rhône. From here it's a long, straight stroll down rue des Fantasques, which joins montée St-Sébastien, returning you to the Place Croix-Paquet.

From there, turn slightly west into rue des Capucins and enter the traboule at number 26, coming out at 2, rue Romarin. Cross the street, enter number 3, and exit at 5, Place du Griffon. On its southwest corner, you'll enter rue St-Claude and go through number 3, emerging at 8, rue du

Griffon. Cross Griffon into number 9, and you will make your final exit at number 21 on the Place Tolozan, where you began.

LEFT BANK OF THE RHONE

The TGV and most other trains deposit travellers at the giant Gare de la Part-Dieu, which has become the center of an entirely new commercial area, with hotels to match and Le Grand Espace Shopping, with movie houses, restaurants and bars, a bowling alley, a discothèque, and more than 200 stores. It's also a central departure point for the local Métro. You could get lost in this modern complex and never find your way out. (Some trains still arrive at the Gare de Perrache on the peninsula; check your ticket at time of purchase.)

North of Part-Dieu, the 42-acre **Parc de la Tête d'Or** (named Golden Head because of a traditional story that a head of Christ worked in gold was found buried here) is graced with Europe's largest rose garden, La Roseraie, with more than five million blossoms in season. It's also a good place to limber up on the huge rowing lake and along jogging paths, and there are outstanding zoological and botanical gardens here as well. From the Gare de la Port-Dieu, the boulevard J. Faure and boulevard des Belges lead north to the park gates.

THE MUSEUMS OF LYON

Few French cities outside Paris possess as large and satisfying a collection of museums as does Lyon; the best known is the **Musée des Beaux-Arts**, located at 20, place des Terreaux in the enormous Palais St-Pierre, built in the 17th century as a Benedictine nunnery for gentle ladies. The 90 rooms are devoted to sculptures of various periods and paintings from all the great ages of European art. There are also some Oriental displays. The **Musée de la Civilisation Gallo-Romaine** (on the Fourvière hill, see above) is the other museum that should on no account be overlooked.

The **Musée Historique des Tissus**, at 34, rue de la Charité, contains the largest collection of textiles in the world, including a wing of 12 rooms devoted to Oriental rugs, fabrics, and tapestries. The French collections are naturally the most important; overall, fabrics date from the fourth century to today. The museum is about halfway between Place Bellecour and the Perrache station and adjoins the **Musée des Arts Décoratifs**. This latter museum is a step back into the 18th century; it is completely outfitted in furniture, objets d'art, faïence, tapestries, porcelain, tableware, and so forth. Especially noteworthy is the Italian Renaissance faïence collection.

In Vieux Lyon near the Place du Change, the **Musée Historique de Lyon** (in the former 15th-century mansion of the Gadagne brothers at 10-14, rue de Gadagne) shows off a remarkable collection of Romanesque sculptures, furnishings, faïence from Nevers, and items illustrating the history of Lyon throughout the centuries. Part and almost parcel of this museum is the **Musée International de la Marionnette**, with an exceptional puppet show of figures from as far away as Cambodia and Java but centered, quite naturally, on the Guignols.

If you are strongly inclined toward museum meandering and have time to spare, also consider the **Musée Guimet d'Histoire Naturelle** at 28, boulevard des Belges (all animals represented from mammoths to humans, with special emphasis on regional finds); the **Musée de l'Imprimerie et de la Banque**, which illustrates the importance of banking and printing through the ages (13, rue de la Poulaillerie), and the **Musée de la Résistance et de la Déportation** (5, rue Boileau), with evidences of the horrors of war and the Nazi death camps, including displays depicting the crimes of Klaus Barbie, who was imprisoned and tried in Lyon and sentenced in 1987 to life imprisonment. The **Musée des Hospices Civils** (in the 17th-century wing of the Hôtel-Dieu on Place de l'Hôpital), contains exhibitions of medical and hospital life from the 17th century on. Visit also the **Musée Africain** at 150, cours Gambetta, and the **Musée St-Pierre d'Art Contemporain** at 11, rue du Dr-Dollard.

Car buffs may wish to make an excursion to the **Musée de l'Automobile Henri-Malartre**, in a 15th-century château and its park on the banks of the Saône. Depart Lyon along the quai J. Gillet to the north and continue on D 433 about 10 km (6 miles) to the suburb of Rochetaillée. Just before entering the village, follow the museum's directional signs to the left. The museum's collection of more than 200 vehicles includes automobiles dating from 1890 to 1968, bicycles, and motorcycles, all in operating condition. It's open every day except Christmas and New Year's Day.

SHOPPING IN LYON

Lyon's chic street is **rue du Président Edouard-Herriot**, which connects Place Bellecour to Place des Terreaux. Here are the shops of Descamps, Charles Jourdan, Alain Manoukian, and Georges Rech, among other ruiners of budgets. **Rue de la République**, in the same area, is also smart.

The one-stop shopping center of **La Part-Dieu** provides a pick of some 220 stores, big and small, including Galeries Lafayette, Jelmoli, Darty, and England's imperishable Marks and Spencer. **Rue St-Jean**, the crowded pedestrian main street of Vieux Lyon, takes the cake and other items for trendy fashions. Stop on the Place du Change at **L'Ateyer de Guignol** for a gift nobody else has: a traditional Guignol puppet handmade to resemble a friend or yourself (take along photographs).

More than 150 galleries offering antiques and high-quality secondhand items are gathered in **Brocante Stalingrad** in the Villeurbanne district, the eastern, industrial part of greater Lyon. It's the third-largest European market for antiques. (*Brocante* is French for "secondhand.")

In the traditional cloth-making quarter of Croix-Rousse, **La Maison des Canuts** is a weavers' cooperative that operates a museum-cum–retail outlet. Old cut-velvets, damask, and portraits woven in silk are on display, as are a Jacquard handloom and a demonstration of silk making. Before the Industrial Revolution, some 60,000 looms clattered away in Lyon's family workshops. This cooperative still creates and sells silks at very reasonable prices: ties, scarves, handkerchiefs, foulards, and more.

Chocolate fiends and their friends should not leave town without visiting **Bernachon Chocolatier** (42, cours Franklin-Roosevelt). Many consider this family-owned firm to be the best artisanal producer of chocolate in France; to achieve such heart-stopping quality they roast their own cocoa beans, extract their own vanilla essence, and work exclusively with top-quality raw ingredients. Gaining access to their truffles and chocolate-dipped fruit would be grounds for homicide. To find the perfect gustatory accessory to your shopping spree here, stop by **La Boite à Dessert** (1, rue de l'Ancienne-Préfecture). The quiches and breads are superb, and the fruit tarts have the still-life-like perfection of Flemish masters, which isn't surprising, since owners Marc and Marie Maloyan are fans of Renaissance painting.

STAYING IN LYON

Lyon's hotels are grouped in nine or ten areas in the city center and its immediate surroundings; most of the best are in Bellecour-Terreaux and Perrache. As is increasingly true elsewhere in France, modern chains that cater to business travellers are taking over the downtown hotels and modernizing them—with rather sad results; you'll find the same lithograph of a weeping clown over your bed in Lille as you do in Lyon. Fortunately, however, in both of the main hotel districts—Bellecour-Terreaux and Perrache—the city does have several wonderful hotels that offer a more indigenous ambience. You'll do well to avoid all of the hotels in the city's La Part-Dieu neighborhood; this is an ultramodern business district, with ultramodern chain hotels, and it's not very convenient to the old city center.

Bellecour-Terreaux

In addition to its excellent location just three steps from the Place Bellecour in the center of the city, the ▶ **Globe et Cécil Hôtel**, at 21, rue Gasparin, offers very good value for the money and particularly warm and helpful service. Madame Nicole Renart is the charming owner/director, and is gradually renovating the hotel's airy, spacious rooms one at a time. Public areas are modern, but room decor varies. Ask for one of the recently renovated rooms, especially number 11, which has a cheerful sort of winter-garden decor.

The handsome 1930s-style lobby of the ▶ **Grand Hôtel des Beaux-Arts**, at 75, rue du Président-Herriot, does not signal what the rooms are like upstairs—they've been done over in a functional but comfortable contemporary style—but this hotel offers very good value in a superb center-city location. Double-glazing keeps down traffic noise from this busy main avenue, but you're still better off asking for a room on one of the top floors.

The ▶ **Hôtel des Artistes**, at 8, rue G.-André, is the preferred hotel of the actors and performers who come to town to perform in the city's main theater across the street, and their presence and the friendly service give this lovely little hotel a distinctive and charming personality. It enjoys a nice location right in the middle of town, overlooking a pretty, quiet square. Rooms are modern and a little small but very comfortable, and the views through the geraniums that hang from the old wrought-iron railings are as much a part of the decor as the gray carpeting and pastel fabrics.

At the ▶ **Hôtel Carlton**, 4, rue Jussieu, you can still see traces of the Belle Epoque grand hotel this once was, especially the caged elevator and coffered lobby, and they add atmosphere to a recent and successful renovation; this is probably the best traditional hotel in the center of town. Decor varies from room to room; best are the sort of English country-house-style rooms, like 214 and 414. Skip the dreary and overpriced breakfast and go to a café instead.

If you want to save your bucks for a big bang at the table, maybe at Paul Bocuse or Léon de Lyon, the ▶ **Hôtel Belle-cordière**, at 18, rue Bellecordière, is a well-located and bearably budget hotel. Rooms are small—so it's better if you're travelling light—and a little spartan but perfectly clean and comfortable. If you're travelling alone, ask for room 601; as two, for room 604.

Vieux Lyon

Until 1987 no hotel in this great ambling-shopping area could be recommended. Then ▶ **La Cour des Loges**, a strikingly modern, almost futuristic, art-filled inn, appeared within a cluster of four 14th- to 17th-century medieval and Renaissance houses. The combined effects are stunning and meld with surprising success. Ancient beamed ceilings have been preserved to look down on bathrooms with two-person tubs. Rooms are opened by electronically coded cards and offer color TVs and videocassette units; the wine cellar is nobly stocked; and there are thermal baths, a restaurant—**Tapas des Loges**—and a private garage. All this comes at a price, and it's worth paying.

▶ **La Tour Rose**, a six-room, six-apartment inn on the rue du Boeuf, offers a second place to stay in Vieux Lyon, although it's better known as a restaurant (a recent, stunning renovation of the rooms may change that, though); its kitchen is presided over by award-winning Philippe Chavent. Try the potato salad with caviar cream. (One-week cooking courses are available.) The mansion dates from the 17th century and each guest room is elegantly decorated by one of the local silk houses. Reserve for meals; Tel: 78-37-25-90.

Environs

The distinguished two-star restaurant ▶ **Alain Chapel**, in the village of Mionnay, 20 km (12 miles) northeast of Lyon, offers 13 rooms in an atmosphere of quiet and rural chic (dining reservations essential; Tel: 78-91-82-02).

Monsieur et Madame Doat welcome guests to ▶ **Château de Bois-Franc**, their two-bedroom residence built in the reign of Napoléon III. In a tranquil setting surrounded by Beaujolais vineyards, it's 7 km (4 miles) outside Villefranche-sur-Saône, which is 31 km (19 miles) north of Lyon.

DINING IN LYON

The Lyonnais probably think more about food than they do about anything else, and the whole city sometimes seems to be one big kitchen/restaurant, with tantalizing aromas wafting out into the street and the clatter of knives and forks coming through open windows. Be forewarned that most local cooking is heavy; a typical meal may begin with a slice of Sabodet (a local sausage that is gently simmered in Beaujolais) served with a potato salad, then maybe continue with a *blanquette de veau* or braised veal in a cream sauce or *quenelles* (dumplings), followed by a serving of St-Marcellin, a deliciously runny and tangy cheese, then maybe a wedge of pear tart. It's just this sort of cooking, though, that has made the city renowned and respected all over France as the country's habitually somewhat conservative and certainly very solid gastronomic capital. Appropriately, too, the famous and somewhat dogmatic gourmet and author Brillat-Savarin was born in the city's environs.

Suddenly, though, Lyon is in the midst of a gastronomic revolution. Beyond the seemingly eternal popularity and hefty prices of the big three chefs, Bocuse, Troisgros, and Chapel—all of whom have assumed a nearly quasi-franchised status as a result of being anointed modern chefs (yesterday a demonstration in Tokyo on how to make an omelette, today an endorsement for mineral water, and tomorrow maybe a line of gourmet frozen foods)—there's a new generation of young lions at home on the ranges of Lyon.

Young chefs such as Daniel Ancel (Le Passage) and Robert Duffaud (Le Vivarais) have applied some of the best ideas of *nouvelle cuisine* to traditional Lyonnaise cooking with superb results. What this means is a lighter version of traditional local cooking with nary a kiwi in sight; a good example is the reworked Lyonnais classic, beef salad, at La Tour Rose—it's been completely brightened up and caloried down by the almost heretical addition of vegetables, including slivers of poached horseradish, and it's delicious.

The leavening impact of these new chefs accents a dining scene that is generally one of the richest and most rewarding in Europe. Not only does one have an ample choice of haute cuisine places—the city and its suburbs boast one three-star, two two-star and 11 one-star restaurants—but also a fine variety of bistros, brasseries, and *buchons* (the word may date from the 16th century, when travellers would stop for a snack while a groom would *bouchonner*—curry—their horses, and today refers to a local hybrid of café, snack bar, and bistro), as well as the pleasures offered by the celebrated *mères lyonnaises,* or lady cooks.

It is thought that the tradition of the "mother chef" was begun almost 250 years ago with La Mère Guy, a fisherman's wife whose fame spread among those who enjoyed her succulent *matelote,* a stew of whatever fish came out of the river. (She is remembered today in the restaurant **Roger Roucou "Mère Guy"** at 35, quai J. J. Rousseau on the bank of the Rhône in Lyon's suburb of La Mulatière; Tel: 78-51-65-37.)

The *mère des mères,* however, was one Mère Fillioux, who

had learned her craft in the kitchens of private homes, then married Louis Fillioux, and in the late 1800s set up a *mère et père* spot on Lyon's rue Duquesne. Père talked politics and served carafes of Beaujolais while Mère Françoise founded 19th-century Lyonnaise gastronomy. A sign over the bar read, "Those who sing at dessert are requested not to stand on the tables." (It is said that when she died in 1925, Mère Fillioux left as her legacy the only two knives she had used in her career and that her children framed them in gold.)

Many other famous mother-chefs have come and gone in the decades since. Perhaps the best regarded was Eugénie Brazier, who worked *chez* Mère Fillioux before she opened a tiny kitchen called **Mère Brazier** at 12, rue Royale and became the saint of local gourmets. (Among her pupils was Paul Bocuse.) Today her modest restaurant is a luxurious retreat at the same address, proud of its one star, where family members still serve such Fillioux specialties as *volaille de Bresse Demi-Deuil,* the chicken in "half-mourning" that's a chicken from heaven (Tel: 78-28-15-49; closed August).

Nobody can consume *haute cuisine* at every sitting, however, and Lyon abounds in satisfying cafés, brasseries, and bistros that prepare the kind of fare even the French don't make at home anymore: stews that simmer for days, handmade potato *gratin,* and the like.

Sometimes reservations are necessary at *bouchons,* sometimes not. Among those not to be overlooked are: **La Meunière**, 11, rue Neuve, where dishes, service, and the paint job haven't changed in 50 years or so (closed mid-July to mid-August; Tel: 78-28-62-91); **Café des Fédérations**, 8, rue de Major-Martin, where the menu is scratched on cardboard and the sausages and *quenelles* are wonderful (closed in August; Tel: 78-28-26-00); and **La Grille**, 106, rue Sébastien-Gryphe, where dishes are huge, serious, and delicious (closed in August; Tel: 78-72-46-58).

Other unforgettable, unpretentious places suited to having a good time include: **Brasserie Georges**, 30, cours Verdun, a stage set from the past that's about the size of New York's Grand Central Station (Tel: 78-37-15-78); and the **Grand Café des Négociants**, 1, place Francisque-Régaud, a spot that's been a café-sitter's café for 110 years (Tel: 78-42-50-05).

Of course, no one should stop in Lyon without dining occasionally amid the stars—for which reservations are mandatory. On most lists the room at the top is that of **Paul Bocuse** in the suburban village of Collonges-au-Mont-d'Or. Bocuse may be the best-known restaurateur in the world (he is surely the most peripatetic), and while it is possible to have a less than memorable meal *chez* Bocuse, it is not probable. Like a person shopping for a yacht, if you have to ask the price, you can't afford it. Just settle into the surprisingly unpretentious dining room and order something familiar—leg of lamb, say, or filet of sole, or chicken from Bresse—and discover how unfamiliar really fine, simple cooking can be. Tel: 72-27-85-85; open year-round.

Virtually all experts agree that a meal should be taken at **Léon de Lyon** (at 1, rue Pleney, near the Musée des Beaux-Arts) for several reasons, the most persuasive of which is its remarkable presentation of Lyonnais classics. In addition, the decor and ambience are warm, welcoming, and not intimidating, with a great display of rare culinary artifacts. Chef Jean-Paul Lacombe is a *maître cuisinier* of France. Tel: 78-28-11-33; closed July 28 to August 20.

Another *maître cuisinier* is Gérard Nandron of **Nandron**, at 26, quai Jean-Moulin, the inheritor of a long cooking tradition in a smart setting. He infuses his traditional cooking with lightness; try the *quenelle de brochet Nantua*. Tel: 78-42-10-26; closed July 27 to August 26.

Refined, friendly, classic, and yet up-to-date, **Orsi** (Pierre Orsi at the helm) lures the discerning to 3, place Kléber in the Left Bank area of Brotteaux, in part, perhaps, to taste his pigeon of Bresse *en cocotte*. The ambience of the little flower-bedecked house is refined and very formal. Tel: 78-89-57-68.

Auberge de Fond-Rose, at 23, quai Clemenceau, gives diners the sensation of having driven into the countryside, with service in a shady, flowery garden complete with an aviary; try the *suprême de dorade* (a sea bream) from October to April. Tel: 78-29-34-61.

To sample some of the city's auspiciously simmering culinary talent, try either Le Layon (52, rue Merciére) or Le Vivarais (1, Place Gailleton). **Le Layon** fronts on the busy and trendy pedestrian rue Mercière, and is a favorite of the chic young crowd here. Chef Jean-Luc Léger is especially talented at adapting classic dishes to contemporary tastes—for example, his succulent rabbit in mustard sauce. During the summer, the sidewalk tables here offer good people-watching, especially if you linger over a bottle of his excellent Coteaux-du-Lyon, the pleasantly fruity local red; Tel: 78-42-94-08. Since chef Robert Duffaud, former pupil and colleague of Alain Chapel, is one of the most talented up-and-comers in town, the 100-franc prix fixe menu at **Le Vivarais** might be the best buy in all of Lyon. The dining room itself is quite plain, maybe because the assumption here is that your attention will remain riveted to your plate. With changing daily specials—maybe a chicken roasted with wild mushrooms or ruddy, nearly bacchanalian beef

stew—this restaurant offers outstanding quality and attention to detail. Tel: 78-37-85-15.

A happy example of how the Parisian Baby Bistro phenomenon—whereby famous chefs with famous and famously
expensive restaurants have been opening lower-priced, often
prix fixe annexes—is occurring in the provinces is **Le Bar du
Passage**, 8, rue du Plâtre. This is the junior restaurant of chef
Daniel Ancel's one-star Le Passage right next door, and it
offers a fine opportunity to sample the expensive restaurant's
superb cooking at moderate prices in a lively setting. Le Bar is
furnished with old red-plush cinema seats and the walls are
painted with trompe l'oeil theater curtains, which creates an
intimate and amusing atmosphere that pulls in a fashionable
crowd all night long. Come here for a light, modern meal,
such as vegetable terrine in a tomato coulis and chicken
breast stuffed with wild rice, especially if you've had a big
traditional feed earlier in the day. Tel: 78-28-11-16.

Vetard-Le Neuf (7, Place Bellecour), the chicest place in
town for lunch, is another good example of the trend to more
classically traditional cooking and more modest checks. Profit-
ing from its strategic location on the Place Bellecour, this
popular two-year-old brasserie serves nonstop from 10:00
A.M. to 9:30 P.M. and is the brainchild of chef Jean Vetard, who
formerly ran a well-known and expensive eponymous restaurant on the same premises. The menu changes daily, but a
perfectly cooked slab of fresh *foie gras de canard* followed by
a delicate Dover sole *en gratin* with homemade noodles
shows how this talented chef has done us a great service in
this new, moderately priced incarnation. Tel: 78-42-07-59.

—*Alexander Lobrano*

AROUND LYON

PEROUGES

Pérouges is one of the most evocative villages in all of
Europe, an outcrop of the Middle Ages atop its hill and
behind its ramparts only 39 km (24 miles) northeast—but
centuries removed—from Lyon. Follow N 84 to Meximieux,
then turn left, uphill on D 4, to Pérouges.

Pérouges owes its name to settlers who arrived from
Perugia, Italy, before the Roman occupation. During the
Middle Ages the lords of the Dauphiné and Savoy squabbled
over the small but rich town (the chief industry was linen
weaving), leading to the major event of its history, the siege
of 1468.

On the exterior of the lower of the two city gates (**Porte d'en-Bas**), an inscription in somewhat bastardized Latin translates as: "Pérouges of the Pérougiens! Impregnable town! Those rogues from Dauphiné wanted to take it, but couldn't. However, they took away the gates, the hinges, and locks, and rolled off with them. The devil take them!"

During the 19th century Pérouges's prosperity ebbed, and by 1910 only 90 souls remained to shelter in the shade of the great and gracious linden trees in the heart of the matter, the **Place du Tilleul**. Owners of ancient houses began to hack them down, and proud Pérouges seemed about to plunge into the past tense.

Then to the rescue came artists and artisans from Lyon and elsewhere, supported in part by government *beaux-arts* funds. A committee for Old Pérouges lured weavers, potters, cabinet makers, and other artisans to build shops along the old streets. A few wealthy investors restored handsome merchants' homes with their beamed and sculpted ceilings, huge fireplaces, and immense rooms once covered with frescoes.

Today you can walk the narrow, sloping, Medieval streets of the town, with rain channels down the center, where once only people of a certain importance could pass under the jutting eaves of houses to keep themselves dry.

At ▶ **Ostellerie du Vieux Pérouges**, a cozy inn with 30 rooms and an excellent kitchen, it is possible to spend a night in the ambience of the past while enjoying the amenities of the present.

VIENNE

In Roman times it was "Vienne the Beautiful"; in the high periods of Christianity, "Vienne the Holy"; in the 19th century Frédéric Mistral wrote of it, "In an elbow of the Rhône, seated like an altar against the buttresses of the noble Dauphiné. . . ."

The fact is, it is the natural site, bathed in light above the river, that makes Vienne attractive. Aside from its Roman ruins, Vienne today is a rather nondescript, small-business town of about 30,000 inhabitants, 30 km (18½ miles) directly south of Lyon on N 7.

La Pyramide

Since the halcyon days between the World Wars, gourmets and gourmands have paraded in pilgrimage to Vienne, however: presidents of the République, food writers, and merchant princes all bound for the door of La Pyramide, that "gastronomic temple" once without peer in France, or anywhere else, for that matter.

Pyramide (named for a Roman marble that stood in the center of the fourth-century circus) was the inspired creation of Fernand Point, the now legendary super-chef who was considered the foremost restaurateur in the world when he died in 1956 at the age of 57. One of his three Michelin stars faded with him (as is Michelin's practice when a great, presumably irreplaceable chef dies). Wonder of wonders: Maintained by Point's crew and his admirable wife, Marie-Louise ("Mado"), Pyramide quickly regained its third star, under the name Chez Point.

Madame Point died in July 1986, and the three-star rating was again reduced to two; and when Chez Point-Pyramide was razed in 1988, the stars disappeared altogether. Today ▶ La Pyramide, back on the old site at 14, boulevard Fernand-Point in its parklike setting, has regained two shiny stars. The inn has 22 fine rooms and four expensive suites.

A very attractive place to stay just outside Vienne is the ten-room ▶ Hostellerie Marais St-Jean, set in a quiet garden in the hamlet of Chonas-l'Amballan, just 9 km (5½ miles) south of town via N 7. It has a good restaurant, and meals are served outdoors in fine weather.

The Cathédrale St-Maurice (honoring a soldier-saint supposedly martyred nearby in the third century) is notable chiefly for its portal sculptures, long nave, and marvelous capital carvings. It's just a short walk east of the Rhône off rue de la Bourgogne. Collectors of antiquities will take time also for the Eglise et Cloître St-André-le-Bas (north of the cathedral off the Place de Jeu-de-Paume) and the former church of St-Pierre, which today houses a lapidary museum.

Roman Vienne

Half a century before Caesar conquered Gaul, Vienne was established as the capital of the tribal Allobroges; under the Romans, the city preceded Lyon as a metropolis and was the home of such magnificent monuments and residences that the poet Martial dubbed it "Vienne the Beautiful."

Among the relics of Roman Vienne, which are scattered throughout the center of the modern town, the grandest is the Temple d'Auguste et de Livie, somewhat reminiscent of the Maison Carrée in Nîmes but smaller in size. Built during the reign of Augustus, it has undergone several permutations, serving as church, Jacobin headquarters during the Revolution, a Temple of Reason, a museum, and a library. It was restored to its original design in the 19th century.

The Roman theater, abandoned as long ago as the fourth century under Emperor Constantine, underwent archaeological work in 1922 and has been returned to excellent condition. It ranks among the largest theaters of Gaul and is only slightly smaller in diameter than the Theater of Marcellus in Rome. Productions are still staged here in summer.

Even more interesting to those who enjoy evidence of daily life in past ages, the ancient towns of **St-Romain-en-Gal** and **Ste-Colombe** have been unearthed across the river from Vienne. Ste-Colombe was the site of giant baths, palaces, and fine residences. St-Romain, today a suburb of almost 1,500 residents, is reached by crossing the Rhône via the Pont Moderne from the Place St-Louis. The archaeological zone, which is the main interest to travellers, is a fairly long walk.

This was almost surely the original town site in Roman times, the Vienne we see today having been born when the riverbed changed over centuries. Visitors are admitted to the Gallo-Roman digs, where they can see the remains of sumptuous villas, the marketplace, warehouses where dyeing and tanning vessels remain, baths, and an impressive network of sewers, heating, and drainage systems. Mosaics from the villas are housed in a little **museum**. A very pleasant restaurant, the **Gallo Romain**, is open near the site year-round except in August; Tel: 74-53-19-72.

SOUTH OF VIENNE

From Condrieu, about 12 km (7½ miles) south of Vienne on N 86, a remarkable route (D 7/ D 8) wiggles south and west along the Crêt (Crest) de l'Oeillon (splendid views over the mountains and valleys of the Rhône country) to **Mont-Pilat** and **Gouffre d'Enfer** (*enfer* means "hell"—here an impressive dam site at the end of a rocky, narrow gorge involving a healthful hike), and then on to the hill hamlet of **Rochetaillée**, with its feudal château ruins.

The end of this particular road comes at St-Etienne, a large industrial town from which you may continue west or cut back to the Rhône route via Annonay and Tournon on N 82, D 206, D 578, and D 532. Continuing south along the Rhône river from Vienne will lead you to Orange, the Rhône wine country, and Provence, all covered in a later chapter.

In Condrieu you should plan to stop at ▶ **Le Beau Rivage**, with 20 rooms and four suites overlooking the river. The lovely terrace restaurant is in fact right on the Rhône; reserve; Tel: 74-59-52-24.

GETTING AROUND

From Paris autoroute A 6 heads southeast to Beaune, with a cutoff via A 38 to Dijon, and continues via Chalon-sur-Saône and Mâcon to Lyon; A 7 continues to Provence. As usual, the back roads are slower and reveal more of the countryside.

The Dijon-Bourgogne airport is linked by daily flights to five international airports in Paris (Charles-de-Gaulle and Orly), Lyon (Satolas), Geneva (Cointrin), and Basel–Mulhouse (Euroairport). Lyon's Satolas Airport receives flights from Paris (12 connections daily) and 33 other cities in France, Fort-de-France and Point-à-Pitre in the French West Indies, London and Manchester in England, 13 other European countries, and ten destinations in Africa.

The TGVs cover Burgundy, with direct service from Paris to Dijon, Montbard, Beaune, and Chalon-sur-Saône. The train for Lyon also stops at Le Creusot and Mâcon-Loché stations. TGVs from Besançon (in the Jura) and Bern and Lausanne, Switzerland, provide service to Dijon, while TGVs from Savoy and Geneva stop at Mâcon-Loché. This swift service is complemented by regular rail services from cities throughout Europe.

In September 1983 the futuristic railway station Lyon Part-Dieu opened to receive new TGV lines that now make the Paris–Lyon run in two hours. Regular Lille–Lyon service, bypassing Paris, runs a few times a day and there are also daily links with Marseille, Valence, and Rouen in France as well as Geneva, Barcelona, Turin, Milan, Rome, Frankfurt, and Munich.

Canal Cruise-Barges

Several companies operate luxury Burgundy canal cruise-barges. These include **French Country Waterways**, P.O. Box 2195, Duxbury, MA 02331, Tel: (800) 222-1236 or (617) 934-2454, Fax: (617) 934-9408; **Abercrombie & Kent**, 1520 Kensington Road, Suite 212, Oak Brook, IL 60521, Tel: (800) 323-7308 or (708) 954-2944, or Sloane Square House, Holbein Place, London SW1W 8NS; **Le Boat, Inc.**, P.O. Box E, Maywood, NJ 07607, Tel: (800) 922-0291 or (201) 342-1838; and **European Waterways**, c/o B&V Associates, 140 East 56th Street, Suite 4C, New York, NY 10022, Tel: (800) 438-4748 or (212) 688-9538, Fax: (212) 688-9467.

In Canada, **France Unlimited** arranges Burgundy barge cruises and apartments in Paris; writen them at 135 Isabella Street, Suite 708, Toronto, Ontario M4Y 1P4; Tel and Fax: (416) 920-6329.

In France contact **Quiztour**, 19, rue d'Athènes, 75009, Paris, Tel: 45-26-16-59, Fax: 42-85-40-43; **Aquarelle**, Port de Plaisance, quai St-Martin, 89000 Auxerre, Tel: 86-46-97-77, Fax: 86-52-55-31; and **Locaboat Plaisance**, quai du Port-au-Bois, 89300 Joigny, Tel: 86-91-72-72, Fax: 86-62-42-41. Inquire at any regional tourist office for information on short-term boat rentals for four to 12 passengers.

One of the newest river-cruisers on the Rhône is the six-cabin, 12-passenger *Napoléon,* which makes six-night cruises between Lyon and Avignon. Equipped with heating and air conditioning, she boasts a comfortable salon, staterooms outfitted with TVs and VCRs, and hotel-like facilities. All gourmet meals on board and a luncheon at an outstanding shoreside restaurant are included. The per-person cabin rate ranges from $3,675 in the low season to $3,950 in the high season. The *Napoléon* also is available for charter for six or 13 nights; make arrangements through Abercrombie & Kent at addresses above. Within Burgundy, Abercrombie & Kent also handles the 22-passenger *L'Abercrombie* between Dijon and Montchanin and the 20-passenger *Litote* between Montbard and Tonnerre.

Ballooning in Burgundy

Ballooning in Burgundy may be arranged through **Bombard Balloon Adventures**, 6727 Curran St., McLean, VA 22101, Tel: (800) 862-8537 or (703) 448-9407; **Société Bombard Air Adventure**, Château de Laborde, 21200 Meursanges, Tel: 80-26-63-30, Fax: 80-26-69-20; and **Air Escargot**, Remigny, 71150 Chagny, Tel: 85-87-12-30, Fax: 85-87-08-84.

Other Tours in Burgundy

City tours, wine tours, gastronomic outings, and float and barge trips throughout the area may be booked through regional tourist offices; for individual guided tours in Lyon, inquire at the Bureau des Guides, 5, place St-Jean. A major U.S. operator of bicycling excursions in Burgundy is **Progressive Travels, Inc.**, 224 West Galer, Suite C, Seattle, WA 98119; in U.S. and Canada, Tel: (800) 245-2229 or (206) 285-1987; Fax: (206) 285-1988. In Canada, comfortable bicycling excursions are the province of **Butterfield & Robinson**, 70 Bond St., Toronto, Ontario M5B 1X3; Tel: (800) 387-1147 (in U.S.), (800) 268-8415 (in Canada), or (416) 864-1354.

Automobile tourists interested in vineyards, architecture, and markets may obtain brochures outlining routes at regional tourism offices in major cities.

ACCOMMODATIONS REFERENCE
The rates given below are projections for 1994. Unless otherwise indicated, rates are for a double room, double occupancy, and do not include meals. As rates are always subject to change, double-check before booking.

▶ **Abbaye Saint-Michel.** Rue St-Michel, 89700 **Tonnerre.** Tel: 86-55-05-99; Fax: 86-55-00-10; in U.S., (212) 856-0115;

Fax: (212) 856-0193. Member, Relais & Châteaux. 750F–1,350F.

▶ **Alain Chapel**. 01390 **Mionnay**. Tel: 78-91-82-02; Fax: 78-91-82-37; in U.S., (212) 856-0115; Fax: (212) 856-0193. Member, Relais & Châteaux. 700F–825F.

▶ **Auberge des Brizards**. 89630 **Quarré-les-Tombes**. Tel: 86-32-20-12; Fax: 86-32-27-40. 270F–750F.

▶ **Le Beau Rivage**. 2, rue du Beau Rivage, 69420 **Condrieu**. Tel: 74-59-52-24; Fax: 74-59-59-36. 500F–820F.

▶ **Belena**. 12, boulevard Foch, 21200 **Beaune**. Tel: 80-24-01-01; Fax: 80-24-09-90. 580F–900F; duplexes 1,300F.

▶ **Bernard Loiseau-La Côte-d'Or**. 2, rue Argentine, 21210 **Saulieu**. Tel: 80-64-07-66; Fax: 80-64-08-92; in U.S., (212) 856-0115; Fax: (212) 856-0193. Member, Relais & Châteaux. 310F–600F (in old building); 950F–1,800F (in new building).

▶ **Le Cep**. 27, rue Maufoux, 21200 **Beaune**. Tel: 80-22-35-48; Fax: 80-22-76-80; in U.S., (212) 254-2217 or (800) 755-9313. 550F–1,000F.

▶ **Chapeau Rouge**. 5, rue Michelet, 21000 **Dijon**. Tel: 80-30-28-10; Fax: 80-30-33-89; in U.S. and Canada, Tel: (800) 528-1234; in U.K., (081) 541-0033. Member, Best Western International. 450F–860F.

▶ **Chapon Fin et Restaurant Paul Blanc**. 01140 **Thoissey**. Tel: 74-04-04-74; Fax: 74-04-94-51. 400F–650F.

▶ **Château d'Ancy-le-Franc**. 89160 **Ancy-le-Franc**. Tel: 86-75-14-63; Fax: 86-75-10-30; in U.S. and Canada, Tel: (800) 438-4748; Fax: (212) 688-9467; in U.K., Tel: (071) 730-9600; Fax: (071) 730-9376. Prices on request only.

▶ **Château de Bois-Franc**. 69640 **Jarnioux**. Tel: 74-68-20-91; Fax: 74-65-10-03. 450F.

▶ **Château de Chailly**. Chailly-sur-Armançon, 21320 **Pouilly-en-Auxois**. Tel: 80-90-30-30; Fax: 80-90-30-00. 900F–2,200F.

▶ **Château du Fey**. 89300 **Villecien**. Tel: 86-63-18-34; Fax: 86-63-01-33. Rates on request, from 700F.

▶ **Château de Gilly**. Gilly-lès-Cîteaux, 21640 **Vougeot**. Tel: 80-62-89-98; Fax: 80-62-82-34. 600F–1,360F.

▶ **Château d'Igé**. 71960 **Igé**. Tel: 85-33-33-99; Fax: 85-33-41-41. 680F.

▶ **Château de Longecourt**. Longecourt-en-Plaine, 21110 **Genlis**. Tel: 80-39-88-76. 700F.

▶ **Château de Malaisy**. Fain-lès-Montbard, 21500 **Montbard**. Tel: 80-89-46-54; Fax: 80-92-30-16. 250F–780F.

▶ **Château de Ste-Sabine**. 21320 **Pouilly-en-Auxois**. Tel: 80-49-22-01; Fax: 80-49-20-01. 300F–550F.

▶ **Château de Saulon la Rue**. 29910 **Saulon-la-Rue**. Tel: 80-36-61-10; Fax: 80-36-91-92. 345F.

► **Château de Vault de Lugny.** Vault-de-Lugny, 89200 **Avallon.** Tel: 86-34-07-86; Fax: 86-34-16-36; in U.S. and Canada, Tel: (800) 438-4748; Fax: (212) 688-9467; in U.K., Tel: (071) 730-9600; Fax: (071) 730-9376. 750F–2,200F.

► **Chez Camille.** 1, place Herriot, 21230 **Arnay-le-Duc.** Tel: 80-90-01-38; Fax: 80-90-04-64. 400F–750F.

► **Côte d'Or.** Rue Charles-Ronot, 21400 **Châtillon-sur-Seine.** Tel: 80-91-13-29; Fax: 80-91-29-15. 420F–560F.

► **La Cour des Loges.** 6, rue du Boeuf, 69005 **Lyon.** Tel: 78-42-75-75; Telex: 330831; Fax: 72-40-93-61; in U.S., (212) 254-2217 or (800) 755-9313. 1,200F–1,700F.

► **Ermitage de Corton.** Route de Dijon, 21200 **Beaune Nord.** Tel: 80-22-05-28; Fax: 80-24-64-51; in U.S., (212) 254-2217 or (800) 755-9313. 750F–950F.

► **L'Espérance.** St-Père, 89450 **Vézelay.** Tel: 86-33-20-45; Fax: 86-33-26-15. 620F–1,350F.

► **Globe et Cécil Hôtel.** 21, rue Gasparin, 69002 **Lyon.** Tel: 78-42-58-95; Fax: 72-41-99-06. 300F–440F.

► **Grand Hôtel des Beaux-Arts.** 75, rue du Président-Herriot, 69002 **Lyon.** Tel: 78-38-09-50; Fax: 78-42-19-19. 350F–600F.

► **Henry II.** 12, rue du faubourg St-Nicolas, 21200 **Beaune.** Tel: 80-22-83-84; Fax: 80-24-15-13. 400F–690F.

► **Hostellerie du Château.** 21320 **Châteauneuf.** Tel: 80-49-22-00; Fax: 80-49-21-27. 170F–500F.

► **Hostellerie Château de Bellecroix.** Route de Chalon, 71150 **Chagny.** Tel: 85-87-13-86; Fax: 85-91-28-62. 500F–900F.

► **Hostellerie des Clos.** 89800 **Chablis.** Tel: 86-42-10-63; Fax: 86-42-17-11. 230F–560F.

► **Hostellerie de Levernois.** 21200 **Beaune.** Tel: 80-24-73-58; Fax: 80-22-78-00. 900F.

► **Hostellerie Marais St-Jean.** 38121 **Chonas-l'Amballan.** Tel: 74-58-83-28; Fax: 74-58-81-96. 550F.

► **Hostellerie du Moulin des Ruats.** 89200 **Avallon.** Tel: 86-34-07-14; Fax: 86-31-65-47. 300F–650F.

► **Hôtel des Artistes.** 8, rue G.-André, 69002 **Lyon.** Tel: 78-42-04-88; Fax: 78-42-93-76. 300F–900F.

► **Hôtel Bellecordière.** 18, rue Bellecordière, 69002 **Lyon.** Tel: 78-42-27-78; Fax: 72-40-92-27. 240F–315F.

► **Hôtel de Bourgogne.** Place de l'Abbaye, 71250 **Cluny.** Tel: 85-59-00-58; Fax: 85-59-03-73. 380F–480F.

► **Hôtel Carlton.** 4, rue Jussieu, 69002 **Lyon.** Tel: 78-42-56-51; Fax: 78-42-10-71. 430F–700F.

► **Hôtel de Greuze.** 5, rue A. Thibaudet, 71700 **Tournus.** Tel: 85-51-77-77; Fax: 85-51-77-23. 770F–1,200F.

► **Hôtel le Home.** 138, route de Dijon, 21200 **Beaune.** Tel: 80-22-16-43; Fax: 80-24-90-74. 285F–340F.

▶ **Hôtel Le Maxime.** 2, quai de la Marine, 89000 **Auxerre.** Tel: 86-52-14-19; Fax: 86-52-21-70. 350F–580F.

▶ **Hôtel du Nord.** Place Darcy, 21000 **Dijon.** Tel: 80-30-58-58; Fax: 80-30-61-26. 300F–400F.

▶ **Hôtel de la Paix.** 47, rue du faubourg Madeleine, 21200 **Beaune.** Tel: 80-22-33-33; Fax: 80-22-84-39. 310F–450F.

▶ **Hôtel Philippe le Bon.** 18, rue Ste-Anne, 21000 **Dijon.** Tel: 80-30-73-52; Fax: 80-30-95-51. 400F–500F.

▶ **Hôtel de la Poste.** 1, boulevard Clemenceau, 21200 **Beaune.** Tel: 80-22-08-11; Telex: 350982; Fax: 80-24-19-71; in U.S., (212) 254-2217 or (800) 755-9313. 750F–1,000F; apartments 1,300F–1,500F.

▶ **Hôtel Poste-Lion d'Or.** 89450 **Vézelay.** Tel: 86-33-21-23; Telex: 800949; Fax: 86-32-30-92. 230F–580F.

▶ **Hôtel Wilson.** Place Wilson, 21000 **Dijon.** Tel: 80-66-82-50; Fax: 80-36-41-54. 360F–420F.

▶ **Lameloise.** 36, place d'Armes, 71150 **Chagny.** Tel: 85-87-08-85; Fax: 85-87-03-57; in U.S., (212) 254-2217 or (800) 755-9313. 500F–1,300F.

▶ **Le Moulin des Templiers.** Pontaubert, 89200 **Avallon.** Tel: 86-34-10-80. 220F–320F.

▶ **Ostellerie du Vieux Pérouges.** 01800 **Pérouges.** Tel: 74-61-00-88; Fax: 74-34-77-90; in U.S., (212) 254-2217 or (800) 755-9313. 700F–980F.

▶ **Du Parc de la Colombière.** 49, cours du Parc, 21000 **Dijon.** Tel: 80-65-18-41; Fax: 80-36-42-56. 280F–330F.

▶ **Le Pontot.** 89450 **Vézelay.** Tel: 86-33-24-40. 500F–850F.

▶ **Le Prieuré.** 49, boulevard de Brou, 01000 **Bourg-en-Bresse.** Tel: 74-22-44-60; Fax: 74-22-71-07. 450F–550F.

▶ **Pullman la Cloche.** 14, place Darcy, 21000 **Dijon.** Tel: 80-30-12-32; Fax: 80-30-04-15; in U.S. and Canada, Tel: (800) 221-4542; Fax: (914) 472-0451. 530F–620F.

▶ **La Pyramide.** 14, boulevard Fernand-Point, 38200 **Vienne.** Tel: 74-53-01-96; Fax: 74-85-69-73; in U.S., (212) 254-2217 or (800) 755-9313. 750F–850F.

▶ **Le Rempart.** 2, avenue Gambetta, 71700 **Tournus.** Tel: 85-51-10-56; Fax: 85-40-77-22. 365F–780F.

▶ **Résidence de la Côte Saint-Jacques.** 14, faubourg de Paris, 89300 **Joigny.** Tel: 86-62-09-70; Telex: 801458; Fax: 86-91-49-70; in U.S., (212) 856-0115; Fax: (212) 856-0193. Member, Relais & Châteaux. 690F–1,650F.

▶ **La Tour Rose.** 22, rue du Boeuf, 69005 **Lyon.** Tel: 78-37-25-90; Fax: 78-42-26-02. 1,050F–2,200F.

THE JURA

By Fred Halliday and Jennifer Quale

Fred Halliday and Jennifer Quale also contribute to other sections of this guidebook.

Where do the smart Swiss go when they want to breathe cool mountain air and wander a hilltop gold and red with wildflowers, or sit down to lunch with a lover, a rich Comté cheese, and a sausage named Jésus? Where do they go for an affordable vacation? And where do these same canny Swiss go to buy a good bottle of inexpensive homemade kirsch, visit an art museum overhanging a trout stream, or watch the cows come home to the barn behind the hotel at *l'heure de l'apéritif?* Why, to the French Jura, *mais oui*. In the Franche-Comté region, the Jura mountain range is bordered by Alsace and Lorraine to the north, Champagne and Burgundy to the north and west, the Savoy to the south, and Switzerland to the east. Although locals may refer to their neck of the woods as a suburb of Geneva, there is nothing suburban about its rustic reaches.

Indeed, it's high time to get over to this land of the Jura, with its old châteaux guarding great gorges, old hotels on gurgling rivers, and old-fashioned menus at old-fashioned prices. In addition to these bucolic blessings, the Jura boasts a beautiful capital—Besançon, just two-and-a-half hours by train (TGV) from Paris. But of all these assets, the Jura's most striking feature is its landscape, dotted with gorges, falls, *cirques* (deep, steep-walled stone canyons), *reculées* (blind valleys), and rivers. The land is a mountain plateau of pressure ridges, a foot table, really, of the Alps, but somehow softer than the Swiss terrain. Its features were cracked, crazed, and chiseled by mountain torrents, underground streams, and grinding glaciers that only recently—geologically speaking—retreated from the region. Covered with trees, the Jura gets its name from the Low Latin word *juria*, meaning forest, and it claims the richest fir forest in Europe; in its most spectacular folds, this region of France calls to mind a verdant Grand Canyon.

MAJOR INTEREST

Besançon
Grande-Rue
Cathédrale St-Jean
Roman ruins
Musée des Beaux-Arts
Citadelle and its museums

The Jura
Wild landscapes
Picturesque villages in the Doubs, Loue,
    and Lison valleys
Musée Courbet in Ornans
Trout fishing
Charcuterie and cheese
Châteaux
Baume-les-Messieurs

BESANÇON

The door to all this fresh air opens in Besançon, the capital of Franche-Comté, some 400 km (250 miles) southeast of Paris and less than a quarter of that distance from Basel, Switzerland. The morning train from Paris arrives in time for a fine stroll before lunch (the Besançon station is a mile from the city center, with buses and taxis going to and fro frequently). Friday is a good day to arrive, as it is in any French provincial capital, because Friday is the liveliest market day. Everybody from the surrounding countryside comes streaming into town with wares to sell in the stalls along the river Doubs beneath the Pont de Battant. Here you can find some of the best food products of the Jura. And as Besançon is the most likely place to rent a car for the trip through the Jura—all the major rental agencies are here—this is an outstanding opportunity to stock up with baskets of food for the road.

The city of Besançon was laid out according to the cardinal principle on which Roman cities were founded: the site. Not only does Besançon have a lariat loop of river to encircle it, making it almost an island, but in practically every direction from its watery ring rise green slope-shouldered hills that

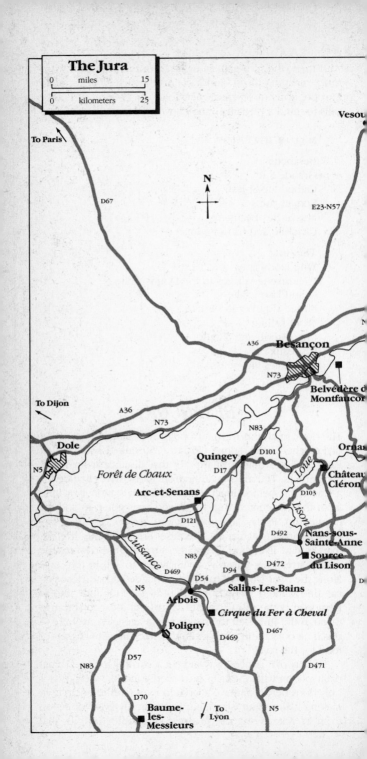

stand as walls before the moat. And beyond these hills are mountains to part the sky and pen up the clouds, bestowing on Besançon a microclimate as fortunate as its site. In summer and fall the days are bright and never stuffy, and there's skiing nearby in winter. But spring, with its abundance of flowers, is the best time for Besançon and the rest of the Jura. Leave your car outside the old city walls. Inside, much of the going is banned to automobile traffic, preserving a seemly atmosphere for walking through antiquity.

CATHEDRALE ST-JEAN
The place in Besançon to begin your tour is the Cathédrale St-Jean, at the far end of the Grande-Rue, the same street that cleaved the old Roman town. Its exterior may seem a patchwork of styles—most of it dates from the 18th century—but the inside is exquisite. On the wall next to the sacristy door is a painting by Fra Bartolomeo of the Virgin with saints, dating from 1512. The cathedral also possesses an astronomical clock, a 19th-century masterpiece composed of 30,000 moving parts and 70 different faces, which generates 122 different bits of information, including time, temperature, and season. (To watch the greatest number of automated clock movements, arrive ten minutes before the hour (e.g., 10:50) between 9:00 A.M. and 5:00 P.M. (the room housing the clock is closed on Tuesdays). Aside from religious services, St-Jean makes a superb venue for the occasional concert.

No one leaving the cathedral gets very far, thanks to the **Square A. Castan**. In front of the cathedral is the **Porte Noire** (Black Gate), a Roman triumphal arch dating from the second century A.D. It was this relic that persuaded the Bisontins (out in the countryside the people are called Comtois) to start digging. What they unearthed on this site—Castan was the chief digger—was a Roman urban center huddled around today's square. Among the ruins is a reservoir for the aqueduct that watered the city, which was growing furiously by Marcus Aurelius's time. The square also contains the remains of a temple or perhaps a bath, prosaically framed by eight Corinthian columns.

ALONG THE GRANDE-RUE
No longer a stranger to Besançon, you're now prepared to poke your nose inside its many courtyards along the Grande-Rue, which runs from Square A. Castan through the center of the city. Number 64, Grande-Rue is a private home with gateless portals well worth strolling through. Inside is the architectural rarity of a courtyard behind a courtyard. The

second of these deserves the longer look. Framed by old wooden stables, it illustrates the provincial town house life-style of the mid-18th century.

Nearby the town house, at number 140, is the birthplace of Victor Hugo, whom the Bisontins never forgave for calling their city "an old Spanish town." They, in turn, referred to Hugo as "a half-breed from Brittany and Lorraine," an epi-thet the writer never disputed. He sought, and found, his adventure elsewhere.

Place du 8-Septembre

Besançon is an outdoor town that owes its spunk and street life less to tourism than to its university. Vest-pocket cafés are planted in open spaces, and the Grande-Rue is so wide and the buildings so uniformly low that there is never the sense of being hemmed in. At the Place du 8-Septembre (also known to Bisontins as the Place St-Pierre, for the church that dominates one flank) the Grande-Rue opens onto the main city square, where stand the separate elements of a superb architectural surprise. Here rise two impressive buildings fronted by a cooling fountain: the 16th-century Italianate **Hôtel de Ville** and, right behind it, the rebuilt **Palais de Justice**. The façade of the latter is conspicuously Burgun-dian, a style imposed by the French crown and a gross injustice, considering that when the original structure was erected, Franche-Comté had long been established as an independent state (*franche* meaning "franchise," or "privi-lege," and *comté* meaning "a fiefdom held by a count," or, more simply, "county").

In 1635 Cardinal Richelieu cast a covetous eye upon the Jura and sent an army to fetch it for the crown of France. It wasn't so easy. Though outgunned and outnumbered, the locals fought fiercely, and the struggle between the French and the Comtois was to last for almost 40 years. When the Bisontins turned back the French armies, Richelieu tried again, this time with Swiss mercenaries who made bonfires of homes and then entombed fleeing partisans in the subter-ranean grottoes where they had sought shelter. Anyone suspected of hiding the family fortune had hot water, hot oil, or worse poured down his throat. But still the Comtois fought on, and the war lengthened over generations until, at last, the French gained the upper hand. They then erected the Besançon courthouse in an obviously French design to show the Comtois what brand of justice they could expect henceforth. Resistance ends when public works to its futility are erected in its midst.

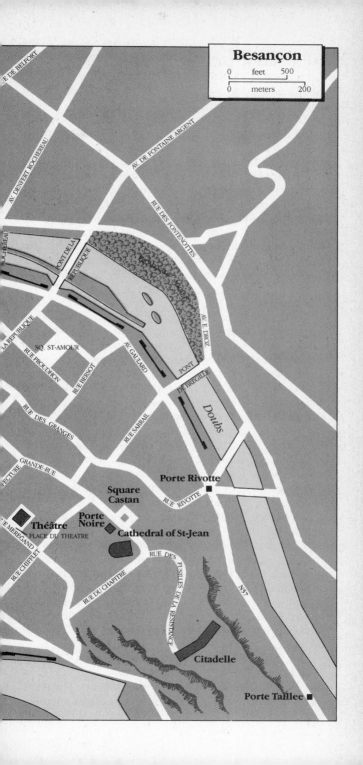

Besançon

| 0 | feet | 500 |
| 0 | meters | 200 |

RUE DE BELFORT

AV. DE FONTAINE ARGENT

AV. DENFERT ROCHEREAU

RUE DES FONTENOTTES

RUE JEHEREAU

PONT DE LA RÉPUBLIQUE

AV. E. DROZ

LA RÉPUBLIQUE

SQ. ST-AMOUR

RUE PROUDHON

RUE BERSOT

AV. GALLARD

PONT DE BRÉGILLE

RUE DES GRANGES

RUE SARRAIL

Doubs

PRÉFECTURE

GRANDE-RUE

Porte Rivotte ■

Square Castan

RUE RIVOTTE

RUE MÉGEVAND

Théâtre

Porte Noire

PLACE DU THÉÂTRE

Cathedral of St-Jean

RUE CHIFFLET

RUE DU CHAPITRE

RUE DES

FUSILLÉS DE LA RÉSISTANCE

N7

Citadelle

Porte Taillée ■

QUARTIER DE BATTANT

From the Place du 8-Septembre the Grande-Rue pushes on past pleasant cafés toward a cheerier perspective: the Battant quarter. Once inhabited by the working class, this ancient enclave in the throes of renovation now draws students and artists. Across the river and up the rue de Battant, part of the original road to Rome, is an old courtyard, at numer 37, of pale rose and blue *grès* (sandstone): the 16th-century **Hôtel de Champagney**, with its sagging zigzag balconies recently restored to show off their unusual mosaic tiling, embracing a thimble park. Near the end of the rue de Battant is a walkway to **Fort Griffon**. Here a long, paved incline, punctuated with flights of steps, leads up a steep hill to the fort, the town gradually falling away to surrounding vistas and gardens. All along the promenade are shops, small hotels, and, out on little setbacks, restaurants and cafés for the weary.

The Market

All varieties of the region's farm produce are sold at Besançon's market, on the Doubs beneath the Pont de Battant. Try the hams, and be sure to pick out a smoked variety. Thinly sliced, it's as good as prosciutto but more savory. Also try the cheeses: the *vacherin,* a soft, orange-rinded cheese (the Mont-d'Or, Haut-Doubs is almost local and made only in the cooler months); or the Gruyère de Comté, the king of French Gruyère, soft and nutty and easily cut by the pocket knife that you can also buy here. (Always buy Opinel when buying pocket knives in France.) There are wonderful fruits, too, particularly apples and pears, and cherries, a specialty of the Jura, which sell for 10 francs a kilo in spring. The Jésus de Morteau, the salami-like sausage that is named for its traditional appearance in the Christmas feast, comes in handy particularly during car trips, as do the *pastilles des Vosges,* candies tasting of pine-scented air. Also tasty, but not so practical for a car trip, are the live ducks and chickens (although some shops do sell chicken fresh off the rotisserie). As with any French market, the best time to drink all this in is before lunch when the *mère de famille* does the shopping and cooks the midday meal. The activity peaks around 11:30 A.M.; arrive much after that and you'll find the market struck and the city quiet, preparing its *déjeuner* behind long rows of windows.

PLACE DE LA REVOLUTION

Just south of the Pont de Battant is Bésançon's premier pâtisserie, **Baud**. Behind the displays of chocolate confections and cherry tarts, a natty salon serves tea to distinguished

Bisontins all afternoon. On the north side of the bridge and down the little hill, hard by the market, is the **Musée des Beaux-Arts et d'Archéologie**, installed in a former granary at Place de la Révolution. The excellent collection of paintings by the masters, ranging from the 16th to the 20th century, includes works by Bellini, David, Bonnard, Matisse, and, of course, local hero Gustave Courbet; the museum's lofty spaces have been restored by students of Le Corbusier, with a sprawl of ramps hinting of New York's Guggenheim. A must to see (closed Tuesdays).

The music conservatory across the street may not grab you, but its festival of classical music, one of the country's oldest, will. The two-week event, including an international competition for young conductors, is held from late August to mid-September.

THE CITADELLE

Follow rue des Granges from Place de la Révolution back across town to the rue Rivotte and the turreted stone gatehouse of the **Porte Rivotte**, the last of the old Comté gatehouses that guarded the city in the war with the French. Down N 57 from Porte Rivotte is the **Porte Taillée**, an opening the Romans chiseled in the rock to allow passage of an aqueduct. This rocky slope is the only overland route into Besançon, and here stands its fortress, the Citadelle, constructed from 1675 to 1711 by Vauban, Louis XIV's military engineer, on the site of the old Roman citadel.

Inside its walls the Citadelle houses three museums. One is the **Musée d'Histoire Naturelle**, a collection of local and other fauna, skeletons, butterflies, shells, and such; the other two—the **Musée Populaire Comtois** and **Musée de la Résistance et de la Déportation**—are far more engrossing. The Comtois is devoted to that most interesting of species, people; here, in particular, the Comtois. The 15 halls start with pottery, weaving, and spinning and go on into an authentic Comtois house with its artifacts, as well as a puppet collection, a vintage 1850 "Théâtre Mécanique." There are farm tools and wine tools and a collection of handcrafted wrought-iron objects, including 16th-century weather vanes. The museum depicting the horrific chapter of history on the Holocaust and Resistance includes German posters announcing the advance of Nazism, as well as a collection of drawings and sculptures created by concentration camp inmates.

Three hundred feet atop the rock rise the walls, ramparts, and towers engineered by the French to protect what was so hard to win. It was on this very hill that Julius Caesar first gazed down upon and appreciated what a marvelous, albeit strategic, spot Besançon occupied in the world. For those who lack the stamina of Caesar's regiment, the petite, three-car **Bisontrain** departs regularly from the Place du 8-Septembre, carrying visitors to its summit.

STAYING AND DINING IN BESANCON

The only hotel in the older part of town is the ▶ **Hôtel Régina**, set back in a courtyard at 91, Grande-Rue. It's somewhat dingy but comfortable, and in keeping with the style of the block; that is, it's built of pastel limestone in late-Renaissance style. The small rooms are high-ceilinged and overlook the wide street; the upper floors are filled with sunlight. A more modish choice would be the large ▶ **Mercure-Altéa Parc Micaud** across the river on avenue E. Droz, with its restaurant, **Le Vesontio**. Off the Promenade Micaud, which runs parallel to avenue E. Droz alongside the river, is the agreeable if touristy barge-restaurant **Le Chaland** (Tel: 81-80-61-61). The menu emphasizes seafood; try the *sandre*. You'll have a lovely view of the town while you dine.

To one side of the Square A. Castan, at 11, rue Victor Hugo, the charming restaurant **Le Castan** preserves that Roman ambience. Ask to eat in the *cave* downstairs, which is at the same level as the excavations—the subterranean Roman wall provides a wonderful backdrop. The food here is home style and heavy, but tasty, especially the goat. Ask for an Arbois wine, or better, an earthy Etoile, a 1986 Pupillin, or a red or rosé put up by Désiré Petit & Fils. At any rate, all are local Jura wines waiting to be discovered and will provide a foretaste of things to come.

There's a perfect little café, the **Restaurant du Champagney**, in the Cour de Champagney in the Battant quarter. Here, regional specialties (for example, *croute aux morilles*) can be had for a relative sou.

INTO THE JURA
The River Doubs

For a refreshing plunge into nature, the wonders of the Jura are ideal. One option is a trip of 200 km (124 miles) along the river Doubs from Besançon, following its sinuous and delectable curves to the northeast along route N 83, past the nearby **Belvédère de Montfaucon** of the verdant views; past **L'Isle-sur-le-Doubs**, where the river splits in three and the lovely 12th-century **Château de Belvoir** overlooks the Sancey Valley; past the curve at the village of Montbéliard and its

famous brown-and-white cows, the most widely distributed
dairy breed in France; and then toward the **Saut-du-Doubs**, a
waterfall with a drop of roughly 100 feet. It is, however, a
long trip, ending, some say, in isolation and souvenir stands.

An alternative is to leave the Doubs at Montbéliard about
85 km (53 miles) from Besançon and continue north on A 36
to Belfort, just 98 km (61 miles) from Besançon.

BELFORT

In its ancient fortress near the Franco-German border lurks
the beast of the keep, the **Lion de Belfort**. Seventy feet long
and 35 feet high, in chunks of red rock, the lion crouches in
the foundations of the town's citadel as if barring the gap in
the hills through which the invaders of France traditionally
came. In 1870 the German army advanced. Like the Celts,
Romans, and barbarians before them, the Germans laid
siege to the rock and fortress that stood in their way, but
with a difference: The Germans had artillery. They fired
5,000 shells a day into the fortress; 400,000 shells in toto fell
on the citadel, and still the garrison held. The defenders
continued to resist for 21 days after the Franco-Prussian War
had ended. This dramatic holdout in the Jura enabled France
to wrest better terms of peace—and a shred of honor—
from her otherwise total defeat.

And so, after the battle, a great sculptor came to the base
of Belfort's citadel and erected this lion in tribute to those
defenders who would not let their enemy pass. For all the
region's wild hills and crags, it is perhaps these blocks of
sculpted stone that best capture the rugged spirit of the Jura.
It is significant that this should have been done by Auguste
Bartholdi, the man who created the Statue of Liberty.

STAYING AND DINING
ALONG THE DOUBS

Belfort now has two stops for the collector of culinary stars:
▶ **Hostellerie du Château Servin** (with ten rooms) at 9, rue
Général-Négrier (Tel: 84-21-41-85) and **Le Sabot d'Annie**, 3
km (2 miles) north of town via D 13 (Tel: 84-26-01-71). For a
truly French culinary extravaganza, though, spend an evening at the **Café de Paris** (within the old Hôtel de Paris, at 1,
avenue Wilson, opposite the train station; Tel: 84-21-58-10).
What the café lacks in "gastronomic" stars it makes up for in
atmosphere. Here is where Old France—the milliner, the
tailor, the old generals and their spouses—comes to dine. It
is one of those places in the provinces that fills up at night
with local luminaries. Enter, and what's put on your plate
matters little next to the all-encompassing swirl of flirtatious-

ness and gentility filling the room. Everyone knows everyone else, and comes to visit at one another's table.

If you're short of time but want to spend a night or two in the countryside, you can also leave the Doubs at Baume-les-Dames, 30 km (19 miles) from Besançon on N 83, and head north 15 km (9 miles) on D 492, D 486, and D 116E to Cubry and just outside the village, the ► **Château de Bournel**. All that's required to appreciate the Jura here is to sit in splendor. Paris prices account for the grandeur (and golf) lacking elsewhere in the region.

The estate has been in the same family for 500 years and the reigning marquis de Moustier is now a master of tourism. With the conversion of the Neo-Gothic castle and the grounds, with their English-style park, gastronomes and golfers clamor at the gates. Never mind the furnishings *ordinaire* in the guest rooms—at the restaurant, **Le Maugre**, the inventive cuisine under the direction of Monsieur le chef and Madame Roy could easily take the region's top honors (save room for the matchless *tarte fine de pommes*).

The River Loue

Meanwhile, there is another river at hand that is just as impressive as the Doubs; the best parts of it can be seen by travelling just 25 miles of its length from its source. To boot, it is the most outstanding trout stream of France.

The Loue river carves a moving itinerary. Its valley has everything: a canyon, falls, châteaux, some of the most picturesque villages in France, irresistible restaurants, memorable accommodations, and a delightful road to lead you through it all. The towns along the Loue, couched safely against the wall of Switzerland, have remained far above the roar of modern artillery. The unscathed streets often bear unsuspected treasures—a stone statue at eye level, a bust of a saint, a piece of wrought-iron artwork.

The source of the Loue is about 50 km (31 miles) southeast of Besançon; follow N 57 southeast about 44 km (27 miles), then follow narrow D 41 and D 443 to the spot where the river bubbles up from a grotto, swells, and goes churning off, carving a rock canyon, now breathtakingly deep. The road, D 67, goes off after the river, zigging around chasms and hopscotching towns nestled in valleys, huddled in coves, or sitting high in the notches between hilltops.

MOUTHIER-HAUTE-PIERRE
The first village you'll come to as you follow D 67 northwest is Mouthier-Haute-Pierre. Six kilometers (4 miles) from the

source and on the curve of a deep gorge of the Loue, Mouthier is built of buff stone, its tile-roofed houses stepping up from the river. On one side of the road Mouthier huddles around its church spire and square, its streets tightly knit; then upward it goes again, a zigzag of road and stone farmhouses and cherry orchards, to the heights of a cliff-toothed mountain, old Hautepierre.

Hautepierre

A climb up Hautepierre provides refreshing exercise, fresh air in big gulps, benches along the way to collapse on, wonderful views of the whole of Mouthier in its valley below, and a nice place to lunch up top. You will find a goat trail through the fields, but unless you're a goat, it works better for descending.

The road on which you will begin your ascent of Hautepierre, D 244, moves upward through Mouthier past a quaint turn-of-the-century school, a village square, and an intact 15th-century church. Behind and to the left of the church, and marked by a little sign, is a path that follows a particular joy of the Jura—kirsch—to its source. Smelling this clear brandy (*eau-de-vie*) distilled from cherries is like having your nose in a barrel of the fruit itself. In fact, it takes 28 pounds of cherries to make a single bottle. Here it is made and sold out of their garage by two retired Parisians.

The path then continues past a *lavoir,* a chiseled stone tub brimming with clear running water. Rarely, however, will you see women on bended knee pounding their linen on a rock; nowadays you are more likely to find couples washing their Renaults or cyclists filling their water bottles. A 4-km (2½-mile) hike up the mountain brings you to Hautepierre's little farm settlement, where you'll be rewarded with a view of the valley and Mont Blanc glistening in its snows beyond, as well as an *épicerie* (French deli) where the omelettes are delicious, the ham is from local pigs, and the Beaujolais is about 60 francs a bottle.

LODS

Back on D 67 and down along the Loue, a couple of kilometers (about a mile) after Mouthier comes Lods, the second pearl of the Loue. (It claims to be the first.) Lods (pronounced Lo) has been designated one of the most beautiful villages in France. Lods is a legitimate gem deserving of such recognition. The parking lot across the Loue provides not just a place for your car but also the best view of the village across the fast-moving stream, except in summer, when the profusion of recreational vehicles tends to spoil the view.

Lods is actually much more appealing in spring and fall, when the camping crowds decamp. A walk through the town on the other side of the river will take about an hour.

About 5 km (3 miles) downstream from Lods is **Vuillafans**, a prosperous little town with prosperous houses, a big church, and one of the prettiest bridges across this prettiest of rivers. In season the Loue is crawling with fishermen in waders, their vest pockets bulging with flies. Those who like their trout freshly cooked head to the café on the river, just beside the 16th-century bridge.

ORNANS

Ornans, about 7 km (4½ miles) from Vuillafans, is the creative and commercial center of the Loue, but don't look for a big town. It's creative because it houses one of the most likable museums of France in the home of one of the leading painters of pre-Impressionist realism. And it's commercial because you can cash a check. Ornans is also very picturesque. Here the river slows down and, having done so, widens. It almost forms a lake, which reflects elongated images of the medieval buildings on both sides.

In warm weather flotillas of neon-colored kayaks flash along the foaming rapids at midday. At the **Pizzeria Le Chavot**, with its open balcony hanging over the the river, you can savor the view as well as good brick-oven pizza. A more soigné choice for dining, just down the main street, **Restaurant Le Corbet** offers a glassed-in terrace above the water.

Gustave Courbet was from Ornans (born to vine-growing parents in 1819), and his house, with its lovely views of the river, has been turned into an appealing museum, the **Musée Courbet**. Stairways lead through the rooms set up as galleries for Courbet's works, and a boutique sells reproductions, periodicals, and postcards. It is not the Picasso Museum in Paris or the van Gogh in Amsterdam, but the visitor comes away with a better idea of who the painter was than is offered by many other museums devoted to the work of a single artist. The museum is closed for lunch and Tuesdays from November to Easter.

The street leaving Ornans, the avenue Président-Wilson, passes a wine shop, an excellent place for picnic provisions and advice on the wines of the Jura. There are whites and reds, and the rosés accompany a mousse rather well.

WEST ALONG THE LOUE

The river road, now D 103, continues to follow the river west past more lovely *belvédères*—riverside places to picnic—to the most enviable of waterside habitations, the **Château de Cléron**. Seldom does the graceful reality of towers, turrets, and crenellations exist in such authentic chunks. The effect is complete; the castle occupies its own island park encircled by a moment of calm in the Loue. It does receive visitors, but only between July 9 and August 19, and then only after lunch, which puts it in the same time zone as Brigadoon.

As the river makes a series of loops up and down, you can stay with it on D 103, then D 102, and finally D 101. You'll lose the river as it makes a big swing north, but regain it at the town of Quingey, where D 17 heads southwest through **Arc-et-Senans** (about 25 km/16 miles from Ornans), sort of an 18th-century theme park more interesting in concept than in reality. Architect Claude-Nicolas Ledoux (1736–1806) envisaged an ideal community laid out in concentric circles. The plan was never fully realized, but the buildings erected for salt production were completed. (In medieval times salt was such a prized commodity that smugglers risked hanging if caught.) Today this national historic monument houses the International Center for Future Studies, a library, and a salt museum—and gives off about as much vitality as a mausoleum. If you pass through here at lunchtime, by all means avoid the deceptively charming Hôtel de Hoop.

STAYING AND DINING ON THE LOUE

Mouthier is a good place to stop, for a decent hotel awaits down on route D 67. Despite its nondescript 1980s architecture and tasteless decor, ► **La Cascade** has the country simplicity that fits in well here, but with sophisticated cuisine, fine views from the restaurant, and balconies overlooking the gorge from the bedrooms. Below, the river twists by, all white and racing. The nights are cool, even in summer. With the balcony doors left open to the roar of the river and the warm perfume of woodfires from the many chimneys below, sleep comes easily.

In **Lods** there is an old restaurant-hotel, the ► **Truite d'Or**, a "Logis de France" well worth visiting for lunch or dinner, especially in the off season, when fireplaces warm the bar and dining rooms. It enjoys a sweet setting between the river and the woods and offers hearty cooking and 13 unassuming rooms.

Directly across the river from the Musée Courbet in **Ornans** is the splendid ► **Hôtel de France**. This superb gray-limestone structure facing the river is an ideal headquarters for visiting the Loue and enjoying the ample charms of Ornans. Oozing with character and old-time comfort, it's the town's social hub, where the Ornanais go for Sunday lunch. But if you prefer to bask in the nearby, tranquil valley of the Brême that was so dear to Courbet, book one of the eight rooms at the charming restaurant-hotel ▶ **Moulin du Prieuré**—a house in the country affecting the chic-*rustique* style of which the French have always been so fond. The beam-ceilinged main house dates from the 13th century, but the current innkeepers built the cottages wedged between the river and woods. The seafood Napoléon is not to be missed here (Tel: 81-59-21-47).

Lodging and Dining around Germigney and Dole

You'll be quite happy if you follow the Loue west on D 7 about 8 km (5 miles) from Arc-et-Senans to Germigney for a meal and a bed. There, tucked alongside the rural road, the old stone **Ferme Auberge du Val d'Amour** plucks chickens and ducks right from the range for roasting or basting in *vin jaune* with local *morilles*. In fact, almost everything on this rustic table is home-grown. That it's off the beaten track guarantees few tourists, although the Comtois from miles around crowd in daily for spirited lunches at rollback prices (Tel: 84-37-60-83).

From here, another 20 km (12 miles) northeast on D 7 just above the Loue brings you to **Dole**, the first capital of the Jura (until Besançon replaced it in 1678, when the old Comté finally became part of France). Despite lost political clout, Dole nonetheless rates a stop on the TGV line and has plenty of historical and architectural attributes. Among them: **Louis Pasteur's birthplace** and the imposing church of Notre-Dame, focal point of the oldest part of town. If you missed church, you can say your blessings steps away at **Les Templiers**, the heaven-sent restaurant housed in a 13th-century crypt on the Grande Rue (Tel: 84-82-78-78). With organ music reverberating from the arched stone walls, this place is more fun than formal and offers both classic and creative cuisine: Try the langoustine with fennel.

For espresso-sipping and people-watching, the terrace of the **Grand Hôtel Chandioux** is the *distingué* place to go. You could easily spend the night there, but you wouldn't want to miss an evening at the ▶ **Auberge du Vieux Moulin**, some 20 km (12½ miles) north in **Aubigney** (D 475 to D 280). Fields of poppies, meadowlands, and avenues of poplars lead the way to Pesmes, yet another "most beautiful village," but this unsung *auberge* on the Haute-Saône border possesses the most winsome setting of all. Constructed as a watermill in 1794, the low, vine-covered building looks as if it grew there, the fancy of some fairy-tale illustrator. One side overlooks cornfields, with the inevitable forest edging the horizon, while the other emerges onto a tangle of woods, streams, and ponds ideal for ambling and angling. Although the *auberge* sits right on the road, the only traffic consists of a passing *deux chevaux* about once an hour. Silence reigns here, with the exception of crickets in the garden and sympathetic souls chatting on the terrace. The warmth of the owners, Madame Mirby and her daughter Betty is such that you'll want to return again and again, as well for their robust cuisine. Be sure to try the carpaccio of foie gras and then work up an appetite for breakfast, with homemade croissants, apricot preserves, honey, and fresh fruit compote, along with *fromage blanc* and eggs for the asking. Chances are you'll even miss the dogs when you leave this place, a rare pocket of *cachet* in the Jura.

Arbois and the Southern Jura

Arbois, 35 km (22 miles) south of Dole via N 5 and D 469, is more of a wine village than a wine center. To the naked eye there looms nothing commercial—no storage vats, no truck parks, no eyesores (although on the first Sunday in September the annual wine festival here would seem to compensate). Arbois has a lovely curl of river, the Cuisance, running through it, as well as old stone arcades buttressing its buildings and culs-de-sac with views through to backyards. The town is also an excellent entry to more spectacular Jura countryside.

Arbois was the home of Louis Pasteur, and his memory is still very much alive here. (And forget about milk: It was his advice regarding fermentation that the local vintners sought on a daily basis.) Anyone with a feeling for Pasteur's contributions to modern science must visit his home on the rue de Courcelles, where his furnishings, laboratory, and instruments remain just as he left them.

From this side of the river the **Eglise St-Just**, its bulbous dome characteristic of the Comté, can be glimpsed through the clotheslines. Also not to be missed, for its arcades and wrought-iron work, is the 18th-century Place de la Liberté, the town hub.

SOUTH OF ARBOIS

Just outside the town are the Arbois vineyards. These may not be the most formidable in the world, but thanks to the site they occupy on a ridge above the Forêt de Poligny, they are certainly among the prettiest. (On the way to the vineyards stop at the **Fruitier d'Arbois**, a local co-op that is the best place to buy Arbois wines.) Seven kilometers (4½ miles) south of Arbois via D 469 is the **Cirque du Fer à Cheval**, a magnificent forested box canyon that rises 655 feet above the springs.

Enroute, about 4½ km (3 miles) along D 469 you'll come to a turnoff for **Reculée des Planches** (the highest blind valley in the Jura) and its endearing village of Les Planches-Près-Arbois, with flowers dripping from every window box and garden wall. The main attraction here is a large *cave* that's open to the public, but you'll also be tempted to rent a bike from the tiny shop on the stream and explore the countryside.

Poligny

If Arbois is the Jura's wine hub, then Poligny is the capital of the Gruyère de Comté. Just 10 km (6 miles) south on N 83, Poligny draws students of the dairy industry, the occasional cheese addict, and few tourists (except perhaps during the Fête de Comté in mid-June). But it's an inviting little town, with cheese and wine shops lining the lanterned central square and bakeries turning out the delectable *pain de comté*. A few blocks beyond the square, the museum of the **Maison du Comté** traces the nearly 1,000-year-old history of this unique cheesemaking process—which still refuses pasteurization and modern methods—and its roots in the *jurassien* culture. Visitors can watch the fabrication of cheese at any number of *fromagères,* such as Arnaud Frères on the avenue de la Gare. And while **Jura Specialités** on the Place des Déportés may not be the biggest emporium, it's a fine old establishment where the *patronne* is full of good cheer and advice regarding not only cheese but its de rigeuer accompaniments, wine and *saucisse.*

Château-Chalon

The vineyard route, stretching about 25 km (16 miles) south of Poligny (on D 68, D 96, and D 204), calls for a stop in Château-Chalon, a village established long ago by Benedictine nuns. Cresting a rocky plateau, Château-Chalon produces a prized yellow dessert wine made exclusively from Savagnon grapes. Aside from a plethora of tasting *caves,* the town—with its soigné town houses and galleries—decants an arty, affluent air. Throughout summer it stages a *son-et-lumière* spectacle to dim all others.

Baume-les-Messieurs

Travelling a few kilometers (a couple of miles) southeast on D 70 brings you to the most magnificent site in the Jura: Baume-les-Messieurs. From the **Belvédère des Roches**, it's as

if the Grand Canyon had been transplanted, sprouted greenery up the cliffsides, and grown a village far below with a
river running through it, a steeple poking upward and stone-
roofed cottages gleaming in the sun. The steeple belongs to
the monastery, founded by the great Irish monk Columban
in the sixth century, at the bottom of the gorge, and even
though the monks have long since departed, the abbey
remains the village's raison d'être, a beautifully preserved
seat of antiquity.

Although some visitors will dutifully pass through the
abbey with its church and museum and hurry on to the
nearby **Grottes de Baume**, the wiser will pause for lunch at
the **Café de l'Abbaye** (what else?) for its salade de l'Abbaye—
greens tossed with Comté cheese, local ham, and walnuts—
and irresistible bread. From the shaded terrace you can watch
the woolly sheep scurrying along the river and the intermit-
tent promenade of villagers along the bank of immense old
linden trees. Should you decide to stay, inquire just above the
café at the crossroads for the tidy room to let (the only one
around) at the home of Rex ▶ **Andrews** and his wife, Marie.
This scholarly Englishman could well be the Jura's answer to
Provence's Peter Mayle, but without the ensuing, gawking
hordes.

EAST OF ARBOIS
One of the loveliest trips out of Arbois—on D 54 to D 94—
climbs northeast for 19 km (12 miles) up to **Salins-les-Bains**,
an old thermal spa and cosmopolitan village. There's a real
saltwater spring bubbling up from the ground (the only one
in the Jura), a thermal hotel, and pharmacies that specialize
in health and beauty products. But today Salins is known
equally for its faïence industry, as you will see by the barrage
of pottery shops. At the **Faïencerie de Salins**, 18, avenue
Aristide-Briand, this year's rage is a line of dinnerware
patterned after Indonesian batik. For one-of-a-kind pottery,
the **Atelier Ludovic**, just outside of town, throws it on the
spot.

The road (now route D 492) plunges east to the lush
Lison river, where trout, their shadows blue in the crystal
eddies, are just waiting for a fly. About 13 km (8 miles) from
Salins, midships in the Lison Valley, you arrive in the village
of **Nans-sous-Ste-Anne**. At the modest 11-room hotel ▶ **Hôtel de la Poste** the cows come home under the verandah at
cocktail hour; the barn is in the back, the roosters in front,
and the price is only 190 francs a day. In the village, not far
from the hotel, is another *fruitier* (in the Jura, a cooperative
cheesemaking center with a shop that sells foodstuffs and

wine). This time the bargain is local Comté cheese, *morbier* and *vacherin*. Across from the store is a billboard with directions to all manner of nature walks, including one to the source of the Lison. The one up to the *belvédère*—here an overlook—starts across the Lison and leads through a pine forest, where you will find wildflowers basking in sunny pools and a great view of the valley.

STAYING AND DINING
IN AND AROUND ARBOIS

If you arrive in Arbois before lunch, be warned: There is a curious dearth of good cafés. Avoid the highly publicized La Finette, unless you warm to cigar smoke, noise, and so-so food. Head instead to the outdoor terrace of **Restaurant La Balance** at 47, rue de Courcelles, for a *salade Bressane*—or a go at *la pierrade,* the popular cooking method in which anything from fish to fruit is sizzled at the table on a smoking granite slab.

Should you stay for dinner and the night, do so at ▶ **Jean-Paul Jeunet** on rue de l'Hôtel de Ville (if the hotel is full, the rooms in the annex a short walk away are cozy and less pricey). Its stylishly smart restaurant gives cause to wish upon its star for better food and service. Among its specialties is *poularde au vin jaune et morilles,* and there is a good selection of regional wines for the tasting that have not taken the trouble you have to get here. Try the famous and seldom tasted (by outsiders) *vin jaune* itself. As the name implies, it is golden, aged at least six years in oak casks topped only with fermenting yeast. This cap serves the double purpose of giving the wine its nutty flavor and keeping it from oxidizing. A neat trick, when it works, for then the wine has much the taste of sherry—a *fino*—from a mass that is heavier. It is this taste that locals crave, and when they get it they claim to feel it down to their toes, crying rapturously as their toes curl, "Ah, that's *jaune.*"

One of the best reasons to visit Poligny is to stay at the family-run ▶ **Hostellerie Les Monts de Vaux** (5 km/3 miles southeast on N 5), which borders one of the loveliest *reculées* in the region. This 19th-century coaching inn embodies a quaint elegance in its warren of comfy rooms that open onto a small park edged in rich forest. The cuisine is classic: Dinner begins with an aperitif of the local version of sherry, *mac-et-vin,* and moves on to the specialty of choice, *turbot au vin jaune*. And, while most other hotels in the Jura seem content to serve canned juices, the Monts de Vaux presses blood oranges in season for an altogether superb breakfast.

GETTING AROUND

TGVs make the 2½-hour run from Paris's Gare de Lyon to Besançon several times a day, some making a 12-minute stop in Dijon. Regular trains also link Paris and Besançon. You can then rent a car in Besançon; all the major rental agencies are here, and driving is the best way to see the Jura.

ACCOMMODATIONS REFERENCE

The rates given below are projections *for 1994. Unless otherwise indicated, rates are for a double room, double occupancy, and do not include meals. As rates are always subject to change, double-check before booking.*

▶ **Andrews** (Rex and Marie). Baume-les-Messieurs, 39210 **Voiteur.** Tel: 84-44-65-72. 150F, including breakfast.

▶ **Auberge du Vieux Moulin.** Aubigney, 70140 **Pesmes.** Tel: 84-31-61-61; Fax: 84-31-21-75. 380F.

▶ **La Cascade.** 25920 **Mouthier-Haute-Pierre.** Tel: 81-60-95-30; Fax: 81-60-94-55. 265F–300F.

▶ **Château de Bournel.** 25680 **Cubry.** Tel: 81-86-00-10; Fax: 81-86-01-06. 890F–970F. (Ask about *demi-pension* and golf packages.)

▶ **Hostellerie du Château Servin.** 9, rue Général-Négrier, 90000 **Belfort.** Tel: 84-21-41-85; Fax: 84-57-05-57. 450F.

▶ **Hostellerie les Monts de Vaux.** Famille Carrion, **39800 Poligny.** Tel: 84-37-12-50; Fax: 84-66-05-67. 850F–1,550F (demi-pension).

▶ **Hôtel de France.** Rue P. Vernier, 25290 **Ornans.** Tel: 81-62-24-44; Fax: 81-62-12-03. 400F.

▶ **Hôtel de la Poste.** 25330 **Nans-sous-Ste-Anne.** Tel: 81-86-62-57. 190F; 350F, demi-pension.

▶ **Hôtel Régina.** 91, Grande-Rue, 25000 **Besançon.** Tel: 81-81-50-22; Fax: 81-81-60-20. 225F.

▶ **Jean-Paul Jeunet.** 9, rue de l'Hôtel de Ville, 39600 **Arbois.** Tel: 84-66-05-67; Fax: 84-66-24-20. 390F–500F.

▶ **Mercure-Altéa Parc Micaud.** 3, avenue E. Droz, 25000 **Besançon.** Tel: 81-80-14-44; Fax: 81-53-29-83; in the U.S. and Canada, Tel: (800) 221-4542; Fax: (914) 472-0451; in the U.K., Tel: (071) 724-1000. 430F–550F.

▶ **Moulin du Prieuré.** Route de Bonnevaux-le-Prieuré (via routes D 67 and D 280), 25620 **Bonnevaux-le-Prieuré.** Tel: 81-59-21-47; Fax: 81-59-28-79. 350F. Closed November 15 to March 1.

▶ **Truite d'Or.** 25930 Lods. Tel: 81-60-95-48; Fax: 81-60-95-73. 230F.

THE SAVOY AND THE FRENCH ALPS

By Mimi Tompkins and Alexander Lobrano

Mimi Tompkins is a freelance print and broadcast journalist who has been based in Paris for the past 11 years. Alexander Lobrano also covers Paris dining and bars and Brittany for this guidebook.

Ever since the first Winter Olympic Games were held at Chamonix in 1924, the French Alps have had global allure as a chic wintertime playground—and this snow-and-sin image has eclipsed to a large extent the mountains' 19th-century reputation as the ideal place for a calm, elegant, and restorative spa holiday. With spectacular scenery and superb recreational facilities, the region today merits both of these reputations. But nearly two hundred years of romantic, leisurely associations and imagery have obscured the fact that this part of France has been a vital European crossroads since even before the Roman general Hannibal first tramped through. As a result of these centuries of transalpine traversing, both for conquest and commerce, this area has been endowed with a variety of cultural and artistic treasures that are found not only in its bustling, prosperous cities of Chambéry, Annecy, and Grenoble, but in the countryside, too, making the Savoy and the French Alps just as rewarding a destination for chain-smoking bookworms as it is for taut-bellied sports buffs. Further, following the massive investment, both public—roads, railroads, and airports—and private—hotels, restaurants, and new ski facilities—that led up to 1992's Albertville-headquartered but regionally staged Winter Olympics, the area is awash in hotel rooms, and so offers a variety of good buys to all tribes of travellers.

MAJOR INTEREST

Skiing (December to April)
Hiking (July and August)
National and regional natural parks

Chambéry
The old city

Abbaye Royale de Hautecombe

Aix-les-Bains (Roman ruins and baths)

Annecy
The old city
Sights relating to Saint François de Sales
Sailing and swimming
Boat tour of the Lac d'Annecy

Cirque du Fer-à-Cheval

Notre-Dame-de-Toute-Grâce (the church at Plateau d'Assy)

Mont Blanc

Grenoble
The Bastille
Centre National d'Art Contemporain
Musée Dauphinois
Musée des Beaux-Arts (new building)

Vauban fortifications at Briançon

More than any other mountain range, the Alps merit a bouquet of adjectives generally awarded only to the world's oceans: The Alps are majestic, immemorial, and awesome. Seeing them for the first or fortieth time is always a stirring, almost startling experience, because they so swiftly shatter our myopic habit of seeing ourselves as the largest thing that looms on any terrestrial landscape. In big and small ways these mountains make you think and react. As you sit on a boat cutting through the waters of Lac d'Annecy on a hot summer afternoon, the waters are pale blue-green and the shores are thickly lined with old trees and bright flowers. Sailboats tack by, and the whole lovely scene has all the drama of a bathtub until you glance skyward and take re-

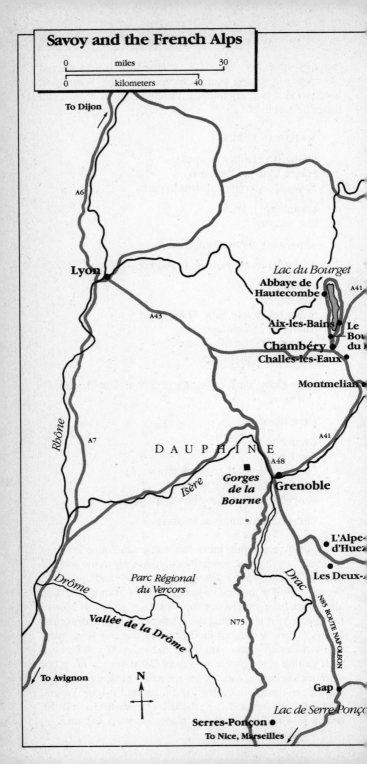

freshment from the snow-capped peaks you see there. It's just plain nice to know that it's cool somewhere, and then you start secretly wondering exactly why it is that the snow there never melts—the altitude, of course, but. . . . In winter the mountains' beauty is more austere, reduced as it usually is to great white plains and planes of snow and pine-scented, shadow-darkened forests, but even as you ski, you can't help but being a little wonder-struck by the purity and simplicity of it all, these extraordinary mountains, and the march of time and the seasons.

Life in the Alps has always had a seasonal quality, though. In pre-tourist times herds of cows and goats moved up to high Alpine meadows for the summer grazing and retreated to the valleys before the first autumn snowfalls. Nowadays the ebb and flow of vacationers marks the change of seasons here. Winter brings skiers to the two breeds of ski resorts: the mountain-village-turned-modern-recreational type (Megève, Chamonix, Morzine, Val-d'Isère) and the integrated vacation complex built from scratch in virgin snowfields (Tignes, Courchevel, La Plagne, Flaine, Avoriaz).

Summer activities are more varied. The ski towns offer golf, tennis, and swimming, and so do the many lakeside villages and campgrounds. Hikers can take advantage of an organized network of trails and mountain shelters that allow the well-provisioned to stay in the wild for days or even weeks on end. Those who prefer more unusual sports can try rock climbing, hang gliding, sailing, and spelunking. Or, those who think strenuous activities are for the birds can head for Annecy, Chambéry, and Grenoble to shop, visit museums and churches, or just sit in cafés.

The French Alps stretch from north to south along the Italian border, bounded by Lac Léman and Switzerland to the north (Geneva and Lausanne are on Lac Léman) and the Mediterranean foothills to the south. While the area is mountainous, not all its mountains were created equal. The rugged 10,000- to 14,000-foot-high peaks around Mont Blanc and Ecrins contrast sharply with the gentler mountains near Annecy and Lac Léman and the sunnier slopes south of Grenoble.

Water is everywhere here, and the Alps, stretching from France to Slovenia, are, in fact, the water towers of Europe, serving as the main watershed for the rivers Rhine, Rhône, Danube, and Po. The Isère, the Arve, the Durance, and the Arc rivers cut deep ravines through the mountains, making the region accessible to trains and cars. The lakes of Léman, Annecy, and Bourget are popular with weekend sailors and big enough for steamships (Bourget is France's largest lake).

Water cascades down the spectacular falls at Cirque du Fer-à-Cheval and forms icy white glaciers on Mont Blanc; medicinal springs soothe the infirm at Aix-les-Bains and St-Gervais-les-Bains, and globally trendy mineral water is bottled and sold at Evian-les-Bains.

A great deal of water also sits behind dams waiting to pass through hydroelectric power turbines. This "white oil" fueled a 19th-century industrial revolution in the Alps, as energy-intensive industries such as chemical manufacturing and metallurgy sought out cheap sources of electricity. While many of these businesses have since relocated or succumbed to deindustrialization, enough remain to create a discouragingly thick smog in some of the major river valleys. This is not a plastic vacation paradise. Rather, it is a prosperous and economically diverse area with a growing population. Local industries include the making of wine and cheese in the hills, aluminum and detergent in the valleys, and everything from microchips to church bells in the larger towns. For better or worse, this once-isolated region is now irrevocably integrated into modern France and Europe. How much more integrated it becomes has, in fact, become a source of heated local debate. A good 15 percent of Europe's freight traffic already passes through the Alps, with almost five million vehicles using the Tunnel du Fréjus connecting France and Italy near Chamonix every year. With this tunnel functioning at near capacity, the European Community planners in Brussels have been urging construction of another, but it is being fought by local residents who say that the town already suffers from the fallout of 25 tons of fuel a day. Such environmental issues will certainly dominate the politics of this region for the rest of the decade.

Not too surprisingly, the mountains look and feel lived-in, and the remote Alpine village untouched by the modern world is pretty much a thing of the past. All this is to say that those seeking a North American–style wilderness in the Alps are likely to be disappointed. What the Alpine towns lack in quaintness, however, they make up for with authenticity.

Historically, the French Alps were divided into two areas: the Savoy to the north and the Dauphiné to the south. The **Savoy**, which occupies the modern administrative departments of the Savoie and the Haute-Savoie, is the newest region of France, a proud and powerful independent kingdom until 1860. The **Dauphiné**, which includes the departments of Isère, Hautes Alpes, and Drôme, has belonged to France since 1349. This pennant-shaped territory includes some of the most varied scenery in France, since it is roughly bounded by the Rhône river, the Alps, and Provence, west, north, and south respectively. While both areas are now firmly French, they retain a subtle Alpine kinship not only with one another but with their Italian and Swiss neighbors across the northern border in the mountains.

SKIING

Skiing in the French Alps is a serious business: The resorts are huge and well equipped, and though they tend to lack charm, they provide an endless variety of slopes. Unlike North American ski centers, they are usually not organized around a single base lodge. Instead, the newer stations have multiple clusters of apartments, shops, hotels, and concessions; ski lifts and restaurants are strewn far and wide across the massive, treeless expanses of snow. The modern stations were developed primarily as real-estate projects and have acres of cheap, small apartments owned by middle-class families. Most visitors rent these apartments when they come to the resorts for stays of more than a weekend; prices start at about 1,500 francs for a studio during a non-holiday week at a midsize resort. Bookings for both apartments and hotels can be made easily through the tourist offices at the individual resorts.

The ski season extends from December to April, but good snow is not ensured outside of January, February, and March. Recent droughts have hit low-altitude resorts and those with exposure to the sun during most of the day hard. Some of the smaller resorts are now closed, and many others have diversified their activities to protect themselves in case of "bad" weather. So you'll find a wide variety of "summer" sports to choose from year-round, ranging from horseback riding to tennis to hiking.

Snow or no snow, if at all possible avoid the Christmas holidays and mid-February, when French schools take their winter break. Weekend ski traffic can be horrendous, especially along the Isère Valley. The only way to avoid it is to travel late at night.

GASTRONOMIC SUMMITS

If you come to this area with no gastronomic expectations beyond a good fondue, you're in for some luscious surprises. This prosperous region eats quite well and produces some of the most famous French cheeses, along with excellent wines and charcuterie—and if you add these elements together you get, of course, an excellent picnic.

The local stars at the *fromagerie* (cheese shop) are Beaufort, Reblochon, Tomme de Savoie, Tamié, and the exceedingly rare Bleu de Gex, a fine, sweet, blue-veined cow's-milk cheese that has been known for over 450 years but is produced by only five small dairies today. Beaufort, which somewhat resembles Gruyère, is a rich, aged cow's-milk cheese with a gentle scent of herbs and flowers that recalls the mountain pastures where the milk is produced. As is true of many popular French cheeses, the mass-produced version has nothing to do with the well-made original; to make sure you're getting the best of this superb cheese, go to a reputable *fromagerie* and ask for a Beaufort *d'été* (summer) or Beaufort *d'alpage* (alpine pasture), which will guarantee that the cheese was made during the best milking period, from mid-June to the end of September. Reblochon, whose name comes from the word *reblochage* (second milking), is an ancient cow's-milk cheese that was once a *fromage de dévotion,* or a votive cheese; the Savoyard peasants offered them to the Carthusian monks who came to bless their fields. As with almost all cheeses, buy only the raw-milk version. Reblochon is at its best from the end of June to the end of November and has a creamy texture with a faint taste of hazelnuts. Tamié resembles a heavier Reblochon, while Tomme de Savoie is made from either cow's or goat's milk and usually has a bumpy, dark-gray rind and a rich, mild flavor.

These cheeses team well with the best-known wines of the region, including Roussette, a pleasant and widely available dry white; Gamay, a light but full-bodied red; and the delicious Mondeuse, a deep, vigorous red with a fruity bouquet. Other gastronomic specialties to look out for are wild mushrooms, especially the tiny *mousserons;* Pormonier, a delicious, spicy sausage; and all the freshwater fish from the lakes, including salmon-trout, pike, perch, and the succulent and expensive *omble chevalier,* also known as *ombre,* a prized lake fish with firm, sweet flesh.

Gastronomically, the most interesting and toothsome dishes in this region are sturdy peasant plates incorporating milk, cheese, and potatoes, the staples most abundant in what had for centuries been a poor part of France. Beyond cheese fondue, you should also try delicious *raclette,* cheese that's sliced, melted in small triangular pans on a special grill, and then eaten with boiled potatoes, *viande de grissons* (air-dried beef), and *cornichons* (tarragon-vinegar-pickled baby cucumbers); or, one day when you're really hungry, try a baked *vacherin,* a strong, creamy winter cheese that comes to the table from the oven deliciously runny; it is best eaten with boiled potatoes. *Gratin dauphinois,* a baked dish of potatoes, onions, cheese, cream, and eggs, and *gratin savoy-*

ard, in which beef bouillon is used instead of cream, are the star potato dishes on local menus.

THE SAVOY

The early history of the Savoy hardly hints at its later glory. The Romans wrested the region from the Celtic Allobroges tribe—who had overrun it in the sixth century B.C.—in 121 B.C. and attached it to the province of Narbonne. It wasn't until the first century A.D. that Rome fully subjugated Savoy. Although settlements sprouted along the Roman road linking Milan and Vienna, notably at Aime and Annecy, no significant ruins from this period remain. A group of Burgundians who migrated here in the fifth century named the region Savoy, from the French *pays des sapins,* or "fir-tree country," and the area became part of the kingdom of Burgundy.

The House of Savoy is the oldest sovereign family in Europe. It was founded at the beginning of the 11th century by Count Maurienne Humbert aux Blanches Mains (White Hands), who received title to the region in exchange for supporting Conrad le Salique's bid to be the Holy Roman Emperor. His new kingdom controlled the Alpine passes to Italy and to the Germanic territories to the east and thus had great geopolitical importance. The later dukes of Savoy fully exploited their position as "porters of the Alps," and many kings were forced to pay humiliating tribute for the right to pass. The kingdom's golden era came in the 14th century when the three Amadeuses—all powerful rulers of the family—extended their domain to Nice, the Jura, Piemonte, and Geneva. At various times the House of Savoy also controlled large chunks of what are now Italy and Switzerland as well as the Mediterranean island of Sardinia. Repeated French invasions—in 1536, in the 17th century (three times), in 1742, and again in 1792—failed to bring the Savoy under the control of Paris. But when the Savoy, weary of war, finally joined France, it did so with some relief; an 1860 plebiscite showed 130,533 votes in favor of the union and just 235 against.

Chambéry

As the historic capital of the Savoy, Chambéry's fortunes rose and fell with those of the House of Savoy. Though it has lost its onetime prominence, the city remains a governmental center. The Château de Chambéry, seat of the dukes of Savoy, is now occupied by the prefecture and the regional council of Savoy. Today Chambéry, 98 km (61 miles) east of Lyon on A 43, remains a stately but animated town. Nearly all the interesting sites lie in the compact old city; the Office de Tourisme, located on the tree-lined boulevard de la Colonne, is exceptionally helpful in directing visitors (it's at number 24; Tel: 79-33-42-47).

THE OLD CITY

The **Château de Chambéry**, actually a collection of buildings on a low, walled hilltop at the southern edge of the old city, dominates Chambéry. Many of the original 14th-century structures burned down in the 18th century, and the massive building that now houses the prefecture was erected then. The church, the dungeon, and the treasure tower, however, retain their original medieval lines. The grounds make for a pleasant walk, but to really see the place the guided tour is a necessity.

The old city has numerous small architectural delights behind its archways and doorways and in its well-proportioned squares. The rue de Boigne, a street of grand façades and Italianate porticoes, begins at the château and cuts through the center of the city past pastry and candy shops that serve tea, continuing to the 15th- to 16th-century **Basilique St-François-de-Sales**, which houses some interesting religious art (especially in the adjoining convent, now the **Musée Savoisien**); the cathedral square is home to fine art galleries. Just north of the cathedral at the intersection of the rue de Boigne and the boulevard de la Colonne stands the slightly bizarre elephant fountain, erected in 1838 in memory of Général Comte de Boigne's trip to India. It has become, to the chagrin of many residents, one of the most popular monuments in town.

Beautiful old houses along the **rue de la Croix d'Or**, at the eastern edge of the old city, are home to many of the groceries and other shops patronized by locals, making this not only the most lovely but also the liveliest street in Chambéry. Nearby, the four-year-old cultural center, **L'Espace André-Malraux**, designed by the prominent young Swiss architect Mario Botta, houses a cinema, a concert hall, meeting rooms, and the library. It is complemented nicely by the **Caserne Curial** next door, a huge, square army barracks that has been transformed into a tasteful shopping center that should please even the most ardent mall-hater.

For a gift of Chambéry origin, try the local chocolate or the famous Opinel knives, available anywhere in town. Another alternative is a bottle of Vermouth. Chambéry has long been a center of Vermouth making, and the distillery of Routin, on rue Emile Romanet, offers guided tours, but only on request. Write or call in advance: Routin, B.P. 9428, 73094 Chambéry, cedex 9; Tel: 79-25-68-76; Fax: 79-25-68-55.

AROUND CHAMBERY

Rousseau's Home in Les Charmettes

On the southern outskirts of town, only a kilometer (less than a mile) on D 4 from the center in the hamlet of Les Charmettes, is a site of great interest to sensualists and literary types—the country retreat of Madame Louise-Eléonore de Warens, the woman who took in writer-philosopher Jean-Jacques Rousseau when he fled his home in Geneva in 1728. The two of them lived here from 1736 to 1742, and in one of his most celebrated accounts, Rousseau describes their passionate and idyllic liaison in book six of his *Confessions*. The attractive 17th-century house has a fine garden with a sweeping view of the Chambéry valley and contains many of its original furnishings, including the contents of Rousseau's bedroom and Madame de Warens's clavicord. (Open from April to September. Tel: 79-33-39-44; call for hours.)

Aix-les-Bains

A Victorian spa town that's been popular with tourists since the Romans began coming here to take the cure in its thermal baths has lost some of its exclusive luster but it's still popular and enjoys a spectacular setting on the shores of Lac Bourget. (Aix is just 16 km/10 miles north of Chambéry on N 201.) In Aix, the **Thermes Nationaux**, just east of the train station overlooking the town and the lake, are open all year. The facilities are ultramodern now, but the ruins of the original Roman baths are still visible in the cellar. Half-hour tours of the ancient baths are given every day, but for those who want to revel in the pleasures of body mud packs, steam baths, and massages, it's better to stay off your feet upstairs.

The ruins of the **Arc de Campanus** and the **Temple de Diane**, the most significant Roman monuments in the Savoy, are housed in the museum behind the tourist office across from the Thermes Nationaux. Aix also has a beautiful lakefront promenade, several fine parks, and many beautiful Victorian buildings. In fact, the beauty of the place inspired the poet Alphonse de Lamartine both to fall in love and to write some of his finest verse here. What he liked has only been enhanced since then, so come down to the lakeside and enjoy the swan-garnished views across the lake's dark blue waters. The **Musée Faure**, next to the Thermes, houses a fine collection of pre-Impressionist art as well as good temporary exhibitions.

Abbaye Royale de Hautecombe

Another nice excursion from Chambéry—and a good historical complement to the château—is a visit to the Abbaye Royale de Hautecombe, a beautiful lakeside monastery where 42 male and female heads of the House of Savoy are buried. Take N 201 north to Aix-les-Bains and then either follow the *tour du lac* around Lac du Bourget or take the boat (from April to October) from the main port to the abbey. There is a recorded tour of the church and tombs in French as well as in English. There is also a museum with displays on the life and history of the abbey. Hautecombe is still used as a burial place—Umberto II, the last king of Italy, was buried here in 1983—but the Benedictine monks fled the grounds in 1990 in the face of the tourist invasion.

STAYING AND DINING IN AND AROUND CHAMBERY

There are not many hotels in Chambéry, so it's a good idea to book ahead in summer. ► **Les Princes**, on rue de Boigne, has a great location and a fine restaurant, which more than compensate for the small rooms and the hotel decor, a somewhat unsuccessful mélange of modern styles. But it is clean and—thanks to double-glazed windows—quite peaceful. The gregarious **Le Tonneau** restaurant, at 2, rue St-Antoine, is a favorite with the locals, and is a good place to try the region's hearty cuisine in an appropriately rustic setting (Tel: 79-33-78-26).

If you prefer a country setting, try the ► **Hôtel de Château de Challes**, 6 km (4 miles) south of town in Challes-les-Eaux. Open all year, this clean and bright hostelry occupies a 15th-century château. Try to book one of the two rooms with the original wood-inlay flooring and 11-foot ceilings. However, all of the 63 rooms in the hotel or the renovated *bergerie* (sheep pen) outside are attractive, and all overlook the courtyard and sculpted gardens in the hotel's private park.

Aix-les-Bains has a selection of good hotels right in the center of town, many with very good restaurants. ► **Le Dauphinois** is a calm, pleasant hotel overlooking a garden; its restaurant serves basic but delicious French fare. For a good view of the lake, try the ► **Hôtel le Manoir**, a country-style hotel that's also close to the national baths.

South of the Abbaye Royale de Hautecombe, perched in

seclusion on a hillside above the Lac du Bourget, rises the
▶ **Ombremont**, a gorgeous 20-room, two-suite inn. With
tranquil gardens and magnificent views from the dining
terrace and most of the rooms, the Ombremont offers an
excellent value in the luxury class. The restaurant is also
first-rate.

Annecy

Annecy, 50 km (31 miles) northeast of Chambéry on A 41, is
one of the most beautiful and charming small cities in
France. With a spectacular setting at the north tip of the
pristine lake of the same name, surrounded by the majesty
of the Alps and possessing splendid views of both lake and
mountains, this lively city has a uniquely appealing personality characterized by a well-balanced blend of Alpine tidiness
and discipline tempered by a good dose of Gallic joie de
vivre. Arriving here from Chambéry, you quickly sense that if
the former is the historic capital of the Savoy, Annecy is the
region's spiritual capital and the real source of its identity.

Its **old city** is almost too charming: 17th-century buildings
painted in pastel oranges and reds line the trickling rivers
and canals, and an excellent flea market takes over the
streets and squares on the last Saturday of every month.

Annecy's **château**, beautifully restored after hundreds of
years of abandonment, sits on a small hill above the old city
and affords excellent views. Along the lakefront are the
public gardens and the refreshingly large and informal (for
France) **Parc du Pâquier**.

Saint François de Sales is the undisputed local hero.
Born to a prominent Savoyard family in 1567, he studied
law in Paris but gave up a promising political career at age
26 to take religious vows. Named head of the Cathédrale St-
Pierre, a large but unremarkable church in the center of
the old city, Saint François led a bitter struggle against
Calvinism in the region. His oratory was said to be "soft as
honey" and was so persuasive that his fame spread throughout France. In 1606 he joined the renowned lawyer Antoine Favre in founding the Académie Florimontane, one of
the earliest literary societies in Europe. It is still headquar-
tered at 18, rue Ste-Claire, its original location.

In 1608, while living in the beautiful Lambert house at 15,
rue Jean-Jacques Rousseau, François wrote *Introduction to
the Devoted Life,* a spiritual treatise that was the 17th-century
equivalent of a bestseller. He was also the sponsor of the
first convent in the region devoted to the Virgin, and he was
canonized in 1665 (at the church that bears his name, just

across from the *mairie*) 43 years after his death. His remains lie at the Basilique de la Visitation, an agreeable 20th-century structure just south of the old city.

Those who like their historical figures a little more profane might want to pay homage to Jean-Jacques Rousseau, who fled here from his native Geneva in 1728; a bust of the writer and philosopher stands in the courtyard of the old episcopal palace.

LAC D'ANNECY
The Lac d'Annecy is unequivocally beautiful and, happily, also unequivocally clean, so dive right in. The lake has been for more than 20 years the object of one of the most stringent and successful antipollution efforts ever made in France or anywhere else in Europe; a drive around it makes a good afternoon's excursion. It's possible to rent sailboats, motorboats, and pedal boats during the summer at Le Petit Port in Annecy-le-Vieux, just east along the lake from the old city, and boat tours of the lake leave from several points along the quais. A floating restaurant in an old steamboat, the **Bateau Libellule**, serves dinner and holds dances as it cruises the lake (from April to October; Tel: 50-51-08-40). For more information on these trips—and on hiking in the nearby mountains—stop by the Office de Tourisme in the Centre Bonlieu, an ugly modern building across from Parc du Pâquier at the corner of avenues Président Faure and d'Albigny (Tel: 50-45-00-33).

The tranquil **Ermitage de St-Germain**, where François de Sales spent his last days, lies about 16 km (10 miles) from Annecy on the east side of the lake, off route D 42. There's a delightful little chapel here and a splendid view of the lake. Just above the church is a nice meadow for picnicking. If you're feeling less rustic, continue up the road to the Col de la Forclaz and have a lunch of traditional French cuisine on the terrace of **La Pricaz** while you watch hang gliders swoop off the ramp next to the restaurant. The drive back down toward the lower lake and Albertville is harrowing but pretty.

STAYING AND DINING
IN AND AROUND ANNECY
Annecy bustles with restaurants, but you should be choosey about where you eat. The renovated **Auberge du Lyonnais**, at 9, rue de la République, has an excellent quai-side location in the heart of the old city and good, straightforward French food. In the same neighborhood, you might also try **Le Petit Zinc**, 11, rue de Pont-Morens, a delicious bistro with

a cozy, beamed dining room that's popular with locals, who come for the cheese croquettes, roasts, and good carafe wines; Tel: 50-51-12-93.

If you're in the mood for something more luxurious, try the **Auberge de l'Eridan**, on the lake about 5 km (3 miles) outside of town in the direction of Thones. This award-winning restaurant is elegant in every respect, with a fine view of the water and food that ranks with the best anywhere. Of special note is the fact that the chef here, Marc Veyrat, working with almost every known variety of seed, shoot, leaf, root, weed, flower, and vegetable, offers what many French gourmet vegetarians believe are some of the best and most interesting veggie dishes in France. Reserve several weeks in advance, and be prepared to spend a fortune; Tel: 50-60-24-00. Note, too, that the best place in town to stock up on picnic supplies, especially for excellent cheeses and sausages, is the market on the rue Sainte Claire (held on Tuesdays, Fridays, and Sundays from 8:00 A.M. to noon).

Should you want to spend a night in town, the ► **Imperial Palace**, 32, avenue d'Albigny, is an enchanting hotel with a lot of fin de siècle nuances and a wonderful site flanking the beautifully planted Parc du Pâquier along the lake; the food's good here, too, even at breakfast, where smoked salmon with dill and goat cheese is a signature dish. Less grand, but comfortable and well located, is the ► **Allobroges Hôtel**, 11, rue Sommellier, just a two-minute walk from the train station. This is a solid, old-fashioned travellers' (as opposed to tourists') hotel that offers good value for the price, even if the decor in many rooms brings to mind Hugh Hefner, circa 1969.

On the lake road, D 909A, just south of the turnoff for route D 42, lies the charming port town of **Talloires**, where there are two excellent inns. The ► **Auberge du Père Bise** has 27 rooms and seven suites, lovely grounds, and one of the most prestigious and expensive restaurants in France, now run by the granddaughter of the original owner and still as good; try the potatoes, foie gras, and truffles in puff pastry, which may be one of the most delicious dishes in France, and note the outstanding wine cellar. It is essential to make reservations far in advance; Tel: 50-60-72-01. The ► **Abbaye de Talloires** occupies a 17th-century abbey. The beauty of its antiques- and tapestry-filled rooms is equaled only by the stunning lakeside location and excellent dining room. A pleasant and more economical alternative is ► **La Charpenterie**. It's a new place built in an ersatz ski-chalet style, but it's clean, comfortable, and friendly.

Into the Mountains

A good place to begin a summertime driving tour of the Haute Savoie is at the top of the region, in **Evian-les-Bains**. This dignified old spa town on Lac Léman, about 80 km (49 miles) northeast of Annecy via the autoroute to Geneva then D 903 and N 5, has special appeal to gamblers, curists, and connoisseurs of fine hotels—the ▶ **Domaine du Royal Club Evian-Hôtel Royal** may be the last real grand hotel in Europe, a stunning palace with remarkable Art Nouveau public rooms and an outstanding kitchen (come for lunch even if you can't afford the steep room rates). Anyone in search of the finely woven fabric of French civilization will delight in this mannered, well-trimmed and planted town, and its fine setting on the kaleidoscopically changing Lac Léman.

From Evian, head south toward Morzine on D 21, D 23, and D 22 to D 902; the route (about 38 km/24 miles) passes through the spectacular **Gorges du Pont du Diable** (Devil's Bridge), a steep valley with a 165-foot waterfall that may be visited in the summer. Rock-climbing expeditions are also available.

From Morzine route D 354 meanders 16 km (10 miles) over the mountains to Samoëns, past the ski trails of Les Gets, providing superb vistas and many good opportunities for walking.

SAMOENS AND ENVIRONS

Samoëns is a perfectly tended village of fewer than 2,000 inhabitants. It is well worth a stop, if only for the **Jaÿsinia**, a remarkable botanic garden devoted to Alpine plants from around the globe. It was the gift of Marie-Louise Jay, a local shepherdess who married a peddler named Ernest Cognacq. Together they made good and founded the Parisian department store La Samaritaine.

From Samoëns it's just 13 km (8 miles) via D 907 up to **Cirque du Fer-à-Cheval**, a flat valley floor surrounded by a near-perfect semicircle of towering cliff walls and angular peaks, the highest of which sit directly on the border with Switzerland. In spring and early summer, an incredible array of some 30 waterfalls spills down the mountains. Hiking opportunities range from a quick jaunt up to one of the falls to a 12-hour trek over the mountains to Chamonix. Bicycles are for rent next to the welcome center.

South of the road leading into the cirque is the Maison de la Réserve at **Sixt-Fer-à-Cheval**. It's open at least a few hours a day all year round and is a friendly place that offers helpful information on the flora and fauna of the nearby nature reserve. Sixt itself is a pleasant, low-key town and a good base for serious exploration of the area. Unfortunately, the only direct route from Sixt to Chamonix is on foot. By car, it's necessary to backtrack through Samoëns to Cluses and take the autoroute.

PLATEAU D'ASSY

To continue south from Samoëns it's necessary to drive 11 km (7 miles) west on D 907, then take D 902 south for 10 km (6 miles) to the autoroute, which in 20 km (12½ miles) comes to the town of Le Fayet and, 3 km (2 miles) north on D 43, the spa town of **Plateau d'Assy**. A major attraction here is **Notre-Dame-de-Toute-Grâce**, a controversial and fascinating church begun in 1937 and consecrated in 1950 and adorned with the work of a remarkable array of prominent 20th-century artists. The huge mosaic on the front of the building is by Fernand Léger; the painting of Saint François de Sales is by Pierre Bonnard and that of Saint Dominique by Henri Matisse; the spectacular tapestry over the altar is by Jean Lurçat; and the ceramic just to the right of the entrance is by Marc Chagall. There are sculptures by Jacques Lipchitz and Germaine Richier and wood carvings by the Savoyard artist Demaison. The overall effect is sacrilegious for some—in part because it is dedicated to the Virgin and her powers of comforting the afflicted (this is a spa town, remember)—but wonderful for lovers of modern art. Be sure to see the crypt, too (entrance in the back).

CHAMONIX-MONT BLANC

The Chamonix–Mont Blanc area (Chamonix is about 20 km/ 12½ miles east of Plateau d'Assy on D 13 and N 205) is a hiker's paradise, a fact not lost on Europe's hordes of hikers. The resulting overcrowding would almost make it a destination worth skipping were not **Mont Blanc**, at 15,771 feet Europe's highest peak, such a truly grand and powerful sight. You'll need a guide to climb the glacier-covered peak itself, but many easier walks yield great views of the massive mountain. If you want to save your strength, take a ski lift up one of the mountains and then walk from there. The Office de Tourisme, located near the church and the *mairie* in the old town square at Chamonix, has hiking information; Tel: 50-53-00-24; Fax: 50-53-58-90. Or contact the Office de Haute Montagne next door; Tel: 50-53-22-08.

The modern town of **Chamonix** may make you wish you'd been there 30 years ago; its charms are somewhat swamped by new development and tourists. The town claims to be the world capital of mountaineering, and its guide school is renowned and exclusive—only recently has the school admitted members not born in Chamonix. The small mountaineering museum, with its display of primitive early equipment, shows just how brave the early climbers were.

STAYING AND DINING IN CHAMONIX

Chamonix has no shortage of restaurants; the best is ▶ Albert Ier, at 119, impasse du Montenvers, with its pleasant dining room, flower-filled garden, and refined traditional cuisine with menus in several price ranges. The address is also home to a friendly family hotel; ask for a room with a view of the mountains. The Tartiffle, at 87, rue des Moulins, is a perfect place for a hearty meal of such regional fare as roast veal with wild mushrooms and potatoes *dauphinois;* Tel: 50-53-20-02. Perched on a hillside just outside Chamonix is the beautiful ▶ Auberge du Bois Prin, an 11-room country inn that boasts tastefully decorated (and pricey) rooms and exceptional views; its fine restaurant is run by the proprietors of the Albert Ier. Advance reservations are crucial in high season; Tel: 50-53-33-51.

SKIING IN CHAMONIX

A family resort in the summer, Chamonix becomes younger and hipper during the ski season. The ski installations are spread across the valley and are not linked with one another, so it's necessary to choose your destination carefully according to your aptitude; Chamonix, therefore, is not ideal for a group including both expert and novice skiers. Les Grands Montets at Argentière, up the valley from Chamonix, is the best all-purpose ski center in the area, with a nice mix of expert, intermediate, and novice runs. The midsize ▶ Les Grands Montets hotel here is comfortable, and it's also located quite close to the slopes.

A special attraction in Chamonix for those who ski reasonably well is La Vallée Blanche, the glacier-covered canyon that tumbles down from Mont Blanc. There are several off-trail runs here that are recommended for advanced skiers only. The strenuous but magnificent descents begin with a 550-yard hike down from the ski lift at 12,466 feet and end near town 15 miles and the better part of the day later. La Vallée Blanche is a glacier, not a ski slope, and thus cannot be negotiated without a guide. The Compagnie des Guides de Chamonix Mont Blanc (Maison de la Montagne, 190, place de l'Eglise, 74400 Chamonix; Tel: 50-53-00-88) offers trips for one to four people. Prices vary with the number of people and difficulty of the trek; the minimum rate is 730

francs per day in summer (two people), while the highest
rates run 5,000 to 6,000 francs per person in peak season.
Individuals and couples can also join group outings.

MEGEVE

From Chamonix take N 205 west back toward Le Fayet, then
D 902 and D 909 south and west 11 km (7 miles) to N 212,
which in 13 km (8 miles) comes to Megève, well worth a
stop if you're curious to see how people play in the snow
when money is no object—or if you are looking for a
luxurious spot to lay your head. This idyllic Alpine village is
not only a major ski resort (and, during the summer, golf
center) with a superb range of facilities, but a jet-setty or
aspiringly jet-setty (same crowd as St-Tropez in August)
winter watering hole popular with movie stars, royals from
near and far, and the gamut of other celebrities and people
with fat checkbooks.

Beyond the grand hotels (pop into the **Loges du Mont
Blanc** to take a look at the Jean Cocteau fresco and drawings
in the bar, and the **Parc des Loges** for a gander at its Art Deco
interior), perhaps the most luxurious place to stay in
Megève is ► **Le Chalais du Mont d'Arbois**. This calm and
beautifully decorated stone-and-wood chalet is perched on
the Mont d'Arbois overlooking Megève, so there are beautiful views from the wonderfully comfortable rooms; they're
decked out with antiques, big, feather comforters, and
homey touches like baskets of lavender tucked in closets
and sheepskin throws scattered here and there. This discreet
and romantic roost is run by French socialite Nadine de
Rothschild, who also created the decor. You'll find the best
gourmet restaurant in Megève here, with classic mountain
dishes (fondues and the like) as well as rotisseried meats
and good game dishes. The excellent wine list features many
bottles from the Rothschild's vineyards in Bordeaux; Tel: 50-
21-25-03.

Another good place to stay here is ► **Les Fermes de
Marie**, a rustic-looking cluster of farmhouses and chalets on
the edge of town that neatly defines the casual chic of
Megève. Inside, the chalets are divided into spacious and
comfortable rooms, almost all of which have either a terrace
or balcony, while the farmhouses—one of which has two
bedrooms, two baths, a fireplace, and a Jacuzzi—are for
rent. Though this delightful place looks antique, it's only
three years old. What creates the illusion is the fact that the
complex was scrupulously built according to traditional local techniques, mostly using timber recovered from old
houses in the region. Whether you are staying on or just

passing through, **La Taverne de Mont D'Arbois** is a fine spot
for a meal. This old wood-beamed farmhouse on the Route
de Mont D'Arbois does an excellent job with all the specialties of the Haute-Savoie, including sausages made with walnuts or pistachios, fondue, *raclette,* and baked *vacherin.* A
local habit might help your digestion of any of these cheese
dishes: a grinding of black pepper. Tel: 50-21-03-53.

After Megève, N 212 continues south through the meandering canyons of the **Gorges de l'Arly.** A turn to the west on
N 508 at Ugine, 23 km (14 miles) south of Megève, will take
you the some 40 km (25 miles) back to Annecy, while
continuing another 8 km (5 miles) south on N 212 will bring
you to Albertville.

ALBERTVILLE AND ENVIRONS

This ugly industrial town has nothing to recommend it except
its convenient location at a train and road intersection; this
situation is what led organizers to choose Albertville as host
of the 1992 Winter Olympic Games, although the town itself is
not a sports center. Those looking for lodging in Albertville
might try the ► **Million**, the nicest hotel in town, or ► **La
Berjann**, a quiet, moderately priced hotel just outside of town.
The elegant restaurant at the Million has made a name for
itself as one of the region's finest, thanks to the refined classic
cuisine prepared by chef Philippe Million, whose family has
been inn-keeping in the region since 1770. Another excellent
restaurant, just over the Arly river, which cuts through Albertville, is **Chez Uginet**. Eric Guillot, the young chef, does
wonderful updates of classic Savoyard dishes like *agnelots,* a
local version of ravioli, which are poached in chicken stock
and garnished with thin slices of foie gras, or taking a *gourée,*
the homely potato cake native to the area, and enriching it
with eggs and bacon. Tel: 79-32-00-50.

From Albertville, a trip up D 925 for 20 km (12 miles) to
the northeast leads through the charming **Beaufort** region,
famous for the cheese of the same name. (The cheese
factory at Beaufort offers tours.) Beaufort is also a good
spot to buy local handicrafts, such as wooden household
items and pewter mugs and plates. The vacation boom has
bypassed this region (although the hydroelectric boom hit
it full force), so it's a bit less crowded than some of the
neighboring areas. The town of **Aime**, 40 km (25 miles)
east via a southward dip on N 80 then north again on N 90,
has a first-rate 11th-century Romanesque church and a
pleasant roadside restaurant called **L'Atre**. At Bourg-St-
Maurice, another 13 km (8 miles) up N 90, where the rail
line terminates, you can head by car toward Italy over Col

du Petit St-Bernard (where Hannibal is supposed to have crossed the Alps) or toward Val-d'Isère (for skiing, see below), the 8,900-foot-high Col de l'Iseran, and the **Parc National de la Vanoise**. The park, in the remotest part of the Savoy, has some 300 miles of hiking paths. You can enter the park from almost any of the towns along D 902 out of Val-d'Isère or from N 6 south of the park. The tourist offices at Modane, Val-d'Isère, and Bourg-St-Maurice are helpful, as is the Maison du Parc in Chambéry.

SKIING AROUND ALBERTVILLE

The Isère Valley just south of Albertville, served by road and rail, is the access route to some of Europe's best ski stations, including Courchevel, Méribel, Val-Thorens, La Plagne, Les Arcs, Tignes, and Val-d'Isère.

Courchevel, Méribel, Val-Thorens

Courchevel, Méribel, and Val-Thorens are linked by ski lifts and together make up an area called **Les Trois Vallées**. This entire area was used for staging various events in the 1992 Winter Olympic Games, with the result that facilities, whether roads, chair lifts, or hotels, are strictly state-of-the-art. **Courchevel** is for the ultra-chic; it boasts many luxury hotels, the fanciest being the ▶ **Byblos des Neiges** (sister to the Byblos in St-Tropez) and the ▶ **Bellecôte**, with an "elegant rustic" decor.

Méribel caters to families and attracts many British visitors; both resorts have skiing to suit every taste. The hotel ▶ **Le Grand Coeur** is many people's favorite spot in the whole area; with a cozy, welcoming lounge area furnished with antique blanket chests, brass pots, and other antiques and sofas pulled up to a huge stone hearth, it achieves a perfect balance between the chic and the casual. It also has an excellent restaurant, where your desire for a quick bowl of soup at noon needn't mean a gastronomic sacrifice—how does beef consommé with slivers of leek and truffle sound? Perhaps followed by a salad of spinach, orange sections, and langoustines?

Otherwise, the number of hotel rooms in Méribel was more than doubled for the recent Winter Olympic Games; three recommended new hotels all have different atmospheres and attractions. The ▶ **L'Antarès** is the most luxurious of the three. Rooms, which are large, handsomely furnished, and have whirlpool baths from which you can view the ski slopes, give out onto a large central atrium. The **Cassiopée**, the formal restaurant here, is one of the best in the area, offering such dishes as lobster with Mediterranean vegetables. L'Antarès also has an indoor pool, and lunch on the deck overlooking the slopes is a chic local custom. The ► Hôtel Le Yeti has a more indigenous feel; its interior is finished in beautifully worked pine, and the rooms are tastefully furnished with rustic but very comfortable, locally made wooden furniture. Fresh-looking fabrics from the stylish Paris decorator Etamine complete the appealing decor. With its big fireplace, the Yeti also has a lobby you might actually want to spend time in, as well as a pleasant bar and a very good restaurant—try the superb cheese fondue. The ► Marie Blanche hotel is the simplest of the group, but still offers substantial comfort. It's a large chalet-style hotel with a fine view of the slopes, a circular hearth in the lobby, and comfortable pine-paneled rooms. The Marie Blanche attracts a younger crowd than do the other hotels, and many clients sign up for half-board, which makes sense because the food is wonderful—trout in a crispy crepe with almond butter, for example.

Val-Thorens has extensive off-trail skiing possibilities and exceptional high-altitude runs, which allow for summer skiing. As in Courchevel and Méribel, there are numerous hotels in Val-Thorens from which to choose, but the best is the elegant chalet-style ► Fitz Roy. For all three resorts remember to pack appropriate après-ski attire; discos, piano bars, concert halls, and movie theaters make for an active nightlife.

La Plagne

La Plagne, 20 km south of Aime and N 90 (the route from Albertville) on twisting D 220 E, is another large, modern resort, especially good for beginning and intermediate skiers. Experts might be frustrated by the abundance of broad, gentle trails; only the spectacular runs from the Bellecôte glacier offer a real challenge. La Plagne also has limited summer skiing. In La Plagne, try to book a room at the charming ► Graciosa hotel, a cozy place with a friendly staff. It has only 18 rooms, and a faithful clientele, so be sure to reserve far in advance. Neighboring **Les Arcs**, accessible by cable car from Bourg-St-Maurice, has 73 ski lifts and attracts many international visitors.

Val-d'Isère and Tignes

Farther up the Isère Valley on N 90 and D 902, Val-d'Isère and Tignes are the best destinations for accomplished skiers. The hometown of Olympic skiing champion Jean-Claude Killy, **Val-d'Isère** (about 80 km/50 miles from Albertville) is a real village that existed long before the skiing boom, and its facilities are second to none. You'll find a variety of hotels here in all price ranges. A good choice is the ▶ **Hôtel le Blizzard**, with comfortable rooms, pleasant service, and a nightclub just downstairs. The mountains above Val-d'Isère are very high and offer many harrowing expert runs and superb off-trail skiing. **Tignes**, which shares much of the same skiing domain, is a newer resort complex 7 km (4½ miles) west. Both are popular with a young, fast crowd, drawn in part by the hopping nightlife in Val-d'Isère. The ▶ **Ski d'Or** hotel in Tignes is one of the top luxury hotels in the region; for a more modest place to stay, try the ▶ **Neige et Soleil**.

THE DAUPHINE

Despite the extensive reach of the Savoyard empire, it never succeeded in absorbing the Dauphiné to the immediate south. The Dauphiné was an independent feudal kingdom from the early 11th century until 1349, when the mercurial King Humbert II, bankrupt after the Crusades, sold his domain to Philippe VI of France. This is not to say that the Dauphiné was a peaceful place. Fierce wars with the Italian kingdoms from 1494 to 1515 brought Pierre Terrail Bayard, the *"chevalier sans peur et sans reproche"* ("the knight without fear and without faults"), to prominence as lieutenant-general of the Dauphiné. Religious wars racked the region in the second half of the 16th century, when the indomitable general and politician François de Lesdiguières ruled as a virtual viceroy. Later the Dauphiné was in the vanguard of the French Revolution; some say the revolution started with the "day of tiles" in 1788, when the Grenoble citizenry erected barricades and fought off royal troops with roof tiles in reaction to edicts from Louis XVI that threatened local sovereignty.

Grenoble

The history of the Dauphiné is inseparable from the history of Grenoble, a bustling and picturesque city at the junction of the Drac and Isère rivers, 55 km (34 miles) south of Chambéry on route A 41, and 104 km (65 miles) southeast of Lyon on A 48. The Romans built an important fortified settlement here called Gratianopolis in honor of the emperor Gratian; from that came the name Grenoble. Today Grenoble is a major regional capital with an important university, budding high-tech industries including computers and advanced nuclear research, and a solid but unimposing tourist infrastructure. It is also a good example of intelligent urban planning, with a sparkling downtown shopping district served by a new tram line, and controlled urban expansion.

THE BASTILLE AND CITY CENTER

While significantly larger than Annecy or Chambéry, Grenoble is still small enough to be navigated easily. If you like to begin your sightseeing with a proper panorama, take the Téléférique de la Bastille—the four Plexiglas bubbles on a wire have become the city's unofficial mascots—from the Isère riverbank north of the old town up to the **Bastille**, a set of early-19th-century fortifications perched on the big hill overlooking the city. On the Bastille you can scramble around the chaotic collection of archways, stairways, and tunnels that once defended Grenoble against invasion from the north, then stroll back down to the city (cable-car tickets are one-way or round trip, but the half-hour walk down is more scenic). If you go by foot, stop at the **Musée Dauphinois**, located in an old cloister on rue Maurice-Gignoux, about halfway down. The museum has a fascinating multimedia exhibit on the evolution of village life in the region, but no English translations are available. However, non-Francophones can still enjoy the paintings that evoke the mystical spirits of the mountains and gain a keener understanding of how very poor and isolated this region was until very recently.

At the bottom of the hill is a pizzeria-lined quai, and just across the photogenic bridge is the **old town**. The Flamboyant Gothic building near the river is the late-15th-century Palais de Justice, home of the original Dauphinois parliament. Across the Place St-André to the right is the home of Lesdiguières, complete with a tower dating from the 14th century. The building now houses the **Musée Stendhal**, with objects and temporary exhibits honoring the novelist (born Marie-Henri Beyle), one of the city's most famous sons.

The 14th-century **Tour de l'Ile**, at the northeastern edge of the old town on the quai Jongkind, is part of Grenoble's early fortifications. The **Musée des Beaux-Arts**, or Musée de Peinture et de Sculpture, houses one of France's better collections of contemporary art, and its classical collections are among the best to be found in a provincial museum, including works by Rubens, Tintoretto, Veronese, and Georges de La Tour. The museum moved into new quarters at 5, place de la Valette, in January 1994. A piece of the city's old **Roman wall** still stands nearby.

Partly because of its large student population—the city is

home to one of the most prestigious and most cosmopolitan universities in France—and partly because of its pride as a long-standing center of enlightened thinking and open-mindedness, Grenoble has a thriving cultural scene. Stop by the **Maison de la Culture**, popularly called Le Cargo, to see what's happening while you're in town; they host everything from film festivals to orchestral concerts, and the building itself, an odd-looking oval structure covered with big white panels so that it vaguely resembles some massive piece of sanitary equipment, is worth a visit. Le Cargo was designed by the architect A. Wogensky and finished in 1968; it's located in the new quarter of the city called Malherbe. Of more recent vintage and a source of great pride to the locals is the **Magasin**, or Centre National d'Art Contemporain, a now-renowned exhibition space for contemporary art that occupies an old cast-iron factory designed by Eiffel at 155, cours Berriat; Tel: 76-21-95-84.

STAYING AND DINING IN GRENOBLE

The city's most luxurious hotel is the modern ▶ **Park Hôtel**, on the Place Paul-Mistral near the Hôtel de Ville. Calm and comfortable, it looks out over the Grésivaudan Valley—so loved by Stendhal—and the Belledonne mountains. The newly renovated ▶ **Hôtel Suisse et Bordeaux** is a good, low-priced option near the train station. Some of the rooms are quite noisy, so be sure to ask for one off the street. The pleasant, friendly, and inexpensive ▶ **Rive Droite** seems to have changed little since its 1968 Olympics-vintage renovation, but this is part of its funky charm. The attic loft rooms are a spacious good buy; good parking and an easy walk into town.

Grenoble is an excellent place to get a reasonably priced top-flight meal. At **L'Escalier**, 6, place de Lavalette, old stone walls combine with ultra-contemporary furniture and fixtures to stunning effect; the atmosphere is informal, the clientele young professionals, and the food excellent (Tel: 76-54-66-16). Try tiny and friendly **A Ma Table**, at 92, cours Jean-Jaurès, for fish specialties (reserve; Tel: 76-96-77-04).

AROUND GRENOBLE

Outside Grenoble, mountains and forests spread out in every direction, making the city an ideal base from which to set off into the Alps.

Parc Régional du Vercors

To the southwest lies the regional park of Le Vercors, which, unlike the national parks, is relatively crowded and not very wild. The park offers courses on the natural features of the area and instruction in rock-climbing, spelunking, and cross-country skiing. The landscape here is gentler and lusher than in the High Alps, and you'll pass through some spectacular scenery, including the **Gorges de la Bourne**, with their steep, twisting crevasses, as you drive south to the park on D 531 and D 103, a trip of about 60 km (37 miles).

Ski Stations Near Grenoble

East of Grenoble is high-mountain country, with several major ski stations, L'Alpe d'Huez and Les Deux-Alpes chief among them. **L'Alpe d'Huez**, one of the oldest ski centers in France and the site of Jean-Claude Killy's heroics in the 1968 Winter Olympics, has completed a 750-million-franc upgrade. About 50 km (31 miles) southeast of Grenoble on D 5, N 91, and D 211, it offers a fine array of long, uncrowded, high-altitude expert trails, as well as a good beginners' area. ▶ **Le Dôme** is a good hotel in L'Alpe d'Huez, with the popular restaurant the **Grand Tétras**. **Les Deux-Alpes**, about 15 km (9½ miles) farther east, is also quite high and has summer skiing.

South Toward Gap

Due south of Grenoble, route N 85 leads 105 km (65 miles) to Gap, following the route Napoléon took when he made his famous return from Elba. However, the highly touted Route Napoléon is actually just a road with an occasional incongruous statue of the general sitting in a field. It's a pretty ride, though, and a good route south to the Mediterranean coast (and therefore crowded in summer). The road skirts the **Parc National des Ecrins**, another high-mountain wilderness area with abundant hiking opportunities.

Briançon

From Gap, if you're not heading for the sea, take N 94 or the train northeast to Briançon, which, at an elevation of 4,300 feet, is the highest town in France. You'll pass Lac de Serre-Ponçon, which has an exceptionally lovely lakeside campground and a number of good picnic spots. Briançon is a spectacular, unsung little town set in a high mountain pass almost on the Italian border. Its strategic position explains the remarkable fortifications, a masterpiece of protection built by Louis XIV's famous engineer Vauban. The old town is surrounded by layered, jutting walls, and a string of nine forts lines ridges around the city like beads on a necklace. The defenses were put to their most serious test in 1815, when an Austro-Savoyard army, which had already seized most of the Dauphiné, laid siege to the town. Briançon held out against an attacking army 20 times as strong for four months, until the treaty of Paris was signed. Since then it's been known as *petite ville, grand renom* (little city, big reputation).

Founded as the Gallo-Roman settlement of Brigantium, Briançon has the feel of a place apart, and indeed its political history is unusual; it was long an autonomous semi-republic, called an *escarton,* which had purchased its right to self-government. Its pure air gave it a minor reputation as a spa; these days Briançon is trying to build its tourist appeal with a new ski lift linking it to nearby ski resorts.

If you're spending the night here, the modest but friendly hotel ▶ **Vauban** is a good choice. Modern yet warm, it backs onto a pleasant tree-filled garden and has its own restaurant, which serves traditional country-style food.

About 16 km (10 miles) northwest of Briançon on N 91 in the resort town of Le Monêtier-les-Bains is the ▶ **Auberge du Choucas,** an 18th-century farmhouse that's been turned into a cozy, rustic retreat. This exceedingly welcoming inn has an excellent restaurant and is a good base for outdoor activities.

GETTING AROUND

Annecy, Chambéry, Grenoble, and Geneva are the gateways to the Alps. Frequent TGV service puts all four cities within three and a half hours of Paris by rail, and the highway connections are also good, if somewhat slower. It's not worth flying from Paris, but if you're starting from outside the country, Geneva, with its international airport, might be the best gateway. From Italy, the tunnels of Mont Blanc and Fréjus, as well as several seasonal mountain roads, provide auto access.

Despite occasional heavy traffic, the Alps are indisputably car country. Trains serve the major river valleys to Chamonix, Bourg-St-Maurice, and Briançon, and there are buses to the big resort towns, but unless you're headed for a single destination you'll be much better off driving yourself. The A 41 autoroute provides the basic north–south link west of the mountains, and from there the Routes Nationales—along with the smaller A 40 autoroute to Passy just before Chamonix—bring you into the high country along the river valleys. A new autoroute was built for the 1992 Olympics, and the N 90 from Albertville to Moûtiers was substantially enlarged. In fact, all major roads around the Olympic sites have been greatly improved. Secondary roads follow all manner of improbable routes through the mountains, where the going tends to be slow but scenic. Outside of

July and August, check with the tourist office before planning an elaborate touring itinerary; any route that doesn't involve extensive backtracking will cross mountain passes that are not open year-round. Tire chains are a good idea in winter even if you're sticking to the main roads, and they're equally advisable in spring and fall if you're planning any high-altitude routes. A word of warning: Something about the mountain air makes people drive like fools on the narrow, winding roads; about all you can do is remain calm.

For information on the facilities, lodging, and transportation at all the French ski resorts, contact the **Association des Mairies des Stations Français des Sports d'Hiver**, 61, boulevard Haussmann, 75008 Paris; Tel: (01) 47-42-23-32; Fax: 42-66-15-94. They do not book accommodations, and not all representatives speak English. Their recording in French of daily ski conditions at major resorts can be heard by calling Tel: (01) 42-66-64-28.

The summer tourist season is short—essentially limited to July and August—and crowded. Hikers can get detailed information on trails and refuges from the **Maison de la Randonnée**, 7, rue Voltaire, 38000 Grenoble (Tel: 76-51-76-00; Fax: 76-42-87-08) and from the various tourist offices mentioned above. Travel in the spring and fall is a mixed bag; there aren't many tourists, but many places are closed and the weather is fickle.

ACCOMMODATIONS REFERENCE

The rates given below are projections *for 1994. Unless otherwise indicated, rates are for a double room, double occupancy, and do not include meals. As rates are always subject to change, double-check before booking.*

▶ **Abbaye de Talloires.** Chemin des Moines, 74290 **Talloires**. Tel: 50-60-77-33; Telex: 385307; Fax: 50-60-78-81; in U.S., (212) 856-0115; Fax: (212) 856-0193. Member, Relais & Châteaux. 520F–1,180F. (Closed January and February.)

▶ **Albert Ier.** 119, impasse du Montenvers, 74400 **Chamonix**. Tel: 50-53-05-09; Fax: 50-55-95-48; in U.S., (212) 254-2217 or (800) 755-9313. 590F–1,150F. (Closed mid-October through November.)

▶ **Allobroges Hôtel.** 11, rue Sommellier, 74000 **Annecy**. Tel: 50-45-03-11; Fax: 50-51-88-32. 330F–600F.

▶ **L'Antarès.** Le Belvédère, 73550 **Méribel**. Tel: 79-23-28-23; Fax: 79-23-28-18. 1,530F–2,460F.

▶ **Auberge du Bois Prin.** 69, Chemin de l'Hermine, Les Moussoux 74400 **Chamonix**. Tel: 50-53-33-51; Fax: 50-53-48-

75; in U.S., (212) 856-0115; Fax: (212) 856-0193. Member, Relais & Châteaux. 860F–1,120F. (Closed April 13–30 and October 24–December 4.)

► **Auberge du Choucas.** 17, rue de la Fruitière, 05220 **Le Monêtier-les-Bains**, Serre-Chevalier. Tel: 92-24-42-73; Fax: 92-24-51-60. 590F–680F; suites 950F. (Closed November to mid-December.)

► **Auberge du Père Bise.** Route du Port, 74290 **Talloires**. Tel: 50-60-72-01; Fax: 50-60-73-05; in U.S., (212) 856-0115; Fax: (212) 856-0193. Member, Relais & Châteaux. 1,000F–1,800F. (Closed November 15 to February 15.)

► **Bellecôte.** 73120 **Courchevel**. Tel: 79-08-10-19; Fax: 79-08-17-16. 1,175F–1,675F. (Closed May through November.)

► **La Berjann.** 873, route de Tours, 73200 **Albertville**. Tel: 79-32-47-88; Fax: 79-37-74-09. 280F–300F.

► **Byblos des Neiges.** Jardin Alpin, 73120 **Courchevel**. Tel: 79-08-12-12; Telex: 980580; Fax: 79-08-19-38; in U.S., (212) 308-2929 or (800) 223-6800. 1,500F–3,460F. (Closed April 18–December 18.)

► **Le Chalais du Mont d'Arbois.** Le Mont d'Arbois, 74120 **Megève**. Tel: 50-21-25-03; Fax: 50-21-24-79. 1,670F–2,000F. (Closed April through December.)

► **La Charpenterie.** B.P. 11, 74290 **Talloire**. Tel: 50-60-70-47; Fax: 50-60-79-07. 300F–420F.

► **Le Dauphinois.** 14, avenue Tresserve, 73100 **Aix-les-Bains**. Tel: 79-61-22-56; Fax: 79-34-04-62. 235F–260F.

► **Domaine du Royal Club Evian-Hôtel Royal.** 74500 **Evian-les-Bains**. Tel: 50-26-85-00; Fax: 50-75-61-00; in U.S., (212) 838-3110. 1,560F–2,740F.

► **Le Dôme.** 38750 L'Alpe d'Huez. Tel: 76-80-32-11; Fax: 76-80-66-48. 400F–460F (low season); 600F–680F (high season).

► **Les Fermes de Marie.** Chemin de Riante Colline, 74120 **Megève**. Tel: 50-93-09-84. 700F per person.

► **Fitz Roy.** 73440 **Val-Thorens**. Tel: 79-00-04-78; Fax: 79-00-06-11. 1,000F–1,400F.

► **Graciosa.** M Cedex B.P. 22, 73214 **La Plagne**. Tel: 79-09-00-18; Fax: 79-09-04-08. 375F–520F; all rates per person, full pension.

► **Le Grand Coeur.** 73550 **Méribel-les-Allues**. Tel: 79-08-60-03; Fax: 79-08-58-38. 900F–1,835F. (Closed May through mid-December.)

► **Les Grands Montets.** 74400 **Argentière**. Tel: 50-54-06-66; Fax: 50-54-05-42. 640F.

► **Hôtel le Blizzard.** 73150 **Val-d'Isère**. Tel: 79-06-02-07; Fax: 79-06-04-94. 500F–750F (low season); 1,050F–1,800F (high season).

► **Hôtel de Château de Challes.** 73190 **Challes-les-Eaux.** Tel: 79-72-86-71; Fax: 79-72-83-83. 410F–550F.

► **Hôtel le Manoir.** 37, rue Georges Ier, 73100 **Aix-les-Bains.** Tel: 79-61-44-00; Fax: 79-35-67-67. 395F–495F.

► **Hôtel Suisse et Bordeaux.** 6, place de la Gare, 38000 **Grenoble.** Tel: 76-47-55-87; Fax: 76-46-23-87. 260F.

► **Hôtel Le Yeti.** B.P. 52, 73553 **Méribel.** Tel and Fax: 79-00-51-15. 900F–1,940F.

► **Imperial Palace.** 32, avenue d'Albigny, 74000 **Annecy.** Tel: 50-09-30-00; Fax: 50-09-33-33. 850F–1,200F.

► **Marie Blanche.** B.P. 55 La Renarde, 73550 **Méribel.** Tel: 79-08-57-07; Fax: 79-08-65-55. 500F.

► **Million.** 8, place de la Liberté, 73200 **Albertville.** Tel: 79-32-25-15; Fax: 79-32-25-36. 650F–700F.

► **Neige et Soleil.** 73320 **Tignes.** Tel: 79-06-32-94; Fax: 79-06-33-18. 370F–550F.

► **Ombremont.** RN 504, 73370 **Le Bourget-du-Lac.** Tel: 79-25-00-23; Telex: 980832; Fax: 79-25-25-77; in U.S., (212) 856-0115; Fax: (212) 856-0193. Member, Relais & Châteaux. 750F–1,700F.

► **Park Hôtel.** 10, place Paul-Mistral, 38000 **Grenoble.** Tel: 76-87-29-11; Telex: 320767; Fax: 76-46-49-88; in U.S., (212) 752-3900 or (800) 888-4747. 595F–1,000F.

► **Au Prince Eugène de Savoie.** Esplanade Curial, 73000 **Chambéry.** Tel: 79-85-06-07; Fax: 79-85-61-01. 495F.

► **Les Princes.** 4, rue de Boigne, 73000 **Chambéry.** Tel: 79-33-45-36; Fax: 79-70-31-47. 390F.

► **Rive Droite.** 20, quai France, 38000 **Grenoble.** Tel: 76-87-61-11; Fax: 76-87-04-04. 315F.

► **Ski d'Or.** 73320 **Tignes.** Tel: 79-06-51-60; Fax: 79-06-45-49. 1,025F (per person, demipension).

► **Vauban.** 13, avenue Général-de-Gaulle, 05100 **Briançon.** Tel: 92-21-12-11; Fax: 92-20-58-20. 245F–420F.

PROVENCE AND THE COTE D'AZUR

By Stephen O'Shea with Georgia I. Hesse

For many people, Provence and the Riviera fuse into a glamorous, sun-splashed picture of the South of France and the good—or perhaps naughty—life. They think of the Fitzgeralds sipping Champagne from slippers, of White Russians imploring roulette wheels, and of sleek jet-setters peeling off to bronze themselves to perfection. All of these images are appropriate, thank God, but they are just a small fraction of what the smiling land of Provence has to offer. For every cosmopolitan treat on the Riviera there is a peaceful hilltop village in the hinterland, and for every sumptuous meal in a swank seaside restaurant there is a simple feast of olives, goat cheese, melons, and wine in a rural paradise.

The Riviera, or Côte d'Azur, comprises the southeastern coast of Provence, a region that stretches from the lower Rhône Valley to the Maritime Alps near the Italian border. A richly diverse land, Provence includes the towering mountains north of Nice and the gentle plains around Arles, the unearthly white cliffs near Marseille and the placid interior valleys east of Avignon. Although the cosmopolitan Côte d'Azur no longer resembles its rustic cousins, it has nonetheless not lost its roots. The traveller has only to step north of Cannes to find a village as sleepily Provençal as anything that sprang from the imagination of playwright Marcel Pagnol.

For our purposes it's best first to compare the two

areas—greater Provence and its wayward, sophisticated Côte d'Azur—and then to treat them separately, for they are, as far as the traveller is concerned, two entirely different places. However, the real problem lies not in which one to choose but in how to leave the southeast of France once you've seen it. Long ago the richest of the Roman Empire's provinces—whence its name and its fascinating classical heritage—Provence remains an ideal place to colonize. Its superb climate and cultural treasures, along with the bounty of its land and the beauty of its nature, make the region one of those rare lands where the sensitive have two pleasant urges: to create or to do nothing at all. While you make up your mind, museums, galleries, festivals, historic cities, ageless villages, and delicious cuisine are all here to help you pass the time.

MAJOR INTEREST

Provence
Art
Roman and Greek ruins
Early Christian antiquities
Vineyards
Village life

Côte d'Azur
Seaside resorts
Perched villages
Gambling
Modern-art museums
Roman ruins

The similarities between Provence and the Côte d'Azur run deep. Even in the glitziest parts of the Riviera there are traces of Provence—a Latin flavor in both food and temperament, a Roman cultural heritage, and a certain laid-back lifestyle that typifies the Mediterranean. When you enter Provence–Côte d'Azur you know you have arrived in the Mediterranean: The intense sunlight, blue skies, dry climate, olive trees, chalky hills, and red-tiled roofs are unmistakable.

But Provence is more than just a Mediterranean land. Provençal is a style, a language, and a history—starting with the Roman Republic and Empire, developing into a kingdom ruled independently of France until the 15th century, and then becoming a special-statute state of the ancien régime—until the French Revolution created Provence as an administrative region in 1790.

If Provence, to the visitor, is the timeless producer of simple joys, the Côte d'Azur is the flashy starlet—and the two have their respective audiences among foreign (that is, non-Provençal) visitors. Resorts such as St-Tropez, Antibes, and Cannes appeal to the practitioners of France's great contribution to civilization, unabashed hedonism. With its spectacular vistas, of both the human and the natural varieties, the French Riviera has deservedly become one of the most popular playgrounds on the Mediterranean. A succession of 20th-century artists, a breed not insensitive to the pleasures of the flesh, have been drawn to the cypress-covered hills overlooking the sea, bequeathing the region an impressive collection of galleries and museums. Sophisticates, cultural connoisseurs of every sort, and the plain old filthy rich made their homes here as well, their influence evident in the excellent jazz and arts festivals that punctuate the Riviera's long summer season. Even Monte-Carlo, its blueblood clientele diluted as exiled European aristocracies grow poorer with each passing generation, still seems the only place in the world where the phrase "Bond. James Bond" might conceivably be uttered in real life.

In Provence proper, however, you hear that the conspicuous worldliness of the *côte* is a trifle vulgar. Admittedly, this sentiment is most often expressed by the Parisian literati who flock southward for their summerlong cocktail parties amid the olive groves of the Alpilles mountains and the Vaucluse valleys, but it does hint at a fundamental difference between the two regions: At its best, the Côte d'Azur is richly sensual; Provence, on the other hand, is uncommonly sensuous. Only the truly oblivious traveller can fail to notice that the striking landscapes of Provence are for the lover of color and smells, the purple fields of lavender mixing with the gentle scent of lime on the outskirts of age-old villages. "This country," wrote one admirer of the plain near Arles, "seems to me as beautiful as Japan for clarity of atmosphere and gay color effects. Water forms patches of lovely emerald or rich blue in the landscape ... the pale orange of the sunsets makes the fields appear blue. The sun is a splendid yellow." The passing of a century has not made Vincent van Gogh's appraisal any less true.

Still, the modern era has not left the region untouched. Along with the Côte d'Azur, the cities of Provence have become France's sunbelt. Millions of northern French have migrated south to escape gray skies and city pressures. Some have been retirees, but a large percentage ranks among the most educated and highest paid workers in France: doctors, lawyers, engineers, and administrators. Even these new Provençaux feel a kinship with those who have been here for generations—united by climate, the proximity of the sea, and the easygoing lifestyle.

LA PROVENCE

James Pope-Hennessy, one of the great observers of the region, wrote in his lyrical *Aspects of Provence:* " . . . this rich countryside has been lived in and lived over for many centuries. Up in the hillside vineyards, down amongst the groves of twisted olive trees, you can smell antiquity." Even the cities conspire to bewitch the traveller, each competing to win admirers with its distinct charms: Roman Arles or papal Avignon, ragged Marseille or elegant Aix.

But it is the village that lies at the heart of Provençal charm. Many hamlets appear to be caught in a lazy trance, just like the inevitable clutch of men playing *boules* in the village square. "I'll come see you in the morning—at about dusk" may be the northern French wisecrack about the unhurried Provençal way of life, but it contains more than a trace of jealousy. Ford Madox Ford, another convert to the cult of Provence, knew the value of indolently sitting with a glass of wine as the sunlight plays on the plane trees and the walls of an ocher village. His poem about just such an afternoon is called "On Heaven."

Although he may have overstated his case, there can be no doubt that Provence, if not perfect, is at least a very magical place. Stories about imaginary beasts abound in its traditional folklore, the best-known being the child-gobbling medieval monster, the *Tarasque,* still seen swimming in the Rhône near Tarascon. The countryside itself adds to the spell. The flower-filled fields of St-Rémy-de-Provence abruptly give way to the stark white peaks of the Alpilles midway between Avignon and Arles, the only pass through them flanked by eerie Roman ruins. An innocuous road south of Vaison-la-Romaine becomes a treacherous defile that opens out suddenly onto the sublime monastery of Sénanque. In the midst of the green orchards of a valley in the Vaucluse east of Avignon stands a gentle abutment that is violently red, its crowning village, Roussillon, a painter's

To
Vienne
and
Lyon

N7

Rhône

A7

D938

D94

St-Auban-sur-l'Ouvèze

Rochegude

Vaison-
la-Romaine

Mollans-sur-Ouvèze

Séguret
Sablet
Gigondas

Malaucène

Mont
Ventoux

Orange

D977

La Roque-Alric

Châteauneuf-du-Pape

D938

D974

Carpentras

VAUCLUSE

D22

Tavel

Venasque

Avignon

D28

L'Isle-
sur-la-
Sorgue

Fontaine de Vaucluse
Abbaye de Sénanque

A9

Gordes

Roussillon
Apt

Rustrel

Cavaillon

Lacoste
Bonnieux

N100

Beaucaire

Oppède-le-Vieux

Lubéron

Tarascon

St-Rémy-de-Provence

ALPILLES

Durance

Maussane

N113

Les Baux-
de-Provence

Vauvenargues

Arles

Salon-de-Provence

Montagne-Ste-Victoire

D570

N7

Aix-en-Provence

D10

A8

Le Tholonet

Rhône

N568

A7

D17

St-Blaise

A51

Fos-sur-Mer

N268

A52

Port-St-Louis-
du-Rhône

A55

To
Toulon

A50

Marseille

Cassis

La
Ciotat

MEDITERRANEAN SEA

N

Provence
(detail)

0   miles   10

0   kilometers   15

palette of 17 different shades from scarlet to orange. Provence stimulates the imagination, even as it rewards the senses with a rosemary-filled breeze, the pungent odor of garlicky *aïoli,* or the soothing sounds from a centuries-old village dovecote. As the sun sets and Vincent's starry night embraces the countryside, the traveller immediately knows why in its long history the kingdom of Provence has been coveted by so many, so often, and so ardently.

Although the Phocaeans (Greeks from ancient Ionia on the west coast of Asia Minor) settled Marseille six centuries before Christ and were soon followed by other Greeks, the conquerors who were first to leave their mark on the land were the Romans. From 102 B.C., the year the consul Marius beat back the Teutons just north of what is now Aix-en-Provence, to the disintegration of the empire five centuries later, this swath of fertile land was one of Rome's wealthiest provinces. Its ancient amphitheaters, aqueducts, arenas, and bridges (the outstanding vestiges are in Arles, Nîmes, St-Rémy, Orange, and Vaison) attest to its importance in classical times. The region was later swept by successive waves of Alemanni, Visigoths, Moors, and just about every other marauding people of the Dark Ages.

When temporary political consolidation came in 972 under Count Guillaume, Provence then entered into centuries of checkerboard development: Part went to the Holy Roman Empire, Orange fell to the Duchy of Nassau, and the counts of Toulouse and Barcelona quarreled incessantly over their rival Provençal fiefdoms. While these medieval princes deployed their armies amid the almond groves and laid siege to fortified villages, such rich cities as Aix became centers of art and poetry. In a great flowering of the Provençal language, 12th-century troubadours composed songs of courtly romance that were performed by itinerant singers—called *jongleurs*—in the castles of the region, most notably at the spectacular site of Les Baux-de-Provence. Such forgotten troubadour poets as Marcabru, Bernard de Ventadour, and Raimbaut d'Orange shaped a new ideal of love between a knight and his lady in what a French historian has aptly termed "the precocious spring of modern Western culture."

However short-lived that spring of the troubadours, politics and religion soon stepped in to add further complexity to the Provençal patchwork. The papal state centered at Avignon became the northern Vatican, as popes and antipopes, having fled the cutthroat politics of Rome, held worldly court by the banks of the Rhône, thus encouraging the development of the arts and sciences. Even after the popes had returned to Rome, their Provençal holdings, known as the Comtat Venaissin, functioned as a refuge for those made unwelcome in the kingdom of France. Refugees poured into this corner of Provence, and the market towns of Carpentras and Cavaillon now possess those rarities of French religious architecture: ornate 18th-century synagogues.

When an expansionist Parisian monarchy finally laid hold of Provence in 1481 (the Comtat Venaissin fell to French revolutionaries in 1791), the same ills of absolutist centralism felt by other provinces of France befell this southern region. During the Renaissance and the Enlightenment, Provençal gradually disappeared as the common spoken language. In the 19th century dramatic economic and social changes—railroads, industry, and tourism—further eroded what was once Provence's dreamy isolation from the bustle of Paris.

In reaction to the changes, a group led by the poet Frédéric Mistral founded a movement—called le Félibrige—advocating a return to the old traditions. The organization tried to revive a Provence of legend: a peaceful, rural community of peasant farmers, bourgeois, and fishermen held together by the Provençal language—and a great faith in the Roman Catholic Church.

Reality lay elsewhere, however. Since the last decades of the 19th century, Provence has developed into a modern and technologically oriented region where the past is nevertheless still stamped on nearly every corner of every town.

It is that living past, where tradition and the love of the good life still abide, that makes Provence so compelling. Although not without its harsh aspects—few things are so demoralizing as the insistent mistral wind that rushes down the Rhône for days on end—Provence is a gentle and beguiling region. To return to the enthusiastic anachronisms of Ford Madox Ford: "[In] a peasantry that has seen many of its sons ennobled because of poetic gifts . . . that has seen painting and sculpture held in high honor, there arose and continued the tradition that occupation with one art or the other is a proper thing for sound men."

MAJOR INTEREST IN PROVENCE

Avignon
Palais des Papes
Rhône wine country to the north

Orange
Roman theater and ruins

The Vaucluse
Vaison-la-Romaine
Abbaye de Sénanque
Villages of Coulon Valley

The Alpilles
Greco-Roman ruins at St-Rémy-de-Provence
Fortress at Les Baux-de-Provence
Abbaye de Montmajour

Arles
Van Gogh colors and landscapes
Roman amphitheater and theater
Eglise St-Trophime

Aix-en-Provence
Cézanne interest
Cours Mirabeau

Marseille
Château d'If
Vieux Port
Bouillabaisse
Excursion to the *calanques* and Cassis

PROVENCAL CUISINE

Sun is one constant in Provence and on the Côte d'Azur. The olive is the other.

In the South of France man has been eating the olive, crushing it for oil, and making salad bowls from its wood for a very long time. The trees along the Riviera are thought to have been introduced by the Greeks more than 2,500 years ago, and nobody knows how long the Greeks had cultivated them before that. Quite simply, the olive gave birth to the art of Provençal cookery. A local saying confirms this: "A fish is an animal that is found alive in water and dead in oil."

Garlic is nearly as pervasive as the olive, as is the tomato. When any dish on a menu appears *à la provençale,* you can be certain it will be served with cooked tomatoes seasoned with garlic.

Following are some of the Provençal dishes that entice travellers to Provence and the Côte d'Azur:

Aïoli. This is simply garlic mayonnaise—*aïl* means "garlic." Called "the butter of Provence," "the soul of the South," and "cream of sun," this wonderful sauce makes an appearance, hot or cold, on vegetable and fish and lobster dishes. In addition to garlic, aïoli contains olive oil (of course), sometimes egg yolks, ground pepper, and perhaps lemon juice.

Aubergine. The word means "eggplant," specifically the small, dark-purple variety. It appears in many guises throughout the region, especially in Nice.

Bouillabaisse. Although everyone agrees this fish stew is the signature Provençal dish, no one agrees on what should be put in it, aside from olive oil, tomatoes, saffron, and fish. The question of what kind of fish is hotly debated, except that *rascasse* (a spiny, coarse fish) must be included; without it, bouillabaisse does not exist. Is lobster included, or is it not? Friendships have broken on the rocks of that decision. As the late food writer Waverley Root describes the two schools of thought: "One holds that a man who would put lobster in bouillabaisse would poison wells. The other is that a man who would leave it out would starve his children."

Bourride. This savory cream soup, made from bass, cod, and other fish, is particularly popular around Nice and is preferred by some to bouillabaisse; unlike the latter, it does not contain shellfish but sometimes uses *aïoli*.

Brandade. This is dried salt cod, usually worked with olive oil, garlic, potatoes, and spices into a kind of mousse. It's a peasant dish, served year-round and traditionally during the "lean dinner" on Christmas Eve.

Daube. On menus it usually appears as *daube de boeuf à la provençale*—a heavy, slowly cooked, infinitely flavorful stew of marinated beef, Cognac, olive oil, onions, carrots, and spices, to which are added bacon, raw mushrooms, tomatoes, garlic, black olives, and bitter orange peel. Daube takes forever to make, and is worth every minute.

Estouffade. Seen mainly around the Camargue region, *estouffade* is another version of beef stew and sometimes includes lamb as well. Home cooks often make it a day in advance of serving; it freezes extremely well.

Loup or *loup de mer*. *Loup* is, literally, "sea wolf." It's really sea bass, tastily served grilled with fennel or vine shoots. *Loup farci à la niçoise* implies the presence of tomatoes, olives, and mushrooms.

Pan bagnat. The name itself is not French, but Provençal. It means, simply, "bathed bread"; the bath is of olive oil. *Pan bagnat* makes a wonderful midday sandwich, a picnic unto itself. A round bread is sliced in half, hollowed out, soaked in oil, and filled with any number of items in the French repertoire: tomato, green pepper, black olives, garlic, red wine vinegar, radishes, and often tuna. Then it's pressed down until squishy. *Pan bagnat* is often sold on the streets of the Riviera.

Pissaladière. In Italy they say *pissaladière* is an Italian gift to France. In Nice they say it's a French invention predating pizza. In any case, it's delicious and appears everywhere. Everyone has his own version, but basically a large, pie-shaped pastry shell is filled with minced onions, olive oil, crushed garlic, spices, puréed black olives, and topped with strips of anchovies. Sometimes tomato sauce is mixed in.

Pistou. Possibly related to the Italian sauce *pesto, pistou* is actually the special seasoning added to a thick vegetable soup made by mashing together a Gruyère-type cheese, small-leaved basil, garlic, and olive oil. Sometimes in Nice this thick soup (also called *pistou*) includes white beans, tomatoes, and *courgettes* (zucchini).

Raïto. Traditionally, this sauce is served hot with grilled fish, but it's also superb with pasta. It involves many of the Provençal *spécialités:* sturdy red wine, garlic, tomatoes, black olives, and many spices.

Ratatouille. Eggplant (*aubergine*) is the essence of this vegetable stew steeped in olive oil: red or yellow peppers, zucchini, tomatoes, onions, garlic, spices, lemon juice, and white wine. It's served both hot and cold, as an accompaniment or a light, complete meal.

Salade niçoise. This is the ultimate salad, a summer feast. As in the case of bouillabaisse, some of its ingredients arouse debate. What it must have are tomatoes cut in quarters, cucumber, *fèves* (limalike beans), artichokes, green peppers, onions, anchovies or *pissala* (anchovies ground into a paste), olives, olive oil, red wine vinegar, and spices. Nowadays, hard-boiled eggs are considered a just addition; purists still frown upon potatoes, but they often appear.

Socca. Made of chick-pea flour, *socca* is usually found in pancake form and is used as a dessert or sold in open-air markets wrapped in brown paper cones. It's also good as an appetizer taken with *apéritifs.*

Tapenade. The apogee of black olive paste, this spread is served on thin toasts, used as a dip for raw vegetables, or diluted with olive oil to serve as a sauce. It is made with capers, garlic, lemon juice, and chopped fresh basil. Ground anchovies are always mixed with the olive paste.

Bon appétit!

—*Georgia I. Hesse*

AVIGNON

Avignon benefits from a strategic geographic location: on a major north–south water route—the Rhône river—halfway

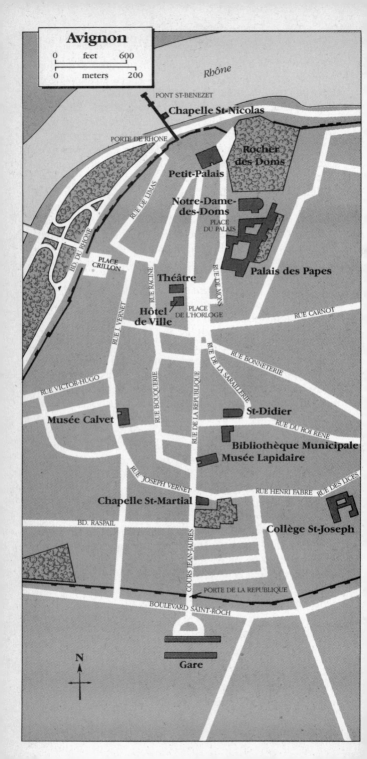

between Spain and Italy. This was partly what led the popes to Avignon in the 14th century. Unfortunately, the city's position also has a climatic disadvantage: the powerful, icy mistral that sweeps down the Rhône Valley, particularly in winter, blowing through Avignon's narrow streets and whipping around its large squares. It is said locally that the mistral can "blow the ears off a donkey." Because Avignon is at the northwestern corner of Provence, it is a good place to start a visit to the region, especially if you are arriving from the north.

The first-time visitor is always awestruck by the city's massive medieval monuments: the imposing Palais des Papes (Popes' Palace), the wall that encircles the city, and the famous bridge where "*on y danse.*" Considering Avignon proper's relatively small size and population (about 90,000), the weight of history can seem heavy. Lawrence Durrell noted: "The past embalmed it, the present could not alter it." A Provençal proverb cautions: "He who leaves Avignon loses his good sense." Avignon leaves no one indifferent.

For centuries the city has been a state within a state, a city of tolerance that has welcomed foreigners and political and religious refugees from around Europe in times when freedom and travel were at a premium. Even today Avignon is among a group of "free" French cities: French law forbids certain released prisoners to live in or near the area of their convicted crime; they must take up residence in a free city— such as Avignon. Political refugees are also sent to live in one of these *villes libres.*

The Walled City

In front of the train station you come face to face with twin stone towers and the outside of the wall that stretches for two and a half miles around the city. Don't be fooled: Despite their medieval appearance, the towers were constructed in 1863, and most of the wall and ramparts were heavily reconstructed at about the same time and again 30 years later. (The original wall went up between 1359 and 1370 under the direction of Pope Innocent VI.) To reach the city center from the station, walk through the gate in the walls facing you and directly down the cours Jean-Jaurès. This becomes rue de la République and leads to the central Place de l'Horloge. If you're driving, enter the Porte de la République and park in the lot just inside; driving in old Avignon is difficult.

RUE DE LA REPUBLIQUE TO
PLACE DE L'HORLOGE

Once you are past the gate, the medieval mirage momentarily vanishes as you confront the bustle of contemporary
Avignon—cafés, restaurants, and shops—along the rue de la
République. Still, amid the clamor of 20th-century commerce, reminders of a rich past are everywhere. Every few
yards a monument or alluring building stands out. One
example: the **Chapelle St-Martial**, a Benedictine monastery
founded in 1378. Major sections of the monastery and its
church were destroyed or rebuilt in the 19th century when
the boulevard was constructed to join the train station with
the Palais des Papes. Avignon's Office de Tourisme now
occupies a corner of one of the old buildings.

Farther down the street is the **Musée Lapidaire**, built as a
chapel for a Jesuit college in 1620. The building is hailed as
one of the most beautiful examples of French Baroque architecture and houses a magnificent collection of antiquities.

Just past the museum and down the rue Prévôt from the
rue de la République is the **Eglise St-Didier**. This fine example of Provençal Gothic style, constructed during the papal
period in 1356, has not been significantly retouched.

On rue Joseph-Vernet, west of rue de la République, is the
Musée Calvet, which occupies an elegant 18th-century mansion and houses an impressive collection of paintings and
archaeological treasures. Of particular interest is the extensive collection of French paintings from the 16th century to
the present.

The rue de la République ends at the large **Place de
l'Horloge**, a pedestrian zone and the center of near-round-
the-clock activity during most of the tourist season and
especially during the Festival d'Avignon theater extravaganza
in July. The square's two monumental buildings—the **Hôtel
de Ville** and the **Théâtre**—were both heavily reconstructed
in the last century. The several unexceptional outdoor café-
restaurants that line one side of the square are constantly
packed, providing a captive audience for street performers.
Avignon is, in fact, a major meeting place for itinerant musicians, especially in the warm months.

During the Festival d'Avignon, a monthlong carnival atmosphere animates this onetime Catholic capital (unlike the
sober ambience at Aix's music festival): The town is invaded
by thousands of theatergoers, actors, performers of all types,
vagabonds, and tourists. The festival has two faces: the official, highly acclaimed Classic Performances at the Théâtre—
Shakespeare, Molière, etc., all in French—and the "Festival
Off," in which dozens of offbeat and less-established troupes

put on performances ranging from one-person shows to traditional plays and experimental theater in various locations around town and in the outskirts (Villeneuve-lès-Avignon; Orange). Avignon has become a showcase for what is best in contemporary French—and European—theater; its only equal is the Edinburgh Festival.

THE PALAIS DES PAPES

The main show in Avignon is nonetheless the Palais des Papes, just north of the Place de l'Horloge. The heavily fortified palace is a reminder that Avignon was—from 1305 to 1378—the capital of Christianity. Contested antipopes stayed until 1417, when the schism between Rome and Avignon ended. Although the revolutionaries of the 1790s stripped the magnificent palace of its secular trappings, the immensity of its now-silent audience halls nevertheless evokes the tremendous power of the medieval papacy. Several vistas from its north windows, looking out over the roofs of Avignon, seem unchanged since the 14th century. The palace is one of the most remarkable buildings in France.

Chance played a part in bringing popes to the city. For years, the popes in Rome consolidated their power over temporal leaders. The new papal position was clear: The pope was the vicar not just of Saint Peter but of Jesus Christ himself. The pope was heir to the spiritual kingdom, directly under God, and therefore was above individual monarchs and territorial rulers. The French kings did not agree and maintained that they were sovereign in matters concerning the Church in France. In 1303 King Philippe le Bel (Philip the Fair) arrested the pope for interfering in the affairs of the French Church. This blow severely weakened the Roman Church.

Two years later Clement V, the former archbishop of Bordeaux, was elected pope. In 1309 he came to Avignon to prepare for a Church council to be held in Vienne, just up the Rhône. Grave security problems in Italy—war and rebellion against the papal state—made his return to Rome unwise.

The next elected pope, in 1316, was John XXII, the bishop of Avignon. He, too, decided to stay in his city, and he was installed as pope in the bishop's palace. His successor, Benoît XII, another Frenchman, also chose Avignon as his residence. He ordered the demolition of the bishop's palace and, in its place, the construction in 1336 of a *demeure* worthy of a pope.

Benoît XII was succeeded by Frenchman Clement VI, who

not only more than doubled the palace's size but in 1348 purchased Avignon itself from Queen Jeanne of Naples, who was also the countess of Provence. From that moment until the French Revolution, Avignon and its hinterland were papal property. Several other important buildings date from the early papal period: The **Petit Palais**, at the northern part of the square in front of the palace, was the residence for archbishops and bishops; during the past few years it has become a superb museum of medieval and Renaissance painting and sculpture, featuring some 400 Italian canvases of the 13th to 16th centuries and regional Avignon paintings from the 14th and 15th centuries. The Italian paintings are special treasures. The **Livrée Ceccano** (now a municipal library), just south of the Eglise St-Didier, was built by Cardinal Ceccano, the archbishop of Naples, in 1330. Some of the original painted ceilings remain intact.

Avignon at Apogee

During the popes' residence Avignon became one of the most important cities of the Western world. Nearly the entire papal administration, including the College of Cardinals, lived here. The city developed significant economic and cultural activities, in part because the Avignon popes were immensely rich from taxes levied on states and church *domaines*. However, Avignon's prestige long outlasted the Avignon popes (the last of them, Grégoire XI, abandoned the city in 1376). The return of the popes to Rome didn't end the story, it only made it more interesting.

After Grégoire's death an Italian pope was elected. Months later the French protested the election, claiming it had been influenced by a menacing Roman population. The French cardinals then elected a second pope (a so-called antipope), who took his seat at Avignon. The Church was now divided in two: England, the German Empire, Poland, Hungary, Bohemia, Flanders, and most of Italy were in favor of the Roman pope; Spain, France, Savoie, Scotland, Sicily, and Portugal were on Avignon's side.

The schism ended in 1417 with the election of a pope seated at Rome. Avignon was governed by the Vatican until it became French during the Revolution in 1791.

THE PONT D'AVIGNON

Standing next to the palace is the 12th-century **Cathédrale Notre-Dame-des-Doms**. Past the cathedral, steps rise to the **Rocher des Doms**, a rocky hill that offers a panoramic view of the valley, the neighboring town of Villeneuve-lès-Avignon, and especially the Pont St-Bénézet, a.k.a. the Pont d'Avignon. To visit the bridge, of which only a partial span and four of the original 22 arches remain, walk westward through the Porte du Rhône, just past the Petit Palais.

Legend has it that an angel appeared before a simple shepherd, Bénézet, and ordered him to build a bridge over the Rhône. Between 1177 and 1185 he built a wooden bridge, which was destroyed by a flood-swollen Rhône in 1226 and then reconstructed in stone. In spanning the river the bridge crossed the small Ile de la Barthelasse. Most of the dancing noted in the song "Sur le Pont d'Avignon" probably took place in taverns located on this island *under* the bridge's arches.

The bridge was also once a place for prayer. The **Chapelle St-Nicolas** still stands on the second pillar and is open daily. Built in the 13th century on Romanesque lines, the chapel was enlarged in 1513. Over the centuries the ravaging Rhône eroded St-Bénézet's arches, and repeated attempts to re-build the fallen supports eventually failed. In 1715 the cha-pel was closed for purposes of worship.

STAYING AND DINING
IN AND AROUND AVIGNON

For those turned off by the throngs, a quiet lunchtime respite can be found at **La Fourchette**, a charming, reasonably priced restaurant at 17, rue Racine, just one block west of the Place de l'Horloge (Tel: 90-85-20-93). East of the *place,* at 10, rue de Mons, is the restaurant **Christian Etienne**. In a town that has more than its share of pretentious restaurants, Christian Etienne is a fine choice. Its owner and chef, Etienne, is a young, energetic Avignon native who learned his trade at the Ritz in Paris. He often comes to the tables to take orders and talk with customers. The fare is light and imaginative, with a Provençal flavor at relatively reasonable prices (Tel: 90-86-16-50). Slightly steeper in price, but universally recognized as one of the best of all Provençal restaurants, is **Hiély-Lucullus** (5, rue de la République; Tel: 90-86-17-07), a gastronomic shrine, especially during the summer theater festival. When not dining there, visiting thespians at Avignon's annual theater festival snooze the afternoons away in the old city's hotel ▶ **Europe**, an ornate 19th-century gem at 12, place Crillon. An excellent, if expensive, way to remain in the shadow of the popes is to stay the night at ▶ **La Mirande**, a former cardinal's palace directly behind the Palais des Papes and a truly beautiful hostelry.

Provence excels in the art of blending sophistication in service and cuisine with country comfort and informality. Two examples near Avignon are ▶ **Hostellerie Le Prieuré**, across the river in Villeneuve-lès-Avignon (in an antique priory), and ▶ **Auberge de Noves**, 13 km (8 miles) to the southeast in an elegantly reworked manor house with a notable kitchen. Both are Relais & Châteaux members, and both are expensive, although not unduly so. Five kilometers (3 miles) to the northeast, at Avignon le Pontet, chef Philippe Boucher has made his ▶ **Auberge de Cassagne** a way station for lovers of Provençal cuisine; Tel: 90-31-04-18.

Rhône Wine Country

"The Rhône is a river of wine," writes Alexis Lichine, and he puts the geography nicely: "It drains vineyards on its broad delta plain, along the steep cliffs above Avignon, in the Cévennes and Jura mountains, and around the Lake of Geneva. Yet the only wines to bear the name are those which come from the central section—the Côtes du Rhône." These *côtes* extend from Lyon in the north to Avignon in the south, a strip about 140 miles long.

In the company of the greatest Bordeaux and Burgundy wines, whose names are shouted aloud, those of the Rhône are whispered: Condrieu, Côte Rôtie, Château Grillet, Gigondas, Hermitage, Saint-Péray, Tavel, and Châteauneuf-du-Pape. Yet the Rhônes have much to recommend them. They are eminently drinkable, for one thing; for another, usually they are reasonable in price.

CHATEAUNEUF

The most famous of these is Châteauneuf-du-Pape, and the *pape* (pope) referred to is generally considered to be Pope John XXII, who from 1316 to 1333 built a new castle (*château neuf*) in the sloping hills about 17 km (11 miles) north of Avignon. Today Châteauneuf, off D 192 halfway between Orange and Avignon and home to about 2,000 inhabitants, most of them wine enthusiasts, is the most interesting village in the valley for the traveller who has time for only one stop. The château was mostly ruined in 1552 during the Wars of Religion, and its remaining keep was wiped out during bombings on August 20, 1944. Only one evocative façade remains to hint at the majesty of the original.

Even among the worldly, extravagant Avignon popes, John XXII was notorious for high living and debauchery. He slept on an ermine-trimmed pillow shared, it was said, by a nearly endless parade of pretty *demoiselles*. Soon his reputation began to enhance that of his wines. As Frederick Wildman, Jr., reminds us in *A Wine Tour of France,* "He let it be known that his Châteauneuf-du-Pape was not only a glory to taste,

but—and he stood as living proof—also a rejuvenator and
aphrodisiac of remarkable potency. The fortunes of Châteauneuf-du-Pape were made."

A few sites in town are worth visiting—notably the **Château des Papes** for its splendid views over the Rhône Valley—but the main attraction is wine: drinking it, fine dining
to accompany it, visiting its vineyards, spending a night in
seductive surroundings.

A wine fair is held in autumn in Châteauneuf; the date
depends on the harvest (usually mid- to late September).

Wine Estates and Villages Around Châteauneuf

The largest estate of Châteauneuf today is **Mont-Redon**, 4 km
(2½ miles) to the north of town on the Route d'Orange
(D 68). Born as Mourredon in the 14th century, it has been a
property of the Plantin family for three generations and is
now the largest producer of little-known white Châteauneuf
as well as the familiar reds and less highly bred bottles
called simply Côtes-du-Rhône. Cellar visits are conducted on
weekdays; the tasting and sales room is open daily.

A lighter, more "modern" Châteauneuf is produced by the
▶ **Château des Fines Roches** domaine, which also, handily,
maintains a fine inn and outstanding restaurant in the highly
picturesque 19th-century château. Just south of the village
via D 17 and a marked private road winding through vineyards, Fines Roches is renowned for lamb dishes perfectly
suited to its wines. The seven rooms are only moderately
expensive; the winery itself is open for visitors daily between March and December.

Travellers who have time to familiarize themselves with
other towns and other bottlings might consider (from north
to south) **Tain-l'Hermitage** (17 km/11 miles north of Valence,
across the Rhône from Tournon), **Gigondas** (see the
Vaucluse section below; 17 km/11 miles east of Orange; only
650 inhabitants but two estates to visit), or **Tavel** (15 km/9
miles northwest of Avignon; there are four estates in its
immediate vicinity).

STAYING AND DINING
IN RHONE WINE COUNTRY

The restaurant **La Mule du Pape**, in the center of Châteauneuf on the Place de la Fontaine, is touted by discerning
gourmets such as Samuel Chamberlain, and serves elegant
meals, though time has slightly dimmed its luster. Two small,
modestly priced inns in attractive settings can be found near
Gigondas: the 15-room ▶ **Les Florets** and the 46-room
▶ **Montmirail**, in the nearby hamlet of that name (see the

Vaucluse section below). Tavel is known for the ▶ **Auberge de Tavel**, a restaurant-hotel with 12 modestly priced rooms and a swimming pool. A more elaborate, and far more refined, alternative is the reasonably priced ▶ **Hostellerie de Crillon le Brave** in the village of the same name. Its 19 rooms and two small houses (one with two rooms and one with three) are decorated with traditional Souleiado fabrics and Provençal country furniture.

—Georgia I. Hesse

Orange

Orange, just 31 km (19 miles) north of Avignon by route A 7 or N 7, shares with Nîmes and Arles important reminders of Roman Provence: a theater, a gymnasium, and a commemorative arch that lived on as evidence of the importance of Roman Arausio long after that city of some 85,000 was trampled by Alemannic and Visigothic invaders. Later, the battered monuments were used as rock quarries for the construction of homes and fortifications.

Orange is one of the most momentous sites in the history of Christianity: In 529 the Council of Orange declared for Augustinian predeterminism and against all forms of Pelagian doctrines of free will. By the 13th century the original Celtic market town upon which the Romans built had become a holding of the German Duchy of Nassau, later joined to the Dutch House of Orange. Thus through the quirks of history this tranquil town lent its name to a king of England, an Irish political faction, and a state of South Africa.

From Celtic days to our own, Orange sat right on France's main north–south route, the commercial Roman road that became Route Nationale 7. Today, however, the town of some 27,500 people has been bypassed by A 7, the Autoroute du Soleil, and it is possible—though not recommended—to hurry by without hesitation.

The plane trees, the sleepy, shady squares, the sidewalk cafés where strollers sit, musing and unmoving, mark Orange as a southern, Provençal town. The works of long-gone Rome remain the major lure.

ROMAN ORANGE

Orange's **Théâtre Antique** is considered by most to be the best-looking and best-preserved classical theater in existence, having been constructed during the last decade of the first century B.C. under Emperor Augustus. It follows the Greek plan of a semicircle of tiers facing the orchestra and stage and was about the same size as that in Arles, with a marble and mosaic backdrop of niches, columns, statues, and other decorations. The backdrop and its supporting wings, as seen from the square behind the theater, were known to Louis XIV as the "finest wall in the kingdom."

The stage lost all its accoutrements long ago, but the acoustics remain unsullied, and classical plays are still performed on a regular basis, watched by the theater's imperial statue—a ten-foot-two-inch-tall Augustus. All Roman theaters had such a statue, but only the one in Orange remains; it was discovered, somewhat the worse for fall and burial, in the orchestra pit.

Near the theater, excavations proceed on an early **temple** and **gymnasium**—the latter is one of only three known in France. Off a courtyard, the gym boasted baths (of course), open and enclosed running tracks, and a dais for the awarding of prizes. Orange's **Arc de Triomphe**, in the triple-arched style, was completed about A.D. 26 and is the third largest, as well as the best preserved, in France.

In 1939 French art collector Count William de Belleroche (whose family had lived for two centuries in Britain) presented to the city some 400 works by one Sir Frank Brangwyn: prints, drawings, watercolors, engravings, all showing town and country activities in France and England and now on display in the **Musée Municipal**, across the street from the excavations.

Orange is the source of some fragrant, long-lasting milled soaps in the French tradition, with scents of lavender, orange, and herbs.

STAYING AND DINING IN AND AROUND ORANGE

The smartest place to stay in the immediate area of Orange is the ► **Château de Rochegude**, about 15 km (9 miles) north via D 976 and D 11. This converted castle—its keep dates from the 12th century—offers a spectacular view of the valley below. The 25 rooms range from expensive to very expensive; the four apartments are in the latter category. Its excellent restaurant specializes in lamb, flavored with the rosemary and thyme that is so assiduously cultivated in Provence.

The ► **Château de Montcaud**, in Combe, about ten minutes outside Orange in the vineyards along D 6, has recently and luxuriously been fitted out as a hotel, with 20 elegant guest rooms and a superb kitchen that makes the most of local produce.

An accomplished but reasonably priced restaurant, **Le Pigraillet** (on the road that enters the hillside Parc de la

Colline St-Eutrope on the south) specializes in duck and local wines (Tel: 90-34-44-25). **Le Forum** is an unpretentious and satisfying restaurant at 3, rue Mazeau, very near the Théâtre Antique (Tel: 90-34-01-09).

—*Georgia I. Hesse*

The Vaucluse

Although Vaucluse is the name of an entire *département* (or French administrative district), for most travellers the Vaucluse conjures up the beautiful villages and gentle valleys that lie east of Avignon and are dominated by the towering Mont Ventoux and the tall Lubéron, an imposing green ridge that cuts off the Vaucluse from Aix-en-Provence. As the region spreads out over several hundred square miles and displays surprising changes of landscape, no one itinerary can be said to be the best. For our purposes we will work from north to south. Aside from a capacity to enjoy the simple things of life, you need a car—or the legs of a champion cyclist.

VAISON-LA-ROMAINE

In contrast to imperial Orange on the plain, Vaison-la-Romaine—27 km (17 miles) northeast of Orange on the vineyard-splitting D 975—presents a glimpse of a prosperous Roman market town nestled in wooded hills. For those whose imagination can rise above the ruins, the ancient neighborhoods thus far excavated—the **Quartier de Puymin** and the **Quartier de la Villasse**—give an indication of how well wealthy Roman families lived in their spacious villas. As with many old Provençal towns, Vaison also possesses a fine amphitheater.

What adds further to the charm of the town is its extensive medieval quarter. The Romans, safe in a secure civilization, built expansively on the flat land of the right bank of the Ouvèze river; their successors in Vaison were less sure of themselves and elected to build a fortified town on the steep hill of the left bank. Reached by a sturdy Roman bridge spanning the river, the upper town is a picturesque warren of sinuous streets that lead up to the ruins of a 12th-century castle.

As the threat of invading armies gradually faded with the passing of time, the people of Vaison moved back across the river and built their town on top of the Roman ruins. Modern Vaison, a small 19th-century grid of wide streets, is now known for its excellent market held on Tuesdays. To sit on the terrace of the otherwise unremarkable **Sporting Bar** and look out over the busy Place du 11-Novembre, which itself overlooks the ruins of the Roman forum, is to realize the antiquity of Vaison's commercial tradition. Of course, it might be more practical to head into the bustle and admire the flowers and herbs on sale, or pick up some truffles and lavender-scented honey for a lazy feast later in the day.

MONTMIRAIL AND MONT VENTOUX
There is no shortage of picnic areas south of Vaison. As wine is the essential lubricant of any impromptu meal in the French countryside, it's advisable to take D 977 out of Vaison and head south on D 88 and D 23 to the nearby vineyards of **Gigondas** and **Vacqueyras**. Vintners there have long adapted themselves to foreign admirers—Pliny spoke warmly of the fruity Gigondas—and roadside tasting stands abound for the thirsty. To the east of these vineyards are the **Dentelles de Montmirail**, eroded, toothlike crags that rise from an irregular terrain of unusual natural beauty. The village of **La Roque-Alric**, perched on a jagged rock, is particularly striking.

   Malaucène, 10 km (6 miles) south of Vaison on D 938, marks the point of departure for the ascent of **Mont Ventoux**, the mountain that can be seen from many parts of Provence. Famous for its wind-whipped summit, Mont Ventoux is also noted for its varied vegetation: European pines grow on its north face; cedars of Lebanon and cypresses climb its southern flank. If the sky is clear and—this is important—the mistral is not blowing, the mountain of the wind is well worth the tortuous 21-km (13-mile) drive up D 974 to the summit. Here, at a height of more than 6,000 feet, all of Provence stretches out to the south and the Alps can be made out in the north. On exceptionally clear mornings, before the heat haze of the warm spring and summer days cuts down visibility, the taller peaks of the distant Pyrénées appear on the horizon to the southwest.

PLATEAU DE VAUCLUSE
South of the grandeur of Ventoux and, in more ways than one, far more down to earth, stretches the uneven Plateau de Vaucluse. A collection of lovely villages and sleepy towns, this area, once part of the papal Comtat Venaissin, is rural France at its best. **Venasque**, the hilltop village that gave its name to the Comtat, typifies Provençal indolence, its narrow streets an oasis of calm. Still, local craftsmen have set up shop in the village for souvenir hunters drawn to the **Eglise Notre-Dame**, part of which dates as far back as the sixth century. The garden of the **Auberge de la Fontaine** here is a

cheerful place to eat a splendid, inexpensive meal; Tel: 90-66-02-96.

From Venasque the traveller has hard choices to make about where next to go. Ten kilometers (6 miles) up D 4 is the town of **Carpentras**, its magnificent 18th-century synagogue awaiting inspection. The region's other major town, **Cavaillon**, 29 km (18 miles) south of Carpentras on D 938, houses another historic synagogue, although its fame in France resides primarily in its production of delicious melons. Cavaillon's immediate neighbor, the **Fontaine-de-Vaucluse**, a bubbling spring that feeds the Sorgue river, is, if not overrated, then certainly overvisited. Still, Petrarch composed sonnets during his 16-year sojourn here in the 14th century, so the site, despite the number of tour buses, is not totally prosaic. Far more pleasurable is a Sunday morning spent at the weekly antiques market at the neighboring **L'Isle-sur-la-Sorgue**, a little town that is a magnet for collectors. A hard morning's shop can be rewarded with lunch at ▶ **Mas de Cure Bourse**, an 18th-century inn 2 km (1 mile) southwest of town; Tel: 90-38-16-58.

Abbaye de Sénanque

Less crowded than the market towns and the Fontaine-de-Vaucluse are the winding D 4 and D 177, which lead from Venasque south to the narrow pocket of land occupied by the Abbaye de Sénanque. Fields of purple lavender defy the arid earth in the defile where the Cistercian monks first decided to settle in 1148. Austere and gracefully Romanesque, the abbey's church and cloisters have not been altered since their construction more than eight centuries ago. To those of a more worldly bent, the monkish guides will gladly sell the distilled specialty of the monastery, an aromatic drink that treads a fine line between elixir and mouthwash. In the buildings open to the public, the history and practices of the monks from Cîteaux (see the Burgundy chapter) are admirably presented in explanatory notes hanging in each room.

Gordes

Just a few kilometers farther south on D 177 stands the town of Gordes, one of the most photogenic in all of Provence. Spilling down a hillside, the tawny-colored houses that make up this Provençal acropolis overlook the Coulon Valley to the south. At the summit is a restored castle, one of its buildings a fine example of decorative Renaissance architecture; it now houses a museum given over to Hungarian artist **Victor Vasarely**.

East and South of Gordes

The Coulon Valley below Gordes is bounded on the south
by the **Montagne du Lubéron**, a lozenge-shaped mountain
that separates rural Vaucluse from the plain leading to the
city of Aix-en-Provence. The area is studded with villages of
arresting beauty, none more so than **Roussillon** (8 km/5
miles east of Gordes), a study in all the different hues of red.
Startling hillsides of brilliant ocher can be seen in the
immediate vicinity of Roussillon. True lovers of the color can
take D 22 from Apt to **Rustrel**, where deserted ocher quarries make for a natural Day-Glo landscape.

South of Roussillon the scenery changes once again:
Where D 108 crosses the Coulon river, the 2,000-year-old
Pont Julien still carries traffic. The handsome villages of
Oppède-le-Vieux and **Bonnieux** overlook the bridge from
the foothills of the Lubéron. Bonnieux has the signal advantage of possessing a bread-making museum. From the medieval heights of Bonnieux the red slash of Roussillon's
hillocks is clearly visible, as are the orchards around the
town of **Apt**. The observant should look out for an anachronism over the ageless landscape: To the northeast jet fighters frequently can be sighted heading back to their base in
the Plateau d'Albion, home to France's nuclear strike force.
Perhaps it would be more cheering to descend from Bonnieux and then climb to neighboring **Lacoste**, where you
can sit in the village café and stare thoughtfully at a ruined
castle—it was here that the marquis de Sade spent much of
his eventful youth.

STAYING AND DINING
IN THE VAUCLUSE

In a romantic setting in **Vaison-la-Romaine** with an arresting
view of the surrounding hills is the intimate hotel ▶ **Le Bef-
froi**, named for the centuries-old belfry perched on the main
gate to the quarter. The hotel, a beautiful town house built in
the 16th century, is tailor-made for people in love.

On the route de Sénanque in **Gordes** are two outstanding,
if pricey, restaurants: ▶ **Les Bories** (reserve; Tel: 90-72-00-
51), with 18 moderately expensive, picturesque rooms, and
the ▶ **Domaine de l'Enclos** (Tel: 90-72-08-22). The latter
includes a deluxe nine-room, four-apartment hotel that, with
its views of the valley, should inspire any well-heeled would-
be painter. This luxury is a far cry from a neighboring
attraction called the **Village des Bories**, a fascinating cluster
of mortarless stone huts thought to have been used by
peasants for storing implements and threshing grain—an
architectural/archaeological wonder not to be missed.

Two other stops may keep you in Gordes country longer than you planned. The first is the ▶ **Bastide de Gordes**, an 18-room enchantment overlooking the Lubéron; the hotel is expensive, as is the outstanding restaurant, with a kitchen that turns out a fine *nage de rouget* (red mullet) *façon barigoule*. Just down the hill in the hamlet of Joucas is the stunning ▶ **Mas des Herbes Blanches**, with 16 rooms done in inspired rustic style, a heated pool, tennis courts, and regional dishes suited to the local wines; expensive, and worth it.

The Alpilles

Midway between Avignon and Arles, a peculiar, 25-km (16-mile)-long range of jagged white hills points up into the blue skies. In some places a brilliant white, the Alpilles range divides the plain of the lower Rhône Valley: The fields to the north, around St-Rémy-de-Provence, are covered in flowers and orchards; those to the south, around Maussane-les-Alpilles, are a succession of almond and olive groves. With the exception of the arid Alpilles themselves, this region has known the hand of human beings, both as creators and destroyers, since the first millennium B.C. Roman and Greek ruins guard the approaches to the north (at St-Rémy), just as an abandoned medieval citadel crowns the range to the south (at Les Baux). Nearby, a magnificent abbey (Montmajour) stands deserted atop a hillock, looking out over the Roman city of Arles and the medieval fair towns of Beaucaire and Tarascon. Add to this sense of history the Provençal climate and slow-moving pace of life, and you may choose to while away weeks beneath the cypresses and plane trees on the village squares.

ST-REMY AND SALON

While the circular old town of St-Rémy-de-Provence has nothing to attract the tourist in search of the spectacular, this flowery Provençal center offers peace of mind—which may be why it, along with Salon-de-Provence, has recently proved so alluring to vacationing pundits from fast-talking Paris. Both towns lay claim to the Provençal seer, Nostradamus, who spent much of his time on earth gazing starward and predicting what would happen when he was gone. Born in St-Rémy, Nostradamus died—he is supposed to have calculated that date, too—in Salon, in 1566. The latter town, by far the busier of the two, lies 32 km (20 miles) southeast of St-Rémy along D 99 (a beautiful tree-lined road) and N 7 (which turns into N 538 at Sénas,

before Salon). Not a pretty place, Salon nonetheless possesses a much-remodeled tenth-century castle that houses
an outstanding military museum and, in late July, plays host
to a jazz festival.

Van Gogh and the Ruins

The true spell of St-Rémy is cast by the quiet monuments to
the south of the town. At **St-Paul-de-Mausole**, a medieval
monastery converted into an asylum during the last century,
a weary Vincent van Gogh spent all but the final months of
his last years in the calm cloister and gardens. It was here
that the penniless artist executed many of the paintings that
now fetch such astronomical prices at auction in London and
New York.

The mausoleum so lugubriously included in the monastery's name refers, in fact, to a non-Christian monument of
considerable archaeological significance. Just before D 5 disappears into the Alpilles, a kilometer (about half a mile) south
of St-Rémy, two odd Roman constructions known as **Les
Antiques** can be seen to the right of the roadway: a triumphal
arch celebrating Julius Caesar's subjugation of Marseille in 49
B.C., and a tall funerary monument (the remarkable mausoleum) commemorating the untimely deaths of two of the
Emperor Augustus's grandsons. Remarkably well preserved,
as well as evocative in their setting near the strangely shaped
hills, these monuments stand across the road from the ruins
of a Greco-Roman city, **Glanum**. Obviously a site of some
importance to Greek settlers—rivaled in the western Mediterranean only by Emporiae in Spanish Catalonia and Marseille—the ruins of Glanum hug the flank of the Alpilles in
testament to the vanity of human pretensions to permanence.
As James Pope-Hennessy warns of this peculiar spot: "The
Plateau des Antiques and the ruins of Glanum are among
several places in Provence that I should not recommend
imaginative persons to visit alone by the light of the moon."

STAYING AND DINING IN ST-REMY

The visitor might profitably linger in St-Rémy. The ▶ **Château des Alpilles**, a 15-room, four-apartment hotel set amid
tall trees, offers a charming, if pricey, respite from the
ardors of sightseeing. So too does the ▶ **Hostellerie du
Vallon de Valrugues**, an extremely comfortable hotel on the
outskirts that is adorned by olive groves, a view of the
Alpilles, and a fine restaurant.

St-Rémy also claims a number of adequate regional restaurants, the most informal being a turn-of-the-century affair
called the **Bistrot des Alpilles** at 15, boulevard Mirabeau

(Tel: 90-92-09-17). Of particular interest to the gourmet is the **Croque Chou** (Tel: 90-95-18-55), located 11 km (7 miles) northeast of St-Rémy along D 30 then D 29 in the village of Verquières. Rather than choosing such habitual regional fare as lamb and rabbit, the adventurous eater may decide to go for a peculiar house specialty—octopus cooked in wine with its ink—while admiring the 11th-century church across the way.

LES BAUX-DE-PROVENCE

A towering rock plateau—a natural fortress—formed of twisted limestone weathered into haunting forms. Below, on either side, two valleys: On one side, a pastoral scene from the tales of Daudet, is the Vallée d'Entreconque; on the other, a tormented landscape, the Val d'Enfer (Valley of Hell) in the cracks of the Alpilles mountains. Atop the rock plateau are ruins of a feudal fortress carved out of stone and long since destroyed by successive wars waged against the castle's powerful and ambitious rulers: This is Les Baux, on the southern slopes of the Alpilles, just 4 windy kilometers (2½ miles) below St-Rémy.

Isolated in the countryside 23 km (14 miles) northeast of Arles, Les Baux still stimulates the imagination as it did 700 years ago when it welcomed troubadours and their ideal of courtly love. Today it is a lively touristic and artistic center of fewer than 500 permanent inhabitants whose main occupations are staffing the few galleries and shops in the upper town and running the celebrated restaurants in the valley below. It is also a meeting place for a segment of France's extreme right, the royalist parties, who hold an annual rally near the village.

While historians debate the exact origins of the name Les Baux—some say it means "high place" in Ligurian, others contend it's Provençal for "cave," and still others believe it's a derivative of Balthazar, one of the three Wise Men—there is no question that Les Baux gave us the word "bauxite," for the mineral mined in the nearby Alpilles chain.

The story of Les Baux is one of a regional feudal power engaged in nearly incessant (and usually lost) wars and rebellions lasting several hundred years. The princes of Les Baux were often cruel and ambitious warmongers. The most notorious of the lot was the 14th-century Raymond de Turenne, who was given the amiable nickname the Scourge of Provence. Given to marauding raids on his neighbors, Raymond had a favorite ploy: He would shove prisoners off the cliffs at Les Baux and laugh diabolically as they plunged to their death. Naturally, he was disliked. The popes at

Avignon raised a mercenary army to dislodge him, but apparently the hired troops imitated Raymond by pillaging everything in sight. The king of France was eventually called in, and *his* army succeeded in forcing the Scourge into exile.

Nevertheless, the court at Les Baux was considered brilliant, especially during the 12th and 13th centuries, when it was home to the troubadours, among them Bernard de Ventadour and Raimbaut d'Orange. Such artists—now, paradoxically, unsung heroes of Western literature—performed regularly at the court of Les Baux, singing of the refinements of love in a rough-and-ready age.

When Provence became French in 1481, Les Baux revolted against Louis XI and the castle was destroyed (not for the first or last time). The Renaissance brought better times for Les Baux; the castle was rebuilt and splendid mansions were constructed, including the **Hôtel de Manville** and the **Hôtel de Brion**—the latter now housing a museum of printing, with artifacts dating from the beginnings of printing in the West.

The renaissance of Les Baux didn't last long. The lords of Les Baux supported the wrong causes all too often: the Protestants, the duke of Orléans against King Louis XIII, and Aixois insurgents rebelling against Cardinal Richelieu. As a result, the king ordered a military occupation of Les Baux, and the castle and city ramparts were torn down for the last time. Les Baux became a ghost town as its 3,000 inhabitants moved to greener pastures.

The writings of Mistral (of the Félibrige movement; see also Arles) and Daudet helped Les Baux regain some of its past glory by rediscovering its historic importance and, above all, its touristic potential. Daudet's tales tell of a peaceful, pastoral village coping with economic hardships and displaying a fervent attachment to the Church and its traditions.

One of his stories describes a centuries-old Christmas ritual still performed today: the midnight Mass procession—the *fête des bergers* (shepherds' festival)—in the now significantly modified 12th-century **Eglise St-Vincent**. Church authorities often forbade the fête because of suspicions that it was rooted in paganism. The procession provides a good show for the several hundred people, mostly visitors, who cram into the small church on Christmas Eve. Provençal music—flute and tambourine—replaces traditional Christmas carols.

Because the village of Les Baux sits on such a small rock plateau—only 2,600 feet long and 650 feet wide—no cars are allowed on its streets. The village is split into two: the

early-medieval ghost town—*ville morte*—and the latter-day
Provençal village, with its arts-and-crafts shops, restaurants,
museums, and exceptional Renaissance mansions.

STAYING AND DINING
IN AND AROUND LES BAUX

The village has few moderately priced restaurants; **Béren-
gère**, in the upper village, is perhaps the best for those
unwilling to splurge (Tel: 90-54-40-00). While you can get a
snack or a decent meal with a spectacular view or charming
ambience almost anywhere in Les Baux, it would be a shame
to come here and not try—budget willing—the ▶ **Oustaù
de Baumanière** (reserve; Tel: 90-54-33-07). The food here
runs to heavy dishes with rich sauces; the house specialty is
local lamb cooked in a crust. Baumanière also has 25 elegantly rustic and comfortable rooms in a restored Provençal
farmhouse and a swimming pool and tennis courts. Do not
expect light-hearted service at either the hotel or the restaurant. Baumanière, as an international stopover for members
of the credit-card set and their voluble companions, tends
toward the stuffy and reserved. Down the road is the less
expensive but charmingly rustic ▶ **La Cabro d'Or**, with 22
rooms and a good restaurant. Baumanière and Cabro d'Or
are both run by M. Charial, grandson of the previous owner,
Raymond Thuilier. The ▶ **Auberge de la Benvengudo**, a
modest hôtel and restaurant, can be found on the D 78 just
outside of Les Baux. Service and ambience here are far less
formal than at Beaumanière.

Just 4 km (2½ miles) south of Les Baux, still along D 5,
away from the constant stream of visitors, is the town of
Maussane-les-Alpilles, a center of olive oil production. Although possessing neither a spectacular site nor a glorious
past, Maussane has that one Provençal trait denied Les Baux:
a large *boules*-playing square with two charming, reasonable
restaurants, **La Pitchoune** and **L'Oustaloun**, and a cranky
café, the **Café de la Fontaine**, frequented by olive growers.
To watch them at work you may visit the oil-pressing cooperative on rue Chaloun and pop olives as you tour the
facility.

MONTMAJOUR

Southwest of the Alpilles, almost on the outskirts of Arles, a
ruined monastery stands on a small hill in the midst of fields
of waving wheat. **Montmajour** is now a ghostly collection of
Romanesque buildings, rendered even more striking by the
precarious state of disrepair of some of the upper floors.
How the Benedictines who settled here in the tenth century

eventually turned worldly and decadent makes a good counterpoint to the successful monastic community at Sénanque.
When Louis XVI suppressed the wanton abbey in 1786, the
fattened monks were not missed by a peasantry ready for
revolution.

Aside from an immense barrel of a church and a well-
restored cloister, Montmajour possesses only one other fully
intact feature—a medieval keep that rises more than 100
feet above the plain. Those willing to make the climb will
see the red roofs of Arles to the south, the Alpilles to the
northeast, and the towns of Beaucaire and Tarascon to the
northwest.

BEAUCAIRE AND TARASCON

These sites merit a brief visit before heading to the wonders
of Arles, for both are medieval towns that were famous for
the great fairs they held for more than six centuries. The
Rhône, though bridged here, separates the two towns, leading visitors in a hurry to ask themselves a soul-searching
question: Do I like my castles in ruin or intact? If you opt for
the former, the ethereal ruin of **Beaucaire**'s castle on the
right (western) bank is a beautiful place to clamber over
stone walls and stare out over the Rhône. Just outside the
walls of the city is a place to stay that is as dreamlike as
Beaucaire itself: ▶ **Les Doctrinaires** (quai du Général-de-
Gaulle), a 17th-century stone *collège* on the side of a tree-
shaded canal, with a pretty outside dining area. Rooms are
moderately priced.

Tarascon, on the other bank, was preternaturally lucky in
backing the right horse during France's dynastic squabbles,
thereby saving its lovely castle from dismantlement by a
wrathful Richelieu. A golden 15th-century gem, the **Château
du Roi René**—Provence's beloved monarch—reflects its
machiolated towers in the waters of the river and stuns
visitors with its interior, which shows the transition from
Flamboyant Gothic to early Renaissance styles. If you've ever
seen French B-movies featuring knights parading for the
edification of their ladies high up on the battlements, you
will recognize Tarascon's castle immediately.

If you should be in the area near the end of June, by all
means reserve the weekend for this town. That is when
Tarascon celebrates its *Tarasque,* a Rhone-dwelling serpent
given to gobbling up children and livestock before the holy
intervention of Saint Martha some 1,500 years ago knocked
some sense into the beast. The festival is a combination of
Loch Ness tomfoolery and Chinese New Year, all under the
sunny skies of Provence.

ARLES

Should you be on the southbound train from Avignon, which stays on the left bank of the Rhône as it goes through the countryside, the words of an artistic genius who took the same journey can guide you: "Before arriving at Tarascon I noticed a magnificent landscape of immense yellowish crags strangely entangled with the most imposing forms. The valleys were lined with small, round trees covered with olive-colored or gray-colored leaves." The train travels farther south, through "magnificent reddish land planted with vineyards," and eventually you, like Vincent van Gogh, will arrive in the lovely town of Arles.

Van Gogh, whose one-year (1888–1889) sojourn here marked a feverish burst of creativity during which he executed more than 200 canvases, may have been ridiculed, persecuted, and interned by intolerant town fathers, yet he immortalized what was already a city of considerable antiquity and charm. Although many of the buildings van Gogh knew have disappeared (his "Maison Jaune" fell to Allied bombs in 1944) or have been curiously reconverted (the hospital in which he was placed in solitary confinement is now a van Gogh center and souvenir mall), the light and colors of this city and its rural surroundings have not changed at all.

Not that van Gogh is Arles's sole claim to fame. Arlésiennes, it will be remembered, have long been celebrated for their manes of dark hair flowing down over shawls of fiery red and deepest black. More impressive for lovers of the inanimate is the city's historical pedigree as capital of Roman Gaul and center of Provençal folklore. Arles, in short, is a city with a past.

Old Arles

To make sense of this compact cluster of sinuous streets, magnificent churches, museums, and massive Roman constructions, it's perhaps best first to sit square in the middle of it all and have a drink. **Place du Forum**, a narrow rectangle of shaded café terraces that face a statue of Frédéric Mistral— Provence's turn-of-the-century cultural savior—and two forlorn Corinthian columns from a long-vanished Roman temple, gives an idea, by its very disorder, of the confusing welter of cultures that is Arles. The temptation is to leave the café and go in three directions at once: To the north a few blocks is the tranquil Rhône riverfront, to the east are the great Roman theaters, and to the south await outstanding museums and medieval churches grouped around the 18th-century Place de la République. For our purposes, we begin with the Arlésiens' most imposing ancestors, the Romans.

THE TWO THEATERS

The amphitheater and the neighboring Roman theater are witnesses to Arles's prestigious place in the Roman world. The name Arles was derived from Arelate (City of Swamps), a reference to the marshes that once surrounded the city (only the Camargue was left untouched by industrious swamp-draining Arlésiens). Despite the inhospitable environment, the Romans developed Arles as an important port and economic center.

The rise of the city dates from 49 B.C., after Julius Caesar had ousted his rival Pompey in a civil war. Neighboring Marseille had the bad luck to have sided with the loser. Consequently, Caesar rewarded his friends in Arles with the lucrative trading connections to Rome that had once been Marseille's source of wealth. A canal was built to join Arles with the Mediterranean, and the city inherited the major portion of Marseille's territory, which extended along the coast to Nice.

During Arles's golden period (first through fourth centuries A.D.) the emperors endowed it with monuments worthy of a major Roman city: a circus, a triumphal arch, a 12,000-seat theater, lavish baths, an aqueduct, temples, and an amphitheater.

Les Arènes, once the haunt of gladiators and now the home of bullfighters, is the largest Roman amphitheater in Provence. Although its uppermost story is conspicuously absent, the massive structure, dating from the first century, is lucky to have survived at all. During the Middle Ages it was used as a military camp and it later became a city within a city, with some two hundred houses and two chapels built inside and outside its walls. The city cleared out the houses and their residents in 1825, and shortly afterward the amphitheater was restored to its original state.

Next to Les Arènes are the ruins of the **Roman theater**, which was constructed before the amphitheater, in about A.D. 30, during the first years of the reign of Augustus. Several artifacts were found here, including the Venus of Arles, a beautiful classical bust that was given to Louis XIV. It is now on view at the Louvre.

Augustus and Caesar weren't the only prominent Roman rulers who supported Arles. Constantine (288–337) adopted Arles as one of his two capitals (Constantinople was the other). He brought family, friends, dignitaries, and treasury here but stayed only for short periods. Constantine ordered new construction at Arles, embellishing the ramparts ordered by Caesar and Augustus and enlarging the city to include the right bank of the Rhône, Trinquetaille.

As a result of Constantine's patronage and Arles's status as capital of the Western Roman Empire, the city is also a treasure trove of ancient Christian art. But to find it, you must leave the great theaters and go west to the Place de la République, where the pagan, patristic, and medieval all share pride of place.

AROUND THE PLACE DE LA REPUBLIQUE

On the western side of the square stands a 17th-century church, which houses the **Musée d'Art Païen**. On display here is a monumental head of Augustus unearthed at the Roman theater, as well as classical statuary, sarcophagi, columns, and friezes from the Arlésien region. Its rival, on the nearby rue Balze, is the **Musée d'Art Chrétien**, which is considered to have the richest collection of sarcophagi after the Vatican Museum. Most of these, dating from the fourth century, were transferred in excellent condition from the late-empire burial grounds at Alyscamps (see below).

To understand what stands on the eastern side of Place de la République, it is necessary to pass through several centuries of history first. After the Germanic tribes overran the Roman Empire, Arles fell into the hands of the Visigoths, then, in succession, the Burgunds, the Franks, the Saracens, and finally the Carolingian Franks—who were later to establish the Holy Roman Empire under Charlemagne. His descendants further divided the new empire with each succession. Arles was first integrated into the kingdom of Provence, then became the capital of the kingdom of Burgundy-Provence (from 934 to 1032). This development was the source of new prosperity for the city. Such was the enduring importance of Arles that Frederick Barbarossa of the Holy Roman Empire (then in effect German) was crowned emperor at the nearly completed **Eglise St-Trophime** in 1178. It is this imposing Romanesque complex that stands across the Place de la République from the Roman museums.

Eglise St-Trophime and Museon Arlaten

St-Trophime is the most interesting of Arles's early-Christian buildings. It was a major stopping point along the medieval Christian pilgrimage route to Santiago de Compostela in

Spain. Built from the ruins of a fifth-century church, St-Trophime is an example of early Provençal Romanesque architecture, strongly influenced by Roman and Greek style. The church's cloisters (12th to 14th centuries), of a rare beauty, exhibit intricately sculptured cornices that recount the resurrection of Christ and the glorification of Arles's patron saints. Also beautiful is the main doorway to the church, which shows a profusion of apostles and saints on the tympanum and is commonly held to be a masterpiece of Provençal Romanesque art.

But this historic neighborhood does not stop here. The subsequent development of Provençal culture—and its revival at the end of the 19th century—is well represented at the **Museon Arlaten**, a few steps away from the square on the rue de la République. Founded by the leader of the Félibrige movement, Frédéric Mistral, with the money he received for winning the Nobel Prize for Literature, the museum traces the history of Arles from prehistoric times to the 20th century with an amazing collection of furniture, local dress, documents, and works of art. The exhibit is in keeping with Mistral's tireless efforts to ensure that Provençal folkways—particularly the Provençal language (preserved in the museum's name)—survived the positivist bulldozing of the late 19th and early 20th centuries.

MUSEE REATTU AND ALYSCAMPS

One of Arles's oldest museums, the Musée Réattu, is on the banks of the Rhône north of the center of town. Formerly a priory of the Knights of Malta, the 15th-century structure now houses works by Picasso and local artists, as well as the city's permanent photographic collection—which serves as a backdrop to the Rencontres Internationales de la Photographie held every June in Arles. This city being what it is, this very modern event takes place in the shadow of the museum's next-door neighbor: the ruins of baths built for Emperor Constantine.

Before leaving Arles, those with a taste for the evocative should visit the **Alyscamps**, the greatest necropolis in the West during the first millennium. Located to the southwest of town, beyond the ramparts, this deserted burial ground is now reduced to a single, shady lane lined with antique sarcophagi and dotted with ancient chapels. It is the best way to take your leave of such a historic city.

STAYING AND DINING IN ARLES

Just south of the Place de la République, the 20th century mercifully takes hold. Like every typical Provençal town,

Arles has its main café-lined avenue, the boulevard des Lices. Here is the reasonably priced ► Jules César, in a rebuilt 17th-century convent. The hotel's restaurant, Lou Marquès, which specializes in Arlesian cooking, provides a relaxed yet somehow fussy atmosphere.

Overlooking the Place du Forum are the balconies of a fine regional restaurant, Le Vaccarès (Tel: 90-96-06-17). In the adjacent rue Sauvage, the hotel ► D'Arlatan, a medieval town house of the local nobility, offers a quiet garden setting and rooms furnished in impeccable 18th-century style (no restaurant). For those who care to venture farther north toward the river—and toward gastronomic adventure— L'Olivier, at 1 bis, rue Réattu (Tel: 90-49-64-88), offers such treats as snails and smoked pork in puff pastry. New to the Arles restaurant world, this establishment has earned an enthusiastic welcome from picky Provençal food critics.

AIX-EN-PROVENCE

It doesn't take an art scholar to understand why Cézanne was captivated by Aix (pronounced "Ex"), a historic inland city just 30 km (19 miles) north of the port of Marseille. All it takes is witnessing an afternoon sun casting a reddish hue on the massive Montagne St-Victoire and reflecting off the city's rose-colored tile roofs and well-groomed orange Baroque buildings.

Aix is a Baroque gem, where sitting on a café terrace and doing absolutely nothing is a worthy calling. Throughout most of its history, Aix has cultivated a noble air and an elitist front. Its reputation for providing the good life, especially among upper-middle-class Parisians, has been responsible for making it one of France's fastest-growing cities. Aix has mushroomed from 30,000 people before World War II to nearly 125,000 today. The growth, however, has taken place outside of what is referred to as Old Aix, which has remained virtually unchanged over the past two hundred years.

In the second and third centuries B.C., Aix was the capital of an important Celtic-Ligurian community. Its ruins can still be visited, at Entremont, just outside the city. In 123 B.C. the Greeks in Marseille (Massilia) called on their Roman allies for military help against the Celtic Ligurians. The Roman armies led by the proconsul Caius Sextius Calvinus defeated the Celts and founded a military outpost on land that contained underground springs. The camp was named Aquae Sextiae, which was eventually shortened to just Aix. Today the Hôtel des Thermes—with its thermal-water cure—stands next to the site of the old Roman baths. The town boasts dozens of fountains, but only one—in the middle of cours Sextius—gives forth mineral water. (A few years ago a scandal struck when it was discovered that the pure water of Aix was not so pure after all.)

Under the Roman Empire, Aix became an important city and was lavishly endowed with temples and amphitheaters. However, successive calamities, including the Moorish invasions of the ninth century, caused the destruction of Aix's fabulous Roman buildings.

Another landmark—the court palace of Provence—fell victim to architectural snobbishness. When Provence lost its independence to the Crown of France in 1481, the old palace was used as the parliament building for the Provence region. By the early 18th century the practical need for more modern facilities and a mania for architectural symmetry led to the demolition of the palace.

Old Aix

The best example of this fashion for symmetry is the **cours Mirabeau**—a short, tree-lined boulevard created in the late 17th century as a promenade based on a triple architectural harmony: the uniform height of the buildings and the length (1,452 feet) and width (145 feet) of the street. It is one of the most attractive streets in France.

Along one side of the *cours* stand a half-dozen majestic *hôtels particuliers* (city mansions) constructed during the 17th and early 18th centuries. Today the buildings house several street-level *pâtisseries* where you can buy Aix's gourmet specialty, *calissons* (a soft almond-paste candy, still handmade in the city's several *calisson* factories).

On the other side of the *cours* are less impressive Baroque buildings, notable only for the numerous large sidewalk cafés that front them. In the summertime trees on both sides of the *cours* form a green roof that shields the cafés from the Provençal sun. During most of the year the café terraces are filled with sippers who spend hours watching the parade of passersby. Buskers, clowns, and other sidewalk performers add spice. The *cours* remains the center of life in Aix, as it was three hundred years ago.

At the bottom of the *cours,* in front of a statue of Good King René—the last great ruler of Provence—stands Aix's most famous café: **Les Deux Garçons.** During the First Empire the café was the meeting place of the "Golden Youth," and after that, under the Restoration, the "Romantic Youth."

Later it became the favorite café of Cézanne, Zola, and others. Now it is protected as a national landmark.

In recent years the *cours* has lost some of its spark. Just as one example, during Aix's music festival, which lasts nearly two months (late June to early August), heavily armed police patrol the street to stop any music played after 10:00 P.M.— which, not surprisingly, has soured the formerly festive atmosphere more than a bit. Still, a recent—and thoroughly unscientific—survey commissioned by a French magazine found that staid old Aix is the "sexiest city in France."

Despite this unexpected distinction, Aix's midsummer music festival is still the city's big draw. It is really two different festivals: **Aix en Musique**, daily free classical and folk concerts in various locations around the city; and the **Festival d'Aix**—the opera festival held in mid-July—which features highly acclaimed performances under the stars in a newly renovated theater at the 17th-century archbishop's palace (on rue Gaston de Saporta, next to the cathedral). Tickets must be reserved months in advance and cost an average of 400 francs for each performance. Aix's festival has become a major stepping-stone for up-and-coming opera stars. The theater runs three different operas per festival and specializes in Mozart. For information, Tel: 42-17-34-00.

Festival time or not, for a break from the more touristy and higher priced *cours,* take a two-minute walk to the majestic **Place de l'Hôtel de Ville** in the center of the old city, **Vieil Aix**, where many of the squares and narrow, crooked streets are closed to automobiles. An almost-enclosed court-yard, the *place* is dominated by the 17th-century city hall and the former Halles aux Grains, now a post office. Just behind it is the small daily produce market—one of the most outstanding in Provence. At the small market you can find a vast selection of Provençal specialties, including braids of garlic, fresh and dried herbs, fresh goat cheese, and melons.

Parallel to the *cours,* on the rue Espariat, is the 17th-century **Hôtel Boyer d'Eguilles**, a natural history museum. The paleontological collection includes dinosaur eggs and ancient seashells.

CATHEDRALE ST-SAUVEUR
Passing through the Place de l'Hôtel de Ville en route to the cathedral, you must go through an arch in the ancient bell tower. The large white stones on the tower's bottom date from Roman times; the rest was built in the 11th century and rebuilt in the 16th.

The tower marks what most historians now believe to be the boundary of ancient Roman Aix. It was perhaps the guard tower of the military outpost, Aquae Sextiae. Beyond the tower and away from the cours begins what was once the main Roman street, now called the rue Gaston-de-Saporta. This is the hub of a part of Aix's student life: The political science building and the foreign student institute sit side by side facing the architecturally interesting Cathédrale St-Sauveur.

The cathedral's mélange of styles clashes with the studied symmetry of the other structures of Aix. While many *hautain* Aixois took swipes at its lack of continuity ("Ugly and irregular," noted one university president in 1739), archaeologists find it a gold mine of information.

Its styles span 2,000 years of Western history, with traces of Roman, early Christian, Romanesque, Gothic, and Renaissance architecture. Recent digs proved that the cathedral was built on the site of a former Roman building, and Roman stones were used to build one wall of the 12th-century Romanesque section. Inside, there is a remarkable triptych of the Burning Bush by Nicolas Froment, King René's court painter. The painting remains shuttered most of the year and you must ask the keeper or guide to open it. The baptistery dates from the fourth and fifth centuries, and the bell tower from the early 15th century. Next to the cathedral, and accessible through the courtyard of the adjoining archbishop's palace, is a small medieval **cloister**, well worth visiting for its sculptured cornices.

In the Place de l'Archevêché is the **Snack Bar Charlie et Maggie**; open during the summer until midnight or later, this is a great place to eat a quick and not too expensive meal outside.

PAUL CEZANNE

Paul Cézanne may be Aix's best-known native, but it's only recently that he has become the city's favorite son. While he lived here the eccentric Cézanne was at odds with the staid Aixois. Children mocked him and his fellow citizens shunned him. Until 1985 no Cézanne painting hung in the city. Today the **Musée Granet**, to the south of the cours Mirabeau off the rue d'Italie, houses several major Cézannes.

Cézanne preferred working away from the city, mostly in the foothills of the imposing Montagne Ste-Victoire, which he painted more than 60 times. He also had a workshop—called **Atelier Paul-Cézanne**—just outside Vieil Aix, past the cathedral, at what is now 9, avenue Paul-Cézanne. American admirers have restored the workshop to the same state it was in at the time of Cézanne's death in 1906.

STAYING AND DINING IN AIX

Despite the fresh food available, Aix is not especially known for its restaurants. The city is filled with eating places, though, and while very few offer gastronomical treats, nearly all of them—except for some chain restaurants—are small, intimate, and charming, or else well situated with comfortable outside terraces. These places are scattered throughout the center of the old city, and you can't go wrong by just wandering around checking out menus and decor until the fancy hits. Try the relaxed and rustic **Comté d'Aix** on the rue de Couronne or the slightly pricier (and fishier) **Le Clam's** on the cours Sextius. The **Clos de la Violette**, at 10, avenue Violette, has one Michelin star and 190-franc and 430-franc prix-fixe menus.

Recently the Aixois committed an architectural faux pas when they tore down the exquisite four-star Hôtel Roi-René to make room for a modern replacement. The loss of the Roi-René has made the ▶ **Augustins** even more appealing. On the rue de la Masse, a side street off the cours Mirabeau, this former convent is intimate, and each room has a charming medieval air. Be sure to ask for one with a balcony (there are only two); they cost about 100 francs more but are worth it, looking out as they do over a small, quiet courtyard with a view of a 15th-century bell tower and a panorama of tiled rooftops.

Another good stopping place, in the center of Old Aix, is ▶ **Le Pigonnet**, a fairly reasonably priced restaurant-hotel that is surrounded by age-old chestnut trees. Just 3 km (2 miles) outside of town, in the northern suburban village of Celony, is the ▶ **Mas d'Entremont**, a fine old Provençal house dispensing honest cuisine and providing restful rooms.

AROUND AIX

The chalky white massif of Cézanne's beloved **Montagne Ste-Victoire**, which received its name in the 16th century as a reminder of the Roman victory over the Teutons in 102 B.C., dominates Aix and the surrounding countryside. At sunset it turns a brilliant red. The summit, with a 17th-century chapel and a panoramic view of the valley, can be reached in about three and a half hours on foot from the village of Cabassols.

Route D 17 runs east from Aix along the southern side of Ste-Victoire; along the route are several lovely villages, including **Le Tholonet** (with its 19th-century Château Noir), **St-Antonin-sur-Bayon**, and **Pourrières**.

Along the route on the northern side of the mountain, D 10, is the village of **Vauvenargues**, where Picasso lived until 1961. This is the Vauvenargues of the early-18th-century marquis de Vauvenargues, author of the famous (in France) *Maximes,* which had a strong influence on Stendhal. The castle of Vauvenargues, unfortunately, is not open to the public.

MARSEILLE

Marseille, a mere 30 km (19 miles) south of elegant, well-heeled Aix, strikes terror in the hearts of some travellers because of its reputation as a nest of gangsters. That's too bad, because this port town is so endowed with charm and beauty that limiting a visit here to changing trains at the Gare St-Charles would be a shame.

Marseille's tarnished reputation is, in fact, part of its attraction. Maverick, mysterious, violent, passionate, and Byzantine, Marseille is a teeming, sprawling, hilly port town of one million inhabitants, most of whom were—or are descended from—immigrants: Italians, Arabs, North African Jews, and Spaniards.

As a major trading and commercial center, Marseille was for centuries focused more toward the Far East and Africa than toward Europe, especially during the Renaissance. To-day sections of the city—Porte d'Aix, for example—are much like the souk in Algiers. A walk along the city's main street, La Canebière, shows that this is more a Mediterranean than a French city. On streets leading south of the Canebière, expect the shops to be selling fragrant jasmine and spicy *harissa* (a condiment made from hot chile peppers and vegetables) rather than wan roses and bland Camembert.

Throughout its long history Marseille has been independent and often rebellious. Neither royalist nor conservative, Marseille has been fiercely democratic ever since it was founded as a republic called Massilia in 600 B.C. by colonizing Greeks from the west coast of Asia Minor.

The story of France's national anthem, "La Marseillaise," is an example. During the Revolution fervent Marseillais revolutionaries marched to Paris, singing a military chant (written earlier in Strasbourg) along the route as a battle cry. The song thereafter became synonymous with the Revolution—much to the chagrin of its composer, who was a royalist.

CHATEAU D'IF AND BASILIQUE DE NOTRE-DAME-DE-LA-GARDE
If nothing else, a quick morning boat ride from the Vieux Port of Marseille to the Château d'If to see the castle made famous by Alexandre Dumas's *Count of Monte Cristo* is well

worth the approximately two-hour round trip. The ride across the harbor lets you view Marseille the right way, from the water, so you can feel a closer identification with the Marseillais, whose town has been linked to the sea for 26 centuries. The château was built as a fort by François I from 1524 to 1528, after Marseille had been held under siege by the armies of Spanish ruler Charles V. It was converted into a prison in 1634 and shut down in 1872 when the Third Republic was established.

The city's most famous monument is no doubt the **Basilique de Notre-Dame-de-la-Garde**, high on a hill above the city. It can be reached from the Old Port—if you've got the legs of a mountain goat—by the rue Fort-Notre-Dame, then the boulevard André Aune and a steep staircase. Done in the Byzantine pastiche that afflicts Paris's Sacré-Coeur basilica, Marseille's cathedral nonetheless commands a breathtaking view of the entire city.

THE VIEUX PORT AND MUSEUMS

The Vieux Port (Old Port) is a protected basin that cuts right into the center of Marseille. The new port, La Joliette, lies at the Marseille end of a 45-mile-long seaside industrial complex that constitutes France's largest, most important port and stretches west to the Port-St-Louis-du-Rhône. Now used by pleasure boaters, tour guides, and fishermen, the Vieux Port is lined with restaurants—most of which are unscrupulous tourist traps that serve bogus bouillabaisse at seemingly reasonable prices. The few honest establishments have banded together and created a bouillabaisse certificate that guarantees authentic traditional quality.

Just behind the Vieux Port is La Bourse de Commerce, a modern shopping complex that nevertheless is near the **Jardin des Vestiges**, an archaeological site with Greek, Roman, and early Christian ruins. (The walls of Marseille's original port have been uncovered here.) Near the gardens is the **Musée d'Histoire de Marseille**, with a collection that includes a well-preserved third-century Roman ship.

Marseille has several other prominent museums and monuments, including the **Musée des Beaux-Arts**, which contains one of France's richest collections of paintings, and the **Centre de la Vieille Charité**, a 17th- to 18th-century hospital that has been converted into a vast cultural center housing a new archaeological museum. **Parc Borély** and its 18th-century château, which houses the **Musée d'Archéologie Méditerranéenne**, France's second-largest collection of Egyptian antiquities (after the Louvre), is south of town on the corniche.

horses, to pretty Collioure, the painter's jewel, and on to Spain in the west. One lovely stretch reaches far inland to encompass the breathtaking gorges of the Tarn river and the grandeur of the Cévennes mountains; the region also encompasses the Parc Régional du Haut-Languedoc and the snowy peaks of the eastern Pyrénées.

In this diverse region you'll find a complexity of different cultures and languages—Languedoc itself is the heritage of the vast lands and the language of the old counts of Toulouse. The language, *langue d'oc,* derives from spoken Latin and was once the tongue of all southern France; it is sometimes called Occitan or, farther east, Provençal. (Oc means *oui* in langue d'oc.)

People in these lands are of strongly independent spirit. Even in the 12th century, when much of Europe was still sunk in the Dark Ages, Raymond V, Comte de Toulouse, cheerfully relinquished his authority to an elected group of councillors. In the southwesternmost part of this region— the old lands of the Roussillon region—you're more likely to see the red-and-yellow-striped Catalan flag than the French *tricolore* flying proudly atop old stone towers. The local language here is Catalan, not *oc*—though if anywhere you come across cheering groups of banner-waving *citoyens,* it's probably a football match or cycling event rather than politics that's firing their fervor.

The region resounds with echoes from across the centuries—the footsteps of marching Romans; the religious wars between the separatist Cathars and the Church of Rome in a crushing alliance with the French king; the struggle for power between France and England. Yet, in history-haunted abbeys like St-Michel-de-Cuxa, close to Prades in the foothills of the Pyrénées, or serene St-Guilhem-le-Désert, in the hills above the graceful town of Pézenas, inspiration to Molière, you'll hear music soaring in the gentle breeze at its many summer festivals. There's a long heritage of Languedoc music: Once, hillsides rang with the melodious songs of knightly troubadours.

In Languedoc-Roussillon you can enjoy walking (or skiing, riding, or climbing) in the massive Pyrénées and, a short drive away, relaxing in sunshine and charm on the clean beaches of Mediterranean resorts. You can indulge a taste for architecture in structures built by Romans, by Louis XIV's great engineer, Vauban, and by the masters of 20th-century architectural design.

You will also observe that even in the most rustic of villages, the residents of the area have accepted that true culture extends to modern plumbing and soft toilet paper,

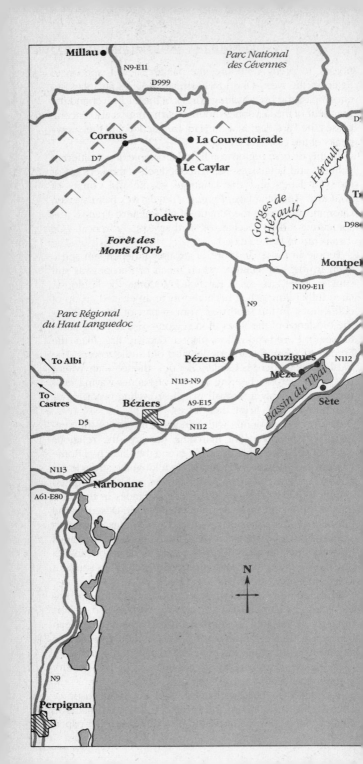

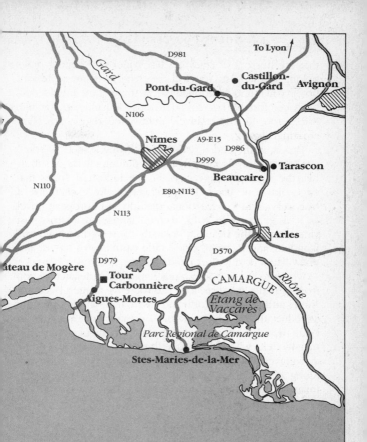

Languedoc-Roussillon
(detail)

| 0 | miles | 20 |

| 0 | kilometers | 30 |

that the horrors of crackling leaf paper and rusting pipes belong in the past. You will never be far from a pleasant hotel (you'll find mentioned below some of the most seductively comfortable) or from delicious food and superb wine. Prices, too, in this relatively untravelled region are often amazingly low.

This is, in the end, a real world, a living France, so you'll see in your travels the predictably dulling effects of suburbia, the signs for supermarkets, the industrial zones that edge old stone cities. But you'll enjoy the excitement of discovery and the exceptional pleasures of European travel as it used to be in wild, scented landscapes, across vast vineyards, in the beauty of lovingly conserved architectural wonders, and in grand cities, little earth-brown towns, and tiny villages dozing under red roof tiles and roses.

Where to begin? You can reach into this variegated region from virtually any direction. The route we suggest begins at Nîmes and leads you north and east to the Pont du Gard, the aqueduct that is one of Rome's greatest achievements in Gaul; then down the curve of the coast to the Camargue, the marshy delta where the Rhône flows into the sea; and to the thriving city of Montpellier and on toward the Pyrénées. Along your journey, easy diversions are proposed to the inland plains and mountain regions.

MAJOR INTEREST

Nîmes
Maison Carrée and other Roman remains

Pont du Gard

Aigues-Mortes

Montpellier
Place de la Comédie and old quarter

The coast west of Montpellier
Sète's Vieux Port and seashore drive
Bassin de Thau
Bouzigues and its oysters

The Languedoc plain
Pézenas
Gorges de l'Hérault and St-Guilhem-le-Désert
Cirque de Navacelles and Cirque de Mourèze
La Couvertoirade, fortress town of the Knights
    Templars
Roquefort: the town, the cheese

The Tarn gorges and Parc National des Cévennes
River and gorge scenery
Corniche des Cévennes
Outdoor activities

Béziers
Cathédrale St-Nazaire
Museums and Roman remains

Haut-Languedoc
Parc Régional du Haut-Languedoc
Castres and its Musée Goya

Narbonne
Cathédrale St-Just and old quarter
Abbaye de Fontfroide
Corbières wines

Perpignan
Cathédrale de St-Jean
Palace of the Kings of Majorca
Castillet fortress and Catalan museum

Eastern Pyrénées
Mountain scenery
Winter and outdoor sports
Prades and the Pablo Casals music festival
Romanesque abbeys of St-Michel-de-Cuxa and
St-Martin-du-Canigou

Collioure and the Côte Vermeille

THE EASTERN LANGUEDOC
Nîmes

The renowned Roman temple, the Maison Carrée (Square House), and other marvels at the heart of this city founded by Caesar Augustus on the eastern edge of Provence, just 30 km (19 miles) northwest of Arles, are like prizes in plain wrapping. To reach the historical center you must first penetrate the modern city's uninspiring outskirts. Nîmes's wealth today springs from textile manufacturing; blue denim, from *bleu de Nîmes,* was invented here in the 19th century to be used for hard-wearing clothes for workers. All the same, there was surely more than a little spite in the remark of the 18th-century British writer Augustus Hare, who said: "There is no beauty in Nîmes, and, after seeing its Roman antiquities, no one will wish to linger there."

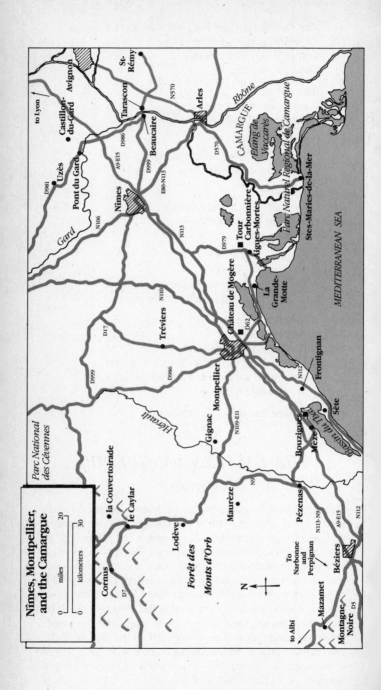

Nîmes, Montpellier,
and the Camargue

Parc National
des Cévennes

miles 0 20
kilometers 0 30

N

to Albi
to Lyon

Montagne Noire
Mazamet
D5
Béziers
N112
A9-E15
N113-N9
Pézenas
To Narbonne
and Perpignan

Cornus
D7
le Caylar
la Couvertoirade
Lodève
Forêt des
Monts d'Orb

Maurèze
N9
Bouzigues
Mèze
Bassin de Thau
Sète
Frontignan
N112
Gignac
Montpellier
N109-E11
D986
Tréviers
D17
Hérault
D999

N110
Château de Mogère
D62
La Grande-Motte
N113
Tour Carbonnière
Aigues-Mortes
D979

Nîmes
N106
N113
Pont du Gard
Uzès
D981
Gard

A9-E15
D999
E80-N113
Beaucaire
D986
Castillon-du-Gard
Avignon
Tarascon
St-Rémy
N570

Arles
D570
Rhône
CAMARGUE
Étang de
Vaccarès
Parc Naturel Régional de Camargue
Stes-Maries-de-la-Mer

MEDITERRANEAN SEA

THE MAISON CARREE

Of several striking Roman antiquities—they include a colosseum that is as well preserved as those in Arles and Orange, and the still-sturdy Tour Magne, France's oldest national monument—the Maison Carrée is the finest. Simply and succinctly described by traveller Tobias Smollett as "ravishingly beautiful," it so stirred Thomas Jefferson, who visited Nîmes when he was the U.S. ambassador to France, that he used it as a model when designing the capitol building in Virginia. Louis XIV's architects wanted to whisk it away to the gardens of Versailles, though ultimately refrained.

The building, perfectly intact, is exactly twice as long as it is wide. Over the years the Maison Carrée has served as a private home, a stable, and a monastery, but for the past 150 years it has been a museum of antiquities, which seems only right.

When the Maison Carrée was built, in A.D. 5, it faced the forum. Today the rue Auguste, one of the city's main shopping streets, runs through the site of the forum. The Office de Tourisme, across from the Maison Carrée at number 6, can provide maps pinpointing city sights (there are many fine 17th- and 18th-century houses).

THE JARDIN DE LA FONTAINE, TOUR MAGNE, AND ARENA

If you head north along rue Auguste for a little more than a block you will come to the watery precincts of the **Jardin de la Fontaine**. The fountain is dedicated to the Roman god Nemausus; before the Pont du Gard (see below) began to bring fresh water into Nîmes, in 19 B.C., this spring supplied the entire settlement. Today the ancient fountain is all but lost in the ornate frippery of gurgling fountains and formal gardens laid out in the 17th century by André Le Nôtre, who also designed the gardens at Versailles.

Next to the central fountain is the crumbling **Temple de Diane**, probably once part of a long-vanished bath complex. A wide staircase leads up a wooded slope (Mont Cavalier) to the **Tour Magne**, one of the best preserved Roman towers in the world and, with the nearby **Porte Auguste**, all that remains of the Romans' four-mile-long system of defensive walls. You can climb 90 feet to a platform at the top of the tower and look out over Nîmes and the rocky countryside that surrounds it.

Nîmes's other great Roman monument, the **arena** (or amphitheater), is a few blocks south of the Maison Carrée on the boulevard Victor Hugo. The arena was built in the first century B.C. to seat 24,000 people, and it is still in such a fine state of repair that the Nîmois consider it a functional rather than ornamental part of their city. In summer the arena is packed with spectators who watch bullfights from the same seats where Roman colonials once cheered the gory contests of gladiators. The arena remains intact because it has always been functional. The Visigoths built a military garrison inside the arena in the 11th century, and it later sheltered as many as 250 houses and thousands of inhabitants.

THE OLD QUARTER

The old quarter of Nîmes stretches just to the north of the arena, and you may well want to spend some time wandering its twisting streets and little squares toward the **Cathédrale de St-Castor**, on Place aux Herbes. The church itself is cold and formidable—most of it is a 19th-century restoration made necessary by the destruction wrought in religious wars. Nîmes was the most important Huguenot city in France, and twice, in 1567 and 1621, the cathedral was the scene of battles between Protestants and Catholics. A Romanesque frieze on the façade, horrifying in parts, seems like a silent shriek from those bloody times.

The museums of Nîmes really don't house much that will keep you from continuing on your way. There are, however, some handsome mosaics and Roman household items in the **Musée d'Archéologie**, next to the cathedral, and some good Roman mosaics in the **Musée des Beaux-Arts**, south of the arena off rue Cité-Foulc.

For a stay in Nîmes you can do no better than the grand ▶ **Imperator Concorde**, wonderfully situated across from the Jardin de la Fontaine, with a garden of its own and very pleasant rooms.

Pont du Gard

The Pont du Gard, the aqueduct constructed by Agrippa around 19 B.C. to supply Roman Nîmes with fresh water, is about 40 km (25 miles) north and east of Nîmes via D 979 and D 981. This route passes through Uzès, a city that owes its beauty not to Imperial Rome but to the Renaissance. Fine 17th-century mansions line the **Place aux Herbes**, named for the commodity that was once this pretty town's mainstay. The fact that the **Duché**, a 16th-century château built around an 11th-century tower, is still occupied does nothing to detract from the sense that Uzès has changed very little since the playwright Jean Racine spent his summers as a young man here visiting his uncle. Parts of the Duché are open to visitors: the *donjon,* from which you get a fine view, some of the furnished rooms, the cellars, and the *oubliettes*—which, fortunately, no longer contain "the forgotten ones." By contrast, if you have time to spare, you'll find just to the west of Uzès on D 982 **Le Musée 1900**, a diverting collection of venerable motor cars, bicycles, cameras, and altogether some 4,000 relics from the turn of this century. Next door is what's claimed to be the world's largest collection of miniature trains.

The Pont du Gard is 16 km (10 miles) southeast of Uzès on D 981. The most refreshing vantage point of what is arguably the best-preserved Roman aqueduct in the world is from the Gard river itself (the waters just below the aqueduct are a popular swimming hole). A path climbs from the east bank of the river to the top of the uppermost of three rows of arches. The lower level of the aqueduct has six arches, the middle 11, and the third level has 35 small arches. What seems like mere decoration is actually an elaborate support system. Many of the stones used to build the aqueduct (quarried nearby) weigh as much as six tons, and the engineers used no mortar. If you make the climb to the top, you cross the 900-foot-long aqueduct a dizzying 160 feet above the river on the narrow, precariously balanced stones of the trough that once carried the water toward Nîmes, 30 miles away.

The countryside here, away from the busy main roads, is peaceful, but the considerable fame of the Pont du Gard attracts busloads of sightseers in the summer. Curiously, by a quirk of nature and skillful marketing, other waters in the area have attained eminence: 13 km (8 miles) southwest of Nîmes, at Vergèze, just off N 113, is where the mineral water Perrier is bottled.

STAYING AND DINING
NEAR THE PONT DU GARD

Just 3 km (2 miles) north of the Pont du Gard via D 19 and D 228, discreetly located in the village of Castillon-du-Gard, is the hotel ► **Le Vieux Castillon**, which has contrived a blend of elegance and comfort in several restored buildings. An olive-tree garden and ochre terraces end where a still-ruined wall artfully sets off the swimming pool. The cuisine, light and subtle, is exemplified by *poitrine de pigeonneau glacé au jus blond* (pigeon breast), one of five *mini-plats* you might find offered in a tasting menu. Among local wines is Château de Belle Coste or the excellent Côtes du Rhône.

The Camargue

Before the Rhône empties into the sea just south of Arles, it broadens and splits into a web of channels that flow across a vast, marshy triangle that covers some 185,000 acres. As you follow D 36 south from Arles along the Grand Rhône, the largest of the river channels, you begin to cut through vineyards, orchards, and eventually rice paddies that have been planted over the northern edge of the marshes. Then you enter a flat, empty land of saltwater lagoons and tall grasses, a land that breeds mosquitoes, black fighting bulls, small, wild white horses, and flamingoes and some 300 other kinds of birds. Not too surprisingly, the promise of seeing these creatures in a wild landscape also attracts visitors in numbers that often exceed any visible wildlife; your excursion into the Camargue could yield nothing more than a frustrating bout with traffic. The Camargue is best seen in the early spring and late fall, when the bird activity peaks and the human influx is at a lull.

A good way to see the Camargue is to follow the narrow D 36B south (pick it up about 5 km/3 miles south of the intersection of D 36 and D 570), which skirts the eastern banks of the Camargue's largest saltwater lagoon, the Etang de Vaccarès. The *étang* and its marshy shores constitute the 40,000-acre **Réserve Naturelle Zoologique et Botanique,** accessible only to professional naturalists who present their credentials at the reserve headquarters on rue Honoré-Nicolas in Arles. Much of the rest of the Camargue is under the auspices of the **Parc Naturel Régional de Camargue.**

If your timing is right (dawn and dusk are best), you'll see a good many birds from D 36B as it threads a course through the salt marshes, especially on the 15-km (9-mile) stretch between the hamlets of Grand Romieu and Le Paradis. Bulls and horses grazing peacefully in the grasslands are easy to spot in the Camargue.

The Camargue's other great attractions are the towns and beaches of Stes-Maries-de-la-Mer and Aigues-Mortes. To visit these you must retrace your route up D 36B as far as Grand Romieu and from there follow D 37 west across the northern shores of the Etang de Vaccarès for about 15 km (9 miles) to D 570, which heads south through the marshes for 23 km (14 miles) to Stes-Maries, or Les Saintes, as it is known locally.

STES-MARIES-DE-LA-MER

Legend has it that a boat without sails or oars made landfall at this spot after drifting across the Mediterranean from the

Holy Land. On board were Mary Magdalen, Mary Jacob (sister of the mother of Christ), Mary Salomé (mother of the Apostles James and John), Lazarus, Martha, Maximinius, Sidonius, and a black Egyptian servant, Sara. Most of the group allegedly set across the marshes to bring Christianity to Provence. The bones of those who remained behind, Mary Jacob, Mary Salomé, and Sara, lie in the town's fortified 12th-century **church**, surrounded by the houses of a medieval fishing village. The church is still the destination for a pilgrimage that brings thousands of Gypsies to town each May to pay homage to the saints, especially Sara.

Outside its quaint center, Les Saintes is a resort with a marina for pleasure craft and a long beach that is very popular in the summer. Aigues-Mortes is 30 km (19 miles) north and west of Stes-Maries on D 570 and D 58.

AIGUES-MORTES

In *Impressions of a Voyage,* Alexandre Dumas *fils* remarked, "We noticed Aigues-Mortes, or rather we noticed its walls, because not one house or building is higher than its ramparts. The Gothic city appears like a jewel carefully wrapped in a case of stone."

Dumas's description still holds nearly a century later. Aigues-Mortes, with a population of not more than 4,500, is one of the few cities in France—Carcassonne is another—whose walls are entirely intact.

Aigues-Mortes was created by King Louis IX (Saint Louis) out of a sandy desert bordered by estuaries and swamps—hence the name, which means "dead waters." Aigues-Mortes's history and fame thus belong to medieval royal France. In fact, for nearly a hundred years Aigues-Mortes enjoyed its status as the kingdom's only Mediterranean port. Louis encouraged neighboring inhabitants to move to his newly created but highly inhospitable town by offering them generous tax breaks. Thousands moved in, and the port was used by traders from throughout the northern Mediterranean coast: Catalonia, Genoa, and Provence. At its height, its population was 15,000.

After Louis chose Aigues-Mortes as his Mediterranean port, he used it twice to embark on crusades to the "Orient," once in 1248 to Egypt and later, in 1270, to Tunis. The king died on that trip, and historians believe the cause of death was malaria contracted in the swampy and mosquito-infested area surrounding Aigues-Mortes.

Most of the ramparts and walls were built by Louis's sons and successors, Philippe III and Philippe IV. Although Aigues-Mortes was heavily fortified, its greatest defensive

asset was the swamps, which rendered the city unapproach-
able by all but one road. To guard that road the king built the
Tour Carbonnière. The fortress tower still stands, virtually
untouched, just out of town on D 46 off D 58 (D 979 from
Aigues-Mortes leads into D 58).

A visit to the **ramparts** begins at the **castle** and the massive
Tour de Constance. The tower—originally isolated by a
ditch—was the centerpiece of Aigues-Mortes's defenses and
contained the city's arsenal.

STAYING AND DINING
IN THE CAMARGUE

Next to the Tour de Constance, in the Place Anatole France,
is the ▶ **Hostellerie des Remparts**, a cozy hotel in a converted two-story 18th-century guardhouse with a view of the
tower.

The main square of this small town is named after its
founder, Saint Louis, and here you'll find restaurants and
café terraces. Unusual for such a small place, Aigues-Mortes
has two fine restaurants, one of which—**Minos**—is also on
the Place St-Louis. The Minos, with its vine-covered terrace
overlooking a statue of the king, offers friendly service and
specializes in fish and *boeuf gardiane,* a local Camargue
dish of bull meat in a black-olive sauce (Tel: 66-53-83-24).
Just off the square on rue de l'Amiral-Courbet is a quiet
hotel, the ▶ **Hôtel Saint-Louis**. Its enclosed private terrace
can be a welcome retreat during the crowded summer
season.

Aigues-Mortes's second major restaurant is **La Camargue**,
at 19, rue de la République. Many people visit the town just
to eat in this centuries-old, converted rustic Camarguais
house and listen to Gypsy and flamenco music. Reservations
are necessary for dining on the terrace in July and August
(Tel: 66-53-86-88). Plaques mark the booths where dignitaries, former president Georges Pompidou among them, have
eaten. The specialties are regional—*tellines* (tiny clams),
shellfish, and *boeuf gardiane*. Pricey, but worth it.

From Aigues-Mortes it's only 8 km (5 miles) to **Le Grau-
du-Roi**, a pleasant drive along an elevated road past salt pans
and with shallow *étangs* on either side where you may easily
see white horses and flocks of flamingoes as well as a touch
of commerce and fleets commercial and pleasurebound. In
this cheerful port town you arrive at one mouth of the Canal
du Rhône as well as at many restaurants. You'll find good
seafood in a tasteful setting at **Le Saint Pierre** at l, quai
Gozioso, beside the Port de Pêche (Tel: 66-53-20-90).

It's only about 30 km (19 miles) from Aigues-Mortes west to Montpellier on D 62. The road skirts La Grande-Motte, a huge vacation complex built in the 1960s as a refuge for the middle classes. Its pyramidal apartment blocks were once seen as futuristic, but as the future has become the past, their allure could be greater for students of architecture or social studies than for travellers seeking a seaside retreat. The beaches, however, remain very fine.

Montpellier

Like Béziers and Narbonne to the southwest (see below), Montpellier was an outpost on the Via Domitia, Rome's major route into Gaul. While nothing of ancient Rome remains in Montpellier, much in evidence are the 16th- through 19th-century mansions, boulevards, and squares that make Montpellier one of the most appealing and livable cities in France.

AROUND THE PLACE DE LA COMEDIE

At the heart of this lively, sun-drenched city is the Place de la Comédie (named for the ornate theater that faces it), a vast sea of white paving stones that is devoid of motorized traffic and filled with café tables, most of them occupied by university students. Montpellier's university is the third oldest in France, after the Sorbonne and the university at Toulouse. Both Rabelais and Nostradamus studied in Montpellier, at a medical faculty founded by the city's tenth-century herb traders, who brought scholars from all over the world to Montpellier to investigate the healing properties of their goods. Many of the university buildings—including the medical research institutes that are still among the most famous in Europe—are in the residential quarters just north of the old center.

Almost any excursion you make in Montpellier will begin on the *place,* known to the locals as *L'Oeuf* (The Egg) because of its vaguely ovoid shape. L'Oeuf is the center of all commerce, entertainment, and, from the looks of it, city life. To one side the paving stones descend stairs past fountains to a modern shopping and office complex, **Le Polygone**. Uninspired as the banal architecture is, the Polygone is always crowded with shoppers and is a fairly good example of how well-planned modern precincts can keep an old city alive. The best and most popular store down here is the chic book and music outlet **FNAC**, with a decent selection of English titles; you might want to stock up here before you venture into the hinterlands of Languedoc-Roussillon.

Just behind Polygone a huge new housing complex, **Antigone**, has taken shape. This stunningly designed Neoclassical collection of buildings is one of several new developments that have gone up near the city center in recent years to house an ever-increasing populace that finds Montpellier and its nearby mountains and beaches so appealing.

The huge **old quarter** of Montpellier stretches over hilly terrain to the west of the Place de la Comédie. To try to follow a logical route through this maze of little streets— locals call the area *lou clapas,* "heap of stones"—is futile. You will probably want to enter it armed with a map from the Syndicat d'Initiative, located on the *place.* Some of Montpellier's best shops, as well as its lively outdoor market, are on and around the busy rue de la Loge, which is also lined with some of the city's best 17th-century mansions.

L'ESPLANADE AND CITADELLE

On its northern end the *place* opens onto **L'Esplanade**, a broad, pedestrians-only avenue shaded by plane trees that stretches a full three-quarters of a mile. The **Musée Fabre**, one of France's best collections of art outside Paris, is about halfway down the esplanade in a 17th-century mansion on the boulevard Bonnes-Nouvelles (signs point the way). The painter François-Xavier Fabre and several other prominent citizens have bequeathed works to the museum over the past two centuries, and the collections now include canvases by Delacroix, Millet, Courbet, and Matisse; some exquisite Italian paintings, including works by Guido Reni and Veronese; and an admirable sampling of works by British and Flemish painters, including a couple by Rubens and Brueghel.

The fortresslike **citadelle**, which occupies much of the east side of the esplanade, was built by Louis XIII in 1624 to keep the city's rebellious Protestants in check. The religious wars here were fierce enough that Montpellier emerged from them scarred; a burst of 17th-century rebuilding shaped the gracious city that you see today.

PROMENADE DU PEYROU AND JARDIN DES PLANTES

One of the great achievements of Montpellier's 17th-century architects is the **Promenade du Peyrou**, a formal garden begun in 1689. From the vicinity of the Musée Fabre you can reach this precinct by heading west on the rue Foch. The promenade begins at an equestrian statue of Louis XIV and follows high ground that affords magnificent views far across the Languedoc vineyards to the Cévennes. The templelike building at the far end of the promenade is Montpellier's *château d'eau* (waterworks), fed by an 18th-century aqueduct modeled on the Pont du Gard.

A few steps north up the boulevard Henri-IV brings you to yet another of Montpellier's fine public spaces, the **Jardin des Plantes**. Created in 1593, it's the oldest botanical garden in France. The poet Paul Valéry and novelist André Gide, both students at the university, used to walk here, and you should, too, as a respite from the Midi sun.

STAYING AND DINING IN MONTPELLIER

If you decide to spend the night in Montpellier—perhaps to pass the evening with what seems to be the entire population of Montpellier sitting at café tables or strolling through the city's public spaces—you will want to find a hotel near the Place de la Comédie. The atmospheric old ▶ **Grand Hôtel du Midi** is at the southernmost corner of the *place,* and is near the train station as well. The elegant ▶ **Hôtel de Noailles** occupies a 17th-century mansion just off the esplanade and is just steps from the Musée Fabre, while the pretty little ▶ **Hôtel Le Guilhem** is in the heart of the old quarter, on rue Jean-Jacques Rousseau.

To eat like a sophisticate but at prices that won't remind you of the Rothschilds, try the riverside **La Réserve Rimbaud** (820, avenue St-Maur; Tel: 67-72-52-53). And for wandering souls who thirst for the grape, **L'Hôtel Montpellieraine des Vins de Languedoc**, a restaurant and tasting bar with more than 80 wines for sale on the rue Jacques-Coeur, just a couple of blocks from the Place de la Comédie, will satisfy even the most extreme craving to explore the enormous range of regional wines. The Minervois and Corbières wines are well known, but the St-Pons is superior. Tel: 67-22-80-80.

Vineyards come right up to the roads just out of town. The **Château de la Mogère** and its vineyards, right on Montpellier's autoroute and only 3 km (2 miles) from downtown at the north exit, offers an excellent opportunity to see an elegant château inside and out, roam typical Languedoc vineyards, take a tour of the *caves,* and taste the estate's wine. Tel: 67-65-72-01.

—*Stephen Brewer*

The Coast West of Montpellier

On a coast shimmering with numerous shallow *étangs,* those flat bays that wind or winter rain can stir to the color of earth or pewter, the sea is many things: bright blue boundary to a shining beach; playground for wind-surfers; breeding ground for succulent shellfish; the end of the road for canals sliced through salty marshes. You can see it in all its moods and roles a short distance from Montpellier.

South of the city, when fringe traffic releases you, D 986 sweeps you a mere 9 km (5½ miles) to the broad, curving beach of the little resort of Palavas-les-Flots, so handy that it's often crowded. Frontignan Plage is another popular beach some 26 km (16 miles) west along D 113 from Montpellier in the Sète direction, then D 112 south to Frontignan (where they grow grapes for a Muscat wine) and a short turnoff to the Plage.

SETE

Changing and growing as you watch, a thickening crust on the slopes of the round bulge of Mont St-Clair, Sète is a commercially important fishing port on the coast. Industry crams its outer zones and traffic crowds approaches, but the city's center, where bridges arching over canals may momentarily remind you of Venice, is attractive. For a visitor, much of Sète's interest is along the quais of the colorful Vieux-Port. The town's most famous recreation is water jousting, staged throughout the summer, in which participants in separate boats try to knock each other into the water with lances.

Rather than standing in crowds watching this spectacle, you'll probably have a more enjoyable time eating at any of the scores of restaurants along the quais. A specialty at all of them is *cigalles de la mer* (literally, "cigars of the sea," spiny crustaceans) and *setois,* a sweet-tasting sole that's only a few inches long and is served sautéed or fried, five or six at a time. Another fish to try is the *dorade,* a foot or so long and resembling, in appearance only, a mackerel. Its sweet flesh is so prized (and expensive) that restaurants often try to pass off a lesser fish in its place. To be sure you're getting the real thing, ask the waiter to serve it with the head on, which should have a mark like a little golden half-moon.

CAP D'AGDE

From Sète, following signs to Agde or Béziers, you will soon reach the gritty, pale-sand beach that stretches unhindered for nearly 20 km (12 miles) beside the long, straight N 112 linking Sète with Agde and the heavily developed resorts of Cap d'Agde. At quiet times, it's a soothing drive along the thin, outer rim of the Bassin de Thau, with the Mediterranean a few paces to your left all the way.

Until about 25 years ago, much of this coastline was malarial and uninhabitable. Now rid of virulent mosquitoes, the beach, the sea, and the Cap d'Agde resorts draw at least a million visitors a year. Many of them are campers lured to the thousands of campsites in Agde, and just as many are nudists. Agde is probably the largest nudist colony in the world, and the sun worshippers don't leave *naturalisme* on the beach: An entire section of Agde, with shops, cafés, apartments, and campsites, is designated the *Quartier Naturiste*.

MEZE AND BOUZIGUES

The built-up mini-city that Cap d'Agde has become can be avoided by turning inland from N 112 toward Marseille and D 51 some 4 km (2½ miles) before you reach the Agde crossroads. D 51 will lead you eastward and, in some 9 km (5½ miles), connect you with N 113 and, to the south, the little oyster town of Mèze facing onto the Bassin de Thau.

Mèze is one of the main cultivators and producers of the Bassin's famous oysters, but the true capital is the much more appealing **Bouzigues**, just 6 km (4 miles) farther east on N 113. A turn off the main road brings you in moments to this graceful little town, where seashore buildings cluster in harmony with a church, the little shops and stands selling the desirable oyster in several varieties (the only pricey one with the flavor, you might be told, of *noisettes,* hazelnuts).

In Bouzigues the oyster rules. Beyond a little yacht basin you'll come to the cream-colored, one-story **Musée de l'Etang de Thau**, well worth visiting. Here you can obtain a leaflet that tells you "*tout tout tout sur les huîtres*" (*all* there is to know about oysters). You may be surprised—did you know, for instance, that France produces annually 140,000 tons of oysters, which you may devour all year round? Or that you would have to eat a hundred oysters before you had consumed the calories in a 100-gram (3½-ounce) steak?

STAYING AND DINING IN BOUZIGUES

There are many restaurants in little Bouzigues. On the waterfront **Le Saint Pierre**, with its stone walls and red-tiled floors, is pleasant. The seaside terrace setting and the superb food of the restaurant at the ▶ **Motel Côte Bleue** draws gourmets from afar, but you can eat more cheaply and as well at **Le Bistrot du Port** beside the little yacht basin. (Both establishments are owned by the oyster-producing Archimbeau family.) Oysters apart, you might enjoy their *moules gratinées* with an *escargot* sauce. Even the modest mackerel, filleted and served in a vinaigrette sauce, has a taste of luxury. An unpretentious light wine to accompany a meal at any restaurant here is the *vin du pays d'Oc*. In summer, the comfortable rooms (the upper, second story with broad terraces) of the Motel Côte Bleue—it also has a swimming pool—are often booked well in advance by fanciers of the basin's renowned oysters and mussels.

INLAND LANGUEDOC AND THE CEVENNES
Vallée de l'Hérault

The best place to begin an exploration of the Languedoc interior is in the fertile valley of the Hérault river, in Pézenas. You'll find this illustrious little town 36 km (22 miles) northeast of Sète, or 23 km (14 miles) northwest of Béziers, on the N 113. From Montpellier, where you can initially follow the A 9 autoroute, it's a distance of 50 km (31 miles).

PEZENAS
In the 13th century Pézenas was a jewel in the crown of the sainted King Louis IX. As the centuries rolled by, it held its appeal and authority—for many of those centuries through the remarkable assembly of the *Etats du Languedoc*. Richelieu played a role in the power struggles in which Pézenas fought the authority of Paris and lost. But Pézenas still possesses the magnificent mansions of the 17th-century nobility. Through ingenuity and pride, the lovely little stone city has resisted the pressures of change so well that to this day Pézenas retains an extraordinary architectural *richesse*.

You might begin a visit to Pézenas in one of the fine mansions, the house of the barber Gély, in the Place Gambetta. Gély was a friend of the playwright Molière, whose patron for a time was Armand de Bourbon, governor of Languedoc. Molière, with his troupe of actors and entertainers, was in Pézenas frequently between 1650 and 1657, hobnobbing with the gentry and collecting anecdotes for his plays. Unfortunately, Bourbon's mood grew bleak and Molière decamped to Paris. Yet there's no escaping him—his name is above the town cinema and any number of other town businesses.

L'Echoppe du Barbier Gély now houses the Office de Tourisme. You can pick up a map here that will lead you through the quiet streets to dozens of beautiful houses, courtyards, and churches, each clearly identified.

Following D 32, which initially runs parallel to the main road out of Pézenas, will bring you through the river valley

The Cévennes Area

0 ——————— miles ——————— 15

0 ——————— kilometers ——————— 25

To Aumont Aubrac

N88

N88

N106

D986

Sévérac-le-Château

Causse de Sauveterre

D907 *bis*

D907

Point Sublime

Tarn

N9-E11

D907

Gorges du Tarn

Causse Méjean

Florac

D996

Millau

Chaos de Montpellier-le-Vieux

St-Laurent-de-Trèves

D996

CORNICHE DES CÉVENNES (D9)

D991

Parc National des Cévennes

D18

D999

Nant

l'Abîme de Bramabiau

▲ *Mont Aigoual*

D7

D986

D48

Cascades d'Orgon

Valleraugue

D999

Cornus

D185

Arre

Le Vigan

D7

la Couvertoirade

Espéries

Cirque de Navacelles

Ganges

N9-E11

D130

D48

D999

D25

Lodève

Prieuré de St-Michel-de-Grandmont

D153

St-Guilhem-le-Désert

Lac du Salagou

Hérault

D986

St-Guiraud

Montpeyroux

Jonquières

D141

St-Jean-de-Fos

D908

Clermont l'Hérault

N

Villeneuvette

D27

N9

N109-E11

D32

Montpellier

to Béziers

for 26 km (14 miles) to the small, faded-brown town of Gignac. North of Gignac an avenue of trees leads northwest, and in almost a catch of the breath, the flat fields of vines disappear and you are set amid the starkly enfolding **Gorges de l'Hérault** (be sure to branch left onto D 27 6 km/4 miles from Gignac) in the village of Aniane.

ST·GUILHEM·LE·DESERT

The dramatic scenery along D 27 provides a striking setting for the captivating village of St-Guilhem-le-Désert, tucked into a gorge of its own. You'll see, high, stark, and solitary, a ruin on a rock and lower, in the arms of the escarpment, the rounded, ribbed profile of the Benedictine **Abbaye de St-Guilhem**, founded in the ninth century and alive and well today. As you go up the hill to the abbey, you'll see gates discreetly stating the modern presence of Carmel St-Joseph and the Presbytre de St-Guilhem. The abbey has always drawn fascinated, or devout, throngs. So popular was it as a pilgrimage site that a new cloister was built in 1206 (parts of this structure—columns and pilasters—were pried away by the Cloisters Museum in New York).

The "Désert" in the name denotes the village's once-isolated location, but you'll find St-Guilhem well prepared for heavy sightseeing visitations in July and August. Yet no crowds can detract from the irresistible charm of this place, with its stone houses, iron balconies bannered with laundry, and the little Verdus river, lined with vegetable patches and red-roofed houses, tumbling down the valley to join the Hérault just below.

You can lunch in the village on an excellent quiche and salad at **Porte de l'Infernet**, a café on the pleasant Place de la Liberté, shaded by a giant plane tree—an *arbre de la liberté* planted in 1848 and measuring, a sign says, fully 5.55 meters (18.2 feet) around.

"Gate of Hell" may be an odd name in this appealing setting, but just 4½ km (3 miles) south of St-Guilhem and below the village of **St-Jean-de-Fos** (the turning is beside La Poste, the post office), is the oldest medieval bridge in France, the 11th-century **Pont du Diable**. You may see youngsters on *motos* racing across it, bridging centuries as well as the river.

CIRQUE DE MOUREZE

From just south of Gignac, a drive west on N 109 then D 908 of 11 km (7 miles) brings you to the prosperous market town of Clermont-l'Hérault, and another 8 km (5½ miles) beyond on D 908 and D 8E lies the very strange landscape of the Cirque de Mourèze, a chaos of jutting limestone that stretches for miles. They are used to tourists here, though—on the outskirts of Mourèze village, for a small charge you have a view of the *cirque* and are shown some of its archaeological trophies. For a glimpse on your own, look in the village for the blue-and-white-tile sign saying *Direction du Cirque*. A gentle walk of less than a fifth of a mile brings you to the dolomitic crags. There's much enjoyment for ramblers here, but if you have a poor sense of direction, don't go too far and keep an eye toward the village rooftops.

You'll see at the junction of D 8E and the larger D 908 a memorial to more than a hundred murdered heroes of Bir Hakeim, the World War II resistance group that fought bravely throughout Languedoc-Roussillon. A moving inscription says (in translation): "Tell your young not to despair of life, for in difficult times we have shown we can live, fight, and die with dignity." Few passing motorists pause here, but older visitors might recall that, were it not for the courage of this group, the course of history might have been very different.

STAYING AND DINING
IN THE VALLEE DE L'HERAULT

From Mourèze it's only 1 km (½ mile) east back toward Clermont-l'Hérault on D 908 to the ▶ **Hôtel-Restaurant La Source** in **Villeneuvette**. French kings and Napoléon kept this one-industry town busy making uniforms for their conquering arms. When the Machine Age took business to the factories of the north, Villeneuvette stood empty for almost a century. Imaginative reshaping of the village has crafted a country hotel occupying what was once a village house or vine-covered cottage, where each room—there are only 15—is quite different from the next. One has an entirely enclosed patio, another a bathroom whose curved stone ceiling shows the room's origin as a *cave*. The hotel has a pool, tennis courts, an impressive vaulted restaurant serving good, fresh food—changing menus include *saumon marine au citron vert* (sea salmon) and *poitrine de canard rotie* (breast of duck)—a wisteria-shaded terrace, and lush gardens where you'll come across flourishing cherry trees and tall bamboo planted long, long ago. Even the French government has obligingly cooperated in making this a stage-setting idyll by damming a nearby river to form the **Lac du Salagou** just to the north.

From Clermont-l'Hérault N 9 will take you north 5 km (3 miles) to a turnoff to a tiny slip of a road, D 130E, which cuts across the vineyards for a few minutes to the hilltop hamlet of St-Guiraud. Follow it, for here, in a big old rustic house beside the town square, is **Le Mimosa**, to many tastes among the best restaurants in Languedoc. The local bounty that enters the kitchen, commanded, incidentally, by an Englishman and his New Zealander wife—oysters from the Bassin de Thau, quail from the surrounding vineyards, vegetables from villagers' gardens—is the basis of daily changing menus that attract local landowners and business executives who drive out here on weekends from Montpellier. The wine list includes the best the region has to offer and excellent labels from all over France. (Reservations are usually necessary; Tel: 67-96-67-96.)

Plans are in the works for a small luxury hotel that will make the most of the view over the plain and vineyards, but right now, should you wish to linger over dinner at Le Mimosa, you'll find handy accommodation at the ▶ **Auberge Le Pressoir** in **St-Saturnin de Lucian**, another delightful wine village with a broad avenue whose great trees shade old houses and dozing dogs, just 2 km (1½ miles) north of St-Guiraud on D 130E. The auberge's *patron,* who runs a cheerful red-gingham restaurant himself behind the bright pink doors of his bar, has lovingly restored a 17th-century town house with modern comforts and plumbing.

The ancien régime built many estates in a wide circle around Pézenas; one of them is now the ▶ **Château Hôtel de Rieutort**. A small, tranquil hotel with spacious grounds and a swimming pool, it is just a short drive north of the town on D 32.

North to the Cévennes

History touches this countryside with infinite grace. On a northward drive up N 9 beyond the cathedral town of Lodève, where the scenery becomes hillier, you'll find both old stone and the beauty of nature.

PRIEURE DE ST-MICHEL-DE-GRANDMONT

From Lodève, which is 20 km (13 miles) north of Clermont-l'Hérault, take D 153 to the right for a winding climb through forest to green plateau until you reach the gates of this 12th-century monastery (the distance is close to 8 km/5 miles), not the 6 km announced on the signpost. Between June 15 and September 3 at 3:00 P.M. and 5:00 P.M., two-hour guided tours will show you not only the monastery but several fine dolmens dating to some 2,000 years B.C.—one, uniquely in France, is quite complete. There are out-of-season tours on Sundays and holidays at 3:00 P.M. You can also dine—by reservation—in the monastery's restaurant, **Le Saint-Etienne**, located below the arched stones of what was surely another *cave* (Tel: 67-44-09-31). Simple *dortoir* (dormitory) accommodation for hikers is also available; contact Domaine de Grandmont, 34700 Soumont par Lodève.

CIRQUE DE NAVACELLES

Another drive takes you east off N 9 onto D 25 (the turnoff is about 5 km/3 miles north of Lodève), which leads for 26 km (16 miles) across a natural landscape where goats graze to the lip of the extraordinary Cirque de Navacelles, an enormous circular depression forming a natural amphitheater with a tiny village and river at the bottom. On a dull day you may find the bowl veiled in mist, but it's a remarkable sight when the drifts of mist open dramatically to reveal the depth and shape of this natural wonder. There's a bar-restaurant at the rim. You'll find refreshments, too, if you wind your way down the 2 km (1¼ miles) to the bottom of the bowl.

On your return to the N 9 you could make a short detour of 3 km (2 miles) with a short walk at the end of the track to see the **Cirque du Bout du Monde**, in English the memorable "End of the World." You'll see lovely wild countryside, another (though less dramatic) depression, a priory ruin, and dolmens—if there's someone around to help you find them.

LA COUVERTOIRADE

Another side trip off the N 9 some 25 km (16 miles) north of Lodève takes you to the well-marked La Couvertoirade, a fortress-town the Knights Templars built in the 12th and 13th centuries as they crossed Languedoc to and from the Crusades (easy access, 4 km/2½ miles, is on D 185). Their walled stone village on an isolated plateau is like a very small, less sophisticated Carcassonne. But it is much less touristic and, unlike that more famous city, has never been reconstructed over the centuries. If you wish, you can pay 15 francs to see the monuments and walk the ramparts, but it's also very pleasant just to wander the byways of this tiny town, looking at ancient doors, windows, and into attractive crafts shops.

If you're there at lunchtime, look for the restaurant **Le Médiéval**, which can squeeze 18 people into a tiny stone-flagged space. Dishes might include Aveyron pâté, trout, and a true Roquefort cheese from Roquefort itself—not far away and interesting to visit. Tel: 65-62-27-01.

ROQUEFORT-SUR-SOULZON

To get there, head back to the N 9 and continue 16 km (10 miles) north as far as the small town of La Cavalerie. Turn left onto D 999, a very pretty drive of 17 km (11 miles) across a flowing landscape of wheat fields sharp-edged with cliffs and crags, to St-Rome-de-Cernon, then follow the signs another 7 km (4 miles) or so to the source of the famous cheese, Roquefort-sur-Soulzon, a small, one-street town.

The cheese, made from ewe's milk, dominates all here, including the Hôtel de Ville (Town Hall) tucked under the great cheese-producing Societé, the largest and oldest of two main producers (Le Papillon is the other). There's also a determined single independent family producer, Le Vieux Berger. Both of the big companies offer guided tours, so popular that buses often crowd the open spaces in town. Tours take about 45 minutes. You're warned to take warm clothing; it's cold in those cliff caves (they'll lend you a blanket, though). For a meal or an overnight stay, the classi-cally styled ▶ **Grand Hôtel** is attractive and comfortable. For other sights and activities in this appealing Aveyron area, among them the Abbaye de Sylvanès, with its international festival of sacred music, a helpful tourist office on the ap-proach to Roquefort will provide maps and information. For Millau, take D 992 north and follow the Cernon river to the Tarn.

The Gorges du Tarn and Corniche des Cévennes

Millau, glossy and prosperous, famous for the manufacture of gloves and a lure for hang-gliding enthusiasts who come here to soar off the surrounding mountainsides, is the gateway to some of the most spectacular scenery in France: the green and glowing gorges of the Tarn river and the mountains of the Cévennes. This is a heaven for outdoor enthusiasts, with hiking (22 nature-discovery trails as well as long-distance footpaths), horseback riding, cycling, climb-ing, canoeing, caving, and kayaking in summer and skiing in winter.

GORGES DU TARN

From Millau you can follow the twists and turns of the Gorges du Tarn for their entirety, almost 70 km (43 miles), on D 907. You may want to join up with D 907 after a side trip from Millau to Montpellier-le-Vieux.

CHAOS DE MONTPELLIER-LE-VIEUX

The name of this landscape of odd rock formations arises from the notion of medieval travellers that the eerily shaped rocks were the ruins of an ancient city called Montpellier (the forerunner to the city to the south), inhabited by devils. It seems a pity, though, that the rocks of this "Chaos" fancifully carved by nature are on private land and a commercial venture. You pay to see the rocks on foot, via a toy train, and more for a tour of the subterranean Aven Armand grotto to the northeast. (Another commercialized grotto in the area, La Grotte Rose, is at Dargilan.) From Millau you can drive northeast 16 km (10 miles) to Montpellier-le-Vieux on the lumpy, steeply uphill D 110 or a little longer and more smoothly on the more easterly D 991, winding eventually alongside the canyon of the Dourbie river.

UP THE GORGES TO POINT SUBLIME

To reach the Gorges du Tarn from Montpellier-le-Vieux, you join the D 907 via **Le Rozier**, a cheerful little town with shops and restaurants 11 km (7 miles) to the north. Or, from Millau, you head 7 km (4 miles) north on the N 9 until you reach the well-marked branch right. Then follow the signs to **Ste-Enimie** along the riverside drive, a narrow but easy road with occasional mini-tunnels and splendid views of the river and cliff scenery, softened by brilliant flowers in spring and chirruping birds, with many well-posted pleasures for walkers, canoers, and rafters. At the village of Les Vignes (about 10 km/6 miles beyond Le Rozier), take the sharp turn left for a rising 11-km/7-mile drive to **Point Sublime** for a huge panoramic view of the gorges and their cliffs, sand-colored and mantled with green trees, or, if you have the head for it, down to the Tarn and thin line of road. Sufferers from vertigo won't much like parts of the access drive to the viewpoint or the thin rail that separates Point Sublime from infinity.

STAYING AND DINING
AROUND THE GORGES

At intervals beside the river you'll find small hotels where you can stop for refreshment. Quite the most compelling, just south of the very picturesque village of Pougnadoires, or 6 km (3½ miles) from cheerful, bustling Ste-Enimie, with numerous cafés and the very pleasant **Auberge du Moulin** restaurant, is the beautifully preserved 15th-century ▶ **Le Château de la Caze**. It still has its battlemented turrets and cobbled entry hall on which knights once rode their caparisoned horses. The dining room is bright and elegant, the food of gastronomic quality—try their *truite souberaine*. Should you stay here, they'll arrange boat trips to the river's grandest places with the experienced Bateliers de la Malène. Seeming so remote from the outside world, here you are only a gentle morning's drive from Millau. A good place to stay in Millau is ▶ **La Musardière**, a distinguished and finely furnished mansion with an extensive garden. Its stylish hall is echoed at the timeworn (and cheaper) ▶ **Le Château de Creissels**, set in a park on the western outsksirts of the city. You can dine agreeably at both hotels—and perhaps try a local wine, a Côtes de Millau.

PARC NATIONAL DES CEVENNES

The gorges of the Tarn form the western edge of the Parc National des Cévennes. Among thousands of enthusiasts who "took possession . . . of a new quarter of this world" was Robert Louis Stevenson. His 1878 classic *Travels with a Donkey in the Cévennes* vividly depicts his 12-day walk in the mountains, his engaging donkey Modestine for company. If times have changed, the Cévennnes are still wild and challenging. Don't think of venturing into the park without stopping at the Maison du Parc in Florac, 27 km (17 miles) on the winding D 907 bis and N 106 east of Ste-Enimie.

In Florac you'll find hotels, among them the 60-room ▶ **Grand Hôtel du Parc**, with pleasing gardens and a pool. The park headquarters, in a château behind the main street, provides maps, books, and booklets on all aspects of the Cévennes (mammals, birds, rocks, flowers, mushrooms, and other flora and fauna) for a small charge. A detailed park map costs 44 francs. The information center is open in July and August every day from 8:00 A.M. to 7:00 P.M.; the rest of the year, Monday through Friday, 8:00 A.M. to noon and 2:00 P.M. to 6:00 P.M. If you want to check the publications list ahead of your visit, write: Parc National des Cévennes, B.P. 15, 48400 Florac. Tel: 66-49-53-00; Fax: 66-49-53-02.

You can get a fair look at the park just by following D 907 to the end of the Gorges du Tarn and staying with it another 50 km (31 miles) as it skirts the **Causse Méjean**, a highland plateau inhabited by sheep and their herders, and, after St-Laurent-de-Trèves, drops down to the D 9, a broad, winding highway widely known as the **Corniche des Cévennes**. While you could spend weeks walking these mountains and valleys without repeating a route, it takes barely an hour to follow this crest route from Florac to St-Jean-du-Gard, 56 km (33 miles) southeast—too soon, perhaps, unless you pause frequently to absorb the views.

You could also cut due south through the park from the

Gorges du Tarn, leaving D 907 on D 986 (the turnoff is about 25 km/16 miles past Point Sublime). After about 30 km (18½ miles) you will come to the village of **Meyrueis**, where there's a wonderful 15th-century château. From here head east on D 996 for 11½ km (7 miles) and turn south on D 18. This road skirts the slopes of **Mont Aigoual**, the tallest peak of the Cévennes, almost a mile high.

If you continue south on D 18 and then D 48 you will come to the pleasant village of **Le Vigan**. (By this route it's about 60 km/37 miles from Meyrueis to Le Vigan.)

From Le Vigan you can drive south and be back on the coast in a little more than an hour on D 999 and D 986.

BEZIERS AND NARBONNE

Béziers

Béziers, 60 km (37 miles) southwest of Montpellier if you take the A 9 La Languedocienne autoroute, looks over the Languedoc plain and the Canal du Midi from a hill crowned by the Cathédrale de St-Nazaire.

THE ROMAN PAST

The city was conquered by Rome in 120 B.C. and became one of the most important outposts on the Via Domitia. Extending from the Rhône to the Pyrénées, the Via Domitia is the oldest road constructed by the Romans in Gaul. Just 10 km (6 miles) southwest of Béziers, 3 km (2 miles) from Nissan on the N 113, at the pre-Roman archaeological site of **Oppidum l'Ensérune**, you'll find the route of the Via vividly explained—with an almost casual mention that it was probably Hannibal who left the place in ruins. There's an exposed fragment you can walk, if you wish—look for the road marked D 37E.

AROUND CATHEDRALE ST-NAZAIRE

You might begin an exploration of Béziers at its hilltop **Cathédrale St-Nazaire**, the site of the city's other great—and tragic—moment in history. The original cathedral was burned to the ground, with as many as 20,000 inhabitants locked inside, when Simon de Montfort ravaged Béziers in 1209 during his tireless crusade against the Cathars. You'll see a plaque outside: "*Le Languedoc—pays de tolérance et de brilliant culture . . . .*" An extract from a Crusade song, the words on the plaque recall, as if it were yesterday, July

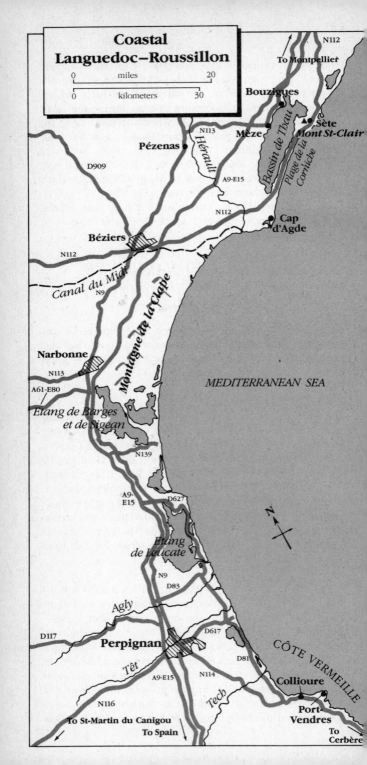

Coastal Languedoc–Roussillon

miles 0 — 20
kilometers 0 — 30

To Montpellier
N112
Bouzigues
Sète
Mont St-Clair
Mèze
N113
Hérault
Pézenas
Basin de Thau
A9-E15
Plage de la Corniche
N112
Cap d'Agde
Béziers
N112
Canal du Midi
N9
Montagne de la Clape
MEDITERRANEAN SEA
Narbonne
N113
A61-E80
Etang de Barges et de Sigean
N139
A9-E15
D627
Etang de Leucate
N9
D83
Agly
D117
Perpignan
D617
Têt
A9-E15
N114
Tech
N
D81
CÔTE VERMEILLE
Collioure
Port-Vendres
N116
To St-Martin du Canigou
To Spain
To Cerbère

22, 1209. The present cathedral, with its frescoed chapels, great red marbled pillars, carved-star stone altar, and fine choir chairs, dates from the 13th and 14th centuries. The treasures in the dusty collections of the **Musée Lapidaire**, reached through the cloisters, include two milestones excavated from the Roman road.

Old Béziers and the shopping district stretches west from the cathedral, toward the lovely tree-lined central avenue that bears the name of the brilliant builder of the Canal du Midi, the baron Paul Riquet. In Béziers—and elsewhere in the southwest—divided loyalties mean that many streets have *two* names, French and Catalan (or Oc). So don't be surprised that Paul Riquet's avenue is also La Passejada— punctuated most days with stalls and populated with shoppers from the surrounding wine-growing countryside.

There's more on Béziers's past in the **Musée du Vieux Biterrois et du Vin** (residents of Béziers are called Biterrois), housed in a 14th-century Dominican convent at 7, rue Massol. Among the most interesting displays are those that explore the construction and colorful shipping history of the Canal du Midi. (And next time you're driving the A 61 autoroute between Toulouse and Narbonne, just west of Béziers, stop at the Port Lauragais service area, a parklike setting in this canal port that includes a **Centre Pierre Paul Riquet**. Among the items displayed is a note from the 1787 diary of a *"touriste américain,"* Thomas Jefferson, who happily travelled the canal "under a cloudless sky" when he was ambassador to the court of King Louis XVI.)

AROUND BEZIERS

The Haut-Languedoc
In the rich variety of Languedoc scenery the Tarn gorges and the Cévennes mountains (see above) are the best known, most visited, most dramatic wild places. But you'll find in the less-travelled 145,000 hectares (nearly 360,000 acres) of the **Parc Régional du Haut-Languedoc** many quiet pleasures and spectacular scenery—especially in the northern Le Sidobre area and, just south of Mazamet, the Montagne Noire, source of the waters that feed the Canal du Midi.

From Béziers to the center of the park it's a panoramic drive west on the N 112 of just over 50 km (31 miles) to **St-Pons-de-Thomières** (signs say St-Pons, or Mazamet, or Castres). You'll pass great vistas of vines, vine-growing towns with catchy names like Puisserguier, and the important wine center of **St-Chinian** before the road rises steeply to traverse forest and wilderness. You can visit or call the

park office in St-Pons (by the cathedral) for information
and route maps; Tel: 67-97-02-10. Or to plan a trip in
advance, write: Parc Régional du Haut-Languedoc, 13 rue
du Cloître, B.P. 9, 34220 St-Pons-de-Thomières.

Castres

The town of Castres, 52 km (32 miles) west and then northwest of St-Pons on N 112, definitely merits a visit. Ignore the
outskirts. In the heart of the city balconied, narrow houses
frame the Agoût River. Fine town houses and formal gardens
line elegant streets, and there's a jolly open market and fine
shopping on the rue Gambetta.

Steps from the helpful tourist office within the grand
Théâtre Municipal, you'll find the **Musée Goya** in a former
Benedictine monastery and bishop's palace. The permanent
exhibition includes early Spanish masters and, above all,
works by Goya: the series of 80 etchings known as *Los
Caprichos,* the horrifying series called The Disasters of War,
40 prints of bullfighting scenes (which Goya adored), and
three very fine paintings, including a surprisingly gentle and
reflective self-portrait. The old ► **Grand-Hôtel** (11, rue de la
Libération) is the place for lunch, in summer on the waterside terrace.

STAYING AND DINING
IN AND AROUND BEZIERS

Béziers is a bright and cheerful town at all times, a good
place to shop and stay. You couldn't do better than to take a
room (preferably overlooking the canal at the back) at the
urbanely old-fashioned ► **Grand Hôtel du Nord**. The hotel
is set in a curve away from the bustle of the Place Jean-Jaurès,
but happily faces the excellent **Le Framboisier** restaurant
(Tel: 67-49-90-00) and is just up the *allées* from the public
gardens, the **Plateau des Poètes**. You might like, too, the
little hotel right beside the park, the ► **Hôtel des Poètes**
(like the Nord, it has no restaurant of its own), which
manages to be in the heart of town and delightfully peaceful—except in mid-August. Unless you're mad about bulls,
bull-running, and the *corrida*—a passion southwest France
shares with Spain—it's best to bypass Béziers on August 15
and the following three days when the entire city, packed
with folk from neighboring wine towns, loudly celebrates
the Fête de la Vierge.

In St-Pons you'll find one of the most soothingly delightful
hotels in all Languedoc, the ► **Château de Ponderach**, a
homely 19th-century mansion set deep in a *domaine* of
forest and greenery. Rooms are quite small, but this is a

place where they still turn down the beds, a salon fire blazes in cool months, and there's terrace dining in summer. The menu includes such dishes as salmon trout, *ris de veau, escalopes de foie de canard poêle,* and *cassoulet Toulousain,* the favorite stew of the closely neighboring Midi. Desserts even in memory are mouthwatering; try the exquisite chocolate mousse or heavenly walnut-and-caramel tart—or both.

Narbonne

From Béziers, Narbonne is 23 km (14 miles) southwest on the N 113/N 9, a route that follows substantially, if not precisely, part of the Via Domitia, the great paved road the Romans blazed between Italy and Spain in 118 B.C. Founded by the Gauls in 600 B.C. and conquered by the Romans in 118 B.C., Narbonne (the Roman Narbo) was the most important town in Gaul until the end of the Empire. It remained an important trading center well into the Middle Ages, until its population of Jewish traders and bankers was expelled and its thriving seaport allowed to silt up in the 14th century.

Physically, Narbonne is dominated by the hulking **Cathédrale St-Just**, begun in the 13th century to help subdue the heretical Narbonnais and never quite completed. The structure you see today is only the choir of what was to have been the largest cathedral in Christendom, had not centuries of war, religious and otherwise, intervened. Yet reminders of Rome are much in evidence, often resting side by side with the town's medieval monuments.

The **Musée Archéologique** occupies several rooms of the archbishop's palace next to the cathedral, and is filled with frescoes, Roman columns and statuary, and other artifacts. Just north at 16, rue Rouget-de-l'Isle is the **Musée de l'Horreum**, an underground Roman grain warehouse that is now filled with coins and other treasures from Rome's presence here. All of these places are on the narrow streets of Narbonne's **old quarter**, known as La Cité; the district to the south of the tree-lined Canal de la Robine is Le Bourg. In its undemonstrative style, Narbonne has many colorful details to catch the eye—few as colorful as the **Maison des Trois Nourrices** in Le Bourg, so called for the ample-breasted caryatids on the façade—and, filling an otherwise empty Sunday morning, a cheerful open market on quai Vallière on the banks of the canal.

STAYING AND DINING IN NARBONNE

A handy and pleasant place to stay is the centrally located ▶ **Hôtel du Languedoc**, a classical town house recently en-

tirely refurbished. From the hotel, you can walk in minutes
to the cathedral and other main points of interest. You'll also
eat well at the hotel.

AROUND NARBONNE

The **Abbaye de Fontfroide**, one of the greatest intact Cistercian abbeys in the world, is just outside Narbonne. Start west
on N 113, turn left after 2 or 3 km (1 or 2 miles) onto D 613
and, in 7 km (4½ miles), left again to the well-signposted
abbey. The abbey church dates to the 12th century, the
cloister to the 12th and 13th centuries. Abandoned during
the religious persecutions of the late 18th century, the abbey
is now almost completely restored. Each tour takes about an
hour and you may have to wait. But if you just walk up the
path behind the abbey, you'll have a fair overall view.

If you have found the area's Corbières wine pleasing,
another agreeable excursion is to the **Musée de la Vigne et
du Vin** in Lézignan-Corbières, 18 km (11 miles) west of
Narbonne on N 113. Its fortress-style church and the building called La Maison de la Maçon are worth seeing, too.
You'll find more good wine if you head southeast of
Narbonne toward its small and rather ordinary beach resort
at **Narbonne-Plage**. On the way there, only 12 km (7½ miles)
from Narbonne's commercial outskirts on D 168, you'll cross
the limestone **Montagne de la Clape**—its wine as memorable as its name. For a different route back, head 10 km (6
miles) south from the Plage to **Gruissan**—it has a pleasant
beach of its own—and another 12 km (7½ miles) inland to
Narbonne.

SOUTH TOWARD SPAIN

Autoroute A 9 speeds south from Narbonne for 65 km (40
miles) to Perpignan, a city that is as Catalan and almost as
Spanish as it is French. En route you will pass the **Fort de
Salses**, guarding what was once the border of French
Catalonia, ceded to Paris in the 1659 Treaty of the Pyrénées.
You are now in the old lands of Roussillon, a region of
startlingly varied scenery and with a style and temperament
all its own.

Perpignan

Perpignan has a Spanish palace, that of the kings of Majorca;
a Spanish cathedral, the Cathédrale de St-Jean; a Spanish
fortress, Le Castillet; and a delightful pedestrian ramble of

streets emanating from the Place de la Loge and winding up toward the palace and down toward the flower-planted banks of La Têt river.

The best place to get an overview of all this and begin a tour of the city is at the 14th-century **Castillet**, a fortress on the north side of the old city, just inside the boulevards that follow the path of the now-demolished city walls. It offers more than panoramic views of Perpignan from its tower, however; inside, the **Musée des Arts et Traditions Populaires du Roussillon** (within the Casa Pairal) provides an intimate room-by-room walk through the popular tastes and folk crafts of Catalonian Roussillon. The heart of the people is visible in the table linens, woodcarvings, and pottery as well as in the tools of their industry—wrought iron and objects connected with the making of wine.

Close by Le Castillet looms the **Cathédrale de St-Jean**, built between 1324 and 1509. This is no French Gothic work but an Iberian one, made of stones from the Pyrénées polished by churning mountain rivers. During Holy Week the mystical procession of La Sanch winds through the streets from the Eglise de St-Jacques to the cathedral, led by a red-robed penitent followed by penitents in black who carry wax and wooden figures representing personages of the Passion.

Across the cathedral square and down delightful twists and turns is the 14th-century **Loge de Mer**. Refurbished in the 16th century in Spanish Renaissance style, it was an early stock exchange. Down the pedestrians-only rue de Loge stands Maillol's statue of Venus, whose longing gaze rests on the Hôtel de Ville. Shops in the surrounding streets are rich in chocolate, thanks to the chocolate factory in nearby Cantalou. Perpignan shops also specialize in all sorts of leather items, particularly shoes. The **Citadelle**, with the curious **Palais des Rois de Majorque** (Palace of the Kings of Majorca) inside its massive hexagonal walls, is on the southern edge of the old city.

STAYING AND DINING IN PERPIGNAN

The ▶ **Hôtel de la Loge**, on the Place de la Loge, is a particularly pleasant place to stay in Perpignan. This 16th-century Catalan mansion is furnished partially with antiques and has a mosaic-tile patio with a gurgling fountain. A couple of good restaurants in town are **Le Chapon Fin**, in the Park Hôtel on boulevard Jean Bourrat (Tel: 68-35-14-14), which serves some of the finest regional food in the Catalan region; and **La Casa Sansa**, at 2, rue des Fabriques d'en Nadal (Tel: 68-34-21-84), with true Catalan specialties including Catalan codfish, hot *bolas* (meatballs), and *parillada* (mixed fish grill). There's also *meli mato* (honey-and-cream-cheese dessert). Inexpensive.

BEACH RESORTS
NORTH OF PERPIGNAN

While Perpignan is a busy and sophisticated city, its northern beach resorts are tranquil and low key. For the nicest, head north on N 9, then turn north onto D 83 after 11 km (7 miles) toward Port-Barcarès. Ignore Port-Barcarès, but continue (the road is now D 627) to **Leucate-Plage** about 25 km (16 miles) from the N 9 turnoff. The drive is a delight, with the blue sea to the right and earthy *étangs* to the left, studded, at times, with the gaudy sails of dashing windsurfers. At Leucate-Plage, you'll find sedate family villas and a long, splendid beach. Another 5 km (3 miles) north on D 627 with a branch right on D 427, where hillside pines meet a broad, flat beach, is the tiny village of **La Franqui**—undeveloped, unfashionable, uncrowded, delightful.

Into the Eastern Pyrénées

The easternmost slopes of the Pyrénées, cloaked with vines and orchards of peaches, apricots, and cherries, drop into the sea just south of Perpignan. Here, below the snowy Pic du Canigou, 9,134 feet high and sacred to the Catalans, you're deep in Roussillon. It's a place for skiing, walking, and riding in the mountains, for taking the waters in still-stylish spas, for boating, for lounging on sunny beaches—and for absorbing fine music in a felicitous setting.

PRADES AND ST-MICHEL-DE-CUXA

Prades, a small town of graceful stone houses 40 km (25 miles) west of Perpignan on N 116, is where cellist Pablo Casals settled when he fled Franco's Spain. Each July and August you can attend the music festival he founded here, and there's a moving display of memorabilia commemorating his life at Prades's tourist office, where you can also buy concert tickets. Contact: Syndicat d'Initiative, 4, rue Victor Hugo, 66500 Prades; Tel: 68-96-27-58; Fax: 68-96-50-95. Many of the concerts are held at the nearby Romanesque **Abbaye St-Michel-de-Cuxa**; the abbey, in a valley of cherry trees under the all-seeing Canigou (see below), was begun in 937, though its beautiful cloister (part of it is in New York's Cloisters Museum) dates to the 12th century.

TO ST-MARTIN-DU-CANIGOU

Another 6 km (4 miles) along N 116 you'll see the sign for
Vernet-les-Bains, a spa that drew the rich and famous in
times past—among them British royalty and Rudyard Kip-
ling—and is still well attended today.

From Vernet-les-Bains you may tire your body but satisfy
your soul if you make the popular pilgrimage, a steep, 40-
minute slog up a half-tarred mountain track, to another
remarkable abbey, **St-Martin-du-Canigou**. (Leave your car in
Vernet-les-Bains or near the Relais St-Martin a little farther
up.) You'll first arrive at St-Martin-le-Vieux, a slate-covered
ossuary. At the abbey, still higher, you can join guided tours
starting at 10:00 A.M., or attend Mass at 11:00 A.M. and sometimes 5:30 P.M. Monks (*béatitudes*) live in the abbey, built in
1007 by Comte Guifred, who took to the mountains to
repent for killing his son. The monks' own privacy in this
ancient place, you'll observe, is guarded by discreet electronically operated doors.

MOUNTAIN SPORTS

Enthusiasts of mountain winter sports will find **skiing** around
Mont-Louis, whose Vauban defenses make it the highest
fortified town in France, or at the major ski station, **Font-
Romeu** (both close to the ski resorts of Andorra). You may
obtain ski passes (by the day or for longer periods, valid at up
to nine stations), and instruction and rental equipment are
available; for more information, contact: Office de Tourisme,
avenue Emmanuel Brousse, B.P. 55, 66122 Font-Romeu Cedex
(Tel: 68-30-68-30; Fax: 68-30-29-70). For **riding** trips in the
mountains, write to: A Cheval en Pyrénées Roussillon, 5 bis,
avenue des Baléares, 66000 Perpignan. If you plan to do much
walking, contact the Association Randonnées Pyrénéennes
for guides and maps: 29, rue Marcel Lamarque, 65000 Tarbes;
Tel: 62-93-57-57.

INTO THE MOUNTAINS BY TRAIN

Don't fancy all that exercise? Much the jolliest way to traverse the lovely eastern Pyrénées it to ride **le petit train
jaune** (the little yellow train), no dinky toy but a veritable
year-round workhorse that's painted bright yellow. The train
runs from **Villefranche-de-Conflent** (6 km/4 miles east of
Prades on N 116) for 63 km (40 miles) on an electrified
narrow-gauge track up the valley of the river Têt to Latour de
Carol. From here, should you choose, you can catch a rather
faster train north to the rest of France or south to Spain. A
compromise could be the ascent to **Mont-Louis** (about an
hour and 20 minutes) and the one-hour descent, in an open-

topped carriage if you want the wind in your hair. You'll still get the benefit of dazzling scenery, amazing viaducts, and sudden tunnels, and have time between arriving and leaving to look around Mont-Louis. Local SNCF stations and the Prades tourist office have timetables.

Allow time, too, to explore the perfect bastion of Ville-franche-de-Conflent, a gem of a medieval town tightly enclosed within its Vauban-constructed fortress walls. The town is linked by subterranean stairway to Fort Liberia high above on the hillside and littered with legends of women, alleged to be poisoners, chained to a wall to rot—and of one who lingered on for 40 years.

STAYING AND DINING
IN THE MOUNTAINS

In Vernet you might stay at ► Le Mas Fleuri, a peaceful place with balconied rooms and a pool, and dine perhaps at the **Hostellerie Au Comte Guifred de Conflent**, where a cookery school within a contemporary building is a guarantee of good eating (Tel: 68-05-51-37). A very pleasant alternative, especially if you plan to spend a little time exploring the area, is to stay at ► Rozinante. This serenely peaceful three-room guesthouse, with the grandeur of Canigou in full view, is near the hamlet of Fuilla, 6 km (4 miles) up the D 6 from **Villefranche-de-Conflent**, 2 km (1¼) southwest of Prades on the N 116. Rozinante is run by the English Mrs. Gene Barter and her family. Breakfast and dinner are provided, if you wish; you may bring your own wine (Fitou and Côtes du Roussillon-Village are among the region's best). For the baking heat of summer there's a large pool and green lawns. If you prefer high style to homely hospitality, by pronounced contrast at **Molitg-les-Bains**, just west of Prades, is the towered domain of the ► **Château de Riell**, a Relais & Châteaux hotel.

Côte Vermeille

Distances are short when you head from mountainside to sea but the change in setting and mood is immense. Fringing the bulk of the eastern Pyrénées is the very pretty coast called Côte Vermeille, which means both vermilion and gilded. Interpret it as you choose—for the vineyards sweeping down to the sea, their leaves a ruddy glow in autumn, or for the glittering beauty of the sea itself.

COLLIOURE

The most sparkling town on this lovely shore is Collioure. You'll find Collioure on the map some 30 km (19 miles) southwest of Perpignan on the N 114. A lively fishing village—anchovies are the prime catch—and immensely popular resort, Collioure has the light, the color, and the charm that have attracted artists over very many years, among them Picasso, Matisse, and Dalí. Walk now into virtually any waterside bar or café and you'll see the impressions of the great, the skillful, and the merely enthusiastic in cheerful exhibition.

STAYING AND DINING IN COLLIOURE

The best show of all is beside the harbor in the famous bar of the ▶ **Hostellerie des Templiers**, whose owners, the Pous family, won't part with any of their treasures, proffered over the years to cover the cost of a bed, a meal, a few drinks. Their collection includes a scene of Collioure, its little bay and lighthouse "on an evening without sails or stars," by Raoul Dufy, painted in 1948.

You can stay near the center of the village at the ▶ **Hostellerie La Frégate**, with a cool waterside terrace. A peaceful place to stay is the ▶ **Relais des Trois Mas**, occupying several restored buildings on the edge of the town. Every room has a view across to the harbor, and some have their own terrace as well. Its restaurant, **La Balette**, wins much justified praise. You'll find numerous little restaurants throughout the village and, with the focus on fresh seafood, will rarely be disappointed. At **La Marinade**, in the little square facing the tourist office, you can taste the famous *anchois* (anchovies) of Collioure and *moules* (mussels) in delicious sauces, or duck or a filet mignon if you prefer. For dessert, try a *crème catalan* or *les pruneaux au Banyuls*—prunes in the delectable sweet wine of Banyuls, a small fishing port that lies farther south on the Côte Vermeille.

NORTH AND WEST OF COLLIOURE

Inland from Collioure you might pause at **Elne**, 16 km (10 miles) north on N 114, to see its ancient cathedral and cloisters (Elne was once the dominant town in the region but is now overshadowed by Perpignan; Romans were here, too). At Thuir, 19 km (12 miles) west of Elne on D 612, you have a small, busy town and a large winery whose notable attraction is the world's greatest oak barrel; visitors are welcome. Continue 23 km (14 miles) on to Vinça on D 615 and you've suddenly left behind vines for orchards. You'll see irrigation canals (people pay around 30 francs a *year* to get water twice a week), and the odd-looking word *vaïna,* Catalan for hamlet, begins to appear on signs. There's a project afoot in this neighborhood to set aside a private reserve for hunting wild boar. If you haven't yet had a chance to see Prades, it is just 15 km (9 miles) west of Vinça on N 116.

To see the coast north of Collioure, head toward Perpignan, then begin back south on D 617 to Canet en Roussillon, a resort conspicuous for its bunkerlike blocks. Continue south on D 81 toward the less daunting resort of St-Cyprien-Plage, with its huge marina and the unified and attractive **port** development at **Argelès Plage**. Watch out for the sign just north of Collioure for charming little **Le Racou**, an unshiny village and peaceable beach.

SOUTH ALONG THE COAST

South of Collioure you will wind along a coastline where the encroachments of holiday development are not yet overbearing. Running atop vineyards clinging to hillsides that dip into a blue-green sea, in 4 km (2½ miles) the road comes to the busy pleasure port of **Port-Vendres**, with a café-lined harbor, then the corniche dips and climbs through vineyards for 20 km (12 miles) to **Banyuls** and its sweet wines, and from there winds on high above the sea for another 10 km (6 miles) to the border town of Cerbère, named for the mythological dog that guarded the gates of Hell.

This coast is as beautiful as the Côte d'Azur, without the glamour or glitz. From Cerbère the road south, now the Spanish C 252, leads you on to the delightful, whitewashed Catalan village of Cadaquez and the northern reaches of the Costa Brava.

GETTING AROUND

Air France and other major airlines will bring you to Paris and on to Montpellier, the largest city in Languedoc-Roussillon. Perpignan also has an airport, and there is a small one between Béziers and Agde as well as other local aerodromes. The domestic airline Air Inter handles regular daily flights from Paris to Montpellier and Perpignan. From London, British Airways and Dan Air fly regularly to Montpellier.

Travellers also have a choice of trains that leave for Montpellier from Paris's Gare de Lyon. There are trains that make the journey at night; arrangements can be made to come south in the same train that brings your car. Additionally, Montpellier and Béziers are on the almost-national TGV fast-train network, and frequent train service also links Paris to Perpignan (via Toulouse) and the main cities, including Narbonne and Béziers, in the southwest.

If you are travelling by car, the A 61 Autoroute des Deux Mers will bring you south via Toulouse from Bordeaux. Or, from Lyon, there is the A 6, then A 7 autoroute, which sweeps down to Nîmes and, as the A 9, calls itself La Languedocienne at Montpellier and La Catalane farther west. Once you are in the south, the autoroutes carry you equally quickly east into Provence, west to Toulouse and the Midi, or southwest to Spain. You'll find the latest autoroute routings—and details of autoroute facilities that include comfortable overnight hotels—at service areas along the way.

Car rental firms have offices in Montpellier and its airport, Fréjorgues, and in Perpignan, Narbonne, and Béziers. Crowded city centers or fast autoroutes apart, this is a region where leisurely motoring is possible and a pleasure. With the yellow Michelin maps for each area you plan to explore, you should have no trouble finding your way onto even the small back roads, where often the true joy of travel lies.

ACCOMMODATIONS REFERENCE

The rates given below are projections *for 1994. Unless otherwise indicated, rates are for a double room, double occupancy, and do not include meals. As rates are always subject to change, double-check before booking.*

▶ **Auberge Le Pressoir.** 34150 St-Saturnin de Lucian. Tel: 67-96-63-59; Fax: 67-96-62-94. 190F–360F. Closed January; reserved for groups only November to April.

▶ **Le Château de la Caze.** D 907 bis La Malène, 48210 **Ste-Enimie.** Tel: 66-48-51-01; Fax: 66-48-55-75. 450F–950F. (Closed November through April.)

▶ **Le Château de Creissels.** Route de St-Affrique, 12100 **Millau.** Tel: 65-60-16-59; Fax: 65-61-24-63. 250F–340F.

▶ **Château Hôtel de Rieutort.** St-Pargoire, 34230 **Paulhan.** Tel: 67-25-00-61; Fax: 67-25-29-92. 520F–750F. (Closed November to Easter.)

▶ **Château de Ponderach.** Route de Narbonne, 34220 **St-Pons-de-Thomières.** Tel: 67-97-02-57; Fax: 67-97-29-75. 395F–460F.

▶ **Château de Riell.** Molitg-les-Bains, 66500 **Prades.** Tel: 68-05-04-40; Fax: 68-05-04-37. 950F–1,510F. (Closed November through March.)

▶ **Grand-Hôtel.** 11, rue de la Libération, 81100 **Castres.** Tel: 63-59-00-30; Fax: 63-59-98-05. 190F–270F.

▶ **Grand Hôtel.** 12250 **Roquefort-sur-Soulzon.** Tel: 65-59-90-20; Fax: 65-59-97-92. 290F–360F. (Closed from October 15 through March.)

▶ **Grand Hôtel du Midi.** 22, boulevard Victor Hugo, 34000 **Montpellier.** Tel: 67-92-69-61; Fax: 67-92-73-63. 620F.

► **Grand Hôtel du Nord**. 15, place Jean-Jaurès, 34500 **Béziers**. Tel: 67-28-34-09; Fax: 67-49-00-37. 430.

► **Grand Hôtel du Parc**. 48400 **Florac**. Tel: 66-45-03-05; Fax: 66-45-11-81. 240F–270F. (Closed January and February.)

► **Hostellerie La Frégate**. 66190 **Collioure**. Tel: 68-82-06-05; Fax: 68-82-55-00. 398F–478F.

► **Hostellerie des Remparts**. 6, place Anatole France, 30220 **Aigues-Mortes**. Tel: 66-53-82-77; Fax: 66-53-73-77. 280F–455F.

► **Hostellerie des Templiers**. Quai de l'Amirauté, 66190 **Collioure**. Tel: 68-98-31-10; Fax: 68-98-01-24. 294F–365F. (Closed January.)

► **Hôtel Le Guilhem**. 18, rue Jean-Jacques Rousseau, 34000 **Montpellier**. Tel: 67-52-90-90; Fax: 67-60-67-67. 300F–350F.

► **Hôtel du Languedoc**. 22, boulevard Gambetta, 11100 **Narbonne**. Tel: 68-65-14-74; Fax: 68-65-81-48. 270F–350F; suite 450F.

► **Hôtel de la Loge**. Place de la Loge, 66000 **Perpignan**. Tel: 68-34-41-02; Fax: 68-34-25-13. 250F–350F.

► **Hôtel de Noailles**. 2, rue des Ecoles-Centrales, 34000 **Montpellier**. Tel: 67-60-49-80; Fax: 67-66-08-26. 415F–470F.

► **Hôtel des Poètes**. 80, allées Paul-Riquet, 34500 **Béziers**. Tel: 67-76-38-66; Fax: 67-76-25-88. 260F.

► **Hôtel-Restaurant La Source**. 34800 **Villeneuvette**. Tel. and Fax: 67-96-05-07. 275F–400F. (Closed January and February.)

► **Hôtel Saint-Louis**. 10, rue de l'Amiral-Courbet, 30220 **Aigues-Mortes**. Tel: 66-53-72-68; Fax: 66-53-75-92. 375F–395F. (Closed January and February.)

► **Imperator Concorde**. Quai de la Fontaine, 30900 **Nîmes**. Tel: 66-21-90-30; Fax: 66-67-70-25. 630F–1,000F.

► **Le Mas Fleuri**. Parc de la Résidence des Baüs, 66820 **Vernet-les-Bains**. Tel: 68-05-51-94; Fax: 68-05-50-77. 300F–680F (breakfast included).

► **Motel Côte Bleue**. 34140 **Bouzigues**. Tel: 67-78-31-42; Fax: 67-78-35-49. 320F.

► **La Musardière**. 34, avenue de la République, 12100 **Millau**. Tel: 65-60-20-63; Fax: 65-61-02-05. 350F–560F. (Closed November to Easter.)

► **Relais des Trois Mas**. Route de Port-Vendres, 66190 **Collioure**. Tel: 68-82-05-07; Fax: 68-82-38-08. 575F–1,550F.

► **Rozinante**. Mrs. Gene Barter, 7, Cami Ribère Enclose, **Fuilla**, 66820 **Vernet-les-Bains**. Tel: 68-96-34-50. 175F.

► **Le Vieux Castillon**. Castillon-du-Gard, 30210 **Remoulins**. Tel: 66-37-00-77; Fax: 66-37-28-17. 680F–1,250F.

TOULOUSE AND THE MIDI

By Stephen Brewer

Stephen Brewer, a New Yorker, has edited several guidebooks in this series. He retreats to the South of France regularly, frequently on assignment for magazines and newspapers.

The Midi, or, in translation of the old French, Midday: This legendary part of France takes its name from the noon-strength sun that shines upon its fields and vineyards year-round. To the French the Midi is, simply, the South—where it is sunnier and warmer than it is in the rest of France, where the food is simple and delicious, where the wine flows freely, where life is easy and the lavender grows in wild abandon.

When Parisians or other northerners announce they are off to the Midi, they will most likely board a southbound train for the Gare Matabiau in Toulouse; this old city, once the most important in all the South, and the countryside around it is where you are most likely to find the spirit of the Midi as it once was. These southwestern lands lie far to the west of Provence and the Côte d'Azur, those more sophisticated places that most non-French travellers are more likely to think of as the South of France (Toulouse is a full 400 km/ 250 miles west of Marseille). You will not find here the worldly attractions of Biarritz, on the Atlantic some 300 km (185 miles) west, nor is the Toulousain Midi as heavily travelled as the Dordogne, just to the north.

The fields and vineyards around Toulouse are among the most bountiful in France. A traveller here can follow narrow

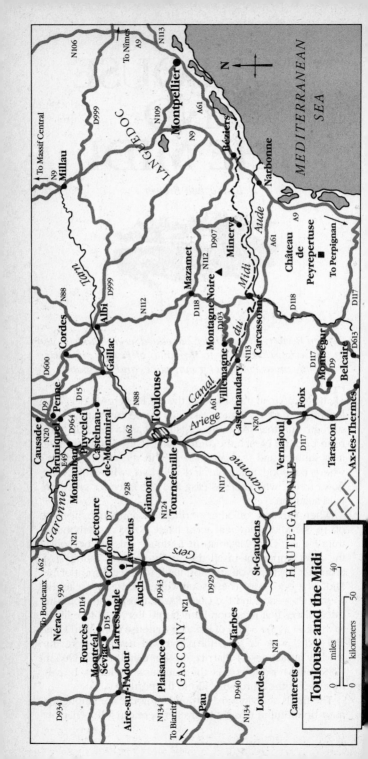

Toulouse and the Midi

MEDITERRANEAN SEA

N

To Nîmes
To Massif Central
To Perpignan
To Bordeaux
To Biarritz

LANGEDOC

GASCONY

HAUTE-GARONNE

Montpellier
Millau
Béziers
Narbonne
Château de Peyrepertuse
Mazamet
Minerve
Montagne Noire
Albi
Cordes
Carcassonne
Gaillac
Penne
Causade
Bruniquel
Puycelci
Castelnau-de-Montmiral
Montauban
Toulouse
Villemagne
Castelnaudary
Foix
Montségur
Belcaire
Tarascon
Ax-les-Thermes
Vernajoul
Tournefeuille
Gimont
Lectoure
Condom
Lavardens
Auch
Nérac
Fourcès
Montréal
Séviac
Larressingle
Aire-sur-l'Adour
Plaisance
Tarbes
St-Gaudens
Pau
Lourdes
Cauterets

Tarn
Garonne
Ariege
Gers
Canal du Midi
Aude

N106
A9
N113
N9
D999
N109
A61
A61
D907
N112
D907
D118
N88
D999
N112
D118
D103
N113
D118
D117
D600
D9
D15
N88
A62
N124
N117
N20
D117
D9
D613
D964
928
D7
N21
930
D114
D15
D943
D929
N21
D940
N134
N20
D934
A62
E49
N9
N88
D117

0   miles   40
0   kilometers   50

roads across rolling countryside and find a meal and a bed in a rustic village that has scarcely changed in several centuries. In the southernmost reaches the vineyards climb the foothills of the Pyrénées. From most of this sun-drenched region—even from the town of Lectoure, almost a hundred miles north of the mountains—you can see these craggy peaks, perpetually snowcapped. And, of course, much of the appeal of this region is gastronomic. Even the simplest restaurant is likely to serve its own variation of foie gras (literally "fat liver") and a good cassoulet, followed by *pruneaux fourrés* (stuffed plums) and an Armagnac.

We begin our coverage in Toulouse, a city that is at once ancient and aggressively modern. From there we follow several itineraries: west to the sophisticated little city of Auch and on into romantic countryside that once comprised the duchy of Gascony; north and east to the medieval city of Albi and the unspoiled towns that surround it; south to Foix, dominated by its hilltop château, and the first of the high peaks of the Pyrénées; and southeast to Carcassonne, the most famous (and touristic) of all French walled cities.

MAJOR INTEREST

Toulouse
Place du Capitole
Basilique St-Sernin
Les Jacobins
Hôtel de Bernuy and other mansions
La Daurade and La Dalbade quarters
Musée des Augustins
Place Wilson and commercial Toulouse

Gascony
Auch
Lectoure, Condom, and the *bastides* (fortified towns)

Albi
Cathédrale Ste-Cécile
Musée Toulouse-Lautrec

Cordes and the hill towns

Foix and the Pyrénées
Grotte de Niaux
Cathar citadels

Castelnaudary (for cassoulet)

Carcassonne, medieval city

Minerve and **Lastours**, medieval strongholds

TOULOUSE

Chances are you will pass through Toulouse on your way to many other places in the Midi. The speedy Autoroute des Deux-Mers (A 61/A 62) skirts its suburbs; its international airport, Blagnac, accommodates nonstop flights from London and many large cities on the continent; and at approximately 7:00 each morning an overnight express train arrives from Paris. Unfortunately, all too often visitors rush through these points of entry for places that are smaller and more immediately appealing.

Granted, with its sprawling modern suburbs, traffic jams, and the somber brick façades of its older sections, Toulouse is a city that reveals its charms only slowly. "A flat, torturous town," is how Henry James described Toulouse on a stopover here in 1882. By the time of his visit Toulousains already numbered 150,000, twice as many as a hundred years before. The city expanded even more rapidly in the 1920s, when local factories began to turn out the first passenger aircraft and the aviator Antoine de Saint-Exupéry commenced his historic transatlantic flights from its new airfield. Since then Toulouse's many immigrants, mostly from Spain and northern Africa, have found work in the city's industrial parks; its factories turn out Concordes and Airbuses, automobile parts and electronics.

Old Toulouse

It would be very easy to miss Toulouse's greatest treasure, one of the largest unspoiled historic quarters in Europe. The oldest parts of Toulouse cluster along the east banks of the Garonne river, which here makes a turn toward the west on its way toward the Atlantic.

PLACE DU CAPITOLE

Old Toulouse can be explored only on foot. The obvious starting point is the Place du Capitole, a vast sea of paving stones that is named for the *capitulari* (magistrates) who ably governed Toulouse through several turbulent centuries. Europe's first step toward democracy was taken here in 1152 when Raymond V, comte de Toulouse, gave this elected body of 24 legislators full power to administer the law and mete out justice.

Even this enormous *place,* a handsome assemblage of brick and stone, has not escaped critics of Toulouse's distinctive brick architecture. Stendhal wrote of the *place*'s enor-

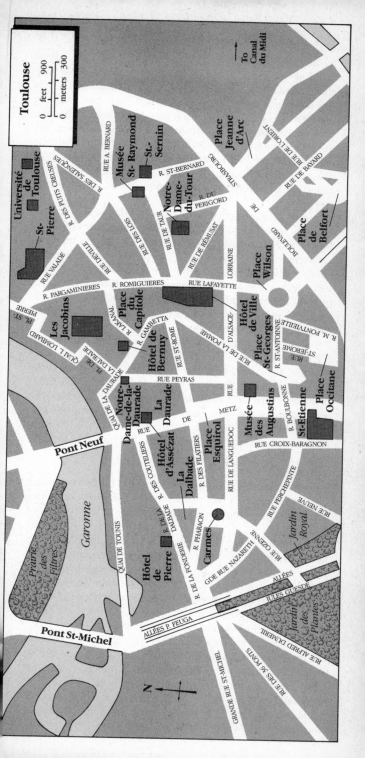

Toulouse

feet 0 — 900
meters 0 — 300

To Canal du Midi

Université de Toulouse

St-Pierre

R. DES PUITS CREUSES

R. DES SALÉNQUES

RUE A. BERNARD

Musée St-Raymond

St-Sernin

Place Jeanne d'Arc

R. ST-BERNARD

Notre-Dame-du-Tour

R. DU PÉRIGORD

RUE DE BAYARD

RUE DE L'ORIENT

RUE VALADE

RUE DEVILLE

RUE DES LOIS

RUE DE TAUR

RUE DE RÉMUSAT

STRASBOURG

LORRAINE

DE

BOULEVARD

Place de Belfort

R. PARGAMINIERES

R. ROMIGUIERES

RUE LAFAYETTE

Place Wilson

R. SAINT PIERRE

QUAI L. LOMBARD

PL. ST. PIERRE

Les Jacobins

PL. DE LA DALBADE

R. LAKANAL

Place du Capitole

Hôtel de Ville

Place St-Georges

RUE ST-ANTONINE

R. M. FONTVIEILLE

RUE ST-JÉROME

R. GAMBETTA

Hôtel de Bernuy

RUE ST-ROME

RUE DE LA POMME

RUE PEYRAS

RUE DE LA DAURADE

Notre-Dame-de-la-Daurade

La Daurade

DE

METZ

RUE

Place Esquirol

RUE DE LANGUEDOC

Musée des Augustins

RUE D'ALSACE

Place Occitane

St-Etienne

R. BOULBONNE

RUE CROIX-BARAGNON

Pont Neuf

Garonne

QUAI DE TOUNIS

R. DE LA DALBADE

R. DES COUTELIERS

Hôtel d'Asséezat

La Dalbade

R. DES FILATIERS

RUE NEUVE

RUE PERCHEPINTE

Prairie des Filtres

R. DE LA FONDERIE

R. PHARAON

Hôtel de Pierre

Carmes

GDE RUE NAZARETH

RUE OZENNE

Jardin Royal

Pont St-Michel

ALLÉES P. FEUGA

ALLÉES JULES GUESDE

Jardin C. des Plantes

GRANDE RUE ST-MICHEL

RUE DES 36 PONTS

RUE ALFRED DUMÉRIL

N

mous **Hôtel de Ville**, constructed in the 1750s: "the ugliest building you could imagine, but the rest of the town is so shabby that this huge structure is quite a pleasant sight." It is the heaviness of Toulousain red brick—the best building material the local soil yields—that many visitors find so unattractive. Toulousains, on the other hand, call their city the Ville Rose (the Pink City) because of the gentle hue the brick takes on in the strong sunlight. The Roman poet Ausonius, who lived in the fourth-century A.D. settlement called Tolosa, referred to the encampment as "a city of rose-red brick."

Pink may also describe the city's political leanings. Toulousains have defied the Crown of England, the Church of Rome, and Paris-based government. Toulouse was the principal city of the 17th-century Etats du Languedoc, a group of southern landholders who attempted to declare their independence from the Crown. Cardinal Richelieu's forces quelled the movement, and the governor of Languedoc was executed in the courtyard of a building that once stood on the site of the Hôtel de Ville.

Before you venture down any of the narrow streets leading off the *place,* walk to the little park in back of the Hôtel de Ville. Here, in a restored 16th-century tower called the **Donjon du Capitole**, the tourist office (Tel: 61-11-02-22) provides maps and English-language pamphlets. You can also make a reservation here for the tours that the Association Toulousain d'Histoire d'Art conducts daily, in French; each covers a particular neighborhood or building.

ST-SERNIN

Your first excursion off the *place* should be down the rue du Taur, a narrow street that leaves the northwest corner of the square and ends several blocks later at the basilica of St-Sernin.

The "street of the Bull" is named for the animal to whose tail the Roman legions tied Saturnin, patron saint and first priest of Toulouse, in A.D. 250. The beast dragged Sernin, as the martyr is known in French, to his death through the streets of the encampment. The rope broke halfway down this narrow street, and the spare brick 13th-century **Eglise Notre-Dame-du-Taur** was built on the spot.

Sernin is entombed at the end of the rue du Taur, beneath the tower of the **Basilique St-Sernin**. For centuries this five-tiered octagonal tower drew pilgrims across the Toulousain plain on their way to Santiago de Compostela, 200 miles away on the other side of the Pyrénées in Spain. (Towers of similar design loom over many other churches in villages

and towns around Toulouse.) St-Sernin's 12th-century builders constructed an extraordinarily long central nave to accommodate these travellers, who worshiped, slept, and set
up temporary marketplaces beneath the high, barrel-vaulted
ceiling. Henry James wrote that this impressively austere
place—the largest Romanesque structure in France, consecrated by Pope Urban II in 1096—"alone was worth the
journey to Toulouse."

Local lore has it that the **Hôtel du Barry**, a handsome
house next to the basilica, now occupied by the Lycée St-
Sernin, was once the home of Madame du Barry. It is
unlikely that Louis XV's worldly mistress, a shopgirl turned
courtesan, ever set foot in Toulouse, though the house did
once belong to her brother-in-law. Closer to the truth is the
city's claim to have educated France's greatest essayist, Michel Eyquem de Montaigne. Though he pursued most of his
studies at the Collège de Guyenne in Bordeaux, for a while
Montaigne attended what is now the **Université de Toulouse**.
Count Raymond VII founded this great center of learning in
1299, and for years it was second in reputation only to the
Sorbonne. The unremarkable buildings of the present-day
institution stretch to the west of Place St-Sernin, and its
17,000 students crowd the cafés in almost every part of old
Toulouse.

The **Musée St-Raymond**, devoted to the city's Roman past,
occupies a 16th-century building and a garden cluttered
with Roman columns directly across Place St-Sernin from
the front of the basilica. Toulouse has few structures to bear
witness to its founders, who pitched a settlement on the
banks of the Garonne in the second century B.C., displacing
the Volques-Tectosages tribe, and maintained a relatively
peaceful presence until their withdrawal in the middle of
the fifth century A.D. But over the centuries the land beneath
the city has yielded a wealth of coins and other artifacts. In
one particularly fruitful dig in the early 1970s, archaeologists
dredging the bottom of the Garonne found 46,000 Roman
coins and other paraphernalia. Many of these are now in the
Musée St-Raymond's rather disorganized collections.

LES JACOBINS

The other great religious presence in Toulouse is the Eglise
des Jacobins, also with a distinctive tower that you can see
from St-Sernin. As with most places in Toulouse, it is not easy
for a first time visitor to find: Retrace your steps up rue du
Taur, cross the Place du Capitole to its southwest corner,
follow rue Gambetta several blocks to rue Lakanal, and turn
right (north).

The Dominicans put up this imposing fortresslike church and cloisters in the late 13th century. In the eyes of the Church, Toulouse was ripe for reform. Count Raymond VI was an ardent follower of the new religion, Catharism, that sparked the Albigensian heresy (this bloody religious war is discussed later in our coverage of Albi, the little city for which it is named). His troops defended Toulouse against the crusaders sent to subdue the rebellion, and Simon de Montfort, Rome's chief crusader against Catharism, was killed in Toulouse in 1218 when a woman hurled a stone at his head from the ramparts.

From the pulpit in Les Jacobins's stark, narrow nave (with an elaborately vaulted ceiling supported by only seven columns that run down the center of the vast expanse), the priests labored relentlessly and, apparently, effectively, to impose the will of Rome upon free-thinking Toulousains. Catholic Toulouse turned on its heretical neighbors repeatedly over the next several centuries—but never so violently as in the awful days of May 1562, when Catholics murdered a thousand Protestants and exiled the survivors.

Napoléon's troops commandeered Les Jacobins as a garrison and stabled their horses in the nave. Only in the past 20 years has Toulouse restored the vast church, housing here one of the city's most prized treasures: a gilded reliquary enshrining the head of Thomas Aquinas. For centuries the skull had been kept in full view of the faithful in a glass case in St-Sernin.

The Bookshop, just down the rue Lakanal from the church's entrance, at number 17, is one of the few places in Toulouse to find English-language literature. This is surprising in light of the fact that Toulouse counts the British among its most noted citizens of the past. Laurence Sterne, wracked with consumption, made a futile journey here for his health in 1767. He spent a year in a rented house, working on *Tristram Shandy.* Adam Smith came to Toulouse in 1764 with his pupil, the duke of Buccleuch. The Scot spent most of his time here holed up in a room writing *The Wealth of Nations.* Actually, Toulouse once belonged to the British, as the city was part of the much-fought-over duchy of Aquitaine. Kings Henry II and Richard the Lion-hearted both laid siege to the city in the 12th century, in their futile attempt to join Aquitaine permanently to Britain.

LA DAURADE

Toulousains like to come to this part of the city to walk along the old quais above the slow-moving Garonne. (A series of delightful murals in the Hôtel de Ville on the Place du Capitole depicts Toulousains' 19th-century ancestors enjoying a Sunday afternoon the same way.) The quarter takes its curious name from the Provençal word *duratta* (gold). Its origins lie behind the heavy doors of the melancholy **Basilique Notre-Dame-de-la-Daurade**, on the Place de la Daurade at the end of rue Gambetta. A few golden mosaics here are all that remains of the Roman temple upon whose ruins the church was built in the 18th century. If you follow quai L. Lombard north for a few blocks you come to the quiet little Place St-Pierre and, just off it a few steps up rue Valade, the Romanesque **Eglise St-Pierre des Cuisines**. The *place* affords a good view across the wide Garonne to the 17th-century **Hôtel-Dieu St-Jacques** on the opposite bank. This large, domed building once housed pilgrims en route to Santiago de Compostela.

Hôtel de Bernuy

The Hôtel de Bernuy, at the end of rue Lakanal at its intersection with rue Gambetta, is just one of the hundreds of mansions that wealthy Toulousains built in the 16th century. By then Toulouse was providing most of Europe with *pastel,* a blue dye. This commodity was much in demand as Europe's increasingly fashion-conscious aristocracy and a growing merchant class were enjoying the luxury of dressing in finery and lavishly furnishing their homes. These prosperous times for Toulouse would soon end when the Spanish began to import indigo from the Far East and the Americas. Until then, though, newly wealthy merchants outdid one another building handsome mansions on twisting lanes in this neighborhood, known as La Daurade, near the Garonne.

Bernuy was the most prosperous Toulousain merchant of his day. A story of rather doubtful authenticity has it that he alone raised the funds to ransom François I when the Spanish took the French king prisoner after the Battle of Pavia. (This is unlikely, as the king quickly handed his two young sons over to the Spanish in his stead. The boys were not released until the Treaty of Madrid was signed two years later.) The hotel now houses the Lycée Pierre de Fermat, and visitors can venture into the columned, ornamented courtyard.

HOTEL D'ASSEZAT

The finest house in Toulouse is the Hôtel d'Assézat, a few blocks from the river along the busy rue de Metz. Having made his fortune in *pastel,* Pierre d'Assézat commissioned

Nicolas Bachelier, a native son and the city's most prominent architect of the period, to build a mansion for him. Assézat never saw his house completed. A Protestant, he was driven from Toulouse in 1557 and died penniless and homeless several years later.

His mansion now houses Europe's oldest literary society. Until the 15th century Toulouse and the rest of the south spoke *langue d'oc,* while the north spoke *langue d'oïl* (both mean roughly "language of yes," and both are variations of the Roman term for "yes," *hoc ille*). *Oïl* has since evolved into *oui,* and the Langue d'oïl into modern French.

Langue d'oc was the lingua franca of the troubadours, poet-musicians whose aristocratic ranks included many of the counts of Toulouse. To preserve their dying language, in 1323 seven Toulousain troubadours founded the Compagnie du Gai Savoir (Company of Gay Learning), which has since become the Académie des Jeux Floraux (Academy of the Floral Games). Every year on May 3, Toulousains gather in the Hôtel d'Assézat's arcaded courtyard to watch the academy's *jeux,* spirited poetry readings. The *langue d'oc* thrives in Toulouse in another way, too: It is on the curriculum at the university.

The public is welcome to enter the mansion's courtyard (as well as those of most of Toulouse's old mansions) and to visit the few rooms of the Hôtel d'Assézat given over to the dusty collections of a museum of medical history.

LA DALBADE

Bachelier also built many of the mansions along rue de la Dalbade, a lovely street that begins at rue de Metz as rue des Couteliers and runs south, changing its name in front of the church of Notre-Dame de la Dalbade. The opulent **Hôtel de Clary**, at number 25, is better known as the "hôtel de pierre" (house of stone). Jean de Bagis had Bachelier cover his house with stone, an extravagance in Toulouse that signified his wealth and success. Here, too, you are welcome to venture into the courtyard. The half-timbered house at number 32 is the Hôtel des Chevaliers de Matte, built in 1665.

Return to the Place du Capitole by retracing your steps to rue de Metz and following that two blocks east to the Place Esquirol (the construction here is for Toulouse's new Métro; the first leg of this extensive system is scheduled to open sometime this year). From the Place Esquirol, the Place du Capitole is about five blocks away up **rue St-Rome**, a pedestrian precinct whose old houses, many of them half-timbered, have been converted into shops.

MUSEE DES AUGUSTINS

Before you turn up rue St-Rome it is well worth your while to walk two more blocks up rue de Metz to Toulouse's favorite museum, the Musée des Augustins.

By the late 19th century the Canal du Midi and new rail connections with Bordeaux promised a bright and prosperous future for Toulouse, and the city began to rebuild to accommodate it. The sacrifice of the city's architectural past was enormous, however: Down came the ramparts to make room for the rue de Metz and other Parisian-type boulevards; the cloisters of St-Sernin and Notre-Dame de la Daurade were destroyed to make room for new buildings. Columns, capitals, and many other victims of the onslaught were brought to this old convent, where they are still on display and, judging by the crowds that fill these rubble-filled galleries, much admired.

CATHEDRALE ST-ETIENNE

From the Place du Capitole, rue de la Pomme leads southeast to pretty, tree-filled Place St-Georges, and from there rue Boulbonne leads south to the **Cathédrale St-Etienne**. This precinct is known as the **Quartier des Antiquaires** for its many wood workshops, furniture restorers, and antiques dealers. There's little for sale here that's readily affordable or easily portable, but these quiet streets are among the most beautiful in Toulouse.

Beautiful is not the word for the hulking cathedral, which presents itself to the Place St-Etienne with a vast, blank wall broken by a single window. Built between the 11th and 17th centuries, St-Etienne is a mishmash of architectural styles, and the result is a church that is likable for its frank ugliness. Inside is an equally eclectic collection of tapestry, statuary, stained glass, and, in the Chapelle des Reliques, 40 gold caskets containing the remains of saints. Among them is King Louis IX, a.k.a. Saint Louis, who died of the plague during a crusade to Tunis in 1270.

SHOPPING IN TOULOUSE

Shopping in Toulouse is concentrated on the busy streets that surround the Place Wilson and is of the fairly ordinary Daniel Hechter and Rodier variety. Given the bounty of the farmland surrounding Toulouse, though, it is not too surprising that the most appealing items to be had are those in any number of food shops and in the city's four public food markets. **Germain**, near the *place* at 6, rue de Rémusat, sells foie gras, cassoulet, crystalized violet roots (a delicious sweet), and other regional specialties in tins and from behind a delicatessen-like counter. The **Marché des Carmes** is only a ten-minute walk south of Place Wilson along rue d'Alsace-Lorraine. The stalls in this marketplace are stocked with all the makings for a meal you can enjoy alfresco in the **Jardins des Plantes**. This trim, palm-shaded patch of greenery is just a few steps down rue Ozenne from the market.

There are few shops that warrant a trip through the shopping center, the Centre Commercial St-Georges, in the bowels of the **Place Occitane**, a shopping/office/apartment complex several blocks east of the Place du Capitole. Most notable among them is an enormous, much patronized branch of the Paris-based book and music store, **FNAC**. Unfortunately, there's only one small table of English-language books, but the range of French titles is exhaustive, as is the selection of CDs and tapes.

STAYING AND DINING IN TOULOUSE

The buildings that surround the Place du Capitole house some of Toulouse's smartest cafés. The **Brasserie le Bibert**, a sparkling, mirror-filled place, is popular with well-dressed patrons who come to eat oysters and drink Sauternes at its sidewalk tables. The ▶ **Grand Hôtel de l'Opéra**, practically next door, is an old post house named for the theater that occupies a wing of the Hôtel de Ville. The hotel houses two fussy restaurants, **Les Jardins de l'Opéra** (Tel: 61-23-07-78) and the **Grand Café de l'Opéra** (Tel: 61-21-37-03). Upstairs, the large guest rooms are nicely appointed with antiques and tasteful fabrics. The Opéra offers a 25 percent discount on Friday, Saturday, and Sunday nights, as do most of Toulouse's better hotels.

Au Chat Dingue, just around the corner from the basilica of Notre-Dame at 40 bis, rue Peyrollières, is an old-fashioned restaurant with an excellent and reasonably priced menu. It's best to make reservations for dinner; Tel: 61-21-23-11. The most popular restaurant along the river is the always-busy **Brasserie des Beaux-Arts**, just down from the basilica at 1, quai de la Daurade (at the corner of rue Metz; Tel: 61-21-12-12). Aproned waiters hurry to and from the canopied sidewalk, where they dish up a vast array of shellfish from ice-filled bins. Windowside tables afford a view of the Pont Neuf (completed in 1659 and the only bridge to withstand the floods of 1875) and, across the river, the Hôtel-Dieu. Upstairs from the brasserie, the ▶ **Hôtel des Beaux-Arts** has recently renovated its 12 reasonably priced rooms in starkly modern style and shades of gray but with an eye to comfort.

Restaurants and Hotels Around Place Wilson and Place St-Georges

Toulousains often end a day of shopping or an evening on the town at one of the many cafés on the Place Wilson, about three blocks east of Place du Capitole via rue Lafayette. The most popular are the busy **La Frégate**, at number 16, and **Restaurant La Bohème**, just off the *place* at 3, rue Lafayette. The best-known restaurant here, and, many would argue, the finest in Toulouse, is the family-run **Restaurant Vanel**, just to the east of Place Wilson at 22, rue Maurice-Fontvieille. The Vanels have been serving pigeon, pig's-feet stew, sweetbreads, and other hearty fare for two generations, and have earned two Michelin stars for their efforts. Reservations are essential; Tel: 61-21-51-82. Seafood and seasonal game, innovatively prepared, are the specialties at **Restaurant Edelweiss**, nearby at 19, rue Castellane. Again, it is wise to reserve; Tel: 61-62-34-70.

The food is remarkably good and the service attentive at the ▶ **Hôtel et le Restaurant d'Occitanie**, 5, rue Labéda. This is a hotel school that sends its graduates to some of the finest establishments in France. As part of their studies, students prepare and serve a five-course dinner at a prix fixe of about 120 francs. Reservations are a must; Tel: 61-21-15-92. Guest rooms are extravagantly large and nicely appointed, and even suites are moderately priced. The slick ▶ **Mercure-Altéa Wilson** next door is popular with business travellers.

The best spot for an easy meal in Toulouse is **Place St-Georges**. Any number of cafés and pizzerias spill out onto the cobblestone pavement of this tree-filled square, several blocks southeast of the Hôtel de Ville via rue de la Pomme and a few blocks due south of Place Wilson on rue St-Antoine.

GASCONY

The old lands of what was once called Gascony, which stretched from the Garonne to the Atlantic, from Bordeaux south to the Pyrénées, and now divided into modern *départements,* run right up to Toulouse's western suburbs. The region is known for its food (especially its rich dishes made from every organ and appendage of ducks, geese, and pigs), its Armagnacs, and for the Gascons themselves. It is no coincidence that the French verb *gasconner* means "to exaggerate." As Edmond Rostand wrote of one very famous, albeit fictional, Gascon, Cyrano de Bergerac, and his colleagues: "They are Gascony cadets, braggers of brags, layers of bets . . . barons who scorn mere baronets, their lines are long and their tempers brief." (Although not a Gascon, Cyrano de Bergerac was a 17th-century adventurer-dramatist on whom Rostand based his 1897 romance.) Gascons are also hospitable, patient with the foreigners who descend upon their peaceful countryside, and eager to lead you to the pleasures of their land.

Gascony is the most rural region of France, and with its fields of wheat and sunflowers, tidy vineyards, little patches of forests, and prosperous farms and small stone villages, it looks today as it must have for centuries past.

A drive into Gascony plunges you into rolling farmland, villages cropping up every few kilometers along the road. As most of the roads follow high ground along the crests of hills, you'll often be able to see for miles in all directions. One of the real joys of travelling here is to choose a distant village and set out for it. We lay out routes to some of Gascony's most appealing towns and villages, but by no means all of them. Don't hesitate to set off on your own and ramble aimlessly—wherever you travel in Gascony you'll never be more than an hour or so away from Auch, the biggest town of the region.

Many of the villages here are *bastides,* fortified towns that were built between the 12th and 15th centuries to protect the citizenry from the ravages of the ongoing wars between the British and the French for control of Aquitaine, which included these lands. The *bastides'* inhabitants worked in the fields by day and returned to the shelter of the stone walls by night.

The other architectural creation of these turbulent times were the *castelnaux,* fortified farms that housed hundreds of people who worked the surrounding lands. Their lord usually lived nearby in a fortified château. You will see many of these imposing little settlements, with their defense towers and rambling brick farm buildings clustered together.

The first town of any size you'll come to after leaving Toulouse on N 124 is **L'Isle Jourdain**, about 35 km (22 miles) west, and becoming a bit of a suburb. Built of the distinctive red-pink brick, L'Isle Jourdain is typical of many of the towns around Toulouse. And, as in most of the towns you will see in Gascony, at its center is a covered marketplace (actually, L'Isle Jourdain has two of these, one just a few blocks away from the other). **Gimont**, 19 km (12 miles) farther west, is another pleasant country town, with a covered marketplace that straddles its main street. Auch, our next destination, is just 24 km (15 miles) farther along on N 124, about 80 km (50 miles) west of Toulouse.

Auch

The first you will see of this small city is its late-15th- to 16th-century **Cathédrale Ste-Marie**, rising high above the green countryside and surrounded by steep lanes known as *pousterles*. Auch is a busy little place, the *préfecture* of the Gers, one of the modern *départements* that now includes parts of the historic lands of Gascony.

The newer town stretches along the tree-lined banks of the river Gers, and from here the **Escalier Monumental** climbs to the old Haute Ville (High Town). Halfway up this broad expanse of 370 steps is a statute of D'Artagnan, trusted friend of the three musketeers and the most famous Gascon of all. He was born near Auch at the Château de Castelmore in the village of Lupiac sometime around 1620, and was christened Charles de Batz. Upon joining the French royal guards he adopted the nobler sounding D'Artagnan, his mother's family name. By the time D'Artagnan was killed in 1673 in a battle of the Thirty Years' War he had been made a captain-lieutenant of the king's musketeers. His career was important and colorful enough to warrant a little biography, *Les Mémoires de Monsieur d'Artagnan;* it was this book that provided Alexandre Dumas with background when he wrote *Les Trois Mousquetaires* in the 1840s.

Your first encounter with a living Gascon may well be inside the cathedral. For a small fee you may enter the choir stalls—along with the stained glass, these are the most notable furnishings in this barnlike place—and obtain the service of a guide. Your lack of French will not deter your host from a loud and very animated description of the 1,500 intricately carved figures that crawl over and above the 132 stalls.

North from Auch

The Syndicat d'Initiative, in a half-timbered house directly in front of Auch's cathedral, will provide you with literature on the countryside and villages that surround Auch.

LECTOURE AND FLEURANCE

A particularly pleasurable trip takes you north from Auch toward Lectoure and the towns and villages surrounding it, all in the heart of Armagnac country. Leave Auch to the west along N 124. After 6 km (3½ miles) there will be a turnoff to the north on a little departmental road, D 930. (This and many other roads around Auch are marked "Circuit des Bastides.") Follow D 930 through golden fields for another

11 km (7 miles), where you will come to a turnoff, D 103, for the little *bastide* of **Lavardens**, a collection of buildings huddled together on a grassy hill in the shadow of an imposing rectangular château. It's possible to visit a few of the château's recently restored rooms, notable for their remarkable tiled floors, but it is the sight of this proud place from afar, watching over the gentle countryside, that you will long remember.

You can complete the 35 km (22 miles) to Lectoure on any number of roads. All are scenic, passing tiny villages, each with its covered market, and properous farms where barn-yards are filled with geese; the most direct route is D 148 to D 123.

Lectoure, situated along the crest of a hill, is an agreeable place with enough sights to fill a few pleasant hours: the 13th-century church; the Promenade du Bastion, from which you can see all the way to the Pyrénées in good weather; the museum in the Hôtel de Ville, where 34 Celtic sacrificial altars from the second century, remnants of the town's first inhabitants, are on display.

It's only 10 km (6 miles) south along N 21 through the wide valley of the Gers river to **Fleurance**. (Another 24 km/ 15 miles through this valley, which becomes lightly industri-alized, will bring you back to Auch.) Fleurance is now a sprawling town with modern outskirts, but its center retains all the character of its origins as a *bastide:* an arcaded central *place,* a timbered market hall, and, in the 14th- to 15th-century Eglise St-Laurent, several exquisite stained glass windows.

CONDOM AND ENVIRONS
Another 20 km (12 miles) west along D 7 brings you to Condom. (The route takes you near the pretty hamlet of **La Romieu**, with a 14th-century church and magnificent clois-ters.) The residents of this busy, appealing place will already have heard any caustic remarks you might make about the name of their town. None other than Vladimir Nabokov once wrote, "There's many a mile between Condom in Gascogne and Pussey in Savoie."

Condom has nothing do to with the manufacture of this seemingly eponymous product, but it is quite famous for the distilling, distribution, and consumption of Armagnac, the regional brandy that is aged in oak barrels. Condom, in fact, is widely considered to be the capital of Armagnac, but historically, and technically, that's not so. The Armagnac-growing territory is divided into three regions: Condom is the center of the Ténarèze region, Auch of the Haut Armagnac, and Eauze (see below) of the Bas Armagnac.

All Armagnac must remain in the barrel for at least a year before it may be sold. Armagnacs marked V.S.O.P. (Very Special Old Pale) have been aged at least four years; Hors d'Age, Napoléon, X.O., and Vieille Réserve have been aged for more than five years, though there are many subtleties within these broad classifications. Depending on the house distilling the Armagnac, many Hors d'Age stay in the barrel around ten years, and X.O.s (also called Très Vieux), about 25 years. Armagnac begins to deteriorate in wood after 30 years or so, though of course it ceases to age once it is bottled. In bars throughout Gascony it's not unusual to see "showpiece" Armagnacs bottled in the 19th century.

You can explore these mysteries in Condom's small **Musée de l'Armagnac**, next to the cathedral, or better yet, in the tasting rooms of the august house of **Ryst-Dupeyron**, on rue Dannou. A 70-centiliter bottle of an Hors d'Age here will cost you about $30, an X.O. about twice that.

Condom's most imposing structure is its Gothic **Cathédrale St-Pierre**. There are enormous, vaulted cloisters to one side, and in front, in the *place* of the same name, an early-Wednesday-morning market.

Around Condom

If you set out in almost any direction from Condom you will come upon other beautiful little *bastides*. After driving northwest from Condom on D 114 for 13 km (8 miles) you come to **Fourcès**, whose half-timbered houses form a circle around a tree-filled *place*. It is only 5 km (3 miles) or so west from Condom along D 15 to **Larressingle**, where ivy and roses creep up the walls of a ruined castle and church.

Séviac is a ruined Roman villa on the southern outskirts of **Montréal**, an old town atop a high hill 15 km (9 miles) west of Condom on D 15. Farmers unearthed mosaics at Séviac in 1868, but it wasn't until 1911 that a Docteur Lammilongue, a Gascon practicing medicine in Paris, returned home and began to excavate in earnest, unearthing baths, a heating system, oval-shaped rooms, and other remnants of the fourth-century Roman villa. None of the findings, though, is quite as compelling as the remains of a man and a woman buried in a single grave. Now the *amants des Séviac* lie in a glass-topped coffin for all to see. How they died, or who they were, remains a mystery.

NERAC

One of the most historically important towns in Gascony is Nérac, 23 km (14 miles) up the river Baïse from Condom on D 930. (You can also reach Nérac along a more scenic route by making a swing through Larressingle, Montréal, and Fourcès, and continuing north for 20 km/12 miles from Fourcès on D 5 and D 656. This way you could also stop at **Mézin**, 7 km/4 miles up D 5 from Fourcès, an enchanting *bastide* completely enclosed within its high walls.)

Nérac is today a sleepy backwater, but in the 16th century it was home to one of the most sophisticated courts in Europe, where Henri d'Albret and Marguerite d'Angoulême (a.k.a. Marguerite de Valois and Marguerite of Navarre) over-saw much of southern France. This forward-thinking couple invited artists, writers, and dissidents out of favor with the Paris court to their Renaissance château at Nérac. Marguerite dabbled in the arts herself. She is best known for the *Heptaméron,* her version of Boccaccio's *Decameron,* and her verses, *Les Marguerites de la Marguerite des Princesses.* Adding to Nérac's literary associations, Shakespeare is said to have set *Love's Labour's Lost* at the Nérac court.

Jeanne d'Albret, Henri and Marguerite's daughter, a fer-vent Protestant, gave birth in 1553 to a son who was to become Henri IV. Raised in Nérac and at the palace in Pau, Henri was one of France's most beloved monarchs and the embodiment of a Gascon. He was a practical man: Presented with the opportunity to assume the crown of France, he renounced Protestantism with the famous line, "Paris is worth a Mass." He was a man of the people: It was he who spoke that democratic line, "A chicken in every pot." And he was blessed with Gascon joie de vivre: An incorrigible wom-anizer, Henri often recounted the story of one of the few times his advances were spurned. When he asked a palace attendant the way to her bedchamber, she replied, "Through marriage, sir."

One wing of the palace still stands, and there are tours of a few sparse apartments. The spectacular palace gardens on the banks of the river are now a park, the **Promenade de la Garenne**; its shaded avenues follow the Baïse for about a mile. Much of the village that sprang up around the court, known as **Petit Nérac**, survives intact, just across the river from the palace.

MOISSAC

There is one reason to make the trip north from Auch or other parts of the region to Moissac, a city at the southernmost edge of the Dordogne region: to see its Eglise St-Pierre.

From Lectoure you can make a trip east through the glorious Gascon countryside on D 7 for 7 km (4 miles) to D 953, then north for 30 km (19 miles) to N 113, which leads 17 km (11 miles) east to Moissac. (At the intersection of D 7 and D 953 you might make a detour of 6 km/4 miles south on D 953 to the incredibly pretty *bastide* of **St-Clar**.) Approaching Moissac on N 113 you will pass the point where the Tarn river flows into the Garonne; to get a better view of this confluence, where the waters of both mighty rivers form a large, placid lake, make a slight detour north of N 113 to the hilltop village of **Boudou**. The vines on the hillsides yield the sweet, delicious Chasselas dessert grape. Most of the harvest goes to Paris, but you may be able to find the grapes in the local markets.

What you see of Moissac's **Eglise St-Pierre** are the remains of a much larger Benedictine abbey founded in the seventh century. By the middle of the 11th century the abbey was one of the most important centers of learning in Europe and a major stop on the route to Santiago de Compostela. St-Pierre was pillaged repeatedly during religious wars over the succeeding centuries, and all that remains is the clumsy, 15th-century church and two of the greatest achievements of the abbey's builders. One is the **tympanum**, from around 1100, one of the world's finest examples of Romanesque sculpture, an exotic depiction of the Apocalypse in which a swirl of biblical figures surround a long-bearded Christ. St-Pierre's other great treasure, the **cloisters**, were barely saved from 19th-century "progressives" who wanted to tear them down to make way for a railway. The Beaux-Arts commission in Paris stepped in to save this serene and beautiful place, surrounded by 76 columns carved with scenes from the Bible.

West from Auch

Another pleasant drive takes you west from Auch along D 943 through a string of picturesque villages toward the town of Plaisance (actually, you pick up D 943 6 km/4 miles out of Auch along N 124). After about 10 km (6 miles) D 943 comes to **Barran**, a handsome *bastide* surrounded by a moat. **L'Isle-de-Noé**, another 6 km farther west, is a quiet village built at the confluence of the rivers Baïse and Petite Baïse. **Montesquiou**, entered through a medieval gate, climbs a hillside 8 km (5 miles) beyond. After another 5 km (3 miles) the road passes down the single street and under the timbered marketplace of **Bassoues**, which is overpowered by the looming tower of its partially ruined château.

D 943 continues along high ground for another 14 km (8½ miles) before dropping into D 3, which in 3 km (2 miles) leads to **Plaisance**, a flat, hot town on the Arros river. To reach countryside that is more scenic, leave Plaisance on D 3 heading northwest and after 2½ km (1½ miles) turn northeast on D 20. Soon you will be surrounded by the Armagnac vineyards. To get a better sense of this pleasant, rolling terrain, after about 10 km (6 miles) turn east onto a small, one-lane farm road, D 157, following the signs for **Vic-Fézensac**, about 15 km (9 miles) from the turnoff. There's not much to see in Vic—except in August, when the town hosts some of France's lustiest bullfights—but the town is pleasant and prosperous, with a good share of half-timbered houses and an arcaded *place* where you should stop for a drink on the terrace of the old-fashioned **Hôtel d'Artagnan**.

If you leave town on D 626, it's about 24 km (15 miles) to **Eauze**, a busy market town and center of the Bas Armagnac appellation. (You can taste the local product in any of the shops around the central Place Armagnac.) Eauze was one of Rome's most important colonies in Gaul, and was known as Elusa. The town shows little evidence of this heritage, but its 15th-century Eglise St-Luperc is built partially of Roman brick, and there are plans afoot to build a museum to display at least part of a local find, a stash of 28,000 coins minted between A.D. 177 and 268.

From Eauze it's only 29 km (18 miles) northeast to Condom on D 931 and a little less than half that to Montréal on D 29.

STAYING AND DINING IN GASCONY

André Daguin, of the ► **Hôtel de France in Auch**, is a larger-than-life Gascon who makes it his business to do justice to foie gras, *confit* (duck, goose, or pork cooked and preserved in its own fat), and other bounty of the region's barnyards. Daguin walks from table to table reassuring his guests from other parts of the world that Gascons eat a steady diet of this cholesterol-rich fare and live to a ripe old age—a boast, incidentally, that French scientists have recently proven to be true, possibly because Gascons wash their meals down with allegedly healthful quantities of sturdy red wines like those in Daguin's cellar. A dinner in the grand, high-ceilinged dining room should include foie gras prepared several ways—the foie gras in lemon and the foie gras with asparagus are sensational—and Daguin's grilled skinless duck breast, a simple but supremely successful preparation. Daguin's cookbook, *Foie Gras, Magret and Other Great Foods from Gascony,* is for sale, along with a good selection of foie gras and regional wines, in a shop in the *caves* of the hotel.

The guest rooms upstairs are flamboyantly done up with upholstered walls and sunken tubs. More modest accommodations are to be had at the ▶ **Relais de Gascogne**, a simple but serviceable hotel at the foot of the Haute Ville on the avenue de la Marne.

Auch's "second" restaurant is **Claude Laffitte**, in an old house at 38, rue Dessoles. (This narrow shopping street, closed to traffic, leads downhill from the Place de la Libération.) As almost anywhere else in this region, your meal here will begin with a *floc de Gascogne* (Armagnac and fresh grape juice) or a *pousse Rapière* (an orange liqueur mixed with Armagnac). These potent apéritifs should sufficiently lessen your inhibitions about eating the duck hearts and stuffed goose neck to follow. Reserve; Tel: 62-05-04-18.

In Lectoure, the ▶ **Hôtel de Bastard**, named for the Toulouse family whose country manor this once was, is an excellent place from which to explore the area. Rooms are small but appealing, and meals—in which the heavy staples of the region appear in some refreshingly light creations, such as a salad of fresh mesclun with strips of duck breast— are served in the lovely salons or on a breezy terrace overlooking the countryside.

Condom's **La Table des Cordeliers** is a true temple of gastronomy, occupying a 14th-century chapel at the edge of the old town on rue des Cordeliers. (As this book went to press the restaurant was in the process of changing chefs, the old one departed and the new one not yet chosen. Tel: 62-68-28-36.) The adjoining ▶ **Logis des Cordeliers** has 21 modern rooms facing a garden and swimming pool. At the **Moulin de Petit Gascon**, about a kilometer (less than a mile) east of town on the Route d'Eauze, you can dine pleasantly alfresco on the banks of the languid river Baïse.

The recently opened ▶ **Hôtel des Trois Lys** occupies a stone mansion on Condom's shopping street, rue Gambetta. The ten rooms here are large and attractively fitted out with bold fabrics, and the swimming pool and lovely garden make this an appealing place to plant yourself for a few days.

There's really only one reason to stop in **Plaisance**, and that is for a meal in the dark-paneled dining room of ▶ **La Ripa Alta**. Chef Maurice Coscuella serves some of Gascony's best stick-to-the-ribs basics: *confit* in white beans, lamb sweetbreads, goose hearts, all accompanied by a wonderful selection of wines and followed by the house Armagnac. The guest rooms upstairs are adequate but a bit shy of character.

The talented Madame Marie-Claude Gracia oversees the

kitchen at ▶ **La Belle Gasconne**, in the tiny village of **Poudenas**, about 15 km (9 miles) northwest of Condom via D 110, D 117, and D 656. Using only the freshest ingredients, Madame Gracia serves true Gascon farm fare, including a hearty duck stew, and when she does get fancy, it's with such marvelous results as her pasta with foie gras and wild mushrooms. The Belle Gascon accommodates overnight guests in six pleasant rooms in an annex across the road.

A trip of about 70 km (43 miles) from Auch across the Gascon countryside on D 943, D 935, and D 2 brings you to the 19th-century spa town of **Eugénie-les-Bains** and one of France's most pleasant country retreats, ▶ **Les Prés d'Eugénie et le Couvent des Herbes**. Michel and Christine Guérard have stunningly restored a 19th-century manor and an old convent, both surrounded by lovely gardens. In the hotel kitchen, the freshest chicken, duck, and seafood are often grilled over an open fire, then beautifully seasoned with homegrown herbs. Monsieur Guérard serves a special 400-calorie *cuisine minceur* menu, popular with curists who take the waters at the hotel spa—but why fuss over calories in the presence of such exquisite cooking?

EAST FROM TOULOUSE

If you request a *vin du pays* in Toulouse, you will probably be served a hearty red or sharp white from a Gaillac vineyard. There are at least 75 producers in the sun-drenched Gaillac region, which stretches from Toulouse northeast toward Albi.

Albi

Route N 88 cuts right through the vineyards, and will deliver you to Albi, only 76 km (47 miles) from Toulouse, in a little more than an hour.

The very name of this pretty little city is associated with the bloodiest religious revolt in Western history, the Albigensian Heresy. The followers of this movement rejected the Church of Rome in favor of Catharism. Between the mid-12th and mid-13th centuries the religion engulfed most of the southwest and spread as far north as England. Cathari believed in two gods: The good god ruled the spiritual world and the evil god ruled the physical world. A good Cathar (known as a *parfait,* "a perfect one") was celibate, ate no food that resulted from sexual union, and did not believe in the Mass, marriage, the organized church, any form of government, and certainly not in the payment of tithes or taxes.

It is easy to understand how the Cathari rankled both the Church in Rome and the Crown in Paris. Pope Innocent III dispatched Domingo de Gúzman to the region. This Span-iard, eventually canonized as Saint Dominic, and his follow-ers (the forebears of the Dominican order) wandered the Toulousain Midi preaching the will of Rome. But it was sheer physical might, wielded by military commander Simon de Montfort, that finally subdued the Cathari. Lords from the north could reap all the benefits of a crusade—plunder, land, and pardon for their sins—without travelling to far-off lands. The bloodshed these crusaders wrought was horrible: Rare is the town in the southwest that does not have a tale of massacre in its past.

Past mayhem aside, it would be hard to find a place better than Albi to spend a few days relaxing. You can wander here at leisure through the magnificent gardens behind the Palais de la Berbie, built along the old ramparts above the Tarn river; in the lovely little cloisters of the **Eglise St-Salvy**; and along crooked streets that are closed to all but pedestrian traffic.

CATHEDRALE STE-CECILE

It was in the best interest of the archbishops of Albi to build a church and residence where they would be safe from their heretical parishioners and that would also intimidate the see into submission. This explains why the Cathédrale Ste-Cécile, begun in 1282 and completed over the next two centuries, has 29 defense towers and battlement walls. The cathedral rises almost directly from the southern banks of the Tarn river, and it is here that most travellers begin a tour of Albi.

One end of the cathedral's nave is covered with an 18th-century fresco of the Last Judgment, a very good one that has been curiously ruined. In subsequent renovations to the church a large opening was cut through the center of the fresco to afford entrance to a chapel; the upper portion has been cut away to accommodate the organ's pipes. All that remain are hundreds of screaming, writhing, doomed fig-ures, with no sign of Christ to provide redemption. The treasure here is the massive **choir**, which is surrounded by a carved limestone screen. As the story goes, 15th-century Albigensians were shocked when these carvings and those above the choir stalls were unveiled: The cherubs and devils bore a striking resemblance to the city's more prominent citizens.

MUSEE TOULOUSE-LAUTREC

Henri de Toulouse-Lautrec was born into an aristocratic Albigensian family in 1864. It has been said that the warm tones of the brick, the profusion of wisteria, and the cobalt blue of the Midi sky greatly influenced the painter's use of color.

An enormous collection of Toulouse-Lautrec's work now hangs in the Musée Toulouse-Lautrec, in the **Palais de la Berbie**, the former archbishop's palace next to the cathedral. The rambling brick house where the painter was born, the **Hôtel du Brosc**, is nearby, at 14, rue Toulouse-Lautrec. His parents, the comte et comtesse de Toulouse-Lautrec, were first cousins. They were prosperous and civilized, and Henri enjoyed a privileged and, until he was crippled in a fall when he was 14, very active childhood. He left Albi for Paris to paint when he was barely 20, and there led a life so debauched that he was dead at 36. A branch of the family still lives in the house, and opens parts of it to the public.

Albi's other famous son is the great Socialist reformer Jean Jaurès, who was assassinated in 1914. Born in nearby Castres, he taught in Albi for many years and created one of France's first worker-owned factories here, the Verrerie Ouvrière (Workers' Glassworks).

Near Albi

CORDES

From Albi you will want to continue to Cordes, just 25 km (16 miles) northwest on D 600. Cordes is built atop a very high hill, and as you approach it from the valley below it is not unusual to see the city floating above the clouds. This all but inaccessible location afforded the Cathari who founded Cordes in 1222 an almost impregnable defense. Indeed, it is said that troops sent to rout the heretics never even attempted to scale the summit. Legend also has it that three inquisitors who managed to infiltrate Cordes were thrown down its 350-foot-deep well, at the very top of the city in the **Place de la Halle**.

Today Cordes is besieged by tourists. Fortunately, most are day-trippers who pour through the gates around noon and leave well before sunset. So if you overnight here, as you should, you will have many quiet hours in which to climb up and down stepped streets that afford dizzying views, sip a beer at a café table in the covered marketplace, or count the mythological creatures that crawl across the façade of the 14th-century **Maison du Grand Veneur** (Master

Huntsman's House) and Cordes's other mansions of the same period. Admittedly, there are no end of boutiques and *brocante* (second hand) shops to service the influx of tourists, but the shops support a number of craftspeople and artists who have established studios in Cordes since World War II, carefully restoring the once-neglected town to its medieval splendor.

Note that if you take the train from Toulouse to Cordes, you will disembark in the countryside and find yourself, surrounded by geese, a good 4 km (2½ miles) from town. Several local car services post their numbers at the little station; alternatively, the walk, with Cordes floating in the distance, is pleasant. During the summer months an open-air *petit train* takes visitors from Cordes's Ville Basse to the Haute Ville above.

Around Cordes

If you are travelling by car, you can venture into the countryside that looks so inviting from on high in Cordes. Much of the land around here is given over to the pretty, hardwood **Forêt de Grésigne**. One circular route, well under a hundred miles all told, takes you west from Cordes through the forest and across upland meadows to a string of wonderful *bastides*. Leaving Cordes on D 600 and driving northwest for 17 km (11 miles), then west on D 115 for 12 km (7½ miles), you come to **St-Antonin-Noble-Val**, enclosed within its medieval walls on the banks of the Aveyron river. The town hall, Maison Romaine, was built in 1125 and is the oldest civic building in France. All of **Penne**, about 16 km (10 miles) south along the river gorge via D 115, seems to cling precariously to a sheer cliff. The impossibly steep streets climb toward a castle perched at the summit, a sight, as the British writer Freda White once observed, "so improbable you do not believe it even as you look at it."

Bruniquel, another 6 km (4 miles) south along the Aveyron, is situated less dramatically but is no less beautiful, with half-timbered houses and a château sitting high above the river. Here you keep to the river and, on D 964, drive south about 11 km (7 miles) to **Puycelci**, a pretty, high hill town, and from there continue another 10 km (6 miles) or so on D 964 south then east to **Castelnau-de-Montmiral**, which has an incredibly beautiful town square surrounded by half-timbered houses. Follow D 964 east and then turn north on D 115A to D 922, which brings you back to Cordes (the distance from Castelnau is about 25 km/16 miles). Services, restaurants included, are difficult to find in these remote towns, so if you set out for an excursion, plan to be back at your hotel before the dining room closes.

Another scenic outing from Cordes takes you 29 km (18 miles) north on D 922 and D 239 through rolling farmland to **Najac**. The countryside around this picturesque village is intriguing, a series of dramatic hillsides that climb out of the deep gorge of the Aveyron river. While D 922 follows high ground, the slower D 47 sticks closer to the winding river. This little stone town climbs the spine of a hill beneath its *fortresse royale*, built by the brother of Saint Louis in 1253. The best way to see the village is to leave your car in the pretty Place des Arcades, lined with slate-roofed cottages that seem to belong in the Cotswolds. From there, simply follow the main street up to the castle and, just beyond it on a ledge high above the Aveyron, its Gothic church.

STAYING AND DINING IN AND AROUND ALBI AND CORDES

There are two especially nice hotels in Albi, both owned and run by the same family. ▶ **La Réserve** (open May to October only), with a swimming pool and tennis courts, is just beyond the northern outskirts of the city in a large garden on the banks of the Tarn. Rooms in this Relais & Châteaux property are large and tastefully decorated, with such amenities as electronically controlled draperies and elegant marble baths. The ▶ **Hostellerie du Grand St-Antoine** is in town, off the animated Place Jean-Jaurès. Rooms here are not as luxurious as those at La Réserve, but they are very comfortable and many overlook a flower-filled garden. The hotel also has a good restaurant, where it is best to reserve a table; Tel: 63-54-04-04. The ▶ **Hôtel Pujol et Restaurant Modern' Pujol**, a little farther out on avenue Colonel-Teyssier, is another good place to dine, and its guest rooms are modern and well appointed; Tel: 63-54-02-92.

It is well worth the trip to **Cordes** to dine and then retire upstairs at the ▶ **Hôtel-Restaurant le Grand Ecuyer** (formerly the residence of the Master Horseman). Rooms are appointed with antiques and replicas and many have bird's-eye views over the tidy farms far below the town. Dinner in the fussily appointed dining rooms is a performance orchestrated by chef Yves Thuriès, who makes an appearance toward the end of every meal and also makes sure there's a copy of the cooking magazine he circulates throughout France in every room. His latest venture in Cordes is the **Musée du Sucre**, just up the street from the hotel, two floors of sea monsters, medieval cities, and other fantastic creations fashioned out of sugar.

Thuriès also runs the ► **Hostellerie du Vieux Cordes**, a homey, comfortable hotel in a medieval mansion with many rooms that enjoy views across the valley below. Unlike that of the Grand Ecuyer, its restaurant, under chef Bernard Laffont, has not earned a Michelin star, but that should not keep you from enjoying a meal in its handsome dining room or alfresco on its wisteria-shaded terrace.

SOUTH INTO THE PYRENEES
Foix

The great marvel of Foix, in the foothills of the Pyrénées only 80 km (50 miles) south of Toulouse along N 20, is its location, hedged in on one side by the Ariège river, on another by the Arget, and on yet another by a craggy hillock topped by the legendary **Château de Foix**.

For centuries the counts of Foix controlled the trade routes over the Pyrénées from their virtually unassailable château, which Bernard Roger, Vicomte de Carcassonne, began in 1012. His successors added towers and halls over the years, and the spectacular castle took its present form with the completion of its distinctive round tower in the 15th century. From behind the thick walls of the château the counts were also able to repel the advances of Simon de Montfort, sent by Rome to quell the town's heretical leanings toward Catharism. The château now houses a museum, its eclectic contents including a rather dull collection of fossils and *pyrénéen* folk costumes.

Wherever you are in Foix, the château looms high above you. It is at its best from the west, as you approach Foix on D 17 from the direction of St-Girons. In the early evening the castle is illuminated by the rays of the setting sun, a stunning sight.

The largest structure on the narrow lanes below the château is the **Eglise St-Volusien**, steeped in a remarkable local legend. Volusien was a sixth-century bishop of Tours who was killed by the Visigoths. Foix requested the body and it was brought here on an ox-drawn cart. When the cortège came to the Ariège, the waters parted, or so the story goes. Roger Bernard erected the church in the 15th century to provide a suitable resting place for the popular saint's remains.

Around Foix

From Foix the busy N 20 follows the pretty gorge of the Ariège southeast into the first of the high Pyrénées peaks. It is only 40 km (25 miles) to the pleasant mountain spa of Ax-les-Thermes (for which see below), and from there only 60 km (37 miles) on to Andorra. It would be a shame, though, to speed up the highway and miss the offerings of this mountainous countryside.

A much-visited attraction near Foix is **Labouiche**, said to be the longest underground river in the world. Visitors descend 250 feet to the river at a point near the village of Vernajoul, about 3 km (2 miles) northwest of Foix on D 1. There they board boats and sail a mile-and-a-half along this eerie waterway.

TARASCON AND THE GROTTE DE NIAUX

Tarascon, not to be confused with the city of the same name on the banks of the Rhône in Provence, is 16 km (10 miles) down N 20 from Foix. Two towers come into view as you approach this small industrial town, an important center for metallurgical works, from the north. The most prominent belongs to the medieval **castle**, on a hillock above the river in the center of town; the other is the 15th-century belfry of the **Eglise St-Michel**. The real attractions here, though, are below ground.

From Tarascon, D 8 leads southwest for 4 km (2½ miles) to Niaux and, in the depths of a mountain above the village, the **Grotte de Niaux**. Here, 10,500 years before Christ, prehistoric man painted bison, horses, and other animals. Most of the images are in the vast **Salon Noir**, a half-mile down a narrow passage. Unlike Lascaux in the Dordogne, the only comparable prehistoric caves in Europe, Niaux can be visited, though with strict restraints to preserve the paintings. The French government allows only 11 groups of 20 people each to enter the cave a day, and each visit must be spaced by 45 minutes. The caves are open daily from 8:30 to 11:30 A.M. and from 1:30 to 5:15 P.M. from July through September, and from 11:15 A.M. to 4:30 P.M. daily from October through June. The entrance fee is 40 francs. Reservations are essential; Tel: 61-05-88-37.

Another cave in the same vicinity, the **Grotte de Lombrives** (off the N 20 just south of the turnoff for the Grotte de Niaux) is the largest in Europe, and also of historical interest. In the 13th century several hundred Cathari took refuge here. Royal troops, discovering their whereabouts, sealed the mouth of the cave, and the heretics starved to death.

ROUTE DES CORNICHES

A slower, even more scenic route down the valley of the Ariège takes you along narrow, winding D 20, aptly called the Route des Corniches because it clings to the mountainside a couple of hundred feet above the valley floor. You can pick up D 20 just south of Foix in the village of Bompas, but to do so would mean missing that incredible sight of the castle tower rising above Tarascon and the Grotte de Niaux. It's better to stay on N 20 as far as Les Cabannes, about 10 km (6 miles) south of Tarascon. From there you can follow D 120 about 5 km (3 miles) up to the Route des Corniches.

The route winds through upland meadows and thick forests and every few kilometers comes to quiet villages where livestock far outnumber the human inhabitants. Trails head off the route in several places, leading to the higher reaches of the slopes of 7,500-foot Montagne de Tabe.

Near Axiat the scenery becomes ugly as the road skirts one of the world's largest quarries, where every year workers extract six million pounds of talc, 8 percent of the world's total. Axiat itself, though, is an appealing little place, with a fine Romanesque church. At Bestiac leave the Route des Corniches and follow D 2 about 5 km (3 miles) to **Unac**, a pleasing little village of steep streets surrounding another beautiful Romanesque church.

From Unac you can descend about a kilometer to N 20 and continue to Ax-les-Thermes, about 8 km (5 miles) south, or you can regain the Route des Corniches and wind down to Ax through the Col de Chioula, a trip of about 20 km (12 miles).

AX-LES-THERMES

Ax-les-Thermes, in the shadow of craggy Pyrénées peaks, is a cheerful town with 80 natural hot springs. The French come here to soak their rheumatic joints in the sulphurous waters and to breathe the clean mountain air. You can test the waters in the large public tub right in the middle of the town square, the Place du Breilh. Regulars bring a newspaper and a pastry, take off their shoes and socks, and soak their feet here for the better part of the morning.

The Office de Tourisme Haute-Ariège, on avenue Delcassé in the center of town, can provide you with reports of ski conditions at **Ax Bonascre**, a resort with 19 runs just 5 km (3 miles) south.

EAST OF THE ARIEGE

The valley of the Ariège is not only the route over the mountains to Spain; from it you can also journey east and west into the Pyrénées. (We travel west from the valley in our chapter The Pyrénées and Pays Basque.) If you travel through the eastern peaks you will drop into the vineyard-clad plains of Languedoc-Roussillon (see the Languedoc-Roussillon chapter). Even if you don't wish to travel all the way to the coast, you may want to make an excursion east to see some magnificent countryside and get your fill of Cathar castles.

You can begin the trip on D 613 through forested mountainsides and bucolic, Alpine-looking valleys to **Belcaire**, 25 km (16 miles) northeast of Ax-les-Thermes. The simple **Hôtel du Bayle** (Tel: 68-20-31-05) here serves a hearty lunch and dinner. From Belcaire your descent begins in earnest. After about 30 km (19 miles) D 613 comes to the rather dull little town of Quillan.

Cathar Strongholds

The rocky, rugged countryside around Quillan, part forested and part covered with low scrub, once provided refuge to thousands of Cathars, and you can see several of their hilltop strongholds here.

From Quillan the route forks: You can take D 118 north through the vineyards to Carcassonne or D 117 east through Corbières wine country toward Perpignan. (We explore both these regions later in this chapter.) If you follow D 117 west (back toward Foix), after 27 km (17 miles) you will come to D 5, which connects to D 549 to bring you, after another 13 km (8 miles) or so, to one of the most magnificent Cathar castles of all, **Montségur**.

In 1242 a party of 60 Cathari set out from Montségur for the town of Avignonet, near Carcassonne, where they killed the papal tribunal responsible for burning their fellow believers at the stake. Rome retaliated: A year later 6,000 soldiers arrived at the foot of the mountain and laid siege. Montségur, with its vast holding tanks for water and large reserves of food, lasted through a summer and a winter. But, come spring, the soldiers hired Gascon mercenaries to show them secret paths up the cliffside. The attackers surrounded the citadel with catapults. Montségur surrendered, and its 215 inhabitants were burned at the stake. Visitors can climb up to the ruined stronghold, a trip of at least an hour on precipitous paths.

If you want to return to Foix from Montségur, continue north on D 9, then west on D 117, for a journey of about 30

km (19 miles). En route you will pass another remote
stronghold of the sect, **Roquefixade**.

South from Quillan, D 117 follows the Aude river beneath
the high cliffs of a spectacular gorge, the **Défilé de Pierre-
Lys**, then opens into the *garrigue,* a wild, rocky landscape
punctuated by green patches of vineyards. About 6 km (4
miles) beyond the gorge you'll see the remote Cathar castle
of **Puilaurens** on a hilltop south of the road on D 22. Another
25 km (16 miles) east there's a turnoff at the wine village of
Maury (center of the eponymous appellation) onto D 19,
which winds north through scrub-covered hills and over the
1,500-foot-high Grau de Maury for about 5 km (3 miles) to
the ruined Cathar **Château de Quéribus**. From there D 123
and D 14 lead west in another 12 km (7½ miles) to the even
more impressive **Château de Peyrepertuse**, reached by a
strenuous 30-minute hike up a steep path. It's well worth the
climb—not only for the closeup look at the evocative ruins,
but for the extensive views over this beautiful countryside.

STAYING AND DINING
IN AND AROUND FOIX

Many visitors to **Foix** remain loyal to the dowdy ▶ **Hostellerie Barbacane**, probably because the old hotel affords
such dramatic views of the château. The ▶ **Hôtel Audoye-
Lons**, among the half-timbered houses of the *vieille ville,* is
much more appealing. Its big, old-fashioned guest rooms
and glass-roofed dining room are directly over the Ariège.

You'll find some of the best bed-and-board in the area in
Unac, at ▶ **L'Oustal**. The glass-enclosed dining room hangs
over the hillside; you can dine well here on such specialties
as spit-roasted pigeon and rabbit snared that morning, then
retire upstairs to a cozy room under the eaves.

Among the many hotels in **Ax-les-Thermes**, a good choice
is the ▶ **Hôtel-Restaurant La Lauzeraie**, reached by its own
footbridge across the Ariège. The hotel is relatively new and
a little short on character, but in compensation you can fall
asleep to the wonderful sound of the river rushing by just
beneath your window.

In the village beneath the Cathar castle at **Montségur**, a
meal and bed can be had at the simple but hospitable
▶ **Hôtel Costes**.

SOUTH TO CARCASSONNE

The easiest way to reach the famous walled city of Carcassonne from Toulouse is to breeze down A 61 (the

Autoroute des Deux-Mers); if you drive like the French it should take you well under an hour to make the trip of 85 km (53 miles). If you're in the mood for a leisurely gambol, you might set off across the Toulousain plain on D 2 through red-brick towns and fields of wheat. One of the most appealing of these towns is hilltop **St-Félix-Lauragais**, about 40 km (25 miles) beyond the Toulousain suburbs and a good place to stop for a glass of wine or lunch on the terrace of the **Café le Cocaigne**, facing the covered marketplace. The road continues for about another 10 km (6 miles) as D 622 to **Revel**, a 14th-century *bastide* that has long since expanded far beyond its arcaded *place*.

The Montagne Noire

The fastest route from here to Carcassonne is on D 624 south to Castelnaudary, and from there east on N 113, a trip of about 50 km (31 miles). But you may want to spend a little more time in this quiet countryside on the edge of the Montagne Noire, a vast forested massif that stretches south and east from Revel. The Syndicat d'Initiative in Revel can load you up with maps and brochures on some of the towns in the midst of the forests.

It's about 5 km (3 miles) from Revel east to **Sorèze**, a pretty village built around two abbeys. One, in ruin, was founded by Pépin le Bref in 758; the other is an abandoned 17th-century Benedictine monastery that dominates the village with an eerie, romantic presence. From D 151, just west of Sorèze, D 44 climbs to high ground and, to the southeast on D 629, past a lake at les Cammazes and through the forest for about 20 km (12 miles) to **Saissac**. This medieval village tumbles down a steep hillside beneath the gloomy ruins of its 14th-century château.

The narrow D 4 takes you north from town for about 5 km (3 miles) through a pine forest to another mountain lake, an appealing side trip on a hot summer day. You can also drop south from Saissac on D 629 to N 113 to Carcassonne. After about 8 km (5 miles) you'll come to **Montolieu**, a small village with big ambitions. Montolieu has designated itself the "Book Town of Southern Europe" and is attempting to attract dealers, binders, and engravers to create a Mediterranean version of England's Hay-on-Wye. There's not yet much evidence the plan is working, but it's an interesting notion.

A drive west from Saissac on D 103 brings you to Castelnaudary in about 22 km (14 miles), with a stop on the way at **St-Papoul**, a serenely beautiful 14th-century Benedictine abbey, and into Castelnaudary.

CASTELNAUDARY

The French Foreign Legion maintains a garrison here, and the legionnaires, walking through the old quarter in their kepis, lend an exotic air to this hot and not particularly attractive backwater. The Canal du Midi opens into a large basin here as well, and bargers and pleasure-boaters stop for provisions, further giving the landlocked town the air of a Mediterranean port.

The real reason to visit Castelnaudary is to eat, because this is the home of cassoulet. (Toulousains claim that they invented cassoulet, which is made in a squat clay pot called a *cassolo,* but most experts give the credit to Castelnaudary.) This blend of beans, pork fat, preserved meats, and sausage is not for the delicate appetite. But when prepared well it is astonishingly tasty, all the more so when accompanied by a light regional wine, such as a Corbières. When Chauriens, as locals are called, wish to dine out on cassoulet, they often go to the ▶ **Grand Hôtel Fourcade**, at 14, rue des Carmes. There are 14 comfortable guest rooms upstairs as well.

From Castelnaudary, Blue Line Midi (whose motto is "Green France in a Blue Boat") makes tours along the Canal du Midi. Contact: Blue Line, 11400 Castelnaudary; Tel: 68-23-17-51.

Carcassonne

Carcassonne, 40 km (25 miles) east of Castelnaudary, is actually two cities separated by the river Aude: the newer Ville Basse (Lower City), a busy agricultural center that is of little interest to travellers, and the Cité, the medieval stronghold surrounded by double walls that stretch for more than a mile.

The most dramatic views of the Cité are those from afar, the best being the one from the rest stop about a mile due east of the Cité, between the exits for Carcassonne Nord and Carcassonne Sud on the Autoroute des Deux-Mers (it is clearly marked as an overlook). As picture-perfect as the Cité looks, much of it has been restored, and much of that clumsily, by the 19th-century architect Viollet-le-Duc. Through political connections he is responsible for so many "restorations" across France that a phrase has actually come into the French language to sit forever in judgment of his efforts: *"Violé par Viollet"* ("raped by Viollet").

THE WALLS OF LA CITE

The original fortress was built by the Romans during the third and fourth centuries. Geographic considerations—the river Aude, the hilltop view, the site's location between Toulouse and the Mediterranean—made Carcassonne an important military garrison. Sections of the original Roman wall may still be seen to the left of Pont Levis (the Roman portion comprises the sections in which the stones are packed more tightly than they are in the others), and several Gallo-Roman relics are on display at the **Musée Lapidaire** in the Château Comtal.

The Visigoths swept into the region in the fifth century and dealt a death blow to Roman control. Carcassonne then became a Visigoth stronghold, and it wasn't until the Arab invasions in the eighth century that the Visigoths forfeited their control. It took nearly a hundred years and all the soldiers of Charlemagne to dislodge the Moors from Carcassonne and the rest of the Narbonne region.

Dame Carcas

Legend has it that Carcassonne owes its name to a Moorish woman, Dame Carcas. In the ninth century the Moors invaded and occupied the fortress. Responding to the invasion, Charlemagne laid siege to the city and captured the Moorish king Balaak. When the Moor refused to convert to Christianity, the French killed him.

Balaak's wife, Dame Carcas, resolutely continued to hold the fortress and kept the Christians outside the walls. The siege lasted five years, during which time nearly all of the Dame's soldiers died of hunger and thirst. Even so, to trick Charlemagne into believing that she had provisions to burn, Carcas showered her last five gallons of water over the walls. She then gathered the last of the remaining wheat and fed it to the last sow, which she also heaved over the walls. The poor beast burst open upon hitting the ground, revealing all of the wheat. Convinced he was defeated, Charlemagne about-faced his army and began a retreat. Wanting an audience with the emperor, Carcas began to sound the bells of the fortress. "Carcas is ringing," the soldiers shouted, or in French, *"Carcas sonne,"* which is how the town got its name.

Carcas met with the emperor and was converted to Christianity. Charlemagne was so taken by the woman's courage, it is said, that he asked her to stay and be the master of the city. He wed her to one of his noblemen, Trencavel, which was then the custom when a great lord wanted to keep a woman for himself without marrying her. Carcas and Trencavel founded the dynasty of the viscounts of Carcassonne.

The Cathar Crusades

By 1209 Carcassonne was a well-protected, prosperous city visited by troubadours and enlivened by tournaments, hunts, and festivals. Most of the festive activities took place in the space between the two encircling walls—the *lices*.

Then began the crusade against the Cathars. Although Raymond-Roger de Trencavel, Carcassonne's lord at the time, was a Catholic, he was a strong believer in protecting the right to worship freely—an opinion that was not shared by many of his fellow lords. Called to Montpellier to an assembly of knights who asked him to chase all heretics from his city, Trencavel replied: "I offer a city, a roof, a shelter, a loaf of bread, and my sword to all those banned who will soon wander throughout Provence, without a city, or a roof, or asylum, or bread." Trencavel's speech led to his downfall. Carcassonne was attacked by 20,000 men; Trencavel was captured, imprisoned, and soon died in one of the towers of his own fortress.

In the 13th century the very Catholic king of France, Louis IX, a.k.a. Saint Louis, ordered the construction of the Cité's outer wall to guarantee the fortress's defensive invulnerability. His son, Philippe III, put the finishing touches on the fortress. Carcassonne became an impregnable stone wonder and a military model for the rest of Europe, earning in the process the title "Maiden of Languedoc." It is no coincidence that no one ever attacked the Cité again.

Looking at the towers, you can see how the defense of the Cité was carried out. Archers were situated on four floors of the major towers behind narrow-slitted openings just big enough to shoot an arrow through but not large enough for enemy arrows to penetrate. Wooden platforms atop the towers were equipped with ramps from which heavy iron balls were rolled and dropped on the hapless invaders below.

INSIDE THE GATES

Two gates give entrance to the Cité, the Porte d'Aude and Porte Narbonnaise. There is surprisingly little to see or do inside, aside from walking through old streets that are still home to 1,000 residents and, as best you can in the crowds, soaking up the history of the place. In addition to its walls, Carcassonne really boasts only two buildings of architectural interest, and one of these, the **Château Comtal** (the Count's Castle, housing the Musée Lapidaire), circa 1125, has been altered horribly over the years. Not so the **Eglise St-Nazaire**, a fine structure with remarkable stained glass from the 14th to the 16th century.

If crowds don't bother you, July is a good time to visit Carcassonne. For all hotels in and near the Cité (see below), reserve well in advance, especially for the Bastille Day (July 14) celebration. The Bastille Day fireworks at the Cité rival the Parisian event. In addition, the outdoor amphitheater on the southern rampart is the scene of various concerts and plays throughout the month-long Festival de la Cité.

NEAR CARCASSONNE:
THE MINERVOIS

The best tonic after a day or two of rubbing shoulders with the crowds in Carcassonne is to head for the hills of the Minervois, the winegrowing region just to the north and east. At the center of this wild, rocky, hilly landscape, covered with scrub and vines, is the village of **Minerve**. Reaching this little place, about 45 km (28 miles) from Carcassonne, can be an adventure. The most direct route takes you east along D 610, which follows the Canal du Midi, to the village of Olonzac and then up D 10.

Like so many other villages in this region, Minerve was a Cathar stronghold. Built atop a rocky plateau and surrounded by the snakelike bends of the river Briant, the village has a location—one of the most incredible you are ever likely to see—that made it virtually unassailable. But in 1210 Simon de Montfort cut off the water supply and 180 Cathars surrendered and willingly walked into the flames of their own funeral pyre. Today the business of Minerve is wine, and you can buy the very pleasant reds and whites at any number of stalls as you stroll the streets of the town.

If this sun-drenched landscape seems appealing, you may want to return to Carcassonne through the hinterlands, stopping at what is arguably the most dramatic Cathar stronghold of all, **Lastours**. This remarkable place is not one castle but four, built next to one another on four separate peaks high above a gorge of the river Orbiel. The best views are from a hilltop about half a mile away (well signposted, and there's a small admission fee to the viewing area), though you can climb up to the ruined châteaux on a well-maintained path.

There are any number of routes you can take from Minerve to Lastours, none of them direct (allow at least an hour, and have a good map at hand). One route follows the Gorges de la Cesse west from Minerve on D 10 and D 182, then drops south on D 55 to D 11 to D 111. Whichever route you take, few drives in France will take you through countryside as remote as this. From Lastours D 411 heads south to D 118 for Carcassonne, only about 25 km (16 miles) away.

STAYING AND DINING
IN AND AROUND CARCASSONNE

Few of Carcassonne's restaurants distinguish themselves, and you are best off with a simple meal at any number of cafés or crêperies. As for lodgings, the ► **Hôtel de la Cité**, just across the *place* from St-Nazaire, is a good choice, with a large garden and antique furnishings. The ► **Hôtel Donjon**, on the other side of the Cité on rue Comte-Roger, is simpler and less costly. But after a day in the Cité, you may well want to retire to a quieter retreat elsewhere in the region, such as the ► **Castel de Villemagne** in the hamlet of **Villemagne**, about 18 km (11 miles) east of Castelnaudary on D 103. The proprietress, Madame Maksud de Vézian, grew up in this comfortable old house, and she puts up her guests in nine antiques-filled rooms and supplies simple, excellent meals. (Villemagne would be a good base from which to explore Carcassonne; the drive takes well under an hour on D 629 and N 113 and you can return in time for a home-cooked meal and an Armagnac in the garden.)

The most elegant place to stay in the immediate vicinity is the 23-room ► **Domaine d'Auriac**, in a restored château just 3 km (2 miles) east of the Cité via N 3 and D 104. Amenities include luxuriously appointed rooms, a golf course, a swimming pool, facilities for helicopter landings, and a dining room where even the cassoulet seems elegant.

GETTING AROUND

Air France will fly you from its North American gateways to Paris and on to Toulouse on one of several daily Air Inter flights. Dan Air and British Airways fly to Toulouse from London.

Travellers also have their choice of a dozen trains that leave for Toulouse at all hours of the day from Paris's Gare d'Austerlitz; Toulouse is also on the ever-expanding TGV system.

For those travelling by car, the Autoroute des Deux-Mers (A 62) connects Toulouse to Bordeaux (near the Atlantic, 240 km/149 miles northwest) and, now called A 61, to Narbonne (near the Mediterranean, 150 km/93 miles southeast). At Bordeaux you may connect with the A 10, which runs north then east toward Paris; at Narbonne, with the A 9, which runs south toward the Spanish border and Barcelona, and north then east through Languedoc-Roussillon toward the Côte d'Azur and Italy. Many French drivers boast that they make the Paris–Toulouse run, a journey of some 700 km (434 miles), in a little more than five hours—a claim that should convince you to take the train.

Toulouse is at the very center of much of the region covered in this chapter, and even the most remote towns and villages are no more than an hour or two away by train or car. From Toulouse's Gare Matabiau an extensive rail network connects the city with Agen, Albi, Auch, Bordeaux, Carcassonne, Castres, Foix, Montauban, Narbonne, Perpignan, Rodez, and most other towns of any size within a radius of 100 miles or so. Many major car-rental firms have offices at either Blagnac airport or in central Toulouse.

Driving in this region is what motoring once was: leisurely excursions along well-maintained, less travelled roads, with stops at village restaurants and hotels. Using departmental roads (marked by the letter "D," followed by a number) almost exclusively, you could make a very scenic "back roads" circuit of the entire region.

ACCOMMODATIONS REFERENCE

The rates given below are projections *for 1994. Unless otherwise indicated, rates are for a double room, double occupancy, and do not include meals. As rates are always subject to change, double-check before booking.*

▶ **La Belle Gasconne. Poudenas**, 47170 Mézin. Tel: 53-65-71-58; Fax: 53-65-87-39. 550F.

▶ **Castel de Villemagne.** 11310 **Villemagne**. Tel: 68-94-22-95. 245F–415F.

▶ **Domaine d'Auriac.** Route St-Hilaire, 11000 **Carcassonne**. Tel: 68-25-72-22; Fax: 68-47-35-54. 600F–1,200F.

▶ **Grand Hôtel Fourcade.** 14, rue des Carmes, 11400 **Castelnaudary**. Tel: 68-23-02-08. 180F–200F.

▶ **Grand Hôtel de l'Opéra.** 1, place du Capitole, 31000 **Toulouse**. Tel: 61-21-82-66; Fax: 61-23-41-04. 850F–1,300F.

▶ **Hostellerie Barbacane.** 1, avenue Lérida, 09000 **Foix**. Tel: 61-65-50-44. 320F.

▶ **Hostellerie du Grand St-Antoine.** 17, rue St-Antoine, 81000 **Albi**. Tel: 63-54-04-04; Fax: 63-47-10-47. 420F–850F.

▶ **Hostellerie du Vieux Cordes.** Rue St-Michel, 81170 **Cordes**. Tel: 63-56-00-12; Fax: 63-56-16-99. 400F.

▶ **Hôtel Audoye-Lons.** 6, place G. Duthil, 09000 **Foix**. Tel: 61-65-52-44; Fax: 61-02-68-18. 225F–350F.

▶ **Hôtel de Bastard.** Rue Lagrange, 32700 **Lectoure**. Tel: 62-68-82-44; Fax: 62-68-76-81. 260F–310F.

▶ **Hôtel des Beaux-Arts.** 1, place du Pont-Neuf, 31000 **Toulouse**. Tel: 61-23-40-50; Fax: 61-22-02-27. 340F–575F.

▶ **Hôtel de la Cité.** Place de l'Eglise, 11000 **Carcassonne**. Tel: 68-25-03-34; Fax: 68-71-50-15. 850F–1,020F.

► **Hôtel Costes.** 09300 **Montségur.** Tel: 61-01-10-24; Fax: 61-03-06-28. 220F.

► **Hôtel Donjon.** 2, rue Comte-Roger, 11000 **Carcassonne.** Tel: 68-71-08-80; Telex: 505012; Fax: 68-25-06-60. 290F–530F.

► **Hôtel de France.** Place de la Libération, 32000 **Auch.** Tel: 62-61-71-84; Fax: 62-61-71-81. 590F–1,250F.

► **Hôtel Pujol et Restaurant Modern' Pujol.** 3, rue Montebello, 81000 **Albi.** Tel: 63-54-02-92; Fax: 63-47-06-16. 270F–310F.

► **Hôtel-Restaurant le Grand Ecuyer.** Rue Voltaire, 81170 **Cordes.** Tel: 63-56-01-03; Fax: 63-56-16-99. 570F–790F.

► **Hôtel-Restaurant La Lauzeraie.** Avenue Delcassé, 09110 **Ax-les-Thermes.** Tel: 61-64-20-70; Fax: 61-64-38-50. 200F–520F.

► **Hôtel et le Restaurant d'Occitanie.** 5, rue Labéda, 31000 **Toulouse.** Tel: 61-21-15-92; Fax: 61-21-36-33. 250F; suite 410F.

► **Hôtel des Trois Lys.** 38, rue Gambetta, 32100 **Condom.** Tel: 62-28-33-33; Fax: 62-28-41-85. 550F.

► **Logis des Cordeliers.** Rue des Cordeliers, 32100 **Condom.** Tel: 62-28-03-68; Fax: 62-68-29-03. 230F–360F.

► **Mercure-Altéa Wilson.** 7, rue Labéda, 31000 **Toulouse.** Tel: 61-21-21-75; Fax: 61-22-77-64; in the U.S. and Canada, Tel: (800) 221-4542; Fax: (914) 472-0451; in the U.K., Tel: (071) 724-1000. 535F–690F.

► **L'Oustal. Unac,** 09250 Ax-les-Thermes. Tel: 61-64-48-44. 195F–350F.

► **Les Prés d'Eugénie et le Couvent des Herbes. Eugénie-les-Bains,** 40320 Geaune. Tel: 58-05-06-07; Fax: 58-51-13-59. 1,100F–1,800F.

► **Relais de Gascogne.** 5, avenue de la Marne, 32000 **Auch.** Tel: 62-05-26-81. Fax: 62-63-30-22. 260F–310F.

► **La Réserve.** Fonvialane, Route de Cordes, 81000 **Albi.** Tel: 63-47-60-22; Fax: 63-47-63-60; in U.S., (212) 856-0115; Fax: (212) 856-0193. Member, Relaís & Châteaux. 480F–1,000F. Closed November through April.

► **La Ripa Alta.** Place de l'Eglise, 32160 **Plaisance.** Tel: 62-69-30-43; Fax: 62-69-36-99. 315F.

THE PYRENEES
AND PAYS BASQUE

By Stephen Brewer

The Pyrénées rise from fertile, southern plains to form a solid curtain between France and the Iberian peninsula. These are noble mountains, soaring to heights of almost 11,000 feet, and they stretch unbroken from the Mediterranean all the way west to the Atlantic, a distance of about 250 miles.

For all their grandeur, the Pyrénées are France's "second" mountains, enjoying but a fraction of the attention lavished on the Alps. Not that the Pyrénées have not had their admirers. The Romans luxuriated in the mountain hot springs; Bagnères-de-Luchon, Cauterets, Pau, and Bagnères-de-Bigorre have been, and to some extent still are, fashionable watering holes. Victor Hugo and George Sand rhapsodized over the sublime beauty of the Cirque de Gavarnie, a vast amphitheater carved by glaciers out of the limestone of the central peaks, and no less a noble personage than the Empress Eugénie put Biarritz, once a little fishing village, on the map as a playground for the aristocracy.

If the Pyrénées have been overlooked, it is a blessing. As far as European mountains go, the Pyrénées have escaped the worst of 20th-century development. There are, of course, modern roads across the peaks to Spain, and ski stations that look best when buried deep in snow. For the most part, though, mountains as unspoiled as these are hard to come by. Travellers in the Pyrénées can stay in simple village hotels, walk through Alpine meadows in solitude, and gaze at peaks unmarred by civilization.

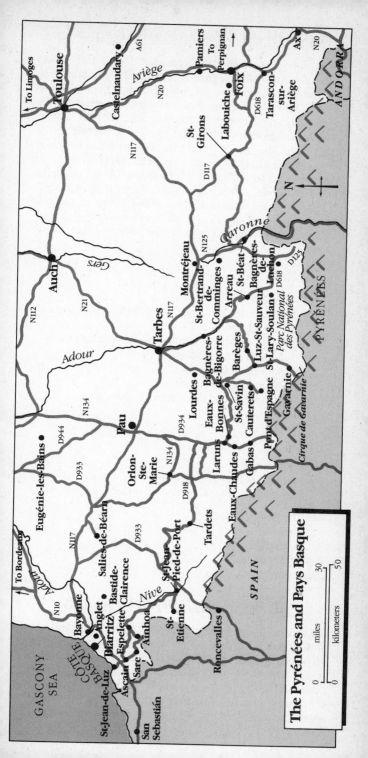

The Pyrénées and Pays Basque

We follow the mountains from east to west. Rather than enter the mountains as they rise, covered with grapevines, from the Mediterranean, we pick them up in the high peaks west of Foix. (We explore Foix and the eastern flanks of the Pyrénées in the chapters Toulouse and the Midi and Languedoc-Roussillon, above). For the most part, we stay to the high roads, the passes (*cols*) that climb and dip their way along the peaks (*pics*), with occasional forays to sights of interest in the foothills and on the plain below, including the cities of Lourdes and Pau. The route crosses the Pays Basque, a region of high mountain peaks, rolling farmland, and tidy villages that is home to one of Europe's oldest and most distinctive cultures, and ends on the shores of the Atlantic Ocean.

MAJOR INTEREST

The Pyrénées
St-Bertrand-de-Comminges, with its Roman ruins and
    medieval cathedral
Bagnères-de-Luchon, fashionable spa surrounded by
    spectacular mountain scenery
The high mountain passes
Parc National des Pyrénées
Luz St-Sauveur and the Cirque de Gavarnie
Cauterets
Lourdes
Pau

Pays Basque
Medieval St-Jean-Pied-de-Port
Sare, Aïnhoa, and other typical villages

The Basque Coast
Bayonne
Biarritz
St-Jean-de-Luz

ACROSS THE HIGH PASSES

We set out on the mountain route from the pretty village of St-Bertrand-de-Comminges, in pastureland that undulates across the foothills in the shadows of the peaks. St-Bertrand is just 8 km (5 miles) south of busy N 117, the much-travelled highway that cuts east and west across southwestern France between Toulouse and the Atlantic. If you are approaching St-Bertrand through the mountains from Foix, follow the Route Vert (D 17), a road that is all views, for about 35 km (22 miles), then continue west on D 618, the route that will take you across the spectacular mountain passes to the west, to D 145 and N 145 for a jog south to St-Bertrand. The trip is about 100 km (62 miles).

St-Bertrand-de-Comminges

St-Bertrand, enclosed entirely within its medieval ramparts atop a hill, has some fine half-timbered houses and the tall, imposing **Cathédrale Notre-Dame**, which dominates the countryside. Two thousand years ago St-Bertrand was the thriving Roman settlement of Lugdunum Convenarum, and ongoing excavations have uncovered baths, temples, and other artifacts of a settlement that probably numbered 50,000 inhabitants. The Vandals laid waste to the city in the fifth century, and Bertrand de l'Isle-Jourdain, a Toulousain aristocrat who was also bishop of the old Pyrénéen county of Comminges, brought civilization back to the district when he began work on the church in the 11th century. When Bertrand was canonized in 1218 the village took his name and became a pilgrimage site. The church evolved over the ensuing centuries in the styles of its different builders—a Romanesque portal, a partially Gothic nave, a Renaissance choir. The cloisters, open to the valley on one side, incorporate elements of all these styles.

St-Bertrand claims another religious presence, the **Basilique St-Just** in the farm village of **Valcabrère**, a pleasant mile-long walk east from St-Bertrand through hay fields. St-Just is a successful example of what has come to be called "found art": Its 11th- and 12th-century builders used materials from an early Christian burying ground as well as what they could scavenge from the remains of Lugdunum Convenarum.

An even earlier attraction lies about 6 km (4 miles) northwest of St-Bertrand on D 26, the **Grottes de Gargas**. Prehistoric man lived in these caves 20,000 years ago and left his mark in the form of the shadowy outlines of hands. Many of the prints seem to have been made with partially amputated fingers, suggesting ritual mutilation or some sort of code. Only a fraction of the hands can be viewed, along with etchings of bison and other prey.

STAYING AND DINING
IN ST-BERTRAND

You can spend a few hours happily in St-Bertrand sitting back with a glass of wine on the wisteria-covered terrace of the ▶ **Hôtel-Restaurant du Comminges** admiring the façade of the cathedral. If you spend a night in one of the simple rooms (many without bath), the only thing likely to disturb your rest is the sound of bleating sheep. The ► **Hostellerie de l'Aristou** is a pleasant country-house hotel with a good restaurant in the nearby village of Barbazan.

Bagnères-de-Luchon to Arreau

The Romans enjoyed the soothing effects of Bagnères-de-Luchon's curative waters, but the fashionable town you see today, at the foot of the highest and most spectacular stretch of the Pyrénées, is an 18th- and 19th-century invention.

Luchon, as the town is commonly known, is still much visited, its popularity due to the mountain scenery that encloses it and the mineral-rich waters that bubble up from deep springs. For about 60 francs you can spend an afternoon sampling the waters at the *thermes,* where a dip in the hot and cold pools is usually followed by a session in a natural, radioactive sauna carved out of the earth beneath the town. Treatments wind down by early evening, in time for the clients to find a seat at a café table on the Allées d'Etigny and watch the light fade on the surrounding peaks.

AROUND LUCHON

Luchon is the jumping-off point for any number of excursions into the high mountains. The best hiking paths lead into high country from the **Hospice de France**, a crude refuge that once provided shelter to travellers crossing the mountains on three paths that meet here, about 11 km (7 miles) south of Luchon through the densely forested Vallée de la Pique on D 125. (The Syndicat d'Initiative on the Allées d'Etigny in Luchon supplies maps and trail information.) A turnoff onto D 46, about 5 km (3 miles) north of the hospice, takes you west through the deep Vallée du Lys (Valley of the Avalanches) as far as the spectacular **Cascade d'Enfer**. From the base of the waterfall a steep trail leads up to another, even more powerful cataract, the **Cascade du Gouffre d'Enfer**, about a half-hour's climb away. Two kilometers (about a mile) before the Cascade d'Enfer there's a turnoff to the north for Luchon's ski resort, **Superbagnères**. With or without snow, the 360-degree views from the resort, taking in a dozen peaks, are amazing.

St-Béat

This stone village, 23 km (13 miles) north of Luchon on D 125 and N 125, is divided in two by the Garonne river. St-Béat was once a place of some significance: Its 12th-century

castle was long known as the "key to France" for the defense
it provided against invasion from the south, and marble
from St-Béat's quarries has found its way as far afield as
Imperial Rome (Trajan's Column) and the gardens of Versailles. For an example of the local product, take a look at
the bridge spanning the Garonne.

OVER THE COL DE PEYRESOURDE

The road west from Luchon, D 618, leads over the first of the
great lateral Pyrénées passes, the **Col de Peyresourde**. There
are several enticements to stop you before the road begins
the real climb to its mile-high summit, though. The first is
the 11th-century Romanesque **Eglise St-Aventin**, in a mountain village of the same name clinging to a nearly vertical
grassy slope just 6 km (4 miles) out of Luchon.

From St-Aventin D 76 leads south through the bucolic Val
d'Oô. Soon after the turnoff onto D 76 there's another
Romanesque church, with 15th-century frescoes depicting
the Old and New Testaments, in the village of Larboust. The
road ends after 7 km (4.5 miles) at the head of the trail to the
serenely beautiful **Lac d'Oô**, about a 45-minute walk beyond
through Alpine meadows dotted with grazing sheep and
cows.

ARREAU AND ENVIRONS

From the summit of the Col de Peyresourde the Neste de
Louron rushes down to Arreau (*neste* is the local term for
"river"); in fact, four rivers flow through this cozy village of
stone houses and slate roofs. Arreau was an important
trading center in the Middle Ages, and its medieval market
hall still accommodates a busy Thursday-morning market.
There is magnificent scenery all around, and the attractive
25-room ▶ **Hôtel d'Angleterre**, a former coaching inn with
a low-ceilinged dining room, is a good base from which to
explore it.

One scenic route leads south from Arreau into the mountains up D 929 through the ski resort of St-Lary-Soulan to a
string of lakes: **Lac d'Orédon, Lac d'Aumar**, and **Lac d'Aubert**.
All of the lakes, snow conditions permitting, are accessible by
car. Two of the highest peaks in the French Pyrénées, the Pic
de Néouvielle and Pic Long, loom just to the west.

Parc National des Pyrénées

The Parc National des Pyrénées is a reserve that follows the
crest of the mountains west from here for 60 miles to the
peaks around the Col du Somport. Vultures, ibex, and a few
remaining Pyrénéen bears and eagles roam the park, where

even the 400 species of wildflowers are protected. The only way into the park is on foot; much of it is crisscrossed by the GR 10, the high east–west hiking route across the mountains. There are no settlements within the park, but Maisons du Parc at towns on the reserve's periphery provide everything you need to know about getting into and enjoying this protected wilderness. There are Maisons du Parc in Arrens, Cauterets, Etsaut, Gabas, Gavarnie, Luz-St-Sauveur, Tarbes, and St-Lary-Soulan.

Arreau to St-Savin

Continuing west from Arreau, D 918 climbs over two more high passes, the pastoral Col d'Aspin and up again into the Col du Tourmalet. In the farming valleys between the two passes there's another spa town, **Bagnères-de-Bigorre**. In the 19th century Bigorre was called, even then with hyperbole, the "Athens of the Pyrénées." Light industry and development detract from some of the charm the town must once have held for Laurence Sterne and other cure-seekers, but with its shops and cafés, Bigorre is a pleasant place to stop.

The **Col du Tourmalet** is the highest of the Pyrénéen passes, climbing to almost 7,000 feet between the craggy **Pic du Midi de Bigorre** to the north and a huge wall of granite, the **Massif de Néouvielle**, to the south. A toll road and funicular lead from the pass to the summit of the Pic du Midi, where one of the world's first astronomical observatories has been operating since 1882.

At its western end the Col du Tourmalet drops through the one-street spa of **Barèges**, where Louis XIV sent his sickly son, the seven-year-old duc du Maine, in 1677. The waters are also said to cure gunshot wounds, a claim that led Napoléon to establish a military hospital here.

Luz-St-Sauveur, in the midst of some of the most magnificent scenery in the Pyrénées, is just 7 km (4½ miles) beyond.

LUZ-ST-SAUVEUR
Luz is a likable, old-fashioned mountain town, with the Gave de Bastan (*gave* is another local term for "river") rushing through it and tall gray and white houses with steep pitched roofs providing a dramatic foreground for the craggy mountain peaks just to the south.

The knights of St. John of Jerusalem established a stronghold here in the 12th century and built the stone **Eglise des Templiers**. They fortified the church with a bell tower that doubled as an arsenal and lookout, and a circle of battlements was added in the 16th century, giving the structure the very solid look of an old military outpost.

St-Sauveur, just west across the Gorge de St-Sauveur, is a 19th-century spa that comprises a single street of old houses clinging to the sides of the deep gorge. The specialty at the baths of St-Sauveur is gynecological complaints, and Louis Napoléon and the Empress Eugénie once stayed here. There's a third village nearby, the 6,000-foot-high ski station of **Luz-Ardiden**, about 12 km (7.5 miles) west up D 12, a twisting, nearly vertical road.

CIRQUE DE GAVARNIE

George Sand, Victor Hugo, Gustave Flaubert, and generations of other travellers have followed the 30-km (18½-mile) route along D 921 up the Gorge de St-Sauveur from Luz. At its end is the **Cirque de Gavarnie**, an imposing semicircular limestone amphitheater carved by glaciers. A modern road that can accommodate busloads of tourists renders Victor Hugo's description of the route, "a black and hideous path," archaic. Nevertheless, mass tourism doesn't detract from the feeling that there is indeed something primordial about the *cirque* and the landscape you encounter en route to it: dense forests that, after the village of Gèdre, give way to a treeless, boulder-strewn wasteland known as the **Chaos de Couméy**.

The village of Gavarnie is the end of the road for vehicular traffic. Visitors continue to the cirque, several kilometers (a couple of miles) beyond, either by foot or on the backs of shaggy Pyrénéen horses. Tourist town that it is, Gavarnie is an appealing place, surrounded by snowcapped peaks and mountain meadows and ringing with the tinkling of cowbells. Gavarnie has erected a statue to one of its 19th-century visitors, Henry Russell (son of an Irish father and Gascon mother). Russell is the most famous climber of the Pyrénées, having made the first ascents of 16 peaks.

Russell climbed 11,000-foot Pic de Vignemale, just to the west of Gavarnie, 33 times. He frequently set up housekeeping in caves near the summit, entertaining guests willing to make the climb and brave the elements.

From Gavarnie a well-maintained path follows a stream across mountain meadows to a mountaineer's refuge, where you can enjoy a beverage on the terrace and look across the stony terrain to the imposing face of the *cirque:* a wall of rock rising as high as 5,000 feet, with Europe's highest waterfall dropping almost 1,400 feet down its flanks to form the Gave de Pau.

Several trails lead up the face of the *cirque*. The most popular route (not strenuous, but an eight-hour round-trip) climbs to a large gap near the top of the wall, known as the **Brèche de Roland** (Cleft of Roland). The knight-nephew of Charlemagne, hero of *Le Chanson de Roland,* is said to have made this indentation with his sword.

Two other cirques lie east of Gavarnie. The nearest, the **Cirque d'Estaubé**, is wild and comparatively virgin, accessible only by mountain trails (equip yourself with maps at the Maison du Parc in Luz). The **Cirque de Troumouse** can be reached by car, but from Gavarnie you must backtrack to the village of Gèdre, then follow the Gave de Héas toward what remains of the hamlet of Héas, which was buried by an avalanche in 1915. Snow conditions permitting, a toll road will take you across wild, rocky meadows to the cirque, a semicircular wall of granite that is almost six miles from end to end.

CAUTERETS

To continue west across the mountains from Luz-St-Sauveur you must follow D 921 north along the Gorge de Luz for 19 km (12 miles). At Pierrefitte-Nestalas, where chemical plants will not encourage you to linger, turn south again and follow D 920 along the Gave de Cauterets for 10 km (6 miles) to Cauterets.

Count Raymond de Bigorre established baths here in 983, and Cauterets became fashionable six centuries later when Marguerite de Navarre, grandmother of King Henri IV, took the cure in the sulfurous waters. The elegant baths at Cauterets, the **Thermes de César**, are said to cure anything that ails you, especially respiratory ailments. This claim, and the spectacular mountain scenery, has attracted numerous visitors over the years. Many have been writers, Rabelais and Chateaubriand among them. Alfred, Lord Tennyson's visits inspired his poem "In the Valley of Cauterets."

PONT D'ESPAGNE AND LAC DE GAUBE

The classic excursion from Cauterets is the 9-km (5½-mile) trek past four spectacular waterfalls to the **Pont d'Espagne**, a historic crossing on one of the most important paths to Spain. Visitors once made the trip up to the bridge on foot, horseback, or sedan chair. Now the narrow D 920 follows the pretty Gave de Cauterets and ends just beyond the **Hostellerie du Pont d'Espagne**, a simple bar-restaurant at the bridge.

The **Lac de Gaube** is tucked in the mountain meadows a few miles above the *pont*. A chairlift makes quick work of the hardest part of the ascent to the lake, which is about 6,000 feet above sea level. Victor Hugo was so stirred by the black depths of Gaube, with the peak of Vignemale soaring above its southern shore, that he mistakenly thought six Notre-Dames could be piled atop one another in it. Gustave Flaubert once ate salmon at the little lakeside refuge-cum-restaurant here, an option for today's visitors as well.

ST-SAVIN

From Cauterets follow the Gave de Cauterets north to Pierrefitte-Nestalas. Just 3 km (2 miles) beyond, on D 13, is St-Savin, yet another pleasant mountain village, surrounded by Alpine meadows. The mountains here are lower than the peaks to the south, 5,000 feet at the highest and covered with forests and emerald green meadows. St-Savin has several half-timbered houses and a fine church from the 12th century, heavily fortified and armed with towers and gun slits. Inside, 15th-century paintings depict the life of the town's saint, the son of a Barcelona nobleman who lived as a hermit on this mountainside.

STAYING AND DINING
BETWEEN ARREAU AND ST-SAVIN

Luz has several simple, pleasant hotels (at most, rooms aren't likely to have baths and furnishings lean more toward functional than stylish). The ▶ Hôtel des Cimes and ▶ Hôtel des Remparts are both in tall, gabled houses near the center of town; the Cimes has a basic restaurant, while at the Remparts you can have the pleasure of awakening to a view of the magnificent Templar church. The ▶ Hôtel de Londres is more citified than the other hotels in town, and its restaurant is the best around.

Gavarnie has several hotels, most of them pretty basic. When the Pyrénéen explorer Henry Russell wasn't holing up in one of his mountaintop aeries, he stayed in Gavarnie at the ▶ Hôtel Vignemale, which has recently been nicely but a little blandly modernized. It's at the foot of the trail up to the *cirque,* so it's handy if you want to scramble into the mountains to see the peaks turn pink in the first rays of the sun.

Cauterets has no shortage of hotel rooms. ▶ Le Bordeaux, the ▶ Hôtel César, and the ▶ Hôtel Etche Ona are old-fashioned, unfussy places in the center of town, all with good restaurants.

St-Savin is a pleasant place to spend a couple of days in the mountains. You can awaken to views over the valley and mountains at either the ▶ Hôtel-Restaurant des Rochers or the ▶ Panoramic Hôtel, and both have restaurants. The views are even better from **Arcizans Avant**, a smaller village about 2 km (1¼ miles) farther up the mountainside. Arcizans also has a hotel, the simple ▶ Auberge le Cabaliros.

Lourdes

The hundreds of thousands of visitors who descend upon Lourdes every year can be divided into the believers and the nonbelievers. For the first group Lourdes is one of the holiest places in Christendom; the latter are likely to find Lourdes tasteless and exploitive and should avoid it. From St-Savin it's only 20 km (12½ miles) north along the valley of the Gave de Pau on D 921 and N 21.

Until 1858 Lourdes was a farming village huddled beneath its somber castle. That year the Virgin Mary appeared to Bernadette Soubirous, an illiterate shepherdess, at least nine times over the course of six months. During one of these visions a spring erupted near where Bernadette stood, and the Virgin instructed the girl to have a church built on the spot. The rest of the story is that of Catholicism's most popular shrine.

Bernadette left Lourdes for a convent in Nevers, in the Loire Valley, where she died at the age of 35. A basilica was built as the Virgin instructed, and the sick began coming to Lourdes seeking cures. Since then, 64 cures have been documented by the shrine's bureau of medical investigation, and millions of other visitors have found enormous comfort here. The religious sites are on the banks of the Gave de Pau in the Cité Religieuse, which consists of an ornate 19th-century basilica, a shrine on the riverbank where the Virgin appeared to Bernadette, and a recent underground church that looks like a stadium and can accommodate 20,000 worshipers at a time.

What any visitor notices first upon entering Lourdes are the shops selling a sordid variety of three-dimensional photos, key chains with glow-in-the-dark likenesses of the Virgin, and other souvenirs. The most popular item sold in Lourdes is a water container shaped like the Virgin, which the faithful fill at Bernadette's spring.

Surprisingly, it is fairly easy to sense the holiness of Lourdes—at the sight of the suffering who leave their sick-beds to come here, for instance, or during the nightly candlelight procession that winds through the Cité Reli-geuse. The worldly attractions of Lourdes are few. There's a fairly decent Musée Pyrénéen in the hilltop castle, and a funicular up the Pic du Jer, a meadow-covered mountain on the outskirts of the city.

Lourdes handles its visitors very efficiently, with streets

full of hotels, hospitals, and a uniformed army of attendants who push the infirm in black canopied chairs and litters. If you are planning a pilgrimage, contact the Office de Tourisme in advance for information on medical care, guides, and accommodations; Place du Champ-Commun, 65100 Lourdes; Tel: 62-94-15-64.

Pau

While visitors to Lourdes set their sights on the heavens, in Pau, about 40 km (25 miles) northwest on D 937, all eyes are on the Pyrénées. This attractive city is not actually in the mountains, but in rolling farmland about 30 miles due north of the peaks. The region's main agricultural product is wine, a rarity in this section of France; Pau's Jurançon wines appear on menus throughout southwestern France. Sweet Jurançons are served as an aperitif, while the dry whites best accompany fish dishes.

The British discovered Pau, with its clement and supposedly curative climate, in the mid-19th century. Vaguely British-looking villas surround Pau's old center, and British retirees still have a penchant for the area.

Pau's main assets are the mountains. To provide a view of them Napoléon laid out a grand avenue on the south side of Pau, the **Promenade des Pyrénées**. The avenue stretches for half a mile, from the town's exquisite château (see below) at one end to the 19th-century **casino** on the other. Modern expansion has robbed the outlook of the romanticism it must have once possessed (a funicular connects the promenade with the newer sections of town that spread out in front of it). In fact, emissions from some of Europe's largest natural gas fields, exploited for the first time in the 1950s, often shroud the view in haze, but the vista is still a grand one.

You might interrupt your walk along the promenade with a stop at the east end to take in the European collections in the **Musée des Beaux-Arts**, just north of the casino through the **Parc Beaumont**. At the western end of the promenade you come first to the city's Anglican cathedral, then to the **château**, started in the 11th century as a crude castle but rebuilt several times since. France's beloved Henri IV was born in the château in 1553. His mother, Jeanne d'Albret, an ardent Protestant, controlled much of southwestern France and northern Spain, then amalgamated as the Kingdom of Navarre. The family's other castle was in Gascony, in the now quiet town of Nérac (see the chapter Toulouse and the Midi, above).

Henri's father, Antoine de Bourbon, supposedly chris-tened the boy who would be king by rubbing Jurançon wine on his lips. For less apparent reasons, Henri's childhood cradle was a tortoise shell, now on display in the Musée National in the castle.

With 85,000 inhabitants, Pau is by far the largest city in the Pyrénées. It has some lively shopping streets around the château, and a university.

After a taste of Pau's civilization you can easily return to the mountains, either back through Lourdes or on D 934, which climbs south and, in fewer than 40 km (25 miles), brings you to the mountain town of Laruns (see below).

Over the Col d'Aubisque

Heading west from Argelès-Gazost (south of Lourdes), D 918 climbs through grazing country and stone villages before ascending in earnest through the Col du Soulor. This pass reaches 4,800 feet before it ends at **la Corniche**, a narrow road carved out of a cliff many thousands of feet above a fertile valley to the north. The route then climbs even higher, over the Col d'Aubisque, before beginning a long descent through the ski resort of Gourette and the spa of **Eaux-Bonnes** (Good Waters). Today a lonely, faded-looking place, in its 19th-century heyday Eaux-Bonnes was one of the more fashionable watering holes in the Pyrénées, popular enough for Napoléon III to want to engineer a "Route Thermale" connecting the spa with Bagnères-de-Bigorre to the east.

The Col d'Aubisque ends at **Laruns**, a pleasant town with several cafés on its square. From here you can continue west or travel south up the **Vallée d'Ossau** on D 934 into the high mountains and, if you wish, on into Spain.

THE VALLEE D'OSSAU
AND COL DE MARIE-BLANQUE

The first village you come to in the heavily forested Vallée d'Ossau is **les Eaux-Chaudes** (Hot Waters), a spa even more faded than Eaux-Bonnes. In another 8 km (5 miles) the road comes to the village of Gabas and a turnoff on D 231 to the **Lac de Bious-Artigues**, set in Alpine meadows beneath the craggy summit of the **Pic du Midi d'Ossau**. From **Artouste**, some 2 km (about a mile) beyond Gabas, you can climb the mountains the easy way: by funicular up the slopes of the Pic de la Sagette to a narrow-gauge railway, which winds for six miles through desolate, high mountain terrain—the most remote you will see in the Pyrénées without hiking—to the pristine Lac d'Artouste.

The route west from Laruns begins with a 7½-km (5-mile) jog north on D 934. At the village of Bièlle turn west onto D 294 and the **Col de Marie-Blanque,** a 3,400-foot-high pass that climbs through beech forests to open meadows, affording fine views south to the higher peaks before dropping down to the N 134.

To the south, N 134 whisks travellers through the Vallée d'Aspe and the Col du Somport into Spain. This is one of the most-travelled north–south mountain passes. A 5-km (3-mile) run north on N 134 brings you to Lurbe-St-Christau, from where it is only 24 km (14 miles) west on D 918 through pleasant farm country to the village of Tardets-Sorholus on the edge of Basque country.

O·LORON·STE·MARIE

This old-fashioned town 8 km (5 miles) north of Lurbe-St-Christau on N 134 is famous for manufacturing the Béarn beret, the natty cap worn throughout France. (The Béarn beret is more compact than the Basque beret donned just to the west of here.) Oloron is a town of rushing water—the Gave d'Aspe and the Gave d'Ossau converge here—and churches. The 11th-century **Eglise Ste-Croix** stands on a summit atop the old quarter of the same name, wedged between the two rivers. The **Eglise Ste-Marie,** on the other side of the Gave d'Aspe, was built in the 12th century as a cathedral. The treasure of Ste-Marie is its portal, where scenes carved in marble depict life both sacred and secular: a deposition, a hunt for wild boar, and the count of Béarn on horseback.

THE PAYS BASQUE

There are no precise geographical boundaries to the Pays Basque. It occupies the southwesternmost corner of France, stretching roughly from the district around Tardets-Sorholus some 50 miles west to the Atlantic, beneath the lands of Gascony and the Landes to the north. Inland, the Pays Basque rolls over foothills and climbs through forests and upland pastures to the western peaks of the Pyrénées. From the short Basque coast, between Hendaye on the Spanish border and the city of Bayonne, the Basques once sent whaling ships as far afield as Newfoundland to establish a reputation as seafarers.

Tardets-Sorholus is the first place you will encounter tall, gabled Basque houses, painted white with dark red trim. Often, lengthy inscriptions on the lintels give the date of construction and list the house's occupants. While other French towns are closely built, Basque villages are usually strung out along a road or river. They are well-kept, with a profusion of hydrangeas and other flowers, and you'd be hard-pressed to find one that didn't have a *frontón,* a court where the Basque game pelota (transported to the United States as jai alai) is played.

The distinctive Basque language, Euskara, was probably passed down from pre-Roman Celtic tribes. Euskara uses "k's" and "s's" liberally, as well as, to the untrained ear, many improbable sounding consonant combinations. French Basques are also fluent in French; many speak Spanish; and, because so many Basque families have sent children to America in search of riches, quite a few are also fluent in English.

TOWARD ST-JEAN-PIED-DE-PORT

A good place on which to set your sights upon entering the Pays Basque is the pretty medieval city of St-Jean-Pied-de-Port, reached by several scenic itineraries from Tardets. The high mountain route takes you south then west via a series of twisting roads (D 57, D 26, D 19, and D 18) through highland meadows and dense forests up the **Col Bagargui**. The popular Basque ski station **Iraty** is on this pass. Another route, following D 117 and D 417, sticks to lower altitudes but passes through a lovely beech forest, the Forêt des Arbailles. Both these routes lead to the village of **Mendive**, about 53 km (33 miles) from Tardets on the high-mountain route, and about 30 km (18 miles) on the other. There's not much to see in this mountain village, or in its neighboring towns, Béhorléguy and Lecumberry. But if you find yourself in Mendive at mealtime, stop in at the **Châlet Pedro**, which serves whatever's fresh that day: trout from the adjacent stream, home-cured ham and cheeses, or wild mountain mushrooms cooked into an omelette. From Mendive it's only about 6½ km (4 miles) northwest on D 18 to St-Jean-Pied-de-Port.

A third route from Tardets to St-Jean follows D 918 north through the rolling grazing land that is so typical of the Pays Basque. About 13 km (8 miles) from Tardets the road comes to **Mauléon-Licharre**. Prettier villages lie ahead, but the markets selling Mauléon's local product, espadrilles, merit a stop, as does the town's 15th-century hilltop castle. St-Jean-

Pied-de-Port is just on the other side of the Col d'Osquich, a gentle ascent to 1,300 feet, with views south to the higher peaks.

St-Jean-Pied-de-Port and Environs

Since the 16th century St-Jean-Pied-de-Port, on the route to Santiago de Compostela, just on the other side of the Pyrénées, has been the largest and most-visited town of the inland Basque country. As St-Jean's church bells tolled, pilgrims from all over France would enter the upper part of the town through the Porte St-Jacques, descend the cobbled rue d'Espagne, cross the river, and leave town through the Porte d'Espagne. The pilgrims continued into the high mountains on the old mountain road, the Port de Cize—hence the name, "Saint Jean at the foot of the pass."

St-Jean is medieval, built of heavy pinkish-brown stone and surrounded by ramparts that France's relations with Spain once rendered necessary. There are a 17th-century citadel (all but the ramparts are closed to the public) at the top of the town and many fine old houses below, including a picturesque string of them overhanging St-Jean's river, the Nive.

St-Jean is a small place, and within a five-minute walk from the center of town you'll find yourself on country lanes that roll across the greenest pastures you've ever seen. The snow-capped Pyrénées are always on the horizon, the air is heavy with the scent of wildflowers and freshly mown grass, and the silence is broken only by a cacophony of cowbells. The Office de Tourisme, hard by the ramparts in St-Jean, makes it easy to explore this delightful countryside with maps to five walking itineraries that range from a couple of miles to day-long gambols. All of the enticing region is within easy reach of St-Jean by car.

ST-ETIENNE-DE-BAIGORRY

Route D 15 takes you due west from St-Jean 11 km (7 miles) to St-Etienne-de-Baïgorry. En route you will pass the Basque country's only vineyards, named for the little village of Irouléguy. These very decent reds and rosés appear on almost every wine list in the region. The other local alcoholic product is *eau-de-vie de poire,* produced by the Etienne Brana family from a little distillery on the rue 11-Novembre in St-Jean.

St-Etienne has tall white Basque houses, a medieval humpbacked bridge over the Nive des Aldudes, and a fine church.

Here, as in most Basque churches, women sit in the nave and men sit on several tiers of balconies, just beneath the wonderfully painted ceiling and finely carved roof beams.

St-Etienne is almost in high mountain country and not far from Spain. If you continue south on D 948 you follow the gorgeous Vallée des Aldudes through highland pastures and up the forested slopes of the high mountains, coming to the Spanish border in about 22 km (13½ miles). If you continue 23 km (14 miles) south from the border you will come to the Spanish Basque village of Zubiri—much less sophisticated than the villages on the French side of the border—then make a return to St-Jean-Pied-de-Port through the **Ronceveaux pass**. If we are to believe *Le Chanson de Roland,* it was here that the Saracens slaughtered Roland and his 20,000 men.

ESPELETTE TO LABASTIDE-CLAIRENCE

As you set out to see more Basque villages, the best route takes you north and west from St-Jean-Pied-de-Port on D 918 through pastureland and forests for some 34 km (21 miles) to the village of Espelette. Here you are only 10 km (6 miles) or so due south of Biarritz and the Basque coast, but there are more fine places to see inland to the west and east.

You may want to stop about 3 km (2 miles) before Espelette in the village of **Itxassou**. In the graveyard of the village's fine church are some of the remarkable Basque headstones called *stèles discoïdales.* These rough-hewn circular stones, carved with a cloverlike Basque cross, rest on tapering stone bases. In spring the hills around Itxassou are pink with cherry blossoms, and by summer the markets are full of the local fruit.

Espelette is a tidy, traditional village with two local products that are much in evidence: *piments d'Espelette* (sweet cayenne peppers) and Pottocks, small, shaggy horses that you see throughout the Pyrénées. The village celebrates both at annual fairs: the Fête du Piment on the last Sunday in October and the Foire aux Pottocks on the last Tuesday and Wednesday in January.

The spa of **Cambo-les-Bains** is just a kilometer or so east of Espelette on the banks of the Nive river. The playwright Edmond Rostand, newly wealthy from his play *Cyrano,* built an oversize Basque-style house on the edge of town in the late 19th century. The dark paneled rooms of **Villa Arnaga** house a collection of Rostand memorabilia, and the vast gardens, with fountains and pools, are as theatrical as the flamboyant character who made Rostand's fame and fortune. (Open every day from May to October, afternoons in October, and Saturdays in November.)

About 5 km (3 miles) northeast from Cambo via D 10 there's a turnoff onto the **Route Impériale des Cimes** (Imperial Route of the Summits), built by Napoléon to move his armies. It follows high ground for about 20 km (12½ miles) to the suburbs of Bayonne. The best views, toward the Pyrénées, are to be had on the return trip.

Route D 10 continues northeast through pleasant farmland to the village of Hasparren (about 10 km/6 miles) from Cambo and from there another 8 km (5 miles) to **Labastide-Clairence**, a 13th-century fortified town with an arcaded square more typical of Gascony, the region just to the north.

AINHOA TO AISCAN

A turn to the southwest from Espelette via D 918 and D 20 brings you after 8½ km (5 miles) to **Aïnhoa**, one of the prettiest Basque villages, with a single street of beautifully preserved 17th- and 18th-century houses and several good hotels.

From Aïnhoa it's 10 km (6 miles) through farms and forests on D 4 to **Sare**, another lovely village with a good church and an animated *place* with several cafés; the surrounding countryside is ideal for walking.

Route D 4 crosses the flanks of Sare's mountain, **La Rhune**, on the 6-km (4-mile) stretch of road to the last of the inland Basque villages, **Ascain**. You can climb the 3,000-foot summit, the last of the French Pyrénées, on a little railway that makes the ascent from a turnoff on the part of the road known as the Col de St-Ignace. Ascain is quiet and quaint, despite its popularity with day-trippers from St-Jean-de-Luz and the coast, just another 6 km (4 miles) beyond.

STAYING AND DINING
IN THE INLAND PAYS BASQUE

There are attractive, pleasant hotels in almost every village in Pays Basque. In St-Jean-Pied-de-Port, the ▶ **Central Hôtel** is a homey, old-fashioned place with big, high-ceilinged rooms where you can fall asleep to the sound of the river Nive tumbling over a falls just beneath your window. The ▶ **Hôtel-Restaurant Ramuntcho** occupies a narrow Basque house inside the ramparts; for a terrace and a view, ask for a room at the end of the house. Even if the dining room at ▶ **Les Pyrénées** is a bit stuffy and slick for this region, the dishes that come out of the kitchen are traditionally

Basque: a thick soup of beans and confit, *garbure aux choux;* wild birds boldly spiced with the local pepper, *piment d'Espelette;* and fresh fish from the nearby Atlantic sautéed *à la Basquaise,* with onions, tomatoes, and green chilis. The guest rooms upstairs are boxy, but there's a pleasant garden and swimming pool in back.

For a setting that's even quieter than St-Jean you need only follow the narrow, wild gorge of the Nive river on D 301 south for 8 km (5 miles) to **Estérençuby**. One of the most comfortable of the several hotels in this mountain village surrounded by deep forests and upland pastures is the ▶ **Hôtel-Restaurant Andreinia-Larramendy**, on the main square.

The ▶ **Hôtel Arcé** is a comfortable and charming hotel, in the same family for five generations, nestled on the banks of the rushing Nive des Aldudes in the pretty village of **St-Etienne-de-Baïgorry**. Several of **Aïnhoa's** tall, old houses have been converted to hotels. The ▶ **Hôtel-Restaurant Ithurria**, in an old coaching inn, has cozily furnished rooms and a pretty, wood-beamed dining room where the menu usually includes bass or other fish caught fresh that day at the nearby fishing port of St-Jean-de-Luz and lamb that graze on the pastures surrounding the village. **Sare** counts among its charms the ▶ **Hôtel Arraya**, an attractive old Basque country mansion on the square. Rooms are tastefully furnished, and many face a quiet, walled garden in the back. The dining room overlooking the village square does a very nice job with seafood and game birds. Sare is a short distance from the port of St-Jean-de-Luz, and the surrounding hills are prime hunting grounds (autumn shooting season is not the time to visit this otherwise peaceful place).

THE COTE BASQUE

The 20-mile strip of land where the Pays Basque meets the Atlantic is one of the most spectacular coastlines in France. The green pastures of the inland meet the sea above rocky cliffs and beaches of fine sand (the best beaches in France, many people say) worn down by the tumultuous surf (sometimes dangerous for swimming but good for surfing). There are three remarkable towns on this short coast, each one vastly different from the other: Bayonne, Biarritz, and St-Jean-de-Luz. From the inland Pays Basque, D 932 (to Bayonne) and D 918 (to St-Jean-de-Luz) are the most direct routes to the sea. Bayonne is just 14 km (9 miles) northwest of Espelette on D 932.

Bayonne

Bayonne, famous for ham, *bayonettes,* and chocolate, is a pleasant, workaday city on two rivers, the wide Adour and the smaller Nive. The Nive separates Grand Bayonne, the busier part of town on the west side, from Petit Bayonne; the Adour is Bayonne's link to the sea, and the Adour shoreline becomes thick with derricks and other equipment of a busy port.

If you set out to explore Bayonne in the morning, you might want to join the well-heeled Bayonnais who begin their day with a cup of hot chocolate at **Cazenave** or **Daranatz**. These elegant shops, selling all varieties of chocolates as well as other candies, are within feet of one another on the same arcaded street in Grand Bayonne, **Arceaux du Port-Neuf.** Jewish refugees brought chocolate-making to Bayonne in the 17th century, and the city still reigns supreme as France's chocolate manufacturer. For libations later in the day, cross the Place de la Liberté to the lively **Café du Théâtre,** in a 19th-century riverside building that, in addition to the theater, houses the Hôtel de Ville and the Syndicat d'Initiative.

The spires of the 13th- to 15th-century **Cathédrale Ste-Marie** are visible from almost anywhere in Bayonne. From the Place de la Liberté it's only a few minutes' walk south on rue Thiers to the cathedral, which was begun in 1253 by the British, who then occupied Bayonne. The most agreeable part of the austere cathedral are the peaceful cloisters.

Almost as dominant as the soaring cathedral is the legend of the Miracle of Bayonne. With the marriage of Eleanor of Aquitaine to Henry II in the 12th century, Bayonne went to the British. It took three centuries of warfare for the French to win it back. In the last of these battles, on August 20, 1451, a large white cross crowned by a fleur-de-lis appeared in the sky, which was readily accepted by both sides as a sign from God that Bayonne was meant to be French.

The massive fortifications to the east and south of the *centre ville* postdate the miracle by a couple of centuries. They were the work of Vauban, the military architect of Louis XVI. The sturdiest structure in these fortifications is the **citadel,** on the opposite shores of the Adour. In the winter of 1813 to 1814 the citadel was the refuge of thousands of Napoléon's troops, driven out of spain by Wellington.

Many of the businesses of Bayonne are situated along the quais of the Nive river, near the market hall. Five bridges cross the Nive to connect Grand Bayonne with Petit Bayonne. There are two fine museums in this quieter section of town, though the more interesting, the **Musée Basque**, on the riverside on rue Marengo, and housing a wealth of artifacts covering every conceivable aspect of Basque life, is closed for renovation until next year. At the **Musée Bonnat**, just around the corner on rue Jacques-Laffitte, paintings by Goya, Constable, and El Greco are among the works collected and bequeathed to Bayonne by a native son, the portrait painter Léon Bonnat, who died in 1922.

Biarritz

The place to see after Bayonne is Biarritz, not because the two have much to do with each other in spirit, but because of their proximity. Their suburbs actually run into one another, and the old center of Bayonne is only about 5 km (3 miles) north of Biarritz's Grande Plage.

Napoléon III built a château in Biarritz on a cliff above the sea for his Spanish-born wife, née Eugénia Maria de Montijo de Guzmán, in 1854. Ever since, Biarritz has enjoyed a rakish reputation to rival that of the Côte d'Azur as a playground of the rich and aristocratic, where European nobility and their followers once came to take the sea air, to gamble, and to partake of other pleasures far beyond the reach of the lower and middle classes. Eugénie's villa is now the ► **Hôtel du Palais**, and a good many of the turreted, 19th-century mansions built by the wealthy habitués of Biarritz remain, as do two churches to remind us of the sort of visitors Biarritz once attracted: an onion-domed Russian Orthodox church near the northern, Hôtel du Palais end of the Grande Plage, and a solid, gray-stone Anglican cathedral past the casino at the other end of the beach.

Today Biarritz is more likely to attract middle-class Parisians than Russian nobles and British aristocrats, and much of the new architecture is of the drab seaside school, but there's still an air of quiet refinement to this city that faces the Atlantic from atop rocky cliffs planted with pines and hydrangeas. From the Palais the smooth sands of the **Grande Plage** stretch to the ornate **Casino Bellevue**. Henry James said the casino, still catering to a crowd that brings the word *louche* to mind, had "quite the air of an establishment frequented by gentlemen who look at ladies' windows with telescopes."

AROUND THE PORT DES PECHEURS

Victor Hugo, the romantic poet and novelist, was a pre-Eugénie visitor to Biarritz. He wrote of the town in 1843, "My only fear is that it will become fashionable." Not only were

Hugo's fears realized, but he so hated the politics of the imperialist emperor and empress who put Biarritz on the map that he fled France in 1851 for 18 years. The old Biarritz that Hugo knew is today called the **Port des Pêcheurs**, separated from the Grande Plage by a rocky promontory, the **Rocher du Basta**.

Many of the simple cottages of the old port contain cafés with tables crowding the quais out front. You can sit here very happily, sipping a wine and watching the surf crash against the seawalls, before climbing the paths to the top of the adjacent Plateau de l'Atalaye, with a little aquarium, the **Musée de la Mer,** and a picturesque watchtower. In Biarritz's fishing-village days, a column of smoke from the tower's chimney signaled fishermen that there was a whale in the local waters. The **Rocher de la Vierge**, a rocky spire with a statue of the Virgin atop it, rises straight out of the sea just beyond the end of the plateau. The **Plage du Port-Vieux**, protected by high cliffs, is on the other side of the plateau, and then begins the mile-long **Plage de la Côte des Basques**, the most popular surfing beach in Europe.

SHOPPING IN BIARRITZ

In addition to the Parisian finery that fills the shop windows around the casino, some of Biarritz's most appealing offerings are edible. The *salon de thé* **Miremont** and the **Pâtisserie Paries**, both on the *place,* have been in business as long as Biarritz has been fashionable. The avenue Victor-Hugo, beginning at Place Bellevue, is given over every morning except Sundays to a lively outdoor market where you can buy strongly scented Basque farmer cheese, a bottle of wine, and a *gâteau Basque* for a picnic on the beach. If you oversleep the market, the selection at **Mille et Une Fromages**, on the avenue at number 8, is as extensive as the name suggests. Try one of the mild Basque *brebis* made from sheep's milk.

STAYING AND DINING IN BIARRITZ

For many Europeans, the only reason to come to Biarritz is to stay at the ▶ **Hôtel du Palais**, one of the last grand hotels, where the service is flawless and guests look across manicured lawns to the sea from gracious rooms where Queen Victoria, Gladstone, and Bismarck once slept. In the hotel's restaurant, **Le Grand Siècle** (a lovely semicircular pavilion at the edge of the sea), you will find yourself surrounded by an impeccably dressed polyglot crowd that seems to be enjoying this slice of *la vie en rose* enormously. The food here is homier than the stiff service would suggest; try the *piperade* *langoustines* (*piperade* is a Basque preparation of soft scrambled eggs with Espelette peppers, onions, and garlic) for a delicious light lunch or dinner. The ▶ **Hôtel Miramar**, a flashy modern hotel just a few steps north of the Palais, may well remind North Americans of the Fontainebleau in Miami Beach; its rooms, each with a terrace facing the sea, and thalassotherapy spa are especially popular with Germans. The ▶ **Hôtel Plaza**, in the center of town just a few steps off the Grande Plage, retains its 1930s charm, with commodious, ornately decorated rooms (no subtle grays and beiges here) that are reasonably priced.

The ▶ **Café de Paris**, for years the most fashionable restaurant in town, was recently renovated and now includes 11 guest rooms. Véronique and Arnaud Daguin are making a great success of their new restaurant, **Les Plantanes**, in a modest house in a residential quarter just east of the city center at 32, avenue Beausoleil. Arnaud is the son of André Daguin, the proprietor of the Hôtel de France in the Gascon capital of Auch and that region's premier chef. The food at Les Plantanes reflects Arnaud's roots: You are as likely to find a hearty cassoulet on the menu here as you are grilled tuna, and the selection of Gascony wines and Armagnac is by far the most extensive in the Pays Basque. Reserve; Tel: 59-23-13-68.

St-Jean-de-Luz

If you found Biarritz and Bayonne lacking in the exotic flavor of the Pays Basque, you'll rediscover it in St-Jean-de-Luz (pronunced "loose"), 15 km (9 miles) south of Biarritz on N 10. You'll also discover just how pleasant and pretty a port and seaside resort can be.

While St-Jean-de-Luz does have some dull apartment blocks (most of these newer buildings face the long sand beach), there are many more high, old Basque houses lining the narrow streets that twist toward the sea. The town's colorful harbor at the mouth of the Nivelle river is home port to a fleet of boats that set out each morning and return with tuna, anchovies, and sardines.

Best of all for those travellers who like a leisurely amble through old towns, the good parts of St-Jean-de-Luz—much of the waterfront and the town's lively, picturesque central section, the **Quartier de la Barre**—are for pedestrians only. Rue Gambetta bisects the quarter and ends near the harbor, in the Place Louis XIV. From a well-situated café table in this pretty square you can see many of the town's most important buildings. Among them is the **Eglise St-Jean-Baptiste**, where Louis XIV married the Infanta María Teresa of Spain in 1660. This is the largest and most beautiful Basque church of all, with a spectacularly painted ceiling and four levels of oak galleries. The only way into the church is through side doors, since the main portals were bricked up after the royal couple's exit, lest mere mortals ever darken the doorway that the Sun King so graced.

For a month before the wedding the Sun King lived in a house on the square, the **Maison Lohobiague**, next to the Hôtel de Ville. (The house is also known as the Maison Louis XIV and is open to the public in the summer.) The future queen lodged in a house on the quai to the north of the *place,* in a red brick and stone building that has ever since been known as the **Maison de l'Infanta** (not open to the public).

At a less favorable time in French history, Wellington and his troops stationed themselves in St-Jean-de-Luz after routing Napoléon's troops from Spain, in 1814. The general's headquarters were just off the *place* in the **Maison Granga Baïta**, at 2, rue Mazarin. This last street is named, of course, for Cardinal Mazarin, the financial minister who helped arrange Louis's politically advantageous marriage.

Any number of shops on rue Gambetta are worth stepping into for their huge selections of Basque table linens, berets, and folksy clothing like sheepskin vests. St-Jean also claims several of the pastry and candy shops with which Basque towns are so well endowed. On Tuesday and Friday mornings, make your way south through the old quarter to the boulevard Victor-Hugo and the town's twice-weekly farmers' market. The selections of cheeses, fruits, and pâtés is overwhelming, and you can eat your fill of the jam- or custard-filled sweet you can find only in these parts, the *gâteau Basque.* For sea views, follow rue Mazarin from the Place Louis-XIV around the narrow spit of land that separates the port from the open sea, then follow the beach on the elevated walkway atop the dike that protects St-Jean from high seas.

STAYING AND DINING IN ST-JEAN-DE-LUZ

▶ **La Devinière** is an especially pleasant hotel in an old Basque house between the church and the sea on rue Loquin. It's quiet and elegantly furnished, and there's a little garden in the back. ▶ **Le Parc Victoria** opened in 1992. The 12 guest rooms in this lovely Victorian mansion in a neighborhood of villas just north of the *centre ville* are decorated with enormous care in 1930s antiques, and all look onto the lush gardens. There's a beautiful swimming pool, and the hotel, one of the most pleasant places to stay on the coast, is only a ten-minute walk from the beach. ► **Chantaco** is a gracious country house in full view of the mountains about 2 km (1¼ miles) east of town. Many guests stay here to golf on the adjoining course, but others come just to enjoy the lush gardens, swimming pool, and relaxing surroundings.

Le Tournasse is a cozy, wood-beamed dining room between rue Gambetta and the sea on rue Tournasse. The food leans toward *pot-au-feu,* sea bass simmered in onions, and other dishes that are as comforting as the surroundings (Tel: 59-51-14-25). The fishing village of **Ciboure**, with its own collection of fine Basque houses and an old church, is just across the Nivelle from St-Jean. At mealtime it's well worth your while to stroll over here to **Chez Dominique**, on the quai Maurice-Ravel (the composer was born in Ciboure). The tiled, informal dining room is really just an extension of the kitchen, which sends out wonderfully grilled fish and other seafood brought into port that day (Tel: 59-47-29-16). After dinner here, cross the Nivelle again and take a seat in the place Louis-XIV for a nightcap beneath a sky full of stars.

SOUTH TOWARD SPAIN

If you follow the coast south from Ciboure on D 912—the so-called **Corniche Basque**, which runs atop limestone cliffs covered with grazing lands that slant into the sea—you'll soon come to **Hendaye**, just 14 km (8.5 miles) south of St-Jean-de-Luz and the last town in France. Hendaye, a fishing village turned resort, is not particularly attractive, but its long sand beach is one of the best along this coast. San Sebastián, Spain, a lovely and fascinating city, is just 23 km (14 miles) farther south. A private, narrow-gauge railway makes the run down to San Sebastián regularly; trains leave from a platform in front of Hendaye's train station.

GETTING AROUND

A car is a necessity in the Pyrénées. There is no east–west bus or train service, and Foix and Luchon are the only towns in the mountains that have regular rail connections to Paris (from the Gare d'Austerlitz). The TGV runs from Paris's Gare Montparnasse to Biarritz, Bayonne, and St-Jean-de-Luz on the Basque coast. Car rentals are available in several of the towns in the foothills of the Pyrénées, including Lourdes and Pau, as well as in Bayonne, Biarritz, and St-Jean-de-Luz.

Toulouse is the major city closest to the mountains, with regular air and train service from London, Paris, and other cities (see Toulouse and the Midi, above). Barcelona, with its international airport, is only half a day's drive from Foix via the autoroute through Perpignan.

Travellers can also approach the mountains from a number of other cities in southwestern France, including Perpignan, Narbonne, and even Bordeaux.

Some of the mountain routes, especially the high passes, are sometimes closed by snow. The dull but speedy N 117, which skirts the foothills, is always open, as are the major north–south passes into Spain.

ACCOMMODATIONS REFERENCE

The rates given below are projections for 1994. Unless otherwise indicated, rates are for a double room, double occupancy, and do not include meals. As rates are always subject to change, double-check before booking.

▶ **Auberge le Cabaliros.** 65400 **Arcizans Avant**. Tel: 62-97-04-31. 240F–260F.

▶ **Le Bordeaux.** 23, rue Richelieu et Gal Leclerc, 65110 **Cauterets**. Tel: 62-92-52-50; Fax: 62-92-63-29. 350F–450F (demi-pension). Closed November 1 to December 1.

▶ **Café de Paris.** 5, place Bellevue, 64200 **Biarritz**. Tel: 59-24-19-53; Fax: 59-24-18-20. 1,000F–1,200F.

▶ **Central Hôtel.** 1, place Charles-de-Gaulle, 64220 **St-Jean-Pied-de-Port**. Tel: 59-37-00-22; Fax: 59-37-27-79. 290F–400F.

▶ **Chantaco.** Route d'Ascain, 64500 **St-Jean-de-Luz**. Tel: 59-26-14-76; Fax: 59-26-35-97. 1,150F–1,800F.

▶ **La Devinière.** 5, rue Loquin, 64500 **St-Jean-de-Luz**. Tel: 59-26-05-51. 500F–600F.

▶ **Hostellerie de l'Aristou.** Route Sauveterre, 31510 **Barbazan**. Tel: 61-88-30-67; Fax: 61-95-55-66. 350F. Closed November and January.

▶ **Hôtel d'Angleterre.** Route de Luchon, 65240 **Arreau**. Tel: 62-98-63-30; Fax: 62-98-69-66. 240F–265F.

▶ **Hôtel Arcé.** 64430 **St-Etienne-de-Baïgorry**. Tel: 59-37-40-14; Fax: 59-37-40-27. 475F–695F. Closed mid-November to mid-March.

▶ **Hôtel Arraya.** 64310 **Sare**. Tel: 59-54-20-46; Fax: 59-54-27-04. 400F–530F. Closed mid-November through April.

▶ **Hôtel César.** 3, rue César, 65110 **Cauterets**. Tel: 62-92-52-57. 260F. Closed October and two weeks in spring.

▶ **Hôtel des Cimes.** Place du Marché, 65120 **Luz-St-Sauveur**. Tel: 62-92-82-03. 200F. Closed October, November, and May.

▶ **Hôtel Etche Ona.** Rue Richelieu, 65110 **Cauterets**. Tel: 62-92-51-43; Fax: 62-92-54-99. 190F–310F. Closed May, October, and November.

▶ **Hôtel de Londres.** 65120 **Luz-St-Sauveur.** Tel: 62-92-80-09; Fax: 62-92-96-85. 210F–240F, demi-pension.

▶ **Hôtel Miramar.** Avenue Impératrice, 64200 **Biarritz.** Tel: 59-41-30-00; Fax: 59-24-77-20. 1,695F–2,635F (high season).

▶ **Hôtel du Palais.** 1, avenue Impératrice, 64200 **Biarritz.** Tel: 59-24-09-40; Fax: 59-41-67-99. 1,300F–2,550F. Closed February.

▶ **Hôtel Plaza.** Avenue Edouard-VII, 64200 **Biarritz.** Tel: 59-24-74-00; Fax: 59-22-22-01. 450F.

▶ **Hôtel des Remparts.** 65120 **Luz-St-Sauveur.** Tel: 62-92-81-70. 150F–160F. Closed October, November, and May.

▶ **Hôtel-Restaurant Andreinia-Larramendy.** Estérençuby, 64220 **St-Jean-Pied-de-Port.** Tel: 59-37-09-70; Fax: 59-37-36-05. 200F. Closed November 15 to December 15.

▶ **Hôtel-Restaurant du Comminges.** St-Bertrand-de-Comminges, 31510 **Barbazan.** Tel: 61-88-31-43. 190F–300F.

▶ **Hôtel-Restaurant Ithurria.** 64250 **Aïnhoa.** Tel: 59-29-92-11; Fax: 59-29-81-28. 450F–600F. Closed mid-November through late March.

▶ **Hôtel-Restaurant Ramuntcho.** 1, rue de France, 64220 **St-Jean-Pied-de-Port.** Tel: 59-37-03-91; Fax: 59-37-35-17. 290F.

▶ **Hôtel-Restaurant des Rochers.** 65400 **St-Savin.** Tel: 62-97-09-52. 240F. Closed mid-October through January.

▶ **Hôtel Vignemale.** 65120 **Gavarnie.** Tel: 62-92-40-00; Fax: 62-92-40-08. 350F–890F. Closed November and December.

▶ **Panoramic Hôtel.** 65400 **St-Savin.** Tel: 62-97-08-22. 210F. Closed mid-October to mid-April.

▶ **Le Parc Victoria.** 5, rue Cèpe, 64500 **St-Jean-de-Luz.** Tel: 59-26-78-78; Fax: 59-26-78-08. 850F–1,400F.

▶ **Les Pyrénées.** 19, place du Général-de-Gaulle, 64220 **St-Jean-Pied-de-Port.** Tel: 59-37-01-01; Fax: 59-37-18-97; in U.S., (212) 856-0115; Fax: (212) 856-0193. Member, Relais & Châteaux. 550F–1,000F.

BORDELAIS AND THE DORDOGNE

By Georgia I. Hesse

Vineyard-rich hills, rising and falling like green swells of ocean, signal the traveller to arrival in the Bordelais, a kingdom of water and wine ruled by the noble city of Bordeaux.

The Bordelais, heart of the old province of Guyenne (sometimes Guienne), covers almost exactly the modern *département* of the Gironde. The department takes its name from the splendid, wide estuary the Gironde, which is formed by the meeting of the Garonne and Dordogne rivers about 35 km (22 miles) north of Bordeaux and joins the waters of the Atlantic near Royan. The limestone plains of the region called Les Charentes stretch north of the Gironde (see the Poitou and Les Charentes chapter). To the south, along the sea, lie the vast, sandy beaches, dunes, and pine forests (studded by those fish-filled pools the English call meres) of Les Landes.

The Bordelais is the linchpin of ancient Aquitaine, the many-rivered "land of waters," which as a region is still clear in the mind of every French citizen, though it no longer exists as an entity on most maps. In Julius Caesar's day it was Aquitania, that part of Gaul lying between the Pyrénées on the south and the Garonne river on the north. A Roman province, then a Frankish duchy, it became the possession of the English kings when Eleanor of Aquitaine died in 1204, and as such it was the principal arena of the Hundred Years War.

The Dordogne, one of France's longest rivers, rises in the

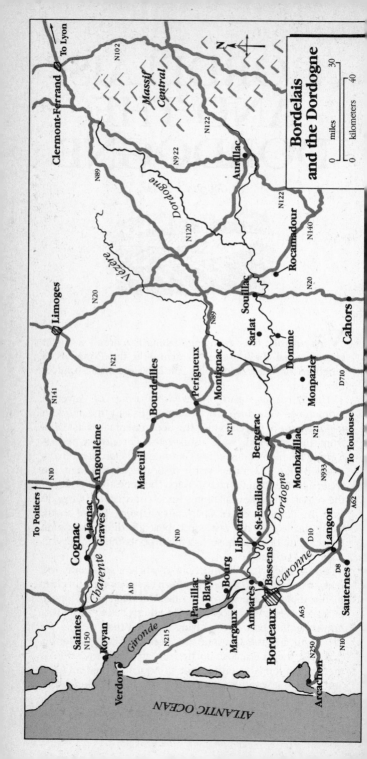

plateau known as the Massif Central; for most of its life tumultuous, it has recently been tamed by dams, artificial lakes, and hydroelectric stations. Still, it remains a capricious river in places, especially along the 38-mile run from Sarlat to St-Cyprien. A journey through the historic, lovely valley of the Dordogne begins 87 km (54 miles) due east of Bordeaux in the town of Bergerac.

The Bordelais and the valley of the Dordogne remain among the lesser-roamed major regions of France, despite their being home to some of the world's greatest wines, most fascinating human antiquities, and most magical landscapes. The best times to visit these areas—as for many parts of France—are May and June or September and October.

MAJOR INTEREST

The Bordelais

Bordeaux
Grand Théâtre
Eglise Notre-Dame
Musée des Arts Décoratifs
Musée des Beaux-Arts
Cathédrale St-André
Musée d'Aquitaine
Basilique St-Michel
Walk from Esplanade des Quinconces along Garonne
    river to Place de la Bourse
La Vinothèque

Wine châteaux and tastings
St-Emilion
Arcachon, seaside

The Dordogne
Prehistoric sites, especially caves
Drive along the Cingle de Trémolat
Les Eyzies-de-Tayac area of prehistoric sites
Monpazier *bastide*
Sarlat-La Canéda, old town for strolling
Domme, La Roque-Gageac, and Beynac-et-Cazenac,
    scenic villages
Rocamadour, scenic medieval religious site
Pech-Merle, prehistoric cave site
Cahors, on the river Lot

In the 12th century Eleanor of Aquitaine inherited lands that stretched north from the Pyrénées to the Loire and east from the Atlantic to central Auvergne, constituting a region at least as large as the kingdom of France itself. When Louis VII married Eleanor in 1137, he gained not only a wife but also a dowry comprising Guyenne, Périgord, Limousin, Poitou, Angoumois, Saintonge, Gascony, Auvergne, and Toulouse. After 15 years of misunderstandings, manipulations, and machinations, Louis VII arranged a divorce from his wife. Two months later Eleanor married Henri Plantagenêt, who himself held Anjou, Maine, Touraine, and Normandy.

The marriage of Eleanor and Henri was disastrous for the ruling house of Capet and for France, which was reduced to half its size with the loss of Eleanor's lands. When, two years later, Henri was crowned Henry II of England (as a descendant of William the Conqueror), England's properties on the continent became equal in size to those of the French kingdom itself. The French-English struggles that ensued were to last almost 300 years, culminating in the Hundred Years War. Everywhere in the Bordelais and the valley of the Dordogne, evidences of this epic antagonism are at hand: fortified castles and churches, walled towns in defensive positions atop hills, and almost 300 *bastides,* small towns designed on a grid plan.

THE BORDELAIS

BORDEAUX

Henry James wrote, "Bordeaux is . . . dedicated to the worship of Bacchus in the most discreet form."

"Take Versailles," Victor Hugo opined, "add Antwerp to it, and you have Bordeaux."

Bordeaux means business, and has since the days of the Romans, who arrived in 56 B.C. to occupy what was then Burdigala (whence, somehow, Bordeaux). The city and the vineyards the Romans planted thrived; of the Romans in Bordeaux, though, there are only scanty remains. During the 14th century and the Hundred Years War the wine trade never slowed, and in the 18th century the keys to Bordeaux's port were the heaviest in the kingdom. Only the Revolution of 1789, followed by the Napoleonic Wars and some miserable harvests, were able to dim the success of the vineyards. Not until after World War II did the suns of success and sales shine fully on Bordeaux again. Today, despite its distance of

60 miles from the sea, Bordeaux, including the outlying towns of Verdon, Bassens, Ambès, Blaye, and Pauillac on the Gironde estuary, is the sixth-largest port in France.

Whether you arrive by train, plane, ship, or car, it is the business of business that you notice first here: the warehouses and cargo sheds that line both banks of the Garonne, the new university area of Pessac-Talence on the outskirts, several industrial zones and the bustling suburbs of Grand-Parc and Benauge, the still-burgeoning fair-sports-convention-hotel-exposition conglomeration known as Le Lac, and Mériadeck, a new commercial quarter. (Much of the current economic expansion of Bordeaux has resulted from the efforts of Jacques Chaban-Delmas in his positions as mayor, president of the regional council, and occasional candidate for the French presidency.)

The center of Bordeaux is a maze of one-way streets best negotiated on foot. Leave your car at any of the quai-side parking lots on the west bank of the Garonne, only a short walk from the center of things civilized, the Place de la Comédie.

Classic Bordeaux

The traveller's Bordeaux is the 18th-century city, a classic design of rich, *bourgeois* mansions set along broad avenues and expansive esplanades with manicured gardens. The ambience is solid and prosperous, like that of a luncheon meeting of worthy burghers settling down to discuss the affairs of the day. The city speaks not of boom and bust, but of old culture purchased with old money.

PLACE DE LA COMEDIE

You should begin your exploration of Bordeaux in the Place de la Comédie, entered by three boulevards—cours du 30-Juillet, the allées de Tourny, and cours de l'Intendance. Today a grand open square with a fine fountain, the elegant *place* was the heart of the Roman town; the forum and temple, both torn down by order of Louis XIV, once stood here.

The Grand Théâtre, one of the most magnificent in France, was built atop the ruins of the temple between 1773 and 1780, to echo ancient Greece in 18th-century stone. (Its staircase and interior served as models during the construction of the Opéra in Paris.) Performances are staged in its sumptuous Salle de Spectacle beneath a sparkling Bohemian crystal chandelier. The most celebrated event is the Mai (May) Musical, with opera, concerts, and recitals; guided

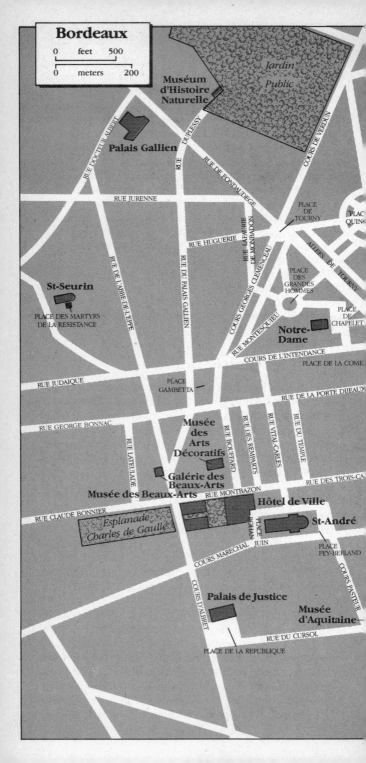

XAVIER ARNOZAN

ES DE CHARTRES

ESPLANADE
ES QUINCONCES

EES D'ORLEANS

PLACE JEAN JAURES

Grand-Théâtre

QUAI LOUIS XVIII

OURS DU CHAPEAU ROUGE

RUE DES PILIERS DE TUTELLE

RUE ST-REMI

PLACE
DE LA BOURSE

PLACE DU
PARLEMENT

RUE BUHAN

QUAI DE LA DOUANE

COURS D'ALSACE ET LORRAINE

Garonne

QUAI DES QUEYRES

Gare

PONT DE PIERRE

PLACE DE
BIR-HAKEIM

PLACE
DURBURG

COURS VICTOR HUGO

**Basilique
et Tour
St-Michel**

QUAI DE LA MONNAIE

PLACE
CANTELOUP

RUE DES MENUTS

N

visits are conducted through the theater on Tuesday through Friday mornings from mid-July through September and on weekday and Saturday afternoons at other times of the year.

Some parks, smart shopping streets, and fashionable sidewalk cafés lie to the north of the *place;* most major museums, churches, and other monumental structures lie to the south.

NORTH OF PLACE DE LA COMEDIE

If you begin north from the Grand Théâtre on the cours du 30-Juillet, you'll soon come to the Office de Tourisme' at number 12. The **Maison du Vin de Bordeaux**, at number 3, offers tastings, brochures, and books on the wines of the region; you may also make reservations to visit those wineries that demand prior arrangements. **La Vinothèque**, nearby at number 8, is a shop the size of a warehouse, its shelves heavy with bottlings and wine paraphernalia.

Two corners north of the Place de la Comédie and across the allées d'Orléans, you arrive at the Esplanade des Quinconces.

Esplanade des Quinconces

This vast expanse of greenery, stretching west of the Garonne and the quai Louis XVIII, claims to be the largest *place* in Europe (Moscow's Red Square not included). Near the western edge of the *place,* the *Monument aux Girondins* (members of a Revolutionary group, many of whom were decapitated in 1792) is an admirable sculptural ensemble incorporating a column topped by the figure of Liberty throwing off her chains and two superb bronze fountains representing the Triumph of Liberty and the Triumph of Concord.

As you face the Garonne at the west end of the esplanade, you can appreciate the two worlds of Bordeaux: Across the river, on the east bank, derricks, ships' funnels, warehouses, and characterless concrete stacks speak of the commercial, workaday world that keeps the city in business. Here on the west bank, harmonious and handsome buildings bespeak the taste of merchants who built one of the most graceful waterfronts in Europe. The gentle, crescent curve of the river here gave Bordeaux its old nickname, Port de la Lune (Port of the Moon).

Quartier des Chartrons and Jardin Public

If you follow the quai Louis XVIII north of the esplanade you'll soon enter the Quartier des Chartrons, an old quarter long devoted to the wine trade and to ships' chandlers. In the 18th century, however, many of the city's great families began building their town houses here.

Some of the finest dwellings still stand along the streets off the quai; among the most attractive examples are the mansions, with classical façades and elegant wrought-iron balconies, that line cours Xavier-Arnozan. Follow this handsome street west to the large **Jardin Public**, laid out in the mid-18th century in formal French (i.e., geometric) fashion but transformed during the Second Empire (1852–1870) into a *parc à l'anglaise*—a style the French call *accidenté,* or as nature, not landscape architects, might have created. Planted with palms and magnolias and brilliant with flowers, it is a lovely spot for strolling and picnicking.

The **Muséum d'Histoire Naturelle** occupies a fine 18th-century mansion at the southwestern corner of the Jardin Public. From the museum, walk south a few yards on rue du Palais-Gallien and turn right on rue E.-Fourcand and rue Naujac toward the **Palais Gallien**, the remains of a third-century Roman amphitheater (never a palace). Built in elliptical form, it once accommodated 15,000 spectators on tiered wooden benches.

If you walk a few steps east from the museum to rue Docteur-Barraud, then turn onto the rue de Fondaudège, a rather long amble southeast will bring you to the Place de Tourny.

Place de Tourny

This *place,* just a few steps west of the Esplanade des Quinconces, is at the apex of a fashionable triangle: The cours Georges-Clemenceau, a flagstone-paved shopping street, leads off to the southwest; the allées de Tourny, which you can follow back to the Place de la Comédie, lead off to the southeast; the cours de l'Intendance, center of upscale business and haute couture, is to the south.

Along these *allées,* chic boutiques elbow sidewalk cafés (a few of the terraces are decidedly patrician, reflecting the excellence of the vintages they serve by the glass) and too-tempting pastry shops and gourmet grocers whose windows form a gallery of epicurean pleasures.

It is a short walk from the Place de Tourny along the allées de Tourny to Place de la Comédie, but it is not made quickly. Keep your eyes open for the **Brasserie de Noailles**; it speaks of the 1930s and is a good place to relax with a seafood snack and a few glasses of dry, snappy Entre-Deux-Mers.

WEST OF PLACE DE LA COMEDIE

Walk a few yards west of the *place* along cours de l'Intendance and turn north one block on rue P.-Sarget to the Place du Chapelet and you'll find before you the unusual façade of **Eglise Notre-Dame**, built at the end of the 17th and beginning of the 18th century in "Jesuit" style (i.e., French Baroque). You may want to step inside to admire the stone carvings, then follow the rue Mably for a block north into the trendy Place des Grands-Hommes, where the **Bar des Grands-Hommes** welcomes you with a Belle Epoque façade that will put you in the mood for a bit of relaxation within.

Eglise St-Seurin

From the Place de la Comédie you can also follow the cours de l'Intendance west several blocks (it soon becomes rue Judaïque) to, with a jog north on rue R.-Pierre, the Place des Martyrs-de-la-Résistance and the Eglise St-Seurin. (At number 57 on cours de l'Intendance, stop for a moment to pay *hommage* to Francisco Goya, the exiled Spanish painter who lived in Bordeaux and died in this house in 1828.)

The treasures of St-Seurin are its 11th-century porch, an alabaster altar screen sculpted with figures from the life of the saint, and Gallo-Roman chapels in the crypt. Next to the church on the *place,* a necropolis, frescoes, and sarcophagi bear witness to the lives of early Roman Christians.

SOUTH OF PLACE DE LA COMEDIE

A walk around the gracious southern reaches of old Bordeaux begins in the Place Gambetta, several blocks west of the Place de la Comédie off cours de l'Intendance. (This is a good place to find yourself when it's time for an apéritif; there are several cafés on the *place.*) The architectural unity of the square is a delight, an ensemble of houses in Louis XV style with arcades on the ground floor and mansard windows at the top. A scaffold stood here during the Revolution.

From Place Gambetta it's a short stroll south on rue Bouffard to the **Musée des Arts Décoratifs**. Of particular interest here are the *pots-Jaqueline,* rustic, traditional pieces from Lille that are reminiscent of English toby jugs.

Around the Hôtel de Ville

Many of Bordeaux's major sights cluster around the Hôtel de Ville, just south of the museum on rue Bouffard in the 18th-century **Palais Rohan**, built for the archbishop and prince of the noted and sometimes notorious Rohan family. You can tour the building on Wednesday afternoons at 2:30, but otherwise be content to admire the gardens and the works in the **Musée des Beaux-Arts** (just behind the Palais Rohan on rue Montbazon), particularly rich in Dutch art and works by three men born in Bordeaux: Odilon Redon, André Lhote, and Albert Marquet. Just "behind" the Musée des Beaux-Arts and west on rue Montbazon (on Place du Colonel-Raynal) the **Galerie des Beaux-Arts** presents contemporary exhibitions.

The **Cathédrale St-André**, almost facing the Rohan Palace, was built in the 11th century and has "endured" several additions, among them the Porte Royale, with its extraordinary 13th-century sculptures, and the curious 15th-century belfry, the Tour Pey-Berland, standing on its own on the grounds. In 1137, the future Louis VII and Eleanor of Aquitaine were married in this cathedral, nearly as long and broad as Notre-Dame in Paris.

The **Centre Jean Moulin**, just north of St-André, off rue des Trois-Conils, houses exhibits that illustrate France's role in World War II, particularly the Resistance and the deportation. Jean Moulin has come to represent the heroic struggle of the French fighters against the Nazis and their collaborators.

The **Musée d'Aquitaine**, at the corner of cours Victor-Hugo and cours Pasteur (which runs south from the Tour Pey-Berland), displays a treasure trove of relics, tools, and artworks ranging from the Paleolithic period to the Renaissance. Among the most famous items here is the fat little Vénus de Laussel, sculpted some 20,000 years before the birth of Christ.

South to the Basilique St-Michel

A walk south along the river brings you first, just south of cours de l'Intendance, to the harmonious architectural ensemble known as the **Place de la Bourse** (*bourse* means "stock exchange"). Flanked by the matched façades of the Hôtel des Fermes (Customshouse) on the south and Palais de la Bourse on the north, the square surrounds a fountain, the work of architects Gabriel, *père et fils*. If you continue south along the quais past the Pont de Pierre (it's a considerable trek) you'll come to the **Basilique St-Michel**, west of the quai de la Monnaie and between Place Duburg and Place Canteloup. Begun in 1350 but not completed for more than two centuries, it boasts a clock tower that at 374 feet is the highest tower in southern France.

SHOPPING IN BORDEAUX

Window shop along cours de l'Intendance and rue Ste-Catherine (they meet at Place de la Comédie) and you'll think you are in Paris. For shopping with a difference, consider everything for your favorite wine enthusiast from **Humbert** on cours Victor-Hugo; cheeses from **Jean d'Alos** on rue Montesquieu off l'Intendance; wines and wine-associated eccentricities plus a museum and tastings at **Badie** on allées de Tourny; and books, many from Great Britain, on everything at **Librairie Mollat**, on rue Vital-Carles.

Sip while shopping at the **Salon de Thé/Pour La Maison**, not far from the Palais Rohan on rue des Remparts; antiques, gifts, tableware, embroideries, and decorative light fixtures can be considered here while you consume a *café filtre*.

Antiques are best found in the area of Notre-Dame, the St-Michel quarter (centered around the old basilica and tower of St-Michel, south of the Pont de Pierre), and around Place Gambetta; flea markets change locations daily—ask at the Office de Tourisme. The best of a handful of covered markets is at **Place des Grands-Hommes**.

STAYING IN AND AROUND BORDEAUX

If you want to be within walking distance of the most important sites and streets, consider the 100-room ▶ **Normandie** on cours du 30-Juillet, neatly situated between the allées de Tourny and the Esplanade des Quinconces. The 50-room ▶ **Majestic** is just across the street from the northeastern corner of the Grand Théâtre. The small but comfortable ▶ **Grand Hôtel Français**, on rue du Temple not far from Place Gambetta, has been handsomely renovated. The ▶ **Sainte-Catherine** is also nicely located south of the Grand Théâtre.

The ▶ **Hôtel Burdigala**, at 115, rue Georges-Bonnac, and the ▶ **Pullman Mériadeck**, at 5, rue Robert-Lateulade, considered to be the two best modern hotels in Bordeaux, are in the quarter west of the Hôtel de Ville.

One of the most relaxing and refreshing countryside retreats near Bordeaux is ▶ **Le St-James**, about 18 km (11 miles) southeast of the city in the suburb of Bouliac (follow D 10 south to Bouliac; the inn is on Place Charles-Hostein, near the village church). The real fame here resides in the kitchen, one of the finest in this region; the shady terrace and views of Bordeaux add to the enjoyment (reserve; Tel: 56-20-52-19). The 18 rooms are innovatively decorated.

The ▶ **Château de Foulon**, a 19th-century country manor, commands a 130-acre park near the Médoc vineyards and shady pine woods; it's about 28 km (17 miles) north of the city via N 215 and D 1 in the direction of Lacanau and Castelnau-de-Médoc. The 19-room ▶ **La Réserve**, 15 km (9 miles) southwest of town near Pessac (follow rue de Pessac

and cours du Maréchal-Gallieni in the direction of Arcachon), is set in a garden and has a fine restaurant on the
premises.

(For other countryside retreats, see also the section on
staying and dining in wine country, below.)

DINING IN BORDEAUX

The cooking of Bordelais is not restricted to a single style,
but covers the range of classical, urbane cuisine. The one
term that reflects local traditions is *à la bordelaise* (simply,
Bordeaux-style), which normally refers to dishes cooked in
sauce bordelaise, a delicious compound of wine, butter,
tomato extract, and marrow seasoned with shallots, thyme,
and nutmeg. *A la bordelaise* usually indicates a dish accompanied by artichokes and potatoes.

The classic beef dish of Bordeaux is *entrecôte à la
bordelaise,* requiring a fine rib steak grilled over dry cuttings
from regional vines, served immediately after being blanketed in *sauce bordelaise.*

Le Chapon Fin was for decades among the top half-dozen
restaurants in France. In the 1960s it fell upon less exalted
days, but *voilà!* It has been returned to excellence by chef
Francis Garcia and, in its original location at 5, rue Montesquieu (near the Place des Grandes-Hommes), has retained
its 1900s Rococo decor. This is a place to try *lamproie à la
bordelaise* (lamprey eel). Always reserve; Tel: 56-79-10-10.
Clustered near the top of the culinary ladder are **Le Rouzic**,
at 34, cours du Chapeau Rouge, right near the Grand Théâtre, where chef Michel Gautier works wonders with such
dishes as curried oyster ravioli (reserve; Tel: 56-44-39-11);
Jean Ramet, at 7, place Jean-Jaurès, near the quai Louis XVIII,
where the *blanquette de veau* is almost required eating
(reserve; Tel: 56-44-12-51); **Pavillon des Boulevards**, at 120,
rue Croix de Seguey, northwest of the city center off avenue
de la Libération—try the fish called *rougets* (reserve; Tel: 56-
81-51-02); and **Le Vieux Bordeaux**, at 27, rue Buhan—try the
duck liver (reserve; Tel: 56-52-94-36).

La Chamade, at 20, rue des Piliers-de-Tutelle, offers elegant service and cuisine in an 18th-century cellar (reserve;
Tel: 56-48-13-74). Sportsmen flock to **Le Clavel Barnabet** at
44, rue Charles-Domercq, across from the St-Jean railway
station, where regulars include members of the local soccer
team (Tel: 56-92-91-52).

La Tupina is a casual and colorful bistro at 6, rue Porte de
la Monnaie. Chef J. P. Xiradakis—a Gascon despite his
Greek-sounding name—is a former president of the associa-

tion for the preservation of southwestern culinary traditions (reserve; Tel: 56-91-56-37).

The highest ranking in the region usually goes to **Le St-James**, southeast of town in suburban Bouliac; see Staying In and Around Bordeaux, above.

Exploring Bordeaux Wine Country

For many oenophiles, the Bordeaux region is simply the greatest winescape on the globe. Here, after all, vines first imported from Greece have grown happily since the beginning of the Christian era. North of Bordeaux blush the noble "red princes" of **Médoc** (the big four are Château Lafite, Château Latour, Château Margaux, and Mouton-Rothschild; others are St-Estèphe, Pauillac, and St-Julien). These are wines that age with grace: "All the angles grow round in the bottle," say the Médociens.

Here, also, mature great whites: the sumptuous **Sauternes**, south of Bordeaux, and the dry and nifty **Graves**, between Sauternes and the city. Across the Garonne and the Dordogne to the east the rewarding reds of **St-Emilion**, **Pomerol**, and **Fronsac** are at home, with Château Pétrus shining the most brilliantly among the Pomerols.

Then there are the crisp whites of **Entre-Deux-Mers**, in the triangle where the two rivers meet to become the Gironde, and the **Côtes de Blaye** on the east bank of the Gironde. These are the delicious everyday wines the French term great *ordinaires*. Other appellations are relatively prestigious in their own right: **Côtes de Bourg**, just south of Blaye, and **Pécharmant**, to name but two.

The prettiest time to wander these winelands is in autumn; however, it is also the hectic harvest time, when visitors are not greeted with glee and frequently are not greeted at all. Except when picking and crushing are in progress, though, it is possible to visit most of the above properties; plan an itinerary with the assistance of wine authorities in Bordeaux. (In general, great Bordeaux châteaux are more chary of welcoming outsiders than are those in other regions of France.)

A few châteaux, such as **Beychevelle** and **Lafite**, operate guided tours on a regular basis. (Beychevelle owes its name to *baisse-voile*, or "lowered sail," a salute demanded by its 17th-century owner, the duc d'Eperon, who demanded both respect and a toll.) To visit others, write or call ahead for an appointment (it's easiest to deal with tourist offices or the Maison du Vin in Bordeaux). The museum in the *caves* of the **Château Mouton-Rothschild** is not to be missed (reserva-

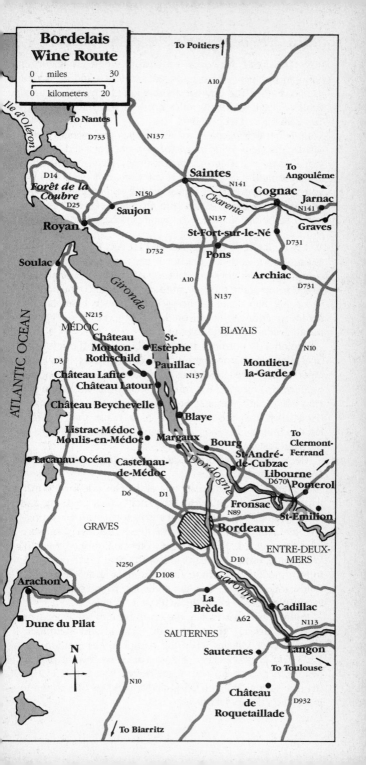

tions required): Artworks from various periods featuring
wine and grapes, and magnificent tapestries and glassware
are on display. The estate is about 2 km (1¼ miles) north of
Pauillac (itself 48 km/30 miles north of Bordeaux); Tel: 56-
59-22-22. Closed weekends.

In general it's easiest to visit estates and wineries that
display the signs *Vente au détail* (loosely translated as "individual sales") or *Dégustation* (tastings). Note that *dégusta-
tions* are held in good faith: If you taste, it is expected that
you will buy, even if it is just a little something. In some
villages and at some estates, the reception center sells light
meals to be accompanied by wine purchased on the spot.

WINE ROUTES AND VILLAGES
Most authorities divide the Bordeaux wine country into five
routes for travellers who want to taste various varietals and
to see some of the most beautiful agricultural countryside in
France. A map detailing the various routes is essential; ask
for information at the Maison du Vin at 3, cours du 30-Juillet
in Bordeaux before setting out.

Region 1 is northern Bordeaux, bordering the left bank
of the Gironde northwest of the city (divided into Haut-
Médoc, the more prestigious, and Bas-Médoc, at the northwestern tip). Among the most famous wine villages in the
Haut-Médoc are Margaux, St-Julien, Pauillac, and St-Estèphe.
(Note that it is the wines that have made their villages
famous, not the reverse. The towns themselves often are of
little interest.)

The round trip from Bordeaux through this region is
about 165 km (102 miles).

Region 2 covers the east bank of the Gironde (also northwest of Bordeaux), including the small Côtes de Bourg and
the Côtes de Blaye. (Blaye is a resort town with an impressive *citadelle*.) Although few of these regional wines are
world-renowned, the reds of the Côtes de Bourg are often of
great value. From Bordeaux follow the river north on D 113,
follow the D 911 turnoff, and, from St-André-de-Cubzac,
follow the signs to Bourg on D 669. The round trip, through
especially nice countryside, is 100 km (62 miles).

Route 3 takes you along the north bank of the Dordogne
east of Bordeaux through pretty Fronsac and St-Emilion,
among other villages. (See the section on St-Emilion, below.) The great vintages of Pomerol come from a plateau
near here; there is no real village center. It's a trip of 130 km
(81 miles) beginning on D 911 and N 10. Via D 670, continue
in the direction of Libourne.

Route 4 goes southeast of Bordeaux through the land known as Entre-Deux-Mers, also the name of some flinty white wines well suited to seafood. (Entre-Deux-Mers means "between two seas," the "seas" being the Dordogne and Garonne rivers.) From here come many of the wines known simply as red or white Bordeaux. The trip of about 130 km (81 miles) begins along D 936 in the direction of Bergerac.

Route 5 explores the vineyards of Graves, Sauternes, and the Premières Côtes de Bordeaux, where some of the most distinctive wines of Bordeaux are produced. This trip of about 125 km (78 miles) begins to the southwest of Bordeaux on N 250 and continues in the direction of Arcachon and Pessac, where one of the most glorious wines in the world (a Graves) is produced at the Château Haut-Brion.

As in the case of St-Emilion (see the next section), a few wine villages and châteaux southeast of Bordeaux are worth visiting in themselves, on separate outings or on one circuit.

Château de Labrède

The Château de Labrède (about 15 km/9 miles southeast of Bordeaux on N 113 and D 108), its severe walls rising from the waters of a wide moat, is the essence of a medieval stronghold. Its appearance hasn't changed since baron de Labrède et de Montesquieu (né Charles de Segondat in 1689) wrote there in his private chambers; it still belongs to his descendants. You can see his study and library, its shelves holding 7,000 volumes, on a guided tour. Concerts are played here during the Mai Musical de Bordeaux.

Cadillac

Cadillac, on the Garonne about 30 km (19 miles) southeast of Bordeaux on N 113 or D 10, has conserved its 14th-century ramparts, and its château of the ducs d'Eperon exemplifies the Henri IV–Louis XIII style. Its huge rooms are outfitted with eight monumental fireplaces, the work of sculptor Jean Langlois; many 17th-century tapestries woven within the château are on display. From Cadillac it's a 35-km (22-mile) run back to Bordeaux.

Château de Roquetaillade

The feudal Château de Roquetaillade (about 50 km/31 miles southeast of Bordeaux on N 113 and D 222), built in 1306, forms a most photogenic composition with its six immense, round, crenellated towers—a sturdy donjon. The interior is a fine example of the restoration of medieval châteaux as conceived by Viollet-le-Duc during the Second Empire.

ST-EMILION

Of all the wine towns in the Bordeaux region, St-Emilion is the most alluring and enticing. (From Bordeaux take avenue de Thiers and N 89 east to Libourne and then veer slightly south on D 243, a total distance of about 40 km/25 miles.) Sitting atop its little limestone hill overlooking the Dordogne, St-Emilion seduces even non-oenophiles.

Two figures step out of history in St-Emilion: the fourth-century Gallo-Roman poet and proconsul Ausonius and the eighth-century Breton monk Emilion. Ausonius, whose poems glorify the joys of food and wine, was a native of Bordeaux who established a sumptuous villa and a vineyard near St-Emilion. Tradition says the wines produced on the estate were served to the Roman emperor; they still command prices that are no less than fabulous. (The vineyards, commanding a splendid site on the southwestern edge of town, escaped the terrible frost of February 1956, when so many other vineyards were destroyed.)

The second historic figure, the hermit Emilion, arrived in the eighth century from Brittany, on pilgrimage to Santiago de Compostela in Spain. Supposedly attracted by a miraculous spring, he established a religious colony upon the spot. Cynics believe the "holy spring" was really the seductive wines of the region, for almost assuredly the little city was already bustling. In any case, the saint lingered; nothing is recorded of his continuing to Compostela.

Today the peace of the golden-stoned village of 3,000 inhabitants belies its bloody history of battles between English and French during the Hundred Years War, between Catholics and Huguenots during the Wars of Religion, and between the radical Jacobins and the moderate Girondists in 1792. (The Girondists were so named because their most persuasive members came from Bordeaux—in the Gironde.)

Churches and Catacombs

St-Emilion sits on two levels. About the only place for drivers to park is on the upper, near the **Eglise Collégiale**, from which the whole village may be explored easily on foot. From the church (the interior is rather disappointing, but its cloister is worth a quick look) a cobbled street winds through the Porte de la Cadène and down to the lower level, the center of town. The **Place du Marché**, the former market-place (the lively Sunday-morning market is actually on Place Bouqueyre), is somnolent most of the time, with the buying and selling (of wines, mostly) proceeding languidly, if at all. (The best wineshop in town is **Le Cellier des Gourmets**.)

St-Emilion's major treasure, the **Eglise Monolithe**, is entered from the Place du Marché; a sign on the door tells which shop is keeping the key. The rare subterranean church, the largest and most important of its kind in France, was hewn from the rock walls of several adjoining caves by Benedictine monks from the end of the ninth to the beginning of the 12th century. Stripped of decorations, treasures, and the bones of the buried monks during the Revolution, it is today a massive, cold, forbidding, almost mystical space. (The hack-marks still show in its bays and vaults and on its pillars.) The tower of this marvel reaches above ground clear to the upper level of the town (on the Place du Clocher, where cars are parked) like "a finger of God [rising] from a sea of vines," as wine writer Ernst Hornickel put it.

At the end of the *place* the 13th-century **Chapelle de la Trinité** stands on top of a grotto known as **L'Ermitage St-Emilion**, supposedly the cave in which the hermit lived, sleeping on a bed cut out of the rock and drinking from a spring that bubbles still, as if the saint were to return by evening. Tombs and an underground chamber known as the **catacombs** have been carved out of a limestone cliff near the chapel. The catacombs were used as a charnel house: From the cemetery on the cliff, bones were dumped through a hole in the top of the chamber. Notice a macabre touch down here: Three children step out of their sarcophagi, holding hands, an image that must have been intended to symbolize resurrection but that alarms, rather than reassures, modern sensibilities. The annual Jurade, a ritual held in late September or early October, depending upon the harvest, dates from medieval times: Several councilmen dressed in ermine-edged scarlet robes parade through town to a hilltop ruin known as **La Tour du Roi** (The King's Tower). From there they pronounce in stentorian chant the result of the year's harvest, echoed by the townsfolk in the square below, who cheer "Hallelujah!" in increasingly excited tones. ("And what would you say if one year the wine was no good?" a *jurat* was asked. "We should pronounce it 'insufficiently fine,'" he answered solemnly.)

STAYING AND DINING IN ST-EMILION AND ELSEWHERE IN WINE COUNTRY
The ▶ **Hostellerie Plaisance** on Place du Clocher is a pleasant, informal, 12-room inn with a kitchen that serves regional fare and boasts an impressive list of St-Emilion wines. For rural, family-style dining, **Logis de la Cadène** is the best in town (Tel: 57-24-71-40), although **Chez Germaine**, across the street from the inn, is also pleasant (Tel: 57-24-70-88). On the main street, rue Guadet, the **Galerie Jean Guyot** offers excel-

lent buys in regional pottery. Between St-Emilion and Pomerol, the **Château Cheval Blanc** (Tel: 57-24-70-70) produces what experts consider the most highly bred of the St-Emilion wines. It is open only by appointment and only on weekdays, as is the equally renowned **Château Figeac** (Tel: 57-24-72-26; phone two days in advance; closed August).

Should you wish to stay a night or so to wander slowly around the Médoc, you could do no better than the ▶ **Relais de Margaux** in the village of Margaux, about 22 km (14 miles) north of Bordeaux on N 215 (follow the signs that mark a right turn to Pauillac and continue on the road reading *Route touristique du Médoc*). The 28 rooms and three apartments are luxurious, the staff pampering, the chef most able, the wine cellar excellent. Expensive, but worth every franc.

The privately owned 19th-century ▶ **Château de Foulon**, mentioned also under Bordeaux, above, welcomes guests in five bedrooms. The château is in a 100-acre park just south of Castelnau-de-Médoc, 21 km (13 miles) north of Bordeaux on D 1.

One of the best country inns in France is ▶ **Claude Darroze**, 48 km (30 miles) southeast of Bordeaux on N 113 in the town of Langon, at 95, cours Général-Leclerc. There are 16 comfortable rooms and a superb kitchen; seafood is a specialty. Reservations are essential; Tel: 56-63-00-48.

Arcachon

The seaside resort town of Arcachon is 64 km (40 miles) southwest of Bordeaux on N 250. The Arcachonnais divide their little city into the *ville d'été* (summer town) and the *ville d'hiver* (winter town). The former looks north across the Bassin d'Arcachon from shaded boulevards and a fine sand beach.

The wide boulevard de la Plage, the summer town's main artery, is lined by smart shops and coffee bars, a **casino** (at the corner of the boulevard and avenue Nelly-Deganne), and an **aquarium-museum**. One section is devoted to oysters, those *huîtres d'Arcachon* that so delighted Rabelais. A disease raged through the oyster beds in 1922 and thereafter, forcing the importation of oysters from Portugal—hence, the widely known *Portugaises*. Since 1972 the crop has been augmented through importation from Japan and Canada, putting Arcachon firmly up front among oyster-producing centers in France.

The winter town, south of city center and sheltered from ocean winds, consists of pretty streets that wander through the pine forests and are lined with late-19th- and early-20th-century homes.

Just 8 km (5 miles) south of Arcachon via D 218 is the **Dune du Pilat**, the highest sand dune in Europe: 317 feet high, 1,640 feet wide, and about a mile and a half long. Rising gently from the ocean on the west, it presents a very steep face inland, on the east. It can be climbed, albeit with some difficulty; inquire about conditions of a fairly well maintained stairway at the Office de Tourisme in Arcachon. The views from the top of the dune at sunset are stupendous.

STAYING AND DINING IN ARCACHON

A very pleasant place to lunch (outdoors, weather permitting) is at **Patio**, 10, boulevard de la Plage (Tel: 56-83-02-72). **Chez Yvette**, at 59, boulevard Général-Leclerc (near the Office de Tourisme on Place Franklin-Roosevelt), specializes in seafood (Tel: 56-83-05-11).

To idle along the sands for a day or so, you might book a room at ▶ **Arc Hôtel sur Mer**, a tranquil 30-room inn with a fine view and its own outdoor swimming pool (but no restaurant). Another good choice is ▶ **Les Vagues**, which has 29 rooms, a restaurant (open only in the evenings), and a pretty garden.

THE DORDOGNE

The green, serene valley of the Dordogne is inexplicably spooky. One tends to drive carefully, as if expecting the mysterious, prehistoric Cro-Magnon man, who 40,000 years ago called this valley home, to materialize in the rear-view mirror.

Perhaps it is the autumnal light-and-shadow haze, a drapery as delicate as a Japanese screen, that hangs above the countryside almost all year long. Maybe it's the flickering forms of willows and poplars reflected in the clear waters of the Dordogne and its tributary, the Vézère. In the Dordogne, artful nature conspires with the works of man—golden stone houses and châteaux, little towns as tempting as pastries—to convince the traveller that this may be the loveliest corner of France.

The Dordogne ranks among the longest rivers in France, taking both its source and its name from the meeting place

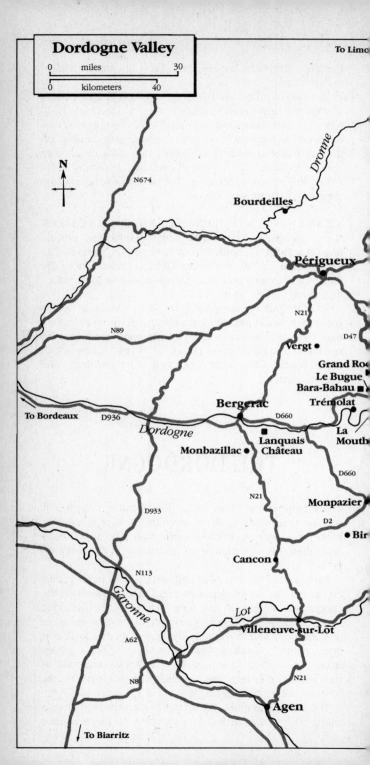

of the Dore and the Dogne near the town of Clermont-Ferrand and the Puy de Sancy—at 6,184 feet the highest peak in the Massif Central. From its headwaters the river used to skip swiftly over its volcanic bed and slice through narrow ravines, but it has been slowed by dams and artificial lakes constructed to turn the turbines of huge power plants. Those who wish to follow the river along (and about and around) its length will start upstream at Bort-les-Orgues and continue down to Libourne, about 500 km (310 miles) to the west.

On the other hand, the Dordogne of lore, legend, and archaeological interest can best be explored by beginning at Bergerac, 87 km (54 miles) east of Bordeaux, and proceeding with measured pace east toward Souillac and the Gouffre de Padirac, making detours north and south en route. The river roams through the regions of Périgord and Quercy, rich in underground caverns.

It is not nature, however, but the mark of humankind that dominates in so many places along the Dordogne and throughout this region. No other place on earth is so rich in evidence of early man, who left behind many outstanding examples of his Paleolithic art and tools. The most intriguing and most advanced of these early peoples were the Cro-Magnons, a tall (about 5 feet 11 inches on average) and erect race that recorded elements of its existence on the cave walls of the Dordogne-Vézère.

The Dordogne West of Sarlat

FROM BERGERAC TO TREMOLAT

There is no compelling reason to visit Bergerac, although from an economic standpoint it is the most important town along the Dordogne. If you arrive at noon, however, there *is* an excellent excuse for stopping: the restaurant known as **Le Cyrano**, in honor of the 17th-century duelist and writer who won fame only posthumously in the writing of Edmond Rostand. (Cyrano was born in Paris, but since his father was a Bergerac the city claims the romantic hero.) The restaurant, at 2, boulevard Montaigne (Tel: 53-57-02-76), offers the regional wines of Bergerac (fruity red, dry or sweet white) to accompany fine local dishes.

After lunch you might visit the **Musée du Tabac**, unique in France, dedicated to the history, influence on society, and growth of the "American weed."

From the vineyards south of here around **Monbazillac** (about 17 km/11 miles round trip) comes the heavy, sweet dessert wine that has made the term "noble rot" a synonym for perfection throughout the centuries. The vineyard's elegant 16th-century château is open as a museum of Calvinism, but photographing its exterior may be satisfaction enough for non-Calvinists. The wine may be tasted and buying is encouraged at the shop near the castle gate.

From Bergerac, D 660 (which becomes D 703, the lovely road that follows the twisting course of the river) runs east toward **Château Lanquais**, an architectural mishmash rising from the ruins of a fortress battered by the English during the Hundred Years War. Students of Louis XIII furniture will appreciate the interiors.

Near the pleasant village of **Trémolat**, 34 km (21 miles) east of Bergerac, the road climbs a coil of white cliffs from which there's a splendid view of the **Cingle de Trémolat** (*cingle* means "meander" in French). Below, the Dordogne bends in remarkable S-curves through fields that look like green or golden chessboards. If twilight is approaching, wait for the sun to set over the ordered landscape.

SOUTH TO MONPAZIER

Not all of the Hundred Years War was devoted to destruction. Constant struggles between the French and English forces necessitated the construction of fortified towns, mostly along disputed frontiers. These *bastides* (the word derives from the old-French verb *bastir,* "to build") are among the most interesting examples of military architecture in France.

Monpazier is among the two or three best-preserved *bastides* still functioning as towns. (To reach Monpazier, leave the river about 19 km/12 miles beyond Bergerac on D 660 south; Monpazier is 26 km/16 miles down the road.) French and English *bastides* once faced each other wall to wall near the rivers Garonne, Lot, and Dordogne. Whether French or English they adhered to an identical plan of straight streets that cut across alleys, and small spaces that acted as drains, firebreaks, or latrines. At the center of each town, a *cornière* (plazalike square) was surrounded by roofed arcades. Nearby stood a church, commonly fortified.

Monpazier was an English *bastide* founded on January 7, 1284, by Edward I. Attackers and defenders often changed roles in those confusing days, and Monpazier was assaulted by both sides with some regularity, depending upon which forces were in power at the time. In 1594 and 1637 Monpazier also served as a center for some of the fiercest peasant revolts in the region.

Remarkably, Monpazier retains its grid pattern, its fortified church (restored in the 16th century), and its roomy square flanked by covered galleries. The sturdy old houses still stand, and the measuring standards for judging weights hang in place in the covered market. Shops selling souvenirs, fruits and vegetables, and arts and crafts snuggle into the arcades, shading themselves from the summer sun, and it seems as though the whole place has been hibernating since the 13th century.

NORTH TO LES EYZIES

High ocher cliffs rise from the narrow green valley that shelters the village of Les Eyzies-de-Tayac, about 10 km (6 miles) northeast of Trémolat on the river Vézère (from Trémolat you can take D 31 and D 31E to Les Eyzies, following the river Vézère much of the time). Prehistoric people lived here during the Ice Age, occupying caves for tens of thousands of years and leaving behind a legacy of tools, weapons, pottery, and—particularly provocative—the marvelous works of art that are their cave paintings. (In ancient times the bed of the Vézère lay some 90 feet above today's level, and the caves were more accessible than they are today.)

Les Eyzies's **Musée National de la Préhistoire** occupies the castle of the barons of Beynac, and from modest beginnings it has grown to rank among the best of its kind in France. Discoveries in the region are described and outlined, while many original objects and reproductions of paintings are displayed. A visit to this museum is mandatory as an introduction to the sites themselves. Nearby, an amusing statue of Cro-Magnon man, as envisioned by sculptor Paul Dardé in 1930, stares out from beneath an overhanging rock.

From Easter through September a lively Monday market fills Les Eyzies's main street.

Prehistoric Sites Near Les Eyzies

The prehistory museum in Les Eyzies provides a list of recommended sites in the immediate neighborhood. It includes the **Grotte de la Mouthe**, the first cave to be discovered (just a croissant's toss south of town), the **Grotte des Combarelles**, with portrayals of nearly 300 animals (a short detour east of town on D 47), and **Bara-Bahau**, with very early flintwork engravings (a short spurt west of Le Bugue along D 703).

Just east of the village (off D 47, where the mouth of the St-Cyprien Valley opens) the **Grotte de Font-de-Gaume** testifies to the creative talents of Paleolithic people. The wall paintings at the grotto form a veritable catalog of creatures of the hunt: bison, mammoths, horses, reindeer, and more. A well-fed horse outlined in black relief thrusts its front legs against a bend in the wall, while another wall forms the hump of a multicolored buffalo.

Stalactites, stalagmites, and more eccentric formations fill the **Grotte du Grand Roc** (to the northwest on D 47), many of them more recent than the paintings within. At the **Grotte de Rouffignac** (just north of Les Eyzies on a spur off D 32), an electric railway passes through two and a half miles of underground galleries, their walls alive with engravings, drawings, and paintings.

Lascaux

Among the most exceptional cave paintings yet found are those at Lascaux, a few miles northeast of Les Eyzies along D 706 near Montignac. These works, dating from about 14,000 to 13,500 B.C., were discovered in 1940 by young boys in search of a dog that had fallen into a hole. The cave, dubbed "the Sistine Chapel of Périgord," was opened to an amazed public in 1948. Alas, despite all precautions, the green sickness (moss and algae) and the white (calcite deposits) proliferated as a result of carbon dioxide and humidity. To preserve the paintings, Lascaux was closed in 1963.

In 1983, after ten years of labor, **Lascaux II**, a brilliant facsimile in a cement shell, opened near the original cave, with archaeological finds from the site as well as ingeniously reproduced paintings, achieved by using the same methods as those employed by the original Paleolithic artists.

The **Centre de Recherche et d'Art Préhistoriques**, south of Montignac, is an excellent one-stop introduction to the animals, environment, cave paintings, and civilizations of the Paleolithic era, employing films, audiovisuals, still photographs, casts, and models. Here, too, you will find a list of recommended sites. The adjoining park is home to animals represented in the paintings, such as the extremely rare Przewalski's horse.

ALONG THE RIVER
FROM BEYNAC TO MONTFORT

Beynac-et-Cazenac, and especially the views from its formidable château, stay in your mind long after you've left. Somehow, a fierce past lies lightly on this pastel, impressionistic countryside. (Beynac is 26 km/16 miles southeast of Les Eyzies on D 706, D 35, D 49, and D 703.)

The Capets and Plantagenêts were rivals here, and Richard the Lion-hearted employed the thuggish Mercadier to pillage the countryside on his royal behalf. He seized Beynac in 1189, but the indefatigable Montfort wiped it out in 1214. A great part of today's **château** dates from the 13th century; the well-restored hall of state is notable, and there's a smashing view from the battlements. In the Middle Ages Beynac was, with Biron, Bourdeilles, and Mareuil, one of the four grand baronies of Périgord.

There is not much to do here except gaze into the distance and imagine Richard's forces attacking. That done, it's time to eat a little something on the terrace of the small inn called **Bonnet**.

Directly south across the sinuous river from Beynac there is a museum of the Middle Ages in **Castelnaud**, one of Europe's finest fortified castles. Its most popular attraction is a reconstructed wooden catapult that in its heyday could hurl a 99-pound stone ball 600 feet with impressive accuracy.

It seems unlikely that **La Roque-Gageac**, 8 km (5 miles) east of Beynac on D 703, should exist at all: Perhaps it and its fewer than 500 Laroquois are figments of an inspired imagination. The flat faces of old stone houses are reflected in the river, while behind them narrow alleyways scale the cliff face and lead to the humble 12th-century church. The castle at the west end of the village is a 19th-century imitation of a 15th-century style; still, it appears very authentic in this setting.

La Roque is best seen and photographed from the west: If you arrive from the east, make sure to see the western approach before leaving.

Domme, 3 km (2 miles) east and across the river from Beynac and La Roque-Gageac on D 46, is a village of fewer than a thousand people whose ancestors were embroiled in the struggles of the Reformation. At a mere suggestion any one of them will tell the tale of Huguenot Captain Geoffroi de Vivans, who with daring (say Protestants) or trickery (say Catholics) took the town in the middle of the night in 1588.

From Domme's Belvédère de la Barre you can look over the rich, crop-checkered valley where the Dordogne eases slowly between its poplar-lined banks. The Château de Beynac, across the river in Beynac, and the great cliff of La Roque-Gageac thrust their silhouettes against the sky. The caves (the entrance is near the covered market) that sheltered the townspeople during the Hundred Years War and the Wars of Religion are rich in stalactites, stalagmites, and bones of Ice Age bison and rhinoceri; the trek through the caves leads to the pretty Promenade des Falaises (Cliff Walk) and then to the Promenade des Remparts.

From La Roque-Gageac or Domme you can snake east on skinny D 703 above the twisting **Cingle de Montfort**. The **Château de Montfort**, just beyond the village of Carsac, sits on its rock outcropping above a wide bend in the Dordogne, its towers and turrets threatening at any moment to teeter over the precipice. Today privately owned, the château has survived a history of sieges, battles, and reconstructions, having been burned to the ground in 1214 by Simon de Montfort in one of his anti-Albigensian crusades. To call its style a mélange is to understate.

From here it's only 9 km (5½ miles) north on D 704 to Sarlat, or you can continue to follow the wiggles of the river east on D 703. You should do both.

Sarlat

It is easy not to stop in Sarlat-La Canéda, 9 km (5½ miles) north of the Dordogne on D 704 (it's 74 km/45 miles east of Bergerac), if you career past on the "modern" rue de la République (built in 1837). The "traverse," as it is called by the locals, cuts unheedingly right through the old quarter and is lined by rather nondescript houses.

Sarlat's most famous son is Etienne de la Boétie, magistrate of the Bordeaux parliament in the 16th century, but better known internationally as a prolific political writer and close friend of Montaigne. His house, with its handsome gables, mullioned windows, and medallions—an exuberance in Renaissance style—still stands right across from the cathedral.

OLD SARLAT

Old Sarlat, the architectural heart of town east of *La Traverse,* was "rescued" when it was selected in 1962 as one of France's experimental projects of restoration. Work began in 1964, and the result is a charming medieval town of *hôtels* constructed from golden limestone with steeply pitched roofs made of weighty limestone slabs (*lauzes*) and often topped by turrets.

A walk begins in the Place du Peyrou in front of the **Cathédrale St-Sacerdos** and near La Boétie's house. Enter the cathedral off the *place* and admire its near-perfect proportions (it is otherwise unremarkable), then leave by the south door. You will find yourself in a courtyard that houses the **Chapelle des Pénitents Bleus** (Chapel of the Blue Penitents). Beyond lie two more courtyards and a cemetery dating from the 12th to 15th centuries.

The curious conical tower off to the right is the so-called **Lanterne des Morts** (Lantern of the Dead), but its purpose is not precisely known. (You will notice these strange, 12th-century constructions throughout the countryside.)

From the garden near the Lanterne, take the short alley into rue d'Albusse, hesitate to admire the Hôtel de Génis, then continue to the rue de Présidial and the **Présidial**, the 16th-century seat of the royal court of justice.

Retrace your steps into the rue de la Salamandre and follow it past the Hôtel de Ville into the Place de la Liberté, Sarlat's main square. Continue north into the **Place des Oies** (Goose Square), where on Saturdays crowds gather to haggle over prices of geese and ducks, fresh goose liver (the famous Périgord *foie gras*), walnuts, and sometimes costly black truffles. This, like all of old Sarlat, is a delicious ensemble of pinnacles, corner staircases, turrets, and mullioned windows.

STAYING AND DINING IN SARLAT AND WEST

In the heart of the Périgord region, 12 km (7½ miles) north of **Bergerac** via skinny back road D 107, the ▶ **Manoir le Grand Vignoble** welcomes visitors who seek a retreat in which to savor the riches of an untrammeled countryside. On the outskirts of the hamlet of St-Julien-de-Crempse, the 44-room inn occupies a country manor constructed in the days of Louis XIV upon the ruins of an ancient English *bastide* and is surrounded by 185 acres of pastures and woods. It offers a heated outdoor pool, tennis, sauna, Jacuzzi, and equestrian center.

For four centuries ▶ **Le Vieux Logis et ses Logis des Champs** in **Trémolat** has been the property of the same family; it was transformed into a 24-room hotel by the mother of the present innkeeper. Each room is elegantly distinct, and there are two attractive dining rooms and a lovely garden.

In **Monpazier** the 13-room hotel ▶ **Edward Ier** is set in a 19th-century manor house with a swimming pool.

Just 5 km (3 miles) outside Le Bugue in the wide spot of Le Réclaud-de-Bouny-Bas, the ▶ **Auberge du Noyer** occupies an 18th-century Périgourdine farmhouse reworked by an English family. The fine meals include hearty breakfasts. Ask for a room with a terrace.

For such a small town, **Les Eyzies** sports an unusually large number of good accommodations. The ▶ **Hôtel du**

Centenaire, with 21 rooms and four apartments, is widely recognized for the finesse of its two-star chef Roland Mazère. (Try such local specialties as the memorable *risotto au foie gras, truffles, et langoustines.*) The grand mansion is surrounded by a splendid garden; Tel: 53-06-97-18.

▶ **Cro-Magnon** was once a relay station for carriages called *diligences* and has been in the Leyssales family for several generations. The most peaceful rooms are those in the annex, with windows giving onto a shaded terrace and the pretty garden with its swimming pool. Local tradition has it that the remains of Cro-Magnon man were found at the site of what is today the hotel's men's room; one of the rooms has been turned into a small museum of prehistory.

Cro-Magnon also is known for its (one-star) kitchen. Try the *lotte aux morilles* (local wild mushrooms) and introduce yourself to fine regional wines, Prayssac and Sigoulès; Tel: 53-06-97-06.

The ▶ **Hôtel Les Glycines** was a post house built in 1862, now shaded by a bower of wisteria and trimmed linden trees. The 25 rooms are contemporary in style and very comfortable; meals may be taken in the dining room or on a veranda overlooking the grassy park; Tel: 53-06-97-07.

▶ **L'Esplanade** is a pleasant, 25-room hotel in **Domme** with great views and a bestarred restaurant. Try the *filet d'agneau en brioche,* and from April to October don't miss the *chaud-froid de fraises* (a strawberry perfection); Tel: 53-28-31-41.

Another excellent restaurant is **Chez Sylvestre** in **Bouzic**, south of Domme, where Yvette Sylvestre concocts such comestibles as surprisingly light meat pies (*tourtières*) and flaky almond desserts; Tel: 53-28-41-01.

In and Near Sarlat

▶ **La Couleuvrine**, a short walk east of the Place de la Liberté, is housed in a 14th- to 18th-century residence set in the city walls that looks as though knights might still call it home. There are 26 rooms and a kitchen that concentrates on regional dishes and market-fresh produce.

To the south of town just 2 km (1¼ miles) via avenue Général-Leclerc in the hamlet of La Giragne, the ▶ **Hôtel La Hoirie** (*hoirie* means "inheritance") is an ancient hunting lodge. It offers 15 rooms, some with fireplaces.

To the northwest, 3 km (2 miles) via D 6, the ▶ **Hostellerie de Meysset** sits at the top of a hill in a wooded park, with 22 rooms and four apartments that exude calm.

Along the same route is the 15th- to 16th-century ▶ **Château de Puymartin**, long open to visitors come to admire its decoration and furnishings. Today the château is both the lordly home of the comte and comtesse de Montbron and an unusual (and unlikely) bed-and-breakfast with two radiant guest rooms in which breakfast is served. Two more rooms are being converted for guests. The château is open from April to the end of October and on weekends; by special arrangement other times.

The Dordogne East of Sarlat

East of Sarlat, moving upstream, you ease out of Périgord Noir (*noir*, or black, because of the density of the forests and the great number of holm oaks with their deep, dark foliage) and enter the region of Quercy. As you go east, the Dordogne (so wide near Bergerac) narrows, becomes less gentle, and cuts dramatically through limestone canyons. This is wonderful country for ambling, with a surprise around every meander. Many travellers prefer it to the better-known, more touristed stretches downriver, west of Sarlat.

Souillac
Souillac sits at the meeting of the Corrèze and the Dordogne rivers 29 km (18 miles) east of Sarlat along D 703.

The Hundred Years War and the Wars of Religion much mutilated old Souillac, particularly its medieval Benedictine abbey. Fortunately, much of the 12th-century **Eglise Ste-Marie** survived; its treasure, the badly damaged doorway, has been placed in the "new" addition dating from the 17th century. It is carved in low relief with episodes from the life of the monk Theophilus and, on what was the central pillar of the door, the wages of human sin in the form of monsters feeding on one another. The masterpiece is the relief of the prophet Isaiah, itself worth a stop in this bustling market town.

Martel
It would be difficult to exaggerate the importance to French history of this little medieval village that today earns its living from canning and the nut trade.

Martel, 15 km (9 miles) northeast of Souillac along D 703, bears the weighty name of Charles Martel, Martel the Hammer, defender of Christian Europe against the Moors, and grandfather of Charlemagne.

After defeating the Moors at the Battle of Poitiers in 732 (see the Poitou-Charentes chapter), Martel chased them south into Aquitaine. Tradition says he exterminated them finally at this site and built a church to celebrate the deed. Later, it is believed, the town grew up around the church. In any case, Martel took as its crest the three hammers that were Martel's favorite weapons.

At the end of the 12th century, the players on the stage were no less personages than Henri Plantagenêt, king of England, Eleanor of Aquitaine, and their four sons. The sons took the part of Eleanor when their father had her locked up in a tower. The most furious was the eldest, Henri Court-Mantel (known in English as Short-Cloak), who was finally driven to plunder the holy places of Rocamadour. Fleeing Rocamadour, Court-Mantel heard the ringing of bells, took it as a warning from God, and fled to Martel. Feverish, fearing death, he made a confession and beseeched his father to forgive him. Henri II, busy at the siege of Limoges, sent a messenger with pardon. Shortly thereafter, agonizing on a bed of cinders, Henri Court-Mantel expired.

Not only that: Just 14 km (8½ miles) to the east, a point named Puy d'Issolud is thought to have been the former Uxellodunum, site of the final Gaulish defense against Julius Caesar after their defeat at Alésia (see the Burgundy chapter).

Today, Martel is as peaceful as a flowery meadow. What action there is takes place on or near the **Place des Consuls** with its 18th-century covered market. On one side stands the Hôtel de la Raymondie, a medieval fortress transformed into a Gothic mansion, now the Hôtel de Ville. On the southeast corner of the place the Fabri mansion with its round tower is supposed to be the place where Court-Mantel died in 1183.

On the eastern edge of the village, the Gothic **Eglise St-Maur** is the very essence of a fortress-church, complete with battlemented towers and a line of machicolations. To reach it from place des Consuls, walk down the rue Droite, lined with lovely old *hôtels*.

Carennac

From Martel it's just a 15-km (9-mile) drive east along D 703 and south across the river at D 20 to tiny Carennac, a village of pretty manor houses. This was the home of François de Salignac de la Mothe-Fénelon, a writer known simply as Fénelon, later an archbishop. The tympanum of the 12th-century Romanesque **Eglise St-Pierre** is carved with a magnificent Christ in Majesty. The chapter house in the cloisters shelters a fine entombment.

A quite different attraction is the **Musée de l'Automate**, a collection of 1,000 automatic objects, mostly toys, that illustrate this arcane art from antiquity to today.

Grottes de Lacave

Deep in the green countryside, on a sinuous bend of the Dordogne, the series of grottoes called Lacave was discovered in 1902. (The site is 9 km/5½ miles southeast of Souillac via route D 43.) The walk through the caves is about a mile long, round trip, past limestone that has been shaped into forms of people, animals, even cities and underground rivers that run into clear, mirrorlike lakes.

East of Carennac, take D 30 and D 43 to the **Château Castelnau-Bretenoux**; it's about 7 km (4 miles). Massive in red sandstone, dominating the valley where three rivers meet (the Dordogne, the Cère, the Bave), the castle of Castelnau-Bretenoux rises above the village of Prudhomat and is one of the finest examples of medieval military architecture in the country. Built in the 11th century as a single, round keep, by the end of the Hundred Years War it was a fortress three miles around with a garrison of a thousand men. Abandoned by the 17th century, Castelnau was pillaged during the Revolution and seemed destined for oblivion. However, in the 1890s it was purchased by one Jean Moulièrat, a tenor at Paris's Opéra-Comique, who restored it with Aubusson and Beauvais tapestries and other fine furnishings and left it to the state in 1932.

St-Céré

The point of journeying to St-Céré, 9 km (5½ miles) southeast of Castelnau on D 940, is usually to visit the château of Montal. Nonetheless, St-Céré, a picturesque gathering of old houses, itself is worth a hesitation.

A first glimpse of the **Château de Montal** reveals a grim, rather forbidding silhouette with pitched *lauzes* roofs and fortresslike towers. But when you walk up the path, you'll find a richness, almost a gaiety, to the decoration of the two-winged facade. (Montal is 6 km/3½ miles west of St-Céré via D 673.) The château was demolished during the Revolution, and the ruins left to vandals. In 1879, the remains were auctioned and distributed worldwide. But in 1908, wealthy industrialist Maurice Fenaille bought the site, conducted a search for the missing stonework, and restored the castle to its past beauty. When he died in 1913, he left it to the state, complete with its period family furniture. Montal today is open every day except Saturdays.

STAYING AND DINING
EAST OF SARLAT

Gourmets will want to make a pilgrimage to ▶ **Pont de l'Ouysse**, a 13-room inn nestled against a green, rocky hillside near Lacave. The rooms are large, light, and comfortable; the dining terrace is hung above a bubbling stream; the menu offers such specialties as roast truffled chicken *en cocotte*.

The ▶ **Château de la Treyne** rises above the intensely green banks of the Dordogne, just 3 km (2 miles) west of **Lacave**. Guest enjoy a refined setting and tennis, swimming, billiards, art exhibitions, hot-air ballooning, and the products of a very good kitchen.

Just 1½ km (1 mile) west of **Cernac** on the road from Sarlat, ▶ **Les Granges Vieilles** is an 11-room inn within a mansion of curious, striped pinkish-brown-and-white appearance, like a building plunked down from Italy and finding itself by mistake in a pretty little park. It's a comfortable place shaded by great trees, with a terrace where meals are served in pleasant weather.

The ▶ **Trois Soleils de Montal** is an attractive hotel in a tranquil setting just 3 km (2 miles) west of **St-Céré** via D 673. It offers dining on a terrace during good weather, an outdoor pool, exercise room, tennis, and other amenities.

Rocamadour

Narrow roads from Les Eyzies, Sarlat, Beynac, or any number of other little towns skitter eastward to Rocamadour, east of N 20 along D 673 and south of the Dordogne, a gathering place for pilgrims in the past and a required stop for tourists today.

Although the site is one of the most stunning in all Europe, Rocamadour is sometimes skipped by travellers who scorn it as overcommercialized. Yet in a sense the town has always been the same, with streets full of buyers and sellers, often dealing in religious trinkets.

It's important to approach from L'Hospitalet (to the east) and to look down and out from the small terrace of the hamlet. Below, the river Alzou wanders through the wide gorge, while houses and shops climb its banks, nearly standing on top of one another as they cling to the steep cliff face, rising to the château on the summit.

Nobody knows who Saint Amadour was, though it is generally acknowledged that he was a pious hermit. The current theory is that he was Zaccheus, who came here with his wife, Saint Veronica (she who wiped the face of Christ on the route to Calvary), and after her death lived on, alone, on the cliff. He first was called *roc amator* ("one who knows and loves the rock"), hence the name Rocamadour. It is said that miracles began to occur as soon as the saint's bones were buried near the altar in the tiny **chapel of the Virgin**.

The resultant pilgrimages attracted thousands of the faithful, some of whom stopped here en route to Santiago de Compostela. French kings, Saint Louis among them, came here, as did England's Henry II, Saint Bernard, Blanche of Castille, and thousands upon thousands of unremembered believers. Repentant sinners were a major source of revenue, paying severe penances in coin and then climbing the 216 steps (the Via Sancta) on bleeding knees to chapels atop the summit, known as the Ecclesiastical City.

Legend has it that during the Wars of Religion, pillaging Protestants dug up the body of Saint Amadour and tossed it into a fire, in which it refused to burn. The abbey finally fell to revolutionaries in 1789. Today the wealth and the splendor have vanished, but Rocamadour lives on, a fascinating witness to history and religious hysteria.

The entrance to the town is through the 13th-century Porte Figuier, where you will find yourself in a swirl of souvenir shops lining rue Roland-le-Preux. It's off-putting but must be braved. The street passes through Porte Salmon and becomes rue de la Couronnerie, growing somewhat less cute and more intriguing along the way.

LA CITE RELIGIEUSE

The point of Rocamadour, however, is La Cité Religieuse, reached either by elevator or by the self-same 216 steps, past shops and hotels situated on terraces along the way. The cluster of buildings at the top (most of them were restored during the 19th century) includes the fort, the seven churches on Place St-Amadour, the Basilique St-Sauveur, the Chapelle Miraculeuse, and the Chapelle St-Michel.

Major treasures include **La Vierge Noire** (The Black Virgin), a wood sculpture above the altar in the Chapelle Miraculeuse; the chapel bell that rings on its own when a miracle is about to occur; and the **iron sword** on the wall of Chapelle Notre-Dame that tradition holds to be Durandal, the weapon of Roland. On the open space in front of the church, a small but rewarding museum is devoted to sacred art.

The delicious regional goat cheese, *chabichou,* should be available at cafés in town. The best is produced by the Ferme

Jean Lacoste between Rocamadour and Gramat. While in Rocamadour and vicinity, be sure to sample the fine plum brandy from the Ségala distillery: *eau-de-vie du Vieux Pigeonnier.*

GOUFFRE DE PADIRAC

If there is time to view only one *gouffre* (chasm) on a trip to France, it should be the Gouffre de Padirac, only a few minutes' drive northeast of Rocamadour on D 673, then D 90. Elevators make the descent into a vast and mysterious—and definitely touristy—underground world of galleries and rivers created by rainwater percolating through porous limestone. After you visit Padirac, on foot and flat-bottomed boat, the legend ascribing it to a face-off between Satan and Saint Martin will seem more probable.

PECH-MERLE

About 40 km (25 miles) south of Rocamadour via Gramat and Labastide-Murat, to the east of N 20 and near the wide spot of Cabrerets, the cave (*grotte*) of Pech-Merle is one of the most exciting of the painted caverns, since Lascaux can no longer be seen. It's entered through a chamber used by prehistoric people 20,000 years ago. Bison and mammoths parade in a frieze, human footprints of 200 centuries past are perfectly petrified, and two horses suffer the stenciled hands of would-be attackers. The **Musée Amédée-Lemozi** at the site is devoted to the prehistory of Pech-Merle and other nearby sites.

STAYING AND DINING
IN AND AROUND ROCAMADOUR

In town, ▶ **Beau Site et Notre Dame** is the choice inn, a 50-room hostelry of agreeable nature and decoration that's always full. Four kilometers (2½ miles) away, on the road leading southeast to Gramat, the unassuming ▶ **Auberge de la Garenne** is one of those warm, welcoming inns in which the French countryside excels, a calm retreat after a day's exploration.

Near Gramat, the ▶ **Château de Roumégouse** offers 14 rooms and three suites to travellers looking for elegance in their home away from the madding crowd. Also near Gramat is the rather new **Parc de Vision** (Safari Park), 94 acres of regional plants and trees that are home to various wild European animals, including some beasts such as wild oxen and bison descended from prehistoric species.

A remarkable hostelry may detain the wanderer in Pech-Merle and the surrounding region: the lordly and extremely fashionable ▶ **Château de Mercuès**, a 12th-century castle of the bishops of Cahors, in Mercuès 9 km (5½ miles) north-west of Cahors on D 911.

Cahors

The perfumed air of the Midi moves ever so slightly in the sleepy streets of Cahors and stirs the plane trees along boulevard Gambetta, which is lined with sidewalk cafés and seductive shops. (Among regional items for sale, the most interesting are the ceramics in brilliant and beautiful shades of gold, green, and a wine red.) The boulevard, the main artery of Cahors, celebrates the favorite local son, Léon-Michel Gambetta, the 19th-century barrister and activist who floated over the German lines in a balloon, became war minister and prime minister, and gave his name to squares and streets all over France.

Cahors sits above a loop in the river Lot south of Roca-madour and serves as an excursion center for the valleys of the Lot and Célé, with their pretty perched villages, fortress churches, troglodyte caves, and châteaux. In town look for the **Pont Valentré**, still a commanding example of medieval military-bridge design, and the admirable tympanum and cloisters of the **Cathédrale St-Etienne**.

Saturday is the best market day in Cahors, as elsewhere in the region, though there is action on Wednesdays as well. The Cahors wines, rich, powerful, and little known outside France, may best be tasted at **La Taverne**. The wines nobly complement the café's renowned dishes, which feature precious truffles. Tel: 65-35-28-66.

GETTING AROUND

Bordeaux usually serves as the starting point for travellers to the region who arrive by air (13 daily one-hour flights from Paris Orly-Ouest or Roissy) or rail (at least ten trains arrive daily from Paris's Gare d'Austerlitz, and there is TGV service from Gare Montparnasse).

Driving is recommended here, as it is everywhere in France when you want to seek out remote valleys, small hotels, and little-known villages. Either pick up a rental car in Bordeaux or drive from Paris via the Loire Valley and Poitiers.

Pleasure boats may be rented in many ports, including Arcachon, Pauillac, Royan, Verdon, and Bordeaux.

In Bordeaux, a guided boat tour shows off the quais of the old city; departures are from quai Louis-XVIII, near the Quinconces.

Bus tours of from four to eight days are sometimes available through the Office de Tourisme in Bordeaux.

ACCOMMODATIONS REFERENCE

The rates given below are projections *for 1994. Unless otherwise indicated, rates are for a double room, double occupancy, and do not include meals. As rates are always subject to change, double-check before booking.*

▶ **Arc Hôtel sur Mer.** 89, boulevard de la Plage, 33120 **Arcachon.** Tel: 56-83-06-85; Fax: 56-83-53-72. 450F–880F.

▶ **Auberge de la Garenne.** Rocamadour 46500 **Gramat.** Tel: 65-33-65-88; Fax: 65-33-61-14. 220F–550F.

▶ **Auberge du Noyer.** 24620 **Le Bugue.** Tel: 53-07-11-73; Fax: 53-54-57-44. 400F per person, demi-pension.

▶ **Beau Site et Notre Dame.** 46500 **Rocamadour.** Tel: 65-33-63-08; Fax: 65-33-65-23; in U.S. and Canada, (800) 528-1234; in U.K., (081) 541-0033. Member, Best Western International. 300F–450F.

▶ **Château de Foulon.** 33480 **Castelnau-de-Médoc.** Tel: 56-58-20-18; Fax: 56-58-23-43. 400F, breakfast included.

▶ **Château de Mercuès.** 46090 **Mercuès.** Tel: 65-20-00-01; Fax: 65-20-05-72; in U.S., (212) 856-0115; Fax: (212) 856-0193. Member, Relais & Châteaux. 750F–1,600F.

▶ **Château de Puymartin.** 24200 **Sarlat.** Tel: 53-59-29-97; Fax: 53-29-87-52. 750F, breakfast included.

▶ **Château de Roumégouse.** RN 140, 46500 **Gramat.** Tel: 65-33-63-81; Fax: 65-33-71-18; in U.S., (212) 856-0115; Fax: (212) 856-0193. Member, Relais & Châteaux. 520F–940F.

▶ **Château de la Treyne.** 46200 **Lacave.** Tel: 65-32-66-66; Fax: 65-37-06-57. 1,200F–1,600F.

▶ **Claude Darroze.** 95, cours Général-Leclerc, 33210 **Langon.** Tel: 56-63-00-48; Fax: 56-63-41-15. 320F–420F.

▶ **La Couleuvrine.** 1, place Bouquerie, 24200 **Sarlat-La Canéda.** Tel: 53-59-27-80; Fax: 53-31-26-83. 190F–340F.

▶ **Cro-Magnon.** 24620 **Les Eyzies-de-Tayac.** Tel: 53-06-97-06; Fax: 53-06-95-45; in U.S., (212) 254-2217 or (800) 755-9313. 350F–550F.

▶ **Edward Ier.** 5, rue St-Pierre, 24540 **Monpazier.** Tel: 53-22-44-00; Fax: 53-22-57-99. 350F–900F.

▶ **L'Esplanade.** 24250 **Domme.** Tel: 53-28-31-41; Fax: 53-28-49-92. 350F–500F.

▶ **Grand Hôtel Français.** 12, rue du Temple, 33000 **Bordeaux.** Tel: 56-48-10-35; Fax: 56-81-76-18; in U.S. and Canada, Tel: (800) 528-1234; in U.K., (081) 541-0033. Member, Best Western International. 330F–550F.

► **Les Granges Vieilles**. Route de Sarlat, 46200 **Souillac**. Tel: 65-37-80-92. 300F–460F.

► **Hostellerie de Meysset**. 24200 **Sarlat-La Canéda**. Tel: 53-59-08-29; Fax 53-28-47-61. 375F–448F.

► **Hostellerie Plaisance**. Place du Clocher, 33330 **St-Emilion**. Tel: 57-24-72-32; Fax: 57-74-41-11; in U.S., (212) 477-1600 or (800) 366-1510. 600F–775F (high season).

► **Hôtel Burdigala**. 115, rue Georges-Bonnac, 33000 **Bordeaux**. Tel: 56-90-16-16; Fax: 56-93-15-06; in U.S. and Canada, (800) 888-4747; in New York, (212) 752-3900; in U.K., (0800) 181-591. 760F–1,350F.

► **Hôtel du Centenaire**. 24620 **Les Eyzies-de-Tayac**. Tel: 53-06-97-18; Fax: 53-06-92-41; in U.S., (212) 856-0115; Fax: (212) 856-0193. Member, Relais & Châteaux. 400F–900F.

► **Hôtel Les Glycines**. 24620 **Les Eyzies-de-Tayac**. Tel: 53-06-97-07; Fax: 53-06-92-19. 370F–420F.

► **Hôtel La Hoirie**. 24200 **Sarlat-La Canéda**. Tel: 53-59-05-62; Fax: 53-31-13-90. 340F–550F.

► **Majestic**. 2, rue de Condé, 33000 **Bordeaux**. Tel: 56-52-60-44; Fax: 56-79-26-70. 360F–500F.

► **Manoir le Grand Vignoble**. 24140 **St-Julien-de-Crempse**. Tel. and Fax: 53-24-23-18. 490F–610F.

► **Normandie**. 7, cours du 30-Juillet, 33000 **Bordeaux**. Tel: 56-52-16-80; Fax: 56-51-68-91. 300F–550F.

► **Pont de l'Ouysse**. 46200 **Lacave**. Tel: 65-37-87-04; Fax: 65-32-77-41. 350F–600F.

► **Pullman Mériadeck**. 5, rue Robert-Lateulade, 33000 **Bordeaux**. Tel: 56-56-43-43; Fax: 56-96-50-59; in U.S. and Canada, Tel: (800) 221-4542; Fax: (914) 472-0451; in U.K., Tel: (071) 724-1000. 520F–950F.

► **Relais de Margaux**. 33460 **Margaux**. Tel: 56-88-38-30; Fax: 56-88-31-73; in U.S., (212) 254-2217 or (800) 755-9313. 800F–1,300F (low season); 975F–1,350F (high season).

► **La Réserve**. Avenue Bourgailh, 33600 **Pessac**. Tel: 56-07-13-28; Fax: 56-36-31-02. 600F–900F.

► **Sainte-Catherine**. 27, rue Parlement Ste-Catherine, 33000 **Bordeaux**. Tel: 56-81-95-12; Fax: 56-44-50-51. 550F–900F.

► **Le St-James**. Place Charles-Hostein, 33270 **Bouliac**. Tel: 56-20-52-19; Fax: 56-20-92-58. 750F–1,350F.

► **Trois Soleils de Montal**. 46400 **St-Céré**. Tel: 65-38-20-61; Fax: 65-38-30-66. 380F–450F.

► **Les Vagues**. 9, boulevard de l'Océan, 33120 **Arcachon**. Tel: 56-83-03-75; Fax: 56-83-77-16. 490F–710F.

► **Le Vieux Logis et ses Logis des Champs**. 24510 **Trémolat**. Tel: 53-22-80-06; Fax: 53-22-84-89; in U.S., (212) 856-0115; Fax: (212) 856-0193. Member, Relais & Châteaux. 680F–1,000F.

POITOU AND LES CHARENTES

By Georgia I. Hesse

Under wide, often opalescent skies, along roads whose remarkable straightness (a legacy of the Romans) slices the deeply rural landscape, a driver's attention tends to wander. Flat fields golden with sunflowers, meandering rivers (notably the Charente), and the occasional village (usually asleep, with shutters closed) contribute to a sense of changelessness, as if the world, heavy with age, had curled up for a Sunday-afternoon nap.

Poitou-Charentes (shared history and geography prompt the sharing of a hyphen) spreads out between the Loire Valley to the north and Aquitaine and the Dordogne to the south, runs to the Atlantic on the west, and leans against the uplands of Limousin in the east. Little known to North American travellers, it is one of the sunniest regions of France.

Poitou, which constitutes approximately the northern half of Poitou-Charentes, has as its main city Poitiers on the Clain river in the east of the region, while Les Charentes lies to the south. Its major metropolitan area is Angoulême, also in the east.

Wherever you wander in Poitou-Charentes you will wonder at the profusion of Romanesque cathedrals, churches, abbeys, and baptisteries: In clear and brilliant limestone they are etched with choruses of carvings, seemingly cut out in a riot of religious frenzy. (They were.)

Like every other region of France, Poitou-Charentes has a solid gastronomic reputation, although its menus are nei-

779

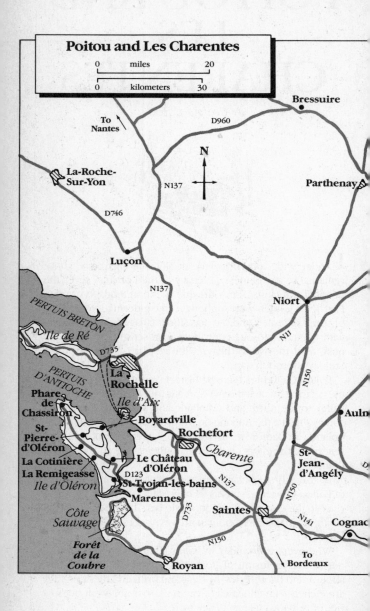

Poitou and Les Charentes

0 | miles | 20
0 | kilometers | 30

Bressuire

To Nantes

D960

N

La-Roche-Sur-Yon

Parthenay

N137

D746

Luçon

N137

Niort

N11

PERTUIS BRETON

Ile de Ré

PERTUIS D'ANTIOCHE

D735

N150

La Rochelle

Ile d'Aix

Phare de Chassiron

Boyardville

Auln

St-Pierre-d'Oléron

Rochefort

La Cotinière

Le Château d'Oléron

Charente

La Remigeasse

Ile d'Oléron

D123

St-Trojan-les-bains

St-Jean-d'Angély

N137

D

Marennes

N150

Côte Sauvage

D733

Saintes

N141

Cognac

Forêt de la Coubre

N150

Royan

To Bordeaux

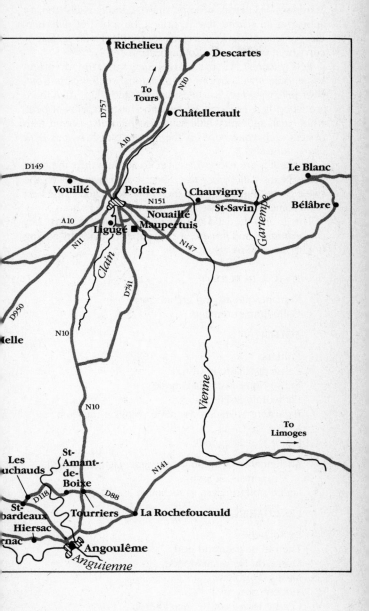

ther so familiar as Burgundy's nor so festive as those of
Provence. Seafood is the sine qua non: oysters from
Marennes or Oléron, shrimps, prawns, and mussels (the last
appearing in *éclade,* that is, grilled, on a bed of pine nee-
dles; or in *mouclade,* a creamy soup spiked with saffron or
curry or, if you're lucky, Cognac).

Eels (*pibales*) and snails (*cagouilles*) attract the adventure-
some; others will stick to the traditional stuffed carp, trout,
river pike (*brochet*), sardines, salmon, and shad. Then there
are fatted hens, capons, geese with chestnuts, ribs of beef,
white veal, and spicy little sausages (*merguez,* served with
oysters and white wine in the sprightly dish *huîtres à la
charentaise*).

Vegetables are everywhere; on no account miss the nutty
white beans called *mojettes.* Special applause goes to the
sweet butter, the garlic, and the *Chabichou* cheese, the best
of 50-some types of goat's-milk cheeses of the region.

This is also the land of Cognac, that triumph of art over
vin ordinaire, and *pineau,* a sweet aperitif made by adding
Cognac to wine musts.

MAJOR INTEREST

Romanesque art and architecture
Gallo-Roman remains

POITOU

Poitiers
Eglise St-Hilaire-le-Grand
Eglise Notre-Dame-la-Grande
Cathédrale St-Pierre
Baptistère St-Jean, today a Merovingian museum
Musée Ste-Croix
Eglise Ste-Radegonde

Ancient abbeys in the countryside: Ligugé, Nouaillé-
    Maupertuis, St-Savin
Literary pilgrimages to Richelieu and Descartes

LES CHARENTES

La Rochelle
The old quarter and port
Musée du Nouveau Monde
Musée d'Orbigny
Modern port area
Coastal islands of Ré, Aix, Oléron
Literary detour to the house of Pierre Loti in
    Rochefort

Cognac country
Royan, seaside resort, coastal drives, casino
Saintes, Roman and medieval sites
The town of Cognac

Angoulême
Cathédrale St-Pierre
A drive or walk around the ramparts

Charentes countryside
Le Moulin de Fleurac (paper mill), La Rochefoucauld
    château, old churches, Gallo-Roman theater
Excursion to Eglise St-Pierre at Aulnay

Though the region, gilded by a luminous light, breathes tranquillity and serenity, war has been a constant across this placid countryside for more than 15 centuries, since Alaric the Hun and his Visigoths were defeated by Clovis, first king of the Franks, in A.D. 507 northwest of Poitiers. In the unforgettable year of 732, Charles Martel, founder of the Carolingian dynasty and grandfather of Charlemagne, inflicted upon the Moorish military machine its first major defeat in Europe, in the so-called Battle of Poitiers. (Actually, it occurred at a point northeast of Poitiers, a few kilometers south of Châtellerault at a spot on the map called Moussais-la-Bataille.)

In 820 the Vikings (Norsemen, or Normands in French) initiated such a fierce series of slaughters, wiping out the entire cities of Saintes and Angoulême, that a panicky populace predicted the world would come to an end in the year 1000. When that year came and went without disaster, a wave of faith swept the land, resulting in an outburst of church building, especially along the great pilgrimage routes to St-Jacques-de-Compostelle (Santiago de Compostela) in Spain.

The battles of the Hundred Years War are generally considered to have begun in 1337 and come to an end only in 1453 at the Battle of Castillon, about 30 miles east of Bordeaux. These struggles included the second battle of Poitiers in 1356, when Edward, the Black Prince, took prisoner Jean le Bon (John the Good), king of France. Exhausted by nearly continual war and ravaged by the Black Death (1347–1351), France rested just longer than a century before beginning the Wars of Religion, which debuted with the Battle of Jarnac (about nine miles east of Cognac) in 1562 and lasted for 36 years, until Henri IV promulgated the Edict of Nantes in 1598, providing safeguards for Protestants (Huguenots) in such places as La Rochelle. Alas, in 1627 Cardinal Richelieu undertook a year-long siege against that seaport, and the edict was revoked in 1685.

Then followed the War of the Vendée (1793–1795) between the Royalists and the adherents of the Revolution (today Vendée is a *département* within Poitou), and World Wars I and II, the latter coming to an end in 1945 with the Allied bombings of German-held Royan.

Echoes of English-French fighting are faint today, existing predominantly in the remains of feudal châteaux, strongholds, and such donjons as that of Niort, begun by Henri II Plantagenêt and completed by his son Richard the Lionhearted. The modern traveller, however, will enjoy conjuring up the past more prosaically in Poitiers's Café Prince Noir (Black Prince).

The Roads to Santiago Through Poitou-Charentes

In the Middle Ages, Europeans expressed their piety and penance, faith, and need for forgiveness by following pilgrimage routes to Jerusalem, to Rome, and to Santiago de Compostela, the tomb of St. James the Apostle, in Galicia in northwest Spain. Four roads began variously in Paris, Vézelay, Le Puy, and Arles. The road from Paris started on the Right Bank from the church of St-Jacques-de-la-Boucherie (near the meat market, or butchery); of the church, only the Tour St-Jacques remains.

After Mass and a blessing of their staffs, pilgrims set out down rue St-Jacques and onto the open road toward Etampes, Orléans, Tours, Poitiers, south in Poitou-Charentes to Melle, Aulnay, St-Jean-d'Angély, Saintes, Bordeaux, and, finally, to Roncesvalles in Spain. A secondary route went via Angoulême.

Churches, hospices, and sanctuaries sprang up along the road like sunflowers in the fields of Poitou. "Sermons in stone," the buildings' façades have been called, sculpted to be "read" like the Bible by the illiterate. The message was always the same: The souls of good and bad are weighed. Good souls rise to live in eternal bliss, watched over by angels; bad ones are damned, pulled down by hideous demons and crushed by evil monsters.

Occasionally the sculptors seem to have been struck by a gay spirit of grotesquerie: Leaves and flowers twist crazily; a fish wears the head of a beast; mysterious creatures mate back to back; elephants are caught by vines; owls wear moustaches. No wonder austere Saint Bernard roared his objections: "For God's sake, if men are not ashamed of these follies, why at least do they not shrink from the expense?"

POITOU

Poitou extends over three *départements:* Vienne, Deux-Sèvres, and Vendée. We begin a tour of the region in its capital, Poitiers, then visit three fascinating, nearby abbeys. We then make pilgrimages to two villages that bear the names of famous writers, Richelieu and Descartes. For North Americans the most interesting aspect of this area may be its association with the Acadians.

The story of the Acadians is a tale of wandering, of the search for Virgil's earthly paradise, Acadia, and of struggle, exile, and migration. It begins in 1603 when Henri IV gave Pierre du Gua de Monts the lands between the 40th and 46th parallels on the continent of North America, lands today known as Nova Scotia, New Brunswick, and Prince Edward Island in Canada. Colonization began, the name Acadia soon came to signify the French New World colony, and in 1632 the treaty of St-Germain recognized the existence of French Acadia.

But Franco-English strife continued unabated, and in 1713 Acadia became English by the treaty of Utrecht. Then in 1755 the British governor issued an ultimatum to the French Acadians: Swear allegiance to the British Crown—or get out.

Thus began the saga called in French *le Grand Dérangement,* the Great Expulsion. By the end of the year half the Acadians had been deported, some to the French West Indies, some to French Louisiana (where they became the Cajuns), and others back to France. In 1773 the first Acadians arrived at Châtellerault, northeast of Poitiers on the plain of Poitou. The plateau soon was transformed into the highly cultivated fields through which we drive today. The Acadians of Poitou still celebrate this period of wandering in an annual festival.

POITIERS

Many travellers find Poitiers drab at first approach, probably because of the haphazardly arranged industrial *faubourgs* that ring the old town. But this initial impression soon disappears as you drive to the city's center on its promontory above the Clain river. (Note that the difficulty of negotiating traffic will put your teeth on edge.) Architecturally, Poitiers is one of the richest cities in France.

The town came to ecclesiastical excellence in the person of Hilary of Poitiers, who was born here in or about A.D. 315, was raised to the bishopric about 353, and is considered today to be the first Christian thinker born and educated in Gaul. He is remembered in the noble church of St-Hilaire-le-Grand (see below).

The saintly line continued in Poitiers with the arrival of Radegonde (sometimes Radegund), the chaste and unwilling wife of Lothair I, king of the Franks and son of Clovis, first ruler in the Mérovingian dynasty. Radegonde founded a convent called Holy Cross, where she served the poor, conducted a deep and spiritual friendship with the Italian poet Venantius Fortunatus, and died in 587. One of the best-loved Poitevins in history, Radegonde lies today in the church of Ste-Radegonde, built over the nuns' burial grounds. (The modern Musée Ste-Croix occupies the site of the ancient convent; see below.)

Poitiers grew rapidly during the 15th century, and during the Renaissance boasted almost 70 churches and a renowned university. Following the Wars of Religion, however, it fell into a long and troubled sleep from which it has only recently awakened, a result of the renewed energies of the university and the arrival of modern industry. Today its population is about 82,900.

Visiting Poitiers

The best way to explore the city is to leave your car at the parking garage on rue Carnot just south of rue Charles Gide. From there walk southwest on rue Carnot and rue de la Tranchée, then turn onto rue du Doyenne, which wriggles around to rue St-Hilaire and the church of St-Hilaire-le-Grand, which is somewhat isolated. You are now in the city's southwestern quarter. After visiting this church, retrace your steps north up rue Carnot. The other architectural treasures are all in the eastern half of Poitiers, within shorter walking distances of one another.

ST-HILAIRE-LE-GRAND

St-Hilaire-le-Grand, begun in 1025 over the small chapel Hilary had erected to house his tomb, ranks among the most noble examples of Romanesque church architecture in France, and connoisseurs of the period consider this the most interesting religious structure in town. The interior spaces range from quite small to enormous; the student of the style will notice some curious rebuilding in the nave, necessitated by a great fire in 1130. Originally, each of the church's three naves had a wooden ceiling. After the fire, stone was used to span the naves. Because stone weighs much more than wood, the naves were reduced in width, the number of aisles was increased, and a series of domes rose on top. The architectural result is interesting and unusual. In the church's crypt, a 17th-century coffin encloses the relics of Saint Hilaire.

Leaving the church, return to rue Carnot and walk north on it for about a third of a mile to Place du Maréchal-Leclerc.

AROUND THE PLACE DU MARECHAL-LECLERC

Flanked by simple but satisfactory sidewalk cafés, this pretty *place* is anchored at its eastern end by the impressive Hôtel de Ville. From the north side of the square, take rue Gambetta and angle into the **pedestrian zone**, an amiable area of modern shops, tearooms, cafés, map- and bookstores, and the like. Beginning here, take a tour of Poitiers's other treasures.

The first of the antiquities, on your right just a few feet beyond the beginning of the pedestrian zone, is the gate and clock tower of **St-Porchaire**, all that remains of an 11th-century church.

The Palais de Justice

A few blocks farther on, at Place Alphonse Lepetit (where an outdoor market may be bustling), is the monumental but unimpressive 19th-century façade of the Palais de Justice (law courts), the former ducal palace. It is much more interesting viewed from the south side and back, reached by turning right (east) on rue des Cordeliers, for the façade simply masks the great hall and donjon of the counts of Poitou.

The immense nave of the Grande Salle and the donjon, called the Tour Maubergeon, reflect the prestige and the good taste of Jean, duc de Berry, who served as governor here from 1368 to 1416. The tower dates from the early 12th century and was later transformed into apartments for Jean.

It was in this palace that Joan of Arc was examined by theologians at the request of Charles VII, who was naturally curious to know whether Jeanne really had heard voices calling her to lead the French armies against the English. After a three-week inquiry Jeanne passed the test and rode away to applause from the citizenry; today her statue, in the small garden near the tower, raises a right hand in triumph.

Notre-Dame to Eglise Ste-Radegonde

From Place Alphonse-Lepetit, return a block to the corner of rue des Cordeliers and take it east for another block to rue du Marché. This leads for one more block to the **Eglise Notre-Dame-la-Grande**, a small but important sanctuary for pilgrims en route to Santiago during the Middle Ages. Its 12th-century façade is a triumph of Romanesque ornamentation, alive with such biblical figures as Adam and Eve, prophets, Saint Joseph, and Nebuchadnezzar, as well as a fantastic bestiary. The interior suggests intimacy, peace, and—above all—immense age. (There's another parking garage on Place Charles-de-Gaulle near Notre-Dame-la-Grande.)

From Notre-Dame cross Grand Rue and take rue de la Cathédrale east for several blocks to the **Cathédrale St-Pierre**, begun near the end of the 12th century but finished in Gothic style, with three wide naves and a vast, soaring apse. Remarkable here are the superbly carved 13th-century choir stalls, among the oldest in France; stained glass of the same vintage; and, on the façade just above the entry doors, the sculpted bodies of the risen dead jumping in haste out of their tombs.

The **Baptistère St-Jean** (Baptistery of Saint John), raised in the middle of the fourth century, is just south of the cathedral on rue Jean-Jaurès. The oldest example of Christian architecture in France, it has settled into the earth, not surprisingly, and is now surrounded by ditches dug in the 19th century to reveal its foundations. Today it houses a collection of Mérovingian sarcophagi, stelae, bas-reliefs, an octagonal baptismal font, and Romanesque frescoes.

Almost elbowing the baptistery is the **Musée Ste-Croix**, a relentlessly modern building atop the now-vanished ruins of Sainte Radegonde's Abbaye Ste-Croix. The archaeological collections housed here concern Poitou from prehistoric times: flints, tools, early jewelry, bronze figures, and Gallo-Roman finds. There are also painting galleries featuring various schools from the 15th to the 19th centuries.

From the back of the cathedral rue de la Mauvinière leads a few yards to one of the most moving of Poitiers monuments, the **Eglise Ste-Radegonde**, built in 552 in Angevin Romanesque style. The interior is dark and dramatic; the crypt beneath the altar shelters the stone slabs of Radegonde's bier. To the right a small room illustrates—with paintings and sketches of Radegonde and her associates as well as contemporary and historical texts—the life of one of the most beloved figures in early Gaul.

The festival **Le Printemps Musical** brings major groups to Poitiers during the first half of May.

STAYING AND DINING
IN AND AROUND POITIERS

Le Saint-Hilaire, at 65, rue Théophraste-Renaudot, is a pleasant little place that serves Poitevin specialties under a 12th-
century vaulted ceiling (Tel: 49-41-15-45). Other choices are
Jack Rolland, at 16, rue Carnot, and **Maxime**, nearby at 4, rue
St-Nicolas. Both are highly rated locally and are just a hop
south of Place du Maréchal-Leclerc.

Diners in the Poitiers region are best served at **Pierre
Benoist** in Croutelle, reached by taking the Poitiers-Sud exit
off N 10 about 6 km (4 miles) south of the city. Specialties
include oysters, scallops, veal sweetbreads, and wines of the
Haut-Poitou. Tel: 49-57-11-52.

Within Poitiers proper the hotel situation is fairly uninspiring, the best of the lot being the 78-room ► **Hôtel de
l'Europe**, at 39, rue Carnot. It has a pleasant garden and a
large garage.

Because of the traffic atop Poitiers's promontory, many
drivers choose to stay outside the city in nearby suburbs.
The inn of choice would be ► **Château de Périgny**, a 14th-
century residence in its own 111-acre park 17 km (11 miles)
west of town via D 149 in Périgny (near Vouillé). Fishing,
horseback riding, and a sauna are offered, and there's golf
nearby.

Somewhat more modest, the ► **Château Clos de la Ribaudière**, 9 km (5½ miles) north via N 10 at the turn east
marked Chasseneuil-centre, offers 19 rooms in a restored
19th-century house set in a riverside park. Following the
same turnoff you'll spot directions to two modern chain
hotels: ► **Novotel**, with 89 rooms, a pool, and tennis courts,
set in its own park; and ► **Mercure Relais de Poitiers**, with
90 rooms, a pool, and a garden. (The last two cater largely to
visitors to Parc Futuroscope, an amusement center with a
cinema in which seats are synchronized to move with the
action on the enormous screen.)

About 8 km (5 miles) south of town on N 10, near Ligugé,
is the ► **Bois de la Marche**, a 53-room, rather commercially
oriented hotel in a wooded setting, only 5 km (3 miles) from
the airport.

Countryside Abbeys Near Poitiers

Of the several ancient abbeys to be visited in Poitou, three of
the most interesting are Ligugé, Nouaillé-Maupertuis, and St-
Savin, all of which may be seen on a one-day excursion from
Poitiers, with time out for lunch. We suggest you visit Ligugé
and Nouaillé-Maupertuis in the morning and St-Savin after

lunch, or you could visit each separately from Poitiers. The best meal in the area is to be had at **L'Ecu** in the town of Bélâbre in the Parc Régional de la Brenne; it is reached most easily from Nouaillé-Maupertuis on D 142, N 147, and D 727, a distance of 42 km (27 miles).

LIGUGE

In the year 360 or 361, a hairy, poorly dressed hermit set up his cell in some Gallo-Roman ruins not far from the banks of the river Clain south of Poitiers, on a spot of land granted him by Hilary of Poitiers, in order to found the first monastery in western Gaul. This was the former Roman soldier and future Saint Martin (see Tours, in the Loire Valley chapter). There he spent ten years performing homely miracles (he could exorcise demons from cows and persuade dogs to cease barking at night) until called to become bishop of Tours.

Since 1953, digs in front of and under the former church have revealed remains of a Gallo-Roman villa, a basilica dated 370 or earlier, a sanctuary, and other structures. Only experts can tell precisely what they're seeing, but it is fine to walk down steps into the shadowy fourth century.

Today you may visit the parish church of St-Martin, very smart and elegant with modern stained glass. About 40 Benedictine monks inhabit the monastery, which holds memories of writer Paul Claudel and painter Georges Rouault, both of whom once lived here. The monks' studio produces beautiful enamel works, some of which are on sale in the little museum. If you are lucky, rain will fall softly outside as the voices of the monks lift in ancient chant.

Ligugé is about 8 km (5 miles) south of Poitiers. To find the abbey, in the heart of the village, follow either D 741 or N 10 south from Poitiers and turn west or east, respectively; the turnoffs are fairly well marked.

NOUAILLE-MAUPERTUIS

In a wooded valley through which the river Moisson meanders, just 11 km (7 miles) southeast of Poitiers, the ancient Benedictine abbey of Nouaillé-Maupertuis overlooks fields where the bloody Battle of Poitiers took place in 1356. Try to paint the bucolic scene with armies, as Jean le Bon, his armor decorated with golden fleurs-de-lis, suffers exhaustion and wounds and is defeated by the Black Prince, son of England's King Edward III. (The Black Prince took his name from the color of his armor.)

You probably will have the 12th-century church to yourself; its treasures include a 17th-century woodwork altar

screen, choir stalls, and a great golden eagle, its wings
spread, that serves as lectern. A massive ninth-century stone
tomb, said to be that of one Saint Junien, and dark, narrow
steps leading to the gloomy crypt where the saint's relics
were venerated add to the lugubrious atmosphere. Romanesque architecture, especially in the country, is not only
admirable but often lonely and moody.

If you are driving directly from Poitiers, follow D 12 down
the valley; from Ligugé take D 87 east through Smarves to its
junction with D 12, then turn south to the abbey. It's about
the same distance either way through fields golden with
flowers.

ST-SAVIN

The charming village of St-Savin, so typical of backroads
France, sits east of Poitiers on the banks of the tree-lined
Gartempe river.

The history of the abbey begins, properly, in legend.
Around the middle of the fifth century, in Macedonia, the
brothers Savin and Cyprien were called before the proconsul because they had refused to worship religious idols.
Imprisoned and condemned to death, they managed to
escape to Gaul. Alas, there the two were seized and decapitated on the banks of the Gartempe. Savin was buried on a
hill not far from the town named after him.

In the ninth century an abbey was built on the holy spot
and Benedictine monks were installed there by order of
Louis I, le Débonnaire (Louis the Kind). Protected by fortifications, the abbey survived Norman incursions in 878; two
centuries later reconstruction was begun, the painted frescoes that once blanketed the entire interior being executed
simultaneously.

The Hundred Years War put an end to the abbey's
prosperity—it suffered at the hands of both the French army
and the soldiers of the Black Prince. During the 16th-century
Wars of Religion it was gutted twice: once by the Protestant
Huguenots, and by the revenge-prone Royalists six years
later. When returned to the Benedictines, the church was so
decrepit that repair hardly seemed worthwhile. The monks
were too poor to do anything but whitewash the interior and
add little edges of flowers. (The whitewash hid the frescoes,
preserving them from Revolutionary zealots.)

The **fresco cycle** of the Apocalypse in the narthex and that
of the Old Testament on the barrel-vault ceiling of the nave
are the most beautiful and complete in all France and
among the greatest (and least known) art treasures in Europe. In simple terms, they are sensational. Their glory is

seconded by the columns painted to imitate marble, a technique rare in France. The "frescoes," having been drawn on already ancient walls, were not executed in the true sense of the medium, which traditionally involves painting on wet plaster. The colors thus could penetrate only the upper layer and form nothing more than a light film. That they exist today, and in such lively, animated form, makes them only the more remarkable.

If you are driving directly from Poitiers, follow N 151 for 41 km (25 miles), passing around Chauvigny on the Vienne river. From Nouaillé, however, the most direct route would follow D 12 south to Nieuil-l'Espoir, then jog east on D 95 to Fleuré, run north on D 2 to Chauvigny, then swing east on N 151 to St-Savin; in all, about the same distance as from Poitiers.

Literary Pilgrimages in Poitou

One of the pleasures of travel in France is making pilgrimages to sites that recall the memory of favorite heroes: writers, painters, warriors, poets. In the area of Poitou there are two especially interesting trips to make.

RICHELIEU

Jean de La Fontaine, poet and fabulist, described Richelieu as "the most beautiful village in the universe." This town of 2,500 people is about 60 km (37 miles) due north of Poitiers. (Leaving Poitiers, take N 147 for a few kilometers; then, at Migné-Auxances, turn north onto D 757 and follow it the rest of the way.)

In 1621 Armand du Plessis, duc de Richelieu, came to a tiny village on the river Mable to establish a château and a small walled town. (In 1622 he became Cardinal Richelieu and prime minister for Louis XIII.) Excessively proud and fond of luxury, he came to own at least eight châteaux. (For more on Richelieu's politics, see La Rochelle, below.)

Built on a classically urban, rectangular plan, the town is sliced by the Grande-Rue and shows off a number of handsome Louis XIII mansions and public buildings. The **Musée Richelieu** in the Hôtel de Ville exhibits documents and artworks belonging to the château and the cardinal's family, although much of the artwork has been dispersed, some of it to the Louvre. Almost nothing remains as witness to the magnificence of Cardinal Richelieu's proud home except the park of more than 1,000 acres shaded by chestnut and plane trees and watched over by a statue of Cardinal Richelieu standing near the entrance. Perhaps justice has been served.

DESCARTES

About 56 km (35 miles) northeast of Poitiers via N 10 and
D 58 lies the town of Descartes, which was called La Haye
in 1596 when favorite son René Descartes was baptized
here. Mathematician, logician, and creator of the Cartesian
Method, he was the son of rich, bourgeois parents.

Educated in a Jesuit school, Descartes spent very little
time in the town that took his name, living for 20 years in
Holland and then, having been summoned by Sweden's
Queen Christina, spending the rest of his life in Stockholm,
where he died in 1650.

Students of Descartes and his philosophy may visit his
natal home on 29, rue Descartes (where else?), which displays documents and memorabilia of his life and work.
Descartes would be a pleasant detour on a trip south from
Tours or Loches to Poitiers.

LES CHARENTES

Les Charentes is composed of the *départements* of Charente
and Charente-Maritime, the ancient provinces of Angoumois
(Angoulême's region), Aunis (the region of La Rochelle),
and Saintonge (around Saintes).

The Charentais admits to being *gueux, glorieux,* and
gourmand (a rascal, a braggart, and a glutton); a proverb
claims: "The Charentais will drink milk when cows eat
grapes."

The best place to begin a tour of the region is the
seductive and historic port of La Rochelle. You may then
want to visit its offshore islands (Ré, Aix, and Oléron), then
return inland to Rochefort. Moving south, in coastal Royan,
you will enter Cognac country and travel in an easterly
direction through Saintes and Cognac itself. Next, the road
turns east again to Angoulême, a major center since Roman
times. Finally, detour into the countryside in search of châteaux and churches of great interest.

LA ROCHELLE

Under a high, porcelain-blue sky or soaked by sudden bursts
of rain, La Rochelle (on the coast southwest of Poitiers) is an

engaging place, a pleasure port not too tourist-ridden, laced with winding arcades that harbor small shops and streets lined with handsome, half-timbered houses. La Rochelle is an example of that rare joining of an animated waterside resort to a city of cultural and historical interest.

A town may have been born on this site as early as the tenth century, when fishermen settled on the rocky, seaside plateau. In the year 1137, when William X, duc de Aquitaine and comte de Poitou, died on a pilgrimage to Santiago de Compostela, the city and its region became the private property of his daughter, the redoubtable Eleanor of Aquitaine. When Eleanor betook herself and her immense properties to Henri II Plantagenêt, later proclaimed king of England, La Rochelle came under the British flag.

It was Eleanor who financed the digging and construction of a major port capable of admitting ships of then-great tonnage. The citizens grew wealthy exporting salt and wine along the expanding trade routes and exploiting the quarrels between England and France. After the opening of the New World the city developed a booming trade in sugar and spices with the West Indies, and in furs with Canada. During the Reformation it was open to Protestant revisionism. The growth of Protestantism, stimulated by monks imbued with the thoughts of John Calvin, prompted La Rochelle's nickname, Little Geneva. (Though born in France, Calvin did most of his work in Switzerland.)

From the early days of the Wars of Religion the Rochelais endured a period of suffering and persecution. In 1573 the royal forces led by the duke of Anjou, later Henri III, besieged La Rochelle, but the citizens defended themselves ferociously; by the time the six-month siege had been lifted 20,000 royal troops had perished.

What we see of La Rochelle today is a product of the prosperity of the late 17th and the 18th centuries, a direct result of dynamic commerce with the young United States. Early in World War II La Rochelle was occupied by German troops. A great submarine base was built and occupation continued until 1945, when the Allies liberated the city on May 8.

The Old Quarter

The old town, center of commercial as well as visitor activity, lies between rue du Palais on the west, rue du Minage on the north, Grande-Rue des Merciers on the east, and quai Duperré and Vieux-Port on the south. The quarter may be seen, shopped in, and photographed in one daylong walk, even if you take time out for lunch.

UP THE RUE DU PALAIS

A good place to begin is at the "foot" of rue du Palais where it meets rue Léonce Vieljeux (named for the Resistance mayor who was deported to Germany and executed there in 1944) at the **Porte de la Grosse Horloge**. This great 13th-century gate that marked the entry to the medieval town from the port was reworked in the 18th century with the addition of a belfry and clock tower. It opens onto the pretty Place des Petits-Bancs, where stands a statue of Eugène Fromentin, the local painter-writer whose chef d'oeuvre, *Dominique,* vividly outlines the life of La Rochelle in the 19th century.

At the corner where rue du Temple enters the square there's a small shop selling delightful hand-printed paper goods and Haitian prints. Shops line both sides of rue du Palais, which is punctuated on the left (west) side by the **Hôtel de la Bourse**, an early Louis XVI–style seat of the Chamber of Commerce with a fine courtyard, and the majestic **Palais de Justice** (both 18th century).

If you detour a couple of blocks left off rue du Palais via rue E. Fromentin to rue de l'Escale, you'll find yourself in front of the handsome **Maison Nicolas Venette**, a 17th-century mansion built for a local doctor, with a rhythmic façade studded with six sculptures of doctors of antiquity. (Rue de l'Escale is paved with stones used as ballast on ships arriving from Canada.)

AROUND THE CATHEDRALE ST-LOUIS

North of rue E. Fromentin, rue du Palais becomes rue Chaudrier, where one ancient house employs slate rather than wood in the half-timbered style, an answer to the vagaries of local weather. (Here enthusiasts of architecture should turn right onto rue des Augustins to admire the luxurious 16th-century residence called **Maison Henri II**.)

The next stop, on the left, is the **Cathédrale St-Louis**, begun during the second half of the 18th century. Sober and heavy, with a remarkably severe exterior, the cathedral is fascinating inside, with many ex-votos and paintings featuring ships and sailors in religious allegories.

Across the street and a couple of blocks north, near rue du Minage, you'll come to the ornate **Café de la Paix**, the last remaining example of the opulent cafés where, at the turn of the last century, locals came to read newspapers and play billiards in surroundings dripping with gilt and mirrors. During the first act of the café's history, around 1709, this dramatic edifice served as a hospital. The second act began in the early 1900s, when salons were in vogue here, with such players as Colette, Henri Bordeaux, Georges Simenon, and the like. In the third act Annie Girardot and Jean Gabin came to town for the café's glory days. Today it's slightly musty and fusty, pleasantly overdone from the banquettes to the painted ceiling. It's a required stop for the sentimental traveller, who can take coffee, a glass of wine, a sandwich, or even a light dinner (*escalope de veau à la crème* is recommended).

PLACE DU MARCHE
AND HOTEL DE VILLE

Follow rue du Minage, where seductive shops selling fashionable clothing, gourmet foods, wine, and antiques lurk beneath irregular arcades and old houses sport sculptures and friezes, east to its end at the Pilori Fountain; then take a few steps south of rue du Pas-du-Minage and you'll find yourself in front of the Place du Marché. This is the epitome of provincial French marketplaces, where, in front of a superb half-timber and a stately Renaissance house, the square is crowded with people and produce: Stalls overflow with the prettiest of produce, merchants shout out their prize tomatoes, and children skitter about creating chaos. Inside the *halle,* fishmongers and meat merchants play out the savory scene until noon.

Leaving the Place du Marché, edge south into the Grande-Rue des Merciers, one of the liveliest arteries in town, lined by shops both chic and commercial installed in 16th- and 17th-century houses resplendent with diverting façades.

At rue de la Grille turn right (west) for the square dominated by the **Hôtel de Ville**. There's a fairy-tale quality to this public structure, which seems less a city hall than a cultural caprice, caught between its medieval wall, its Rapunzel-like belfry, its Flamboyant Gothic entryway, and an elegant little pavilion. At the center of the *place* strides a statue of Jean Guiton, the tough, fanatical, and determined mayor who held off the famous siege of La Rochelle (1627–1628), conducted by the crafty Cardinal Richelieu. There's a handy sidewalk café suited to contemplation of the past.

Just west of the old town is the **Parc Charruyer**, an ambler's retreat where birds come to settle by the little river and trees stand along old *allées;* there is a gaming casino here as well.

THE VIEUX-PORT

South of the Hôtel de Ville lies La Rochelle's Vieux-Port (Old Port), one of the most picturesque on the Atlantic coast of France. Situated at the inner end of a great bay, it is too small to accommodate industrial traffic. It forms a small rectangle to the south of town and the quai du Perré. Evenings here, they say, are best for contemplation of the comings and goings of decorated fishing boats while passing the time in the open-air cafés along the **quai Duperré**; fragrant breezes blow in from the sea and the fading light outlines the Tour de la Chaîne and the Tour St-Nicolas. The Vieux-Port is by far the best place to eat in La Rochelle, and you can enjoy this scene over a plate of seafood; see the dining section, below. To the right across the Vieux-Port, which is usually busy with private yachts, sailboats, and countless tiny pleasure craft, stands the splendid 14th-century **Tour de la Chaîne**, an arsenal with a great chain that at night linked it to its sister tower, **Tour St-Nicolas**, across the entrance to the harbor. In itself Tour St-Nicolas constitutes a fortress; it frequently served as a prison. Rue Sur-les-Murs leads west from the Tour de la Chaîne along the medieval ramparts to the **Tour de la Lanterne**, which served as a kind of lighthouse for navigators. From a platform halfway up there's a fine view.

In season, small boats depart the Vieux-Port at frequent intervals for excursions to the islands of Aix, Ré, and Oléron (see below), and upriver on the Charente.

THE MODERN PORT

The modern port of La Rochelle, southwest of the Vieux-Port, is most easily reached by car. It still ranks among France's major ports, particularly for the catching and distribution of fresh seafood. A substantial fleet from La Rochelle fishes south along the French coast, into the gulf of Gascony, off the Portuguese coast, and near the coasts of England and Ireland.

In addition to serving the fishing fleet, the modern port handles freighters and other heavy-tonnage shipping; the newest area, Minimes, is reserved for pleasure craft. Regattas and boat races of various kinds attract a wide audience, and each year ten days before Pentecost (the seventh Sunday after Easter) an International Sail Week provides for day-and-night action on both sea and land.

LA ROCHELLE'S MUSEUMS

It's a bit disorienting but most educational for an American to visit the **Musée du Nouveau Monde**, at 10, rue Fleuriau.

(The building is in the middle of the block between rue Albert Ier and rue St-Yon, several blocks south of the Place du Marché). Opened in 1978 to illustrate the evolution of the relationship between France and America since the 16th century, it discloses a double vision: the reality of America and the Europeans' image of America.

La Rochelle, having been a cradle of commerce and immigration to Acadia, Canada, Louisiana, the French West Indies, and Brazil, is a perfect place for such study. Installed in a beautiful 18th-century *hôtel,* the museum displays 500 works: paintings and drawings, maps, engravings, sculptures, American copies of English furniture, and decorative *objets d'art.* As portrayed, Native Americans seem to fulfill Rousseau's own vision of the "noble savage." The whole turns American eyes right around.

Just a block north of this museum at 28, rue Gargoulleau, the **Musée des Beaux-Arts** illustrates the history of painting from the primitives until today. Most interesting are the 20th-century views of the port as seen by Signac and a group of lesser-known regional artists.

The **Musée d'Orbigny**, at 2, rue St-Côme, is devoted to the history of La Rochelle and of ceramics. There are souvenirs of the Siege of La Rochelle and objects of archaeological interest, but most important is the exceptional series of faïence, including superb vases and lovely pieces from other parts of France.

The **Muséum d'Histoire Naturelle** is located at the entrance of the Jardin des Plantes (Botanical Gardens), several streets north of the place de Verdun along rue Albert Ier. Two buildings house fine collections of antique furnishings, primitive art, and scientific, prehistoric, and zoologic exhibits. In other words, it's eclectic.

Three other museums are located in the Ville-en-Bois quarter near the modern port. They may be reached by taxi (say, from the railroad station) or, in summer, by water taxi from the Vieux-Port.

The **Musée des Automates**, on rue de la Désirée, reveals the world of automatons, with more than 300 animated figures performing on a musical stage: clowns, musicians, a snake charmer, various animals, and such. All are designed to re-create as closely as possible the natural movements of human beings and creatures.

Next to the Musée des Automates, on rue de la Desirée, the **Aquarium R-Coutant** displays fish from tropical seas and marine animals from nearby coasts.

At the Port des Minimes, in the Bassin du Lazaret, the **Musée Océanographique** houses skeletons of seagoing mammals (whales and seals, for example), and live seals splash in a small pool. Water buses regularly connect the Port des Minimes to the Vieux-Port.

STAYING AND DINING IN LA ROCHELLE

Most of the town's top restaurants are found in the Vieux-Port area. Just west of the Tour de la Lanterne on the beach named Concurrence, the Michelin-rated **Richard Coutanceau** serves *mouclade* (a creamy mussel soup spiked with saffron, curry, or Cognac; available June to November), sea bass, or Breton lobster (Tel: 46-41-48-19). Inland from the Tour de la Chaîne at 14, rue St-Jean-du-Pérot, elegant **La Marmite** (also a "Michelin restaurant") offers *mouclade* as well as, for example, skate-stuffed ravioli with shallots (Tel: 46-41-17-03). A few steps away at 46, cours des Dames, **Serge** specializes in fish and crustaceans (Tel: 46-41-18-80).

Right near La Marmite at 22, rue St-Jean-du-Pérot, **l'Entracte** satisfies at a reasonable price (Tel: 46-50-62-60). On the same popular street at number 49, **Les Quatre Sergents** is unpretentious in its pleasant winter-garden setting (Tel: 46-41-35-80).

The ▶ **Hôtel de France-Angleterre et Champlain** is nicely located near the old quarter at 20, rue Rambaud, just a block north of the Place de Verdun. Of the 33 rooms and four suites, many are spanking new, while the antiques-filled public rooms occupy a restored town house. There's parking nearby and a breakfast room, but no restaurant.

Perhaps the most pleasantly situated hotel is the 48-room ▶ **Les Brises**, a short drive west of the city center and just north of the modern harbor. It also lacks a restaurant.

The ▶ **Hôtel de la Monnaie** is a restored 17th-century house that sits near the entry to the Vieux-Port at the foot of the Tour de la Lanterne. It has 32 rooms, four apartments, a bar—but no restaurant—and an enclosed garden. Nearby on the Place de la Chaine is the slightly less expensive 57-room ▶ **St-Jean d'Acre**; it does have a restaurant, **Au Vieux Port**, as well as a lovely garden. The 38-room ▶ **François Iᵉʳ** occupies an ancient house not far from the Hôtel de Ville on rue Bazoges (no restaurant).

The Coastal Islands

It would be possible to touch on all three islands off the coast of La Rochelle in a day: from north to south, Ré, Aix, and Oléron. More practical, though, would be to cover both Ré and Oléron as full-day trips, while a trip to Aix might be combined with a visit to Rochefort (for which see below).

These islands are not oriented toward tourism. They do cater to the French, who come to enjoy the sun, beach, and quiet for weeks at a time. Most travellers from overseas are content with a daylong trip to one of the three.

ILE DE RE

Excursion boats from La Rochelle's Vieux-Port take you to the island; there are also a few car ferries departing from La Pallice, a commercial port area about 5½ km (3½ miles) west of the Vieux-Port. The most practical approach, however, is via the Pont de l'Ile de Ré, a highway toll bridge on D 735.

Only about 18 miles from east to west, Ile de Ré today is little more than a summer seaside resort, where many fruits and vegetables are grown. Much of its quaintness exists only in memory—donkeys dressed in trousers to protect them from flies and mosquitoes when working in saline marshes, and women dressed in the *quichenotte,* a headpiece to protect them from the sun.

On the northwesternmost reach of the island, the wetlands around the bay of Fier d'Ars constitute good bird-watching country. On the south side of the island, a long stretch of sand dunes lies behind a rough and rocky coast.

The little town of **La Flotte**, 18 km (11 miles) from La Rochelle and 5½ km (3½ miles) from the end of the Ile-de-Ré bridge, is the best place to stop if you want to lunch on the island. Its ▶ **Richelieu Hôtel** (37 rooms, three apartments) has an outstanding dining room and is a natural place in which to order seafood: grilled lobster, langoustines, or turbot (usually prepared in the fashion of sole); Tel: 46-09-60-70. Should you plan to spend the night, you can enjoy the outdoor pool and tennis courts.

The main town of this nearly somnolent isle is **St-Martin-de-Ré**, about 5½ (3½ miles) west of La Flotte, where students of military architecture will admire the fortifications created by the master of the art, Sébastien le Prestre de Vauban. A couple of other attractions are worth a stop, chiefly the **Musée Naval et Ernest-Cognacq**; the collections of faïence and furniture recall the recently reopened Musée Cognacq-Jay Museum in Paris. To lunch in a pretty setting, try **Les Terrasses du Galion**, at 3, cours Pasteur.

Farther west along the island's one main road, the village

of **Ars-en-Ré** is notable for narrow streets with houses that almost touch across the walkway, and the pretty, old church of St-Etienne.

ILE D'AIX

Napoléon is the past and present attraction on little Ile d'Aix (pronounced "eye"), which floats in the Pertuis d'Antioche (*pertuis* means "narrow passage"). Wooded with oaks, pines, and tamarisks, the island is home to only 173 Aixois.

The easiest way to reach Aix is on one of the excursion boats from La Rochelle. From June through September they make the hour-long sailing two or three times a day; they make three trips a week the rest of the year. For tickets and information, inquire at Croisières Inter Iles, 14 bis cours des Dames, right on the western quai of the Vieux-Port; Tel: 46-50-55-54.

Drivers follow N 137–E 602 south of La Rochelle for 21 km (13 miles) to the marked D 214 turnoff west for the fort of Fouras and beyond to the Pointe de la Fumée, another 8 km (5 miles). From here, it's a 20-minute ferry crossing to the island. (No cars are allowed on the island; there's ample parking near the ferry slip.)

Once fortified by Vauban, who designed the citadel Fort de la Rade, Aix became important historically when Napoléon Bonaparte arrived on July 8, 1815, following the disastrous defeat at Waterloo. He had planned to escape to America, but the presence of the English fleet kept him sequestered and finally forced him to throw himself on England's mercy. After spending his final hours on French soil, he sailed off toward exile on Ste-Helena on July 15.

Aix often has served as a prison: to Russian soldiers during the Crimean War, to Prussians in the War of 1870, to insurgents of the Commune during the Revolution, and to Russians again during World War I.

It takes only about two hours to visit the main attractions of the island's only village (also called Aix): the **Musée Napoléonien**, in a large home built to Bonaparte's order in 1808 when, at the height of his power, he inspected the defenses. It is one of the few houses in town with more than one story, and it is still topped by the imperial eagle. Today ten rooms here are crowded with souvenirs of the emperor, his family, and his entourage: artworks, furniture, arms, clothing, portraits, and the like. Napoléon's bedroom has been left as it was when he watched from his balcony as British ships approached to take him away.

The **Musée Africain**, housed in military barracks, shows

off interesting ethnographic and zoologic collections of one Baron Gourgaud, assembled from 1913 to 1931, including some rare animal specimens. Most notable is the (now stuffed) white dromedary ridden by Napoléon during his Egyptian campaign; it was moved here from the Jardin des Plantes in Paris in 1933.

ILE D'OLERON

The largest French coastal island, Oléron (about 18 miles long by 4 miles wide) is suggestive of the Mediterranean, with its wooded sand dunes, white houses surrounded with mimosa, rose-laurel, tamarisks, fig trees, and agave, and the occasional arms of an old windmill. It is a popular summer retreat for families who come to enjoy the seaside, the sun, and the pine-scented air.

Oléron is reached by a 20-minute boat ride south from Aix; boats depart from the jetty south of Fort de la Rade on Aix and call at Oléron's north coast port of Boyardville. However, an easier route (especially for those who wish to drive around the island) is via the longest bridge-viaduct in France (about two miles long), which connects Oléron to the mainland near Marennes. From La Rochelle, take N 137 south to Rochefort, then go southwest on D 733 for 11½ km (7 miles) and follow the D 123 turnoff another 15 km (9 miles) in the direction of Marennes.

Oléron offers outstanding examples of successful aqua-culture, including oyster farming and the cultivation of clams, trout, and eel. Fishing is important to the economy, as is the farming of spring vegetables and grapes. (The local wine, white or rosé, is agreeable.)

In 1199, in the twilight of her remarkable life, Eleanor of Aquitaine arrived, at the age of 76, at her château on Oléron, preparing to retire from the world to the abbey of Fontev-raud, where she would die in 1204. Here she promulgated a series of rules ordering the life of the sea, a maritime code governing ships and their masters, sailors, and merchants. The so-called *Rôles d'Oléron* served as a basis for all such laws in the future.

Following Eleanor's reign the island's ownership was vigorously contested between British and French, with the French winning out in 1372.

Around the Ile d'Oléron

The natural place to begin the daylong drive of about 85 km (53 miles) around Oléron is St-Trojan-les-Bains on the south-ern tip of the island, a pleasant seaside resort with pretty villas set among pine forests and a permanent population of

1,470. Four fine-sand beaches here are bathed by the warming Gulf Stream. A little train takes tourists from St-Trojan to the **Pointe de Maumusson**, an isolated point along the Côte Sauvage (Wild Coast).

From St-Trojan take D 126 to **Château-d'Oléron**, a town gathered around the remains of an old stronghold that was rebuilt in 1666 to help protect La Rochelle and the mouth of the Charente. There's an Office de Tourisme on the attractive Place de la République.

From here follow the signs to the tiny settlement of Les Allards along D 734 and D 126 through oyster-farming country and continue to **Boyardville** along the eastern coastline.

Leaving Boyardville, continue on D 126 as it winds along the coast, then follow signs to St-Georges d'Oléron to admire the 11th- to 12th-century **Romanesque church**, its façade bearing fine geometric decorations.

Rejoin D 126 to the northern tip of the island and the **Phare de Chassiron** (*phare* means "lighthouse"). If you climb the 224 steps you'll be rewarded by a panoramic view of the entire island as well as of the islands of Aix and Ré and as far as La Rochelle, weather permitting.

Route D 734 will take you south again to **St-Pierre-d'Oléron**, the island's metropolis. In season, the pedestrian heart of the town swarms with summer people (although the town's inns are unimpressive). Two stops should be made here on rue Pierre-Loti: first at number 13, where romance writer Pierre Loti (see Rochefort, below) spent holidays with his grandparents; Loti was buried in 1923 in the family garden, his childhood bucket and shovel placed by his side. The other is at number 23, the **Musée Oléronais Aliénor-d'Aquitaine**, which displays traditional arts and crafts, along with a reconstructed rural kitchen. A copy of Eleanor's effigy from her tomb at Fontevraud lies in repose.

Before leaving Oléron don't fail to take the scenic one-way circular route through the sand dunes, beginning and ending at the hamlet of **Vert-Bois**, then take D 126 again back to St-Trojan.

Staying and Dining on Ile d'Oléron

St-Trojan offers a major hotel, the 80-room ▶ **Novotel**, set in a forest near the sea, with an indoor pool, a nearby beach, and tennis courts.

In Boyardville, **La Perrotine** (Tel: 46-47-01-01) and **Bains** (Tel: 46-47-01-02), both right by the pleasure-craft port, are good places for light meals; the latter has an outdoor terrace.

From St-Pierre, you can also find good food and lodging by heading seaward on D 274 in the direction of **La**

Cotinière, a lively little port on the Côte Sauvage. Try local shrimp (called *bouquets d'Oléron*), sole, lobster, or crab, perhaps at **L'Ecailler**, right at the port.

Continue south along the sea on D 126 to La Remigeasse, where, right above the beach, sits the top inn on the island, ▶ **Le Grand Large**, with 21 rooms, five apartments, a fine restaurant, a covered and heated pool, and tennis courts.

Rochefort

This pleasant little city is 32 km (20 miles) south of La Rochelle via N 137–E 602.

Rochefort was built in the 17th century as a river port for the defense of the Atlantic coast; it's nine miles upstream from the mouth of the Charente. Today it's a businesslike town where the wide, straight streets that replaced the ramparts meet one another at right angles. Families and students from the local naval college stroll along the linden-shaded promenades through formal gardens to the east and west of the downtown area.

Visitors with a literary bent will want to see the **Maison de Loti** on the street that bears his name. (It's in the south of town, not far from the bus station.) Pierre Loti (1850–1923), born Julien Viaud, military officer, sports enthusiast, and world traveller, became an author of romances in exotic settings and attracted an international audience. His "house" is really two: his birthplace and a structure next door that was purchased later. To step inside is to enter a sumptuous, ornate, almost imaginary world; his own bedroom suggests a Turkish mosque. If you haven't read his works before a visit, you'll feel compelled to do so afterward.

The **Musée d'Art et d'Histoire de la Ville**, a five-minute walk north of the Maison de Loti on rue de Pierre Loti at the corner of avenue Charles de Gaulle, houses paintings of several schools, ethnographic displays, natural-history collections, and automatons.

The 17th-century Corderie Royale (a *corderie* is where ship's ropes were made), on the eastern edge of town just beyond the Jardin de la Marine, today houses the **Centre Internationale de la Mer**, where there are permanent and changing exhibitions illustrating France's maritime tradition.

If you are staying overnight in Rochefort, consider the 50-room ▶ **La Corderie Royale**, located in a restored gunnery station on the banks of the Charente river; it has a pool, a terrace, and a restaurant. A pleasing restaurant in the area is **Le Soubise**, 3 km (2 miles) to the southwest in the town of the same name (Tel: 46-84-92-16).

COGNAC COUNTRY
Royan

You will thoroughly enjoy or completely deplore Royan, an ancient port at the mouth of the Gironde, depending upon your views of what is or is not typically French. Royan is almost precisely south of La Rochelle via N 137 to Rochefort, then D 733 (about 78 km/48 miles in all).

Almost nothing remains of the old port of Royan. During the battles to liberate the region in the autumn of 1944, German troops holed up here and in other nearby pockets, only to be bombed by Allied forces in April 1945, less than a month before the armistice of May 8.

Today Royan is nicknamed Reine de la Côte de Beauté (Queen of the Beautiful Coast); it is the largest and most modern sea resort between La Baule to the north in Brittany and Biarritz to the south on the Spanish border. There are those who wax nostalgic about old Royan, the Royan of elegant cliff-side chalets, of breezy Victorian hostelries with wide corridors and intimidating façades and concierges, of palatial casinos in Renaissance or Baroque dress. Some sense of the olden days may be glimpsed in the smart suburb of Pontaillac, although most visitors stop there not because of nostalgia but to play at the Sporting-Casino.

Today expressions such as *resto en vogue* (trendy restaurant) are more suggestive of Royan than *aristocratique* or *traditionnel*. Indeed, the top tourist attraction in town is a triumph of reinforced concrete dating from 1958, the **Eglise Notre-Dame**. Seen from the front, the soaring belfry (almost 215 feet high) suggests the giant prow of a ship sailing into town from the Atlantic.

The heart of the modern town curves around the Grande Conche, a large bay flanked on the north by a fine sandy beach and a seafront promenade backed by shops, banks, and apartment houses. Across the bay, the port is filled with resting trawlers, sardine-fishing boats, and pleasure craft, right at the foot of the **Grand Casino**. (In European fashion, the casino visitor is expected to be properly dressed, quiet, and serious, and to respect an atmosphere utterly unlike that in Reno, Las Vegas, or Atlantic City.)

The Côte Sauvage

The resort setting may best be admired by driving northwest of town on the coastal road to the **Forêt de la Coubre**, about 20 km (12 miles) along D 25 to the Pointe de la Coubre and

its lighthouse. Rounding the various *conches* (bays, coves)
on cliffs above or down by sandy dunes where sea pines
bow, you will begin to appreciate the natural beauty that
brings inland souls to this place. The best type of day along
La Grande-Côte between Royan and the lighthouse in the
Forêt de la Coubre is a cold, windy one, when waves batter
the shore and spray drenches the windshield.

From the lighthouse you have the choice of retracing your
route to Royan or of continuing north with the Forêt de la
Coubre on the east and the appropriately named Côte
Sauvage on the west. At the northern point of the peninsula,
you can swing around and return south on D 14 along the
wetlands and marshes of the Charentes. From Royan to
Royan, the total distance is 62 km (39 miles).

STAYING AND DINING IN ROYAN

Overlooking the beach, the ► **Family Golf Hôtel** is the best
in town, though it's quite modest and has no restaurant.
Better is the ► **Résidence de Rohan**, just a couple of miles
north along the coast; a 41-room inn occupying a handsomely furnished 19th-century home, it's comfortable but
far from ostentatious (no dining room).

For dining, **La Coraline** (at 102, avenue des Semis, right in
the heart of things back of the seafront; Tel: 46-05-51-34) and
Le Chalet (at 6, boulevard La Grandière, in the southeastern
part of town near the main city park; Tel: 46-05-04-90) are
good choices. Both are solid, middle-ground restaurants
offering such dishes as salmon in a parsley cream sauce,
grilled sole, and oysters. You might also try **Trois Marmites**,
right in town at 37, avenue Regazzoni; Tel: 46-38-66-31.

Saintes

Saintes, an ancient and attractive town of about 27,500
Saintais, or Santons, 38 km (23 miles) east of Royan on N
150, comes as a complete surprise to the traveller in Poitou-
Charentes; it is a remnant of the powerful presence of Rome
in southwestern France. Today it is cut in two by the
Charente, but in Roman days it was a major trading city
called Mediolanum Santonum, and was confined mainly to
the river's left bank.

In medieval times, under Plantagenêt domination, the
town watched year in and year out as thousands of pilgrims
passed through the Roman Arc de Germanicus and crossed
the bridge, bound for the shrine of Santiago de Compostela
in Spain. Today a regional center of industry, agricultural

markets, and crafts, Saintes well deserves at least one day of exploration.

Saintes seems pleasant enough—animated, well supplied with shops, but relatively anonymous—as you sweep along avenue de Saintonge and turn north on cours Reverseaux to its meeting with cours National, on the edge of the *vieille ville* (old town).

THE OLD TOWN

In its old town, however, and in what were once suburbs on the right bank, Saintes is far more impressive, boasting witnesses to every age since that of the Romans. As usual, touring begins best in the old town, which surrounds the **Cathédrale St-Pierre** and **Place du Marché**. The cathedral, built atop a Roman structure, owes its appearance mainly to the 15th century and is of only passing interest. Three corners north on rue St-Michel and half a block left on rue Victor-Hugo is the **Musée des Beaux-Arts**, housed in the classic, 17th-century Hôtel Présidial in the center of an attractive pedestrian district. Beautifully restored in the modern manner (i.e., the exhibitions can be seen clearly), the Présidial's six rooms house Saintonge ceramics from the 11th century to today, as well as paintings from the 15th through 19th century.

The **Musée Dupuy-Mestreau**, an example of the regional collections in which France excels, is south from the cathedral. Take rue R. G. Clemenceau four blocks to rue Monconseil. The *hôtel* itself abounds in handsome woodwork, fireplaces, and ceilings, and the displays include items of maritime importance, stamps, peasant headdresses and costumes, weapons, and reconstituted rooms in regional style. From here it's a pleasant walk back along the quai de Verdun, with its handsome 17th- and 18th-century mansions sporting gardens and wrought-iron balconies.

EGLISE ST-EUTROPE
AND ROMAN SAINTES

From the *vieille ville,* continue to explore the left bank of the Charente. Begin just west of the Musée Dupuy-Mestreau at Place Blair. Follow rue Berthonnière, then rue St-François and rue St-Eutrope to the western rim of the old city. Here, about 3 km (2 miles) from the museum, sits the **Eglise St-Eutrope**.

This church ranks among the most important in western France. Long a place of pilgrimage, it was erected above the grave site of Eutrope, the first bishop of Saintes in the third century. In the 11th century two churches were superimposed on this site: the grand pilgrimage church on top and the parish church below. It is the crypt of the latter that has survived, half buried, second only to that of Chartres in size. The body of the saint, twice "lost" over the centuries, rests securely in its sacrophagus in the area of the choir, surrounded by sturdy Roman pillars.

About 200 yards north of St-Eutrope, via rue St-Eutrope to the west and then rue Lacurie to the north, sits an **amphitheater**, almost the size of that in Nîmes, that once held 20,000 spectators; today grass grows over the tiers. Built in the first century, it is among the oldest remaining from the Roman world, and it is a moving setting for the musical performances staged here on many summer nights.

The rest of the essential sights in Saintes sit on the right bank of the Charente. From the amphitheater, take the cours National (the Office de Tourisme is at number 62; Tel: 46-74-23-82) east across the river via Pont B. Palissy. (Here, cours National becomes avenue Gambetta.)

You are now in the place Bassompierre; the **Arc de Germanicus**, in its center, has been standing on the right bank of the river, the Gambetta side, since 1842, when the Roman bridge on which it originally stood had to be demolished. (Prosper Mérimée, author of the *Carmen* on which Bizet's opera was based and an inspector of historical monuments, insisted it be saved.) The wonder of this arch, built of local limestone in the year A.D. 19, is that its inscriptions, by one Caius Julius Rufus, may still be read in dedication to Germanicus, Emperor Tiberius, and his son Drusus.

A few feet south of the arch, on the southern edge of the *place,* the **Musée Archéologique** is installed in a former faïence factory. Down an *allée* lined by ancient Doric columns, you walk to the museum, which houses exciting remains from the local Gallo-Roman military camp. Inquire at the museum about visiting some of the archaeological digs that continue (though not on a daily basis) in the vicinity of Saintes. The large public gardens south of the museum are studded with antiquities.

ABBAYE AUX DAMES

From the museum, walk southeast a few yards down the rue Gautier and turn north (left) onto rue du Pont-Amilion and the Abbaye aux Dames.

Consecrated in 1047 to house Benedictine nuns, the abbey soon became prosperous under the influence of Agnès of Burgundy, wife of Geoffroy Martel, Comte d'Anjou. Handsomely restored, it is one of the finest examples of the style called Saintonge (for the region of Saintes) Romanesque.

First, admire the rich ornamentation of the façade. On just one part of the central portal, no fewer than 54 sagacious men wearing crowns face each other, two by two, and play musical instruments. To the right, there is a wonderful depiction of the Last Supper.

The interior retains its 12th-century appearance; the nave, transept, and choir are of particular interest to enthusiasts of medieval architecture. The entire visit will take about half an hour. To see other examples of Saintonge Romanesque, take an excursion of about 72 km (45 miles) around the countryside near Saintes. Ask for a map at the Office de Tourisme.

From the north wing of the abbey, take rue St-Pallais for a short walk east to rue Denfert-Rochereau, then walk one block north and turn right to the Musée Educatif de Préhistoire. Here, exhibits are dedicated to the life of prehistoric man and his use of tools.

STAYING AND DINING IN SAINTES

There are two good hotels in Saintes, the ► **Messageries**, on the street of the same name, and the ► **Relais du Bois St-Georges**, past the amphitheater on rue Royan via D 137. The St-Georges has 30 rooms, three apartments, and its own park.

For a light luncheon try the **Logis Santon**, at 54, cours Genêt, two streets north of the amphitheater. **La Rôtisserie François** opened recently on the site of the old hotel Commerce Mancini, on Rue Messageries; Tel: 46-94-15-01.

Cognac

"The Charente is a rolling patch of French countryside just north of Bordeaux where the actinic quality of the sunlight is extraordinary, and where the majority of rural postmen have liver trouble." So Samuel Chamberlain prefaces his study of the world-famous brandy from Cognac, a small port city on the Charente river where the great château builder François I was born in 1494. From Saintes it's a drive of 26 km (16 miles) east along N 141 to Cognac.

Arriving in Cognac from Saintes, you will cross the Charente river and follow boulevard Denfert-Rochereau right to Place François Ier. In the center of the *place* is a pretty fountain into which children and dogs are always threatening to fall. If you want only to hesitate and explore for an hour or two, find a metered parking place here. If that proves impossible, follow the signs to the Office de Tourisme just to the west on the Place Jean-Monnet. It's a natural starting place for finding out which *chais* (wine sheds or storage places) are open to the public on what days: **Otard** (in the former château where François was born), **Polignac**, **Martell**, **Hennessy**, and others. The office can provide information about *son-et-lumière* performances in nearby châteaux and can also arrange visits to the respected glass factory of **St-Gobain**.

On Place Jean-Monnet, a **Cognathèque** provides information about Cognacs and sells an enormous selection of them at reasonable prices. Also available for purchase are the blue tasting glasses used by professional tasters. The fascinating **Musée du Cognac**, in the Dupuy d'Angeac town house (set in the kind of unmanicured park the French term *accidenté*), joins archaeology to art to the eau-de-vie industry. Fossils, ceramics, tools for viticulture, paintings—all are displayed in this entirely engaging museum.

The making of Cognac leaves its mark everywhere in the town (about 21,000 Cognaçais), even on many buildings near distilleries, which have assumed a curious brown shade imparted by a fungus that lives on the vapors of the distillation process. Aside from visits to the *chais* and museum, your primary pastime in Cognac will be walking along Grande-Rue, with its 15th-century half-timbered houses, and the more aristocratic rue Saulnier, with town houses of the 16th and 17th centuries. Right at the edge of the old quarter, the **Eglise St-Léger** boasts a beautiful rose window in Flamboyant style.

COGNAC THE SPIRIT

Wines have been grown in the region of the river Charente since the Romans planted vines there in A.D. 300; in addition to salt, the Roman wines were a major export to England, the Netherlands, and Scandinavia. However, the white table wines have never been very good, and even today they tend toward tartness, meanness, and cloudiness, so that the postman who stops to take an occasional glass on his rounds will not only make the mail tardy but will give himself a *crise de foi*.

More than three centuries ago, though, it was discovered that the same spirits, when distilled, metamorphose into an elixir permitting no competition for excellence from any quarter except Armagnac. Besides, the government had begun to exact a heavy tax on wine exports that did not extend to distilled, or "concentrated," wines.

It was the English and the Dutch who in the 17th century began to import this *vin brûlé,* or burnt wine (from the distillation process), which in Dutch is *brandewijn* and was long ago Anglicized as *brandy*.

The production of Cognac is complicated; travellers who wish to make a short study of it will find more than enough information in the Office de Tourisme in the town of Cognac. Suffice it to say that the name Cognac may be put on the label only if the grapes have been grown in an area comprising about 150,000 acres outside the town. Aging is all-important, as is the use of Limousin oak for the casks.

The seven grades of Cognac come from territories spreading out from the towns of Cognac and Jarnac in concentric circles: Closest in is *Grande* or *Fine Grande Champagne* (nothing to do with the region of the bubbly), followed by *Petite Champagne, Borderies,* the rings of *Fins Bois, Bons Bois,* and *Bois Ordinaires.* Finally, on the coast and islands of Oléron and Ré, there is *Bois à Terroir*.

The star device on labels began about a hundred years ago when the first three-star Cognac was designated for the Australian market. (Today 50 percent of Cognacs sold are of the highest quality.) Younger and less worthwhile spirits have no stars and, as wine connoisseur Alexis Lichine puts it, "are best drunk with soda." The third type is designated V.S.O.P. (Very Superior Old Pale). For export, some firms add such names as Réserve, Extra, X.O., and Cordon Bleu to the label.

Because Cognacs don't age after bottling, a Cognac made in 1814 but bottled in 1815 would now be only a year old, or younger than one produced in 1983 and bottled today. While V.S.O.P.'s must be at least five years old and sometimes ten, increasingly high costs of production for older ones means that one day they will be priced out of the market. A sweet liqueur made in the Cognac region, Pineau des Charentes, may be drunk as an aperitif.

STAYING AND DINING IN COGNAC

A pretty, indoor-outdoor restaurant you might choose for lunch is **Pigeons Blancs**, northwest of downtown at 110, rue J. Brisson (Tel: 45-82-16-36), but the best answer for both dining and staying the night in the Cognac area is ▶ **Moulin de Cierzac**, about 13 km (8 miles) south near St-Fort-sur-le-Né. The Moulin is a peaceful 17th-century country house that offers ten rooms and a marvelous collection of Cognacs. In the dining room, from October to April, order oyster *cassolette à la Fine Champagne*. An informal atmosphere prevails here, and the Moulin is a good value per franc (for reservations, Tel: 45-83-01-32).

Angoulême

From Cognac continue 44 km (27 miles) east along N 141 to this city, "the balcony of the Southwest," as it has been called. (You may want to pull off at one of the roadside stands en route to buy Cognacs or Pineau des Charentes to take along. The prices are quite reasonable.) Angoulême sits atop a plateau dividing the Charente and the Anguienne rivers. The rampart that girdles this city of about 50,000 people encloses the upper town, the one the traveller comes to see: the winding pedestrian dining and shopping streets near the old covered market; the Hôtel de Ville, with its château towers of the 13th and 15th centuries; and, most notably, the Cathédrale St-Pierre. (The lower town is commercial, industrial, and residential in an almost suburban sense.)

That illustrious Renaissance woman Marguerite de Valois, known variously as Marguerite d'Angoulême, Marguerite of Navarre (she became its queen), and, by her brother François I (the master builder of the châteaux on the Loire), as "the Marguerite of Marguerites," was born in Angoulême in 1492 in the round tower that is now a part of the **Hôtel de Ville**. She is said to have spoken Spanish and Italian as smoothly as French; she wrote in Latin, Greek, and Hebrew; and she gave French literature the *Heptaméron,* a series of tales that were takeoffs on Boccaccio's *Decameron.* Today, alas, she is called to mind most often when one munches the local chocolate bonbons called *marguerites.*

Two Balzacs add literary tone to Angoulême: Guez de Balzac, born here in 1597, whose devotion to courtly belles lettres gained him the admiration of language purists and devotion of the Académie Française; and novelist Honoré de Balzac, who lovingly described the town in *Illusions Perdues.*

OLD ANGOULEME

An exploration of Angoulême begins naturally at the **Cathédrale St-Pierre**. Handily, just across the street at 2, place St-Pierre, is the Office de Tourisme, which can supply information about the city including a helpful brochure (in English) called "Discovering Old Angoulême by Foot."

The Cathédrale and Environs

The 12th-century cathedral is the city's *chef d'oeuvre.* Its remarkable façade is intricately sculpted, with striking scenes of the Last Judgment (told with more than 70 figures), Christ in Majesty, and an episode from the *Chanson de Roland.* Badly damaged by the Calvinists in 1562 and restored in 1634, and again in 1866 by local architect Paul Abadie *fils* (responsible for Paris's Sacré-Coeur), the church is a triumph of Poitevin Romanesque. Unfortunately, the interior is unattractive and uninteresting.

Neighboring the cathedral on its northern wall in a former bishopric at 1, rue Friedland, the **Musée Municipal** (sometimes called the Musée des Beaux-Arts) contains a rich collection of African art gathered by a local doctor; it is said to be the third most important such collection in France. Contemporary exhibitions and African musical performances are often held here as well. The museum's collection of original illustrations for comic strips (*bandes dessinées*) is unrivaled in the country. An international festival celebrating such cartoon strips is held annually in Angoulême.

From the Hôtel de Ville to Rue de Genève

From the museum, walk east along rue Tison d'Argence one block to the rue Prudent. Turn left, and you will find yourself almost immediately in Place F. Louvel facing the Palais de Justice. Walk to your right (east) along the rue des Postes, which at the second corner opens into the place de l'Hôtel de Ville.

This is an area bustling with shops and cafés, full of action at lunchtime and at the end of the working day. Gardened on its east and south sides (the latter plantings constitute the Square J. Kennedy), the *hôtel* is a curious but satisfying construction in Gothic-Renaissance style built on the site of the former château of the counts of Angoulême. What remains of that, incorporated in the "new" structure, are the 13th-century keep, from the top of which is a fine panoramic view, and the round 15th-century tower in which Marguerite d'Angoulême was born.

From this busy *place* and the northeast corner of the Hôtel de Ville, take rue du Général-de-Gaulle for its short length to Place des Halles and its central Marché Couvert (covered market). This is a very colorful scene Tuesday through Sunday from 7:00 A.M. to 12:30 P.M.

From the west side of the Place des Halles, take rue de Genève into a pedestrian zone of several blocks where little streets lead off to left and right, alive with cafés, bars, and small, trendy shops. Rue de Genève ends in lively little Place du Palet.

Promenade des Remparts

The Promenade des Remparts, which you may begin from the Place des Halles or the Place du Palet, is a highly recommended walk for the fairly hardy with plenty of time; you may prefer to drive it in the counterclockwise direction. The promenade affords dramatic views of the countryside, especially from Place Beaulieu, below which stretches a parklike garden.

STAYING AND DINING
IN ANGOULEME

On a warm evening the Genève pedestrian zone is excellent dining and people-watching territory. The best of the restaurants here is probably **Le Margaux**, a handsome house with a fine menu (seafood specialties) at 25, rue de Genève (Tel: 45-92-58-98). Also good is **La Ruelle**, at 6, rue des Trois Notre-Dame (Tel: 45-95-15-19).

Motorists might want to check into the 90-room ▶ **Mercure-Altéa Hôtel de France**, the epitome of a modern, business-oriented hotel on the Place des Halles, where a large underground garage provides easy parking. Most of the city that is of interest can best be seen on foot. A second choice would be the 32-room ▶ **Européen** on Place G. Pérot, but it is not quite so handy for walking and has no restaurant.

A fine place to base yourself for country wandering and for exploring Angoulême is ▶ **Hostellerie du Moulin du Maine Brun,** just outside Hiersac, itself 11 km (7 miles) west of Angoulême on N 141. (From St-Cybardeaux take D 18 and D 14 south to Hiersac, a trip of about 15 km/9 miles.) A renovated old mill on the banks of the little river Nouère, the 20-suite inn, with individual terraces, is decorated with 18th- and 19th-century French furniture; the bar is cozy, the swimming area gardened. The kitchen has earned one Michelin star.

NERSAC

In the suburb of Nersac, 10 km (6 miles) west of Angoulême on D 699, the 17th-century craft of papermaking is still practiced. The **Moulin de Fleurac** is a remnant of about 100 mills that in the 17th century furnished fine, hand-printed papers to Holland (for books and superb illuminated manuscripts of the period), where many manufacturers had gone after the revocation of the Edict of Nantes. Here at Nersac the techniques invented in China in the second century have scarcely changed.

The public is admitted to seven workrooms on guided tours (lasting an hour) every day except Tuesdays. A museum at the site illustrates the history of paper, and a boutique sells fine samples. In the summer, boats will take you there via the Charente river; ask your hotel concierge or at the Office de Tourisme.

The Charentes Countryside

From Angoulême you can enjoy a pleasant day of idle
motoring along back roads and through seductive little
towns of special interest to enthusiasts of history and religious architecture: Churches, chapels, and shrines dot the
landscape.

LA ROCHEFOUCAULD

Leaving Angoulême in a northeasterly direction via N 141,
you arrive after only 22 km (14 miles) at La Rochefoucauld,
on the banks of the Tardoire river.

Sometime in the tenth century a man named Foucauld,
father of the bishop of Angoulême, came to this site on the
frontier between Poitou and Aquitaine to construct a fort atop
a rocky hill. Soon the spot was called *la roche à Foucauld*
(Foucauld's Rock); its inhabitants, in Latin, Rupificaldiens.

Thus was born one of the distinguished family trees, that of
La Rochefoucauld, of which line the head always has been
named François. (François I of La Rochefoucauld was the
godfather of François I, the great Renaissance king of France.)
The most familiar to us today is the 17th-century François VI,
duc de La Rochefoucauld and author of the reflections on
morality colloquially called *Les Maximes*.

The Château

Today's Château de La Rochefoucauld was begun in 1622 by
François II and his wife, Anne de Polignac. Its Italian Renaissance appearance probably results from the fact that Anne
had lived in Italy and was a friend of Leonardo da Vinci. Seen
from below and from across the river, it is the very picture of
a medieval castle, with vestiges of the donjon and 15th-
century towers. Much of this side of the castle is still under
reconstruction as the result of extensive damage caused by
an underground river in January 1960.

Despite the ongoing restoration, many parts of the château are open to the public: the courtyard; the part Neo-
Gothic, part Renaissance chapel with coats of arms on the
ceiling and a figure of Saint Jacques on his way to Santiago;
three salons with 17th-century paneling (the furniture will
be returned when repairs are complete); the delightful
boudoir with paintings attributed to Marguerite d'Angoulême; a beautiful example of an Italian Renaissance staircase;
and the kitchens.

The La Rochefoucauld family occupies some rooms in the
donjon. The Duchess Edmée de La Rochefoucauld is a writer
and essayist and president of the Femina literary jury, while

the present generation is represented by François Alexandre de La Rochefoucauld, the 38th François in the line.

A *son-et-lumière* show, *La Perle de l'Angoumois,* is staged here at nightfall several times during July and August, bringing a thousand years of history to life.

EGLISE ST-AMANT-DE-BOIXE

This is one of the most exciting religious sites in Les Charentes. To go directly there from La Rochefoucauld, take D 88 northwest to Tourriers, then D 32 through Villejoubert, always following the signs to St-Amant; in all about 26 km (16 miles). From Angoulême, follow D 737 and D 508 north 16 km (10 miles) to the village of Montignac; St-Amant-de-Boixe is 1½ km (1 mile) northeast on D 15.

The tranquil village named for a seventh-century hermit sits near a forest studded with megalithic stones. One's initial impression of the church is that it's almost the size of the entire town. Nearly 230 feet long, with a Romanesque nave and a Gothic choir, the church was reconstructed in the 15th century. A stunning, modern stained glass window over the altar only adds to the sense of wonder.

From St-Amant follow signs to D 737, go north as far as Le Fouilloux, cross the Charente on D 118, continue to Les Bouchauds near St-Cybardeaux, and follow the signs for the **Gallo-Roman theater.** The total distance is about 17½ km (11 miles). Stand in the wooded countryside (it's likely that you'll have the site to yourself), look up at rows of stone seats, now overgrown, and try to imagine the Romans, ever building—even so far from home.

AULNAY

It is difficult to summon up the sensations medieval pilgrims must have felt as they trudged toward Spain and Santiago across a France empty of highways, hotels, and inns, through lands that were sometimes dangerous and always uncomfortable. The great churches we visit today are often now in the hearts of cities that subsequently grew up around them, and thus we sense mere echoes of their importance in other days.

The **Eglise St-Pierre-de-la-Tour** in Aulnay is an exception, sitting far off the major travel routes, almost as lost in isolation as it was in the past. Its melancholy setting in an old cemetery surrounded by cypresses and untended tombstones inspires the kind of brooding dear to artists and historians.

To get to Aulnay from Angoulême, follow D 939 northwest in the direction of St-Cybardeaux and St-Jean-d'Angély. At a wide spot in the road signposted for the two churches of Matha and Marestay (about 48 km/30 miles), take little D 121 north for 19 km (12 miles) and Aulnay.

A triumph of Poitevin Romanesque architecture, built in one sweep in the 12th century and left all but untouched for 800 years, St-Pierre still lures us to study in detail its "sermons in stone." Edwin Mullins puts it perfectly in *The Pilgrimage to Santiago:* "Even separated in time from us by the Renaissance, by the Reformation and the Age of Reason, by the medieval revival in the Romantic era, by centuries of comfortable agnosticism and now by the dispassion of tourism, the heart thumps at such a vision of an alternative world."

Getting to Aulnay is half the fun for those whose pleasure it is to wander through rural landscapes dotted with small, old villages, humble shrines, and tiny cafés where the locals fall silent at the sound of an outsider's footsteps. The nearest town of any size, **St-Jean-d'Angély**, is about 17 km (11 miles) southwest of Aulnay on D 950. The best place for lunch in town is **Le Scorlion**, at 8, rue Gallerand, near the covered market.

Aulnay is a somewhat shorter excursion from Saintes (approximately 37 km/23 miles) or Cognac (some 46 km/29 miles).

GETTING AROUND

From Paris, A 10 (motorway) and N 10 (national highway) lead to Poitiers; it's a three- to four-hour drive. From Poitiers N 11 continues to La Rochelle. From there the main route is N 137 to Saintes, Cognac, and Angoulême; N 10 leads back to Poitiers.

TGVs run from Paris's Gare Montparnasse to Poitiers in one hour, 35 minutes; to Angoulême in two hours, 20 minutes; and to La Rochelle in three hours, 11 minutes. From Paris's Gare d'Austerlitz, Corail trains serve Poitiers, Niort, and La Rochelle, and also Angoulême with connections to Cognac, Saintes, and Royan.

This region is particularly well served by the France Rail'N Drive Pass, which involves four days of travel by rail and three days by rental car (Avis) within a 15-day period, or nine days by rail and three days by auto within one month. For example, you might take the train to Poitiers, see the city on foot, rent a car for travel in the country, continue to La Rochelle by train, and so on, finally returning from Angoulême to Paris by train.

TAT Airlines flies twice weekly during July and August from London-Gatwick to Poitiers. There is daily service from

Paris's Orly-Ouest to La Rochelle year-round. TAT makes weekend flights in July and August from Orly-Ouest to Royan.

Poitou-Charentes makes good use of its waterways by offering boat rentals, cabin-cruiser rentals, or houseboats. In La Rochelle various companies offer **rental boats** with or without skipper: Loch 2000, Rivage, and Coloma. To find the one best suited to your needs, see the Régie du Port (Port Authority) in La Rochelle; Tel: 46-44-41-20.

Houseboats on the Charente are available out of Cognac through Charente Plaisance, 1, place Solençon, Tel: 45-82-79-71; from La Rochelle through CMP Rivières, 20, rue Newton, Rytré; Tel: 46-44-88-57.

There are 18-hole **golf courses** in Cognac, Royan, Poitiers, La Rochelle, Saint-Cyr (near Poitiers), and in smaller centers such as Loudun, Mazières-en-Gatine, and La Roche-Posay, and nine-hole courses in Angoulême, Saintes, Ile d'Oléron, Ile de Ré, Niort, and Montbron. A brochure about facilities in Poitou-Charentes is available at Maison de France offices.

ACCOMMODATIONS REFERENCE

The rates given below are projections for 1994. Unless otherwise indicated, rates are for a double room, double occupancy, and do not include meals. As rates are always subject to change, double-check before booking.

▶ **Bois de la Marche.** 86240 **Ligugé.** Tel: 49-53-10-10; Fax: 49-55-32-25; in U.S., Tel: (800) 927-4765; Fax: (212) 689-5435; in U.K., Tel: (071) 287-3231. Member, Inter-Hotel. 305F–475F.

▶ **Les Brises.** Avenue Philippe Vincent, 17000 **La Rochelle.** Tel: 46-43-89-37; Fax: 46-43-27-97. 400F–580F.

▶ **Château Clos de la Ribaudière.** 86360 **Chasseneuil-du-Poitou.** Tel: 49-52-86-66; Fax: 49-52-86-32. 320F–620F.

▶ **Château de Périgny.** 86190 **Vouillé.** Tel: 49-51-80-43; Fax: 49-51-90-09; in U.S., Tel: (800) 927-4765; Fax: (212) 689-5435; in Canada, Fax: (418) 452-3240. Member, Relais du Silence. 490F–1,350F.

▶ **La Corderie Royale.** Rue Audebert, 17300 **Rochefort.** Tel: 46-99-35-35; Fax: 46-99-78-72. 475F–700F.

▶ **Européen.** Place G. Pérot, 16000 **Angoulême.** Tel: 45-92-06-42; Fax: 45-94-88-29. 330F–420F.

▶ **Family Golf Hôtel.** 28, boulevard F. Garnier, 17200 **Royan.** Tel: 46-05-14-66; Fax: 46-06-52-56. 350F–450F.

▶ **François Ier.** 15, rue Bazoges, 17000 **La Rochelle.** Tel: 46-41-28-46; Fax: 46-41-35-01; in Canada, Fax: (418) 452-3240. Member, Relais du Silence. 170F–495F.

▶ **Le Grand Large.** Baie de la Remigeasse, 17550 **Dolus-d'Oléron**. Tel: 46-75-37-89; Fax: 46-75-49-15; in U.S., (212) 856-0115; Fax: (212) 856-0193. Member, Relais & Châteaux. 660F–1,530F.

▶ **Hostellerie du Moulin de Maine Brun.** RN 141-La Vigerie, 16290 **Hiersac**. Tel: 45-90-83-00; Fax: 45-96-91-14; in U.S., (212) 856-0115; Fax: (212) 856-0193. Member, Relais & Châteaux. 550F–750F.

▶ **Hôtel de l'Europe.** 39, rue Carnot, 86000 **Poitiers**. Tel: 49-88-12-00; Fax: 49-88-97-30. 240F–480F.

▶ **Hôtel de France-Angleterre et Champlain.** 20, rue Rambaud, 17000 **La Rochelle**. Tel: 46-41-34-66; Fax: 46-41-15-19; in U.S. and Canada, Tel: (800) 528-1234; in U.K., (081) 541-0033. Member, Best Western International. 300F–450F.

▶ **Hôtel de la Monnaie.** 3, rue de la Monnaie, 17000 **La Rochelle**. Tel: 46-50-65-65; Fax: 46-50-63-19. 450F–850F.

▶ **Mercure-Altéa Hôtel de France.** 1, place des Halles, 16000 **Angoulême**. Tel: 45-95-47-95; Fax: 45-92-02-70; in U.S. and Canada, Tel: (800) 221-4542; Fax: (914) 472-0451; in U.K., Tel: (071) 724-1000. 430F–630F.

▶ **Mercure Relais de Poitiers.** 86360 **Chasseneuil-du-Poitou**. Tel: 49-52-90-41; Fax: 49-52-51-72; in U.S. and Canada, Tel: (800) 221-4542; Fax: (914) 472-0451; in U.K., (071) 724-1000. 400F–530F.

▶ **Messageries.** Rue Messageries, 17100 **Saintes**. Tel: 46-93-64-99; Fax: 46-92-14-34. 250F–300F.

▶ **Moulin de Cierzac.** 17520 **Cierzac**. Tel: 45-83-01-32; Fax: 45-83-03-59. 380F–540F.

▶ **Novotel.** 86360 **Chasseneuil-du-Poitou**. Tel: 49-52-78-78; Fax: 49-52-86-04; in U.S. and Canada, Tel: (800) 221-4542; Fax: (914) 472-0451; in U.K., (071) 724-1000. 385F–495F.

▶ **Novotel.** Plage de Gatseau, 17370 **St-Trojan-les-Bains**. Tel: 46-76-02-46; Fax: 46-76-09-33; in U.S. and Canada, Tel: (800) 221-4542; Fax: (914) 472-0451; in U.K., (071) 724-1000. 750F.

▶ **Relais du Bois St-Georges.** Rue Royan, 17100 **Saintes**. Tel: 46-93-50-99; Fax: 46-93-34-93. 350F–1,100F.

▶ **Résidence de Rohan.** 17640 **Vaux-sur-Mer**. Tel: 46-39-00-75; Fax: 46-38-29-99. 400F–630F.

▶ **Richelieu Hôtel.** 17630 **La Flotte**. Tel: 46-09-60-70; Fax: 46-09-50-59. 800F–2,000F.

▶ **St-Jean d'Acre.** 4, place de la Chaîne, 17000 **La Rochelle**. Tel: 46-41-73-33; Fax: 46-41-10-01; in U.S., Tel: (800) 927-4765; Fax: (212) 689-5435; in U.K., Tel: (071) 287-3231. Member, Inter-Hotels. 320F–600F.

CHRONOLOGY OF THE HISTORY OF FRANCE

PREHISTORY

Sea caves on the Côte d'Azur may be the oldest inhabited sites in Europe, occupied by Neanderthal man and his predecessors a million years ago. Following these ancient, Acheulean, cultures, the main ones evidenced in France are the Mousterian (60,000–39,000 B.C.), Châtelperron (33,000 B.C.), Aurignacian (30,000 B.C.), Gravettian (24,000 B.C.), Solutréan (17,000 B.C.), and Magdalenian (15,000 B.C.).

- **15,000–10,000 B.C.:** Cave art in sites around Les Eyzies in the Dordogne: Lascaux, Font-de-Gaume, Cap Blanc, La Mouthe, Les Combarelles, and many cave shelters (*abris*).
- **3,800–2,000 B.C.:** Tombs and stone alignments (avenues of upright stones called menhirs, some 14 to 20 feet high), tumuli (earth-covered tomb mounds), megaliths. The Ménec alignment, near Carnac in Brittany, boasts more than a thousand standing stones.
- **3,500 B.C.:** Megalithic tombs in southern France, particularly the Grotte des Fées near Arles.
- **600–50 B.C.:** The *oppidum* (hilltop fort) of Vix, in Burgundy near Châtillon-sur-Seine.

THE CELTIC PERIOD

Beginning about 1,000 B.C., the Celts, an Indo-European race, arrive in waves from the east, bringing decorative La Tène art (the Basse-Yutz flagon, the Janus head from Roquepertuse); hilltop strongholds (*oppida*); a warrior aristocracy; and many divinities as well as the Druids. Eventually they are driven out by the Romans, though they keep a toehold in Brittany.

GREEKS, ROMANS, GALLO-ROMANS

- **About 600 B.C.:** Founding of the trading colony of Marseille (Massilia) by the Phocaeans of Ionia.

- **From c. 400 B.C.:** Greeks establish a chain of trading posts along the Mediterranean coast, including Antibes (Antipolis) and Nice (Nikaia).
- **121 B.C.:** Romans establish Gallia Narbonensis (present-day Narbonne in Provence).
- **58–51 B.C.:** Caesar conquers Gaul.
- **52 B.C.:** Vercingétorix battles Caesar, loses.
- **A.D.162:** Arrival of the first Alemannic hordes.
- **c. 250:** Christianity comes to the Gallo-Romans.
- **c. 355:** Invasions of Gaul by Franks, Alemanni, Saxons.
- **373–397:** Saint Martin is bishop of Tours.
- **418–507:** The Visigoths rule the south, out of Toulouse.
- **443:** The Burgundians establish themselves in the Rhône Valley.
- **451:** Attila and his Huns are defeated by the Romans and their allies in the Battle of the Catalaunian Fields near Troyes.
- **481:** Mérovingian Clovis I crowned king of the Franks.
- **c. 496:** Clovis is crowned at Reims and the Franks become Christian.
- **c. 511:** Gaul is divided into three parts: Austrasia, Neustria, Burgundy.
- **c. 630:** The first Benedictine monasteries are built.
- **732:** Charles Martel (the Hammer), son of Pépin of Herstal, defeats the Moors at the Battle of Poitiers.
- **751:** Pépin le Bref (the Short), father of Charlemagne, is proclaimed king.
- **788:** Death of Roland, in the Pyrénées, when Charlemagne's army, returning from Spain, is ambushed. He is immortalized in the medieval epic *La Chanson de Roland*.
- **800:** Charlemagne is crowned emperor in Rome.
- **843:** After Charlemagne's death, the Frankish empire is partitioned among three grandsons by the Treaty of Verdun.

THE ROMANESQUE ERA

- **910:** Founding of the abbey of Cluny in Burgundy.
- **From c. 950:** Expansion is the theme, with clearing of lands, growth of population, broadening of trade with fairs, movement of people on pilgrimages, building of new towns. Romanesque art is exemplified in Vézelay, Autun, Conques, and Sénanque,

among other towns. Old French moves away from Latin in this time; monks at Jumièges add vocalizations to traditional Gregorian chants.

- **987**: Hugues Capet ("Little Cloak") is crowned king of the Franks, creating the Capetian dynasty (direct line to 1328, collateral until 1848).
- **1066**: William the Conqueror (Guillaume le Conquérant), duke of Normandy, conquers England.
- **1095–1099**: First Crusade, led by Raymond IV, comte de Toulouse, and Godefroi de Bouillon (now a town in Belgium). The Crusades continue periodically until 1250.
- **1115**: Saint Bernard founds Cistercian abbey of Clairvaux.
- **1122**: Birth of Eleanor of Aquitaine, queen consort first of Louis VII of France, then of Henry II of England; mother of many children, including English kings Richard the Lion-hearted and John Lackland of Magna Carta fame. She dies in 1204.
- **c. 1132**: Cathedrals begun at Vézelay and Autun.
- **1137**: Start of construction of cathedral of St-Denis, first monumental Gothic structure.
- **1137–1180**: Major conflicts between Louis VII and English king Henry II.
- **c. 1140**: Development of Catharism, one of the Albigensian heresies.
- **1147–1149**: Disastrous Second Crusade, preached by Saint Bernard at Vézelay.
- **1150–1167**: Universities founded at Paris and Oxford.
- **1154**: Henry II becomes king of England (Henri II in France), to begin the House of Plantagenêt. (His father, Geoffroi, comte d'Anjou, created the name by sticking a sprig of broom—*genêt*—into his hatband.) The Plantagenêts will rule England and battle over French inheritances until the death of Richard II during the Hundred Years War, in 1400.
- **1163**: Cornerstone of Notre-Dame de Paris laid.
- **1189–1192**: Third Crusade, led by France's Philippe Auguste, England's Richard the Lion-hearted, and Holy Roman Emperor Frederick I.

GOTHIC AND LATE GOTHIC

- **c. 1200–1300**: Medieval France in full flower; trade and population expansion continue. Gothic art gives birth to cathedrals at Amiens, Beauvais, Chartres,

Reims; stained glass brings light to those at Bourges, Laon, Notre-Dame, and others. Polyphonic music is heard at Notre-Dame.

- **1202–1204:** Fourth Crusade; Constantinople seized.
- **1208:** Beginning of the Albigensian Crusade.
- **1210–1294:** Construction of Reims's cathedral of Notre-Dame.
- **1226:** Accession of Louis IX, king and crusader; reigns 44 years; canonized as Saint Louis, 1297.
- **1233:** Start of the Papal Inquisition.
- **1246–1248:** Construction of Sainte-Chapelle, one of the finest examples of Gothic architecture, on Ile de la Cité, Paris.
- **1253:** Founding of the Sorbonne, which will become the nucleus of the University of Paris, by Robert de Sorbon.
- **1270:** Gothic cathedrals begun in Toulouse, Narbonne.
- **1300–1400+:** Decorative ornamentation comes to architecture in Radiant Gothic (cathedrals of Strasbourg, Metz) and Flamboyant Gothic (flowing, flame-like forms), mostly in Normandy and Picardy.
- **1309–1378:** The "Babylonian captivity" of the popes in Avignon.
- **1328:** Accession of Philippe VI, first of the House of Valois.
- **1333:** Edward III of England claims the French crown.
- **1337–1453:** The Hundred Years War, which begins with dynastic squabbles between France and England.
- **1348–1351:** The Black Death kills as many as half the inhabitants of Europe.
- **1349:** The heir to the throne inherits the Dauphiné region; each kingly heir is afterward known as the Dauphin.
- **1356:** Edward, the Black Prince, son of England's Edward III, captures King Jean II le Bon (the Good) in the Second Battle of Poitiers.
- **c. 1360:** The portrait of Burgundian duke Jean le Bon (now in the Louvre) marks the debut of French portraiture.
- **1378–1417:** The Great Schism; rival popes in Rome and Avignon.
- **1407:** War breaks out between the Burgundians and the Armagnacs.
- **1415:** The Battle of Azincourt (Agincourt in English) in northern France, won by Henry V of England.

- **1429**: Joan of Arc raises the English siege of Orléans and accompanies Charles VII to Reims and his coronation.
- **1431**: Joan of Arc is burned at the stake in Rouen on May 30; she will be canonized in 1920.

THE RENAISSANCE

- **c. 1450**: Somewhere about here the Renaissance begins, moving out of the so-called Dark Ages with burgeoning trade, improving economy, renewed interest in building and the arts. The influence of Italy is a dramatic force in architecture (François I imports Italian artisans of every stripe), and Italian Mannerism influences painting and music.
- **1451**: Financier and minister Jacques Coeur is arrested and accused of having poisoned Agnès Sorel, Charles VII's mistress; he will die fighting the Turks in 1456.
- **1453**: The Hundred Years War comes to a shaky end as England loses all its possessions in France except Calais.
- **1455–1485**: The Wars of the Roses in England between Houses of Lancaster and York, involving Henry IV's queen, Margaret of Anjou, daughter of René le Bon.
- **1469–1470**: Founding of France's first printing house.
- **1477**: Charles le Téméraire, duke of Burgundy, dies; Burgundy and Picardy pass to the Crown, other lands go to Emperor Maximilian I, and the France-Hapsburg quarrels begin.
- **1484**: Meeting of the Estates-General in Tours; town representatives join clergy and nobility as the Third Estate.
- **1515**: Accession of François I of Angoulême, who reigns for 32 years, fights four major wars, and becomes the greatest master builder and art patron in French history with the help of Cellini, Leonardo, et al.
- **1517**: Martin Luther posts his 95 theses on the door of the castle church in Wittenberg.
- **1524**: Italian Giovanni da Verrazano, sailing under the French flag, explores the New England coast and becomes the first European to enter New York harbor.
- **1534–1542**: Jacques Cartier departs St-Malo and ven-

tures up the St. Lawrence in what is now Canada, giving France claims to the region.

- **1547**: Henri II, husband of Catherine de Médicis, lover of Diane de Poitiers, ascends to the throne.
- **1547–1559**: Henri II persecutes the Huguenots.
- **1561**: Persecution of Huguenots stopped, briefly, by Édict of Orléans.
- **1562–1598**: Wars of Religion—Catholics led by the Guise family, Protestants by the Bourbons.
- **1572**: Saint Bartholomew's Day Massacre (of Protestant Huguenots), August 24, on orders of Catherine de Médicis.
- **1589**: Henri of Navarre becomes Henri IV, first of the House of Bourbon; becomes a Catholic in 1593 and claims "Paris is worth a Mass."
- **1598**: The Edict of Nantes grants freedom (conditional) to the Huguenots.
- **1609**: Samuel de Champlain establishes a French colony in Quebec.

LOUIS XIII

- **1610**: Henri IV is assassinated, succeeded by Louis XIII with his great ministers, Cardinals Richelieu and Mazarin.
- **c. 1630–1700**: Art styles in France reflect serenity, i.e., Poussin; classical values in literature are expressed by Racine's tragedies; Montaigne creates the essay (from 1571).
- **1635**: The Académie Française is founded to promote education and the arts. France involves itself in the Thirty Years' War on the side of Denmark and Sweden against Germany.

LOUIS XIV AND THE CLASSIC CENTURY

- **1643**: Louis XIV becomes king, and will reign for 72 years.
- **1648–1653**: *La Fronde* is a series of outbreaks caused by the efforts of Parlement to limit royal authority; eventually, Parlement will be joined by the nobility and the people of Paris.
- **1661–1715**: Louis XIV's Sun King period sees a flowering of Baroque art and architecture (Versailles, with Le Vau, Le Nôtre, Le Brun, others); painting (Georges de La Tour, Claude Le Lorrain, others);

literature (Corneille, Racine, La Fontaine, Molière, La Rochefoucauld, others); music (Lully, Couperin); and philosophy, science, and mathematics (Pascal and many others).

- **1685**: Revocation of the Edict of Nantes; half a million Huguenots leave France.
- **1700–1800**: The French Enlightenment is born in the works of Montesquieu, Voltaire, Rousseau, Diderot. In art, Rococo emerges with Watteau, Neoclassicism with David.
- **1701–1714**: War of the Spanish Succession; the duke of Anjou and grandson of Louis XIV becomes Spanish king Felipe V over other European claimants.

LOUIS XV AND THE ENLIGHTENMENT

- **c. 1715**: The economy booms, inspiring increasingly sophisticated salons and receptions, the construction of more châteaux, and a passion for knowledge.
- **1715**: Death of Louis XIV, succeeded by Louis XV, who loses Canada to the English and enjoys such favorites as Madame de Pompadour and Madame du Barry.
- **1751**: First volume of Denis Diderot's *Encyclopédie* is published.
- **1768**: France buys Corsica from Genoa.
- **1769**: Napoléon Bonaparte (Buonaparte) is born in Ajaccio, Corsica.
- **1774**: Louis XVI ascends to the throne.
- **1777**: Marie-Joseph-Paul-Yves-Roch-Gilbert du Motier, marquis de Lafayette, arrives in America, is made a major-general by the Continental Congress, and serves in many battles. (In 1789 Lafayette will create the modern French flag.)
- **1783**: First manned free-balloon flight by brothers Joseph-Michel and Jacques-Etienne Montgolfier, over Paris.

THE REVOLUTION

- **1789**: Outbreak of the French Revolution; Louis XVI and Marie Antoinette beheaded in 1793. This is followed by the continent-wide French Revolutionary Wars until 1802.
- **1792**: France is declared a republic, but the wars, uprisings, and massacres go on.
- **1794**: Maximilien François Marie Isidore de Robes-

pierre, chief architect of the Terror, dies on the guillotine.

- **1796–1804**: Napoléon's successes against the Austrians, Milan, Genoa, Mamelukes of Egypt, etc.

THE 19TH CENTURY

- **1800–1840**: Romanticism replaces Neoclassicism and Rococo: Théodore Rousseau leads the Barbizon school of painting; Victor Hugo expresses in his novels the new desire for freedom, Eugène Delacroix in his paintings the appeal of exotic locales.
- **1803–1815**: Napoleonic Wars against European powers.
- **1804**: Napoléon is crowned Emperor of the French, and civil law is codified in the *Code Napoléon*.
- **1805**: Napoléon crowns himself King of Italy; Viscount Horatio Nelson defeats combined French and Spanish forces at Battle of Trafalgar; Napoléon triumphs over Russians and Austrians at Austerlitz.
- **1812**: Napoléon's disastrous Russian campaign.
- **1814**: Continent-wide Wars of Liberation against Napoléon.
- **1814**: Napoléon abdicates, receives the island of Elba as a principality; the Bourbon dynasty is restored with Louis XVIII as king.
- **1815**: The 100 Days: During the Congress of Vienna, Napoléon lands at Cannes and marches to Paris. Louis XVIII flees and Napoléon rules until beaten by the British and Prussians in the Battle of Waterloo; he is then exiled to the British island of St. Helena, where he dies in 1821.
- **1815–1816**: The White Terror—Royalist uprisings, persecutions of Jacobins and Bonapartists.
- **1824**: Charles X, brother of Louis XVIII, ascends to the throne.
- **1825**: Louis Braille invents script for the blind..
- **1830**: The July Revolution forces abdication of Charles X; he is succeeded by Louis-Philippe and the House of Orléans.
- **1840–1880**: The official Beaux-Arts school of Paris sets an international style for public buildings and sculpture with such examples as the Paris Opéra and Bartholdi's Statue of Liberty. Realist painting is influenced by Daguerre and photography. Balzac provides a realistic look at social classes.
- **1848**: The February Revolution brings about the

abdication of Louis-Philippe and installation of Louis Napoléon Bonaparte (nephew of Napoléon I) as president of the Second Republic.

- **1852:** The president becomes Napoléon III, emperor of the French, to begin the Second Empire.
- **1854–1870:** France takes part in the Crimean War, takes Nice and Savoy from Austria, extends her possessions in Southeast Asia, aids in the construction of the Suez Canal, and sees the collapse of the Mexican Empire established for Archduke Maximilian of Austria.
- **1870–1871:** Franco-Prussian War—Napoléon III is defeated at Sedan, taken prisoner; the Third Republic is proclaimed, with Louis-Adolphe Thiers as president.
- **1874:** First exhibition of the Impressionists opens April 15; canvases by Cézanne, Degas, Monet, Morisot, Pissarro, Renoir, Sisley, 21 others; the school is named for Monet's *Impression, Soleil Levant* (Sunrise).
- **1879–1896:** France expands into parts of Central Africa, Tunis, Indochina, and Madagascar.
- **1880–1900:** *Fin-de-Siècle* period in literature and art—Flaubert, Zola, Verlaine, Rimbaud; Cézanne, Gauguin.
- **1889:** Paris International Exhibition stars the Eiffel Tower.
- **1890:** Birth of Charles de Gaulle.
- **1895:** The brothers Louis-Jean and Auguste Lumière patent first device for making and projecting films.
- **1894–1906:** The Dreyfus Affair, a case revolving around supposed treason, brings the left wing to power, raises issues of anti-Semitism, and helps split Church and State (Alfred Dreyfus exonerated in 1906).

THE 20TH CENTURY

- **1900–1909:** France is the center of experimentation in the arts; Fauvism (Matisse a leader, 1905), Cubism (Picasso et al.); Diaghilev in Paris alters classical ballet; new sounds of music (Debussy, Satie, Stravinsky).
- **1909:** Louis Blériot is the first man to fly an airplane across the English Channel.
- **1913:** Igor Stravinsky's *Le Sacre du Printemps* (The Rites of Spring) debuts on May 29 and, some say, the modern age is born.

- **1914**: World War I is occasioned by the murder of Archduke Francis Ferdinand, heir to the Austro-Hungarian throne, at Sarajevo, Yugoslavia, June 28.
- **1916**: Beginning of Dada movement in arts (Arp, Tzara).
- **1918**: Allied counteroffensive begins; Franco-German armistice at Compiègne, November.
- **1919**: Treaty of Versailles returns Alsace and Lorraine to France, gives her mandate over other lands; France becomes a founding member of the League of Nations.
- **1925**: Exhibition of Surrealists, now in their heyday: Breton, de Chirico, Dalí, Ernst, Magritte, Tanguy; in literature, Eluard, Cocteau, heirs of Baudelaire, Rimbaud, and, eventually, Freud.
- **1929**: Beginning of worldwide Depression.
- **1936**: Germany occupies the demilitarized Rhineland; no action from France or England.
- **1939**: World War II; after a series of unanswered German takeovers culminating in an attack on Poland, France declares war on Germany on September 3.
- **1940**: German army occupies Paris, June 14; Vichy government headed by Henri Philippe Pétain; Third Republic ends; Charles de Gaulle forms a government in exile in England; Resistance is formed.
- **1942–1943**: Existentialism in literature and philosophy; publication of Albert Camus's *The Stranger* and Jean-Paul Sartre's *Being and Nothingness.*
- **1944**: Allies land in Normandy on June 6 and in the South of France on August 15 to liberate France; Charles de Gaulle forms a provisional government.
- **1945**: Germany capitulates.
- **1946**: De Gaulle resigns, succeeded by Félix Gouin and Georges Bidault.
- **1948**: Proposed by the U.S., the Marshall Plan for the recovery of Europe begins.
- **1954–1956**: France loses Equatorial Africa, Indochina, Morocco, Tunisia, and West Africa to independence movements and wars.
- **1957**: European Common Market comes into being with France as a founding member.
- **1959**: Having dealt with the Algerian question as prime minister under René Coty, de Gaulle becomes president of the Fifth Republic.
- **1962**: Algeria is granted independence.
- **1969**: De Gaulle retires from the presidency, succeeded by Georges Pompidou.

- **1970**: De Gaulle dies and is buried near his home at Colombey-les-Deux-Eglises.
- **1974**: Valéry Giscard d'Estaing is elected third president of the Fifth Republic.
- **1981**: François Mitterrand is elected president of France.
- **1986**: Jacques Chirac, mayor of Paris, is elected France's premier by a center-right coalition, instituting the continuing period of *cohabitation* with Socialist President Mitterrand.

  The Musée d'Orsay, the Museum of Art of the 19th Century, opens in the renovated Orsay train station on the Left Bank.
- **1987**: Klaus Barbie tried in Lyon for war crimes and sentenced to life imprisonment.
- **1988**: François Mitterrand is elected president of France for a second seven-year term.
- **1989**: Year-long celebrations are staged around the country in celebration of the bicentenary of the French Revolution.

  The Grand Louvre reopens after completion of the controversial I. M. Pei glass pyramid in the central courtyard and the first phase of the excavations of the 12th-century castle in the Cour Carrée.

  The Grande Arche de la Défense is completed.
- **1990**: In April the Opéra de la Bastille opens with Hector Berlioz's *Les Troyens*.
- **1991**: Edith Cresson becomes first woman to serve as prime minister of France. She is dismissed in 1992.
- **1992**: French voters narrowly approve the European united currency treaty.
- **1993**: The Socialist party is routed in March elections, and with the new conservative majority there is much discussion as to France's future political bent. The Richelieu wing of the Louvre opens in November, nearly doubling the museum's capacity.

—Georgia I. Hesse

INDEX